1 → 1-37
  & stuff on syllabus, websites etc.
7-26 - 7-60   8-47 - 8-58   + 3 cases (not done yet) A 97.50
4-70 → 4-129 + cases

4-7 → 4-18 + cases

4-40 → 4-70
4-172 → 4-194

E-Business Legal Handbook

5-1 → 5-52
5-69 → 5-78 & 5-91 → 5-100
3-3 → 3-50, 3-54 → 3-66 (briefed all set)
5-76 - 5-78
5-91 - 5-100
3-76 → 3-97

E-Business Legal Handbook

2003 Edition

Michael L. Rustad
Cyrus Daftary

ASPEN LAW & BUSINESS
A Division of Aspen Publishers, Inc.
New York   Gaithersburg

This publication is designed to provide accurate and authoritative information in regard to the subject matter covered. It is sold with the understanding that the publisher is not engaged in rendering legal, accounting, or other professional services. If legal advice or other professional assistance is required, the services of a competent professional person should be sought.

—From a *Declaration of Principles* jointly adopted
by a Committee of the American Bar Association
and a Committee of Publishers and Associations

Printed in the United States of America

1 2 3 4 5 6 7 8 9 0

Library of Congress Cataloging-in-Publication Data

Rustad, Michael.
E-business legal handbook / Michael L. Rustad, Cyrus Daftary.
p.   cm.
Includes bibliographical references and index.
ISBN 0-7355-1726-6
ISBN 0-7355-2953-1 (2003 Edition)
1. Electronic commerce—Law and legislation—United States. I. Daftary, Cyrus, 1969–
II. Title.

KF889.3.R87   2000
343.7309'944—dc21   00-053127

About Aspen Law & Business

Aspen Law & Business—comprising the former Harcourt Professional Publishing, Prentice Hall Law & Business, Little, Brown and Company's Professional Division, and Wiley Law Publications—is a leading publisher of authoritative treatises, practice manuals, services, and journals for accountants, auditors, attorneys, financial and tax advisors, corporate and bank directors, and other business professionals. Our mission is to provide practical solution-based how-to information keyed to the latest legislative, judicial, and regulatory developments.

We offer publications in the areas of accounting and auditing; banking and finance; bankruptcy; business and commercial law; construction law; corporate law; pensions, benefits, and labor; insurance law; securities; taxation; intellectual property; government and administrative law; real estate law; matrimonial and family law; environmental and health law; international law; legal practice and litigation; and criminal law.

Other Aspen products treating intellectual property and technology law issues include

Business to Business Internet Exchanges
The Commercial Law of Intellectual Property
Corporate Partnering
Drafting License Agreements
Federal Telecommunications Law
Guide to Registering Trademarks
Intellectual Property for the Internet
Internet and Technology Law Desk Reference
Law and the Information Superhighway
The Law of Electronic Commerce
Law of the Internet
Scott on Computer Law
Scott on Multimedia Law
Software Patents
Technology Transfer Guide

ASPEN LAW & BUSINESS
A Division of Aspen Publishers, Inc.
A Wolters Kluwer Company
www.aspenpublishers.com

For Chryss, James, and Erica

M.L.R.

To my wife, Faranak, and my parents Jaleh and Ali Daftary
for their guidance and support.

C.D.

SUMMARY OF CONTENTS

Contents

About the Authors

Acknowledgments

Overview: The Rise of the Internet

Chapter One   Introduction

Chapter Two   Establishing and Maintaining an Identity on the Internet

Chapter Three Internet Security

Chapter Four   Protecting Intellectual Property in Cyberspace

Chapter Five   Civil Liability in Cyberspace

Chapter Six   The Law of E-Commerce Transactions

Chapter Seven Exposure to Lawsuits in Distant Forums: Jurisdiction

Chapter Eight   Global E-Business Legal Issues

Chapter Nine   Conducting a Legal Audit and Managing Risk

Chapter Ten   E-Mail and Internet Usage Policies

Appendix A: The Business Plan: Legal and Strategic Guidance for
                      Writing a Business Plan for Your Dot-Com Venture

Appendix B: Internet Resources for Lawyers

Glossary

Index

CONTENTS

A complete table of contents for each chapter is included in the beginning of the chapter.

About the Authors

Acknowledgments

Overview: The Rise of the Internet

Chapter One
INTRODUCTION

§ 1.01   Overview
§ 1.02   The Evolution of Internet Law
§ 1.03   What Is the Internet?
§ 1.04   What Are People Doing on the Internet?
§ 1.05   Accessing and Using the Internet

Chapter Two
ESTABLISHING AND MAINTAINING
AN IDENTITY ON THE INTERNET

§ 2.01   Overview
§ 2.02   Doing Business in Cyberspace
§ 2.03   Funding a Startup
§ 2.04   Purpose of the Web Site
§ 2.05   Developing and Maintaining a Commercial Web Site
§ 2.06   Staking a Claim in Cyberspace: How to Choose a Corporate Identity
          for the Internet
§ 2.07   Advertising Your Products and Drawing Traffic to Your Web Site
§ 2.08   Preventive Law Pointers

Chapter Three
INTERNET SECURITY

§ 3.01   Overview
§ 3.02   Auditing Internet Security Technologies
§ 3.03   The Radius of Risk

§ 3.04   Implementing Information Security Systems
§ 3.05   Remedies for Computer Abuse
§ 3.06   Preventive Law Pointers

Chapter Four
PROTECTING INTELLECTUAL PROPERTY IN CYBERSPACE

§ 4.01   Overview
§ 4.02   Copyrights in Cyberspace
§ 4.03   Trademarks in Cyberspace
§ 4.04   Trade Secrets in Cyberspace
§ 4.05   E-Commerce-Related Patents
§ 4.06   Globalization of Intellectual Property Rights

Chapter Five
CIVIL LIABILITY IN CYBERSPACE

§ 5.01   Overview
§ 5.02   General Principles of Tort Law
§ 5.03   Intentional Torts in Cyberspace
§ 5.04   Business Torts in Cyberspace
§ 5.05   Internet Torts
§ 5.06   Publishing Torts in Cyberspace
§ 5.07   Privacy in Cyberspace
§ 5.08   Negligence in Cyberspace
§ 5.09   Strict Liability in Cyberspace
§ 5.10   Immunities and Privileges
§ 5.11   Regulation of Cyberspace
§ 5.12   Preventive Law Pointers and Supplemental Checklists Aimed at
          Avoiding Cyberspace Liability

Chapter Six
THE LAW OF E-COMMERCE TRANSACTIONS

§ 6.01   Overview
§ 6.02   E-Business Models
§ 6.03   Sources of E-Commerce Law
§ 6.04   Electronic Contracting Rules
§ 6.05   Software and Internet-Related Licenses under the Uniform Computer
          Information Transactions Act
§ 6.06   License Agreements
§ 6.07   Internet Taxation
§ 6.08   Internet Payment Systems
§ 6.09   Preventive Law Pointers

Chapter Seven
EXPOSURE TO LAWSUITS
IN DISTANT FORUMS: JURISDICTION

§ 7.01   Overview
§ 7.02   Two Paradigms of Personal Jurisdiction
§ 7.03   Cyber-Jurisdiction Cases
§ 7.04   Preventive Law Pointers and Internet Jurisdiction Guides

CHAPTER 8
GLOBAL E-BUSINESS LEGAL ISSUES

§ 8.01   Introduction: The Global Legal Marketplace
§ 8.02   International E-Business Legal Audit
§ 8.03   International Business Issues
§ 8.04   Resolving International Disputes and Preventive Law Pointers

Chapter Nine
CONDUCTING A LEGAL AUDIT AND MANAGING RISK

§ 9.01   Overview: Risk Management
§ 9.02   Legal Audit Checklists
§ 9.03   Insurance Policies
§ 9.04   Online Dispute Resolution
§ 9.05   Preventive Law Pointers

Chapter Ten
E-MAIL AND INTERNET USAGE POLICIES

§ 10.01   Overview
§ 10.02   Risks from E-Mail and Internet Usage
§ 10.03   Risk Management
§ 10.04   E-Mail and Internet Usage Policies
§ 10.05   Sample E-Mail and Internet Usage Policy
§ 10.06   Launching an E-Mail and Internet Usage Policy
§ 10.07   Preventive Law Pointers
Appendix 10-1:   Department of Commerce Internet Use Policy

Appendix A: The Business Plan: Legal and Strategic Guidance
                for Writing a Business Plan
                for Your Dot-Com Venture

Appendix B: Internet Resources for Lawyers: Legal Research, Issues,
                and Practice

Glossary

Index

ABOUT THE AUTHORS

Michael L. Rustad, Ph.D., J.D., LL.M, is the Thomas F. Lambert Jr. Professor of Law and Director of the Intellectual Property Law Concentration at Suffolk University Law School in Boston. He is a core faculty member in Suffolk's new LL.M. program in Global Technology. He also teaches in Suffolk's summer program at the University of Lund in Sweden. Prior to joining the Suffolk law faculty, he was an associate with the Boston law firm Foley, Hoag and Eliot. He clerked for the late Honorable William E. Doyle of the Tenth Circuit U.S. Court of Appeals. He is a member of the American Law Institute's consultative group for the Restatement (Third) of Torts and the revision of the Uniform Commercial Code. He is the co-editor of the *Bi-Monthly Review of Law Books*. His numerous law review articles and books have been cited by state supreme courts, federal district and appellate courts, and the United States Supreme Court. He is the author of *Women in Khaki: The American Enlisted Woman* (Praeger 1981), *The Concepts and Methods of Sales, Leases and Licenses* (Carolina Academic Press 1999), and *In Defense of Tort Law* (NYU Press 2002).

Cyrus Daftary, J.D., LL.M., is a Tax Partner at PricewaterhouseCoopers and an adjunct faculty member in Suffolk University Law School's Intellectual Property Law Concentration, at Suffolk University's Frank Sawyer School of Management, and in Northeastern University's Master of Taxation program. He received his J.D. from the University of Dayton School of Law and an LL.M. in Corporate Tax from Temple University. Mr. Daftary has served as a corporate counsel and consults with law firms and companies throughout the country on the use of technology in their businesses. He was the founder of Suffolk University Law School's first course in cyberspace law.

He teaches and lectures students and lawyers throughout the country in the uses of electronic research methods, cyberlaw-related issues, e-commerce, and taxation of the Internet. He is a member of the bars of Indiana, U.S. District Court, and the U.S. Supreme Court.

ACKNOWLEDGMENTS

2003 EDITION

Many people contributed their time and talents to the 2003 Edition, and we greatly appreciate their help. We would particularly like to thank James F. Ewing, a technical specialist for Mintz Levin Feris Cohn Glovsky and Popeo, P.C. in Boston, who authored the section on e-commerce patents. Dr. Ewing will join Mintz Levin as an associate in the fall of 2002. We would also like to thank Fred Sroka, a Tax Partner at PricewaterhouseCoopers, who updated the tax section. Next, we would like to acknowledge the extraordinary contribution of Todd Krieger, Esq., an adjunct faculty member in Suffolk University Law School's Intellectual Property Law Concentration and an attorney with the Bose Corporation, and Dawn McGuire, Esq., a solo practitioner located in San Francisco. A special thanks to our law student assistants for their valuable help: Beth Brown, Brett Boskiewicz, Christina Filleti-Sheridan, Kenneth W. Loock, Cynthia Montolve, Jessica M. Natale, Anne-Marie Paone, Punam Sharma, Gina Takemori, and Anna Zubova. Jessica, Anne-Marie, and Cynthia also authored valuable practice pointers in this edition. Michael L. Rustad would like to thank his wife, Chryss Knowles, and Professor Andy-Beckerman-Rodau for their editorial work on this edition. We would like to thank Brian Flaherty, Elizabeth McKenzie, and Susan Sweetgall, who provided excellent reference librarian support. Finally, we would like to thank Frank Quinn and Larry Wexler of Aspen Law & Business for their extraordinary support of the 2003 Edition.

October 2002   Michael L. Rustad and Cyrus Daftary
                                                                Boston, MA

OVERVIEW:
THE RISE OF THE INTERNET

[The] Internet's pace of adoption eclipses all other previous technologies. Radio was in existence thirty-eight years before fifty million people tuned in; television took thirteen years to reach that benchmark. Fifty million people were using desktop computers only sixteen years after the first personal computer (PC) kit came out.[1]

The number of people with Internet access from home worldwide is nearing five hundred million, according to the Neilsen/NetRatings.[2]

Although the World Wide Web did not begin to become an integral part of the popular culture until 1995, it is now difficult to imagine a world without bandwidth, browsers, and bytes. Today people across the globe are accessing the Internet through their cell phones, pagers, personal digital assistants (PDAs), and computers. These digital communications devices have generated a number of video/audio-enhanced web sites, which are offering new Internet-related products and services. Cable operators report a dramatic increase in digital cable and high-speed Internet access, which is a necessity to access video/audio-enhanced web sites.

The rise of the Internet has dramatically changed the ways in which business and personal communications are conducted. More specifically, cyberspace is increasingly the place where millions of people pay bills, do their banking, consult professionals, shop for gifts, communicate electronically, and make connections with family and friends. Internet use in the United States is growing at a rate of 2 million new Internet users each month, according to a study by the National Telecommunications and Information Administration and the Economics and Statistics Administration.[3] The study, "A Nation Online: How Americans Are Expanding Their Use of the Internet," found that 143 million Americans (50 percent of the U.S. population) used the Internet in September 2001.[4] That is a 26 percent increase over August 2000.[5]

---

[1] United States Dep't of Commerce, Emerging Digital Economy 12 (Apr. 1998).

[2] Michael Pastore, The World's Online Population (visited June 15, 2002), http://cyberatlas.internet.com/big_picture/geographics/articles/0,,5911_986431,00.html.

[3] A Nation Online: How Americans Are Expanding Their Use of the Internet (visited June 15, 2002), http://www.ntia.doc.gov/ntiahome/dn/index.html.

[4] Id.

[5] CyberAtlas Staff, U.S. Internet Population Continues to Grow (visited June 15, 2002), http://cyberatlas.internet.com/big_picture/ geographics/articles/0,1323,5911_969541,00.html.

As of March 2002, an estimated 561 million people around the globe were connected to the Internet.[6] Six out of ten of these Internet users are not native English speakers. The Internet sites that are visited vary based on individual interests, but most people frequent commercial web sites. Amazon.com and eBay.com are probably two of the most heavily visited web sites in the United States. As more and more people come online, the corporate demand to reach these potential consumers will continue to increase. Jupiter Media Metrix predicts online advertising will exceed $15 billion worldwide by 2006.[7] Besides online advertising, online business will utilize e-mail campaigns, print media, and search engines to tap into these potential customers.

Startup dot-com companies were the success stories of the late 1990s. Now many of those dot-coms are affectionately referred to as "dot bombs" or "flops."[8] Nevertheless, these companies and the Internet have revolutionized the online selling of goods and services. According to the U.S. Census Bureau, retail e-commerce sales in the United States increased to $11 billion in the fourth quarter of 2001, up from $9 billion in the fourth quarter of 2000, which amounts to an increase of 18 percent in one year.[9]

Consumers are shopping on the Internet for a broad range of goods and services, and companies have been eager to take advantage of this new sales channel. On the weekend of Christmas 2001, online shopping reached an industry high of 345 million in sales, up 73 percent compared to the same weekend the year before.[10] E-commerce rebounded in 2002 as companies found ways to commercialize the Internet, with consumers increasingly willing to pay subscription or license fees for software, music, and other transfers of data.[11] This is evidenced by the fact that online orders increased one-third in the first quarter of 2002, an increase of 23 million purchases from the first quarter of 2001.[12]

Those dot-com companies that have been able to successfully establish themselves as legitimate long-term online companies are working to further their brands by expanding into new markets. For example, Amazon.com, already the world's largest online bookstore with nearly a million volumes in stock, expects its online music store to grow to a comparable size. Besides having products that have a market demand, dot-com companies must provide their consumers with

---

[6] Global Internet Statistics (visited June 15, 2002), http://www.glreach.com/globstats/index.php3.

[7] Online Ad Spending to Rebound and Reach Over 15 Billion Dollars by 2006, But Will Eventually Be Outpaced by Other Digital Marketing Initiatives, Predicts Jupiter Media Metrix, PR Newswire, Aug. 8, 2001.

[8] Dot.com to Dot.bomb (visited June 15, 2002), http://news.bbc.co.uk/hi/english/in_depth/business/2000/review/newsid_1069000/1069169.stm.

[9] United States Dep't of Commerce News (visited June 15, 2002), http://www.census.gov/mrts/www/current.html.

[10] Michael Pastore, Shoppers Show Confidence in Internet for Holidays (visited June 15, 2002), http://internetnews.com/ec-news/article.php/4_947401.

[11] Making Money Online: The Internet Sells Its Soul, Economist, Apr. 20, 2002, at 68.

[12] Beth Cox, E-commerce Goes on a Roll, Cyberatlas (visited June 15, 2002), http://cyberatlas.internet.com/markets/retailing/article/0,,6061_1016641,00.html.

various purchasing and payment options. Ninety percent of commercial web sites now accept credit card payments.[13] In addition, many companies have embraced PayPal as a viable alternative to accepting payment for online purchases.[14]

With a sales volume five times that of consumer transactions, business-to-business transactions play a much larger part in e-commerce. Dell Computers now processes orders worth $5 million every day from its web site,[15] and Intel processes $2 billion in electronic orders per month.[16] Cisco, Dell, and IBM are the three major players in business-to-business transactions, accounting for billions of dollars' worth of online transactions per year.[17]

Some analysts predict that the Internet will be the most important techno-logical development since the Industrial Revolution.[18] The Internet continues to grow faster than we could have imagined. The information superhighway is so vast that it has become an integral part of our daily personal and professional lives. Corporations are using sophisticated Internet-based communications services to tie together traditional corporate phone systems with mobile phones, wire LANs, and web-based controls.

Mobile web applications will be the next Internet-based revolution. Innova-tive uses of mobile web applications will surface. The proliferation of voice-browsing technology and portals has many positive effects for users and e-businesses. The hands-free operation of voice browsing is ideal for using wire-less devices while on the go. As the usability of these devices increases, so will the number of transactions on the Internet. For instance, some organizations are nearly all virtual, giving them a broad range of benefits in terms of time, money, and quality of life. Virtual companies will be able to

- save money on office space,

- take advantage of a nationwide (or even worldwide) labor force,

- save on relocations costs,

- attract skilled employees who want to telecommute,

- offer flexible time for all employees whose job functions permit it, and

- offer employees the ability to travel and/or work from anywhere they please.

With broadband connectivity in every home becoming a reality, it is likely that attorneys, surgeons, construction workers, and other professionals using the

---

[13] Visa's Online Security Program (visited June 15, 2002), http://advisor.com/Articles.nsf/aid/OLSEE172.

[14] *See generally* PayPal.com (visited June 15, 2002), www.paypal.com.

[15] David Jaachim, E-Biz Efforts Pay Huge Dividends for Intel (visited June 15, 2002), http://www.internetweek.com/story/INW20001011S0006.

[16] *Id.*

[17] *Id.*

[18] Harvard Conference on the Internet and Society 67 (O'Neill & Associates 1996).

Internet will be able to access vital information at any time to increase their effectiveness and productivity. The spectacular adoption of the Internet has spawned instantaneous communication and commerce and resulted in a radical paradigm shift to a truly interconnected global marketplace never before seen in the world economy. This paradigm shift can be attributed to several separate but distinct changes:

1) **Technology.** Phenomenal technological advances have been achieved in the last 30 years. On one level, we have moved from a noncomputer to a mainframe computer environment and leaped to a PC-network-based society. Accelerating this movement is the fact that the cost of change has become relatively low. State-of-the-art PCs are now available for as little as $500.

2) **Community.** There has been a radical change in the way society perceives itself. We have moved from a national to a global focus; our sense of community has been extended to cover larger territory than our own backyards. Some individuals find they have more in common with those in a worldwide Internet community than with their next-door neighbors. There are many examples of this global focus, from the introduction of the Euro to NAFTA.

3) **Economy.** Finally, the economics of our world have changed. The world has moved from an industrial-based economy to an information-based economy. As barriers to global trade fall, goods and services are exchanged in a global economic system.[19]

These recent trends stemming from the rapid development and adoption of technology and the Internet have revolutionized the way society interacts and does business.

1. Legal Challenges

The rise of the information society is displacing the traditional legal paradigm that matured as a response to an economy based on the national distribution of durable goods. As the Internet continues to become an integral part of our lives, business professionals and their legal advisers must address many new challenges. The following is an example of a dialogue that you might face in your practice or company:

Mike: Cyrus, I need some legal advice. One of my largest commercial customers claims that I violated their privacy rights because I shared their sales activities with one of my trusted business partners. This customer, with which I have done in excess of $500,000 worth of sales in the first quarter of this year, now threatens to take legal action to obtain a refund of the purchase price

---

[19] David Johnston et al., Cyberlaw: What You Need to Know About Doing Business Online 11 (1997).

of all items previously purchased and damages for the harm that they have encountered resulting from my trusted business partner spamming their employees' e-mail accounts, which required the company e-mail system to be shut down for three days.

Cyrus: I didn't realize that you had a computer store. Where is it located?

Mike: Suffolk Personal Computers (SPC) is a virtual storefront on the Internet . . . you know, one of those "dot-com" businesses.

Cyrus: Do you maintain a privacy policy on the web site?

Mike: I don't have a privacy policy posted on the web site. I wasn't sure how we wanted to profile our customers based on their purchases, so I drafted a privacy policy, but opted to wait to post it, so that the policy would not be too limiting. In the interim, one of my trusted business partners offered me $1 million for my customer account profiles.

Cyrus: Have you spoken with the customer to find out how you might be able to resolve this problem?

Mike: We have only communicated via e-mail. My customer is in France and wants to sue under some European law. They claim to have jurisdiction since my web site can be accessed from anywhere in the world and SPC fulfilled their orders by shipping the products into France. What can I do to avoid being sued in a European court?

This dialogue illustrates how technology and the Internet have drastically changed the way businesses and customers interact. For many businesses, a web site or an e-mail address has become more important than a telephone number. Although several years ago this kind of legal dilemma would have been foreign to most people, the increasing popularity and power of the Internet, coupled with the affordability and dependability of personal computers, have made problems like this all too routine. The third edition of this book will help you deal with some of the more common issues confronting e-businesses, such as licensing, privacy, webvertisements, business method patents, employee policies, and e-mail usage policies.

What makes the Internet different as a legal landscape? Much of the commercial law governing Internet transactions was conceived 50 to 100 years ago, decades before the rise of the information age. The Uniform Commercial Code (UCC) is based on a legal paradigm conceived 50 years ago, long before the rise of the software industry, and in its day was a new paradigm that displaced nineteenth-century "horse law and haystack law."[20] But legal principles that made sense when people signed contracts on paper cannot be applied easily to online contracts that parties do not sign but expect to be enforceable.

Traditional commercial law principles are being overhauled to accommodate the global Internet. State legislatures in the vast majority of states are enacting or considering digital signatures to facilitate electronic commerce. The entire UCC is being revised to adapt to cyberspace law, software licensing, and information

---

[20] Grant Gilmore, Note, On the Difficulties of Codifying Commercial Law, 57 Yale L. J. 1341 (1948).

access contracts. The state legislatures in 40 states have enacted or are contemplating legislation to validate electronic forms signing or digital signatures. The 52 countries of the Hague Convention have drafted new rules for international jurisdiction and the enforcement of foreign judgments that will dramatically change the rules for consumer transactions and give consumers a right to litigate any e-commerce-related disputes in their own countries, which takes away the home jurisdictional advantage for companies like Microsoft and America Online. In addition, other areas of law—intellectual property rights, data privacy, data security, consumer protection, and regulations affecting public network operators—are also evolving at an exponential pace as a result of the Internet.

Doing business on the Internet raises a host of challenging issues relating to how to deal with electronic cash, online banking, commercial transactions in digital information, and digital signatures. Privacy regulation and jurisdiction questions, too, have been especially pressing. For example, Yahoo!, which has 230 million users, revised its privacy policy to exploit the personal information of its users in an effort to market its own products and services as well as those of its business partners.[21] The European Commission is investigating Microsoft's Passport online identification and authentication system. The EPIC filed complaints with the Federal Trade Commission in July and August 2001 alleging that the system is designed to profile users and that Microsoft engaged in unfair and deceptive business practices.[22] Testimony in Microsoft's antitrust trial revealed that the company intended to build the largest database of profiles to facilitate targeted advertising campaigns.[23]

The global nature of the Internet raises difficult problems of sovereignty and jurisdiction, both because the Internet is not governed by any single entity and because many online activities cut across multiple jurisdictions and could potentially be regulated by hundreds of jurisdictions.[24] These challenges are compounded by the fact that every country has its own unique and complex legal system. None of these legal systems anticipated the development of the Internet, and a number of them are rethinking how their existing laws apply to the Internet. Consumer protection rules, global privacy standards, and of course taxes are just a few of the issues being debated and decided by many jurisdictions.

Traditional concepts of jurisdiction must be adapted to the global nature of the World Wide Web. The Internet, by its very nature, involves cross-border transactions involving radically different legal and cultural traditions as to the meaning of civil liability, criminal law, consumer privacy, intellectual property, free speech, and the appropriate role of governments in Internet governance. The U.S. federal

---

[21] Making Money Online: The Internet Sells Its Soul, Economist, Apr. 20, 2002, at 68.

[22] Microsoft in EU Commission Privacy Probe, N.Y. Times, May 25, 2002.

[23] *See generally* Supplemental Materials in Support of Pending Complaint and Request for Injunction, Request for Investigation, and for Other Relief (visited June 15, 2002), http://www.epic.org/privacy/consumer/MS_complaint2.pdf.

[24] Betsy Rosenblatt, Principles of Jurisdiction (visited June 15, 2002), http://cyber.law.harvard.edu/property/domain/Betsy.html.

government is increasing its regulatory scrutiny of online commerce. The Federal Trade Commission (FTC) has begun to investigate the use and abuse of personal data of consumers who use the Internet and is proposing greater consumer protection in international online transactions. Businesses will have to be aware of any new FTC regulations. A number of other agencies are also considering increased regulation of Internet commercial transactions.

The European Union's approach to privacy illustrates how privacy and sovereignty concerns can intersect. The United States has traditionally had a free-market approach to information privacy, which conflicts with the individual-rights-based approach of the European Union (EU). The enactment of the EU Data Protection Directive, the consequent creation of national enforcement agencies, and new reporting requirements and restrictions on collection of personal information threatened to hamper the ability of American companies to conduct business in Europe.[25] After much negotiation, the U.S. Commerce Department and the EU agreed on a set of safe harbor privacy principles that permit American businesses to comply with the EU data protection principles.[26] Such conflicts are likely to arise in other countries also; the Global Internet Liberty Campaign surveyed 50 industrialized countries and concluded that most had either enacted or were considering new protection for the privacy of individual data.[27] Companies not complying with the privacy principles outlined by these directives face the risk of loss of consumer loyalty and damage to their online brand as well as prosecution for any violations.

Increasingly, the law of the Internet is found in industry standards such as those formulated by the International Standards Organization (ISO). To the business community, self-control is the most effective form of social control. The Internet Law and Policy Forum (ILPF) argues that Internet industry standards will create a predictable legal environment for e-commerce and are a desirable alternative to government regulation.[28] The ILPF urges that Internet law be market- and industry-standard driven rather than strong public regulation.[29] The recent ILPF report on authentication acknowledges a traditional role for government in consumer protection and fraud prevention,[30] but industry "accreditation is preferred to licensing . . . which should be consistent with or rely on private sector practices."[31]

---

[25] *See* U.S. Dep't of Commerce, Welcome to the Safe Harbor (visited June 15, 2002), http://www. export.gov/safeharbor/.

[26] *Id.*

[27] Global Internet Liberty Campaign (GILC), Privacy and Human Rights: An International Survey of Privacy Laws and Practice (visited June 15, 2002), http://www.gilc.org/privacy/survey/.

[28] Internet Law & Policy Forum, Bibliography of Internet Self Regulation (visited June 15, 2002), http://www.ilpf.org/groups/index.htm#authentication.

[29] *Id.*

[30] Internet Law & Policy Forum, Legislative Principles for Electronic Authentication (visited June 15, 2002), http://www.ilpf.org/ groups/bib4_15.htm.

[31] *Id.*

2. Organization of the Book; the SPC Hypothetical Example

E-Business Legal Handbook serves as a guide to the rapidly evolving laws and industry standards governing online transactions. E-business transforms more than business; it is imperative to understand and embrace how the online environment is changing the law. This book is designed for corporate counsel, general practitioners, business professionals, and corporate executives who want to harness the power of the Internet and need a basic understanding of the various legal issues that may be encountered in this new medium. In providing a detailed review of specific legal and business issues, each chapter peels back the layers of traditional law as well as global Internet legal developments, to help firms avoid liability and protect their rights in cyberspace.

To better illustrate the legal issues and challenges confronting us, the chapters will use this hypothetical example for demonstrative purposes.

> In 1996, cofounders Mike Rustad and Cyrus Daftary, along with four employees, launched Suffolk Personal Computers (SPC), a C Corporation, with its headquarters at 120 Tremont Street, Boston, MA. Within two years, SPC had achieved phenomenal growth, with revenues in excess of $4 billion in 1998. SPC owned 65 percent of the Northeast PC market and employed 4,000 professionals. SPC sold and distributed custom-built PCs through its own retail stores, catalogs, and third-party retail stores like Circuit City and CompUSA. To expand SPC's existing client base and compete against the likes of Dell and Gateway Computers on a national level, Mike and Cyrus decided that it was time for SPC to engage in electronic commerce.
>
> SPC has diversified its products and services to include partnerships with prominent portals such as Yahoo!, AOL, and Microsoft. SPC's business model involves substantial online advertising costs. Recently, SPC has purchased search-terms for key search engines that are emblematic of its best-selling products. SPC has also decided to target users based on user profiles compiled from its own customer profiles.

Chapter One provides an overview of the Internet, its related terminology, and the accelerating pace of related legal developments. Each succeeding chapter seeks to guide the reader through difficult legal and business issues that arise during each stage of conducting business online. We examine the broad range of Internet activity and discuss how individuals, companies, and firms access and use the Internet. This is the third edition of this book, and with each new edition the intent is to add new substantive content as well as update each chapter. Each chapter reflects the latest case law, statutory, and industry developments along with an enhanced glossary, legal audit checklists, and preventive law pointers. These materials will aid companies in resolving legal dilemmas that frequently arise out of Internet-powered business activity.

A word about preventive law pointers: The business community is ill served when legal liability on the web is portrayed as casino-style random lightning strikes. Since the first edition, torts on the Internet have evolved, as old causes of action are adapted to the Internet. In our view, legal liability stems from a firm's failure to anticipate legal problems before they arise, and lack of planning is the hallmark of liability. Much of our country's common law is based on common sense: balancing the risk of harm against the cost of prevention. Like preventive medicine, the logic of preventive law is that it is cheaper to prevent the conditions leading to liability or the loss of rights in cyberspace. The lesson of our common law is that liability is avoidable and preventable even in the uncertain legal landscape of cyberspace.

Our thesis is that the rational corporate response to the risks posed by doing business on the Internet is to carry out a high-level legal audit. The type of risk analysis will vary depending on the type of online activity and the type of products or services offered on the Internet, but a thorough legal audit serves the interests of the company in a number of ways. The recordkeeping necessary to measure and avoid Internet liability may help the firm not simply to prevent liability but also to uncover management and other problems. Without centralized safety audits, a firm may not spot a pattern of developing dangers until it is in a protracted legal war fighting for its life, not just its market share.

Preventive law is less expensive than financing litigation that can bankrupt a business. The goal of preventive law is to anticipate and resolve problems before they become full-blown corporate crises as in the Enron debacle. As the information economy expands its global reach, new risk factors must be anticipated. The checklists and preventative law pointers in the 2003 edition are designed to help companies conduct their own internal legal audits. Companies that do not conduct legal audits before and after conducting business in cyberspace do so at their peril.

CHAPTER ONE

INTRODUCTION

§ 1.01   Overview

§ 1.02   The Evolution of Internet Law
          [A]   The Development of the Internet
          [B]   Leading Cases and Statutes

§ 1.03   What Is the Internet?
          [A]   How Does the Internet Work?
                 [1]   Backbone
                 [2]   Internet Exchange Point
                 [3]   Point of Presence
                 [4]   Servers
                 [5]   Protocols

§ 1.04   What Are People Doing on the Internet?
          [A]   Who Is Using the Internet?
                 [1]   Charting Internet Results
                 [2]   Surveying the Digital Future
                 [3]   So, Where Do We Stand?
                 [4]   Money Matters
                 [5]   Privacy, Please
                 [6]   Wired Kids
          [B]   E-Mail and Online Service Providers
          [C]   Electronic Bulletin Boards
          [D]   Mailing Lists
          [E]   Private Systems
          [F]   Computer Networks/Protocols
                 [1]   DNS
                 [2]   Telnet
                 [3]   HTTP
                 [4]   FTP
                 [5]   POP3
                 [6]   PPP
                 [7]   SSL
          [G]   Publishing and Research
          [H]   Electronic Commerce

§ 1.05   Accessing and Using the Internet
          [A]   Internet Service Providers (ISPs)
          [B]   Internet Connections

      [1]   **Modem Access**
      [2]   **ISDN**
      [3]   **Cable Modems**
      [4]   **DSL**
      [5]   **T1 and T3 Lines**
      [6]   **Satellite Connections**
[C]   **Web Browser**
[D]   **Navigating the Web**
[E]   **Portals**
[F]   **Looking to the Future**
      [1]   **Internet2**
      [2]   **Internet-Enabled Devices**
      [3]   **Voice Browsing**
      [4]   **PDAs**
      [5]   **Web Pads**
      [6]   **Identity on the Internet**

§ 1.01   OVERVIEW[1]

Many companies are integrating the Internet into their business strategies and objectives. In an online world, the business strategy and objective of doing business and selling products and services is to enter new markets, reduce operating costs, and increase revenues, which in turn increases shareholder value. The term *e-business* refers to a company's organizational changes to conduct business transactions on the Internet. The use of computers and electronic communications in business transactions is referred to as *e-commerce*. As of early 1998, more than one-fourth of U.S. businesses with more than ten employees had established an Internet presence.[2] Today, companies that fail to harness the potential of the Internet may lose current customers and market share, while companies that use the Internet may reach new markets and raise their market share. E-commerce is evolving rapidly as a business tool as companies try to reach the rapidly increasing number of Internet users.[3]

Although many companies have successfully established a presence on the Internet, relatively few have completed a legal audit of the risks and liabilities stemming from e-commerce. Generally speaking, legal issues are considered very late in the business process and usually result from some negative situation. In the online world, those companies that are successful will establish themselves and their businesses by using legal strategies to transform the businesses to gain a competitive advantage. Failure to do so could result in a business being doomed. This book covers the full range of Internet-related issues, including the following:

1. *Creating and establishing a corporate identity*: Balancing the current corporate name and identity with the selection of an appropriate domain name; protecting and establishing trademark and other related intellectual property issues. These things contribute to a company's commercial reputation, which in the case of the online business is ultimately created by its web site.

2. *Going online*: Developing an Internet site and accessing the Internet via an Internet Service Provider (ISP). The web site itself must be protected with effective contracts, policies, and terms of use. Furthermore, effective contracts must be in place to protect its creation, hosting, and third-party relationships.

3. *Entering into and enforcing contracts*: Identifying the parties, determining the location of parties, selecting the applicable law, and enforcing agreements (such as webwrap, web linking, and web development

---

[1] We would like to thank Manish Vashist of PricewaterhouseCoopers for his written, strategic, and editorial contributions to this chapter.

[2] PricewaterhouseCoopers, Technology Forecast: 1999, at 182 (1999).

[3] How Many Online? (visited May 16, 2002), http://www.nua.ie/surveys/how_many_online/ (noting that for the week ending May 15, 2002, there were an estimated 544.2 million Internet users).

agreements); limiting liability for damages and warranties; using digital signature technology as necessary to permit the electronic "signing" of documents.

4. *Collecting revenue*: Establishing payment systems, digital cash; encryption; establishing merchant accounts; setting up a virtual store-front.

5. *Establishing a marketing presence while protecting the corporate name and reputation*: Creating links to and from a corporate web page; drafting a disclaimer of endorsement of and liability for linked sites.

6. *Distributing products*: Expanding corporate presence by distributing software products; developing and distributing corporate software: licensing, clickwrap, complying with UCC and other laws limiting warranties, excluding consequential damages, and limiting remedies; complying with the Uniform Information Transfer Act, the Uniform Computer Information Act (UCITA), and the Uniform Electronic Trans-actions Act (UETA); drafting clickwrap or webwrap agreements that comply with UCITA and webwrap agreements that condition access to the site on agreement with terms of service.

7. *Complying with legal guidelines and planning for taxation*: Contem-plating tax planning opportunities: value added tax (VAT), products ver-sus services, sales and use, nexus, and the federal Internet Tax Freedom Act.[4]

8. *Anticipating jurisdiction*: Planning for strategic use of jurisdiction, venue, conflict of interest, and choice of law, and selecting choice of law, forum, and venue provisions.

9. *Expanding into foreign markets and forming alliances*: Extraterritorial legislation and legal issues surrounding international sales; complying with European Union directives regarding data protection and privacy, consumer protection, and distance selling.

10. *Protecting intellectual property and other intangible assets*: Protecting domain names, use of metatags and hyperlinks, and the copyrightability of a web site; disclaimers of liability for infringement claims for materi-als posted by third parties.

11. *Drafting and implementing privacy policies*: Disclosures of privacy practices of web sites; the Federal Trade Commission as the chief fed-eral agency policing the collection of consumer information over the Internet; compliance with best industry practices for privacy.

12. *Employee training and content control*: Devising an Internet usage and e-mail policy; training employees on the proper use of facilities; enforcement of usage policies.

---

[4] For a discussion of the moratorium on Internet taxation, *see* § 6.07.

§ 1.02 THE EVOLUTION OF INTERNET LAW

[A] The Development of the Internet

Many people are credited with making the Internet what it is today. This section provides a brief, general summary of the evolution of the Internet from a legal perspective.[5] To paraphrase Oliver Wendell Holmes, we must study history in order to understand the path of the law.

The precursor to the Internet was established when the U.S. Department of Defense wanted to link its network, ARPANET, to various radio and satellite networks.[6] The goal of the network was to ensure that the U.S. defense communications system could withstand a nuclear strike. This vision of a robust network and the investment that went into its creation enabled the Internet to grow, unrestricted by boundaries, regulations, or preconceived notions of what it should look like.[7] Today, the Internet is comprised of sophisticated protocols such as XML; improved programming languages and utilities such as Java and Java Beans/Script; and interactive databases such as Oracle, Sybase, and SQL.

The cooperative effort and vision of many creative minds in the U.S. government and at corporations such as Genuity (formerly BBN), IBM, MCI World-Com, AT&T, Microsoft, Oracle, and Intel have influenced and shaped the evolution of the Internet. Internet law is rapidly evolving as industry groups, governments, and international organizations formulate new standards and as new regulatory initiatives, statutes, and case law arise.

[B] Leading Cases and Statutes

In this section of prior editions of this book, we noted selected cases and statutory highlights in the development of Internet law. However, Internet-related cases and legislation have evolved quickly from the Wild West of the mid-1990s to the more codified, but still contentious, environment of the early 2000s. The environment is still shifting rapidly, and some cases that were once valid precedent from a legal and business perspective have been overturned or superseded by new case law. Today, rather than risk compiling cases that could be obsolete before this book is even printed, we offer the following list of dynamic resources which can provide more recent insight and direction.

- Perkins Coie Internet Case Digest (*www.perkinscoie.com/casedigest/default.cfm*): summarized and categorized by topic

- Phillips Nizer Internet Law Library (*www.phillipsnizer.com*): summarized and categorized by topic

---

[5] For a comprehensive overview of the history of the Internet, see Stephan Segaller, Nerds 2.0.1: A Brief History of the Internet (1998).

[6] The Law of the Cyberspace I. Introduction, 112 Harv. L. Rev. 1574 (May 1999).

[7] Forerunner of Today's Internet (visited May 16, 2002), http://www.bbn.com/arpanet/index.html; *see also* All About Internet (visited May 16, 2002), http://www.isoc.org/internet/.

- Internet Law Library (*www.internet-law-library.com*): articles, statutes, cases, and resources

- Internet Public Library (*www.ipl.org/ref/QUE/PF/netlaw.html*): resources, articles, and analysis

- Electric Law Library (*www.lectlaw.com/111.html*): resources for online legal issues and disputes

- Bitlaw Internet Law (*www.bitlaw.com/internet/index.html*): articles and analysis

- Gigalaw (*www.gigalaw.com*): articles categorized by topic, including Internet-related issues

- UCLA Online Institute for Cyberspace Law and Policy (*www.gseis.ucla.edu/iclp/hp.html*): cases, articles, and resources

- KEYTlaw (*www.keytlaw.com*): legal information for owners, operators, and developers of web sites

- Netlitigation (*www.netlitigation.com/netlitigation/*): cases, news, and discussion information

Figure 1-1 shows the number of cases mentioning the Internet from 1991 to 2002, pointing to an overall spurt in "mentions" since 1995.

§ 1.03   WHAT IS THE INTERNET?

The Internet (often referred to as the Net) is a vast configuration of interconnected computers, a network of networks in which users at any one computer can, if they have permission, get information from any other computer (and sometimes talk directly to users at other computers). It consists of computers, peripheral components, telephone lines, satellites, and an assortment of other infrastructure devices.

The Net was conceived by the Advanced Research Projects Agency (ARPA)[8] of the U.S. government in 1969 and was first known as the ARPANET.[9] The original aim was to create a network that would allow users of a research computer at one university to be able to "talk to" research computers at other universities.[10] A side benefit of ARPANET's design was that, because messages could be routed or rerouted in more than one direction, the network could continue to function even if parts of it were destroyed in the event of a military attack or other disaster.

---

[8] Whatis.com, ARPA (definition) (visited May 16, 2002), http://searchwebmanagement.techtarget.com/sDefinition/0,,sid27_gci213781,00.html (noting that Advanced Research Projects Agency is an agency of the U.S. Department of Defense that developed technology for the military. ARPANET, which was one of its projects, grew into the Internet.).

[9] Development in the Law—The Law of the Cyberspace I. Introduction, 112 Harv. L. Rev. 1574, 1578 (May 1999).

[10] *Id.*

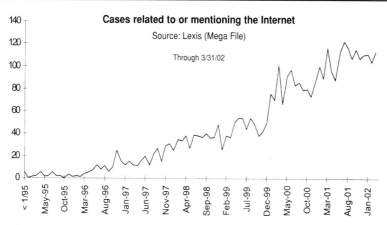

FIGURE 1-1. Cases Mentioning the Internet

In 1985, the National Science Foundation (NSF) created NSFNET,[11] a series of networks for research and education communication. Based on ARPANET protocols, the NSFNET created a national backbone service, provided free to any U.S. research and educational institution.[12] At the same time, regional networks were created to link individual institutions with the national backbone service. NSFNET grew rapidly as people discovered its potential and as new software applications were created to make access easier. Corporations such as Sprint and MCI began to build their own networks, which they linked to NSFNET. As commercial firms and other regional network providers took over the operation of the major Internet arteries, NSF withdrew from the backbone business. By 1995 the Internet was a wholly commercial structure, dominated by major telecommunication companies including AT&T, Sprint, and MCI WorldCom.[13] Much has changed with the Internet since its inception. Perhaps what has changed the most, however, is our perception of it. Society now views the Internet as a wide assortment of content and broad base of end users.

[A] How Does the Internet Work?

The Internet has transmission channels and interconnected points. The transmission channels come in various sizes and speed limits. Many different companies and institutions to which users may be required to pay subscription fees own

---

[11] A high-speed network funded by the National Science Foundation that formed the original backbone of the academic part of the Internet, NSFNet extends across the continental United States and outward to Canada, Central and South America, Europe, and the Pacific Rim. Midlevel networks are attached to this backbone, and university and local networks attach to those.

[12] Edward L. Rubin, XML and the Legal Foundations for Electronic Commerce: Computer Languages as Networks and Power Structures: Governing the Development of XML, 53 SMU L. Rev. 1447, 1450 (Fall 2000).

[13] See generally A History of Computer: Network (visited May 16, 2002), http://www.pbs.org/nerds/timeline/network.html.

the Internet. To truly understand the Internet infrastructure, one must understand the various components that hold it together.

[1] Backbone

Figure 1-2 illustrates the various components utilized within the Internet infrastructure. Backbones are the high-speed transmission channels that provide the fastest and most direct paths for data to travel. They are bonds that tie together multiple networks. Backbones are typically built around fiber optic cables called optical carriers or digital carriers. Optical carriers support transmission capacities as high as 10 Gbps (Gigabits per second), and digital carriers such as T1[14] carriers support data transmission of around 45 Mbps (Megabits per second). These lines provide high-speed transmission capabilities to outlying cities and businesses that are off the backbone path. In this way, the largest backbone networks may be accessible to an entire country or even several countries.

Backbone networks are developed and maintained by national backbone operators such as Sprint, MCI WorldCom, and AT&T.[15] These operators secure each end of the backbone with devices called routers[16] that receive and forward incoming transmissions to specified destinations via the shortest possible route. The operators own the routers, but they may not own the lines that constitute the backbone itself. They must lease these lines from local and long-distance telephone service providers instead.

[2] Internet Exchange Point

A single backbone network cannot provide access to all the data currently available online. It must have some means of connecting to other networks. The Internet exchange point is a designated point where backbones and smaller regional networks can peer with one another. These points are mostly owned and managed by private businesses and public institutions such as Ameritech and MCI WorldCom.[17]

---

[14] Whatis.com, T1 (definition) (visited May 16, 2002), http://searchnetworking.techtarget.com/sDefinition/0,,sid7_gci213084,00.html (noting that a T1 is a telephone line connection for digital transmission that can handle 24 voice or data channels at 64 kilobits per second, over two twisted pair wires. T1 lines are used for heavy telephone traffic or for computer networks linked directly to the Internet. Small and medium-sized companies with heavy network traffic normally use T1 lines. They can send and receive very large text files, graphics, sounds, and databases very quickly.).

[15] Internet Backbone Maps (visited May 16, 2002), http://www.nthelp.com/maps.htm.

[16] Whatis.com, Router (definition) (visited May 16, 2002), http://searchnetworking.techtarget.com/sDefinition/0,,sid7_gci212924,00.html (noting that a router is a device that finds the best path for a data packet to be sent from one network to another. A router stores and forwards electronic messages between networks, first determining all possible paths to the destination address and then picking the most expedient route, based on the traffic load and the number of hops.).

[17] Exchange Point Information (visited May 16, 2002), http://www.ep.net/.

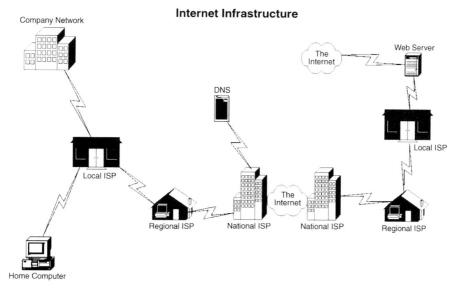

FIGURE 1-2. Internet Infrastructure

[3] Point of Presence

Points of presence are the points where individuals connect to the Internet. They are maintained by ISPs, which typically charge a small subscription fee as a toll for accessing the Internet. Telephone-modem lines, television cable lines, DSL circuits, or wireless airwaves can make a connection to point of presence. Some of the larger ISPs are America Online (AOL), AT&T (WorldNet), and Microsoft Network (MSN).

[4] Servers

The computers that store the content are also a part of the Internet infrastructure. These computers, called servers,[18] are identified by the type of content they contain. For example, web servers contain hyperlinked web content, mail servers contain e-mail messages, etc. Any computer can act as a server, and servers can exist anywhere in the Internet infrastructure. Most servers, however, are located at the point of presence.

[5] Protocols

Protocols[19] are the rules that govern the Internet. They dictate how the infrastucture components interact with one another to carry data. So how does the

---

[18] Whatis.com, Server (definition) (visited May 16, 2002), http://searchnetworking.techtarget.com/sDefinition/0,,sid7_gci212964,00.html (noting that a server is a computer in a client/server architecture that supplies files or services).

[19] Whatis.com, Protocol (definition) (visited May 16, 2002), http://searchnetworking.techtarget.com/sDefinition/0,,sid7_gci212839,00.html (noting that a communications protocol is a set of rules or standards designed so that computers can exchange information with a minimum of errors).

information get passed from computer to computer? And why can different computers, like Macs and PCs, talk to each other so easily? The secret is in a networking protocol called TCP/IP.[20] TCP/IP is the language of the Internet.[21] If a computer has TCP/IP installed, it is able to talk to any other computer on the Internet. It is a standard that transcends computer types (PCs, Macs) and operating systems (Windows, DOS, UNIX).

§ 1.04 WHAT ARE PEOPLE DOING ON THE INTERNET?

Internet activities can be categorized into five main types: (1) e-mail, (2) online services, (3) private networks, (4) publishing, and (5) e-commerce. E-mail[22] is by far the most common, with 90 percent of all Internet users claiming to be e-mailers.[23] For the most part, the Internet today is a giant public library with a decidedly commercial tilt. The most widespread use of the Internet today is as an information search utility for products, travel, hobbies, and general information. Virtually all users engage in one or more of these information-gathering activities. A little over one-third of all Internet users report using the web[24] to engage in entertainment such as computer games (such as online chess, role games, and the like). Thus, the current Internet is also emerging as an entertainment utility.

Chat rooms[25] are for the young and the anonymous.[26] Many young Internet users claim to have used chat rooms, but this activity substantially decreases after age 25. The people who chat report that the overwhelming portion of their chat room interaction is with anonymous other users whose identities remain unknown.

Consumer-to-business transactions such as purchasing, stock trading, online auctions, and e-banking are engaged in by much smaller fractions of Internet users, with only one-quarter purchasing online and less than 15 percent doing any of the other transactional activities. Despite all the sound and fury, business-to-consumer commercial online transactions are still in their earliest stages.

---

[20] Whatis.com, TCP/IP (definition) (visited May 16, 2002), http://searchnetworking.techtarget.com/sDefinition/0,,sid7_gci214173,00.html (noting that TCP/IP was developed by the Defense Advanced Research Projects Agency (DARPA) to enable communication between different types of computers and computer networks).

[21] When a computer loads TCP/IP, it specifies a network number for itself, called an IP address. Every computer on the Internet has a unique IP address, of a defined numerical form, for instance, 147.9.10.7. Think of this number as being like a phone number. When someone wants to communicate with another web site, the computer needs to know the IP address of the web site. Without it, there is no communication, other than the link.

[22] Whatis.com, E-mail (definition) (visited May 16, 2002), http://searchnetworking.techtarget.com/sDefinition/0,,sid7_gci212051,00.html (noting that e-mail is a service that sends messages on computers via local or global networks).

[23] NUA Internet Surveys (visited May 16, 2002), http://www.nua.com/surveys/.

[24] *Id.* (noting that it is named the web because it is made of many sites linked together; users can travel from one site to another by clicking on hyperlinks).

[25] Chat rooms are online, real-time conversations conducted by typing messages by turns.

[26] Ian Ansdell, Don't Talk to e-Strangers, Herald (Scotland), Nov. 24, 2002, *available at* http://www.peelcom.com/os/herald/chat.htm.

[A]   Who Is Using the Internet?

It's a rainy Sunday, and you've just crossed off the last item on your "to do" list. With the afternoon looming ahead, do you grab the remote and make a bee-line for the easy chair and some channel surfing or head into the den toward the PC and some Net surfing? Chances are, the TV will come out the winner (especially if you're a sports fan). Yet according to the *UCLA Internet Report 2001*, the Internet is making inroads into America's TV-viewing time. Internet users—and more than 72 percent of Americans[27] who had Internet access in 2001—watched 4.5 hours less television each week than those who are not web surfers.[28] If an anti-social, geeky image arises in your mind, banish it. The study also found that Internet users get more exercise and spend more time with their families than do nonusers.

[1]   Charting Internet Results

The last time a new technology with the potential to change the way our society interacted, learned, shopped, and was entertained—namely, television—was introduced, not many people viewed it as an instrument that would change the very fabric of our culture. No one bothered to embark on a comprehensive study of the impact it would have on our lives and our society. Researchers at the University of California Los Angeles (UCLA) are making sure the early years of Internet use do not go unexamined. In June 8, 1999,[29] UCLA launched an in-depth exploration of how computers, information technology, and their users are shaping and changing society. "The UCLA study will provide the first long-term exploration of how life is being transformed by computers and the Internet, with year-to-year comparisons of the social and cultural changes produced as people use this extraordinary technology," said Jeffrey Cole, director of the UCLA Center for Communication Policy and principal investigator of the study.[30] Dubbed "Surveying the Digital Future,"[31] this study is also the first to analyze these broad questions about the Internet on a global scale. Funded by the National Science Foundation, AOL, Microsoft, Disney, Sony, GTE, Pacific Bell, and the National Cable Television Association, the study will survey Internet use in over 2,000 American households and, in conjunction with international partners, in Europe, Asia, Latin America, and Africa, as well. UCLA's Center for Communication Policy will conduct the U.S. survey and will coordinate the global partner projects to be directed by teams in each country.

---

[27] The UCLA Internet Report 2001—Surveying the Digital Future (visited May 16, 2002), http://www.ccp.ucla.edu/pdf/UCLA-Internet-Report-2001.pdf.

[28] A web surfer is a person who explores a sequence of web sites in a random, unplanned way to get some information.

[29] Internet Project, UCLA Center for Comm. Pol'y (visited May 30, 2002), http://www.ccp.ucla.edu/pages/internetstudy.asp.

[30] *Id.*

[31] *Id.*

[2] Surveying the Digital Future

In the U.S. study, the same 2,000 households will be surveyed each year, tracking changes in Internet use as the technology evolves and noting both direct and indirect effects of the Internet on life and society. "For example, the automobile initially made it easier to visit grandma on Sunday afternoons; before long, it contributed directly to the suburbanization of America. The Internet will have direct effects on the behavior of individuals, but will also inspire a host of other changes, many of which are unimaginable today."[32] Of special interest are those households currently unconnected, which will provide before and after scenarios once they begin using the Internet. Although the overall study was designed as a long-term project, annual reports will analyze current findings and trends. The UCLA Internet Report 2001,[33] titled *Surveying the Digital Future*, compares the responses of Internet users and nonusers, and newbies (less than one year online), experienced, and "very experienced" (five or more years) users. It also compares 2001 results with those from the previous year's report. The survey covers five major areas: who is online and who is not, media use and trust, consumer behavior, communication patterns, and social and psychological effects.

[3] So, Where Do We Stand?

Internet use is widespread and growing: 72.3 percent of Americans have access to the Internet (up from 66.9 percent in 2000), and users spend an average of 9.8 hours per week online (up from 9.4 hours).[34] On a scale of 1 (not at all satisfied) to 5 (completely satisfied), the Net rated an overall score of 4. The most satisfying feature of the Internet is users' ability to communicate with others. Teenagers in particular find the Internet an easy way to interact with friends and strangers. Users in every age group said that e-mail made it easier to keep in touch with people they don't usually speak to otherwise. In addition, the 18.8 percent of users who said that they had met someone in person whom they had originally met online averaged six new friends met in person in 2001, up slightly from 2000.[35] Of those households that are not online, most cited "no computer" or "lack of access to a computer" as the reason—and 44 percent of nonusers expect to be online within the next year.[36] Only 21.4 percent said they had no interest in using the Internet.[37]

---

[32] *Id.*

[33] The UCLA Internet Report 2001 — Surveying the Digital Future (visited May 16, 2002), http://www.ccp.ucla.edu/pdf/UCLA-Internet-Report-2001.pdf.

[34] *Id.*

[35] *Id.*

[36] *Id.*

[37] *Id.*

[4]   Money Matters

Of course, the dot-com crash cannot be ignored. Some of the issues considered in the 2001 study were: How did a backdrop of economic meltdown affect users and nonusers of the Internet? Would Internet users lose faith in online technology? Would Internet use decline? Did the collapse of the Internet boom affect online purchasing and other use?[38] Internet shopping remains strong, despite the dot-bomb turmoil. In 2001, 48.9 percent of Internet users made a purchase online.[39] Shifts away from traditional retail buying were substantially lower in 2001, with 52.8 percent saying that online purchasing has "somewhat reduced" or "reduced a lot" their purchases from retail stores.[40] Fewer Internet shoppers said they expect to eventually make many more purchases online.[41] Not surprisingly, 43.3 percent agree or strongly agree that adding sales tax for online purchases would reduce their Internet shopping. The study also noted that several trends about online buying continue to develop—especially regarding credit card security—that could have major effects on the evolution of Internet commerce. In both 2000 and 2001, users expressed deep concerns about credit card security. Nearly all new users had some worries about credit card safety when shopping online.[42] Very experienced users are somewhat more comfortable, but not much: 89.1 percent express some concern, and 57.2 percent remain very or extremely concerned.[43] The study noted that Americans have widely divergent views about credit card security when used in traditional purchasing compared to online shopping. Although restaurant patrons often think nothing of leaving a signed credit card receipt on a table in a busy café, they are nevertheless extremely concerned about online security. Without question, broad shifts in perceptions about Internet security must occur before online purchasing can truly flourish.[44]

[5]   Privacy, Please

Privacy is an issue that transcends credit card security. More than half of Internet users and close to three-quarters of nonusers agree or strongly agree with the statement that people who go online put their privacy at risk. When or if they purchase goods online, 94.5 percent of all surveyed express some concern about the privacy of their personal information.[45] Worrying about fraud and deception rank among the top reasons that users cite for putting off their first online purchase, and 10 percent of ex-users say that they stopped using the Internet entirely due to privacy concerns.[46]

---

[38] *Id.*
[39] *Id.*
[40] *Id.*
[41] *Id.*
[42] *Id.*
[43] *Id.*
[44] *Id.*
[45] *Id.*
[46] *Id.*

[6] Wired Kids

When the researchers asked adults for their opinions on their children's use of the Internet, the results were largely favorable. For example, 88.2 percent said the kids were spending the right amount of time or too little time online; 96.5 percent said that their children's grades had stayed the same or improved since using the Net; and 91.8 percent felt the children spent the same amount of time, or more time, with friends.[47] However, both users and nonusers agreed that children could gain access to inappropriate material online. In most cases, family time has not been aversely affected by Internet use. Only the "more experienced" users reported spending less time with family than before they went online. New users, very experienced users, and nonusers all reported about the same amount of time spent in family activities such as eating dinner and playing games or sports together. In fact, the only "family" activity that appears to suffer from Internet use is television viewing.[48] In 2001, 23 percent of the adults reported that their kids now watch less TV than before they began using the Internet.[49] Nonusers watch the most TV (10 hours per week). Newbies clock 9.4 hours, and very experienced users watch only 6.7 hours of TV per week.[50]

[B] E-Mail and Online Service Providers

It is estimated that electronic mail (e-mail) messages outnumber regular mail by ten to one. E-mail is a form of text communication that allows people to send and receive messages from almost anywhere in the world. Generally speaking, a user with access to a telephone line and an e-mail account with an ISP can access e-mail messages at any time and from any place. E-mail has become more widely used than fax machines because it is relatively inexpensive (not requiring an additional, dedicated piece of machinery, the fax machine), and it is an efficient medium that can be employed throughout an organization. E-mail messages also have the advantage of enabling an individual to send text messages instantly and simultaneously to multiple recipients.

E-mail systems range from those that carry only simple text messages to other, more complex systems that allow users to incorporate typed memos, spreadsheets, photographs, and video clips in their messages. Senders can also "carbon copy" or "blind carbon copy" multiple recipients. This flexible functionality provides users with an audit trail that can be followed, should the need arise. E-mail messages create electronic records that can be traced to assist the sender or to provide a smoking gun in lawsuits.[51] E-mail smoking guns were star witnesses in the government's antitrust case against Microsoft, and they are frequently invaluable

---

[47] *Id.*

[48] *Id.*

[49] *Id.*

[50] *Id.*

[51] See Chapter Ten for a detailed discussion of e-mail messages and smoking guns.

in bolstering a client's position in a lawsuit.[52] E-mail messages are delivered using an address scheme specific to computer networks. Sending an e-mail to Cyrus Daftary at Suffolk University, for example, would require the sender to type *cdaftary@acad.suffolk.edu* in the address line. This e-mail address can be broken down into its components, much as the address on the envelope of a letter indicates both local and regional points. *Cdaftary* identifies the specific user, Cyrus Daftary. The @ symbol[53] connects the e-mail recipient's username to the computer network of which the user is a member. The *acad.suffolk.edu* indicates that Cyrus is affiliated with Suffolk University; the *.edu* suffix identifies the organization as being an academic institution.

Likewise, the e-mail address for Michael Rustad, *ProfRustad@aol.com*, can be broken down as follows: *ProfRustad* is the naming convention used to indicate Professor Rustad; *aol* indicates that Michael Rustad is a member of AOL; *.com* shows that AOL is a commercial institution. The primary endings of e-mail addresses in the United States include *.com, .edu, .mil, .net, .org, .gov, .biz, .pro, .aero, .museum, .coop, .info,* and *.name.*

After an e-mail message is sent, it is broken into packets of data and routed through a network of computers until it arrives at its final destination, where all the packets come together and are reassembled. Despite the many wonderful things that can be said about e-mail, it is vulnerable at two points. Messages are sometimes lost, and hackers may compromise the message or network security.

For lawyers exchanging confidential or sensitive information with clients, the risk of interception raises particular concern. One way companies and lawyers can protect against having their e-mail intercepted is by using encryption[54] software, or a system of codes. Encryption and encoding scrambles the contents of a message so that only a recipient that has the keys can decipher the message needed to unscramble the message. Many governments, including the United States, place limits on the use of encryption, particularly restricting the import and use of cryptographic products.[55]

Many people have access to e-mail either through their employers or through affiliations with organizations that provide members with free e-mail accounts. Many employers, however, restrict how their employees may use e-mail. Consequently, for personal use, most Americans look to third-party Online Service Providers (OSPs) to obtain e-mail and other online services. OSPs provide an infrastructure in which subscribers can communicate with each other, by e-mail

---

[52] *See* America Online, Inc. v. IMS, 24 F. Supp. 2d 548 (E.D. Va. 1998).

[53] For the origin of its use in this context, see The @ Sign: Icon for the Digital Age (visited May 16, 2002), http://www.bbn.com/@sign/index.html.

[54] Whatis.com, Encryption (definition) (visited May 16, 2002), http://searchsecurity.techtarget.com/sDefinition/0,,sid14_gci212062,00.html (noting that encryption is the translation of data into a secret code and the most effective way to achieve data security. To read an encrypted file, one must have access to a secret key or password that enables decryption. Unencrypted information is called plain text; encrypted data are referred to as cipher text.).

[55] Crypto Law Survey (visited May 16, 2002), http://rechten.kub.nl/koops/cryptolaw/.

messages or through online conferences, forums, or chat rooms. In addition, most OSPs offer proprietary content, developed either in-house or through licensing arrangements, and can connect users with an unlimited number of outside information and service providers through the Internet.

Subscribers can receive up-to-date stock quotes, news stories, articles from magazines and journals, and any other information available in electronic format. Accessing all this information carries a price, of course, but it is a price that many subscribers pay happily. Collectively, the three largest online services, America Online (AOL), CompuServe, and Microsoft Network (MSN), provide approximately 300 million people with access to the Internet.[56]

The landscape of commercial online services changes almost daily, so comparison shopping is important. Companies are constantly merging or buying each other out. America Online purchased CompuServe, one of its main competitors, in 1998,[57] and in early 2000, in a move of historic proportions, "little" America Online purchased the publishing powerhouse Time Warner.[58]

[C] Electronic Bulletin Boards

Computer bulletin boards (BBS)[59] and Internet newsgroups provide sites on which anyone may post text, photographs, software, and videos to share with the larger Internet community. Most bulletin boards are a part of a system called USENET,[60] a global system that hosts more than 30,000 newsgroups. Bulletin boards function similarly to e-mail, but whereas an e-mail message is private, intended for a specific individual or group of individuals, a bulletin board posting is intended to reach a larger, nonspecific audience. Newsgroups broadcast and publish messages and related responses for any and all members of the newsgroup to read.

Many observers of the Internet have said that the collective knowledge of humankind is posted and transmitted each day on USENET. Each day, over 25 million users participate in USENET's public newsgroups to share ideas, trade advice, and conduct research.[61] Each individual USENET discussion is called a newsgroup, and individual postings are called articles. Newsgroups vary in the

---

[56] AOL and CompuServe have respectively 34 million and 3 million members. AOL (visited May 16, 2002), http://corp.aol.com/whoweare.html. MSN claims to serve 270 million unique users worldwide. Microsoft Network (visited May 16, 2002), http://advantage.msn.com/home/audienceprofile.asp.

[57] CompuServe (visited May 16, 2002), www.compuserv.com/corporate/cs-info.html.

[58] AOL Time Warner (visited May 16, 2002), http://media.aoltimewarner.com/media/testpress_view.cfm?release_num=50251353.

[59] BBS is shorthand for a dial-in computer service that is used for exchanging e-mail, reading notices, and other services.

[60] Newsgroup A to Z: A Primer on the Still Useful USENET, USA Today, Mar. 13, 2001 (noting that USENET is a worldwide bulletin board system that can be accessed through the Internet or through many online services. USENET contains more than 36,000 forums, called newsgroups, covering every imaginable interest. USENETs are accessed daily by millions of people around the world.).

[61] USENET (visited May 16, 2002), http://www.usenet-server.com/faqs.htm.

subjects they treat, which can range from world hunger to e-commerce to a popular culture movie phenomenon like *Star Wars*. Anyone can create a newsgroup or participate in a newsgroup. In today's rapidly changing world, newsgroups on the hot topic of the day can quickly flower, flourish, and then die as people gain and lose interest in it and no more messages are posted. Since many web sites have created their own discussion areas, many people within the United States have stopped using USENETs, but overseas USENETs are still popular.[62]

[D] Mailing Lists

Mailing lists function similarly to newsgroups, but they require membership. In essence, a mailing list is an automated e-mail notification service that brings together, via e-mail, groups of people who share a common interest.[63] Lists require individuals to send an e-mail note to the list manager asking to "subscribe."[64] Once a user has successfully subscribed, the subscriber, like other members of the list, will automatically receive whatever e-mail messages are posted to the list. The recipients of these e-mails may, in turn, respond with a message to the entire group or by private e-mail to the original sender.

To avoid disruptive or unrelated messages, some lists may have moderators who filter out inappropriate messages. Those lists that do not have moderators will have no way to filter out unwanted messages. Consequently, a member of the list may post inappropriate commercial solicitations, or spam.[65] If this occurs frequently, subscribers who find this unacceptable may withdraw from the list; members have the option of suspending (for vacations and so on) or canceling their subscriptions at any point.

[E] Private Systems

A server or file server is a "computer in a network that stores application programs and data files accessed by the other computers in the network."[66] Private

---

[62] Newsgroup A to Z, *supra* note 60.

[63] Mailing lists are sometimes referred to as "listservs," but LISTSERV is a registered trademark of L-Soft International, Inc., which distributes software for managing mailing lists. LISTSERV (visited May 16, 2002), http://www.lsoft.com/manuals/1.8d/user/user.html.

[64] To subscribe to the CYBERIA-L listserv on the law and policy of computer networks, for example, interested parties must subscribe by sending an e-mail to listserve@eagle.birds.wm.edu.

[65] Spam is an unsolicited posting, usually off the topic, sent to many newsgroups or lists simultaneously. Spam e-mail ranges from online advertisements proclaiming ways users can get rich fast to political messages or commentaries to pleas for help in finding missing children. One court has defined spam as "unauthorized bulk e-mail advertisements." FTC (visited May 16, 2002), http://www.ftc.gov/bcp/conline/pubs/online/inbox.htm.

[66] Whatis.com, File Server (definition) (visited May 16, 2002), http://searchnetworking.techtarget.com/sDefinition/0,,sid7_gci212964,00.html (noting that a file server is a computer in a client/server architecture that supplies files or services. The computer that requests services is called the client. The client may request file transfer, remote logins, printing, or other available services.).

systems consist of local (LANs) or wide area networks (WANs), client server applications, UNIX[67] machines, and intranets.[68] Each of these systems is a series of personal computers connected to each other through a common server[69] linked by fiber optic cable or connected by the Internet.

Private networks can be used to create what is called an *intranet*, not to be confused with the Internet. The purpose of an intranet is to increase communication in a business or corporate environment, to coordinate projects and tasks, and to coordinate schedules—all using the same interface or "look." An intranet consists of all HTTP nodes on a private network, such as a LAN,[70] which may or may not be connected to the Internet. An intranet connects clients using standard protocols such as TCP/IP[71] or HTTP.[72] An intranet can deliver such services as an institutional directory, e-mail, filing, printing, and network management to those connected to it. Intranet software also includes application and development tools and utilities; databases; e-commerce; and distribution capabilities, messaging, and groupware software. Using any or all of these tools raises security concerns, just as with e-mail. Institutions utilizing an intranet generally invest in a separate software application to provide the requisite security.[73] Standard protocols make it possible to bridge the gaps between browsers with different configurations.

Extended intranets, or extranets,[74] function in the same manner as intranets, but they allow access through the Internet to people outside the enterprise, such as

---

[67] Whatis.com UNIX (definition) (visited May 16, 2002), http://searchsolaris.techtarget.com/sDefinition/0,,sid12_gci213253,00.html (noting that UNIX is an operating system developed by Bell Telephone Laboratories. UNIX was developed originally as a portable program development environment that could be ported to many different computers so that Bell engineers designing telephone switching systems could move easily among machines made by IBM, Digital, Hewlett Packard, or any other manufacturer without needing retraining.).

[68] Whatis.com, Intranet (definition) (visited May 16, 2002), http://searchwebmanagement.techtarget.com/sDefinition/0,,sid27_gci212377,00.html (noting that an intranet is a network of computers accessible only by individuals within a particular enterprise via a local area network.).

[69] Whatis.com, Server (definition) (visited May 16, 2002), http://searchnetworking.techtarget.com/sDefinition/0,,sid7_gci212964,00.html (noting that a server is a computer, attached to the Internet, capable of offering one or more Internet services).

[70] Intranet Design Magazine, Intranet FAQ: Intranet Basics (visited May 16, 2002), http://www.intranetjournal.com/faqs/whatis/.

[71] Indiana University Knowledge Base, What Does TCP/IP Mean? (visited May 16, 2002), http://kb.indiana.edu/data/abkr.html?cust=12632 (noting that TCP/IP is an abbreviation for Transmission Control Protocol/Internet Protocol, which permits computers to communicate on a network. "TCP/IP was developed by the Department of Defense for the Defense Data Network and has since been widely adopted as a networking standard.").

[72] Whatis.com, HTTP (definition) (visited May 16, 2002), http://searchsystemsmanagement.techtarget.com/sDefinition/0,,sid20_gci214004,00.html (noting that HTTP stands for Hypertext Transfer Protocol. When the abbreviation appears as part of an Internet address or URL, that is the Internet protocol being used. Hypertext is a "standard web formatting language.").

[73] One of the leading intranet security application companies is Guardeonic Solutions, a Siemens company. Guardeonic Solutions (visited May 16, 2002), http://195.30.241.193/index_cross.php?go=consultancy. Other leading intranet software companies are Applix, Inc., INTERSHOP, Netegrity, Open Text, and Wallop.

[74] Extranets are based on TCP/IP network and on Internet standard protocols and services.

customers or suppliers.[75] An extranet is essentially a "web-based analog of LAN and WAN."[76] Industry-specific extranets have been designed for the automobile industry, health care, financial services, telecommunications, and other industries. A corporate web connecting trading partners is known as a business-to-business web or extranet.[77] Because of relatively low maintenance costs, it is not unusual to find corporations that maintain intranets, extranets, and a public Internet web site.

Traditionally, company computer networks at different locations have been connected by dedicated lines or switched dial-up lines. A dedicated line, sometimes called a leased line,[78] is a "telecommunications path between two points available twenty-four hours a day for use by a designated user." A dedicated line is a nonswitched line, as opposed to a switched dial-up line, used by many users. A company may lease lines from a carrier or use public switched lines with secure message protocols.

A virtual private network (VPN) is an innovation that allows secure exchange of information among multiple locations via the Internet, rather than through more costly dedicated lines or switched dial-up lines. VPNs are usually supported and maintained by ISPs to enable secure Internet-based access to computer networks. VPNs permit organizations to use the Internet as a "private enterprise backbone infrastructure to provide secure access to telecommuting employees, business partners and customers."[79] At a minimum, a VPN must have the following features: authentication, data encryption, user access control, and event logging. Data may be transmitted from a telecommuting employee's PC to a firewall, where the data are encrypted and transmitted through the company's access line to the company's ISP. The information is then "tunneled"[80] through the Internet to arrive at the receiver's firewall, where it is decrypted. A remote receiver can then dial into the VPN and gain access to the decrypted data via a remote server. VPNs are a cost-effective and secure way of delivering business information using the Internet.

---

[75] Commerce One (visited May 16, 2002), http://www.commerceone.com. Commerce One works with many companies to set up extranets. General Motors and Commerce One are working on a proposed product, to be proprietary to GM and intended as a marketplace for GM suppliers to which those wanting to enter must enroll as members.

[76] Intranet Design Magazine, Intranet FAQ: What Is an Extranet? (visited May 16, 2002), http://idm.internet.com/faqs/whatis/10.html.

[77] Intranet Design Magazine, Intranet FAQ (visited May 16, 2002), http://idm.internet.com/faqs/whatis/2.html.

[78] Whatis.com, A Leased Line (definition) (visited May 16, 2002), http://searchnetworking.techtarget.com/sDefinition/0,,sid7_gci212470,00.html (noting that a leased line is a telephone line that has been leased for private use. Typically, large companies rent leased lines from the telephone message carriers (such as AT&T) to interconnect different geographic locations in their companies. The alternative for these companies is to buy and maintain their own private lines.).

[79] Tim Armstrong, How Virtual Private Networks (VPNs) Save Money and Improve Security, Electronic Security University (visited May 16, 2002), http://www.v-one.com/.

[80] Whatis.com, Tunnel (definition) (visited May 16, 2002), http://searchsecurity.techtarget.com/sDefinition/0,,sid14_gci213230,00.html (noting that the term "tunnel" refers to encapsulating and encrypting of information through Internet Protocol packets).

[F]   Computer Networks/Protocols

[1]   DNS

When a computer loads TCP/IP, it specifies a network number for itself, called an IP address. Every computer on the Internet has a unique IP address of a defined numerical form of four groups of three digit numbers, with each group of three digit numbers ranging from 0 to 255, for instance, 147.9.10.7. The IP address of a computer may change with every connection made to the Internet. Think of this number as being like a phone number. When a user wants to communicate with a particular web site, that computer needs to know the IP address of that particular web site. Without it, there is no communication, just as you can't talk to your friend in California without knowing that person's phone number.

It would be pretty miserable if everyone had to memorize numbers for every web site visited. That's why the Domain Name System (DNS) was created.[81] DNS translates an IP address like 207.25.71.5 into an alphanumeric domain name that is easier to remember, in this case, *www.cnn.com*. The Domain Name registry and distribution is handled by InterNIC.[82]

[2]   Telnet

Telnet[83] provides a means to access and obtain data from another computer. Telnet makes it possible for users to log into a remote computer and use programs and data made available by the remote owner. Telnet is a "user command and an underlying TCP/IP protocol"[84] permitting the user to log into mainframes,[85] midrange systems, or UNIX servers.

Telnet, although still used by many educational institutions and universities, is no longer widely used by corporations. Many library catalogs are available only by Telnet, although libraries are gradually converting to web-based catalogs. Through Telnet, researchers at another university can connect to the Suffolk University e-mail server (Pine) or to the Suffolk University Law School Library Online Catalog, for example. An example of a Telnet command request is *telnet the.libraryat.Suffolk.edu*. These Telnet sites permit a remote user to request data from anywhere in the world, assuming the user has a password or user ID.

---

[81] Whatis.com, DNS (definition) (visited May 16, 2002), http://searchwebmanagement.techtarget.com/sDefinition/0,,sid27_gci213908,00.html (noting that DNS is a database system that translates an IP address into a domain name).

[82] *See* § 2.06[B] for a complete discussion of the Domain Name System.

[83] A terminal emulation protocol that lets a user log in remotely to other computers on the Internet; it has a command line interface.

[84] Whatis.com, Telnet (definition) (visited May 16, 2002), http://searchnetworking.techtarget.com/sDefinition/0,,sid7_gci213116,00.html.

[85] Mainframes are very large computers that can perform a huge number of instructions per second, servicing a large user group so quickly that all appear to be receiving service simultaneously.

[3]   HTTP

Hypertext Transfer Protocol (HTTP) is a protocol that that determines how computers will communicate over the Internet; in fact, it is the protocol most often used to transfer information, such as web pages and documents, from World Wide Web servers to browsers, which is why web addresses begin with *http://*.[86] It lays down the rules for how a computer and the computer on the other end of the transfer will exchange text, graphics, sound, video, and other multimedia elements. Whenever *http:* is typed as part of the URL in the address field of the web browser window, the web browser and the server from where the information is retrieved adhere to HTTP rules.

[4]   FTP

Transferring files and sharing data are the heart and soul of the Internet. The types of files that can be transferred include documentation, graphics, software, sound, and video. These files can contain megabytes of information.[87] One method of receiving such files is to use a program called File Transfer Protocol (FTP).

FTP is an Internet protocol that permits users to transfer files between two systems.[88] FTP provides a medium through which two computers can retrieve copies of files and place new files online as needed. When using FTP software to log into a specific site, users are prompted for and must enter a username and a password to gain access. Some sites will allow users to identify themselves as "anonymous."

[5]   POP3

This is the most recent version of the Post Office Protocol,[89] which governs the storage of e-mail messages on a mail server. POP3 is a client/server[90] protocol in which e-mail is received and held for a recipient by the Internet server. Periodically, client e-mail receivers check the mailbox on the server and download any mail. POP3 is built into the Netscape and Microsoft Internet Explorer browsers. POP3 complements SMTP (Simple Mail Transfer Protocol),[91] which governs the

---

[86] Whatis.com, HTTP (definition) (visited May 16, 2002), http://searchsystemsmanagement. techtarget.com/sDefinition/0,,sid20_gci214004,00.html.

[87] A megabyte is 1,048,576 bytes of data, the rough equivalent of 1,000,000 characters, or the text on 33,000 typewritten pages. Data transfer rates are often described in megabytes per second, or Mbps.

[88] Whatis.com, FTP (definition) (visited May 16, 2002), http://searchnetworking.techtarget. com/sDefinition/0,,sid7_gci213976,00.html (noting that FTP stands for File Transfer Protocol. FTP is a set of standard codes for transferring files over the Internet. FTP is usually used for retrieving large files or files that cannot be displayed through a browser.).

[89] Whatis.com, Protocol (definition) (visited May 16, 2002), http://searchnetworking.techtarget. com/sDefinition/0,,sid7_gci212839,00.html (noting that a protocol is a set of rules by which a client machine can retrieve mail from a mail server).

[90] Client/server describes the relationship between two computer programs in which one program, the client, makes a service request from another program, the server, which fulfills the request.

[91] A server-to-server protocol for delivering electronic mail.

transmission of electronic messages across the Internet. However, since SMTP is limited in its ability to queue messages at the receiving end, it's usually used with one of two other protocols, POP3 or Internet Message Access Protocol,[92] that let the user save messages in a server mailbox and download them periodically from the server.

[6] PPP

Point-to-Point Protocol (PPP)[93] is a protocol for communication between two computers using a serial interface, typically a personal computer connected by phone line to a server. For example, the ISP may provide a PPP connection so that the provider's server can respond to the client's computer requests, pass them on to the Internet, and forward the requested Internet responses back to the client's computer.

[7] SSL

The Secure Socket Layer (SSL)[94] is a popular online encryption protocol that protects web data during transmission. The SSL is a commonly used protocol for managing the security of message transmission on the Internet. SSL has recently been succeeded by Transport Layer Security (TLS),[95] which is based on SSL. SSL uses a program layer located between the Internet's HTTP and Transport Control Protocol (TCP) layers. SSL is included as part of both the Microsoft and Netscape browsers and most web server products. Developed by Netscape, SSL also gained the support of Microsoft and other Internet client/server developers as well and became the de facto standard until evolving into TLS. The "sockets" part of the term refers to the sockets method of passing data back and forth between a client and a server program in a network or between program layers in the same computer. SSL uses the public-and-private key encryption system from RSA,[96] which also includes the use of a digital certificate.[97]

---

[92] A protocol that allows a user to perform certain electronic mail functions on a remote server rather than on a local computer. Through IMAP the user can create, delete, or rename mailboxes; get new messages; delete messages; and perform search functions on mail.

[93] A protocol for communication between computers using TCP/IP, over standard telephone lines, ISDN, and other high-speed connections.

[94] Whatis.com, SSL (definition) (visited May 16, 2002), http://searchsecurity.techtarget.com/sDefinition/0,,sid14_gci343029,00.html (noting that SSL is a protocol from Netscape Communications Corporation, which is designed to provide secure communications on the Internet.).

[95] Whatis.com, TLS (definition) (visited May 16, 2002), http://searchsecurity.techtarget.com/sDefinition/0,,sid14_gci557332,00.html (noting that TLS is a protocol that ensures privacy between communicating applications and their users on the Internet.).

[96] Whatis.com, RSA (definition) (visited May 16, 2002), http://searchsecurity.techtarget.com/sDefinition/0,,sid14_gci214273,00.html (noting that RSA is an Internet encryption and authentication system that uses an algorithm developed in 1977 by Ron Rivest, Adi Shamir, and Leonard Adelman). Encryption is the conversion of data into a form that cannot be easily understood by unauthorized people.

[97] A digital certificate is an electronic "credit card" that establishes your credentials when doing business or other transactions on the web.

By convention, URLs that require an SSL connection start with *https:* instead of *http*. Almost all web-based online purchases and monetary transactions, including online bank transactions and other credit card transactions, are now secured by SSL.

[G] Publishing and Research

The ease of creating a web site has allowed a large number of people to publish information cheaply and easily. An Internet web page can be built using free applications, such as Hotdog,[98] Notepad, or WordPad, or by using a sophisticated web-publishing tool, such as Microsoft's Front Page. These publishing tools convert information into HTML, the universal language understood by computers connected to the Internet. Most of the information that constitutes the World Wide Web exists as HTML files. HTML is a formatting language that defines the presentation of the information. HTML allows web developers to position images and text so that they appear in specific locations in the viewing field. HTML also supports popular online programming languages such as Sun Microsystem Java[99] and Microsoft .NET platforms.

The mere ability to publish information is no guarantee of the ability to do it well. Before a company sets up a web site, it should establish goals for the site and minimize its risks of liability. In the corporate world, the various corporate stakeholders, including marketing, sales, management information systems (MIS), finance, tax, and legal departments need to determine and agree on the goals for the web site.

The content of a web page or pages can be designed either in-house or off-site. In either case, it has been observed that there is an abundance of poor quality web page design on the Internet, and finding good quality designers is not always easy. To build an effective corporate web site, a design team familiar with corporate goals, led by a sophisticated webmaster or designer, is crucial. The Internet itself constitutes a valuable source of ideas for content design and provider resources. The Sun Microsystems web site,[100] for example, provides many relevant guides and links.

The cost of setting up a web site depends on the level of complexity desired for the site. A novice using an off-the-shelf HTML design software package such as Net Fusion or Microsoft Front Page can design a "passive" page that simply provides information. A sophisticated linked set of pages that includes online shopping, security functions, and interactive multimedia, such as streaming video, will require an experienced web site designer.

Although complex graphics and multimedia files work well on some sites, they can detract from the chief goal of most business web sites: disseminating the

---

[98] Sausage (visited May 16, 2002), http://www.sausage.com.

[99] Whatis.com, Java (definition) (visited May 16, 2002), http://searchsolaris.techtarget.com/s Definition/0,,sid12_gci212415,00.html (noting that Java is a cross-platform programming language from Sun Microsystems that can be used to create animations and interactive features on World Wide Web pages. Java programs are embedded into HTML documents.).

[100] Sun Microsystems (visited May 16, 2002), http://www.sun.com.

company's message quickly to site visitors. Many users will not wait for memory-heavy graphics to load, especially if they are accessing the Internet at low speeds over telephone lines; they will simply leave the site in frustration.

Like other forms of publishing, information publishing on the web can create liability. Before publication, an attorney knowledgeable about an Internet business should review the costs and benefits of being online and its associated content. An intellectual property attorney can examine the proposed web site and give advice on whether linking, framing,[101] metatags,[102] or references to a competitor's trademarks are advisable. The attorney can offer guidance on a variety of other issues, including the most beneficial corporate structure of the web business, its tax implications, and any corporate liabilities that may stem from ineffective or absent postings on privacy policies, disclaimers, and other web-related agreements.

[H]   Electronic Commerce

The Internet offers today's businesses a global marketplace that operates 24 hours a day, 365 days a year. An organization can now modify every aspect of its business operations to harness the potential of the Internet. Companies can now, for example, (1) enable their customers to price, submit orders, and monitor the distribution and processing of their orders online; (2) respond to customer inquiries; (3) increase professional staff efficiency; (4) recruit new professionals online; (5) reduce operating costs; (6) expand sales opportunities and clientele; and (7) connect various business operations together in real time meetings. By utilizing the full potential of the Internet, customers, suppliers, employees, and business partners can collaborate in ways that allow them to be more productive, to adapt rapidly to change, and to make more effective business decisions. With these capabilities, the Internet has penetrated all parts of the globe, making it possible to reach customers and achieve efficiencies that were unimaginable just a few years ago.

Coined by Lawrence Livermore in 1989, the phrase "electronic commerce," or e-commerce as it has come to be called, refers to the electronic network of commercial transactions that bring the entire supply chain (suppliers, customers, and vendors) online through an electronic infrastructure.[103] More specifically, e-commerce is the use of computer networks—the Internet, intranets, extranets, and private networks—to engage in business transactions.

Great opportunities abound for both small and large businesses that are able to gain worldwide access to millions of consumers by effective use of the Internet.

---

[101] The practice of displaying content from another site while still maintaining advertisements from the original site.

[102] Metatags are HTML tags, which provide information that describes the content of the web pages a user will be viewing.

[103] David Johnston et al., CyberLaw: What You Need to Know About Doing Business Online 37 (1997) (defining *e-commerce* as "the consolidation of technology, material, people, and processes on an electronic network for commercial transactions").

E-commerce is attractive to companies because of its relatively low operational costs, its convenience, its potential for customization, and the astounding access it provides to a global marketplace never before realizable on this scale. Moreover, e-commerce now enables a corporation to advertise, sell products, and even exchange goods with a larger client base while maintaining lower operational costs than is possible using traditional methods. For consumers, e-commerce enables them to shop for a variety of products and services from their own homes and offices using their credit cards.

E-commerce transactions can be broken down into segments: business-to-consumer (B2C), business-to-business (B2B), business-to-government (B2G), and peer-to-peer (P2P). Business-to-consumer refers to using the Internet to sell products or services to consumers just as through a retail store, direct sales, or catalog or phone ordering. One of the primary goals of B2B is to provide a more efficient distribution model. The most successful e-commerce businesses include Cisco Systems, Dell Computers, eBay.com, and Amazon.com, which respectively report *daily* sales in the millions of dollars.

Cisco Systems reported net sales of $4.82 billion for the third quarter of fiscal 2002.[104] Cisco has a multifaceted business model and is expanding into the service provider marketplace as well as the optical market, the enterprise market, and small and medium-sized business markets. Cisco's Internet products are for data, voice, and video communications. Its horizontal business model is built upon "internal development, acquisitions and partnerships."

Dell Computer Corporation has become the "world's largest direct computer systems company with revenues of $31.168 billion for the fiscal year ending February 01, 2002."[105] Dell's direct business model delivers custom-built computer systems, eliminating the network of wholesalers, retailers, and distributors interposed elsewhere between the computer customer and seller. Dell expanded its Internet business by creating an online store for 30,000 competitively priced products. Its use of direct customer service is coupled with customer paperless purchase orders, approved product configurations, global price, real-time order tracking, purchasing history, and account team information.

Founded in 1995, eBay created a powerful platform for the sale of goods and services by a passionate community of individuals and businesses. On any given day, there are millions of items across thousands of categories for sale on eBay. eBay enables trade on a local, national, and international basis with customized sites in markets around the world. It has a total of 42 million registered users. Net revenues for 2001 are a record $245.1 million, a 59 percent increase over the $154.1 million generated in the same period the previous year. eBay users transacted a record $2.735 billion in gross merchandise sales during the fourth quarter of 2001, representing a 69 percent year-over-year increase from the $1.616 billion reported in the fourth quarter of the year 2000.[106]

---

[104] Cisco (visited May 16, 2002), http://newsroom.cisco.com/dlls/fin_050702.html.

[105] Dell Computer Corporation, Form 10-K, Annual Report for the Fiscal Year Ended Feb. 2, 2002 (visited May 16, 2002), http://www.dell.com/downloads/us/corporate/sec/10k-01.htm.

[106] eBay (visited May 16, 2002), http://www.shareholder.com/ebay/annual.cfm.

Amazon.com opened its web site in July 1995 and has since sold products to millions of online shoppers in more than 220 countries.[107] It does $3 billion in sales yearly. Amazon's net sales for the quarter ended March 31, 2002, were $847 million, compared with $700 million in the first quarter of 2001, an increase of 21 percent. The company recorded a first quarter 2002 operating profit of $2 million, compared with a loss of $217 million a year ago.

These four companies have in common one highly successful sales strategy, which allowed three of them to vault to the top of the Fortune 500 rankings in a very short time by cutting out the middleman. Each of these companies has offered its products and services to the global marketplace. By doing so, these companies have achieved several objectives:

- Create an immediate connection with the customer.

- Offer every visitor a relatively unlimited selection of products, without being constrained by floor space, store hours, or advertising costs.

- Create targeted marketing efforts that entice visitors to buy products and services that they may not have been looking for.

- Implement a detailed transaction record allowing increased ease in post-sale dialogue with the customer.

- Reduce inventory.

Although Cisco, Dell, eBay.com, and Amazon.com are regarded as some of the most successful e-commerce businesses, many other corporations have experienced phenomenal revenue growth through effective use of business-to-consumer e-commerce. The Disney Store, for example, currently sells as much merchandise online as it sells in eight of its traditional stores combined.

Business-to-business e-commerce integrates the use of private networks and the Internet to automate business transactions between companies. B2B can be subdivided into electronic data interchange (EDI),[108] "buy side" procurement,[109] and "sell-side" catalog-based sites.[110] Companies that opt to engage in business-

---

[107] Amazon.com (visited May 16, 2002), http://www.corporate-ir.net/ireye/ir_site.zhtml?ticker=AMZN&script=1801&layout=8.

[108] EDI is the electronic transmission of documents from one company to another using a set of standard forms, messages, and data elements. Following is a partial list of EDI service providers: GEIS, IBM Global Services, Sterling Commerce, Harbinger, TranSettlements, AT&T, MCI, Railnc, EC Company, and Sprint.

[109] Buy-side procurement involves linking all the individuals or organizations involved in the procurement process. Each entity plays a distinct role, for example, requesting or approving the expenditure, negotiating the purchase, processing the payment, or keeping financial records. Buy-side procurement companies include Ariba, Commerce One, Fisher, and Harbinger.

[110] Sell-side sites accomplish the steps needed to track and record the various elements of a transaction's life cycle. These elements include product description and pricing, tracking inventory, processing and filling orders, and financial reporting.

to-business e-commerce agree to enter into a contractual relationship to do business either by extending a line of credit or by implementing a purchase order process.

Inherent in these business activities is the need to provide a secure and reliable mechanism so that buyers and sellers can confidently undertake these transactions and safely transfer funds. Requirements include a secure payment gateway for processing the transaction and transferring funds, a back office system for tracking core business components, and a storefront system.

The success of business-to-consumer e-commerce and of business-to-business e-commerce has had a profound effect on the American workforce. Recent reports indicate that 14 million people are working from home full-time, and another 13 million part-time. This number is increasing by almost 600,000 per year.[111]

§ 1.05   ACCESSING AND USING THE INTERNET

Individuals and corporations can access the Internet in a number of ways. To determine the best option for accessing the Internet in a particular situation, one must consider such things as the purpose for being on the Internet, the potential number of users, the types of sites to be visited and transactions to be made, and the required response time needed. Access to the Internet requires access to a computer with a web browser, a modem, or some similar connection and a subscription with an ISP.

[A]   Internet Service Providers (ISPs)

ISPs[112] offer Internet access to businesses and consumers. Small office and residential consumers typically connect to the Internet via a 56 Kbps modem, which carries data over analog (telephone) lines or Integrated Services Digital Network (ISDN) lines. In the event that users or small businesses need higher speed access to the Internet, Asymmetric Digital Subscriber Lines (ADSL) or cable modems serve as faster options and can provide an uninterrupted Internet connection. Large enterprises link to ISPs through dedicated connections on larger pipelines.

Regardless of which access option an enterprise or consumer chooses, ISPs generally assess a monthly fee. This fee varies depending on the size of the connection needed, for example, whether the user is a corporation purchasing access for conducting its private enterprise or an individual using the service for personal

---

[111] HomeEmployed.com (visited May 16, 2002), http://www.homeemployed.com.

[112] Whatis.com, ISP (definition) (visited May 16, 2002), http://searchwebmanagement. techtarget.com/sDefinition/0,,sid27_gci214028,00.html (noting that the term "ISP" stands for Internet Service Provider. An ISP is a company that provides individuals and other companies access to the Internet and other related services such as web site building and hosting solutions.).

home access. Fees for personal use (by individual(s) for nonwork-related purposes) usually fall between $9.99 and $19.99. Fees for analog service (accessing/connecting to the Internet with a standard telephone line connection) can be as much as $32 per month, with fees for cable lines and DSL approaching $50 monthly. In general, costs depend on the service, access, and technical support desired. Some plans do not allow unlimited Internet access, imposing a time limit on use per pay period. Notwithstanding the hardware costs, the perception that the Internet is essentially free is a misperception. The minimum cost is the monthly ISP access fee.

[B] Internet Connections

[1] Modem Access

The least expensive method of connecting a user to the Internet is via modem,[113] a connection between a computer and an ISP via an analog telephone line. Over the past several years, modem speeds have improved, enabling users to transfer data at a faster rate. Today, most computers connect to the Internet with a 56 Kbps modem. Modems capable of 56 Kbps transmission range in cost from $40 to $150. Once a user has a computer and a modem, no additional hardware is necessary to connect to the Internet. In recent years, computers have been designed with built-in modems.

[2] ISDN

The clamor for faster connections brought about the introduction of ISDN (Integrated Services Digital Network).[114] ISDN delivers high-speed data and voice over a single telephone line. At 128 Kbps, ISDN lines are considerably faster than modem connections. An ISDN connection differs from a modem connection in that it can transfer data in its original digital format end-to-end, whereas a modem connection requires converting data from a digital to an analog signal for transmission over telephone lines. Because ISDN requires no such conversion, data can

---

[113] Whatis.com, Modem (definition) (visited May 16, 2002), http://searchsystemsmanagement. techtarget.com/sDefinition/0,,sid20_gci212583,00.html (noting that a modem (aka a modulator/ demodulator) is a simple analog data communications device for transmitting data over a POTS (Plain Old Telephone Service) line. Digital signals are converted to analog signals and vice versa.).

[114] Whatis.com, ISDN (definition) (visited May 16, 2002), http://searchwebmanagement. techtarget.com/sDefinition/0,,sid27_gci212399,00.html (noting that the term "ISDN" stands for Integrated Services Digital Network. ISDNs are digital telecommunications lines that can transmit both voice and digital network services up to 128 Kbps.).

be transmitted and received four times faster than using a modem. Unfortunately, the same factors that limit modem connections ("line noise") affect ISDN subscribers in the same way. One additional problem arose when ISPs failed to make ISDN connections readily available. Today, ISDN is a very expensive ancestor of the newer technologies being offered.

[3] Cable Modems

The real limit faced by modems has always been the fact that digital information had to be converted into analog signals for transmission and then converted back to digital for use by the computer. Cable modems make this a moot issue since there is no conversion of signal required and the information is transferred digitally. In the last year or so, cable companies have moved into the Internet service field by offering cable modems. Using the same wiring that provides viewers with ESPN, MTV, and CNN, cable companies also allow the computer to connect to the Internet. The computer needs a cable modem (similar to a Network Interface Card) that connects to the coaxial cable line running all the way back to the local cable company office. Unlike standard modems, cable modems are always on and connected (just like the TV).

In early 2002 there were 7.2 million cable modem subscribers in the United States, according to data released by the National Cable & Telecommunications Association (NCTA).[115] The cost of cable is already down to about $50 for installation and $50 per month, and even cheaper in some areas, making cable an attractive option for the average Internet consumer.

[4] DSL

DSL[116] is a technology that enables high-speed transmission of digital data over regular copper telephone lines. DSL technology opens up the phone line for fast transmission of data. A special DSL modem is needed, and one must be within a certain radius (5.5 kilometers) of a major DSL connection point (beyond this distance, the DSL signal cannot be reliably maintained). Individual connection speeds range from 512 Kbps to 1,500 Kbps. Purchasing certain guaranteed bandwidths of DSL service may be possible in certain areas, but in practice, the telecommunications companies have had difficulty keeping up with the demand for this service. Verizon has been an important player, developing solutions for the problems the industry has encountered in trying to meet consumer demand.

---

[115] NCTA (visited May 16, 2002), http://www.ncta.com/press/press.cfm?PRid=238&show Articles=ok.

[116] Whatis.com, DSL (definition) (visited May 16, 2002), http://searchnetworking.techtarget.com/ sDefinition/0,,sid7_gci213915,00.html (noting DSL is a technology that enables high-speed transmission of digital data over regular copper telephone lines).

[5]   T1 and T3 Lines

A T1[117] or T3[118] connection is a dedicated point-to-point connection that runs from an enterprise or user site directly to the ISP's communication center. The data transmitted on a T1 or T3 line travel on fiber optic wires, enabling data to travel 100 times faster than through a modem connection. T1 and T3 can handle voice conversations and videoconferencing between two different networked locations. The T3 line has enough bandwidth to transmit full-motion real-time video and very large databases over a busy network. T3 lines are generally installed as a major networking channel for a large corporation or university with high-volume network traffic. Establishing a T1 or T3 connection requires installing a dedicated physical line, at a cost in excess of $1,000. Recently, however, these costs have decreased greatly in some areas. In addition, the monthly access charge may run in excess of $1,000 per month, depending on the location of the enterprise and the distance to the ISP's communication center.

[6]   Satellite Connections

Satellite brings Internet access to areas not served by other types of connections. Satellite access works in a continuous circuit between land-based Internet connections, the satellite, and the user. When a user makes a request for web content, the request is routed through the user's dish antenna onto the satellite. The satellite also has a direct connection with the ISP; thus the information is retrieved with this connection and sent back to the user.

[C]   Web Browser

A web browser enables a user to browse HTML pages and Internet newsgroups and to communicate with standard e-mail services that conform to POP3 or IMAP standards. Today two products dominate the web browser market, Microsoft's Internet Explorer (IE) and America Online's Netscape Navigator. Both products have essentially equal market share and process web pages similarly, since web sites are published in a fairly standard format.

---

[117] Whatis.com, What Is . . .T1 (definition) (visited May 16, 2002). http://searchnetworking. techtarget.com/sDefinition/0,,sid7_gci213084,00.html (noting that a T1 is a telephone line connection for digital transmission that can handle 24 voice or data channels at 64 kilobits per second, over two twisted pair wires. T1 lines are used for heavy telephone traffic or for computer networks linked directly to the Internet. Small and medium-sized companies with heavy network traffic normally use T1 lines. They can send and receive very large text files, graphics, sounds, and databases very quickly.).

[118] Whatis.com, What Is . . .T3 (definition) (visited May 16, 2002), http://searchnetworking. techtarget.com/sDefinition/0,,sid7_gci213096,00.html (noting that a T-3 connection is made up of 28 T1 carriers, used to transmit digital signals on fiber optic cable at 44.736 megabits per second.T3 can handle 672 voice conversations or one video channel.).

[D] Navigating the Web

Depending on the type of access, users have the ability to transmit or receive data in various media. The most common network on the Internet is the World Wide Web.[119] Its outstanding feature is hypertext, a method of instant cross-referencing. In most web sites, certain words or phrases appear in text of a different color than the rest; often this text is also underlined. When users select one of these words or phrases, they will be transferred to the site or page that is relevant to this word or phrase.

The Internet provides access to millions of pages of information. To access these pages, a user can type in the IP address[120] or Universal Resource Locator (URL)[121] of the desired destination directly or use a search engine.[122] The URL is a

---

[119] Whatis.com, WWW (definition) (visited May 16, 2002), http://searchcrm.techtarget.com/sDefinition/0,,sid11_gci213390,00.html (noting that the World Wide Web is a network of computers on the Internet that maintains documents that users can read and transfer with a variety of programs. These documents may include graphics, full-motion video, and sound, as well as text. Users access the web through a computer program known as a browser, which creates the graphical interface necessary to view images as well as text.).

[120] See Chapter Two for a more detailed explanation of IP addresses.

[121] A URL is an address through which to gain access to World Wide Web pages. It generally consists of a protocol or program (such as http, gopher, or telnet), followed by a colon or a colon and two slashes, followed by the address of the site. Suffolk University Law School's home page, for example, is http://www.law.suffolk.edu. A home page is the gateway to the site; it often serves as a main menu, listing documents or graphics (such as product data or legal treatises) that a company, association, or individual maintains in a computer as part of its World Wide Web site.

[122] Searches on the Internet can be conducted in various ways. Following is a partial list of search engines and their web addresses:

AOL	http://netfind.aol.com
AltaVista	http://altavista.com
Ask Jeeves! Smart Answers Fast	http://askjeeves.com
CNN Webspace Search Engine	http://cnn.com/SEARCH/index.html
Direct Hit	http://www.directhit.com
Dog Pile	http://www.dogpile.com
Excite	http://www.excite.com
Fast	http://www.alltheweb.com
Google	http://www.google.com
HomeWiz	http://www.800go.com/homewiz/homewiz.html
HotBot	http://www.hotbot.com
Infoseek	http://www.infoseek.com
Jump City	http://www.jumpcity.com/NEWHOME.html
LawCrawler	http://www.lawcrawler.com
LookSmart	http://www.looksmart.com
Lycos	http://www.lycos.com
Magellan	http://www.mckinley.magellan.excite.com
MetaCrawler	http://www.metacrawler.com
News Index	http://www.newsindex.com
Northern Light	http://www.northernlight.com
OpenText	http://www.opentext.com
Snap	http://home.snap.com

combination of *http://*, the DNS name for the computer on the Internet, and a specific web page on that computer. The URL of Suffolk University Law School is *http://www.law.suffolk.edu*, but the URL for a specific page on our site, for instance, the Spring 2002 Cyberlaw course web page, is *http://www.law.suffolk.edu/academic/hightech/classes/Spring02/index.html*. URLs are advertised everywhere nowadays. A good way to find a company is to type in the name of the company, surrounded by the *http://www.* and *.com*.[123] For instance, the CNN television network's URL is *http://www.cnn.com*.

Search engines are often characterized as spiders, worms, or crawlers, by analogy to the way some creatures move in the real world, and as indexes, subgrouped according to how they index web pages. Not all search engines index words in the same way. Some index each visible word on every web page, whereas others also index by *metatags*,[124] words that are *not* visible. Irrespective of the indexing technique, once a search request has been entered, the search engine will traverse the Internet in search of the information or sites requested.

Two of the more popular search engines are Yahoo! and Google. Yahoo! functions like an Internet Yellow Pages; it is organized to allow users to search for web sites conceptually, as well as by text. Numerous web sites are listed under each category. Web sites related to the Supreme Court, for example, can be found under the category Government: U.S. Government: Judicial Branch: Supreme Court. Users can input several key terms and search categories, or, if they are uncertain about the correct category, all listed sites.

In contrast, Google searches millions of web pages by specified search terms. A simple search can be conducted by typing in key words, and a more advanced search can utilize Boolean search logic. Boolean search logic on the web resembles that used by the legal databases LexisNexis™ and WESTLAW®.

[E] Portals

Portals[125] are often the first page your web browser loads when you start up your web browser. The term "web portal" began to be used to describe mega sites

---

| Starting Point | http://stpt.com |
| Yahoo! | http://www.yahoo.com |

Other search tools include Wide Areas Information Server (WAIS), Gopher, Archie, Jughead, and Veronica.

[123] See § 2.06[B][2] for a discussion of the value of easily found domain names.

[124] A metatag is a special HTML tag that provides information about a web page. Unlike normal HTML tags, metatags do not affect how the page is displayed. Rather, they provide information about who created the page, how often it is updated, what it is about, and the key words that best represent the page's content. Many search engines use this information when building their indexes. *See* Chapter Two for a detailed discussion of metatags.

[125] Whatis.com, Portal (definition) (visited May 16, 2002), http://searchebusiness.techtarget.com/sDefinition/0,,sid19_gci212810,00.html (noting that "portal" is a term, generally synonymous with "gateway," for a World Wide Web site that is or purports to be a major starting site for users when they get connected to the web or that users tend to visit as an anchor site. There are general portals and specialized or niche portals. Some major general portals are Yahoo!, Excite, Netscape, Lycos, CNET,

such as Yahoo!, Excite, MSN, Netscape Netcenter, and AOL because many users used them as a "starting point" or "entry point" for their web surfing. Portals offer a wide range of customization options and functionality, including Internet search and navigation; e-mail; customized news, weather, sports, and horoscopes; planners, calendars, and contact managers; bookmark managers to save favorite web sites; real-time chat; message boards; original content on every imaginable topic; shopping; free home pages; "clubs" that function as makeshift intranets; small business services; and much more.

Increasingly, major portals are seeing to it that vital content such as news, stock prices, and messages can be accessed with wireless devices and phones. Portals, like all emerging companies in the technology field, come with a range of innovative business models and expect to earn revenue from a variety of revenue streams. An attentive, registered base of users is seen as a valuable asset. On average, a loyal user will spend a certain amount of money on e-commerce for emerging branded services like online banking or other services. Portals hope to exploit their sales opportunities with these loyal users, which in turn open the door for online advertising.

Internet analysts suggest that the larger and more influential Internet companies act as "platforms" for e-commerce. As platforms they decide what to do with their loyal users. Some Internet companies deliberately resist revenue-generating opportunities so that their growth in market share is not impeded or shared by others. As portal companies cement their market dominance, they will have many revenue opportunities that are not apparent in today's balance sheets. Yahoo!, for example, is now highly profitable after several years of losing money, partially due to advertising revenues. Given its size and strong brand, Yahoo! is likely to become even more profitable in the future because there are likely many unrealized revenue opportunities associated with its vast audience.

[F] LOOKING TO THE FUTURE

[1] Internet2

The incubator for some of the emerging technologies that are shaping the future is known as Internet2.[126] Formed in 1996 and administered by the University Corporation for Advanced Internet Development (UCAID), Internet2 is a partnership among universities, corporations, and government agencies. The project's goals are to create new applications that can't run over the existing Internet and to develop the infrastructure that supports those applications. Internet2 is not a single network but rather a consortium of hundreds of high-speed networks linked by fiber optic backbones that span the United States and link to other countries. It transmits data at speeds up to 2.4 gigabits per second—45,000 times faster than a

---

Microsoft Network, and America Online's AOL.com. Examples of niche portals are Garden.com (for gardeners), Fool.com (for investors), and SearchNetworking.com (for network administrators).).

[126] Internet2 (visited May 16, 2002), http://www.internet2.edu.

56 Kbps modem, allowing scientists to test their laboratory discoveries in the real world.

The next-generation network went online in February 1999, linking a number of universities around the world. It should be available for commercial use in a few years, when we are likely to see 21st-century services like interactive television, virtual 3-D videoconferencing, movies-on-demand, and much more. High-speed networks will make it possible for professionals to work in ways never before possible. For instance, scientists around the world can share specialized equipment like electron microscopes. NASA has developed a Virtual Collaborative Clinic that connects medical facilities around the United States, allowing doctors to manipulate high-resolution, 3-D images of MRI scans and other medical imaging. Not only can doctors consult and diagnose, but they also can simulate surgery by using a "Cyber-Scalpel."[127] Virtual surgery gives surgeons an opportunity to practice before ever entering the operating room, reducing the time required for the actual procedure. Using this kind of virtual technology, local hospitals can access resources and skills only available at larger institutions. NASA plans to use the technology to provide remote health care to astronauts on extended space journeys.

[2]   Internet-Enabled Devices

Although PCs were once the primary means of accessing the Internet, there are Internet-enabled devices such as pagers and cell phones that send and receive e-mail and access the Internet. Soon, everything from cars to the home refrigerator will be connected to the global network, communicating with each other wirelessly.

Wireless devices have particular needs when it comes to accessing the Internet. The protocol most services use today is called WAP[128] (Wireless Application Protocol) and its associated web page language called WML (Wireless Markup Language). WAP uses WML[129] to code or recode web pages for use on what are known as "micro browsers."[130]

---

[127] The CyberScalpel is an instrument developed at NASA's Ames Center for Bioinformatics that can be used to operate on 3-D simulations on a computer screen so that surgeons can test or rehearse procedures virtually before carrying them out on the patient. Paroma Basu, Space Medicine Gets Smart, Technology Rev. (June 20, 2001), http://www.techreview.com/articles/basu062001.asp.

[128] Whatis.com, WAP (definition) (visited May 16, 2002), http://searchnetworking.techtarget. com/sDefinition/0,,sid7_gci213337,00.html (noting that WAP is a global standard for developing applications over wireless communication networks).

[129] Whatis.com, WML (definition) (visited May 16, 2002), http://searchwebmanagement. techtarget.com/sDefinition/0,,sid27_gci214129,00.html (noting that WML is an XML-based markup language designed for specifying the content and user interfaces of narrowband wireless devices, such as pagers and cellular phones).

[130] Whatis.com, Micro browser (definition) (visited May 16, 2002), http://searchwebmanagement. techtarget.com/sDefinition/0,,sid27_gci214129,00.html (noting that a micro browser is an Internet browser designed for use with a wireless handheld device such as a mobile phone. Micro browsers have small file sizes to accommodate the low memory available to handheld devices and the low-bandwidth constraints of the wireless-handheld networks.).

[3]   Voice Browsing

Companies are working to expand access to the Internet to allow people to interact via keypads, spoken commands, listening to prerecorded speech, synthetic speech, and music. This will allow any telephone to be used to access appropriately designed Internet-based services and will be a boon to people with visual impairments or those needing Internet access while keeping theirs hands and eyes free for other things. It will also allow effective interaction with display-based web content in the cases where the mouse and keyboard may be missing or inconvenient.

Many more people today have access to a telephone than have access to a computer with an Internet connection. In addition, sales of cell phones are booming, so many of us have already or soon will have a phone within reach wherever we go. Voice browsers offer the promise of allowing everyone to access Internet-based services from any phone, making it practical to access the web any time and any where, whether at home, on the move, or at work.

It is common for companies to offer services over the phone via menus traversed using the phone's keypad. Voice browsers offer a great fit for the next generation of call centers, which will become voice web portals to the company's services and related web sites, whether accessed via the telephone network or via the Internet. Users will be able to choose whether to respond by a key press or a spoken command. Voice interaction holds the promise of naturalistic dialogues with web-based services, particularly in cases where hands-free operation is required, for instance in automobiles where hands/eyes free operation is essential. Voice interaction can escape the physical limitations on keypads and displays as mobile devices become ever smaller.

[4]   PDAs

A personal digital assistant (PDA)[131] is a handheld computer that allows users to store, access, and organize information. Most PDAs work on either a Windows-based or a Palm operating system. PDAs can be screen-based or keyboard-based, or both. Basic PDAs allow one to store and retrieve addresses and phone numbers, maintain a calendar, and create to-do lists and notes. More sophisticated PDAs can run word processing, spreadsheet, money manager, games, and electronic book reading programs and also provide e-mail and Internet access. Some PDAs come with all of the programs included. For others, users have to acquire or purchase extra software. Some PDAs play stereo-quality music and record voice memos, while some others can with additional hardware.

---

[131] Whatis.com, PDA (definition) (visited May 16, 2002), http://searchbusiness.techtarget.com/sDefinition/0,,sid19_gci214287,00.html (noting that PDAs usually can store phone numbers, appointments, and to-do lists. Some PDAs have a small keyboard, others have only a special pen that is used for input and output. A PDA can also have a wireless fax modem. Files can be created on a PDA that are later entered into a larger computer.).

Most PDAs can exchange information with a desktop or laptop computer, although users may have to buy additional accessories. These devices include Pocket PCs and handheld PCs, although handheld devices are more robust than the Pocket PCs.

Wireless connectivity with PDAs can be achieved from the following:

- PC cards[132]: Local area networks can be accessed using PC cards.

- Cell phone: A data-ready cell phone can be used as a modem for a handheld. The phone can be connected to the handheld PC with a cable such as the Digital Phone Card or wirelessly using the Infrared port on certain cell phones.

- Modem: Some handheld PCs come with an integrated 56 Kbps modem.

- ISPs: The high-speed data network provides guaranteed bandwidth of 128 Kbps with raw data throughput up to 1 Mbps in a growing number of major metropolitan areas.

[5] Web Pads

Web pads are the next generation of information appliances and fall somewhere between a notebook and a PDA in terms of functionality and power. The device will be more useful to professionals who frequently need instant information but are always on the go, with very little or no time to sit in front of their computers. Web pads work on a 802.11b transceiver.

Wireless technologies, and 802.11b[133] in particular, are making it easier and cheaper to connect large numbers of people through over-the-air networks. Large amounts of information can now be sent for miles at very little cost, without ever involving a telephone or cable company. A speed of 11 Mbit/s is achievable with a wireless connection. With more security and bandwidth in place, wireless is the way to go in the future.

[6] Identity on the Internet

The ability for a user to log on once to a network and be able to access all authorized resources within the enterprise can be achieved by defining the identity of the user on the Internet. A *single sign-on program* accepts the user's name and

---

[132] Whatis.com, PC Card (definition) (visited May 16, 2002), http://searchsystemsmanagement. techtarget.com/sDefinition/0,,sid20_gci212758,00.html (noting that a PC Card (previously known as a PCMCIA card) is a credit card-sized memory or I/O device that fits into a personal computer, usually a notebook or laptop computer. Probably the most common example of a PC Card is the 28.8 Kbps modem for notebook computers. There are 16-binary digit and 32-bit (CardBus) varieties of PC Cards.).

[133] 802.11 is a family of specifications for wireless local area networks (WLANs) developed by a working group of the Institute of Electrical and Electronics Engineers (IEEE).

password and automatically logs on to all appropriate servers. Single sign-on services such as Microsoft's Passport are increasingly being used for web sites.

These services help individual consumers and businesses to maintain personal information securely. Online identity promises consumers convenience and control over their interactions with online destinations and with other consumers. For vendors, an identity system provides clearly identified marketing "targets" with open online wallets.

CHAPTER TWO

ESTABLISHING AND MAINTAINING AN IDENTITY ON THE INTERNET

§ 2.01 Overview

§ 2.02 **Doing Business in Cyberspace**
    [A] **Preparing to Go Online**
    [B] **Management Support**
    [C] **Benefits of Being Online**
    [D] **Choice of Business Entity**
        [1] **Sole Proprietorship**
        [2] **Partnership**
            [a] **General Partnership**
            [b] **Limited Partnership**
            [c] **Limited Liability Partnership**
        [3] **Corporations**
            [a] **C Corporations**
            [b] **S Corporations**
            [c] **Limited Liability Companies**
            [d] **Professional Corporations**

§ 2.03 **Funding a Startup**
    [A] **Funding Sources**
        [1] **"Friends and Family"**
        [2] **Federal and Local Grant Programs**
        [3] **U.S. Small Business Administration (SBA)**
        [4] **Bank Loans**
        [5] **Corporate Funds**
        [6] **Venture Capital**
            [a] **Levels of Funding**
            [b] **Process for Applying for Venture Capital Funding**
            [c] **Trends among Venture Capitalists**

§ 2.04 **Purpose of the Web Site**
    [A] **Business Requirements**
    [B] **Organizing Your Web Site**
    [C] **Web Site Content**
    [D] **Validating the Purpose of the Web Site**

§ 2.05   Developing and Maintaining a Commercial Web Site
          [A]   Internal versus External Development and Maintenance
                 [1]   An Example of Building a Web Site Internally
          [B]   Updating Your Web Site

§ 2.06   Staking a Claim in Cyberspace: How to Choose a Corporate
          Identity for the Internet
          [A]   Registering Names
          [B]   Selecting and Registering a Domain Name and Resolving
                 Domain Name Disputes
                 [1]   Trademarks
                 [2]   Registration Process: Domestic and Foreign
                        Registrations
                 [3]   Registering Multiple Names
                 [4]   Resolving Domain Name Disputes
                        [a]   Legal Remedies
                        [b]   Legal and Statutory Causes of Action
                        [c]   Purchasing a Domain Name
                        [d]   Registering a Name in Another Domain
                        [e]   Monitoring Expirations of Domain Names
                        [f]   Registering with Search Engines

§ 2.07   Advertising Your Products and Drawing Traffic to Your
          Web Site
          [A]   Introduction
                 [1]   Banner Ads
                 [2]   Interstitial and Pop-Up Advertising
                 [3]   Web Page Sponsorship
                 [4]   Other Advertising Strategies
                 [5]   Editorial and Search Engine Priority
                 [6]   Ad-Blocking Software Applications
          [B]   Internet Advertising Law
                 [1]   Federal Trade Commission
                        [a]   Claim Substantiation
                        [b]   Deception and Unfairness
                 [2]   Misrepresentation and False Advertising
                 [3]   National Advertising Division of the Council of the
                        Better Business Bureau
                 [4]   Other Considerations
                 [5]   Advertising to Children
          [C]   Linking
                 [1]   Introduction
                 [2]   Legal Implications of Linking
                        [a]   Direct Linking
                        [b]   Third-Party Links
                 [3]   Linking Precautions—Look Before You Link

[D]   Framing
    [1]   Advantages of Framing
    [2]   Legal Issues in Framing
    [3]   Resolving Framing Controversies
        [a]   Protecting Your Web Site
        [b]   Framing Other Web Sites
[E]   Marketing Through E-Mail
    [1]   Advantages of E-Mail
    [2]   Opt-In versus Opt-Out E-Mailing
    [3]   Legal Challenges to E-Mail Marketing
    [4]   Solutions for E-Mail Marketing
[F]   Metatags
    [1]   What to Include in Metatags
    [2]   Tips on Using Metatags Effectively
    [3]   Legal Issues and Limitations

§ 2.08   Preventive Law Pointers
[A]   Sample Legal Disclaimer on Web Site
[B]   Sample Privacy Policy Statement
[C]   Sample Security Policy
[D]   Sample Cease and Desist Letter
[E]   Sample Linking Terms and Conditions
[F]   Sample Linking Agreement
[G]   Sample Web Site Hosting Terms
[H]   Sample Terms of Service Agreement
[I]   Sample Online Disclosure Regarding Terms of Service

§ 2.01   OVERVIEW*

The evolution and acceptance of the Internet in recent years has forever changed how the world does business. Despite the fact that some people think that the dot-com bubble has burst, it seems as if everyone is still talking about e-business. On any given day, newspaper and magazine headlines and influential personalities tout the value of and opportunities and risks possible with an e-business. See Figure 2-1.

People lack many things: jobs, shelter food, health care and drinkable water. Today, being cut off from basic telecommunications service is a hardship almost as acute as these other deprivations, and may indeed reduce the chances of finding remedies to them. Kofi Anan, U.N. Secretary General

"Seeking Profits, Internet Companies Alter Privacy Policies – Online companies searching for profits are increasingly selling access to user's portal mail address and phone numbers, as well as sending junk e-mails. New York Times – 04/11/02

"The capacity of the Internet – yet to be fully imagined – to eliminate forever the knowledge gap between rich and poor countries may be the single most important determinant of what our world will look like in fifty years. Whether it be linking rural villages in India with one another, health clinics in Kazakhstan to hospitals in Paris, or farmers in Ukraine to commodity markets in Chicago, we have the power to accelerate development by generations." James D. Wolfensohn, President, World Bank Group

"As we leave the Industrial Age and enter the Information Age, it's clear that despite all of the technical advances and globalization, the formula for economic success has remained the same: Economic prosperity relies on high speed access to the critical network of information and commerce. That network is the Internet, and the type of access needed is broadband."

William Kennard, Chairman of the Federal Communications Commission

"Credit Card Theft Thrives Online as Global Market Losses Grow – Thousands of stolen credit card numbers are being offered for sale every week over the Internet in membership-only cyberbazaars. " N.Y. Times - 05/13/02

" A Libel Suit May Establish E-Jurisdiction – A Virginia prison warden's libel suit against publishers from another state is the nub of a legal dispute that could reverberate nationally and internationally. N.Y. Time – 05/27/02

"House votes to fund cyber-security: The U.S. House of Representatives voted to boost federal spending on computer security, overwhelmingly passing a bill that would pay $880 million over five years for research scholarships and other incentives." MSNBC 02/02/02

Beta version of new Napster is ready: Napster launched a test version of its new copyright-compliant service in a bid to restart the once widely popular song-swap web site that was shut down by a recording industry lawsuit.
MSNBC 01/10/02

"Yahoo updates privacy policy: The web portal says it has revised its privacy policy to more clearly describe how user data will be treated in certain circumstances." MSNBC 03/28/02

FIGURE 2-1

These headlines capture the attention of management in all organizations. Consequently, management teams have become convinced that to increase revenues and enter new markets, their organizations must establish a presence on the Internet. On the World Wide Web, any company can market its products in a virtual shopping center 24 hours a day, 7 days a week, to a global market.[1] The opportunities seem endless, and failing to establish a presence on the Internet could be detrimental to your company's existence. Practically speaking, the brick and mortar world functions in a manner similar to the online world. Stores that are located via a uniform resource locator (URL) have replaced physical storefronts. Products that are normally found in aisles or on shelves are now accessible via databases or

---

* We would like thank Dawn McGuire, Esq., and Manish Vashist of PricewaterhouseCoopers for their written, editorial, and strategic contributions to this Chapter.

[1] Businesses learn quickly: "If superstores don't get you, cyberstores will." *See* Iven Patterson, A Bookseller Gives Up in Battle with Internet, N.Y. Times, June 27, 1999, at 24.

online catalogs. Cash registers have been replaced by e-payment systems, and instead of being able to carry the product out the door, the purchased good can either be shipped or downloaded.

Although the environments function in the same manner, they are radically different from each other from an implementation perspective. Before engaging in e-commerce, an organization should address a number of issues ranging from the goals of a web-based presence to the type of legal entity needed. Proper strategic planning can help ensure a successful e-business site that is enabled by the Internet and other connected networks.

This chapter explores the business issues and legal challenges of going online. Section 2.02 of this chapter introduces the basic requirements of doing business in cyberspace. In an effort to streamline strategic and tactical issues, two tables provide practical guidance. The first table addresses potential management and organizational challenges and considerations. The second discusses the value of being online and its tangible benefits. Section 2.03 outlines the various funding options that companies might want to explore before launching their businesses. Sections 2.04 and 2.05 outline the basic purposes of a commercial web site and offer guidance on how to organize a web site and what considerations ought to be given to develop and maintain a web site's content. Section 2.06 examines how companies can stake a claim in cyberspace and what considerations should be given when choosing a corporate identity for the Internet. The issues discussed center around registering domain names and protecting them for continued use. Section 2.07 focuses on how to advertise your products and draw traffic to a web site. The topics addressed include methods of and restrictions on advertising, framing and linking considerations, and the use of metatags. Section 2.08 provides several preventive law pointers which include model language and sample forms.

§ 2.02   DOING BUSINESS IN CYBERSPACE

[A]   Preparing to Go Online

At the height of the dot-com revolution, many young companies leveraged the Internet in an attempt to make their startups a corporate juggernaut. Very few of the dot-com startups were successful in penetrating the Fortune 500 rankings, as Amazon.com did.[2] Despite their failure to revolutionize the corporate world, dot-com companies showed that smaller teams without the traditional corporate bureaucracies were able to innovate and bring new products to market faster. Although the business world may never see the likes of the dot-com revolution any time soon, this attribute was not overlooked by established companies.

Many brick and mortar companies took a wait and see attitude about the Internet. Now that things have settled down, and the Internet has proven to be a

---

[2] The Fortune 500, Fortune, Apr. 15, 2002, at F-62 (Amazon.com ranked 492 out of 500 as a specialty retailer.)

viable medium, most companies recognize that if they haven't already, they must find some way to integrate the Internet into their overall corporate strategies. Established brick and mortar companies recognize that to make this transition, they must take advantage of things like their scale, goodwill, loyal customers, and long-standing business relationships and alliances. Each of these strengths can potentially be as valuable online as it is offline. To sustain companies' current marketplace positions and sustain growth, a presence on the Internet is needed to survive.[3] Moreover, the question is no longer *if* a business should have a web site, but *how* and *what kind.* More and more people will be online, and they fully expect that any business they deal with will have a working commercial web site. This fact alone indicates that the Internet remains a very powerful business medium that companies must leverage to their advantage.

New technologies have made building a web site easy. However, turning a web site into a profit center is more challenging, since businesses are asking how they can establish a web site while avoiding liabilities and protecting their legal rights. Becoming a successful online business is a challenging task requiring a careful balance of costs and benefits. The benefits may seem endless and obvious: finding new customers and the opportunity to reach new markets, enhance customer service, attract new employees, and create new sales distribution channels. On the other hand, the costs may seem daunting because there are many issues to resolve, such as content, scalability, advertising, security, bandwidth, and keeping everything manageable and up to date. To meet all of these challenges requires that senior management support the online initiative and that important executives play an integral part in formulating the corporate vision as it will be represented in the online business. Management must answer the following questions: (1) What is your web site about?, (2) Who is the target audience?, and (3) How will the company measure its success?

For most businesses, going online represents a significant paradigm shift; thus, unless corporate goals and expectations are focused and managed, the online venture could fail just as many of the dot-com startups did. Accomplishing every objective or fulfilling everyone's needs is impossible. A well-thought-out vision, coupled with a comprehensive strategic business and tactical plan, can help ensure success. For a sample business plan, see Appendix A.

[B] Management Support

Strong support from senior management is vital to the long-term viability of a commercial web site. Management must fulfill five core functions and document their understanding in a well-thought-out business plan that will be the roadmap for a successful experience on the Internet (for a sample plan, see Appendix A): (1) companies should conduct an impact analysis on the business rationale for creating a web site; (2) if the impact analysis concludes that an Internet presence is

---

[3] *Number of Massachusetts Software and Interactive Firms Continues to Climb,* Mass High Tech (Sept. 20-26, 1999), at 23 (reporting boom in "dot-com" companies).

needed, then the company must define its marketing and sales objectives; (3) companies need to put some structure around the impact analysis finding and marketing/sales objectives by creating a dot-com proof of concept and conducting a beta test; (4) the company must assess the legal risks of being an online company; and (5) the company must define how success will be measured. (For sample questions to consider under each phase, see Table 2.1.)

First, an independent team must scrutinize the initiative. The findings of the independent team should be summarized in a document for management's review. The table of contents[4] of such a document might include the following:

- Executive Summary

- Introduction

- Assumptions

- Definition of Project Scope and Audience

- Current Operational Processes

- Proposed Operational Methodology

- General Business Decisions and Issues

- Functional Requirements

- Proposed Architecture

- Proposed System Design

- Costs

- Appendices/Supporting Documents

This analysis must cover a broad range of issues to ensure that the online plan is well defined and manageable. One important topic that must be addressed is the cost of the initiative. To be successful, the initiative must receive adequate funding, including both startup costs and the ongoing costs associated with updating and maintaining the web site as the business continues to grow.

Second, management must decide what the sales and marketing objectives are. Such decisions, among other things, will define the type of content and offerings that management wishes to make available to prospective customers. Information is a powerful tool, and the type and quality of information published on a commercial web site can make or break a business.

Third, create a proof of concept. This allows various interested parties to see how the vision may unfold without incurring all of the costs upfront. A solid proof

---

[4] Potential investors and management teams typically read dozens of reports daily. Use a table of contents as a means to provide easy access to information they want. *See generally* HierosGamos E-Commerce Resource Center (visited June 15, 2002) http://www.hg.org/busecommerce.html.

TABLE 2.1
The Internet Roadmap—Potential Management
and Organizational Issues to Address

Phase I—Conducting an Impact Analysis

Challenges	Considerations
What kind of web site is needed?	Why a web site? What would the goal or purpose of this web site be? • Will you be a B2B, B2C, B2G, C2C, or a combination of these? Prioritize the needs. • What is the singular business purpose? • What are the top two or three objectives of the web site? • What are the top five or ten drivers that will allow the dot-com business to achieve these objectives (i.e., increasing traffic, increasing customer loyalty, cutting costs, providing technical and customer support, obtaining better customer/marketing information, leveraging expertise, reducing sales and marketing costs, opening new sales channels or distribution networks, enhancing customer service, learning more about your customers'/market's needs, making a stronger first impression for new product launches)? • Consider phased approaches. • What will be the competitive advantage?
Who are your targeted customers?	What is the desired client profile? • Are there current geographical boundaries that have impeded your current scalability? • Will the web site cater to a different audience than the brick and mortar store? • How do the demographics of your brick and mortar clients differ from those of your online clients?
How will a web site enhance customer service? • Can the site provide sales support? • Can it provide product information and support? • How can order tracking be managed?	How is the organization currently servicing clients? • How are clients served, where, and by whom? • Is traffic monitored? • Is content updated?

continued

TABLE 2.1
The Internet Roadmap—Potential Management
and Organizational Issues to Address (Continued)

Phase 1—Conducting an Impact Analysis

Challenges	Considerations
• How will orders be fulfilled, and by whom?	
• Do clients care about other current clients: is benchmarking and other "what if" analysis needed to enhance the site's value?	
Will your brick and mortar customers buy online?	What makes your brick and mortar business successful?
	• Is it location?
	• Is it the personal touch provided by each service or sales advisor?
	• Will the online business hamper the brick and mortar business?
	• Can the brick and mortar business be complemented by the online business?
What technologies should be used?	Build or buy?
	• Should the company build it all (a lot of flexibility and control but high costs)?
	• Should the company buy (less flexibility but lower costs)?
	• Is there a middle ground?
Does the initiative have adequate funding?	What are the benefits of being online?
What are the costs of building a web site?	• Cost-effective means of reaching new markets: global reach.
• Software, people, hardware, graphics, security, databases, web servers, vendors, ISPs, experienced graphic designers.	• Cost-effective and enhanced customer service.
• Build internally or externally.	• Inexpensive means of promoting the company's products.
	• The ability to test new product ideas and assess customer needs.
	• The ability to attract and help retain customers.
	• The ability to improve communications with and among employees, subsidiaries, consultants, and trading partners.
	• Provide customers with the means to order goods and services from their homes, offices, or in remote locations around the globe.

continued

TABLE 2.1
The Internet Roadmap—Potential Management
and Organizational Issues to Address (Continued)

Phase I—Conducting an Impact Analysis

Challenges	*Considerations*
	• Provide product demonstrations and vital up-to-the-minute product information in an attempt to simplify the customer's purchasing decision-making process.
	• Automate and/or outsource inefficient business processes; improve core business processes by streamlining marketing, procurement, and chain management.
	• Enhance media and investor research by publishing company information, financial reports, and news releases.
	• Easy communication and coordination of orders with suppliers and/or distribution channels.
What is your competition doing?	How will you distinguish yourself from the competition? • Better content? • Free value-added services? • Flexibility? • Price?
Who will manage the web site? • Is there a central team? • Should the group include sales, marketing, corporate communications, legal, tax, security officer, and information technology? • What is the scope of each business unit's responsibility?	Why a web site? What would be the goal of this web site? • Management needs to decide the potential value of the web site. • Most companies know they need to go online, but they must prioritize activities.

Phase II — Marketing and Sales Objectives

Challenges	*Considerations*
What are the marketing and sales objectives? • Will your product or service be viable online? • Should the site offer product information?	Will the traditional marketing and sales strategy work in an online environment? • Can direct mailings, mass media ads, and fliers be leveraged online? • Is it possible to integrate traditional marketing and sales techniques in an online environment?

continued

TABLE 2.1
The Internet Roadmap—Potential Management
and Organizational Issues to Address (Continued)

Phase II — Marketing and Sales Objectives

Challenges	Considerations
• Should the site preview future product offerings? • How will the information on the site be updated, and by whom? • What information will be required from customers? • What information will be of value to customers? • What information will the site contain about competitors, if any?	• Can an online customer lead be profiled and managed using some of the same techniques used in the brick and mortar world?
What role will your site play in the overall sales strategy? How will revenue be generated? • Sales of products and services? • Banner ads? • Third-party click-through? • Will all sales be conducted online? • Who will manage credit card transactions? Will the "back office" functions like accounting, invoicing, reconciliations, and payments be outsourced? • Must customer service representatives be available 24 hours a day, 7 days a week?	What are the qualities of the new sales model? • Should sales still be made by phone or by a traditional sales force team? • Should the sales model be geared toward servicing a global market?
How will the revenues be collected? • Will advertising be used as a source of revenue?	How do you protect against fraud? • Should third-party vendors be utilized? • Will you accept credit cards or merchant accounts?
Is there a way to extend your reach via search engines?	How are search results generated? Is there a way to register your site with all of the search engines or select search engines? How does one increase visibility by being one of the first companies displayed with the search results? What role do metatags play in the search request process?

continued

TABLE 2.1
The Internet Roadmap—Potential Management
and Organizational Issues to Address (Continued)

Phase II — Marketing and Sales Objectives

Challenges	Considerations
What are the potential uses, misuses, and abuses of online advertising?	Is online advertising better than print or other traditional forms of advertising?
• What value do links offer?	• How deep should a link be?
• Are metatags useful?	• Are a lot of links a plus for users or an annoyance?
• What personal data are collected about each visitor? Are cookies used to track visitors? Do advertising practices comply with privacy regulations and best industry practices?	• Can the inclusion of metatags cause liability because they include trademarks of competitors?
	• Can the site give the appearance of false advertising or misrepresentation?
Is selecting a domain name important?	What does the domain name really represent?
	Should it be simple to remember?
	What happens if the desired name is already taken?
	Should the domain name relate to the corporate offering(s)?
How do you keep the store open 24 hours a day, 7 days a week?	How do you select the right web host?
• What is the impact of a web site not being accessible 24 hours a day?	• Based on reputation?
	• Based on cost?
	• Based on up time?
How do you monitor site usage?	How do you measure usage statistics?
	• Should the site be built in multiple platforms?
	• Should the site be built to handle multiple browsers?
	• Should cookies and/or a registration process be utilized with each visit to the web site?
	• Can profile data be utilized to generate focused sales leads?
Who is responsible for the web site?	How time-consuming is site management?
	• Does the information have to be kept current?
	• How often can the site be updated: monthly, weekly, daily, or hourly?

continued

TABLE 2.1
The Internet Roadmap—Potential Management
and Organizational Issues to Address (Continued)

Phase II — Marketing and Sales Objectives

Challenges	*Considerations*
	• Should the prices of the goods and services be posted? What happens if the price list is not up to date?
	• Should other costs be listed, such as shipping and taxes, if applicable?
Should a separate marketing leader be appointed to manage the online business?	What should the marketing leader concentrate on?
	• Ensuring that online product strategies have been applied to the web?
	• Analyzing competitor sites as well as their product and/or service offerings?
	• Preparing marketing budgets?
	• Negotiating with other sites to utilize advertising banners and registering with search engines?
	• Mandating that the dot-com's URL is included in all company correspondences, press releases, advertisements, business cards, brochures, etc., for both the dot-com and brick and mortar entities?
Can a web portal be advantageous to the dot-com business?	Should Excite, Yahoo!, and other portals be explored as a way to have the business be part of their web directories? Are the categories within the portals too limited or broad?

Phase III — Proof of Concept

Challenges	*Considerations*
What is the corporate message/online mission?	What do you want to tell your current clients and potential clients?
	• Can you keep the message simple, yet appealing?
	• Does your online mission statement have to match that of your traditional corporate message?
	• Is there value in having a message from the CEO?
	• How does that corporate message complement the content of the web site?

continued

TABLE 2.1
The Internet Roadmap—Potential Management
and Organizational Issues to Address (Continued)

Phase III — Proof of Concept

Challenges	*Considerations*
What content and offerings will be delivered? How should the site be organized?	
• What are the logical categories?	
• Who is the target audience being sought?	
• What are the design considerations?	
• How will the site keep pace with the e-business initiatives?	
• How can navigation and consistent "look and feel" issues be managed?	
• Will music, video, or virtual tours be included? Will it be easy for visitors to turn off music, video, graphics, or other multimedia if the load time is too long?	
• What programming languages should be used?	
• Will the site have a contact person, feedback form, or real-time customer service contact person?	
• Does the overall "look and feel" of the site attract and maintain visitors?	
What kind of a user experience will be created?	What type of interactivity should be established between the web site and your customers?
What are the security and quality control issues?	What are the goals for network security?
Should an information security officer be appointed?	• Local area networks.
	• Storage area networks.
• Can the site be compromised by competitors, hackers, or other intruders?	• Operating systems, personal computers in the networked environment, telecommuters.
• What third-party tools will be required to protect the company from security risks? Consider firewalls, passwords, biometrics systems, encryption, virtual private networks, security audit products, and physical security products. Is physical security calibrated to the risks specific to online companies?	• Audit of online security risks for the business.
	• Attractiveness to hackers, corporate espionage, computer crimes, denial of service, viruses, protection against imposters, natural disasters, social engineering.
	• Emergency response to intrusions, viruses, and other data disasters.

continued

TABLE 2.1
The Internet Roadmap—Potential Management
and Organizational Issues to Address (Continued)

Phase III — Proof of Concept

Challenges	Considerations
• Should the site be hosted by the company or by a third-party vendor?	• Assessing potential liabilities due to Internet intrusion or viruses.
• What should the disaster recovery plans include?	
• Should there be a backup site in the event the web site goes down?	
• Is the information up to date and accurate?	
• Are the correct data and prices being published?	

Phase IV — Legal Risks

Challenges	Considerations
Should the dot-com company be a separate legal entity?	What about shared intellectual property interests? What about sharing of customer information between the brick and mortar company and the online company?
	Should the dot-com company be incorporated in the same state/location as the brick and mortar company?
What is the preferred legal entity choice?	Should the online company be a separate legal entity? If so, which corporate entity isolates the entity and its related entity from liability? • Partnership • General partnership • Limited partnership • Corporation • Professional corporation • S Corporation • Limited liability company Depending on which legal entity is chosen, which structural model should be used for the corporate decision-making process? • Parent company with multiple interdependent operating companies. • Parent company with multiple independent operating companies.

continued

TABLE 2.1
The Internet Roadmap—Potential Management
and Organizational Issues to Address (Continued)

Phase IV — Legal Risks

Challenges	*Considerations*
	• Operating company with multiple divisions or business units.
	• Single company with multiple functions or processes.
How do you protect your intellectual property?	Should a third legal entity be created to hold all intellectual property rights and license the use of such property to the brick and mortar and online companies?
What jurisdiction(s) will the online business service?	Is it necessary to have the web technology hosted in the same state/location where the corporation is registered?
How does a company deal with the myriad of privacy issues?	What information should be kept private? Can online data gathered during each visit to the web site be aggregated, mined, and/or sold?
How many legal agreements should be executed, and with whom?	Can in-house corporate counsel prepare all of the necessary documents?
	Should the company engage outside counsel? If so, does the current outside counsel team have subject matter expertise in all facets of the online world?

Phase V — Measuring Success

Challenges	*Considerations*
How will the dot-com business be measured?	Is success measured by profitability of the web site?
• Review the monthly operating reports.	• What is a reasonable return on investment?
• Review industry and economic indicators on a quarterly basis.	• Does the site have to be constantly updated to reflect the corporate vision, strategies, and tasks?
• Annually review all steps mentioned herein.	• Are there intangible success factors that warrant keeping the web site, such as keeping in touch with the customers, potential customers, and vendors, or staying ahead of market demands?
• Have an independent review summarize and document results, commenting on what was successful and not so successful.	What review function will the strategic team have over the dot-com business?
	• Strategy formulation and budgetary control?

continued

TABLE 2.1
The Internet Roadmap—Potential Management
and Organizational Issues to Address (Continued)

Phase V — Measuring Success

Challenges	Considerations
	• Strategy implementation process review?
	• Strategy evaluation process review?
	• Should an advisory board be brought in to review the progress instead of the strategic team and/or in conjunction with the strategic team?
Will the dot-com business be a separate company?	What governance model is the executive team using for the dot-com business?
	• A shareholder model, in which the primary purpose of the business is to create wealth.
	• A stakeholder model, in which the purpose of the business is not wealth creation but rather enhancing current market presence.
How will the employees be rewarded? What type of organizational chart will be established?	Will the compensation level be commensurate with the level of commitment expected from each employee?
	• Do what is expected and no more; feel no ownership interest or stake.
	• Do more than what is expected to make it happen.
	• Do more than what is expected to make it happen and receive an ownership interest or stake.

of concept will allow people to refine their expecations and/or expand requirements that were not fully analyzed.

Fourth, someone within the organization must review the legal risks associated with the venture. Minimizing the legal risk upfront will prove to be essential in the years ahead. Risks can be managed in a number of ways, including, but not limited to, terms and conditions, license agreements, contracts, and insurance.

Finally, management must decide how it will measure the success of the venture. Such an assessment will require that management constantly update its vision, strategies, and tasks. Having an online presence requires that organizations keep in touch with customers, potential customers, vendors, and market demands on a daily basis. Internet business strategies will evolve and continually change.

Corporate leaders must decide what they want to accomplish by being online. Irrespective of the strategic motives, organizations must more than ever be responsive and flexible in meeting changing market demands. Table 2.1 identifies some of the organizational strategy issues that management must review and document in its business plan.

When examining some of the management and organizational issues listed in the table, companies must also recognize that the Internet will bring many new challenges. These include new marketplaces; new technologies; new distribution channels; new product offerings; enhanced business processes; new client and revenue expectations; new organizational priorities; new partners; and new insights. Without proper planning, a flexible business plan, and a well-thought-out strategy, these challenges can cause chaos in companies, disrupting their current business operations.

[C] Benefits of Being Online

Addressing the organizational strategies may seem like a daunting task. As each issue is considered, however, numerous benefits of being an online company will immediately become apparent. If done right, web commerce can help companies increase revenue, reach new markets, and improve customer service. The benefits will vary by company, but will ultimately enhance shareholder value. Table 2.2 outlines some common value drivers.

To identify some key organizational issues, assume we've been hired by SPC, our business model, to handle all legal matters and provide business advice for its web site launch. As you recall (Overview, page xli), SPC's product line consists of personal computers built to customer specifications.

In an effort to assist SPC with its desire to develop an online presence, we have prepared a preliminary business plan.[5] At a minimum, the business plan requires that SPC address the following:

1. Decide on the business purpose for the web site and what peripheral information should be published on it. Branding, positioning, marketing, and sales strategies must be clearly addressed and expressed by the site. Who should be the contact person for the public? Will real-time customer service be available 24 hours a day, 7 days a week?
2. Determine whether or not a third-party consultant should be hired to develop and maintain the commercial web site.
3. Choose and register a domain name encompassing the company's valuable trademark and not infringing on similar marks owned by others.
4. Determine what products to advertise and what sales or services to offer.
5. Plan for sales of products via a secure web server.[6]
6. Develop an Internet model that satisfies the firm's needs.

---

[5] For an example of a comprehensive model business plan, *see* Appendix A–SPC Business Plan.

[6] *See* Chapter Three for an in-depth discussion of product sales via a secure web server.

TABLE 2.2
Value of Being Online

Business Value	Tangible Benefits
Increased competitiveness: Demonstrates that your company is up to date, aware of the potential of e-business, and able to harness technology to improve its business processes while reducing operational costs.	• Effective way to promote products and their value to client base. • Online catalog and pricing is always current. • Pricing can be changed at any time.
Expanded sales opportunities: Encourages potential customers to learn more about company products and services. Reaching new markets and clients enables businesses to achieve higher market share.	• Products and services can be sold 24 hours a day, 7 days a week. • Access to a global marketplace without the need for offices in numerous locations. • Shorter sales cycles and faster delivery of goods. • Ability to electronically profile customers' needs and purchasing habits.
Improved access to customer information and dissemination of company information: Gathering customer information leads to more pointed contact with customers. Newsletters and product explanations help educate consumers.	• Ability to publish whatever is deemed necessary. • Quality information can be made readily available. • Information can be distributed independent of user platform. • Information can be shared instantaneously. • Information can be shared with business partners. • Supplemental or updated product information can be made available.
Reduction in costs: Costs decline while mechanisms to distribute information and provide better customer service and sales support improve.*	• Online catalogs only need updating when changes occur relative to particular items. • Reduced cost of paper, publications, mailing, and distribution. • Consistent "look and feel" can be achieved for all communications. • Core information can be accessed faster.
Enhanced customer service: Service, customer loyalty and trust, and improved name and brand recognition grow simultaneously.	• Better service for less money than can be provided by a customer service staff required to be available 24 hours a day. • Time is never a factor: Service is always available. • Answers to frequently asked questions can be posted. • Sites can provide access to internal resources or experts.

*Gail L. Grant, *Business Models for Internet and New Media*, 505 PLI/Pat 49 January 1998.

[D]   Choice of Business Entity

Once a decision has been made that the opportunity exists to create a viable business, consideration must be given to the legal and tax form of the new entity. In many ways, the formation of an e-business is similar to the formation of any other kind of business in the brick and mortar world. It is a complex decision surrounded by a host of tax, legal, financial, and management structure considerations. Although there are a number of factors that ought to be considered when choosing the appropriate entity type, some of the more important are (1) the tax treatment of the entity, (2) the tax treatment of the founding and management members, (3) limiting liability, and (4) opportunities and ramifications for the owners to participate in the management of the new entity. Generally speaking there are three basic legal entity structures that are considered when creating a new business: the sole proprietorship, the partnership, and the corporation. Partnerships and corporations can be further subcategorized.

[1]   Sole Proprietorship

A sole proprietorship[7] is a business entity that is established and conducted by a single individual called a sole proprietor. Income and losses from the business are reported on the individual's income tax return (Schedule C). The sole proprietor is fully liable for all debts and liabilities of the proprietorship. This entity type is relatively simple and inexpensive to establish and maintain. Given the complexities of jurisdiction and taxation laws in the online environment, this entity type may not be a feasible option.

[2]   Partnership

A partnership is a type of business entity that is owned by two or more individuals who voluntarily agree to carry on a business as co-owners for profit. The parties entering a partnership may contribute money, labor, and so forth to the partnership with the understanding that there will be a proportional sharing of the profits and losses. Partnerships are not subject to tax, for federal purposes; rather the income, gains, losses, deductions, and credits are passed on to the partners equally unless otherwise provided for in the partnership agreement.

In certain instances, the partnership is recognized as a separate legal entity for federal tax purposes. For example, the partnership is allowed to make certain elections such as the accounting method and accounting year. Some states recognize the flow-through nature of a partnership for state income tax purposes, while others tax the partnership itself in a manner similar to a corporation. Similar to sole proprietors, given the complexities of jurisdiction and taxation laws in the

---

[7] *See generally* Mitchell F. Crusto, Extending the Veil to Sole Entreprenuers: A Limited Liability Sole Proprietorship Act (LLSP), 2001 Colum. Bus. L. Rev. 381 (2001) (Describing the characteristics of a sole proprietorship).

online environment, partnerships may not be the entity type to select. Nevertheless, there are three common types of partnerships: general partnerships, limited partnerships, and limited liability partnerships.

[a]   General Partnership

General partnerships allocate the profits, losses, management, and liability equally.[8] Moreover, all of the partners in a general partnership may participate in the management and each may act as an agent for the others. This type of partnership can be created by the intent of the partners, and there are no formal filing requirements.

[b]   Limited Partnership

Limited partnerships have two tiers of partners: general and limited.[9] There must be at least one general partner, who is personally liable for claims against the partnership. Limited partners contribute cash but are not legally responsible for the liabilities of the partnership beyond their initial cash contribution and are not involved in the management of the partnership.

[c]   Limited Liability Partnership

A limited liability partnership is a variation on the general partnership that provides only partial liability.[10] More specifically, partners are not liable for negligence, wrongful acts, and misconducts of other partners. However, they remain personally liable for business obligations caused by their own negligence, wrongful acts, or misconduct of those under their direct supervision.[11]

[3]   Corporations

Corporations are the most common, with various legal rights. Corporations are viewed as entities separate from their owners. This separation limits owner liability for debts and taxes. More specifically, the corporation itself is liable for any liabilities or claims against it rather than the individual shareholders, absent any fraudulent activities. Corporations also provide for the transfer of shares of stock and survive the death of their owners. There are four common types of corporations: C corporations, S corporations, limited liability companies, and professional corporations.

[a]   C Corporations

Drafting by-laws and filing articles of incorporation in the appropriate state office initiate the formation of a C corporation.[12] For legal and tax purposes, the C

---

[8] Richard A. Westin, Tax Dictionary 261 (1996).

[9] *Id.* at 341.

[10] Delaware Limited Liability Partnership Act, Del. Code Ann. tit. 6, Ch.15 (2002).

[11] *Id.* tit. 8, § 1515(b).

[12] *See, e.g.*, Del. Code Ann. tit. 8, §§ 101-02 (2002).

corporation[13] is treated as a separate entity from its shareholders. The taxable items of the incorporated business are reported on the corporate return and the corporation pays any federal taxes owed. A second level of taxation occurs when the shareholders pay tax on earnings from the corporate dividends.

From a management control perspective, shareholders have the ability to elect a board of directors, or serve as directors, officers, or employees. Depending on the role assumed, a shareholder could be exposed to some fiduciary duties of care and loyalty and managerial liability for his or her actions. Practically, if a business can afford the expenses and requirements associated with maintaining a C corporation, this is probably one of the best options for a dot-com venture.

[b]   S Corporations

From a legal standpoint, an S corporation[14] functions in a similar manner to a C corporation. However, an S corporation is treated as a pass-through entity (like a partnership), and the shareholders are responsible for the tax liabilities for federal tax purposes. In addition, an S corporation has a limited number of shareholders, restrictions on the type of shareholders, and limitations on the type of stock that can be issued.[15]

[c]   Limited Liability Companies

A limited liability company[16] combines the pass-through attributes of the partnership with the corporate characteristics of limited liability.[17] Generally speaking, two or more persons form an LLC. To be an LLC, it must lack two of four corporate characteristics: (1) continuity of life, (2) centralization of management, (3) limited liability, and (4) free transferability of interest.[18]

[d]   Professional Corporations

A professional corporation is a specialized type of corporation that is organized by those rendering personal services to the public of the type that requires a license or other legal authorization, such as certified public accountants, architects, and attorneys.[19]

When deciding which business entity option to select, entrepreneurs should consider tax and nontax factors. The tax consideration is whether the entity will be

---

[13] C corporations are defined as having (1) continuity of life, (2) centralization of management, (3) liability for corporate debts limited to corporate property, and (4) free transferability of interest. I.R.C. §§ 301.7701-2 (2002).

[14] The name S corporation refers to the particular subchapter of the Internal Revenue Code (I.R.C.) that governs the taxation of this particular type of corporation. *See generally* I.R.C. §§ 1361-1378 (2002).

[15] I.R.C. § 1361 (b) (1)(A), (b) (1) (B), (b) (1) (D), (c) (4) (2002).

[16] *See generally* David Cartano, Federal & State Taxation of Limited Liability Companies (1999).

[17] Treas. Reg. § 301.7701-1.

[18] Treas. Reg. § 301.7701-2(a)(1)–(2).

[19] *See, e.g.,* N.Y. Bus. Corp. Law § 1501(d).

subject to tax or merely be a conduit entity, which will pass the tax consequences on to each individual owner. Entrepreneurs and their lawyers should consult with accountants to decide which entity makes sense from a tax perspective while considering the tax consequences to the entity and the entrepreneurs.

The most critical nontax consideration is how to limit liability. Limited liability is defined as liability that is limited to the contributed capital.[20] If the entrepreneurs are contemplating a risky business venture and are of modest means, it is imperative to limit potential personal liability in the event the entity should be subject to a lawsuit or subsequently fail. Another critical consideration is the ownership structure because it affects whether the business entity should be a private or public company. Although it is difficult to choose the right entity type, it is strategically one of the most important decisions a company must make.

§ 2.03   FUNDING A STARTUP

Funding a new enterprise is always a challenge. During the heyday of the "Internet bubble," a little technology and a business plan were enough to land financing through an initial public offering (IPO). There was a rush in Silicon Valley to come up with some sort of business—any business—to cash in on the money to be made on an Internet IPO. Then the bubble burst. Investors realized that an Internet startup with few hard assets, an outrageous cash burn rate, and no hopes of profitability was not an investment but a money pit. Stock market and mutual fund investors as well as venture capitalists and institutions lost a great deal of money once the demand for technology stock plummeted. Today, financing is a tougher game, particularly for Internet-related ventures. Financing will remain difficult until the IPO market begins to improve.

Some entrepreneurs, however, believe that now is the best time to seek funding. Many venture capitalists also believe that now is a good time to invest.[21] The number of valid investment opportunities is smaller because there are fewer people out there willing to work hard to get funding and keep their business alive. Also, investors see that businesses still seeking funding deeply believe in their companies and products and have reasonable cash burn rates and a plan for profitability.

[A]   Funding Sources

Several sources of funding are available to entrepreneurs. The following resources may cost money in the form of interest but may not require the business owner to give ownership equity to the source of the funds.

---

[20] Westin, *supra* note 8, at 340.

[21] Matt Marshall, Menlo Park Venture Firm Keeps Up Investing Pace: New Enterprise Associates Thinking Long Term, Mercury News, May 18, 2002 (visited May 20, 2002), http://www.siliconvalley.com/mld/siliconvalley/3290532.htm.

[1] "Friends and Family"

"Friends and family" is the term used to describe funds raised from personal connections. Remember to include in your list of potential financers those of your acquaintances who are accredited investors (typically those with $1 million or more in net worth.) Do not comingle personal funds and business entity funds. Particularly when receiving funds from family, be sure to define and properly document the transaction. Is the money a loan, or is it an investment in exchange for equity in your enterprise? If it is an equity investment, be careful. Even small businesses must comply with securities regulations. Retain counsel to ensure that appropriate procedures are observed and documented. If this is not done and the business later needs another round of funding from other sources, expensive and troubling legal costs arise. This also leads to a great delay in gaining funds from those other sources.

[2] Federal and Local Grant Programs

As a way to encourage economic growth and development, the U.S. government gives grants to business owners. Matching funds and interest subsidies on loans may also be available. For instance, there may be federal, state, or local government or private grant money available to create jobs in certain areas of town. Grants do not have to be paid back, but they do come with strings attached. Low-interest loans or interest subsidies on loans may offer more flexibility. Tax breaks may also be negotiated between business owners and taxing authorities, if the number of jobs your venture will bring into the area is significant to the local authorities. Also, be sure to contact local and state economic development agencies. A grant writer may be a helpful resource for government as well as private funds. Check U.S. government as well as state web sites for more information. For federal funds, check the *Federal Register for Notices of Funding Availability* (NOFA), printed each business day by the federal government. NOFAs invite applications for federal grant programs.[22]

[3] U.S. Small Business Administration (SBA)

The SBA does not offer loans directly but does act as guarantor for certain loans obtained through its lending partners. Repayment terms and interest rates can be attractive. See the SBA web site at www.sba.gov for more information.

[4] Bank Loans

Banks are more conservative in their lending practices these days. Credit standards have tightened. Traditional asset-based financing may not be the easiest

---

[22] *See* http://ocd.usda.gov/nofa.htm (visited July 9, 2002) for a search engine that generates a customized list of NOFAs.

for the entrepreneur to achieve, but these loans should not be overlooked as a potential source of funding.

[5] Corporate Funds

Private corporations have venture funds. These funds are multipurpose for the corporation. They invest available company funds in private companies, hoping, like other investors, that the private companies will go public and they will reap rewards. In addition, these funds help nurture businesses that may be complementary to the corporation. Large technology companies tend to have venture funds. When applying, try to reach the business development director of the fund.

Entrepreneurs should be prepared to write to dozens of such funds. These funds are inundated with multiple requests and may not respond in a timely manner. Nevertheless, never give up the quest. It is possible, given market indicators and economic conditions, for a fund to contact an entrepreneur months after receiving the original funding request. In the event a business development director of a corporate fund calls, be prepared to succinctly respond to targeted questions and show the potential for the business offering and the target market.

However, before discussing your intellectual property in depth, always have the investing organization sign a nondisclosure agreement (NDA).[23] These contracts can be brief and are standard practice for protecting the intellectual property of your organization. Be sure to obtain good counsel from a knowledgeable lawyer, and do not rely on your own understanding of a nondisclosure agreement drafted by the corporation. Many entrepreneurs have run into trouble without this simple protection properly negotiated.

[6] Venture Capital

Why go through a venture capitalist (VC)? Many of these financial services firms are known to nurture innovation. Entrepreneurs say that the top four things VCs provide are strategic guidance, money, introductions to customers and partners, and introductions to investors.[24] Investment bankers do much the same thing but also have such frequent interactions with large public companies that they bring a useful public market perspective to the entrepreneur.[25]

Generally, institutional investors are reluctant to invest more money with venture capitalists' funds until the market for IPOs returns.[26] This means that new money that the VCs have available to invest is not coming into the VCs as fast.

---

[23] *See* Appendix A, Confidentiality Agreement for a sample NDA.

[24] Julie Landry, Enabling Innovation, Red Herring (online) (June 20, 2002), http://www.redherring.com/vc/2002/0620/innovation062002.html.

[25] *Id.*

[26] *See* Matt Marshall, Austin VC Firm Halts Fund Raising, Mercury News, Apr. 30, 2002 (visited May 15, 2002), http://www.siliconvalley.com/mld/siliconvalley/business/financial_markets/venture_capital/2954280.htm.

However, VCs still have such large sums of money to invest that they are seeking good investments currently.

[a]   Levels of Funding

1. Seed capital. The initial money to begin a business is termed seed capital. This is the earliest round of funding, and therefore has the highest risk. These funds are raised from "angel" investors. Angels invest based on the passion of the entrepreneur and the potential of the technology. Professional angel groups are being more aggressive these days, requiring a large block of equity in exchange for investment.[27]

2. Early stage financing/early institutional round of funding. Provided by many VCs. To receive funds at this stage, a company must have, at the least, positive beta-test results with happy beta-test customers.

3. Later institutional rounds of funding. In later rounds of financing, the company will have to show happy, paying customers, and good prospects for more paying customers.

[b]   Process for Applying for Venture Capital Funding

Generally, VCs prefer to receive a two-page executive summary of the business. Venture fund managers receive hundreds of proposals per week. They will not read a 60-plus-page business plan until and unless the executive summary sparks some interest. If the executive summary is of interest, VCs will ask for a full-blown business plan. If the full business plan—with its detailed explanation of the business, management, technology, competitive landscape, and reasonable financial plan—is also of interest, the VCs will ask for a meeting. To get to this point, however, the entrepreneur must use all of his or her networking skills. A business development professional with a wide range of contacts may be helpful.

[c]   Trends among Venture Capitalists

1. Entrepreneurs in residence. VCs cannot know all nuances of the start-up's marketplace, so they now rely on entrepreneurs. Many VCs have hired entrepreneurs-in-residence (EIRs) who were successful entrepreneurs in sectors in which the VC wishes to invest. The VCs rely on the EIR's judgment and ideas.[28] The goal is for the VC firm to invest in a startup where the EIR can be a major contributor to the success of that startup. The EIR of a VC firm can go into the portfolio company to help that company change direction, more fully develop ideas, or raise other funds.

---

[27] Mark Calvey, Firms with No Cash, No Clients Get Creative, San Francisco Bus. Times, June 14-20, 2002, at 12.

[28] Marshall, *supra* note 26.

2. More VCs are sharing deals. Previously, there was immediate buy-in so that the VCs could take more for themselves. Now, VCs are spreading the risks among themselves and are willing to share the investment opportunity with others. The money invested must be meaningful enough for the VCs to have some sway with the company, but not so much that the entrepreneur's zeal is dampened. VCs generally shoot for 20 percent ownership interest in a target company.

3. Investments tied to milestones. Investments are allotted over time, tied to the achievement of predetermined milestones. This is particularly true with early-stage investments. When milestones are not reached, VCs are quick to withdraw funding.

4. Higher scrutiny and full due diligence. Standards have been raised. VCs are careful to take their time these days doing full due diligence before they invest. Businesses most likely to be funded must show several things:

- Management team: A management team with a successful track record and a passion for the business.

- Technology: A disruptive or powerful technology that is more powerful than options currently available, or that will solve a problem efficiently for the masses.[29] In addition, investors consider competitive products in development by others (the "competitive landscape").

- Traction with customers: Paying customers who are using the product strategically with good results are critical to gaining later-stage financing.[30]

- Market size validation: How large is the target market? Be sure to express how this was determined.

- Financial plans: Include headcount and product development plans and costs based in reality.

5. Three to five years for exit value. Instead of looking for immediate IPO value in a hot and rising market (which is now history), VCs are expecting a three- to five-year time horizon for achieving exit value via IPO, sale, or merger. This gives companies a longer time to solidify their business. However, the time horizon for expected positive cash flow is still tight, at about 18 months.[31]

6. Smaller markets. New ideas focusing on smaller defined markets seem more favored by VCs and have the best potential for investment. Many innovations come from smaller markets. Village Ventures built a national network of early-

---

[29] Bill Roberts, Getting Real: It's the Only Way to Build a Company During Economic Adversity, Electronic Bus. Online, Apr. 1, 2002 (visited May 12, 2002), http://www.e-insite.net/eb-mag/index.asp?layout=article&stt=000&articleid=CA202931&pubdate=4/1/2002.

[30] *Id.*

[31] *Id.*

stage VC funds in emerging markets, raising national and local funds where there was a "relative lack of competitive sources of venture capital . . . readily accessible source of intellectual capital . . . a low cost of doing business . . . and a high quality of life."[32] Entrepreneurs in smaller markets should explore Village Ventures' funds and other sources in their area. The national players are not the only venture funds available.

7. Network. To increase the likelihood of funding, network. Get to know the VC community. Ask everyone you know for connections to their capital resources. Once connected with a VC firm, entrepreneurs must find one of the partners to be their champion with the rest of the VC partners. The value of this networking cannot be overstated. Each entrepreneur must have a strong advocate inside the venture capital group, as the vote to fund an organization generally must be unanimous among the VC partners. Most of all, do not give up. In this very changed and difficult funding market, entrepreneurs must be persistent to succeed.

§ 2.04 PURPOSE OF THE WEB SITE

The Internet has rapidly expanded with the promise of changing business processes and increasing business opportunities. The question of what to include on a web site is a very difficult one to answer. Most users who surf the Internet casually spend, on average, from thirty seconds to two minutes at a given web site. This short time does not allow the web site owner, or host, to distribute much information. Companies must meet the challenge of finding creative ways to translate surfing into online orders and to engender brand loyalty. The accomplishments will require making difficult decisions about what and how much information to include on the site. One way to manage the decision-making process is to put together a business requirements document.

[A] Business Requirements

Most companies concentrate on what they want to say or show but spend little time considering who might be viewing their pages and how these viewers will access the site. To ensure that the web site benefits the business and users, goals and objectives should be noted in a business requirements document. Every organization must first know who its target audience is and then design and advertise the web site accordingly. Some of the key questions that arise when organizing a site and preparing the business requirements include the following:

---

[32] Brian Taptich, Village Ventures Brings Innovation to Venture Capital, Red Herring (online) (Apr. 28, 2002), http://www.redherring.com/vc/2002/0428/2676.html.

Customer-Related Issues

- Which customers are you trying to attract?

- Are your target customers currently using the web?

- How can the web be used to keep customers? (Repeat customers generally cost less to service than acquiring new customers—thus, retaining and maintaining customers through web presence can be highly advantageous to your business.

- Does your web site provide the information your customers need?

- Who else might be in your target web audience that is not currently part of your target audience? Should you adjust your offerings for this new audience?

- How will your site maintain information on customers' profiles and preferences?

- Does the web site make purchasing a good or service simple and easy?

- Should online brochures be used?

- How can the web site be used to provide the highest level of customer support in a digital world?

- Are customer needs at the forefront of the online mission?

Connection- and Access-Related Issues

- How will users access or enter your site? Will the site have multiple access points?

- What kind of network connection will users have?

- What methods of payment will your site accept?

Product- or Service-Related Issues

- What information or products will users be looking for?

- How will you organize your site and your operations to build brand loyalty?

- Will your site allow for commercial sales? For advertising?

- Could your site be used to communicate with third parties, such as banks (e.g., payment processing), business partners, or suppliers?

Web Site Considerations-Related Issues

- Who will build the web site?

- Who will host the web site?

- Once the initial site has been built and hosted, who will modify the software design to update the site as necessary?

- Who will process credit card orders?

- Who will manage the order and fulfillment process?

Evaluating the foregoing issues will result in a well-thought-out business requirements document. The business requirements analysis should also identify the business risks, the profit opportunities, and the resources required to truly establish a solid commercial presence on the Internet. Creating an e-commerce-related site is a collection of many complex business decisions. Failure to fully analyze each decision can prove to be extremely costly down the road.

[B] Organizing Your Web Site

After completing the business requirements, a company must complete a functional requirements analysis to determine how to organize its site. Generally speaking, a company should organize its site into logical sections. A commercial web site may be broken down into sections such as Welcome, About the Company, Services and Products, Order/Response Form, and FAQs (Frequently Asked Questions). Depending on the company, a variety of other categories may make sense, such as pricing, service guarantees, performance, professional staff profiles, markets, locations, competition, ancillary products or services, and so on.

Each section should note appropriate disclaimers and disclosures, the company contact person, acceptable use policies, and indemnity statements. The Practice Pointers at the end of this chapter contain sample policies and disclosures. Irrespective of how a web site is organized, the site must reflect the image the company wants to project, as illustrated in Figure 2-2. A well-constructed web site will provide visitors with various levels of information, ranging from brief overviews to thorough specifications or other details.

[C] Web Site Content

The two most important pieces of information on a site are the products and services the sponsor sells and how customers can reach the seller. The web site should interest viewers enough that they browse through the site, buy goods, and return as repeat customers.[33] Web sites use images, illustrations, designs, icons, graphics, and streaming audio and video to convey a corporate image and to enhance good will. In addition to selling to customers, web sites offer an unprecedented opportunity for companies to seek feedback, criticism, suggestions, and ideas *from* customers. Virtual focus groups can provide invaluable feedback. You may want to include information promoting the company and its products and services, testimonials of successes, and competitive analyses. Keep in mind that both investors and competitors often use web sites as a starting point for research about

---

[33] For an example, *see* the Gap's web site at http://www.gap.com (visited May 15, 2002).

FIGURE 2-2

a company. Listing alliance partners, high-profile customers, and press coverage are useful marketing tools made possible by the Internet. The options are endless if branding can be maintained. Consider the following approaches:

- Start each page with a short paragraph summarizing the content displayed on that page. On every page, the most useful information should appear at the top.

- Incorporate corporate logos, branding look-and-feel, or other intellectual property notices into the site.

- Provide multiple access sources for your customers (phone, e-mail, site).

- Keep the site up to date.

- Avoid long download times.

- Provide detailed product, service, and pricing information.

- Include hypertext links to other pages within your site or to other ancillary sites (but avoid deep-linking liabilities with respect to third-party sites).

- Provide current information, such as new product releases, press releases, press coverage, or information about job openings.

- Include persuasive sales literature promoting products and specials, including online catalogs, ordering information, and order systems.

- Maintain and manage consumer registration and profile information.

- Provide a statement on the site relating to company policy, annual reports, and quarterly reports or include a corporate mission statement.

- Minimize the number of mouse clicks needed to get to useful information.

- Make navigation easy and information useful, so that viewers will have a reason to return. Always have your home page one click away from any location on your site.

- Make ordering simple and straightforward.

- State when the web site was last updated and provide contact information.

- Provide an on-site search engine to allow customers to be able to quickly find something in the event they are not familiar with your site.

- Insert metatags so that search engines will be drawn to your site.[34]

[D] Validating the Purpose of the Web Site

Creating and managing a web site is a never-ending task. Management needs to assign review roles to several different individuals once the site is in production. Specifically, a marketing lead and information technology lead must be engaged to validate that the site satisfies the goals and objectives of the organization. Table 2.3 lists some areas that need to be analyzed and validated.

§ 2.05 DEVELOPING AND MAINTAINING A COMMERCIAL WEB SITE

The procedures for establishing a commercial presence on the Internet have evolved rapidly since 1991, when the ban on commercial use of the Internet was lifted. But creating a web site that attracts and maintains potential customers is not easy. Companies should visit many other web sites to see how others are doing it. By analyzing various sites and business models, you can determine what works and what to avoid. Companies have spent as little as $500 and as much as $1,000,000 or more to establish and maintain their sites. Commercial web sites should have enough content to interest new as well as existing customers. A successful commercial web site, from a content perspective, helps its users learn enough about products to make them comfortable buying from that site. If the customer happens to buy the product, the entire experience must be enjoyable. Moreover, the transaction should be easy to complete and efficient. Users are usually hesitant to do any transaction on the web due to the fear of having their data compromised. A commercial site should articulate its privacy and security policies on the site. The site should let the users know what information the company is collecting and what it intends to do with it.

---

[34] *See* § 2.07[F] for a more in-depth discussion of metatags.

TABLE 2.3
Validating a Web Site's Purpose

Items That Need to Be Validated by the Marketing Lead

Issues	Consideration
Who is responsible for managing the web site?	Managing the overall content of a commercial web site is a full-time job. Different parts of the organization need to actively participate in the site's content. Interested groups must be identified and someone must assume final editorial control over the site.
Is the information on the site up to date?	It is important to have repeat visits to your site. Keeping your content fresh and new does this. Update the content with new images, articles, press releases, and offerings as necessary. Out-of-date content and prices will result in lost sales opportunities. Sites need to be frequently updated; certain pages may need to be updated on a daily or weekly basis.
Has the web site been integrated into the core business?	Maximize the integration of the online world with the brick and mortar world. Ensure that all company correspondence, marketing materials, e-mails, business cards, and advertisements promote the dot-com's URL.
Are the metatags effective?	Search engines are a great way to generate traffic. Metatags indicate what your web site is about. Common metatags include keywords and descriptions.
What steps should be taken to continue generating traffic?	Besides search engines and corporate literature, other steps must be taken to generate traffic. This can be done by banner ads, linking agreements, or mining customer data.
Are customer service needs being met?	To have repeat customers, it is imperative that proactive steps be taken to give the customers the best possible customer service. This means that the customer service is first rate in all instances: order processing, the shipping process, the return process, and the customer support process.

continued

TABLE 2.3
Validating a Web Site's Purpose (Continued)

Items That Need to Be Validated by the Marketing Lead

Issues	Consideration
What type of experience is created for each user?	Selling things on the web often means that you will do business with people that you have never met. The impersonal nature of the technology could result in lost sales. Examine what information is available: does the site have a nice user interface, does the site load fast, does the site provide alternative means to contact the organization?

Items That Need to Be Validated by the Information Technology Lead

Issues	Consideration
Is the site secure?	Security is critical. Businesses must protect themselves from hackers compromising critical data. Digital certificates, passwords, secure socket layer protocols, and the like may be required to keep the site safe and sound.
Is there a disaster recovery site/plan?	
How is the navigation process?	Ensure that the site is easy to navigate. Make sure that within your site you have the ability to return the user to the home page. In addition, a site map will also improve upon the accessible needs and interests.
What software tools should be used?	Technology changes fast. Many companies want to use bleeding-edge technology on their site. However, it is better to using leading-edge technology. C++, Domino, .Net, Java, HTML, and XML can all be used to do incredible things, but make sure that the software tools employed serve a practical and functional purpose.
Has the site been tested and retested?	If something doesn't work or the site is not stable, do not make it accessible to the outside world. See what the site looks like on various monitor settings and browser versions. Verify that all links work. Try to break the site: try to anticipate common user mistakes and see what impact, if any, they have on the site. Try every process: registration, ordering, fulfillment, FAQs, e-mail, etc. When updating the site, apply the update on a test site, prior to putting it in production, to ensure that it does not cause something else within the site to become inoperable.

continued

TABLE 2.3
Validating a Web Site's Purpose (Continued)

Items That Need to Be Validated by the Information Technology Lead

Issues	*Consideration*
How is the bandwidth?	Too much traffic is a great problem to have. However, the problem could become detrimental if the site cannot handle high volumes. Ensure that the site has enough bandwidth, server space, and high-speed connections.
How long does it take for a given web page to load?	Speed is always an issue. Since the web is impersonal, you may only have seconds to keep a customer engaged at your site. Set maximum sizes for each page.
How are the data being managed?	
Is the site easy to maintain?	Expect changes to be the one constant. Highly inflexible code will make maintaining the site a nightmare. Make sure that when designing the site consideration is given to each web page from a maintenance perspective.
How do you manage relationships with third parties?	Connectivity may be a key issue between your site and merchant accounts, in processing centers, or within different parts of the organization. Their may be some incompatibility issues based on the technologies between the different sites. The site may have to be redesigned to ensure seamless integration with other sites.

Another important attribute of a successful commercial web site is the ability to quickly load the web pages into the user's web browser. Sites that take too long to load are not visited often due to the time it takes the browser to load their contents. Users will be frustrated if the site is too slow to respond. Practically speaking, the site should be compatible with at least two major web browsers, such as Internet Explorer and Netscape Navigator versions 5.0 or higher.

Commercial sites should avoid script errors. A script error is a common programming error that renders the application inoperabile due to faulty code. If the site uses scripts and interactive databases, there is nothing worse for the user than receiving a script error. Script errors are annoying and can often cause the user's browser to crash. Another downfall of scripting errors is that hackers can use script errors to exploit the web server operating system. This can jeopardize the security of the personal information and the site itself.

In short, a commercial web site should have a professional approach throughout. This starts from the opening page and continues through every page visited. A professional look is difficult to define but is appreciated as users repeatedly visit the web site and also encourage others to do so. Moreover, companies that have successfully branded themselves on the web have done so by creating web sites that provide potential visitors with a reason to come, to stay, and ultimately to buy a particular product or service.

[A]   Internal versus External Development and Maintenance

After deciding to create a web site, the next critical decision a company must make is whether to outsource the web site development or to develop the site internally. Firms have several options. First, they may have the personnel and resources in-house to construct an effective web site. An Internet-based company may have better design capabilities than the average site developer. This viable option is considerably less expensive as long as the internal resources are capable of handling the fundamentals of going and staying online, including both technical and marketing savvy. Second, a company may decide to hire a third-party consultant to build and maintain the web site. The danger with this option is that a consultant may use a cookie-cutter approach, resulting in a web site that looks and feels like all the others developed by that consultant. For some companies, however, this may be appealing, since outside vendors specializing in such services can build efficient, creative web sites and maintain them for reasonable fees. Third, a company may elect to use a combination of internal resources and outside consultants. Depending on deadlines, resources available, and costs, this option may be best.

Keep in mind that if your organization chooses an option involving outside vendors, management should negotiate contracts that allow for appropriate transition and retention of ownership rights. One of the key negotiating points is ownership of the copyright and virtual trade dress of the web site. If content is provided by consultants, indemnification agreements with bullet-proof hold harmless clauses are also vital. The contract with the web site developer must, at a minimum, cover payment, pricing, warranties, and remedies and dispute resolution, as well as "address company growth, changes in company direction, even downturns."[35]

[1]   An Example of Building a Web Site Internally

For purposes of our hypothetical case, assume that since SPC is a computer company, senior management has decided to build the web site in-house.[36] Some

---

[35] Daniel Tully, Hammering Out a Contract? Hit These Points for a Good Deal!, Mass High Tech (Sept. 20-26, 1999), at 27.

[36] A firm setting up a web site needs IT professionals who can plan, design, build, test, launch, and maintain the site. A firm should not attempt to create a web site internally unless it has the required knowledgeable, experienced personnel within the organization.

of the advantages of building a web site internally are the ability to have full control over the entire site (flexibility in page, content, and site design), customization of each aspect of the site, ability to readily integrate a corporate brand, and lower ongoing maintenance costs. The executives at SPC, having established the corporate vision for the web site, met with their programmers to talk specifically about building SPC's web site. Senior management requests that the programmers inform them of the tools they need to build a web site. Accordingly, the programmers present the following list:

1. *Either a Mac or a PC.* The faster the machine and the more memory it has, the better. A solid Apple Macintosh should have at least a PowerPC G4, 700 MHz, 512 MB RAM, 40GB hard drive and a Mac OS X. An IBM clone should have at least a Pentium III, 1.3 GHz, 512 MB RAM, 40GB hard drive, and a Windows 2000 operating system.

2. *A web design tool.* A successful web site design appeals to sensory, conceptual, and reactive needs. In general, three types of web design tools are useful: a word processor; a web authoring tool; and a web site management tool. Word processors like Microsoft Word or WordPerfect may be used to create a simple web site using Hypertext Markup Language (HTML), a nonproprietary language that enables users to create web pages using simple commands. Web authoring tools differ from word processors, in that they allow design of web pages without an understanding of HTML code.[37] The site management tools used by sophisticated designers can help you create much faster web sites that are easier to maintain. Two of the more popular site management tools are Cold Fusion and NetObjects Fusion.

3. *A web browser.* Anyone developing a web site should design it to work with at least Microsoft Internet Explorer 5.0+ and Netscape Navigator 4.6+. Not all code renders the same output with a given browser.

4. *A graphics editor.* The developer must be able to manipulate the graphic images featured in most commercial web sites. Popular graphic editor programs include Adobe PhotoShop and Paint Shop Pro.

5. *A database tool.* A database tool is necessary to sell products or services or to manage customer data. A company may elect to build such a database in Oracle or Sybase or to tie into an existing database offered by a third-party vendor.

6. *A web server or host server.* In order to make the contents of the web site accessible to the world, a web server is required. The web server manages all of the HTML pages, databases, and credit card transactions needed to manage a commercial web site. If a company chooses to hire a web hosting company to host its site, it should consider the following:

---

[37] Some of the more popular web authoring tools include AOLPress; Microsoft's Front Page; Netscape's Navigator Gold; Adobe PageMill; and Sausage Software's Hot Dog.

the hosting company's available technical support, services, and bandwidth; the speed of its connections and peering; the quality of its site administration, security, and customer service; service level agreement; and the price it charges.[38]

In short, building a commercial web site internally involves a number of costs as well as benefits that should be carefully analyzed before beginning. A number of effective tools[39] may be used, but regardless of which software packages, graphics design tools, web server hardware and hosting, network connections, and ISP are utilized, each will have its associated expenses—and these can become very high. Failure to manage these expenses may affect the core business decisions that a company subsequently makes about its site.

[B] Updating Your Web Site

Web sites, like the products they sell, have a short shelf life. Firms need to stay at the leading edge and to market creatively dynamic content, products, and services. It makes absolutely no sense to build a commercial web site and then never update it. Is a customer likely to return to, let alone buy a product from, a company web site still advertising a Spring 2000 products list?

Maintaining a web site can become a full-time job, considering the range of tasks involved. These include removing outdated content; continually posting changes and updates; responding to customer demands; developing new content on a weekly basis; and redesigning enhancements to the site for things like personalized web pages or messages. The corporate webmaster must be familiar with the latest web site tools, web technologies, and security vulnerabilities, and be aware of and responsive to marketing programs, press releases, and other company news. The webmaster ought to be in the loop for all sales and marketing programs.

In developing the web site, the programmers at SPC came up with a few questions for the management team:

- What does management want to use as a domain name? Should the domain name incorporate an existing registered trademark? Other companies have already registered *www.SPC.com*, *www.suffolk.com*, and a few other obvious selections. An individual in Batesville, Indiana, has already registered *www. suffolkpcs.com*, but is willing to part with it for $50,000. Should SPC license or share the domain name?

- SPC is spending a lot of money to be on the Internet. How will it get people to visit the site?

---

[38] For a detailed discussion of host qualifications, *see* http://www.exeat.com/host.html (visited May 15, 2002).

[39] Tools include Adobe Acrobat, browsers, databases, diagnostic tools, editors, filters, firewalls, forms, gateways, graphics libraries, Java applets/scripts, Real Audio, search tools, security, Shockwave, tracking tools, viewers, and VRML, to name a few.

- Should SPC provide links to its software vendors, even though some of them have links directly to SPC's competitors?

- Should SPC create new pages for the technical specifications of its products or can it just frame the web sites of its suppliers? What about other web sites that will frame SPC's site just to do price comparisons?

- Is SPC willing to pay money to protect its proprietary data, intellectual property, and consumer data? What are the risks if SPC fails to do this?

The remaining sections within this chapter address the various issues raised above and provide some guidance in resolving them.

§ 2.06   STAKING A CLAIM IN CYBERSPACE: HOW TO CHOOSE A CORPORATE IDENTITY FOR THE INTERNET

With the explosive growth of e-business and the projected number of companies slated to establish a presence on the Internet, many existing and new companies are uncertain about how best to inaugurate their presence on the Internet.[40] Before jumping online and engaging in business transactions, the first thing a company needs is an address on the Internet, that is, an IP address or domain name. Unlike a traditional street address, the Internet address generally reflects the corporate name or identity.[41]

The best domain names are easy to remember and help brand a company's products or services. Where possible, in an effort to maintain their corporate identity, companies register a domain name in the form of "corporatename.com." Companies must take great care to register an appropriate domain name. Failure to procure the proper identity may result in a loss of potential customers, business partners, or other opportunities, which can translate into lower earnings.

Domain names arise from the Internet Protocol that makes the Internet possible. Every computer connected to the Internet has a unique Internet Protocol (IP) number, which allows connected computers to receive information through the network.[42] Because the IP number is a difficult-to-remember string of digits, the Domain Name Service provides a means for associating the number with a more easily remembered alphanumeric address. Corporations and individuals may regis-

---

[40] Network Solutions, Inc. registered more than 8,000,000 domain names between 1994 and 1999. Beth Fitzgerald, "Loans.com" Is the Latest Domain Name to Draw Big Bucks, Star Ledger, Jan. 28, 2000, available in LEXIS, News Library, Curnws file. Individuals and companies creating an online presence are registering domain names at a rate of 15,000 per day; by 2003, the total number of registered names is expected to reach 100,000,000. *Id.*

[41] *See* Gayle Weiswasser, Domain Names, The Internet, and Trademarks: Infringement in Cyberspace, 13 Santa Clara Computer & High Tech L.J. 137, 163 (1997) (noting domain name may include trademark).

[42] 63 Fed. Reg. 8826. *See also* Josh Goldfoot, Note, Antitrust Implications of Internet Administration, 84 Va. L. Rev. 909, 913 (1998).

ter unique domain names for their web sites.[43] Domain names thus generally have two addresses. The first is a series of numbers, separated by a period or a dot, such as "123.456.543.21,"[44] and the second an alphanumeric address, such as *microsoft.com*.[45] Numerical addresses are assigned by the Internet Corporation for Assigned Numbers and Names (ICANN), which allocates blocks of numerical addresses to regional registries. Entering the alphanumeric address *microsoft.com* in a web browser triggers a data transmission that obtains the IP number associated with that domain name (such as 206.111.111.11). This transmission ultimately engages Microsoft's host server, which renders Microsoft's home page for display on the inquiring user's computer screen. The alphanumeric names are assigned for ease of use, but they are not necessary to access a specific site.

Domain names are hierarchical and consist of two levels, the top level domain (TLD) and the second level domain (SLD).[46] In *microsoft.com*, for example, the top level domain, *.com*, indicates that the domain name owner is a commercial entity. The second level domain, *microsoft,* is the name of the commercial entity. Together, the TLD and SLD create the specified domain name *microsoft.com*.[47] The most common TLDs in the United States are *.com* (commercial organizations), *.net* (network service providers), *.gov* (government entities), *.mil* (military organizations), and *.edu* (schools, colleges, and universities), although other generic TLDs exist.[48] Country-specific domain names are administered in many different nations. Country code TLDs are often two characters representing the country or origin of the domain name, such as *.uk* for the United Kingdom or *.fr* for France.

Companies try to register domain names that reflect their corporate trademark[49] since the domain name symbolizes their corporate identity and can carry good will. The purpose of trademarks is to prevent consumer confusion as to the source of goods and services, and trademark rights relate to the mark as used with particular goods or services. As a result, different companies can have different trademarks that share the same name. The search engine Alta Vista, for example,

---

[43] *See* Dale Dallabrida, Companies Vying for Internet Domain Names, Gannett News Service, Sept. 15, 1997, at S12 (defining domain name).

[44] The first number signifies the computer's geographic region; the second number, a specific ISP; the third number, a specific group of computers; and the fourth number, a specific computer within that group. G. Peter Albert, Jr., Eminent Domain Names: The Struggle to Gain Control of the Internet Domain Name System, 16 J. Marshall J. Computers & Info. L. 781, 784 (1998).

[45] Hearst Corp. v. Goldberger, 96 Civ. 3620 (PKL) (AJP), 1997 U.S. Dist. LEXIS 2065, at *7 (S.D.N.Y. Feb. 26, 1997).

[46] Department of Commerce, Management of Internet Names and Addresses, 63 FR 111 (June 10, 1998).

[47] Guy T. Donatiello, Internet Domain Names: What's All the Confusion?, Legal Intelligencer Intell. Prop. Supp., Mar. 24, 1997, at 3.

[48] Other top-level domains (TLDs) include .aero, .agent, .arts, .auction, .biz, .chat, .church, .club, .family, .free, .game, .golf, .inc, .info, .kids, .law, .llc, .llp, .love, .ltd, .med, .mp3, .name, .school, .scifi, .shop, .soc, .sport, .tech, .travel, .tv, .video, and .xxx. Newnet (visited June 15, 2002), http://www.new.net.

[49] Trademarks are defined as words, symbols, or devices used to denote one's products or services as a way to distinguish them from all others.

has a separate and distinct trademark from that of Alta Vista Sports.[50] In their respective markets, however, consumers are not likely to be confused between the two companies.

While multiple trademarks may exist contemporaneously in different countries and in different product classes in the United States, Internet domain names are unique worldwide.[51] Consequently, alphanumeric domain names that incorporate trademarks have created into a litigation explosion pitting trademark owners against domain name registrants.[52]

[A] Registering Names

Commercial use of the Internet has led to a domain name gold rush with a colorful cast of cybersquatters, pirates, and scoundrels. Traditionally, domain names have been assigned on a first-come, first-served basis, which allows a registrant to register any desired name as long as it is available at the time. Consequently, nothing guarantees that a trademark owner will be able to register the desired domain name.[53] When Hess Oil Corp., for example, wanted to register *hessoil.com*, it found

---

[50] *See* http://www.altavistasports.com (visited May 15, 2002).

[51] *See* Legal Update, Brand Strategy, Sept. 19, 1997, at 21 (identifying Internet domain name trademark conflicts). Multiple owners of identical trademarks are also a source of domain name conflicts in the United States. *See* Bob Woods, Spree.com Sues Sprint in Preemptive Move Over Domain Name, Newsbytes, Sept. 18, 1997, available in LEXIS, News Library, Curnws File (outlining conflict between Internet retailer Spree.com and Sprint's Spree telephone cards). Internet addresses are unique, allowing only one "spree.com" site address. *See id.*

[52] *See* Kurt A. Wimmer, E-Litigation, What's in a Net Name, Nat. Law J., Dec. 4, 2000, at A23 (observing increase in domain name litigation due to broader options for trademark holders); Electronic Intellectual Property Protection: Hearings on H.R. 3163 Before the Subcomm. on Courts and Intellectual Property of the House Comm. on the Judiciary, 105th Cong. (1998) (testimony of Theodore H. Davis, Jr., Chairman, Federal Trademark Legislation Committee of the Section of Intellectual Property Law of the American Bar Association) (noting tension between business community's trademark interests and needs of overall Internet community). *See also* Sharon Schmickle, Slumberland's Legal Battle Over Internet Site Name Is Indicative of Larger Unrest, Minneapolis Star Trib., Apr. 19, 1998, at 1A (questioning whether commercial entities can register premium domains while individuals must settle for second rate names).

[53] *See* Dallabrida, *supra* note 43 (listing multiple trademark owners who would want same Internet address). Many domain name registrars operate on a first-come, first-served basis. *See* David Noack, Newspapers Sue Over Net Domain Names, Editor and Publisher, Nov. 22, 1997, at 28. Network Solutions, for example, does not determine which domain names infringe trademarks; it relies on the trademark owner to enforce his or her rights. *See id.* Trademark holders who find an infringing Internet site that was registered by NSI may request that NSI put the domain name on hold until the domain name owner and the trademark holder resolve the dispute. *See id.*

Other countries also favor the first registrant of a domain name in their domain name systems. *See* Rob Hosking, New Zealand: Internet Name Case Favours Earlybirds, Nat. Bus. Rev., June 6, 1997, available in LEXIS, News Library, Curnws File (noting New Zealand's first-come, first-served Internet domain name registration policy); British Court Says First Domain Name Registrant Gets to Keep It, Computer & Online Industry Litig. Rep., July 15, 1997, at 24431 available in LEXIS, News Library, Curnws File (detailing results of dispute between two trademark holders in United Kingdom); Heiner Buenting, The New German Multimedia Law—A Model for the United

the soil-testing company HES Soil had already registered the domain.[54] Similarly, *delta.com* was originally owned by a small technology firm, not by Delta Air Lines, which used *delta-air.com* as its domain name until it acquired rights to *delta.com*.[55] Because the Internet does not have a comprehensive directory and users may have difficulty finding a company's web site, companies usually want a memorable Internet address like *www.fedex.com* rather than the more unwieldy *www.suffolk.edu/ law/hightech/classes/spring01/course/index.html*.[56]

Another advantage to registering a distinctive domain name is that consumers tend to guess when trying to find a particular company's web site.[57] Several cases have recognized that people surfing the Internet guess at a company's domain name by entering the company name between *www* and *.com*.[58] Having the right domain name is, therefore, essential to an effective marketing strategy that reaches the desired customer base; it is also likely to prove to be a valuable organizational asset.[59]

When guessing at a domain name, consumers do not know what company they have reached until the vendor's web site is opened, showing who is actually using the domain name.[60] A few years ago, for example, users who entered *AltaVista.com* were surprised to learn that they had not reached the Alta Vista search engine but had stumbled on another company that had registered Alta Vista as its domain name. The search engine company Alta Vista ultimately bought the domain name for over $3,000,000.[61] Shopping on the Internet can at times be analogous to walking into

---

States?, Computer Lawyer, Sept. 1997, at 17 (illustrating trademark conflicts under Germany's first-come, first-served domain name registration system); Chu Moy, Trademark Strategies and Offensives in E-Commerce, E-Business Advisor, Nov. 1998, at 12 (noting Belgian court's adoption of first-come, first-served domain name policy for companies).

[54] *See* Ron Fluery et al., Inadmissible, N.J.L.J., Nov. 24, 1997, at 3 (noting Hess Oil's domain name lawsuit).

[55] *See* Eryn Brown, The Net Name Game, Fortune, Feb. 16, 1998, at 124 (highlighting concern about Internet governance); *see also* Morning Business Report: ABC World News This Morning (ABC television broadcast, transcript # 98021604-j03, Feb. 16, 1998) (commenting on Nabisco's challenge to individual's registration of www.oreos.com).

[56] *See, e.g.,* Leora Herrmann & Andrew T. Tarshis, Domain Names and the Courts, Conn. L. Trib., Oct. 6, 1997, available in LEXIS, News Library, Arcnws file (explaining value of easy to find web address); *see also* Arun Natarajan, The Utility of a Bouncing Web Address, Bus. Line, Oct. 8, 1997, at 7, available in LEXIS, News Library, Arcnws File (recognizing brand benefits and ease of memorizing exclusive domain name).

[57] *See* Trademark Confusion Is Tangling Up the Web, Companies Decry Net Address Chaos, Online Buyers Are Left Guessing, St. Louis Post-Dispatch, Feb. 18, 1998, at A5 (comparing process of looking for company on Internet to "shopper's roulette").

[58] *See generally* Cardservicec Int'l, Inc. v. McGee, 950 F. Supp. 737, 741 (E.D. Va. 1997).

[59] Panavision Int'l v. Toeppen, 1998 U.S. App. LEXIS 7557, at *32 (9th Cir. April 17, 1998). The court held that "a domain name mirroring a corporate name may be a valuable corporate asset, as it facilitates communication with a customer base." *Id.*

[60] *See* Paul Carlyle, Why Squatters Aren't Budging from the Domain, Scotsman, Dec. 17, 1997, at 7 (explaining that companies may resort to litigation to resolve domain name confusion issues). Although consumers may not be confused between a sporting goods company and a software manufacturer, they may not know which company they are accessing until they are already in the Internet site. *See id.*

[61] Briefs: Microsoft Files Suit Over Cybersquatting/Online Organizing for Living and Work, Ventura County Star, Jan. 4, 1999, at E01.

what one thought was a grocery store, only to find automobile parts on the shelves.[62]

[B] Selecting and Registering a Domain Name and Resolving Domain Name Disputes[63]

Internet sites clearly represent valuable commercial commodities for companies because they offer 24-hour-a-day exposure to potential customers.[64] By using domain names identical to their corporate names, companies facilitate communication with potential customers.[65] In addition to reaching domestic customers, a domain name can be a corporation's "passport across the border into cyberspace."[66]

Popular domain names have increased in value, with some selling for many times the $100 registration price.[67] *Business.com*, for example, sold for $7.5 million in 1999,[68] which may have been a reasonable price at the time, considering the traffic and attention the domain name may have generated. Many domain names have lost much of their value, however, in the wake of the myriad online business failures, aka "dot-com bombs." Still, many Internet users in the United States represent a desirable demographic profile. An easy to find and remember domain name can facilitate corporate access to those users.[69] Popular trademarks

---

[62] *See supra* note 55 (comparing Internet shopping to finding computer software for sale at fast food restaurant).

[63] Trademarks and domain name legal issues are explored extensively in § 4.03. This section is intended to provide a strategic overview.

[64] *See* Haelan Products Inc. v. Beso Biological, No 97-0571, 1997 U.S. Dist. LEXIS 10565, at *10 (C.D. La. July 14, 1997) (comparing temporary nature of magazine and television advertisements to Internet); SF Hotel Co. v. Energy Inv. Inc., 985 F. Supp. 1032, 1034 (D. Kan. 1997) (recognizing Internet facilitates worldwide commerce from desktop computer).

[65] *See* MTV Networks v. Adam Curry, 867 F. Supp. 202, 204 n.2 (S.D.N.Y. 1994) (identifying domain name as potentially valuable corporate asset); Gary W. Hamilton, Trademarks on the Internet: Confusion, Collusion or Dilution?, 4 Tex. Intell. Prop. L.J. 1, 5 (noting that many may argue that domain names function as trademarks).

[66] David Post, Breaking Up the Domain Name Monopoly, Recorder, Sept. 25, 1997, Business and Technology, at 4 (warning that without a domain name, one becomes invisible on Internet).

[67] Memorable domain names are now selling for millions of dollars. Dot-Com Squatters Lose Cyberwars, Toronto Star, Jan. 23, 2000, available in LEXIS, News Library, Curnws File. One observer noted that a name on the Internet may be worth the $100 it cost to register it as a domain name, but in court it is worth "damages in an amount to be determined at trial." Gina Fann, Country Stars' 'Net Suit Eyed; First Amendment Rights an Issue, Tennessean, Apr. 11, 1998, at 1E.

[68] For a list of the top prices paid for domain names, see Domain Mart (visited June 15, 2002), http://www.domainmart.com/interact/most-valuable.htm. *See also* Prices Skyrocket for Choice Internet Sites, Deseret News, Jan. 23, 2000, at M5 (noting competition for popular domain names). The domain name *business.com* originally set a price record in 1997 when it sold for $150,000. USA: Record Price Paid for Internet Name, Computergram, June 6, 1997, available in LEXIS, News Library, Arcnws File.

[69] *See* Luxury Items Attract Upscale Web Shoppers; Consumers Graduate from Buying Books and Baubles Online, San Jose Mercury News, Dec. 20, 1999, at 2 (noting Internet users tend to be better educated and wealthier than the average population). As more individuals obtain access to the Internet, however, the demographics migrate more toward the general population. Shannon Obern-

such as McDonald's or Marlboro are valued in the billions of dollars, so it should come as no surprise that related domain names are also becoming valuable corporate assets.[70]

Corporations must also consider in which top level domain their name will reside.[71] The most popular Internet domains, such as *.com* or *.net*, are in high demand, while country code alternatives, such as *.us* and *.jp,* are not commonly used.[72] Newly added domain names include *.aero*, *.biz*, *.coop*, *.info*, *.museum*, *.name*, and *.pro*.[73]

[1]   Trademarks

Businesses must protect their valuable trademarks in cyberspace.[74] Trademark owners in the United States can enhance their domestic protection by registering with the Patent and Trademark Office.[75] Not every trademark, however, can be registered, and this should be considered by an entity looking to create an identity online.[76] Examples of some restrictions include the refusal of the Patent and Trademark Office to register a descriptive trademark (such as *tissues.com*), a trademark similar to another registered mark,[77] or an immoral or scandalous mark.[78] Domain names already in use, such as *yahoo.com*, can be registered as trademarks,[79] but domain names that do not have a corresponding Internet site may

---

dorf, Know Thy Buyer, Customer Profiles Differ by Medium, Catalog Age, Oct. 1999, available in LEXIS, News Library, Curnws File.

[70] *See* GreatDomains.com, which offers to assist clients in buying and selling domain names: http://www.greatdomains.com (visited April 26, 2001).

[71] *See* Andrew Craig, U.S. Domain Extension May Ease Shortage, TechWeb News, Feb. 21, 1998, available in LEXIS, News Library, Curnws File (explaining popularity of some top level domains and lack of interest in others).

[72] *See id.* (noting business risk of using *.us* instead of *.com*).

[73] New Top Level Domains, http://www.ICANN.org. *See also* Mark Wigfield, Congress Unlikely To Reverse ICANN Internet Names, Dow Jones Newswires, 02/08/2001 (last visited April 26, 2001), http://www.dowjonesnewswires.com.

[74] A trademark is a distinctive "word, name, symbol, device," or combination that identifies goods or services and distinguishes them from other goods and services. Restatement (Third) of Unfair Competition § 9 (1995).

[75] *See* Lanham Act § 1, 15 U.S.C. § 1051 (1996) (delineating trademark registration procedures in the United States).

[76] *See* Lanham Act § 2, 15 U.S.C. § 1052 (1996) (listing grounds for refusing trademark registration).

[77] *But see* Park 'N Fly, Inc. v. Dollar Park & Fly, Inc., 469 U.S. 189, 191 (1985) (defining incontestable, descriptive trademark that has acquired secondary meaning). A registered trademark can become incontestable after five continuous years of use.

[78] *Id.*

[79] *See* Sabra Chartrand, Patents; The Process of Filing an Application Is Slowly Catching Up with the Technology Available, N.Y. Times, Jan. 26, 1998, at D2 (explaining applicants registering domain names as trademarks must show that Internet site exists for name). One observer noted a large increase in the number of applications to register domain names as trademarks. *See* Molly Buck Richard, It's Easier to Protect Some Intellectual Property, Texas Lawyer, Nov. 30, 1998, at 34 (noting Patent and Trademark Office's recognition that domain names may function to identify source of goods or services).

not be registered as trademarks unless the domain name has another use in commerce.[80]

A visible brand name, by fostering consumer recognition and differentiating its products from others in the marketplace, can be a competitive advantage for a company.[81] By registering a trademark, the trademark holder helps to protect its valuable brand name.[82] Popular trademarks may be worth billions of dollars in sales because of the value of brand recognition.[83]

In our earlier example, SPC could register a domain name that reflects its trademark, provided that the domain name were available. *SPC.com*, a natural choice, has already been taken, so SPC would need to consider other possible names. SPC might use a name with broad reach, such as *www.personalcomputers. com*, as its domain name, but this name, because it is generic, is not afforded trademark protection.[84]

[2]   Registration Process: Domestic and Foreign Registrations

Once a company has chosen a domain name, or collection of domain names, it must register the domain name(s). In the early to mid-1990s, Network Solutions, Inc. (NSI) had an exclusive government contract to build a database and registry system for the *.com*, *.org.*, *.net*, *.gov*, and *.edu* domain names.[85] NSI was awarded this authority under a contract from the National Science Foundation (NSF).[86] NSI established InterNIC to carry out this process, and ICANN succeeded InterNIC. Under the NSI system, in order to register a domain name, applicants had only to pay a $70 registration fee for the domain name they sought to be assigned to them for the two-year period then allowed.[87]

This process and the associated fees have changed, now that the U.S. government has deregulated the sales of domain names. Registrants can now choose

---

[80] *Id.* (outlining restrictions on registering domain names as trademarks). To qualify for registration, the domain name must identify and distinguish the goods or services and indicate their origin. *See id.* Domain names that are only "directional references," such as addresses or telephone numbers, may not be registered as trademarks. *See id.*

[81] *See* James Saunders, How Best to Keep Rivals' Hands Off Your Brands, Scotsman, Oct. 22, 1997, at 7 (citing additional benefits of having Internet presence). Trademark protection on the Internet protects both trademark holders and Internet users by ensuring credibility. *See* IPR Protection on Net to be Discussed, Businessworld, Apr. 2, 1998, available in LEXIS, News Library, Curnws File (quoting World Intellectual Property Organization).

[82] *Id.* (advocating brand owners to protect their trademarks).

[83] The Coca-Cola brand was assessed for $72 billion for the year 2000. Kohli Chiranjeev & Lance Leuthesser, Brand Equity; Capitalizing on Intellectual Capital. *See* Category Charts, Superbrands, Ad Week Supplement, Oct. 20, 1997, at 110 (listing sales revenue and total advertising by brand).

[84] The U.S. Patent and Trademark office published a helpful article on registering domain names as trademarks at http://www.uspto.gov/web/office/tac/notice/guide299.htm (last visited April 26, 2001).

[85] *See* Kelly Flaherty, NSI Focus of Internet Talks in Congress, Recorder, Oct. 2, 1997, at 1 (detailing NSI's Internet address domain).

[86] *Id.*

[87] Applicants can visit InterNIC's web site at http://rs.internic.net (visited May 15, 2000). *See also*, Domains 'R' Us, Communications Today, Apr. 22, 1999.

among a number of domain name registrars, many of which offer different options for pricing and web site hosting.[88]

To start the registration process, the applicant should first assess whether the desired domain name is available, which can be done through Network Solutions' 'whois' database[89] or through another registrar.[90] The 'whois' database also contains a record of registrants for existing domain names. Secondly, the applicant should select a registrar. Many have different prices, terms, and options, ranging from hosting to bulk registration. Additionally, the applicant needs to decide on the term of the registration. Registration terms can vary from one year to ten years, or even longer.[91] Finally, the applicant fills out a registration application, usually completed online at a registrar's web site, and submits the completed application to the registrar. Applicants may receive written or e-mail confirmation, depending on the particular requirements of the individual registrar.

Once approved, the applicant must pay the registration fee or the domain name may be revoked, leaving it vulnerable to registration by another party.[92] Additionally, accredited registrars will transfer domain names to other owners if requested to do so by the registered owner, upon an order from a court or tribunal, or based on a decision from an administrative panel.[93] A word of caution—unfortunately, there are cybersquatters/hackers out there that try to register domain names that you may be interested in. By typing in a desired domain name at a registrar to see if it is available, you may be making that name available to hackers. Some hackers have even created automated searches that note all search attempts at registrars resulting in available names, and then automatically register those names. This is cybersquatting, and could be expensive to fight or settle. When seeking a domain name from a registrar, be prepared to immediately pay for the registration once you have found your desired domain name available.

[3] Registering Multiple Names

In today's competitive marketplace, given the importance of domain names, companies should consider registering multiple domain names. Our hypothetical

---

[88] For a list of domain name registrars accredited by ICANN, visit http://www.icann.org/registrars/accredited-list.html (last visited June 15, 2002).

[89] *See* http://www.netsol.com (last visited June 15, 2002).

[90] *See* John Hill, Stake Your Claim with a Domain Name, Columbian (Vancouver, Washington), Feb. 11, 1998, at C1 (explaining "who is" Internet query to see if someone has registered domain name). Alternative whois databases, such as http://www.betterwhois.com (visited June 15, 2002), may also provide helpful research tools for establishing a domain name.

[91] Patricia Jacobus, Register.com to Offer 10-Year Net Name Registrations, CNET News.com, Jan. 5, 2000 (visited April 26, 2001), http://www.register.com/domain-news/jan052000.cgi?1[843279433].

[92] Real Life Corporate Domain Name Challenges, http://www.verisign.com/rsc/wp/domain-Name_wp.html (last visited April 26, 2001).

[93] The current domain name dispute resolution policy is available at http://www.icann.org/udrp/udrp.htm (visited June 15, 2002).

company, SPC, for example, might want to consider registering *www.spc.com*, *www.suffolkpc.com*, and *www.suffolkpersonalcomputers.com*. Absent a challenge, any or all of these domain names can be readily assigned, ensuring that several different domain names lead consumers to SPC.[94]

Several other important reasons exist for companies to register multiple domain names. First, they may need to reserve the names for future products or services. Nothing requires that the registered domain name be used immediately or within a specified time period. The lack of such a restriction allows companies as yet unprepared to create an Internet presence to reserve domain names for future use,[95] and many companies reserve or register names for products under development.[96]

Another popular reason to register multiple domain names is to capture users who inadvertently misspell or use variants of a domain name. Domain names registered by other firms that exploit typing or other errors could arguably dilute a company's online value.[97] Fidelity Investment, for example, owns *www.fidelitu.com* and other variations.[98] Large companies with valuable names should register potential name variations and misspellings to assist consumers in finding the site and to prevent others from exploiting these errors.[99]

Finally, a company may want to avoid negative publicity deriving from parody sites or sites that may cause confusion.[100] Not all use of trademarks in domain

---

[94] Many companies try to register as many domain names as possible, including domain names that would result from commonly made typographical errors or other mistakes. Lotus, for example, has registered Lotus.com as well as Lotus.net.

[95] *See* $50 for Domain Name Register & Free Domain Name Research Tool, Business Wire, Sept. 30, 1997, available in LEXIS, News Library, Arcnws File (advertising service reserving domain names pending customer activation on Internet).

[96] *See* Dallabrida, *supra* note 43 (noting Dupont registers products in development).

[97] *See* Lawrence Magid, Sex Sites Capitalizing on Misleading URLs, L.A. Times, Mar. 2, 1998, at D3 (listing now defunct *www.disnie.com* and *www.nasa.com*, adult web sites). A current list of such so-called stealth sites is available at http://www.webchaperone.com/stealthlist.html (visited Sept. 16, 1999). *See id.* New sites, however, quickly replace those that have been shut down. *See* Jon Swartz, Government Parasites; "Stealth" Web Pages Feed Off Addresses, San Francisco Chron., June 3, 1998, at D1 (noting proliferation of such sites has prompted legislation). While NASA was successful in eliminating "nasa.com," for example, other registrants created *nassa.com*, filling the site with pornographic photos. *See id.*

[98] *See* Todd Wallack, If It's Rude, They Want It—Companies Eat Up Internet Names, Boston Herald, Dec. 30, 1997, at 1 (noting another company registered misspellings of "Fidelity" to try to increase traffic to its web site).

[99] *See id.* (suggesting Fortune 500 companies should register almost anything relating to their trademarks). Domain name registrants trying to exploit misspellings of trademarks may face legal action. Copy-Cat Domain Names Can Spell Trouble, Deutsche Presse-Agentur, Jan 23, 2000, Available in LEXIS, News Library, Curnws File.

[100] *See id.* (illustrating corporate preemptive strike to avoid angry customer's registration of pejorative domain name). In addition to exposure to confusion or criticism, some trademark holders have discovered that hate groups registered their trademarks as domain names and sent visitors to a white supremacist web site. *See* Mary McLachlin, Internet Surfers Hijacked to West Palm Hate Site, Palm Beach Post, Dec. 21, 1998, at 1A (noting hate group registered name variations of fourteen newspapers). Following legal action, the newspapers were able to have the infringing sites transferred or shut down. *See id.*

names, however, is infringing: news commentary and other noncommercial uses of a trademark, for example, are not actionable under the Lanham Act.[101] Individuals have registered Microsoft parody sites, including *www.microsnot.com* and *www.microsos.com*.[102] Bell Atlantic registered *bellatlanticsucks.com* and *bigyellowsucks.com*, after discovering that an individual had registered *nynexsucks.com*.[103] Unfortunately, when Bell Atlantic let the domain name expire, critics quickly posted a new web site at *bellatlanticsucks.com*.[104] In one similar case,[105] a federal district court held that the defendant's use of "Bally Sucks" neither constituted federal trademark infringement nor diluted the plaintiff's mark, because the defendant's criticism was not a common use of Bally's mark.[106] Of course, there have been instances where critics, finding *www.xxxsucks.com* already registered by the company in question, have registered *www.xxxreallysucks.com*. Balance the need for multiple registrations with good judgment.[107]

In short, every company could potentially face one or all of the aforementioned issues, which would point to multiple registrations. Absent economic constraints, registering multiple domain names is a sound business decision.

[4] Resolving Domain Name Disputes

Before companies were fully aware of the value of domain names, entrepreneurs registered many names, including some using valuable trademarks, and then

---

[101] *See* Lanham Act § 43(c)(4), 15 U.S.C. § 1125(c)(4) (1996). Compare Cliff Notes, Inc. v. Bantam Doubleday Dell Pub. Group, Inc., 886 F.2d 490, 497 (2d Cir. 1989) (finding no infringement in Spy magazine's Cliff Notes parody "Spy Notes," which was marked "satire"), and L.L. Bean, Inc. v. Drake Publishers, Inc., 811 F.2d 26, 34 (1st Cir. 1987) (allowing High Society parody of L.L. Bean Catalog, "L.L. Beam's Back to School Sex Catalog"), with Anheuser-Busch, Inc. v. Balducci Publications, 28 F.3d 769, 796-97 (8th Cir. 1994) (concluding Snicker magazine's "Michelob Oily" parody advertisement infringed "Michelob Dry" because trademarks not sufficiently altered), and Mutual of Omaha Ins. Co. v. Novak, 836 F.2d 397, 403 (8th Cir. 1987) (finding likelihood of confusion with antinuclear protester's "Mutant of Omaha" T-shirts and Mutual of Omaha Insurance).

[102] *See* Rebecca Quick, In High Jeer; Home-Page Parodies Proliferate on Free-Wheeling Web, Pittsburgh Post-Gazette, Mar. 23, 1998, at D3 (comparing parody sites and corporate responses); *see also* Hormel Foods Corp. v. Jim Henson Prods., 73 F.3d 497, 507 (2d Cir. 1996) (finding puppet "Spa'am" did not infringe "Spam" because likable character did not cause negative associations). *But see* Deere & Co. v. MTD Prods., Inc., 41 F.3d 39, 45 (2d Cir. 1994) (finding fearful deer parodying Deere logo in competitive advertisement diluted trademark).

[103] *See* Wallack, *supra* note 98 (discussing Bell Atlantic's alarm at vulgar Internet sites using company name).

[104] *See id.* (claiming company focuses on customer service rather than preventing customers from creating forums for complaints). Unfortunately, derogatory terms are too numerous for companies to hope to register every one. *See id.*

[105] Bally Total Fitness. v. Faber, 23 F. Supp. 2d 1161 (C.D. Cal. 1998).

[106] Microsoft's Law & Corporate Affairs, Summary of Global Internet Legal Developments 63 (April 1999) (reporting decision).

[107] Gwendolyn Mariano and Evan Hansen, Parody Sites Sucked into Cybersquatting Squabbles, CNET News.com, Aug. 24, 2000 (visited Aug 25, 2000), http://yahoo.cnet.com/news.

offered to sell them to the trademark holders for a lucrative premium.[108] These registrants are referred to as cybersquatters.

Other domain name disputes which do not necessarily involve cybersquatters may include:

- Generic terms that have meaning beyond the trademarked name;

- Intentional misspelling of trademarks in the hopes of drawing traffic through typographical errors;

- Acronyms that have meanings for multiple groups;

- Parody, criticism, and "sucks" site;

- Reverse cybersquatting wherein a corporation late to register sues a lawful registrant.

Both parties may have legitimate rights in some of the disputes listed above, and before pursuing any legal action, trademark holders should seek the advice of competent counsel.

[a] Legal Remedies

The first line of defense against an infringing domain name registrant is a cease and desist letter from legal counsel requesting the transfer of the disputed domain name. This is an inexpensive remedy and may be effective against infringers who do not want to risk the potential expense and penalties of litigation. Often, as a good-faith gesture, trademark holders will offer to pay for reasonable expenses associated with the transfer. Registrants may not be willing to part with their domain names, and more firm legal remedies can be necessary. Even as early disputes arose, however, courts in the United States and other countries provided

---

[108] *See* Panavision Int'l. v. Toeppen, 938 F. Supp. 616, 618 (C.D. Cal. 1996) (returning *panavision.com* to Panavision International), *aff'd,* 141 F.3d 1316 (9th Cir. 1998). Toeppen demanded $13,000 to discontinue using *panavision.com* after Panavision asked to use the domain name. *See id.* at 619. Rather than returning the name, Toeppen registered another Panavision trademark, *panaflex.com. See id.* Toeppen had registered other trademarks as domain names, including *lufthansa.com, neiman-marcus.com,* and *intermatic.com. See id.; see also* Intermatic Corp. v. Toeppen, 947 F. Supp. 1227, 1229 (returning *intermatic.com* to Intermatic Corp.); American Standard, Inc. v. Toeppen, No. 96-2147, 1996 U.S. Dist. LEXIS 14451, *2-3 (C.D. Ill. Sept. 3, 1996) (granting American Standard's request for preliminary injunction against use of *americanstandard.com* domain name); Tom Campbell, Reynolds Domain Is Foiled for Now; Trademark Lawsuit Focuses on Web Site, Richmond Times Dispatch, Dec. 30, 1997, at A1 (examining Reynolds Metals discovery that another company had registered *reynoldswrap.com*). The World On Net, Inc. had registered *reynoldswrap.com* in addition to *davematthewsband.com, tysonscornercenter.com,* and *dustinhoffman.com. See id.* World On Net, Inc. claimed it had registered the names for noncommercial commentary and parody. *See id.* Noncommercial use, news reporting, and news commentary are not actionable under federal false description of origin or dilution claims. *See* Lanham Act § 43 (c)(4), 15 U.S.C. § 1125(c)(4) (1996) (listing federal trademark infringement exceptions).

relief from individuals who registered infringing domain names for the sole purpose of reselling the domain name to others.[109]

In earlier disputes, trademark owners often sought the transfer of the domain name as a remedy. More recently, however, courts have been imposing substantial damages against egregious cybersquatters. For example, a cybersquatter who has earnings close to $1 million per year in advertising hosted on his infringing domain names was ordered to pay $530,000 in damages to one trademark holder.[110] Overseas, in one landmark case, two British domain name dealers were ordered by the United Kingdom High Court to pay £65,000 (U.S. $110,000) in legal costs and to transfer the infringing domain names to the trademark owners.[111] Cybersquatters in the United States may be liable for $1,000 to $100,000 per infringing domain name, thus diminishing the incentive and increasing the risk to the cybersquatter.[112] A trademark holder may, therefore, reasonably pursue litigation to obtain the infringing domain name and even, potentially, to recover attorneys' fees and damages.[113]

In the United States, trademark owners may employ a variety of causes of action to pursue cybersquatters and other infringers. Keep in mind that trademark law is designed to protect consumers and not to provide businesses with a monopoly on the English language. Gateway 2000, for example, was unable to convince a judge that *gateway.com* infringed on its famous trademark, since there was no evidence that Gateway 2000 had used the term "gateway" independently.[114]

---

[109] *See* American Standard, 1996 U.S. Dist. LEXIS 14451 at *1-3 (citing trademark owner's redress against infringing domain name registrant in United States); Judge Bans Internet Name Dealers, Irish Times, Dec. 1, 1997, at 18 (noting U.K. court's ruling against registrants of trademarks as domain names); Germany: Internet Domain Name Dealers Challenged, Handelsblatt, June 10, 1997, available in LEXIS, News Library, Curnws File (discussing German court's support of victims of domain grabbing).

[110] Electronics Boutique Holding Corp v. Zuccarini, No. 00-4055, 2000 U.S. Dist. LEXIS 15719 (E.D. Pa., Oct. 30, 2000).

[111] *See* Terence Shaw, Internet Dealers' Name Game Ended, Daily Telegraph, Nov. 29, 1997 at 9 (citing numerous domain names registered by dealers). The domain name dealers had registered many trademarked names through their company, One in a Million, including *buckinghampalace.org*, *marksandspenser.com*, and *burgerking.co.uk*. *See id.* One in a Million had approached Burger King and offered to sell it the name *burgerking.co.uk* for £25,000 (U.S. $40,000). *See id.* The judge found that "[t]he threat of passing off and trademark infringement, and the likelihood of confusion arising from infringement of the mark, are made out beyond argument." Internet Pair Lose Trade Names Case in Highcourt.co.uk., Herald (Glasgow), Nov. 29, 1997, at 3 (quoting Deputy Judge Jonathan Sumption QC).

[112] *See* United Greeks, Inc. v. Klien, No. 00-CV-0002, 2000 U.S. Dist. LEXIS 5670 (N.D. N.Y., May 2, 2000) (awarding $10,000 damages to trademark owner).

[113] *See* New York State Society of Certified Public Accountants v. Eric Louis Associates, 99 Civ. 3030 (LBS) 1999 U.S. Dist. LEXIS 18543 at *79 (S.D. N.Y., Dec. 2, 1999) (assessing $46,818 in attorneys' fees against domain name registrant exploiting trademark); Britain Puts End to Net Scam Involving Sale of Site Names, Straits Times (Singapore), Dec. 2, 1997, available in LEXIS, News Library, Curnws File (discussing U.K. court's award of legal fees and return of domain names containing trademarks).

[114] Gateway 2000, Inc. v. Gateway.com, Inc., No 5:96-CV-1021-BR (3), 1997 U.S. Dist. LEXIS 2144, at *10 (E.D. N.C., Feb. 6, 1997).

Domain name registrants have broad rights in fair use of trademarks, including descriptive terms, criticism, and commentary, although some of these rights may have retreated in arbitration.[115] Again, trademark holders should seek competent counsel before contemplating a suit against a domain name holder who may have a legitimate claim to the name. Conversely, domain name owners who registered names in good faith should not cede their names to a business threatening to sue without the advice of legal counsel.[116]

[b] Legal and Statutory Causes of Action

Trademark holders whose names have been exploited online have a veritable toolbox of legal actions, ranging from a federal trademark dilution suit to the ICANN domain name dispute resolution policy. Some of these causes of action may not apply to domain names registered in other countries not adhering to the ICANN domain name dispute resolution policy. A list of the various remedies and their applications appears in Table 2.4.

Prior to the Anticybersquatting Consumer Protection Act[117] and the modification of the dispute resolution policy, trademark holders often had little recourse against foreign or unknown registrants of infringing domain names or cybersquatters who did not use the names in commerce. Porsche Cars of North America, for example, was unable to sue registrants of several infringing domain names, since the company could not identify the defendants.[118] The Federal Trademark Dilution Act did not allow individuals to sue domain names directly in *in rem* proceedings. Now trademark holders can obtain recourse through the ICANN Dispute Resolution Policy or the Anticybersquatting Consumer Protection Act.[119] Liability begins at the point of registration, and statutory damages can range from $1,000 to $100,000.[120]

Another possible avenue for relief is through ICANN's Domain Name Dispute Policy.[121] Certified domain name registrars require registrants to agree to the ICANN policy. Prior to the new policy, a trademark holder could get an infringing domain name suspended until the resolution of the dispute. While this was effective at getting the attention of the registrant, domain name suspension became a disruptive tool used against legitimate online businesses.[122]

---

[115] David King, Dot.squatters Law Doesn't Hamper All, San Antonio Express-News, Jan. 16, 2000, at 1C; Henry C. Dinger, Cybersquatters May Still Have Some Rights, Mass High Tech, Oct. 30, 2000, at 27.

[116] Henry C. Dinger, When You Hang Your Web Shingle, Don't Be Bullied, Mass High Tech, Oct. 25, 1999, at 24.

[117] 15 U.S.C. § 1125(d).

[118] Porsche Cars North America, Inc. v. Porsh.com, 51 F. Supp. 2d 707 (E.D. Va., 1999).

[119] Henry C. Dinger, New Anti-Cybersquatting Act Still a Bit Fuzzy, Mass High Tech, Jan 3, 2000, at 15.

[120] Sporty's Farm LLC v. Sportsman's Market, Inc., 202 F. 3d 489 (Cir. 2000).

[121] Available at http://www.icann.org (visited June 15, 2002).

[122] Juno Online Services v. Juno Lighting, Inc., 979 F. Supp. 684 (N.D. Ill. 1997).

TABLE 2.4
Trademark Holders' Causes of Action/Remedies in Domain Disputes

Cause of Action	Statute	Effective Against	Limitations	Notes
Federal Trademark Dilution Act	15 U.S.C. § 1125 (c)(1)	Dilution of famous trademarks	Only applies to famous mark; infringement must be in commerce	State cause of action may be similar
Federal Trademark Infringement Act	15 U.S.C. § 1114 (1)	Infringement of trademarks	Infringing mark must be likely to cause confusion, in the same product class, and in commerce	State cause of action may be similar
Federal Unfair Competition Act	15 U.S.C. § 1125 (a)	Domain names that cause mistakes in terms of affiliation, connection, or association with another mark—i.e., bait and switch domain names	Domain name must be in commerce	Also effective against web sites that allege endorsement
Anti-Cybersquatting Consumer Protection Act	15 U.S.C. § 1125 (d)(1)	Domain names registered in bad faith that are identical or confusingly similar to a trademark	Damages available only for marks registered after 11/29/99	Provides a broad cause of action and substantial damages
ICANN Dispute Resolution Policy	www.domain-magistrate.com/disputepolicy	Domain names registered in bad faith that are identical or confusingly similar to a trademark	Must be registered through top level domain that subscribes to the policy	Arbitration mechanism provides an alternative to litigation

The new policy does not allow suspension, but it does permit trademark holders to submit a dispute to an administrative proceeding to determine if the domain name is infringing and registered in bad faith. The World Wrestling Federation, for example, was able to recover *www.worldwrestlingfederation.com* from a cybersquatter by employing the new dispute policy.[123] Use of the procedure can cost approximately $1,000 or more, and results may take several months, which should be more cost-effective and expeditious than litigation.[124] Parties still have the option of appealing an unfavorable decision in federal court.[125]

[c] Purchasing a Domain Name

Companies would have little legal recourse against good-faith registrants of domain names who have the same or similar trademarked names or those who registered a term that is descriptive or have had prior use. Therefore, purchasing a domain name may be a viable option.[126] Although potentially expensive, purchasing the domain name could prove to be a more effective way to attract customers or a cost-effective alternative to litigation.[127] It should be noted, however, that a company will have little legal recourse against a domain name registrant who actually owns the same trademarked name in a different product class.[128]

Despite all of the discussion of cybersquatters, most of them have not profited from their vacant web sites and may be willing to part with them for a reasonable price.[129] Reasonable domain name prices can range between $500 and $2,000, which could be less than the potential legal expense and effort of filing a lawsuit.[130] The web site *www.farside.com*, for example, was sold for $225 by a domain name broker.[131] Companies should consider negotiating through an undisclosed agent or anonymous e-mail to avoid giving the seller the impression that they are negotiating with a buyer who has substantial financial resources.[132] Also keep in mind that while some companies have paid more than $10,000 to purchase infringing domain names from cybersquatters, companies now are less likely to pay huge sums than to assert their trademark rights in a legal forum.[133]

---

[123] Ed Hore, Lawyers Weekly (Canada) Jan. 21, 2000, available in LEXIS, News Library, Curnws File.

[124] Roger Harris, Domain Duels, Ventury County Star, Oct. 23, 2000, at D01.

[125] Kenneth A. Alder, Robert D. Gilbert & Susan L. Crane, Domain name registrants have new rules to follow, Nat'l Law J., Jan. 31, 2000.

[126] *See* William A. Tanenbaum, Rights and Remedies for Three Common Trademark-Domain Name Disputes, Computer Law., Sept. 1997, at 9 (noting lack of established case law for common trademark domain name dispute).

[127] *See* Stephen McGookin, Name Best Kept to Yourself, Fin. Times, June 3, 1998, at 12 (recommending companies purchase domain names instead of resorting to time-consuming and costly legal action); James Saunders, How Best to Keep Rivals' Hands Off Your Brands, Scotsman, Oct. 22, 1998, at 7 (indicating legal costs may put smaller companies at a disadvantage).

[128] See Tanenbaum, *supra* note 126.

[129] *See* Damon Darlin, I Got Here First, Forbes, Dec. 16, 1996, at 326 (explaining lawyers are real winners in legal disputes over domain names).

[130] *See id.*

[131] *See id.* According to one web site, most domain names can be purchased for under $1,000. A to Z of Domain Name Selection (visited June 15, 2002), http://www.domainguru.com/dgb.php/AtoZ.html.

[132] Getting That Cool Name On the Cheap, Internet World, May 1, 2001, at 24.

[133] Dot-Com Squatters Lose Cyberwars, *supra* note 67.

Some registrants may not want to sell their validly held domain names for a reasonable sum, with the hopes that the value will appreciate in the future. Parties may consider a domain name licensing agreement as a potential solution.[134] While this may not provide an ideal long-term solution, domain name licensing can be a cost-effective first step for a company looking to create an online presence.

[d]   Registering a Name in Another Domain

After exploring every option, it is possible that a corporation may not be able to register or purchase the domain name it desires. Indeed, with registrants grabbing domain names at the rate of one every five seconds, much of the pool of unregistered names has dried up.[135] Although this may be disappointing, it does not mean all is lost. Companies encountering this problem still have two choices. The first is to obtain their desired domain name through another top level domain or an alternative registry, such as *www.tonic.to*, which registers the domain *.to*, for Tonga.[136] Other countries also sell domain names, although these countries may have lengthy application processes or exorbitant registration fees.[137] Registrants looking to register at *.tv* when it first became available had to pay at least $2,500 or more per name, although many names are now available on *.tv* for $35 per year.[138]

[e]   Monitoring Expirations of Domain Names

With the downturn in online ventures and diminished incentives for cyber-squatters, some domain name owners prefer to let their registration expire, rather than pay an additional $70 for 2 more years.[139] Therefore, domain names that were initially unavailable may become available again. Those looking to create an online presence with a memorable address may consider registering or buying an initial domain name and monitoring the expiration of suitable names that are prone to expiration.[140]

[f]   Registering with Search Engines

Another option for companies unable to secure a desirable domain name is to rely on search engines. Recall that consumers can still find a specific business

---

[134] Johnathan Bick, The Advantages of Licensing (Not Selling) Domain Names (visited Jan. 15, 2001), http:www.gigalaw.com/articles/bick-2000-12-pl.html.

[135] Matt Lake, How to Get Your Own Domain Name, PC World, June 8, 2000, http://www.cnn.com/2000/TECH/computing/06/08/get.own.domain.idg/.

[136] *See* Elizabeth Corcoran, Tiny Tonga Expands Its Domain; A Web Site Offering Internet Addresses Puts the Islands on the Online Map, Washington Post, July 1, 1997, at C1 (noting Tongan domain registry reserved popular trademarks to avoid trademark controversies occurring in other domains).

[137] *Id.* More than 70 countries permit nonresidents to register domain names. See Peter H. Lewis, The Great Domain Name Hunt, N.Y. Times, June 4, 1998, at G1 (explaining that some countries only require some sort of local presence to register domain name).

[138] *See* http://www.tv (visited June 15, 2002).

[139] Susan Stellin, Rivals Say VeriSign Still Has Advantage, N.Y. Times, April 9, 2001, at C04.

[140] Expiration dates are listed in the whois database: http://www.netsol.com.

by using a search engine, rather than by typing in the domain name. This choice requires every company to carefully consider the content of its web page.[141] By giving serious thought to each word and to all possible metatags,[142] companies assist in directing customers to their corporate web sites.

Irrespective of how a consumer arrives at a company's web site, the next hurdle to overcome is providing easy access to the desired information. Failure to do so may result in potential customers turning elsewhere for goods or services.[143] More specifically, a web site should serve the target audience and reflect the business strategies of the company.[144] With the right focus, a company that goes online can improve its corporate image and service, find prospective clients, and expand into new markets.[145] Domain names can become a significant strategic asset of a company and an important component in a marketing plan.[146]

§ 2.07   ADVERTISING YOUR PRODUCTS AND DRAWING TRAFFIC TO YOUR WEB SITE

[A]   Introduction

You need to buy a disk drive for your computer at work and decide to gather information from the Internet. After you type a few words into a search engine, an advertisement from a disk drive manufacturer dances across the top of your browser, offering an inexpensive solution. Intrigued, you ignore the search results, click on the ad, and go to the manufacturer's web page.

After exploring this site, you return to the search engine and are surprised to find some unknown manufacturers listed in the results before the national brands. It turns out that the unknown brand paid the owner of the search engine for the privilege of being listed first in an appropriate search.

Later, you find a web site in which a columnist makes recommendations for several manufacturers, accompanied by links to their sites. The editor of the online publication fails to disclose that the recommended web sites paid for their endorsements.

---

[141] *See* Neil Winton, Corporate Web Sites Ubiquitous But Feeble—Report (visited Feb. 23, 1998), http://biz.yahoo.com/finance/980222 /computers_1.html (observing corporate web sites were often disappointing).

[142] Metatags enable web site owners to slip key words or phrases onto the web site; these are invisible on the web site itself, but can be found using the indexing mechanism of the various search engines.

[143] *See* Central Corporation Redefines Internet Navigation, Bus. Wire, Mar. 12, 1998, available in LEXIS, News Library, Curnws File (citing study showing 15.9 million Americans canceled their Internet service because of difficulty finding information).

[144] *See id.* (arguing Internet is more than passing fad).

[145] *See* Linda Tsang, Weaving Trade from the Web, Lawyer, Feb. 17, 1998, at 45 (suggesting Internet strategies).

[146] *See* Epoch Internet Becomes Domain Name Registrar Approved by the Internet Council of Registrars, Bus. Wire, Nov. 18, 1997, available in LEXIS, News Library, Curnws File.

Welcome to the world of Internet advertising. Advertising on the Internet can appear in many different forms and may provide a company with an inexpensive conduit to new customers. Online advertisements may create brand awareness or invite customers to visit a web site or to try a product that they might not have found on their own.

The bottom line is, to get people to visit your site, you must advertise. Failure to do so will mean no visitors, no matter how great the web site. Web advertising has also become critically important to site owners as a way to recoup the costs of maintaining their site. Most site owners prefer to fund web site development costs by selling advertising space on a portion of their site, rather than charge visitors a fee.[147] Internet marketers have measured the success of advertising initiatives based on the length of time visitors spend at the site in addition to actual sales or brand awareness.[148] Table 2.5 identifies several different ways to advertise products or services on the Internet. Regardless of which method you use, online advertising is constantly evolving. Although the table identifies certain methods of advertising, the primary revenue-generating forms of Internet advertising include banners, interstitials, and web page sponsorship.

[1] Banner Ads

Banner ads appear at the top, side, or bottom of many web pages and are currently the most common form of advertising on the Internet. Many companies employ animated banners to grab a web site visitor's attention. The ads often provide a link to a company's web site, where the customer can learn more about what was advertised on the banner.

Internet users are growing more sophisticated, however, and advertisers have had to resort to different approaches to advertising, ranging from larger ads to ads placed more prominently within content. New banner strategies focus on simplifying the purchase process for consumers, allowing them to buy items without clicking out of the host site.[149] Still, banner ads are an inexpensive way to help generate traffic to a web site.

[2] Interstitial and Pop-Up Advertising

Interstitial advertisements fill the browser window while another web page downloads. The ad may have a banner at the top and links to other pages. Since

---

[147] *But see* the Wall Street Journal Interactive Edition (visited January 28, 1999) http://www. wsj.com.

[148] The average time spent at any given site varies from between three to five minutes. Charles Papas, Don't Just Count Hits—Generate Hits that Count and Turn into Sales, Home Office Computing, January 1999, p. 90. Enticing visitors to stay at your site for a given length of time is called *stickiness*. Stickiness can be defined as "[t]he quality of attracting longer and more frequent repeat visitors to a web site." *Id.*

[149] Dean Tomasula, Taking the 'Click' out of Click-Through Banner Ads, Imarketing News, April 6, 2001, http://www.imarketingnews.com.

TABLE 2.5
Methods of Advertising on the Internet

Method	How It Works
Search Engines	Search engines are the primary ways in which people find information on the Internet. For each page included in a site, decide on a few key words that, when searched for, will return that page. You may register your web site using either *Submit-It* or *Add Me*. Other popular search engine sites include: • Alta Vista • Excite • Infoseek • Lycos • Yahoo!
E-Mail	E-mail various online magazines with details about your site.
Exchange Links	Look for third-party vendors with which you do business and ask if you can post links from their site to yours, and vice versa. Additionally, you may want to find companies that sell services similar to yours and ask if they would help promote your site and services.
Free Web Link Sites	There are sites that will allow you to post your web site free of charge. These sites may provide a surge of temporary visitors. Such sites include: • WebStep Top 100 • Free Links: The Ultimate Web Site Traffic Builder
Internet Link Exchanges	Advertise your site for free using banners that are displayed on other people's sites.
Newsgroups	Feel free to advertise your site in newsgroups related to your business or corporate mission.
Signature Files	At the end of your e-mail or newsgroup messages, advertise your site. The things to include would be: • "Check us out . . ." • Company Name • URL (e.g., *www.suffolk.edu/law*)

they usually consume the entire screen, interstitial ads are hard to ignore and may be more effective than banner ads.[150]

A variation of the interstitial is the pop-up ad, which appears in a new browser window. Pop-up ads usually contain links and are more elaborate than

---

[150] Matthew Reed, Going Beyond the Banner Ad, Marketing, Apr. 29, 1999, at 25.

banner ads. Though intrusive, pop-up ads will certainly generate more traffic than will a banner ad. Some Internet users do not like to have pop-up ads interfere with their web surfing. Both interstitial and pop-up ads require programming knowledge and may be beyond the technical capacity of many web site hosts.[151]

[3]   Web Page Sponsorship

Web page sponsorship is similar to television advertising. Sponsors pay to have their links and logos on a popular web site. This provides the sponsor with potential exposure and the web site with revenue with which to generate content. For example, Areaguides.com, a host of online community guides, lists pricing for community guide sponsorship on its web site.[152] While it is difficult to directly attribute specific profitability to web page sponsorship, it may be a facet of successful Internet campaigns.[153]

[4]   Other Advertising Strategies

Many successful Internet ad campaigns are coordinated with traditional advertising media.[154] Lotus, for example, successfully launched a new product in the United Kingdom by combining traditional newspaper advertising with Internet banner ads.[155] Procter & Gamble created an effective campaign in the United States by coordinating television and Internet ads.[156]

Other Internet advertisers have fully integrated online strategies that include e-mail advertising, banner ads, and site sponsorship. To obtain new customers, for example, First USA paid Microsoft $90,000,000 for the exclusive right to advertise its credit cards across Microsoft's MSN Internet network for five years.[157] The credit card company hoped to reach customers who do not respond to traditional media, such as mail or telemarketing campaigns.[158]

[5]   Editorial and Search Engine Priority

While banner ads are popular and overt, advertising pervades many other facets of the Internet. Some advertising is subtly placed within editorial content.

---

[151] *Id.*

[152] http://areaguides.com/webrates.htm (visited June 15, 2002).

[153] Irv DeGraw, Don't Change That Channel, On Wall Street, Sept. 1, 1998, available in LEXIS, News Library, Curnws File.

[154] Adam Woods, A Software Company Saw a Positive Response to the Launch of Its All-In-One Intranet Package Through a Web and Conventional Press Push, Precision Marketing, Apr. 20, 1998, at 10.

[155] *Id.*

[156] Alasdair Reid, P&G Looks Beyond Banner Ads to Boost Its Web Presence.

[157] Largest Internet Ad Deal Signed, Bank Marketing Int'l, Dec. 1998, at 7.

[158] *Id.*

Search engines are a necessary component in online advertising. The highest quality of traffic probably will not be derived from search engines, but this access point is nonetheless important. Potential visitors may find your site by using a search engine like Google, AltaVista, or Yahoo!. Companies should affirmatively add their URLs to the search engine indexes by clicking on the link that allows them to submit a site on the bottom of most search engine home sites and submitting the request information.[159] Advertisers may also purchase key words within search engines so that their links receive priority in any relevant search. Advertisers may also purchase banner ads that appear on search engines any time the key word is used in a search,[160] allowing more targeted banner advertising.

In one example of subtle sponsorship, publishers paid the online bookstore Amazon.com for prominent placement of favorable book reviews.[161] Visitors to the Amazon.com site who looked at reviews under the heading "What We're Reading" were likely to see book reviews subsidized by the books' publishers. Such hidden sponsorship, if deceptive, may run afoul of the law and will likely be received unfavorably by the public.[162]

[6]   Ad-Blocking Software Applications

As online advertising becomes more popular and aggressive, so does consumer frustration. Interstitial ads or banner ads, for example, can increase the amount of time needed to load a particular web page. It is estimated that the average Internet user spends thirty seconds to two minutes at a particular web site. If the visitor has to wait thirty seconds for the ad to load, he or she is likely to be frustrated and/or leave the site. Ad-blocking software companies like webswasher.com, InterMute, or Guidescope have created software tools that filter ads from reaching the visitor's screen similar to the way anti-virus software filters viruses. These applications are currently free to home users and are sold to corporate customers for a fee. While these applications prevent ads from being displayed, they will not totally eliminate advertisements. Rather, they may make banner ads or interstitial ads less popular and in turn increase web sponsorships or links.

---

[159] AltaVista allows users to submit a site by clicking on a link entitled "Submit a Site." *See* AltaVista, Submit a Site (visited June 15, 2002), http://www.altavista.com/addurl. Yahoo! allows users to submit a site by clicking on a link entitled "Suggest a Site." *See* Yahoo!, How to Suggest Your Site (visited June 15, 2002), http://docs.yahoo.com/info/suggest/.

[160] *See supra* note 135.

[161] *See* Saul Hansell and Amy Hoarmon, Subtly Trolling for Online Shoppers, National Post, Feb. 27, 1999, at D11.

[162] It is possible that the Federal Trade Commision may file an enforcement action if the "hidden sponsorship" is considered to be an unfair and deceptive trade practice.

[B]   Internet Advertising Law

The Internet is no longer like a developing country or the Wild West, with informal frontier justice governing advertising. Because of the many different forms of advertising, many different regulatory agencies become involved, and a wide variety of issues arise.[163] Many jurisdictions are now devoting resources to protecting consumers online, and agencies worldwide are working together to punish offenders and deter advertising scams across jurisdictions.[164] The Federal Trade Commission (FTC) has a special bureau that combs the Internet for deceptive advertising.[165]

[1]   Federal Trade Commission

Consumer protection that applies to traditional commercial activities has been extended to cyberspace. The FTC rules, guidelines, and disclosures developed for other media apply to the Internet.[166] To reduce confusion, the FTC has devoted a great deal of attention to educating business and consumers through Internet-specific news releases and publications.[167] Mandatory disclosures must, for example, be clear and conspicuous. The FTC's enforcement of online advertisement focuses on three key issues: claim substantiation, deception, and unfairness.[168]

[a]   Claim Substantiation

Advertisers must have a reasonable basis for their advertised claims.[169] Advertisers or web site designers who are unable to substantiate claims may be subject to fines or other remedies levied by the FTC. If Suffolk Personal Computers advertised on the Internet that it had the fastest computers available, then, it must have proof substantiating the claim, or it may be exposed to a possible enforcement action.

---

[163] Mark Sableman, Business on the Internet, Part II: Liability Issues, 53 J. MO. B. 223, (1997).

[164] See Special Report—Protecting the Consumer: To Boldly Go into Space Chasing Rogues, London Daily Telegraph, Dec. 7, 1998, at 28 (illustrating cooperative pursuit of Japanese company advertising miracle cures).

[165] See supra note 143.

[166] Federal Trade Commission, Dot.Com Disclosures (visited June 15, 2002) http://www.ftc.gov/bcp/conline/pubs/buspubs/dotcom; Federal Trade Commission, Advertising and Marketing on the Internet: The Rules of the Road (visited June 15, 2002), http://www.ftc.gov/bcp/conline/pubs/buspubs/ruleroad.htm (describing how FTC Act's prohibition on "unfair or deceptive acts or practices" applies to Internet advertising, marketing, and sales).

[167] James E. Schatz, FTC Regulates Online Ads to Ensure Truthfulness, Nat'l Law J., Mar. 5, 2001, at B14.

[168] Arent Fox, Advertising Law Internet Site (visited June 15, 2002), http://www.arentfox.com/quickGuide/businessLines/advert/advertisingLaw/advertisinglaw.html.

[169] FTC Policy Statement Regarding Advertising Substantiation Program (visited Apr. 28, 1999), http://www.webcom.com/~lewrose/adsubpol.html.

Subjective claims or opinions, such as "At Suffolk Personal Computers, we have the best looking keyboards in the world,"[170] are permitted. Such sales talk or puffery requires substantiation only when it suggests the company has consumer support or agreement, as in phrases such as "More PC users prefer Suffolk PC's keyboards." Companies advertising on the Internet should endeavor to separate seller's talk or puffery from factual claims.

[b] Deception and Unfairness

"Unfair advertising" is a catch-all classification for advertising that offends public policy or injures consumers or competitors. Deceptive acts in Internet advertising can subject a company to FTC or state enforcement against unfair or deceptive advertising. A deceptive act is one that misleads consumers and influences their behavior or decision to purchase the product.[171]

Both failure to disclose material facts and affirmative acts may constitute deception. If Suffolk Personal Computers advertises a new computer for $100, but forgets to mention that the offer is only good with the purchase of a $2,000 monitor, the advertisement is deceptive. Internet advertisers should be clear about what they are offering, and they must avoid any hidden charges or "bait and switch" sales tactics, that is, advertising one item with the intent of selling another. In one case, Virgin Atlantic Airways had to pay a $14,000 fine to the U.S. Department of Transportation for failing to clearly disclose a $38.91 tax applicable to tickets it had advertised on the Internet.[172] Indeed, 26 percent of consumer fraud complaints to the FTC involved the Internet.[173]

[2] Misrepresentation and False Advertising

FTC regulations are not the only guidelines for advertisers. The Lanham Act imposes liability for advertisers who misrepresent their own or someone else's products to the consuming public.[174] Any comparisons or representations of competing brands should not be disparaging or false. If Suffolk Personal Computers employed a false banner ad showing defective circuits and phantom bugs in a competitor's computers, it may be liable to that company if it found itself to be damaged by the misleading ads.

---

[170] Roscoe B. Starek, III, Regulatory Enforcement of Your Web Site, Who Will Be Watching? (visited Apr. 28, 1999), http://www.ftc.gov/speeches/starek/onlinweb.htm.

[171] *See* Frances Katz, Atlanta Tech; IXL's IPO Scheduled to Come Next Week, Atlanta Journal and Constitution, May 12, 1999 at 9D.

[172] Lewis Rose and John P. Feldman, Internet Marketing: Practical Suggestions for International Advertising and Promotions (site visited on May 25, 1999), www.webcom.com/lewrose/article/intl.html.

[173] Fraud Could Curb Growth of Internet (visited April 26, 2001), http://www.ftc.gov/opa/2001/04/senfinance.htm.

[174] Lanham Act § 8, 15 U.S.C. § 1125 (a)(1)(B) (1996).

[3] National Advertising Division of the Council of the Better Business Bureau

The Better Business Bureau (BBB) has a national advertising division (NAD) with guidelines for voluntary self-regulation of advertising. Like the FTC, the NAD is concerned with consumer protection and the corrosive effects of false or misleading advertising.[175] NAD investigates truth in national advertising and may ask noncomplying advertisers to modify or discontinue unsubstantiated claims.[176] Since Internet advertising may be considered national in scope, online advertisers should conform to the NAD's guidelines and recommendations.

[4] Other Considerations

Since Internet advertising regulations are still evolving, many companies are cautious in their approach. IBM, for example, announced that it would advertise only on web sites with a clear privacy policy.[177] Additionally, advertising techniques popular in the United States may also be contrary to local laws in other countries. Now that more traffic to web sites in the United States originates from international visitors, companies need to be more cautious.[178] For example, while comparative advertising is a popular practice in the United States, other countries impose broad restrictions. Since the Internet is a worldwide medium, advertisers should proceed conservatively with any comparisons. The following are a few of the countries that place restrictions on comparative advertising: Australia, Argentina, China, The Czech Republic, El Salvador, Germany, Greece, Italy, Japan, Malaysia, The Philippines, and Switzerland.[179]

Companies selling their products and services on the Internet are in a complex legal environment where there is a risk of violating some local advertising regulation. Advertising only in English and stating that any offer is available only in the United States may minimize the risk of liability. Advertisers who venture into other countries should engage local counsel to assess the local advertising regulatory landscape. In Denmark, for example, advertising targeting children is prohibited.[180] In another interesting example, Italian clothing designer Benetton was held liable in both German and French courts for print advertising that was held to exploit emotions.[181]

---

[175] Better Business Bureau, Promoting Honest Advertising (visited May 28, 1999), http://www.bbb.org/advertising/index.html.

[176] National Advertising Division (visited May 28, 1999), www.caru.bbb.org/advertiserAssist.html.

[177] Jeri Clausing, I.B.M. Vows to Pull Ads From Web Sites that Lack Clear Policies on Protecting Consumer Privacy, N.Y. Times, Apr. 1, 1999, at C4.

[178] Dean Tomasula, Report: U.S. Sites Get Majority of Traffic From Outside Country, Imarketing News, April 25, 2001, http://www.imarketingnews.com (visited Apr. 26, 2001).

[179] Stephen P. Durchslag, Comparative Advertising Doesn't Always Work Overseas, Promo, Jan. 1, 1999, available in LEXIS, News Library, Curnws file.

[180] Roscoe B. Starek, III, Unfairness, Internet Advertising and Innovative Remedies, (visited Apr. 28, 1999), http://www.ftc.gov/speeches/starek/aaffub.htm.

[181] *See supra* note 152.

[5]   Advertising to Children

Although children represent a substantial portion of the Internet surfing population, Internet advertising aimed at children is carefully monitored and should be approached with caution.[182] The Better Business Bureau has a children's advertising review unit to help prevent advertisers from taking advantage of children's naiveté.[183] The review unit has published self-regulatory guidelines to provide advertisers with a framework to help avoid exploiting children.[184] The guidelines and principles articulate the NAD's concerns about children's advertising and suggest reasonable solutions for making parents and advertisers comfortable.[185]

The Children's Online Personal Protection Act (COPPA) imposes federal restrictions for collecting personal information on children. COPPA requires any site that targets and collects information on children under the age of thirteen to have a conspicuous privacy policy and to obtain parental consent for any personal data collected, among other requirements.[186] COPPA applies only to commercial web sites or online services directed to children under thirteen. At minimum, the web site operator must post a clear and conspicuous privacy policy. Verifiable parental consent is required prior to collecting, using, or disclosing personal information from a child. The FTC fined three web sites a total of $100,000 for illegally collecting personally identifiable information from children under thirteen without parental consent.[187] A web site should comply with self-regulatory programs that have been granted "safe harbor" status by the Federal Trade Commission.

While other state and federal regulations are emerging slowly, web site operators should be careful in collecting personal information about anyone under eighteen; they should either obtain parental consent or correlate the data to a screen name rather than a real-world identity.[188] By using screen names, children are guaranteed anonymity within the web site, yet the web site operator can still keep a

---

[182] Denise Caruso, A Push to Provide "Safe Playgrounds" in Cyberspace, International Herald Tribune, Feb. 19, 1999, at 10.

[183] *See* Children's Advertising Review Unit (visited May 28, 1999), http://www.bbb.org/advertising/childrensmonitor.html (defining the review unit and its jurisdiction).

[184] Guidelines for Children's Advertising (visited May 28, 1999), http://www.caru.bbb.org/caruguid.html.

[185] *Id.*

[186] 15 U.S.C. §6501 et seq. (2000). The FTC filed its first COPPA enforcement action against an insolvent Internet toy retailer that offered to sell its customer database to pay creditors. Federal Trade Comm'n v. Toysmart.com, 17 Computer & Online Indus. Litig. Rptr. 9 (Aug. 2000) (charging Toysmart.com with collecting personal information from children under age 13 without obtaining parental consent).

[187] FTC Announces Settlements with Websites That Collected Children's Personal Data Without Parental Permission (visited Apr. 20, 2001), http://www.ftc.gov/opa/2001/04/girlslife.htm.

[188] Richard Raysman and Peter Brown, Privacy and the Internet, N.Y.L.J., May 12, 1998, at 3. The Direct Marketing Association also provides advice to advertisers about online data collection at www.the-dma.org.

record of the user's activities. The Children's Advertising Review Unit has developed advertising guidelines geared toward protecting children.[189] These guidelines include the following points:

1. Advertisements should not mislead about the performance of a product.
2. Do not exploit a child's imagination.
3. Products should be shown being used in safe ways and environments.
4. Children should not be urged to ask parents or others to buy products.
5. The name of the sponsoring company should be prominently displayed.
6. Claims should be presented in ways a child can understand.
7. Some act should be required to represent an intentional joining of a club or acceptance of an offer.
8. Parents may not be obligated to fulfill sales contracts entered into by children.
9. Ordering instructions must clearly state that a child must have a parent's permission to order.
10. Mechanisms should be clear for cancelling an order after it has been placed.[190]
11. Privacy measures must be implemented to protect the identities of children.
12. Words that create a sense of urgency should not be used (for example, "Call now!").

[C]   Linking

[1]   Introduction

Linking, or hyperlinking, is one of the primary methods of navigating the Internet.[191] By clicking on highlighted text or an image, Internet users can move quickly and directly to the linked web site, file, or segment of the current web page. Many business web sites use links extensively, allowing visitors to move quickly among pages within the site or to connect easily to another company's web site for further resources or information. If linking were not available, companies on the Internet would have to do more to educate the public about their web addresses and web site content through traditional advertising media. This would raise a cost barrier for smaller companies seeking to do business on the Internet.

---

[189] *See* Better Business Bureau, The Children's Advertising Review Unit, 1997 Self Regulatory Guidelines for Children's Advertising. *See also* Federal Trade Commission, How to Comply with The Children's Online Privacy Protection Rule, Nov. 1999 (visited Sept. 15, 2000), http://www.ftc.gov/bcp/coline/pubs/buspubs/coppa.htm.

[190] *Id.*

[191] The other methods of connecting to a web site, by typing in the desired address or URL in the address bar of the Internet browser or returning to a site that the user had "bookmarked" earlier, are effective only if the Internet user already knows the web site's address.

A web page with useful links serves as a valuable tool for web users while generating traffic for the site's host. Although simple linking is generally unobjectionable, some practices may create legal liabilities.

Linking is useful: An Internet user searching for a new computer monitor, for example, might use a search engine to find computer equipment vendors and reviews. The search results would be composed primarily of a list of links to vendors' web sites. The user can enter the vendor's web site by clicking on the hyperlink in the search results.

The first page of the web site is usually the home page or "front door," and links to a vendor will often lead to the home page. In the case of a vendor, the home page often contains many image and text links to other pages describing products, specials, company policies, and technical support. Each successive link may lead the viewer deeper into the web site. The site might also provide links to software vendors, who in turn might provide links back to the original computer equipment company. These links are symbiotic, increasing the traffic to both sites, which usually results in increased sales.

A link to a web site that bypasses the web site's home page is called a deep link. The link to the software company may be a "deep link" that goes right to a discount page or other targeted page. For example, Suffolk PC's home page may be located at *www.suffolkpcs.com* while a deep link could bypass the home page and link to *www.suffolkpcs.com/specials/clearance.htm*. Deep links cause greater legal hazards than do regular links.

[2]   Legal Implications of Linking

For several years, courts were relatively silent in linking disputes, and cases did not yield a clear legal direction. Recent cases, however, illustrate that judges in the United States are often reluctant to impose liability for links.[192] Despite this reluctance, several linking controversies overseas have illustrated how some links can create legal hazards.[193]

The most controversial question is whether permission is needed to link to another site. A web site linking agreement serves as a good preventive measure. Most Internet companies believe that web site hosts, merely by publishing their sites, are making those sites available for linking—provided the linking site acts in good faith.[194] This widespread belief is largely based on two theories, both of

---

[192] *See* Ticketmaster Corp. v. Tickets.com, Inc, No. CV 99-7654 HLH (BQRx), 2000 U.S. Dist LEXIS 4553 (C.D. CA, Mar. 27, 2000) (finding deep link does not amount to unfair competition); Kelly v. Arriba Soft Corp., 77 F. Supp. 2d 1116 (C.D. CA S.D. 1999) (finding no evidence of harm from search engine's deep link to plaintiff's web site).

[193] Courts in Germany and the United Kingdom have both issued preliminary injunctions in deep linking cases: http://www.steptoe.com/WebDoc.NSF/Law+&+The+Net+All/E-Commerce+Law+Week,+Issue+138?OpenDocument (visited Apr. 26, 2001).

[194] Richard Raysman and Peter Brown, Dangerous Liaisons: The Legal Risks of Linking Web Sites, N.Y. L.J., April 8, 1997, Computer Law, at 3.

which are independent of whether the owners of the linked pages are aware of the links.[195]

Under the first theory, creating a hyperlink does not entail reproduction of content, only reproduction of the site address or Uniform Resource Locator (URL).[196] The URL itself is not subject to copyright protection because it lacks creative elements.[197] Some legal commentators take the position that providing a hyperlink is no different from providing a phone number or street address.[198] Other commentators make the novel argument that the link may potentially infringe the copyright owner's right to distribute its work by delivering the linked page.[199]

A growing number of academics argue that courts should not hold the owner of the linking site directly liable for infringement absent evidence of copying or distributing the material.[200] The linking site may be liable, however, for contributory infringement for providing the means by which the viewer can copy the work.[201]

The second theory is based on an implied license or estoppel.[202] Subscribers to this theory cite strong public policy reasons to preserve the web's virtually uninhibited navigation system.[203] Commentators argue that parties who voluntarily post copyrighted material on the web do not have a reasonable expectation of being free from unwelcome linking.[204] This does not mean that web site owners have no intellectual property protection for materials or content on the web site. Rather, site proprietors may disclaim implied licenses by placing an express warning on their home pages denying access by hyperlink.[205] Sites that have expressed warnings or "terms of use" usually incorporate language that binds the visitors to its terms in exchange for viewing its contents.[206]

Linking controversies have largely been decided under copyright law, though a link often highlights a trademarked symbol or company logo.[207] Trademark law,

---

[195] Donald Sovie, Downloading from the Net Is Dangerous, Nat'l L. J., December 14, 1998, at B5.

[196] Id., citing Echerou, Linking to Trouble: Legal Liability Emanating from Hyperlinks on the World Wide Web, 10 No. 2 J. Proprietary Rts. 2, 3 (1998) (referring to a Uniform Resource Locator as an Internet address that identifies the type and location of an Internet resource).

[197] Kara Beal, The Potential Liability of Linking on the Internet: An Examination of Possible Legal Solutions, BYU L. Rev. 703, 724 (1998).

[198] Id.

[199] Sovie, *supra* note 195.

[200] Id.

[201] Id. Proof of contributory infringement, however, requires that the owner of the linking site have knowledge of the infringement and actively aid that infringement. Carl S. Kaplan, Can a Web Link Break Copyright Laws?, N.Y. Times, September 25, 1998, at B10.

[202] Sovie, *supra* note 195, at B5 (referring to an estoppel theory where the linked party would be barred from alleging harm because of that party's own act of publishing on the Internet).

[203] Id.

[204] Id.

[205] Id.

[206] Id. See, e.g., http://www.real.com/company/legal.html (visited June 15, 2002).

[207] Lisa Green and Heather Meeke, Hyperlinking License; It Is Common for Hyperlinking License Provisions to Be Reciprocal, Intell. Prop. Strategist, October 1998, at 2; *see, e.g.,* Intellectual Reserve, Inc. v. Utah Lighthouse Ministry, Inc., 75 F. Supp. 2d 1290 (D. Utah 1999) (linking to

on the other hand, lends itself more easily to the Internet than does copyright law because trademark law does not unreasonably restrict the flow of information any more than it restricts information presented in more traditional media.[208] Linking cases may also be recast as state unfair competition or federal trademark infringement or dilution claims.[209]

Trademark claims come in two forms: infringement[210] and dilution.[211] Links created with a proprietary name, image, or logo may be subject to a trademark infringement claim.[212] Liability turns on whether a perception of "sponsorship" arose.[213] Even the appearance of sponsorship between the two linked sites, whether that link incorporates a logo or text, may be sufficient to bring an action for trademark infringement against the linking company.[214] Without sponsorship, some lawyers argue, unauthorized linking is not a true instance of trademark infringement.[215] Nevertheless, a cautious site owner should obtain a trademark license before implementing such a link.[216] Links that incorporate a distinctive mark, such as a trademark logo or icon, are more egregious than those that simply use a text trade name in the URL.[217] Moreover, use of the trade name in a URL may constitute a fair and descriptive use of the mark.[218]

Most trademark claims that concern unwelcome links, however, arise under a dilution theory.[219] The Federal Trademark Dilution Act of 1995[220] makes dilution

---

site containing infringing materials did not constitute copyright infringement); *cf.* Playboy Enterprises, Inc. v. Universal Tel-A-Talk, Inc., No. Civ. 96-CV-6961 1998 U.S. Dist. LEXIS 8331 (E.D. Pa., June 1, 1998) (holding that defendant's use of a federally registered trademark "Playboy" in a link did not constitute trademark counterfeiting).

[208] Beal, *supra* note 197, at 727.

[209] *Id.*

[210] A party with rights in a particular mark can bring a trademark infringement claim against a third party if the third party's use of the mark creates a "likelihood of confusion." 15 U.S.C. § 1114 (1998). Specifically, the use of a trademark in connection with the sale of goods constitutes infringement if it is likely to cause consumer confusion as to the source of those goods or as to the sponsorship or approval of such goods. For a more detailed discussion, *see* § 4.03[F].

[211] Under federal law, a party with rights in a particular mark can bring a dilution claim to protect "famous" marks. A court will consider the following factors in deciding whether a mark is famous: (1) the degree of inherent or acquired distinctiveness; (2) the duration and extent of use; (3) the amount of advertising and publicity; (4) the geographic extent of the market; (5) the channels of trade; (6) the degree of recognition in trading areas; (7) any use of similar marks by third parties; (8) whether the mark is registered. 15 U.S.C. § 1125(c) (1998). For a more detailed discussion, *see* § 4.03[G].

[212] Beal, *supra* note 197, at 727.

[213] Green and Meeke, *supra* note 207.

[214] *Id.*

[215] *Id.*

[216] *Id.*

[217] Beal, *supra* note 197, at 727.

[218] *Id.*

[219] *Id.*

[220] Trademark Dilution Act, 15 U.S.C. § 1125 (1998).

of "famous" trademarks actionable.[221] Liability arises under the act when site owners use links, images, or framed materials in a way that diminishes the value of the mark.[222] The value of a mark is measured by its capacity to identify and distinguish goods or services.[223] Since the Internet is a global medium, companies must be aware of major trademarks and be ethical in selling advertising, or it can cost companies dearly, not only here, but in defending or settling lawsuits abroad as well. Estee Lauder sued Excite, Inc. and iBeauty and won in German court during March 2000, but settled out of court in the U.S. on Dec. 11, 2000. Excite sold the Estee Lauder trademark as keywords to advertiser iBeauty to trigger iBeauty's banner ads for competing products. Estee Lauder commenced suit, and the parties settled in the U.S. after two years of attorney involvement. Do not sell keywords that are trademarks to advertisers to trigger ads.

[a]   Direct Linking

Many web site operators want to control who links to their sites and to which of the site's web pages the link connects.[224] In a high-profile case, Ticketmaster sued Microsoft over a deep link from a Microsoft online entertainment guide.[225] The link bypassed Ticketmaster's main web page, which contained Ticketmaster's logo and third-party advertising.[226] Ticketmaster claimed that the link from the Microsoft page exploited Ticketmaster's trademarked name.[227] Ticketmaster also alleged that, through the link, Microsoft was displaying and publicly distributing the content of Ticketmaster's copyrighted web site.[228] Microsoft removed the link when the complaint was filed, and the parties settled before the court could issue an opinion.[229] Ticketmaster also pursued Tickets.com

---

[221] *Id.*

[222] *See supra* note 194. The Direct Marketing Association also provides advertisers with insight into online data collection at www.the-dma.org (visited May 15, 2000).

[223] *Id.* In a dilution claim, plaintiffs argue that the link creates an association between the two organizations that tarnishes the plaintiff's image in the eyes of the consumer. Beal, *supra* note 197, at 727. As many practitioners recognize, the Federal Trademark Dilution Act gives plaintiffs a big stick with which to obtain judicial recourse. Trademark Dilution Act, 15 U.S.C. § 1125 (1998). Steven E. Shapiro, Use of "Mead Data" Test Dilutes the Dilution Act, Nat'l L.J., May 12, 1997, at C02. Courts seem willing to grant summary judgment on trademark dilution while denying a summary judgment on trademark infringement, for example, which further illustrates the Act's power. *Id.*; *see, e.g.,* Intermatic Inc. v. Toeppen, 40 U.S.P.Q.2d 1412 (N.D. Ill. 1996); Panavision International, L.P. v. Toeppen, 938 F. Supp. 616 (C.D. Cal. 1996), *aff'd*, 141 F.3d 1316 (9th Cir. 1998).

[224] Sean M. Mead, The Internet—Legal Resources, Legal Issues (visited May 6, 1999), http://www.blueriver.net/~wyrm/iclef/98Iclef.html.

[225] Ticketmaster Corp. v. Microsoft Corp., No 97-3055 DDP (C.D. Cal. filed 4/29/97).

[226] Beal, *supra* note 197, at 713.

[227] *Id.* at 714.

[228] Nichole M. Bond, Linking and Framing on the Internet: Liability Under Trademark and Copyright Law, 11 DePaul Bus. L.J. 185, 198 (1998).

[229] The Perkins Coie Internet Case Digest (visited May 3, 1999), http://www.perkinscoie.com/resource/ecomm/netcase/Cases-27.htm.

over deep linking, including the argument that deep linking violated Ticketmaster's term-of-use policy.[230]

A more compelling case against linking was that of Shetland Times Ltd. v. Wills.[231] The Shetland News posted links using headlines from the competing Shetland Times.[232] The headlines linked directly to the Shetland Times articles, bypassing its home page and advertising, leading readers to believe that they were still at the Shetland News page.[233]

Yet another potential pitfall in linking to a web page at another site is the possibility that a company will subject itself to the personal jurisdiction of a remote state.[234] Most courts have held that operating a web site does not in itself subject the operator to the jurisdiction of any state in which the site is viewed when the basis for exercising jurisdiction is the web presence alone.[235] Some plaintiffs have attempted to erode this trend, however, by arguing that the creation and use of a hyperlink constitutes a tort and, accordingly, subjects the operator of the site to jurisdiction on the basis that the tort was committed within the jurisdiction.[236]

[b]   Third-Party Links

The Suffolk Personal Computer web site contains links to third-party web sites. SPC's disclosures should state that SPC neither endorses nor has control over the content of linked sites. SPC is only providing these links as a convenience, and does not imply an endorsement of the linked site. Is the use of third-party links valuable to entities on the Internet? A California court dismissed a case against a web site operator for a third party's infringing web site, which was connected by a link.[237] If the plaintiff had been successful, the case would have resulted in potential liability for all web sites containing links, thus reducing the use of links on the Internet.[238] In another case, a United States district court held

---

[230] Ticketmaster Corp. v. Tickets.com, No. CV 99-7654 HLH (BQRx), 2000 U.S. Dist. LEXIS 4553 (C.D. Cal., Mar. 27, 2000). The court dismissed the case, finding that Ticketmaster could not show any injury from the deep links, and in fact, the links from Tickets.com were creating revenue for Ticketmaster. *Id.*

[231] 1997 F.S.R. 604 (Ct. Sess. O.H.) (Ireland Oct. 24, 1996).

[232] Perkins Coie Digest, *supra* note 229.

[233] *Id.*

[234] For a complete discussion of jurisdiction, *see* Chapter Seven.

[235] Minimum Contacts in Cyberspace: A Taxonomy of the Case Law, 35 Hous. L. Rev. 453, 469, 474, 476, 480 (1998).

[236] Bensusan Restaurant Corp. v. King, 126 F.3d 25 (C.A.2, 1997). Although the Court in Bensusan found that there was no personal jurisdiction, the decision was based upon an inferred requirement in New York's Long Arm Statute that a defendant must be physically present in order to commit a tortious act within the state. Many courts do not require physical presence, however. *See, e.g.,* United Conveyor Corp. v. King, 1992 WL 265852 (N.D. Ill.).

[237] Bernstein v. J.C. Penney Inc., No. 98-2958 R (ex) 1998 U.S. Dist. LEXIS 19048, at *2 (C.D. Cal. Sept. 30, 1998).

[238] CA Judge Dismisses Copyright Claims Based on Linking, Software Law Bulletin, Nov. 1998, at 213.

that the operator of a "visual search engine" did not commit a copyright infringement by displaying a "thumbnail image," lacking copyright management information, as a means of linking to larger versions of the image, located on another web site.[239] The court stated that the "Plaintiff's images are vulnerable to copyright infringement because they are displayed on Web sites."[240]

Congress enacted the Digital Millennium Copyright Act (DMCA)[241] to implement two copyright law treaties promulgated by the World Intellectual Property Organization (WIPO). The DMCA is an attempt to merge technical remedies with legal remedies. Section 512(a) of the DMCA provides a safe harbor for web sites that transmit allegedly infringing material. The DMCA may be used to limit the liability of any party that transmits, routes, or provides connections for infringing materials.[242] While businesses operating on the web should take precautions to ensure that their directly linked pages are noninfringing, they are not expected to monitor third-party links that connect to linked pages.

[3] Linking Precautions—Look Before You Link

Linking is a great way to add value to your web site and to generate traffic. Nevertheless, prudent web site operators should obtain permission from other sites before linking.[243] While Microsoft can afford to test the court's opinion regarding linking without permission, most businesses cannot afford the expense of litigation. Even sites that permit unlimited linking to their home page may object to deep links that bypasses their identification or content.

Conversely, if a web site you do not want associated with your business links to your site, you must send it a request to remove the link. If the site refuses, you may be able to thwart the link by slightly modifying the address of the linked page. This is especially helpful in eliminating unwanted deep links. Ticketmaster, for instance, modified the web page targeted by Microsoft's unwanted link. Internet users who clicked on the link would see a message informing them that the link was unauthorized.

Since the courts have not issued opinions regarding linking, legal action should be a last resort. A simple cease-and-desist letter from counsel will probably deter most unwanted links.

---

[239] Kelley v. Arriba Soft Corp., 1999 WL 1210918 (C.D. Cal.).

[240] Id., at 6.

[241] 17 U.S.C. § 1202, et seq.

[242] Alan J. Hartnick, The New Limitations on Online Copyright Liability, N.Y. L.J., Feb. 5, 1999, at 5.

[243] The American Bar Association published a book of model web linking agreements and policies. The book, Web-Linking Agreements: Contracting Strategies and Model Provisions, is available at http://www.abanet.org/buslaw/catalog/5070311.html (visited May 15, 2000). Additionally, some companies may give permission to link to their web sites. See http://www.batesville.com/html/link.htm (visited June 15, 2002).

Web sites should contain a clear policy regarding linking. Unless your business is unconcerned with who may be linking to your web page, you should post a clear policy requiring written permission for all links. Finally, make sure that all links start at your home page and do not bypass whatever content or advertising you want all visitors to see when they enter your site.

[D] Framing

Frames are used to display portions of multiple web pages within a single page. This allows Internet users to navigate through the content of different web pages while still maintaining the original frame and menu of the framing page. Frames may be employed seamlessly, giving visitors the illusion that they never left the original web page, even though they have clicked through numerous web sites.

[1] Advantages of Framing

Frames aid the Internet user by facilitating navigation. Internet pages with frames often contain various navigation buttons, allowing users to search the web site or to explore other pages while still maintaining the frame. Web page operators can maintain a consistent look across the web site and beyond. Framing sites can keep their logo and advertising in front of the viewer longer than would be the case if the user continued through the Internet via other links.[244]

Suffolk PCs, for example, may want to provide technical information about the computers it sells online. Rather than recreating the manufacturer's information, a web page within the Suffolk PC site can frame the latest technical information straight from the manufacturer's web site. SPC may also want to frame many of its own web pages. Through the frame, any changes to the site navigation menu would require only a change to a few web pages rather than every page on the site. This would be advantageous, for example, if Suffolk PCs wanted to have dynamic links to a few special offers on the side of every web page.

[2] Legal Issues in Framing

Since framed pages can be made to look like part of the original page, some web site owners object to framing, and several legal theories support that position. Unauthorized framing may violate the framed page's copyright by creating a derivative work,[245] defined in the Copyright Act as "work consisting of editorial revisions, annotations, elaborations, or other modifications."[246] A derivative works

---

[244] Beal, *supra* note 197, at 717.

[245] Daniel A. Tysver, Linking and Liability (visited May 6, 1999), http://www.bitlaw.com/internet/linking.html.

[246] 17 U.S.C. § 101 (1998).

claim in a framing case is an especially viable approach for plaintiffs because evidence of copying is not necessary to support such a finding.[247]

A framed link may also invoke liability under trademark infringement and dilution.[248] Under infringement principles, liability would result from the unauthorized use of proprietary marks for commercial purposes, however they appear on the framed page.[249] Dilution principles also apply to framing when the display of the trademarks within the framed page includes the logo and URL of another organization.[250] Framing tends to create great confusion over the owner of the site and can mislead a user into inferring a commercial relationship between the two organizations.[251]

The frame may also infringe upon a web site's trademark by causing confusion and diminishing the value of a protected mark.[252] While courts have not provided decisive precedent regarding framing, web operators should take precautions to avoid the expense of initiating or defending against a lawsuit.

The most notable framing dispute was Washington Post v. TotalNews, Inc.[253] The TotalNews Internet page provided links to the web sites of hundreds of newspapers.[254] Visitors to the web page could view the newspapers' web sites through the TotalNews frame by clicking on links containing their trademarked names and logos.[255] The frame contained TotalNews' advertising and links while providing the content of other web sites.[256]

The TotalNews frame obscured or eliminated the advertising from the target newspapers' framed pages.[257] While some web sites were eager to be linked to the TotalNews page, others objected to the use of trademarked logos as links, to the frame obscuring their advertising, and to the commandeering of content.[258] Parties in the controversy settled before the court could issue a ruling. TotalNews agreed to remove the frame and to eliminate links containing stylized logos, leaving only plain text links.[259] As a small web site, TotalNews had little chance of success going against several large newspapers, each of which could afford a lengthy battle.

---

[247] Mirage Editions, Inc. v. Albuquerque A.R.T. Co., 856 F.2d 1341 (9th Cir. 1988) (holding that mounting copyrighted artwork onto ceramic tiles is a derivative work for copyright purposes).

[248] Beal, *supra* note 197, at 727.

[249] *Id.*

[250] *Id.*

[251] David Mirchin, Liability for Hypertext Linking: Recent Cases, Internet News: Legal & Bus. Aspects, May 1998, Vol. 3, No. 2, at 5.

[252] *Id.*

[253] 97 Civ. 1190 (PKL) (S.D.N.Y., Feb. 20, 1997).

[254] David L. Hayes, Application of Copyright Rights to Specific Acts on the Internet, Computer Lawyer, Aug. 1998, at 1.

[255] Nichole M. Bond, Linking and Framing on the Internet: Liability Under Trademark and Copyright Law, 11 DePaul Bus. L.J. 185, 196 (Fall/Winter, 1998).

[256] Carol Ebbinghouse, Webmaster Liability, Searcher, Feb. 1998, at 19.

[257] Hayes, *supra* note 254.

[258] Beal, *supra* note 197, at 718.

[259] Online Advertising? Beware of Dangers (visited April 28, 1999), http:www.lgu.com/cy45.htm.

[3] Resolving Framing Controversies

[a] *Protecting Your Web Site*

The first step in avoiding costly litigation over framing is to post a clear framing policy. Web sites that violate the policy should respond to a well-crafted cease-and-desist request. Unwanted frames may also be side-stepped through proper programming of the web site.[260]

[b] *Framing Other Web Sites*

Before you frame another web site, obtain its host's written permission. If you are already framing other sites, and they object, eliminate the links and determine whether the other sites object to unframed links. Frames can be a very effective way of providing content that keeps visitors within your web site for a long time. SPC, for example, may want to give its customers access to Intel's web site whenever it makes reference to its use of the Pentium III chip. Framing Intel's web site within SPC's web site enables SPC to leverage Intel's content without any rewriting. With a few legal precautions, companies can take advantage of Internet framing technology.

[E] Marketing Through E-Mail

E-mail is a marketer's dream. For minimal cost, a company can communicate with thousands of prospective and current customers. E-mail advertising ranges from informative messages directly requested by the recipients to bulk "spam," which can be a convoy of unsolicited messages clogging the information superhighway.

[1] Advantages of E-Mail

As the response rates to banner ads and other advertising formats on the Internet diminish, e-mail marketing is becoming an important medium.[261] E-mail can be used to develop traffic to a web site and to distribute information about new products and special promotions.[262] Sending an advertisement via e-mail is similar to mailing traditional solicitations, without the high costs of designing, printing, and postage. Unlike printed advertisements, potential customers may receive e-mails within minutes of their transmission. E-mail ads may contain direct links

---

[260] Andrew J. Hollander, Do-It-Yourself Source-Code Firewalls, Internet Newsletter: Legal and Business Aspects, May 1998, at 4. The code to avoid frames is available online at www.netscapeworld.com/netscapeworld/nw-05-1997/nw-05.html (visited May 14, 1999). *Id.*

[261] *See* Ian Oxman, Opt-In E-mail—Who's the Fool?, DM News, Mar. 22, 1999, at 24 (comparing e-mail advertising to other methods of Internet marketing).

[262] *See* Marketing News and Resources, Marketing Department Management Report, Feb. 1999, at 8 (illustrating economics of e-mail advertising).

to the advertised web site or even enclosures of pictures, movies, or other media to intrigue customers.

[2] Opt-In versus Opt-Out E-Mailing

The most effective method of e-mail advertising is to send messages to people who have registered at the host's Internet site to be on its e-mailing list; this allows the host to target mailings based on the recipients' interests and needs, and it eliminates unwanted messages. Many Internet users have a positive view of e-mail that allows them choose to participate or "opt-in."[263] Even Internet groups who oppose traditional e-mail solicitations agree that the "opt-in" model is an acceptable form of e-mail advertising.[264]

In one creative example, Calvin Klein Cosmetics incorporated opt-in e-mail advertising into a traditional television, print, and radio campaign.[265] The ads in traditional media contained an e-mail address for the various featured characters.[266] Those who sent e-mails to the advertised addresses received a fictitious correspondence from the characters.[267] This campaign illustrated many of the benefits of e-mail advertising by combining an "opt-in" mailing list culled from traditional advertising media with an intriguing correspondence that subtly advertised products.

Opt-out e-mail advertising, on the other hand, is considered offensive and in bad taste.[268] Opt-out advertising requires the recipient of an unsolicited advertisement to send an e-mail to a specific address to be removed from the mailing list. Since e-mail marketing is so inexpensive, some companies are willing to risk irritating thousands of people in order to get a few respondents.[269]

[3] Legal Challenges to E-Mail Marketing

When the technology for bulk e-mailing was developed, advertisers were quick to recognize its value. Unlike traditional mailed advertisements, however, e-mail solicitations are viewed as intrusive and unwelcome. The first bulk e-mail incident, in 1994, aroused an uproar across the Internet community.[270]

---

[263] Stacey Lawrence, Marketing Spotlight: E-Mail Spruces Up Its Reputation, Industry Standard, Feb. 14, 2000.

[264] See Roberta Fusaro, Groups Eye Model for E-Mail Ads; Antispam Summit, Computerworld, Dec. 21, 1998, at 47 (reporting agreement between direct marketing group and antispam coalition).

[265] Patrick Allossery, You've Got E-Mail: An Internet Soap Opera from Calvin Klein: New Medium Carries the Storyline for the Campaign, National Post, Dec. 14, 1998, at C4.

[266] Id.

[267] Id.

[268] Erika Rasmusson, Spam Gets Slammed, Sales & Marketing Management, Dec. 1998, at 56.

[269] Kimberly Patch and Eric Smalley, E-mail Overload; Companies Risk Getting Crushed by All Those Messages If They Don't Devise Strategies for Handling the Burden, Network World, Oct. 26, 1998, at 1.

[270] Margaret Loftus, Great Moments in E-mail History, U.S. News and World Report, Mar. 22, 1999, at 56.

Compared to printed advertisements, unsolicited bulk e-mails may be burdensome to the recipient and costly and time-consuming for Internet Service Providers. Unsolicited e-mail advertising may be likened to selling products via collect telephone calls.[271] Recipients of e-mail still pay the Internet connection charges and phone line rental whether or not they requested the advertisement.[272] According to one estimate, large companies lose $500,000 annually as a result of spam.[273]

Unsolicited e-mail represented five percent to thirty percent of America Online's e-mail traffic,[274] and AOL actively filters incoming e-mail.[275] Other ISPs face similar spam burdens, which slow down servers, consume disk space, and cost money to filter out. America Online, Compuserve, and other ISPs have successfully sued several intrusive e-mail marketing companies on a variety of legal theories, ranging from the common law tort of trespass to the Computer Fraud and Abuse Act.[276]

Unscrupulous e-mail marketers have also aroused the ire of ISPs by forging return addresses. This practice, known as "spoofing," benefits the e-mail sender by keeping its return address unknown while masking its identity with an address that looks innocuous. Additionally, recipients have no way to reply to the e-mail and little hope of tracing its origins. Spoofing was once a popular method for trying to draw traffic to shady web sites purveying get rich quick schemes or pornography.[277] Recent state and federal laws, however, have prohibited false return e-mail addresses. America Online used trademark law and local computer statutes, among other theories, to win a substantial legal victory against a bulk e-mailer who sent unsolicited e-mails with false return addresses to AOL subscribers.[278]

As spam becomes more burdensome to companies, individuals, and ISPs, plaintiffs are employing state and federal laws to protect themselves.[279] States have been adopting legislation requiring caution on the part of any company planning to use e-mail for advertising.[280] Virginia, for example, passed a law imposing statutory damages of $10 per message or up to $25,000 per day for falsifying a return

---

[271] Rasmusson, *supra* note 268.

[272] Four Reasons Why It's Wrong to Spam, Computimes (Malaysia), Apr. 15, 1999, available in LEXIS, News Library, Curnws file.

[273] Patch and Smalley, *supra* note 269.

[274] *Id.*

[275] Rachel Ross, Spam Blocker Wipes Out E-Mail, Toronto Star, Mar. 21, 2001, available in LEXIS, News Library, Curnws File.

[276] *See* The Perkins Coie Internet Case Digest: Spam (Junk E-Mail) (visited May 3, 1999), http://www.perkinscoie.com/resource/ecomm/netcase/Cases-23.htm (listing e-mail controversies).

[277] Court Rulings Give AOL Three New Victories in the Battle Against Junk E-Mail, Business Wire, Dec. 21, 1998, available in LEXIS, News Library, Curnws file.

[278] American Online, Inc. V. LCGM, INC., 1998 U.S. Dist. LEXIS 20144 (E.D. Va Nov. 10, 1998). *See also* Court Rulings Give AOL Three New Victories, *supra* note 277 (listing legal victories against bulk e-mailers and return address forgers).

[279] For a comprehensive list of current a proposed legislation, *see* Existing and Emerging Anti-Spam Law (visited May 19, 1999), http://www.tigerden.com/junkmail/laws.html.

[280] For a comprehensive list of state laws, visit http://www.spamlaws.com.

address.[281] The Washington Supreme Court overruled a lower court decision holding that Washington's Unsolicited Electronic Mail Act was unconstitutional because it violated the Commerce Clause.[282] California and Tennessee have several requirements for bulk e-mail, including providing a toll-free telephone number or an e-mail address through which to request removal from the e-mailing list.[283] California also requires entities that send out mass commercial e-mailings to begin the subject line with "ADV" for advertisement, and it gives ISPs standing to sue spammers.[284] While these statutes raise free-speech implications and may have a limited scope, companies should heed the current laws rather than testing them, since they make sense from a business and legal perspective.[285]

[4]   Solutions for E-Mail Marketing

Companies using e-mail marketing should limit mailings to individuals who ask to be put on their mailing lists.[286] Sending unsolicited e-mail detracts from a company's image and could result in retaliatory bulk e-mail responses, which can slow down or cripple a server.[287] Since e-mail advertising is not as well accepted as printed advertising, companies should proceed cautiously in utilizing their e-mailing list. Using e-mail to support traditional mass marketing strategies can backfire and result in a robust e-mailing list of customers who ignore your e-mails.[288] Start slowly and on a small scale to test how consumers respond.

Additionally, all e-mail advertisements should follow the laws of the most restrictive state. Advertisers should use the following checklist as a precaution:

1. Use only opt-in advertising and archive all consumer requests to be part of the e-mailing list. If a recipient claims that the e-mail was unsolicited, you may need to prove that the recipient actively sought to be on the list.

2. Minimize the number of e-mail advertisements sent at one time to avoid burdening the ISPs and recipients' servers.

3. Make sure that your return e-mail address is accurate.

---

[281] Mark Grossman, No Matter How You Slice and Dice It, Spam's a Problem, Broward Daily Bus. Rev., Apr. 30, 1999, at B1.

[282] State v. Heckel, 24 P.3d 404 (2001) (finding Act to be sufficiently limited).

[283] California Laws 1999, LA Times, Jan. 1, 1999, at A3.

[284] Rob Turner, Relief From Online "Spam" Attacks?, Money, Dec. 1998, at 104. For an analysis of the California e-mail regulations, see California's New Anti-Spam Laws (visited May 19, 1999), http://www.wsgr.com/resource/intprop/pubs/articles/spam.htm.

[285] Kelly Hearn, Will U.S. Crack Down on Rising Volume of E-Mail 'Spam'?, Christian Science Monitor (visited June 15, 2002), http://www.csmonitor.com/durable/2000/04/17/p13s1.htm.

[286] Consumers can volunteer to have their names put on a mailing list by registering at a given web site. But consumers have found their names on mailing lists for which they had not specifically registered. This happens primarily because many companies sell their customer lists to other marketers.

[287] Four Reasons Why It's Wrong to Spam, supra note 272.

[288] Erika Rasmusson, What Price Knowledge? Marketers Should Understand Consumer's Wish for Privacy, Sales and Marketing Management, Dec. 1998, at 56.

4. Put 'ADV' in the subject line, along with an accurate description of the e-mail's contents.

5. Provide your company's name, address, e-mail address, and telephone number clearly within the body of the e-mail.

6. Provide recipients with an e-mail address or toll-free number to contact should they wish to be removed from the e-mailing list.

7. Never sell your e-mailing list or purchase one from others.

8. Check your own ISP's policy regarding distribution of e-mail solicitations. You may have certain restrictions within your contract.

9. Keep the content of e-mail advertising brief. The e-mail should contain a link to your web site for those looking for more information.

10. Define a clear, corporate-wide e-mail advertising policy. This will help prevent recipients from receiving multiple e-mails from different departments of the same company.

11. Make sure that your e-mail policy is compatible with the privacy policy on your web site. The opt-in web page should state exactly why personal information is being collected and the use you intend to make of it.

[F] Metatags

Web site owners are always looking to find ways to generate traffic to their site. Traditional advertising, or web advertisements, can prove to be very costly for some organizations. One way to get free advertising or at least direct traffic to one's web site is through the use of metatags. When companies create a home page and register the URL with a search engine, or a number of search engines, their web-searching tools will eventually find your site and attempt to index it. Each of the search engines does this slightly differently. Alta Vista, for example, will grab everything from your web site and index it, but will only show the first 250 characters in its description. Consequently, if a site included a dedication right at the beginning, this is what Alta Vista would then show in its description, and it would not give the viewer any idea of what the site actually has. However, not all search engines work in this manner.

Web site owners have used metatags as a way to exert some control over how their site might be indexed.

Metatags are hidden HTML codes in the head portion of your various web pages; they are not visible to site visitors, but they contain key words, phrases, or descriptions used by many search engines. Search engines will provide a higher search result ranking to your site if the metatag used is the proper one for your content. Every page, therefore, should include a metatag.

[1] What to Include in Metatags

As a general rule, web designers suggest that every metatag on a given web page include a title, a few keywords, and a brief description. Titles are generally created by HTML editing programs. If the tool you use does not create a title for each page, be sure that you otherwise include one. Keywords represent a subjective list of concepts relevant to a site or page. Metatags should also include brief descriptions. Internet searches return the URLs of relevant sites along with a brief description of each. This description, if compelling, helps convince people that the site is worth a click. This is often the only chance site owners have to attract potential customers.

[2]   Tips on Using Metatags Effectively

Metatags are invaluable for generating traffic to a site, and their use can be enhanced in a number of ways.

- Some search engines prefer shorter metatags composed of relevant keywords.

- Metatags should also be provided for on frames.

- Do not cut-and-paste a metatag from one page to another.

- Do not use a competitor's name or products as a metatag.

[3]   Legal Issues and Limitations

In the past, some web site operators exploited metatags by using other company's trademarks and company names to siphon off visitors looking for another site.[289] Courts have ruled against such metatag abuse.[290] Metatag users should, therefore, use the following precautions against the appearance of misuse.

1. In creating metatags, do not use anyone else's trademark without permission.
2. Never mention the names or products of competitors in a metatag, even if the names are not trademarked.
3. If you carry third-party products, get permission before using other brand names or products in metatags.
4. Include your own brand name and product names in metatags.
5. Use descriptive terms for your products or service in metatags. (Suffolk PCs, for example, might use the terms "computer, monitor, CPU, hard drive," among other words, in its metatags.)

A carefully written metatag can be effective in drawing web traffic without inciting a legal dispute. For a complete discussion of the legal issues related to metatags, see § 4.03[M][6].

---

[289] *See* Playboy Enterprises, Inc. v. Calvin Designer Label, 985 F. Supp. 1220, 1221-22 (N.D. Cal. 1997) (prohibiting use of Playboy trademark in computer code that indexed page on Internet search engines).

[290] Intellectual Property Court Watch Roundup of Recent Developments, Intell. Prop. Strat., Nov. 1997, at 10. The court focused on the defendants' unauthorized use of the registered trademark.

§ 2.08   PREVENTIVE LAW POINTERS

[A]   Sample Legal Disclaimer on Web Site

This web site's purpose is to provide users with information about the SPC. Though we believe this information to be accurate at the time of its posting, there may be omissions or inaccuracies in this information.

Further, laws and regulations change, and the application and impact of such laws and regulations may vary based on the jurisdiction and the specific facts and circumstances. Accordingly, the information on this web site is provided with the understanding that SPC is not herein engaged in rendering legal or professional advice or services. As such, this web site should not be used as a substitute for the user's consultation with its professional advisors.

SPC is not responsible for any errors or omissions in the information contained in this web site, or for the results obtained from the use of any information contained herein. All information in this web site is provided "as is," with no guarantee of completeness, accuracy, timeliness, or of the results obtained from the use of this information. SPC makes no warranty of any kind, express or implied, including, but not limited to, warranties of performance, merchantability, or fitness for a particular purpose. SPC also makes no representations or warranties with respect to the accessibility or availability of the web site to any user. In no event will SPC, its affiliated entities, or their officers, directors, partners, or employees be liable to any party for any damages of any kind whatsoever, including consequential damages, arising from any use of or inability to use this web site, or any information provided herein, or decision made or action taken in reliance upon such information.

Certain links in this web site connect to other web sites maintained by third parties. SPC has no control over these web sites or the information or goods or services provided by such third parties. SPC shall have no liability for any use or reliance of a user on these third-party web sites.

[B]   Sample Privacy Policy Statement

About Our Privacy Policy

SPC is committed to your right to privacy and to keeping your personal information private. Because our web site includes areas in which individuals can provide personally identifying information, we have developed the SPC Privacy Policy below to inform you of our policies and practices regarding information we collect about you on this site. If you have further questions about our privacy policies or practices after reading this Privacy Policy, please contact us at the following address:

Suffolk Personal Computers
120 Tremont Street
Boston, MA 02110

This Privacy Policy governs the URL http://www.spc.com. The information about you described in this document is controlled by SPC professionals.

SPC Privacy Policy

1. How we gather information about you
2. The ways information about you is collected
3. The ways information about you is used by SPC
4. What information about you is shared
5. Implications of collecting and sharing information about you
6. Ways you can control the information collected about you

Additional Information

1. Protection of children's online privacy on SPC.com
2. Additional Privacy Rights and Resource
3. Changes to the SPC Privacy Policy

1. How we gather information about you

SPC.com collects and maintains certain personal information about you when you send us e-mail or complete any of our online forms such as Application Form or Contact Us. The personal information you provide can identify you and your business individually, and includes items such as your name and e-mail address, job title, company name and address, phone number, IRS not-for-profit certificate number, web site address, and contact details of the web site administrator.

SPC.com also collects, or logs, certain other information that cannot identify you personally when you visit our web site. This information includes your Internet Protocol ("IP") address and your domain name. An IP address is a number that is automatically assigned to your computer by the ISP computer through which you access the web and a domain name is the name of the ISP computer itself through which you access the web.

SPC.com logs these IP addresses and domain names and aggregates them for system administration and to monitor the use of our site. We use the aggregated information to measure the number of visits to our site, the average time spent on our site, the number of pages viewed, and various other site use statistics. This monitoring helps us evaluate how our web site is used and continuously improve the content we provide. While we may report aggregated IP address information to SPC program participants, SPC.com does not link IP addresses or domain names with any personally identifiable information, which means that a visitor's session will be logged on our servers but the visitor will always remain anonymous.

SPC.com does not purchase or otherwise obtain any supplemental personal information about you from any third parties.

2. Ways information about you is collected

We may actively collect information about you from the following sources: applications, forms, and other information that you provide to us, whether in writing, in person, by telephone, electronically, or by any other means, and by public sources and credit reporting agencies. This information may include your name, address, billing information, and recent purchases. If you choose to send e-mail messages to SPC, we may retain the content of your e-mail message, your e-mail address, and our subsequent responses. Please be careful about the information that you provide us by e-mail; as with any public web site, this channel of communication is not necessarily secure against interception.

In addition, we may utilize passive information collection means. As you navigate through SPC's web site, certain information can be passively collected (that is, gathered without your actively providing the information) using various technologies and means, such as navigational data collection. This site may use Internet Protocol (IP) addresses. An IP address is a number assigned to your computer by your Internet service provider so you can access the Internet and is generally considered to be nonpersonally identifiable information, because in most cases an IP address is dynamic (changing each time you connect to the Internet), rather than static (unique to a particular user's computer). We use your IP address to diagnose problems with our server, report aggregate information, determine the fastest route for your computer to use in connecting to our site, and administer and improve the site.

A "cookie" is a bit of information that a web site sends to your web browser that helps the site remember information about you and your preferences. "Session" cookies are temporary bits of information that are erased once you exit your web browser window or otherwise turn your computer off. Session cookies are used to improve navigation on web sites and to collect aggregate statistical information. This site **does not** use cookies and/or session cookies.

"Internet tags" (also known as Web Bugs, single-pixel GIFs, clear GIFs, invisible GIFs, and 1 by 1 GIFs) are smaller than cookies and tell the Web site server information such as the IP address and browser type related to the visitor's computer. We **do not** use Internet tags at this site.

"Navigational data" ("log files," "server logs," and "clickstream" data) are used for system management, to improve the content of the site, market research purposes, and communicate information to visitors. This site **uses** navigational data.

If you have joined the SPC.com, we may send you, via e-mail or post, our bi-weekly newsletter as well as other information impacting online customer relationships that we think you might find useful. If you do not wish to receive these communications, please opt-out by sending an e-mail to spcremove@spc.com, stating that you would like to be removed from our mailing list.

We do not collect any information from you online other than the personal information described above. SPC.com does not use cookies to collect information about you for any reason. A cookie allows SPC to determine that a visit has occurred within our site, as well as which pages were viewed. A cookie is NOT used to identify you and will not collect personal information. You remain anonymous throughout your visit. Cookies are commonly used on web sites and do not harm your PC. You can decide if and how your computer will accept cookies by configuring your preferences option within your web browser.

3. Ways information about you is used

We use the information you provide us to contact you in response to any requests, complaints, or comments you may have about SPC.com or SPC. If you have used our Register form and have elected to join our mailing list, we may also use the information you have provided to us to contact you in the future regarding SPC.

4. What information about you is shared

Under certain circumstances SPC.com may share personal information that you have provided us with other service lines within SPC. SPC.com does not collect or compile personal information for distribution to parties outside of SPC. Except as described below, SPC.com does not share any information about you with any parties outside of SPC.

If you send us e-mail or use our Register form to send us a request, complaint, or comment relating to any web site that displays the SPC logo, we may forward your request, complaint, or comment to the appropriate web site.

We will disclose personal information to comply with valid legal processes such as a search warrant, subpoena, or court order, judicial process or regulatory authorities, to prevent fraudulent transactions, or to protect our rights and property. We will disclose information when we believe in good faith that the law requires it. Absent a legal or internal SPC corporate need, your information may be shared with consumer reporting agencies or in connection with a proposed or actual sale, merger, or transfer of all or a portion of a business or an operating unit.

With respect to limiting employee access, SPC has policies and procedures to limit employee access to information to only those employees with a business reason for accessing such information. SPC educates its employees about the importance of confidentiality and customer privacy. We take appropriate disciplinary measures to enforce employee responsibilities regarding customer information.

5. Implications of collecting and sharing information about you

If you send us e-mail or use our Register form, we will send you an online acknowledgment that we have received your contact. If, when you complete our Register form, you elect to join our mailing list, you may also receive other contact from us regarding SPC or other topics we feel may be of interest to you.

As previously mentioned above, under certain circumstances SPC.com may share personal information you provide us, such as your e-mail address, job title, or company name and address, with other service lines within SPC. These service lines may contact you, via e-mail or post, to provide you information about their services and products that you may find useful.

You will not receive any contact from third parties outside of SPC as a result of providing information to us, with the possible exception of contact from a web site to which we have forwarded a request, complaint, or comment that you have sent to us.

6. Ways you can control the information collected about you

When you submit an inquiry, request, complaint, or comment to SPC.com, you have the opportunity to join our mailing list. If at a later time you wish to change your participation in our mailing list, please use an e-mail request and our staff will make the appropriate change for you. You will receive an immediate confirmation that we have received your communication.

If you would like to update information previously submitted to SPC.com or request to have outdated information removed, please e-mail your request.

7. E-mailing SPC

This Web site allows you to send e-mail to SPC and certain designated individuals. Information you send us will be considered nonconfidential and may be used by SPC or its affiliates without restriction. DO NOT SEND INFORMATION THAT YOU CONSIDER CONFIDENTIAL OR PROPRIETARY, INCLUDING BUSINESS PLANS OR IDEAS, INVENTIONS, AND THE LIKE. If you send a resume or other personal information to SPC or its career contact, the company reserves the right to disclose this information to its affiliates and to third parties such as employment agencies or search consultants used by the company; third parties that conduct background checks; and government agencies, including police departments, as permitted by law. If you send personal information in a request for shareholder services or investor information, the company may use that information or disclose it to third parties the company uses to respond to such inquiries. We may use the information to provide you with marketing information about SPC, including investor/shareholder materials, as permitted by law. Certain countries place restrictions on the collection and use of personal information that are more restrictive than permitted under the laws of Indiana and the United States. IF YOU RESIDE IN THE EUROPEAN UNION (EU) OR EUROPEAN ECONOMIC AREA (EEA), DO NOT SEND PERSONAL INFORMATION TO SPC BY E-MAIL UNLESS YOU SPECIFICALLY CONSENT TO ITS USE AS DESCRIBED ABOVE.

8. Security

SPC takes reasonable steps to protect your personally identifiable information as you transmit your information from your computer to our site and to protect such information from loss, misuse, and unauthorized access, disclosure, alteration, or destruction. You should keep in mind that no Internet transmission is ever 100 percent secure or error-free. In particular, e-mail sent to or from this site may not be secure, and you should therefore take special care in deciding what information you send to us via e-mail. Moreover, where you use passwords, ID numbers, or other special access features on this site, it is your responsibility to safeguard them.

Additional Information

1. Protection of children's online privacy on SPC.com

SPC.com understands the importance of protecting children's privacy, especially in an online environment. Protecting children's identities and information online is important. SPC does not knowingly solicit data from children online, nor does SPC market online products and services to children.

2. Additional Privacy Rights and Resources

You may have other privacy protections under state laws, and SPC will comply with applicable state laws with regard to our information practices. For a brief list of resources that provide privacy and other information about online activities, click here.

3. Changes to the SPC's Privacy Policy

SPC reserves the right to modify or amend this Privacy Policy at any time and for any reason. Any changes to this Privacy Policy will be preceded by a notice posted to this Privacy Policy at least ten (10) days prior to the effective date of such change. Please check back periodically, and especially before you provide any personally identifiable information. This Privacy Policy was last updated June 15, 2002.

4. How to Contact Us

If you have any questions or concerns about this Privacy Policy or the information practices of this site, please contact us as follows: Public Affairs, Suffolk Personal Computers, Inc., 120 Tremont Street, Boston, Massachusetts, 02110. You may also contact us by e-mail at public.affairs@spc.com.

[C]   Sample Security Policy

Security Policy

SPC is committed to your right to security and to keeping your personal information secure. That is why we have documented our security policy to allow you to make an informed decision when submitting identifying data to us or communicating with our site. After you have read our policy, if you have further questions, please contact us.

This Security Policy governs the URL http://www.spc.com and applies to both consumer- and business-related information.

SPC Security Policy

1. Site certificate information
2. User identification, where necessary
3. Protection of information being transmitted
4. Protection of stored information

Additional Information

1. Additional security resources
2. Changes to the SPC Security Policy

1. Site certificate information

SPC understands that the security of your personal information and business details is important to you. Whenever you submit personally identifiable or business identifiable information through our site, you will be doing so through our secure server.

The SPC site only allows secure browsers access to the secure areas of our site. The browser's "secure mode" is in place only when it is needed—when you are submitting a Registration Form or using our 1441 Compliance applications. You will be able to tell you are in a secure mode when your browser displays a special icon on the lower bar of your browser window. Specifically:

- On Netscape Navigator™ 1.x, 2.x, and 3.x, you will see a picture of a solid key
- On Netscape Communicator™ or Netscape Navigator™ 4.x and Microsoft Internet Explorer™, you will see a picture of a closed lock
- The web site address will start with "https" instead of "http".

Every secure page on http://www.spc.com has been secured with a digital certificate. This is shown via the "site certificate" that sits on all secure pages. To view this certificate, click on the image of the closed lock or the solid key on the bottom bar of your browser window. A small frame displaying site security information will pop up. Click on the word "Subject" to verify that you are on http://www.spc.com. Click on "Issuer" to verify the site certification authority.

2. User identification, where necessary

You do not need to set up a user id and password to use http://www.spc.com because we do not require you to establish your identity when you visit our site. Any information that you submit to us through this site is not retrievable by you after it is submitted.

3. Protection of information being transmitted

When you use a secure browser, all information you submit to us through the Registration Form is transmitted to us over the Internet in a protected form. Your browser provides security by allowing us to use Secure Socket Layer (SSL) encryption when transmitting your information. You may click on the closed lock or solid key to verify that we are using this encryption product. A small frame displaying site security information will pop up. Click on the word "Security Protocol" to view that we are using SSL v.3.0 and that we support up to 128-bit key length.

4. Protection of stored information

All information that you submit to us is transmitted directly to our highly secure internal database server, both for processing and as an SPC business record. We take many measures to protect this information while it is stored, including:

- Monitoring system and application activity logs to identify any unusual activity, from authorized and/or unauthorized individuals accessing our systems and/or making changes to stored information, for investigation.
- Housing internal computer systems in a secure building to provide additional protection against unauthorized access and changes to stored information.

Additional Information

1. Additional security resources

For a brief list of resources that provide security and other information about online activities, click here.

2 Changes to the SPC Security Policy

SPC reserves the right to modify or amend this Security Policy at any time and for any reason. Any changes to this Security Policy will be preceded by a notice posted to this Security Policy at least ten (10) days prior to the effective date of such change.

[D]   Sample Cease and Desist Letter

April 26, 2001
Via e-mail (tkrieger@suffolkpersonalcleaners.com)
Confirmation via First Class Mail
Suffolk Personal Cleaners
129 Vine Street
Boston, MA 02110
Attn: Todd Krieger

Re: SPC's Objection to Registration and Use of amex-activity.com and
    amexactivity.com

Our File No. SPC-GCOR-2001-04-26:

Dear Mr. Krieger:

We represent the Suffolk Personal Computers, Inc. in matters involving trademarks and unfair competition. It has come to our attention that Suffolk Personal Cleaners

LLC has registered the domain names spc-shines.com and spcproduces.com with AOL, Inc. Copies of the registration information from AOL, Inc. are enclosed with the confirmation copy of this letter for your review.

Please be advised that our client is the owner of a federal trademark registration for SPC, specifically Registration No. 2,341,988 registered on January 2, 2000. SPC began using the SPC mark in 2000, and has continuously and extensively used and advertised its SPC trademark since that time, making the SPC mark famous in the United States and worldwide. As such, the SPC trademark is a valuable asset of our client, one it will take all reasonable steps to protect.

Unauthorized registration and use of SPC and spc-shines.com and spcproduces.com is likely to cause confusion, mistake, or to deceive the public and is a violation of our client's federally protected rights under 15 U.S.C. §§ 1114 and 1125. Indeed, the registration of spc-shines.com and spcproduces.com appears to be clearly intended to falsely create the impression that Suffolk Personal Computers is the owner of or associated with these domain names. Additionally, the Anticybersquatting Consumer Protection Act, which amends the Federal Trademark Act, states that a domain name registrant is liable in a civil action if the registrant has a bad faith intent to profit from registration of the trademark as a domain name and registers, traffics in, or uses a domain name that is identical or confusingly similar to another party's trademark or dilutes a famous trademark. Under the Act, the trademark owner can recover damages of $1000 to $100,000 per domain name registration.

Accordingly, we request that Suffolk Personal Cleaners LLC withdraw the spc-shines.com and spcproduces.com domain name registration from AOL, Inc. within 10 days, and that Suffolk Personal Cleaners LLC cease and desist all current and future use of spc-shines.com and spcproduces.com, or anything else confusingly similar thereto, in connection with a domain name or in any other manner. If we do not receive confirmation of the withdrawal of the domain name from AOL, Inc. and your assurances within 10 days that Suffolk Personal Cleaners LLC will cease and desist all use of spc-shines.com and spcproduces.com, we will recommend to our client that it take the necessary legal steps to protect its rights.

Very truly yours,

Suffolk Law, LLP.

[E]   Sample Linking Terms and Conditions

SPC welcomes and encourages links to spc.com (the "Web Site")—however, prior to linking to our web site, please visit spc.com to view its Linking Terms and Conditions. You may link only to www.spc.com provided you agree to the conditions described below. Links may not be established to any other pages of the web site without SPC's prior written permission. If you establish a link to the web site, you will be deemed to have agreed to these Linking Terms and Conditions.

- You may link only to the homepage of www.spc.com.
- If you link to the web site, SPC grants you a limited, nonexclusive, non-transferable, royalty-free license to use the SPC service mark and Internet icon(s), if available, (the "Licensed Marks") solely for the purpose of serving as a link from your web site to spc.com. Except for the limited license to use the Licensed Marks granted in this paragraph, you may not use any of SPC's trademarks or service marks (the "Marks") for any reason without SPC's prior written permission.
- You acknowledge that all rights to the Marks, the content appearing on the web site and the look and feel of the web site belong to SPC and/or its third-party licensors. You will not at any time directly or indirectly contest or infringe these rights.
- If you link to spc.com, your web site:
  - May not create frames around spc.com or use other techniques that alter the visual presentation of the web site.
  - May not imply that SPC is endorsing you or your products or services.
  - May not imply an affiliation between your company and SPC without prior written consent by SPC.
  - May not misrepresent your relationship with SPC or present false or misleading impressions about SPC's products or services.
  - May not contain materials that may be interpreted as distasteful or offensive and should be appropriate for all age groups.
- SPC shall have no responsibility or liability for any content appearing on your web site.
- SPC—at any time, in its sole discretion—may immediately terminate your license to use the Licensed Marks and your right to link to spc.com, with or without cause. If SPC exercises this right, you must immediately remove all links to the web site and cease using the Licensed Marks.
- SPC may amend these Linking Terms and Conditions at any time. You agree to abide by these Linking Terms and Conditions and other legal terms and conditions on the web site, as amended from time to time. All terms and conditions related to the use of spc.com will be construed according to the laws of Massachusetts, United States of America, without regard to its conflict of law provisions. By using the web site, you consent to the exclusive personal jurisdiction and venue of courts located in Massachusetts regarding all disputes related to the web site.

[F] Sample Linking Agreement

THIS AGREEMENT, dated as of _____ (the "Effective Date"), is by and between the Suffolk Personal Computers ("SPC"), a Massachusetts corporation, and _____, a _____ corporation/an individual ("Linking Site Owner").

SPC and Linking Site Owner agree as follows:

1. *Grant of License:* SPC grants a nonexclusive license to Linking Site Owner to provide a link from the web site at URL _____ ("Linking Site") to the web site at URL http://www.spc.com ("web site") pursuant to the terms of this Agreement. Linking Site Owner grants a nonexclusive license to SPC to provide a link from the web site to the Linking Site.

2. *Terms of License:*

   a. *Acceptable Links.* Linking Site Owner agrees to link only to the home page of the web site. The acceptable format for links consists of the name of the web site in plain text, which may be highlighted and/or underlined.

   b. *Prohibited Links and Use of SPC Marks.* Linking Site Owner shall not "frame" any portion of the web site. SPC and other graphics, logos, trademarks, and service names of SPC are trademarks of SPC ("SPC Marks"). Linking Site Owner may not use on any web site, as hyperlinks or in any other way, any SPC Marks (except as described in Section 2(a) above), nor may Linking Site Owner otherwise link in any manner reasonably likely to: (i) imply affiliation with, endorsement or sponsorship by SPC; (ii) cause confusion, mistake, or deception; (iii) dilute or tarnish SPC's Marks; (iv) disparage or discredit SPC; or (v) otherwise violate state or federal law. SPC may immediately terminate this agreement if SPC believes Linking Site Owner's use of SPC Marks or Linking Site Owner's link to the SPC site violates any of the prohibitions in this Section 2. Linking Site Owner agrees not to take any action inconsistent with SPC's ownership of the SPC Marks. Nothing in this Agreement shall be deemed to grant to Linking Site Owner an ownership interest in SPC's Marks.

   c. *Other Prohibited Uses of Web Site.* Linking Site Owner further agrees not to reproduce, retransmit, publicly display, perform, sell, or rent any content of the web site, including logos, text, graphics, button icons, images, video or audio material, and software, all of which are protected under U.S. and international copyright, trade dress, and other laws. The compilation (meaning the collection, arrangement, and assembly) of all content on the web site is the exclusive property of SPC and protected by U.S. and international copyright, trade dress, and other laws. Commercial use of the web site, or any material located on it, is strictly prohibited.

3. *Revocability of License to Link:* SPC's Agreement to permit linking by Linking Site Owner remains revocable on 15 business days' notice in accordance with SPC's sole discretion. If Linking Site Owner refuses to cease linking upon notice, Linking Site Owner acknowledges that such refusal shall result in immediate irreparable and irremediable damage to SPC. Linking Site Owner agrees that, in the event of such refusal, there is no

adequate remedy at law and pursuant to Section 7 of this Agreement, SPC shall be entitled to relief in the way of temporary or permanent injunctions and such other and further relief as an arbitrator may deem just and proper.

4. *Control Over Linking Site:* SPC takes no responsibility for the content or information contained on the Linking Site and does not exert any editorial or other control over the Linking Site.

5. *Disclaimer of Representations and Warranties:* SPC IS PROVIDING INFORMATION AND SERVICES ON THE INTERNET AS A BENEFIT AND SERVICE IN FURTHERANCE OF SPC'S BUSINESS PURPOSES. SPC MAKES NO REPRESENTATIONS OR WARRANTIES OF ANY KIND, EXPRESS OR IMPLIED, AS TO THE OPERATION OF THE WEB SITE, THE INFORMATION, CONTENT, MATERIALS, OR PRODUCTS, INCLUDED ON THE WEB SITE. TO THE FULL EXTENT PERMISSIBLE BY APPLICABLE LAW, SPC DISCLAIMS ALL WARRANTIES, EXPRESS OR IMPLIED, INCLUDING BUT NOT LIMITED TO, IMPLIED WARRANTIES OF MERCHANTABILITY, FITNESS FOR A PARTICULAR PURPOSE, TITLE, AND NON-INFRINGEMENT. SPC OFFERS NO ASSURANCE OF UNINTERRUPTED OR ERROR-FREE SERVICE. SPC DOES NOT WARRANT THE ACCURACY OR COMPLETENESS OF THE INFORMATION, TEXT, GRAPHICS, LINKS, OR OTHER ITEMS CONTAINED ON THE WEB SITE. SPC MAY CHANGE ANY OF THE INFORMATION FOUND ON THE WEB SITE OR CEASE PROVIDING THE WEB SITE AT ANY TIME WITHOUT NOTICE. SPC MAKES NO COMMITMENT TO UPDATE THE INFORMATION FOUND AT THE WEB SITE. SPC WILL NOT BE LIABLE FOR DAMAGES OF ANY KIND ARISING FROM THE USE OF OR INABILITY TO USE THE WEB SITE, INCLUDING BUT NOT LIMITED TO DIRECT, INDIRECT, INCIDENTAL, PUNITIVE, AND CONSEQUENTIAL DAMAGES.

6. *Indemnification:* Linking Site Owner shall defend, indemnify, save, and hold harmless SPC, SPC's registrants, officers, directors, agents, and employees from any and all third-party claims, demands, liabilities, costs, or expenses, including reasonable attorneys' fees, resulting from the Linking Site Owner's breach of any material duty or representation contained in this Agreement or resulting from any third party's use of the Linking Site. SPC reserves the right, at its own expense, to participate in the defense of any matter otherwise subject to indemnification by Linking Site Owner.

7. *Dispute Resolution:* SPC and Linking Site Owner agree that any dispute(s) between them shall be submitted promptly for binding resolution in accordance with the Federal Arbitration Act, 9 U.S.C. §§ 1-15, by a single arbitrator with specific expertise in Internet and electronic communications matters. The arbitrator shall conduct the arbitration under the then current rules of the American Arbitration Association, and all expedited procedures in the AAA rules shall apply. The arbitration shall be heard in Boston, Massachusetts, or another mutually agreeable location. The arbitrator's award shall be final and binding and may be entered in any court having

jurisdiction thereof. The prevailing party, as determined by the arbitrator, shall be entitled to an award of reasonable attorneys' fees and costs. If any party hereto files a judicial or administrative action asserting claims subject to arbitration, as prescribed herein, and another party successfully stays such action and/or compels arbitration of said claims, the party filing said action shall pay the other party's costs and expenses incurred in seeking such stay and/or compelling arbitration, including reasonable attorney's fees. It is expressly agreed that the arbitrator shall be authorized to issue injunctive relief pending an award in arbitration and either party may seek relief in an appropriate court of law to enforce such determination by an arbitrator.

8. *Notice:* Any notice, approval, request, authorization, direction, or other communication under this Agreement shall be given in writing and shall be deemed to have been delivered and given for all purposes (i) on the delivery date if delivered by electronic mail and confirmed by U.S. First Class Mail, return receipt requested, postage and charges prepaid; (ii) on the delivery date if delivered personally to the party to whom the same is directed; (iii) one (1) business day after deposit with a commercial overnight carrier with written verification of receipt; or (iv) five (5) business days after the mailing date if sent by U.S. First Class Mail, return receipt requested, postage and charges prepaid. Notice shall be sent to:

Cyrus Daftary, President
SPC
120 Tremont Street
Boston, MA 02110

9. *Binding Effect:* This Agreement shall be binding upon and inure to the benefit of the parties hereto and their respective successors and permitted assigns.

By: _____	By: _____
Cyrus Daftary,	Name:
President	Title:
SPC	Company:
120 Tremont Street	Address:
Boston, MA 02110	City, State, Zip:

IN WITNESS WHEREOF, this Agreement has been duly executed and delivered on behalf of each party hereto as of the date first above written.

[G]   Sample Web Site Hosting Terms

If as a part of SPC's service offering it were to host applications for third parties, some of the sample clauses it should consider including in the Agreement would include:

1. *Lawful Purpose:* The Client account and/or related electronic services can only be used for legal purposes under all international, federal, provincial, and municipal laws. Violations of this or any other provision of this Agreement can result in a 30-day notice to terminate service or an immediate termination of service depending upon the severity of the violation. SPC reserves the right to refuse service if the content of information provided is deemed illegal, misleading, or obscene, in the opinion of SPC. Client agrees not to store, transmit, link to, advertise, or make available any images containing nudity or semi-nudity or target advertisements to children under the age of 14. SPC will make the final decision in any dispute over unacceptable context, and Client agrees to accept SPC's decision.

2. *Connectivity Requirements:* Any access to other networks connected to SPC's network must comply with the rules appropriate for that other network. Connectivity is provided for Client only.

3. *"Netiquette" Responsibilities:* The Client agrees to follow generally accepted rules of "Netiquette" when sending e-mail messages or posting to newsgroups. Client is responsible for security of the password. SPC will not change passwords to any account without proof of identification which is satisfactory to SPC, which may include written authorization with signature. In the event of any partnership break-up, divorce, or other legal problems that includes Client, Client understands that SPC will remain neutral and may put the account on hold until the situation has been resolved. Under no circumstances will SPC be liable for any losses incurred by Client during this time of determination of ownership, or otherwise.

4. *Billing & Fees:* Billing for SPC's service will normally commence when Client data files are installed on the SPC server and can be accessed from the Internet. Service is invoiced monthly in advance and may be cancelled in writing within 30-day notice with no penalty. SPC reserves the right to increase prices at any time, but will notify Client 30 days in advance of the effective date of the change.

5. *Hold Harmless:* The Client agrees not to harm SPC and its vendors, its reputation, computer systems, programming and/or other Client using SPC. SPC and authorized vendors reserve the right to select the computer for Accountholders' web site for best performance. If Client breaches this agreement, then SPC has the right to terminate service without any refunds of the unused portion prepaid by Client. The Client agrees to indemnify and hold harmless both SPC and any other Client from any and all claims and/or costs resulting from the Client use or abuse of their service in any manner.

6. *Shared Servers:* Client understands this service is provided on a shared server. This means that one web site cannot overwhelm the server with heavy CPU usage from highly active CGI scripts or chat scripts. If Client's web site overwhelms the server and causes complaints from the other users, it has outgrown the realm of

shared servers, and will need to relocate your web site. SPC will refund any unused portion of prepaid services. If at any time Client breaches any part of this contract and SPC must engage the services of an attorney, then Client will pay any and all of SPC's and its vendors' reasonable attorney fees and court costs. The Client's rights and privileges cannot be sold or transferred without written consent from SPC.

7. *Unsolicited Commercial E-mail:* This contract represents the complete understanding between the parties. If Client sells or resells advertising or web page space to a third party, then Client will be responsible for the contents of that advertising and the actions of that third party. SPC and its vendors have the right to reject any illegal or offensive content. The e-mail distribution by the Client of "SPAM," "JUNK MAIL," or "UNSOLICITED COMMERCIAL E-MAIL" is expressly prohibited and may be cause for immediate termination of this Agreement. If Client refuses to remove any content found objectionable by SPC, SPC may terminate this Agreement. Client agrees to pay SPC its reasonable expenses, including attorney and system administration fees, incurred in responding to complaints and damages caused by the actions of sending unsolicited commercial e-mail.

8. *Uptime:* SPC will use its best efforts to maintain a full-time Internet presence for Client. The network may be down due to, but not restricted to, utility interruption, equipment failure, natural disaster, acts of God, or human error. Client agrees that these events may or may not occur and Client will hold SPC, its vendors, employees, owners, and contractors free and harmless from any damages incurred in any event of any type of loss resulting from any reason whatsoever. SPC's total liability under all circumstances will never exceed the amount paid by Client for duration of this agreement. If Client selects the option for 12 months prepaid service, then any amounts prepaid cannot be refunded by SPC in the event Client stops using this service.

Other clauses that ought to be included are: financial terms; taxes; trademark and copyrights; acceptable use policies; termination; limited liability; indemnification; domain name ownership dispute and use; and acceptance.

[H]   Sample Terms of Service Agreement

As a part of SPC's service offering, it should outline the terms of service: Some of the sample clauses it should consider including in the agreement follow.

1. Terms of Service

Welcome to Suffolk Personal Computer. SPC provides its service to you, subject to the following Terms of Service ("TOS") Agreement, which may be updated by us from time to time without notice to you. You can review the most current version of the TOS at any time at http://www.spc.com/legal/terms. In addition, when using particular SPC services, you and SPC shall be subject to any posted guidelines or rules applicable to such services, which may be posted from time to time. All such guidelines or rules are hereby incorporated by reference into the TOS.

2. Description of Service

Your use of the Service will be subject to the terms of this TOS Agreement. SPC grants to you a nonexclusive license to use and display the Service, and to download materials available through the Service, all solely for your personal, noncommercial use. You may not transfer, assign, sublicense, lend, or resell the rights granted under this license. The Service and all materials published therein, including but not limited to articles, graphical images, interactive applications, audio clips, and video clips (collectively, the "Content"), are protected by copyright and are owned by SPC or its licensors. You may not modify the Content or republish, retransmit, or otherwise distribute any Content to any third person. You may copy and display the Content solely for your personal, noncommercial use, as permitted by the license granted above. All trademarks on the Service are the property of their respective holders.

3. Exclusions of Warranty and Liability

THE SERVICE AND MATERIALS PROVIDED THROUGH THE SERVICE ARE PROVIDED "AS IS" AND WITHOUT WARRANTY OF ANY KIND, AND ALL EXPRESS OR IMPLIED WARRANTIES ARE HEREBY EXCLUDED, INCLUDING, WITHOUT LIMITATION, THE WARRANTIES OF MERCHANTABILITY AND FITNESS FOR A PARTICULAR PURPOSE. SPC IS NOT RESPONSIBLE FOR THE ACCURACY OF OR ERRORS OR OMISSIONS IN ANY MATERIAL. SPC WILL NOT BE LIABLE FOR ANY DIRECT, INDIRECT, SPECIAL, INCIDENTAL, OR CONSEQUENTIAL DAMAGES ARISING OUT OF THE USE OR INABILITY TO USE THE SERVICE OR MATERIALS OBTAINED THROUGH THE SERVICE, EVEN IF SPC HAS BEEN ADVISED OF THE LIKELIHOOD OF SUCH DAMAGES. SOME STATES DO NOT ALLOW EXCLUSION OR LIMITATION OF IMPLIED WARRANTIES OR LIMITATION OF LIABILITY FOR INCIDENTAL OR CONSEQUENTIAL DAMAGES, SO THE ABOVE LIMITATIONS MAY NOT APPLY TO YOU.

This Agreement states the entire agreement between the parties with respect to the Service, and all prior or contemporaneous agreements are merged herein and superseded hereby.

4. SPC Privacy Policy

Passive and actively collected information and certain other information about you is subject to our Privacy Policy. For more information, see our full privacy policy at http://www.spc.com/legal/privacypolicy.

5. Links

The Service may provide, or third parties may provide, links to other World Wide Web sites or resources. Because SPC has no control over such sites and resources, you acknowledge and agree that SPC is not responsible for the availability of such external sites or resources, and does not endorse and is not responsible or liable for any Content, advertising, products, or other materials on or available from such sites or resources. You further acknowledge and agree that SPC shall not be responsible or liable, directly or indirectly, for any damage or loss caused or alleged to be caused by or in connection with use of or reliance on any such Content, goods, or services available on or through any such site or resource.

6. Modification/Termination of Service

SPC reserves the right at any time and from time to time to modify or discontinue, temporarily or permanently, the Service (or any part thereof) with or without notice. You agree that SPC shall not be liable to you or to any third party for any modification, suspension, or discontinuance of the Service.

7. Miscellaneous

The TOS constitute the entire agreement between you and SPC and govern your use of the Service, superseding any prior agreements between you and SPC. You also may be subject to additional terms and conditions that may apply when you use affiliate services, third-party content, or third-party software. The TOS and the relationship between you and SPC shall be governed by the laws of the State of Massachusetts without regard to its conflict of law provisions. You and SPC agree to submit to the personal and exclusive jurisdiction of the courts located within Suffolk County in Boston, Massachusetts.

The failure of SPC to exercise or enforce any right or provision of the TOS shall not constitute a waiver of such right or provision. If any provision of the TOS is found by a court of competent jurisdiction to be invalid, the parties nevertheless agree that the court should endeavor to give effect to the parties' intentions as reflected in the provision, and the other provisions of the TOS remain in full force and effect. You agree that regardless of any statute or law to the contrary, any claim or cause of action arising out of or related to use of the Service or the TOS must be filed within one (1) year after such claim or cause of action arose or be forever barred.

8. Section Headings

The section titles in the TOS are for convenience only and have no legal or contractual effect.

[I]   Sample Online Disclosure Regarding Terms of Service

SPC may want to consider placing this language at the bottom of various pages of the web site to alert visitors that the use of the site is governed by a Terms of Service Agreement.

The use of this site, and the terms and conditions for the sale of any goods or services, is governed by the Terms of Service Agreement. By using this site you acknowledge that you have read the Terms of Service Agreement and the disclaimers and caveats contained in this site, and that you accept and will be bound by the terms thereof.

CHAPTER THREE

INTERNET SECURITY

§ 3.01   Overview

§ 3.02   Auditing Internet Security Technologies
    [A]   Assessing Internet Security Technologies
        [1]   Network Security
            [a]   Local Area Networks
            [b]   Storage Area Networks
        [2]   Routers/Gateways and Bridges
        [3]   Operating Systems
        [4]   Firewalls
            [a]   Packet Filters
            [b]   Proxy Server or Application Gateway
            [c]   Hybrid Firewalls
            [d]   Special Problems with Firewalls
            [e]   Firewall Administrators
        [5]   Passwords
        [6]   Biometrics Systems
        [7]   Encryption
        [8]   Public-Key Cryptography
        [9]   Digital Signatures
        [10]   Certificate Authorities
        [11]   Export Controls on Encryption
        [12]   Virtual Private Networks
        [13]   Security Audit Products
        [14]   Physical Security
    [B]   Mass-Market Security Products
    [C]   Owner-Distributed Security Products
    [D]   Customized Security Products
    [E]   Emerging Trends in Security Products
        [1]   Elliptic Curve Cryptography
        [2]   Smart Cards

§ 3.03   The Radius of Risk
    [A]   Hackers
        [1]   Corporate Espionage
        [2]   Hackers as the "Enemy Within"
        [3]   E-Delinquents and Nonutilitarian Web Site Vandalism
        [4]   Anti-Corporate Hacktivism

[B] Cyberextortion
[C] Computer Crimes
[D] Distributed Denial of Service (DDoS) Attacks
[E] Computer Viruses
[F] Virus-Worm Hybrids
[G] Integrity of Data
[H] Proection Against Impostors
[I] Natural Disasters
[J] Social Engineering Hazards
[K] Privacy and the Corporate Criminal

§ 3.04 Implementing Information Security Systems
[A] Emergency Response to Data Disasters
[B] Qualified Webmasters
[C] Allocating Security Risks
[D] General Guidelines for Internet Security Policy
     [1] Sample Information Security Guidelines

§ 3.05 Remedies for Computer Abuse
[A] Criminal Remedies for Computer Abuse and Hacking
     [1] The Electronic Communications Privacy Act
     [2] Computer Fraud and Abuse Act
[B] Private Corporate Policing
     [1] eBay's Private Policing
     [2] Private/Public Policing
     [3] Software Publishers' Software Police
     [4] ICC's Commercial Crime Bureau
[C] Common Law Negligence
[D] Professional Malpractice

§ 3.06 Preventive Law Pointers
[A] Continuous Security Improvement—Where to Find Your
     Hacker "Huggy Bear"
[B] Computer Emergency Response Team/Coordination Center
     (CERT/CC)
[C] Hacker Insurance
[D] Denial of Service Protection
[E] Antivirus Protection
[F] Protecting Consumer Privacy
[G] Hold Harmless Clauses
[H] Sample Notice to Users
[I] Responding to a Computer Intrusion
[J] Wireless LAN Risks

§ 3.01   OVERVIEW

Internet security remains a top concern for companies. A survey of Australian companies found that "more than a quarter of executives felt e-business was not secure with those saying it was reasonably secure and reliable dropping to 45 per cent, down from 64 per cent in 2001."[1] A survey of U.S. companies "concluded that the average number of cyber-attacks against businesses increased 79 percent from last July to December. Companies faced an average of 20 attacks per week in July, but by December it increased to 35 a week."[2]

Credit card security has a major impact on Internet commerce. In a 2001 survey, nearly all new users (98.6 percent) had some worries about credit card safety when shopping online.[3] In the wake of September 11, 2001, "Internet users are increasingly concerned about the security of e-government, with 65 percent 'very concerned' about identity theft."[4] Sixty-two percent of information technology managers reported that spending on security would increase in 2002 after the September 11, 2001, terrorist attacks. It is estimated that "corporations and governments worldwide will invest a total of $30 billion a year by 2005 in IT security."[5]

The National Infrastructure Protection Center of the FBI (NIPC) has documented that Pakistani hackers have been active in hacking into U.S. web sites. A single hacker defaced web sites numbering in the thousands by compromising an ISP domain name server and redirecting those sites to a page entitled "Fluffi Bunni Goes Jihad." This one anti-U.S. hacking incident is the largest single defacement act in the history of the Internet.[6] With a click of the mouse, hackers can potentially disrupt Internet service, steal trade secrets, or deface web sites.[7] Hackers on

---

[1] Net Safety Fails Business, Courier Mail, Feb. 22, 2002, at 2.

[2] William Glanz, Survey Foresees Increase in Attacks on Computers, Wash. Times, Jan. 28, 2002, at D4.

[3] Who's Using the Net? Prototype, Poptonics, Apr. 1, 2002, at 11.

[4] John Yaukey, Americans Want e-Government If It's Secure, Gannett News Serv., Mar. 4, 2002, at 1.

[5] Christine Winter, Data Security Goes to War, Sun-Sentinel (Fort Lauderdale, Fla.), Jan. 13, 2002, at 1G.

[6] National Infrastructure Protection Ctr., FBI, Cyber Protests Related to the War on Terrorism: The Current Threat, Nov. 2001, http://www.npic.gov.

[7] Hacking is broadly defined as "the act of penetrating computer systems to gain knowledge about the system and how it works." Loa/Ash, The Ultimate Beginner's Guide to Hacking and Phreaking (visited Apr. 18, 2001), http://www.members.aol.com/angband/starthak.txt. The motives to "hack" into computer systems are diverse. Ethical hackers, in contrast to dark-side hackers or cybercriminals, hack into networks to learn about computer security. See, e.g., Legion of Ethical Hacking, A Hacking Group With Ethics (visited Apr. 18, 2001), http://www.geocities.com/SiliconValley/Circuit/2644/LEH. Hacktivism is a relatively recent form of computer crime motivated by anti-global and anti-corporate protest. Hactivists typically place political messages, thus defacing corporate sites. See, e.g., Stuart Millar, For Hackers, Real Political Heroes of Cyberspace, The Guardian (London), Mar. 8, 2001; see also Hacktivists Motto: Oppose a Policy? Hack the System, The Economic Times (India) (Feb. 9, 2001).

the Internet have launched various Internet crime waves which include IP spoofing,[8] piggybacking,[9] data diddling,[10] viruses,[11] salami-type,[12] e-mail flood attacks,[13] and scavenger-like "password sniffing,"[14] and other information heists. The NIPC of the FBI warned companies about the increased incidence of distributed denial of service (DDoS) attacks that would be launched by cyberterrorists. The typical DDoS attack is launched through the use of remote access Trojans, or RATs. A RAT can be placed on an unsuspecting user's machine in a variety of ways: through an infected file download, via an infected e-mail attachment, or through Internet Relay Chat (IRC).[15] Once a RAT is embedded in the system, it "phones home to its controller to let it know it is in place."[16] A computer system infected with a RAT is called a zombie, and a large number of zombies "are all directed to begin flooding specific sites with traffic. Under the deluge, the sites are crippled and thus unable to handle any additional traffic."[17] In addition to the risk of cyberterrorism, cyber protests and hacktivism have been on the increase since September 11.[18] At times, hackers have even coordinated with each other to launch a denial of service attack against targeted sites. In February 2000, such a coordi-

---

[8] "IP spoofing occurs when an attacker compromises the routing packets to direct a file or transmission to a different destination." Ken Brandt, Cracker Exploits, Information Security, Mar. 2001, at 86.

[9] Piggybacking occurs when malicious code enters a computer system riding on the back of a legitimate program. Back Orifice is one of the best known examples of "piggybacking." Akweli Parker, Welcome to the High-Tech World of Corporate Spying, The Virginian-Pilot, Jan. 18, 1999, at D1.

[10] "Data diddling" is entering false entries or data generally by employees or insiders to embezzle funds or perpetrate other fraudulent schemes. Those Wacky Employees, Datamation, July 15, 1995.

[11] "A virus is a piece of software that installs itself on your computer without your knowledge. Once resident on your computer, the virus replicates itself and does its best to spread to other computers." The University of Melbourne, Its InfoSheet 125: Computer Viruses: How to Keep Yourself Nice (visited Sept. 17, 1999) (defining computer virus), http://www.its.unimelb.edu.au/InfoSheets/InfoSheet_125.html. In the mid-1990s, macro viruses appeared which were attached "to a document, not an application, and you can become infected simply by opening an infected document." Id. One of the most highly publicized macro viruses affected Microsoft Word documents. Id. The rate of computer viruses is increasing at an exponential rate. The National Computer Security Association reported that its members suffered a threefold increase in computer viruses from 1998 to 1999.

[12] "Salami" is defined as a series of minor computer crimes—slices of a larger crime—that are difficult to detect and trace. Logophilia, Tech Word Spy (visited Apr. 28, 2002), http://www.logophilia.com/TechWordSpy/S.html.

[13] Ken Brandt, Battle Plans, Information Security, Mar. 2001, at 86 (describing e-mail flooding as an attempt to overwhelm a server by repeated e-mails in a concerted attack).

[14] Crime on the Internet, Password Sniffers, Jones Telecommunications & Multimedia Encyclopedia (visited Apr. 27, 2002), http://www.digitalcentury.com/encyclo/update/crime.html.

[15] How Strong Is the Web? Can Internet Communications Be Crippled, About.com (visited April 1, 2001), http://ads.x10.com/?c2Fib3V0MS5kYXQ=1017445335080>compute.

[16] Id.

[17] Id.

[18] Wayne Matus et al., Now More Than Ever, Cybersecurity Audits Are Key, Nat'l L. J., Mar. 11, 2002, at C8.

nated denial of service attack was launched against Yahoo! E*Trade, Amazon.com, and eBay.[19]

On any given day, a sampling from newspaper and trade publications reports that the information highway has devolved into a road to suspicion:

1. "Cyber Assault Hits Global Leaders' Summit."[20]
2. "Two Men Plead Guilty in Internet Piracy Scheme."[21]
3. "FTC Plans Crackdown on Deceptive Junk E-Mail."[22]
4. "Teen Was Million-Dollar Scammer Online, SEC Says."[23]
5. "Hacker Attack Shuts Down British ISP CloudNine."[24]
6. "Net Provider Faces Data-Leak Inquiry."[25]

In December 2001, security experts uncovered security vulnerability "in Microsoft's new Windows XP operating system that could allow attackers to wreak havoc on or gain complete control of a user's computer."[26] Hackers are then free "to run the malicious code of their choice on the vulnerable system."[27]

Besides the headlines, there are public broadcast shows like TechTV, a weekly 30-minute cable television show, which features topics like fraud, hacking viruses, cybersex crime, and web privacy.[28] These headlines give reason for SPC and other online companies to be concerned about Internet security. SPC's information security professionals need to monitor "cybervulnerabilities, malicious scripts, information security trends, virus information, and other infrastructure-related business practices."[29] In short, information security is critically important to protect the intellectual property and other intangible assets of an e-business.[30]

---

[19] The term "denial of service" refers to the use of "rogue programs to bombard the target site with nonsense data. This bombardment soon causes the target site's server to run out of memory, and thus causes it to be unresponsive to the queries of legitimate customers." United States Department of Justice, Computer Crime Policy and Programs, Distributed Denial of Service Attacks (visited Apr. 27, 2002), http://www.usdoj.ov/criminal/cybercrime/ccpolicy.html.

[20] Yahoo! News (visited Feb. 1, 2002), http://dailynews.yahoo.com/h/nm/20020201/tc/forum_hackers_dc_1.html.

[21] CNN.com (visited Feb. 3, 2002), http://www.cnn.com/2002/TECH/internet/02/03/cyberspace.arrests.ap/index.html.

[22] Yahoo! News (visited Feb. 4, 2002), http://dailynews.yahoo.com/h/nm/20020131/wr/tech_spam_dc_2.html.

[23] Steven Bonisteel, Teen Was Million-Dollar Scammer Online, SEC Says, Newsbytes (visited Feb. 4, 2002), http://www.newsbytes.com/news/02/173466.html.

[24] Bernhard Warner, Hacker Attack Shuts Down British ISP CloudNine, Yahoo! Finance (visited Feb. 4, 2002), http://biz.yahoo.com/rf/020201/l31487325_2.html.

[25] Joan Yip, Net Provider Faces Data-Leak Inquiry, Hong Kong Mail (Aug. 9, 2001) (reporting that Hong Kong ISP negligently released e-mail addresses of 70,000 users).

[26] Brian Krebs, Severe Security Hole Discovered in Microsoft XP, Newsbytes (Dec. 20, 2001), http://www.newsbytes.com/news/01/173164.html.

[27] Id.

[28] TechTV, Cybercrime (visited Apr. 17, 2001), http://www.techtv.com/tvshows.

[29] National Information Protection Center, Issue #2001-04 (Feb. 26, 2001).

[30] This chapter updates themes found in Michael Rustad & Lori Eisenschmidt, The Commercial Law of Internet Security, 10 High Tech. L.J. 213 (1995).

Because the Internet has the potential to compromise mission-critical information, such as databases, customer lists, and other inside information, network security is a critical area for any dot-com company.

According to the Computer Security Institute/Federal Bureau of Investigation (CSI/FBI) report, Issues and Trends: 2001 CSI/FBI Computer Crime and Security Survey, 91 percent of responding companies surveyed reported employee abuse of Internet access privileges, and 26 percent reported theft of proprietary information. For those companies that could put a dollar figure on their losses, the amount totaled over $120 million. Losses of proprietary information accounted for losses of $151,230,100. Ninety-four percent detected computer viruses, a 9 percent increase from 2000.[31] Over the next few years, these statistics are bound to increase as companies rely more on their technology infrastructure. Despite the increasing number of computer intrusions and service attacks, no one is suggesting that companies seal off their networks and lock their laptops. The greater the risk of cybercrime, the greater the duty of precaution. Courts applying a premises liability analogy would find it highly probative to find that a company failed to take prompt remedial steps after computer intrusions.

This chapter reviews the information security measures that a networked company must adopt to protect its fuel supply of information. The concepts and methods of information security are illustrated by references to Suffolk Personal Computers (SPC), our hypothetical e-business. Because SPC has product divisions in a networked world, its information security is especially difficult to implement. The Internet's interconnected nature offers SPC great potential benefits, but it also poses great dangers. SPC has a duty to provide security capable of protecting its trade secrets, proprietary and confidential information, customer lists, and personal data about its employees and customers. SPC realizes that the Internet and its virtual store require it to make a fundamental change in its computer security.

Section 3.02 of this chapter introduces the basic principles underlying internetworking technologies, explores the various components of network security, and assesses information security technologies. Client and server computers, mass-market security products, owner-distributed security products, customized security, and the basics of the Internet security audit are explained. Information security technologies introduced include firewalls, passwords, biometrics security devices, encryption, virtual private networks, and customized security products.

Section 3.03 examines the radius of the risks to information security. Threats can come from hackers, computer criminals, viruses, impostors, or information thieves; each is examined and relevant suggestions made for reducing the radius of that risk. Section 3.04 examines the elements of a comprehensive information security program. The evolving information security law for common law negligence, professional malpractice, product liability, sales warranties, and other legal

---

[31] Computer Security Institute/Federal Bureau of Investigation (CSI/FBI) reports, Issues and Trends: 2001 Computer Crime and Security Survey (visited Mar. 5, 2002), http://www.gocsi.com/prelea/000321.html.

issues are explored in § 3.05. Section 3.06 provides several preventive law pointers, which range from continuous security improvements to responding to a computer intrusion.

§ 3.02   AUDITING INTERNET SECURITY TECHNOLOGIES

[A]   Assessing Internet Security Technologies

[1]   Network Security

Information security differs from home security in two important respects. Home security is primarily designed to prevent the theft of *tangible* personal property, such as jewelry, electronics, computers, and other valuables. In contrast, network security addresses the theft of *intangibles*, such as software, customer lists, and intellectual property. An information heist may occur without leaving a trace, unlike most burglaries of a home or business. Uncovering digital fingerprints often requires the efforts of a computer forensic expert. Consumers without adequate security protection for their computers leave their systems vulnerable to attack. If a user leaves a "home computer running Apple's Mac OS or Windows 95 or 98 without the maker's latest security updates or additional security software, it is the closest thing to an unlocked door they are likely to find."[32]

The six fundamental elements of information security are confidentiality, control (or possession), integrity, authenticity, availability, and utility.[33] There are basically three overlapping types of risks that every company must counter:

- Bugs or misconfiguration problems in the web server that allow unauthorized remote users to

  - steal confidential documents not intended for their eyes;

  - execute commands on the server host machine, allowing them to modify the system;

  - gain information about the web server's host machine that will allow them to break into the system; or

  - launch denial-of-service attacks, rendering the machine temporarily unusable.

- Browser-side risks, including

  - active content that crashes the browser, damages the user's system, breaches the user's privacy, or merely creates an annoyance; or

---

[32] Ian Austen, High-Speed Lines Leave Door Ajar for Hackers, N.Y. Times, July 8, 1999.

[33] M.E. Kabay, The Year in Review, Info. Security, Dec. 1998, at 16.

- the misuse of personal information knowingly or unknowingly provided by the end user.

- Interception of network data sent from browser to server or vice versa via network eavesdropping. Eavesdroppers can operate from any point on the pathway between browser and server, including

  - the network on the browser's side of the connection;

  - the network on the server's side of the connection (including intranets);

  - the end user's Internet service provider (ISP);

  - the server's ISP; or

  - either ISP's regional access provider.[34]

At a basic level, threats to network security can be classified into three general areas: (1) unauthorized access to information; (2) unauthorized modification of information; and (3) unauthorized denial of service. The term "unauthorized" implies that the release, modification, or denial occurs contrary to some security policy. To combat these threats, network security architecture should be put in place. This architecture consists of the following components:

1. Access Control. Access control mechanisms ensure that information is controlled and access is granted by predetermined security policy. There are numerous approaches to achieving access control. These range from simple password protection to token-based mechanisms, to more advanced biometric encryption technologies.

2. Privacy. The goal of privacy is to ensure that unauthorized people on the network cannot see the contents of the message being sent. Privacy is synonymous with confidentiality and secrecy.

3. Authentication. The purpose of authentication is to enable principals to communicate in confidence, knowing that the communication originates with one principal and is destined for the other. Principals can be people, machines, organizations, and network resources such as printers, databases, and file systems. All authentication schemes ultimately reduce to enabling each principal to obtain or possess some information that uniquely identifies the other. "Identification is when your customer tells you who they claim to be; authentication is when you verify that they are in fact who they claim to be."[35]

4. Integrity. Data integrity addresses the unauthorized alteration or destruction of data. To ensure data integrity, one must have the ability to detect data manipulation by unauthorized parties. Data manipulation includes activities like insertion, deletion, and substitution. "Less capable systems, such as Macin-

---

[34] W3C, World Wide Web Security FAQs (visited Mar. 5, 2002), http://www.w3.org/Security/faq/wwwsf1.html#GEN-Q2.

[35] Glenda Barnes et al., Cyber Risks and Financial Institutions, *in* Fidelity Coverage in the Age of E-Commerce, ABA Tips Section (Jan. 26, 2001).

toshes and special-purpose Web server boxes are less easy to exploit. The safest Web site is a bare-bones Macintosh running a bare-bones Web server."[36]

5. Management and Audit. Constant administration is essential to ensure the continued success of a network security system. This is achieved through maintaining detailed records and audit trail information. A security audit should also include a review of any prior computer hacking attacks or intrusions.

Companies without adequate security are vulnerable to attacks by hackers or employees that can threaten to compromise proprietary information. For SPC, inadequate security threatens the integrity of its trade secrets, which, by definition, require reasonable security measures. Failure to implement reasonable security also exposes SPC to the possibility of lawsuits by third parties whose data, confidential information, or personal data is stolen or compromised by hackers.

Even though software may travel on physical disks or CD-ROMs, it is the intangible collection of magnetically fixed electronic impulses and optically stored data that constitutes the value of digital information. Network security must, therefore, not only prevent access to data but also protect magnetic data from unwanted intrusion and theft. If this were not the case, security for computers would be limited to prevention of physical harm and theft, much like security for computer hardware. Precautions and safeguards correlate directly with the level of risk. The greater the danger or economic impact, the greater the burden of precaution.

Just as products, devices, and methods (that is, steel doors, locks, bars, security monitors, and guards) have been developed against unwanted physical intrusion, a growing information security industry has arisen to deter electronic invasions of computer systems. Unlike a home burglar, a cybercriminal does not need physical access to a computer to accomplish an unauthorized entry; electronic access is sufficient. Intrusion-detection systems are emerging as a critical tool for bridging the gap between the Internet and internal networks.[37] Computer crime statutes punish and deter intrusions even if computer files are not altered, corrupted, or otherwise damaged. Another difference between home security and network security has to do with the interconnectivity of the Internet and of computer networks in general.

Remote computers connect with one another via the Internet by transmitting packets of data over wires, modems and telephone lines, optical fibers, and radio waves. Once computers are connected to the Internet, their precious intangible assets of information and stored data become vulnerable. The first step in preventive law for information security is to survey the basic principles of networking technologies. The probability of an intrusion depends on the type of computer hardware used, the degree of connectivity to external networks, the number and

---

[36] W3C World Wide Web Security FAQs (visited Apr. 15, 2002), http://www.w3.org/Security/faq/wwwsf1.html#GEN-Q2.

[37] Security Tools and Technology for Locking Up Agency Networks, Federal Computer Week (visited Apr. 28, 2002), http://www.fcw.com/ref/hottopics/security.htm.

type of security devices in use, and the nature of the users (that is, nonprofit educational institution, governmental entity, or Fortune 500 company).

The events surrounding the World Trade Center and Pentagon disasters have heightened security in government agencies. Internet security is a necessity for government agencies, as shown by a federal court's shutting down of the Department of Interior's web site because it lacked standard security measures.[38] A Special Master concluded that the government site had "no firewalls, no staff currently trained/capable of building and maintaining firewall devices, no hardware/software solution for monitoring network activity including but not limited to hacking, virus and worm notification . . . [and] a serious lack of wide area networking and security personnel in general."[39]

Class actions may result in private networks being shut down if security holes recklessly endanger proprietary data or vulnerabilities allow attackers to launch third-party attacks from inadquately protected web sites. The burden of precaution is great given the radius of the risk.

6. The Importance of Backups. Information security may also be compromised by unauthorized or accidental modification of operational data;[40] for example, "[a]t the Stanford University Graduate School of Business, sysadmins installed additional disk capacity to their servers. They then reloaded files from a corrupt backup tape, destroying many faculty and graduate student research files."[41] A company must have reasonably adequate backups or face almost unlimited liability for the consequences.

[a]   Local Area Networks

Network is a broad term referring in the information technology context to computers and communications equipment connected so that users may share data, programs, and peripheral devices. A local area network (LAN) is a specific kind of network that connects computers, software, and communication channels within a limited or local area. As its name suggests, a LAN is a local, delineated network, as opposed to the Internet's global network.

SPC may find it cost-effective to have a LAN, which allows employees to share data, programs, and peripheral devices. A LAN does not pose a risk from external hackers, because it has no connection to the Internet, being a stand-alone internal network. A LAN can be hacked into remotely, however, by or from any other computer connected to or able to connect to the LAN, if it is connected to other networks or to the Internet. This is the essence of the security threat known as remote intrusion. The LAN, without Internet connectivity, simply limits physical access to SPC's server to trusted personnel, thus preventing in-house security

---

[38] Jon Baumgarten, Court Shuts Down Federal Web Site Because of Inadequate Security, Cyberspace Law., Feb. 2002, at 14.

[39] *Id.*

[40] Kabay, *supra* note 33, at 16.

[41] *Id.*

threats. LAN operating systems are "secure" or "insecure," depending on how hardware or software is configured. A company that complies with best industry practices for network security is unlikely to be held liable if a hacker gains entry.

A properly secured LAN network permits work groups to "send memos, letters, and documents in electronic form to other users,"[42] allowing an efficient use of shared software, fax machines, storage devices, and other communications resources.[43] A server refers broadly to any device that offers a service to network users. The LAN client/server architecture employs high-speed, high-capacity workstations, called servers, to manage the activities of the network and to distribute data and programs as requested by client desktop computers.[44]

An *intranet* is a way of using Internet-based technologies within an organization via the LAN network to facilitate communication access to information. Within an intranet, users are able to share programs, data files, electronic publishing, and e-mail.[45] Hence, intranets are an integration mechanism for people, process, and information within the enterprise. Sensitive data including salary information, strategic plans, and intellectual property requires extra protection. Advanced operating environments within the intranet provide multiple levels of file protection and logging utilities to track users who access, or attempt to access, the data. Whereas extranets permit trusted outsiders to connect to company computers as though they were apart of the intranet. The Department of Defense, for example, permits potential bidders, suppliers, and vendors to learn the details of requests for proposal through its extranet.

The way users connect to the LAN depends on physical location. Desktop computers connect to the corporate intranet using network interface cards and "network police." Access is also dependent on recognition of the hardware address of the network card[46] and the user's log-on account and password, and it is screened by the use of firewalls.[47] A personal computer at home may be connected

---

[42] *Id.*

[43] *Id.*

[44] *Id.*, at 561.

[45] *Id.*, at 561.

[46] Most systems will only log the network address of a client. An attacker may easily spoof the network address by binding a legitimate address to its network card or interface. Computers connected to a LAN or intranet in a corporate environment will use a Network Interface Card (NIC). Each NIC will have a unique Media Access Controller number "stamped" into the firmware. Auditing the MAC address will require attackers wishing to spoof a network administrator to have access to the physical system for the MAC address.

[47] "Although firewalls are usually placed between a network and the outside untrusted network, in large companies or organizations, firewalls are often used to create different subnets of the network, often called an Intranet. Intranet firewalls are intended to isolate a particular subnet from the overall corporate network. . . . The decision to use an Intranet firewall is generally based on the need to make certain information available to some but not all internal users, or to provide a high degree of accountability for the access and use of confidential or sensitive information." National Institute of Standards Technology, Internet Firewall Policy, Internet Security Policy (Washington, D.C.: NIST, 1999): A Technical Guide (Dec. 14, 1999), (visited Apr. 28, 2002), http://csrc.nist.gov/isptg/html/ISPTG-6.html.

to an ISP server and other servers on the Internet through a telephone or cable connection. The ISP's computers function as servers, providing news and mail services as well as routing data between the client computer and the rest of the Internet.

Every metropolitan city in the United States has at least one ISP with dial-up services. In the Boston metropolitan area, for example, Internet connectivity services are available from a number of ISPs, including, to name just a few, North Shore Access, of Lynn; Novalink, of Westborough; The Internet Access Company, of Bedford; and the Complete Internet Access Company, of Newton. In recent years, America Online, CompuServe, cable companies, and other commercial services have offered Internet access for their customers, some over digital subscriber lines (DSL), which provide users with a fast, constant link to the Internet. DSL lines are increasingly targets of hackers using probing, scanning, and sniffing techniques.[48]

Popular wisdom has it that a pure client computer or client computer network is "bulletproof" and invulnerable to hackers. An intermediary—the ISP server computer—shields it. Even if the ISP server is compromised, the client computer is still safe, this reasoning goes, because it lacks the communications protocols necessary to enable the hacker to establish a connection with it. Yet, if the client computer connects to the ISP computer via a Serial Line Internet Protocol (SLIP) or Point-to-Point Protocol (PPP) connection, it *is* vulnerable—because it is connected to the Internet. This vulnerability, however, does not arise unless the client computer itself runs programs downloaded from the Internet or attempts to act as a server. A client can act like a server by running programs referred to in computer jargon as a daemon.[49] These daemons run in the background without user interaction, waiting to respond to packets of data received over a network.

The greatest threat to the security of client computers is not the Internet hacker, but the enemy within, the in-house hacker. Insiders who have otherwise nominal access privileges can invade the computer system by "shoulder surfing,"[50] intercepting the passwords of individuals with higher-level clearance or access to additional network resources. Screen-locking programs are critical for reducing the risk of shoulder surfing.

In this context, PC and Mac-based LANs are more vulnerable to Internet security attacks than are mainframe computers: mainframe computer systems have traditionally had a department of Management Information Systems (MIS) dedicated to backups and security; no such well-established practices were institution-

---

[48] *Supra* note 2.

[49] Windows NT refers to daemons as services or server processes. The term *server process* may be more familiar to devotees of the Microsoft operating systems. In mythology, a *daemon*, according to Webster's, was "an attendant power or spirit." *Daemons* can be confused with *demons*, which has a different but similar meaning. The New Hacker's Dictionary describes a *daemon* as a program that runs by itself directly under the operating system; a *demon*, however, is part of a larger application program. What Is . . . a Daemon (A Definition) (visited Apr. 28, 2002), http://www.whatis.com/daemon.htm (quoting Eric S. Raymond, The New Hacker Dictionary).

[50] Looking over another person's shoulder, or "shoulder surfing," is a means of gaining credit card numbers as well as passwords.

alized in the LAN environment.[51] Most large corporate network and MIS groups, however, are now concerned with security and with providing backups for a company's servers. To reduce maintenance costs, some corporations have been concentrating their server resources into fewer, more powerful computers in a single location, which is reminiscent of the mainframe-computing environment.

Social engineering is a serious security threat that cannot be solved by purely technological fixes such as firewalls or a password program. Social engineering occurs when insiders wishing to gain more than nominal access privileges engage in "soliciting unwitting participation from a person inside a company rather than breaking [in]to the system independently"[52] Effective countermeasures include maintaining a strong security policy and architecture and employee education.

[b]   Storage Area Networks

In the late 1990s, network storage evolved as a method of managing large storage requirements on the LAN, versus the traditional host-connected storage systems.[53] This method of data storage evolved into what is generally known as the SAN. The Storage Area Network, or SAN, is a "high-speed channel storage network relying on hubs, switches and gateways."[54] The SAN adds a new dimension to information security as well as to the capacity for a common storage-sized system.[55] The online company cannot afford to be without a backup in the event the company's computer systems fail because of natural disasters, viruses, or computer crimes.[56] Three decades ago, companies stored data files on magnetic disks and tapes, which were connected to mainframe computers. Mass storage devices evolved in the mid-1980s and were used primarily by companies with large online databases.[57] Computer systems were traditionally backed up by online disk and tape library systems.

An off-line traditional business, let alone a web-based business, cannot afford to be without a backup for data and storage accessibility. Online companies may decide to have a hot site computer facility geographically far away from the main office. A hot site is ready and able to transfer all data processing in the event of a disaster to the principal computer system. In contrast, a cold site has hardware

---

[51] Network Help Desk, Network World, Nov. 21, 1994, at 2.

[52] Malcolm Allen, The Use of Social Engineering as a Means of Violating Computer Systems (visited Feb. 18, 2002), http://rr.sans.org/social/violating.php.

[53] David Doering, Up the SAN BOX, E-Media Professional, July 1999, at 54.

[54] Id.

[55] IBM Enters. Storage Server is an example of a SAN product developed in the late 1990s for high capacity, reliable off-site storage.

[56] "To support recovery after failure or natural disaster, a firewall like any other network host has to have some policy defining system backup. Data files as well as system configuration files need to have some backup plan in case of firewall failure." Firewall Failure, Internet Security Policy (Washington, D.C.: NIST, 1999): A Technical Guide (visited Apr. 28, 2002), http://www.csrc.nist.gov/isptg/html/ISPTG-6.html.

[57] Larry Long, Introduction to Computers and Information Processing 147 (1984).

ready to develop an alternative site.[58] The SAN permits a company to recover from a disaster that threatens mission-critical databases. IBM, for example, has a storage hub that supports data speeds as high as 100 MBps. IBM's storage server "starts with 18 [gigabytes] of storage capacity and can handle as much as 16 terabytes using six expandable storage units."[59]

The median cost for a single network outage is "$140,000 in the retail industry and over $450,000 in the securities sector."[60] Backups are thus critical to any information security policy. The traditional means of backing up company data was to add tape drives to traditional servers. One problem with traditional host-attached storage was that when something went wrong with the server, the storage also became inaccessible.[61] Today's storage area networks are chiefly based upon "fibre channel."[62] Fibre channel, approved by the American National Standards Institute (ANSI), enables gigabits/sec connectivity.[63]

A SAN is a centrally managed repository or centrally managed networked pool[64] that creates a dedicated storage network, versus a multiple application storage system.[65] Compaq, EMC, IBM, StorageTek, and Sun are a few of the major storage vendors.[66] A company like SPC needs to keep its virtual store open 24 hours a day, 7 days a week. A denial of service attack could result in significant lost revenues. SPC needs to have available a backup of its web-based information should its site be compromised. SPC needs to consider setting up a dedicated network to offload storage traffic.[67] SPC may save money now by replacing departmental backup with a large-scale centralized storage model.[68] SPC should also review its business insurance policy to determine what computer disasters are covered.

[2]   Routers/Gateways and Bridges

Routers and *bridges* transmit information from one network area to another. A *gateway* is the network point that acts as an entrance to another network. A *switch* is a "network device" that selects how data gets to the next destination. These devices may be used to transmit data from the Internet to LAN destinations and vice versa. When SPC evolves into a full-grown e-business, it may connect

---

[58] Monique C.M. Leahy, Tort Liability for Failure to Provide Computer Disaster Recovery Measures, 29 Am. Jur Proof of Facts 53 (1995).

[59] IBM TotalStorage FAStT500 Storage Server Specifications (visited Apr. 18, 2002), http://www.storage.ibm.com/hardsoft/products/fast500/fast500-spec.htm.

[60] SAN Summit '99 (visited Aug. 2, 2000), http://www.creative-expos.com/san.html.

[61] *Id.* at 52.

[62] Brian Robinson, Is Fibre Channel Losing SAN Dominance? Fed. Comp. Wk. (Dec. 6, 1999) (visited Apr. 28, 2002), http://www.fcw.com/pubs/fcw/1999/1206/fcw-specfibre-12-06-99.html.

[63] *Id.*

[64] Thomas Hughes, Special Report: Storage Area Networks: Shifting SANs, Global Tech. Bus. 31 (June 1999).

[65] *Id.*

[66] *Id.*

[67] Robinson, *supra* note 39.

[68] *Id.* at 33.

many LANs together in a Wide Area Network (WAN). The WAN will utilize routers to transmit data between LANs.

Web servers constitute a serious risk to network security because inadequately configured networks give the entire world a window onto a computer system. "The general goal of network security is to keep strangers out. Yet the point of a Web site is to provide the world with controlled access to your network. Drawing the line can be difficult. A poorly configured Web server can punch a hole in the most carefully designed firewall system. A poorly configured firewall can make a Web site impossible to use."[69]

Gateway nodes are traffic cops for a company's computer network and the Internet.[70] A gateway may also be used if the LAN does not recognize Internet protocols such as the Transmission Control Protocol/Internet Protocol (TCP/IP).[71] An IP switch using this protocol is based upon packet switching. *Packet switches* divide data messages into bytes.

Gateways convert diverse and disparate network protocols to a single protocol compatible with its network system. This can be done using either a router or a bridge. Additional protocols can be added to allow error detection and connections for bookkeeping functions. Routers are necessary if companies are to directly access the Internet. Routers/gateways filter messages destined for recipients outside the local network and receive messages from remote networks to be delivered locally on the LAN. Just as a group of computers in an office can be linked together to share files and e-mail through a LAN, so can they be networked on a worldwide scale.

SPC, which is headquartered in Massachusetts, may link to computers located in offices around the world through secure Internet connections. Any company using a router or gateway to send and receive messages from the Internet is potentially vulnerable, since the router is a single, obvious access point into the corporate network. If SPC's systems administrator does not take proper security precautions, the router/gateway may become a vulnerable link in a computer network. SPC's security policy should state who has responsibility for managing the company's computer system.[72] "CGI scripts are a major source of security holes. Although the CGI (Common Gateway Interface) protocol is not inherently insecure, CGI scripts must be written with just as much care as the server itself."[73]

---

[69] W3C World Wide Web Security FAQs (visited Apr. 25, 2002), http://www.w3.org/Security/faq/wwwsf1.html#GEN-Q2.

[70] Whatis.Com, Definitions (visited Apr. 25, 2002), http://whatis.com/gateway.htm.

[71] Most modern network Operating Systems (NOS) and mainframe hosts now support TCP/IP. Previously, the network administrator would have to connect mainframe systems that used the System Network Architecture (SNA) and proprietary LAN protocols, such as Novell's IPX/SPX protocols.

[72] The Chief Information Security Officer may also designate persons responsible for managing firewalls. "Each firewall administrator shall provide their home phone number, pager number, cellular phone number and other numbers or codes in which they can be contacted when support is required." NIST, Firewall Administration, Internet Security Policy (Washington, D.C.: NIST, 1999): A Technical Guide (Dec. 14, 1999) (visited Apr. 28, 2002), http://csrc.nist.gov/isptg/html/ISPTG-6.html.

[73] W3C World Wide Web Security FAQs (visited Mar. 5, 2002), http://www.w3.org/Security/faq/wwwsf1.html#GEN-Q2.

[3] Operating Systems

An *operating system* (OS) is the systems software designed to operate many of the essential processes of the computer. For example, GNU/Linux operating system is an e-business computing platform. If SPC implements Linux for its business applications, it will need to test for vulnerabilities and monitor security alerts closely. SPC's network administrator will want to subscribe to mailing lists to monitor problems in "open source" software identified by users or programmers. "Unix systems, with their large number of built-in servers, services, scripting languages, and interpreters, are particularly vulnerable to attack because there are simply so many portals of entry for hackers to exploit."[74] One in four "Internet application service providers (ASPs) were found to have substandard protection against security breaches and viruses."[75]

One of the original PC operating systems was the Disk Operating System, or DOS, an operating system sold by Microsoft (MS-DOS), IBM (PC-DOS), and Digital Research (DR-DOS).[76] IBM's PC-DOS "was developed by Microsoft at IBM's behest."[77] The DOS operating systems were character-based: users would interact with the system by typing commands to a command interpreter. Most modern operating systems include a graphical user interface (GUI), which permits users to interact with the computer through pictorial metaphors, known as *icons*.

Today's most widely used PC operating system is Microsoft's Windows. Microsoft Windows contains operating system functions, a graphical user interface, and network connectivity capability.

Security on the Internet is inseparable from the security of the computers that access and/or serve the Internet. Operating systems frequently contain security "soft spots," which can be exploited by cybercriminals. At the operating system level, security can be breached on several fronts.

The majority of the computers connecting through the Internet use UNIX-based or compatible standardized operating systems. UNIX-based operating systems were not originally designed with security in mind; they contain scores of well-known security loopholes. Hackers exploit these security soft spots to infiltrate the OS. UNIX-based operating systems do not have a monopoly on hacker

---

[74] *Id.*

[75] Quarter of ASPs Have Substandard Security, Agence France-Presse (Mar. 8, 2002), http://www.inq7.net/inf/2002/mar/09/inf_3-1.htm (citing worldwide "survey of 50 ASPs, finding that 25% lacked fundamentals such as user authentication, virus protection, network security and firewall services").

[76] DOS and its variants were born from a clone of Digital Research's CP/M written by hacker Tim Patterson of Seattle Computer Products. MS-DOS Jargon Dictionary, DOS (visited Sept. 19, 1999), http://www.netmeg.net/jargon/terms/m/ms-dos.html. The original name for the product was QDOS for Quick and Dirty Operating System. *Id.* A rather interesting history exists surrounding IBM's choice of DOS over CP/M for their PC line of products. It is well documented in the PBS special "Triumph of the Nerds." The full transcript is available at http://www.pbs.org/nerds/transcript.html.

[77] Nat Gertler, Computers Illustrated 204 (1994).

interest, however; Windows-NT based servers are also a frequent target of hacker attacks. For example, both Windows NT, 4.0 and 2000 UNIX have bugs in their input commands, which permits "a malicious user [to] gain access to database resources."[78] Hence, SPC's primary vulnerability lies in its ISP server's OS.

Finding the front door secured, hackers use the back door to break into Internet sites. The back door in the send-mail feature, for example, has been used to break into UNIX operating systems. A hacker may be able to exploit these loopholes to access and copy a list of the server's accounts (that is, the computers and companies that utilize that ISP to access the Internet); browse e-mail stored on the computer for some or all of the accounts; or disclose or damage ISP data files. In cases of severe breach, the hacker can actually disrupt or halt the operation of the server's programs and may be able to extend this destructiveness to other computers by introducing a malicious routine, such as a computer virus or worm.

Since UNIX-based operating systems have numerous inherent security flaws, the industry has filled the gaps with informal trade usages or the owner of the operating system will issue patches. A patch, for example, was issued for Commerce CGI 2.0.1 Software, which operates on a Windows 95/98 NT platform. The patch corrects a vulnerability that permitted unauthorized users or hackers to "gain read access to directories and files outside the root directory."[79] Some of the widely used industry practices include monitoring for hacker programs, worms, and viruses; blocking repetitive failed access attempts; maintaining adequate log-in and audit trail records; and trolling for suspicious activities or possible trouble. Now that extensive means are available to overcome the original security loopholes, operating system security is a "reasonable" proposition.[80] SPC has a duty to keep informed about ways to take prompt remedial measures once a security hole is found.

The federal government certifies agencies' operating systems as secure if they meet the federal standards for C2 security classification.[81] Certified C2 systems include NetWare 4.x, Windows NT Server, Trusted Network Computing Environment, and Cordant's Assure.[82] Companies that contract or partner with federal agencies may be required to comply with C2 certification as a condition of doing business. At a minimum, SPC will need to enact network security systems that comply with reasonable industry standards. If it intends to register with the Defense Department's online procurement system, for example, it will need to be certified as C2 compliant.

---

[78] National Infrastructure Protection Center, NPIC Cybernotes #2001-04 (Feb. 26, 2001).

[79] *Id.*

[80] The other main tenets of network security—survivability and availability—are not addressed in this chapter. *Survivability* refers to the ability to maintain or restore hardware, software, and data integrity in the event of an electronic or natural disaster. *Availability* refers to the consistency and continuity of network functioning.

[81] *Cf.* Roger Addelson, Making Your Customer's Network Secure, Stacks: The Network Journal, Dec. 1994, at 27.

[82] *Id.*

Operating systems, such as Digital Equipment Corporation's Open VMS/VAX 6.0 and Security Enhanced VAX/VMS, were evaluated by the Department of Defense's National Computer Security Center (NCSC) and were rated as meeting or exceeding security specifications for C236 security classification.[83] These O/S systems, however, comprise only a small part of the backbone of the Internet.

Individual workstation security is also related to LAN security because workstations can be used as unauthorized ports of entry. Disk, screen, and keyboard locking mechanisms can be used to prevent unauthorized access when employees have stepped away from their computers. It is also critical that laptops be equipped with functionally equivalent locking mechanisms to protect the business traveler. In addition, certain programs prevent unauthorized alteration of configuration and startup files.[84] Programs may automatically notify SysAdmins of any attempts to change program initiation (that is, authorization specification) files. Finally, armoring products prevent either computer booting through the floppy disk drive, where password security could be bypassed, or resetting computer clocks to make former passwords or SuperUser access retroactive.[85] Fischer International Systems Corp. markets a suite of products that perform these and other protective functions.[86] Many companies hire information security consultants who are expert in pricing security products and who may also provide negotiating tips.

Client computers and LANs that have modems are also vulnerable to external intrusion from outside the local network. The *modem* "acts as an interface between your computer and a phone line."[87] Computers communicate with other computers via telephone lines, with the help of modems or dedicated communication equipment.[88] A common, and effective, method of preventing intrusions employs a "call-back" protocol. An authorized user who wishes to dial into an office computer first dials up the computer via its modem. The computer, programmed to allow remote use from only certain, preauthorized phone numbers,

---

[83] Bob Melford, "Six-O" for Security and Things That Take Six Years, Digital News & Rev., Sept. 27, 1993, at 11.

[84] Important configuration files for PC-based systems are CONFIG.SYS and AUTOEXEC.BAT. "Most large programs now come with installation programs (usually called INSTALL.BAT or SETUP.EXE or something similar) that automatically set up their own directories on your hard disks, copy the files, etc. Many of these will alter your AUTOEXEC.BAT and CONFIG.SYS files without you knowing about it." Nat Gertler, Computers Illustrated (1994). AUTOEXEC.BAT is "a batch file program that is run by DOS at startup. *Id.* at 72. Batch files "are programs (easily changed by the user) which are interpreted by the operating system. Generally they're made up mostly of commands just like you would type at the DOS prompt. When you load MS-DOS, it automatically looks for the batch program AUTOEXEC.BAT, and runs that." *Id.* at 73. Newer operating systems may have a variety of configuration files that could be targeted by virus makers. The Back Orifice Trojan virus, for example, developed by the Cult of the Dead Cow, attached itself to the Windows registry, enabling it to restart each time the computer was rebooted.

[85] *See* Horace Labdie, Digital Crime Watch: Developing an Effective Security System, Comp. Shopper, Mar. 1994, at 594.

[86] *Id.*

[87] Gertler, *supra* note 50.

[88] *Id.* at 227.

receives the call-in and immediately terminates the connection; it then checks the number from which the call came against its list of authorized numbers and calls the user's computer back if the number is found to be an authorized one. While effective, this procedure may be problematic for the telecommuting employee who may dial in from a variety of different client sites or hotel telephones.

When the connection is reestablished, the user must log in and successfully complete the rest of the user identification and authentication challenges to initiate the remote session with the computer.[89] Security products exist that permit centralized security administration, user management, and access controls to LANs. One company has developed software agents installed on protected application servers "designed to create the authenticated, secure connection from the desktop to the application server."[90] Organizations will frequently hire security consultants that provide turnkey solutions for protecting a LAN as well as extranet and intranet applications.

[4]   Firewalls

Firewalls authenticate data and identify users, while "hiding information like system names, network topology, network device types, and internal user ID's from the Internet."[91] The purpose of a firewall is to prevent intruders from accessing computers. A firewall is the point at which a company's private company network and a public network, such as the Internet, connect. A firewall system is a hardware/software configuration which sits at this perimeter, controlling access into and out of a company's network. While in theory firewalls allow only authorized communications between the internal and external networks, new ways are constantly being developed to compromise these systems. Firewall upgrades may be implemented to allow network administrators to remotely control and monitor users' activities such as using video streaming media.[92]

Router-based firewalls do not require user identifications or user authentication, whereas *host-based firewalls* provide for different kinds of authentication, such as (1) usernames and passwords, (2) one-time passwords, and (3) digital certificates.[93] Organizations should design the architecture of their firewalls to match their risk profile.[94] SPC will install firewalls as gatekeepers between its computers

---

[89] This concept *authentication* refers to the identity of a computer user. Authentication, for example, is required before a user can access a company computer.

[90] Security Dynamics and RSA Unveil Enterprise Application Security Strategy, RSA Data Security Conference, San Jose, California, Jan. 18, 1999 (visited on Apr. 28, 2002), http//www.rsa.com/pressbox/html/990118-1.html.

[91] NIST Special Publication 800-10, Keeping Your Site Comfortably Secure: An Introduction to Internet Firewalls (visited Apr. 28, 2002), http://www.csrc.nist.gov.

[92] Security Holes Found in Windows Media Player, Unix Insider, Nov. 2000.

[93] NIST, Internet Firewall Policy Internet Security Policy (Washington, D.C.: NIST, 1999): A Technical Guide (visited Apr. 28, 2002), http://csrc.nist.gov/isptg/html/ISPTG-6.html.

[94] *Id.* at Firewall Architecture.

and the Internet, which will serve to block unwanted traffic, hide vulnerable computer systems, and log traffic to and from the web site. SPC may configure its firewalls using a number of different architectures and various levels of security, choosing among three basic types of firewalls: (1) packet filters, (2) proxy servers, and (3) stateful inspection.[95]

Although there are different options for configuring a firewall, if properly implemented, firewalls are very effective means of preventing unauthorized users from having access and stopping unwanted activities on an internal network. Firewalls can also be deployed within an enterprise network to compartmentalize different servers and networks, in effect controlling access within the network. For example, an enterprise may want to separate the accounting and payroll server from the rest of the network and only allow certain individuals to access the information.

[a] *Packet Filters*

The File Transfer Protocol (FTP) was developed to move information by breaking files into packets ensuring that "each packet arrives with its data intact."[96] Firewalls create a shell of protection between a computer network and possible intruders. Although they are commonly used to restrict information from leaving or entering a company's computer or LAN via a modem, firewalls are increasingly being designed and integrated into routers/gateways to regulate the flow of information between the LAN and the Internet. Firewalls are increasingly being designed to perform packet filtering, for example. Firewalls may be conceptualized as part of system-wide computer policy used in conjunction with password protection, data encryption, and workstation security or biometrics security devices.

The firewall, typically housed on the router, functions by filtering all the electronic data packets sent to it from the LAN and the outside connection. Routers attached directly to the Internet employ "packet filters," which are essentially rule-based programs that instruct a router to accept only certain types of traffic from specified network addresses.[97] The firewall permits only verified electronic data packets to be passed on by its packet filter. The firewall must be properly configured to screen electronic data packets; for example, a firewall must be configured to accept and process only e-mail type communications data packets and to accept mail for only a particular set of addresses. In such a case, an intruder attempting to initiate a file-transfer request would be thwarted, as the firewall would detect the unauthorized communications protocol and reject it. In fact, without the proper server program on the host computer, the computer would have no mechanism for responding to such a request.

---

[95] Brian Robinson, Special Report on Security: Firewalls: The First Line of Defense, Fed. Comp. Wk., Mar. 29, 1999.

[96] *Id.*, at 182.

[97] Ted Doty, The Whole Truth About Network Security, Data Comm., Nov. 1994, at 150.

Packet filters use Internet Protocol (IP)[98] addresses or other identifiers to control information in the network. Access is granted or denied based on source address, destination address, or port. Packet filters may block designated sites or IP addresses. The security risks inherent in packet filtering include (1) IP or DNS address spoofing, (2) attacks with direct access to any host after getting past the firewall, (3) lack of strong user authentication, and (4) weak or nonexistent logging capability.[99]

[b] Proxy Server or Application Gateway

The *proxy server,* or *application gateway,* runs on the firewall. One advantage of application gateways is that they perform user authentication and logging. Application gateways are strongly recommended for medium- to high-risk sites such as the military.[100] The proxy acts as an intermediary point between user programs, application programs, and Internet content. Specific proxies check for security information.[101] The firewall can be configured "as the only host address that is visible to the outside network, requiring all connections to and from the internal network to go through the firewall."[102]

[c] Hybrid Firewalls

Hybrid or *complex gateways* combine different types of firewalls and implement them in series to enhance security.[103] The National Institute of Standards and Technology (NIST) describes the hybrid gateway as the best solution for a high-risk environment.[104]

[d] Special Problems with Firewalls

Firewall architecture is based on variables such as desired level of security, cost of installation, and the number of network interfaces.[105] A *multi-homed host* is defined as a host "that has more than one network interface, with each interface connected to logically and physically separate network segments."[106] A *dual-homed host,* for example, has two network interface cards (NICs).[107] With a dual-homed host, the firewall "must always act as an intermediary."[108] If the

---

[98] For more on Internet Protocols, *see* § 1.04[E].

[99] Internet Firewall Policy, Internet Security Policy (Washington, D.C.: NIST, 1999): A Technical Guide (visited Apr. 28, 2002), http://csrc.nist.gov/isptg/html/ISPTG-6.html.

[100] *Id.*

[101] *Id.*

[102] *Id.*

[103] *Id.*

[104] *Id.*

[105] *Id.*

[106] "Multi-homed Host," *Id.*

[107] *Id.*

[108] *Id.*

dual-homed firewall allows "traffic coming in from the untrusted network to be directly routed to the trusted network," the firewall is circumvented, and the intruder will gain access to the system.[109] Firewalls may also employ a firewall architecture that uses a "bastion host to which all outside hosts connect, rather than allow direct connection to other, less secure internal hosts."[110] The *bastion host* is also sometimes called a *screened host.*

[e]   Firewall Administrators

The firewall is the chief means of information security. Accordingly, it requires well-trained firewall administrators, appointed by the online company's chief information officer. The firewall administrator needs the following qualifications:

1.   Understanding of network concepts such as TCP IP protocol,
2.   Understanding of LAN administration,
3.   Hands-on experience configuring and designing firewalls, and
4.   Training in network security.[111]

The firewall administrator needs to ensure that "operational procedures for a firewall and its configurable parameters be well documented, updated, and kept in a safe and secure place"[112] and must provide for physical firewall security, handle firewall incident reporting, upgrade the firewall, and revise or update the firewall policy.[113] The administrator of the firewall is also responsible for logging traffic on the firewall's audit trail logs.[114]

[5]   Passwords

Firewalls are only secure as long as strong authentication systems, such as passwords, are used to control access. Subject-oriented security generally permits users to gain access or permission to access a computer system based on passwords.[115] Remote access over the Internet, for example, requires "strong authentication such as one-time passwords."[116] Passwords were one of the earliest developed security devices, having first evolved in the mainframe-computing environment. Windows 98, for example, requires a network password for Microsoft

---

[109] *Id.*

[110] *Id.*

[111] These guidelines are drawn from Qualification of the Firewall Administrator, Internet Security Policy (Washington, D.C.: NIST, 1999): A Technical Guide (visited Apr. 28, 2002), http:// csrc.nist.gov/isptg/html/ISPTG-6.html.

[112] *Id.*

[113] *Id.*

[114] *Id.*

[115] David M. Kroenke, Database Processing: Fundamentals, Design, and Implementation 506 (4th ed. 1992).

[116] NIST, Remote Firewall Administration, in Internet Security Policy (Washington, D.C.: NIST, 1999): A Technical Guide (visited Apr. 28, 2002), http://csrc.nist.gov/isptg/html/ISPTG-6.html.

Networking. Passwords are frequently easy to crack because many people choose passwords easy for hackers to guess, such as their own first names. Windows 98 for Dummies recommends keeping "your password short and sweet: the name of your favorite vegetable, for example, or the brand of your dental floss."[117] It is estimated that more than half of the passwords in use are the first names of spouses or children, dates such as birthdays and anniversaries, or the names of popular culture "super-heroes."[118] Some companies routinely run a program, such as Cracker, to detect easy-to-break passwords. Systems administrators may install electronic agents that force e-mail computer users to change their cracked passwords.

In general, the shorter the password, the faster it will be cracked. Hacker dictionary programs operate by trying every word in the dictionary (including variant spellings of words and names) until a password match is found. Given the comprehensiveness of these dictionary programs and the high speed of today's computers, most common passwords can be cracked within a few minutes or less. If the vulnerable password is on a router/gateway computer, then the weak password risks the integrity of information assets the equivalent of corporate crown jewels. A company's security system is vulnerable not only from unauthorized company employees, but from outside Internet hackers as well. A successful password system requires employee training and support.

Passwords are frequently subverted by a cavalier corporate attitude about their significance. Trade secrets remain trade secrets only if they are kept secret. The same may be said about passwords. A security expert illustrated poor organizational attitudes toward passwords in a demonstration in which he posed as a computer-room operator. He was able to get a telephone company switchboard operator to give him a critical, top-secret password to the company's computer, thereby gaining access to the names and addresses of all of the company's customers.[119] Such socially engineered dial-in access is the result of failing to train employees in the importance of keeping passwords secret.

Socially engineered lapses of security have no technological remedy. More passwords are lost through employee carelessness than are stolen across the Internet. A successful password system thus requires full employee training and support. One expert suggests emphasizing the following principles to achieve a good password system:

• Good password management will stop most security attacks.

• Common words, such as last or first names, are bad passwords, since they are easily guessed.

---

[117] Andy Rathbone, Windows 98 for Dummies 62 (1998).

[118] Eric H Steele, Software Review: Security, 5 Comp. Couns. 39 (Aug. 1993).

[119] Susan Watts, The BT Hacker Scandal: BT "Flouted Its Own Advice to Government," Consultants Are Fighting a Losing Battle to Persuade Companies to Protect Their Computer Systems, Network World, Feb. 13, 1995, at 37.

- Since passwords are often stored in an encrypted state in a publicly readable file, passwords appearing in a common dictionary may be open to offline dictionary attacks.

- To create strong but still user-friendly passwords, convert an easily remembered personal saying. "Suffolk Law is A number 1," for example, would yield the password of "SLiAn1." This fanciful password is not in any dictionary and thus will be difficult to guess.[120]

The British hacker Paul Bedworth was able to enter numerous government and corporate computers because of their inadequate security. Many of these facilities were protected only by a password established by the installing engineer. A number of computers were accessible merely by typing in the simple default supplied by computer hardware or software licensors. Passwords are sometimes written down or posted in conspicuous places, such as on the computer monitor or a whiteboard above it.

Corporations must institute comprehensive programs to protect passwords. Information security consultants can recommend security programs that detect attempts to "crack" passwords and set off an alarm. Another technique is to install software that requires employees to change their passwords regularly. Increasingly effective password-protection programs are available for a moderate price. Vendors have a variety of technological solutions for password protections.

Some of the more useful solutions, however, are sociological. One expert recommends choosing "hard to guess, but easy to remember passwords [by] concatenat[ing] unrelated words: WhatINow or letters of a nonsense phrase: MhalGwhw (Mary had a little Goat with hairy wool)."[121] The use of uppercase letters and numbers is a simple technique that makes "dictionary attacks more difficult."[122]

Another simple protective measure is to use a *passphrase*, as opposed to a *password*. Another option is to use a two-factor identification, rather than a mere password. The two-factor ID method requires a user to insert a card or token belonging to the user alone and then to give the proper password. "A cryptocard is a physical token or program which: authenticates via a cryptographic exchange; each exchange is unique and cannot be guesses or snooped; eliminates the risk of password interception or eliminates the risk of password guessing."[123]

Companies need security systems to protect computers that are left unattended.[124] The best password programs assign different passwords that permit the user to access different levels of data or information, depending on their need to know. Norton Disklock 3.5 for Windows and DOS provides "password protection

---

[120] Carl-Mitchell Smoot, Internet Security 2.8 (1999).

[121] *Id.* at 2.12 (1999).

[122] *Id.*

[123] *Id.* at 2.14.

[124] Symmantec, Norton Disklock 3.5 for Windows and DOS: Easy-to-Use Password Security, File Locking, and Encryption (visited Apr. 20, 2002), http://www.symantec.com/region/can/eng/product/disklock/fs_dsklpc.html.

against unauthorized system access, selective file locking and encryption." Norton's Disklock also automatically activates a screen-saver to block access when an employee steps away from the computer for a few moments. Such a feature would be useful for the business traveler, helping to defeat snoops or business spies. Disklock also calibrates file protection for different levels of security.[125] Norton's For Your Eyes Only provides similar protection for Windows 95 but implements the more secure public/private key encryption.[126]

The Department of Defense has long used dynamic synchronized password schemes that change the password in both the host and the user token every few seconds. The DOD's classified computer system, which stores this nation's most sensitive data, is not connected to the Internet.[127] The greatest threat to the DOD is employees within the DOD having access to classified information. The DOD, however, has detected and thwarted internationally coordinated hacker attacks. The Pentagon denies that hackers have penetrated its secret networks.[128]

Another relatively new product is the software-token-based challenge-response system, which uses strong encryption to ensure the security of all transactions.[129] An example of an advanced password product is one combining two-factor identification with dynamic synchronization. The password on the synchronized card changes every 30 to 60 seconds, and thus is good only for the duration of a single log-on session. This smart card is called SecurID and is manufactured by Security Dynamics, Inc., of Cambridge, Massachusetts.

SecurID is a password authentication program, used as a unique personal identification number that restricts network access to authorized users. These programs are available in various forms, including credit card-sized hardware tokens and key fobs, as well as software tokens.[130] Each SecurID form is based upon an "algorithm that generates a one-time, pseudo-random code that changes every 60 seconds."[131] The SecurID is an all-purpose network resource restricting user access to those with the "one-time Code with a PIN."[132] "The 6 digit password changes each minute and may be synchronized with a server. A user enters a 4-8 digit PIN followed by the 6 digit number displayed on the card."[133] Another smart card

---

[125] *Id.* (describing how different kinds of encryption offer different levels of security; DES for maximum security and a lesser standard security).

[126] Symantec, A Clearer Image of Norton For Your Eyes Only (visited Apr. 25, 2002), http://service1.symantec.com/SUPPORT/disklock.nsf/docid/199732612310.

[127] CNN, DOD Confirms Cyberattack "Something New," Mar. 6, 1999 (visited on Apr. 28, 2002), http:\\www.cnn.com/TECH/computing/9903/06/dod.hacker.update.idg/.

[128] *Id.*

[129] *See generally* Winn Schwartau, New Keys to Network Security, Infoworld, May 15, 1995, at 51 (reviewing a number of password security products).

[130] Security Dynamics Technologies, Inc. Press Release, Security Dynamics Breaks the Barrier for Outsourced Network Security, Dec. 8, 1998 (visited Apr. 25, 2002), http://www.securitydynamics.com/press/pr/pr 1998-12-15.html.

[131] *Id.*

[132] *Id.*

[133] Smoot, *supra* note 120.

vendor is Enigma Logic, Inc., which produces a competing product called Safe-word.[134] But each year a new generation of secure methods for authenticating user identity appears.

Even a computer armed with state-of-the-art security will not remain impregnable for long if the institution does not support training for corporate employees in how to maintain good security. No bulletproof security systems exist, however, even in the most rationally managed organization. High-tech hackers will continually find new means by which to obtain unauthorized access to computer systems. Like automobile antitheft devices, Internet security devices must continue to evolve over time. Steps must be taken so that the technological fixes stay ahead of enemies both inside and outside the organization. A future enhancement to password protection, for example, might be the use of biometrics. A best practice by SPC's security administrator would be to run a dictionary attack periodically, and warn users who have insecure passwords. SPC consumers will be warned to choose a password that they will remember but that is not obvious.

[6] Biometrics Systems

SPC may decide to install biometrics technology for personal authentication by retinal scanning, fingerprint identification, signature recognition, or voice recognition. Biometric security products are so sophisticated that they recognize the unique way a user inputs his or her password or passphrase. Biometric devices are increasingly replacing passwords or ID cards to protect computer networks.[135] Electronic fingerprint-authentication technologies are available to protect networks, laptops, cell phones, and even credit cards.[136] Biometrics devices can recognize the "imprint of a human finger, offering . . . a new way to protect laptops, cell phones, and even credit cards from unauthorized use."[137] Veridicom of Santa Clara, California, for example, has patented software that "checks the imprint against a mathematical representation or template stored in a compact memory bank or computer database."[138]

Face recognition is increasingly being used in retail, financial, security, health care, and e-business applications[139] to thwart fraud in check cashing, theft, piracy, and counterfeiting.[140] Hand geometry can also be used to verify a person's identity.[141] Hand geometry reads an individual's hand three dimensionally, computing a number of different measurements "including length, width, thickness,

---

[134] *See generally* Tom McCusker, Take Control of Remote Access, Network Security Measures Datamation, Apr. 1, 1994, at 62.

[135] Schwartau, *supra* note 129.

[136] How to Let Your Fingers Do the Walking and Talking, 2 Business Vision for the Entrepreneurial Spirit, Magazine for Key Bank Clients (Time, Inc., Mar. 1999).

[137] *Id.*

[138] *Id.*

[139] Michael Kuperstein, Biometrics, SC Magazine, Mar. 1999, at 19.

[140] *Id.* at 37.

[141] *Id.*

and surface area."[142] The scanning of the hand by the reader results in a mathematical representation that can be retrieved and compared to an exemplar.[143] Hand geometry readings may also be transferred to a computer or other media.[144] Biometrics security devices such as hand geometry are used in high-security operations such as nuclear power plants.[145] Since many biometric devices have retail costs under $200 per unit,[146] it may be economically feasible to install fingerprint readers at each desktop. Retinal scans may be coded and maintained by accessible servers as a reliable method for authenticating transactions.[147] For highly secure systems, SPC may combine biometrics and passphrase authentication for system access.

[7] Encryption

Cryptography is the science of secret writing, "a science that has roots stretching back hundreds, and perhaps thousands of years."[148] Encryption "involves running a readable message known as 'plaintext' through a computer program that translates the message according to an equation or algorithm into unreadable 'ciphertext.'"[149] Decryption translates ciphertext back to plaintext.[150] The two generic types of encryption are "conventional or symmetric and public-key or asymmetric cryptography."[151] *Symmetrical cryptography* uses a single key to encrypt and decrypt messages.[152] *Public-key cryptography* employs a pair of complementary keys: a private key and public key,[153] and is based on algorithms such as RSA and DSA.[154]

Global sales of encryption products reached approximately $184 million in revenue in 2000 and are expected to reach $364.6 million by 2005.[155] Encryption

---

[142] *Id.*

[143] *Id.*

[144] *Id.*

[145] *Id.* (noting that more than 90 percent of U.S. nuclear plants do have hand geometry systems on their main entrances).

[146] *See* ACT, SecureTouch Fingerprint Reader (last visited Apr. 28, 2002), http://www.altcomp. com/products/bac/securetouchannounce.htm.

[147] Tyler Prochnow, From John Hancock to Retinal Scans, What Is Your Signature on the Internet?, 17 E-Commerce 6 (July 2000).

[148] Bernstein v. United States Dep't of Justice, 1999 WL 27411 (9th Cir. May 6, 1999).

[149] *Id.* at *1.

[150] *Id.*

[151] Lorijean G. Oei, Primer on Cryptography, Chapter 31 in Thomas J. Smedinghoff, ed., Online Law: The Spa's Legal Guide to Doing Business on the Internet 497 (1996) (describing basic concepts of cryptography).

[152] *Id.* at 499.

[153] *Id.* at 500.

[154] Oei notes that RSA is named after Rivest, Shamir, and Adelman; DSA stands for Digital Signature Algorithm. *Id.* at 501.

[155] Brian Burke et al., Worldwide Encryption Software Market Forecast and Analysis, 2001-2005, Internet Security Bull. (visited Feb. 26, 2002), http://www.mediacrypt.com/engl/News/IDC%20 Encryption%20SW%20Market%20FC%2001-05.pdf.

products are available from more than 900 companies in 30 countries.[156] Encryption is the principal tool for ensuring the authenticity and integrity of data and messages transmitted on the Internet. Electronic checks, for example, currently being developed in Singapore, will contain a private digital signature code.[157] Encryption in a company's information infrastructure protects its "software databases, network products, telecommunications equipment, computer peripherals, electronic commerce and financial services."[158] Digital signatures employ the technology of encryption and "provide users the ability to certify and authenticate the message and therefore trust that the message is authentic."[159] In addition to ensuring secrecy, data integrity, and authentication, encryption facilitates nonrepudiation, which is the process of linking a specific message to a specific sender.[160] Once the plaintext messages are transformed into coded messages, a key is required to decrypt them.

The federal government has used Data Encryption Standard (DES), a 56-bit single key encryption technology, since the mid-1970s for its sensitive, but not classified, information. Encryption works by "converting plaintext into ciphertext, an unreadable string of numbers and letters."[161]

DES was developed by the National Security Agency (NSA) to protect the confidentiality of classified military information that could be transmitted in digital form.[162] The National Bureau of Standards, predecessor to the National Institute of Standards and Technology (NIST), worked with NSA, the Department of Commerce, and IBM to develop DES.[163] NIST is currently developing the Advanced Encryption Standard (AES), scheduled to replace DES later in the century.[164] NIST selected the Advanced Encryption Standard (AES) to replace DES on October 2, 2000.[165] AES provides on the order of 1,021 times more AES 128-bit keys than DES 56-bit keys.[166]

Encryption algorithms can be used to secure a corporate computer network that would otherwise be subject to cyberattacks. With the help of encryption, corporate computer networks may be "configured to control access, authenticate users, hide some or all of a corporate network from the public and to protect live corporate data."[167]

---

[156] *Id.*

[157] Microsoft Law & Corporate Affairs, Summary of Global Internet Legal Developments (for the period Jan.-Mar. 1999), Apr. 1999.

[158] *Supra* note 136.

[159] *Id.*

[160] *Id.* at *2.

[161] Mai-Tram B. Dinh, The U.S. Encryption Export Policy: Taking the Byte Out of the Debate, 7 Minn. J. of Global Trade 375 (1998).

[162] RSA Laboratories, Frequently Asked Questions About Today's Cryptography (visited Apr. 25, 2002), http://www.rsa.com/rsalabs/faq/html/1-6.html.

[163] *Id.*

[164] *Id.*

[165] National Inst. of Standards and Tech., Overview of the AES Development Effort (visited Apr. 27, 2002), http://csrc.nist.gov/encryption/aes/index2.html#overview.

[166] Morris Dworkin, Security and Maintenance of the AES (Feb. 27, 2002), http://csrc.nist.gov/encryption/aes/round2/aesfact.html.

[167] Joanie Wexler, Users Send Out an SOS to Internet Providers, Network World, Feb. 13, 1995, at 37.

Different kinds of encryption may be tailored for different types of business applications. High-speed but lower strength algorithms may suit some messages. StorageTek's BorderGuard employs four different encryption algorithms: "DES (Data Encryption Standard), 3DES (triple DES), IDEA (International Data Encryption Algorithm) and NSC1 (a proprietary, high-speed algorithm)."[168] StorageTek's software uses different encryption for different purposes: "one type of encryption for suppliers and another for customers."[169] Selective encryption makes it possible to tailor security according to the standard of care required. A firm may decide to use encryption selectively or to use high-speed algorithms, depending upon the business activity.

The Department of Defense policy of overclassifying information had the unanticipated consequence of devaluing the currency of secrecy. A business that uses strong encryption for every data transmission may unwittingly fall into the same trap. On the other hand, a lackadaisical attitude toward security may create unnecessary risks in the cyberworld. If information security software is difficult to use and locks employees out of their workplace, serious problems will result. The information audit must, therefore, include connections to trusted business partners, suppliers, remote sites, and any other party sharing access.

Entities with high security requirements will need to employ bulletproof measures to assure that security. One company has announced that it would incorporate a more complex coding formula, along with a coding string 10 times longer than its predecessor—the equivalent of a 50-digit RSA key.[170] A law student may not be concerned with the possibility that a foreign government might attempt to use brute force to crack a 64-digit RSA key; on the other hand, a defense contractor may want to employ a 170-digit RSA key. As with home security, the "haves" will require stronger security programs than the "have-nots."

[8] Public-Key Cryptography

The concept of public-key encryption is a technology built upon trust. Public-key encryption is the Swiss Army knife of Internet security technology in that it provides an all-purpose solution to the problem of ensuring secure e-business, extranet, and Internet applications. Public-key cryptography was first conceptualized in 1975, when Whitfield Diffie published an article describing the dual key system. RSA's public key/private key encryption technology uses a private key, known only to the sender, and a widely published public key. Assuming that the private key is not inadvertently disclosed or stolen, the result is message confidentiality as well as secure transmission of data or information. Assume that sender A transmits a message using the recipient B's public key; only the proper recipient, B, has the private key necessary to decode it.

---

[168] StorageTek, BorderGuard: Can You Trust Your Network?, Press Release, Feb. 5, 1999.

[169] Id.

[170] John Markoff, Software Security Flaw Put Shoppers on Internet at Risk, N.Y. Times, Sept. 19, 1995, at A1.

Conversely, when sender A transmits a message encoded with her own private key, any recipient with sender A's public key can decode it; the private key acts as a digital signature, authenticating that A is, in fact, the sender and that the message has not been altered. Barring what is known in the security trade as a "man in the middle" security breach, recipient B knows that the message could only have been sent by A. RSA's implementation of a Public Key Infrastructure (PKI) has an additional level of security not available under DES. With DES, each party had to have knowledge simultaneously of the secret key. With an RSA-based PKI, only one person holds the private key.

SPC may choose from a number of software vendors that market public-key infrastructure products. Security Dynamics Technologies Inc., for example, developed Keon Desktop, a PKI-ready security software program, for worldwide distribution. The Keon software features a certificate server as well as "PKI system interoperability . . . and PKI-enabled application including e-mail, virtual private networks and Internet-based and e-business applications."[171] Currently, PKI processing is much slower than that of DES: 100 times slower in software and 1,000 times slower in hardware.[172] Vendors, however, are working to find ways to speed it up.

One solution to the slow speed problem is to use RSA primarily to transmit short messages. RSA encryption can be used for longer messages if sent to the recipient with a one-time single-key encryption scheme, which can then be used to send longer messages.[173] Since the single key encryption scheme is used only one time, the security of the transmission is not compromised. Digital envelopes that combine DES and RSA can also speed up transmission. A message is first encrypted using a "random DES key and then, before being sent over an insecure communications channel, the DES key is encrypted with RSA. Together, the DES-encrypted message and the RSA-encrypted message are sent."[174]

Any encrypted key can be broken with enough "brute force." To do this, one or more computers are programmed to try every combination of numbers, letters, or symbols conceivable until the key is unlocked. Now that many governments and private entities have the resources to crack a 64-digit RSA key, most RSA keys are made many times longer than that. The longer the key, the greater the security. Entities with great security needs will have longer keys and will combine them with additional security software to gain as much security as possible. The company StorageTek, for example, uses strong encryption in conjunction with filters. Companies now also have the ability to construct "private sleeves," which protect data as it goes across the Internet or another network and prevent it from being

---

[171] Security Dynamics Technologies, Security Dynamics and RSA Unveil Enterprise Application Security Strategy, Press Release, Jan. 18, 1999 (visited Apr. 28, 2002), http://www. securitydynamics.com/press/pr/pr1999-1-18_2.html.

[172] Public Key Cryptography Algorithm (visited Feb. 27, 2002), http://www.softforum.com/english/learningcenter/learningcenter_06.html.

[173] Id.

[174] RSA, RSA's Frequently Asked Questions About Today's Cryptography (visited Apr. 28, 2002), http://www.rsa.com.

sent by others. Private sleeves also authenticate that data is from an authorized transmitter or user.[175] StorageTek's BorderGuard, for example, employs filters to segment users by group and to prevent access to hosts on the Internet.[176]

Company employees using encryption should be required to use key-recovery or escrow in the event that the company needs to access information during the absence or after the death of an employee.[177]

[9] Digital Signatures

The American Bar Association's Science and Technology Committee defines *digital signatures* as an electronic signature "created and verified by means of cryptography, the branch of applied mathematics that concerns itself with transforming messages into seemingly unintelligible forms and back again."[178] Digital signatures use two different keys. "Public key or asymmetric cryptography uses two keys that are mathematically tied together. If one key is used to encrypt a message, the other must be used to decrypt the same message (and vice-versa). One of the keys is kept secret. The other key made available to the general public, is known as the public key."[179]

A private key can transform a real message or data into a gobbledygook string of characters and/or numbers in a process called *encryption*. The public key can be used to transform the gobbledygook back into a real message. This is called *decryption*.[180] A private key and encryption technology can be used to transform another real message or data into an additional string of gobbledygook characters, thus generating a digital signature. This additional string of characters, the digital signature, can be appended to the primary data or message and will serve to authenticate it as to its source and contents, an authentication confirmable by using the public key. These public-key applications permit the safe conduct of e-business transactions. Web browsers, web servers, e-mail, and databases may be protected through public key cryptography.

Digital signatures, designed to insure against falsification or alteration, are well established in the information security industry. Digital signatures have an evidentiary, authenticating, and ceremonial role in electronic commerce.[181] Paper-based signatures may be authenticated by watermarks, semipermanent ink, time

---

[175] StorageTek, BorderGuard: Can You Trust Your Network? Press Release, Feb. 5, 1999.

[176] *Id.*

[177] Vincent Polley, Electronic Communication Guidelines, Joint Presidential Presentation, ABA Section on Business Law, American Bar Association Annual Meeting, Toronto, Ontario, Aug. 2, 1998.

[178] Information Security Committee, American Bar Association, Committee on Science and Technology, Digital Signature Guidelines with Model Legislation (Chicago: American Bar Association, 1995).

[179] Information Security, All Eyes on PKI (visited Apr. 28, 2002), http://www.infosecuritymag.com/oct/pki.htm.

[180] *See, generally, id.*

[181] Nabil R. Adams, Electronic Commerce: Technical, Business & Legal Issues 123 (1999).

stamps, post-marks, and examination for erasures, modifications, or deletions.[182] Functionally equivalent safeguards are necessary for digital messages and signatures. Digital messages "are simply strings of bits—zeros and ones—represented by fractions of a volt. The problem is how to distinguish your volts from my volts."[183] At least 36 states have enacted or are considering enacting legislation legitimating digital signatures. By October 2003, the federal government will require all transactions to be electronic, and it is studying electronic signatures, electronic authentication, and privacy issues to this end.[184]

[10] Certificate Authorities

A *certificate authority* (CA) is a third-party entity whose business it is to issue and revoke certificates that establish the validity of public keys. This entity is the trusted third party that vouches for the user's identity and issues public-key certificates.[185] Certificate authorities are the equivalent of a passport office for Internet commercial transactions.[186] The CA, a trusted intermediary between two trading partners, issues digital certificates that certify a holder's identity and authority. The CAs "embed an individual's or an organization's public key along with other identifying information into each digital certificate and then cryptographically 'sign' it as a tamper-proof seal, verifying the integrity of the data within it and validating its use."[187] VeriSign is the world's largest CA and has issued more than 100,000 certificates validating the identity of the user and the integrity of the data.[188] VeriSign's method for issuing digital signatures is the "electronic equivalent of a business license."[189] A public key certificate contains (1) a subject name, (2) a subject public key, (3) an issuer name, (4) notice of the validity period for the information, (5) a serial number, and (6) an issuer's signature.[190]

VeriSign issues what it calls a Server ID, vouching for the users' rights to use a company name and serial number web address. The function of the CA is roughly analogous to what a "Secretary of State does when it issues Articles of Incorporation."[191] The role of the CA is to review an applicant's credentials to

---

[182] Michael S. Baum, Secure Electronic Commerce, Doing Business and Avoiding Liability in Cyberspace, Suffolk University Law School, May 10, 1996.

[183] *Id.*

[184] Office of Management and Budget, Implementation of the Government Paperwork Elimination Act (visited Feb. 27, 2002), http://www.whitehouse.gov/omb/fedreg/gpea2.html.

[185] *Id.*

[186] Netscape, Certificate Authority Program (visited Apr. 28, 2002), http://home.netscape.com/security/caprogram/index.html (comparing certificate authorities to the digital world's equivalent of passport offices).

[187] *Id.*

[188] VeriSign, Inc., White Paper—Securing Your Web Site (visited Apr. 22, 2002), http://www.verisgn.com/whitepaper/server/secure/secure.html.

[189] *Id.*

[190] *Supra* note 182.

[191] *Id.*

ensure that the organization's agents are who they claim to be. When a CA issues a certificate, it is, in effect, "an electronic credential that a business can present to prove its identity or right to access information."[192] In concept and methods, the CA's role is that of trusted intermediary, one who can verify the credentials or identity of online trading partners. Trust is essential to an online business, and the CA's rigorous authentication practice plays a role as important as the implementation of physical security for databases or networks. Corporate subscribers should carefully examine the certification authority's statement of the practices it uses in issuing certificates.

[11]   Export Controls on Encryption

In November 1999, the Clinton administration released proposed regulations to control the export of encryption products.[193] Prior to this, companies had to obtain a license for key lengths of 56+ bits before exporting them to any country. Encryption has many positive business applications. RSA Data Security, Inc., is a leading vendor of encrypted software and has supplied "more than 330 million copies of RSA encryption and authentication technologies."[194]

"The length of its key, which is measured in bits and the complexity of the algorithm measure the strength of DES. Each bit doubles the number of possible key sequences; thus, as the number of bits increase, the encryption becomes dramatically stronger."[195] The Bureau of Export Administration of the Department of Commerce has a web site describing the latest export rules,[196] regulations, and lists.[197] The Bureau develops export control policies, issues export licenses, and prosecutes violators.[198]

In May 1999, the Ninth Circuit U.S. Court of Appeals held that the government's ban on the export of encryption codes violated free expression.[199] *Bernstein v. United States Department of Justice*[200] dealt with the situation of an Illinois mathematics and computer science professor who had developed an encryption method based upon a one-way hash function he dubbed "Snuffle."[201] The State

---

[192] *Id.*

[193] Nancy Weil, United States Grants PGP Encryption Export License, Infoworld.com (Dec. 13, 1999).

[194] Security Dynamics Technologies, Security Dynamics Breaks the Barrier for Outsourced Network Security, Press Release, Dec. 8, 1998 (visited Apr. 28, 2002), http://www.securitydynamics.com/press/pr/pr1998-12-15.html.

[195] *Id.*, at 376.

[196] An export of software includes any release, including an oral exchange of information, to a foreign country or a foreign national within the United States. 15 C.F.R. § 734.2(b)(2) & (3).

[197] Home page, Bureau of Export Administration, Welcome to the Bureau of Export Administration Web Site (visited May 12, 1999), http://www.bxa.doc.gov.

[198] *Id.*

[199] Bernstein v. United States Dep't of Justice, 1999 WL 274111 (9th Cir. May 6, 1999) (holding that the government's Export Administration regulations operated as a prepublication prior restraint offending the First Amendment).

[200] *Id.*

[201] 1999 WL 274111, *1 (9th Cir. 1999).

Department told Professor Bernstein that he would need a license to export his research paper, source code, and instructions on using Snuffle. Bernstein and the government were unable to agree on the scope and application of the export regulations applicable to Snuffle, and Bernstein filed an action challenging the constitutionality of the export regulations. The district court held that the regulations were facially invalid as a prior restraint on speech. The Ninth Circuit affirmed, holding that the challenged regulations violated the First Amendment.

The court was concerned that export regulations allowed the government to restrain speech indefinitely with no clear criteria for review.[202] The court observed that prior restraints on speech are viewed "with suspicion because such restraints run the twin risks of encouraging self-censorship and concealing illegitimate abuses of censorial power."[203] The *Bernstein* court found that the source code used by cryptographers parallels the expression of scientific ideas used by mathematicians and economists.[204] The court concluded that source code is expressive for First Amendment purposes and entitled to the protections of the prior restraint doctrine.[205]

In September 1999, the Clinton administration liberalized export controls further, in a policy decision applauded by the software industry. The new policy permits software products of any key length to be exported without a license, except to countries considered terrorist states.[206]

The software industry struggled with the Clinton administration over U.S. government encryption controls since the early 1990s.[207] The Bush administration will be forced in the ensuing years to deal with encryption, security, and privacy issues. The Federal Bureau of Investigation (FBI) seeks "real-time access to all encrypted data without notifying the user or the company that owns the lines for the data."[208] The FBI seeks legislation that would require all companies to hand over private keys to "encrypted data stored on drives."[209]

The NSA designed the so-called Clipper Chip using the single-key based algorithm SKIPJACK to defeat cellular-based security breaches.[210] The Clipper Chip had the single purpose of defeating private parties from using encrypted cellular-based communications for drug deals, spying, and other illegal activities.[211]

---

[202] *Id.* at *8.

[203] *Id.* at *4.

[204] *Id.* at *5.

[205] *Id.*

[206] The Industry Standard's Intelligencer, Encryption Prescription, The Week in the Internet Economy, Sept. 17, 1999.

[207] Jim Kerstetter, Key Uprising: Tighter Crypto Limits Shake IT, PC Week Online, Sept. 29, 1997 (Feb. 9, 1999), http://www.zdnet.com.au/pcweek/news/0929/29crypt.html.

[208] *Id.*

[209] *Id.*

[210] Privacy Issues in the Telecommunications Industry: Testimony Before the Subcommittee on Technology and the Law of the Senate Committee on the Judiciary, 103d Congress, 2d Session (1994) (statement of Stephen T. Walker, President, Trusted Information Systems).

[211] *See* Stephanie Stahl (with Mary E. Thyfault), About Face on Clipper—Privacy Advocates Draw Conflicting Conclusions on Encryption Policy, Info Week, Aug. 8, 1994, at 24.

Inaugurating the Clipper Chip involved a complex balancing of interests. On the one hand, the government would provide the private sector with a strong encryption technology, certified by the NSA as "unbreakable." Recipients, however, would need to allow selected government enforcement agencies to hold the secret keys to this "unbreakable" encryption in escrow.[212]

The Clipper Chip initiative was meant to establish a complex system in which the keys would be divided into two parts and housed with escrow agents at two different government agencies, the Treasury Department's Automated Systems Division and the U.S. Department of Commerce's NIST, both executive branch offices.[213] The government's key escrow recovery system would permit keys to be obtained for law enforcement purposes in the face of valid warrants.[214] The secret keys would then permit law enforcement officials to decode any Clipper-encrypted communications. A functionally equivalent system of key escrow, entitled the Capstone algorithm, was envisioned for database information.[215] The Clipper Chip and Capstone were opposed by civil libertarians, who viewed the government's role as an escrow agent able to break strong cryptography at will as the first step toward Big Brother.[216] Legal academics, too, challenged the Clipper Chip as violative of the right to privacy, freedom of association, free speech, and unreasonable search and seizure.[217]

Government agencies such as the Securities and Exchange Commission, the Food and Drug Administration, and the Atomic Energy Commission, however, argued that they also had a compelling law enforcement interest in the Clipper Chip and Capstone secret keys. Regulatory agencies would like access to encrypted materials to have "the capability to eavesdrop on the industries they watch over under hostile circumstances."[218] The federal government has endorsed the public/private key encryption technology, but seeks its own exclusive access to deter and punish terrorists seeking to unleash an "Electronic Pearl Harbor."

[12]   Virtual Private Networks

A *Virtual Private Network* (VPN) uses the Internet as a backbone for connecting company computers, servers, databases, and other key infrastructure. The VPN gives off-site employees, telecommuters, business partners, and other trusted

---

[212] A. Michael Froomkin, The Metaphor Is the Key: Cryptography, the Clipper Chip, and the Constitution, 143 U. Pa. L. Rev. 715-16 (1995).

[213] *See* Rochelle Garner, Clipper's Hidden Agenda, Open Computing, Aug. 1994, at 54.

[214] *Id.*, at 54.

[215] Allan McDonald, Federal Bureau of Investigation, Protecting Enterprise Information in the Digital Age: Digital Telephony, Privacy and Security, Presentation at the American Bar Association, Section of Science & Technology, Annual Meeting, Chicago, Illinois (Aug. 7, 1995).

[216] Rochelle Garner, Clipper's Hidden Agenda, Open Computing, Aug. 1994, at 54.

[217] *See* Froomkin, *supra* note 212, at 810.

[218] *See* Rochele Garner, Clipper's Hidden Agenda, Open Computing, Aug. 1994, at 52 (quoting Donn Parker, program manager of information and security, SRI International, Menlo Park, California).

parties secure access or a tunnel into a company's network.[219] A VPN makes it possible for a company to communicate on the Internet in a secure private environment through the technology of strong user authentication. Businesses with telecommuting employees are on the increase, as are companies with remote sites. A company must know that those entering its systems are authorized employees, not impostors. Businesses must ensure that only authorized users can gain access to the company's information assets. The traditional network, however, by not permitting business partners, customers, or telecommuters to access company computers over the Internet, can sometimes leave them marooned.[220] VPN technology replaces "costly leased communications facilities with encrypted channels across public networks, such as the Internet."[221]

The common hazard of the VPN is the exposure of company assets to hackers and unauthorized users. The Internet Architecture Board issued a 1994 directive that concluded that any Internet-based system required security "from unauthorized monitoring and control of network traffic as well as the need to secure end-to-end traffic using authentication and encryption."[222] A VPN may be vulnerable to cyberattacks such as IP spoofing, in which intruders give packets false IP addresses, eavesdropping, and packet sniffing, which cyberthieves use to read information transmitted over the Internet.[223] IP spoofing would be foiled by a filtering router, which drops "outside" packets with an "inside" source address.[224] Proposed Internet standards, such as IPSec, are evolving "to secure communications across LANs, private and public WANs and the Internet."[225] The IPSec standard uses encryption to authenticate all traffic and applications including "remote logons, client server, e-mail, file transfer and Web access."[226]

A number of vendors are implementing the IPSec industry standards with an array of new products. One way to achieve a VPN is to use an encrypted point-to-point tunnel to transmit company data and applications.[227] The tunnel model mode provides protection in the following way:

---

[219] GTE, Virtual Private Networks-VPN (visited Apr. 27, 1999), http://www.bbn.com/groups/vpn/service/.

[220] An extranet allows access to company computers over the Internet.

[221] Edward Skoudis, Fire in the Hole, Information Security: A World of Information for the Security-Conscious (visited Apr. 23, 2002), http://www.infosecuritymag.com/fire.htm.

[222] William Stallings, A Secure Foundation for VPNS Information Security: A World of Information for the Security-Conscious (visited Feb. 9, 1999), http://www.infosecuritymag.com/vpn.htm.

[223] Id.

[224] Security First Network Bank, Security Issues: A Closer Look at SFNB's Security Architecture (1996).

[225] Id.

[226] Id.

[227] Security Dynamics Technologies, Inc., Security Dynamics and Aventail Enter Strategic Relationship to Provide Secure Remote Access and Extranet Solutions, OEM Licensing and Distribution Agreement to Enhance Security Dynamics' Enterprise Security Solutions, Press Release, July 7, 1998 (visited Apr. 28, 2002), http://www.securitydynamics.com/press/pr/pr1998-07-07.html.

To achieve this, after the ESP [Encapsulating Security Payload] fields are added to the IP packet, the entire packet along with its security field is treated as the payload of a new outer IP packet with a new outer IP header. The entire original, or inner, packet travels through a "tunnel" from one point of an IP network to another; no routers along the way are able to examine the inner IP header. Because the original packet is encapsulated, the new packet may include different source and destination addresses, adding to the security. Tunnel mode is used when one or both ends are a security gateway, such as a router or firewall that implements IPSec.[228]

Authentication and encryption give "highly secure remote access and extranet uses" in business-to-business commerce.[229]

The risk factor is far less for SPC's private computers accessing the Internet through a dial-up ISP than it is for a corporate network with Internet access provided directly by an Internet backbone company. The larger the company, the more likely it is to be targeted by hackers. Government offices are the second most likely targets for security crimes, followed by educational institutions. At least for now, the private home is the least likely target for a security attack. Technologies such as the VPN, however, make it possible to thwart many security attacks.

[13]   Security Audit Products

To help determine if there is a violation of a security policy, companies should take advantage of the tools that are included with their computer and networks. Most operating systems store numerous bits of information in log files. Examination of these log files on a regular basis is often the first line of defense in detecting unauthorized use of the system. System logging facilities, such as the UNIX "syslog" utility, should be checked for unusual error messages from system software. For example, a large number of failed login attempts in a short period of time may indicate someone trying to guess passwords. Operating system commands that list currently executing processes can be used to detect users running programs they are not authorized to use, as well as to detect unauthorized programs which have been started by an intruder.

SPC must make critical policy choices about how it will implement information security at the operating system level. One possibility is to hire a computer consulting firm or a consultant specializing in information security. SPC should complete a security audit to determine what holes it has in its system and then research ways to patch its particular security soft spots. A number of products have been developed for making security audits. Internet Security Systems, Inc., for example, markets Internet Scanner, which they claim is the most comprehensive

---

[228] *See* Stallings, *supra* note 222.

[229] *Id.* (quoting Chuck Stuckey, president, chairman, and CEO of Security Dynamics).

"attack simulator" available;[230] it has the capacity to perform audits for more than 100 security vulnerabilities.[231] Internet security consultants, too, can provide multifaceted audits that tell a company where its network is vulnerable, what holes it has, and how to plug them.[232]

The information security industry is one of the fastest growing sectors of the information-based economy. Diagnostics products include the controversial Security Administrator Tool for Analyzing Networks (SATAN) program, COPS, Omni-Guard/Enterprise Access Control UNIX, and NetProbe. SATAN is controversial because of its dual nature: It functions by probing its target across the network from another host, and thus can be used to crack systems as well as to defend them.[233] Using SATAN, a hacker can systematically exploit any system weakness it discovers.[234] SATAN and COPS can be downloaded from various servers on the Internet for no charge. The other products, available commercially, run directly on the target host and operate as self-diagnostics.[235] These products enable a systems administrator to find and plug O/S security holes before hackers can exploit them.

[14] Physical Security

The online company must also provide for adequate physical security to prevent unauthorized use of its equipment or other information intrusions. The firewall, for example, must be protected by physical controls to preclude unauthorized use. In a high security environment, "the company firewall should be located in a controlled environment, with access limited to the Network Services Manager, the firewall administrator, and the backup firewall administrator."[236] Adequate physical security measures are calibrated on the basis of how critical a company finds it to protect sensitive data and information.[237] Trade secret protection requires physical access controls such as placing confidential information in locked cabinets and electronic access controls by computer security measures.[238] Computer

---

[230] Thomas Noonan Joins Internet Security Systems as President, Business Wire, Aug. 30, 1995.

[231] Id.

[232] Internet Security Systems: Plugging Network Holes: New Network Security Software Uses Simulator to Scan Network for Vulnerabilities, Wall Street & Technology, Jan. 1, 1997, at 28.

[233] Jason Levitt, Techview: Dealing with the Devil, Information Week, Apr. 17, 1995, at 2.

[234] See Winn Schwartau, The Key to Defeating SATAN Is Understanding How It Can Bedevil You, Network World, May 1, 1995, at 32.

[235] Rutrell Yasin, Vendors Fire Up Wares to Vie with SATAN, Communications Week, Apr. 10, 1995, at 4.

[236] Physical Firewall Security, in NIST, Internet Security Policy (Washington, D.C.: NIST, 1999): A Technical Guide (NIST, 1999), (visited Apr. 25, 2002), http://www.csrc.nist.gov/isptg/html/ISPTG-6.html.

[237] Traditionally, mainframe computers were so heavy that the computer room was located in the basement, making the systems prone to flooding. In a PC environment, it may make sense to locate computers on upper floors. The physical security of the computer system should not necessarily be based on traditional methods.

[238] Jennifer L. Blackman and M. Patricia Thayer, Avoiding Trade Secret Problems When Hiring, 16 Computer Law. 8 (Nov. 1999).

systems must be protected adequately from fire, water hazards, electric power supply losses, shifts in humidity, natural disasters, and magnetic surges; finally, good housekeeping procedures protect against damage from dust and dirt.[239] Additional measures must be tailored to the specific physical, human, or environmental risks.

[B]   Mass-Market Security Products

Most information security products consist of sets of instructions for performing designated security functions housed on diskette or CD-ROM. Norton Anti-Virus and MCA Anti-Virus are examples of mass-marketed information security products that perform a single primary security function, patrolling for viruses and controlling viruses. Norton's Internet Security 2002 is a comprehensive security product that can be used on a single computer or in a network to restrict access to hard drives, provide firewall protection and privacy controls, and provide antivirus protection.[240] Businesses as well as consumers use mass-market products that are distributed to the desktops and updated automatically.

Mass-marketed firewall software products include FireWall-1, sold by CheckPoint Software Technology, Inc., of Lexington, Massachusetts. FireWall-1 is installed like any other mass-market software, without any customized modifications. Firewalls for UNIX-based software gateways are increasingly being designed to perform packet filtering. (A packet is "[a] group of characters transferred from one computer to another, including control information."[241])

Vendors offer a wide array of firewalls to protect Internet routers/gateways.[242] Network Systems, for example, markets BorderGuard for the protection

---

[239] These standard environmental safeguards should be implemented for all computer systems. "Even with an onsite backup solution in place, companies are still in a vulnerable state. The backup media is kept in the same location. If your computer is ruined due to fire, flood or other natural disaster, or if it is stolen, then the backup tapes or discs will be lost too. Your tape and Zip drives are the most common point of failure in a system." Jeff and Marc Slutsky, BizSmart Column (Street Fighter Inc.), Aug. 27, 2001.

[240] Symantec, Norton Internet Security™ 2002 (visited Feb. 27, 2002), http://www.symantec. com/sabu/nis/nis_pe/.

[241] Webopedia, Dedicated to Computer Technology, "Packets" (visited Apr. 28, 2002), http:// webopedia.internet.com/SHARED/search_action.asp.

[242] "Most organizations insert *firewalls* between their publicly accessible Web servers and the remote clients who can access those servers, blocking incoming traffic according to various criteria. Firewalls partition the Internet in *security cells*, whose boundaries are difficult to penetrate for remote service invocations." Ernesto Damiani, Fine Grained Access Control for SOAP E-Services, The Tenth International World Wide Web Conference Proceedings, Hong Kong, May 1-5, 2001.

The revenues for security products have increased in response to well-publicized intrusions and viruses such as Code Red. The leading security vendors include market leaders such as Checkpoint (CHKP), intrusion-detection systems from Internet Security Systems (ISSX), and antiviral software from McAfee. Nokia is rapidly becoming a market leader for firewalls and other security technologies, challenging Cisco Systems and other major players. Alex Salkevery, Nokia's Security Connection, The Finnish cell-phone giant is threatening to overtake even Cisco in the hot area of firewall appliances. Business Week, Aug. 29, 2001, reprinted at SecurityFocus.com (visited Sept. 3, 2001), http://firewall.com/cgi-bin/jump.cgi?ID=249.

of remote sites. Another product employs proxies, which are "slimmed-down versions of applications that are open to outside users and serve to protect the 'real' application behind the firewall from bugs."[243] IBM's NetSP Gateway enforces network access rights based on user-determined rules. It also takes action if hacking is suspected, based on an analysis of address pairs and requested services.[244] Harris Corp. makes a computer safeguard called CyberGuard Firewall, which places a computer between a company's LAN and its outside connections.[245] Trusted Information Systems, Inc., developed Gauntlet, a firewall based on Pentium hardware, using a modified version of UNIX.

Custom-designed security products or systems may be necessary where the mass-market product provides insufficient protection. The firewall industry is changing rapidly as companies seek firewalls that serve as Internet gateway filters.

An inference of negligence may be predicated on a company's failure to implement adequate Internet security measures. "Weak security of a company may actually subject that company to a lawsuit where an attack is involved,"[246] although there are not yet decided cases on this issue. Netscape Navigator and Microsoft Internet Explorer are two of the most popular mass-marketed web browsers used to read documents on the Internet. Mosaic was the first mass-distributed web browser, written by researchers at the National Center for Supercomputing Applications (NCSA).[247] " 'Secure' browsers and servers are only designed to protect confidential information against network eavesdropping. Without system security on both browser and server sides, confidential documents [are] vulnerable to interception."[248]

[C] Owner-Distributed Security Products

A number of network-security products are not mass-marketed but distributed by the developers or their authorized distributors. Developer-distributed secu-

---

[243] Joanie Wexler, Users Send Out a SOS to Internet Providers, Network World, Feb. 13, 1995, at 37. *See also* Mike Fratto, Multisite Firewall Management: Not Enterprise e-Read," Network Computing (Apr. 3, 2000) (noting that "proxy-based firewalls examine and enforce security at the application layer and beyond, thus offering more stringent access controls").

[244] Wexler, Users Send Out a SOS to Internet Providers, *id.*

[245] Frank Ruiz, ECI to Build E-Mail Security Chip for U.S., Tampa Tribune, June 8, 1995, at 1.

[246] Ara C. Trembly, Instant Messaging Leaves Firms Exposed, 106 Nat'l Underwriter Prop. & Casualty-Risk & Benefits Mgmt. 28 (Mar. 4, 2002); *see also* They Shoot Trojan Horses, Don't They? An Economic Analysis of Anti-Hacking Regulatory Models, 89 Geo. L.J. 171 (2000) (arguing for a negligence standard applied to inadequate security in computer systems); *see also* Note, The Doors Are Locked But the Thieves and Vandals Are Still Getting In: A Proposal in Tort to Alleviate Corporate America's Cyber-Crime Problem, 16 J. Marshall J. Computer & Info. L. 167 (1997) (same).

[247] Boutell.com, Web Browsers, Open FAQ (visited Apr. 25, 2002) http://www.boutell.com/openfaq/browsers/1.html.

[248] W3C World Wide Web Security FAQs (visited Apr. 25, 2002), http://www.w3.org/Security/faq/wwwsf1.html#GEN-Q2.

rity products include Ace/Server and ACM, from Security Dynamics Technologies, Inc., and properly configured network servers, such as SecureManager from Cylink Corp. The typical owner- or developer-distributed product tends to have more complex functions than do mass-marketed products. Frequently, these products combine hardware and software and have more detailed installation and update procedures. The trend in the information security industry is to license these products with a services component.

[D] Customized Security Products

Network security professionals may also custom-design security products or systems for companies. The network security professional may custom-develop a security product or system in response to a request for a proposal (RFP) or another software contract. The role of the security consultant is to conduct an internal investigation of security solutions for a business. A consultant may determine that the online business faces the potential of intrusions or other information security risks and then custom-designs a solution. As with preventive law, it is best to hire a consultant to forecast a security problem as opposed to being forced to plug a hole after a security breach has occurred. Information security professionals can aid companies in determining the presence of security dangers and can suggest solutions. Because businesses vary significantly in form and function, the information security consultant should be experienced in a given industry. The International Organization for Standardization (ISO) is in the process of proposing a set of minimum standards for assessing the security features of computer products.[249]

[E] Emerging Trends in Security Products

[1] Elliptic Curve Cryptography

Recent improvements in integer factorization and parallel processing have resulted in a requirement for longer key sizes for most current public-key systems. Unfortunately, longer key sizes make these public-key systems even slower and more cumbersome. Use of Elliptic Curve Cryptography (ECC) allows increases in strength at the same time as decreasing overhead and latency. ECC is a new cryptographic system that uses the algebraic system defined on the points of an elliptic curve to provide public-key algorithms. These algorithms can be used to (1) create digital signatures, (2) provide secure distribution of secret keys, and (3) provide a secure means for the transmission of confidential information. Applications such as financial transfers or wireless data transmissions requiring intensive use of

---

[249] International Organization for Standardization (visited Sept. 3, 2001), http://iso.org/iso/en/ISOOnline.frontpage. (describing information security standard). *See also* NIST, International Organization for Standardization (IS0) (visited Apr. 28, 2002), http://www.csrc.nist.gov/cc/cerm/cemlist.htm@CEM2.

signing, authentication, high speed, and limited bandwidth will benefit from the advantages offered by elliptic curve implementations.

It is anticipated that ECC will be valuable in a variety of circumstances:

- Where computational power is limited (smart cards, wireless devices, and PC cards)

- Where space is limited (smart cards, wireless devices, PC Cards)

- Where high speed is required

- Where intensive use of signing, verifying, or authenticating is required

- Where signed messages are required to be stored or transmitted

- Where bandwidth is limited (wireless communications)

A company called Certicom began licensing its implementation of elliptical curve cryptography algorithm in September 2000. Vendors of handheld devices and mobile gateway makers used the algorithm in their VPNs to provide security to mobile communities.[250]

[2] Smart Cards

A smart card is like an electronic safe deposit box. The size of a credit card, a smart card contains a semiconductor chip with logic and nonvolatile memory. The software within the card detects attempts at intrusion and tampering and monitors abnormal usage. Billions of smart cards have been made since their introduction in 1977. Smart cards have long been popular in Asia and Europe, and are gaining popularity in the United States. Some of the many applications of smart cards include:

1. Stored value card: This type of smart card minimizes the need to carry cash. It can be used in stores, vending machines and pay phones.

2. Health care: Health care smart cards provide a portable, customized health care file with medical emergency data, HMO, and insurance information.

3. Access control in offices and hotels: These smart cards can store information such as the time entered and exited, access conditions, and identity.

4. Contactless tickets for ski resorts and airlines: These smart cards increase the speed, convenience, and security of ticketing, and facilitate baggage checking.

Smart cards can be read using conventional contact readers or interrogated remotely by microwave or infrared signals. They offer superior security and lower

---

[250] Joanie Wexler, Securing Wireless IP VPNs, Network World Wireless in the Enterprise News., Sept. 6, 2000.

life cycle costs than alternatives such as coins, paper money, or magnetic stripe cards. MasterCard Cash, Mondex, Visa Cash, and Wells Fargo P-ATM are examples of smart cards currently being introduced in the United States.

Security in smart cards is typically ensured by a combination of digital signature and public-key technology. There are many different algorithms in use for smart cards, but all act to verify the authenticity of cards and to prevent misuse or fraud. Smart cards incorporate write-once memory that cannot be modified once it has been programmed. This allows each card to contain a unique identification number. Limits are typically placed on the number of erroneous attempts, preventing brute-force access.

§ 3.03   THE RADIUS OF RISK

The only way a company can prevent potential legal problems is by formulating and implementing a comprehensive information security policy. The online company must fulfill basic security requirements to comply with its duty of care to customers, third parties, and the general public. The policy must emphasize the high standard of care with which employees should treat confidential information. A company should also appoint a systems administrator in charge of information security. The system administrator should construct a Frequently Asked Questions (FAQ) document for employee reference. The company should conduct regular training seminars to make employees aware of the dangers of breaches in information security, as well as the proper use of the technologies available to protect sensitive information. Our hypothetical company, SPC, will need to appoint a rota of contact persons to provide coverage 24 hours a day, 7 days a week, so that SPC will be able to take prompt remedial steps in the face of a computer intrusion, virus, or denial of service attack. When a company has notice of a security flaw, it needs to implement additional security measures to avoid a finding of negligent security. When a company has prior similar security incidents, it needs additional security measures. The greater the radius of the risk of intrusions, the higher the duty to implement additional remedial measures.

Companies might consider installing e-mail firewalls, which permit administrators to enforce security policies.[251] Employees should be warned of the risk of Internet e-mail attacks, such as address spoofing, in which a cybercriminal uses false headers to obtain proprietary information. Another danger is the potential interception and alteration of an e-mail message. Companies should consider using message encryption, sometimes referred to as Privacy Enhanced Mail or

---

[251] "E-mail firewall server that allows administrators to enforce an array of security and content policies." Ralph S. Larsen, "Framework: Turning the Challenges of Change into Opportunities for Growth; Johnson & Johnson's Management Process, Chief Executive (May 1, 1999) at 10. Companies need to implement e-mail policies "that preclude the transmission of sensitive company information to external e-mail addresses without verification and approval." Louise Kehoe, Watch Out for Spoofers: Falsified E-Mails Can Be Damaging: The Only Defense Is to Use Your Common Sense, Financial Times (London), June 27, 2001 at 16.

PEM. Message encryption should be used for all sensitive information transmitted by e-mail.

Security policies have little value if the supporting infrastructure does not enable a company to implement its plan. SPC must not choose its security products randomly. A viable security solution must not overemphasize functionality at the expense of the sociology of application. Information security depends on educating and socializing employees, consultants, and customers to follow security protocol. Careful attention must be given to how each security component will be implemented. This section describes the various components of a typical network, the associated security issues (as identified by SPC), and some insights into differentiating among competing products. Information security must be tailored for the specific computer systems, including servers, all systems for data storage and applications, and routers, hubs, and networks. The security audit should review each computer component or application.

For SPC, its formal security audit or assessment should be tailored to its Internet-based virtual store. An online company attracts web users to its site to increase business and advertising revenue. SPC faces liability risks from materials posted online or generated by its site's users. SPC must also prevent its employees, consultants, and other users from exchanging or distributiing materials deemed harmful to children. In particular, the company needs some mechanism to report violations of federal child pornography laws.[252]

If an online company employs a "reward" program that entitles users to receive points redeemable for merchandise, such as books or music, it must provide security measures to prevent fraud.[253] Further, the online company must protect its payment systems and the privacy of its customers.[254] SPC sells computer software and hardware directly over the Internet. Customers entering SPC's web site need to be assured that its payment system is secure. SPC incorporated a

---

[252] Increasingly, "the Internet is a channel for the dissemination of child pornography and used an instrumentality for crimes against children and adults. Harris N. Miller, E-Commerce Security Risks, Testimony Before the Senate Commerce, Science and Transportation Committee, Science, Technology and Space Subcommittee, July 16, 2001, reprinted at FDCH Congressional Testimony (July 16, 2001). South Carolina, for example, has enacted a new law making it a felony to send child pornography by e-mail. The new criminal statute requires computer technicians to report child pornography if they find it on a coworkers' machine. Sandra Swanson, You Be the Judge, Information Week (Aug. 6, 2001) at 18. There is a growing problem of employees trading child pornography in the electronic workplace. *Id.*

[253] Jerry Sumner, Advances in Loyalty Programs Keep Customers Coming Back, 4 Card Marketing 22 (Dec. 18, 2000) (arguing need to protect customer's information with the latest security technology in the interactive clicks 'n' mortar environment); *see also* Carol Angrisani, The Cyber-Coupon Connection, Supermarket News, July 16, 2001 (noting the importance of a security system and fraud-prevention system for online coupons).

[254] *See* Peter Lucas, ACH Payments Hit the Web, 14 Credit Card Management 34 (Sept. 2001) (arguing that security and a fraud-detection system are critical to payments over the Internet); The New York Clearing House, B2B Clearing & Settlement Project Announced; New Universal Payment Identification Code Will Become Industry Standard for I-Enabled Payments, PR NewsWire, Apr. 24, 2001 (announcing development of Universal Payment Identification Code protecting against fraud in electronic payments to the Internet).

secure ordering system that protects the integrity of the credit card numbers it is given. SPC employs a "1-Click" technology, providing customers with a secure, streamlined ordering process.[255] SPC and all online businesses must address online fraud by professional thieves and amateurs. One method is to monitor ordering logs to detect fraudulent orders. Internet fraud may originate from anywhere in the world—Pakistan, Russia, Israel, the United Kingdom, Mexico, or a host of other countries.

SPC needs security that will protect its numerous site management, customer interaction, and transaction-processing services. Any online company's process of accepting, authorizing, and charging customer credit cards must be protected. Systems security must be tailored to protect its rapidly evolving virtual businesses. A company such as SPC has "a real need for contingency planning, sometimes dubbed business-continuity planning or disaster-recovery planning [where] disaster-recovery plan easily can mean the difference between smooth operations and complete collapse."[256]

[A] Hackers

Steven Levy's book *Hackers: Heroes of the Computer Revolution,* documented how hackers share common values and endorse what he called a "hacker ethic."[257] Hackers form a distinctive subculture based upon a belief that a computer is a tool for understanding the world rather than a tool of corporate capitalism. "Access to computers—and anything which might teach you something about the way the world works—should be unlimited and total. Always yield to the Hands-On Imperative!" Levy identified the following counterhegemonic values of hackers: "(1) All information should be free; (2) Mistrust Decentralization; (3) Hackers should be judged by their hacking, not bogus criteria such as degrees, age, race, or position; (4) You can create art and beauty on a computer, and (5) Computers can change your life for the better."[258]

Empirical studies of computer hackers confirm that hackers are not a monolithic threat but instead reflect diverse subcultures ranging from ethical hackers to organized crime networks and cultural radicals.[259] Dorothy Denning's empirical study of hackers concluded "they were a diffuse group with complex values."[260]

---

[255] SPC will need to adopt an authentication technology to provide a secure site for its e-tailer operations. VISA USA has adopted a new web authentication system making the checkout process more secure for the online business such as SPC. Dennis Callaghan, Visa Upgrades Its Web Authentication, ZDNET eWeek (May 14, 2001) at 17.

[256] Scott Leibs, E-Business: An Executive Guide to IT; Bracing for the Big One, Industry Week, (Dec. 6, 1999).

[257] Steven Levy, The Hacker Ethic, *in* Hackers: Heroes of the Computer Revolution 26-36 (1984).

[258] *Id.* at 27.

[259] Dorothy E. Denning, Concerning Hackers Who Break Into Computer Systems, Paper Presented at the Thirteenth National Computer Security Conference, Washington D.C. (visited Apr. 28, 2002), http://www.cpsr.org/cpsr/privacy/crime/denning.hackers.html.

[260] *Id.*

Denning's surveys confirmed that many of her respondents were ethical in the sense that they were not generally engaged in financial crimes. Ethical hackers were primarily motivated by the intellectual satisfaction gained by greater understanding of how computer security and systems function.[261]

Criminologists confirm that hackers are not all ethical and may be subdivided diverse subcultures reflecting different motivations, cultural values, norms, and practices.[262] Paul Taylor, an English criminologist, views hacking as a product of "conflict and contestation between various social groups."[263] Taylor argues that "computer cognoscenti are split into two camps: those who either come from or are prepared to co-operate with the computer underground and those to whom the computer underground is an anathema." Corporate network security administrators need to be aware that political hacktivists have different motives for committing intrusions than corporate spies or foreign terrorists. Information security needs to be calibrated to the type of hacker. Hacktivists pose a different threat to information security than organized criminals operating in an offshore haven.

The HBO series "The Sopranos" is a fictional account of a contemporary New Jersey crime family that used illicit means to attain the American dream. During the Great Depression, Al Capone, Bugsy Seigel, and John Dillinger were innovators, as were the networks of criminals who developed Las Vegas, Nevada, as America's gambling and prostitution capital. Finding the front door to American financial success blocked, organized criminals achieved financial success by breaking in through the back door. Dark-side innovators use illegitimate means to attain easy riches or better living through hacking.[264] East European gangs of cybercriminals are the functional equivalent of "The Sopranos" for Internet wrongdoing. Corporate network administrators need to understand the subcultures of cybercrime to determine the best information security to protect their site.

The law enforcement community reports that a large number of Internet crimes originate in Eastern Europe and certain Russian Commonwealth states. Russia, for example, has an estimated 6.6 million Internet users and is ranked twelfth in Internet use in the world's online population.[265] Hackers in Kazakhstan have been

---

[261] The earliest hackers were so-called ethical hackers who hacked computers to understand computer systems. Ethical hackers are sometimes contrasted with dark-side criminals or cybercriminals as a means for gaining wealth through computer intrusions.

[262] A hacker was traditionally defined as "[a]ny person who derives joy from discovering ways to circumvent limitations." Matt Pfeifer's Hacking Page (visited Apr. 18, 2001), http://members. aol.com/angband/hacking.htm.l (quoting Robert Bickford). Hackers today have differentiated into diverse subcultures, including hacktivists, computer radicals, e-delinquents, and organized cybercrime gangs.

[263] Paul A. Taylor, Hackers: Crime in the Digital Sublime xi (1999).

[264] The term *dark-side hacker* is "a criminal or malicious hacker; a cracker. . . . [The term is derived] from George Lucas's Darth Vader, seduced by the dark side of the Force. . . . The implication that hackers form a sort of elite of technological Jedi Knights is intended." Definition, Dark-Side Hacker, Denis Howe, The Free Online Dictionary of Computing (Apr. 21, 2001), http://burks.brighton.ac.uk/burks/foldoc/63/27.htm.

[265] Cyberatlas, The World's Online Population (visited Apr. 25, 2002), http://www.cyberatlas.internet.com/big_picture.

charged with hacking, extortion, and computer intrusion resulting from an unauthorized intrusion into Bloomberg's computer network. The Russian Republics, for example, have been a popular venue for a number of innovative scams involving stolen credit card numbers from web sites.[266] Organized hacker groups in the Ukraine gained access to e-commerce computer systems, stealing credit card information.[267] There is a poverty of empirical data on the incidence of Internet crime from "have not" nations in the world's online population.[268] It is hypothesized that organized cybercriminals in less developed countries constitute a significant segment of online fraud. One of the difficulties facing corporate web sites is that cybercrimes can originate in any country and even from offshore data havens.

Financial institutions will often be the target of cybercriminals seeking credit card information. In December 2000, an unknown hacker broke into Creditcards.com web site, stealing confidential credit card information.[269] Cybercriminal innovators use the Internet as an instrumentality or target for committing crime.[270] Some of the so-called phone phreaks break into telephone networks for Internet wealth, not intellectual curiosity. Phone phreaks are frequently well-organized gangs of criminals who hack into telephone systems using sophisticated computer programs to unscramble cellular-telephone codes.[271] A leading security expert described how one enterprising information security expert absconded with $10.2 million in a funds-transfer fraud from a bank where he had served as a security

---

[266] John Leyden, Extradition Hearing in Bloomberg Hack/Extortion, The Register (visited Apr. 14, 2001), http://www.theregister.co.uk/content/8/18196.html.

[267] Anecdotal reports indicate that a large number of Internet cybercriminal gangs work on servers located in Eastern Europe. A network administrator needs to pay particular attention to Internet communications originating from this region. Frequently, Internet communications will be disguised and sometimes originate in offshore data havens. *See, e.g.,* United States Department of Justice, NIPC ADVISORY 01-003 Press Release, Mar. 8, 2001 (visited Apr. 18, 2001), http://www.usdoj.gov/criminal/cybercrime/NIPCpr.htm (noting that "several hacker groups from Eastern Europe, specifically Russia and the Ukraine, have penetrated U.S. e-commerce computer systems by exploiting vulnerabilities" in Microsoft software). Christine Winter, Scams Are Thriving in World of E-Business, Sun-Sentinel, Feb. 4, 2001, at 1.

[268] The world's online population is now extending to less developed countries. The United States has 36 percent of the Internet users worldwide with 135.7 million users. However, China now has 15.8 million users. *See* CyberAtlas, The Big Picture: The World's Online Populations (visited Apr. 14, 2001), http://www.cyberatlas.internet.com/big_picture/geographics/article/0,1323.5911_151151,00.html.

[269] Dick Kelsey, Creditcards.com Hacked, Data Exposed, Infowar.com (visited Apr. 28, 2002), http://www.infowar.com/hacker/00/hack_121300a_j.shtml.

[270] The ideology of ethical hackers is that their main goal is to learn about computers, telephones, or communities. Hacking is portrayed in romantic terms as a form of higher learning by committing computer crimes. The Legion of the Apocalypse, for example, states that its "main goal is to show the public what hacking and phreaking [are] all about and to reveal confidential information to the hacking/phreaking community so that we can learn more about computers, telephones, electronics etc." Revelation Loa-Ash, The Ultimate Beginner's Guide to Hacking and Phreaking (visited Apr. 28, 2002), http://membes.aol.com/angband/starthak.txt.

[271] Michael Myer et al., Stop! Cyberthief! Technology: Don't Be Alarmed, But the Law Can't Cope With Computer Crime, Newsweek, Feb. 6, 1995, at 36.

system analyst and consultant.[272] Banks and other financial institutions will need to have maximum security of their sites.

The CSI/FBI Computer Crime and Security Survey found that financial losses due to computer breaches were $265.6 million. This amount was double that from 1998.[273] "The grand total of losses reported in the period 1997-2001 was $1,004,135,495."[274] The hundreds of millions of dollars in losses due to computer crime fall into two components: (1) the actual financial gain by cybercriminal innovators and (2) the cost of hiring information security experts who can help a company recovery from an intrusion or the havoc caused by a computer breach.

[1] Corporate Espionage

Hacker attacks on corporate web sites appear to be "motivated by a desire to steal information or to extort money."[275] Industrial espionage frequently takes the form of hiring a hacker to break into a competitor's computer systems.[276] Netspionage is broadly defined as "using networks, computers and associated capabilities to steal corporations' secrets.[277]

The ECHELON network, which includes the United States, "in cooperation with its closest allies, the United Kingdom, Australia and Canada," is supposed to track all telephone conversations, electronic mail messages, and faxes.[278] If Big Brother has such a network, there is little question that Little Brother (private corporations) engages in "wholesale [data] collection efforts."[279] Network-enabled espionage in the "black zone" is accomplished by a wide variety of tools, including Trojan horse software, BackOrifice2000, digital dead drops, computer elicitation, steganography, Van Eck Interception, Network Mapping, and other attack tools.[280] Sexpionage or sex-related blackmail is another technique for gaining information for firms.[281] Netspionage may result in a wide variety of legal risks, including:

---

[272] Donn B. Parker, Fighting Computer Crime: A New Framework for Protecting Information 19 (1998).

[273] Curtis E.A. Karnow, Computer Network Risks: Security Breaches and Liability Issues, Computer Law Strategist (Feb. 1999) at 1; *see also* David Hughes, Hackers Help Insurers Lead the Way: Risk Management Fundamentals in Cyberspace, 14 Andrews Del. Corp. Litig. Rep. 12 (Oct. 2, 2000).

[274] Richard Power, Computer Security Inst., 2001 CSI/FBI Computer Crime & Security 6 (Spring 2001).

[275] Karnow, *supra* note 273, at 1.

[276] Power, *supra* note 274, at 1.

[277] William Boni and Gerald L. Kovacich, Netspionage: The Global Threat to Information 93 (2001).

[278] *Id.*

[279] *Id.*

[280] *Id.* at 101-16.

[281] *Id.* at 109-12 (describing how corporate spies employ sex-related techniques based on the individual target's profile and sexual preferences to accomplish netspionage).

[1] Disclosure or theft of company trade secrets liability to contractual parties as a result of exposure of data that is subject to a nondisclosure commitment.

[2] Financial losses from deleted, corrupted, or copied data, possible insurance claims for loss of data, property damage, business interruption, or employee fraud or dishonesty

[3] Shareholder suits against directors and officers for share price drops due to network disruptions.

[4] Liability to "downstream" victims of a network attack perpetrated through your company's network.

[5] Customer or employee lawsuits for violation of their privacy rights or exposure of financial information.[282]

Corporate networks may be at risk from (1) investors and potential investors; (2) competitors interested in intercepting data on customers, vendors, and potential employees; (3) governments intercepting data; (4) terrorists, ideologues, and political opponents; (5) opportunists using corporate networks to distribute spam e-mail; and (6) insiders including current and former employees and consultants seeking to damage the company.[283] Hackers have diverse motives for attacking networks, which range from thrill-seeking to calculated motives.

The purpose of corporate espionage is to gain an illicit competitive advantage by breaking into competitors' computer systems. Like electronic robbers, corporate spies seek to steal information from competitors to gain financial rewards or increases in market share.[284] Corporate competitors or foreign terrorists could be responsible for denial of service attacks.

[2] Hackers as the "Enemy Within"

The typical computer criminal is described as a trusted insider, usually an employee or ex-employee.[285] Insiders familiar with the computer network carry out most computer intrusions. Unauthorized use, disruption, and breaches of security by insiders are common forms of computer abuse.[286] An ex-employee of a New Jersey engineering firm used his password to destroy data, software, and other intellectual property worth more than $10 million. The ex-GTE employee

---

[282] NETSPIONAGE.COM: What Every Lawyer Should Know About Minimizing and Responding to Attacks on Corporate Information Infrastructures (presentation by the Netspionage.com Working Group at the ABA Annual Meeting, Aug. 4, 2001).

[283] *Id.*

[284] *Id.* (citing Computer Security Institute Report entitled Issues and Trends: 2000, CSI/FBI Computer Crime and Security Survey).

[285] David Neal, Security Threats Begin at Home, Warns KPMG Study, Apr. 9, 2001 (visited Apr. 28, 2002), http://www.zdnet.co.uk/news/2001/14/ns-22143.html.

[286] Lois Forcht et. al., Computer Crime: Assessing the Lawyer's Perspective, 8 J. Bus. Ethics 243 (1989).

pleaded guilty to violating a federal computer crime statute by intentionally damaging protected computers.[287] A 1999 survey by a consulting firm concluded "more than 75 percent of all attacks come from within the organization."[288] The *2001 CSI/FBI Computer Crime and Security Survey* found the Internet connection to be the point of attack in 70 percent of computer intrusions.[289]

A recent IBM advertisement for Internet security features two 20-something hackers who have infiltrated the computer network containing confidential executive compensation information.[290] The young woman hacker observes that the other company vice presidents would be surprised at what one of the other vice presidents made. Her arrogant accomplice says: "They know. I just sent an e-mail to everyone in the company." The IBM advertisement is designed to use fear to sell its information security software. The fear is that a company will lose their trade secrets and valuable proprietary information at the click of the mouse by an insider. One of the greatest threats to the security of client computers is not the Internet hacker, but the enemy within—trusted company employees, consultants, or other insiders.[291]

Software applications are freely available on the Internet as a tool to exploit instant messaging. Cybercriminals may use instant messaging "to execute 'arbitrary commands,' such as formatting your hard drive or controlling your computer [to launch] more insidious denial-of-service attacks.'"[292] E-businesses have been faced with a growing number of cybertortion claims in which ex-employees or other knowledgeable insiders threaten to release sensitive financial data or proprietary information unless the company pays a bribe.[293] Increasingly companies are focusing on cybercriminal insiders, and the number of incidents of unauthorized access by "insiders" dropped from 71 percent in 2000 to 49 percent in 2001.[294]

---

[287] United States Department of Justice, Ex-GTE Employee Pleads Guilty to Intentionally Damaging Protected GTE Computers, Mar. 20, 2001 (visited Apr. 18, 2001), http://www.usdoj.gov/criminal./cybercrme/VentimigliaPlea.htm.

[288] *Id.* (reporting that "IDC, a global technology research and consulting firm based in Framingham, Massachusetts, reported late in 1999 that more than 75 percent of all attacks come from within the organization").

[289] Power, *supra* note 274, at 6.

[290] The term *hacker* was first coined at MIT in the 1960s, meaning that the person was a computer virtuoso. A hacker was someone who could design innovative ways around difficult problems. Wade Rousch, Hackers: Taking a Byte Out of Computer Crime, Tech. Rev., Apr. 1995, at 32. Corporate web site hackers are another form of computer abuse. *See* Attrition.org, Attrition Defacement Statistics, http://www.attrition.org/mirror/attrition/stats.html (visited Apr. 28, 2002). *See also* Hacker Crashes e-Bay's Web site, CNN Financial News, Mar. 22, 1999.

[291] Companies may reduce the incidence of cybercrimes committed by employees by better screening and supervising of employees, as well as enforcement of Internet usage or e-mail policies.

[292] Ara C. Trembly, Instant Messaging Leaves Firms Exposed, 106 Nat'l Underwriter Prop. & Casualty-Risk & Benefits Mgmt. 28 (Mar. 4, 2002).

[293] Joia Shillinford, Insuring Against Cybercrime, Fin. Times (London), Sept. 5, 2001, at 6; *see generally* Computer Crimes, 38 Am. Crim. L. Rev. 481 (2001) (discussing recent trends in computer crimes).

[294] Power, *supra* note 274, at 1, 8.

[3]   E-Delinquents and Nonutilitarian Web Site Vandalism

The 1995 movie *Hackers* starring Kiefer Sutherland was a "cyberpunk thriller" about teenage hackers outwitting government agents.[295] The movie portrayed an elite group of teenage hackers with handles like Zero Cool, Cereal Killer, and Acid Burn. A 20-year-old Northeastern University student from Nigeria was charged with hacking into NASA, the Defense Department, and a commercial Internet service. The student was charged with spraying "cybergraffiti calling for the release of fellow hackers from jail and for war against the FBI."[296]

Mail flooding or denial of service attacks frequently are motivated by non-utilitarian thrill-seeking, as is the tagging of web sites with "electronic graffiti."[297] A large number of computer-related crimes involve non-utilitarian motives such as "exhibiting technical expertise, highlighting weaknesses in computer security systems, punishment or retaliation, computer voyeurism, asserting a belief in open access to computer systems or sabotage."[298]

Electronic pranksters vandalize web sites for the fun of it. A group of hackers posted "a picture of a jolly fat man wearing nothing but a Santa hat and a smile" on a corporate site.[299] A Brazilian hacker "cracked into more than 100 Brazilian Web sites" in January 2001 to impress his girlfriend.[300] The computer hacker group called "globalHell" goes far beyond mere pranks with its public defacement of web sites.[301] It is hypothesized that many nonutilitarian computer crimes are authored by young male "e-delinquents."[302]

Denial of service attacks do not seem to be motivated by economic gain but rather by a form of cultural retreatism. Hackers that break into corporate computer networks seem primarily motivated by thrill-seeking rather than economic gain.[303] "Recreational hackers break into computer networks for the thrill of the challenge

---

[295] 18 Hackers, United Artists, released 1995, MovieWeb (visited Jan. 3, 2001), http://movieweb.com/movie/hackers.

[296] David E. Kaplan, Hacking: Ain't No Joke? U.S. News & World Report, Aug. 28, 2000 (visited Apr. 23, 2002), http://www.usnews.com/usnews/issue/000828/nycu/hackers.htm.

[297] Jose Martinez, Experts Say It's a Rush to Hack Into Some Sites, Boston Herald, Feb. 24, 2000, at 6 (describing nonutilitarian hacking by Boston area college students).

[298] Michael Hatcher et al., Computer Crimes, 36 Am. Crim. L. Rev. 397, 400 (1997).

[299] Jennifer McKee, Hackers of a Different Color, Albuquerque Journal, Feb. 11, 2001, at 1.

[300] *Id.*

[301] *See* United States Department of Justice, News Release, Computer Hacker Sentenced (visited Apr. 22, 2002), http://www.ussdoj.gov/criminal/cybercrime/gregorysen.htm (noting that the global-Hell hackers stole access devices, traded in credit cards, and maliciously disrupted computer services).

[302] A 20-year-old defendant was found guilty of hacking into NASA computers and using stolen credit card numbers in a November 2000 case. *See* United States Department of Justice, News Release: Orange County Man in Federal Custody for Hacking into Government Computers (visited Apr. 18, 2001), http://www.usdoj.gov/criminal/cybercrime/diekman2.htm.

[303] Attrition.org, Attrition Defacement Statistics (visited Apr. 28, 2002), http://www.attrition.org/mirror/attrition/stats.html.

or for bragging rights in the hacking community."[304] A 22-year-old "cracker," for example, compromised eBay's security system, causing the online auction's web site to crash and resulting in the loss of revenue.[305] In another case, a 16-year-old high school student hacked into a Massachusetts Internet Service Provider, gaining access to over 15,000 customer accounts.[306] Some of the authors of viruses, like other computer abusers, are motivated by the thrill of outwitting law enforcement authorities worldwide. Criminal law statutes do not take into account whether a hacker is motivated by thrill-seeking or financial gain.

[4]   Anti-Corporate Hacktivism

Hacktivism is a form of political activism against globalism and corporate control of the Internet.[307] Criminologist Paul Taylor observes that the targets of hacktivists are typically political messages placed upon the web sites of powerful corporations.[308] The computer hackers who developed the computer program called DeCSS that circumvents the protection system for DVDs containing motion pictures refer to their hacking as a form of "electronic civil disobedience."[309] The countercultural radicals of the late 1960s, like electronic radicals, eschewed dominant culture, positing alternative values, norms, and institutions. Counterculture radicals rejected traditional nuclear families and experimented with alternative extended family groups with communal ways of living.[310]

Electro-hippies collectives hit corporate sites with a range of electronic weapons, from viruses to e-mail bombs, which crash web sites by bombarding them with thousands of protest messages. The Swiss hactivist Virtual Monkey-wrench described the computer intrusion as hacking for a cause against the "well-oiled running of the corporate machine."[311] Hacktivists broke into the World Trade Organization's computer system during an online press conference[312] of the World Economic Forum. The political activists downloaded the phone numbers and addresses of 1,400 business and political leaders, including personal information on Bill Gates, during their concerted attack.[313] Italian hacktivists protesting the

---

[304] Eric J. Sinrod and William P. Reilly, Cyber-Crimes: A Practical Approach to the Application of Federal Computer Crime Laws, 16 Santa Clara Computer & High Tech L. J. 177 (2000).

[305] Hacker Crashes e-Bay's Web site, CNN Financial News, Mar. 22, 1999.

[306] ISP Hacked by 16-Year Old, Geek News, Mar. 22, 1999.

[307] Stuart Millar, For Hackers, Read Political Heroes of Cyberspace, The Guardian (London), Mar. 8, 2001, at 4.

[308] *Id.*

[309] Universal City Studios, Inc. v. Reimerdes, 111 F. Supp. 2d 294 (S.D.N.Y. 2000).

[310] *See generally* Charles Reich, The Greening of America (1970).

[311] *Id.*

[312] Hacktivists Motto: Oppose a Policy? Hack the System, The Economic Times (India), Feb. 9, 2001, at 1.

[313] Aoife White, Hackers Adopt Political Causes to Legitimize Their Targets, Network News, Feb. 21, 2000, at 18.

increased role of government on the Internet launched a protest attack against an Italian online share-dealing web site in April 2001.[314]

Recently, hacktivism has been extended to politically motivated viruses. A virus similar to the Kournikova strain was released along "with a message attacking Israeli security forces and calling for an end to violence in the Middle East."[315] Software applications are available for detecting unauthorized changes to web sites and restoring original content.[316]

Internet hacktivists, like the hippies and yippies of an earlier generation, are a protest movement against corporate America and technological society. The Internet rebel, for example, rejects societal definitions of what constitutes intellectual property.[317] Cultural radicals challenge the legitimacy of copyright law in favor of a counterculture value that "information should be free."[318] In November 2001 in *Universal City Studios, Inc. v. Corley*,[319] the Second Circuit affirmed a finding that enjoining publication of DeCSS did not violate the First Amendment, even though the code was considered speech, because the Digital Millennium Copyright Act prohibition affected the nonspeech aspects of the computer code.

[B] Cyberextortion

A *Wall Street Journal* reporter described the unknown and possibly unknowable dangers of Internet threats as an "eerily quiet day at the beach. [W]e're standing on the shore, wondering what the weather's going to be like, while a 300-foot tidal wave is mounting unseen at sea."[320] The unseen tidal wave represents the possible loss of marketable information products, such as software, but also proprietary information, such as customer lists, product designs, marketing plans, and other material protected by trade secrets. Malicious hackers, white-collar criminals, career criminals, members of organized gangs, and terrorists could thwart the growth of e-business. Many business executives fear that the potential Internet gold rush will suddenly veer into the Infobahn Hell of unknown or unknowable

---

[314] Cyberdigest, 13 Jane's Intelligence Review 1, Apr. 1, 2001.

[315] *Id.*

[316] CIMCOR, Stop Hackers from Tampering with Your Web Site (visited Mar. 5, 2002), http://www.cimcor.com/ct_wse.htm?source=overture (describing application called CimTrak Web Security Edition).

[317] A group of hackers posted a computer program called DeCSS that circumvented the devices that used encryption software to protect motion pictures on DVDs in Universal City Studio v. Reimerdes, 111 F. Supp. 2d 294 (S.D.N.Y. 2000). The *Reimerdes* court ruled that the motion picture studios were entitled to injunctive relief against the hackers that enjoined their posting DeCSS or linking to other sites posting the software. The court rejected the defendants' claim that the Digital Millennium Copyright Act's prohibition of anti-circumvention devices violated the First Amendment of the U.S. Constitution.

[318] *See* Gary D. Robson, Am I a Hacker? (visited Apr. 18, 2001), http://www.robson.org/gary/writing/hacker.html (articulating the hacker ethic and its belief that "information should be free").

[319] 273 F.3d 429 (2d Cir. 2001).

[320] Frederick Rose, ModaCad Aims to Bridge Gaps in Virtual Mall, Wall St. J., May 14, 1998.

cybercriminals who infiltrate corporate computer networks. Consequently, companies on the Internet must ensure that their sites are secure and that they have a comprehensive information security policy in place. Information security is to e-business what having a parachute is to skydiving. "If at first you don't succeed in e-business, so much for skydiving."[321]

A recent IBM advertisement for Internet security features two hackers who have infiltrated a computer network containing confidential executive compensation information.[322] The young woman hacker notes that the other company vice presidents would be surprised to know what one of the other vice presidents made. Her accomplice says: "They know. I just sent an e-mail to everyone in the company." Advertisements similar to this one use fear to sell information security software. The fear is that a company will lose its trade secrets and valuable proprietary information at the click of the mouse.

[C] Computer Crimes

As mentioned earlier, an empirical study of Internet security found that nearly 70 percent of surveyed companies had experienced at least one episode of information theft,[323] and half of the responding companies reported at least one theft of property of $10,000 or more.[324] Trusted company employees, both consultants and insiders, committed nearly one in five of these crimes.[325] SPC may build technological solutions, such as firewalls, to help keep external threats at bay, but it must not fail to monitor internal threats, such as the violation of SPC company security policies. The enemy within poses the most serious risk management problem for SPC. "Financial losses from unauthorized insider access are 30 times greater than from system penetrations."[326]

The rise of e-business as a significant sector of our economy is likely to attract organized criminals, as well, and to keep white-collar criminals interested. Donn Parker describes how one enterprising information security expert absconded with $10.2 million in a funds-transfer fraud from a bank at which he had served as a security system analyst and consultant.[327] Some cybercriminals break into computers for the same reason Willie Sutton robbed banks: "That's where the money is." Carnegie Mellon University researchers found a statistical

---

[321] I attribute this quotation to Victor O'Reilly, Games of the Hangman (1992).

[322] Hackers generally have a negative reputation. The term *hacker,* however, at first designated someone who was a computer virtuoso. At MIT in the 1960s, a hacker was merely someone who could design innovative ways around difficult problems. Wade Rousch, Hackers: Taking a Byte Out of Computer Crime, Technical Review, Apr. 1995, at 32.

[323] *Id.* at 183-84 (reporting survey of COMEEC BBS).

[324] *Id.* at 184.

[325] *Id.*

[326] Consul Risk Management, Inc., Your Greatest Security Threat, an advertisement in SC Magazine, Mar. 1999, at 26 (citing 1998 CSI/FBI Computer Crime and Security Survey).

[327] Donn B. Parker, Fighting Computer Crime: A New Framework for Protecting Information 19 (1998).

association between intrusions into Internet hosts and the monthly increase in Internet connections.[328]

The escalation of computer crime and its damage to confidence in Internet commerce have not been lost on the U.S. government. In mid-2000, Senator Kay Bailey Hutchison (R-Texas) proposed new legislation that would double the five-year penalty for "fraud or related activity in connection with computers."[329] This new revision to Title 18 of the U.S. criminal code would also double sentences for second offenses to 20 years and establish a "National Commission on Cybersecurity."[330] The executive branch of the U.S. government has also begun efforts to combat cybercrime. Both legislative and executive efforts, however, will likely stop short of full-scale Internet regulation. While the executive branch has called for increased expenditures for protecting the critical infrastructure, Department of Commerce Secretary William Daley quickly pointed out that "this is not about the [U.S.] government regulating this."[331]

[D]   Distributed Denial of Service (DDoS) Attacks

Traditional denial of service (DoS) attacks cause the crash of a "computer or network by overloading it with a large amount of network traffic using TCP, UDP (User Datagram Protocol), or ICMP (Internet Control Message Protocol) data packets."[332] The distributed denial of service attack overwhelms the computer system by increasing the density of packets at a server. Police in the United Kingdom and the FBI are investigating reports that an American spam e-mailer highjacked the domain name of UK firms to send spam.[333] It is often difficult to prove that competitors launched denial of service attacks to gain an unfair competitive advantage. In March 2002, the Kazaa.com web site sustained a severe denial of service attack that prevented users from accessing the site or downloading software for about five hours. "The Kazaa.com Web site was being bombarded by hundreds of thousands of HTTP (hypertext transfer protocol) requests, and our HTTP logs indicate that these requests were referred by the (Morpheus) ad server."[334]

---

[328] April Streeter, Don't Get Burned by the Internet, LAN Times, Feb. 13, 1995, at 58.

[329] Robert MacMillon, Sen. Hutchinson Seeks to Double Hacker Sentences, Newsbytes (visited Feb. 21, 2000), http://www.newsbytes.com/pubNews/00/143996.html.

[330] Id.

[331] Micheal Perine, White House Cybersummit Yields Pledge of Cooperation, The Standard (visited Apr. 26, 2002), http://thestandard.com/article/display/0,1151,10428,00.html.

[332] Why Distributed Denial of Service Attacks Are Hacker Tools of the Trade, Ins. Day, Jan. 16, 2002 (describing how distributed DoS attacks use "an array of compromised systems to launch a distributed flood attack against a single target, which is accomplished by loading software on compromised machines located on different corporate or public institution networks").

[333] Lisa Kelly, Spam Scam Wreaks Havoc, VNU NET, Mar. 11, 2002, at 4.

[334] Steven Bonisteel, Kazaa Says Servers "Attacked," Denies Role in Morpheus Roles, Newsbytes (Mar. 5, 2002), http://www.newsbytes.com/news/02/174963.html.

Denial of service attacks take diverse forms, including buffer overflows, SYN flooding, directed broadcast attacks, Ping of Death, teardrop, and UDP flooding attacks.[335] Buffer flow attacks prey on the capacity of the memory of the server to respond to incoming packets. The buffer overflow attack crowds out legitimate requests for service with a flood of ersatz requests.[336] Recently there has been a steady stream of attacks on DNS name services using TCP SYN flooding.[337] SYN flooding results from a soft spot in TCP/IP connections between clients and servers.

The TCP/IP suite allocates a socket for a connection by sending a message to the client "advising it that the socket is ready to establish the connection."[338] The client then responds to the message from the server by sending a final message confirming it synchronized with the server.[339] The problem occurs when the server continues "to hold the socket open, waiting for the establishment of the connection. If a client sends a flood of unresolved connections, legitimate requests will also be turned down."[340] Computer systems need "mitigation settings specifically against, SYN flooding, IP spoofing, and port scans."[341]

The directed broadcast attack (DDoS), like the SYN attack, uses address spoofing as the instrumentality for its attack. The DDos attacker will use a Smurf tool or similar device to send repeated

> echo requests to the directed broadcast address of a victim network. By using the directed broadcast address, the attacker's ICMP packets are routed across the Internet to the victim's network. Once in the target network, most IP stacks respond to a broadcast address by replying. In the Smurf attack, the computers in the victim network send ICMP echo replies back to the source (which is the other victim, as the source address used was spoofed).[342]

The directed broadcast attack, like the SYN flood, overwhelms the computer network. Firewalls need to be configured to block directed broadcasts.[343] The attacks that crippled the leading Internet sites in February 2000 were attributed to "dis-

---

[335] Kevin J. Connolly, Law of Internet Security and Privacy, 44-51 (2001) (describing the necessity of protecting computer networks "from attacks such as SYN Flood, ICMP Flood, UDP Flood, Tear Drop Attack, Smurf Attack, Ping of Death, Fraggle, IP Spoofing, Port Scanning, IP Source Route Attack, Address Sweeping, LAND and WinNuke"); *see also* ServGate Technologies Adds Web Caching and DoS Attack Protection to Its SG200 and SG300 Security Gateways, PR News, Feb. 19, 2002.

[336] Connolly, *supra* note 335, at 45.

[337] Geoff Huston, It's a Trust Thing, Satellite Broadband, Dec. 2001.

[338] David Ludlow, Technology: First Line of Defense, Network News, Feb. 27, 2002, at 1.

[339] Connolly, *supra* note 335, at 46.

[340] *Id.* at 46-47.

[341] *Id.*

[342] Rik Farrow, Network Defense: Internet Security: Trouble in the Stock; Denial of Service, an Internet-based Attack, Network, May 1, 1998.

[343] *Id.*

tributed Smurfing attacks."[344] One difficulty of staving off Smurf attacks is that the system to be reconfigured is the one that is exploited to originate the attack.[345]

The Ping of Death draws its name from an Internet utility known as PING "that tests whether a host machine is 'live' and 'reachable.' "[346] Ping flood vulnerabilities permit attackers to shut down computer systems by transmitting a large number of data packets to them.[347] "Macs were vulnerable, however, to the so-called Ping of Death attacks that crashed all kinds of operating systems a few years ago."[348] The teardrop attack is similar to the Ping of Death in that it exploits the target computer's attempts to assemble the transmittal of ICMP fragments.[349] Finally, UDP flooding exploits a soft spot in the User Datagram Protocol. UDP flooding preys on two systems, "the first of which it hit with requests for the character generation (chargen) service."[350] The requests are then spoofed with the address of the target system, "so that the first system sends the stream of characters it generates to that second, targeted system."[351] Enterprise firewalls configured to deflect each of these attacks should be implemented.

Even though the February 2000 DDoS attacks gained headlines because of the large e-commerce companies whose businesses ground to a halt, the real hack victims went largely unnoticed.[352] DDoS attacks occur when Internet sites are flooded with so much traffic that legitimate users cannot gain access.[353] To conceal the source of the attack, hackers may break into and launch their attacks from corporate, small business, or educational computers,[354] using Trojan horse programs or distributed denial of service (DDoS) agents. Simon Perry, the director of security at Computer Associates International (CA), described the three characteristics of computers most vulnerable for use in cyberattacks: "They are turned on all of the time and connected to the Internet; they have high bandwidth access; and they are located at places like universities, small businesses, and increasingly in homes with Digital Subscriber Lines (DSL) or cable modem services."[355]

The battle against DDoS attacks must be fought on two fronts. First, the web site must be protected from facial DOS attacks. Second, the internal computer infrastructure must be protected against being used as a pawn in the hacker's plan. CA's InnoculateIt and eTrust Intrusion detection products can help to detect DDoS

---

[344] Connolly, *supra* note 335, at 48.

[345] *Id.* at 49.

[346] *Id.*

[347] News Briefs: Patch Issues for BlackIce Firewall Hole, Computerworld, Feb. 18, 2002, at 14.

[348] J. D. Biersdorfer, Protecting the Macintosh: A Lesser-Known Victim, N.Y. Times, Dec. 27, 2001, at 5.

[349] Connolly, *supra* note 335, at 50.

[350] *Id.*

[351] *Id.* at 50-51.

[352] Nancy Weil, Real Denial-of-Service Hack Victims Weren't Web Sites, Computerworld (visited Apr. 26, 2002), http://computerworld.com/home/print.nsf/all/00211E986.

[353] *Id.*

[354] *Id.*

[355] *Id.*

programs such as Trinoo, Tribal Flood, and tntf2k.[356] The FBI's National Infrastructure Protection Center (NIPC) has also released a program for scanning for DDoS programs running on Linux or Solaris servers.[357] Cisco, Inc. markets an intrusion detection system that attempts to prevent and react to detected unauthorized activity in the network.[358] Although firewalls are generally used to block unauthorized traffic from flooding networks in DOS attacks, IDSs are often placed inside the network to assist in protecting against the second threat. Since IDSs can monitor both incoming and outgoing packets, they provide protection against hackers who have successfully gained unauthorized access, as well as internal against threats from "trusted" sources.

[E] Computer Viruses

The number of computer viruses "grew in 2001, and will continue to do so moving into the foreseeable future. Corporations, in fact, were hit with a monthly average of 113 virus infections for every 1,000 computers they owned in 2001, according to the seventh annual survey of virus prevalence in the enterprise conducted by ICSA Labs, a division of security services firm TruSecure."[359] Damages caused by viruses cost U.S. businesses $7 billion in the first half of 1999.[360] Of the survey respondents, 43 percent had experienced at least one virus disaster, defined as infection of 25 or more personal computers or of a server.[361] One in four respondents had experienced infections caused by outside diskettes brought into the workplace.[362] Two out of three virus disasters "were caused by macro viruses infecting Microsoft Word and Excel files."[363] A few respondents took up to 1,000 hours to recover following a virus disaster. The median response was that recovery took five person-days.

The U.S. media warned the country about the destructive virus Chernobyl, which was set to strike on April 26, 1999, the anniversary of the Russian nuclear disaster. Chernobyl disabled computers in Hong Kong, and despite the warnings, it also infected computers in the United States. The Computer Emergency Response Team (CERT) tracks viruses such as Chernobyl much as the U.S.

---

[356] CA, CA's InoculateIT and eTrust Solutions Protect e-Businesses against Windows Zombie Attacks (visited Apr. 26, 2002), http://www.cai.com/press/2000/02/etrust_zombie.htm.

[357] NIPC, National Infrastructure Protection Center Information; Trinoo/Tribal Flood Net (visited Feb. 21, 2000), http://www.fbi.gov/nipc/trinoo.htm.

[358] Cisco Intrusion Detection, Products and Technologies (visited Apr. 7, 2002), http://www.cisco.com/warp/public/cc/pd/sqsw/sqidsz/.

[359] Sam Costello, Virus Problem Expanded in 2001, Continued Growth Expected, InfoWorld Daily News, Mar. 7, 2002.

[360] Aidan Turnbull, Don't Let the Hackers Beat Your Bank Security, Shore to Shore, Winter 1999/2000, at 27 (quoting Michael Vatis, FBI's National Infrastructure Protection Center).

[361] *Id.*

[362] *Id.*

[363] *Id.*

Weather Service tracks hurricanes. Many viruses, like hurricanes, have first names, for example, the virus Melissa, which crippled corporate servers around the world on March 26, 1999. Melissa exploited an e-mail program, Microsoft Outlook, and Microsoft Word. "CERT reported that at least 300 organizations and 100,000 machines were affected" by the Melissa virus.[364] "Virus-planting pirates" are continually creating new viruses.[365] A recent corporate survey concluded, "Melissa was more than 38 times more frequent as the cause of virus disasters" and caused greater server down-time than any other virus.[366] The Melissa virus of March 1999 caused $80 million damages to computers worldwide, affecting 1.2 million computers in 1 out of 5 American businesses.[367] Federal prosecutors reached a plea agreement with David Smith, the author of the Melissa virus, after he was charged with violating the Computer Fraud and Abuse Act.[368] Bubble Boy "is the first e-mail virus that could activate by simply being read or previewed in a computer user's Microsoft Outlook or Outlook Express e-mail program."[369]

Many viruses masquerade as useful programs. Trojan horses received their name from the Trojan horse in Homer's *Iliad*, delivered by the Greeks to the gates of the city of Troy.[370] One type of Trojan horse, for example, is "a program that is advertised as something desirable, but is actually something undesirable." The group calling itself Cult of the Dead Cow wrote one of the most infamous Trojan horse programs, Back Orifice. Back Orifice would invade a system through a benign program, such as an animated greeting card attachment. After the user ran the benign program, Back Orifice would copy itself to the computer's hard driver.[371] Back Orifice would then log computer activity and open a back door for malicious users to usurp control of the system and read confidential information.[372]

The prosecution of the creators of computer viruses has been stymied by the failure of many nations to have adequate criminal statutes. The Philippines had no statute to charge the author of the ILOVEYOU virus. The prosecutors dismissed all charges "due to a lack of evidence and a lack of a specific law criminalizing

---

[364] Steven Levy, Biting Back at the Wily Melissa, Newsweek, Apr. 12, 1999, at 62.

[365] *Id.*

[366] Michael E. Kabay et. al., Fifth Annual ICSA Survey, Anti-Virus Prevalence Survey (1999) (visited Apr. 26, 2002), http://www.icsa.net.

[367] Keith Bowers and Iolande Bloxsom, CIH "Chernobyl" Set to Detonate, ZDTV, Apr. 26, 1999 (visited Apr. 26, 2002), http://web-e6.zdnet.com/zdtv/cybercrime/viruswatch/story/0,3700,2246676,00.html.

[368] United States Department of Justice, The Melissa Virus (visited Apr. 28, 2002), http://www.usdoj.gov/criminal/cybercrime/ccpolicy.html.

[369] Carlene Hempel, Anatomy of a Virus (visited Apr. 26, 2002), http://www.techserver.com/noframes.

[370] VWA Glossary, Trojan Horse (visited Apr. 26, 2002), http://members.aol.com/mmxbytes/glossary.htm.

[371] NW Internet, The Back Orifice Backdoor Program (visited Apr. 26, 2002), http://www.nwinternet.com/~pchelp/bo/bo.html.

[372] *Id.*

computer hacking."[373] The United States has not fared much better. The first successful criminal prosecution of the creator of a computer virus did not occur until 1991.[374] To date, there have been only a handful of computer virus cases nationwide. Few cybercrime cases in any substantive field other than online pornography have been successfully prosecuted.[375]

Cyberspace criminals have also constructed viruses that permit the introduction of destructive code into computer systems. Electronic mail attachments were used to transmit the virus known as Chernobyl, which struck hard drives on machines running Microsoft Windows 95 and 98.[376] The Melissa virus also struck through e-mail attachments.[377] Many other documented cases demonstrate the misuse of legitimate protocol for destructive purposes.[378]

SPC's systems administrators should perform periodic spot checks for viruses using antivirus software. Further, before a visitor is allowed to download anything from SPC's web site, he or she should be warned (using a pop-up window) about the risks involved and the necessity of running antiviral software on all files downloaded from the site. SPC's antivirus software should be updated often, as new viruses are spread almost daily. Already, experts have found "more than 45,000 known viruses, and many new and altered viruses [are] discovered every day."[379] In the rapidly changing Internet, some risks will continue to be unknown and unknowable. Yet many Internet security risks *are* known and knowable. Only the risk of known viruses can be reduced by state-of-the art antivirus programs, hence the need for continual updating. The risk of property damage from a newly developed virus cannot be eliminated entirely.

---

[373] Miguel Deutch, Computer Legislation: Israel's New Codified Approach, 14 J. Marshall J. Computer & Info. L. 461 (2001) (describing new Israeli criminal statute that penalizes introducing or transferring computer viruses and making it a crime to launch a viral attack even if there is no documented damage).

[374] Bradley S. Davis, It's Virus Season Again, Has Your Computer Been Vaccinated? A Survey of Computer Crime Legislation as a Response to Malevolent Software, 72 Wash. U. L. Q. 411 (2001) (describing case in which malevolent software was introduced into a company computer by an ex-employee who gained access by using his revoked password and security clearance).

[375] Ralph Clifford found that the term *cybercrime* had not yet been used in a state or federal case as of February 10, 2001. Ralph D. Clifford, Cybercrime: The Investigation, Prosecution and Defense of a Computer-Related Crime 1 n.1 (2001).

[376] Keith Bowers and Iolande Bloxsom, CIH "Chernobyl" Set to Detonate, ZDTV, Apr. 26, 1999 (visited Apr. 26, 2002), http://web-e6.zdnet.com/zdtv/cybercrime/viruswatch/story/0,3700,2246676,00.html.

[377] *Id.* (noting that the Melissa virus caused an Internet traffic slowdown, whereas the CIH "Chernobyl" destroyed data by disabling flash bios).

[378] The Internet depends on standardized protocol to permit millions of host computers to communicate across diverse cultures and diverse programming languages. Examples of protocols are those rules developed by the International Organization for Standardization (ISO) and the standard ASCII character set for transmitting data. The misuse of protocols can result in widespread destruction not previously possible in the prehistory of the Internet.

[379] "Now there are around 45,000 known viruses. This time last year there were 25,000." Mark Ward, "Cornered: Virus Alert Over New Years Day," The Daily Telegraph (England), Dec. 23, 1999, at 2.

[F] Virus-Worm Hybrids

A computer worm's sole purpose is to self-reproduce; it differs from a virus mainly in that the worm has no attack phase.[380] The worm uses valuable system resources but does not exploit the infected system as a virus would, by deleting files, changing data, writing over existing files, and so on.[381] Recent worms and viruses, however, have combined the characteristics of the classic infections, causing concern that the next wave of infections will be hybrids that propagate faster and cause greater harm.[382] The Nimda worm that began infecting systems in September 2001 is an example of this new hybrid infection. Combining the characteristics of standard worms and viruses, Nimda had advanced propagation and a harmful attack phase that exploited bugs in system software to damage files and create vulnerabilities on the infected system.[383] Unlike either a standard worm or virus, Nimda had four methods of infection, one of which would infect a machine that happened to browse the web site of a previously infected machine.[384] Simply by clicking on a link to a web page, a user could infect his or her machine and the entire corporate network.[385] The risk of damage increases with these hybrids, and it becomes increasingly crucial for companies to maintain the policies, procedures, and education levels that will protect their networks from these vulnerabilities.

[G] Integrity of Data

SPC has also made the decision to maintain an internal network, or intranet, not connected to the Internet, to help counter some of the potential problems of insecure data transfers. SPC's intranet is located behind the company's firewall and is dedicated to performing internal transactions. SPC has also established an extranet to handle transactions between vendors and other trusted suppliers. Isolating transactions with intranets and extranets will help prevent external wrongdoers from using network analysis tools to snatch passwords, credit card numbers, and other information.

Originally developed by Network General and now sold by Network Associates,[386] Sniffer was the first network capture and analysis tool. It became so popular that all similar tools became known as "sniffers." SPC's security precautions

---

[380] Worms, Virus Tutorial (visited Apr. 7, 2002), http://www.cknow.com/vtutor/vtworms.htm.

[381] Virus Behavior, Virus Tutorial (visited Apr. 7, 2002), http://www.cknow.com/vtutor/vtbehave.htm.

[382] Edward Hurley, Nimda: Setting a Sinister Standard?, Win2000 News & Analysis (Apr. 7, 2002), http://searchwin2000.techtarget.com/originalContent/0,289142,sid1_gci772655,00.html.

[383] The SANS Institute, Nimda Worm Virus Report (Apr. 7, 2002), http://www.incidents.org/react/nimda.pdf.

[384] Id.

[385] Id.

[386] Network Associates, Inc., Sniffer Total Network Visibility (visited Apr. 11, 2002), http://www.sniffer.com/asp_set/products/tnv/intro.asp.

need to be calibrated to guard against the theft of proprietary and confidential information.

[H]   Protection Against Impostors

Forgers, impostors, and other wrongdoers specialize in altering data. A payment order, for example, may be altered or compromised by adding extra zeros or changing the name or address of the beneficiary. The security administrator needs object and subject-oriented authentication and access controls to protect data integrity. Object authentication will authorize a user to use a specific component of the information system, such as a parcel of data or a specific server; it allows companies to define who can use an object and how that object can be used.[387] Subject authentication authorizes an individual to use an application system or set of resources; it is typically implemented by a username/password combination.

[I]   Natural Disasters

One in ten companies have a comprehensive contingency plan for recovering their computer system in the event of a natural disaster.[388] Most data losses occur due to system malfunction, but they can also result from natural disasters, such as hurricanes or earthquakes.[389] A disaster contingency plan should establish a contact person within the company who will be responsible for coordinating emergency responses to disaster. Well-constructed contingency plans will also include provisions for the off-site backup of data, continuity of business, and computer restart procedures.

SPC needs a comprehensive system of Internet security to communicate securely over the Internet. Information security is only as good as its implementation. Scott Adams' "Dilbert" describes how a company purchased laptop computers for their employees to use while traveling—then the chief information officer permanently attached the laptops to the employees' desks to prevent theft.[390] SPC's chief information officer must tailor the security policy to the organization's culture. A growing number of companies are finding it more cost effective to outsource the building of an information infrastructure, such as a private network. Genuity, Sprint, and AT&T all offer services that provide Virtual Private Networks to businesses and individuals seeking to outsource this aspect of their security solution.[391]

Many ISPs now offer VPN services to their customers. The World Wide Web version of *InternetWeek* magazine dedicates a section of its web site to tracking the

---

[387] Object Level Security (visited Apr. 26, 2002), http://as400.rochester.ibm.com/tstudio/ca400/odbobj.htm.

[388] Jo Faragher, Special Report Disaster Recovery, Dealing with Disaster, Global Tech. Bus., June 1999, at 37.

[389] *Id.*

[390] Scott Adams, Dilbert Principles 11 (1996).

[391] Tim Greene, VPN Service Providers, Network World (visited Mar. 7, 2002), http://www.nwfusion.com/research/2000/0814featsideone.html.

VPN industry.[392] The site includes information on hardware vendors, service providers, and other news about the VPN industry. Whether Internet security is designed in-house or is outsourced, a company must take an active role in implementing effective security. No magic silver bullet exists for solving Internet security issues.[393] No technological fix can, for example, prevent employees from stealing trade secrets.

A comprehensive security policy supplements a technological infrastructure with employee hiring, training, and education procedures. Before rolling out a web site, an online business needs to develop policies and practices to protect the integrity and confidentiality of information assets. As one security expert notes: "You cannot secure what you don't understand."[394] The online company needs to implement, test, fix, and again test its security.[395]

[J]   Social Engineering Hazards

Social engineering refers to the use of deception or artifice to gain illicit access to computers. SPC may have the most sophisticated firewalls available, but it will still be infiltrated by a cybercriminal able to convince a low-level SPC employee that he is a computer or telephone repairman. Well-organized criminals have been able to gain unauthorized access to the computer system at the San Diego Supercomputer Center, compromising programs belonging to Tsutomu Shimomura and to the center itself.[396] Increasingly, companies are testing their systems by hiring hacker-gurus to attempt to break down ISP security measures.

Since confidential information is increasingly transmitted on the Internet, business executives must ask the critical question: Just how secure is the World Wide Web? An SPC telecommuter, for example, may give his child a company computer password. The SPC employee's child may in turn give the password to his entire online buddy list, which may result in an unknown third party gaining illicit access to SPC's trade secrets and other computer information. Comprehensive technological security solutions will likely fail without proper employee training. The social engineering aspects of firewalls and other information technologies cannot be ignored in the search for comprehensive information security.[397]

---

[392] InternetWeek Online, VPN Source Page (visited Apr. 28, 2002), http://www.internetwk.com/VPN/default.html.

[393] Evan I. Schwartz, Digital Darwinism: Strategies for Surviving in the Cutthroat Web Economy 5 (1999) (noting the tendency of the business community to seek magic bullet solutions to the problems of e-business).

[394] Bruce Schneier, "A Plea for Simplicity: You Can't Secure What You Don't Understand" (visited Apr. 26, 2002), http://www.infosecurity.mag.com.

[395] Id.

[396] Id.

[397] Firewalls serve as gatekeeper between company computers and the Internet. The purpose of a firewall is to prevent intruders from accessing SPC's computers. A knowledgeable insider may, however, bypass a seemingly bulletproof firewall.

[K] Privacy and the Corporate Criminal

In a world of hackers, crackers, careless employees, and corporate espionage agents, it can be difficult to stay on top of computer security. Forgetting about any potential security breach may expose a business to incredible losses both tangible and intangible. Even faced with this degree of risk, many companies remain negligent in providing proper security. Yet even the most diligent company often forgets one very important protection—protection against its own actions.

Long before the Internet was opened to commerce and our vocabulary enriched with words such as e-business, deep linking, and cyberspace, businesses knew the value of information. Information was harvested and fed into computer systems to quickly determine new competitive advantages and potential market entry points. The Internet has merely expanded the reach of companies into the homes and lives of billions of potential consumers. With this new channel of information, new problems are born. How much can a company do with the information it gathers? How much information can they require from consumers? What are the ethical limits in the use of information? What are the contractual rights of each party when collecting and disseminating consumer information?

The world of legislation and policy around consumer privacy continues to evolve. The Electronic Privacy Information Center (EPIC) catalogues many of the current initiatives that shape this movement.[398] Recently, the FTC has become more active and has begun to investigate such heralded e-commerce giants as DoubleClick, eBay, eToys, and Amazon.com.[399] EPIC has filed suit against DoubleClick for "unfair and deceptive industry practices."[400] The complaint against DoubleClick alleges that consumers do not know that their web behavior is being tracked, and in response, DoubleClick has changed its privacy policies over the last two years.[401] Perhaps the largest concern was the merger of DoubleClick's data acquisition mechanisms with the tracking capability of Abacus Direct, one of the nation's largest catalog shopping database firms.[402]

The FTC ended the DoubleClick investigation, concluding that the company never used personally identifying information in any way that breached the privacy policy.[403]

The DMA, the oldest and largest trade association for users and suppliers in the direct, database and interactive marketing field,[404] has taken steps to help its

---

[398] *See generally* EPIC, EPIC Archive (visited Apr. 24, 2002), http://www.epic.org/security.

[399] Patricia Jacobus, FTC Investigates DoubleClick's Data-Collection Practices, CNET News.com (visited Apr. 21, 2002), http://news.cnet.com/news/0-1005-200-1551521.html.

[400] *Id.*

[401] *Id.*

[402] *Id.*

[403] FTC Ends Investigation of DoubleClick, Previous Top News (visited Mar. 14, 2002), http://www.epic.org/news/#2000.

[404] The DMA, Privacy—Privacy Promise (visited Apr. 26, 2002), http://www.the-dma.org/library/privacy/privacypromise.shtml.

members regulate policies regarding consumer privacy.[405] In October 1997, the DMA issued a privacy promise assuring that all of its member organizations would comply with a set of rules regarding the collection and use of consumer data.[406] The DMA promise contains four provisions:

1. Provide customers with notice of their ability to opt out of information exchanges;
2. Honor customer opt-out requests that their contact information not be transferred to others for marketing purposes;
3. Accept and maintain consumer requests to be placed on an in-house suppress file to stop receiving solicitations from the member company; and
4. Use the DMA Preference Service suppression files, currently available for mail and telephone lists and soon to be available for e-mail lists.[407]

The details of each provision may be seen at the DMA's web site.[408]

Although company security administrators will not want to thwart the decisions of management or counsel, they should make sure that information exchanges among departments conform to corporate guidelines. Furthermore, SAs must evaluate the possible impact on corporate security whenever any new data management resource is introduced into the infrastructure.

There are new privacy policy laws in place that regulate the collection, use, and sale of personal information about customers. Corporations need to be informed of these regulations and maintain privacy policies that comply with the regulations. For companies deemed to be financial institutions, the Gramm-Leach-Bliley (GLB) Act of 2000 requires that the institutions provide customers with annual notices regarding the company's privacy policy that explain how the customer information is collected and shared and provide a method for customers to opt out of the information collection and sharing process.[409]

In December 2000, the U.S. Department of Health and Human Services implemented the privacy provisions of the Health Insurance Portability and Accountability Act of 1996 (HIPAA). Under this Act, health plans, health care providers, and health care clearinghouses and the third parties they work with must inform individuals that they intend to use or disclose protected health information for marketing or fund-raising purposes.[410] Companies that qualify must comply by April 14, 2003.[411] Compliance means providing both consent and

---

[405] Id.

[406] Id.

[407] Id.

[408] See id.

[409] Direct Markting Ass'n, What Must a Gramm-Leach-Bliley Privacy Policy Notice Include? DMA Privacy Policy Generator (visited Mar. 11, 2002), http://www.the-dma.org/cgi/registered/privacy/glbppg.shtml#requirements.

[410] Direct Markting Ass'n, Frequently Asked Questions, The Privacy Provisions of the Health Insurance Portability and Accountability Act (HIPAA) (visited Mar. 11, 2002), http://www.thedma.org/government/hipaafaqs.shtml#I1.

[411] Id.

authorization forms to the individual whose personally identifiable information is at risk.[412]

The DMA also provides companies with a web site that generates a personalized privacy policy for the company. A company representative would go to http://www.thedma.org/glb/createprivacy.shtml and fill in the online questionnaire; DMA will then send him or her a policy via e-mail shortly afterward. If the policy satisfies the elements in the questionnaire, the policy will be GLB compliant. Even if our hypothetical company, SPC, does not believe that it works in the financial or health industries, it should research its compliance with this policies if it works with other companies in those industries, since it may be considered a third-party entity that must comply with these acts. SPC should develop workplace privacy policies to explicitly describe its rights and the rights of employees using SPC equipment.

In *United States v. Slanina*,[413] the Fifth Circuit stated that unless there is a computer use policy to the contrary, a municipal employee has a constitutionally protected privacy interest in materials stored on his or her office computer. In *United States v. Angevine*,[414] the Tenth Circuit held that, given the privacy policies disseminated by the university, an Oklahoma State University professor had no expectation of privacy. In *Bourke v. Nissan Motor Corp.*[415] a California court held that employees had no expectation of privacy regarding stored e-mail, since the corporation had explicitly informed employees of the privacy policies in place. Even though SPC is a private, nongovernmental organization, unlike the entities in *Slanina* or *Angevine*, having a workplace privacy policy is critical so that it is clear to employees what expectations they should have regarding privacy and what rights SPC intends to reserve and enforce.

§ 3.04   IMPLEMENTING INFORMATION SECURITY SYSTEMS

The security risks of a business connecting to the Internet are not merely anecdotal horror stories. Real companies' computer networks may have holes in their electronic-mail systems that permit network break-ins.[416] Companies that have implemented off-the-shelf e-mail and other Internet applications without having a security plan may be at greater risk since they do not even consider them-

---

[412] *Id.*

[413] 2002 WL 247141 (5th Cir. 2001) (holding that the defendant had a reasonable expectation of privacy but that the search was reasonable).

[414] 281 F.3d 1130 (10th Cir. 2002) (holding that professor did not have reasonable expectation of privacy regarding university computer).

[415] 1 ILR (P&F) 109 (Cal. Ct. App. 1993) (holding that employees did not have reasonable expectation of privacy).

[416] Patrick Thibodeau, Security Experts Warn of Christmas Day Hack Attacks, ComputerWorld, Dec. 16, 1996, at 1.

selves vulnerable to attack.[417] Many mass-marketed network security products take a "one size fits all" approach to the problems of the Bad Network.[418] They make great claims, as well. One new security product was described as being close to "bullet proof."[419] Other information security products are represented as being "hacker-proof."[420] One marketing director stated that his company had comprehensive solutions "to provide hacker-proof security across any network."[421]

SPC's systems administrator needs to probe for unauthorized devices, such as modems connected to user PCs.[422] CERT also recommends that the systems administrator conduct daily audits for anomalies or unauthorized devices. SPC's systems administrator should conduct a monthly inspection of the computer system to search for any other anomalies.[423] Companies need a contingency plan in the event of a disaster, a hacker attack, or any other security problem. Disaster recovery, emergency preparedness, and backup facilities are critical to retrieving any data lost during a computer outage and are vital for all companies.[424]

[A] Emergency Response to Data Disasters

SPC needs to discover as quickly as possible the name of the ISP through which the hacker attack is made and should keep on hand as many ISP emergency telephone numbers as it can. If a hacker infiltrates SPC's web site using AOL or MSN, for example, the ISP will typically be able to provide records useful in investigating and dealing with the breach. The faster SPC acts after an attack, the greater the probability that the intruder will be detected. Some hackers, however, use anonymous services to conceal their identities, or commit their attacks using another person's identity. Law enforcement agencies profile hackers based upon the methods used to compromise the target site and the type of damage done to the target computer system.

---

[417] A large number of network security products exist to provide firewalls, antivirus checks, and plug-ins for Internet security. Terrisa Systems, for example, sells plug-ins for Internet security, as do Symantec and Norton, which both specialize in plug-ins for detecting and disinfecting computer systems affected by viruses and other malicious codes.

[418] *See* Anne Knowles, UUNET Suite Tightens Security: System Offers Firewall, Encryption for Virtual Private Networks, PC Week, May 29, 1995, at 14; Erica Roberts, Network Systems to Secure Hubs, Routers, Comm. Wk., Feb. 20, 1995, at 1.

[419] Network Systems, Network Systems Offers Public, Private Network Data Security, Network Management Systems & Strategies, Nov. 15, 1994, at 1043.

[420] Roberts, *supra* note 418 (statement of Tom Gilbert, marketing director at Network Systems Corp).

[421] *Id.*

[422] Modem banks, a key part of the information infrastructure of many businesses, are not the problem. The problem is unauthorized modems that can provide wrongdoers with access to company computers.

[423] *See generally* Carnegie-Mellon Computer Emergency Response Team (CERT) Advisories at www.cert.org.

[424] Two kinds of companies are doing e-business today: companies who *have* experienced computer failure due to viruses, hacking, or natural disasters, and companies who *will* experience such a computer disaster.

[B]   Qualified Webmasters[425]

SPC's webmaster needs to monitor its web site, especially because SPC has a substantial computer network. The webmaster needs to be a dedicated position or the likes of a systems administrator. The webmaster will have root, or superuser, access to the computers that comprise the Internet infrastructure. Each server should generate log files recording the Internet address of each visitor to the site. A special administrative computer may be configured that consolidates the log files from each SPC web server and application computer. This administrative computer may also contain defensive programs that generate statistics from the log files and monitor specific attacks against the SPC web site. SPC's webmaster must examine log files to determine potential intruders and to promptly uncover security risks.

[C]   Allocating Security Risks

The use of indemnification agreements, hold harmless clauses, and other contractual devices may limit the online company's exposure for liability claims arising out of information security incidents. A webwrap "click through" agreement, in which visitors click an "I accept" or "I decline" icon before entering the web site, may be used to limit security claims from web site visitors.

The webwrap agreement is the e-business equivalent of a contract. A vendor or licensor of a product or service will display an information screen containing the terms of the license or agreement. The consumer will be asked to assent to the terms of the agreement before completing the sale, entering into the license agreement, or using the service. This agreement forms the basis of an offer and indicates acceptance of the contract terms. Unfortunately, the matter may not always be resolved so simply. Serious questions may arise over whether the consumer actually understood the terms of the agreement sufficiently well to bind both parties.

As of the fall of 2002, webwrap agreements had not undergone significant litigation; their predecessors, however, the software shrinkwrap agreements, have progressed through the court with mixed results.[426] Software shrinkwrap agreements generally accompany a program's installation disk, and they are most often found on the media envelope inside a sealed package.[427] Early court decisions were very conservative and reluctant to restrict parties to terms they had not been aware of when forming the initial contract.[428] More recent holdings have liberalized this attitude, holding shrinkwrap agreements to be more binding than had previously been held.[429]

---

[425] Vincent J. Froio, Jr., a former computer systems administrator, contributed to this section.

[426] For a complete discussion of shrinkwrap and webwrap agreements, *see* § 6.03[A][2].

[427] *See* Brian Covotta and Pamela Sergeeff, Intellectual Property: A Copyright: 1. Preemption: (b) Contract Enforceability: ProCD, Inc. v. Zeidenberg, 13 Berkeley Tech. L.J. 35 (1998).

[428] *Id. See also* Step-Saver Data Systems, Inc. v. Wyse Tech., 939 F.2d 91 (3d Cir. 1991).

[429] *Id.* Discussing a comparison between Step-Saver, 939 F.2d at 104 (shrinkwrap licenses found invalid by Third Circuit), with ProCD II, 86 F.3d at 1447 (shrinkwraps deemed enforceable contracts by Seventh Circuit).

Both webwrap and shrinkwrap agreements are used to limit liability beyond the standard protection offered by copyright law or the UCC. The shrinkwrap agreement differs from the webwrap agreement in that the online consumer usually has an opportunity to read and assent to the terms before completing the contract. If consumers cannot understand the terms, however, either because they are expressed confusingly or because the consumers do not read English well, this difference will evaporate.

SPC may still need to draft such an agreement. One strategy SPC may use is to place a link to the agreement, translated into various languages, on the webwrap page. SPC may also want to place a large notice on the webwrap page indicating that all questions regarding the terms of the agreement should be forwarded to its customer service department. A hyperlink with the customer service e-mail address could also be provided.

Each of these options will be considered and reviewed by SPC management. When it took its business to the Internet, SPC immediately entered the global marketplace. A small investment in planning could save costly litigation in the future. To prevent large opportunity costs, SPC could incrementally make the other language agreements available based on the demographics of its consumers, information that could be gathered through a simple questionnaire. Additionally, SPC could reduce its customer service costs by publishing a listing of FAQs with corresponding answers on its web site.

[D]   General Guidelines for Internet Security Policy

Why does an online company need a security policy for Internet-related issues? First, the Internet is a networked world "not designed to be very secure."[430] The Internet is based upon open and interoperable standards. It is relatively easy to eavesdrop, spoof, and monitor e-mail, passwords, and file transfers.[431] In a six-month period in 1999, 60 federal World Wide Web sites were hacked and defaced because of a hole in a Microsoft product.[432] An e-business should incorporate the following World Wide Web Consortium (W3C) industry standards in its security policy:

- Who is allowed to use the system?

- When are they allowed to use it?

- What are employees allowed to do (different groups may be granted different levels of access)?

- What are the procedures for granting access to the system?

---

[430] National Institute of Standards, Internet Security Policy: A Technical Guide (Washington D.C.: NIST, 1999) (visited Dec. 14, 1999), http://csrc.nist.gov/isptg/html/ISPTG-1.htm.

[431] Id.

[432] Win2000 Gives Security Boost, Federal Computer Week, Nov. 15, 1999 (visited Apr. 26, 2002), http://www.fcw/com/ref/hottopics/security/background/fcw-mktwin20000-11-15-99.html.

- What are the procedures for revoking access (e.g., when an employee leaves)?

- What constitutes acceptable use of the system?

- Does the company permit remote as well as local login methods?

- What computer system monitoring procedures are in place?

- Have protocols been developed for responding to suspected security breaches?[433]

SPC needs an overall security policy for maintaining the security of its electronic transactions. SPC's company employees need to be trained in the following protocol for reducing information security hazards:

1. SPC employees should not leave computers running unattended. Screenlock may prevent unauthorized access.[434]
2. SPC's computer users should be instructed to make frequent backups. SPC's systems administrators need an overall backup and disaster recovery plan.
3. SPC's antivirus systems must be updated regularly, and their use mandated, to reduce the risk of viruses from downloaded software or data.
4. SPC needs to complete security audits to determine whether all software is licensed.
5. Outdated databases or information should be discarded under a formal record retention policy.

SPC's security policy must be tailored to the security risks unique to its organizational culture. SPC's systems administrators will need to implement general security precautions, especially regarding known hazards with web browsers, Java, and web servers.

SPC's Internet security needs and standards should be made part of its training and education programs. The amount and type of training necessary will depend upon the policy instituted. SPC's executives, for example, will need to know about policy-level Internet security principles if they are to make informed decisions about what computer and security programs the company will implement. Internet security has a significant economic impact on any online business. Senior executives must be on board so security policies are given sufficient financial support. Managers, on the other hand, need to understand the chief threats and vulnerabilities of SPC's web site and automated information resources. The chief information officer or equivalent will need to design, execute, and evaluate Inter-

---

[433] W3C World Wide Web Security FAQs (visited Apr. 25, 2002), http://www.w3.org/Security/faq/wwwsf1.html#GEN-Q2.

[434] Screenlock differs from commercial or operating system screen-savers. A screen-blanker is generally part of a comprehensive security package that refuses system access without a password. A screen-saver is a product originally designed to preserve the life of a computer monitor. Rebooting the system may easily defeat whatever security it provides. If no other security measures against unauthorized access are present during a system reboot, a cybercriminal may easily gain access to the data on the computer's hard drive.

net security procedures and practices. SPC must publish its information security guidelines for all employees.

Each SPC employee should receive a copy of the information security policy and should be asked to acknowledge their responsibility for complying with it. SPC's policy should make it clear that any employee's violation of SPC's network security or information security policy may result in disciplinary action. SPC's policy should also make it clear that security violations may also carry criminal or civil liability, as well as sanctions including dismissal. The information security officer should audit records and transmissions and should try to determine whether users are following the guidelines. In addition, the policy should be posted on SPC's intranet, extranet, and web site. Finally, the policy should be periodically reviewed and updated to prevent it from becoming a dead-letter regulation.

[1]   Sample Information Security Guidelines

1. Publish authorization rules. SPC must publish its computer authorization rules in its employee handbook, on its web site, and in its training materials. After determining what security policies it needs to protect its valuable information, SPC must publish them in a publicly conspicuous manner. In addition to posting a hardcopy in a common area such as near the water cooler, SPC should have a senior manager e-mail a softcopy to every person in the organization.

2. Provide information about company procedures and policy regarding basic security, authentication, and authorization. SPC's policy should explain its security technology and guidelines for safeguarding the company's information assets. SPC employees should be trained in using any newly-acquired technologies as they are instituted. SPC's corporate culture must support information security: A bulletproof firewall will be useless if SPC's employees are lackadaisical about security measures.

3. Involve senior management in formulating security policies. Responsibility for assessing risk levels and determining the resources and support necessary to ensure computer security should fall to senior management.

4. Block any potential interference with or disruption in Internet service. Although denial of service may be less destructive than other security attacks, the downtime resulting from these attacks can be costly for the company. Specific steps should be taken to prevent denial-of-service attacks.

5. Prohibit the downloading of any illegal or obscene content or the excessive use of bandwidth by employees who download unauthorized video or massive amounts of data. Large amounts of data can flood SPC's computer network and result in downtime. If SPC has a low bandwidth network, large downloads should be scheduled during nonpeak hours. SPC employees need to be warned about the negative consequences of occupying bandwidth with noncritical data.

6. Implement automatic antiviral program to detect worms, viruses, Trojan horses, and other destructive code. SPC employees must be trained in how to avoid posting or transmitting files containing destructive code; they must also be instructed not to bypass security procedures. If viruses or other malicious code is detected or suspected, prompt reporting may minimize their consequences.

7. Require employees to use their own names in online communications. SPC employees should know, understand, and use forms of communication considered acceptable to the company. An employee's online conduct affects the image of the employer.

8. Maintain both hardware and software security. A number of information security protections can be built into a company's hardware and software. Users may, for example, be given limited access to files, or may have only specific devices allocated to them. Software may also be engineered to incorporate security features. Operating system software should control user access to authorized resources and capabilities. Both programs and data areas may be restricted.

9. Give notice that the company will cooperate with the investigations of local, state, and federal law enforcement agencies whenever security violations are suspected. Company policy should inform employees that SPC will adhere to industry standards and all laws applying to Internet use and commerce.

10. Hire and supervise personnel with security goals in mind. All online companies need personnel policies and procedures that emphasize the security of trade secrets, business plans, and other confidential information. A printed and circulated copy of company policy should include the names of a contact person who can answer questions about Internet security. Because "insiders" commit 90 percent of e-business security breaches, background investigations of employees and access limited to information and devices employees need to do their jobs are as important to information security as are firewalls and other technological barriers to invasion from outside. Finally, employees must be trained and supervised to ensure proper security.

11. Hold individuals accountable for proper information security. The online company must train its employees in the proper use of its information technology systems. As security technology improves and company security policies and procedures change, employees will require periodic security updates. SPC's web site, too, must be updated so that its security policy statements reflect its current practice. The company should give employees notice that from time to time the company will change its Internet security procedures and that employees will be expected to abide by amended rules.[435] Employees that violate security procedures should lose access privileges and face sanctions, including termination.

---

[435] The President's Commission on Critical Infrastructure Protection (PCCIP) studies the radius of the risk of cyberattacks on the government's operating systems. The U.S. government has a Computer Emergency Response Team (CERT) that tracks vulnerabilities and warns systems administrators to fix them. CERT provides technical assistance, security alerts, technical documents, and seminars relating to computer security problems. The CERT Coordination Center evolved out of a computer emergency response team formed by the Defense Advanced Research Projects Agency (DARPA) in 1988 in response to the first reports of Internet worms. The center works with private computer consultants and vendors to develop patches or workarounds for known computer security problems.

By subscribing to CERT's free mailing lists, SPC can have CERT's security advisories sent directly to its e-mail account. SPC's chief information officer must regularly consult CERT's alert

12. Report incidents and violations promptly. The online company must implement procedures for minimizing the costs and effects of an intrusion, virus, or security breach. Timely detection and reporting of actual or suspected security breaches can help to mitigate damages.

13. Develop contingency and disaster recovery plans. The online company needs to undertake contingency planning for the following emergency response activities: (a) backup and retention of data and software; (b) selection of alternate operations strategy; (c) emergency response actions; and (d) efficient resumption of normal operations.[436]

§ 3.05   REMEDIES FOR COMPUTER ABUSE

Each episode of the 1940s radio program "The Shadow" commenced with a mysterious-sounding voice asking: "Who knows what evil lurks in the hearts of men? The Shadow knows."[437] A sinister laugh followed this statement of the Shadow's omniscience. That sinister laugh is emblematic of lack of security on the Internet. The anonymity provided by the Internet has led hackers to create web sites the sole purpose of which is to post software for launching attacks.[438]

[A]   Criminal Remedies for Computer Abuse and Hacking

"Cybercrimes are often described as falling into three categories: crimes in which the computer is the target of the criminal activity, crimes in which the computer is a tool used to commit the crime, and crimes in which the use of the computer is an incidental aspect of the commission of the crime."[439] The first appellate court decision to mention the Internet was the 1991 case of *United*

---

list and advisories. (CERT advisories may be accessed at http://www.cert.org.) CERT also publishes vendor-initiated bulletins on their products' security problems. In addition to subscribing to CERT's advisory mailing lists, SPC's system administrators should attend relevant CERT presentations, workshops, and seminars.

As Internet horror stories multiply, so, too, does the need for comprehensive network security. One malevolent cyberspace netizen, for example, set up a site called INFES-Station BBS, an anonymous File Transfer Protocol (or FTP, which permits transfers of files between internetworked computers) with the sole purpose of distributing virus codes. The abuse of this FTP, which normally ensures the orderly and reliable transfer of data, and the resulting undetected transfer of infected data caused substantial harm to many company computer networks.

[436] These principles are based on Defense Department policies implemented by DOCT IT security managers. *See* Contingency and Disaster Recovery Planning (visited Apr. 28, 2002), http://csrc.ncsl.nist.gov/secplcy/doc-poli.txt.

[437] John M. Carroll, Confidential Information Sources: Public and Private xi (2d ed. 1991) (comparing the loss of privacy due to the government's assembling of data files with the loss of privacy inherent in the concept of "The Shadow").

[438] The number of cyberattacks increased from 2,000 in 1997 to 8,000 in 1999. News Analysis & Commentary, Bus. Wk., Feb. 28, 2000, at 34.

[439] Susan Brenner, *Defining Cybercrime: A Review of State and Federal Law, in* Ralph D. Clifford, Cybercrime: The Investigation, Prosecution and Defense of a Computer-Related Crime 12 (2001).

States v. Morris.[440] The defendant in that case was Robert Morris, a Cornell University computer science doctoral student. Morris's research was in the field of information security. One of his research projects was to design an "Internet worm" or virus that would test the security of computer networks. Morris's computer code would copy itself into computer systems and reproduce. He tested his worm by releasing it from a computer science laboratory at MIT. Due to a defect in the program, the worm replicated at a high rate of speed, shutting down computers in universities, medical facilities, and defense facilities throughout the United States

One of the difficulties of cybercrime enforcement is Internet crimes frequently involve multiple jurisdictions. One of the difficulties of cybercrime legislation is to enact statutes to punish and control cybercrimes that are in effect a moving target. The difficulty of prosecuting cybercrimes is illustrated by the first Internet criminal case of *United States v. LaMacchia.*[441] David LaMacchia, an MIT student, was prosecuted for distributing software over the Internet. LaMacchia had a computer bulletin board where anyone could copy copyrighted computer software for free.

The criminal action against David LaMacchia was ultimately dismissed because the federal court held that the criminal penalties of wire fraud could not be imposed because there was no proof that LaMacchia had received any financial gains or profits from the infringing acts of illegal copying. It was not until the end of 1997 that the LaMacchia loophole was eliminated by the No Electronic Theft Act of 1997 (NET).[442] NET broadens criminal liability for copyright infringement even where no financial gain or profit is involved. To date, there is no caselaw construing NET, which may mean that Congress patched a statutory loophole for a problem that no longer exists.[443]

[1] The Electronic Communications Privacy Act

Computer crime statutes were first enacted decades after the invention of computers. More than 40 federal statutes have at least some relevance to the prosecution of Internet-related crimes.[444] Federal legislation tends to target specific forms of wrongdoing such as "hacking, cracking, virus dissemination, using computer to commit fraud and using computer equipment to create and disseminate child pornography."[445] The term *computer crime* is defined by the Department of Justice to include "any violations of criminal law that involve a knowledge of computer technology for their perpetration, investigation, or prosecution." The

---

[440] 928 F.2d 504 (2d Cir. 1991) (upholding a criminal conviction under the Computer Abuse and Fraud Act for releasing a computer worm which shut down computers throughout the United States).

[441] 871 F. Supp. 535 (D. Mass. 1994).

[442] The No Electronic Theft Act of 1997, 17 U.S.C. § 506 (2001) (amending § 506 of the U.S. Copyright Act).

[443] A LEXIS search completed on April 20, 2001, for all state and federal cases reveals only one mention of the NET, in Eldred v. Reno, 74 F. Supp. 2d 1 (D.D.C. 1999) (rejecting challenge to the Sonny Bono Copyright Term Extension Act).

[444] Brenner, *supra* note 439, at 16.

[445] *Id.* at 17.

Electronic Communications Privacy Act (ECPA) was enacted as an amendment to the Omnibus Crime Patrol and Safe Streets Act Title III of 1968. The ECPA was enacted before the rise of the Internet and software industry and applied to wire communications. Title II of the ECPA "aims to prevent hackers from obtaining, altering, or destroying certain stored electronic communications."[446]

The ECPA prohibits the disclosure of the contents of an electronic communication to any person or entity. The ECPA states that "a person or entity providing an electronic communication service to the public shall not knowingly divulge to any person or entity the contents of a communication while in electronic storage by that service."[447] The ECPA provides civil and criminal remedies against hackers who intercept wire communications, whether from company voicemail or e-mail.[448] The contents of any wire, oral, or electronic communication includes any information concerning the "substance, purport or meaning of that communication," but not information concerning the identity of the author of the communication.[449] The ECPA sanctions access to, or alteration of records or stored wire or electronic communications where the defendant has no authority to access the computer. The ECPA was intended to provide a cause of action against hackers and other electronic trespassers.[450] Web sites are "users" of Internet access under the ECPA.[451]

Section 2707 creates a civil action against violators of the ECPA by "any provider of electronic communication service, subscriber, or other person aggrieved by a violation of [the Act] in which the conduct constituting the violation is engaged in with a knowing or intentional state of mind."[452] The ECPA is often used as a civil remedy against the search and seizure of computer systems or computer messages by law enforcement officers.[453] Employers and corporate entities frequently use the ECPA as a civil cause of action for the illegal seizures of computer systems or the interception of computer communications.[454] A federal

---

[446] *In re* Doubleclick Privacy Litig., 2001 U.S. Dist. LEXIS 3498 (S.D.N.Y. Mar. 29, 2001).

[447] 18 U.S.C. § 2702 (a) (2000).

[448] United States v. Smith, 155 F.3d 1051, 1057 (9th Cir. 1998) (noting that "a hypothetical hacker could be sued for civil damages and criminally prosecuted under the ECPA").

[449] Jessup-Morgan v. America Online, Inc., 20 F. Supp. 2d 1105 (E.D. Mich. 1998) (dismissing ECPA action against service provider, holding that disclosure of identity of subscriber who posted messages on AOL system did not violate the ECPA).

[450] State Wide Photocopy Corp. v. Tokai Fin. Servs., Inc., 909 F. Supp. 137, 145 (S.D.N.Y. 1995) ("It appears that the ECPA was primarily designed to provide a cause of action against computer hackers (i.e. electronic trespassers.)."

[451] *In re* Doubleclick Privacy Litig., 2001 U.S. Dist. LEXIS 3498, *34 (S.D.N.Y. Mar. 29, 2001).

[452] 18 U.S.C. § 2707 (2000).

[453] *See, e.g.,* Steve Jackson Games v. United Secret Service, 816 F. Supp. 432 (W.D. Tex. 1993), *aff'd,* 36 F.3d 457 (5th Cir. 1994) (discussing case in which ECPA was used as a cause of action for computer hackers whose computer equipment was seized by federal law enforcement authorities).

[454] There were only 76 cases in which the term "Electronic Communications Privacy Act and computer" is mentioned in cases in LEXIS' state and federal caselaw database. Only 5 of the 76 cases involve computer hacking. Private litigants file many of the ECPA cases for civil damages for improper access of computer systems, web sites, or networks. *See, e.g.,* Konop v. Hawaiian Airlines, Inc., 236

court recently considered the question of whether the use of Internet "cookies" which collect potentially personally identifiable profiles to build demographic profiles of web site visitors violated the ECPA.[455] Despite its statutory aim, the ECPA is seldom used to successfully prosecute computer hackers for the unauthorized access to stored electronic communications.[456] The Electronic Communications Privacy Act (ECPA) is the principal federal statute governing law enforcement surveillance of electronic communications.[457] In general, the government requires a warrant or consent of the customer. Although the ECPA applies principally to law enforcement, provisions may apply to ISPs.[458] Section 7 of the ECPA requires law enforcement to obtain court orders or consent to intercept real-time electronic communications.[459] Section 6 requires a warrant for electronic communications in storage less than 180 days, a subpoena for storage of more than 180 days, or the parties' consent.[460] A customer record includes basic subscriber information, such as an AOL customer's name or address. A provider may not release customer records absent a subpoena for subscriber information under Section 3.[461] A court order or consent is required for other records.[462] "However, the ECPA does not in any way restrict a provider from disclosing records about a customer (e.g., customer user names, other identification information and transactional records related to the account) to any entity other than a governmental entity."[463] A provider may implement more stringent standards for when it discloses records to nongovernmental entities.[464]

[2]   Computer Fraud and Abuse Act

The Computer Fraud and Abuse Act (CFAA) and its amendments punish and deter computer hacking, viruses, and other forms of computer crime. The federal

---

F.3d 1035 (9th Cir. 2000) (involving a case brought by employee against employer airline during a labor dispute); Coronado v. BankAtlantic Bancorp, Inc., 222 F.3d 1315 (11th Cir. 2000) (ruling in a case where a defendant bank was sued by his customer for unauthorized disclosure of customer's account records); Lopez v. First Union Nat'l Bank, 129 F.3d 1186 (11th Cir. 1997) (same).

[455] *In re* Doubleclick Privacy Litig., 2001 U.S. Dist. LEXIS 3498 (S.D.N.Y. Mar. 29, 2001) (granting defendants' motion to dismiss ECPA claim that use of cookies collecting personally identifiable information violated the Act).

[456] The ECPA is frequently asserted as a cause of action against law enforcement officers and corporations monitoring employee e-mail and Internet-related communications.

[457] Clint N. Smith, The Electronic Communications Privacy Act: A Primer for Service Providers (distributed at NETSPIONAGE.COM: What Every Lawyer Should Know About Minimizing and Responding to Attacks on Corporate Information Infrastructures (presentation by the Netspionage.com Working Group at the ABA Annual Meeting, Aug. 4, 2001)).

[458] *Id.*

[459] *Id.*

[460] *Id.*

[461] *Id.*

[462] *Id.*

[463] *Id.* (citing 18 U.S.C. § 2703(c) (1) (A)).

[464] *Id.*

statute broadly extends to all computers in interstate commerce.[465] "While the CFAA is a good first line of defense for e-commerce businesses and financial institutions, its coverage is not broad enough to address the growing trend in general computer-related economic espionage being waged against all types of businesses and industries."[466] The CFAA was enacted in 1984 and amended in 1986 and 1990. It is a violation of the CFAA for persons to obtain unauthorized access to the computer networks of government agencies, financial institutions, or computers used in interstate or foreign commerce. Such a broad jurisdiction covers the Internet.

It is a violation of the CFAA to intentionally infect a computer system with a virus, causing damage to a computer system. The CFAA prohibits any person from knowingly causing the transmission of information, which intentionally causes damage, without authorization, to a protected computer. Section 1030 punishes those who "knowingly accessed a computer without authorization or exceeding authorized access, and by means of such contact having obtained information."[467]

The CFFA criminalizes access to a computer without authorization or exceeding authorized access and obtains a record of a financial institution or an issuer of a credit or debit card.[468] A prima facie criminal case requires proof that the person intentionally or recklessly caused damage to a computer system.[469] The state of mind required is that the defendant knowingly causes the transmission of information with the intent to defraud. The value of the unauthorized use of the computer must be at least $5,000 in any one-year period.[470] The CFAA provides for civil liability for intentionally introducing viruses or malicious codes into a computer system.[471] The federal computer crime statute also punishes conduct committed "in furtherance of any . . . tortious act in violation of the . . . laws of the United States or of any State."[472] A person who intentionally accesses a computer without authorization and causes damage is criminally liable under the CFAA.[473]

The use of a computer to "extort from any person, firm, association, educational institution, financial institution, government entity, or other legal entity, any money or other thing of value," is also a violation of the CFAA.[474] The CFAA punishes criminal attempts as well acts that caused damage to a computer.[475] The

---

[465] 18 U.S.C. § 1030 (2000).

[466] Mark A. Rush and Lucas G. Paglia, Preventing, Investigating and Prosecuting Computer Attacks and E-Commerce Crimes: Public/Private Initiatives and Other Federal Resources, 18 Computer & Online Industry Litig. Rep. 12 (July 17, 2001).

[467] 18 U.S.C. § 1030(a)(1) (2000).

[468] 18 U.S.C. § 1030(2)(A) (2000).

[469] 18 U.S.C. §§ 1030(a)(5) (A)-(C) (2000).

[470] 18 U.S.C. § 1030(a)(4) (2000).

[471] 18 U.S.C. § 1030(g) (stating that "[a]ny person who suffers damage or loss by reason of a violation of this section may maintain a civil action against the violator . . .").

[472] 18 U.S.C. § 1030(c)(2)(B)(ii) (2000).

[473] 18 U.S.C. § 1030(5)(B) (2000).

[474] 18 U.S.C. § 1030(7) (2000).

[475] 18 U.S.C. § 1030(b) (2000).

CFAA punishes threatening national defense or foreign relations "by a fine . . . or imprisonment for not more than ten years or both."[476] Repeat offenders endangering national defense or foreign relations may receive a fine or imprisonment ". . . for not more than twenty years or both . . . after a conviction for another offense."[477] The CFAA punishes the trafficking of computer passwords or similar identifiers to facilitate unauthorized access.[478] The CFAA sanctions unauthorized access to nonpublic computers with a fine or imprisonment of one year or both and repeat offenders may be fined or imprisoned for up to five years.[479]

The CFAA has been expanded to encompass evolving technologies. The National Information Infrastructure Protection Act of 1996 was enacted to extend federal computer crime statutes to the Internet.[480] It was the 1996 amendments to the CFAA that extended the scope of the statute from "federal interest computers" to "protected computers."[481] The amendments to the CFAA specifically addressed the subject of computer hacking, making it a federal crime "to cause damage intentionally to a protected computer . . . or to cause damage recklessly, negligently or otherwise if the protected computer was intentionally accessed without authorization."[482] The 1996 amendments had the effect of punishing company insiders for intentional damage and hackers for intrusions "even if the transmission was only reckless or negligent."[483] Congress passed the Economic Espionage Act in 1996 that made it a federal crime to steal or receive trade secrets placed in interstate commerce.[484] The USA PATRIOT Act of 2001 was enacted in the wake of the September 11, 2001, attacks on New York City and Washington, D.C.[485] The PATRIOT Act is a direct response to the September 11 terrorist attacks. The PATRIOT Act expands the ECPA's pen register and trap and trace provisions to grant the government greater access to Internet address information but not content.[486] Online piracy of copyright is punishable by § 506 of the U.S. Copyright Act.[487] It is a federal crime to infringe a copyright for financial gain "by reproducing or distributing, during any 180-day period, one or more copies or phonoecords of one of more copyrighted works having a total retail value in excess of $1,000."[488] Criminal penalties are also imposable under the Trademark Counter-

---

[476] 18 U.S.C. § 1030(c)(1) (2000).

[477] 18 U.S.C. § 1030(c)(1)(B) (2000).

[478] 18 U.S.C. § 1030(6) (2000).

[479] 18 U.S.C. § 1030(c)(2) (2000).

[480] 32 Pub. L. No. 104-294, Title II, § 201, 110 Stat. 3488, 3491-94 (1996), codified in 18 U.S.C. § 1030 (2000).

[481] 18 U.S.C. § 1030(e)(2) (2000).

[482] Michael Hatcher et. al., "Computer Crimes," 36 Am. Crim. L. Rev. 397, 405 (1999).

[483] Id.

[484] 18 U.S.C. §§ 1831 et seq. (2001).

[485] U.S. PATRIOT Act, Pub. L. 107-56 (2001).

[486] Ronald L. Plesser, USA Patriot Act for Internet and Communications Companies, 19 Computer & Internet Law. 1 (March 2002)

[487] 17 U.S.C. § 506 (2001).

[488] Brenner, *supra* note 439, at 19.

feiting Act.[489] The 1996 Act permits prosecutions of outside hackers and trusted insiders who exceed the scope of their duties as well as those who spread viruses.

[B]   Private Corporate Policing

[1]   eBay's Private Policing

The Internet has become a haven for cybercriminals because of the possibilities for instant wealth without detection or prosecution. In this section, I argue that a strong regime of private enforcement is needed to supplement public law enforcement. Private enforcement in the form of e-cops is already becoming well established on the Internet. eBay, the online auction house, employs private police to patrol its web site.[490] eBay's private police, for example, uncovered the online sale of a human kidney.[491] eBay's web site has 22.4 million members and 6 million items for sale at any one time, which makes it impossible for law enforcement to enforce all bad acts on the site.

[2]   Private/Public Policing

Another example of private enforcement is the Internet Fraud Watch, a watchdog group formed by the National Consumers League.[492] Federal agencies such as the Department of Energy educate consumers on self-help measures for online fraud such as e-mail chain letters and pyramid schemes.[493] State attorney generals in a growing number of states have similar programs to help consumers uncover and report online fraud and other cybercrimes.

[3]   Software Publishers' Software Police

Private enforcement by the Software Publishers Association (SPA) is a well-funded, worldwide e-police force that is actively detecting and prosecuting copyright infringement and software piracy.[494] The software industry employs private investigators to investigate companies and individuals that make unauthorized or

---

[489] *Id.* at 29 (discussing Trademark Counterfeiting Act, 18 U.S.C. § 2320).

[490] Joelle Tessler, "E-Cops Patrol Web Site: Former Federal Officers Take Lead Roles on Issues Ranging from Criminal Investigations to Setting Rules," Mercury News (April 7, 2001), in Silicon-Valley.com (visited Apr. 28, 2002), http:www.siliconvalley.com.

[491] *Id.*

[492] *Id.*

[493] The Department of Energy, for example, has a web page devoted to "Hoaxbusters" to help consumers take self-help measures against fraudulent schemes, viruses, and other forms of Internet wrongdoing. *See* Hoaxbusters (visited Apr. 28, 2002), http://fullcoverage.yahoo.com/fc/Tech/Cybercrime_and_Internet_Fraud.

[494] Dan Bricklin, "The Software Police vs. the CD Lawyers," Dan Bricklin's Web Site (visited Apr. 15, 2001), http://www.bricklin.com/softwarepolice.htm.

counterfeit copies of software.[495] Software private police participate in raids on companies where unlicensed copies of software are confiscated. The SPA claims that $7.5 billion of American software is illegally copied and distributed.[496] The SPA's campaign of private enforcement is to thwart software pirates who are unlikely to be prosecuted for criminal copyright infringement.[497]

The SPA mounted an educational campaign to create new norms against illegal copies. The SPA created a rap video entitled "Don't Copy That Floppy" used in schools and companies.[498] The SPA claims that its campaign of private policing and education has slowed down the rate of piracy. As a result of the difficulty of obtaining a successful criminal prosecution, the victims of cybercrime often seek civil redress.

[4]   ICC's Commercial Crime Bureau

An online banking fraud was detected and shut down on the basis of the investigative work of the International Chamber of Commerce's Commercial Crime Bureau (ICC).[499] The private investigators uncovered a complex financial scheme involving false bank guarantees and financial documents on 29 web sites potentially worth $3.9 billion.[500] The web sites had the "look and feel" of Euroclear Bank, which is the international clearinghouse for the settlement of securities sales and Eurobonds.[501] The ICC routinely polices financial and intellectual property offenses on the Internet and has uncovered a number of fraudulent financial sites ranging in value from $50 million to over $400 million.[502]

Hackers operating in former Russian Republics victimized Bloomberg Financial News.[503] The hackers were able to impersonate Bloomberg employees and collect personal information such as personal credit card numbers from the corporate web site.[504] The perpetrators sent an e-mail message to Michael Bloomberg requesting $20,000 for security services and if the "consulting fee" was not paid, it would expose the security weaknesses of Bloomberg's network to the press and public.[505] Bloomberg's security experts worked with the FBI to construct a sting that resulted in the arrest and extradition of the perpetrators.

---

[495] Id.

[496] Crime on the Internet, "Software Piracy," Jones Telecommunications and MultiMedia Encyclopedia (visited Apr. 18, 2001), http://www.digitalcentury.com/encrclo/update/crime.html.

[497] Id.

[498] Id.

[499] Online Banking Scam Shut Down by ICC Commercial Crime Bureau, Pike & Fischer Internet Law & Regulation, Document 42 (Apr. 13, 2001).

[500] Id.

[501] Id.

[502] Id.

[503] John Leyden, "Extradition Hearing in Bloomberg Hack/Extortion," The Register (visited Apr. 28, 2002), http://www.theregister.co.uk/content/8/18196.html.

[504] Id.

[505] Id.

[C] Common Law Negligence[506]

A business may be liable for negligence if its conduct falls below the standard established by law for protecting others against an unreasonable risk of harm. Negligence "is a departure from the conduct expected of a reasonably prudent man under like circumstances."[507] Businesses are held to the standard of the reasonable business, while professionals in a given business are held to the "diligence ordinarily possessed by well-informed members of the trade or profession."[508] A company has a duty to implement the level of security found in similar entities in the same industry. When attempting to apply these standards to parties in the information economy, however, little authority exists on the standard of care expected from Internet security professionals and consultants. Professionals in the field of information security have a duty to keep up with security alerts so that they have the skill and training to respond to security breaches with the appropriate patches and upgrades. The evolving standard holds businesses liable for the failure to implement effective computer systems.

One starting point for extending the doctrine of negligence into this new type of conduct is that consultants are expressly or impliedly promising to perform security audits in a diligent and reasonably skillful manner. Therefore, the appropriate standard of care must be calibrated to the level of risk. One question is whether a company has a duty to protect the plaintiff from the type of harm that occurred from a given breach of Internet security. Is the risk of harm causing injury to a plaintiff beyond the scope of any duty to provide protection? A prior history of similar security breaches may establish foreseeability. In the absence of a history of similar intrusions and security breaches, foreseeability is based on all facts and circumstances.

This situation could arise from SPC's implementation of a telecommuter program through which its employees work from home via an Internet connection to the SPC internal network. If adequate security measures are not taken, hackers could gain access to the SPC network and harm SPC or any other parties with confidential or valuable information on its network. Third parties may thus have causes of action in the event of an attack, holding that SPC let "their [computer] systems be commandeered."[509]

In general terms, SPC would not have a duty of care arising out of a company telecommuting program. More typical circumstances involve plaintiffs who suffer a physical injury, such as from a slip and fall on the sidewalk of a telecommuter's house. Courts have found that SPC would not be liable where the major

---

[506] For a complete discussion of negligence in the Internet context, *see* § 5.08. Mark Maier, Esq., drafted the practice pointers in this section.

[507] Pence v. Ketchum, 326 So. 2d 831, 835 (La. 1976).

[508] Data Processing Servs, Inc. v. L.H. Smith Oil Corp., 492 N.E.2d 314, 319 (Ind. Ct. App. 1986); *see also* Young v. McKelvey, 333 S.E.2d 566 (S.C. 1985) (employee expressly or impliedly promising to perform work in a diligent and reasonably skilled manner).

[509] News Analysis & Commentary, Bus. Wk., Feb. 28, 2000, at 34 (quoting James Dempsey, General Counsel for Democracy and Technology).

use of the telecommuter's house was residential. Only where the property had a predominately commercial use could vicarious liability be extended to SPC.[510]

The analysis differs, however, where the injury arises out of the telecommuter's Internet connection to the SPC network. In this case, SPC could be found to have additional duties arising out of the use of its network by the Internet telecommuter, beyond those of any employee. These new duties could be based on telecommuting being a hazardous situation in plain view, or the employer itself creating the peril, or from a contractual relationship.[511]

The duty arises from the fact that the Internet connection is a separate, external pipe used predominately by employers such as SPC in telecommuter programs. Since this pipe would be paid for and provided by SPC to access the SPC internal facilities, it is similar to providing a company car to employees or to opening a retail store to the public. As such, employers would be held directly liable for inadequate maintenance, insurance, and control of its equipment.[512] Likewise, SPC could be directly liable for inadequate security and control of the Internet connections that lead to the injury.[513]

Once a duty has been established, SPC's particular standard of care must be calibrated or set. These standards could be found by applying a risk-utility analysis or a professional malpractice standard. The risk-utility analysis is discussed in this section, and the malpractice standard in the following section.

The risk-utility analysis was initiated by Judge Learned Hand in the hallmark case *Carroll Towing*,[514] in which a barge suffered damage because a crew member, known as a "bargee," was not stationed onboard during the night. Had a bargee been onboard, the damage could have been avoided. To answer the question of whether the bargee should have been on board, Judge Hand introduced the economic formula of identifying three factors:[515] one, the liability (L) of the potential damage without precautions; two, the probability (P) that the damage would actually occur; and three, the burden (B) of the cost of reasonable precautions adequate

---

[510] *See* Wasserman v. W.R. Grace & Co., 656 A.2d 453 (N.J. Super. Ct. App. Div. 1995), where the plaintiff was injured on the sidewalk in front of the telecommuter's house. Since the home had only a single-room office for telecommuting, and thus the majority of the home's use was residential, the house was not a commercial property of W.R. Grace, and the company had no vicarious liability. *See also* Hungate v. United States, 626 F.2d 60, 62 (8th Cir. 1980), where the U.S. government, as property owner, was not found liable due to an absence of some special use or conversion of the sidewalk.

[511] Mark J. Maier, The Law and Technology of Internet Telecommuting, SMU Computer L. Rev. & Tech. J. 28 (Fall 1999).

[512] For premise liability analysis, *see* Tillman v. Great Lakes Steel Corp., 17 F. Supp. 2d 672, 679 (E.D. Mich. 1998), and Gellerman v. Shawan Road Hotel Ltd. Partnership, 5 F. Supp. 2d 351, 353 (D. Md. 1998).

[513] *See* Maier, *supra* note 511, at 29-30.

[514] United States v. Carroll Towing Co., 159 F.2d 169, 173 (2d Cir. 1947).

[515] "[I]t serves to bring this notion into relief to state it in algebraic terms: if the probability be called P; the injury, L; and the burden, B; liability depends upon whether B is less than L multiplied by P: i.e., whether B is less than PL." *Id.*

to prevent the damage from occurring. The product of the liability and the proba-bility, known as the risk, is compared to the burden. If the risk is less than the bur-den, the standard of care does not require the investment in the precautions. If the risk is greater than the burden, however, the standard of care does require the investment in the precautions.

In the case of SPC telecommuters, the liability (L) of the potential damage would be based on the value of the information to which the telecommuter has access. On one side of the scale would be placed items of little to no value, such as the ten-tative schedule of employee mid-morning coffee breaks, while on the other side of the scale would be placed important trade secrets and confidential information worth thousands or millions of dollars, such as the secret recipe of a popular soft drink.[516]

The probability (P) that damage will actually occur must be calculated on a case-by-case basis. In the case of an SPC telecommuter, the probability can be determined with the following multiset process. First, most Internet domains[517] experience approximately one attack incident per year, and of these attacks, 57.9 percent[518] are successful. This is expressed as 0.579. The probability that an attack would come via the telecommuter would be 0.0001236.[519] Taking the product of these two numbers (0.579 × 0.0001236) reveals a probability that damage would occur to information stored on SPC's internal network of 0.0000715.[520]

The burden (B) to protect these SPC telecommuters varies with how secure one could make them. For telecommuters without access to valuable information, a proportionately small amount of security would be necessary. To protect infor-mation with a modest value, however, basic tunnel protection, which encrypts the information, is readily available from vendors such as AltaVista or Microsoft.[521] The cost to implement this type of protection for 1,000 telecommuters would be approximately $5 per telecommuter.[522] For a higher level of advanced tunnel secu-rity, products available from Altiga, 3Com, and Cisco encrypt information as well as prevent access to the telecommuter's computer. The cost for this kind of pro-tection for 1,000 telecommuters would be approximately $55 per telecommuter.[523]

To identify the necessary standard of care, risk of harm from a telecommuter attack is first determined by taking the product of the liability and probability

---

[516] See Maier, *supra* note 511, at 21-22.

[517] An Internet domain is a group of computers within the same organization, such as all the com-puters in the *suffolk.edu* domain. For information on Internet domains, see John D. Howard, An Analysis of Security Incidents on the Internet: 1989-1995, Carnegie Mellon University (1997), at Chapter 2, http://www.cert.org/research/JHThesis/Chapter2.html.

[518] The 57.9 percent accounted for root break-ins of 31.0 percent and account break-ins of 26.9 percent. The percentage of unsuccessful attacks was 42.1 percent. *Id.*, at Chapter 7, http://www.cert.org/research/JHThesis/Chapter7.html.

[519] See Maier, *supra* note 511, at 23.

[520] *Id.*

[521] Microsoft Corp., Virtual Private Networking: An Overview (May 29, 1998) (visited Apr. 28, 2002), http://msdn.microsoft.com/workshop/server/feature/vpnovw.asp.

[522] See Maier, *supra* note 511, at 25.

[523] *Id.*, at 27.

(0.0000715). This value is then compared to the burden (B). Starting with the case of information of little or no value, the risk would be approximated by multiplying $0 by 0.0000715, which gives a result of $0. Thus, in this case, no protection would be required. For more important information, however, valued at $100,000, for example, multiplying that amount by 0.0000715 would give a result of $7.15. Since this is greater than the cost of basic tunnels ($5), but less than the cost of advanced protection ($55), the standard of care would require only basic tunnel protection. Finally, for highly valuable information, the risk to which could amount to $1,000,000, that amount multiplied by 0.0000715 would give a result of $71.50. Since this is greater than the cost for both basic tunnels ($5) and advanced tunnel ($55) protection, the standard of care would require advanced tunnel protection.

[D] Professional Malpractice

The common law imposes a higher duty of care on professionals. Computer professionals are increasingly certified and render services that may be assessed against industrywide good practices.[524] No general professional standard exists, but industries such as hospitals, insurers, banks, and other regulated institutions may have a statutory duty to protect the confidentiality of client records.[525] A plaintiff injured by a disclosure of confidential information may be able to maintain an action against an information security professional for failing to provide adequate security. Such an action would be analogous to *Cruz v. Madison Detective Bureau, Inc.*,[526] in which a movie theater usher assaulted by a patron was permitted to maintain a negligence action against a contract security system for failing to provide adequate security. In that case, the security company was held to be negligent for failing to provide adequate security and for failing to follow its own security procedures. It may similarly be sufficient to raise an issue of negligence if an information security company fails to meet industry standards or otherwise fails to provide adequate security.[527] To prevail in a negligence action, the plaintiff must prove that the consultant's conduct was a cause-in-fact of the harm to plaintiff caused by the disclosure of private information. Moreover, the defendant must be shown to have owed the plaintiff a duty of care to protect against the risk involved and that the defendant breached the duty, resulting in harm. To find professional malpractice for security professionals, the elements are even more

---

[524] See Restatement (Second) Torts § 299A (1979).

[525] *See* Holtz v. J.J.B. Hilliard W.L. Lyons, Inc., 185 F.3d 732, 744 (7th Cir. 1999), where the special relationship between the parties created a duty to act in a reasonable manner.

[526] Cruz v. Madison Detective Bureau Inc, 528 N.Y.S.2d 372 (Sup. Ct. of N.Y., App. Div., 1st Dept. 1988).

[527] *See* Stanford v. Kuwait Airways Corp., 89 F.3d 117, 123 (2d Cir. 1996), where the standard was to have such as "superior attention . . . knowledge, intelligence, and judgment . . . ," as well as, Heath v. Swift Wings, Inc., 252 S.E.2d 526, 529 (N.C. App. 1979).

challenging. Plaintiff would have to show the existence of minimum educational requirements,[528] a certification process, and a prevailing discipline, and that the employer held itself as a professional organization.[529]

Computer professionals must have the same skills, competence, and training as others in the industry.[530] One such organization working to change the lack of standards is the International Information Systems Security Certification Consortium, or (ISC)2, which promotes the Certification for Information System Security Professional (Cissp) certification exam to aid in the evaluation of personnel performing information security functions.[531]

The (ISC)2 was established in 1989 as an independent, nonprofit corporation whose charter is to develop and administer a certification program for information security practitioners.[532] The (ISC)2 is well established in North America and gaining international acceptance.[533] Cissp applicants must adhere to a code of ethics; have at least three years of work experience in one or more of ten test areas; and pass an examination testing them on a common body of knowledge, which includes access control systems, cryptography, and security management practices.[534] The greater the professionalization of Internet security, the higher the likelihood that a court will recognize the functional equivalent of computer malpractice. The standard of care for computer malpractice for security breaches will be based on computer industry standards.

In regard to the entrance requirement, a number of technical certification bodies with challenging requirements exist,[535] but certification is optional and is not required of any organization prior to its claiming to offer professional security.[536]

---

[528] Michael Rustad and Lori E. Eisenschmidt, The Commercial Law of Internet Security, 10 High Tech. L. J. 213, 249 (1995).

[529] Steiner Corp. v. Johnson & Higgins of California, 135 F.3d 684, 688 (10th Cir. 1998), where a professional that held himself out as a professional is liable for the negligent performance of duties undertaken. *See also In re* Daisy Systems Corp., 97 F.3d 1171, 1175 (9th Cir. 1996), where a duty of professional care required the plaintiff to show the defendant should have used such skill, prudence, and diligence as other members of his or her profession commonly possessed and exercised. *See also* Hospital Computer Systems, Inc. v. The Staten Island Hospital, 788 F. Supp. 1351, 1361 (D.N.J. 1992).

[530] *See* Patricia DiRuggiero, The Professionalism of Computer Practitioners: A Case for Certification, 25 Suffolk Univ. L. Rev. 1139 (1991) (arguing for the extension of the professional standard of care to computer specialists).

[531] Cissp Home Page (visited Apr. 18, 2002), http://www.cissp.com.

[532] Cissp, Exam (visited Apr. 18, 2002), http://www.cissp.com/Exam/exam.html.

[533] *Id.*

[534] *Id.*

[535] Certifications exams are provided by Cisco Systems, Inc., Cisco Certified Internetwork Expert (CCIE) (visited Apr. 18, 1999), http://www.cisco.com/warp/public/625/ccie/; Microsoft Corp., Microsoft Certified Professional (MCP) (visited Apr. 28, 2002), http://www.microsoft.com/mcp/; and Novell, Inc., Certified Novell Engineer (CNE) (visited Apr. 18, 1999), http://education.novell.com/cne/cnebroch.htm.

[536] *See* Maier, *supra* note 511, at 39.

§ 3.06   PREVENTIVE LAW POINTERS

[A]   Continuous Security Improvement—Where to Find Your Hacker "Huggy Bear"[537]

Another recent development is online businesses employing rehabilitated cybercriminals as computer consultants to test the security of their sites. Ex-hacker members find their skills in demand and are increasingly hired by companies as consultants and employees to test the security of computer systems. This section explores the advantages and disadvantages of employing hackers as consultants.

SPC must make a decision as to which of its company officers will have complete access to confidential data or information. As with any information-based company, SPC's confidential data and trade secrets are its crown jewels or lifeblood. Some security choices offer low risk. Implementing a firewall or virus protection product from an established vendor, for example, does not require exposing information to any third party. Vendor selection may be done with the help of outside consultants or through an internal technology selection process.[538]

At some point, companies must establish a trust relationship with an in-house security administrator (SA) or choose a reputable external security auditor to assist in setting up their IT security policy. Turning over the keys to the kingdom may be scary; however, relying on references or certifications can make the choice easier.[539] Unfortunately, this is but the first step in a long process. Technology changes rapidly, and the procedures designed to stop today's intruders will offer little resistance to tomorrow's invaders. Staying protected means keeping the company's Information Security Program current. Staying current requires a channel to information about the latest advances in security breaches and remedies.

Large resources will be earmarked for keeping hackers out, but a small sum should be allotted to letting a few in. Despite the noble attempts of security consulting companies, hackers still remain the best security oversight service in the industry. Their efforts will expose any software security loopholes that could leave a firm's data prone to a variety of malicious attacks. Even though the Back Orifice software from Cult of the Dead Cows has been used for malevolent purposes, it has also helped to expose the security flaws in user access rights and procedures in Windows 95. Attrition.org's errata page provides an excellent resource for determining the true radius of risk, as opposed to media hysteria.[540]

---

[537] Bobby Hazelton, an information technology consultant and certified information systems auditor, drafted the tips contained in this section.

[538] ISACA, an independent security assurance corporation, maintains a list of security products having an objective minimum of the necessary specifications. *See* ISACA, Product Certification (last visited Sept.22, 1999), http://www.icsa.net/services/product_cert/products.shtml.

[539] The Information Audit and Control Association has established a set of universal Control Objectives for Information and Related Technologies (CobiT). The Certified Information Systems Auditor (CISA) must possess comprehensive knowledge of these objectives and adhere to a strict guideline of professional ethics. *See* ISACA (last visited Sept. 22, 1999), http://www.isaca.org.

[540] Attrition.org, Errata (last visited Sept. 22, 1999), http://attrition.org/errata/.

It is natural to want to keep hackers away from information resources. Additionally, the hacker culture may not be compatible with the corporate environment. Their choice of language, graphics, and political messages may be contrary to the desired workplace image. One way to insulate a company from both problems is to view hacker web sites and to communicate with hackers through a low-risk meeting place. Maintaining dial-up ISP accounts for security administrators allows contact to be made without compromising or even divulging the location of the corporate network. Maintaining a security test lab on the public side of a firewall will allow security administrators to experiment with new hacks without inadvertently causing harm to actual production resources.

The 1970s TV show "Starsky and Hutch" featured two street-wise detectives who knew their way around the criminal underworld. Although capable police officers, they still relied on Huggy Bear, an informant who was even closer to the criminal element. Thankfully, SAs do not need bright orange Ford Torinos to find their hacker Huggy Bears. Hackers are building security-related sites everywhere. Choosing the sites and/or persons with which to maintain contact, however, will be an individual decision for each SA.[541]

The hiring of reformed hackers may create additional legal risks if confidential information is shared with other hackers. Hiring someone with a record of hacking would be analogous to hiring someone with a criminal record to screen baggage in an airline terminal. "If a company hires a consultant who performs a vulnerability assessment, and anything goes wrong . . . the company may be liable."[542] However, even Microsoft Corporation met with a Dutch hacker who hacked into some of the software giant's web servers.[543]

[B] Computer Emergency Response Team/Coordination Center (CERT/CC)[544]

The CERT/CC is a federally funded research and development facility located at Carnegie Mellon University. The main function of CERT/CC is incident response, but it also provides training to incident response professionals, conducts research into the causes of security vulnerabilities, and provides suggestions for improving network and Internet security.

SPC's administrators may contact CERT/CC by telephone, fax, e-mail, or through the Internet. To use CERT/CC's services, SPC's administrators will need

---

[541] A few of these sites can be found at http://attrition.org/, http://www.cultdeadcow.com/, http://astalavista.box.sk/, and http://neworder.box.sk/. Potential visitors should be warned that the content at some of these sites may be explicit.

[542] George V. Hulme, Vulnerabilities Beckon Some with a License to Hack, InformationWk., Oct. 23, 2000, at 1.

[543] Joris Evers, IDG News Serv., Amsterdam Bureau, Microsoft Hacker Secretive About Meeting, Unix Insider, Nov. 2000.

[544] Written by Kim Vagos, Suffolk University Law School Class of 2002 and expert in cybercrime.

to conduct an internal investigation to gather the following information: (1) all general contact; (2) the name of SPC's host; (3) the IP address and timezone of the affected machine(s); (4) the IP address and timezone of the source of the attack; (5) information on contacts, if any, between the attack and the victim; and (6) a description of the incident, including (a) the date(s), (b) the methods of intrusion, (c) the intruder tools used, (d) software versions and patch levels in use on the target computer(s), (e) intruder tool output, (f) details of the vulnerabilities exploited, and (g) any other relevant information.

CERT officials will review and research the information provided by SPC, prioritizing the report. CERT officials will then give SPC various patch tools with which to remedy the vulnerability. Patches have been devised to plug most known holes in mass-marketed software programs, such as Windows 98 or 2000. If no patches exist for a particular software or specific type of intrusion, CERT will notify the commercial vendors of the software of the existence of the vulnerability so they can addres the problem and prevent similar attacks in the future. CERT/CC's web site, *http://www.cert.org*, provides the latest information on various types of incident response resources.

CERT distributes reports and studies covering Internet security vulnerabilities, available training and education opportunities, survivability research, technical tips, and various advisories on current security issues. CERT/CC is an important resource that SPC should utilize to help it in maintaining a commercially reasonable information security.

[C]   Hacker Insurance

IBM and Sedgwick, a London-based insurance company, have combined to provide Internet security consulting and insurance services. A corporate client that implements their information security tools may also insure for loss of business revenues. Sedgwick offers insurance covering business interruption losses from $5 million to $15 million. Coverage may be available for $50 million or more for losses due to information security intrusions. Security consultants who implement or install firewalls or other information security products may be required to obtain third-party liability insurance as a precaution.[545]

[D]   Denial of Service Protection

SPC's corporate culture should guard against DOS attacks by implementing procedures designed to thwart DDoS agents. SPC's employees need to be instructed to actively scan for viruses, Trojan horses, and other breaches in PC security. Additionally, employees should be instructed to log-off their systems and

---

[545] Kurt D. Baer and Carl E. Metz, Cyber Subrogation Claims: The Next New Things, e-Business Ins. Legal Rep., Feb. 7, 2001, at 7 (noting that cyberinsurers include Lloyd's of London Syndicate).

to shut down their computers for any periods of prolonged inactivity. Company antibreach software programs should be updated frequently, and systems administrators should constantly monitor NIPC alerts and messages from other security periodicals for possible planned hacking activities. New scanning software should be downloaded and implemented, as it becomes available.

If SPC encounters a facial DOS attack, a response team should implement a response plan and continuity of business plan. The response plan should include steps for identifying the offending IP addresses, notifying the offending party of discovery and, potentially, terminating their service, and reporting the attack to state and local authorities. The continuity of business plan should provide for maintaining essential business functions without the aid of Internet resources, alternative processing facilities, and where applicable, alternative methods for customer service and fulfillment.

[E] Antivirus Protection

Antivirus rules need to be instituted as part of SPC's corporate culture. Avoiding viruses is a more effective means than allocating responsibility for the consequences of viruses. Scanning every disk, program, or data file may combat viruses. SPC's employees need to be instructed not to load any application, program, or data file without scanning them first for viruses. Antivirus software programs should be updated frequently.[546] Systems administrators should look for "strange occurrences" to minimize the effects of viruses.[547] Strange or anomalous occurrences include program loading that takes longer than anticipated, unusually large program files, or a sudden reduction in available disk space.[548]

Worms and viruses are programmed to propagate havoc automatically, ad infinitum.[549] A *worm* is a program that travels from one computer to another without attaching itself to the operating system of the computer it infects.[550] A *virus*, on the other hand, while also a migrating program, attaches itself to the operating system of any computer it enters and can affect any other computer that uses files from the infected computer.[551] Technicians may also differentiate a virus from a worm according to how the malicious program implements itself on the computer.

---

[546] Symantec Corporation, Norton AntiVirus Product Information (visited Feb. 27, 2002), http://www.norton.com/nav/index.html.

[547] *Id.*

[548] *Id.*

[549] A Cornell University student released an Internet worm in 1999. Worms are "self-contained programs containing malicious code that copy versions of themselves across electronically connected nodes." Michael D. Scott, Internet and Technology Law Desk Reference 555 (1999) (quoting U.S. General Accounting Office, Information Superhighway).

[550] United States v. Morris, 928 F.2d 504, 505 n.1 (2d Cir.), *cert. denied*, 502 U.S. 817 (1991).

[551] *Id.*

In this sense, a worm is a type of virus or replicative code that situates itself in a computer system in a place where it can do harm.[552] A virus is a piece of programming code inserted into other programming that causes some unexpected and, for the victim, usually undesirable event.[553] A 2001 survey of companies found that nearly one-third reported at least one instance of a virus disaster, defined as "any event in which a single virus infects more than 25 machines, files or pieces of storage media in roughly the same time."[554]

The United States Department of Energy has developed a database of viruses, a project of the Computer Incident Advisory Capability (CIAC). The National Institute of Standards and Technologies of the Commerce Department also compiles an antivirus database. It is estimated that several hundred new computer viruses come online each month, rendering virus databases quickly outdated. Companies that purchase antivirus programs must have the latest version. Even so, new viral attacks may not yet have been detected by even the latest antiviral programs.

[F] Protecting Consumer Privacy

SPC has resolved to maintain the highest standard of ethics when dealing with consumer information. SPC's data collection and use policies will be clearly posted on its web site, and these rules will not be altered unless a compelling advance in technology, legal, or social policy emerges. Whenever SPC changes its data collection policy, it will provide reasonable and fair notice to all its consumers before implementing the change.

SPC will not sell consumer data, nor will it collect any data on consumer behavior that does not directly relate to its ability to improve its service to its customers. In any instance in which consumer data may be collected, SPC will provide a clear and easy mechanism for the consumer to opt out of the data collection procedure. If SPC must collect data to complete its contractual duty, it will offer consumers an alternative means of providing information with the assurance that no information will be obtained or used beyond the purpose of fulfilling the transaction and maintaining normal business records for accounting, regulatory, or other legal purposes.

SPC will ensure that all personal data dealing with consumer behavior will not be provided to any employee not having a business-related need for the information. SPC will apply all security mechanisms used to forestall external attacks to prevent inadvertent access to information by nonauthorized employees. SPC's security manager will be part of an infrastructure team that will review the implementation of any new hardware or software that provides data management, data

---

[552] Whatis.com, What Is a Worm (A Definition) (visited Apr. 14, 2002), http://whatis.com/wormviru.htm.

[553] *Id.*

[554] Sam Costello, Virus Problem Expanded in 2001, Continued Growth Expected, InfoWorld Daily News, Mar. 7, 2002.

mining, or other data analysis services for possible breaches of its stated privacy policies.

If SPC requires consumer data collected by other parties, it will ensure that the data is processed and filtered by a trusted third party. At no time will SPC request or accept consumer behavior data that does not assist it with improving its customer service. Information needed for marketing or increasing business development will be gathered from published industry sources or through clearly marked polls on the SPC web site. All polls will state the underlying business rationale for acquiring the data, and SPC will guarantee that the information will be used only for that purpose.

All SPC security management and regulatory counsel will review industry sources, such as EPIC, The DMA, and the Electronic Frontier Foundation, to ensure that its privacy policy addresses consumers' concerns. Should SPC discover that its privacy policy does not meet the high standards of these organizations, it will adjust its policy in favor of consumer protection and provide the proper notification to its customers. SPC could also consider hiring a chief privacy officer to conduct audits of privacy issues and reduce the risk of consumer privacy lawsuits.[555]

[G] Hold Harmless Clauses

SPC management will not limit its planning regarding webwrap service agreement to contracts with its consumers. SPC might also want to seek special assurances in its paper-based contracts with suppliers. SPC may also wish to enter into agreements with trading partners about allocating the risks of information security. SPC may seek indemnification from its ISP, for example, if the corporate web site is hacked by unknown parties. (A thorough legal audit of the ISP's security protection mechanisms would be a prudent precondition for an agreement.) The following indemnification clause is a simple "hold harmless" adaptable to most information security agreements:

INDEMNIFICATION

_____, at your own expense, agrees to defend, indemnify and hold harmless Suffolk Personal Computer (SPC), its affiliates and their respective officers, directors, employees and agents, from all actions, claims, liabilities, losses, damages, and expenses, including reasonable attorneys' fees, arising out of or relating to the use of any material supplied by _____ including, without limitation, claims arising out of or relating to the content provided by _____, and the use of the domain name provided by _____ to Suffolk Personal Computers (SPC) for use with the _____ web site.[556]

---

[555] John Schwartz, First Line of Defense: Chief Privacy Officers Forge Evolving Corporate Rules, N.Y. Times, Feb. 12, 2001, at 1B.

[556] Vincent Froio, Jr., Esq., drafted this clause.

[H]   Sample Notice to Users

> This computer system is the property of Suffolk Personal Computers. It is for authorized use only. Users (authorized or unauthorized) have no explicit or implicit expectation of privacy. Any or all uses of the SPC computer system may be disclosed to or intercepted, monitored, recorded, copied, audited, or inspected by, any authorized site supervisors.
>
> Unauthorized or improper use of the SPC system may result in administrative disciplinary action and civil and criminal penalties. By continuing to use this system, you indicate your awareness of and consent to these terms and conditions of use. LOG OFF IMMEDIATELY if you do not agree to the conditions stated in this notice.

[I]   Responding to a Computer Intrusion[557]

Private enforcement of cybercrime is a rapidly evolving legal institution that is filling the public law enforcement gap. The role of the Computer Emergency Response Team (CERT) at Carnegie Mellon University is the first line of defense against many forms of cybercrime such as computer intrusions and viruses.[558] CERT officials review material provided by the victims of cybercrime to develop ways to address attacks. CERT also develops software designed to patch software soft spots and other vulnerabilities.[559] A new security alliance was recently launched between CERT and the Electronic Industries Alliance to provide reports on risk management, computer vulnerabilities, computer viruses, and data crimes.[560] CERT also issues advisories to assist network administrators in rapidly responding to computer crimes by audits for anomalies or unauthorized devices.[561] Private enforcers are de facto the first line of offense against fraud, hacking, and viruses by criminals within and outside the organization. In the words of one computer forensics expert: "First you find out who did it. Then get legal advice. And if you can't get it stopped, file a civil suit."[562] It is critical to understand the method

---

[557] Kim Vagos, a 2002 graduate of Suffolk Law School, provided research assistance for this section.

[558] The CERT is located at Carnegie Mellon University and on the web at http://www.cert.org. The Department of Justice frequently works with CERT in developing advisories on software vulnerabilities or reports of new forms of cybercrime. The victims of cybercrime are also encourageed to report computer crime to the NIPC Watch of the Department of Justice. United States Department of Justice, NIPC ADVISORY 01-003 (Mar. 8, 2001) (visited Apr. 22, 20022), http://www.usdoj.gov/criminal/cybercrime/NIPCadvisory.htm.

[559] New Internet Security Alliance Is Born (visited Apr. 19, 2001), http://www.newsbytes.com/news/01/164661.html.

[560] An anomaly is a general information security term that refers to any suspicious or unusual activity or code in a computer system.

[561] Love Bug Suspect Can Still Face Civil Suits Philippine Prosecutor, Agence France Presse, Aug. 23, 2000.

[562] William M. Landes and Richard R. Posner, The Economic Structure of Tort Law 160-61 (1987).

of computer attack. Common methods of intrusion include computer viruses, denial of service, distributed denial of service, Trojan horses, trapdoors, and other known vulnerabilities.[563]

SPC has recently been victimized by a computer intrusion and a series of denial of service attacks. SPC is willing to prosecute computer intruders to deter future hackers who might be tempted to tamper with its computers or digital information in the future. Prosecution is worthwhile for the company because of the time and resources it must expend to remedy the effects of security intrusions. Corporate espionage places SPC's future at stake if the loss of business models, customer lists, trade secrets, or other confidential information impedes its ability to become a fully developed e-business.

Until recently, companies victimized by computer crime have been reluctant to report intrusions to law enforcement agencies because of adverse publicity. A growing number of high-profile online companies, however, are now cooperating with law enforcement officials to prosecute intruders to deter other computer criminals. Successfully combating a computer intrusion or denial of service attack requires prompt remedial measures following the attack. The compromise of a computer system or network often causes confusion in a company, making it all the more important to take quick decisive action.

SPC should designate a person in charge of dealing with security intrusions. This emergency response team head should maintain a chronological log of all events. Systematic documentation helps prevent key evidence from being dispersed, overlooked, or misplaced. A well-documented log helps law enforcement officials and prosecutors obtain convictions.

Network security managers should be notified immediately following the discovery of a computer intrusion. At SPC and other online companies, the network security managers have the best knowledge of company computer systems. The network security manager will be the key person to assist law enforcement in seizing and protecting evidence as well as in understanding the nature of the intrusion.

SPC will need to document the amount of damage that occurred before reporting the security intrusion to law enforcement. Law enforcement is far more likely to be willing to become involved in the case if the damage is great. SPC's network security manager should calculate the costs of the time needed for post-attack recovery. Both law enforcement and prosecuting officials will need these figures to proceed with the investigation. State and federal laws governing computer intrusion incidents observe certain damage thresholds, and only cases reaching these thresholds can be tried in court.

SPC's managers must consult with security officers, legal counsel, or law enforcement on how to proceed once an estimate of the damage from the intrusion

---

[563] National Infrastructure Protection Ctr., Cyberthreat & Computer Intrusion Incident Reporting Guidelines 3 (2001).

has been calculated. The head of SPC's disaster recovery team should then contact the state police and the local Federal Bureau of Investigation (FBI) office. Telephone numbers for the state police and FBI are located on the inside cover of every phonebook, and the offices for both are open 24 hours a day. When contacting the state police, the head of SPC's internal investigation team should ask to speak with an officer on the High Technology or Computer Crime Unit. Most states have specific units devoted to computer crime, and an increasing number of states have units devoted to Internet-related crime.

In many computer intrusions, the FBI will have jurisdiction, due to federal computer crime statutes. The Computer Fraud and Abuse Act is the key federal statute governing intrusions, viruses, or unauthorized access.[564] In addition, the Electronic Communications Privacy Act of 1986 prohibits the interception of electronic messages.[565]

SPC's head of its internal investigation should request to speak with one of the National Infrastructure Protection Center (NIPC) agents, who have specialized knowledge of computer crimes. An agent will likely conduct an interview with SPC's internal investigation chief. The FBI investigates only violations of federal laws. If it is not clear which law enforcement entity has jurisdiction over the situation, the FBI is a good place to start. State officials may prosecute a computer intrusion if the FBI decides against a full-scale investigation.[566]

SPC's administrators must take steps to secure physical evidence, such as copies of intruder-damaged files and system audit logs. Companies often overwrite valuable system logs automatically after a certain period of time, destroying evidence needed for their case. SPC needs to limit access to evidence of the intrusion in the event that it is a trusted insider acting in concert with an outsider. In any case, all evidence, including backup tapes, needs to be secured, with limited authorized access, until the case is closed.

SPC must be aware of the hazards of transmitting or receiving e-mail from a compromised system. Many companies respond to an intrusion by replacing the computer system. SPC's managers must avoid corresponding via e-mail about the computer intrusion incident. Computer hackers often maintain access to the compromised system for some time following the incident and can intercept these communications. If SPC sends e-mails on a compromised e-mail system, it may unwittingly be providing a hacker with information about its computer system and emergency response and the criminal investigation.

If SPC documents each step and preserves evidence at every stage, it will increase the probability of a successful conviction. A successful prosecution of a computer criminal, resulting in a 10-year prison sentence in a federal facility for maliciously unleashing a computer virus, will both deter the individual criminal

---

[564] 18 U.S.C. § 1030 (West Supp. 1999).

[565] 18 U.S.C. §§ 2510 et seq. (Law. Co-op LEXIS 1999).

[566] Every state has enacted a computer crime statute. Many of the states model their statutes after the Computer Fraud and Abuse Act.

and signal to others that such destructive behavior will not be tolerated. Deterrence depends upon certain and severe punishment following actions that threaten the social order. Criminal punishment expresses societal disapproval by ratcheting up the price of wrongdoing. The message of deterrence is that computer crime does not pay.

[J] Wireless LAN Risks*

It has become possible for a company such as SPC to create a network on its premises that employees may use to access the corporate intranet wirelessly. At minimal cost, companies can now deploy networks providing employees with Internet/intranet access via radio waves instead of traditional wire-line methods. The 802.11 standard for deploying wireless ethernet networks has become very popular and provides great mobility for company employees. The major problem with using wireless LANs in a corporate environment is that no security can be afforded to the data on the network at this time. There was initially an algorithm in place to provide some protection, but the Wireless Equivalent Privacy (WEP) algorithm was broken almost as soon as it was released and provides no security to wireless LANs.[567] The lack of security means that it is easy for a third party to compromise data on wireless LANs. An innocent third party trying to access its own data via its own wireless LAN can instead be given wireless access to the wrong LAN or improper access to machines on the appropriate LAN.

Many wireless LANs are improperly configured, or may even be intentionally configured as open networks, making improper access by an unwitting individual easy. It is also simple for a malicious third party to access an unauthorized wireless LAN since there is no security in place to enforce "authorized" versus "unauthorized" access. Then, using existing computer software to read the data on that wireless LAN, the malicious third party may quickly misappropriate and misuse data, damaging the company, perhaps irreparably.

In spite of these dangers, wireless LANs are gaining popularity and, as costs fall, more and more wireless LANs are being implemented. The first common scenario in which these LANs are being used is the corporate scenario. SPC would implement a wireless LAN and provide employees with wireless cards for use at work. The motivation behind this action includes visions of employees accessing the company intranet throughout the site, while away from their desks, in areas that do not generally provide the employee with Internet access, such as cafeterias, conference rooms, and other offices. The employees then use the wireless LAN to send and receive company data of varying levels of importance (private, confidential, proprietary, trade secret). Then, as described above, a third party maliciously (via electronic eavesdropping) or unwittingly (by wandering into range

---

*This section was written by Cynthia Montalvo, network security technologist and Suffolk University Law School student.

[567] Nikita Borisov et al., Security of the WEP Algorithm (visited Apr. 25, 2002), http://www.isaac.cs.berkeley.edu/isaac/wep-faq.html.

from a separate and distinct wireless LAN) gains access to the company information. The information is, at best, in the hands of the public and, at worst, in the hands of a competitor practicing corporate espionage.

The second common scenario is one in which an independent company implements a wireless LAN and provides clients with access to the LAN while on company premises. Many hotels and public places have been offering for-fee wireless LANs since at least the summer of 2001.[568] In the Northwest, Starbucks has been offering wireless LAN access to customers in their coffeehouses since 2001.[569] The threat in this scenario is that an SPC employee would use the for-fee wireless LAN to work remotely, from a hotel while on a business trip, for example, and send and receive company data of varying levels of importance (private, confidential, proprietary, trade secret). The third party, again maliciously or unwittingly, gains access to the company information. The information is once again at risk.

The e-business providing for-fee access (for instance, the hotel or the Starbucks) will most likely have little or no liability for lost data, since it will have presumably protected itself by providing notice to users of the inherent dangers involved in accessing the LAN. It is most likely that SPC will have full liability for any data lost to third parties since it did not safeguard the data properly. Using wireless networks may in and of itself be deemed negligence and SPC, having brought the damage upon iself, may have no legal recourse against those third parties that misuse the information and cause damage (economic or otherwise) to SPC.

In terms of employee liability, the employee will probably not be liable for loss or misuse of the data in the scenario where SPC provided the wireless access and encouraged employee use of the network. However, if the employee negligently accessed a non-SPC wireless LAN for the purposes of performing work for SPC and the data are stolen, then the employee may be liable because of negligence. A reasonable employee should have known better than to use an inherently insecure network for work-related activities. However, if SPC is employing a wireless LAN at work and the employee has been told to use that LAN, absent training or direction to the contrary, it might be reasonable for an employee to assume that SPC sanctions the use of wireless LANs in general.

The third party that took the information ought to be held responsible for misappropriation and misuse of the data. However, realistically speaking, it will be almost impossible to find such a third party and punish him or her in any way. Therefore, even if SPC is not found to be negligent and the third party is held to be liable, there will be no third party against which to enforce a judgment. Even if the third party is known and found, the damage already done to SPC may be irreparable.

---

[568] Mark Gibbs, Less Wires, More Connections, Network World (visited Apr. 25, 2002), http://www.nwfusion.com/columnists/2001/1029gearhead.html.

[569] *Id.*

As of early 2002 there were few, if any, cases litigating these issues. It is difficult to predict how the courts will define liability and how these issues will be resolved. The technology is still new, and the issues of responsibility and liability are still being debated. Companies like SPC would do well to avoid wireless LAN implementation until the issues are better defined.

CHAPTER FOUR

PROTECTING INTELLECTUAL PROPERTY IN CYBERSPACE

§ 4.01   Overview

§ 4.02   Copyrights in Cyberspace
    [A]   Overview
    [B]   Constitutional and Statutory Authority
    [C]   The Copyright Act of 1976
        [1]   Copyright Terms and Extensions
        [2]   Copyright Term for Joint Works
        [3]   Copyright Renewal
        [4]   Exclusive Rights of Copyright
            [a]   What Is Copyrightable?
            [b]   Originality
            [c]   Fixation
        [5]   First Sale Doctrine and Licensing
        [6]   Derivative Works
        [7]   Notice
        [8]   Works Made for Hire
        [9]   Collective Work
        [10]   Joint Works
        [11]   Online Music
    [D]   Copyright Infringement
        [1]   Direct Infringement
        [2]   Contributory Infringement
        [3]   Vicarious Infringement
        [4]   Remedies for Infringement
    [E]   Defenses to Copyright Infringement
        [1]   Fair Use
        [2]   Fair Use in an Online Setting
    [F]   Linking Issues
        [1]   Linking
        [2]   Deep Linking
        [3]   Liability for Remote Links
        [4]   Framing

*We would like to thank Todd Krieger, Esq., of Bose Corporation for his written and editorial contributions to this chapter, and James Ewing, who wrote § 4.05 on E-Commerce-Related Patents.

[G]   Digital Millennium Copyright Act
    [1]   ISP Limited Liability: Section 512
        [a]   Transitory Digital Network Communications
        [b]   Immunity for System Caching
        [c]   Information Residing on Systems or Networks at Direction of Users
        [d]   Information Location Tools
    [2]   Copyright and Management Systems
    [3]   Digital Copies for Libraries
    [4]   DMCA Caselaw
[H]   Noncopyright-Related Issues
    [1]   VARA Moral Rights
    [2]   Right of Publicity
[I]   Software Copyrights
[J]   Online Copyright in Practice
    [1]   Notice of Copyright
    [2]   Benefits of Copyright Registration
    [3]   Registration Procedures
    [4]   Who May File an Application Form?
    [5]   Internet Copyright Searches
    [6]   Content Licenses
        [a]   Granting Clause for Content License Agreements
        [b]   Payment/Royalty Reports
        [c]   Warranties and Infringement
        [d]   Acceptance Testing
        [e]   Choice of Law and Forum/Dispute Resolution
        [f]   Franchise Rules
    [7]   Linking Agreements and Disclaimers
    [8]   Disclaimers
    [9]   Content Posted on SPC's Services
[K]   Streaming Media and Copyright Law

§ 4.03   Trademarks in Cyberspace
[A]   Overview
[B]   Types of Marks
    [1]   Trademark
        [a]   Strength of Trademarks
        [b]   Distinctive Marks
[C]   Other Marks
    [1]   Service Mark
    [2]   Collective Mark
    [3]   Certification Mark
    [4]   Trade Name
    [5]   Trade Dress
[D]   Concurrent Use in Cyberspace
[E]   Trademark Infringement

[1] Likelihood of Confusion Test
[2] Dilution
    [a] Federal Trademark Dilution Act of 1996
    [b] State Antidilution Remedies
[F] Unfair Competition
[G] Defenses to Trademark Infringement
    [1] Noncommercial and First Amendment-Related Defenses
    [2] Statutory Fair Use
    [3] Parody
    [4] Other Defenses
[H] Trademark Registration
    [1] Trademark Searches
    [2] The Benefits of Federal Registration
        [a] Actual Use
        [b] Intent to Use
    [3] International Registration
[I] Protecting Trademarks
[J] Use and Abandonment of Trademarks
[K] Internet Domain Name Issues
    [1] Domain Name Registration Procedure
    [2] Management of Internet Names and Addresses
    [3] UDRP Domain Name Arbitration
        [a] Uniform Domain Name Dispute Resolution Policy (UDRP Policy)
        [b] Rules for Uniform Domain Name Resolution Policy (UDRP Rules)
    [4] Anticybersquatting Consumer Protection Act of 1999
    [5] Domain Name Caselaw
        [a] Infringement
        [b] Federal Dilution
        [c] State Dilution
    [6] Dislodging Cybersquatters
    [7] Metatags
        [a] *Insituform Technologies v. National Envirotech*
        [b] *Playboy Enterprises, Inc. v. Calvin Designer Label*
        [c] *Playboy Enterprises, Inc. v. AsiaFocus International*
        [d] *Playboy Enterprises, Inc. v. Terri Welles*
        [e] *Oppedahl & Larson v. Advanced Concepts*
        [f] *Nettis Environmental Ltd. v. IWI, Inc.*
        [g] *Brookfield Communications, Inc. v. West Coast Entertainment Corp.*
        [h] *Trans Union LLC v. Credit Research, Inc.*

        [i]   *Ty, Inc. v. Baby Me, Inc.*
        [j]   *Oyster Software, Inc. v. Forms Processing Inc.*
        [k]   *Caterpillar, Inc. v. TeleScan Technologies, L.L.C.*
    [8]   **Key Words in Banner Advertisements**
  [L] **Metatag Dispute for SPC**
    [1]   **Metatags**
        [a]   **Potential Causes of Action**
        [b]   **Limitations of Current Law**
        [c]   **SPC's Best Course of Action**

§ 4.04   **Trade Secrets in Cyberspace**
  [A] **Overview**
    [1]   **Uniform Trade Secrets Act**
        [a]   **Misappropriation of Trade Secrets**
        [b]   **Definition of Trade Secret**
        [c]   **"Improper Means" Test**
        [d]   **Reasonable Efforts to Maintain Trade Secrets**
        [e]   **UTSA Remedies for Misappropriation**
        [f]   **Potential UTSA Defendants**
    [2]   **Alternative Claims**
        [a]   **Restatement of Torts**
        [b]   **Breach of Confidence**
    [3]   **Criminal Prosecution for Trade Secret Theft**
    [4]   **Preventing Losses: Nondisclosure Agreements**
    [5]   **Trade Secrets and the Internet**
  [B] **Trade Secrets on the Internet in Practice**
    [1]   **Drafting Nondisclosure Agreements**
        [a]   **Checklist for Nondisclosure Agreement for Web Sites**
        [b]   **Sample Clauses**
    [2]   **Web Site Trade Secrets**
    [3]   **Security Measures to Protect Trade Secrets**
    [4]   **Confidentiality of Trade Secret Litigation**
    [5]   **Inevitable Disclosure/Noncompetition Agreements**

§ 4.05   **E-Commerce-Related Patents**
  [A] **Patent Law Basics**
  [B] **The Patent and Trademark Office Procedure**
    [1]   **Patentability and Patent Examiners**
    [2]   **Patent Prosecution**
  [C] **Anatomy of a Patent**
    [1]   **Specifications**
    [2]   **Drawings of Inventions**
    [3]   **Oath**
    [4]   **Examination of Application**
  [D] **Software Patents**

      [E]   Patent Infringement
      [F]   Patents in Cyberspace
            [1]   Patents for Push Technologies
            [2]   Internet-Related Patents
                 [a]   Roundup of Internet-Related Patents
                 [b]   The Impact of *State Street*
                 [c]   Licensing E-Commerce Patents

§ 4.06   Globalization of Intellectual Property Rights
      [A]   World Intellectual Property Organization (WIPO)
      [B]   Copyright and National Origin of the Work

§ 4.01 OVERVIEW

Intellectual property can represent a significant portion of a company's assets. Aside from start-up capital, the entire value of many online ventures is vested in their trademarks, patented processes, copyrighted content, and domain names. Coupled with the value of intellectual property online is the unfortunate ease of online infringement, both accidental and intentional. This chapter is designed to help a company protect its intellectual property rights (see Table 4.1) while conducting e-commerce. Copyright, trademarks, trade secrets, and patent law comprise the four primary branches of intellectual property law, and this chapter will discuss each in turn.

Section 4.02 addresses copyright issues in cyberspace. Copyright law is the federal law that protects original works of authorship: literary, dramatic, musical, artistic, software, and other works. Traditional copyright law is being challenged on several fronts by the rise of the Internet, and any company operating online must be aware of these issues. Section 4.03 focuses on a host of trademark-related issues, including Internet-related unfair competition. Trademarks like domain names[1] are also important components of intellectual property on the Internet. If a competitor registers and uses trademarks of another company as a domain name, that company may have an action for trademark infringement and false designation of origin under § 43(a) of the Lanham Act. Section 4.04 exposes companies to laws designed to protect trade secrets in cyberspace in the form of business plans, customer lists,[2] and other proprietary information. Section 4.05 reviews e-commerce patents and the licensing agreements, as patents are a critical factor for an online company, which must be aware of the latest developments in computer-based business method patents. Finally, § 4.06 covers the globalization of intellectual property rights.

Throughout the chapter, references will be made to Suffolk Personal Computers (SPC), our hypothetical dot-com company, which will be used to demonstrate the practical impact of intellectual property issues. SPC maintains a hypothetical web site on the Internet at *http://www.spc.com* (the SPC site) that permits users to search for and access content that it has developed for its site. The reader should assume that SPC's web site consists of digital content including software, photographs, databases, and streaming video, all of which is classifiable as intellectual property. We will demonstrate how the company should protect its copyrighted software, trademarks, domain names, trade secrets, and patents while selling goods and services on its web site and also how SPC has rights not only in

---

[1] A *domain name* means any alphanumeric designation registered with domain name registrars or other authorities.

[2] Courts are sharply divided on whether trade secret protection is available for customer lists. H. Ward Classen, General Counsel, CSC Intelicom Inc., Fundamentals of Software Licensing, Presentation at Fourth Annual High Technology Law Conference: Licensing in a Network Environment, Mar. 10, 2000, Suffolk University Law School.

TABLE 4.1
Summary of Intellectual Property in Cyberspace

Intellectual Property	What Is Protected?	Length of Term/Registration
Copyright rights are provided by the U.S. Copyright Act of 1976.	To be copyrightable, digital works must be (1) an "original work of authorship;" and (2) be "fixed in a tangible medium of expression . . ." 17 U.S.C. § 102(a) (2000). The requirement that a work be "fixed in a tangible medium of expression" is satisfied by computer software. Copyright protection extends to source and object code. Copyright works apply to diverse works of authorship on the Internet (i.e., clip-art, video games, thumbnails of copyrighted images, music, DVD movies, and photographs). A copyright owner of a web site has exclusive rights to produce the work, distribute copies, prepare derivative works, rights to public performance, display and make digital performances. 17 U.S.C. § 106 (2000).	Author's life plus 70 years, works made for hire, 120 years from creation for works made for hire; term for joint work: 70 years after death of last surviving author; Registration in the United States Copyright Office. Copyrights may also be registered in foreign countries. The Digital Millennium Copyright Act of 1998 provides new rules for Internet-related copyright activities. The Sonny Bono Copyright Term Extension Act of 1998 increased the copyright term by 20 years.
Trademarks (federal and state) The Lanham Act governs the federal registration of trademarks. Section 43(a) governs unfair competition. Trademark registration is also made in the states, though protection is quite limited.	A trademark is a distinctive symbol used in commerce to identify goods and services. SPC may trademark symbols, designs, and names. Trade dress protection for web site design may also be available under section 43(a) of the Lanham Act. The more distinctive the trademark, the greater the protection. Fanciful or coined marks such as EXXON or KODAK have the highest degree of protection. Generic terms are not protectible. The likelihood of confusion is the touchstone of trademark infringement and means roughly that a customer is	Trademark protection is indefinite, unless abandoned. Federal trademark protection is obtained by registering a trademark application in the U.S. Patent and Trademark Office (USPTO). A trademark applicant may also register trademarks in individual states. Protection may be obtained under the unfair competition provisions of the Lanham Act, federal or state anti-dilution law. Foreign registration may be advisable since registration with the USPTO applies only within the United States. A single registration for European Union countries is made in Alicante, Spain. State trademark protection provides only limited protection.

TABLE 4.1
Summary of Intellectual Property in Cyberspace (Continued)

Intellectual Property	What Is Protected?	Length of Term/Registration
	confused about the source of goods or services. The use of another's trademark in a domain name may also dilute the trademark through tarnishment or blurring.	
Trade secrets (state only)	Commercially valuable secret information such as customer lists, business models, formulas, or business methods.	Trade secret protection is indefinite so long as reasonable efforts are made to maintain secrecy and the information does not become generally known. Protection lasts until the information is disclosed and no longer secret. Most states have adopted the Uniform Trade Secrets Act. There is no provision for registering trade secrets.
Patents Patents are registered with the United States Patent & Trademark Office ("USPTO").	Patents protect inventions securing a monopoly for a limited period in return for disclosure of the invention. To qualify for patent protection, inventions must be novel, utilitarian, and non-obvious ("one-click" method) of ordering goods and services online, methods for the real-time processing of loans. Processes, products, and plants may be patentable subject matter. Patent protection is for inventions which are nonobvious, useful, and novel.	Exclusive rights for 20 years from the date of application. Patent protection is obtained by registering a patent claim with the USPTO. The three statutory requirements for obtaining a patent are (1) novelty, (2) utility, and (3) nonobviousness.

Protections and Remedies for Copyrights

Method for obtaining protection	An infringer may be found liable for direct infringement for unauthorized copying. Direct copyright infringement is a strict liability offense, whereas contributory infringement requires proof of a defendant's knowledge. A defendant is liable for vicarious liability even if the defendant did not know of the infringing activity of a third party. To prevail on a contributory or vicarious copyright claim, a plaintiff must show direct infringement by a third party. A court found that visitors to Napster site

continued

TABLE 4.1
Summary of Intellectual Property in Cyberspace (Continued)

	engaged in direct infringement and that Napster had knowledge of the infringing activity and contributed to infringing conduct of site visitors. The court also found Napster was vicariously liable because it had a direct financial interest in the visitor's infringing activities.[a] A federal court does not have jurisdiction of a copyright infringement claim until the copyright is registered.
Remedies for infringement	Copyright infringement occurs if there is copying done without copyright owner's authorization. Remedies for infringement include (1) injunction; (2) seizure of infringing articles; (3) actual damages plus profits and statutory damages; (4) costs; and (5) criminal penalties. The No Electronic Theft Act of 1997 permits federal prosecution for willful copyright infringement even if the infringer does not act for a commercial purpose or for private financial gain.[b]

[a] Contributory infringement results when a defendant knowingly contributes to infringing conduct of another party. Vicarious copyright infringement occurs if a defendant has a right to supervise the direct infringer and financially benefits from the direct infringer's conduct. SPC is vicariously liable for an online partner's infringing conduct if SPC had a right to supervise and receive profits from the infringing activity. An employer such as SPC could be directly liable for its own infringement and be liable for vicarious or contributory infringement for the acts of its employees, coventurers, or partners.

[b] The No Electronic Theft Act closed the loophole in United States v. Lamacchia, 871 F. Supp. 535 (D. Mass. 1994) (holding that a defendant could not be prosecuted for criminal copyright infringement under the wire fraud statute where no commercial purpose or financial gain was proven).

the digital information sold on its web site, but also in the web site itself. Unlike other chapters, there is not a section devoted to preventive law pointers. Instead, examples are embedded where appropriate within a given topic section.

As the 2003 edition of this book is being prepared, there have been a number of high-profile intellectual property cases involving the Internet. A critical debate is being mounted in Congress and the courts over copyright law in a digital age. In *Eldred v. Ashcroft*, the U.S. Supreme Court granted certiorari in a challenge to the Copyright Extension Act.[3] The Court will determine whether Congress exceeded its power under the Patent and Copyright Clause in enacting the Copyright Term Extension Act, which retrospectively increased the terms of existing copyrights. The petitioners also raise a First Amendment challenge to extensions of present and future copyrights.

Copyright law's fair use doctrine is being updated for the Internet. In *Kelly v. Arriba Soft Corp.*,[4] the Ninth Circuit considered a case in which the operator's

---

[3] 122 S. Ct. 1062 (2002).
[4] 280 F.3d 934 (9th Cir. 2002).

search engine displayed its results as small pictures. It obtained its database of pictures by copying images from other web sites. By clicking on one of these "thumbnails," the user could view a large version of that same picture in the context of the operator's web page. The Ninth Circuit held that the use of the thumbnails was a fair use but that the operator's inline linking to and framing of full-sized images infringed upon the photographer's exclusive right to display the copyrighted work publicly.

Big media companies are seeking new copyright protections in the wake of massive bootlegging of music and video facilitated by services such as Napster. A new type of copyright protection currently being tested on tens of thousands of new CDs prevents the consumer from burning the CD or transferring a copy of the CD onto a hard drive for personal use or distribution on the Internet.[5] This anticircumvention technology has created an uproar among consumers, because the ability they previously enjoyed of making copies or putting a copy on their hard drives has been stripped away.[6]

In the past year, there have been a large number of multimillion-dollar verdicts arising out of intellectual property disputes over digital rights. A Delaware jury found that Broadcom Corp. did not infringe two Intel patents related to networking and digital video in an $82 million patent infringement lawsuit.[7] The jury invalidated Intel's networking patent, and the court will rule on whether Intel is liable for patent misuse and inequitable conduct. In another case, a court granted summary judgment in favor of eBay, ruling that it was not subject to vicarious or contributory copyright infringement by sales by unaffiliated third parties on the auction site.[8] The court ruled that § 512(c) of the Digital Millennium Copyright Act (DMCA) immunized service providers from copyright infringement claims so long as they do not have actual knowledge of the infringing activity and promptly block allegedly infringing sales once notified.

Consumers argue that the anticircumvention provisions of the DMCA need to be balanced against their rights to (1) time-shift, or play back at a later time, audio or video content; (2) space-shift, or copy material to blank CDs and use it on different players at different locations; (3) make backup copies; (4) use content on any platform, for example, on a Windows PC or DVD player; and (5) translate

---

[5] John Borland, Compromise for CD Copying Is in the Works, C/Net News (Sept. 28, 2001), http://www.news.cnet.com/news/0-1005-201-7320279-0.html.

[6] Id.

[7] Drew Cullen, Broadcom Brushes Aside Intel Patent Suits, The Register (Dec. 17, 2001), http://www.theregister.co.uk/content/3/23421.html (stating that "if Intel's claims had been upheld, the patent would have covered the products shipped by nearly every computer networking company in the world").

[8] Hendrickson v. eBay, Inc., 165 F. Supp. 2d 1082 (C.D. Cal. 2001) (holding that a web site and its employees were protected under the safe harbor provision of the Digital Millennium Copyright Act against copyright claims, and the Lanham Act claim was moot since injunctive relief had already been provided).

content into different contents.[9] There is a growing sentiment that the DMCA's anticircumvention rights need to give way to consumer rights.

In *Gucci America Inc. v. Hall & Associates*,[10] plaintiff Gucci owned the trademark and trade name used on jewelry, apparel, and related services. Mindspring is an Internet Service Provider (ISP) that provided web page hosting services to an individual who infringed Gucci's marks. Gucci notified the ISP twice by e-mail that the individual was using the ISP's services to aid in acts of trademark infringement and unfair competition, including advertising jewelry that bore Gucci's trademark on the web site. Gucci alleged that, despite the e-mails, Mindspring continued to permit the defendant individual to use the defendant's Internet services to infringe the plaintiff's trademark rights. The court rejected Mindspring's argument that the First Amendment and the Communications Decency Act of 1996 barred Gucci's claims.

§ 4.02   COPYRIGHTS IN CYBERSPACE

[A]   Overview

The federal law of copyright protects original works of authorship fixed in a tangible form,[11] and a copyright owner has the exclusive right to reproduce copyrighted work, distribute copies, and display the copyrighted works publicly.[12] Courts have had little difficulty ruling that copyright protection extends to electronic materials.[13]

The Internet has made it easier to copy artwork, photographs, streaming video, text computer software, and other information, and recent changes in copyright law are accommodating changing technologies. Web sites are a collection of data, video, sounds, and images accessible to hundreds of millions of Internet users. Many of these materials have their own copyrights, and a web site as a whole may also have copyright protection as a work of authorship.[14]

---

[9] Walter S. Mossberg, Consumers Must Protect Their Freedom to Use Digital Entertainment, Wall St. J., Mar. 14, 2002, at B1 (discussing Digital Consumers bill of rights for consumers' use of digital content).

[10] 135 F. Supp. 2d 409 (S.D.N.Y. 2001) (ruling that neither the First Amendment nor the Communications Decency Act of 1996 immunized web site from claims arising out of trademark infringement, false designation of origin and false descriptions and representations, and unfair competition).

[11] *See* A&M Records, Inc. v. Napster, Inc. 2000 U.S. Dist. LEXIS 11862 (N.D. Cal., Aug. 10, 2000) (enjoining Internet company because of a reasonable likelihood of success on contributory and vicarious copyright infringement claims for assisting site visitors in copying plaintiffs' copyrighted music).

[12] 17 U.S.C. § 106 (2000).

[13] A *domain name* means any alphanumeric designation registered with domain name registrars or other authorities.

[14] Copyright Act, 17 U.S.C. § 401(D) (2002).

A company operating online must register its copyright to protect the original elements of its own web site. The company will also be subject to direct copyright infringement for using images, music, clip art, video, and other copyrighted materials on its web site without the owner's permission or authorization,[15] or even if one of its employees uploads or downloads copyrighted materials without permission.

[B] Constitutional and Statutory Authority

The United States Constitution provides for the protection of intellectual property by granting Congress the power to "promote the Progress of Science and useful Arts, by securing for limited times to Authors and Inventors the exclusive Right to their Writings and Discoveries."[16] The power to determine the duration of copyright terms rests with Congress. Congress extended the length of the copyright term four times in the past century. It is crucial to be aware of the length of the copyright terms because, after expiration, the copyright work descends into the public domain, where it may be freely copied.

[C] The Copyright Act of 1976

Copyright is a federal statutory privilege that applies to works "fixed in a tangible medium" that satisfy a minimum threshold of creativity. Copyright protects literary and dramatic works but not facts, ideas, systems, or mechanics of operation. Section 102(a) of the Copyright Act provides:

> Copyright protection subsists . . . in original works of authorship fixed in any tangible medium of expression, now known or later developed, from which they can be perceived, reproduced or otherwise communicated, either directly or with the aid of a machine or a device.[17]

Copyrights vest immediately upon fixation of an original work of authorship in a tangible medium of expression. However, to bring legal action for infringement of copyrights, the work or works sought to be protected must be registered with the United States Copyright Office ("Copyright Office"). A prima facie case for infringement is made when a copyright owner shows proof of ownership and copying. Third parties may be liable for vicarious or contributory infringement even if they have not copied or displayed protected material,[18] although copyright infringement that occurs solely outside the territorial boundaries of the United

---

[15] *See, e.g.,* Marobie-FL., Inc. v. National Assoc. of Fire Equip. Distributors, 983 F. Supp. 1167 (N.D. Ill. 1997) (finding defendant liable for using copyrighted clip art on web site without permission or authorization).

[16] *See* U.S. Const. art. I, § 8, cl. 8.

[17] 17 U.S.C. § 102 (2002).

[18] *See* § 4.02[D] *infra.*

States is outside the scope of federal copyright protection.[19] Chapter Eight provides a discussion of how residents in member states such as the United States receive copyright protection in the other nations that are signatories to the Berne Convention as well as to Trade-Related Aspects of Intellectual Property (TRIPS).

[1]   Copyright Terms and Extensions

The history of copyright has evidenced a continuous expansion in the copyright term. Copyrighted works created after January 1, 1978, are protected for the life of the author plus 70 years. For joint works, protection is life of the last surviving author plus 70 years. If a work was created (fixed in tangible form for the first time) on or after January 1, 1978, it is automatically protected from the moment of its creation and is ordinarily given a term enduring for the author's life plus an additional 70 years after the author's death. For works created, published, or registered before January 1, 1978, the copyright lasts for a first term of 28 years from the date it was secured. During the last (twenty-eighth) year of the first term, the copyright was eligible for renewal.[20]

Table 4.2 describes the copyright term *after* the Sonny Bono Copyright Term Extension Act of 1998 (CTEA), which became law on October 27, 1998.[21] The CTEA extends the copyright duration for individual and corporate entities by an additional 20 years. Individual authors now receive copyright protection for life plus 70 years.[22] Corporate entities receive copyright protection for a "work made for hire" to 95 years from publication or 120 years from creation, whichever is shorter. These rights apply to works created on or after January 1, 1978. The CTEA also immediately extends copyrights still in their renewal term at the time the Act was passed. The effect of the law is to delay the entrance of copyrighted material into the public domain.

The U.S. Supreme Court granted a writ of certiorari to consider the constitutionality of the Copyright Term Extension Act in *Eldred v. Ashcroft*.[23] The petitioners claim that Congress's retrospective extension of current and future copyright terms exceeded its powers under the Patent and Copyright Clause of the U.S. Constitution. This issue had been considered and dismissed summarily by a federal district court and also by the court of appeals in *Eldred v. Reno*[24] and then again by the court of appeals in *Eldred v. Ashcroft*.[25] The plaintiffs argued that the

---

[19] Subafilms v. MGM-PATHE Communications Co., 24 F.3d 1088 (9th Cir. 1999), *cert. denied*, 513 U.S. 101 (1994) (holding that copyright laws have no application to extraterritorial infringement).

[20] The basic copyright rules described in this section are based upon the publication of the United States Copyright Office, Questions Frequently Asked in the Copyright Office (visited Mar. 1, 2000), http://www.lcweb.loc.gov/copyright/faq.html.

[21] Sonny Bono Copyright Term Extension Act of 1998, Pub. L. No. 105-298, 112 Stat. 2827 (1998).

[22] *Id.*

[23] 122 S. Ct. 1062 (2002).

[24] 74 F. Supp. 2d 1 (D.D.C. 1999).

[25] 239 F.3d 372 (D.C. Cir. 2001).

TABLE 4.2
Copyright Terms

Type of Work and Date of Creation	Length of Term
Single author: On or after 1/1/78	Life of author + 70 years after the author's death
Joint authors: On or after 1/1/78	Life of last surviving author + 70 years
Works made for hire: On or after 1/1/78	95 years from first publication or 120 years from creation, whichever is shorter
Work originally created before 1/1/78, but not published or registered by that date	Duration is same as for work created on or after 1/1/78: author's life + 70 or 95/120-year terms apply to them.
Work originally created and published or registered before 1/1/78	Extends renewal term of copyrights still subsisting on that date by an additional 20 years (renewal term of 67 years and a total term of 95 years).*

* If a work is unpublished as of January 1, 1978, protection lasts for the life of the author plus 70 years, but the term expires no earlier than December 31, 2000. If a previously unpublished work is published between January 1, 1978, and December 31, 2002, the term extends until December 31, 2047.

CTEA is a violation of the First Amendment and the Copyright Clause of the Constitution.[26]

The plaintiffs "maintained only that the substantive grant of power in the Copyright Clause—authorizing the Congress to grant copyrights for "limited Times"—does not authorize the Congress to extend the terms of copyrights as it did in the CTEA."[27] Congress has extended the term of copyrights "eleven times since 1962, compared to only twice from 1790 to 1962." The plaintiff argued that the concept of copyright's limited protection loses all meaning if Congress is empowered to endlessly extend the reach of the copyright term. The relentless expansion of the copyright term is inconsistent with the concept of a limited copyright.[28] The major policy question is whether constitutional limits should be placed on the power of Congress to extend copyright terms.

[2] Copyright Term for Joint Works

Joint works are works created by "two or more authors with the intention that their contributions be merged into inseparable or interdependent parts of a unitary whole."[29] The duration of a joint work not classified as a work for hire is 70 years after the last surviving author's death. The duration of copyright in joint works is

---

[26] 255 F.3d 849 (D.C. Cir. 2001).
[27] *Id.* at 850.
[28] *Id.*
[29] 17 U.S.C. § 303(a) (2002).

generally computed in the same way as for works created on or after January 1, 1978: the life-plus-70 or 95/120-year terms apply to them as well. The Copyright Act provides that in no case will the term of copyright for works in this category expire before December 31, 2002, and for works published on or before December 31, 2002, the term of copyright will not expire before December 31, 2047. The CTEA expanded copyright an additional 20 years.

[3] Copyright Renewal

The Copyright Act states that the parties entitled to the renewal and extension of copyrights are (1) the author of such work, if the author is still living; (2) the widow, widower, or children of the author, if the author is not living; and (3) the author's executors, if the author, widower, or children are not living; or (4) next of kin.[30] The 1976 Act extended the renewal term from 28 to 67 years for copyrights. Pre-1978 copyrights restored under the Uruguay Round Agreements Act (URAA) are eligible for a total term of protection of 75 years.[31] The CTEA further extended the renewal term of copyrights still subsisting on that date by an additional 20 years, providing for a renewal term of 67 years and a total term of protection of 95 years.[32]

The Copyright Act creates copyright protection for the author's life, plus 50 years for individual works, and 75 years for commissioned works or works for hire.[33] When an author dies before the renewal period begins, his or her executor is entitled to the renewal rights unless the author has assigned those rights to another party, such as a publisher.[34]

[4] Exclusive Rights of Copyright

The Copyright Act grants the copyright owner the right to display "literary, musical, dramatic, and choreographic works, pantomimes, and pictorial, graphic, or sculptural works, including the individual images of a motion picture or other audiovisual work, publicly."[35] Copyright ownership refers to the exclusive rights granted by § 106 of the 1976 Copyright Act (1) to reproduce the copyrighted work in copies or phonorecords; (2) to prepare derivative works based upon the copyrighted works;[36] (3) to distribute copies or phonorecords of the copyrighted work to the public by sale or other transfer of ownership, or by rental, lease, or lending;

---

[30] 17 U.S.C. § 304(a)(1)(c) (2002).

[31] 17 U.S.C. § 304 (2002).

[32] 17 U.S.C. § 304(b) (2002).

[33] 17 U.S.C. § 302 (2002).

[34] 17 U.S.C. § 304(b) (2002).

[35] *Id.*

[36] A *derivative work* is a work based upon a preexisting work. A motion picture version of *Oliver Twist* is a derivative work.

and, (4) in the case of literary, musical, dramatic, and choreographic works, pantomimes, and motion pictures and other audiovisual works, to perform the copyrighted work publicly. A *performance* or *display* of a work means to perform or display it at a place open to the public.

The extent of the rights afforded to a copyrighted work depends somewhat on the type and nature of the work. The 1909 Copyright Act, for example, provided no protection for a particular performer's rendition of a musical work. The Court in *Sony Corp. of America v. Universal City Studios, Inc.*[37] determined that the manufacturers of videocassette recorders (VCRs) that consumers used to record respondents' programming did not constitute copyright infringement. The Court noted that when Congress enacted the Sound Recording Amendment of 1971, Congress extended copyright protection to sound recordings. Once it is determined that a work is in fact copyrightable and in what category that work belongs, the scope of protection for that work may be fully ascertained. In the *Sony* case, the Court determined that Congress did not intend to prohibit the private home use of either audio or video tape recording equipment in its holding that VCR manufacturers were not liable for contributory infringement.[38] The Copyright Office determined in a rulemaking proceeding that the transmission of an AM/FM radio broadcast over the Internet is not exempt from copyright liability under the exemption to the digital performance rights in sound recording. The Copyright Office initiated the rulemaking proceeding as a response to a petition from the Recording Industry Association of America (RIAA).[39] The RIAA's position was that broadcasting transmission of an AM or FM radio station over the Internet is not exempt from copyright liability under § 114 of the Copyright Act. The courts may ultimately determine whether the § 114(d)(1)(A) exemption covers a digital transmission over the Internet.

In *ILOG Inc. v. Bell Logic LLC*,[40] a federal court in Massachusetts ruled that software with added features to help implement business policies was outside the scope of copyright protection because it was classified as an idea and methods. In granting summary judgment of noninfringement, the court held that the literal copying of nonliteral elements of a copyrightable program was not protectable. Although the computer software program was protectable, the enhancements were not. The court applied the abstraction, filtration, and comparison test of *Computer Associates International Inc. v. Altai Inc.*[41] to this case of nonliteral copying. The court found that mere expressions of methods of operation are not copyrightable. In *ILOG* the copied elements included enhancements such as having dual editors for writing rules (one for computer trained persons and one for nontechnical users), context-sensitive pop-up menus, and the color-coding of key words. The

---

[37] 464 U.S. 417 (1984).

[38] *Id.* at 438.

[39] Public Performance of Sound Recordings: Definition of a Service, 37 C.F.R. pt. 201, 65 Fed. Reg. 77292 (Dec. 11, 2002).

[40] 181 F. Supp. 2d 3 (D. Mass. 2002).

[41] 982 F.2d 693 (2d Cir. 1992).

court found that individually, the elements were uncopyrightable ideas and collectively constituted methods of operation. Federal copyright law did not protect either the ideas found in the elements or the aggregate methods of operation.

[a] What Is Copyrightable?

Copyright law protects "original works of authorship" that are "fixed" in a tangible medium of expression."[42] In other words, copyright protects expression but not ideas, facts, nonoriginal databases, and public domain and government materials. Quantum theory is not copyrightable. A book describing how quantum theory explains the periodic chart of the elements, however, is copyrightable.[43] Inventions, based upon quantum theory, such as the laser or microchip, are patentable. Einstein's general theory of relativity is an idea not copyrightable, but a book on Albert Einstein's thought experiments in the 1930s is copyrightable. In an online environment, a company must obtain copyright protection for all created works of authorship, including software code, images, clip art, text, software, audio, HTML, and other digital information.

The Copyright Act recognizes eight categories of authorship, all of which may be displayed in an Internet transmission: (1) literary work; (2) musical works, including any accompanying words; (3) dramatic works, including any accompanying music; (4) pantomimes and choreographic works; (5) pictorial, graphic, and sculptural works; (6) motion pictures and other audiovisual works; (7) sound recordings; and (8) architectural works.[44] Section 106 of the 1976 Copyright Act sets forth the six exclusive rights of copyright owners (would apply to online content):

1. *To reproduce* the work in copies or phonorecords;
2. To prepare *derivative works* based upon the work;
3. *To distribute copies or phonorecords* of the work to the public by sale or other transfer of ownership, or by rental, lease, or lending;
4. *To perform the work publicly,* in the case of literary, musical, dramatic, and choreographic works, pantomimes, and motion pictures and other audiovisual works;
5. *To display the copyrighted work publicly,* in the case of literary, musical, dramatic, and choreographic works, pantomimes, and pictorial, graphic, or sculptural works, including the individual images of a motion picture or other audiovisual work; and
6. In the case of *sound recordings, to perform the work publicly* by means of a *digital audio transmission.*

Several categories of works are generally not eligible for federal copyright protection. Works so fleeting and ephemeral that they are not fixed in a tangible

---

[42] 17 U.S.C. § 101 (2002).

[43] *See, e.g.,* J.P. McEvoy & Oscar Zarate, Introducing Quantum Theory 3 (1997).

[44] 17 U.S.C. § 102 (2000) (defining the categories of works of authorship).

form of expression are not copyrightable. No copyright covers works written in the sands of a Cape Cod beach or etched on a frosty windshield. An unrecorded improvisational speech is not copyrightable. Titles of books or periodicals are not copyrightable. Short phrases and slogans such as "Got Milk?" are not copyrightable, but they may be trademarked. Familiar symbols, designs, and variations in typographic lettering or coloring are not copyrightable. Lettering or colorings are not copyrightable. Federal copyright law does not protect:

1. Ideas, procedures, methods, systems, processes, concepts, principles, discoveries, or devices, as distinguished from a description, explanation, or illustration.

2. Works consisting *entirely* of information that is common property and that contains no original authorship (for example, standard calendars, height and weight charts, tape measures and rulers, and lists or tables taken from public documents or other common sources).[45]

In *Schoolhouse Inc. v. Anderson*,[46] the Eighth Circuit ruled that a web site's selection and arrangement of topics in a table similar to a copyrighted magazine did not constitute copyright infringement. The plaintiff Schoolhouse Inc. is the publisher of a magazine addressing the quality of schools in various neighborhoods of Minneapolis and St. Paul and marketed to homebuyers. The defendant was a real estate agent who created a web site including information from Schoolhouse's table. The court concluded that "the selection and arrangement of facts . . . [we]re as a matter of law, not substantially similar to the selection[s]" in the defendant's web site.[47] The *Schoolhouse* court found that the ratio of similar topics was not probative as to originality. Rather, the selection and arrangement of topics was the key factor in the test for copyrightable originality.

[b] Originality

A work needs some minimum degree of originality to qualify for copyright protection, and a work is original if it was independently created by the author and possesses some minimal level of creativity. Copyright law protects any content a company places on its web site as well as postings by visitors, although most compilations of data lack the creativity necessary for protection. In *Feist Publications, Inc. v. Rural Telephone Service Co.*,[48] the Supreme Court found that a telephone directory consisting of white and yellow pages lacked the minimal originality to receive copyright protection. The Court rejected a "sweat of the brow" theory that

---

[45] 17 U.S.C. § 102(b) (2002).

[46] 275 F.3d 726 (8th Cir. 2002).

[47] *Id.* at 731.

[48] 499 U.S. 340 (1991).

the time and effort in compiling and organizing a database satisfied the originality requirement for copyright protection.[49]

Since *Feist*, there has been intense lobbying to create additional database protection.[50] The European Union adopted database protection in a directive that requires individual signatory countries to develop conforming amendments. In fall 1999, the House Judiciary Committee considered a bill, H.R. 354, "that would grant copyright protection to collections of computerized data and make it illegal for competitors to copy, repackage, and sell information obtained over the Internet or from CD-ROMS." The bill would impose civil and criminal liability for the unauthorized extraction of a database, providing that the extraction adversely affected the market for the product or service incorporating the database.[51]

[c] Fixation

The second requirement is that the work be fixed in a tangible medium of expression. A work is fixed in a tangible medium of expression when it is sufficiently permanent or stable to permit it to be perceived, reproduced, or otherwise communicated for a period of more than transitory duration.[52] The Copyright Act provides that copyright protection may be obtained "in original works of authorship fixed in any tangible medium of expression, now known or later developed, from which they can be perceived, reproduced, or otherwise communicated, either directly or with the aid of a machine or device."[53] Software inscribed on a diskette or CD-ROM is sufficiently tangible to meet the fixation requirement.[54]

Material on a web site is fixed because it may be perceived, reproduced, downloaded, or transmitted. The Ninth Circuit, in *MAI Systems Corp. v. Peak Computer*,[55] held that simply loading a computer operating system into RAM constituted the making of a copy for purposes of the Copyright Act. The act of transmitting e-mail or viewing a web page also stores copies in the user's computer operating system and creates copies. The web site visitor makes a temporary copy each time a browser visits a web site.

---

[49] The supporters of the Digital Millennium Copyright Act introduced a provision for database protection added to the Conference Report. Jonathan Band, Digital Millennium Copyright Act (visited Apr. 23, 2002), http://www.dfc.org/issues/graphic/2281/JB-Index/JB-Memo/jb-memo.html.

[50] Federal Legislation: Collections of Information Antipiracy Act, H.R. 354: Congress Introduces Database Piracy Bill for Third Time, 12 Software Law Bull. 185 (Sept. 1999) (discussing proposed bill granting copyright protection to computer databases). The statutory purpose of the proposed Collection of Information Antipiracy Act is to revive the "sweat of the brow" doctrine struck down in *Feist*.

[51] Microsoft Law & Corporate Affairs, Summary of Global Internet Legal Developments (for the period Jan.-Mar. 1999) 56 (Apr. 1999).

[52] 17 U.S.C. § 101 (2002).

[53] *Id.*

[54] MAI Sys. Corp. v. Peak Computer, Inc., 991 F.2d 511 (9th Cir. 1993) (holding that loading a program in a computer's random access memory constituted a copy for purposes of the Copyright Act).

[55] 991 F.2d 511 (9th Cir. 1993).

[5] First Sale Doctrine and Licensing

The *first sale doctrine* of § 109 of the Copyright Act provides that the *owner* of a copy lawfully acquired may use, dispose of, or display it without risk of infringement.[56] Copyright owners have exclusive distribution and display rights. Copyright is therefore licensed to circumvent the "first sale doctrine" of the Copyright Act. If a copyright owner licenses a copyrighted work, the owner retains rights of distribution and display. A licensee of computer software may, for example, own the physical diskette or CD-ROM but not the copyrighted information inscribed on the diskette.

Courts distinguish between copyright protection for books and e-books transmitted in a digital format. A licensor must include electronic rights as well as book rights if seeking to distribute copyrighted materials in an electronic format. When the owner of a copyright transferred "the right to 'print, publish and sell the works in book form,'" a court ruled that the transfer of rights in book form did not include e-book rights.[57] In *Random House, Inc. v. Rosetta Books, LLC*, the publisher contracted with the authors to publish their books in book form, but the defendant contracted with some of the same authors to publish their books on the Internet.[58] Random House brought an action of copyright infringement against the defendant. The court held that Random House could not develop a prima facie case for the claim because "the phrase itself ['print, publish and sell the works in book form'] distinguishes between the pure content—i.e. 'the work'—and the format of display—'in book form.'"[59] In addition, the court found that in custom, the phrase is understood by the industry to not include publishing the works in e-book format.[60]

[6] Derivative Works

A *derivative work* arises out of a preexisting work and includes translations, arrangements, films, recording, or condensations, and an owner of a copyright has the right to prepare derivative works of preexisting works such as "a translation, musical arrangement, dramatization, fictionalization, motion picture version, sound recording, art reproduction, abridgment, condensation, or any other form, recast, transformed, or adapted."[61]

A Spanish translation of a Robert Parker novel is a derivative work, as is a French translation of the American film *Eyes Wide Shut*. New versions of e-commerce software or enhancements to search engines constitute derivative works.

---

[56] 17 U.S.C. § 109 (2002). *See also* Bobbs-Merrill Co. v. Straus, 210 U.S. 339, 349-350 (1908) (holding that owner has no exclusive rights after first sale of a copyrighted work).

[57] 150 F. Supp. 2d 613, 614 (S.D.N.Y. 2001).

[58] *Id.*

[59] *Id.* at 620.

[60] *Id.* at 621.

[61] 17 U.S.C. § 101 (2002) (defining derivative works).

[7]   Notice

Companies should always include a copyright notice on their works in such a manner that will give reasonable notice of the claim of copyright. Proper notice precludes a defendant in a copyright infringement lawsuit from using an "innocent infringer" defense to mitigate actual or statutory damages. Section 401 of the Copyright Act lists the proper form for a copyright notice as consisting of the following three elements: (1) the copyright symbol ©, the word "Copyright," or the abbreviation "Copr."; (2) the year of first publication of the work; and (3) the name of the owner of the copyright. For example, on SPC's web site, the copyright notice should read © 2001 Suffolk Personal Computers.

The proper affixing of copyright notice gives global Internet users around the world notice that its web site and content is protected by copyright.

[8]   Works Made for Hire

The Copyright Act treats works prepared for an employee within the scope of employment as a work for hire, which means that the company for which the work is prepared is considered the author. Works for hire include a work specially ordered or commissioned for use as a contribution. Section 101 of the Copyright Act defines a "work made for hire" as:

(1)   A work prepared by an employee within the scope of his or her employment; or

(2)   A work specially ordered or commissioned for use as a contribution to a collective work, as a part of a motion picture or other audiovisual work, as a translation, as a supplementary work, as a compilation, as an instructional text, as a test, as answer material for a test, or as an atlas, if the parties expressly agree in a written instrument signed by them that the work shall be considered a work made for hire. . . .[62]

Whether an author is an employee acting within the scope of his or her employment is determined by the common law rules of agency. Therefore, for a company to be the owner of the copyright in a work, the employee must have created the work within the scope of his or her employment, or the work must be one that is specifically listed in part 2 of the definition of a work made for hire.

[9]   Collective Work

A web site is a *collective work* if it includes separate contributions from different content providers. Copyright in collective work vests initially with the author of the contribution and includes the whole work. A co-branded site may include contributions from at least two creators of content, each of which has an

---

[62] Copyright Act, 17 U.S.C. § 101 (2002).

ownership interest in the site as a collective work. Each author contributing copyrighted text, photographs, images, or other material to the web site may have a copyright ownership interest to the web site if it is a collective work. If a visitor posts photographs or text in publicly accessible areas of a web site, for example, the site owner needs to obtain worldwide, royalty-free, and nonexclusive licenses to reproduce, modify, adapt, and publish such content.

The court in *Greenberg v. National Geographic Society*[63] held that National Geographic could not republish a freelance photographer's work in a CD-ROM collective work without receiving permission by "rul[ing] that the CD-ROM set was not a mere revision of a prior collective work, but instead was an entirely new product."[64] In *National Geographic*, the plaintiff's photographs were used in its magazine and the copyright transferred back from the publisher. The magazine created a compact disc program that included all of its published magazines and an animated clip featuring one of the plaintiff's photographs. The district court granted summary judgment to the magazine, holding that the revision of the prior collective work was privileged. The Eleventh Circuit disagreed, holding that the CD-ROM was a new collaborative product not protected by fair use and was not a mere revision of the magazines.

[10] Joint Works

The Copyright Act defines a *joint work* as "a work prepared by two or more authors with the intention that their contributions will be merged into an inseparable or interdependent parts of a unitary whole."[65] The intention that two works be merged must exist at the time of the creation of the work. A joint work is created even if the collaborative efforts or contributions of the authors are unequal. The authors of a joint work are considered to be co-owners of the copyright in the work. The joint owners of a copyright are analogous to "tenants in common, with each co-owner having an independent right to use or license the use of a work, subject to a duty of accounting to the other co-owners for any profits."[66] A joint owner cannot be held liable for copyright infringement to his or her co-owner. In the absence of a web development agreement, a web site created by several parties may be classifiable as a joint work. Joint authorship is a distinct possibility where a dot-com company hires a site developer and designer to construct the site and there is no "work for hire" agreement or transfer of ownership. The term of the copyright for a joint work is "the life of the last surviving author and seventy years after such last surviving author's death."[67]

---

[63] 244 F.3d 1267 (11th Cir. 2001).

[64] Kendra Mayfield, Freelance Victory Blurs Picture, Wired (Oct. 10, 2001), http://www.wired.com/news/politics/0,1283,47430,00.html.

[65] 17 U.S.C. § 201 (2002).

[66] Prepared Testimony of Marybeth Peters, Register of Copyrights, U.S. Copyright Office, Testimony Before the House Judiciary Committee, Subcommittee on Courts and Intellectual Property, Sound Recordings as Works Made for Hire (May 25, 2000), reprinted in Federal News Service, May 25, 2000.

[67] 17 U.S.C. § 302(B) (2000).

Lack of a formal agreement regarding web site content ownership can lead to litigation. For example, the publisher of Scientific American failed to formalize its contractual arrangement to develop a web site in *Holtzbrinck Publishing Holdings, L.P. v. Vyne Communications, Inc.*[68] Holtzbrinck is the parent company of *Scientific American* (SA) and a number of other publications. Holtzbrinck hired Vyne, a web site developer, to construct and maintain its web site. The parties had an oral agreement for the developer to create files, code, graphics, and other necessary components for the web site.[69] Vyne created and maintained the site from sometime in 1995 to March of 1996. Late in 1995, Holtzbrinck negotiated with Vyne to create the SA site with the provision that the site would not be developed and serviced until it could be transferred in-house.

As the SA site became more complex and additional features were added, the parties discussed the need to formalize their web site developer agreement. Holtzbrinck sent Vyne a draft web site development agreement containing a "work for hire" clause. The developer objected to the clause and claimed that he owned all the coding, programming, and graphics for the SA site. Vyne threatened to shut down the SA site unless additional fees were paid and no written development agreement was ever formalized. Vyne not only claimed ownership of the SA site, but the right to deny Holtzbrinck use of materials on the site.[70] Holtzbrinck filed a certificate for copyright registration for the web site after negotiations broke down between the publisher and site developer. The published filed a motion for declaratory judgment in federal district court to determine ownership to the site. The federal district court granted the publisher's motion in part and denied it in part. The court held that Holtzbrinck had, at minimum, a nonexclusive license in the programs and files created by Vyne. The court found it ambiguous whether the publisher and developer intended the SA web site to be a joint work with both parties sharing ownership.

The *Holtzbrinck* case illustrates the necessity for a written web site development and maintenance agreement. It is critical that the development agreement vest sole ownership in the online company. If a site is considered to be a joint work, either co-owner could transfer the site to a third party, accounting only for the profits of such a transfer. A web site development agreement prevents disputes over respective rights and responsibilities, including ownership of the site. The web site development agreement will also address the issue of whether a developer gives warranties on whether components are inoperable. It is important to address the issue of whether the site is a "work made for hire" as the online company wants ownership of the site. The development agreement will also address whether the site developer may use the "look and feel" of a site or components on the site for other projects. If independent contractors are used to perform any of the work on the site, there must be some agreement as to ownership of the content or the components.

---

[68] 2000 U.S. Dist. LEXIS 5444 (S.D.N.Y., Apr. 26, 2000).
[69] *Id.* at *3.
[70] *Id.* at *7.

[11] Online Music

The Internet has dramatically changed the dynamics of music distribution. An entire generation that did not grow up with vinyl records now has little reason to visit a music store to buy compact discs. Consumers can sample music online, create custom CDs, upload their own garage band recordings, visit virtual music communities, or even transform their computers into virtual jukeboxes. Music file compression formats and faster communication tools have reduced the speed of downloading a music track from hours to minutes. MP3 is a file compression format that permits the rapid compression of CDs into electronic files. Once posted online or listed on a file swapping network, the files can be copied by Internet users. Copyrights may attach to the written music and lyrics as well as the performance.

 A consumer who buys a CD has a limited right to transfer the contents to other media, such as cassette tape or a computer file, for his or her own use. When the consumer transfers the file to a friend, it is violating its limited right and infringing the copyright of the CD. Some web sites, such as MP3.com,[71] were embroiled in copyright disputes since they exceeded the scope of permitted use of CDs by allowing different degrees of public access to tracks without the permission of the record companies or artists. Peer-to-peer networking technologies like Napster had further complicated matters by letting users search, upload, and download tracks directly from other participants' computers. A court rejected Napster's argument that it was not liable for direct or contributory copyright infringement because it was immunized by the Digital Millennium Copyright Act's safe harbor provision.[72] Napster's service of enabling Internet users to copy digitized files of copyrighted music without payment or permission constituted contributory and vicarious infringement. Rights to use video clips may be retained by syndicators, and may only be licensed to a network.[73] Napster is an online application that permits the downloading of MP3 music from the Internet. New technologies for the downloading and sharing of DVDs, movies, and music are being used by millions of Internet users. "Three companies, MusicCity.com, Grokster and Consumer Empowerment B.V., employ decentralized technologies to permit Internet users to share music."[74] The decentralized file-sharing system permits Internet users to use their own computer as an instrumentality for trading and searching for music to download. Napster, in contrast, was designed so that users would use Napster's computer system to search for titles and their own computers to trade music with other Internet surfers.[75] The music industry would find it difficult to

---

[71] UMG Records, Inc. v. MP3.Com, Inc., 2000 U.S. Dist. LEXIS 13293 (S.D.N.Y., Sept. 6, 2000) (concluding that MP3.com was a willful infringer and imposing statutory damages of $25,000 for each copyrighted compact disc in the defendant's online database).

[72] A & M Records, Inc. v. Napster, Inc., 2000 U.S. Dist. LEXIS 11862 (N.D. Cal., Aug. 10, 2000).

[73] James R. Burdett, et al., A Wake Up Call From Virtual Reality, Mid-Winter Inst., The Law of Computer Related Tech. 131 (1995).

[74] Matt Ritchel, A New Suit Against Online Music, N.Y. Times (Oct. 4, 2001), http://www.nytimes.com/2001/10/04/technology/04MUSI.html?todayheadlines.

[75] Id.

restrain the activities of the post-Napster companies as their subscribers could continue to trade and search for titles even if the companies were permanently enjoined.[76]

[D] Copyright Infringement[77]

Copyright infringement is the legal cause of action used to protect and enforce the exclusive rights of copyright owners. Copyright infringement occurs when any of the copyright owner's rights are violated by another party. The posting of unauthorized copyrighted pictures on a web site violates the exclusive rights of the copyright owner. A prima facie case for direct copyright infringement is made by demonstrating (1) the plaintiff's ownership of a valid copyright and (2) the defendant's violation of at least one of the exclusive rights of the copyright owner.[78] There is no copyright infringement if the copyright owner has given permission to use copyrighted information in cyberspace. There is no copyright infringement if online publication constitutes fair use or there is some other defense. The law recognizes three types of infringement: (1) direct infringement, (2) contributory infringement, and (3) vicarious infringement (see Table 4.3).

This section uses a recent case, *A&M Records v. Napster,*[79] to illustrate copyright infringement in an online setting. The defendant, Napster, was an online service that facilitated the transmission of MP3 digital music files between users through a "peer to peer" file-sharing technology. The Napster service allowed its users to copy MP3 files that were stored on other user's hard drives. Users could search for MP3 files stored on other users computers. Napster users created a list of the song files. These files were then uploaded to the Napster server while that user was connected to the Napster system. The Napster service maintained a current list of available song titles based on the song lists of users that were connected to the system at any given time. In the *Napster* case, the plaintiffs were record companies that brought a copyright infringement action against Napster for facilitating the exchange of copyrighted songs. To establish Napster's liability for contributory and/or vicarious infringement, the plaintiffs first had to demonstrate that the Napster *users* were direct infringers.

To obtain song files, a Napster user first had to search the index of available song file names. The Napster server then returned a list of available songs that matched the search criteria. Once the user selected the song that he or she desired, the Napster service transfered a copy to the user's computer from another user's computer. The file was copied directly from the transferor's machine to the recipient's machine, hence the term "peer-to-peer" software.[80]

---

[76] John Borland, Suit Hits Popular Post-Napster Network, C/Net News (Oct. 3, 2001), http://news.cnet.com/news/0-1005-200-7389552.html.

[77] Brett Boskiewicz authored this section.

[78] 17 U.S.C. § 501(a) (2002).

[79] A&M Records v. Napster, 114 F. Supp. 2d 146 (N.D. Cal. 2000), *aff'd in part, rev'd in part,* 299 F.3d 1004 (9th Cir. 2001) (amending opinion reported at 2001 U.S. App. LEXIS 5446 (9th Cir., Feb. 12, 2001).

[80] A&M Records v. Napster, 299 F.3d 1004, 1011-13 (9th Cir. 2001).

TABLE 4.3
Types of Copyright Infringement

Type of Copyright Infringement	Primary Exposure and State of Mind
Direct Infringement	Company is *strictly liable* for copies infringed by its employees committed within the scope of employment. Intent or knowledge is not an element of infringement.
Contributory Infringement	Company or its employees *knowingly contribute* to an act of infringement by another party.
Vicarious Infringement	Company is liable for a primary infringer's activities based upon the company's right to control and receiving a direct financial benefit derived from the infringing activities.

The federal district court granted a preliminary injunction enjoining Napster from engaging in or facilitating others in copying all copyrighted music owned by the record company plaintiffs. The online music web site was enjoined by a preliminary injunction ordering that all copyrighted music be removed from its network. Judge Marilyn Patel, a federal district judge, ruled that the recording industry had a strong likelihood of prevailing on its claim that Napster was liable for copyright infringement.[81]

The Court of Appeals for the Ninth Circuit issued a stay of the preliminary injunction issued by the district court because Napster had raised substantial questions of first impression.[82] The court, however, on appeal, affirmed the district court's injunction in part but stated that the injunction was overbroad because it placed the entire burden on Napster to ensure that no "copying, downloading, uploading, transmitting, or distributing" of copyrighted works occur on the system. The court found that the plaintiffs must "provide notice to Napster of copyrighted works and files containing such works available . . . before Napster has the duty to disable access to the offending content."[83]

Contributory infringement requires a finding of knowledge of the infringing activity of another as well a finding that the defendant induced, caused, or materially contributed to the infringing activities of another. *Vicarious infringement* is a form of third party liability, which requires the right and ability to supervise infringing activities by the direct infringer and a direct financial benefit. The Ninth Circuit held that Napster had potential liability for contributory and vicarious infringement and was not insulated by the Digital Millennium Copyright Act (DMCA)'s safe harbor. The DMCA immunizes Internet Service Providers for copyright infringement provided that it is provided by third parties. The court did

---

[81] A&M Records v. Napster, 114 F. Supp. 2d 146 (N.D. Cal. 2000) (enjoining Napster from facilitating the unauthorized transfer of copyrighted song files).

[82] A&M Records v. Napster, 299 F.3d 1004, 1013-14 (9th Cir. 2001).

[83] *Id.*

not find the DMCA safe harbor inapplicable *per se*, but that the issue should be more fully developed at trial. On remand, the district court limited the preliminary injunction so as to require the record companies to provide the title of the work; name of the artist performing the sound recording; the name of a file available on Napster; and certification that the record companies own or control the rights being infringed.

[1] Direct Infringement

To present a prima facie case for direct copyright infringement, a plaintiff must prove (1) that the plaintiff is the owner of the copyright for the allegedly infringed material and (2) that the defendant violated one of the exclusive rights afforded copyright owners.[84] If a company, for example, posts a copyrighted photograph on its web site without permission of the copyright owner, the company may be liable for copyright infringement for violating the copyright owner's exclusive right to reproduce, display, and distribute its photograph. In the Napster case, the court had little difficulty determining that Napster users directly infringed the copyrights owned by the record companies by making copies of the songs and distributing those copies to other Napster users.[85] The plaintiffs, however, did not sue the Napster users for direct copyright infringement, since the case would have been unwieldy due to the enormous number of users and could have resulted in substantial negative publicity for the recording industry.

[2] Contributory Infringement

Contributory infringement occurs when a party has knowledge of a directly infringing activity and "induces, causes or materially contributes to the infringing conduct of another[.]"[86] The definition of *knowledge* in this context is the same as if it were applied in a common law tort context; the party either has actual knowledge or has reason to know of the direct infringement. In the *Napster* case, the court determined that, based on the record, Napster had actual knowledge and constructive knowledge. Internal communications referencing "pirated music" and communications from the Recording Industry Association of America informing Napster of more than 12,000 infringing files constituted actual knowledge; moreover, Napster executives had experience in the recording industry and had "enforced intellectual property rights in other instances."[87] The Napster court explicitly stated that "if a computer system operator learns of specific infringing material available on his system and fails to purge such material from the system,

---

[84] 17 U.S.C. § 501(A) (2002).

[85] A&M Records v. Napster, 299 F.3d 1004, 1013-14 (9th Cir. 2001).

[86] *Napster*, 199 F.3d at 1019 (citing Gershwin Publishing Corp. v. Columbia Artists Mgmt., Inc., 443 F.2d 1159, 1162 (2d Cir. 1971)).

[87] *Id.* at 1020, n.5

the operator knows of and contributes to direct infringement."[88] However, without specific information of an infringing activity, a computer system operator cannot be held liable as a contributory infringer merely because "the structure of the system allows for the exchange of copyrighted material."[89]

[3] Vicarious Infringement

Vicarious liability for copyright infringement is another application of a common law tort theory of liability—respondeat superior. *Respondeat superior* is commonly applied in an employer/employee relationship to impute legal liability to an employer for the acts of an employee acting within the scope of employment.[90] To establish vicarious liability in the copyright context, the defendant must (1) have the right and ability to supervise the infringing activity and (2) have a direct financial interest in such activities.[91]

In the *Napster* case, both of these requirements were satisfied. Napster expressly reserved the right to control its service and terminate accounts in situations where "Napster believes that user conduct violates applicable law" and failed to "police" its system within the limits of its technology.[92] The financial interest requirement was satisfied by the fact that the availability of infringing material attracted users and that Napster's future revenue directly depended on increasing the number of users.[93]

Adobe Systems Inc. v. Canus Productions, Inc.[94] is an example of a digital rights-related case confronting issues of contributory infringement and vicarious liability. In this case, Adobe claimed that the defendants, proprietors of computer fairs, were liable for vicarious liability and contributory infringement because of the sale of unauthorized Adobe software at their fairs.[95] Adobe notified the defendants that unauthorized sales might be occurring at their fairs, and the defendants promised to remove those vendors from the fairs; subsequently Adobe and the U.S. marshal seized about 100 unauthorized copies of Adobe's software from one fair.[96] Adobe then sued the defendants for vicarious liability and contributory infringement.[97]

As to the vicarious liability claim, the court held that a direct financial interest in the infringing activities must be found on the part of the defendants, and the direct financial interest must be that the infringing activity is the "draw" of the

---

[88] *Id.* at 1021.

[89] *Id.*

[90] *See* Restatement (Third) of Torts § 13 (2002) (explaining doctrine of vicarious liability).

[91] *Id.* at 1022 (quoting Gershwin Publishing Corp. v. Columbia Artists Mgmt., Inc., 443 F.2d 1159, 1162 (2d Cir. 1971)).

[92] Id. at 1023-4.

[93] *Id.* at 1023.

[94] 173 F. Supp. 2d 1044 (C.D. Cal. 2001).

[95] *Id.* at 1046-47.

[96] *Id.* at 1047.

[97] *Id.* at 1048.

customers to the fair to support the financial benefit, which is the entrance and booth fees that the defendant received from the fairs.[98] The advertising of the sale of inexpensive software, Adobe claimed, is what "draws" the crowd to the fair because the customers believe that they will be able to purchase cheap Adobe software.[99] The court, however, held that is insufficient evidence because advertising that states inexpensive software can be purchased does not constitute that the customers are drawn to the fair to purchase cheap Adobe software.[100] The court also held that the defendants did not have enough control over what the vendors sold at the fairs to constitute vicarious liability because the defendants did not monitor the booths, only maintained guards for the security of the premises.[101] As for contributory infringement, the court held that the notification by Adobe to the defendants that there were possible unauthorized sales and the one seizure of unauthorized software was not sufficient evidence to prove that the defendants were on notice about the infringing activity.[102]

[4] Remedies for Infringement

Prior to instituting an action for copyright infringement, it is important to consider the available remedies. The Copyright Act provides for injunctive relief, seizure and disposition of infringing articles, damages, and criminal penalties.[103] The availability of injunctive relief creates leverage for negotiating a licensing agreement between the infringer and copyright owner. A copyright owner may recover any actual damages incurred as a result of the infringement, and any profits that the infringer made from the infringement that are not included in the amount of actual damages.[104] Since actual damages are often difficult to prove in copyright situations, however, the Copyright Act provides for statutory damages. The statutory damages are determined by the court and can range from $750 to $30,000 for all infringements by the infringer per each copyrighted work.[105] The court may increase damages for willful infringement up to $150,000.[106] Costs and attorney's fees are also available to the prevailing party at the discretion of the court.[107] Certain actions may also be subject to criminal sanctions. For example, willful copyright infringement is a criminal offense if committed either (1) for purposes of commercial advantage or private financial gain or (2) by reproduction or distribution, during any 180-day period, of one or more copies of phonorecords or

---

[98] *Id.* at 1052.
[99] *Id.*
[100] *Id.* at 1052-53.
[101] *Id.* at 1053-54.
[102] *Id.* at 1056.
[103] 17 U.S.C. § 502-6 (2002).
[104] 17 U.S.C. § 504(b) (2002).
[105] 17 U.S.C. § 504(c)(1) (2002).
[106] 17 U.S.C. § 504(c)(2) (2002).
[107] 17 U.S.C. § 505 (2002).

copyrighted works that have a total retail value of more than $1000.[108] Other criminal offenses include providing fraudulent information in copyright notice, fraudulent removal of a copyright notice, and making false representations of material facts in the application for a copyright registration.[109]

[E] Defenses to Copyright Infringement

[1] Fair Use

Fair use evolved as a judicial doctrine and was codified in § 107 of the Copyright Act of 1976. Fair use is an exception to the copyright owners' exclusive right "to reproduce the copyrighted work in copies."[110] The defendant has the burden of proving that its copying constitutes fair use.[111] Four factors are considered in determining whether use of a copyrighted works constitutes fair use:[112]

> (1) "the purpose and character of the use including whether such use is of a commercial nature or is for nonprofit educational purposes; (2) the nature of the copyrighted work; (3) the amount and substantiality of the portion used in relation to the copyrighted work as a whole; and (4) the effect of the use upon the potential market for or value of the copyrighted work."[113]

If a company's use of the copyrighted work on a web site is to carry out a commercial function, this statutory factor weighs against fair use. If a company's use of copyrighted works benefits science or scholarship, this factor would weigh in favor of a defense of fair use.

The second statutory factor is the nature of the copyrighted work. This factor focuses on whether the copyrighted work is published and informational or

---

[108] 17 U.S.C. § 506(a) (2002).

[109] 17 U.S.C. § 506(c)-(e) (2002).

[110] 17 U.S.C. § 106(1) (2002).

[111] Sega Enters. Ltd. v. MAPHIA, 857 F. Supp. 679, 683 (N.D. Cal. 1994) (holding computer bulletin board operator directly liable for copyright infringement where it solicited subscribers to upload files containing copyrighted video games). *See also* Playboy Enters., Inc. v. Webbworld, 968 F. Supp. 1171 (N.D. 1997), *aff'd*, 168 F.3d 486 (5th Cir. 1999) (upholding direct and vicarious infringement); American Geophysical Union v. Texaco, Inc., 60 F.3d 913, 918 (2d Cir. 1995). Houghton Mifflin was enjoined from publishing *The Wind Done Gone* in a copyright infringement suit filed by the owner of the copyright to *Gone With the Wind*. *See* Houghton Mifflin Is Enjoined From Publishing "The Wind Done Gone," 22 Entertain. L. Rptr. 1 (May 2001). The court rejected the fair use defense, finding that as a matter of fact the amount and substantiality of what was copied weighed against fair use. *Id.* The court found the work to be partially transformative and partially commercial, and that it would have a negative impact on the market value of *Gone With the Wind*. *Id.* The Eleventh Circuit vacated its injunction against the publication of *The Wind Done Gone* in May of 2001.

[112] UMG Recordings, Inc. v. MP3.com, 92 F. Supp. 2d 349 (S.D.N.Y. 2000) (rejecting fair use defense of Internet company for copying recordings and replaying them for subscribers on its computer system).

[113] 17 U.S.C. § 107 (1999).

creative.[114] In other words, is the nature of the work being copied close to the core of intended copyright protection?[115]

The third fair use statutory factor is the amount and substantiality of the copyrighted work copied and displayed. The amount and substantiality element focuses upon whether the portion constitutes the essence of the work.

The fourth factor is the effect of the display of copyrighted materials upon the potential market for the work. Will posting works on the Internet, for example, have a negative effect on the copyright owner's market? If so, this will be a factor against a finding of fair use.

[2]　Fair Use in an Online Setting

Section 117 of the Copyright Act permits an owner of a copy of software to make a new copy if it is an "essential step" in the utilization of the program.[116] It is not an infringement for the owner of a copy of a computer program to make or authorize the making of another copy or adaptation of that computer program provided (1) that such a new copy or adaptation is created as an essential step in the utilization of the computer program in conjunction with a machine and that it is used in no other manner or (2) that such copy or adaptation is for archival purposes only and that all archival copies are destroyed in the event that continued possession of the computer program should cease to be rightful.[117] Section 117 is a narrow exception, which applies only to backup copies of computer programs, but does not extend to copying for commercial purposes.[118]

Fair use is an affirmative defense which applies equally to online disputes. A corporate web site's use of a copyrighted work for purposes such as criticism, comment, news reporting, teaching, scholarship, or research may constitute fair use.[119] If a web site adds a further purpose or constitutes a different character to the work, there is a higher likelihood of fair use.[120] If the infringing use does not qualify as criticism, commentary, news reporting, or teaching, the court may address whether the web site publication of a copyrighted work is "transformative."[121] If so, the "transformative" nature weighs toward a finding of fair use.

---

[114] Religious Tech. Ctr. v. Netcom On-Line Communications Servs., Inc., 907 F. Supp. 1361 (N.D. Cal. 1995).

[115] Campbell v. Acuff-Rose Music, 510 U.S. 569, 586 (1994).

[116] Section 117 was enacted in response to MAI Systems Corp. v. Peak Computer, Inc., 991 F.2d 511, 518 (9th Cir. 1993), in which the Ninth Circuit held that a repair person was not authorized to use a computer owner's licensed operating system and infringed an operating system when he turned on the computer loading the operating system into RAM. The court held that infringement occurred when the operating system was loaded into the computer.

[117] 17 U.S.C. § 117 (2002).

[118] Mark A. Lemley et. al., Software and Internet Law 201 (2000) (citing ProCD v. Zeidenberg, 908 F. Supp. 640 (W.D. Wis. 1996), rev'd on other grounds, 86 F.3d 1447 (7th Cir. 1996)).

[119] 17 U.S.C. § 107 (2002).

[120] See, e.g., American Geophysical Union v. Texaco, Inc., 60 F.3d 913 (2d Cir. 1994).

[121] Campbell v. Acuff-Rose Music, 510 U.S. 569, 585 (1994).

Another consideration of this factor is whether the use is for commercial or non-commercial purposes. A web site providing information designed to educate the public, as opposed to selling goods or services, weighs in favor of fair use. While not conclusive, a commercial use by an alleged infringer weighs against a finding of fair use. Additionally, the alleged infringer does not necessarily need to receive some economic benefit from the infringement. "[R]epeated and exploitative copying of copyrighted works, even if the copies are not offered for sale, may constitute a commercial use."[122]

The underlying theory of copyright protection is the focus of the second inquiry. This theory is based on the concept that the "useful arts and sciences" benefit society as a whole and that providing authors with exclusive rights to their works for a period of time will be an incentive for authors to create works, and therefore society will benefit. In the fair use context, highly creative works, such as paintings or works of fiction, are typically afforded more protection than works that have an informational purpose, such as news articles or other fact-based works.[123]

The third factor of substantiality of the portion copied is easy to apply in an online setting. How much of the copyrighted work was posted on a web site, and of what significance is the copied portion to the entire work? Use of the entire copyrighted work often weighs against a finding of fair use.[124] Even if the alleged infringer uses only a portion of the copyrighted work, however, if that portion is the essence of the copyrighted work, then the scales tip away from fair use.[125]

The fourth factor attempts to determine the effects the alleged infringing work will have on the market for the copyrighted work. Will posting works on the Internet, for example, prevent people from purchasing those works? A trailer for a film, for example, may actually increase ticket sales. On the other hand, the posting of photographs from a magazine may diminish sales. If sales are negatively impacted by posting materials on the web site, this will be a factor against a finding of fair use.

In *Kelly v. Arriba Soft Corp.*,[126] the Ninth Circuit considered the application of the fair use doctrine to the world of the Internet and Internet search engines. The plaintiff was a professional photographer who held copyrights for many of his images of the American West. Some of these images were located on his web site or other web sites with which the plaintiff had a license agreement. The defendant operated an Internet search engine that displays its results in the form of small pictures rather than the more usual text. The defendant obtained its database of pictures by copying images from other web sites. By clicking on one of these small pictures, called "thumbnails," the user can then view a large version of that same picture within the context of the defendant's web page. In finding that the operator's actions constituted fair use, the district court determined that the character

---

[122] *Napster*, 299 F.3d at 1015.
[123] *Acuff-Rose*, 510 U.S. at 586.
[124] *Napster*, 299 F.3d at 1016.
[125] *Acuff-Rose*, 510 U.S. at 589.
[126] 280 F.3d 934 (9th Cir. 2002).

and purpose of the operator's use were significantly transformative and did not harm the market for or value of the photographer's works.

The Ninth Circuit found that although the photographer had established a prima facie case of copyright infringement, analysis of the four factors of the fair use test weighed in favor of the operator, and the court concluded that the operator's use of the images as thumbnails was a fair use. However, the defendant operator's inline linking to and framing of full-sized images infringed upon the photographer's exclusive right to display the copyrighted work publicly and was not protected by fair use.

[F]   Linking Issues

[1]   Linking[127]

A *hyperlink* is a link from one site to another on the Internet. A web site is a specific location on the World Wide Web identified by the Universal Resource Locator (URL). The URL can be a string of letters, such as *http://www.spc.com*, or it may include letters, numbers, or slashes.[128] Links permit Internet users to click on highlighted text and surf from web page to web page without typing in URLs.[129]

A simple link between sites will not normally be problematic, but it may be a violation of netiquette[130] not to request permission to link. In fact, many web sites welcome linking. An adult entertainment web site that linked to the Papal Visit web site owned by the Archdiocese of St. Louis, however, was found liable for trademark dilution by tarnishment.[131] A company should give a notice that it has no control over linked sites and resources and does not endorse or is not otherwise liable for materials on linked sites. In *Playboy Enterprises, Inc. v. Universal Tel-A-Talk, Inc.*,[132] a court ruled that an adult web site that posted Playboy's logo to link to the Playboy web site diluted Playboy's trademark by association.

---

[127] For an analysis of linking from a marketing perspective, see § 2.05[C].

[128] Webnovice.com, Reading Internet Addresses (visited Apr. 25, 2002), http://www.webnovice.com/web address.htm (explaining that a Universal Resource Locator, or URL, is a string of letters, numbers, slashes, or others symbols that "point to a specific place on the Internet").

[129] Intermatic, Inc. v. Toeppen, 947 F. Supp. 1227 (N.D. Ill. 1996).

[130] *Netiquette* is a term used to describe informal norms that have evolved among Internet users as to what is proper online conduct. When an Arizona law company deluged listservers with spam e-mail about immigration services, it was considered a gross violation of netiquette. Internet users responded by a counterattack of spam mail that shut down the law company's web site. Those who violate important Internet-related norms may face similar self-help measures.

[131] Archdiocese of St. Louis v. Internet Entertainment, Inc., 34 F. Supp. 2d 1145 (E.D. Mo. 1999) (holding that the use of the domain names "papalvisit1999.com" and "papalvisit.com" by adult entertainment web site was likely to tarnish the marks' image and that the plaintiffs were likely to prevail on their federal and state claims). The opinion was withdrawn by the court by 34 F. Supp. 2d 1145 (E.D. Mo. 1999).

[132] 1998 WL 767440 (E.D. Pa. 1998).

The practice of simple linking is "unlikely to constitute copyright infringement, because it is probably protected either by an implied license or under the copyright doctrine of fair use."[133] Linking, however, may infringe trademarks by implying an association between the initial site and the linked site. It is unlikely that a company would be liable for copyright infringement if it links to a web site that contains infringing materials.[134] To establish a claim of copyright infringement, a plaintiff must prove, first, that he owns a valid copyright in a work and, second, that the defendant copied original elements of that work. To prevail on a claim of trademark infringement, a plaintiff has the burden of showing (1) that he had a valid trademark and (2) that the defendant had adopted an identical or similar mark such that consumers were likely to confuse the two. The display of a simple hyperlink does not implicate either copyright or trademark infringement theories.[135]

Anticorporate web sites present difficult strategic issues because of a policy concern with free speech. In *Ford Motor Company v. 2600 Enterprises*,[136] the defendant operated a web site, *www.fuckgeneralmotors.com,* which automatically redirected users from that site to *www.ford.com,* a web site operated by Ford.[137] The defendant used Ford's trademark in its programming code to link to their site, but the court held that use of the trademark by the defendant would not entitle Ford to succeed in a federal trademark dilution action, because the defendant's use of the trademark was not use in commerce, which is a requirement for a federal trademark dilution action.[138] In addition, Ford could not succeed on a trademark infringement claim either because Ford could not show that the defendant used the mark "in connection with the sale, offering for sale, distribution, or advertising of any goods or services."[139] The court distinguished between using the trademark as a domain name and using the trademark in programming code; since the defendant

---

[133] *See* Maureen O'Rourke, Fencing Cyberspace: Drawing Borders in a Virtual World, 82 Minn. L. Rev. 609 (1998).

[134] Archdiocese of St. Louis v. Internet Entertainment, Inc., 34 F. Supp. 2d 1145 (E.D. Mo. 1999) (holding that the use of the domain names "papalvisit1999.com" and "papalvisit.com" by adult entertainment web site was likely to tarnish the marks' image and that the plaintiffs were likely to prevail on their federal and state claims). The opinion was withdrawn by the court by 34 F. Supp. 2d 1145 (E.D. Mo. 1999).

[135] *See, e.g.,* Ticketmaster Corp. v. Tickets.com, Inc. (C.D. Cal., Aug. 10, 2000), *aff'd,* 2001 U.S. App. LEXIS 1454 (9th Cir., Jan. 8, 2001) (holding that ticket broker was not entitled to injunction against ticket clearing house under copyright infringement since time, place, venue, and price of public events were not protected by copyright); Playboy Enters., Inc. v. Universal Tel-A-Talk, Inc., 1998 U.S. Dist. LEXIS 8231 (E.D. Penn., June 1, 1998) (holding that use of federally registered trademark in a hypertext link that took users from web site to another web site did not constitute trademark counterfeiting); Lyons Partnership v. Giannoulas, 179 F.3d 384 (5th Cir. 1999) (holding that links to anti-Barney web sites did not constitute a violation of Copyright Act or Lanham Act and finding that Barney caricature was a parody).

[136] 177 F. Supp. 2d 661 (E.D. Mich. 2001).

[137] *Id.* at 662.

[138] *Id.* at 663-64.

[139] *Id.* at 665.

was using the trademark in programming code, it was not competing with the trademark owner's goods or services.[140]

[2] Deep Linking

When web site visitors click on a deep link, they are transferred to an interior web page, bypassing the home page of the second site. Deep linking occurs when a web site creates a link from its site to a web page deep within the second web site. *Deep linking* has been the subject of litigation based on copyright infringement or unfair competition. A federal court in *Ticketmaster Corp. v. Tickets.com, Inc.*[141] dismissed Ticketmaster's claim that Tickets.com's deep-linking practices violated the federal copyright act. Ticketmaster has a web site that permits customers to purchase tickets to various events through an Internet connection with its pages. Ticketmaster had exclusive agreements with the events on its web pages so that tickets were not generally available except under the web site. Tickets.com, the defendant, operated a web site performing a different ticketing service. Tickets.com sells tickets at its site, but it also provides visitors with information on how to obtain tickets to events. If Ticketmaster is the exclusive ticket broker, the visitor is transferred to an interior page in Ticketmaster's site; that is, Tickets.com has a "deep link" into Ticketmaster's site.

The federal court granted Tickets.com's motion to dismiss the infringement complaint because copyright cannot protect factual data. In this case, Tickets.com extracted factual data from Ticketmaster and placed it in its own form. The court rejected Ticketmaster's argument that there may be copyright infringement on base facts from publicly available web pages. The court observed that "hyperlinking does not itself involve a violation of the Copyright Act . . . since no copying is involved, the customer is automatically transferred to the particular genuine web page of the original author."[142] The court also noted that it may not have had jurisdiction over the copyright infringement claim because it was unclear whether Ticketmaster's event pages were registered in the Copyright Office.[143]

The Supremacy Clause of the U.S. Constitution mandates that the federal copyright law overrides any state contract or tort causes of action with which it conflicts.[144] In *Ticketmaster*, the court found many of the plaintiff's contract and

---

[140] *Id.* at 663-65.

[141] Tickermaster Corp. v. Tickets.Com, Inc., 2000 U.S. Dist. LEXIS 4553 (C.D. Cal., Mar. 27, 2000), *aff'd*, 2001 U.S. App. LEXIS 1454 (9th Cir., Jan. 22, 2001). *See also* Ticketmaster Corp v. Tickets.Com, Inc., 2000 U.S. Dist. LEXIS 12987 (C.D. Cal., Aug. 11, 2000) (holding that ticket brokerage businesses were not entitled to injunction against Tickets.com under copyright infringement theory).

[142] *Id.* at *6.

[143] A federal court does not have jurisdiction of a copyright infringement claim unless the owner registers its copyright with the U.S. Copyright Office. The web site of Ticketmaster Corp. was registered with the U.S. Copyright Office. However, "the events pages changed from day to day as old events are dropped out, and new ones are added." The court found an ambiguity in the scope of copyright registration: the court found it unclear whether the copyright registration covered only the home page or the event pages as well. *Id.* at *6.

[144] U.S. Const., art. VI, cl. 2.

torts claims overridden by the Copyright Act. The court also denied Ticketmaster's breach of contract claim, noting that simply placing terms and conditions on the web site without requiring the visitor to take further action does not create an enforceable contract.[145] The court also rejected the Lanham Act claim and ruled that Ticketmaster's misappropriation and trespass claims were preempted.[146]

Deep linking was also the issue in the litigation between Ticketmaster and Microsoft. Microsoft deep-linked Ticketmaster's site through its Sidewalk city guides. Ticketmaster sued Microsoft, alleging that the deep linking deprived it of advertising revenues, caused its trademark to be diluted, and hence created an atmosphere of unfair competition.[147] After the settlement of the case, Microsoft stopped deep linking and now links to Ticketmaster's home page.[148]

Kelly v. Arriba Soft Corp.[149] is one of the deep linking cases where there was no pretrial settlement. In that case, Arriba was importing Kelly's images straight from Kelly's web site, creating thumbnail and full images on Arriba's web site, which constituted inline linking.[150] The importing of the images was not copying the images from Kelly's site, which is a violation of 17 U.S.C. § 106(5), but was instead considered a violation of the owner's public display rights, because any visitor to Arriba's web site could view the images creating the infringement.[151] There was no prior caselaw stating that this activity constituted a violation of the owner's public display rights, but this court held that this use did infringe the owner's right.[152]

[3]   Liability for Remote Links

The practice of linking to sites containing infringing or illegal content may also make a site susceptible to criminal prosecution in a foreign venue. Germany, for example, has criminal laws against the publication of materials on National Socialism. A federal court found that no liability could be imposed for deep linking to a web site that contained materials that allegedly infringed a copyrighted work.[153] In some circumstances, however, a court may enjoin a party from providing a link to a site that contains material that might violate applicable laws. For example, a federal court enjoined a computer hacker from electronically linking

---

[145] *Id.* at *8.

[146] The court also found the plaintiff's stated unfair business practices claim preempted to the extent that it covered Tickets.com's taking and publication of factual data. *Id.* at *9. The court also found the plaintiff's unjust enrichment claim to be preempted. The court did not, however, rule out the possibility of tortious interference with prospective business advantage. *Id.* at *12.

[147] Ticketmaster Corp. v. Microsoft Corp., No. 97-3055 (C.D. Cal., complaint filed Apr. 28, 1997, settled Jan. 22, 1999).

[148] Glasser Legal/Works, Update, 11 Cyberspace Law 18 (Feb. 1999).

[149] 280 F.3d 934 (C.D. Cal. 2002).

[150] *Id.* at 944.

[151] *Id.* at 944-45.

[152] *Id.* at 945.

[153] Bernstein v. J.C. Penney, Inc., 1998 U.S. Dist. LEXIS 19048 (C.D. Cal. 1998) (dismissing complaint of copyright infringement against perfume manufacturer because its product was posted on a web site linked to another web site containing an infringing photograph of actress Elizabeth Taylor).

its site to others that posted a computer program called DeCSS that allowed motion pictures on DVDs to be copied.[154] According to one writer, there is a greater risk of a claim of Internet trademark infringement than copyright infringement.[155] In *Intellectual Reserve, Inc. v. Utah Lighthouse Ministry, Inc.*,[156] the defendants posted links to the Mormon Church's *Church Handbook of Instructions*. The court found that the defendant actively encouraged the infringement of the plaintiff's copyright. After being ordered to remove the *Handbook* from their web site, the defendants posted the addresses of three web site addresses where the *Handbook* could be downloaded. The plaintiff was unable to specifically identify persons who have infringed its copyright but would likely be able to do so after discovery. The court ordered an injunction ruling that the plaintiff only needs to show that the defendants' actions induced or materially contributed to the infringing conduct of another. At a minimum, companies should prohibit links to sites containing illegal or objectionable content to avoid the loss of good will.

[4] Framing

Framing is commonly used to refer to the practice of drawing the content of a web site into another, so that the content of the imported site is surrounded by the importing site's content. The propriety of framing has been bandied about the Internet and the courts for the past several years. Although no published decision has made any definitive statements about the legality of framing, there are strong indications that framing can form the basis for intellectual property violations.[157] Plaintiffs in framing cases have argued that framing may constitute trademark infringement by creating a likelihood of confusion as to source. A second argument is that the "placement of one Web site within a frame comprised portions of another Web site can create an unlicensed derivative work" constituting copyright infringement.[158]

The practice of *framing* causes the plaintiffs' web site to appear in a form other than the one envisioned by the web site developer. Framing permits a party to superimpose its content on a frame around all the web sites to which links are made. The practice of framing goes well beyond deep linking by creating a frame around the web site that hides the target site's advertising and substitutes the framer's advertising. Framing was "introduced by Netscape in Version 2 of its Navigator product. A framing site, by virtue of certain commands in its HTML code, links to another site, and displays that site within a window or frame."[159] In

---

[154] Universal City Studios, Inc. v. Reimerdes, 111 F. Supp. 2d 294 (S.D.N.Y. 2000).

[155] Jonathan Bick, 101 Things You Need to Know About Internet Law 196-198 (2000).

[156] 75 F. Supp. 2d 1290 (Utah 1999).

[157] Hillel I. Parness, Framing the Question: How Does *Kelly v. Arriba Soft* Advance the Framing Debate?, Cyberspace Law., Mar. 2002, at 9.

[158] *Id.*; *see also* Mark Sablmen, Link Law Revisited: Internet Linking Law at Five Years, 16 Berkeley Tech. L.J. 1273 (2001) (reviewing possible causes of action for deep linking and framing).

[159] *See* Maureen O'Rourke, Fencing Cyberspace: Drawing Borders in a Virtual World, 82 Minn. L. Rev. 609 (1998).

Washington Post v. TotalNews, Inc.,[160] the newspaper contended that TotalNews infringed its copyrights and trademarks and misappropriated its news material by framing various newspaper sites.[161]

The plaintiffs included diversified communications channels, such as *Time Magazine, Entertainment Weekly,* and *The Los Angeles Times,* all of which had online versions of their publications. These and other publications were displayed in a *TotalNews* frame. The plaintiff in the *TotalNews* case argued that framing was a parasitic practice that diverted advertising revenues generated by online publications.[162] The plaintiffs also argued that framing was the "Internet equivalent of pirating copyrighted materials from a variety of famous newspapers, magazines, or television news programs."[163] In the *TotalNews* case, the plaintiffs' objection was that the defendant's framing method made its web sites appear in an altered form:

> The totalnews.com web site consists of lists of numerous "name-brand" news sources, including the famous trademarks exclusively associated with Plaintiffs in the public mind. When a user of totalnews.com "clicks" on one of those famous trademarks with the computer mouse, the user accesses a Plaintiff's corresponding web site. . . . Plaintiff's site, however, does not then fill the screen as it would had the user accessed either plaintiff's site directly or by means of a hyperlink from a web site that does not "frame" linked sites. Nor does Plaintiff's URL appear at the top of the screen as it normally would. Instead, part of the site is inserted in a window designed by the defendants to occupy only a part of the screen. Masking part of Plaintiff's site is the totalnews.com "frame," including . . . the "TotalNews" logo, totalnews.com URL, and advertisements that others have purchased from Defendants.[164]

Each of the named plaintiffs in *TotalNews* had registered trademarks and were copyright owners as well.[165] The court ordered *TotalNews* "not to directly or

---

[160] Washington Post Co. v. TotalNews, Inc., No. 97-1190 (S.D.N.Y., filed Apr. 28, 1997, settled Jan. 22, 1999).

[161] *Misappropriation* is the acquisition of a "trade secret by 'improper means' or from someone who has acquired it through 'improper means.'" National Conference of Commissioners on Uniform State Laws, The Uniform Trade Secrets Act: A Summary (visited Apr. 26, 2002), http://www.nccU.S.l.org/summary/utsa.html.

[162] The plaintiff argued: "Although Defendants, too, derive revenue by selling advertisements placed within the totalnews.com web site, defendants provide little or no content of their own. Instead Defendants have designed a parasitic web site that republishes the news and editorial content of others' web sites in order to attract both advertisers and users." *Id.*

[163] Washington Post v. TotalNews, Inc., Complaint ¶ 8 (visited Apr. 28, 2002), http://www.ljx.com/Internet/complain.html (reprinting complaint filed by Debevoise and Plimpton on behalf of the plaintiff).

[164] *Id.* at ¶ 30.

[165] The plaintiffs' lawsuit was based upon misappropriation, federal trademark dilution, trademark infringement, false designations of origin (false representations and false advertising), dilution under state law, deceptive acts and practices, copyright infringement, and tortious interference. Counts I-X of Plaintiff's Complaint.

indirectly cause any Plaintiff's web site to appear on a user's computer screen with any material . . . and to permanently cease the practice of 'framing' Plaintiffs' web sites."[166] The parties eventually agreed to permit linking through non-stylized links.

A federal appeals court upheld a district court's denial of a preliminary injunction to restrain the defendant from employing a framed link to a plaintiff's web site in *Futuredontics, Inc. v. Applied Anagramic, Inc.*[167] The plaintiff's argument was that the framed link falsely implied an association between the parties. The court found no evidence that the defendant had caused the plaintiff to lose business or goodwill due to the framing.

For a discussion of framing as a marketing strategy, see § 2.05[D].

[G]   Digital Millennium Copyright Act

The DMCA amended the Copyright Act to comply with copyright treaties of the World Intellectual Property Organization (WIPO) and adapt to Internet-related technologies. The DMCA added § 512 to the Copyright Act to provide limitations of the liability of Internet service providers (ISPs) for copyright infringement, and Chapter 12 to protect against the circumvention of copyright protection technologies and tampering with copyright management information.[168]

[1]   ISP Limited Liability: Section 512

Section 512 provides a "safe harbor" for ISPs for intermediate and temporary storage of digital copies. The amendment is essentially a codification of the principles and analysis applied in *Religious Technology Center v. Netcom On-Line Communication Services, Inc.*[169] For the purposes of § 512, a "service provider" is generally defined as a "provider of online services or network access, or the operator of facilities therefore."[170] In addition, to qualify for any of the limitations provided for in § 512, the service provider must (1) adopt and reasonably implement a policy for terminating the accounts of subscribers who are repeat infringers and (2) accommodate and not interfere with standard technical measures that are used by copyright owners to identify or protect copyrighted works.[171] There are four sit-

---

[166] Washington Post v. TotalNews, Inc., No. 97 Civ. 1190 (PKL) (S.D.N.Y. 1997) (order granting settlement and dismissal).

[167] Futuredontics, Inc. v. Applied Anagramic, Inc., 1998 WL 417413 (9th Cir. July 23, 1998) (unpublished opinion reported in Perkins Coie Internet Case Digest (visited May 26, 1999), http://www.perkinscoie.com/resource/ecomm/netcase/Cases-04.htm.

[168] For a general overview of the Digital Millennium Copyright Act, *see* The Digital Millennium Copyright Act of 1998, U.S. Copyright Office Summary (Dec. 1998). The summary is available on the U.S. Copyright Office's web site at http://www.loc.gov/copyright/legislation/dmca.pdf.

[169] ALS Scan, Inc. v. RemarQ Communities, Inc., 239 F.3d 619, 622 (4th Cir. 2001) (citing H.R. Rep. No. 105-551(I) at 11 (1998)).

[170] *Id.*

[171] 17 U.S.C. § 512(I) (2002).

uations where ISP liability for copyright infringement may be limited by § 512: (1) transitory communications, (2) caching, (3) content of web sites hosted by the ISP, and (4) information location tools.[172]

[a] Transitory Digital Network Communications

Section 512(a) limits the liability of a service provider for copyright infringement in situations where the ISP merely transmits digital information, which may include infringing material, from one point to another at the request of a third party. For this specific limitation, the definition of a service provider is narrowed to "an entity offering the transmission, routing, or providing of connections for digital online communications, between or among points specified by a user, of material of the user's choosing, without modification to the content of the material as sent or received."[173] In addition to meeting the more narrow definition of a service provider, the ISP must meet the following criteria to qualify for the limitation of liability:

1. The transmission was initiated by or at the direction of a third party;
2. The transmission, routing, provision of connections, or copying must be carried out through an automatic technical process without selection of the material by the service provider;
3. The service provider cannot select the recipients of the material;
4. Any copies made by the service provider cannot be accessible to anyone other than the anticipated recipients and cannot be maintained on the service provider's system for longer than reasonably necessary; and
5. The material must be transmitted without modification of its content.[174]

[b] Immunity for System Caching

Caching is the practice of replicating identical web pages to improve the speed of access to the web pages by reducing "the need to re-transmit information from the source server."[175] The three types of caching are (1) PC or browser caching, (2) proxy server caching, and (3) mirror image caching.[176] PC caching stores images of web pages on the user's own computer. A cached copy on a proxy server copies and stores web pages on a separate server.[177] Mirroring or mirror caching sets up identical web sites, on different servers.[178] Replication is the practice of duplicating data on servers at several points on the network, in anticipation of unusual user demand.[179] As of March 2000, there were "nearly a quarter-billion

---

[172] Id.

[173] 17 U.S.C. § 512(k)(1)(A) (2000).

[174] 17 U.S.C. § 512(a) (2002).

[175] Jon Knight and Martin Hamilton, Cashing in on Caching (visited July 5, 2001), http://www.ariadne.ac.uk/issue4/caching/.

[176] Id.

[177] Id.

[178] Id.

[179] Global Internet Project, presented by America Online at the Fourth Annual High Technology Law Conference, Suffolk University Law School, Boston, Mass. (Sept. 1998).

computer users online worldwide, that number [is] expected to grow to just over 500 million by 2003."[180]

The limitation of liability for system caching applies in circumstances where the material is made available online by a person other than the service provider, is transmitted to a user at the user's direction, and is carried out through an automatic technical process for the purpose of making the material available to users upon their request.[181] For example, our hypothetical dot-com company, SPC, makes a big business announcement that results in a substantial increase to the usual heavy traffic to the SPC web site. SpeedyNetAccess, a hypothetical ISP, has technology that recognizes the increased traffic and automatically generates copies of the SPC web pages to accommodate the increased demand by its users. This reproduction of SPC's copyrighted material is a violation of SPC's exclusive copyrights and could constitute copyright infringement. However, since the material is made available online by SPC, is transmitted in response to requests by users of SpeedyNetAccess, and SpeedyNetAccess generated the copies of the SPC web pages through an automatic technical process to accommodate its users, SpeedyNetAccess would not be liable for copyright infringement of SPC's copyrighted web pages because of the § 512(b) exemption.

While this provision benefits and protects ISPs, the statute also protects content providers by requiring the ISP to meet the following conditions to qualify for the § 512(b) limitation of liability.[182]

1. The material must be transmitted in its original form without any modifications by the ISP.
2. The ISP must periodically update the cached copy according to the specification of the content provider, which must be in accordance with generally accepted industry standards.
3. The ISP must not interfere with the content provider's ability to obtain information that it would normally have available to it had the user accessed its site directly (for example, the number of hits).
4. If the content provider has imposed any conditions to access to the material, such as passwords, payment of fees, etc., the ISP must only permit access to the information to users who satisfy the conditions.

If the content provider has posted material that infringes the copyright of a third party, the ISP must "expeditiously" remove or disable access to the infringing material upon receipt of notification that the material has been removed or ordered to be removed from the content provider's site. To qualify for the "safe harbor" for liability related to Internet materials, the provider must designate an agent for notification of claimed infringement. SPC needs to designate an agent to

---

[180] Caching Technology: Preventing Internet Bottlenecks and Enhancing the User Experience, Global Internet Project (March 2000) (visited Apr. 28, 2002), http://www.gip.org/publications/papers/gipcache.asp.

[181] 17 U.S.C. § 512(b)(1) (2002).

[182] 17 U.S.C. § 512(b)(2) (2002).

receive notification of claimed copyright infringement. The Copyright Office does not have a specific printed form for filing an Interim Designation of an Agent but does have a suggested format.[183]

The minimum information that must be submitted about the designated agent includes (1) the name, address, phone number, and electronic mail address of the agent; (2) legal name and address of the Internet Service Provider (ISP); (3) all names under which the ISP does business; (4) a filing fee of $20; and (5) display of the agent's name and contact information on the web site.

[c] Information Residing on Systems or Networks at Direction of Users

The DMCA also addresses the liability of an ISP for the content of web sites, bulletin board systems, or other sources of information the ISP hosts. The service provider is not liable for content stored on its systems provided that the ISP:

1. Does not have actual or constructive knowledge of the infringing material or activity; and upon obtaining such knowledge, acts "expeditiously" to remove or disable access to the infringing material upon obtaining knowledge or awareness of said material;

2. Does not receive a financial benefit directly attributable to the infringing activity in situations where the ISP has the right and ability to control such activity; *and*

3. Upon notification of claimed infringement, acts "expeditiously" to remove or disable access to the material that is claimed to be infringed or to be the subject of the infringing activity.[184]

Note that to qualify for this safe harbor, the ISP must comply with all three of the requirements of § 512(c)(1) and "a showing under the first prong—is prior to and separate from the showings that must be made under the second and third prongs."[185]

The requirements for the safe harbor indicate that qualifying for relief is highly dependent on what circumstances the ISP is aware of or what the ISP knows to be infringing material. "The DMCA's protection of an innocent service provider disappears at the moment the service provider loses its innocence, i.e., at the moment it becomes aware that a third party is using its system to infringe."[186] Therefore, the statute provides requirements for providing effective notice to the ISP of a claim of infringement.

---

[183] U.S. Copyright Office, Designation by Service Provider of Agent for Notification of Claims of Infringement (visited Apr. 22, 2002), http://www.loc.gov/copyright/onlinesp.

[184] 17 U.S.C. § 512(c)(1) (2000).

[185] ALS Scan, Inc. v. RemarQ, Inc., 239 F.3d 619, 623 (4th Cir. 2001).

[186] *Id.* at 625.

Section 512(3)(A) establishes the elements of notification as follows:

To be effective under this subsection, a notification of claimed infringement must be a written communication provided to the designated agent of a service provider that includes substantially the following:

(i) A physical or electronic signature of a person authorized to act on behalf of the owner of an exclusive right that is allegedly infringed.

(ii) Identification of the copyrighted work claimed to have been infringed, or, if multiple copyrighted works at a single online site are covered by a single notification, a representative list of such works at that site.

(iii) Identification of the material that is claimed to be infringing or to be the subject of infringing activity and that is to be removed or access to which is to be disabled, and information reasonably sufficient to permit the service provider to locate the material.

(iv) Information reasonably sufficient to permit the service provider to contact the complaining party, such as an address, telephone number, and, if available, an electronic mail address at which the complaining party may be contacted.

(v) A statement that the complaining party has a good faith belief that use of the material in the manner complained of is not authorized by the copyright owner, its agent, or the law.

(vi) A statement that the information in the notification is accurate, and under penalty of perjury, that the complaining party is authorized to act on behalf of the owner of an exclusive right that is allegedly infringed.[187]

Interpretation of this requirement is still relatively unsettled. The Fourth Circuit U.S. Court of Appeals addressed the notification issue in *ALS Scan v. RemarQ*.[188] *ALS Scan* involved a creator and marketer of "adult" photographs that displayed its photographs on the Internet, ALS Scan, and an ISP, RemarQ.[189] ALS Scan discovered infringing photographs in two of RemarQ's newgroups and sent a letter to RemarQ demanding the removal of ALS Scan's copyrighted works. The letter specified the RemarQ newsgroups that contained the copyrighted material and directed RemarQ to ALS Scan web sites where it could identify their models and review applicable copyright information.[190] RemarQ responded by refusing to remove the items unless they were identified with "sufficient specificity."[191] As a result, ALS Scan filed a copyright infringement action, which the district court dismissed for, inter alia, ALS Scan's failure to comply with the notice requirements set forth in 17 U.S.C. § 512(c)(3)(A).[192]

The Fourth Circuit reversed the district court's ruling regarding the notification issue. The court found that the statute does not require copyright holders to identify "every infringing work—or even most of them—when multiple copyrights are involved."[193] The statute requires "substantial" compliance with the noti-

---

[187] 17 U.S.C. § 512(c)(1) (2002).
[188] 239 F.3d 619 (4th Cir. 2001).
[189] *Id.*
[190] *Id.* at 620-21.
[191] *Id.* at 621.
[192] *Id.*
[193] *Id.* at 625.

fication[194] that the copyright holder provide a "representative" list in cases of multiple infringements,[195] and the copyright holder "provide information that is 'reasonably sufficient' to permit the service provider to 'locate' [the infringing] material."[196] The court concluded that "when a letter provides notice equivalent to a list of representative works that can be easily identified by the service provider, the notice substantially complies with the notification requirements."[197] Therefore, ALS Scan substantially complied with the notification requirement because it (1) identified the newsgroups where the infringing material was located, (2) asserted that almost all of the material in the identified newsgroups infringed ALS Scan's copyrights, and (3) directed RemarQ to ALS Scan web sites where it could obtain copyright information and identify ALS Scan models.[198] The Fourth Circuit reversed summary judgment in favor of the defendant, finding an issue of material fact whether it knowingly allowed infringement. The DMCA immunity is only available to innocent infringers without knowledge of the infringement. An ISP loses its immunity when it fails to take action after it becomes aware that a third party is using the service to commit infringing acts. The DMCA requires the provider to disable the infringing matter, thus providing incentives to take prompt remedial steps once it discovers infringing material on the network.

In *Hendrickson v. eBay, Inc.*[199] the copyright owner of a documentary film entitled *Manson* sent eBay a cease and desist letter in December 2000 alleging that pirated copies of the film in digital video disc (DVD) format were being offered for sale to the highest bidder on eBay's site. The plaintiff requested that eBay stop "any and all further conduct that violated the copyright owner's rights as well as trademark claims."[200] But the letter from the copyright owner did not explain which copies were at issue or provide evidence of plaintiff's copyright interest in the allegedly infringing materials.[201] After receiving this letter, eBay repeatedly asked the copyright owner for more information, including a proper notice under the Digital Millennium Copyright Act (DMCA). The plaintiff instead filed suit.[202] The court held that under the Safe Harbor section, "the service provider's duty to act is triggered only upon receipt of proper notice" (described above) which it held eBay did not receive.[203] The letter did not give "sufficient information to identify the various listings that purportedly offered pirate copies of [the DVD] for sale."[204]

When eBay requested the specific listings, the plaintiff answered that "it is not his job to do so once he notified eBay of the existence of infringing activity by

---

[194] *Id.* at 625 (citing 17 U.S.C. § 512(c)(3)(A)).

[195] *Id.* (citing 17 U.S.C. § 512(c)(3)(A)(ii)) (2002).

[196] *Id.* (citing 17 U.S.C. § 512(c)(3)(A)(iii)) (2002).

[197] *Id.*

[198] *Id.*

[199] Hendrickson v. eBay, Inc., 8 ILR (P&F) 573 (2001).

[200] The court held that the plaintiff's trademark claim was mooted. *Id.*

[201] *Id.*

[202] *Id.*

[203] *Id.*

[204] *Id.*

eBay sellers," but the court disagreed. The court found that it was the plaintiff's burden to give specific listings in order for eBay to take steps to prevent sales of infringing copies.[205] The court found that eBay did not have actual notice of the infringing activity, could not control illicit transactions, and had no received proper notice under the DMCA.[206] The court also found that eBay took down all advertisements for illicit sales identified by the copyright owner and therefore substantially complied with the DMCA. The court granted eBay's motion for summary judgment and dismissed contributory and vicarious copyright infringement claims, holding that eBay was entitled to protection under 17 U.S.C. § 512(c), which limits liability for "infringement of copyright by reason of the storage at the direction of a user of material that resides on a system or network controlled or operated by or for the service provider." This statute offers protection to those facing liability because of the posting of materials online as well as liability arising out of the use of such materials to further infringing activities.

To qualify for such protection, a service provider must meet three requirements: (1) The service provider either must lack both actual knowledge of the infringing activity and an awareness of facts or circumstances from which infringing activity is apparent or must promptly, upon gaining such knowledge, move to prevent the use of its service to further such infringing activity; (2) the service provider must not receive a financial benefit directly attributable to infringing activity it has the ability to control; and (3) the service provider must expeditiously remove material from its service on receipt of an appropriate written notice. The court dismissed the infringement claim against eBay because it satisfied the three requirements for a DMCA safe harbor. The court found that the online auction house did not have notice of the infringement. Moreover, because of its defective nature, the notice could not be relied upon to establish that eBay had actual notice of infringing activity on its site.

[d] Information Location Tools

Section 512(d) limits ISP liability for linking to or referring users to a site that contains infringing materials through hyperlinks, search engines, and other information location tools. Similar to § 512(c), § 512(d) also includes provisions regarding knowledge and notification of the ISP, and references the § 512(c)(3) notice requirements.[207]

[2] Copyright and Management Systems

Chapter 12 of the DMCA, entitled "Copyright and Management System," proscribes the circumvention of copyright protection systems.[208] The DMCA

---

[205] Id.

[206] Id.

[207] Id.

[208] 17 U.S.C. § 1201(a) (2002) (noting that the circumvention of a technological measure is to "descramble a scrambled work, to decrypt an encrypted work, or otherwise avoid, bypass, remove, deactivate, or impair a technological protection measure").

makes it a crime to create or sell technologies to circumvent copyright protection devices. Section 1201(b) of the DMCA prohibits the manufacture of anticircumvention devices, which bypass technical measures controlling access to copyrighted works.[209] A prohibited device has three attributes: (1) it is primarily designed for circumvention; (2) it has limited uses for legitimate commercial purposes (other than circumvention); and (3) it is marketed for use in circumventing copyright protection. Section 1201(f) permits software developers to reverse-engineer circumvention devices to achieve interoperability of independently-created computer programs.[210]

The first criminal prosecution of a defendant under the DMCA stemmed from the arrest of Dmitry Sklyarov, a Russian developer indicted on charges of violating the DMCA. Sklyarov was the developer of software (Advanced eBook Processor) that circumvented Adobe's "copy-control technologies."[211] Sklyarov's software broke the encryption that Adobe was using to protect its software, allowing users of his software to make the copies that Adobe's software was trying to prevent.[212] Sklyarov claims that his software is allowing fair use of Adobe's software. He is presently awaiting trial to see if he will be fined heavily or serve a jail sentence for the circumvention.[213]

Section 1201 of DMCA prohibits technological measures to bypass copyright protection. Such measures are defined as means to descramble a scrambled work, to decrypt an encrypted work, or otherwise to avoid, bypass, remove, deactivate, or impair a technological measure, without the authority of the copyright owner. A technological measure "effectively controls access to a work" if the measure, in the ordinary course of its operation, requires the application of information, or a process or a treatment, with the authority of the copyright owner, to gain access to the work.

Section 1201(b) makes it a violation to manufacture, import or traffic in devices with a predominant purpose of circumventing technological measures for copyright protection. A court will examine the degree to which circumvention devices have commercial uses other than bypassing technological measures protected copyrighted materials in determining whether there is a violation of the DMCA. Section 1202(b) of the DMCA prohibits, unless authorized, several forms of knowing removal or alteration of copyright management information.[214] A violation of § 1201 may result in civil and criminal penalties, provided there is proof

---

[209] DMCA, § 1201.

[210] DMCA, § 1201(f).

[211] Jovi Yam Tanada, Does Dmitry Sklyarov Belong in Jail?, Sept. 13, 2001 (visited Apr. 28, 2002), http://itmatters.com.ph/columns/yam_09062001.html.

[212] Robert Lemos, Russian Cryto Expert Arrested at Def Con, C/Net News (July 17, 2001), http://www.news.cnet.com/news/0-1003-200-6592390.

[213] Id.

[214] Section 1202(b) of the DMCA provides that "No person shall without the authority of the copyright owner or the law—(1) intentionally remove or alter any copyright management information . . . (3) distribute . . . copies of works . . . knowing that copyright management information has been removed or altered without authority of the copyright owner or the law, knowing, or, with respect to civil remedies under section 1203, having reasonable grounds to know, that it will induce, enable, facilitate, or conceal an infringement of any right under [federal copyright law]."

that a competitor made copies of copyrighted work separated from a copyright information management measure.

In the wake of September 11, 2001, some U.S. senators proposed a registration model in which there would be a "backdoor key" for every encryption method. The backdoor key would be held in escrow and be used to decrypt the encryption, if there was a public necessity.[215] The holding of keys in escrow is justified on the grounds that the government must prevent terrorists' plots by decrypting terrorists' encrypted e-mail messages.[216] Although this may sound like a safe and worthwhile idea to some, opponents argue that there could be "millions or billions of keys" the government body would have to keep track of and have control over.[217] Moreover, it would be an enticing target for either terrorists[218] or any hacker with a desire to have control of such powerful information.[219] Another concern is that of bribery by someone with control over the information for access to the keys.[220]

[3] Digital Copies for Libraries

Title IV of the DMCA amends § 108 of the Copyright Act to permit libraries to digitize analog materials without the permission of the copyright owner for archival purposes. Libraries may make up to three digital copies of copyrighted materials for archival purposes. The DMCA permits libraries to reproduce published works in their last 20 years of protection for the purposes of scholarship, research, and preservation.

[4] DMCA Caselaw

In *Kelly v. Arriba Software*,[221] the owner of copyrighted thumbprint photographs displayed on an Internet web site sued the operator of a visual search engine for copyright infringement. In *Arriba*, the defendant operated a "visual search engine." Like other Internet search engines, the user obtained web content in response to a search query. The Ninth Circuit found that a search engine's reproduction of a photographer's images for use as "thumbnails" was a fair use under the Copyright Act. However, its display of the photographer's full-sized images violated his exclusive right to publicly display his works. The appellate court found that there was a prima facie case of copyright infringement since "[the

---

[215] Brian Krebs, Techies Urge Senator to Drop Encryption Key Plan, Newsbytes (Oct. 27, 2001), http://www.newsbytes.com/news/01/170592.html.

[216] *Id.*

[217] *Id.*

[218] *Id.*

[219] High-Tech Leaders Slam Encryption Back Door Bill, Newsbytes (Oct. 4, 2001), http://www.newsbytes.com/news/01/170839.html.

[220] *Id.*

[221] 280 F.3d 934 (9th Cir. 2002).

plaintiff] owned the copyright to the images and that [the defendant] copied those images."[222]

The court found that the separation of the image from the plaintiff's copyright management information did not constitute a violation of § 1202(b)(3) of the DMCA since there was no reasonable basis that this action would cause copyright infringement. The *Arriba* court found that the thumbprint index was protected by fair use since it was "transformative" of and "very different" from the original copyrighted images. The court also found that the purpose of the visual thumbnail index was to provide a comprehensive index to images posted on the Internet and not a form of expression.

In *Universal City Studios, Inc. v. Reimerdes*[223] (*Reimerdes II*), a federal district court issued a preliminary injunction enjoining hackers from making available on their web site the software utility program DeCSS, which permitted users to bypass copyright protection on digital versatile discs (DVDs). The defendants were publishers of *2600*, a publication geared to hackers, and also maintained a web site with content oriented to hackers. The plaintiffs in *Reimerdes* were eight major United States motion picture studios that distributed many of their copyrighted motion pictures for home use on DVDs.[224] The DeCSS program permits users to bypass CSS, which is a copy protection system for movies in a digital format.[225] The hackers quickly posted the DeCSS to its web site. The plaintiffs' sought a preliminary injunction against the 2600 Magazine, a hacker quarterly, that was distributing DeCSS on its web site.

The plaintiffs filed suit under the DMCA seeking to enjoin the 2600 web site from posting DeCSS or linking its site to others posting the descrambling software.[226] The 2600 Magazine contended that its actions did not violate the DMCA or the DMCA "as applied to computer programs violated the First Amendment."[227] The defendants argued that the DMCA as applied to computer software would prevent "fair use" of technologically protected programs.

The hackers were accused of violating § 1201(a)(2) in its posting and linking to other sites posting DeCSS, "and not of using it themselves to bypass plaintiffs' access controls."[228] The hackers voluntarily removed the DeCSS software after an issuance of a preliminary injunction but continued to electronically link to other sites with the descrambling software. An electronic disobedience campaign

---

[222] *Id.*

[223] 117 F. Supp. 2d 294 (S.D.N.Y. 2000) (*Reimerdes II*); *see also* 115 F. Supp. 2d 346 (S.D.N.Y. 2000) (*Reimerdes I*).

[224] *Id.* at 303.

[225] "CSS involves encrypting, according to an encryption algorithm, the digital sound and graphics files on a DVD that together constitutes a motion picture. An appropriate decryption algorithm that employs a series of keys stored on the DVD and the DVD player can decrypt a CSS-protected DVD. In consequence, only players and drives containing the appropriate keys are able to decrypt DVD files and thereby play movies." *Id.* at 309-400.

[226] *Id.* at 304.

[227] *Id.*

[228] *Id.* at 316.

against the motion picture studios resulted in more than 500 sites offering downloads of DeCSS. The court rejected the defendants' fair use argument, as well as defendants' First Amendment defense asserting that the anti-circumvention provisions of the DMCA were a content-neutral restriction on speech that advanced important government interests of preventing the piracy of copyrighted works. The court also rejected the defendant's overbreadth challenge to DMCA's anti-circumvention provisions.

The court held that the motion picture studios met the requisite showing of irreparable injury given that the hackers were offering the descrambling software that facilitated copyright infringement. In *Universal City Studios v. Corley*,[229] the Second Circuit affirmed the district court order enjoining the defendants from posting DeCSS and from linking to other web sites containing the software. The court found the computer code to be content neutral, surviving the constitutional standard of intermediate scrutiny. The defendant's appeal centered on the First Amendment protection enjoyed by software capable of cracking encrypted DVDs in light of technical measures protection provisions found in the DMCA.[230]

[H]　Noncopyright-Related Issues

[1]　VARA Moral Rights

Moral rights are the rights of artists to prevent works from being modified, even after the works have been sold and transferred to another party. While moral rights have been applied primarily to works of art created in a tangible medium, they can apply to online modifications as well. Unless they already have permission or a license, companies altering an artist's work of recognized stature online must obtain clearance for authors' moral rights associated with digital information displayed on its web site. Visual artists contributing to a web site have moral rights of attribution and integrity, as described in § 106(A) of the 1976 Copyright Act. On an international level, the Berne Convention gives authors moral rights even if they are employees or contractors.[231] A French court, for example, might find that the digitalization of a photograph constitutes an alteration of an author's moral rights.[232]

---

[229] 2001 U.S. App. LEXIS 25330 (2d Cir. May 30, 2001) (holding that injunction against posting of DeCSS targeted only the nonspeech component of the software or computer code).

[230] Michael Geist, BNA's Internet Law News, May 1, 2001 (citing http://www.newsbytes.com/news/01/165121.html; http://www.wired.com/news/digiwood/0,1412,43450,00.html; http://www.siliconvalley.com/docs/news/tech/022538.htm; and http://www.inside.com/jcs/Story?article_id=29720).

[231] 134 H. Ward Classen, Fundamentals of Software Licensing, Fourth Annual High Technology Law Conference: Licensing in a Network Environment (Mar. 10, 2000). *See generally* M. Holderness, Moral Rights and Authors' Rights: The Keys to the Information Age, 1998(1), J. of Information, L. & Tech. (visited Aug. 16, 2000), http://elj.warwick.ac.uk/JLT/intosoc/98_/bold/.

[232] France recognizes four separate moral rights: (1) the right of disclosure assures that the artist is the sole judge of whether his or her work is a completed creation, and whether it should be submitted to the public; (2) the right of withdrawal; (3) the right of paternity; and (4) the right of integrity. This issue, however, has yet to be brought before a court in an online context.

The term *droit morales* is a French term that "refers not to 'morals' . . . but rather the ability of authors to control the eventual fate of their works."[233] The doctrine of *les droits morales* refers to "the belief that an artist injects his spirit into a work (s)he creates and that the integrity of the work—and therefore the artist's spirit and personality—should be protected and preserved."[234] The right of attribution, integrity, and *droit de suite,* or the right to resale, are well-developed moral rights in the French legal system.[235] The doctrine of moral rights accords the author a continuing interest in the integrity of his or her artistic work after it is sold or assigned.

The right of integrity is "inalienable and perpetual," protecting the artist against "any distortion or alteration of his or her creation once the completed work has been transferred or made the subject of publication or performance."[236] The Berne Convention for the Protection of Literary and Artistic Works protects artists' moral rights.[237] Article 6(b) of the Berne Convention provides that "the means of redress for safeguarding the [right of integrity] shall be governed by the legislation of the country where protection is claimed."[238] Article 6(b) recognizes principles of paternity and integrity as inalienable personal rights of the artist.[239]

The United States is a signatory of the Berne Convention, but it has been slow to recognize the concept of moral rights of authors. If a work is first published in the United States, or simultaneously in the United States and another nation, the "country of origin" under the Berne Convention would be the United States. A work is governed by the Berne Convention if the authors are nationals, domiciles, or habitual residents of the United States.[240]

The United States' implementation of the Berne Convention in 1988 did little to protect artists' moral rights.[241] American copyright law, unlike the law in many countries in the European Union which have a civil code tradition, does not protect the author against destruction, mutilation, or even attribution of her works of authorship. The Second Circuit Court of Appeals in *Gilliam v. American Broadcasting Co.*[242] held that ABC's mutilation of the British Broadcasting Service's "Monty Python's Flying Circus" was precluded by the Lanham Act. Few U.S.

---

[233] Betsey Rosenblatt, Moral Rights Basics (visited Mar. 13, 1998), http://cyber.law.harvard.edu/property/library/moralprimer.html.

[234] Patrick W. Begos, Artists' Moral Rights (1997) (visited Apr. 27, 2002), http://www.molton.com/artlaw/artlaw.html.

[235] *Id.*

[236] *Id.*

[237] *Id.*

[238] *Id.*

[239] Flore Krigsman, Section 43(a) of the Lanham Act As a Defender of Artists' 'Moral Rights,' 73 Trad. Rep. 251 (May-June 1983).

[240] 17 U.S.C. § 101(3)(A)(B)(1)(A)-(D)(2)(3) (2002).

[241] *Id.*

[242] 538 F.3d 14 (2d Cir. 1975) (holding that altering an artist's work and attributing the new creation to the artist can violate the Lanham Act); *see also* Leigh v. Warner Bros., Inc., 212 F.3d 1210 (11th Cir. 2000) (refusing to follow Second Circuit holding in *Gilliam* in case involving Internet icons).

courts would subsume moral rights under the Lanham Act. Moral rights are generally recognized under copyright law, not trademark law. Canada, for example, recognizes the concept of moral rights of authors under its copyright law.[243] It is advisable to obtain written waivers of moral rights to prevent claims that change to a web site "distorts" or "mutilates" the owner's original creation.[244]

The moral rights of artists were fortified when Congress passed the Visual Artists Rights Act of 1990 (VARA). VARA protects the artist's moral rights that a visual work will not be revised, altered, or distorted, even if sold or assigned to another party. "The author of a work of visual art . . . shall have the right . . . to prevent any destruction of a work of recognized stature, any intentional or grossly negligent destruction of that work is a violation of that right."[245] VARA protects only works of visual art, which have attained the status of "recognized stature."[246] Under VARA, a creator may restrain the alteration of the work in a manner that is prejudicial to his or her literary or artistic reputation. Section 106A recognizes "rights of certain authors to attribution and integrity."[247]

In a nondigital example, the Second Circuit determined in *Carter v. Helmsley-Spear, Inc.*[248] that a sculpture made from recycled materials was not of "recognized stature."[249] The sculpture in that case was made from recycled materials affixed to the walls and ceiling. The work "included a giant hand fashioned

---

[243] Rina Elster Pantalony, NAFTA Kills Copyright Protection for Databases, IP Worldwide (Sept. 1998/Oct. 1998) (noting that Canada's concept of moral rights is tied to copyright law).

[244] E. Perle, Electronic Publishing and Software, 17 Computer Law 27 (Mar. 2000); *see generally* Mark Fischer, E. Gabriel Perle, John Taylor Williams, Perle and Williams on Publishing Law (Aspen Law & Business 2001).

[245] 17 U.S.C. § 106A(a)(3)(b) (2000).

[246] The court in Carter v. Helmsley-Spear, Inc., 861 F. Supp. 303 (S.D.N.Y. 1994), *aff'd in part, vacated in part, rev'd in part,* 71 F.3d 77 (2d Cir. 1995) (defining meaning of "recognized stature" under VARA).

[247] 17 U.S.C. § 106A (2002). Section 106A provides:

Rights of attribution and integrity—Subject to section 107 and independent of the Exclusive rights provided in section 106, the author of a work of visual art—
(1) shall have the right—
(A) to claim authorship of that work, and
(B) to prevent the use of his or her name as the author of any work of visual art which he or she did not create;
(2) shall have the right to prevent the use of his or her name as the author of the work of visual art in the event of a distortion, mutilation, or other modification of the work which would be prejudicial to his or her honor or reputation; and
(3) subject to the limitations set forth in section 113(d), shall have the right—
(A) to prevent any intentional distortion, mutilation, or other modification of that work which would be prejudicial to his or her honor or reputation, and any intentional distortion, mutilation, or modification of that work is a violation of that rights, and
(B) to prevent any destruction of a work of recognized stature, and any intentional or grossly negligent destruction of that work is a violation of that right.

[248] 71 F.3d 77 (2d Cir. 1995).

[249] *Id.* at 83.

from an old school bus, a face made of automobile parts, and a number of inter-active components."[250] To qualify as a work of "recognized stature" requires:

> that the visual art in question has "stature," i.e. is viewed as meritorious, and that this stature is "recognized" by art experts, other members of the artistic community, or by some cross-section of society. In making this showing, plaintiffs generally, but not inevitably, will need to call expert witnesses to testify before the trier of fact.[251]

Most corporate web sites are unlikely to qualify as works of "recognized stature," either.

In *Martin v. City of Indianapolis*,[252] a creator of a large outdoor stainless steel sculpture filed a lawsuit under VARA after the City of Indianapolis demolished the sculpture as part of an urban renewal project. The federal district court granted the plaintiff's motion, awarding him statutory damages under VARA. The Seventh Circuit affirmed the finding that the sculpture was of "recognized stature."[253] The court did not find the city's conduct to be willful, effectively precluding the plaintiff from receiving enhanced damages.[254]

Canadian authors have a moral right of integrity in all literary, dramatic, musical, and artistic works as well as sound recordings.[255] Digital modification of a photograph posted at a web site, for example, may constitute an infringement of copyright and a violation of a photographer's moral rights.[256] As a preventive law measure, companies should enter agreements with authors permitting materials to be digitized or modified on their web sites.

[2] Right of Publicity

The *right of publicity* is an individual's right to control the commercial value of his or her likeness, name, or voice. A web site audit should determine whether all materials posted on the site are owned or licensed by the company. The audit should determine whether any photographs, voices, or images on its web site potentially violate a right to publicity or privacy. The online company needs to obtain rights to use names, faces, images, voices, or other likenesses in photographs, video clips, or other images of living persons. One of the other privacy-based torts may apply to displaying photographs of living persons on its web site.

---

[250] *Id.* at 80.

[251] Carter v. Helmsley-Spear, Inc., 861 F. Supp. 303, 325 (S.D.N.Y. 1994), *aff'd in part, vacated in part, rev'd in part,* 71 F.3d 77 (2d Cir. 1995).

[252] 192 F.3d 608 (7th Cir. 1999).

[253] *Id.* at 609.

[254] *Id.* at 617.

[255] Brian MacLeond Rogers and Sheldon Burshtein, The Information Highway: The Canadian Perspective on the Bumps in the Road, Software L. Bull. (Mar. 1996), at 46.

[256] *Id.*

Section 5.06 in Chapter Five covers Internet-related privacy torts, including the right of publicity.

hold
nlas

In a recent case, a California court denied summary judgment in a right-of-publicity claim by Dick Clark, the host of American Bandstand.[257] The right-of-publicity claim arose from the use of Clark's name in an AOL mailing to members of the American Association of Retired Persons. The court dismissed Clark's claim of trademark infringement and dilution claims, agreeing that AOL's use of Clark's name constituted fair use under trademark law.

The right of publicity is a transferable interest,[258] and an online company may decide to license or become an assignee of publicity rights. In *Gridiron.Com, Inc. v. NFL*,[259] a court granted summary judgment in favor of the National Football League's player's union because the defendant was violating a license agreement covering the right of publicity for NFL players on its web site.[260] Additionally, according to one writer, a right of publicity action may also be filed for "digital transformations of a person's likeness; and the use of a person's name in a Web site's metatags."[261]

[I] Software Copyrights

By the mid-1980s, as the consumer and business demand for software exploded it was clear that software could be protected by copyright.[262] By then, the trend in the law was for courts "to accord software a relatively thin protection," as one circuit after another followed the abstraction-filtration-comparison test.[263] Courts will examine the program at various levels of abstraction from the most detailed to the most general. The court makes a decision as to which aspects of the software are not susceptible to copyright protection at each level of abstraction from specific to general. After filtering out all of the nonprotectible elements, the court compares the original to the copy to determine whether there is a "substantial similarity."

---

[257] Clark v. America Online, Inc., No. CV-98-05650 (C.D. Cal., Dec. 4, 2000), reported in 18 Computer & Online Industry Litig. Rptr. 10 (Jan. 3, 2001); *see generally* Mark D. Robins, Publicity Rights in the Digital Media, 17 Computer & Internet Lawyer 29 (Dec. 2000); CA Woman's Class Suit Alleges Corel Used Her Photo Without Her Okay, 11 Software L. Bull. 238 (Dec. 1998) (reporting case of *Lyon v. Corel Corp.*).

[258] First Nat'l Bank v. United States, 620 F.2d 1096 (5th Cir. 1980).

[259] 106 F. Supp. 2d 1309 (S.D. Fla. 2000).

[260] *Id.* at 1315.

[261] *See* Mark D. Robins, Part I: Publicity Rights in the Digital Media, 17 Computer & Internet Law 1 (Nov. 2000).

[262] Raymond T. Nimmer and Patricia Ann Krauthaus, Software Copyright: Sliding Scales and Abstracted Expression, 32 Houston L. Rev. 317, 320 (1995) (nothing that "[e]arly court opinions focused on whether any copyright protection exists for computer programs," but the "question was resolved: software is copyrightable").

[263] Stephen M. McJohn, Software Copyright Developments, presented at the Fourth Annual High Technology Law Conference, Suffolk University Law School, Boston, Mass. (Sept. 1998); *see generally* Stephen M. McJohn, Fair Use of Copyrighted Software, 28 Rutgers L.J. 1 (1997).

For example, the United States Supreme Court, in *Lotus Development v. Borland International*,[264] let stand the First Circuit's holding that the "look and feel" of the menu command structure of the 1-2-3 Lotus spreadsheet program are not copyrightable under § 102 of the Copyright Act. The First Circuit compared the Lotus 1-2-3 menu to the buttons on a VCR: "Just as one could not operate a buttonless VCR, it would be impossible to operate Lotus 1-2-3 without employing its menu command hierarchy. Thus, the Lotus commands are not equivalent to the labels on the VCR's buttons, but are instead the equivalent of the buttons themselves."[265] If a copycat developed a web site with the same feel as a company's site, the company may have a possible action for unfair business competition or trademark dilution. Dilution occurs when a trademark loses its distinctive quality because of unauthorized use by another party.[266]

Copyright infringement issues are beginning to be litigated for shareware. In a recent shareware case,[267] developer Storm licensed its shareware solely for noncommercial use on the Internet. Storm filed a copyright infringement against Software of the Month Club (SOMC) because it violated a clause of the license agreement prohibiting charging for the distribution of Storm's software.[268] Although SOMC argued that "by publishing its shareware . . . Storm impliedly consented to SOMC's distribution," the court disagreed because Storm "place[d] the material on the Internet, allow[ed] limited distribution for free, and attempt[ed] to restrict this free distribution to non-commercial use."[269] SOMC also argued that the shareware was transformative and thus protected under the fair use doctrine of copyright law. The court, however, held that "a shareware version of a copyrighted computer program is not transformative within the meaning of fair use."[270] The court also rejected SOMC's claim that its copying was comparable to a book review because it copied the software line for line.[271] The court ruled in favor of Storm, holding "that SOMC's copying and distribution of Storm's products did not constitute fair use and that SOMC has infringed Storm's copyrights by exceeding the terms of the license." The court granted Storm $20,000 in statutory damages for its copyright infringement claims."[272]

---

[264] Lotus Dev. v. Borland Int'l, 49 F.3d 807 (1st Cir. 1995), *aff'd,* 116 S. Ct. 817 (1996) (accompanied by a 4-4 vote).

[265] *Id.* at 816.

[266] Trademarks are divided into five general categories of distinctiveness: (1) generic, (2) descriptive, (3) suggestive, (4) arbitrary, and (5) fanciful. Spear, Leeds & Kellogg v. Rosado, 2000 U.S. Dist. LEXIS 3732 (S.D.N.Y., Mar. 24, 2000).

[267] Storm Impact v. Software of the Month Club, 13 F. Supp. 2d 782 (N.D. Ill. 1998).

[268] *Id.*

[269] *Id.* at 791.

[270] *Id.* at 788.

[271] *Id.*

[272] *Id.* at 792.

[J]   Online Copyright in Practice

It is late one Friday afternoon and SPC executives need advisory opinions on a number of copyright issues arising out of the launch of the SPC site: *http://www.spc.com.* SPC recently launched a web site with streaming video, music, software, and an online ordering system.[273] SPC's web site contains a wide range of copyrightable text, artwork, audiovisual material, sounds, and music. The section that follows provides the executives with the necessary guidance.

[1]   Notice of Copyright

SPC should affix proper copyright notices on its web site even though copyright notice is no longer required after the United States adhered to the Berne Convention on March 1, 1989. Also, because prior law did contain such a requirement, the use of notice is still relevant to the copyright status of older works. Notice was required under the 1976 Copyright Act. This requirement was eliminated when the United States adhered to the Berne Convention, effective March 1, 1989. Although works published without notice before that date could have entered the public domain in the United States, the Uruguay Round Agreements Act (URAA) restores copyright in certain foreign works originally published without notice. The Copyright Office does not take a position on whether copies of works first published with notice before March 1, 1989, which are distributed on or after March 1, 1989, must bear the copyright notice.

A *copyright notice* is notice that the work is protected by copyright; it identifies the copyright owner, and it is evidence of the year of first publication. Furthermore, in the event that a work is infringed, if a proper notice of copyright appears on the published copy or copies to which a defendant in a copyright infringement suit had access, then no weight shall be given a defense based on innocent infringement. Innocent infringement occurs when the infringer does not realize that the work was protected before making a copy.

The notice for visually perceptible copies should contain the following three elements:

1. The symbol © (the letter C in a circle), or the word "Copyright," or the abbreviation "Copr."
2. The year of first publication of the work. In the case of compilations or derivative works, incorporating previously published material, the year date of first publication of the compilation or derivative work is sufficient. The year date may be omitted where a pictorial, graphic, or sculptural work, with accompanying textual matter, if any, is reproduced in or on greeting cards, postcards, stationery, jewelry, dolls, toys, or any useful article.

---

[273] Suffolk Personal Computer (SPC) is a hypothetical company. Our use of the SPC™ is for illustration purposes only and is not affiliated with SPC Software of Walled Lake, Michigan, or Software Professional Consultants or the Software Productivity Center (SPC).

3.   The name of the owner of copyright in the work, or an abbreviation by which the name can be recognized, or a generally known alternative designation of the owner.

An example of a copyright notice is © 2002 SPC or Copyright © 2002 by Michael L. Rustad and Cyrus Daftary.

The "C in a circle" notice is used only on "visually perceptible copies," which is a copyright law concept. The "visually perceptible copy," for example, does not apply to certain kinds of copyrighted works, such as a sound recording. Certain kinds of works—for example, musical, dramatic, and literary works—may be fixed not in "copies" but by means of sound in an audio recording. If SPC employs sound, music, or spoken words on its web site, it will need to comply with the special rules for the form of notice for sound recording. Sound recordings include musical, spoken, or other sounds, but not sounds accompanying a motion picture or other audiovisual work. Common examples include recordings of music, drama, or lectures.

A sound recording, however, is not the same as a phonorecord. A phonorecord is the physical object or medium in which works of authorship are embodied, and includes tapes, CDs, LPs, 45 r.p.m. disks, and other sound formats. The "C in a circle" notice, therefore, is not used to indicate protection of the underlying musical, dramatic, or literary work recorded, and a separate notice is required. The notice for phonorecords embodying a sound recording should contain all the following three elements:

1.   The symbol ℗ (the letter P in a circle);
2.   The year of first publication of the sound recording; and
3.   The name of the owner of copyright in the sound recording, or an abbreviation by which the name can be recognized, or a generally known alternative designation of the owner. If the producer of the sound recording is named on the phonorecord label or container, and if no other name appears in conjunction with the notice, the name of the producer shall be considered a part of the notice.

An example of a phonorecord notice is ℗ 2002 SPC.

Copyright registration is a predicate to obtaining statutory damages or attorneys' fees.[274] Registration is also a means of proving ownership of a copyright, though it is not a requirement of copyright ownership. The owner of a copyright, or the assignee of the exclusive right of publication, must deposit within three months of the date of publication two complete copies of the best edition.

[2]   Benefits of Copyright Registration

SPC should "register with the Copyright Office to obtain statutorily prescribed benefits, including eligibility for statutory damages and legal fees in the

---

[274] U.S. Copyright Act, 17 U.S.C. § 412 (2002).

event of infringement."[275] For SPC, copyright registration is a simple and inexpensive means of protecting its copyrightable materials. When SPC registers its copyright, it is essentially staking a public claim in the Copyright Office. Copyright registration is highly recommended because SPC seeks the certificate of copyright registration, which will be useful in case of a copyright infringement lawsuit. If SPC files a copyright registration at the time of first publication, it may use the registration as prima facie evidence of ownership of a copyright. SPC has an exclusive right to obtain a copyright registration during the period of copyright protection.[276]

SPC should register its web site and copyrighted materials posted at its web site. Copyright registration is a legal formality intended to make a public record of the basic facts of a particular copyright.[277] Copyright registration is not a predicate for SPC obtaining copyright protection but is strongly recommended.[278]

Despite the fact that registration is not required for protection, it provides SPC with several strategic advantages. First, registration serves as a public record for establishing the date of copyright creation. Second, copyright registration is a prerequisite if SPC wishes to file a copyright infringement lawsuit. Third, copyright registration is also evidence to establish the validity of the copyright. If registration is completed before or within five years of publication, registration is treated as prima facie evidence of the validity of the copyright and the facts stated in the copyright registration certificate. Fourth, if registration is completed within three months after publication of the work or before an infringement of the work, statutory damages and attorneys' fees will be available to the copyright owner in court actions.

If no copyright registration is completed three months after publication or before infringement, the copyright owner may not seek statutory penalties against

---

[275] Carey R. Ramos and David S. Berlin, Three Ways to Protect Software, 16 Comp. Law 16 (Jan. 1999) (noting that copyright law only protects against copying of the work and that if "someone independently creates a similar or even identical work, he or she does not violate the copyright").

[276] Copyright Act, 17 U.S.C. § 408 (1999).

[277] Information on registering copyrights is available through the Copyright Office web site. The Copyright Office provides copies of all circulars, announcements, regulations, other related materials, and all copyright application forms on its web site. The registrant may access all of these forms at the Copyright Office homepage at http://www.loc.gov/copyright. In addition, information (but not application forms) is available by Fax-on-Demand, at (202) 707-2600. For general information about copyright, call the Copyright Public Information Office at (202) 707-3000. The TTY number is (202) 707-6737. Information specialists are on duty from 8:30 A.M. to 5:00 P.M. eastern time, Monday through Friday, except federal holidays. Recorded information is available 24 hours a day. Specific application forms and circulars can be requested from the Forms and Publications Hotline, at (202) 707-9100, 24 hours a day. Information on registration is also available by regular mail: Library of Congress, Copyright Office, Publications Section, LM-455, 101 Independence Avenue, S.E., Washington, D.C. 20559-6000.

[278] Registration may be made at any time within the life of the copyright. Unlike the law before 1978, when a work has been registered in unpublished form, it is not necessary to make another registration when the work becomes published, although the copyright owner may register the published edition, if desired.

the infringer. If there is no copyright registration, the total remedy is limited to an award of actual damages and profits. One of the essential issues to understand is whether the registration will extend to the entire scope of SPC's online work. Registration for all online works extends only to the copyrightable content of the work as received in the Copyright Office and identified as the subject of the claim. The Copyright Office has different forms that correspond to the type of work registered. Because a web site contains many different types of work, the form used for a web site containing more than one type of authorship will be the form that corresponds to the predominant material (see Table 4.4).[279]

Finally, SPC is a multinational dot-com company, which needs to protect others from importing infringing copies of its software. When SPC registers its copyrights, it should also record the copyright registrations with the United States Customs Services for confiscating infringing copies.[280]

[3] Registration Procedures

Copyright registration transforms a particular copyright into a public record. An original registration of copyright is made in the Copyright Office of the Library of Congress. A work may be registered any time during the life of the work of authorship. It is advisable, however, that copyrighted material be registered early in the life of the copyrighted work. An online work may be registered using any of the Copyright Office forms, with the sole exception that sound should be registered using Form SR. The applicant needs to describe the nature of authorship being registered.

The applicant should use terms that refer to copyrightable authorship, such as text, music, artwork, photographs, audiovisual material, and sound recordings. The Copyright Office advises the applicant not to refer to elements not protected by copyright, such as "user interface," "format," "layout," "design," "lettering," "concept," or "game play."[281] The Copyright Office's definition of *publication* does not "specifically address online transmissions."[282] The paper-based definition of publication refers to the distribution of copies to the public for sale or other transfer of ownership by rental, lease, or lending. A public performance or display of a work does not constitute publication.[283]

---

[279] U.S. Copyright Office, Copyright Registration for Online Works (Circular 66) (visited Apr. 22, 2002), http://lcweb.loc.gov/copyright/circs/circ66.html.

[280] Registration allows the owner of the copyright to record the registration with the U.S. Customs Service for protection against the importation of infringing copies. For additional information, request Publication No. 563 from Commissioner of Customs, ATTN: IPR Branch, U.S. Customs Service, 1300 Pennsylvania Avenue, N.W., Washington, D.C. 20229 (visited Apr. 14, 2002), http://www.customs.gov.

[281] U.S. Copyright Office, Copyright Registration for Online Works (Circular 66) (visited Apr. 29, 2002), http://www.lcweb.loc.gov/copyright/circs/circ66.html.

[282] *Id.*

[283] 17 U.S.C. § 101 (2002).

TABLE 4.4
Copyright Application Forms

For Original Registration

Form PA	For published and unpublished works of the performing arts (musical and dramatic works, pantomimes and choreographic works, motion pictures and other audiovisual works).
Form SE	For serials, works issued or intended to be issued in successive parts bearing numerical or chronological designations and intended to be continued indefinitely (periodicals, newspapers, magazines, newsletters, annuals, journals, etc.).
Form SR	For published and unpublished sound recordings.
Form TX	For published and unpublished nondramatic literary works.
Form VA	For published and unpublished works of the visual arts (pictorial, graphic, and sculptural works, including architectural works).
Form G/DN	A specialized form for registering a complete month's issues of a daily newspaper, when certain conditions are met.
Short Form/SE and Form SE/GROUP	Specialized SE forms for use when certain requirements are met.
Short Forms TX, PA, and VA	Short versions of applications for original registration. For further information about using the short forms, request Circular SL-7.
Form GATT and Form GATT/GRP	Specialized forms to register a claim in a work or group of related works in which U.S. copyright was restored under the 1994 Uruguay Round Agreements Act (URAA). For further information, request Circular 38b.

For Renewal Registration

Form RE	For claims to renew copyright in works copyrighted under the law in effect through December 31, 1977 (1909 Copyright Act) and registered during the initial 28-year copyright term.

For Corrections and Amplifications

Form CA	For supplementary registration to correct or amplify information given in the Copyright Office record of an earlier registration.

For a Group of Contributions to Periodicals

Form GR/CP	An adjunct application to be used for registration of a group of contributions to periodicals in addition to an application Form TX, PA, or VA.

The application requires the online publisher to determine whether the work is published with the complete date and nation of first publication.[284] It is unclear when an online publication is published or if it is published. The country where the work was first uploaded defines the nation of publication for an online publication.[285] If the online applicant determines that work is unpublished, the Copyright Office requests that the applicant leave the nation of first publication blank rather than fill the space with *Internet* or *homepage*.[286] It is unclear how works transmitted online should be deposited with the Copyright Office. The Copyright Office is developing new rules for depositing online materials. The deposit requirement for registered software on a CD-ROM is to deposit the CD-ROM, operating software, and manual.

The three elements of a copyright registration are (1) a completed application, (2) a filing fee of $30,[287] and (3) a deposit copy of the work being registered. The Copyright Office requires the applicant to place the copyright registration application, filing fee, and deposited work in the same envelope or package and to send them to the following address.

Library of Congress
Copyright Office
Register of Copyrights
101 Independence Avenue, S.E.
Washington, DC 20559-6000

SPC's copyright registration is effective on the date the Copyright Office receives all the required materials in acceptable form. The time that it takes to process SPC's application and mail the certificate of registration does not affect the date of copyright registration. The Copyright Office acknowledges that the time that it takes to process an application varies considerably.

In 1999, the Copyright Office reported it was averaging over 600,000 applications each year. The Copyright Office does not acknowledge the receipt of an application. The Copyright Office issues a certificate of registration upon acceptance of the copyrighted materials. The Copyright Office cites statutory reasons if it rejects a copyright application. SPC should send its application, filing fee, and deposited material by registered or certified mail to obtain a return receipt.

[4] Who May File an Application Form?

SPC's web site is a collective work protected by copyright. SPC's copyrights in the materials that compose the web site are distinct from copyright in the web

---

[284] For revised works, the publication date is the date the revised version was first published, not the date of the original version. Circular 66, *id.*

[285] *Id.*

[286] Space 3b should not be filled in if the work is published. *Id.*

[287] All remittances should be in the form of drafts, that is, checks, money orders, or bank drafts, payable to: Register of Copyrights. The Copyright Office does not accept cash.

site as a collective work. SPC's web site may also be protected by trademark, if the "look and feel" of the web site is distinctive, to obtain trade dress protection under the federal Lanham Act.[288] If SPC's employees develop the web site, it is quite likely that the work qualifies as "work for hire." If SPC employs consultants or outside developers to develop its web sites, however, it is advisable that SPC enter into agreements that would make SPC the owner of the copyrighted content.

The Copyright Office considers the following persons to be legally entitled to submit an application form: First, the author who is the creator or, if the work was made for hire, the employer or other person for whom the work was prepared can claim copyright. Second, the *copyright claimant,* as defined in Copyright Office regulations, may be either the author of the work or a person or organization that has obtained ownership of all the rights under the copyright initially belonging to the author.[289] The owner of a copyright may not necessarily be the original creator. Third, a publisher or an authorized agent of an author or of the owner of exclusive right(s) may register copyrights. Any person authorized to act on behalf of the author, another copyright claimant, or the owner of exclusive rights may apply for registration.

[5]   Internet Copyright Searches

SPC may wish to conduct a search before attempting to register its copyrights. The records of the Copyright Office are open for inspection and search by the public. In addition, the Copyright Office will conduct a search of its records at the statutory hourly rate of $65 (effective through June 30, 2002) for each hour or fraction of an hour. The Copyright Office publishes Circular 22, "How to Investigate the Copyright Status of a Work," and Circular 23, "The Copyright Card Catalog and the Online Files of the Copyright Office." Another option is for SPC to conduct an Internet search through the Copyright Office's web site. The Copyright Office has copyrights in a machine-readable form, cataloged from January 1, 1978, to the present, including registration and renewal information and recorded documents.[290]

[6]   Content Licenses

If SPC hires consultants or other non-employees to provide content for its web site, it needs to obtain ownership or assignments to use copyrighted materials, since the "work for hire" doctrine does not automatically confer ownership rights onto SPC. If SPC's web site incorporates text, video, audio, pictures, or

---

[288] The leading case for trade dress is Two Pesos, Inc. v. Taco Cabana, Inc., 505 U.S. 763 (1992).

[289] Copyrights are freely transferable, assignable, or conveyed. Anyone who has obtained the right to a copyright may register it with the Copyright Office.

[290] The Copyright Office web site is at http://www.loc.gov/copyright/rb.html. The Telnet site can be found at locis.loc.gov.

other content protected by a third party's copyright, it will need to enter into content license agreements. If SPC employs outside consultants, artists, or other content providers, it will need that party to assign or transfer ownership for all copyrighted materials.

SPC may decide to enter a content license agreement with the copyright owners. The content license agreement, however, does not provide the same degree of control for the licensee as copyright ownership or assignment and may require regular royalty payments. A content license agreement may be as simple as an authorization giving permission to use the materials. The effective date for the license is an important term to include in every agreement and should have the authorized signatures of the licensor and the licensee.

It is essential that SPC's content licenses clearly extend the scope of the agreement to include the Internet as well as print media. What is being transferred or licensed? What is the geographic scope of the license agreement? If SPC is the licensee, it should seek to obtain the right to use the content for all media worldwide.

In *New York Times Co. v. Tasini*,[291] the Supreme Court affirmed the Second Circuit Court of Appeals' reversal of the district court's dismissal of a copyright infringement claim by a number of freelance authors. The Second Circuit held that in the absence of an agreement to do so, periodical publishers did not have the right to publish articles on electronic services or CD-ROMs.[292] The lower court held that, in the absence of any agreement, newspapers and magazine publishers had the presumptive right to publish periodicals electronically, as well as in paper versions.[293]

[a]   *Granting Clause for Content License Agreements*

The *granting clause* is the heart of the content license agreement and defines the scope of the agreement. A licensor will typically want to grant limited rights in nonexclusive agreements, while the licensor will frequently want an exclusive license to use the content for all purposes at all locations. Other considerations include whether the license is exclusive, semiexclusive, or nonexclusive and whether the content license is extended to any subsidiaries of the licensee or just the main entity.

A content license agreement may commence at the execution of the agreement or on the date of delivery of the content and needs both a termination date and a list of designated events of default that constitute grounds for termination. Each party to SPC's content licenses will have a right to cancel the agreement in the event of a material breach. The failure to pay license royalties is a standard event of termination in license agreements. Insolvency of either party is another standard event of default in a content license agreement. The parties should also decide whether there should be a period in which to cure defaults as well.

---

[291] No. 00-201 2001 U.S. LEXIS 4667 (S. Ct., June 25, 2001).

[292] *Id.*

[293] 972 F. Supp. 804 (S.D.N.Y. 1997).

[b]   Payment/Royalty Reports

A licensee may agree to pay a licensor a set fee for content, even if it is a nominal fee. A vast number of payment options are available, depending upon the type of content agreements. The company may require the developer of the content to assign all exclusive rights to the company in return for compensation. Another option is to enter a license agreement with the author of the content. This may involve the need for up-front fees, annual fees, royalties, or fees based upon the number of web site visitors viewing or downloading content. A multitude of methods can be used to compute royalties. A licensor, for example, may receive a given percent of the net sales.

Payment streams are generally greater if the license agreement is exclusive. The licensee may want to obtain warranties and an indemnity to protect it from claims for intellectual property infringement. The danger is that a licensee may be subject to a copyright or trademark infringement lawsuit if a third party believes that the licensed material infringes its rights.[294]

[c]   Warranties and Infringement

SPC must have permission to use all copyrighted materials on its web site that it does not own or it may be liable for damages for copyright infringement. For example, the web posting of model building codes resulted in a copyright infringement action in *Veeck v. Southern Building Code Congress International, Inc.* (SBCCI).[295] In *Veeck,* the defendant operated a nonprofit web site that posted the text of local building codes.[296] The Fifth Circuit ruled that the SBCCI held copyrights to the building Codes and that the web site copied the copyrighted materials without permission.[297] The court rejected the defense that the public had a due process interest in free access to the building codes.[298]

SPC should audit its content to reduce the potential for contributory infringement arising out of SPC's unknowing participation in infringing activities. A company may otherwise be liable for contributory infringement if copyrighted materials from a third party's sources are posted without an appropriate license or assignment. Even if contributory infringement is not proven, SPC may be liable for vicarious infringement because of its relationship with a primary infringer.[299] A company is

---

[294] To succeed in a trademark infringement lawsuit, SPC must establish that it has a protectable trademark and that the infringer's use of that trademark is likely to cause confusion in the same channel of trade.

[295] No. 99-40632 (5th Cir., Feb. 2, 2001), reported in 18 Computer & Internet Law. 27 (Apr. 2001).

[296] *Id.*

[297] *Id.*

[298] *Id.*

[299] The leading vicarious liability case is Shapiro, Bernstein & Co. v. H.L. Green Co., 316 F.2d 304 (2d Cir. 1963) (articulating the doctrine of vicarious infringement).

liable for vicarious infringement where it (1) has the right and ability to control the infringer's acts and (2) receives a direct financial benefit from the infringement.

To further reduce the likelihood of liability for infringement, SPC should obtain content licenses from all third-party providers. The content licensee will typically require the licensor to warrant that it owns all rights in the content. The licensee will seek indemnification for infringement of a third party's intellectual property rights in a content license agreement. A licensee will want the licensor to indemnify and "hold harmless" the licensee for liabilities or claims arising from claims of infringement. A common warranty is that the content will conform to the specifications in the license agreement.

A licensor will typically want to limit what it warrants. For example, the licensor will typically limit liability for express or implied warranties such as the warranty of merchantability and fitness for a particular purpose. The licensor will often seek to limit liability for express or implied warranties, or consequential damages, for example. Many licensors substitute an exclusive remedy of a refund of fees paid instead of all express or implied warranties.

[d]   Acceptance Testing

It is customary in the software industry to have a 30-day acceptance period. A licensor will find it advantageous to have a long acceptance period during which to cure any defaults. A licensee will want a broad license to use content that allows the transfer of content to backup computers.

[e]   Choice of Law and Forum/Dispute Resolution

As with every other web site agreement, it is critical that parties determine the applicable law and/or method for resolving disputes. The case law on Internet jurisdiction is uncertain as to which law is applicable in a situation that involves multiple jurisdictions. The parties should tailor their agreements to include a specific choice of forum and law, otherwise, in the event of a dispute, they may have to bear the cost of litigating in an inconvenient, out-of-state court.

[f]   Franchise Rules

If SPC licenses its trademark to other sites, it may be subject to franchise rules. An agreement between a licensor and a licensee to license a trademark, trade name, service mark, or advertising may be deemed a franchise. A franchise may include a commercial relationship in which a franchisee sells or distributes products on the Internet using SPC's trademarks. If a franchisee uses SPC's trademarks, service marks, or trade names, it may create a franchise.

The Federal Trade Commission (FTC) regulates franchise sales, whether on the Internet or in the brick-and-mortar world. The FTC requires compulsory disclosures in "Franchising and Business Opportunity Ventures," 16 C.F.R. § 436. SPC may also have to comply with state laws governing franchise sales.

[7] Linking Agreements and Disclaimers

Web linking agreements are recommended for activities which go beyond simple linking, such as advertising, outsourcing, framing, or more complex links.[300] Web site linking agreements are also advisable when framing a linked site with a company's own trademarks and materials.[301]

SPC may permit free linking to its site, but it will thus risk links from adult entertainment sites or other sites that may tarnish the company's good will. This can be done through a linking clause on a web site's terms of use agreement. The following language is an example of a linking clause:

> You are free to establish a hypertext link to this site as long as the link does not state or imply any endorsement or sponsorship of you, your company, or your site by SPC.com. However, without the prior written permission of SPC.com, you may not frame any of the content of SPC.com nor incorporate into another web site or other service any intellectual property of SPC or its licensors. You may not, without prior written permission of SPC, deep link into the interior of SPC's site. You must link directly into the home page of SPC, which is the first page of its web site, unless you have written permission from SPC. Requests for permission to frame alternatively or to deep link our content may be sent to our Customer Service Manager, either by e-mail or at the SPC address. Reciprocal promotional linking and affiliate agreement inquiries should be directed to the Affiliate Manager at the SPC address.

SPC will need to determine whether other web linking license requirements are necessary. An affiliate revenue-sharing agreement will spell out web link specification, commissions, reporting, ownership, termination, representations, and indemnification. Even if SPC does not enter into promotional or affiliate linking agreements, it will need a linking policy for web sites that maintain links to its web site. SPC may require, for example, notification of links to its web site and the linkers' acceptance of SPC's terms and conditions. As an alternative, SPC may use "click through" web site license agreements to reduce transaction costs, rather than negotiating each linking agreement.

SPC may also enter web-linking agreements to promote its web site or to share resources with another web site through linking. Model provisions for web linking agreements are available through the American Bar Association's Business Law Section.[302] The following terms are common in web-linking agreements: (1) granting clauses of the right to link; (2) details about the integrity and operation of the sites; (3) descriptions of ownership rights to information in sites; (4) indemnification and disclaimers noting that the parties are agents for named or unnamed

---

[300] William F. Swiggart, Web Linking Agreements: Quasi-Licenses in Interactive Media, 6 Cyber. Law. 2 (Mar. 2001).

[301] *Id.*

[302] Subcommittee on Interactive Services, Committee on the Law of Commerce in Cyberspace, ABA Section of Business Law, Web-Linking Agreements: Contracting Strategies and Model Provisions (1997).

principals; and (5) term limits, termination, and limitations on warranties, liability, and remedies.[303] A linking agreement could be modeled on the following language:

SPC grants to XYZ Company a nonexclusive, nontransferable license to hyperlink ("link") your Internet web site to SPC's link logo and/or SPC's web site, provided XYZ Company accepts all of the following terms and conditions. To indicate XYZ's acceptance of all of the terms and conditions of this web linking agreement, an authorized representative of XYZ Company must click the button marked "XYZ Company Accepts" after its review of the terms and conditions. If XYZ does not agree to all the terms and conditions of this agreement, their authorized representative should click the button "XYZ Company does not accept" the terms and conditions. To link to the SPC web site and/or use SPC's link logo, XYZ must agree to all of the following terms and conditions:

XYZ company must include the following notice on any World Wide Web page it creates which includes the SPC link or SPC link logo: SPC and the SPC link logo are licensed trademarks of SPC, Inc. XYZ Company has no rights to the intellectual property of SPC, and in particular, has no rights to distribute SPC hardware or software.

XYZ may not use the name "SPC," the SPC link, and/or the SPC link logo to disparage SPC, its personal computers, software, and/or services.

XYZ company is not permitted to tarnish or diminish SPC's trade name, trademarks, service marks, logos, or good will by linking it to web sites, including but not limited to content such as pornography, obscene materials, political commentary, hate speech, or web sites that incite unlawful activity.

XYZ may not change the appearance of the SPC logo on its web site. The SPC logo must not be attached to any XYZ or third party's logo and must have a minimum amount of 30 pixels of empty space around it. SPC's link logo may not be used as the design element of any XYZ logo or third party's logo or link logo.

XYZ may not use the name SPC, the link, and/or the SPC link logo in any way that implies SPC sponsorship or endorsement of XYZ's product services, and/or SPC's web site.

You may not display the name "SPC," the SPC link, and/or the SPC link logo more prominently than XYZ's product, Internet web site name, or logo. Links from the SPC web site do not constitute an endorsement from SPC.

SPC reserves the right to alter, modify, or discontinue the SPC web site and/or SPC logo at any time, at its sole discretion. SPC makes no warranties, whether express or implied, and specifically disclaims the implied warranty of merchantability and fitness for a particular purpose related to SPC's web site and/or services. SPC is not liable for any damages or losses arising out of this web linking agreement with XYZ.

XYZ agrees to defend, indemnify, and "hold harmless" SPC, its officers, directors, employers, agents, and any of its affiliated companies for any loss

---

[303] Bruce Gaylord, Web Linking Agreements: Understanding Unique Legal Issues: The Judicial System Is Only Starting to Address Related Privacy Matters, 15 Comp. L. Strat. 1 (Mar. 1999).

or damages caused to SPC arising out of XYZ's use of the name "SPC," the SPC link, and the SPC link logo. XYZ acknowledges that it is responsible for the contents of its web site and acknowledges that SPC is not liable for the defamatory, offensive, or illegal conduct of other users, links, or third parties. SPC is not responsible for hypertext links to web sites that are defamatory, offensive, or illegal.

SPC is not responsible for the contents of XYZ's web site or off-site page references by the XYZ web site.

SPC reserves the right to review XYZ's use of the name "SPC," the SPC link, and the SPC link logo. SPC is hereby granted unrestricted access to XYZ's web site in order to review XYZ's use of the name "SPC," the SPC link, and the SPC link logo.

SPC has the sole discretion to cancel XYZ's use of the trade name SPC, the SPC link, and the link logo for any reason.

XYZ agrees that the laws of the Commonwealth of Massachusetts govern construction of the disclaimers above and resolution of disputes.

Please fill out the following information:

Name of XYZ's authorized representative _____

Title of XYZ's authorized representative _____

Company name and mailing address_____

URL of link to SPC's web site _____

Web site/company _____

Please click "I Accept" if the above information is correct and you agree to the terms of the SPC web link and logo license agreement. If you do not agree to the terms, click "I Do Not Accept" to clear the form and leave the SPC web site.

I Accept   I Decline

[8]   Disclaimers

SPC's web site should also contain corporate disclaimers of links made to corporate home pages or subsequent pages. SPC's disclaimer should state that links are made available by the company's home page, which permits the user to go to other Internet sites. The disclaimer should make it clear that the linked sites are not the property of the company or under its control. The company should emphasize that the company makes no express or implied endorsement of linked sites, and it should conspicuously post on its web site a disclaimer similar in language to the following:

CORPORATE DISCLAIMER

NOTE: Some of the links made available to you through Suffolk Personal Computer's (SPC's) home page and subsequent pages will allow you to leave the SPC web site. Please be aware that the Internet sites available through these links, and the material that you may find there, are not under the control of SPC. SPC cannot and does not make any representation to you about these sites or the materials available there. The fact that SPC has made these links available to you is not an endorsement or recommendation to you by SPC of any of these sites or any material found there. SPC provides these links only as a convenience to you.[304]

[9]   Content Posted on SPC's Services

If SPC has a computer bulletin board or other service in which third parties post materials about products or services, it may be advisable to obtain a content license agreement as depicted below:

> YOU AGREE THAT UPON POSTING ANY MATERIAL ON THE SPC "SPC" [SPECIFY SERVICE], YOU GRANT SPC AND ITS SUCCESSORS AND ASSIGNEES A NONEXCLUSIVE WORLDWIDE ROYALTY-FREE, PERPETUAL, NONREVOCABLE LICENSE TO USE, MODIFY, OR RETRANSMIT MATERIAL YOU POSTED. YOU HEREBY GRANT SPC THE RIGHT TO DOWNLOAD, DISTRIBUTE, DISPLAY, REPRODUCE, AND PRINT IN WHOLE OR IN PART ANY MATERIAL YOU HAVE POSTED [TO THE SERVICE]. YOU AGREE TO TAKE ANY NECES-SARY STEPS TO PROTECT WHATEVER OTHER INTELLECTUAL PROPERTY RIGHTS YOU HAVE IN SUCH CONTENT, INCLUDING POSTING APPROPRIATE COPYRIGHT NOTICES.

[K]   Streaming Media and Copyright Law

Streaming is "when the same broadcast [as allowed in 17 U.S.C.S § 14] is transmitted digitally over the Internet."[305] The U.S. Copyright Office has ruled that streaming media is not covered by 17 U.S.C. § 114, which permits "an FCC-licensed AM or FM radio broadcaster, who is now exempt from paying royalties to record producers and recording artists when it broadcasts a recording in its FCC-licensed geographic area."[306] In a case challenging the U.S. Copyright Office ruling, the court held that the copyright office had the authority to make such a rul-ing, stating that "Congress implicitly, if not explicitly, entrusted the Copyright Office with the task of determining which entities and means of transmission would be exempted by section 114 from the public performance rights of section 106."[307] The court also held that the Copyright Office's ruling was reasonable because the Copyright Office determined that "Congress used the term 'over-the-air' to identify those broadcasts it sought to exempt from the public performance right, and made no mention of any other type of transmission made by an FCC-licensed broadcaster," which would eliminate streaming.[308] In addition, the Copy-right Office, when looking at policy considerations, held "that it was illogical to permit broadcasters to stream under an exemption but impose liability on a third

---

[304] The example adapts language from the GTE Internetworking Legal Documentation, *id.*
[305] Bonneville Int'l Corp. v. Peters, 153 F. Supp. 2d 763, 764 (E.D. Pa. 2001).
[306] *Id.*
[307] *Id.* at 773.
[308] *Id.* at 782.

party when it retransmits the very same programming," which the court also found reasonable.[309]

§ 4.03   TRADEMARKS IN CYBERSPACE[310]

[A]   Overview

"A trademark is a word, name, symbol, device or other designation, or a combination of such designations, that is distinctive of a person's goods or services and that is used in a manner that identifies and distinguishes them from the goods or services of others."[311] Trademarks are used to distinguish the source of goods for a consumer. Thus, a consumer buying a Hershey chocolate bar knows that it can expect the degree of quality consistent with the Hershey brand. Any company operating a web site needs to understand how trademark law impacts its choice of a domain name, its development of a brand, and its relations with competitors, cybersquatters, or other entities who want to exploit its name. On a practical level, the company must know how to register its trademarks and domain name and be aware of what remedies are available if someone infringes on its mark (*see* Table 4.5).

[B]   Types of Marks

A *trade name* "means any name used by a person to identify his or her business or vocation."[312] A *trademark,* in contrast, is "any word, name, symbol, or device . . . used by a person in commerce."[313] A trademark must distinguish a source of origin or it does not qualify for federal or state trademark protection.[314] From a legal perspective, trademarks are classified in terms of degree of trademark protection along a spectrum from weakest to strongest: generic, descriptive, suggestive, and arbitrary or fanciful. Four types of trade symbols are (1) trademark, (2) service mark, (3) certification mark, and (4) collective mark. In the United States, anyone who claims rights in a mark may use the ™ (trademark) or SM (service mark) designation with the mark to alert the public to the claim. It is not necessary to have a registration, or even a pending application, to use these designations. The claim may or may not be valid. The symbol ® may only be used

---

[309] *Id.* at 783.

[310] For a discussion of trademark issues from a business perspective, *see* § 2.04[B][1] *supra.*

[311] 15 U.S.C. § 1127 (2000); *see* A&H Sportswear, Inc. v. Victoria's Secret Stores, Inc., 237 F.3d 198 (3d Cir. 2000) (stating that to prove either trademark infringement or unfair competition, a plaintiff must demonstrate that (1) it has a valid and legally protectable mark; (2) it owns the mark; and (3) the defendant's use of the mark to identify goods or services causes a likelihood of confusion). *See also* Lanham Trademark Act, §§ 32, 43(a)(1)(A) (2002).

[312] Trademark Act of 1946, 15 U.S.C. § 1127 (defining "trade name" and "commercial name").

[313] *Id.* (defining trademark).

[314] Restatement (Third) of Unfair Competition § 18, cmt. d (1995).

TABLE 4.5
Protection and Remedies for a Trademark

Method for Obtaining Protection	Trademarks, service marks, certification marks and collective marks, are registered in the USPTO. Registration is also available in states.
Remedies for Infringement	SPC must prove that its mark is entitled to protection and that the defendant's use of SPC's mark will likely cause confusion with its mark. SPC may seek injunctive relief under the Lanham Act, profits, damages, costs, and attorneys' fees; courts balance (1) threat of irreparable harm to the moving party against (2) the state of the balance between this harm and the injury to the other party; (3) the probability of success on the merits; and (4) public interest in determining whether to grant injunction. The Federal Trademark Dilution Act of 1995 provides protection against dilution for "famous" marks. It also protects against dilution for nonfamous marks under state trademark laws, under theories of blurring and dilution by tarnishment.

by SPC if the mark has been registered in the USPTO.[315] The ™ symbol should be displayed even if a company has not yet registered its trademarks.

Trademarks identify goods made by sellers and distinguish them from those of other companies. A trademark must create "a separate and distinct commercial impression, which . . . performs the trademark function of identifying the source of the merchandise to the customers."[316] When two or more companies adopt the same mark, basic rules of trademark priority apply. *Trademark priority* is based generally upon the first to use a mark in interstate commerce. To determine superior ownership a court considers the following factors: (1) which party invented and first affixed the mark onto the product, (2) which party's name appeared with the trademark, (3) which party maintained the quality and uniformity of the product, and (4) with which party the public identified the product and to whom purchasers made complaints. In addition, courts look at which party owns the goodwill associated with a product.[317] Ford Motor Company is a trade name used in commerce. CBS is a trade name, whereas CBS marks include CBS™ and the CBS "eye" design. CBS also has an Internet web site, *CBS.com*, as well as television, radio, cable, and other Internet web sites.

If a company's marks are not inherently distinctive, they are not registrable on the USPTO's Principal Register. A mark not qualifying for the Principal Register, however, may be registered on the Supplemental Register if it is capable of

---

[315] *Id.*

[316] *In re* Chemical Dynamics, Inc., 839 F.2d 1569, 1571 (Fed. Cir. 1988).

[317] Tactic Int'l, Inc. v. Atlantic Horizon Int'l, Inc., 2001 U.S. Dist. LEXIS 5162 (S.D.N.Y. 2001).

acquiring distinctiveness or secondary meaning. The question of whether SPC's marks have acquired distinctiveness is a matter of fact. The Lanham Act's remedies for infringement will apply only to a company's registered marks.

On the web, trademark information on a company's logos, products, service name, and trademarks should be included on a company's terms-of-service page. The trademark notice should state that the trademarks are the intellectual property of the company and are not to be used without the company's prior permission. The clickwrap or webwrap "terms of service" agreement should include a clause that the site visitor or user agrees not to display or use a company's trademarks in any unauthorized manner.

[1]   Trademark

The law of trademarks is comprised of international, federal, and state law. Chapter 8 addresses how the online company files for international trademarks. Your company should register its trademarks in the core countries where it is rendering online sales and services. Trademark ownership, however, is based upon the first to use a mark rather than the first to register the mark. Federal trademark rights are strengthened by registration of a trademark in the USPTO. Common law trademark rights arise when a mark is used to identify goods or service but is not federally registered. Finally, all states have trademark registration statutes for marks used within a state. Increasingly, lawsuits are based upon the claim that Internet domain names infringe trademarks. Internet domain name and trademark infringement litigation frequently centers on whether a defendant registered an Internet domain name that is confusingly similar to a trademark with the intent to profit from the protected mark.[318]

Trademark owners have a wide array of federal and state remedies provided they have a distinctive trademark worthy of protection. Federal trademark registration creates a presumption that the registrant is the owner of the mark.[319] In addition a certificate of registration constitutes prima facie evidence that a plaintiff's mark is distinctive. The federal trademark statute is the Lanham Act, which provides remedies for false advertising, trade libel, and trademark infringement for registered and unregistered marks. Federal trademark law provides special statutory protection against the dilution of famous and distinctive marks. Trademarks not sufficiently famous to warrant federal dilution protection may qualify

---

[318] *See, e.g.,* Virtual Works, Inc. v. Volkswagen of Am., Inc., 238 F.3d 264 (4th Cir. 2001) (holding that registration of Internet domain name with intent to profit from a protected mark to which the domain name was confusingly similar violated the federal anticybersquatting statute); *see also* Northern Light Tech., Inc. v. Northern Lights Club, 236 F.3d 57 (1st Cir. 2001) (affirming injunction against domain name infringer partially on theory that registration of multiple domain names was evidence of bad faith and intent to profit in dispute over two similar Internet domain names by two separate entities).

[319] America Online, Inc. v. AT&T Corp., 243 F.3d 812 (4th Cir. 2001) (holding that certificate of registration from USPTO constituted prima facie evidence that plaintiff's mark was suggestive, establishing a question of material fact that could not be disposed as a summary judgment).

for protection under state antidilution statutes or the common law. If a competitor or other third party registers an Internet domain name partially with the intent to profit from a protected mark to which the domain name is confusingly similar, there are remedies under the federal anticybersquatting statute. The anticybersquatting statute does not impose liability upon registrars of Internet domain names that infringe trademarks. There are no trademark rights in the absence of a distinctive trademark unless the mark has acquired secondary meaning.[320] The stronger and more distinctive the mark, the greater the protection. Distinctiveness is traditionally calibrated on a scale ranging from the least to the most distinctive: (1) generic, (2) descriptive, (3) suggestive, (4) arbitrary, or (5) fanciful.

The level of a trademark's distinctiveness is the strength of the mark and considered to be an issue of fact. If a trademark is classified as descriptive or arbitrary, it may be regarded as a "weak" mark, especially if used with a number of different products.[321] If products are directly competing and the trademarks are very similar, a court will determine whether a likelihood of confusion exists in a trademark or unfair competition case. Suffolk Personal Computers will need to choose trademarks that distinguish its sales and services in the online marketplace. This section covers the law for protecting trademarks in cyberspace.

[a] Strength of Trademarks

Suggestive, arbitrary, and fanciful marks are deemed inherently distinctive; descriptive marks receive protection only upon a showing that they have acquired secondary meaning; and generic marks are not protectable.[322] The "strength" of a particular trademark refers to the distinctiveness of the mark or "more precisely, its tendency to identify the goods sold under the mark as emanating from a particular source."[323] *Arbitrary* or fanciful marks have the highest level of strength, or distinctiveness. *Suggestive marks* are inherently distinctive, whereas *descriptive marks* are slightly more distinctive than generic marks. A *generic* term can never receive trademark protection, although it may acquire a secondary meaning.[324] Terms such as onions.com or toiletpaper.com are generic domain names.

Although a trademark may be found distinctive, it may not be protected by the Lanham Act if it "comprises immoral, deceptive or scandalous matter, or consists of matter which may disparage or falsely suggest a connection with persons,

---

[320] *See, e.g.*, Park 'n Fly, Inc. v. Dollar Park & Fly, Inc. 469 U.S. 189 (1985) (noting descriptive mark is still protectable).

[321] A&H Sportswear, Inc. v. Victoria's Secret Stores, Inc. 237 F.3d 198 (3d Cir. 2000); *see also* TCPIP Holding Co., Inc. v. Haar Communications, Inc., 2001 U.S. App. LEXIS 2867 (2d Cir., Feb. 28, 2001) (holding that the mark, "The Children's Place," for stores selling children's merchandise was not sufficiently distinctive to qualify for trademark protection).

[322] United States Patent and Trademark Office, Basic Facts About Registering a Trademark (Apr. 9, 2000), http://www.uspto.gov/web/offices/tac/doc/basic/basic_facts.html.

[323] Northern Light Technology, Inc. v. Northern Lights Club, 97 F. Supp. 2d 96 (D. Mass. 2000).

[324] 1 J. Thomas McCarthy, McCarthy on Trademarks and Unfair Competition § 12:47 at 12-92 and 12-93 (1996, 1999).

living or dead, institutions, beliefs, or national symbols or bring them into contempt or disrepute."[325] An adult entertainment site, for example, will not be permitted to register obscene trademarks.

Courts impose a variety of tests to distinguish suggestive marks from merely distinctive ones. If a mark is not inherently distinctive, acquiring secondary meaning in the minds of consumers may protect it. A company should choose inherently distinctive marks so that they may be registered on the Principal rather than the Supplemental Register. A descriptive mark that has the potential of acquiring distinctiveness or secondary meaning is registered on the Supplemental Register.

Ford is a surname that has built up secondary meaning. Descriptive marks are not protectible as trademarks unless they acquire secondary meaning. Secondary meaning is acquired in the marketplace, rather than emanating from its natural meaning.[326] The New Ford Explorer is an example of a Ford trademark. The Cadillac car company uses the trademarked slogan "Creating a higher standard." Trademarks prevent consumers from confusing Donald Trump's luxury hotels with the Holiday Inn or Motel 6. Pier 1 Imports is a trade name for a chain of stores selling stylish but inexpensive home furnishings and accessories. The Dollar Stores, on the other hand, is a chain of stores catering to the less affluent. Both use trademarks to identify the types of goods they offer for sale.

A federal court found AOL's "Instant Message" and "You Have Mail" phrases to be generic and not entitled to trademark protection.[327] Branding of distinctive goods and services is occurring in cyberspace at a rapid pace. Amazon.com is an example of one of the most famous marks in cyberspace, being used for the sale of books, music, and videos.

[b] Distinctive Marks

The greater the distinctiveness of a mark, the higher the level of trademark protection. The hierarchy of distinctiveness has five descending levels, ranging from the most distinctive to the least distinctive marks: (1) fanciful or coined, (2) arbitrary, (3) suggestive, (4) descriptive, and (5) generic. Fanciful or coined marks have the highest level of protection, followed by arbitrary, suggestive, and generic marks, which reside at the bottom of the distinctiveness hierarchy. A coined or fanciful trademark consists of a made-up phrase or words that have no purpose other than to identify the goods or services.

---

[325] 15 U.S.C. § 102(b) (2002).

[326] Arthur R. Miller and Michael H. Davis, Intellectual Property: Patents, Trademarks, and Copyrights 165 (2d ed. 1990).

[327] America Online, Inc. v. AT&T Corp., *aff'd in part, remanded in part*, 2001 U.S. App. LEXIS 2866 (4th Cir. 2000) (finding a genuine issue of material fact and remanding as to the validity of AOL's "Buddy List" mark).

[i]   Fanciful or Coined Trademarks

A company should choose a fanciful word that identifies the source of its computer products but that is not descriptive.[328] Coined phrases enjoy the highest level of protection. Kodak is an example of a *fanciful* or *coined* mark that enjoys the highest level of protection. Polaroid, Exxon, and Vaseline are also fanciful trademarks that enjoy strong trademark protection. The name "Vornado," combining the words "vortex" and "tornado," is an example of a fanciful mark. Vornado also has descriptive content when used to market a household fan.[329] Prozac® is a fanciful word that carries no meaning apart from its use to identify a product.

[ii]   Arbitrary Trademarks

An *arbitrary mark* is unlike a real word or phrase that can be remembered and associated in the public's mind with the mark's owner. The essence of an arbitrary trademark, however, is that it uses an ordinary word in an extraordinary way. Banana Republic, GAP, Express, and Polo are arbitrary trademarks for clothing. Morningside No-Load Funds is an arbitrary mark used for financial services. Apple is an arbitrary trademark for computers. An arbitrary mark may not be used without permission if the use refers to the product it identifies.

[iii]   Suggestive Trademarks

A *suggestive trademark* is a word that describes qualities of a product or service (*see* Table 4.6). The use of Greyhound for a bus line, for example, suggests speed, since the greyhound is the fastest of all dog breeds. Suggestive trademarks "suggest" but do not directly describe a feature of a product. Coppertone, for example, is a suggestive trademark, as is Cap'n Crunch cereal. Coppertone's "Bug-Sun" is a suggestive trademark for sunscreen combined with insect repellent.

[iv]   Descriptive Trademarks

The fourth level of trademarks is the *descriptive trademark,* which enjoys the least amount of protection. "A suggestive mark is one that may be partly descriptive but is primarily distinctive. If a mark conveys the nature of the product only through the exercise of imagination, thought and perception, it is suggestive."[330] The boundary between suggestive and descriptive trademarks "is not altogether clear and ultimately . . . is a question of fact."[331] Descriptive terms are not inherently distinctive, and they are entitled to protection only if they acquire secondary meaning.

A descriptive mark directly describes an ingredient, quality, or use of goods or services. New York taxi drivers have the Wooden Bead Seat, which helps them sit for long periods without discomfort. A geographic term like Vermont Maple

---

[328] The Seventh Circuit in Polaroid Corp. v. Polaroid, Inc., 319 F.2d 830, 837 (7th Cir. 1963) stated that a fanciful word is entitled to the greatest trademark protection.

[329] Vornado Air Circulation Systems, Inc. v. Duracraft Corp., 58 F.3d 1498, 1501 (10th Cir. 1995).

[330] Arthur R. Miller and Michael H. Davis, Intellectual Property: Patents, Trademarks, and Copyright 164 (1990).

[331] Shade's Landing, Inc. v. Williams, 76 F. Supp. 2d 983 (D. Minn. 1999).

TABLE 4.6
Examples of Suggestive Trademarks

"LA"	Low alcohol beer[a]
Dietene	Food supplement for people on a diet[b]
"Roach Motel"	Suggestive mark for anti-roach product[c]
"Coppertone"	Suggestive mark for suntan oil
Nair	Suggestive mark for hair removal product

[a] Anheuser-Busch, Inc. v. Stroh Brewery Co., 750 F.2d 631, 635 (8th Cir. 1984).

[b] Dietene Co. v. Dietrim Co., 225 F.2d 239, 243 (8th Cir. 1955) (holding that Dietene is more suggestive than descriptive for diet product).

[c] American Home Prods. Corp. v. Johnson Chemical Co., Inc., 589 F.2d 103, 106 (2d Cir. 1978) (holding that "roach motel" was a suggestive mark for anti-roach product).

Syrup is a descriptive mark, as is a trademark using a surname such as Colonel Sander's Kentucky Fried Chicken. These marks are not registrable on the Principal Register of USPTO until they have acquired secondary meaning. Kool is a descriptive mark that suggests qualities of that brand of cigarettes. Cabot, Vermont, is a descriptive mark that describes geographic origin. "The Heart of Snow Country" is a descriptive trademarked phrase used by Sugarbush and Mad River Glen ski resorts.

[v] Generic Terms

A *generic mark* is in general use in a trade or industry. Generic means that a term refers to the genus of which the particular product is a species. The concept of a trademark identifies a unique source for goods or services. The term "shredded wheat" was held to be a generic term generally known to the public in *Kellogg Co. v. National Biscuit Co.*[332] Generic terms are so common that they do not differentiate goods or services in the minds of Internet users. America Online's "Instant Message or IM" and "You Have Mail" have been deemed generic.[333]

Companies using Internet trade names seek to build up goodwill, protect business identity, and prevent confusion in the global marketplace. Trademark law can never protect generic marks. A famous or distinctive trademark can descend into the disfavored generic category if it comes to describe a general class of goods rather than an individual product. Companies should prevent competitors or others from using their trademarks in a generic way, to avoid the fate of marks such as aspirin, thermos, or the phrase "March Madness," which have all been ruled generic.[334]

---

[332] 305 U.S. 111 (1938).

[333] America Online, Inc. v. AT&T Corp., No. 98-1821-A, 1999 U.S. Dist. LEXIS 12615 (E.D. Va., Aug. 13, 1999), *aff'd in part, vacated in part, remanded in part*, 2001 U.S. App. LEXIS 2866 (4th Cir., Feb. 28, 2001) (holding that the district court erred when it granted summary judgment as to the invalidity of the "Buddy List" trademark because the certificate of registration, issued by the USPTO, was enough to establish a question of material fact as to the mark's validity).

[334] Illinois High School Ass'n v. GTE Vantage, Inc., 99 F.3d 244, 247 (7th Cir. 1996) (finding that "March Madness" was generic and citing examples of "aspirin" and "thermos").

A federal court reversed an earlier decision by an arbitrator from the Uniform Domain Name Dispute Resolution Policy (UDRP), and ordered the web site, eReferee.com, to stop using the word "referee" in any of its domain names.[335] The judge ruled in favor of Referee Magazine, which claimed that the use of the word "referee" would likely cause consumer confusion in thinking the site was affiliated with the magazine.[336] The web site targeted referees, offering news stories and forums where people could discuss refereeing tips and rule changes.[337] One concern is that the domain name system is permitting trademark rights to vest in commonly used, generic words, which may undermine trademark law.

[C] Other Marks

[1] Service Mark

A *service mark* is a word, name, symbol, or device used in commerce "to identify and distinguish the services of one person."[338] In the off-line world, Midas is a service mark for automobile mufflers. America Online registered its "Buddy List,"[339] "You Have Mail," and "Instant Message" features as service marks. When AT&T used the phrase "Buddy List"[340] on its competing service, AOL filed a lawsuit for unfair competition. A federal court found AOL's "Buddy List" to be generic and not entitled to protection.[341]

The title of a television program such as "Dawson's Creek," "Friends," or "The Awful Truth" may be registered as service marks. Garrison Keillor's "Prairie Home Companion," a syndicated radio program produced by Minnesota Public Radio, is a syndicated service mark. An Internet company that provides classified advertising for products and services will register its service mark identifying its information services. Call numbers for radio and television stations, such as KNOX or KCND, may be service marks. Like trademarks, service marks are the intellectual property of the owners and may only be used with permission.

[2] Collective Mark

A *collective mark* is a trademark or service mark used by the members of a cooperative, an association, or another collective group or organization. The

---

[335] Lisa M. Bowman, Judge approves domain name penalty on eReferee, CNET News.com (Feb. 16, 2001), http://news.cnet.com/news/0-1005-202-4839749-0.html.

[336] Id.

[337] Id.

[338] United States Patent and Trademark Office, Basic Facts About Registering a Trademark (Apr. 9, 2000), http://www.uspto.gov/web/offices/tac/doc/basic/basic_facts.html.

[339] A Buddy List provides for real-time chat between two or more persons simultaneously using the AOL Service. Its members refer to "instant messages" or "IM" to signify the real-time chat component.

[340] A buddy list permits real-time chat between "Buddy List" AOL members.

[341] America Online, Inc. v. AT&T Corp., No. 98-1821-A 1999 U.S. Dist. LEXIS 12615 (E.D. Va., Aug. 13, 1999).

National Fluid Milk Processor Promotion Board is a collective mark. The slogan "Got milk?" is a trademarked slogan owned by the board. The Cabot Cooperative of Cabot, Vermont, has a collective mark. The Cabot Co-op produces trademarked products under the mark Cabot of Vermont. The Humboldt Elevator Association of Humboldt, Minnesota, could file for a collective mark for its grain, seed, and fertilizer products. Collective marks differ from trademarks and service marks only in ownership; they may also only be used with the permission of the owners.

[3]   Certification Mark

"The term 'mark' includes any trademark, service mark, collective mark or certification mark."[342] Collective works are separately-created works which are combined. The International Standards Organization (ISO) has certification marks which were at issue in *Cadwell Industries v. Chenbro America, Inc.*[343] Chenbro America was deemed to be holding itself out as a computer case manufacturer when it used ISO 9001, ISO 9002, and ISO 40000 on its stationary and business cards.[344] Certification marks may be used for many products and services sold on the Internet.

The e-Trust mark is one of the most notable certification marks in Internet-related commerce. Web sites that display the e-Trust mark follow certain minimum privacy standards. A *certification mark* is a "word, name, symbol or device used to certify regional or other characteristics of such person's goods or services, or that the work or labor on the goods or services was performed by members of a union or other organization."[345] The French, for example, could apply for a certified mark for Roquefort cheese or Burgundy wines.[346] A labor union such as the AFL/CIO may apply for a certification mark. Consumers rely upon certification marks for information about goods and services. The failure to observe formalities in the use of certification marks may result in cancellation of the registration.

The Lanham Act does not permit self-application for a certification mark because of the potential problem of the lack of objectivity in owners acting as certifiers of their own marks. Owners of certification marks must police their marks or lose them. The Vermont Maple Syrup producers are vigilant in protecting their mark against producers who make syrup with high proportions of cane sugar or other deviations in quality.

[4]   Trade Name

A *trade name* is a name, word, or phrase employed in identifying the source of products or services. Trademarks at common law require that the mark be

---

[342] JTH Tax, Inc. v. H&R Block Eastern Tax Servs., 128 F. Supp. 2d 926 (E.D. Va. 2001).

[343] 119 F. Supp. 2d 1110 (E.D. Wash. 2000).

[344] *Id.* at 1112.

[345] America Online, Inc. v. AT&T Corp., No. 98-1821-A, 1999 U.S. Dist. LEXIS 12615 (E.D. Va., Aug. 13, 1999).

[346] *See, e.g.*, Community of Roquefort v. Faehndrich, 303 F.2d 494 (2d Cir. 1962).

affixed to the goods. Surnames are not a good choice for trademarks, since there is a "judicial reluctance to enjoin use of a personal name."[347] A court will be reluctant to register surnames, such as Rustad or Daftary, because all persons bearing those surnames should have an equal opportunity to utilize the surnames as distinguishing marks. The Fairbanks Brothers of St. Johnsbury, Vermont, however, obtained trademark protection for their scales because the geographic meaning of the marks was deemed to be as great as the surname Fairbanks. Marks that are primarily a surname may be registered on the USPTO's Supplemental Register.

The Vermont company Ben & Jerry's Ice Cream uses first names as a trade name and a surname in its brand, Cherry Garcia. Ford and Dodge are surnames that have acquired secondary meaning as trade names for automobiles. "Secondary meaning indicates that through 'long and exclusive use and advertising in the sale of the user's goods, [the mark] has become so associated in the public mind with such goods that it serves to identify the source of the goods and to distinguish them from the goods of others.' "[348]

Secondary meaning in this context means that a surname has "developed a quality that distinguishes the goods of the producer."[349] Louis Vuitton and Nissan are surname trademarks that have "secondary meaning." Giorgio Armani, Calvin Klein, Ralph Lauren, and Walt Disney are surnames that have gained secondary meaning. Consumers associate luxury leather goods with Louis Vuitton and well-made cars with Nissan, which has been a registered mark since 1959. The Nissan mark benefits from the presumption of incontestability.[350]

Hermès Paris trademarked the term "*Caleche Soie de Parfum*," meaning silk calash perfume or silk bonnet perfume. The Lanham Act permits the registration of foreign words or phrases as trademarks. The Lanham Act defines the "trade name" or "commercial name" to "mean any name [used] by a person to identify his or her business or vocation."[351]

Courts will frequently focus on whether a product is sufficiently similar to create a likelihood of confusion regarding the source of origin when sold under the same trade name.[352] For example, in *GOTO.COM v. Walt Disney, Co.*,[353] the district court issued a preliminary injunction against Walt Disney for its use of similar Internet logos for similar Internet services.[354] The plaintiff's Internet logos consisted of the words "GO" and "TO" in white, stacked vertically within a green

---

[347] Nissan Motor Co., Ltd. v. Nissan Computer Corp., 2000 U.S. Dist. LEXIS 3718 (C.D. Cal., Mar. 23, 2000) (citing Gallo Winery v. Gallo Cattle Co., 967 F.3d 1288 (9th Cir. 1992)).

[348] Shade's Landing, Inc. v. Williams, 76 F. Supp. 2d 983 (D. Minn. 1999) (citation omitted).

[349] Arthur R. Miller and Michael H. Davis, Intellectual Property: Patents, Trademarks, and Copyright 164 (1990).

[350] *Id.* at 165 (noting that "[A] user who comes to the Patent and Trademark Office with a mark he has used for five continuous years may benefit from a presumption despite the fact that the mark is facially descriptive or nondescriptive in some other way").

[351] *Id.*

[352] GOTO.COM, Inc. v. Walt Disney Co., 202 F.3d 1199 (9th Cir. 2000).

[353] *Id.*

[354] *Id.* at 207.

circle, often against a square yellow background. To the right of "TO" were the characters ".com" in black. Disney's Internet logos resembled a traffic light: a green circle within a yellow square. Within the green circle, the word "GO" appeared in white; next to the traffic light, the word "Network" appeared in black.[355] The court concluded that competing Internet search engines using similar logos created a high likelihood of confusion regarding the source of origin.[356] Functional product design is not protected by trade dress by the Lanham Act.[357]

[5] Trade Dress

Section 43(a) of the Lanham Act protects against infringement of unregistered marks and trade dress as well as registered marks.[358] *Trade dress* is the overall image, design, or appearance of a product and its packaging, but does not include functional elements.[359] *Functional trade dress* that serves to enter Internet commands does not identify the origin of products and services and is therefore not protected by trademark law. Trade dress of a product may serve as a trademark if it identifies the goods or services in its package, distinctive shape, or color.

Examples of trade dress include the shape of the Coca-Cola bottle, Ralph Lauren's tapered square perfume bottle, and McDonald's golden arches. Color may be used as a type of product ornamentation, as with Owens-Corning's use of pink in its fiberglass insulation. A company may obtain trademark registration of the overall color scheme of its web site if it can prove the look and feel of color scheme is an accepted symbol in the trade. Color may only be protected if the trademark owner demonstrates that it has acquired secondary meaning.[360] Examiners will determine whether the colors used as ornamentation on a company's web site function as trademarks. The color scheme of a company's web site may be protected as a mark depending upon the number of color combinations and how color is used in marketing for hardware and software sales. If a company's web site uses distinctive colors, color combinations, graphics, icons, or other features, for example, and someone else uses the same design and layout for a different site, the company may bring a trade dress action.

---

[355] *Id.*

[356] *Id.*

[357] Tactica Int'l, Inc. v. Atlantic Horizon Int'l, Inc., 2001 U.S. Dist. LEXIS 5162 (S.D.N.Y., Apr. 27, 2001) (rejecting plaintiff's trade dress claim because functional product design was not protected by the Lanham Act).

[358] GOTO.COM, Inc. v. Walt Disney Co., 202 F.3d 1199 (9th Cir. 2000) (prohibiting Disney from using a logo confusingly similar to GOTO's mark.).

[359] Pecos, Inc. v. Taco Cabana, Inc., 505 U.S. 763, 765 (1992).

[360] Qualitex Co. v. Jacobson Prods. Co., 514 U.S. 159 (1995) (holding that color can be protected as a trademark, but only upon a showing of secondary meaning).

However, the Supreme Court has held that in an action for infringement of unregistered trade dress, a product's design is protectible only upon a showing of secondary meaning.[361] A clothing retailer was held liable for trade dress infringement for making "knock offs" of Wal-Mart Store's dress designs. The Supreme Court reversed the Second Circuit's denial of the retailer's motion for judgment as a matter of law.

[D] Concurrent Use in Cyberspace

Trademark law evolved in a market economy in which goods and services were sold in markets separated by physical distance. Before the rise of a national economy, identical trademarks could be used in geographically dispersed marketplaces. Two trademark owners could sell essentially the same products in different markets using the same marks. The concept of *likelihood of confusion* occurs only when two identical or similar marks are competing in the same market.[362] The Lanham Act permits *concurrent registration* when more than one party is entitled to use the mark and the likelihood of confusion is low.[363] An owner may establish priority rights with registration on the Principal Register, which places the world on notice that it claims exclusive rights in a mark.[364] The USPTO presumes that the first user is entitled to priority.[365]

In *In re Beatrice Foods Co.*,[366] the U.S. Court of Customs and Patent Appeals developed rules for concurrent use proceedings. The *Beatrice Food* court acknowledged the rule that, in the typical case in which neither party has a federal registration, the senior trademark user is entitled to a registration covering the entire United States, except areas of proven use by the junior user.[367] A senior user holding a federal trademark registration is subject to limited concurrent rights of junior user.[368] The court refused to affirm the "district court's conclusion that an injunction prohibiting Allard's use of the mark in a specific geographic area necessarily precludes any use of the mark by Allard on the Internet."[369]

---

[361] Wal-Mart Stores, Inc. v. Samara Bros., 529 U.S. 205, 216 (2000).

[362] Polaroid Corp. v. Polarad Elecs. Corp., 287 F.2d 492, 492 (2d Cir. 1961) (measuring likelihood of confusion by eight factors).

[363] Arthur R. Miller and Michael H. Davis, Intellectual Property: Patents, Trademarks, and Copyright 164 (1990).

[364] Paul J. Cronin, Tea Roses, and Donuts in Cyberspace: Is the Concurrent Use of Trademarks Possible on the Internet? High Technology Law Program Thesis, Spring 1997, Suffolk University Law School.

[365] *Id.*

[366] 429 F.2d 466 (C.C.P.A. 1970).

[367] *Id.* at 474.

[368] Allard Enters. v. Advanced Programming Resources (APR), 2001 U.S. App. LEXIS 8508 (6th Cir. 2001).

[369] *Id.*

Concurrent use of trademarks on the Internet has the potential of creating misperceptions about a site's ownership.[370] In *Brookfield Communications, Inc. v. West Coast Entertainment Corp.*,[371] the court discussed the different ways an Internet surfer might be confused by the concurrent use of trademarks on the Internet. The concept of concurrent uses of the same trademark in different classes of goods and geographical areas is difficult to apply to the Internet. The key factors that courts consider include consumer misperceptions about the site's ownership, the incorrect inference of an agreement between the parties, and a belief that the plaintiff's services were no longer offered.[372] Concurrent use of trademarks focuses on the "uncontestable similarity between the products for which the mark is used."[373] Creating an exact match between Internet addresses and trademarks will require overcoming the problem of concurrent uses of the same trademark in different classes of goods and geographical areas.[374] A potential solution may be a "graphically-based Internet directory [which] would allow the presentation of trademarks in conjunction with distinguishing logos."[375]

The Internet creates the possibility that concurrent use of trademarks will create confusion. Under the common law, the trademark owner's protection extended to any area in which the goods and services became associated with the use of the mark.[376] The rise of the Internet leads to the possibility that consumers may be confused by two identical yet previously geographically remote trademarks.

The Internet "erases geographic boundaries and blurs the boundaries between different products and services," stated the court in *Simon Property Group L.P. v. mySimon Inc.*[377] "In cyberspace, a junior user's registration of an Internet domain name and establishment of a Web site under an identical or confusingly similar mark—in any field—can represent an encroachment on the rights of the senior user in a manner that a geographically isolated use would not."[378]

[E]   Trademark Infringement

Trademark law provides remedies against the use of marks by persons or entities other than the trademark registrant. A plaintiff alleging causes of action for

---

[370] Network Network v. CBS, Inc., 2000 U.S. Dist. LEXIS 4751 (Jan. 16, 2000). In Allard Enters. v. Advanced Programming Resources (APR), 174 F.3d 1036 (9th Cir. 1999), the court held that APR had superior rights to use its mark, at a minimum, in central Ohio.

[371] 174 F.3d 1036 (9th Cir. 1999).

[372] *Id.* at 1047.

[373] AT&T Corp. v. Synet, Inc. 45 U.S.P.Q.2d 1656 (N.D. Ill. 1997).

[374] Lockheed Martin Corp. v. Network Solutions, 985 F. Supp. 949 (C.D. Cal. 1997).

[375] *Id.* at 968.

[376] Paul J. Cronin, Tea Roses, and Donuts in Cyberspace: Is the Concurrent Use of Trademarks Possible on the Internet? High Technology Law Program Thesis, at 29, Spring 1997, Suffolk University Law School.

[377] 104 F. Supp. 2d 1033, 1037 (S.D. Ind. 2000).

[378] Bruce A. McDonald, Progressive Encroachment Theory Is Weakening, Nat'l L.J., Dec. 12, 2000.

trademark infringement and unfair competition must prove (1) that it possesses a mark; (2) that the defendant used the mark; (3) that the defendant's use of the mark occurred "in commerce"; (4) that the defendant used the mark in connection with the sale, offering for sale, distribution, or advertising of goods or services; and (5) that the defendant used the mark in a manner likely to confuse consumers.[379]

Sections 32(1) and 43(a) of the Lanham Act generally govern trademark infringement in the United States.[380] Trademark law prevents competitors from "free-riding on their rivals' marks and capitalizing on their rivals' investment of time, money, and resources."[381] Trademark infringement may be based on the simultaneous use of two trademarks "likely to cause confusion" or dilution. To prove trademark infringement, "a trademark owner must prove that the competing use of the mark is capable of generating a likelihood of confusion concerning the source of its product."[382] The parties' lines of business need not be the same, as long as their products or services are "the kind the public attributes to a single source."[383]

Trademark infringement may occur on the Internet when users of "plaintiffs' services who mistakenly access defendants' web site may fail to continue to search for plaintiffs' web site due to confusion or frustration. Such users, who are presumably looking for the services provided by the plaintiffs on their web site, may instead opt to select hyperlinks contained in defendants' web site"[384] A web site owner's action in appropriating a plaintiff's mark has a connection to the plaintiffs' distribution of its services over the Internet.

[1] Likelihood of Confusion Test

To recover for trademark or trade dress infringement under § 43(a) of the Lanham Act, a plaintiff must prove "(1) that its trademark or dress is protectable because (a) it is inherently distinctive or (b) it has acquired distinctiveness by achieving 'secondary meaning' in the marketplace; and (2) that there is a likelihood of confusion between its product and the defendant's product."[385] The unauthorized use of a trademark infringes the trademark holder's rights if it is likely to confuse an "ordinary consumer" as to the source or sponsorship of the goods. A court makes a determination whether a given web use, in its entirety, creates a likelihood of confusion.[386] The distinctiveness inquiry is truncated if a validly registered federal trademark becomes 'incontestable" after five years of continuous use

---

[379] 15 U.S.C.S. §§ 1114, 1125(a) (2001).

[380] *Id.*

[381] New Kids on the Block v. New Am. Publ'g, Inc., 971 F.2d 302, 306 (9th Cir. 1991).

[382] Stratus Computers, Inc. v. NCR Corp., 2 U.S.P.Q.2d (BNA) 1375, 1378 (D. Mass. 1981), cited in Michael D. Scott, Internet and Technology Law Desk Reference 505 (1999).

[383] Eli Lilly & Co. v. Natural Answers, Inc., 86 F. Supp. 2d 834 (S.D. Ind. 2000).

[384] People for the Ethical Treatment of Animals v. Doughney, 263 F.3d 359 (4th Cir. 2001).

[385] Samara Bros., Inc. v. Wal-Mart Stores, Inc., 165 F.3d 120, 124 (2d Cir. 1998) (citation omitted).

[386] People for the Ethical Treatment of Animals v. Doughney, 263 F.3d 359 (4th Cir. 2001).

subsequent to its registration. Evidence of actual consumer confusion is difficult to establish. In *Online Partners.Com, Inc. v. AtlanticNet Media Corp.*,[387] the defendant proved a likelihood of confusion between an Internet domain name and its plaintiff by demonstrating instances of actual confusion. Courts permit plaintiffs to prove confusion by scientific surveys establishing the statistical likelihood of consumer confusion.[388] There is little authority on how potential Internet consumers are to be surveyed. Care must be taken to sample the proper Internet universe to establish a finding of consumer confusion.[389]

Products must be similar at the time they enter the market or there is no consumer confusion as to source.[390] If there is insufficient proof of confusion, a claim for trade infringement will fail.[391] In *People for the Ethical Treatment of Animals, Inc. v. Doughney*,[392] a web site owner was enjoined from using an animal protection organization's registered service mark in defendant's Internet domain name since the organization proved its case for trademark infringement and dilution.

The use of similar trademarks on different web sites creates a *likelihood of confusion* for site visitors.[393] The test used to measure a likelihood of confusion is whether "the similarity of the marks is likely to confuse customers about the source of the products."[394] Courts consider the following factors in determining whether a likelihood of confusion or unfair competition exists: (1) strength or weakness of plaintiff's mark, (2) the degree of similarity with defendant's mark, (3) class of goods, (4) marketing channels used, (5) evidence of actual confusion, and (6) intent of the defendant.[395] No one factor is determinative, as the likelihood of confusion test considers the totality of facts under the circumstances.[396] Likelihood of confusion relies heavily on whether web sites offer similar goods or services and use the Internet as a channel for advertising.[397]

---

[387] 2000 U.S. Dist. LEXIS 783 (N.D. Cal., Jan. 18, 2000) (finding that defendant's Internet domain name infringed on plaintiff's trademark because defendant's domain name was similar, and plaintiff showed a likelihood of confusion by demonstrating instances of actual confusion).

[388] W.E. Bassett Co. v. Revlon, Inc., 435 F.2d 656, 662 (2d Cir. 1970); Sterling Drug, Inc. v. Bayer AG, 14 F.3d 733, 741 (2d Cir. 1994).

[389] Courts will not admit survey data unless probative and meaningful. "To be probative and meaningful . . . surveys . . . must rely upon responses by potential consumers of the product in question." Public Performance of Sound Recordings: Definition of a Service, 37 C.F.R. pt. 201, 65 Fed. Reg. 77292 (Dec. 11, 2000).

[390] *See, e.g.,* M2 Software, Inc. v. Viacom, Inc., 119 F. Supp. 2d 1061 (C.D. Cal. 2000) (finding no actual confusion where products were extremely different at the time music television company entered the market and there had been no actual confusion as to the source of company's software product).

[391] Planet Hollywood, Inc. v. Hollywood Casino Corp., 80 F. Supp. 815 (N.D. Ill. 2000).

[392] 263 F.3d 359 (4th Cir. 2001).

[393] GOTO.COM v. Walt Disney Co., 202 F.3d 1199 (9th Cir. 2000).

[394] E.&J. Gallo Winery v. Gallo Cattle Co., 967 F.2d 1280, 1290 (9th Cir. 1992).

[395] *See, e.g.,* Americana Trading, Inc. v. Ross Berrie & Co., 966 F.2d 1284, 1287 (9th Cir. 1992).

[396] Hotmail Corp. v. Van$ Money Pie, Inc., 47 U.S.P.Q.2d 1020 (N.D. Cal. 1998).

[397] The Third Circuit devised a 10-factor test to determine the likelihood of confusion for direct confusion claims between goods that do *not* directly compete in the same market. A&H Sportswear, Inc. v. Victoria's Secret Stores, Inc., 237 F.3d 198 (3d Cir. 2000) (articulating factors in Interpace

Actual confusion between marks is often demonstrated through empirical studies. A company will be more likely to obtain a remedy for infringement if it produces evidence of actual confusion. Empirical evidence such as questionnaires filled out by consumers may establish that trademarks are confusingly similar. If trademarks are being used in the same market, the likelihood is greater that consumers will be confused between the two marks.

An ISP's web-hosting agreement and acceptable use policy needs to address the issue of customers who post materials that infringe on the trademarks of third parties. A host will typically disclaim liability for the infringing activities of customers. In *Gucci America, Inc. v. Hall & Associates*,[398] the plaintiff owned the famous Gucci trademark and trade name that was used to sell jewelry, apparel, and related services. The defendant was an ISP who provided web page hosting services to an individual defendant using the ISP to advertise jewelry on the web site that bore the Gucci trademarks. The court held that the ISP was not an innocent trademark infringer, even though the actions were of a third party. The court found that the ISP acted with (1) knowledge of the infringement or (2) reckless disregard as to whether the material infringed the trademark owner's rights.

The ISP was notified by Gucci with two e-mail notices about the individual defendant's infringing advertising sales and failed to take action against the infringing material. The federal court denied the defendant's motion to dismiss, holding that Gucci's trademark infringement action against the web site was not barred by the First Amendment and that the Communications Decency Act of 1996 did not immunize defendant corporations from liability for information posted on the web site by defendant individuals. The hosting and acceptable use policies need to address the question of indemnification for infringement claims against a company. If a company mounts an online advertising campaign mentioning competitors' trademarks, service marks, or logos, it may be sued by competitors. The use of similar marks selling similar products may trigger an infringement claim based on consumer confusion.

A trademark owner may seek a preliminary injunction to prevent a web site from using its trademarks, but first it must show that its mark is entitled to trademark protection. For example, Labrador Software filed a lawsuit against an Internet search service, which used a black Labrador retriever image in its Internet search product. The court denied the injunction, holding that Labrador Software's

---

Corp. v. Lapp, Inc., 721 F.2d 460, 463 (3d Cir. 1983)). The *Lapp* factors include (1) degree of similarity between owner's mark and alleged infringing mark; (2) strength of owner's mark; (3) price of goods and other factors indicative of care and attention expected of consumers when making a purchase; (4) length of time defendant has used mark without evidence of actual confusion arising; (5) intent of defendant in adopting the mark; (6) evidence of actual confusion; (7) whether goods, competing or not competing, are marketed through the same channels of trade and advertised through same media; (8) extent to which targets of parties' sales efforts are the same; (9) relationship of goods in minds of consumers, whether because of near-identity of products, similarity of function, or other factors; and (10) other facts suggesting that consuming public might expect prior owner to manufacture both products, or expect prior owner to manufacture a product in defendant's market, or expect that prior owner is likely to expand into defendant's market. *Id.*

[398] 135 F. Supp. 2d 409 (S.D.N.Y. 2001).

trademark was only descriptive and not entitled to protection absent a showing of secondary meaning.[399]

[2] Dilution

[a] Federal Trademark Dilution Act of 1996

There are two recognized forms of dilution: blurring and tarnishment. *Blurring* means lessening the distinctiveness of a trademark, such as another party's use of Microsoft sneakers. *Tarnishment* occurs when another party creates a negative association with a mark, such as "adults'r us.com" tarnishing Toys "R" Us's famous mark. The Federal Trademark Dilution Act (FTDA)[400] provides new remedies for the trademark dilution of famous trademarks. To meet the famousness element of protection under the FDTA, a mark must be prominent and renowned.[401] The owner of a "famous mark" may obtain an injunction against another "person's commercial use in commerce of a mark or trade name, if such use begins after the mark has become famous and causes dilution of the distinctive quality of the mark. . . ."[402] Eight factors determine whether a mark is famous: (1) the degree of inherent or acquired distinctiveness of the mark; (2) the duration and extent of use of the mark in connection with the goods or services with which the mark is used; (3) the duration and extent of advertising and publicity of the mark; (4) the geographical extent of the trading area in which the mark is used; (5) the channels of trade for the goods or services with which the mark is used; (6) the degree of recognition of the mark in the trading areas and channels of trade used by the mark's owner and the person against whom the injunction is sought; (7) the nature and extent of use of the same or similar marks by third parties; and (8) whether the mark was registered on the principal register.[403]

Distinctive trademarks identify origins of goods and services. For example, in *Avery Dennison Corp. v. Sumpton*,[404] the Ninth Circuit held that the trademarks "Avery" and "Dennison" on the USPTO Register were insufficiently famous for purposes of the Federal Trademark Dilution Act. The federal district court originally held that Sumpton's domain name registrations for "avery.net" and "dennison.net" diluted two of Avery Dennison's separate trademarks, "Avery" and "Dennison." The district court ordered the defendant to transfer the domain name registrations to Avery Dennison in exchange for $300.

The Ninth Circuit reversed the district court's summary judgment which was in favor of Avery Dennison, ruling that the domain names did not dilute Avery

---

[399] Labrador Software, Inc. v. Lycos, 32 F. Supp. 31 (D. Mass. 1999).

[400] 15 U.S.C. § 1125(c) (2002).

[401] Avery Dennison Corp. v. Sumpton, 189 F.3d 868 (9th Cir. 1999) (holding the Avery and Dennison trademarks were not sufficiently distinctive to warrant a federal cause of action for dilution).

[402] 15 U.S.C. § 1125(c)(1) (2002).

[403] *Id.*

[404] 51 U.S.P.Q.2d 1801 (9th Cir. 1999).

Dennison's trademarks within the meaning of the Federal Trademark Dilution Act. The court found the plaintiff's trademarks acquired secondary meaning but were not famous marks entitled to dilution protection. "Dilution is a cause of action invented and reserved for a select class of marks—those marks with such powerful consumer associations that even noncompeting uses can impinge on their value."[405] To meet the "famous" element of the federal statute, the "mark must be truly prominent and renowned."[406]

To qualify as a famous mark requires something greater than mere distinctiveness, whether inherent or acquired. The court found both "Avery" and "Dennison" to be used as trademarks on and off the Internet, with no conflict between channels of trade. Sumpton, the defendant, was in the business of selling vanity e-mail addresses, whereas Avery Dennison sold office products and industrial fastenings. The court found no evidence that Sumpton was focusing on Avery Dennison's customer base.

No one factor is determinative in establishing whether a mark is famous, and a court may receive evidence beyond the statutory factors in the federal antidilution statute.[407] Unlike state antidilution acts, the federal antidilution statute does not require a plaintiff to show injury or a likelihood of confusion. A company can establish that its mark is distinctive by pointing to national or international advertising providing strong, unobtrusive evidence of consumer recognition.[408] A defendant, in turn, may assert a defense of a valid registration under the 1881 or 1905 Trademark Act, or on the Principal Register. The Trademark Act exempts use of a famous mark in comparative advertisements, promotions, news reports, or in noncommercial uses.[409]

The FTDA gives a remedy for the gradual attenuation of the value of a famous trademark where there is unauthorized use even in the absence of a likelihood of consumer confusion.[410] To establish a prima facie case for relief, the plaintiff must plead and prove that (1) the plaintiff is the owner of a mark that qualifies as a famous mark in light of the totality of the eight factors listed in 15 U.S.C. § 1125(c)(a); (2) the defendant is making commercial use in interstate commerce of a mark or trade name; (3) the defendant's use began after the plaintiff's mark became famous; and (4) the defendant's use causes dilution by lessening the capacity of the plaintiff's mark to identify and distinguish goods or services.[411] In *Eli Lilly & Co. v. Natural Answers*,[412] a federal court affirmed a preliminary injunction of "HERBROZAC," a dietary supplement, ruling that it would cause dilution of Lilly's trademark Prozac. The court found the "causes dilution" element of the FTDA satisfied by evidence of a mere likelihood of dilution.

---

[405] *Id.*

[406] The court cited I.P. Lund Trading Aps v. Kohler Co., 163 F.3d 27 (9th Cir. 1998) (quoting Thomas McCarthy, McCarthy on Trademarks).

[407] 15 U.S.C. § 1051(c)(1) (2002).

[408] *Id.*

[409] 15 U.S.C. §§ 1125(c)(3) & 1125(c)(4) (2002).

[410] Times Mirror Magazine, Inc. v. Las Vegas Sports News, 212 F.3d 157 (3d Cir. 2000).

[411] *Id.*

[412] 233 F.3d 456 (7th Cir. 2000).

Trademark owners claiming protection under the FTDA must establish that their trademarks possess a minimum distinctive quality in order to state a claim for distinctiveness.[413] If a trademark is sufficiently famous for the FTDA, anti-dilution protections attach. A preliminary injunction is appropriate where a plaintiff's famous trademark would be diluted by a defendant's junior use of a similar mark. In *Ringling Bros.-Barnum & Bailey Combined Shows, Inc. v. Utah Division of Travel Development*,[414] the plaintiff circus had to prove that the state of Utah's similar slogan brought about a mental association that caused an actual economic harm by lessening the famous mark's selling power. Before the passage of the FTDA, a trademark owner's only recourse for dilution was to seek relief in the state courts for blurring or tarnishment.

[i] Blurring of Internet trademarks. The FTDA applies to the Internet, if a web site blurs a famous trademark by using it in a domain name or in metatags.[415] *Blurring* whittles away the capacity of a distinctive and famous mark to identify and distinguish goods or services, regardless of the presence or absence of competition between the owner of the famous mark and other parties. Aspirin, for example, was once a distinctive mark. Gradually, however, the word lost its distinctive qualities.

[ii] Tarnishment of Internet trademarks. *Tarnishment* occurs when "a famous mark is linked to products of poor quality or is portrayed in an unwholesome manner."[416] A company must prove four elements to establish a tarnishment or blurring federal trademark dilution claim: (1) the company's mark is famous; (2) a competitor adopted its mark after the original company's mark became famous; (3) the competitor diluted the company's mark; and (4) the competitor used the company's mark in commerce. In *Toys "R" Us, Inc. v. Akkaoui*,[417] the defendant used the Barbie trademark in its adult entertainment web site. The court held that the use of the Barbie trademark combined with particular fonts and a particular color scheme tarnished the mark.[418] In contrast, blurring may occur when a

---

[413] TCPIP Holding Co. v. Haar Communications, Inc., 2001 U.S. App. LEXIS 2867 (2d Cir., Feb. 28, 2001) (holding that trademark was not sufficiently distinctive or famous to warrant dilution protection and certain Internet domain names were dissimilar to mark, but similarity of certain names to mark was likely to cause consumer confusion).

[414] 170 F.3d 449 (4th Cir. 1997).

[415] 15 U.S.C. § 1125(c) (2002).

[416] Panavision Int'l, L.P. v. Toeppen, 945 F. Supp. 1296, 1304 (C.D. Cal. 1996), *aff'd*, 141 F.3d 1316 (9th Cir. 1998).

[417] 48 U.S.P.Q.2d 1467, 1996 U.S. Dist. LEXIS 17090 (S.D.N.Y., 1996); Mattel v. Internet Dimensions, 2000 U.S. Dist. LEXIS 9747 (S.D.N.Y., July 13, 2000) (enjoining defendants from the commercial use and infringement of Barbie trademarks because the similarities made the web site and its domain name confusingly similar and directing transfer of registration of domain name to Mattel); *see also* Hasbro v. Internet Entertainment Group, Ltd., 1996 U.S. Dist LEXIS 11626 (W.D. Wash., Feb. 9, 1996) (finding adult entertainment web site tarnished distinctive mark of famous board game).

[418] *Id.*

company's mark is used on a number of different goods and services and, though distinctive, loses its association with the company.[419]

In *Mattel v. Internet Dimensions, Inc.*,[420] for example, Mattel brought an action against the defendant alleging trademark infringement, trademark dilution, and violation of the Anti-Cybersquatting Consumer Protection Act of 1999 for the use of the name "Barbie," which is the same name as Mattel's famous toy doll. The court found that the defendant's use of the Barbie trademark diluted the trademark in violation of the Federal Trademark Dilution Act of 1995. The court found that the defendant's web site created "negative associations with BARBIE and that there is a likelihood of confusion under the tarnishment theory of dilution."[421] The court found that the defendant's bad-faith intent was to "cash in on a favorable image of the Barbie dolls in the use of the mark BARBIE's PLAYPEN in its adult Internet site" which diluted the BARBIE trademark.[422]

Many of the successful tarnishment lawsuits involve the incorporation of marks into the domain names for adult web sites. In *Lucent Techs. v. Johnson*,[423] for example, the plaintiff stated a claim under the Anticybersquatting Consumer Protection Act for the incorporation of the plaintiff's mark into a domain name for a web site that offered pornography for sale. In *Ford Motor Co. v. Lapertosa*,[424] the automobile manufacturer was able to enjoin a web site which used its trademark in a domain name for a hard core pornography web site.

The federal Act restrains those who use similar trade names as domain names on the Internet. However, the Act may be ineffective against non-commercial web sites that are critical of a company's products or services. For example, Bally's Total Fitness filed a lawsuit against a former member who created a web site entitled "Bally sucks." The theme of the anti-Bally web site was criticism of the health chain.[425] Bally's sued for trademark dilution because the defendant was using its trademarks in an unauthorized manner.[426] The federal court in California granted summary judgment in favor of the defendant, holding that "no reasonable person would think Bally's is affiliated with or endorses" the anti-Bally site.[427] The court also found "fair use" in the anti-Bally site's use of the plaintiff's trademarks. Finally, the court found the anti-Bally web site did not tarnish Bally's mark simply because of the name link between the sites. The court also upheld the use of Bally's metatags to promote the anti-Bally site.[428]

---

[419] Hormel Foods Corp. v. Jim Henson Prods., Inc., 73 F.3d 497, 506 (2d Cir. 1996).

[420] 2000 U.S. Dist. LEXIS 9747 (S.D.N.Y., July 13, 2000).

[421] *Id.* at *26.

[422] *Id.*

[423] 522 U.S. 977 (1997).

[424] 126 F. Supp. 2d 463 (E.D. Mich. 2001).

[425] Bally Total Fitness Holding Corp., 29 F. Supp. 2d 1161 (C.D. Cal. 1998). *See also* Lucent Technologies, Inc. v. Lucentsuck.com, 95 F. Supp. 2d 528 (E.D. Va. 2000) (dismissing claim because plaintiff failed to satisfy due diligence clause of the Anticybersquatting Consumer Protection Act).

[426] *Id.*

[427] *Id.*

[428] *See* § 4.02[J][1] *infra* for a further discussion on permissible trademark uses and defenses to infringement claims.

In a more successful tarnishment case, an adult web site used the domain names "papalvisit1999.com" and "papalvisit.com" to draw more visitors to its adult entertainment sites. The Archdiocese of St. Louis and Papal Visit 1999 discovered that the adult web sites were using their marks in adult-oriented sites.[429] A federal judge ruled in favor of the plaintiffs and issued an order enjoining the link of the trademarks to the adult entertainment sites. The federal judge found the plaintiffs' marks to be famous, triggering the protection of the Federal Trademark Dilution Act as well as state dilution law.[430]

[b]   State Antidilution Remedies

State antidilution statutes provide remedies for the dilution of the distinctive quality of trademarks. The concept of dilution is that a mark's uniqueness or selling power is gradually lost over time. Plaintiffs are required to prove a likelihood of *dilution* that will diminish the economic value of a mark versus actual dilution under the FDTA.

State antidilution statutes vary with the requirement of whether a mark must have a degree of distinctiveness as well as be famous. California's statute, for example, requires that marks be both distinctive and famous.[431] The Texas antidilution statute, on the other hand, requires distinctiveness, not fame.[432] Courts applying state antidilution statutes consider many of the same factors used in the FTDA analysis: "Whether the mark is arbitrary, the length of time the user has employed the mark, the scope of the user's advertising, and promoting the nature and extent of the first user's business, and the scope of the first user's reputation."[433] The FTDA comes "very close to granting rights in gross in a trademark."[434]

State antidilution laws protect a prior or senior user's mark even when the later or junior user is not a competitor and no likelihood of confusion exists between the two users' products or trademarks.[435] To prevail on a state antidilution claim, the senior user must demonstrate that it has a senior mark and that the junior user's conduct damages the senior's interest in the mark "by blurring its product

---

[429] Archdiocese of St. Louis and Papal Visit 1999 v. Internet Entertainment Group, Inc., 34 F. Supp. 2d 1145 (E.D. Mo. 1999) (enjoining adult web site from using domain names PapalVisit.com and PapalVisit 1999.com on grounds of federal state law claims for trademark infringement, dilution, and unfair competition). The court found that the adult entertainment web site's use of the plaintiff's marks as diluted the distinctive quality of the marks and tarnished the image of the papal visit. The court held that the plaintiffs established the likelihood of success on their dilution claims but withdrew the opinion at 34 F. Supp. 2d 1145 (E.D. Mo. 1999).

[430] *Id.*

[431] Avery Dennison Corp. v. Sumpton, 189 F.3d 868 (9th Cir. 1999).

[432] Advantage Rent-A-Car, Inc. v. Enterprise Rent-a-Car Co., 238 F.3d 378 (5th Cir. 2001) (applying Texas law and stating that distinctiveness but not fame is required).

[433] *Id.* at 381.

[434] *Avery Dennison Corp.*, 189 F.3d at 875.

[435] The FTDA provides that possession of a valid federal trademark registration is a complete bar to a dilution claim "under the common law or a statute of a State." 15 U.S.C. § 1125(c)(3) (2000).

identification or by damaging positive associations that have been attached to it."[436]

If a company's brand names do not qualify as famous marks, they may be protected under state antidilution statutes or state common law. State antidilution claims, whether under statute or the common law, provide a remedy when there is similarity between two marks that either tarnishes or blurs the senior mark, even though the marks are noncompeting and do not create a likelihood of confusion. A state antidilution claim may be filed under the common law or by statute.

State antidilution statutes vary in their provisions. The Illinois Antidilution Act, for example, provides a remedy for a prior trademark user who proves that "its mark is distinctive and that the subsequent user's use dilutes that distinctiveness."[437] Illinois does not require the prior user to prove "competition between the users or confusion."[438] Ohio also recognizes state common law antidilution claims.[439]

[F] Unfair Competition

Section 43(a) of the Lanham Act provides rights and remedies for unfair trade practices such as the "false designation of origin, false or misleading description of fact, or misleading representation of fact."[440] Section 43(a) covers false or misleading misrepresentations of fact "likely to cause confusion, or to cause mistake, or to deceive as to the affiliation, connection or association of such person with another person, or as to the origin, sponsorship, or approval of his or her goods, services, or commercial activities by another person."[441] The test for trademark infringement and unfair competition under the Lanham Act is essentially the same as that for common law unfair competition.[442] A web site that falsely alleges endorsement, for example, may be liable for federal unfair competition.

Section 43(a) also covers unfair trade practices in the form of false or misleading advertising. The essence of a false or deceptive advertising claim under the Lanham Act is an advertisement that "misrepresents the nature, characteristics, qualities, or geographic origin of his or her or another person's goods, services, or commercial activities."[443]

---

[436] Ameritech, Inc. v. American Info. Technologies Corp., 811 F.2d 960, 961 (6th Cir. 1987) (applying Ohio Law).

[437] Eli Lilly and Co. v. Natural Answers, Inc., 86 F. Supp. 2d 834 (S.D. Ind. 2000) (citation omitted).

[438] Id.

[439] See, e.g., Guild & Landis, Inc. v. Liles & Landis Liquidators, Inc., 207 N.E.2d 798, 800 (Ohio Com. Pl. 1959) (comparing similar marks). See Ringling Bros.-Barnum & Bailey Combined Shows v. Utah Div. of Travel Dev., 170 F.3d 449 (4th Cir. 1999) (noting that courts applied the [state antidilution] statutes reluctantly and many states found it difficult to apply the dilution concept).

[440] Id.

[441] 15 U.S.C. § 1125(a)(1)(A) (2002).

[442] People for the Ethical Treatment of Animals v. Doughney, 263 F.3d 359 (4th Cir. 2001) (applying Virginia law).

[443] 15 U.S.C. § 1125(a)(1)(B) (2002).

[G]   Defenses to Trademark Infringement

[1]   Noncommercial and First Amendment-Related Defenses

The use of a trademark is not actionable where such use, even if dilutive, is part of a public commentary or journalistic report. An e-commerce publication, for example, may use a company's trademarks in a feature story about how its web site became an e-business success story. Editorial comment is constitutionally protected expression, as is comparative advertising in which another company's marks are mentioned.[444] Anticompany or critical non-commercial web sites may be protected by the First Amendment and the news commentary exemption to trademark infringement. The use of trademarks in journalistic reports, comparative advertising, and other noncommercial uses developed as a common law "fair comment" or fair use defense.[445] For example, in *Patmont Motor Works, Inc. v. Gateway Marine, Inc.*,[446] a federal court held that the use of a trademark owner's product name in the text of search engines constituted fair use.

Yahoo! Inc. has an auction web site, where items can be posted online for others to bid on and purchase. Certain users had offered for sale Nazi paraphernalia, which French law prohibits.[447] The defendant, who took Yahoo! to court in France, was granted an order from the French court requiring that Yahoo! not allow French citizens to "access" any of these items, not just through *yahoo.fr* but also *yahoo.com*. Yahoo!, realizing that it is it impossible to prevent access through *yahoo.com*, sought relief in the U.S. courts. The district court held that although the context that the paraphernalia embodies is "one of the worst displays of inhumanity in recorded history," the court could not enforce the French order without interfering with and threatening Yahoo!'s free speech rights under the First Amendment. It is quite likely that U.S. courts will refuse to enforce foreign judgments that conflict with the First Amendment or other important public policies in trademark or copyright law as well. Courts in the United States would not likely enforce a foreign court attempting to enjoin a U.S. web site for publishing parodies or comparative advertisements.

[2]   Statutory Fair Use

The Lanham Act also recognizes a *fair use* defense, "the concept that a trademark registrant or holder cannot 'appropriate a descriptive term for his exclusive use and so prevent others from accurately describing a characteristic of their

---

[444] *See* Seuss Enter, L.P. v. Penguin Books USA, Inc., 924 F. Supp. 1559 (S.D. Cal.), *aff'd,* 109 F.3d 1394 (9th Cir.), *cert. denied,* 118 S. Ct. 27 (1997) (holding uses of a trademark not to be actionable as dilution where the commentary is on an issue of public importance).

[445] *See* Arthur R. Miller and Michael H. Davis, Intellectual Property: Patents, Trademarks, and Copyright 164 (1990).

[446] 1997 U.S. Dist. LEXIS 20877 (N.D. Cal., Dec. 17, 1997).

[447] Yahoo!, Inc. v. La Ligue Contre Le Racisme et L' Antisemitisme, 169 F. Supp. 2d 1181 (N.D. Cal. 2001).

goods.' "[448] The Lanham Act's fair use defense permits the use of registered marks in a descriptive and fair way to describe the goods and services of the trademark owner. The defendant's use of a trademark owner's trademarks must not be used in conjunction with the sale of goods and services.[449]

Similarly, the FTDA extends the common law fair use doctrine to famous trademarks. Section 1125(c)(4) states that: "All forms of news reporting and news commentary" are classified as fair use.[450] The use of a competitor's advertisement in a comparative advertisement was also validated by § 1125(c)(4) of the FTDA: "[A] fair use of a famous mark by another person in comparative advertising or promotion to identify the competing goods or services of the owner of the famous marks."[451]

A federal court found fair use was a defense to liability under the Lanham Act in *Playboy Enterprises v. Welles*.[452] Terri Welles, a former Playboy playmate, opened a web site including photographs of herself and a heading entitled "Terri Welles: Playmate of the Year 1981." Ms. Welles also used Playboy and Playmate as keywords in the metatags. The court found Ms. Welles's use of the Playboy and Playmate marks in web site advertisements descriptive and used in good faith. Another court found the descriptive use of a trademark owner's marks in the URL of a web address to be protected by fair use.[453]

[3] Parody

A *parody* is a "simple form of entertainment conveyed by juxtaposing the irreverent representation of the trademark with the idealized image created by the mark's owner."[454] The Internet is a haven for parodies and other noncommercial speech, with its potential for a global audience and inexpensive publishing capabilities. L.L. Bean sued an adult magazine for dilution when it featured a section called "L.L. Bean Back to School Sex Catalog."[455] The court stated that the antidilution statute could not be used to enjoin the noncommercial use of a trademark.[456]

---

[448] Playboy Enters. v. Welles, 1999 U.S. Dist. LEXIS 21047 (S.D. Cal., Dec. 1, 1999).

[449] Sealed Indus., Inc. v. Chesebrough-Ponds USA Co., 125 F.3d 28 (2d Cir. 1997).

[450] 15 U.S.C. § 1125(c)(4) (2002).

[451] *Id.*

[452] 1999 U.S. Dist. LEXIS 21047 (S.D. Cal., Dec. 1, 1999).

[453] Teletech Customer Care Management, Inc. v. Tele-Tech Co., Inc., 977 F. Supp. 1407-14 (C.D. Cal. 1997) (holding that domain name did not confuse web site visitors when placed in the context of web site content).

[454] L.L. Bean, Inc. v. Drake Publishers, Inc., 811 F.2d 26, 34 (1st Cir. 1987); *see also* Cliffs Notes, Inc. v. Bantam Doubleday Dell Publ'g Group, Inc., 886 F.2d 490, 494 (2d Cir. 1989) (noting that a parody must convey two contradictory images simultaneously: that it is the original and it is also a parody; Jordache Enters., Inc. v. Hogg Wyld, Ltd., 828 F.2d 1482, 1486 (10th Cir. 1987) (holding in parody of jeans manufacturer that an effective parody diminishes the risk of consumer confusion "by conveying [only] just enough of the original design to allow the consumer to appreciate the point of parody").

[455] *Id.* at 27.

[456] *Id.* at 32.

A federal court held that the use of the domain name *www.compupix.com/ ballysucks* did not infringe Bally's trademark because the use of the mark did not identify goods or promote a service, but instead showed current Bally members how to cancel their memberships.[457]

The Fourth Circuit affirmed a lower court ruling that a defendant registering the domain name *peta.org*, which contained a trademark of an animals rights group, was not protected by parody doctrine. The defendant argued that its web site, *People Eating Tasty Animals*, was a parody of the plaintiff's organization, the People for the Ethical Treatment of Animals (PETA).[458] Web site visitors accessing the site "would see the title 'People Eating Tasty Animals' in large, bold type. Under the title, the viewer would see a statement that the web site was a 'resource for those who enjoy eating meat, wearing fur and leather, hunting, and the fruits of scientific research.'"[459] PETA requested that the defendant transfer the domain name, and when he refused, filed a lawsuit "asserting claims for service mark infringement, unfair competition, dilution and cybersquatting."[460] PETA did not seek damages, but sought only to enjoin the defendant's use of the *PETA* trademark and an order requiring the defendant to transfer the *peta.org* domain name to PETA. The defendant's answer to the lawsuit was that his web site was a constitutionally protected parody of PETA. The district court found that the web site simply copied PETA's trademark and did not constitute a parody. The district court granted PETA's motion for summary judgment on the infringement and unfair competition claims. The Fourth Circuit affirmed the district court's finding that the defendant's use of PETA's trademark in the domain name of his web site was likely to prevent Internet users from reaching PETA's own Internet web site and was not constitutionally protected as a parody.

[4] Other Defenses

In *Gucci America, Inc. v. Hall & Assoc.*,[461] the court held that neither the Communications Decency Act nor the First Amendment immunized an Internet hosting company from potential liability under the Lanham Act for hosting a third-party web site that allegedly infringed Gucci's trademark.[462] Section 230(e) of the Communications Decency Act provides that "nothing in this section shall be construed to limit or expand any law pertaining to intellectual property." The court therefore held that § 230(c)(1) could not be held to grant the ISP immunity from

---

[457] Bally Total Fitness v. Faber, 29 F. Supp. 2d 1161 (1998).

[458] People for the Ethical Treatment of Animals v. Doughney, 263 F.3d 359 (4th Cir. 2001 (affirming district court and ruling that defendant was liable for service mark infringement and unfair competition and violated the Anticybersquatting Consumer Protection Act).

[459] *Id.* at 363.

[460] *Id.*

[461] 00 Civ. 549 (S.D.N.Y., Mar. 19, 2001).

[462] *Id.*

the claims brought under the Lanham Act, because to do so would then be limiting a law pertaining to intellectual property.

[H]   Trademark Registration

[1]   Trademark Searches

Before a trademark is registered, counsel must conduct a trademark search to determine whether a selected mark or confusingly similar mark is already being used. The trademark search begins with the USPTO's federal register; it is also possible to search some state registers. Other possible ways to search a trademark include the following:

1. The Principal and Supplemental Registers of the USPTO. The Principal Register is for marks that are or will become distinctive, while the Supplemental Register is for descriptive trademarks. Notice of registration is published in the USPTO's Official Gazette. Notice of opposition to a pending mark must be filed within 30 days of the mark's publication in the Official Gazette.

    Companies may also use an Internet Jumpstation, which permits searches of scores of trademarks. Keep in mind that trademark law is national or state, and the Internet is transnational. It may too expensive to register trademarks for every country connected to the Internet. A company's trademark should be registered in countries where the company is currently or is planning on doing business.

2. Industry trade publications for similar marks. After completing initial searches, it is possible to hire a search company, such as Thomson & Thomson, to do a complete trademark search of other sources.

3. Internet domain names. The same domain name may be used with a different high-level domain. *Suffolk.edu* and *Suffolk.org* may coexist. Most domain name battles are fought over "the right to use the same domain."[463] Only one owner can possess the domain *Suffolk.edu*. [464]

    (a) If a trademark is being used, it may be possible to purchase, license, or assign trademark rights. A growing number of trademark owners are filing lawsuits against holders of domain names that contain their registered trademark or similar marks.

---

[463] Linda A. Heban, Live and Let Live: Tips for Sharing Domain Names, 5 Intell. Prop. Strat. 1 (July 1999).

[464] Should a trademark owner decide to purchase a corresponding domain name, the trademark owner should draft a contract for the sale. The contract should include certain provisions to protect the purchaser from future liability. Such provisions should include an indemnity clause and specific representations and warranties regarding the seller's rights and ability to enter into the sale of the domain name. In addition, a transfer form, which can be obtained from the registrar of the domain name, should be filed with the appropriate registrar.

An owner of a mark must apply to the federal Patent and Trademark Office in Washington, D.C., to register it nationally for trademark or service mark protection. The USPTO Act specifies that the application must state "the date of applicant's first use of the mark, the date of applicant's first use of the mark in commerce, the goods in connection with which the mark is used, and the mode or manner in which the mark is used in connection with such goods." The trademark applicant must attest that she or he owns the mark, that it is used in commerce, and that there is no similar mark that will create confusion.

The requirements for an application include the name of the applicant, citizenship of the applicant, domicile, and post office address of the applicant. The applicant must also describe the class of goods or services the mark is for, according to the USPTO international classification system. The USPTO recognizes 34 classes for trademarks. An applicant may register for more than a single class in a single application. The date of the applicant's "first use of the mark as a trademark or service mark must be noted on the application."[465] The filing date is the date on which the elements of an application are received in the USPTO.[466]

The federal registration of trademarks is governed by the Trademark Act of 1946, as amended, 15 U.S.C. § 1051 *et seq.*; the Trademark Rules, 37 C.F.R. Part 2; and the Trademark Manual of Examining Procedure (2d ed. 1993). The USPTO uses the terms "trademark" and "mark" to "refer to both trademarks and service marks whether they are word marks or other types of marks. A trademark owner will use trademarks on the product and its packaging, while service marks advertise services."[467] The application and all other correspondence should be addressed to The Assistant Commissioner for Trademarks, 2900 Crystal Drive, Arlington, Virginia 22202-3513. The initial application should be directed to Box NEW APP/FEE. An Amendment to Allege Use should be directed to "Attn. AAU." A Statement of Use or Request for an Extension of Time to File a Statement of Use should be directed to Box ITU/FEE. The applicant should indicate her or his telephone number on the application form. Once a serial number is assigned to the application, the applicant should refer to the serial number in all written and telephone communications concerning the application.

The owner of a trademark may theoretically file his or her own application for registration before the Patent and Trademark Office. Corporate counsel will likely hire a trademark company specializing in prosecuting trademark applications. A trademark application is given a filing date once all of the elements of an application have been filed.[468]

In addition to registration, companies must remember to obtain permission to use any trademarks owned by others.[469] A company should not use its trade-

---

[465] 37 C.F.R. § 2.33(v).

[466] 37 C.F.R. § 2.21 (stating requirements for receiving a filing date).

[467] *Id.*

[468] *See* Rules of Practice in Trademark Cases, 37 C.F.R. §§ 2.1-2.189.

[469] The licensing of trademarks is typically the method of obtaining rights. Trademarks, however, are frequently assigned or purchased.

marks online in a manner likely to cause consumer confusion with another party's trademarks. Internet sales make trademark disputes more likely because sales on the Internet are made on the same channel of trade and are directed to the same class of consumers.[470] A federal court refused to cancel the trademark registration for "Ecash" on defendant's request merely because the plaintiff failed to notify the USPTO during the registration process of the defendant's use of the "Ecash" mark as a domain name.[471] A trademark applicant has a duty to inform the USPTO of the issue of mark by others when the user of the same mark's rights are "clearly established."[472] The court determined that the registration of the ecash.com domain name did not create "clearly established rights."[473]

[2]   The Benefits of Federal Registration

A trademark registration may be applied for by filing an application with the USPTO. The USPTO sends a filing receipt to the applicant approximately six months after filing. The filing receipt includes a serial number of the trademark application. Registrations issued after November 16, 1989, have a 10-year term and may be renewed every 10 years forever. However, an Affidavit of Use must be filed between the fifth and sixth year following registration and within the year before the end of every 10-year period after the initial registration. Information on registering trademarks is available free of charge from the U.S. Patent and Trademark Office at http://www.uspto.gov or 1-800-786-9199. The Official Gazette is the official journal of the USPTO relating to trademarks and contains information about registered trademark.

Federal registration is not required to establish rights in a mark, nor is it required to begin use of a mark. Federal registration, however, can secure benefits beyond the rights acquired by merely using a mark. The owner of a federally registered trademark, for example, is presumed to be the owner of the mark for the goods and services specified in the registration and is entitled to use the mark nationwide.

Each trademark application must be filed in the name of a company as owner of the mark. If a company is listed as the owner of the mark, it is responsible for the nature and quality of the goods or services identified by the mark. A company should remember to register trade name, trademarks, service marks, collective

---

[470] It is uncertain whether courts will classify the Internet as the same channel of trade involving sales to the same class of consumers.

[471] Ecash Techs. v. Guagliardo, 127 F. Supp. 2d 1069 (C.D. Cal. 2000) (stating such rights are "clearly established when set forth in a court decree, settlement agreement, or a trademark registration").

[472] Id.

[473] Id.

marks, and certification marks promptly.[474] The first user of a mark to file is conferred "a right of priority, nationwide in effect."[475] The right of priority to federal registration does not necessarily mean the right of priority to use the mark nationwide. The nationwide right to use a mark could, for example, be impeded by the common law right of an earlier use.

Unlike copyrights or patents, trademark rights can last indefinitely if the owner continues to use the mark to identify its goods or services. A trademark receives protection when it is used in commerce in connection with the sale of goods or services. The definition of being "in commerce" may refer to interstate commerce or foreign commerce.

The Lanham Act permits two types of use application: (1) actual use and (2) intent to use. The Trademark Commissioner may accept evidence that an applicant has used a mark "in commerce" for five years as prima facie evidence of distinctiveness.[476] Alternatively, an applicant may attest that the mark will be used in the future. The applicant must state how the mark is (or will be) used in the course of the sale of goods or the rendering of services. The applicant must attest that she or he is the owner of the mark and that the mark is (or will soon be) used in commerce.[477]

[a] Actual Use

If a company has already used its marks in selling, for example, computer software or hardware, it will file an "actual use" application. The elements of an application consist of a page with the mark drawing, an application form, documentation of use, and the application fee of $325 per class.[478] If an examiner determines that the mark is distinctive, and it thus passes the examination stage, then the examiner will issue a registration. If no opposition arises following publication in the registry, the trademark registration is issued.

[b] Intent to Use

A company may also file an intent-to-use application, which allows an applicant to register a trademark prior to the actual use of the goods or services in com-

---

[474] SPC's marks can be in the form of a word, design, symbol, or device that fulfills the purpose of differentiating its goods and services. SPC plans on using its marks on labels on its software, tags on its monitors, screen-savers for its personal computers, brochures, magazine advertisements, and its web site, to name just a few of its uses in commerce.

[475] 15 U.S.C. § 1057(c) (2002).

[476] 15 U.S.C. § 1054(f) (2002) (stating that the Commissioner may accept as *prima facie* evidence that the mark has become distinctive, as used on or in connection with the applicant's goods in commerce . . . for the five years before the date on which the claim of distinctiveness is made").

[477] *Id.*

[478] SPC will file a multiple-class application to cover the wide breadth of goods and services. It may decide to apply for use of a trademark on its personal computers, for example, and another for use with its online services division. The classification of goods and services is in accordance with the World Intellectual Property Organization (WIPO) categories. For more information, visit www.USPTO.gov.

merce. This means that if a company files its trademarks before other filers, it has a claim on use of the mark.[479] However, this would not trump another party's prior usage. In an intent-to-use application, the applicant must provide a drawing of the mark and attest to a bona fide intention to use the mark on goods that are to be sold.[480] The intent-to-use application states that the applicant has a bona fide intention to use the mark in commerce regulated by Congress.[481] The dates of first use of the mark in Internet commerce will be noted on the application to prove use in commerce.[482] After a company files an intent-to-use application, an examination and opposition stage follows. The company's marks are not registered until the mark is used, although the registration date is the filing date of the intent-to-use application.

Federal trademarks may be renewed every 10 years as long as the mark is used in commerce. A company's trademark counsel must remember to keep the registration alive by filing an affadavit with the USPTO between the fifth and sixth year after the date of initial registration. The failure of the registrant to provide the affidavit will result in the cancellation of the trademark registration.

[3]   International Registration

The owner of a trademark registered with the USPTO has exclusive rights only in the United States. An online business may wish to file trademark registrations in foreign countries as well. Trademarks may be registered in different countries, especially those where goods and services are sold on the Internet. In the United Kingdom, for example, trademarks are regulated under the Trademark Act of 1938. A subsequent body of laws, the Trade Description Act of 1968, deals with false trade descriptions and imported goods bearing trademarks of U.K. manufacturers. Trademark registration in the United Kingdom is for 7 years initially and may be renewed for periods of 14 years. Germany also permits trademarks to be registered in the German Federal Patent Office. Most U.S. law firms specializing in intellectual property will have affiliations with trademark counsel in essential countries where protection is required. Registrants may also file to protect their trademarks in all European Union member states.

The House of Representatives has also approved the Madrid Protocol Implementation Act, which would make it easier to file for an international registration

---

[479] The filing date constitutes a constructive date of first use.

[480] 37 C.F.R. § 2.52 (2000) (stating requirement for drawings in patent application).

[481] 15 U.S.C. § 1051(b) (2002).

[482] SPC must have clear documentation of the date of first use in commerce, although technically the owner does not have to show the exact date to the USPTO. If the filing date of the first use fails, the entire application fails. With an intent-to-use application, SPC may amend its application to include the first use in commerce. SPC's safest course is to file an intent-to-use application if any doubt might arise as to when first use in commerce occurred.

of marks by filing an international application with the USPTO.[483] Madrid Union signatory countries have agreed to a method for the international registration of marks. The Madrid Protocol formed the International Bureau of the World Intellectual Property Organization. The application for international registration of a mark is filed with the International Bureau.[484] The Foreign Relations Committee of the U.S. Senate approved the Madrid Protocol, paving the way for companies to be able to obtain trademark protection globally.[485] The Madrid Protocol permits a U.S. company that has filed in the Trademark Office to seek trademark protection not only in the United States but any signatory country. The single application significantly decreases the cost of obtaining international protection.

[I]   Protecting Trademarks

Trademark holders must take reasonable steps to protect their marks from misuse or risk losing trademark protection. A company can monitor the use, misuse, and abuse of trademarks on the Internet by hiring a search service. Counsel will frequently send "cease and desist" letters and threaten legal action where a company's trademarks are infringed on the Internet. A distinctive trademark may descend into the generic abyss if many others in Internet commerce misuse the mark in a manner that diminishes its distinctiveness. Other ways to protect the marks include using private policing resources such as brand cops, loyal employees, outsourcing, and in house and outsourcing.[486]

Many owners of famous marks assert that similar terms are causing consumer confusion in Internet commerce. In one legendary case, the father of a young girl named Veronica registered the domain name of Veronica.com. Archie Comics, whose comic character, Veronica, was a trademarked term, sued Veronica and her father. The owner of the trademarks dropped its lawsuit and settled the case after purchasing the Veronica.com domain name.[487]

A WIPO Panel employing UDRP procedures ruled that the name *La Caixa* was "an international famous trademark."[488] La Caixa claimed that the respondent had registered the domain name *lakaixa.com* in bad faith, but the respondent

---

[483] Microsoft Law & Corporate Affairs, Summary of Global Internet Legal Developments (for the period Jan.-Mar. 1999) 56 (Apr. 1999) (reporting that H.R. 769 would permit a U.S. trademark owner to seek registration of its mark internationally by filing an international application with the U.S. Patent and Trademark Office, but the U.S. has yet to ratify the Madrid Protocol).

[484] Protocol relating to the Madrid Agreement Concerning the International Registration of Marks, art. 2 (entitled "Securing Protection Through International Registration").

[485] Arent-Fox, E-Tipsheet, Senate Foreign Relations Committee Approves Madrid Protocol (Dec. 2001), http://www.arentfox.com/publications/E-TIPSheet/e-tip2001-11/e-tip2001-11.html.

[486] The Food Institute Report, Brand Police, Techniques Used to Monitor Brands on the Web (Nov. 13, 2000).

[487] Archie Comics may have saved itself from a public relations debacle by trying to find a business solution prior to filing a lawsuit.

[488] Caixa d'Estalvis y Pensions de Barcelona ("La Caixa") v. Namezero.com, 8 ILR (P&F) 532 (WIPO Arb. & Mediation Ctr. 2001).

claims it registered the domain as "a political and cultural criticism of Complainant's activities."[489] Although in Latin countries it is understood that changing the letter *C* to the letter *K* is considered to "express a left-wing or anarchist protest,"[490] outside of Latin America that is not understood, and it was found to be confusingly similar to the complainant's mark.

Trademark infringement and counterfeiting is increasing at an exponential rate for products and services sold on the Internet and in traditional retail channels. Companies selling trademarked goods need to keep in contact with the U.S. Customs Service (Customs), which polices the importation of counterfeited goods into this country. Customs recently published guidelines on restraining the importation of "gray market" goods bearing genuine trademarks but that are different from goods authorized for importation.[491]

[J] Use and Abandonment of Trademarks

Trademarks must be used "in commerce," or they will be treated as abandoned and not entitled to protection. The rule for trademark protection is to "use it or lose it." The concept of use means that the mark is used in the ordinary course of trade. A mark is presumed abandoned if it is discontinued or if a company shows intent not to resume use of a mark. Intent not to resume use is determined from the circumstances. The trademark owner's failure to use a trademark for three consecutive years is *prima facie* evidence of abandonment. Trademark applications may also be abandoned if "an applicant fails to respond, or to respond completely, within six months after the date an action is mailed; the application shall be deemed to have been abandoned."[492]

[K] Internet Domain Name Issues

[1] Domain Name Registration Procedure

Domain names, like the real estate market, are all about "location, location, location." The choice of a domain name is one of great strategic importance. Consumers are more likely to find an entity with a memorable domain name in a common top level domain, like SPC.com compared with SuffolkPersonalComputers.nu. Companies need to register their domain names with one of the Internet Corporation for Assigned Names and Numbers (ICANN) accredited registrars. International domain name issues are covered in § 8.02[B][4][c]. Chapter Eight provides

---

[489] *Id.*

[490] *Id.*

[491] U.S. Customs Service, Gray Market Imports and Other Trademarked Goods, 19 C.F.R. pt. 133 (T.D. 99-21) RIN 1515-AB49 (Sept. 29, 1999), http://www.customs.UStreas.gov/fed-reg/notices/914486.htm.

[492] Rules of Practice in Trademark Cases, 37 C.F.R. § 265 (describing abandonment of trademark applications).

a detailed discussion of the new top-level domains, country-level domain issues, and resolving global domain name disputes in the WIPO Arbitration and Mediation Center and other UDRP arbitration panels.[493] Additionally, the choice of a Domain Name Registrar may also be an important consideration in light of the potential dire consequences if a domain registrar becomes insolvent.[494] In one dispute, a successor to a bankrupt registrar failed to notify the original domain name registrant that the registration had lapsed and another party registered the name in the interim. When registering, applicants must represent that (1) the registration is complete and accurate; (2) the domain name does not infringe trademarks of third parties; (3) the domain name is not registered for unlawful purposes; and (4) the domain name owner will not knowingly use the domain name to violate any laws or regulations.

Many companies will want to use their trade name as a domain name, if it is available. The fee for registration varies by registrar and top level domain name.[495] According to the terms of service and the rulings in several lawsuits, a registrar of Internet domain names is not liable for direct, contributory, or vicarious infringement for accepting registrations of Internet domain names confusingly similar to a plaintiff's service or trademark.[496] The online company will be required to provide contact and technical information for a central directory or registry. "This registry provides other computers on the Internet the information necessary to send you e-mail or to find your web site. You will also be required to enter a registration contract with the registrar, which sets forth the terms under which your registration is accepted and will be maintained."[497] The online company should be aware that all contact information is public information and published on the "Whois" site.[498] In the event of a dispute over rights over a domain name, trademark owners can readily locate domain name registrants by searching the Whois

---

[493] A list of all the accredited registrars is available at www.internic.net/origin.html. The Internet domain name system (DNS) consists of a directory, organized hierarchically, of all the domain names and their corresponding computers registered to particular companies and persons using the Internet. When you register a domain name, it will be associated with the computer on the Internet you designate during the period the registration is in effect. Domain names ending with .com, .net, or .org can be registered through many different companies (known as "registrars") that compete with one another. An alphabetical listing of these companies appears in the InterNIC Registrar Directory on the InterNIC site. The online company is free to choose any accredited registrar. See ICANN, Domain Name Registration Questions (visited Apr. 28, 2002), http:www.icann.org/general/faq1.htm.

[494] Michael Geist, Internet Law News, May 1, 2000, citing http://www.theregister.co.uk/content/6/18619.html.

[495] ICANN (visited Apr. 28, 2002), www.icann.com.

[496] The leading case is Lockheed Martin Corp. v. Network Solutions, Inc., 985 F. Supp. 949 (C.D. Cal. 1997) (granting summary judgment in favor of registrar of Internet domain names because the registrar's use of Internet domain names was not connected with their trademark functions; acceptance of domain names is not a commercial use and thus does not infringe trademark law).

[497] ICANN, Frequently Asked Questions About Domain Name Registration (visited Apr. 28, 2002), http://www.icann.org/general/faq1.htm.

[498] Id.

database.[499] Many desired domain names have already been taken as over "[o]ver 11 million domain names have already been registered worldwide."[500]

ICANN recommends that the domain name applicant compare accredited registrars to determine the best price.[501] A registry will have the IP addresses of all domain names in a given TLD. "The .org registry databases, for example, contain the Internet whereabouts—or IP address—of icann.org."[502] In November 2000, ICANN approved seven new top-level domains (TLDs): (1) *.aero* (air-transport industry); (2) *.biz* (businesses); (3) *.coop* (cooperatives); (4) *.info* (unrestricted use); (5) *.museum* (museums); (6) *.name* (for registration by individuals); and (7) *.pro* (accountants, lawyers, and physicians). These are the first new TLDs (other than country-code TLDs) to be introduced to the Internet since 1988.[503]

The root servers contain the IP addresses of all the TLD registries, both the global registries such as *.com, .org,* etc., and the 244 country-specific registries such as *.fr* (France), *.cn* (China), and registries in other countries.[504] Currently, there are 244 top-level domains (TLDs) denoting different countries. The internationalization of the domain name system creates the potential for disputes over the meaning of words used in domains. For example, there is a debate over the meaning of *.us*: whether kids should have their own domain and if so whether it should be *.kids.us* or just *.kids*.[505] Since the registration process started for the *.info* TLD, a major concern has been raised about TLDs that have been registered by "applicants with no rights to the names at all." A recent dispute, for example occurred between DuPont, which registered *science.info,* and Russ Smith, who already had the *science.net* web site.[506] In April 2002, U.S. Internet users registered more than 200,000 names. Consumer groups are critical of NeuStar's "policy that permitted public interest related addresses to be sold on a first-come, first-served basis."[507]

---

[499] *Id.*

[500] John O'Dwyer, Web 101—Domain Names, O'Dwyer's PR Services Report (Sept. 2001), http://www.odwyerpr.com/web_sitings/2001/september.htm.

[501] *Id.*

[502] InterNIC, Domain Name FAQs (visited Apr. 28, 2002), http://www.internic.net/faqs/authoritative-dns.html.

[503] ICANN, New TLD Program (visited Apr. 28, 2002), http://www.icann.org/tlds (noting that the new TLDs constitute two types: .biz, .info, .name, and .pro are intended to be relatively large, "unsponsored" TLDs, and the other three proposals (.aero, .coop, and .museum) are for smaller "sponsored" TLDs).

[504] InterNIC, The Domain Name System: A Non-Technical Explanation—Why Universal Resolvabilty Is Important (visited Apr. 28, 2002), http://www.internic.net/faqs/authoritative-dns.html.

[505] O'Dwyer, *supra* note 500; *see also* Andy Sullivan, NewStar Inc. to Administer '.us' Domain (Oct. 29, 2001), http://www.siliconvalley.com/docs/news/reuters_wire/16087101.htm; David McGuire, Government Awards '.us' to NeuStar, Newsbytes (Oct. 29, 2001), http://www.newsbytes.com/news/01/171604.html; David McGuire, LawMakers Consider ".Kids.US" Compromise, Newsbytes (Oct. 30, 2001), http://www.newsbytes.com/news/01/171670.html.

[506] Charles Arthur, Cybersquatters Accused of Trying to Hijack New. Info Web Addresses, The Independent, Aug. 28, 2001.

[507] David McGuire, Consumers Decry "Dot-Us" Policies, Wash. Post, Apr. 29, 2002, http://www.newsbytes.com/news/02/176214.html.

ICANN's policies have also been castigated by practitioners, academics, and Internet users. Esther Dyson, the former chair of ICANN, described the organization as a "cesspool mired in disputes about authority, accountability, and openness."[508] ICANN policies and country-level and other global domain name issues are discussed in detail in § 8.02[B][4][c].

The last several characters, or top-level domain (TLD), of a domain name refer to the type of organization that runs the site. The *.gov* in the following URL for the Census Bureau denotes a government site: *http://www.census.gov/*. The URL for ABC television is *http://www.abc.com/*. The *.com* signifies a commercial site. Suffolk University Law School has an *.edu* at the end of its URL: *http://www.suffolk.acad.edu*, which signifies that this URL is an educational institution. National Public Radio has an organization top-level domain: *http://www.npr.org*. The *.org* signifies a noncommercial organization. An address with a *.mil* at the end signifies a military site. A two-character code at the end of an address signifies a particular country: *au* (Australia), *br* (Brazil), *ca* (Canada), *uk* (United Kingdom), and *jp* (Japan) are examples.[509] In November 2000, ICANN granted seven new domain names, including *.biz* (businesses), *.museum* (museums), *.info* (unrestricted use), *.aero* (air-transport industry), *.coop* (cooperatives), *.name* (individuals), and *.pro* (accountants, lawyers, and physicians).[510] Domain names may be canceled, transferred, or changed if (1) the owner requests it, (2) there is an order from a court or tribunal, or (3) there is a decision from an administrative panel. A domain name may be canceled or changed in a lawsuit or arbitration proceeding if the plaintiff proves the domain name: (1) is identical or confusingly similar to trademarks or service marked owned by another, (2) is owned by a party with no legitimate interests to the name, and (3) was registered in bad faith.

[2] Management of Internet Names and Addresses

The management of the Internet was originally a project of the U.S. government. Dr. Jon Postel, a UCLA graduate student, developed the original list of host names and addresses while the Internet was a project of the Defense Communications Agency.[511] Dr. Postel's publication of the technical protocol for the Internet evolved into the Internet Assigned Numbers Authority (IANA). In the early 1990s, The National Science Foundation (NSF) developed connections between the government Internet (NSFNET) and commercial network services.

NSF awarded a contract to Network Solutions (NSI) to register domain names. National or country-codes TLDs were administered by governments or by

---

[508] Esther Dyson on Internet Privacy, C/Net News (Apr. 27, 2002), http://news.com.com/2009-1017-893537.html.

[509] Bruce J. McLaren, Understanding and Using the Internet 37, 38 (1997).

[510] ICANN, The Internet Corporation for Assigned Names and Numbers, New LTD Program (posted Nov. 16, 2000) (visited Apr. 28, 2002), http://www.icann.org/tlds/.

[511] United States Department of Commerce, Management of Internet Names and Addresses, National Telecommunications and Information Administration (visited Apr. 26, 2002) at 2, http://www.ntia.doc.gov/ntiahome/domainname/6_5_98dns.htm.

private entities. NSI administered the domain name registration for second-level domains (SLDs) which included .com (commercial), .org (not-for-profits), and .net (network service providers). By the mid-1990s, there was widespread dissatisfaction with the absence of competition in domain name registration.[512] As Internet domain names developed commercial value, conflicts between trademark holders and domain name holders reached an epidemic level.[513]

A United States Green Paper called for the creation of "a new private, not-for-profit corporation responsible for coordinating specific DNS functions for the benefit of the Internet as a whole."[514] The system of private competition called for competitive registrars. The Green Paper also called for the creation of new generic top-level domains (gTLDs). One of the most difficult issues was for the new entity to develop policies for the addition of new domains by consensus. Another difficulty was establishing a remedy for the misuse and abuse of domain names, such as when a trademark is used as a domain name without the trademark owner's consent.[515] Trademark owners had no practical remedy when a cybersquatter registered its trademark as a domain name, especially if the cybersquatter was located in an inconvenient jurisdiction.

A new entity was needed to offer the Internet community remedies for domain name misuse or abuse. On February 20, 1998, the National Telecommunications and Information Administration published for public comment a proposed rule regarding the domain name registration system.[516] The United States government worked with the World Intellectual Property Organization in developing a set of procedures for resolving trademark/domain name disputes.[517] During the transition from the NSI monopoly to competition in the domain name system, the Internet Assigned Numbers Authority (IANA), the NSF, and other entities worked cooperatively to assure a transition to control by a nonprofit entity.[518] The United States government relinquished control of the DNS in an agreement with the Internet Corporation for Assigned Names and Numbers (ICANN).[519]

The Internet domain name system is now administered by ICANN and the Internet Assigned Numbers Authority (IANA).[520] IANA staff members assign IP

---

[512] *Id.* at 5.

[513] *Id.*

[514] *Id.* at 8.

[515] *See* Barcelona.Com, Inc. v. Excelentisimo Ayuntamiento de Barcelona, 2002 WL 359759 (E.D.Va., 2002) (noting that "the process by which these domain names [i.e., first level domain name ".com"] are registered is almost completely automated. NSI's registration system does not check to see whether the domain name sought to be registered is subject to a trademark, nor does it check to see how similar the proposed domain name is to a previously registered domain name.").

[516] *Id.* at 17.

[517] *Id.* at 23.

[518] *Id.* at 23-25.

[519] The ICANN web site provides detailed information on the formation of the entity. *See* www.icann.org.

[520] Internet Corporation for Assigned Names and Numbers, Internet Assigned Numbers Authority, Internet Domain Name System Structure and Delegation (visited Apr. 28, 2002), http://

addresses, autonomous system numbers, top-level domains (TLDs), and manage the unique parameters of the DNS and its protocols.[521] IANA delegates the root or highest level of the domain name system to individual country managers. TLDs are divided into classes based on rules that have evolved over time. TLDs are designated by county-code top-level domains (ccTLDs). In addition, there are a limited number of "generic" top-level domains (gTLDs), which do not have a geographic or country designation. The domain name system was transferred to the Internet Corporation for Assigned Names and Numbers (ICANN) in 1999.

Network Solutions was once a quasi-public entity that administered all domain name registrations. ICANN was created as a nonprofit public sector corporation to serve the operational standards of the Internet. VeriSign, parent company of the domain name registrar Network Solutions, is only one of the ICANN-accredited registrars and remains a dominant domain name stakeholder because of its comprehensive database. Prior to the formation of ICANN, Network Solutions had a dispute resolution policy which placed domain names on hold if challenged by trademark owners.

Under Network Solutions' original dispute resolution policy, corporate plaintiffs who held registered trademarks could restrain a registrant's use of a domain name as long as the plaintiff could produce a trademark registration predating the domain name registration. The Network Solutions dispute resolution policy has been supplanted by the ICANN dispute resolution policy for trademark/domain name disputes. ICANN's board of directors adopted a dispute resolution policy applicable for all ICANN-accredited registrars in the .com, .net., and .org top-level domains.[522] ICANN utilizes a procedure partially online designed "to take less than 45 days and expected to cost about $1,000 in fees."[523] The attorney representing an online company can learn about ICANN and its activities by visiting the following web sites:

1. *www.icann.org*: ICANN's main web site;
2. *www.internic.net*: information on the domain name system, the domain name registration process, and domain name registrars
3. *www.iana.org*: the Internet Assigned Numbers Authority (IANA), which manages "top-level domains (including ccTLDs) within the Internet's domain name system" and oversees "the technical operation of the Internet's root-nameserver system"
4. *aso.icann.org*: ICANN's Address Supporting Organization (ASO), which "develops recommendations for global policies concerning allocation of IP addresses and autonomous system (AS) numbers"

---

www.icann.org/icp/icp-1.htm (summarizing practices of the Internet Assigned Number Authority (IANA)).

[521] *Id.*

[522] ICANN, The Internet Corporation for Assigned Names and Numbers, Frequently Asked Questions (FAQ), FAQ on Uniform Dispute Resolution Policy (posted Sept. 13, 1999) (visited Apr. 26, 2002), http://www.icann.org/general/faq1.htm.

[523] *Id.*

5. *dnso.icann.org*: ICANN's Domain Name Supporting Organization (DNSO), which "develops recommendations for global policies concerning the Internet's domain-name system (DNS)"

6. *forum.icann.org*: a "web-based forum for community comment on various ICANN-related topics"

7. *members.icann.org*: presently dormant

8. *www.pso.icann.org*: ICANN's Protocol Support Organization (PSO), which advises ICANN's board on the "assignment of parameters for Internet protocols"

[3] UDRP Domain Name Arbitration

[a] *Uniform Domain Name Dispute Resolution Policy (UDRP Policy)*

The e-business will register its domain name with an ICANN-accredited registrar. All ICANN-accredited registrars are required to follow a uniform dispute resolution policy (UDRP).[524] The UDRP resolves disputes over domain names by deferring to court resolution between the parties claiming conflicting rights to the registration. The UDRP requires the registrar to abide by a court ruling as to rights to a registration.[525] The UDRP policy provides an expedited administrative procedure to resolve disputes over abusive practices such as "cybersquatting" and cyberpiracy that permits the resolution of domain name disputes "without the cost and delays often encountered in court litigation."[526] If SPC learns that a domain name registrant is cybersquatting, it may file a complaint with a dispute-resolution service provider.[527] The dispute-resolution service providers are (1) the CPR Institute for Dispute Resolution, (2) the National Arbitration Forum, (3) the World Intellectual Property Organization, and (4) the Asian Domain Name Dispute Resolution Centre. The purpose of the UDRP policy is to "establish a uniform and mandatory administrative dispute-resolution system to address cases of bad faith cybersquatting."[528] Under the dispute policy, most trademark-based domain name

---

[524] The Uniform Dispute Resolution Policy is available at http://www.icann.org/udrp/udrp.htm. There were more than 4,500 cases filed under the UDRP Policy as of October 2001. Steven Bonisteel, WIPO Arbitrators Stern in Domain Hijacking Rulings, Newsbytes (Oct. 19, 2001), http://www.newsbytes.com/news/01/171338.html.

[525] ICANN, "Frequently Asked Questions About Domain Name Registration (visited Dec. 3, 2001), http://www.icann.org/general/faq1.htm.

[526] *Id.*

[527] ICANN, Approved Providers for Uniform Dispute Resolution Policy (visited Dec. 3, 2001), http://www.icann.org/udrp/approved-providers.htm.

[528] WIPO Press Release, First Cybersquatting Case Under WIPO Process Just Concluded, PR/2000/204 (Jan. 14, 2000) (visited Apr. 14, 2002), http://www.wipo.org/eng/pressrel/2000/p204.htm.

disputes are resolved by agreement, court action, or arbitration before a registrar cancels, suspends, or transfers a domain name.[529]

The Uniform Domain Name Dispute Resolution Policy (UDRP Policy), the Rules for Uniform Domain Name Dispute Resolution Policy (UDRP Rules), and the Supplemental Rules for Providers are posted at *http://icann.org*.[530] The UDRP "Policy is between the registrar (or other registration authority in the case of a country-code top-level domain) and its customer (the domain-name holder or registrant)."[531]

The UDRP Domain Name Dispute Resolution Policy has been "adopted by all accredited domain-name registrars for domain names ending in .com, .net, and .org. It has also been adopted by certain managers of country-code top-level domains (e.g., .nu, .tv, .ws)."[532] The UDRP proceedings are less expensive than a federal court proceeding. However, federal courts have the power to award statutory damages and attorney's fees, whereas UDRP proceedings have only the limited power to transfer or cancel domain name registrations, and such transfers or cancellations can be appealed in federal court.[533]

The UDRP Policy is incorporated into all Registration Agreements and sets the terms and conditions of any dispute between a customer and a third party. Registrants warrant that information on domain name registrations is "complete and accurate."[534] Registrants also warrant that the "registration of the domain name will not infringe upon or otherwise violate the rights of any third party."[535] In addition, registrants must represent that they are "not registering the domain name for any unlawful purpose" or using the domain name in violation of any applicable laws or regulations.[536]

A registrar is permitted to cancel, transfer, or change a domain name registration upon "receipt of written or appropriate electronic instructions from the customer or agent."[537] Registrars do not appear in any administrative proceeding and "do not participate in the administration or conduct of any proceeding before an Administrative Panel."[538] In addition, a domain name registration may be can-

---

[529] ICANN, Uniform Domain Name Dispute Resolution Policy (visited Feb. 10, 2000), http://www.icann.org/udrp/udrp.htm.

[530] The implementation scheduled for the UDRP policy is posted at www.icann.org/udrp/udrp-schedule.htm. The material in this section is largely drawn from ICANN, Uniform Domain Name Dispute Resolution Policy. For the complete UDRP Policy and rules, *see* http://www.icann.org/udrp/udrp-policy-24oct99.htm.

[531] *See* ICANN, Notes to Uniform Domain Name Dispute Resolution Policy, Implementation Document Approved Oct. 24, 1999 (hereinafter UDRP Policy).

[532] *Id.* at n.2.

[533] *See generally* Christopher F. Schulte, The New Anticybersquatting Law and Uniform Dispute Resolution Policy for Domain Names, 36 Tort & Ins. L.J. 101 (2000) (comparing advantages of UDRP proceedings to federal court litigation); *see also* Tamara Loomis, Domain Names: Disputes Get Swift Resolution Under UDRP, N.Y.L.J. (July 27, 2000) at 5.

[534] UDRP Policy, ¶ 2.

[535] *Id.*

[536] *Id.*

[537] UDRP Policy, ¶ 3.

[538] UDRP Policy, ¶ 4(h).

celled, transferred, or otherwise changed by an "order from a court or arbitral tribune."[539] In addition, changes may be made to a domain name registration in accordance with the terms of the Registration Agreement.[540] Registrants are required to "submit to a mandatory administrative proceeding conducted before an administrative-dispute-resolution service provider."[541]

Mandatory arbitration is normally triggered by complaints by third parties to a Provider that a registrant's "domain name is identical or confusingly similar to a trademark or service mark in which the complainant has rights."[542] The complainant must prove three elements in the administrative proceeding: (1) the registrant's domain name is identical or confusingly similar to the trademark or service mark in which the complainant has rights; (2) the registrant has no rights or legitimate interests in respect of the domain name; and (3) the domain name has been registered and is being used in bad faith.[543] The key element causing a domain name to be cancelled or transferred in a UDRP proceeding is the registrant's bad faith in the registration and use of a domain name.[544]

Evidence of registration and use in bad faith includes (1) "[if the registrant] acquired the domain name primarily for the purpose of selling, renting, or otherwise transferring the domain name registration to the complainant who is the owner of the trademark or service mark or to a competitor of that complainant, for valuable consideration in excess of documented out-of-pocket costs directly related to the domain name"; (2) registration of a domain name in order to prevent the owner of the trademark or service mark from reflecting the mark in a domain name; (3) registration of a domain name for the purpose of disrupting or interfering with a competitor's business; and (4) using a domain name to divert Internet users to the defendant's web site by creating a likelihood of confusion or implied endorsement.[545]

A domain name registered with the intent to profit indicates cybersquatting. The ownership of multiple domain names containing famous trademarks owned by others strongly indicates bad faith. UDRP panels have issued opinions that resolved the "reverse hijacking" of domain names. The panels found that Nestle and Aspen Grove were found to be trying to "reverse hijack" Internet addresses.[546] Both companies had claimed that the owners of the two Internet addresses were cybersquatters, but the arbitrators disagreed.[547] The Panel for Nestle held that Nestle "avoided the whole story by "fail[ing] to even mention [the owner's] alleged personal interest in the Domain Name," which was a legitimate personal interest;

---

[539] UDRP Policy, ¶ 3(b).

[540] UDRP Policy, ¶ 3(c).

[541] UDRP Policy, ¶ 4.

[542] UDRP Policy, ¶ 4(a)(i).

[543] UDRP Policy, ¶ 4(b).

[544] Id.

[545] UDRP Policy, ¶ 4(b)(I) (iv).

[546] Steven Bonisteel, WIPO Arbitrators Stern in Domain Hijacking Rulings, Newsbytes (Oct. 19, 2001), http://www.newsbytes.com/news/01/171338.html.

[547] Id.

therefore Nestle acted in bad faith.[548] The Panel for Aspen held that the owners of the Internet address had registered the address two years before Aspen Grove formed its business, and thus it could not have registered it in bad faith and Aspen Grove had no trademark rights in the address.[549]

The best defense to a complaint in an administrative proceeding frequently turns on demonstrating a legitimate interest or right to the domain name.[550] A defendant's use of or preparations to use a domain name to sell goods or offer services prior to the notice of the dispute demonstrate a legitimate interest.[551] Evidence of rights may also be established by proof that an individual or entity is known by its domain name even in the absence of trademark or service mark rights.[552] One WIPO arbitrator even held that there was a "general, legitimate interest in allowing citizens to use descriptive names to publish criticism about their government" after deciding that a citizen could retain the use of two Internet addresses, *DorsetPolice.com* and *DorsetPolice.net*, to "expose alleged police corruption."[553] Defendants may also have a fair use defense where there is no intent for commercial gain.[554]

The complainant submits its complaint directly to the Provider, not the respondent. The selected provider administers the proceeding and has general authority to consolidate multiple cases between the parties.[555] Arbitration fees are paid by the complainant for single arbitrator panels.[556] If the respondent requests three panelists on the panel, then the fees are split between the parties.[557] The median filing fee is $1,500 and varies depending on whether there is a single complaint involving one domain name and the size of the panel.[558] Of course, the fees do not include the attorney's fee if the complainant retains counsel to file a complaint or respond to proceedings. Even with attorneys' fees, the UDRP proceedings are far less expensive than litigation in federal courts or in a foreign court.[559] Fee schedules are available at the web sites of the UDRP providers' web sites.[560]

---

[548] WIPO Arbitration and Mediation Center, Administrative Panel Decision, Societe des Produits Nestle S.A. v. Pro Fiducia Treuhand AG, Case No. D2001-0916.

[549] WIPO Arbitration and Mediation Center, Administrative Panel Decision, Aspen Grove Inc v. Aspen Grove, Case No. D2001-0798.

[550] UDRP Policy, ¶ 4(c).

[551] UDRP Policy, ¶ 4(c)(i).

[552] UDRP Policy, ¶ 4(c)(ii).

[553] Steven Bonisteel, Cops' Critics Can Keep Dorset Police Domain Names, Newsbytes (Oct. 25, 2001), http://www.newsbytes.com/news/01/171529.html.

[554] UDRP Policy, ¶ 4(c)(iii).

[555] UDRP Policy, ¶ 4(c)(f).

[556] UDRP Policy, ¶ 4(g).

[557] Id.

[558] One commentator noted that UDRP fees "range from $750 to $4,500, depending on the provider and panel size and fee." See Steve Jarvis, ICANN Sets Rules for Resolving Disputes, Marketing News ™ (Oct. 23, 2000) at 5.

[559] Total costs including attorneys' fees "should not exceed the mid-to-high four figures." UDRP Policy, ¶ 4.

[560] See, e.g., World Intellectual Property Organization site at http://www.arbiter.wipo.int. See also The National Arbitration Forum at http://www.arbforum.com, eResolution Consortium at

The Provider will notify the Registrar of a decision made by an Administrative Panel, and the decisions are published on the Internet.[561]

ICANN's mandatory arbitration proceedings do not preclude the trademark holder from filing an action in federal court seeking redress for cybersquatting or other domain name issues.[562] Unlike the previous dispute resolution policly, the UDRP has no provision for injunctive relief which enjoins, cancels, transfers, activates, deactivates, or otherwise enjoins a domain name registration until a dispute is resolved.[563] Neither party may transfer a domain name to a new holder during a pending administrative proceeding.[564] Similarly, the domain name registrant may not switch to another registrar during a pending administrative proceeding. Finally, the policy may be modified at any time by a Registrar and the sole remedy for the registrant is cancellation of the domain name.[565]

[b] Rules for Uniform Domain Name Resolution Policy (UDRP Rules)

The UDRP administrative proceeding is initiated by the complainant (trademark holder) against the respondent (domain name registrant).[566] The administrative proceedings are governed by the UDRP Rules and the Supplemental Rules of the Provider (or dispute resolution panel).[567] Providers are permitted to supplement UDRP as long as the supplemental rules are not inconsistent with the policy. Each provider's supplemental rules cover "topics such as fees, word and page limits [of complaints] and guidelines, and the means for communicating with the Provider."[568] It is the duty of the provider to achieve actual notice with the respondent in a domain name dispute. Rule 2 of the UDRP Policy states that:

> (a) When forwarding a complaint to the Respondent, it shall be the Provider's responsibility to employ reasonably available means calculated to

---

http://www.eresolution.ca, and the CPR Institute for Dispute Resolution Inc., at http://www.cpradr.org. A list of providers is available at www.icann.org/udrp/approved-providers.htm.

[561] UDRP Policy, ¶ 4(j).

[562] UDRP Policy, ¶ 5.

[563] UDRP Policy, ¶ 7.

[564] UDRP Policy, ¶ 8

[565] UDRP Policy, ¶ 9.

[566] UDRP Policy, ¶ 3.

[567] The four authorized providers are (1) the World Intellectual Property Organization, (2) the National Arbitration Forum, (3) Disputes.org/eResolution Consortium, and (4) CPR Institute for Dispute Resolution, Inc. See Steve Jarvin, ICANN Sets Rules for Resolving Disputes, Marketing News (Oct. 23, 2000) at 5. Each provider develops its own roster of panels — "judges, corporate lawyers or academics, for example — and they are all trained and authorized by ICANN as UDRP experts." Id.

[568] Preamble to Rules for Uniform Domain Name Dispute Resolution Policy (visited May 15, 2001), http://www.icann.org/udrp/udrp-rules-24oct99.htm.

achieve actual notice to Respondent. Achieving actual notice, or employing the following measures to do so, shall discharge this responsibility:

> (i) sending the complaint to all postal-mail and facsimile addresses (A) shown in the domain name's registration data in Registrar's Whois database for the registered domain-name holder, the technical contact, and the administrative contact and (B) supplied by Registrar to the Provider for the registration's billing contact; and
>
> (ii) sending the complaint in electronic form (including annexes to the extent available in that form) by e-mail to:
>
>> (A) the e-mail addresses for those technical, administrative, and billing contacts;
>>
>> (B) postmaster@<the contested domain name>; and
>>
>> (C) if the domain name (or "www." followed by the domain name) resolves to an active web page (other than a generic page the Provider concludes is maintained by a registrar or ISP for parking domain-names registered by multiple domain-name holders), any e-mail address shown or e-mail links on that web page; and
>
> (iii) sending the complaint to any address the Respondent has notified the Provider it prefers and, to the extent practicable, to all other addresses provided to the Provider by Complainant under *Paragraph 3(b)(v)*.[569]

Rule 3 of the UDRP policy states that the administrative procedure is triggered "by submitting a complaint in accordance with the Policy and these Rules to any Provider approved by ICANN."[570] Complaints are submitted in hard copy and electronic form.[571] The properly drafted UDRP complaint is required to contain the following:

> (i) Request that the complaint be submitted for decision in accordance with the Policy and these Rules;
>
> (ii) Provide the name, postal and e-mail addresses, and the telephone and telefax numbers of the Complainant and of any representative authorized to act for the Complainant in the administrative proceeding;
>
> (iii) Specify a preferred method for communications directed to the Complainant in the administrative proceeding (including person to be contacted, medium, and address information) for each of (A) electronic-only material and (B) material including hard copy;
>
> (iv) Designate whether Complainant elects to have the dispute decided by a single-member or a three-member Panel and, in the event Complainant elects a three-member Panel, provide the names and contact details of three candidates to serve as one of the Panelists (these candidates may be drawn from any ICANN-approved Provider's list of panelists);

---

[569] UDRP Policy, ¶ 2.
[570] UDRP Policy, ¶ 3.
[571] *Id.*

(v) Provide the name of the Respondent (domain-name holder) and all information (including any postal and e-mail addresses and telephone and tele-fax numbers) known to Complainant regarding how to contact Respondent or any representative of Respondent, including contact information based on pre-complaint dealings, in sufficient detail to allow the Provider to send the com-plaint as described in *Paragraph 2(a)*;

(vi) Specify the domain name(s) that is/are the subject of the complaint;

(vii) Identify the Registrar(s) with whom the domain name(s) is/are reg-istered at the time the complaint is filed;

(viii) Specify the trademark(s) or service mark(s) on which the com-plaint is based and, for each mark, describe the goods or services, if any, with which the mark is used (Complainant may also separately describe other goods and services with which it intends, at the time the complaint is submit-ted, to use the mark in the future.);

(ix) Describe, in accordance with the Policy, the grounds on which the complaint is made including, in particular,

(1) the manner in which the domain name(s) is/are identical or confusingly similar to a trademark or service mark in which the Com-plainant has rights; and

(2) why the Respondent (domain-name holder) should be consid-ered as having no rights or legitimate interests in respect of the domain name(s) that is/are the subject of the complaint; and

(3) why the domain name(s) should be considered as having been registered and being used in bad faith

(The description should, for elements (2) and (3), discuss any aspects of *Para-graphs 4(b)* and *4(c)* of the Policy that are applicable. The description shall com-ply with any word or page limit set forth in the Provider's Supplemental Rules.);

(x) Specify, in accordance with the Policy, the remedies sought;

(xi) Identify any other legal proceedings that have been commenced or terminated in connection with or relating to any of the domain name(s) that are the subject of the complaint;

(xii) State that a copy of the complaint, together with the cover sheet as prescribed by the Provider's Supplemental Rules, has been sent or transmitted to the Respondent (domain-name holder), in accordance with *Paragraph 2(b)*;

(xiii) State that Complainant will submit, with respect to any challenges to a decision in the administrative proceeding canceling or transferring the domain name, to the jurisdiction of the courts in at least one specified Mutual Jurisdiction;

(xiv) Conclude with the following statement followed by the signature of the Complainant or its authorized representative:

"Complainant agrees that its claims and remedies concerning the regis-tration of the domain name, the dispute, or the dispute's resolution shall be solely against the domain-name holder and waives all such claims and remedies against (a) the dispute-resolution provider and panelists, except in the case of deliberate wrongdoing, (b) the registrar, (c) the reg-istry administrator, and (d) the Internet Corporation for Assigned Names and Numbers, as well as their directors, officers, employees, and agents."

"Complainant certifies that the information contained in this Complaint is to the best of Complainant's knowledge complete and accurate, that this Complaint is not being presented for any improper purpose, such as to harass, and that the assertions in this Complaint are warranted under these Rules and under applicable law, as it now exists or as it may be extended by a good-faith and reasonable argument;" and

(xv) Annex any documentary or other evidence, including a copy of the Policy applicable to the domain name(s) in dispute and any trademark or service mark registration upon which the complaint relies, together with a schedule indexing such evidence.[572]

Complaints may cover more than one name as long as "the domain names are registered by the same domain-name holder."[573] Complaints are submitted to providers who conduct a first level of review to determine whether the complaint complies with the UDRP policy and the rules. A Provider reviews a complaint for administrative compliance with the Policy and these Rules. If the complaint complies with the Rules, the Provider (in compliance with UDRP Policy) "shall forward the complaint (together with the explanatory cover sheet prescribed by the Provider's Supplemental Rules) to the Respondent . . . within 3 calendar days following receipt of the fees to be paid by the Complainant in accordance with *Paragraph 19*."[574]

"If a Provider determines that a Complaint is defective, it notifies both parties of the nature of deficiencies identified."[575] The Complainant (Plaintiff in Administrative Proceeding) has five (5) calendar days within which to correct any such deficiencies. If the deficiencies in the complaint have not been corrected, the administrative proceeding will be deemed withdrawn without prejudice to submission of a different complaint by Complainant. An administrative proceeding commences on the date a complaint is forwarded to the Respondent. Upon commencement of the proceeding, the following are notified: "the Complainant, the Respondent, the concerned Registrar(s), and ICANN."[576] The Respondent has 20 days after commencement of the administrative proceedings to respond to the Provider.[577] Under UDRP's Rules, the complaint as well as the response are submitted in hard copy as well as electronic form. The Response requires the defendant to:

(i) Respond specifically to the statements and allegations contained in the complaint and include any and all bases for the Respondent (domain-name holder) to retain registration and use of the disputed domain name (This portion of the response shall comply with any word or page limit set forth in the Provider's Supplemental Rules.);

---

[572] UDRP Policy, ¶ 3, (b)(i)-(xv).

[573] *Id.*

[574] *Id.*

[575] UDRP Policy, ¶ 4(b).

[576] *Id.*

[577] UDRP Policy, ¶ 4(c).

(ii) Provide the name, postal and e-mail addresses, and the telephone and telefax numbers of the Respondent (domain-name holder) and of any representative authorized to act for the Respondent in the administrative proceeding;

(iii) Specify a preferred method for communications directed to the Respondent in the administrative proceeding (including person to be contacted, medium, and address information) for each of (A) electronic-only material and (B) material including hard copy;

(iv) If Complainant has elected a single-member panel in the Complaint (see *Paragraph 3(b)(iv)*), state whether Respondent elects instead to have the dispute decided by a three-member panel;

(v) If either Complainant or Respondent elects a three-member Panel, provide the names and contact details of three candidates to serve as one of the Panelists (these candidates may be drawn from any ICANN-approved Provider's list of panelists);

(vi) Identify any other legal proceedings that have been commenced or terminated in connection with or relating to any of the domain name(s) that are the subject of the complaint;

(vii) State that a copy of the response has been sent or transmitted to the Complainant, in accordance with *Paragraph 2(b)*; and

(viii) Conclude with the following statement followed by the signature of the Respondent or its authorized representative:

"Respondent certifies that the information contained in this Response is to the best of Respondent's knowledge complete and accurate, that this Response is not being presented for any improper purpose, such as to harass, and that the assertions in this Response are warranted under these Rules and under applicable law, as it now exists or as it may be extended by a good-faith and reasonable argument."; and

(ix) Annex any documentary or other evidence upon which the Respondent relies, together with a schedule indexing such documents.

(c) If Complainant has elected to have the dispute decided by a single-member Panel and Respondent elects a three-member Panel, Respondent shall be required to pay one-half of the applicable fee for a three-member Panel as set forth in the Provider's Supplemental Rules. This payment shall be made together with the submission of the response to the Provider. In the event that the required payment is not made, the dispute shall be decided by a single-member Panel.

(d) At the request of the Respondent, the Provider may, in exceptional cases, extend the period of time for the filing of the response. The period may also be extended by written stipulation between the Parties, provided the stipulation is approved by the Provider.

(e) If a Respondent does not submit a response, in the absence of exceptional circumstances, the Panel shall decide the dispute based upon the complaint.[578]

The arbitrators are chosen according to the following rules:

---

[578] UDRP Policy, ¶ 5(a).

(a) Each Provider shall maintain and publish a publicly available list of panelists and their qualifications.

(b) If neither the Complainant nor the Respondent has elected a three-member Panel (*Paragraphs 3(b)(iv) and 5(b)(iv)*), the Provider shall appoint, within five (5) calendar days following receipt of the response by the Provider, or the lapse of the time period for the submission thereof, a single Panelist from its list of panelists. The fees for a single-member Panel shall be paid entirely by the Complainant.

(c) If either the Complainant or the Respondent elects to have the dispute decided by a three-member Panel, the Provider shall appoint three Panelists in accordance with the procedures identified in *Paragraph 6(e)*. The fees for a three-member Panel shall be paid in their entirety by the Complainant, except where the election for a three-member Panel was made by the Respondent, in which case the applicable fees shall be shared equally between the Parties.

(d) Unless it has already elected a three-member Panel, the Complainant shall submit to the Provider, within five (5) calendar days of communication of a response in which the Respondent elects a three-member Panel, the names and contact details of three candidates to serve as one of the Panelists. These candidates may be drawn from any ICANN-approved Provider's list of panelists.

(e) In the event that either the Complainant or the Respondent elects a three-member Panel, the Provider shall endeavor to appoint one Panelist from the list of candidates provided by each of the Complainant and the Respondent. In the event the Provider is unable within five (5) calendar days to secure the appointment of a Panelist on its customary terms from either Party's list of candidates, the Provider shall make that appointment from its list of panelists. The third Panelist shall be appointed by the Provider from a list of five candidates submitted by the Provider to the Parties, the Provider's selection from among the five being made in a manner that reasonably balances the preferences of both Parties, as they may specify to the Provider within five (5) calendar days of the Provider's submission of the five-candidate list to the Parties.

(f) Once the entire Panel is appointed, the Provider shall notify the Parties of the Panelists appointed and the date by which, absent exceptional circumstances, the Panel shall forward its decision on the complaint to the Provider.[579]

Panelists must represent to the Provider that they are "impartial and independent and shall have, before accepting appointment, disclosed to the Provider any circumstances giving rise to justifiable doubt as to the Panelist's impartiality or independence."[580] The panelist has a responsibility to disclose to the Provider "any new circumstances arise that could give rise to justifiable doubt as to the impartiality or independence" during the pendency of the proceeding to promptly disclose such circumstances to the Provider. The Provider "has the discretion to

---

[579] UDRP Rules, ¶ 5(b)(I)-(ix)(e).
[580] UDRP Policy, ¶ 6.

appoint a substitute Panelist."[581] The UDRP Rules prohibit ex parte communications between the parties and the panel. "No Party or anyone acting on its behalf may have any unilateral communication with the Panel. All communications between a Party and the Panel or the Provider shall be made to a case administrator appointed by the Provider in the manner prescribed in the Provider's Supplemental Rules."[582]

The complaint, response, and supporting documents ("the file") is forwarded to the panel after the last member is appointed.[583] The panel is given broad power to conduct the proceedings. The UDRP rules provide for broad standards of fairness rather than precise rules of procedure.[584] The UDRP rules for conducting the proceeding provide:

> (b) In all cases, the Panel shall ensure that the Parties are treated with equality and that each Party is given a fair opportunity to present its case.
>
> (c) The Panel shall ensure that the administrative proceeding takes place with due expedition. It may, at the request of a Party or on its own motion, extend, in exceptional cases, a period of time fixed by these Rules or by the Panel.
>
> (d) The Panel shall determine the admissibility, relevance, materiality and weight of the evidence.
>
> (e) A Panel shall decide a request by a Party to consolidate multiple domain name disputes in accordance with the Policy and these Rules.[585]

The language of the proceeding is the language of the domain name registration. There is no provision for in-person hearings of any kind except "hearings by teleconference, videoconference, and web conference, unless the Panel determines, in its sole discretion and as an exceptional matter, that such a hearing is necessary for deciding the complaint."[586] Respondents not complying with time deadlines risk default and a summary disposition on the complaint.[587]

The UDRP rules for publishing decisions are as follows:

> (a) A Panel shall decide a complaint on the basis of the statements and documents submitted and in accordance with the Policy, these Rules and any rules and principles of law that it deems applicable.
>
> (b) In the absence of exceptional circumstances, the Panel shall forward its decision on the complaint to the Provider within fourteen (14) days of its appointment pursuant to Paragraph 6.
>
> (c) In the case of a three-member Panel, the Panel's decision shall be made by a majority.

---

[581] UDRP Policy, ¶ 7.
[582] *Id.*
[583] UDRP Policy, ¶ 8.
[584] UDRP Policy, ¶ 9.
[585] UDRP Policy, ¶ 10.
[586] *Id.*
[587] UDRP Policy, ¶ 13.

(d) The Panel's decision shall be in writing, provide the reasons on which it is based, indicate the date on which it was rendered and identify the name(s) of the Panelist(s).

(e) Panel decisions and dissenting opinions shall normally comply with the guidelines as to length set forth in the Provider's Supplemental Rules. Any dissenting opinion shall accompany the majority decision. If the Panel concludes that the dispute is not within the scope of *Paragraph 4(a)* of the Policy, it shall so state. If after considering the submissions the Panel finds that the complaint was brought in bad faith, for example in an attempt at Reverse Domain Name Hijacking or was brought primarily to harass the domain-name holder, the Panel shall declare in its decision that the complaint was brought in bad faith and constitutes an abuse of the administrative proceeding.[588]

Decisions are communicated to the parties from the Provider within three calendar days.[589] The Registrar then communicates "to each Party, the Provider, and ICANN the date for the implementation of the decision in accordance with the Policy."[590] The parties may agree to settle their domain name dispute and terminate the administrative proceeding prior to the panel's decision. If there are also legal proceedings initiated "prior to or during an administrative proceeding in respect of a domain-name dispute that is the subject of the complaint, the Panel shall have the discretion to decide whether to suspend or terminate the administrative proceeding, or to proceed to a decision."[591]

Most complainants prevail under the UDRP: over 80 percent of UDRP domain name disputes have been resolved in the complainant's favor.[592] Professor Milton Mueller's study of domain name arbitration proceedings concluded that the approved providers are unduly favoring trademark holders.[593] Mueller's 2000 study was based on the 2,166 proceedings involving 3,938 domain names decided in the first year of the implementation of the UDRP Policy and Rules.[594]

Still, the rate of complaints remains low. For every domain name registration dispute, approximately 3,500 new names are registered.[595] Professor Mueller found that the UDRP policy and rules are generally fair but there are systematic biases in the interpretation of the guidelines and a clause that permits forum shopping and complainant bias.[596] Another key finding of the Mueller study is that the World Intellectual Property Organization (WIPO) and the National Arbitration

---

[588] UDRP Policy, ¶ 15.

[589] UDRP Policy, ¶ 16.

[590] *Id.*

[591] UDRP Policy, ¶ 17.

[592] Summary of Proceedings Under Uniform Domain Name Dispute Resolution Policy (June 27, 2001), http://www.icann.org/udrp/proceedings-stat.htm.

[593] Milton Mueller, Rough Justice: An Analysis of ICANN's Uniform Dispute Resolution Policy (visited May 16, 2001), http://dcc.syr.edu/roughjustice.htm.

[594] *Id.* at 1.

[595] *Id.*

[596] *Id.* at 3.

Forum (NAF) attracted the vast majority of the complaints (61 and 31 percent, respectively).[597] Mueller explains that the low market share of cases going to eResolutions was the result of its greater likelihood of finding for defendants.[598]

Mueller recommends a change in ICANN policy that would allow domain name registrars rather than complainants to select the providers.[599] Respondents fared best under the E-Resolution provider, winning 41.9 percent of the cases versus only 16.6 percent under WIPO and 17.5 percent under NAF.[600] Another key finding was the time span between domain name registration and commencement of a UDRP proceeding. "The average UDRP challenge occurs 477 days after the name was registered."[601] Another interesting finding is that more than a third of respondents defaulted in the first year of proceedings.[602]

The first UDRP decision resulted in a ruling in favor of the World Wrestling Foundation (WWF) in a dispute over ownership of the domain name *worldwrestlingfederation.com*. The WWF commenced a proceeding with the WIPO provider under the UDRP against a California resident who registered the domain name and then offered to sell it to WWF for a large sum.[603] The panel ruled that the California registrant had acted in bad faith by offering to sell the domain name for a significant profit. In addition, the arbitrator found the domain name was confusingly similar to WWF's trademark and service mark. Finally, the respondent was found to have no legitimate interest or other rights in the domain name. The arbitrator ruled that the domain name be transferred to WWF.[604]

Personal names have been frequently at issue in domain name disputes. In another high-profile case, Mohamed Al Fayed, whose son Dodi was killed in a 1997 Paris car crash with Britain's Princess Diana, won control of the Internet domain name dodiaafayed.com.[605] WIPO's panel ruled that "Robert Boyd of Dayton, Ohio, who registered the domain and offered it for sale for $400,000 had no 'legitimate interest in the domain name.' "[606]

Companies considering UDRP proceedings will find a variety of practice forms on the web sites of UDRP providers. The NAF, for example, has an excellent library of model forms for UDRP complaints, complaint transmittal sheets,

---

[597] *Id.*

[598] Mueller praises Disputes.org/eResolutions of Canada for its careful following of the UDRP policy in contrast to WIPO panelists who frequently give a liberal interpretation of trademark rights. *See* News Release, Study Finds Bias in Internet Domain Name Dispute Resolution (visited May 16, 2001), http://dcc.syr.edu/udpnews.htm.

[599] *Id.* at 10.

[600] *Id.* at 11.

[601] *Id.* at 9.

[602] *Id.* at 11.

[603] Joe Borders, New Process Can Dislodge Cybersquatters, Texas Law. (Mar. 14, 2000) at 1.

[604] *See also* WIPO Arbritrators Deny Bruce Springsteen Right to Domain Name, 18 Computer & Online Indus. Litig. Rptr. 17 (Feb. 27, 2001).

[605] Reuters Inc., Dodi's Still His Father's Son, Mar. 17, 2000 (visited Mar. 17, 2000), http://www.wired.com/news/print/0,1294,35031,00.html.

[606] *Id.*

requests to withdraw complaints, model responses to complaints, response extension requests, pre-panel requests to withdraw complaints, joint requests to withdraw complaints, joint requests to stay administrative proceedings, and requests to remove stays of administrative proceedings.[607]

Famous performers, including Bruce Springsteen and Sting, were unsuccessful in UDRP actions to have their respective domain names transferred or cancelled.[608] The administrative panel in the Sting case held that although the name "Sting," an unregistered trademark, is world famous, and the complainant is known as such, "Sting" is also a common word in the English language and therefore it does not follow that he has rights in "Sting" as a trademark or service mark. The Administrative Panel ultimately held in favor of the respondent because Sting had failed to show that the domain name *www.sting.com* was registered or being used in bad faith. Similarly, the WIPO also held that the domain name *www.brucespringsteen.com* was not registered in bad faith by the owner of the web site *www.celebrity1000.com.* The panel espoused four nonexclusive circumstances in which bad faith may be shown:

(i)   Registrant obtained the domain name for the purpose of selling, renting, or otherwise transferring it to the legitimate owner of the mark or to a competitor;

(ii)   Registrant obtained the domain name in order to prevent the owner of the trademark or service mark from reflecting that mark in a corresponding domain name;

(iii) Registrant obtained the domain name primarily for the purpose of disrupting the business of a competitor;

(iv) The Registrant, by using the domain names, has intentionally attempted to attract for commercial gain, internet users to his web site or other online location, by creating a likelihood of confusion with the Complainant's mark as to the source, sponsorship, affiliation or endorsement of the web site or of a product or a service on the web site.[609]

In the Bruce Springsteen dispute, the panel noted that the registrant did not attempt to sell the domain name, nor did he prevent Bruce Springteen from registering a corresponding domain name as Mr. Springsteen's record company registered brucespringsteen.net and brucespringsteen.org in 1998. In addition, the panel went on to hold that an Internet user who searched for Bruce Springsteen would receive thousands of hits, and even if they did come across registrant's web site, they would soon realize that the site was not the official Bruce Springsteen site. The panel found no likelihood of confusion under the circumstances.

---

[607] *See* National Arbitration Forum, Dispute Resolution for Domain Names (visited May 15, 2001), http://www.arbforum.com/domains.

[608] *See* ICANN, Decisions in Proceedings Under the Uniform Domain-Name Dispute-Resolution Policy (visited Apr. 29, 2002), http://arbiter.wipo.int/domains/decisions/html/2000.

[609] *Id.*

[4] Anticybersquatting Consumer Protection Act of 1999

President Clinton signed the Anticybersquatting Consumer Protection Act of 1999 (ACPA) on November 29, 1999.[610] (See Table 4.7.) Part of an omnibus appropriations bill, ACPA was passed to deter the unauthorized registration or use of trademarks of others as Internet domain names. The Senate Committee Report stated that the bill was "to protect consumers and promote electronic commerce by amending certain trademark infringement, dilution and counterfeiting laws."[611] The Act is a response to the trafficking in domain names where there is a bad-faith intent to profit from the goodwill of another's marks.[612] The ACPA amends § 43 of the Trademark Act of 1946, 15 U.S.C. § 1125, and applies to domain names registered before, on, or after the date of enactment. The ACPA creates *in rem* jurisdiction over domain names that are registered in bad faith.

Cybersquatters register the trademark of another company for the purpose of selling it when the company seeks to develop a presence on the Internet. Congress enacted the Anticybersquatting Consumer Protection Act (ACPA) to deter this practice. To prove an ACPA violation, a plaintiff is required to prove (1) that the defendant had a bad faith intent to profit from using a domain name and (2) that the domain name was identical or confusingly similar to, or dilutive of, the distinctive and famous mark.[613] A violation of the ACPA occurs when someone "registers, traffics in, or uses a domain name that . . . is identical or confusingly similar" to a "famous" or "distinctive" mark and "has a bad faith intent to profit from that mark."[614] The ACPA lists nine nonexclusive factors to determine bad faith:

> (I) the trademark or other intellectual property rights of the person, if any, in the domain name;
>
> (II) the extent to which the domain name consists of the legal name of the person or a name that is otherwise commonly used to identify that person;
>
> (III) the person's prior use, if any, of the domain name in connection with the bona fide offering of any goods or ser vices;
>
> (IV) the person's bona fide noncommercial or fair use of the mark in a site accessible under the domain name;
>
> (V) the person's intent to divert consumers from the mark owner's online location to a site . . . that could harm the goodwill represented by the mark, either for commercial gain or with the intent to tarnish or disparage the mark . . .

---

[610] Congress passed S. 1948 (incorporated in H.R. 3194). The Anticybersquatting Act will create a new cause of action under § 43(d) of the Lanham Act, 15 U.S.C. § 1125(d) (2002).

[611] The Anticybersquatting Consumer Protection Act, Hearings on S. 1255 Before the Committee on the Judiciary, 106th Cong., 1st Sess. (1999).

[612] *Id.* at § 2.

[613] People for the Ethical Treatment of Animals v. Doughney, 263 F.3d 359 (4th Cir. 2001) (citing 15 U.S.C.S. § 1125(d)(1)(A)).

[614] Sporty's Farm, L.L.C. v. Sportsman's Market, Inc., 202 F.3d 489, 499 (2d Cir. 2000).

TABLE 4.7
Anticybersquatting Consumer Protection Act of 1999 (ACPA)

Who is defined as a cybersquatter?	A person who registers a domain name that "consists of the name of another living person, of a name substantially and confusingly similar thereto, without that person's consent, with the specific intent to profit from such name by selling the domain name for financial gain to that person or any third party, shall be liable in a civil action by such person." Section 47 of the ACPA; 15 U.S.C. § 1129(1)(a) (2000).
What is the test for bad-faith intent?	(1) Trademark or intellectual property rights of the person in the domain name; (2) extent to which the domain name consists of a legal name of the person or a name that is commonly used to identify that person; (3) person's prior use of the domain name for offering of goods and services; (4) person's noncommercial or fair use of the mark in a site accessible under domain name; (5) intent to divert consumers from the trademark owner's online location; (6) offer to transfer, sell, or assign domain name to the mark owner; (7) material and misleading false contact information; (8) registration and acquisition of multiple domain names identical or confusingly similar to the marks of others or to famous marks; and (9) extent to which the mark incorporated in the person's domain name registration is not distinctive and famous. 15 U.S.C. § 43(d)(1)(B).
Who is given cyberpiracy protection?	All entities or individual that own trademarks not just individuals with famous trademarks.
What damages and remedies are available?	An *in rem* remedy is available where the owner is not able to find a defendant after due diligence. The *in rem* remedy applies retroactively. *See* 15 U.S.C. § 1125(d)(2)(A) (2000). "A court may order the forfeiture or cancellation of the domain name or the transfer of the domain name to the owner of the mark."[a] The ACPA permits a plaintiff to "elect at any time before final judgment is rendered by the trial court, to recover, instead of actual damages and profits, an award of statutory damages in the amount of not less than $1,000 and not more than $100,000 per domain name, as the courts consider just."[b]
What defenses and limitations on liability are available?	In the event of good-faith registering of a domain name or name of another living person that is substantially or confusingly similar, the domain registry is not liable for monetary relief.

[a] 15 U.S.C. § 1125(d)(1)(C) (2002).

[b] If the plaintiff does not opt for statutory damages, the court may award damages under 15 U.S.C. § 117(a)(b) based on damages, profits, and the cost of the action. 15 U.S.C. § 1125(d)(1)(C) (2002).

(VI) the person's offer to transfer, sell, or otherwise assign the domain name to the mark owner or any third party for financial gain without having used . . . the domain name in the bona fide offering of any goods or services . . .

(VII) the person's provision of material and misleading false contact information when applying for the registration of the domain name . . .

(VIII) the person's registration or acquisition of multiple domain names which the person knows are identical or confusingly similar to marks of others . . . ; and

(IX) the extent to which the mark incorporated in the per son's domain name registration is or is not distinctive and famous.[615]

The determination of bad faith depends on the facts and circumstances of each case. The ACPA has a safe harbor in which bad faith cannot be found where the "person believed and had reasonable grounds to believe that the use of the domain name was a fair use or otherwise lawful."[616] The ACPA was intended to prevent "cybersquatting," an expression that has come to mean the bad faith, abusive registration, and use of the distinctive trademarks of others as Internet domain names, with the intent to profit from the goodwill associated with those trademarks. Under the ACPA, successful plaintiffs may recover statutory damages in an amount to be assessed by the district court in its discretion, from $1,000 to $100,000 per domain name, as well as attorneys' fees in "exceptional" cases.[617]

The Anticybersquatting Consumer Protection Act provides two avenues for suing a defendant in a trademark action. A trademark owner may proceed either *in personam* against an infringer, or in certain circumstances where this cannot be done, the owner may proceed *in rem* against the domain name; a mark owner may not proceed against both at the same time. A trademark owner may file an *in rem* cause of action only where a district court finds that the owner of the mark (1) is not able to obtain *in personam* jurisdiction over a person who would be a defendant in the action or (b) through due diligence is not able to locate the person who would be a defendant in the action.[618]

The *in rem* provisions of the ACPA allow, under limited circumstances, the owner of a federally registered trademark to sue the domain name directly. This provision may have been in response to the pre-ACPA dispute of *Porsche Cars North America, Inc. v. Porsche.com.*[619] In that case, Porsche, the owner of the

---

[615] 15 U.S.C. § 1125(d)(1)(B)(i) (2001).

[616] Domain Name Clearing Co., LLC v. F.C.F. Inc., 2001 U.S. App. LEXIS 15619 (4th Cir., July 12, 2001) (citing ACPA).

[617] 15 U.S.C.S. § 1117(a), (d); *see* Shields v. Zuccarini, 254 F.3d 476 (3d Cir. 2001).

[618] 15 U.S.C. § 1125(d)(2)(A)(i)-(ii); *see* Goldstein v. Gordon, 2002 U.S. Dist. Lexis 3348 (N.D. Tex. Feb. 27, 2002).

[619] Porsche Cars North Am., Inc. v. Porsche, 51 F. Supp. 2d 707 (D. Va. 1999) (dismissing federal antidilution action since the FTDA did not provide for *in rem* remedy). *See* Porsche Cars North Am., Inc. v. Porsche, 2000 U.S. App. 12843 (4th Cir. 2000) (applying ACPA's *in rem* remedy retroactively); *see also* Lucent Techs. v. Lucentsucks.Com, 95 F. Supp. 2d 528 (E.D. Va. 2000) (dismissing plaintiff's *in rem* action because personal jurisdiction was possible).

trademarks "Porsche" and "boxster," filed an action against 128 domain name owners claiming that they had diluted Porsche's famous trademarks. The actions were filed *in rem*, rather than as *in personam* actions against the registrants. The court observed that even if the federal antidilution act permitted *in rem* actions against domain name holders, such a procedure might be unconstitutional because there is no requirement of minimum contacts. In addition to the new *in rem* and injunctive remedies, the ACPA provides for statutory damages between $1,000 and $100,000 for each domain name that has been encroached by cybersquatters.[620]

The *in rem* remedy may only be sought in the judicial district in which the domain registry, registrar, or other domain authority is located. The Cable News Network (CNN), for example, filed an action against a Chinese firm in the district where Network Solutions was located. A Virginia federal court denied the defendant's motion to dismiss the *in rem* action, finding that the plaintiff satisfied the procedural requirements of the ACPA.[621] In contrast, in *Standing Stone Media, Inc. v.Indiancountrytoday.com*,[622] a media corporation sought *in rem* jurisdiction under the ACPA after a former employee registered, in his name, defendant Internet domain names in which the *corporation* asserted trademark ownership. The employee did not appear in the action or oppose the corporation's motion to transfer the name. Since there was no basis for personal jurisdiction, the corporation sought to establish *in rem* jurisdiction over the domain names.

The *Standing Stone* court found that *in rem* jurisdiction was limited to the judicial district in which the domain name registrar was located. The courts found that the plain meaning of the ACPA did not permit the *in rem* action to be filed in another district. The *Standing Stone* court, like all other courts, strictly construed the procedural requirements of the ACPA's *in rem* remedy.[4623]

Although the ACPA "does not explicitly address whether the alleged mark owner must disprove the existence of *in personam* jurisdiction over the defendant in any judicial district in the United States or only in the forum where the domain name registrar is located, courts have held that the alleged mark owner must show the absence of *in personam* jurisdiction in any judicial district in the United States."[624] If such a showing can be demonstrated, the ACPA statute provides an avenue for relief against foreign-resident cybersquatters.

Courts have carved out a number of limits to the exercise of *in rem* jurisdiction over an Internet domain name dispute under the ACPA. In *FleetBoston Financial Corp. v. FleetBostonFinancial.com*,[625] for example, a federal district court held that the ACPA did not provide for *in rem* jurisdiction except in the judicial

---

[620] *Id.*

[621] Cable News Network, L.P. v. CNNews.com, 162 F. Supp. 2d 484 (E.D. Va. 2001).

[622] 2002 U.S. Dist. LEXIS 4519 (N.D.N.Y. Mar. 20, 2002).

[623] *See also* Goldstein v. Gordon, 2002 U.S. Dist. Lexis 3348 (N.D. Tex. Feb. 27, 2002) (setting aside default judgment and invocation of *in rem* jurisdiction because of plaintiff's failure to show that personal jurisdiction was unavailing).

[624] *Id.*

[625] 2001 U.S. Dist. LEXIS 4797 (D. Mass., Mar. 27, 2001).

district in which the domain name registry, registrar, or other domain name was located.[626] In the *FleetBoston* case, a Rhode Island financial institution with offices in Boston brought an *in rem* action in the United States District Court for the District of Massachusetts against an Internet domain name that allegedly violated the financial institution's trademark.[627] In *Alitalia-Linee Aeree Italiane*,[628] a district court held that a mark owner may file an *in rem* cause of action only where the court finds that the owner of the mark was unable to obtain *personam* jurisdiction over a person who has been a defendant in a civil action under 15 U.S.C. § 1125(d)(1) (A), or through due diligence was not able to find a person who would have been a defendant under 15 U.S.C. § 1125(d)(2)(A).[629] In *Hartog & Co. v. Swix.com*,[630] a federal court refused to transfer a domain name that was confusingly similar to the plaintiff's mark because the plaintiff did not show bad faith on the defendant's part.

The ACPA has also been extended to international domain name disputes in *Barcelona.Com, Inc. v. Excelentisimo Ayuntamiento de Barcelona*.[631] Plaintiff Barcelona.Com is a U.S. corporation that registered the domain name *barcelona.com*. The City Council of Barcelona, Spain received a determination in a WIPO hearing that Barcelona.com infringed on the defendant's trademark *Barcelona*.[632] The U.S. company then appealed the determination, and the court determined that neither party had registered the trademark *Barcelona* in the United States or Spain. However, the city had registered trademarks that included the word *Barcelona*, which under Spanish law was sufficient to be considered a trademark of the defendant, as the dominant element of the mark was "Barcelona."[633] The U.S. court then concluded that

> [w]hen an individual registers a domain name on the Internet, the initial act of registration may take place within the United States, but the effects of such a registration can be felt worldwide. An Internet site registered in the United States can be viewed by anyone with Internet access anywhere in the world. Further, while the registration may be in the United States, a party need not be in the United States to actually register a domain name. Registration itself occurs over the Internet, thereby permitting an individual to register a U.S. domain name from anywhere in the world. It is untenable to suppose that Congress, aware of the fact that the Internet is so international in nature, only intended for U.S. trademarks to be protected under the Anticybersquatting statute. Indeed, the federal government established ICANN, which, in turn, authorized the World Intellectual Property Organization to resolve Internet

---

[626] *Id.*

[627] *Id.*

[628] 128 F. Supp. 2d 340 (E.D. Va. 2001).

[629] 2001 U.S. Dist. LEXIS 3568 (E.D. Va., Apr. 3, 2001) (refusing to permit *in rem* transfer of Internet domain name in absence of a showing of bad faith on defendant's part).

[630] 136 F. Supp. 2d 531 (E.D. Va. 2001).

[631] 2002 WL 359759 (E.D.Va. 2002).

[632] *Id.* at 2.

[633] *Id.* at 4.

domain name disputes. This authorization was granted, in part, precisely because of the international nature of these disputes. For these reasons, this Court is of the opinion that the Spanish trademark "Barcelona" is valid for purposes of the ACPA.[634]

The court set aside any question as to whether the ACPA applied to foreign trademarks, which had been a controversial issue up until this decision.[635] Since the defendant's mark would be protected in the United States, the WIPO panel needed to determine if there was bad faith involved in the registering of the domain name and whether confusion existed as to the trademark and the domain name. Bad faith was based upon evidence that the U.S. firm approached the city to purchase the domain name; that it was subsequently incorporated under the name Barcelona.Com, Inc.; that is was incorporated in Delaware, not Spain; and that it was a shell with no employees, separate bank accounts, rents, or even a telephone number.[636] The court also found that the domain name was confusingly similar to the trademark because the web site contained information regarding Barcelona, Spain; when it was viewed, the visitor would be confused into thinking it the official site for Barcelona, Spain.[637] The federal court refused to override the WIPO panel's decision, agreeing that there was possible consumer confusion.[638]

Sporty's Farm, LLC v. Sportsman's Market, Inc.[639] was the first appellate case considering the applicability of the ACPA. In that case, Sportsman's Market, Inc. was the owner of the Sporty's federal trademark. Sportsman's is a mail-order catalog company selling products tailored to aviation. Sportsman's used the logo "Sporty" to identify its catalogs and products. In 1985, Sportsman's registered the trademark Sporty's with the USPTO. Sporty's was used on the cover of Sportsman's catalogs, and Sportsman's spent $10 million per year advertising its Sporty's logo.

Sporty's Farm sold Christmas trees and advertised its trees on a *sportys.com* web page. Sporty's Farm filed suit seeking a declaratory judgment that it owned the domain name *sportys.com*. The federal district court determined that Sporty's was distinctive as well as a famous trademark and that Sporty's Farm's use of *sportys.com* diluted the famous mark owned by Sportsman's. The lower court found no infringement, however, since Sportsman's and Sporty's Farms were in different lines of business. While the appeal was pending, President Clinton signed the federal ACPA. The Second Circuit ruled that the ACPA applied, not the FTDA,

---

[634] *Id.* at 5.

[635] Steven Bonisteel, U.S. Court Stakes Out New Turf in Barcelona.com Ruling, Newsbytes (Mar. 2, 2002), http://www.newsbytes.com/news/02/174913.html.

[636] 2002 WL 359759 at *7.

[637] *Id.* at *8.

[638] *Id.*

[639] 202 F.3d 489 (2d Cir. 2000).

and ordered the transfer of the sportys.com domain name to Sportsman's Market, finding it to be distinctive and declining to rule on whether it was famous.

In *Shields v. Zuccarini*,[640] a court found that a wholesaler of Internet domain names was liable under the ACPA. The plaintiff registered *www.joecartoon.com* as his web site and sold Joe Cartoon merchandise. The defendant in *Zuccarini* registered five World Wide Web variations on the plaintiff's site: *joescartoon.com*, *joecarton.com*, *joescartons.com*, *joescartoons.com*, and *cartoonjoe.com*. Zuccarini has been the defendant in at least 60 cybersquatting cases arising out of his bad faith or abusive registrations of domain names of famous trademark owners. He is the most notorious "typo-squatter" for his registration of dozens of misspelled versions of names of famous trademarks.[641] Recently, he was named as a defendant in a case in which he allegedly registered 41 different versions of "Britney Spears" and 15 variations of "cartoonnetwork." It is estimated that Zuccarini has registered 5,500 copycat web domain names.[642] But because all he needs to "operate this entire scheme [is] a laptop . . . and an Internet connection," he continues his bad-faith practices.[643] The Federal Trade Commission plans to make Zuccarini pay back the estimated $800,000 to $1 million he earned from his scheme.[644] The defendant "mousetrapped" web visitors seeking the plaintiff's site *http://www.joecartoon.com*. A mousetrap does not permit the visitor to exit without clicking through a succession of ads. The defendant received between 10 and 25 cents from the advertisers for each click. The court issued a preliminary injunction against the defendant's site based on the ACPA. The court found the defendant's domain mark to be confusingly similar to the plaintiff's domain name. The court also found that the defendant intended to profit from the plaintiff's distinctive and famous mark, Joe Cartoon. The court ordered the defendant to deactivate the infringing domain names.

Harvard University brought suit against a domain name entrepreneur who registered 55 domain names relating to the Harvard and Radcliffe trademarks.[645] Harvard received an e-mail from a principal officer of Web-Pro offering to sell the university domain names incorporating the Harvard and Radcliffe trademarks. Harvard charged Web-Pro with federal trademark cyberpiracy, trademark infringement, unfair competition, and trademark dilution under the Lanham Act, as well as trademark dilution, unfair methods of competition, and deceptive practices and unfair competition under Massachusetts state law. Harvard charged the defendant

---

[640] 2000 U.S. Dist. LEXIS 3350 (E.D. Pa., Mar. 22, 2000).

[641] Brian Krebs, FTC Cracks Down on Porn Site "Mousetrapping," Newsbytes (Oct. 01, 2001), http://www.newsbytes.com/news/01/170695.html.

[642] *Id.*

[643] Reuters, FTC Shutters Thousands of Web Sites, C/Net News (Oct. 01, 2001), http://www.news.cnet.com/news/0-1005-200-7371736.html.

[644] *Id.*

[645] Harvard Uses Cybersquatting Law for Infringement Suit, E-Commerce Law Weekly, Dec. 1999 (reporting on President and Fellows of Harvard College v. Michael Rhys, No. 99CV12489RCL (D. Mass., filed Dec. 6, 1999).

with "willfully adopting, registering, maintaining and offering to sell or license numerous Internet domain names incorporating these marks."[646]

The First Circuit decided a case that involved a conflict between the ACPA and the World Intellectual Property Organization (WIPO) dispute resolution procedures under the UDRP.[647] The court was asked to intercede in a dispute between Jay D. Sallen, a resident of Brookline, Massachusetts, and Corinthians Licenciamentos LTDA, a Brazilian corporation, over Sallen's registration and use of the domain name *corinthians.com.* Sallen had lost the right to use the domain name in a WIPO dispute resolution proceeding that declared him a cybersquatter. The issue before the court was whether the finding of the UDRP panel precluded Sallen from seeking a declaratory judgment that he was not in violation of the ACPA. The case raised the issue of whether a domain name registrant, who has lost in a WIPO-adjudicated UDRP proceeding, may bring an action in federal court under § 1114(2)(D)(v) seeking to override the result of the earlier WIPO proceeding.

The district court held that federal courts lack jurisdiction over such claims, but the First Circuit reversed, holding that there was federal jurisdiction over such claims. The First Circuit found that the ACPA provided that a registrant whose domain name has been "suspended, disabled, or transferred" may sue for a declaration that the registrant is not in violation of the act and for an injunction returning the domain name.[648] The court found Sallen to be a registrant, his domain name transferred by a prior UDRP proceeding, and declaratory relief available to determine whether the ACPA statutory provision afforded relief such as a return of his domain name.[649]

In another case, Mattel, the owner of numerous trademarks, including the word *Barbie,* brought suit against a defendant who had registered the domain names *barbiesbeachwear.com* and *barbiesclothing.com.* Neither site was the destination site; each redirected the user to another web site not including the word *Barbie.*[650] Since Barbie is a famous trademark, the court found that both web sites caused dilution to Mattel's trademark.[651]

After balancing the nine factors used to determine bad faith, the court also found that the defendant registered the name in bad faith, even though the defendant claimed he registered the web sites for use as parody. The court disagreed because the defendant made the destination web site its retail web site.[652]

The web site Greatdomains, which traffics in domain names, was sued for cybersquatting, trademark dilution, and trademark infringement. In *Ford Motor*

---

[646] Harvard seeks to restrain Web-Pro from using domain names or offering them for sale. The domain names that were the subject of the litigation included: *www.harvard-lawschool.com, www.harvarddivinity.com, www.harvardgraduateschool.com,* and *www.radcliffecollege.com.*

[647] Sallen v. Corinthians Licenciamentos Ltd., 2001 U.S. App. LEXIS 25965 (1st Cir. Dec. 5, 2001).

[648] *Id.* (citing 15 U.S.C. § 1114(2)(D)(v)).

[649] *Id.*

[650] Mattel, Inc. v. Adventure Apparel, 2001 U.S. Dist. LEXIS 13885, 2-3 (S.D.N.Y 2001).

[651] *Id.* at 7.

[652] *Id.* at 12.

Co. v. Greatdomains.com Inc.[653] a federal district court dismissed all claims, finding no violation of either the ACPA or Lanham Act for offering domains for sale. The court found that Greatdomains had not registered any of the domain names, and the ACPA requires that the defendant be a domain name registrant or that registrant's authorized licensee.[654] The court also found that a web site that warehoused, trafficked, and registered domain names did not violate the Federal Trademark Dilution Act since these activities did not constitute the use of trademarks in connection with goods or services. The court rejected a claim that a site that auctioned domain names had contributory liability under the ACPA absent evidence that the auction site knew about the infringement. The court ruled that the trademark owners must show that the "'cyber-landlord' knew or should have known that its vendors had no legitimate reason for having registered the disputed domain names in the first place."[655] Finally, the court refused to dismiss ACPA claims against individual defendant registrants selling their names on Greatdomains, ruling that the plaintiff had set forth a prima facie case of bad faith and intent to profit.[656]

[5] Domain Name Caselaw

Domain name disputes are litigated under diverse causes of action, including (1) federal trademark infringement, (2) federal trademark dilution, (3) state dilution, and (4) other state common law causes of action.

[a] Infringement

A Massachusetts federal district court found the use of the domain name *energyplace.com* to be infringement of the plaintiff's service mark, "Energy Place."[657] On the other hand, a California court found the use of the plaintiff's trademark in the "path" or "second level" of a domain name did not constitute trademark infringement, since the second level does not identify the origin of the web site; it only describes the site's type of organization.[658] The court found the defendant had limited use of the plaintiff's federally registered mark describing a product that was being sold. This use constituted "nominative fair use of the mark" and was not infringing. The court took notice that the plaintiff's product was one not readily identifiable without the use of the mark.

---

[653] 177 F. Supp. 2d 635 (E.D. Mich. Mar. 30, 2001).

[654] 15 U.S.C. § 1125(d)(1)(D) (2001).

[655] 177 F. Supp. 2d at 648.

[656] *Id.* at 644.

[657] Public Serv. Co. of N.M. v. Nexus Energy Software, Inc., 36 F. Supp. 2d 436 (D. Mass. 1999).

[658] Patmont Motor Works, Inc. v. Gateway Marine, Inc., 1997 U.S. Dist. LEXIS 20877 (N.D. Cal., Dec. 8, 1997) (ruling that use of mark in path or second level of the domain name was not likely to cause confusion).

In *Cat Internet Systems, Inc. v. Providence Washington Insurance Co.,*[659] the owners of the domain name *magazine.com* sued the owner of the domain name *magazines.com*. The defendant is the insurer of the plaintiff. Magazines.com, Inc. filed trademark infringement suit against the plaintiffs because they felt the domain name was confusingly similar to theirs. The owner of magazine.com had either used the domain name as a site for pornography or as a site for a competitor of magazines.com, Inc., which sells magazine subscriptions.[660] The plaintiffs claimed that the allegations brought by magazines.com, Inc. were covered by their insurance policy under "advertising injury," but the defendant never defended them in this claim.[661] Magazines.com, Inc. claimed that "its domain name was a registered trademark identifying 'the source of origin of its services,'" and the court agreed by holding that it was misappropriation of their trademark.[662] The court held it was an "injury that was complete in the advertisement, requiring no further conduct."[663] The defendants tried to argue that *magazine* is not an "original, novel advertising idea" so it would not be covered under the policy, but the court held that "although 'magazines' is not a novel word, magazines.com is a trademarked domain name." Magazines.com Inc. alleged infringement on their trademark that identified "the source of origin of its services," not merely the misuse of a common phrase.[664]

In another domain name case, the plaintiff registered the name "Chambord" for food products, while the defendant used the name Chambord for coffee and makers.[665] The plaintiff instituted a trademark infringement claim, which ended with a decree that stated that the defendants should not be able to use the trademark for coffee products but could continue to use the trademark for coffee makers.[666] The defendant proceeded to register its trademark, including the word *chambord,* as a trademark for coffee makers, and then it registered *chambord.com* for a web site that sold and advertised its coffee makers.[667] The issue then became that both parties had a valid trademark in the word *chambord.* The court found that the defendant could continue use of the domain name because it did not use bad faith when registering the domain name because it had a valid trademark in the domain name.[668] In addition, the court held that since the goods between both parties were not competing goods, there was no trademark infringement.[669] Furthermore, the court held that there was no trademark dilution because the plaintiff's mark was not famous, which is a requirement for dilution.[670]

---

[659] 153 F. Supp. 2d 755 (E.D. Pa. 2001).

[660] *Id.* at 758.

[661] *Id.* at 759.

[662] *Id.* at 762.

[663] *Id.*

[664] *Id.* at 762-63.

[665] Chatam Int'l, Inc. v. Bodum, Inc., 157 F. Supp. 2d 549, 551 (E.D. Pa. 2001).

[666] *Id.* at 552.

[667] *Id.* at 552-53.

[668] *Id.* at 554.

[669] *Id.* at 556.

[670] *Id.*

In another case, it was held that a domain name similar to the plaintiff's trademark does not necessarily mean the defendant will lose its right to the domain name. In *A.B.C. Carpet Co., Inc. v. Mehdi Maeini*, the defendant registered "abc-carpetandhome.net" as a domain name for his business, American Basic Craft Carpet and Home Restoration, after the defendant had previously done business with the plaintiff, A.B.C. Carpet Co., which had a registered trademark, "ABC Carpet & Home."[671] The defendant, however, claimed to have registered the domain name because it was an abbreviation for his business and the business had been in operation since 1980. Although the defendant had done business with the plaintiff prior to the registration and the domain name was similar to the plaintiff's trademark, the court could found that there was a genuine issue of fact as to whether there was a bad faith registration of the domain name, so the court denied the plaintiff's motion for summary judgment on the trademark infringement claim and the ACPA claim.

[b] Federal Dilution

Trademark dilution is "the lessening of the capacity of a famous mark to identify and distinguish goods or services."[672] Dilution is "not intended to serve as a mere fallback protection for trademark owners unable to prove trademark infringement."[673] "Tarnishment occurs when a famous mark is associated improperly with an inferior or offensive product or service."[674] Dilution corrodes the trademark by blurring its product identification or by damaging positive associations that have attached to it. "To establish dilution, plaintiff must show that: (1) [defendants have] made use of a junior mark sufficiently similar to the famous mark to evoke in a relevant universe of consumers a mental association of the two that (2) has caused (3) actual economic harm to the famous mark's economic value by lessening its former selling power as an advertising agent for its goods and services."[675] Dilution can occur even where the products are not in competition and no likelihood of consumer confusion is present. For example, a court found that the use of the name HERBOZAC diluted the plaintiff's mark, PROZAC, by blurring the mark through sales over the Internet.[676]

---

[671] 2002 U.S. Dist. Lexis 1129, *5-*6 (E.D.N.Y. Jan. 22, 2002).

[672] 15 U.S.C. § 1127 (2000).

[673] I.P. Lund Trading Co. v. Kohler Co., 163 F.3d 27, 48 (1st Cir. 1998).

[674] Playboy Enters., Inc. v. Netscape Communications Corp., 55 F. Supp. 2d 1070 (C.D. Cal. 1999) (denying plaintiff's motion for preliminary injunction and holding that plaintiff failed to show a likelihood of success on the merits for using key words in search engines containing plaintiff's trademarks).

[675] *Id.* at 1076.

[676] Eli Lilly & Co. v. Natural Answers, Inc., 86 F. Supp. 2d 834 (S.D. Ind. 2000) (granting injunction against defendant herbal treatment manufacturer prohibiting defendant from continuing to market a product with a name similar to plaintiff's registered trademark and from referring to plaintiff's trademark in advertising).

Net entrepreneurs register thousands of domain names, including famous trademarks, in the hope of selling them to the trademark owners. The new generation of domain case is based on the tendency of web surfers to make careless typographical errors when typing in URL addresses. Domain name entrepreneurs are registering domain names that are a letter or space different from those of famous trademarks; those who do this are called *typosquatters*. In one recent case, a defendant registered the domain name of WWWPainewebber.com, capitalizing on the mistake made by some users who fail to type the period after WWW when looking for the PaineWebber site.[677] A Virginia federal court enjoined the defendants from operating the confusingly similar web site, stating that it was tarnishing the plaintiff's trademark.

In *Panavision v. Toeppen*[678] the Ninth Circuit held that the Federal Trademark Dilution Act was implicated because the defendant was registering domain-name combinations using famous trademarks and seeking to sell the registrations to the trademark owners.

In a notorious cybersquatting case, Dennis Toeppen registered scores of domain names containing the trademarks of famous companies and then sought to sell them to the owners of the marks. Toeppen attempted to show legitimate use of the Panavision domain name by posting aerial photographs of Pana, Illinois, at the web site *Panavision.com*. The Ninth Circuit found Toeppen was misappropriating the trademark of Panavision through his practice of registering trademarks as domain names and then selling them to the trademark owners.[679]

[c] State Dilution

Federal dilution occurs when a defendant's "junior mark," adopted after a plaintiff's mark became famous, dilutes the famous mark either by "tarnishment" or by "blurring."[680] The requirements for a state dilution claim, however, vary by state and may not require that the infringed mark is considered famous. For example, a defendant's registration of plaintiff's trademark as an Internet domain name made commercial use of the mark and diluted it within the meaning of the California Anti-dilution statute as well as the FTDA.[681] "In order to dilute a more

---

[677] PaineWebber, Inc. v. WWWPainewebber.com, 1999 U.S. Dist. LEXIS 6552 (E.D. Va., Apr. 9, 1999), http://www.phillipsnizer.com/int_synopses.htm.

[678] 945 F. Supp. 1296 (D.C. Cal. 1996), *aff'd*, 141 F.3d 1316, 1324 (9th Cir. 1998).

[679] 141 F.3d at 1325.

[680] Ringling Bros. Barnum & Bailey Combined Shows, Inc. v. Utah Div. of Travel Dev., 955 F. Supp. 605, 613 (E.D. Va. 1997).

[681] Panavision Int'l, L.P. v. Toeppen, 141 F.3d 1316 (9th Cir. 1998) (holding that registration of domain name made commercial use of the plaintiff's trademark and diluted it within the meaning of the FTDA and the California anti-dilution statute); *see also* Toho Co. v. Sears, Roebuck & Co., 645 F.3d 788, 793 (9th Cir. 1981) (refusing to give a broad interpretation to California dilution statute "lest it swallow up all competition in the claim of protection against trade name infringement").

senior mark, the junior mark must be sufficiently similar."[682] In *Planned Parenthood v. Bucci*,[683] a federal court ordered an injunction against a pro-life web site that used the domain name *plannedparenthood.com*. The injunction of the court was based on a finding that the domain name would cause confusion and dilute the plaintiff's mark, Planned Parenthood Federation of America, in violation of state law. Planned Parenthood had a diametrically opposed mission to that of the plannedparenthood.com web site, which was put up by an anti-abortion activist.

Musician and television personality John Tesh sued Celebsites, a Nevada corporation, and its officers. Celebsites operated a celebrity and entertainment web site, *Celebsites.com*, a site dedicated to celebrities. In addition, the site also offered advertising, contests, reports, and news.[684] *Celebsites.com* registered the domain name *JohnTesh.com* and offered to sell it back to Tesh for a large sum. Tesh filed an action under the federal trademark act, the Anticybersquatting Act, and California state law. Tesh charged the defendant with marketing the *JohnTesh.com* web site as the official site for Tesh and, as a result, creating a substantial risk of confusion for Internet users.

[6] Dislodging Cybersquatters

Cybersquatting is the practice of registering domain names for the purpose of reselling them for a profit. The mere fact that another party registered *SPC.com* for use as a domain name does not necessarily support an infringement or dilution claim. In addition, evidence must exist showing that a defendant is acting in bad faith.[685] Assume SPC timely registered the domain name *www.SPC.com*, but not *www.spc.net* or *www.spcsucks.com*. SPC has several options. First, it can pay the domain name owner to assign or sell the domain names *SPC.net* or *www.SPCsucks.com*.

Second, it may file a trademark or unfair competition lawsuit if the registrant is a speculator in domain names. A number of courts have ruled that a cybersquatter's registration of a domain name incorporating a well-known tradename or trademark blurs or dilutes the famous mark. Evidence must exist, however, that the SPC mark met the standard for protection as famous and that the defendant's use would cause dilution.[686] SPC will seek the assignment or transfer of the domain name incorporating its trademarks from the defendant to the company. SPC may

---

[682] Victoria's Secret v. Victor Moseley d/b/a Victor's Little Secret, 2000 U.S. Dist. LEXIS 5215 (E.D. Ky., Feb. 9, 2000) (granting injunction under the federal antidilution act because user of the mark "Victor's Little Secret" diluted the "Victoria's Secret" mark as it had a tarnishing effect).

[683] Planned Federation of America, 42 U.S.P.Q.2d 1430 (S.D.N.Y. 1997) (granting preliminary injunction finding sufficient likelihood of confusion and false designation of origin).

[684] John Tesh Sues for Trademark Infringement and Cybersquatting, E-Commerce Law Weekly (Jan. 1999).

[685] HQM, Ltd. & Hatfield, Inc. v. Hatfield, 1999 U.S. Dist. LEXIS 18598 (D. Md., Dec. 2, 1999).

[686] In Avery Dennison v. Sumpton, 1999 U.S. App. LEXIS 19954 (9th Cir., Aug. 23, 1999) the plaintiff held that the trademarks "Avery" and "Dennison" were distinctive but not famous for purposes of the federal antidilution act.

have an action under ACPA if a cybersquatter registered domain names, such as *www.suffolkpersonalcomputers.com,* and attempted to sell them.

A great deal of uncertainty persists as to whether ACPA would apply to a cybersquatter located in another country. Suppose a cybersquatter located in Russia registered the domain name *www.spc.ru* to divert business to its site. In a similar case involving Kodak, the Russian Institute of Public Networks ruled that United States' intellectual property rules do not apply in Russia.[687]

[7] Metatags

"Metatags are HTML codes intended to describe the contents of the web site. There are different types of metatags, but those of principal concern to us are the 'description' and 'keyword' metatags. The description metatags are intended to describe the web site; the keyword metatags, at least in theory, contain keywords relating to the contents of the web site."[688] Increasing the traffic to one's site has a high priority to site owners, especially for commercial sites. "The more often a term appears in the metatags and in the text of the web page, the more likely it is that the web page will be 'hit' in a search for that keyword and the higher on the list of 'hits' the web page will appear."[689]

Increasing the traffic to one's web site has a high priority to site owners, especially for commercial sites. Some webmasters surpass acceptable levels of creativity when they resort to deception by embedding popular, nonrelevant words such as *sex* and the trademarks of others in their web site's metatags. Such webmasters deceive users because they use words that may be of interest to the users to divert them to sites that may be of no interest to the user. For example, a user seeking to purchase a "Healthy Ways" product would not likely be interested in viewing a pornographic site for which "Healthy Ways" is used in the pornographic site's metatags to draw visitors.[690] Such misuse of trademarks, whether by competing or noncompeting businesses (including providers of add-ons and complementary products or services), may be termed "invisible infringement."[691] Such misuse of trademarks, whether by competing or noncompeting businesses (including providers of add-ons and complementary products or services), may be termed "invisible infringement" or "metatag bending."[692]

These webmasters engage in a pursuit of attention and divert web traffic from the rightful trademark owner's site. They intend to increase their business or

---

[687] John T. Aquino, Why Foreign Internet Laws Are So Important, 4 The Internet Newsltr (Feb. 2000) at 1.

[688] Brookfield Comm., Inc. v. West Coast Entm't Corp., 174 F.3d 1036, 1045 (9th Cir. 1999).

[689] *Id.*

[690] Healthy Ways is a hypothetical company used to illustrate the problem with metatags.

[691] Inventor of the term *invisible infringement* is unknown; the term is widely used.

[692] Andy McCue, Search Engine Cheats Risk Jail, Computing (Dec. 14, 2000), http://www.computing.co.uk/news/1115464.

the advertising value of their sites, which is similar to the advertising value of television shows: The more "hits" a site has, the greater its sales will be or the more its owners can charge for advertising on it. Often, these webmasters deliberately manipulate search engine results to profit commercially from the reputation of another.[693] This tactic may help the unscrupulous webmaster, but it is a detriment to the public because the resulting metatags do not always accurately reflect the content of the web page, making it more difficult for users to find the information they seek. For such behavior "one in four companies risks prosecution and even jail" time.[694]

Some search engines do not have any explicit policies for policing the use of trademarks to prevent misuse.[695] Other search engines, however, such as Excite, may inadvertently benefit the trademark owners because they do not use keyword metatags, hoping in this way to protect users from unreliable information and to avoid influencing a site's ranking in the search results.[696] Where no metatags are used, as in the indexing at Excite, unscrupulous webmasters cannot confuse potential customers by diverting web traffic to their sites by using others' trademarks in the metatags.

Many search engines automate the indexing process by using programs called "spiders" that search the Web and pull keywords from the text within a site and/or from the web pages' invisible metatags. These spiders index and rank the relevant web sites using algorithms proprietary to the search engine, with the most relevant site having the highest rank. The frequency of words also influences the ranking, such that a word that appears in a web page or its metatag five times will give that web site a higher rank than is achieved by the web page that contains that word only three times. Thus, webmasters use controllability of metatags as a tool to influence the ranking and increase the likelihood of "hits" on their web site.

Not all search engines index the same way. Some will take the contents of a document and index it, but if the search engine limits its examination to the first 250 characters, the site will not be accurately indexed if those characters do not contain anything of relevance to the major part of the site's contents. Metatags serve a useful purpose by allowing such search engines to more accurately list the web site in their indices.

There are growing number of metatag disputes, but most cases are settled or result in an injunction. Metatag litigation is generally predicated upon trademark causes of action seeking remedies for trademark infringement, trademark dilution, and unfair competition. Most of the metatag cases have little precedential value, rarely resulting in an appellate opinion.

---

[693] *See* Robert Scheinfeld and Parker Bagley, Emerging Issues on the Internet, N.Y.L.J. (Nov. 26, 1997), http://www.ljx.com/Internet/1126netissue.html.

[694] McCue, *supra* note 692.

[695] *See* Elizabeth Gardner, Trademark Battles Simmer Behind Sites (Aug. 8, 1997) (visited Oct. 28, 1998), http://www.web week.com/current/news/19970825-battles.html.

[696] *See* Understanding Metatags—What is a Metatag? (visited Apr. 29, 2002), http://www.excite.com/Info/listing7.html.

[a]   *Insituform Technologies v. National Envirotech*[697]

National Envirotech, an industrial plumbing supplier, used the registered trademarks—*Insituform*® and *Insitupipe*®—of its competitor, Insituform, as metatags in its web site.[698] The contents of the infringing site did not refer to Insituform or its products, even in a comparative advertising manner. Defendant's act caused search engines to link Insituform's trademarks with National Envirotech's site, and searches for plaintiff's site, via its trademarks, returned a list of matching sites, including defendant's site. Insituform filed suit and brought a motion for a preliminary injunction against National Envirotech.

Insituform argued that defendant's conduct constituted unfair competition. Insituform analogized defendant's conduct to an alteration in Directory Assistance's database such that potential customers requesting Insituform's telephone number would be given National Envirotech's number.[699] These potential customers would then call National Envirotech and purchase its plumbing supplies rather than purchasing Insituform's products. Misdirecting potential customers to its web site appears the sole plausible reason for National Envirotech's conduct. Insituform suffered damages of lost potential sales and profits because of National Envirotech's action.

The suit was resolved with a settlement, and a court issued a permanent injunction.[700] National Envirotech agreed to remove Insituform's trademarks from its web site's keyword metatag section, to notify all the search engines of the court's order in order for them to delete from their databases the links that associated plaintiff's trademarks with the defendant, to resubmit their web pages for indexing, and to file a report evidencing their compliance. National Envirotech, however, did not stipulate that it was suggesting an affiliation with Insituform or that it was attempting to deceive anyone.[701] Nevertheless, this case has significance for having the first judicial order leading to a metatag settlement.

[b]   *Playboy Enterprises, Inc. v. Calvin Designer Label*[702]

Playboy Enterprises sued an adult web site operator for using its registered trademarks, Playboy® and Playmate®, in the offensive web site's domain name, metatags, and contents.[703] Defendant's unauthorized acts resulted in the retrieval

---

[697] *See* Insituform Technologies v. National Envirotech, No. 97-2064 (E.D. La., July 1, 1997).

[698] *See id.*, Complaint.

[699] *See* Cowan, Liebowitz and Latman, P.C., CL&L Successfully Stops a Competitor's New Form of Web Site Unfair Competition (visited Apr. 28, 2002), http://www.cll.com/keyword.htm.

[700] *See* Insituform Technologies v. National Envirotech, No. 97-2064 (E.D. La. order, Aug. 27, 1997) (visited Oct. 28, 1998), http://www.cll.com/case1.htm.

[701] *See* Danny Sullivan, Metatag Lawsuits (visited Apr. 28, 2002), http://searchenginewatch.com/resources/metasuits.html.

[702] *See* Playboy Enters., Inc. v. Calvin Designer Label, 44 U.S.P.Q.2d (BNA) 1156 (N.D. Cal. 1997).

[703] *See id.* at 1157, Complaint (Sept. 8, 1997) (visited Apr. 28, 2002), http://www.patents.com/ac/playcpt.sht.

of the offensive web site whenever a search was conducted to locate plaintiff's site using "Playboy" or "Playmate." Plaintiff claimed that defendant acted with knowledge and intent to cause confusion, mistake, or deception, and that defendant's unauthorized use of its famous trademarks would dilute their distinctive quality and destroy the public's association of the marks with Playboy Enterprises.

Plaintiff sought a permanent injunction prohibiting defendant from using Playboy marks, or terms similar to these marks, in any domain name, directory address, metatags, or web page content. Playboy also sought $5 million in damages, any profits defendant made, and punitive damages. The trial court, however, limited the remedy to an immediate preliminary injunction enjoining defendant from using Playboy's trademarks or similar terms in its domain name, directory address, metatags, or web page. The injunction also prohibited the use of Playboy's trademarks in connection with retrieval of data or with advertising the defendant's products in a manner that would create a likelihood of confusion. Metatags should not have been used to convey the impression that the defendant's web site was authorized or licensed by Playboy.[704] Although favorable to trademark owners, this ruling does not have a significant effect on wrongful metatag use because it also involved other issues, such as wrongful use of trademarks in domain names.

[c]   *Playboy Enterprises, Inc. v. AsiaFocus International*[705]

Playboy Enterprises sued two Hong Kong-based web site operators for using its federally registered trademarks Playboy® and Playmate® as metatags embedded in their web sites.[706] Defendants' sites existed as click-through sites, where defendants earned money whenever users clicked on banners that routed them to pornographic web sites. As the web pages did not contain any references to the trademarks, it appears that the sole purpose of defendants' act was to capture traffic using Playboy's established reputation in its trademarks for commercial gain.

Playboy claimed trademark infringement, due to customer confusion, and dilution by blurring of its well-known marks. A federal judge in Virginia ruled that Playboy's marks have acquired goodwill through Playboy's national and international advertising, causing the public to associate these marks only with the plaintiff, and awarded Playboy $3 million in damages, plus costs.[707]

[d]   *Playboy Enterprises, Inc. v. Terri Welles*[708]

Not all uses of trademarks in metatags are actionable. Playboy Enterprises sued its former playmate, Terri Welles, for using the terms *Playboy* and *Playmate*

---

[704] *See id.* at 1158, Order (Sept. 27, 1997) (visited Apr. 28, 2002), http://www.patents.com/ac/playord.sht.

[705] *See id.*

[706] *See id.*

[707] *See* Courtney Macavinta, Playboy Wins Piracy Suit (Apr. 4, 1998) (visited Apr. 28, 2002), http://www.news.com/News/Item/0,4,21370,00.html.

[708] 279 F.3d 796 (9th Cir. 2002).

of the Year in her commercial web site's metatags and content. Welles uses her web site to sell erotic photographs of herself and her services as a spokesmodel. Plaintiff asserted federal trademark infringement, false description of origin, and dilution causes of action and asked for an injunction plus damages of $5 million. Although Welles was not contractually restricted from using these terms, Playboy brought this action to stop her from competing with its CyberClub subscription web site.

Courts look to the factual circumstances relating to the use and intention of the defendant rather than automatically declaring against the unauthorized use of trademarks as metatags. The judge in this case refused to grant an injunction based on fair use because the law allows descriptive use of a trademark.[709] Ms. Welles' use constituted descriptive use because the plaintiff gave the title to her, and it became a part of her identity to the public. Thus, she had the right to use these marks to describe herself and to catalog her web site appropriately with the search engines. The judge also stressed that by using disclaimers in the web pages, the defendant did not use plaintiff's marks to mislead users to believe that her site belonged to Playboy. Implications of this case are quite limited due to the narrow facts; the Lanham Act can easily be used because the fair use exception applies. The court found the use of Playboy's metatags in Ms. Welles' lawsuit to constitute fair use because the marks were used to describe her status as a former Playmate, not Playboy's goods and services.

The Ninth U.S. Court of Appeals affirmed the district court's grant of summary judgment in favor of Terri Welles as to the claims for trademark infringement, trademark dilution, and breach of contract but reversed as to the use of the abbreviation "PMOY."[710] The court concluded that the model's uses of the publisher's trademarks were permissible, nominative uses and implied no current sponsorship or endorsement by Playboy, Inc.[711] In fact, Welles specifically disavowed any such sponsorship.

Her use of the title "Playmate of the Year" did not dilute or tarnish Playboy's trademarks. Welles' use of the abbreviation "PMOY" on the wallpaper of her site, however, was not nominative because the abbreviation's use was not necessary to describe the model. The court noted that the restrictions Playboy proposed for use of its trademarks on the site would have a chilling effect on criticism online.

[e] *Oppedahl & Larson v. Advanced Concepts*[712]

Oppedahl & Larson, an intellectual property law firm, sued Advanced Concepts, Code Team-LBK, Inc., Professional Web Site Development, MSI Market-

---

[709] *See* 15 U.S.C. § 1115(b)(4).

[710] Playboy Enters., Inc. v. Welles, 279 F.3d 796 (9th Cir. 2002).

[711] The court applied the test for nominative uses set forth in New Kids on the Block v. New American Publ'g, 971 F.2d 302 (9th Cir. 1992): a trademark use is nominative if (1) the product or service is not readily identifiable without use of the mark, (2) only so much of the mark is used as is reasonably necessary to identify the product or service, and (3) the user does nothing to suggest sponsorship or endorsement by the trademark holder.

[712] No. 97-Z-1592 (D.C. Colo. 1997).

ing, Inc., and Internet Business Services based on misuse of trademarks. The law firm conducted an Internet search on their names, and respondents' web sites appeared on the search results.[713] No references to the plaintiff were found in the offensive web site. Examination of the site's underlying source document revealed that the names Oppedahl and Larson were each used eight times as metatags. Plaintiff brought its cause of action under federal unfair competition and trademark dilution, as well as state unfair competition and trademark infringement.[714]

The law firm and Carl Oppedahl have an established reputation in the domain name area. Plaintiff stated in the complaint that although Advanced Concepts is not a competitor, it willfully intended to trade on that reputation or to cause dilution of its trademark.[715] Defendants were charged with using the plaintiff's trademarks to draw traffic to their site and commercially advertise their services. Defendants intended to profit from Oppedahl & Larson's established good name. Plaintiff alleged that defendants' practice would confuse and mislead users into believing that plaintiff endorsed or sponsored defendants' site. Oppedahl & Larson claimed that defendants' acts would injure its business reputation and diminish the distinctive quality of its mark.

Plaintiff sought an injunction against the defendants to enjoin them from using its trademarks or any colorable imitation in its web pages or in advertising or promotions. Plaintiff also sought destruction of any materials containing the marks, award of damages greater than three times defendants' profits or plaintiff's damages, reasonable attorneys' fees, and punitive damages. The court entered judgment in favor of Oppedahl & Larson, limiting it, however, to the granting of a permanent injunction against the defendants.[716]

[f] *Nettis Environmental Ltd. v. IWI, Inc.*

In *Nettis Environmental Ltd. v. IWI, Inc.*,[717] a competitor used the plaintiff's name Nettis in metatags on its web site. When the defendant registered its web site with hundreds of search engines, it submitted the term *Nettis* and *Nettis Environment* as keywords. The federal district court enjoined the defendant from using the Nettis® trademarks as metatags. The defendant complied with the injunction and removed the metatags from its web site. The defendant, however, was found to be in contempt of court for failing to remove the Nettis keywords in its registrations with the search engines. The court imposed sanctions against the defendant and awarded attorneys' fees to the plaintiff.

---

[713] *See id.*, Complaint, July 23, 1997 (visited Apr. 28, 2002), http://www.patents.com/ac/complaint.sht.

[714] *See* Jeffrey Kuester, Link Law on the Internet: A Panel Discussion, 38 IDEA 197 (1998).

[715] *See* Oppedahl and Larson LLP, General Information About Patents (visited May 27, 1999), http://www.patents.com/patents.sht.

[716] *See* Oppedahl & Larson, *supra*, Order (Dec. 19, 1997), http://www.patents.com/ac/welchord.sht.

[717] No. 1:98 CV 2549, 1999 U.S. Dist. LEXIS 5655 (N.D. Ohio, Apr. 14, 1999).

[g]   Brookfield Communications, Inc. v. West Coast Entertainment Corp.

In *Brookfield Communications, Inc. v. West Coast Entertainment Corp.*[718] the Ninth Circuit reversed the district court's denial of an injunction prohibiting a competitor's use of another company's trademarks in the domain name as well as metatags on its web site. Brookfield is an information content provider for the entertainment industry. West Coast is a video rental store chain which used terms similar to Brookfield's trademark "MovieBuff" in metatags and buried code. The Ninth Circuit was asked to determine whether trademark and unfair competition law prohibited West Coast from using Brookfield's trademark (or similar terms) in the domain name and metatags of the video store's web site.

The case arose out of Brookfield's failed attempt to register the domain name *moviebuff.com* with Network Solutions, a domain name registrar. Network Solutions informed Brookfield that the *moviebuff.com* name was already registered by West Coast. Brookfield then registered the domain names *brookfieldcomm.com* and *moviebuffonline.com*. Brookfield used its web sites to sell "MovieBuff" software and to market its "MovieBuff" database. In 1998, Brookfield applied to the U.S. Patent and Trademark Office for a federal registration of "MovieBuff" as a mark to designate its goods and services. The federal trademark registrations were issued in September 1998.

In October 1998, Brookfield learned of West Coast's plans of launching a web site at *moviebuff.com,* also offering a searchable computer database. Brookfield sought an injunction in the federal district court alleging that West Coast's online services using the term *moviebuff.com* constituted trademark infringement and unfair competition. Brookfield sought a temporary restraining order against any use of the mark "MovieBuff" or similar term likely to cause confusion. Brookfield objected to West Coast's use of "MovieBuff" in its metatags as well as the video stores's use of the domain name *moviebuff.com.*

West Coast opposed the injunction on the grounds that it was the senior user of "MovieBuff," not Brookfield. West Coast also argued that it was the first user of "MovieBuff" because it had used the term in its federally registered trademark "The Movie Buff's Movie Store" since 1986. West Coast also claimed common-law rights in the mark in using the domain name *moviebuff.com* prior to Brookfield's use of the term in marketing its electronic data base. Finally, West Coast argued that its use of *moviebuff.com* would not cause confusion with Brookfield's MovieBuff mark. The district court refused to order an injunction. The Ninth Circuit reversed and remanded the case to the district court with an order to enter the injunction in favor of Brookfield.

---

[718] 174 F.3d 1036 (9th Cir. 1999). SNA, Inc. v. Array, 51 F. Supp. 2d 554 (E.D. Pa. 1999); New York State Society of Certified Public Accountants v. Eric Louis Assocs., Inc., 79 F. Supp. 2d 331 (S.D.N.Y. 1999); N.V.E. Pharm., Inc. v. Hoffman-LaRoche, Inc., 1999 U.S. Dist. LEXIS 20204 (D.N.J., Dec. 27, 1999) (holding that use of competitor's trademarks in metatags unfairly diverted traffic from mark owners' sites).

The Ninth Circuit began its opinion by establishing that Brookfield, not West Coast, was the senior holder of the "MovieBuff" trademark. The court granted the injunction on the grounds that West Coast's use of MovieBuff and similar terms in its domain name and metatags was likely to cause "initial interest" confusion. Even though consumers would not be confused as to source, they would initially be confused by West Coast's use of "MovieBuff" and related terms in metatags and the domain name. The court found that a web surfer entering "MovieBuff" into a search engine was likely to turn up the West Coast as well as Brookfield's site. The court reasoned that West Coast's use of "moviebuff.com" in metatags would divert traffic from Brookfield. Some web users would use West Coast's site while looking for Brookfield. The court stated that some users would be diverted to West Coast's site because of "initial interest confusion." The court acknowledged that West Coast's misuse of metatags (and domain name) did not constitute source confusion. However, initial interest confusion could constitute unfair competition and infringement.

The court acknowledged that West Coast could make "fair use" of the "MovieBuff" in describing Brookfield's products. However, West Coast caused initial interest confusion by using the term "movie buff" in metags and this use of Brookfield's mark was not protected by fair use. The Ninth Circuit used a hypothetical to explain how that use by West Coast of Brookfield's mark in a metatag could constitute unfair competition:

> Using another's trademark in one's metatag is much like posting a sign with another's trademark in front of one's store. Suppose West Coast's competitor (let's call it "Blockbuster") puts up a billboard on a highway reading—"West Coast Video: 2 miles ahead at Exit 7"—where West Coast is really located at Exit 8 but Blockbuster is located at Exit 7. Customers looking for West Coast's store will pull off at Exit 7 and drive around looking for it. Unable to locate West Coast, but seeing the Blockbuster store right by the highway entrance, they may rent there. . . . Customers are not confused in the narrow sense; they are fully aware that they are purchasing from Blockbuster and they have no reason to believe that Blockbuster is related to, or in any way sponsored by, West Coast. Nevertheless, the fact that there is only initial consumer confusion does not alter the fact that Blockbuster would be misappropriating acquired goodwill of West Coast.[719]

The court acknowledged that use of competitors' trademarks for nondeceptive comparative advertising would be protected by the doctrine of fair use. An online company may use another's trademark in a web site to describe a competitor's products and services, but may not use marks in metatags or domain names to divert traffic. Online companies risk claims for infringement and unfair competition by using metatags to divert traffic looking for their competitor's site.

---

[719] *Id.* at 1063.

[h] Trans Union LLC v. Credit Research, Inc.

Credit Research was charged with misuse of Trans Union's trademarks on the Internet in *Trans Union LLC v. Credit Research, Inc.*[720] Credit Research displayed the Trans Union logo on its Internet web site and used its trade name in metatags. Transunion argued that Credit Research's use of the Trade Union trade name in their web site's metatags was likely to create a false impression that Trans Union endorsed or was affiliated with Credit Research.[721] Credit Research's web site's metatags contained the terms "credit," "credit report," and "residential mortgage credit report," as well as "trans union," "equifax," and "experian."[722] The court held that the defendants' use of the term "trans union" in a web site metatag constituted fair use of the trade name.[723] The court found it significant that only one "trans union" metatag was embedded in the web site, which indicates that Credit Research was not "engaged in 'cyber-stuffing,' the practice of repeating a term numerous times in a web site's metatags in order to lure the attention of internet search engines."[724] The court granted a preliminary injunction in part ordering Credit Resarch to cease using certain domain names, the plaintiff's log, and ordering it to transfer ownership of certain domain names.[725]

[i] Ty, Inc. v. Baby Me, Inc.

In *Ty, Inc. v. Baby Me, Inc.*,[726] Ty brought an action for copyright, trade dress, and trademark infringement against Baby Me for copying its trademark *beanies* in its metatag.[727] Ty sent a cease and desist letter, but Baby Me responded by saying it was going to continue selling its toy.[728] Baby Me claimed it was not subject to personal jurisdiction because the owner of Baby Me created the web site as a convenience for visitors to Hawaii to purchase its toys after visiting Hawaii.[729] The court, however, held that Baby Me was subject to personal jurisdiction under the state's long arm jurisdiction because it operated a web site that targeted "its products to anyone anywhere in the world who wished to purchase a Baby Me bear,"[730] even if it only intended to target those who visited Hawaii; those it targeted could be from anywhere in the world.

---

[720] 2001 U.S. Dist. LEXIS 3526 (N.D. Ill., Mar. 27, 2001).

[721] *Id.* at *30.

[722] *Id.* at *17.

[723] *Id.* at *18.

[724] *Id.; see also* National Baseball Hall of Fame & Museum, Inc. v. All Sports Promotions Group, Inc., 2001 U.S. Dist. LEXIS 1592 (S.D.N.Y. 2001) (finding that use of metatags containing the words "Baseball Hall of Fame" and "National Ball Hall of Fame" in web site metatags was insufficient to establish bad faith in a federal and state trademark infringement lawsuit).

[725] *Id.* at *37-39.

[726] 2001 U.S. Dist. LEXIS 5761 (N.D. Ill. 2001).

[727] *Id.* at *3.

[728] *Id.*

[729] *Id.* at *13.

[730] *Id.*

In addition, the court held that Baby Me was subject to personal jurisdiction under federal due process because the state's interest in protecting its citizens from intellectual property claims outweighed the inconvenience it would cause the small company, which freely chose to establish a web site on the Internet, thereby creating opportunity to establish contacts with other states.[731] The court held that since a web site is accessible around the world, the potential to injure the trademark holder around the world is created, and the defendant cannot claim it did not target its customer no matter where that customer originated from.[732]

[j] Oyster Software Inc. v. Forms Processing Inc.[733]

Oyster claimed trademark infringement and copyright infringement against a defendant who copied Oyster's metatags from its web site and copied Oyster's trademarks by posting them on its own web site.[734] After Oyster informed the defendant about the infringement, the defendant removed the infringing material, but Oyster brought suit claiming that there was still a triable issue, because the infringing activity could happen again.[735] Even though Oyster tried to show that it had a loss of profits during the period in which the trademark infringement occurred by showing fewer hits to its web site, the court held that was not sufficient to show lost profits because Oyster did not provide sufficient evidence to show that it ever obtained profits through its web site.[736] Since Oyster could not show lost profits or the "track record" required to calculate lost profits, Oyster's trademark infringement claim was dismissed.[737]

The copyright infringement claim, on the other hand, survived. The defendant argued that since the infringed material was not registered at the time of filing, the copyright infringement claim should be dismissed. The court disagreed, holding that since Oyster stated that it had begun the filing for registration, the court would allow Oyster to amend its complaint,[738] but because all of the activities occurred prior to the registration, Oyster would be allowed only "actual damages and profits," not statutory damages or attorneys' fees.[739]

[k] Caterpillar, Inc. v. TeleScan Technologies, L.L.C.[740]

Caterpillar, Inc. filed an action against TeleScan Technologies, L.L.C. to prevent TeleScan's use of the *CATERPILLAR* and *CAT* word and design marks as

---

[731] *Id.* at *19-*21.

[732] *Id.* at *23.

[733] 2001 U.S. Dist. LEXIS 22520 (N.D. Cal. 2001).

[734] *Id.* at *2-*5.

[735] *Id.* at *5, *12-*13.

[736] *Id.* at *15-*16, *18.

[737] *Id.* at *20-*21.

[738] *Id.* at *30-3*2.

[739] *Id.* at *31-*33.

[740] 2002 U.S. Dist. LEXIS 3477 (C.D. Ill. Feb. 22, 2002).

trademarks and domain names in connection with heavy equipment and related services[741] The court found that TeleScan's verbatim incorporation of the trademark holder's marks in the disputed domain names and use of the trademark holder's marks on the disputed web sites conveyed an overall commercial impression that would confuse consumers and also found that the use of Caterpillar's trademarks in metatags created initial interest confusion.

Initial interest confusion occurs when web site visitors or potential customers believe that the sites and services to be provided to them were approved, authorized, or otherwise endorsed by the trademark holder. The court found that the defendant's use of the trademark holder's marks in connection with heavy equipment and motor vehicle sales, advertising, or listing services and the infringer's use of the trademark holder's marks within the disputed domain names constituted trademark infringement, unfair competition, dilution, and cybersquatting. Finally, the infringer's registration of the disputed domain names and intent to use the domain names to direct traffic to its web site constituted bad faith and entitled the trademark holder to its attorneys' fees related to the action.

[8]   Key Words in Banner Advertisements

Key words sold to advertisers of Internet web sites are an increasing source of revenue for search engines. When a web site visitor types in the keywords, banner advertisements appear along with the search results. If a user types the key word *beer,* the search results include web sites for "Guinness Global," "Pub-Crawler," "Labatts Beer.\\," and an advertisement for Amazon.com with a hyperlink for books on beer. Similarly, a user typing the key word *automobile* on the Excite search engine receives banner advertisements along with the search results. Autotrader.com is the banner advertisement that comes with the key word *automobile.* The selling of banner advertisements for key words is a means of generating revenue for search engines.

Many companies, such as Lycos, sell advertisements on the web pages of their search engines. Lycos, for example, enters advertising contracts that take one of the following forms:

1. A *run of site* contract, under which a customer is guaranteed a number of impressions;
2. A *key word* contract, in which a customer purchases the right to advertise in connection with specified word searches; or
3. A *targeted* contract, where the customer purchases a specified number of impressions in one of the targeted categories, or on a specified page or service.[742]

---

[741] *Id.*

[742] Lycos, Inc., Notes to Condensed Consolidated Financial Statements (visited Apr. 28, 2002), http://www.sec.gov/Archives/edgar/data/1007992/0000927016-99-002346.txt.

Playboy sued the Excite and Netscape search engines for selling a preselected package of search queries containing terms such as *playboy* and *playmate* to banner advertisers operating adult entertainment web sites.[743] Playboy Enterprises argued that the key words *playboy* and *playmate* were confusingly similar to the trademarks Playboy® and Playmate®. The Ninth Circuit found no trademark infringement or evidence of dilution because of the practice of keying banner ads with words similar to trademarks. The court observed that the firms offering Web portal services were not in competition with Playboy's adult entertainment publications. Moreover, the search engines were not using Playboy's trademarks to identify the source of any goods or services. The court found a user of Excite or Netscape could easily find Playboy Enterprises on the search result pages for "playboy" and "playmate." The court found "no evidence that the banner advertisements on Excite's and Netscape's Search Results pages 'keyed' to the words 'playboy' or 'playmate' are likely to cause confusion as to source, sponsorship, or affiliation."[744] Finally, the court noted that if Playboy was granted an injunction, it would essentially restrain the use of the words *playboy* and *playmate* on the World Wide Web.

[L] Metatag Dispute for SPC[745]

[1] Metatags

It's late Friday afternoon. Maxwell A. Turney, general corporate counsel of SPC, Inc., calls its outside intellectual property counsel, Amanda Adams, for advice. When one of their marketing people conducted an Internet search using their trademarks SUFFOLK 2000 and MILLENIUM-II, the search retrieved a web site that ranked higher on the list than did SPC's site. That site belonged to Neeto Corporation, a manufacturer of a low-quality line of computer peripherals. Helga Hunter, SPC's chief computing and information systems officer, examined the contents of the site and found no references to SPC or its trademarked products. Neeto's site, however, contained invisible source code that used each of SPC's trademarks, SUFFOLK 2000 and MILLENIUM-II, seven times.

Metatags comprise the HTML code and contain information about the contents of a web page.[746] Of the several types of metatags, key word and description tags provide the most useful information.[747] *Description tags* contain the description of the site, and *key word tags* specify key words or synonyms that pertain to

---

[743] Playboy Enters., Inc. v. Netscape Comm. Corp., 55 F. Supp. 2d 1070 (9th Cir. 1999).

[744] *Id.* at 1086.

[745] Copyright (c) 2000 Lucy Elandjian. All rights reserved. The author is an alumnus of Suffolk University Law School High Technology Law Concentration and a corporate patent attorney, practicing in Cincinnati, Ohio.

[746] *See* David Loundy, Hidden Code Sparks High-Profile Lawsuit, Chicago Daily Law Bulletin (Sept. 11, 1997), http://www.Loundy.com/CDLB/Meta_Tags.html.

[747] *See* Danny Sullivan, How To Use Metatags (visited Nov. 12, 1998), http://searchenginewatch. Internet.com/web masters/meta.html.

site contents, in addition to words that appear in the text of the site.[748] Metatags of SPC's web site are written as follows:

> <META NAME="description"=content="world's largest manufacturer of personal computers">
>
> <META NAME="keywords"=content="personal computers, SUFFOLK 2000, MILLENIUM-II">

Moreover, Neeto's keyword metatag was discovered to be the following:

> <META NAME="keyword"=content="peripherals, computers, NEETO, SUFFOLK 2000, SUFFOLK 2000, SUFFOLK 2000, SUFFOLK 2000, SUFFOLK 2000, SUFFOLK 2000, SUFFOLK 2000, MILLENIUM-II, MILLENIUM-II, MILLENIUM-II, MILLENIUM-II, MILLENIUM-II, MILLENIUM-II, MILLENIUM-II">

Webmasters use metatags for indexing web pages to enable the retrieval of sites during searches. Terms that appear in metatags are invisible because the page that a web browser opens does not display the metatags.[749] One can, however, view them using the "view page source," or an equivalent command from the browser; the lines that start with "<meta" contain the hidden terms.[750]

[a]   *Potential Causes of Action*

Mr. Turney believes that SPC's growing reputation for quality computer products, along with its recent successful IPO (initial public offering of stock), are being used by Neeto to bring traffic to Neeto's site. He has also heard rumors that Neeto is planning to enter the personal computer business. He wants to know what SPC's rights and remedies are with respect to its trademarks, business, and reputation. This scenario focuses on federal and state causes of action that SPC may have against Neeto regarding unauthorized use of its trademarks as metatags.

SPC's complaint will be for (1) trademark infringement for Neeto's violation of the Lanham Act; (2) unfair competition under the Lanham Act; (3) unfair competition under Massachusetts tort law (tort of misappropriation); and (4) dilution of the distinctiveness of plaintiff's trademarks, trade names, and logos in violation of the federal antidilution act. SPC will need to prove that its marks are famous to qualify for protection under the federal antidilution act. SPC may seek an injunction to enjoin Neeto from using its trademarks in metatags.[751]

---

[748] *See* Web Developer's Virtual Library, Metatagging for Search Engines (visited Nov. 11, 1998), http://www.stars.com/Search/Meta/Tag.html.

[749] *Id.*

[750] *See* Marcelo Halpern, Meta-tags: Effective Marketing or Unfair Competition? 7 Cyber L. 2, 3 (1997).

[751] *See, e.g.*, Niton Corp. v. Radiation Monitoring Devices, Inc., 27 F. Supp. 2d 102 (D. Mass. 1998).

[i] Trademark infringement. The use of SPC's trademarks in a metatag may divert traffic away from SPC's web site and violate the Lanham Act. If SPC's trademarks, trade names, and logos are used as "metatags" on a competitor's web site, there may be a trademark infringement or dilution action. The more times the trademarked terms appear in the metatags, the greater the likelihood that consumers will find the site through a search engine.[752]

SPC can argue that upon Neeto's entry into the personal computer business, Neeto will be infringing SPC's trademarks because Neeto will be confusing potential purchasers by luring them to Neeto's site, using SPC's marks as metatags, to sell them similar products. In such a situation, Neeto will be intentionally riding on SPC's goodwill and the strength of its trademarks to compete in the same markets.

[ii] Unfair competition. In our example, Mr. Turney is particularly concerned that Neeto is unfairly competing against SPC. A federal cause of action for unfair competition provides remedies for common law passing off, unfair competition, and state statutory unfair trade practices.[753] The Lanham Act prohibits anyone from misleading or misrepresenting facts in commerce that are likely to cause confusion, mistake, or deception as to origin, sponsorship, affiliation, or endorsement of the unauthorized user's products by the trademark owner.[754] A finding of passing off requires an association between the mark and its owner in the mind of the consumer and a likelihood of consumer confusion when the mark is used with the goods or services of another.[755] *Passing off* rests on the premise of misappropriation of the skill, labor, and investment of another.[756]

Neeto deceives potential customers as to the origin of its site, as well as the origin of the products featured on the site, when it lures these customers to its web pages using SPC's trademarks as its web site's metatags; Neeto leads customers to think that SPC is somewhat associated with Neeto. These customers may then associate Neeto's computer-related products with SPC. Thus, Neeto's act results in the passing off of its low-quality computer peripherals on the tails of SPC's standards of high quality and its goodwill, earned through significant investment of time and money. Unfair competition usually accompanies trademark infringement and dilution causes of action.

[iii] Misappropriation. In our example, SPC may argue that Neeto's action constitutes misappropriation. The tort of misappropriation is governed solely by state law, as there is no federal statute providing remedies for misappropriation.

---

[752] Brookfield Communications, Inc. v. West Coast Entertainment Corp., 174 F.3d 1036, 1045 (9th Cir. 1999).

[753] *See* Federal Unfair Competition Statute derived from Lanham Act § 43(a).

[754] *See* 15 U.S.C. § 1125(a)(1) (1998).

[755] *See* Jeffrey Kuester, Link Law on the Internet: A Panel Discussion, 38 IDEA 197, 250 (1998).

[756] *See* American Footwear Corp. v. General Footwear Co., 609 F.2d 655, 662 (2d Cir. 1979) (defining passing off).

Misappropriation is a tort exclusively governed by state law. A successful misappropriation claim requires the trademark owner to prove that the owner has invested time, money, and effort in the mark, that the unauthorized user appropriated the mark at insignificant cost, and that the unauthorized user's act injured the trademark owner, as by loss of profits or royalties.[757] Misappropriation, a judge-constructed legal hybrid of unfair competition, fills in the gaps where patent, copyright, and traditional trademark laws do not provide an adequate remedy for the protection of intellectual property right.[758]

Assuming SPC invested significant amounts of time, money, and effort in building its goodwill in the marks, Neeto's unauthorized use injured SPC's business because potential customers were diverted to Neeto's site. Although the marks were used invisibly, Neeto accomplished its purpose of using them to help its business at the cost of SPC, thereby misappropriating SPC's trademarks.

[iv] Trademark dilution. SPC can also seek relief under the Federal Trademark Dilution Act of 1995 (FTDA), which added § 43(C) to the Lanham Act, and under the more limited state antidilution statutes. Trademark dilution differs from infringement because it does not require proof of confusion.[759] The FTDA provides remedies for trademark dilution of well-known marks.[760] The Act defines *dilution* as "the lessening of the capacity of a famous mark to identify or distinguish goods and services without regard to competition between the owner of the mark and others or to likelihood of confusion, deception or mistake."[761] Dilution is an "erosion of the distinctiveness and prestige of a trademark caused by the sale of other goods or services under the same name . . . although there is no confusion as to source."[762]

Dilution would be a desirable legal cause of action to SPC in this situation, because there is no requirement that the potential customers be confused between marks. SPC may argue that Neeto's use of SUFFOLK 2000 and MILLENIUM-II constitutes dilution by blurring because Neeto uses these trademarks to lure potential customers to its site. The potential customers who are led to Neeto's site may no longer think that SPC's marks are exclusively associated with SPC. SPC may claim that Neeto's conduct is also dilution by tarnishment. Potential customers,

---

[757] *See* 1 J. Thomas McCarthy, McCarthy on Trademarks and Unfair Competition, at 10-90 (1996, 1999).

[758] *Id.* at 10-90.

[759] *See* McCarthy, *supra* note 757, at 24-117.

[760] Section 43(C)(1) provides:

> The owner of a famous mark shall be entitled, subject to the principles of equity and upon such terms as the court deems reasonable, to an injunction against another person's commercial use in commerce of a mark or trade name, if such use begins after the mark has become famous and causes dilution of the distinctiveness of the mark, and to obtain such other relief as is provided in this subsection.

15 U.S.C. § 1125(c) (2002).

[761] 15 U.S.C. § 1127 (2002).

[762] Eli Lilly & Co. v. Natural Answers, 86 F. Supp. 2d 834 (S.D. Ind. 2000) (citation omitted).

who expect to see high-quality computers, enter Neeto's site and find instead low-quality computer peripherals. Neeto's action will reduce SPC's goodwill and high standard of quality in the mind of those potential customers because they may think that SPC is somewhat associated with these low-quality computer peripherals. It is unlikely that SPC's mark is famous or distinctive enough to qualify for protection under the federal dilution act, but it may become famous through online advertising and publicity.

[b] Limitations of Current Law

The confusion of SPC's customer may be considered similar to the point-of-sale confusion claims in traditional business practices. Thus, if the initial interest confusion subsides before the consumer makes a purchase at Neeto's site, there is arguably no commercial injury.[763] This is a narrow view, however, because it does not take into consideration the uniqueness of Internet commerce, such as when potential consumers are misled to other sites and never return to the trademark owner's site. Others may claim that it is not the customer but the search engine that is being misled, thus there is no consumer confusion violating the Lanham Act.

The original misrepresentation to the search engine, however, may have caused the customer's confusion, with the misuse of the trademark causing the original confusion. Arguably, in both of these scenarios the damage is done to the potential customers because the manipulative metatagging has increased their search costs (primarily in time), and it may be considered a goal of trademark law to reduce consumer search costs.[764] Current laws do not specifically define such a violation of trademarks. Perhaps some courts may extend trademark protection to redress the inconvenience of increased search costs. Such interpretive process can result in different outcomes in different jurisdictions; hence, it can lead to forum shopping by the parties. Furthermore, different jurisdictions may interpret differently the degrees of confusion in traditional analysis of infringement, or the degree of fame ("fame" not defined in statute) required for protection, which may also lead to forum shopping.

The federal dilution act limits action to misuse of famous marks. This leaves start-up companies and owners of nonfamous marks without a remedy. Misuse of a nonfamous mark may be just as damaging to its owner as misuse of a famous mark would be to its owner. SPC's marks SUFFOLK 2000 and MILLENIUM-II may not be famous, like IBM™ or MOBILE™, but SPC has every right to the protection of these marks because it has expended great effort and resources to gain recognition for them in conjunction with its products.[765] The use of SPC's marks in connection with poor-quality computer peripherals dilutes the value and whittles away the selling power of those marks as applied to SPC's products. Where the federal dilution act is the primary source of remedy for misuse of trademarks

---

[763] See Jeffrey Kuester, Link Law on the Internet: A Panel Discussion, 38 IDEA 197, 218 (1998).

[764] See McCarthy, supra note 757, at 2-3.

[765] IBM is a registered trademark of IBM Corp.; Mobile is a registered trademark of Mobil Corp.

in noncompeting situations (as infringement or unfair competition may not be on point), its limitation to famous marks prevents a fair application of the law to all marks.

A plaintiff may be limited in finding a viable remedy due to the gaps in current trademark and unfair competition law. For example, some courts have determined that the utilization of a plaintiff's descriptive marks in web site metatags may be insufficient alone to constitute trademark infringement or unfair competition. A competitor is generally permitted to include a competitor's trade name in a metatag where the use is simply descriptive. A defendant "can legitimately use an appropriate descriptive term in its metatags under the fair use doctrine."[766] Consequently, a plaintiff in an online dispute has to bring multiple causes of action, such as trademark infringement, trademark dilution, unfair competition, and misappropriation, and hope that at least one cause of action will provide him with a remedy. Thus, if SPC is not able to persuade the court that Neeto's conduct constitutes trademark infringement, dilution, or unfair competition, SPC would not have a remedy nor a means of protecting its business, its trademarks, and its customers. Many potentially unfair uses of metatags may go undeterred in the event that no remedy applies.

[c]   SPC's Best Course of Action

Ms. Adams informs SPC that they can bring action against Neeto under traditional theories of protection, such as federal and state trademark infringement, trademark dilution, and unfair competition. She advises that these theories have limitations when applied to new and nebulous areas, such as metatags, and that SPC may be unable to secure an injunction. Ms. Adams mentions that use of trademarks invisibly in metatags is one of the newer ways of misusing trademarks, and that there is a weak fit between the misuse of metatags and traditional intellectual property remedies. Interpretations of the available laws are similar to a coin toss, differing from court to court. Thus, SPC may be left a victim of the electronic age.

§ 4.04   TRADE SECRETS IN CYBERSPACE

[A]   Overview

An Internet company can acquire four broad categories of information, which are classified as (1) public domain, (2) proprietary, (3) confidential, and (4) trade secrets.[767] *Public domain* information, as its name suggests, consists of common knowledge or easily available information; it is available for anyone's use without permission. Government documents, such as state and federal statutes, agency hearings, and Congressional Reports, are in the public domain. Copy-

---

[766] *Brookfield*, 174 F.2d at 1065-66.

[767] Fenwick and West, Trade Secrets: A Practical Guide for High Technology Companies 2-3 (1995).

righted works go into the public domain after the term of copyright expires. Thus, the works of Louisa May Alcott, Oliver Wendell Holmes, and Robert Louis Stevenson are in the public domain, because the copyright has expired on them. Similarly, inventions go into the pubic domain after the patent term has expired.

A second type of information is *proprietary information*. The predicate of proprietary information is some claim of ownership. Patent and copyright law may protect proprietary information.[768] The third form of information is *confidential information*, "that is restricted from unlimited disclosure by the person or entity who knows it."[769]

The fourth category of information is *trade secrets,* which are protected by state tort law. Trade secret laws protect against the misappropriation of proprietary information by third parties, including competitors.[770] For a company to recover for misappropriation of a trade secret, it must prove that the defendant put the proprietary information in question to some commercial use. A trade secret is neither known by others nor readily ascertainable by proper means.

The classic example of a trade secret is the formula for Coca-Cola, which has been a closely held secret for more than a century. An Internet company's software, hardware design, computer networking technology, and future design specifications may be protected as trade secrets. Also protectable as trade secrets is proprietary information such as financial data, including pricing, cost information, customer lists, buyer contacts, and vendor information.

Trade secrets in the online world need to be protected just as in the "bricks and mortar" world.[771] The first step in a trade secrets audit is to classify information classifiable as a trade secret. Information that is transmitted on the Internet may become "generally known" and destroy the information's trade secret status. Information both disclosed in public court files and made "generally known" by Internet publication will likely lose its trade secret status.[772]

Trade secrets may not be patentable or subject to copyright, since these require disclosure in return for a limited monopoly.[773] That said, there is no requirement that trade secrets be trademarked, patented, or copyrighted, and no

---

[768] *Id.* at 2.

[769] Fenwick and West, *supra* note 584.

[770] 415 University Computing Co. v. Lykes-Youngstown Corp., 504 F.2d 518 (5th Cir. 1974).

[771] Monster.com settled a trade secret lawsuit against its former President and 18 ex-employees who left the company to join a rival firm and paid the employees' legal fees. Monster.com Drops Suit Against Ex-employees, N.Y. Times (May 2, 2001) (visited May 1, 2001), http://www.nytimes.com/2001/05/01/technology/01MONS.html.

[772] Merely describing trade secrets does not destroy their status as a secret. For example, a company sued a competitor alleging that the competitor had misappropriated its trade secrets. The court rejected the defendant's argument that a description of these trade secrets in an unsealed court file destroyed the information's trade secret status. Hoechst Diafoil Co. v. Nan Ya Plastics Corp., 174 F.3d 411 (4th Cir. 1999) (rejecting argument that a document's presence in public files destroyed its secrecy and reasoning that public disclosure in court documents alone did not make information "generally known").

[773] National Conference of Commissioners on Uniform State Laws, The Uniform Trade Secrets Act: A Summary (visited Apr. 28, 2002), http://www.nccU.S.l.org/summary/utsa.html.

registration procedure exists for doing so. A trade secret is protected by keeping it secret, not by disclosing it through a registration process. For SPC, a trade secret would be any information used in the operation of its online business that is valuable and that gives the company a competitive edge, such as profit margin, sales training methods, and long-term growth plans. Judge Richard Posner has stated that trade secrets are "of growing importance to the competitiveness of American industry . . . [and] the future of the nation depends in no small part on the efficiency of industry, and the efficiency of industry depends in no small part on the protection of intellectual property. Trade secrets have become part of the currency of the services and software-based economy built upon an infrastructure of information assets."[774]

The trade secret owner must use reasonable means to protect its trade secrets (see Table 4.8). The principal dangers to trade secrets are from insiders who have access to a company's confidential information. To qualify as a trade secret, confidential information must be not readily ascertainable by proper means and not generally known. Typically, companies require employees to sign agreements to transfer creative works on the web site to the company, and these "work for hire" agreements generally contain a duty of confidentiality that continues to protect trade secrets after the termination of the employment relationship.

[1]   Uniform Trade Secrets Act

[a]   *Misappropriation of Trade Secrets*

The Uniform Trade Secrets Act (UTSA) defines *misappropriation* as the use of improper means, such as misrepresentation or breach of a duty, to maintain secrecy.[775] UTSA is a model statute that provides a statutory state law remedy in all but a few states.[776] One of the broadly stated policies behind trade secret law is "the maintenance of standards of commercial ethics."[777] A trade secret owner has the right to control use and access and to take measures to prevent disclosure. If reasonable measures are in place to prevent disclosure and a wrongdoer uses improper means to access or use information, the owner will have a remedy for the tort of misappropriation; there may also be a crime of computer fraud if the information was gained by means of unauthorized access.

---

[774] Rockwell Graphics Sys. v. DEV Indus., 925 F.2d 174, 180 (7th Cir. 1991).

[775] UTSA, § 1(1)(2).

[776] Uniform Trade Secrets Act (UTSA) § 1 (2002). The UTSA was approved by the National Conference of Uniform State Laws (NCCUSL) in 1979 and amended in 1985. Forty-four states have adopted UTSA: Alaska, Arkansas, Alabama, Arizona, California, Colorado, Connecticut, Delaware, District of Columbia, Florida, Georgia, Hawaii, Idaho, Illinois, Indiana, Iowa, Kansas, Kentucky, Louisiana, Maine, Maryland, Michigan, Minnesota, Mississippi, Missouri, Montana, Nebraska, Nevada, New Hampshire, New Mexico, North Dakota, Ohio, Oklahoma, Oregon, Rhode Island, South Carolina, South Dakota, Tennessee, Utah, Vermont, Virginia, Washington, West Virginia, and Wisconsin.

[777] Kewanee Oil Co. v. Bicron Corp., 416 U.S. 470 (1974).

Table 4.8
Overview of Trade Secrets

Method for obtaining protection	Use of commercially reasonable means to protect secret; nondisclosure agreements with employees and consultants; information security
Remedies for infringement	Injunctive relief and damages; tort of misappropriation; punitive damages and compensatory damages

[b]   Definition of Trade Secret

Internet trade secrets are often more vulnerable because the interconnected system of computers makes it possible for hackers, competitors, and experts in corporate espionage to steal information without leaving physical evidence. The Internet economy is known for a rapid turnover in employees, and online companies face the constant danger that an ex-employee will appropriate trade secrets for use in a competitor's business.

The first requirement for a plaintiff suing under the UTSA is that its claim involve an actual trade secret. The UTSA defines *trade secrets* to include "information, including a formula, pattern, compilation, program, device, method, technique, or process, that:

(i) derives independent economic value, actual or potential, from not being generally known to, and not being readily ascertainable by proper means by, other persons who can obtain economic value from its disclosure or use, and (ii) is the subject of efforts that are reasonable under the circumstances to maintain its secrecy.[778]

[c]   "Improper Means" Test

The second requirement is that the information derives actual or potential economic value from not being disclosed or readily ascertainable by improper means[779] by other persons.[780] Since a trade secret is lost through public knowledge,

---

[778] UTSA § 1(4).

[779] Comment 1 to UTSA sets forth five legitimate means of obtaining knowledge of trade secrets: "1. Discovery by independent invention; 2. Discovery by 'reverse engineering,' that is, by starting with the known product and working backward to find the method by which it was developed. The acquisition of the known product must, of course, also be by a fair and honest means (i.e., purchase of the item on the open market for reverse engineering to be lawful); 3. Discovery under a license from the owner of the trade secret; 4. Observation of the item in public use or on public display; and 5. Obtaining the trade secret from published literature." UTSA, § 1, comment.

[780] The comment to UTSA, § 1 states:

The definition of "trade secret" contains a reasonable departure from the Restatement of Torts (First) definition which required that a trade secret be "continuously used in one's business." The broader definition in the proposed Act extends protection to a

the unauthorized disclosure of a trade secret also constitutes the tort of misappropriation.[781] Unlike patents, there is no requirement that trade secrets be novel. Mathematical algorithms, not protectable by patents, may be protected as trade secrets if not readily ascertainable or known.

For example, an ex-employee who bypasses a company's information security procedures to appropriate trade secrets is using improper means. An ex-employee who sells confidential information to a foreign competitor is also using an improper means to appropriate trade secrets. Another example of an improper means would be intercepting an e-mail message containing trade secrets.[782] The concept of acquiring trade secrets by "improper means" is key to obtaining relief under UTSA. Section 1(1) of UTSA defines *misappropriation* as acquisition of trade secrets by improper means, including "theft, bribery, misrepresentation, breach or inducement of a breach of a duty to maintain secrecy, or espionage through electronic or other means."[783]

The UTSA requires that information that is the subject of a trade secret be protected by means that are "reasonable under the circumstances to maintain its secrecy."[784] Theft, bribery, fraud, or other improper means may constitute misappropriation.

Trade secret law does not restrain an employee, competitor, or third party from acquiring confidential information through proper means. If so-called confidential information is freely available on the Internet or otherwise readily ascertainable, it is not classified as a trade secret. If a company's employees publish confidential information on the Internet, the information is available through proper means. If information was previously disclosed in court proceedings, it is no longer secret and may be freely used.

Reverse engineering is a *proper* method of learning about trade secrets. Competitors are free to "reverse engineer" a company's software, hardware, and web site to learn about its methods of doing business. Trade secret law only restrains insiders and outsiders from using *improper* means of appropriating SPC's trade secrets.

---

plaintiff who has not yet had an opportunity or acquired the means to put a trade secret to use. The definition includes information that has commercial value from a negative viewpoint, for example the results of lengthy and expensive research which proves that a certain process will not work could be of great value to a competitor.

UTSA § 1, comment.

[781] For liability to exist under UTSA, a § 1(4) trade secret must exist and either a person's acquisition of the trade secret, disclosure of the trade secret to others, or use of the trade secret must be improper under § 1(2). The mere copying of an unpatented item is not actionable.

[782] Improper means could include otherwise lawful conduct which is improper under the circumstances; e.g., an airplane overflight used as aerial reconnaissance to determine the competitor's plant layout during construction of the plant. E.I. du Pont de Nemours & Co., Inc. v. Christopher, 431 F.2d 1012 (5th Cir. 1970), *cert. denied,* 400 U.S. 1024 (1970).

[783] UTSA § 1(1).

[784] UTSA § 1.4(ii).

[d] *Reasonable Efforts to Maintain Trade Secrets*

A company must use reasonable efforts to protect its trade secrets, not every possible or conceivable step.[785] The UTSA requires that a trade secret owner use reasonable efforts to maintain the secrecy of its information. The efforts required to maintain secrecy are those "reasonable under the circumstances." The courts apply a negligence-based formula, in which the burden of precaution need not be greater than the radius of the risk in protecting trade secrets. For example, if trade secrets are transmitted on the Internet, it may be reasonable to encrypt the message. Competitors or unknown hackers may also intercept trade secrets if transmitted in an unencrypted form. Digital signatures with encrypted messages may be the only reasonable means of protecting electronically transmitted trade secrets. Therefore, it may be reasonable to transmit confidential information in an encrypted envelope with a digital signature providing proof of authorship and privacy.[786] A court might find, however, that it is unreasonable to transmit trade secrets on the Internet since hackers may launch cryptographic attacks against the algorithms used to encrypt trade secrets. The measures used to protect trade secrets will depend on the value of the Internet.

[e] *UTSA Remedies for Misappropriation*

The UTSA provides a wide array of remedies for trade secret misappropriation, including preliminary injunctive relief, monetary damages, lost profits, consequential damages, lost royalties, attorneys' fees, and punitive damages. Section 3 of UTSA, entitled "damages," provides:

> a) Except to the extent that a material and prejudicial change of position prior to acquiring knowledge or reason to know of misappropriation renders a monetary recovery inequitable, a complainant is entitled to recover damages for misappropriation. Damages can include both the actual loss caused by misappropriation and the unjust enrichment caused by misappropriation that is not taken into account in computing actual loss. In lieu of damages measured by any other methods, the damages caused by misappropriation may be measured by imposition of liability for a reasonable royalty for a misappropriator's unauthorized disclosure or use of a trade secret.
>
> (b) If willful and malicious misappropriation exists, the court may award exemplary damages in an amount not exceeding twice any award made under subsection (a).[787]

UTSA adopts a three-year statute of limitations, and it is uncertain whether courts will apply the "continuing wrong" theory to extend it to determine when the time limit for a cause of action has expired. A court may toll the trade secret cause

---

[785] Rockwell Graphic Sys., Inc. v. DEV. Indus., Ind., 925 F.2d 174, 180 (7th Cir. 1991).

[786] Bruce Schneier, Applied Cryptography: Protocols, Algorithms, and Source Code in C 227 (2d ed. 1996).

[787] UTSA § 3.

of action at the "initial misappropriation."[788] The UTSA statute of limitations is three years after the misappropriation is discovered or after it should have been discovered, had reasonable diligence been exercised.[789]

The remedies for the misappropriation of trade secrets include damages,[790] injunctive relief,[791] and attorneys' fees if bad faith is proven.[792] A reasonable royalty may be obtained for the loss of revenue attributable to the misappropriation of a trade secret. Punitive or exemplary damages are capped at twice compensatory damages.

Preliminary injunctive relief is also available under the UTSA, which permits the owner of a trade secret to seek an injunction for actual or threatened misappropriation.[793] The purpose of injunctive relief is to preserve the status quo and to prevent defendants from destroying "smoking gun" evidence.[794] A temporary

---

[788] Section 6 of UTSA states that "[a]n action for misappropriation must be brought within 3 years after the misappropriation is discovered or by the exercise of reasonable diligence should have been discovered. For the purposes of this section, a continuing misappropriation constitutes a single claim." The Comment to UTSA § 6 states: "There presently is a conflict of authority as to whether trade secret misappropriation is a continuing wrong." Compare Monolith Portland Midwest Co. v. Kaiser Aluminum & Chemical Corp., 407 F.2d 288 (9th Cir. 1969) (not a continuing wrong under California law—limitation period upon all recovery begins upon initial misappropriation) with Underwater Storage, Inc. v. U.S. Rubber Co., 371 F.2d 950 (C.D. Cal. 1966), *cert. denied,* 386 U.S. 911 (1967) ("continuing wrong under general principles—limitation period with respect to a specific act of misappropriation begins at the time that the act of misappropriation occurs").

[789] *Id.* at § 6 (noting that the statute of limitations is within three years after the discovery of misappropriation).

[790] UTSA § 3 (explaining that damages may be recoverable for misappropriation of trade secrets).

[791] UTSA § 2 (noting that actual or threatened misappropriations may be enjoined).

[792] *Id.* at § 4 (noting that attorneys' fees may be recoverable where a claim of misappropriation is made in bad faith, a motion to terminate an injunction is made or resisted in bad faith, or willful and malicious misappropriation exists).

[793] The Comment to § 3 notes that damages are set for the period in which information is entitled to protection, "plus the additional period, if any, in which a misappropriator retains an advantage over good faith competitors because of misappropriation." UTSA § 3, Comment. The measure of damages then includes actual damages plus the unjust benefit to a misappropriator caused by misappropriation during this time alone. *Id.*

The comment further notes that "[a] claim for actual damages and net profits can be combined with a claim for injunctive relief, but, if both claims are granted, the injunctive relief ordinarily will preclude a monetary award for a period in which the injunction is effective." *Id.*

[794] Scott D. Marrs, Trade Secrets: Preliminary Relief in Trade Secret Cases, Texas Bar J. (Oct. 1998) at 880. Section 2, titled injunctive relief, provides:

> (a) Actual or threatened misappropriation may be enjoined. Upon application to the court, an injunction shall be terminated when the trade secret has ceased to exist, but the injunction may be continued for an additional reasonable period of time in order to eliminate commercial advantage that otherwise would be derived from the misappropriation.
> (b) If the court determines that it would be unreasonable to prohibit future use. In exceptional circumstances, an injunction may condition future use upon payment of a reasonable royalty for no longer than the period of time for which use could have been prohibited. Exceptional circumstances include, but are not limited to, a material and prejudicial change of position prior to acquiring knowledge or reason to know of misappropriation that renders a prohibitive injunction inequitable.
>
> In appropriate circumstances, affirmative acts to protect a trade secret may be compelled by court order.

UTSA § 2.

restraining order or other injunctive relief is ordered if a disclosure threatens harm to the trade secret owners.[795]

UTSA permits the owner of a trade secret to recover exemplary damages up to two times the actual amount of damages if the misappropriation is willful and malicious.[796] Exemplary (or punitive damages, as they are called in most states) are designed to punish and deter the defendant. If an ex-employee has sold trade secrets to a competitor, punitive damages may be sought against both parties. The legal standard of willfulness and malice must be met before statutory punitive damages are recoverable. Attorneys' fees are also recoverable if the misappropriation is willful and malicious.[797]

[f] Potential UTSA Defendants

Employees have a duty not to disclose trade secrets acquired in the employment relationship independent of any express nondisclosure agreement.[798] Information may be disclosed to employees, business partners, or others in the normal course of doing business without loss of trade secret protection. Companies frequently require that their employees sign nondisclosure agreements to maintain secrecy. If a current employee or ex-employee discloses a trade secret to a competitor without permission, civil and criminal liability attaches for the theft of trade secrets. Even if there is employment without a nondisclosure clause, the employee may nevertheless be bound by a duty not to disclose confidential information.

Where there is a First Amendment issue, courts will frequently apply a balancing test in determining whether trade secrets should be protected. In a case where the defendant posted trade secret information, the court held that "[plaintiff]'s statutory right to protect its economically valuable trade secret is not an interest that is 'more fundamental' that the First Amendment right to freedom of speech or even on equal footing with the national security interests and other vital government interests that have previously been found insufficient to justify a prior restraint."[799]

---

[795] Section 2(a) permits threatened misappropriations to be enjoined, and it is common to seek injunctions restraining future harm from use and disclosure of misappropriated trade secrets, UTSA § 2(a), Comment.

[796] The comment to § 3 states:

> If willful and malicious misappropriation is found to exist, Section 3(b) authorizes the court to award a complainant exemplary damages in addition to the actual recovery under Section 3(a) an amount not exceeding twice that recovery. This provision follows federal patent law in leaving discretionary trebling to the judge even though there may be a jury; compare 35 U.S.C. Section 284 (1976).

UTSA § 3, comment.

[797] UTSA § 4 permits a court to award attorneys' fees: "If (i) a claim of misappropriation is made in bad faith, (ii) a motion to terminate an injunction is made or resisted in bad faith, or (iii) willful and malicious misappropriation exists, the court may award reasonable attorney's fees to the prevailing party." UTSA § 4.

[798] Scott D. Marrs, *supra* note 611.

[799] Shannon Lafferty, Trade Secrets Lose Out to Speech, The Recorder, Nov. 2, 2001 (discussing DVD Copy Control Ass'n v. Bunner, 2001 Cal. App. Lexis 1179 (Cal. Ct. App. Nov. 1, 2001)), at http://www.law.com.

[2] Alternative Claims

[a] *Restatement of Torts*

Under the tort of misappropriation, the Restatement of Torts is an influential source of law in the states that have yet to adopt the Uniform Trade Secrets Act. The Restatement defines a *trade secret* as information used in the operation of a business or other enterprise, "that is sufficiently valuable and secret to afford an actual or potential economic advantage over others."[800]

[b] *Breach of Confidence*

In addition to the tort of misappropriation for trade secrets, a company may also have a *breach of confidence* claim. To prevail in a breach of confidence claim, the plaintiff must show that (1) it conveyed confidential and novel information, (2) defendants had knowledge that the information was being disclosed in confidence, (3) there was an understanding between plaintiff and defendants that the confidence be maintained, and (4) there was disclosure or use in violation of the understanding.[801]

[3] Criminal Prosecution for Trade Secret Theft

The Economic Espionage Act of 1996 (EEA) criminalizes the theft of trade secrets,[802] by making the theft of trade secrets a federal crime. An individual whose misappropriation of a trade secret benefits a foreign government, instrumentality, or agent may be sentenced to a federal prison for up to 15 years and fined up to $500,000.[803] An entity that steals a trade secret benefiting a foreign government can be fined up to $10 million.[804] The theft of trade secrets for the benefit of "anyone other than the owner" is also punishable by criminal and civil penalties.[805]

The defendant must knowingly have stolen, duplicated, downloaded, or received trade secrets belonging to an owner.[806] Individuals found guilty of trade secret theft benefiting parties other than foreign governments may be fined or imprisoned for not more than 10 years, or both.[807] Any organization that know-

---

[800] The Restatement (First) of Torts § 757 and § 758 (1939) provided tort remedies for the misappropriation of trade secrets. In 1995, the National Conference of Commissioners on Uniform State Laws approved the Restatement (Third) of Unfair Competition § 39 (1995) (providing tort remedies for misappropriation of trade secrets).

[801] Cinebase Software v. Media Guaranty Trust, Inc., 1998 U.S. Dist. LEXIS 15007 (D.N.D. Cal., Sept. 21, 1998).

[802] Economic Espionage Act of 1996, 18 U.S.C. §§ 1831-1839 (2002).

[803] 18 U.S.C. § 1831(a)(5) (2002).

[804] 18 U.S.C. § 1831(b) (2002).

[805] 18 U.S.C. § 1832 (2002).

[806] 18 U.S.C. § 1832(1)(5) (2002).

[807] 18 U.S.C. § 1832(5) (2002).

ingly transmits, receives, or possesses misappropriated trade secrets not benefiting foreign governments may be fined "not more than $5,000,000."[808]

Like the UTSA, the EEA defines *trade secrets* broadly to include the following:

> All forms and types of financial, business, scientific, technical economic or engineering information, including patterns, plans, compilations, program devices, formulas, designs, prototypes, methods, techniques, processes, procedures, programs or codes, whether tangible or intangible, and whether or not stored, compiled, or memorialized physically, electronically, graphically, photographically, or in writing if: (A) the owner thereof has taken reasonable measures to keep such information secret; and (B) the information derives independent economic value, actual or potential, from not being generally known to, and not being readily ascertainable through proper means by the public.[809]

The EEA applies to any individual who transmits, receives, or possesses stolen trade secrets.[810] Individuals convicted of violating the EEA may be punished by fines of $500,000 and up to 10 years in prison.[811] Corporate defendants may be fined up to $5,000,000.[812] The standard of proof for criminal prosecution is "beyond a reasonable doubt that an individual or corporation knowingly received, bought, or possessed misappropriated or stolen trade secrets."

The EEA criminalizes the knowing theft of trade secrets, as well as attempts or conspiracies to steal trade secrets. The EEA does not apply unless an online company employs reasonable measures to keep its trade secrets secret. The EEA "protects a wider variety" of information than most civil laws; however, "it is clear that Congress did not intend . . . to prohibit lawful competition such as the use of general skills or parallel development of a similar product,"[813] The EEA applies to conduct occurring outside the United States if the offender is a U.S. citizen or permanent resident alien or an organization (corporation, LLP, etc.) organized under the law of the United States.[814] The Third Circuit in *Hsu* observed that the purpose of the EEA was to punish "the disgruntled former employee who walks out of his former company with a computer diskette full of engineering schematics."[815] The EEA does not preempt civil or criminal remedies for the misappropriation of trade

---

[808] 18 U.S.C. § 1832(b) (2002).

[809] 18 U.S.C. § 1839(3) (2002).

[810] 18 U.S.C. § 1832(a)(3) (2002).

[811] 18 U.S.C. § 1838 (2002).

[812] 18 U.S.C. § 1832(a) (2002).

[813] United States v. Hsu, 155 F.3d. 189, 193 (3d Cir. 1998); *see also* United States v. Hsu, 982 F. Supp. 1022 (E.D. Pa. 1997) (denying protective order to prevent disclosure of trade secrets to defendant, since existence of trade secrets was an element of case charging theft and attempted theft of trade secrets in violation of Economic Espionage Act).

[814] 18 U.S.C. § 1837 (2001).

[815] *Id.* at 201 (citing H.R. Rep. No. 104-788, at 7).

secrets.[816] The First Circuit in *United States v. Martin*[817] observed that the EEA "was not designed to punish competition, even when such competition relies on the know-how of former employees of a direct competitor. It was, however, designed to prevent those employees (and their future employers) from taking advantage of confidential information gained, discovered, copied, or taken while employed elsewhere."[818] Criminal penalties for stolen trade secrets may also derive from violation of the federal wire and mail fraud statutes.[819] The Justice Department has brought 27 cases under the EEA.[820] Civil tort actions are also frequently brought for trade secret theft. Trade secrets disputes can result in multimillion-dollar judgments. Cargill, for example, agreed to pay $100 million to settle a claim for the theft of genetic materials by a former researcher at a biotech firm.[821]

In addition, every state has a computer crime statute. A wrongdoer who steals trade secrets may be liable for criminal fraud, for theft, or for computer crimes. In a recent case a high technology company sued a rival, accusing it of stealing software, copyright infringement, and conspiracy.[822] Trade secret theft is increasingly prosecuted as a criminal offense. A former vice president of Borland and a chief executive officer of Symantec Corporation, a competitor of Borland, were indicted by a California court for criminal theft of trade secrets.[823]

Trade secret litigation is sometimes misused or abused to create a cloud around a competitor's business. The mere threat of a trade secret lawsuit may have a chilling effect on client developments, new customers, or employee recruitment.

[4] Preventing Losses: Nondisclosure Agreements

High technology employers should require their employees to sign standard nondisclosure agreements, which are evidence that a company is taking reasonable

---

[816] 18 U.S.C. § 1838 (2001).

[817] 228 F.3d 1 (1st Cir. 2000).

[818] *Id.* at 20.

[819] In United States v. Martin, 228 F.3d 1 (1st Cir. 2000), the defendants were convicted under the EEA as well as of wire fraud and mail fraud. *See* 18 U.S.C. §§ 2 (aiding and abetting), 1341 (mail fraud), 1343 (wire fraud), and 1346 (honest services fraud). To prove wire or mail fraud, the government must show (1) a scheme to defraud by means of false pretenses, (2) the defendant's knowing and willing participation in the scheme with the intent to defraud, and (3) the use of interstate wire or mail communications in furtherance of the scheme. *Id.* at 33 (citing United States v. Montminy, 936 F.2d 626, 627 (1st Cir. 1991) (defining elements of federal mail fraud statute)).

[820] Douglas Pasternak, In the DNA Vials, Secrets to Steal, 130 U.S. News & World Report 42 (May 21, 2001).

[821] *Id.*

[822] Lawrence M. Fisher, Avant Wins Ruling in Cadence Copyright Suit, N.Y. Times (Sept. 10, 1999) at C2.

[823] People v. Eubanks, 38 Cal. App. 4th 114, 44 Cal. Rptr. 2d 846 (1995).

steps to protect its trade secrets.[824] Keep in mind, however, that an overly restrictive covenant in an employment contract may actually be counterproductive by limiting a plaintiff's right to enjoin a defendant.[825]

The Comment to § 2 of the UTSA states:

> Finally, reasonable efforts to maintain secrecy have been held to include advising employees of the existence of a trade secret, limiting access to a trade secret on "need to know basis," and controlling plant access. On the other hand, public disclosure of information through display, trade journal publications, advertising, or other carelessness can preclude protection.[826]

A written agreement is proof that a company's employees had notice of their duty to maintain confidentiality. A defendant may argue that a company's failure to secure a nondisclosure agreement reflects a too casual attitude toward secrecy, potentially destroying the trade secret status of software or other information.[827]

Nondisclosure agreements may be customized to cover employees, contractors, trade partners, licensees, consultants, grantees, bidders, or government entities who have access to a company's trade secrets. Trade secrets should be marked with a notice that they are confidential. As with military intelligence, however, there is a danger when either too much or too little information is classified as confidential. Most importantly, a company's security policy must be enforced.

A nondisclosure or confidentiality agreement, frequently used by trading partners, can take diverse forms. A nondisclosure agreement must address the question of who owns confidential or copyrighted information. Nondisclosure agreements must be customized to the type of business activity and the form of corporate organization they address. A Fortune 500 company with subsidiaries in

---

[824] Companies may also want to consider entering *noncompete* agreements to establish that they are taking reasonable efforts to protect their trade secrets. Courts will enforce reasonable *noncompete* agreements as long as the agreement does not restrain commerce or does not impede an ex-employee's ability to earn a livelihood. Whether a noncompetition agreement is reasonable depends upon

> (1) the agreement's geographic and temporal limits; (2) whether the employee represents the sole customer contact; (3) whether the employee possesses confidential information or trade secrets; (4) whether the agreement seeks to restrain ordinary, rather than unfair, competition; (5) whether the agreement stifles inherent skills of the employee or whether employee's talents were developed during the employment; (6) the balance of the agreement's detriment to employer and employee; (7) whether the agreement restricts employee's sole means of support; and (8) whether the restricted employment is merely incidental to the main employment.

LEXIS-NEXIS v. Beer, 41 F. Supp. 2d 950 (D. Minn. 1999).

[825] EarthWeb, Inc. v. Schlack, 71 F. Supp. 2d 2999 (S.D.N.Y. 1999) (holding that onerous restrictive covenant in at-will employment contract limited plaintiff's right to enjoin defendant from pursuing other employment through reliance on the theory of inevitable disclosure).

[826] UTSA § 2, Comment.

[827] Weseley Software Dev. Corp. v. Burdette, 977 F. Supp. 137 (D. Conn. 1996) (noting defense argument that failure of plaintiff to demand nondisclosure agreement was evidence of lax attitudes about confidential information).

many countries should tailor its nondisclosure agreements to take into account cultural and regulatory differences.

[5]   Trade Secrets and the Internet

Web sites may contain secrets in the form of data on log files and information obtained from an audit of what visitors do at a corporate web site. If a web site developer is building a specialized company web site, corporate counsel may wish to draft noncompetition and nondisclosure agreements. An appropriate use of a *noncompetition* agreement would be to prevent a web site developer from disclosing information on the web development project to competitors and third parties when working on their projects.[828]

Companies must make reasonable efforts to maintain the secrecy of information. The use of encryption and the other information security tools described in Chapter Three is essential in protecting trade secrets on the Internet. The Internet and e-mail usage policies described in Chapter Nine also contain useful information on protecting trade secrets on the Internet. It may not be enough to have a formal policy regarding confidentiality of documents if there is no mechanism of enforcement. At minimum, documents should be labeled with a confidential and proprietary mark as evidence that they are confidential.

Amazon.com and Wal-Mart Stores settled a trade secrets case in which the online bookseller was charged with hiring Wal-Mart's essential computer systems managers to steal trade secrets.[829] The Church of Scientology sued the Washington Post for misappropriating and publishing portions of church doctrine entitled "Advanced Technology Works" which were claimed as trade secrets. The Post's defense was that the Advanced Technology Works were not trade secrets when it obtained copies of them because they had been in public court files for 28 months and were published on the Internet.[830] In *Religious Technology Center v. F.A.C.T. Net, Inc.*,[831] the Church of Scientology sued former members for copyright infringement and trade secret misappropriation for posting Church trade secrets and copyrighted material on the Internet. The federal district court denied injunctive relief, finding that the defendants' actions were primarily covered by the fair use doctrine and that the disputed documents lost their status as trade secrets.[832] The court held that despite the best efforts of the Church to maintain the secrecy

---

[828] Geoffrey G. Surgis, Web Site Development Agreements: A Guide to Planning and Drafting (visited May 20, 1999), http://www.digidem.com/legal/wda/wda.html.

[829] Associated Press, Amazon and Wal-Mart Settle Accusations Online Bookseller Stole Trade Secrets, Boston Globe (April 5, 1999).

[830] *Id.* at 1368.

[831] Religious Tech. Ctr. v. F.A.C.T. Net, Inc., 901 F. Supp. 1519 (D. Colo. 1995) (denying preliminary injunction where balance of harms weighed against plaintiff in case involving trade secrets of church).

[832] *Id. See also* Religious Tech. Ctr. v. Lerma, 908 F. Supp. 1362 (D. Va. 1995) (holding newspaper's publication of church's confidential documents protected by "fair use" defense).

of the works, Internet publication of the documents by other parties destroyed the trade secret.

Publication of information on the Internet eviscerated a trade secret in *DVD Copy Control Association v. Bunner*.[833] In *Bunner*, the DVD Copy Control Association claimed that its trade secret had been violated because a decryption software called DeCSS, which defeated the CSS encryption used for DVDs, was published and posted on Bunner's web site and linked to many other web sites on the Internet. Bunner argued that he had no knowledge that the software was classifiable as a trade secret and that he had a right under Norwegian law to reverse engineer the code. Norwegian copyright law permits users of software to reverse engineer to create "interoperability" of different operating systems. The California court nevertheless issued an injunction requiring Bunner to remove the software from his web site.[834] Bunner also claimed that the First Amendment protected his posting of the decryption software code to the Internet; he has been granted an appeal of this case.[835]

[B] Trade Secrets on the Internet in Practice

[1] Drafting Nondisclosure Agreements

Courts have long recognized that trade secrets of an employer, customer goodwill, and specialized knowledge acquired from an employer are all protectable through a restrictive covenant. Restrictive covenants must be "supported by adequate consideration" and be "limited in time and geographic scope and . . . be reasonably necessary to protect legitimate business interests."[836] SPC should consider an employment agreement containing a noncompete clause to protect its interests when employees leave the company.

The purpose of a *nondisclosure agreement* is to emphasize to the employee or other party that SPC is providing them with access to confidential company documents, which must be kept in confidence. The nondisclosure agreement should set forth the responsibilities that employees and others have in protecting trade secrets. The nondisclosure agreement should include a general obligation to protect information, as well as set forth any specific responsibilities. The nondisclosure agreement should also state the possible sanctions for breaching a nondisclosure agreement, and there should also be a termination clause, which requires the return or destruction of all copies of confidential documents held by the signer.

---

[833] 93 Cal. App. 4th 648, 651-52 (Cal. Ct. App. 2001).

[834] *Id.* at 652-55.

[835] DVD Copy Control Association v. Andrew Bunner, 2002 Cal. LEXIS 614 (Cal. 2002).

[836] National Bus. Servs. v. Wright, 2 F. Supp. 2d 701, 709 (E.D. Pa. 1998) (holding that plaintiff proved that ex-employee will break the restrictive covenants by working for competitor and that covenants were ancillary to employment, supported by adequate consideration, are reasonably limited in time and geographic scope, and the covenants are reasonably necessary to protect legitimate business interests).

Each nondisclosure agreement should have a choice of law and forum clause and should include an integration clause stating that this agreement supersedes all prior or contemporaneous agreements.

SPC also needs nondisclosure agreements for all nonemployees working on its web site and related technologies. Nondisclosure agreements should be included for web site development contracts, web site service and maintenance agreements, web site consulting agreements, sales agreements, and for all other joint venturers granted access to SPC trade secrets. In the event of litigation, SPC should seek a court order early in the litigation to protect its trade secrets. A court, for example, can use *in camera* inspections of SPC's trade secrets. A nondisclosure agreement must be included in the employee handbook as well as posted on the company's intranet site. Confidential documents should be stamped with a notice that the employee has a duty to guard the secrecy of the document. It is critical that the nondisclosure agreement have a continuing obligation not to disclose information after termination of employment. The nondisclosure agreement should set forth what constitutes a breach or violation of the agreement by a terminated employee. It is also advisable to include a provision in the employee's agreement stating that the company may file for injunctive relief in case of default. This may be an important clause, since many nondisclosure agreements require the plaintiffs to resolve disputes by arbitration.

Employees violating nondisclosure agreements should be warned that violating a confidentiality agreement may subject them to criminal as well as civil liability. Employees who breach nondisclosure agreements also may be punished with a punitive damages award for misappropriating trade secrets. Moreover, a breach of fiduciary duty may result in lawsuits for trade secrets theft, conversion, tortious interference, unfair competition, and other business torts. The Economic Espionage Act of 1996, for example, as discussed earlier in this chapter, applies to anyone who receives, buys, or possesses trade secrets knowing that they have been stolen or misappropriated.

SPC will need to enter into confidential and nondisclosure agreements to provide a contractual remedy against the misappropriation of trade secrets and unauthorized disclosure of confidential information. Nondisclosure agreements will also be appropriate when making confidential information available to customers, potential customers, consultants, independent contractors, and vendors. A nondisclosure agreement is a safeguard that can help satisfy the secrecy element key to the existence of a trade secret. The essential clauses of the agreement are:

1. What information is considered confidential? Is the confidentiality agreement tailored to the objectives of the e-business? Are confidentiality agreements customized to protect the e-business's interests with respect to employees, independent contractors, consultants, trading partners, and others having access to information classifiable as trade secrets?

2. What are the exceptions?

3. Is each party bound to hold the other's information confidential in reciprocal confidentiality agreements?

4. Does the information have to be marked "confidential"? Do conversations and visual information have to be reduced to a written disclosure?

5. What is the term of the agreement?

6. What is the duration of the obligation to maintain confidentiality (during and beyond the expiration of the agreement)?

7. Granting clause with mutual consideration.

8. What are the responsibilities of the parties upon breach or termination?

9. Who gets to review, examine, inspect, or use confidential information, and for what purposes?

10. What are the conditions for various levels of access?

11. Who is authorized to sign the nondisclosure agreement?

12. Which employees, co-venturers, or third parties are classifiable as trustworthy insiders and need access to perform their jobs?

13. Who has a "need to know"? Closely-held subsidiaries of parent corporations may be classifiable as trusted insiders with access to confidential information.

14. What are the potential consequences if the nondisclosure agreement is violated?

15. What remedies are available to the disclosing party in the event of breach? Is the remedy at law inadequate? Does the balancing of equities weigh in favor of injunctive relief to enforce a nondisclosure agreement?

16. What state's law will apply and in which forum?

17. Are there any warranties with respect to the disclosed data?

18. Do the parties have any other obligations to each other?

19. Who owns the data? Has notice of ownership of data and the need for confidentiality been clearly communicated to employees, independent contractors, consultants, and third parties?

[a] *Checklist for Nondisclosure Agreement for Web Sites*

I. What is the subject matter that is not to be disclosed?

❐ Technical specifications for software

❐ Source code

❐ Customer lists

❐ Business plans

❐ Online business methods

❐ Technical data for software and hardware

❐ HTML code and method of monitoring web site traffic

❐ Information security controls

❏ Other web business information (please list)

❏ Other technical information (please list)

II. What is the nature of the obligation to keep information secret?

❏ Clear definition exists of what information is encompassed within the agreement

❏ Access limited to "need to know" basis in recipient company

❏ Recipient indemnifies SPC and holds SPC harmless for harming interests of third parties if proprietary information disclosed

❏ Proprietary information furnished by either party has been marked with "Confidential," "Trade Secret," or "Proprietary Information— Not to Be Disclosed"

❏ Recipient of proprietary information has agreed not to make copies except as needed to perform web site tasks

III. Who should be subject to a nondisclosure agreement?

❏ Employees and ex-employees

❏ Web site designers

❏ Web site maintenance contractors

❏ Web site service personnel classified as independent contractors

❏ Co-venturers or partners

❏ Web site contractors

❏ Web site sales agents at co-branded sites

❏ Parties to litigation

IV. What clauses are essential for the nondisclosure agreement?

❏ **Recitals:** In order to protect SPC's confidential information, Suffolk Personal Computers and its [subsidiaries, co-venturers, etc.] disclose to _____.

❏ **Effective date:** Effective Date _____ 2002.

❏ **Disclosure period:** The agreement pertains to SPC's confidential information in Attachment A that is disclosed between Effective Date _____ and _____.

❏ **Duration:** The obligations herein shall endure ____ years from the date of disclosure.

❑ **Granting clause:** In consideration of the promises and the mutual promises made in this agreement, _____ and _____ agree to be mutually bound. The parties agree to protect SPC's proprietary information in Attachment A. All proprietary information supplied to _____ [recipient] must be marked with the legend "Confidential."

❑ **Mutual promises or consideration clause.**

❑ **Warranty:** Each discloser warrants that it has the right to make the disclosures under this agreement. No other warranty is given including the warranty of merchantability, fitness for a particular purpose, or warranty of title or infringement. Neither SPC nor _____ makes any other warranty.

❑ **Standard of performance:** SPC requires _____ [recipient of disclosed information] to protect the disclosed proprietary information by using the same degree of care, but no less than a reasonable standard of care, to prevent the unauthorized use or disclosure of the confidential information as _____ [recipient] will use in protecting its own confidential information of similar importance.

❑ **Ownership rights:** Neither party to this agreement acquires any intellectual property rights under this agreement except the limited rights necessary to carry out this agreement.

❑ **Court-ordered disclosure by receiving party:** Neither party shall be restricted from disclosing proprietary information of the other party pursuant to a judicial or governmental order.

❑ **Non-assignment and delegation clause:** The agreement does not permit the obligations or duties under this agreement to be assigned or delegated.

❑ **No partnership clause:** This agreement does not create an agency, partnership, or joint venture.

❑ **Modifications in writing:** This agreement does not permit additions or agreements except in writing signed by both parties.

❑ **Choice of law:** This nondisclosure agreement is governed by the Commonwealth of Massachusetts.

❑ **Choice of forum:** Disputes concerning this nondisclosure agreement are adjudicated in the state and federal courts of Suffolk County, Massachusetts.

❑ **Events of termination:** Either party may terminate the use of its proprietary information by the receiving party at any time without liability upon written notice to the other party. The recipient of proprietary information must return all copies of information.

❑ **Integration clause:** This nondisclosure agreement supersedes all prior or contemporaneous agreements, whether oral or written, between the parties.

❑ **Discloser's authorized representative:** [Name; title; date; contact information, including e-mail address], signature.

❑ **Disclosing party's authorized representative:** [Name; title; date; contact information, including e-mail address], signature.

❑ **Appendix A:** Proprietary information included in nondisclosure agreement between SPC and _____ [recipient]. Effective Date: _____.

[b]　*Sample Clauses*

[i] RFPs. The following is a nondisclosure agreement to bind bidders on contracts for requests for proposal (RFPs):

IMPORTANT: This agreement, including Attachment A hereof, entered into and made effective as of _____ [date], is between Suffolk Personal Computers (SPC) and _____ [prospective bidder]. The prospective Bidder [name], by receipt of specifications and information provided by SPC, acknowledges that such specifications and information which may subsequently be supplied by SPC have been, or will be disclosed to it in strictest confidence. The Bidder acknowledges that SPC has a continuing proprietary interest in all such specifications and information. The Bidder [name] acknowledges that SPC has the sole right and privilege to use, patent, manufacture, or otherwise exploit the processes, ideas, and concepts described or revealed as belonging to SPC. In consideration of SPC's disclosure of specifications and information disclosed to Bidder [name], Bidder agrees that all precautions will be taken to ensure that such specifications and information will not be revealed or divulged to any third party at any time, through the use of copies, summaries, or like material, made without the knowledge or consent of SPC. All such specifications, information, and materials, including any copies, summaries, or the like, will be promptly returned to Suffolk Personal Computer without demand.

[ii] SPC's Nondisclosure Agreement.

This agreement is entered into and made effective on the date of the last signature affixed by SPC, a Massachusetts corporation having a place of business at: 120 Tremont Street, Boston, Massachusetts 02108-4977 and [employee]. In consideration of being employed by SPC, the undersigned [employee] acknowledges that: During the course of my employment at SPC, there may be disclosed to me certain Confidential Information, which may consist of, but is not necessarily limited to, how SPC (1) designs its distinctive software, computer systems, business plans, and online marketing models; (2) manufactures, assembles, designs, and tests its software; (3) designs, tests, and monitors its web site; (4) solves clients' problems; (5) markets its products online; (6) implements its metering software; (7) answers customers' inquiries online; (8) arrives at strategies for prices, discounts, and rebates; (9) develops customer lists as well as lists of potential customers; (10) develops its source code; (11) analyzes its potential and actual Internet customer list and market; and (12) develops its other business and strategic planning information.

[iii] Duty of Confidentiality Clause.

The employee agrees to maintain the confidentiality of all Confidential Information and to take all reasonable precautions to prevent disclosure, use, duplication, reverse engineering, and/or reverse compilations of any Confidential Information or any part or parts thereof for any purpose whatsoever. Upon termination of employment, and/or any other time that employment ends, the employee agrees to turn over to SPC any confidential information in his or her possession.

[iv] Restrictive Covenants.

As an employee of SPC, I agree not to solicit (or assist any third party in soliciting) on behalf of myself or on behalf of any third party, any "business opportunity" from any customer.[837] This agreement defines a business opportunity to mean and include any matter, which SPC, in its reasonable judgment, deems competitive or potentially competitive to its business or to the relationship between SPC and the subject customer.[838]

[2] Web Site Trade Secrets

Material published on a web site cannot qualify as a trade secret because it is no longer secret. SPC's trade secrets must remain secret during the period of exploitation. If SPC permits third parties to have access to trade secrets, reasonable means must be taken to maintain secrecy. Hidden aspects of web sites or software may be deemed as trade secrets provided reasonable steps are taken to keep information secret. In many trade secrets claims, adequate protection has been

---

[837] A *customer* means and includes (1) any Licensee of a Company product or service; (2) any person or entity for whom the Company provided or was obligated to provide, within six (6) months prior to such Termination Date, maintenance or other services, or a fee, pursuant to a formal agreement or otherwise; (3) any person or entity to whom, within six (6) months prior to such Termination Date, the Company had made a presentation or solicitation wholly or partially in writing, or for whom the Company had performed or provided, a "savings analysis"; and (4) any joint venturer or subcontractor of the Company. *See* Weseley Software Dev. Corp. v. Burdette, 977 F. Supp. 137 (D. Conn. 1996) (discussing employment agreement with definition of customer).

[838] This clause tracks the restrictive covenant discussed in *Weseley Software, id.*

questionable. Employees or consultants who have access to computer applications with software should be required to sign nondisclosure agreements. Web site trade secrets "should be marked with legends which alert a reader of the nature of the document as proprietary."[839] Software applications may be protected by license agreements prohibiting reverse engineering. A European Union Directive, however, gives residents in member states a "right to reverse engineer" to encourage the interoperability of computer systems.[840]

[3]   Security Measures to Protect Trade Secrets

SPC must take measures to guard the secrecy of information transmitted on the Internet; business espionage on the Internet has become an illicit means of stealing trade secrets. Foreign governments, foreign corporations, competitors, independent hackers, or disgruntled employees may use the Internet to steal trade secrets.[841] SPC may also face the threat of losing its trade secrets if disgruntled ex-employees post confidential information to the Internet anonymously, using false return addresses.[842]

Once a trade secret is transmitted on the Internet, potentially viewable by millions of users, it is no longer secret. Trade secrets may consist of technical and nontechnical information, such as processes, recipes, plans, strategies, data, systems, sketches, technology, customer lists, and client lists. The security measures used to protect SPC's trade secrets should be calibrated to the value of the information and the adverse consequences if the information is disclosed. Risk analysis is a quantitative means of determining whether expenditures for information security are cost-effective. An effective security policy has the best available technologies, coupled with a workplace culture committed to safety.

Trade secret protection lasts as long as the information is kept secret. The online company needs to establish physical security reasonably calculated to prevent the theft of trade secrets. Information security may consist of relatively simple access devices, such as a lock and master key or a checkpoint guard to protect a trade secret. Chapter Three provides a description of security tools used to protect trade secrets; these include digital signatures; repeat-back passwords; keyboard and screen locks; date/time stamps; trusted third parties; double-key and single-key encryption; digital signatures; mass-marketed security products; audits of computer systems; and a company-wide policy for using security protocol.

---

[839] David B. Himelstein, Web Sites and Software as Trade Secrets (visited Mar. 19, 2000), http://www.himels-computer-law.com/trdscrt.htm.

[840] European Union Software Directive 91/250 (1991).

[841] Computer Security Institute, The 1998 Computer Crime and Security Survey (1998) (reporting the most likely sources for Internet attacks).

[842] *Id.*

[4] Confidentiality of Trade Secret Litigation

Section 5 of UTSA places a duty on a court in a trade secret litigation to "preserve the secrecy of an alleged trade secret by reasonable means, which may include granting protective orders in connection with discovery proceeding." Section 5 also notes that the court may hold *in camera* hearings and seal the records of trade secrets proceedings to protect confidentiality. If SPC is involved in trade secret litigation, it should file pretrial motions for *in camera* hearings and sealed records and an order imposing confidentiality on all persons involved in the litigation.

[5] Inevitable Disclosure/Noncompetition Agreements

SPC may be able to prevent a former employee working for an online competitor by invoking the "inevitable disclosure" doctrine. Under this doctrine, an ex-employee's disclosure may be considered inevitable, even if the employee takes measures to prevent accidental disclosure. Courts, however, have been reluctant to enforce similar clauses in noncompetition agreements because of the public policies of free competition, the mobility of skilled labor, freedom to change jobs, and the freedom to take one's skill and experience to new employers.

In *LEXIS-NEXIS v. Beer*,[843] for example, a court found a noncompetition agreement that prevented a low-level employee from engaging in "competitive activity" for one year after leaving the company overly broad. The clause in question included the following language:

> As used herein, the term "competitive activity" shall include acting directly or indirectly as an agent, employee, officer, director . . . partner or in any other capacity whatsoever, in any business, venture, association, or organization which engages in programming, designing, or marketing computerized information retrieval systems, or system components anywhere in the United States of America, the United Kingdom, Canada, France, or any country in which LEXIS-NEXIS offers services or products to the public.[844]

Notably, the employee would have been precluded from "working in any capacity anywhere in the world."[845] The court found the agreement failed "to sensibly identify the kind of competitive businesses that an employee . . . must stay out of in order for LEXIS-NEXIS to protect its legitimate business interest."[846]

Courts are reluctant to permit companies to use trade secret law as a vehicle for unreasonable restraints on competition.[847] In some cases, though, if the

---

[843] 41 F. Supp. 2d 950 (D. Minn. 1999).

[844] *Id.* at 957.

[845] *Id. See also* Earthweb, Inc. v. Schlack, 71 F. Supp. 2d 299 (S.D.N.Y. 1999) (denying injunction against former employee preventing him from pursing employment with competitor).

[846] *Id.*

[847] *See, e.g.*, Cudahy Co. v. American Labs, Inc., 313 F. Supp. 1339, 1343 (D. Neb. 1970) ("The status given trade secrets is not to be used as a sword to prevent employees from rendering their services,

employee in question is at a senior level, it is more likely that a court will enforce a noncompetition agreement that has reasonable limits on time and geography. Courts balance the purposes of trade secret law against the strong public policy against inhibiting competition in the marketplace.[848] The common law of trade secrets distinguished between an employee's "head knowledge" and "trade secrets."

Courts consistently refuse to enjoin an employee's use of his or her "head knowledge" in competition with the former employer when there is no evidence that the employee misappropriated any of the former employer's documents containing business information.[849] Courts refuse to restrain "head knowledge" because it is unrealistic to require employees to forget what they learned on the job. A New Jersey court, for example, held that an employee's knowledge of price and cost data could not be enjoined since the employee need not "force himself to forget."[850] In general, a former employee's use of his memory of former employer's data and information may not be restrained.

§ 4.05   E-COMMERCE-RELATED PATENTS*

This section examines legal and business issues for online businesses seeking e-commerce patents. The Federal Circuit held a business method to be patentable subject matter in *State Street & Trust Co. v. Signature Financial Group, Inc.*[851] As shown in Table 4.9, this seminal judicial decision incited a stampede of patent activity in the e-commerce area.[852]

---

based on knowledge and experience, to somebody other than that one employer."). *See also* DoubleClick v. Henderson, 1997 N.Y. Misc. LEXIS 577 (App. Div. 1997) (declining to grant injunction for a full year in forming own Internet company given rapidly evolving Web advertising business).

[848] Fleming Sales Co. v. Bailey, 611 F. Supp. 507, 511-12 (N.D. Ill. 1985).

[849] *See, e.g.*, Metal Lubricants Co. v. Engineered Lubricants Co., 284 F. Supp. 483, 486-88 (E.D. Mo. 1968) (refusing to enjoin competition where former employees took no documents containing confidential data).

[850] Midland Ross Corp. v. Yokana, 185 F. Supp. 594, 604 (D.N.J. 1960).

* James F. Ewing, Ph.D., who serves as a technology specialist for Mintz Levin Ferris Cohn Glovsky and Popeo, P.C. in Boston, recently revised this section. Dr. Ewing graduated with high honors from the intellectual property law concentration from Suffolk University Law School in May 2002 and will join Mintz Levin as an associate in September 2002. An earlier version of the section was written by Peter Stecher, a member of the patent bar and a student at Suffolk University Law School.

[851] 149 F.3d 1368, 1107 (Fed. Cir. 1998), *cert. denied*, 199 S. Ct. 851 (1999) (holding business methods patentable subject matter). Signature Financial Group, Inc. patented a method for pooling assets of individual mutual funds. *Id.* After licensing negotiations with Signature Financial Group, Inc. deteriorated, State Street Bank & Trust Co. filed a declaratory judgment to invalidate the patent. *Id.* The federal district court for Massachusetts granted State Street's motion for summary judgment and found Signature's patent invalid on the ground that the claimed subject matter was not encompassed by 35 U.S.C.S. § 101. *Id.* The Court of Appeals for the Federal Circuit disagreed, holding "that declaratory judgment plaintiff State Street was not entitled to the judgment of invalidity . . . as a matter of law, because the patent claims are directed to statutory subject matter." *Id.*

[852] Peter R. Lando, Business Method Patents: Update Post State Street, 9 Tex. Intell. Prop. L.J. 403, 406-10 (2001) (asserting State Street created stampede to USPTO). "Quickly, State Street created a stampede to the PTO to 'stake out a claim' in the e-commerce landscape." *Id.* at 406. In 1997,

TABLE 4.9
Class 705 Application Filing and Patents Issued Data

Class 705	1995	1996	1997	1998	1999	2000
Applications Filed	330	584	927	1340	2821	7800
Patents Issued	126	144	206	420	585	899

The U.S. Patent and Trademark Office (USPTO) is the government agency that examines e-business methods and all other patent applications.[853] The USPTO has developed new guidelines for examining e-commerce and other business method patents.[854] The Business Method Patent Improvement Act of 2000 was introduced in October 2000 as a response to skyrocketing numbers of methods of doing business patents.[855] The proposed bill requires the USPTO to determine whether a patent application qualifies as an application for a "business method." If

Class 705 for e-business method patents derived from the business and cost/price sections of computer Classes 395 and 364. *Id.* at 410. *See also* Patents.Com: Exclusivity for E-Commerce, 16 Computer Law. 10 (Dec. 1999) (noting a 40 percent increase in the number of software-related inventions after 1998); USPTO, Class 705 Filing and Patents Issued Data (visited Apr. 28, 2002), http://uspto.gov/web/menu/pbmethod/application filing.htm (summarizing Class 705 patent application and issued patent statistics). Eight hundred ninety-nine business method patents were issued in FY 2000, compared with 585 business method patents issued in FY 1999. *Id.*

[853] Lando, *supra* note 852, at 406-14 (noting adverse impact of *State Street* on Patent and Trademark Office). The flood of patent applications following the *State Street* decision had a strong impact on the U.S. Patent and Trademark Office. *Id.* at 406.

[854] *Id.* at 408-09. Critics suggested that the USPTO struggled unsuccessfully to ensure adequate review and quality of patents in the business method area. *Id.* at 407. In response, on March 29, 2000, the USPTO announced a "new 'step' initiative." *Id.* at 408; *see also* USPTO Office of the Solicitor, Business Methods Patent Initiative: An Action Plan (2000) (visited Apr. 28, 2002), http://www.uspto.gov/web/offices/as/ahrpa/opa/ptotoday/mar2001.pdf (announcing Business Method Patents Initiative). It was announced that the USPTO would first reach out to industry to establish a "Customer Partnership" with the software, Internet, and electronic commerce industry. *Id.* These quarterly meetings with industry experts were intended to create a forum for the USPTO to share efforts in the technology area and to brainstorm common problems. The USPTO would solicit input on shoring up information collections and electronic databases in order to expand and enhance prior art collections. There was also a renewed emphasis on issuing quality patents in the e-commerce area. To that end, the USPTO would increase technical strength among examiners and continue training efforts in partnership with industry associations and select corporate sponsors. Business practice specialists in the areas of banking/finance, general e-commerce, insurance, and Internet infrastructure were sought to serve as a resource to examiners. The USPTO also targeted the Examination Guidelines for Computer-Related Inventions for revision in light of recent case law. The scope of prior art searches was expanded to provide for a better prior art record. A new second level of review was created for all allowed applications in the business method patents class along with increased sampling of applications reviewed by the Office of Patent Quality Review and a new in-process review of office actions in the technology area.

[855] H.R. 5364, Business Method Patent Improvement Act of 2000, 106th Cong. (Oct. 6, 2000) (introduced by Reps. Howard Berman (D-Calif) and Rick Boucher (D. Va)); *see also* House Bill Would Change PTO Procedures for Business Method Patents, 13 Software L. Bull. 216 (2000) (reporting that bill has been "immediately referred to the House Committee on the Judiciary").

such a determination is made, the USPTO must comply with special rules for "business method" patents.[856] The proposed statute would establish a special administrative opposition process that could be used by anyone to challenge the validity of a business patent.[857] Challenges would be filed with 18 special administrative opposition judges.[858] Publication of business method patent applications must be made 18 months after filing.[859] The proposed statute lowers the burden of proof for challenging a business patent's validity and creates a rebuttable presumption that an invention is obvious if it is simply a computerization of a known business practice.[860] The USPTO has a web site devoted to its present methods for evaluating business method patents applications.[861] The site has a wide variety of materials relevant to patent business methods. John J. Love, director of the USPTO's Technology Center 2100, has developed a business method web site to provide information on business method-related patent issues. The site has downloadable reports on Trilateral Business Methods, a Business Methods White Paper, Class 705 Classification Definitions, the Class 705 core database and filing dates, and a list of 705 Managers and contacts within the USPTO. The web site also has a downloadable copy of the Revised Examination Guidelines for Computer Implemented Inventions, 103 Rejection Examples for Business Method Inventions, links to legal decisions, and the training materials for patent examiners assessing patents for business methods.

A patent gives the patent holder the right to exclude others from making, using, or selling an invention in the United States.[862] The subject matter for a patentable invention may consist of useful processes, machines, articles of manufacture, and the composition of matter and material.[863] Patents provide stronger protection for intellectual property but are "more difficult, time consuming and expensive than other forms of intellectual property protection."[864] A patent is a property right held by an inventor constitutionally mandated in Article I, Section 8, Clause 8 of the United States Constitution, which states:

---

[856] Lando, *supra* note 852, at 412 (outlining changes proposed under 'Business Method Patent Improvement Act of 2000'). "The bill defines the term 'business method' as: '(1) a method of administering, managing, or otherwise operating an enterprise or organization (including a technique used in doing or conduction business) or processing financial data; (2) any technique used in athletics, instruction, or personal skills; and (3) any computer-assisted implementation of such methods or techniques." *Id.* The bill also proposes that business methods applications be made public and subject to public scrutiny during prosecution. Furthermore, the bill proposes to reduce "the challengers burden of proof to invalidate issued patents to a preponderance of the evidence" standard. *Id.*

[857] *Id.*

[858] *Id.*

[859] *Id.*

[860] *Id.*

[861] The United States Patent and Trademark Office web site is located at http://www.uspto.gov.

[862] 35 U.S.C. § 101 (1999).

[863] 17 U.S.C. § 101(b) (2000).

[864] Carey R. Ramos and David S. Berlin, Three Ways to Protect Computer Software, 16 Computer Law. 16 (1999).

> Whoever invents or discovers any new and useful process, machine, manu-
> facture, or composition of matter, or any new and useful improvement thereof
> may obtain a patent therefore, subject to the conditions and requirements of
> this title.[865]

[A]   Patent Law Basics

An online company may seek protection under the Patent Act for Internet-
related inventions. If a company holds the patent on an e-commerce business
process, it can file an infringement lawsuit against competitors who copy the
process. The patent owner can also raise revenues by licensing its patents. If a
company, for example, invents a method of Internet payment, it may receive patent
protection provided the business process is novel, useful, and nonobvious.

To obtain patent protection, a company must file an application with the
Patent and Trademark Office (USPTO), an office of the Department of Commerce.
The USPTO is the repository for "records, books, drawings, specifications, and
other papers and things pertaining to patents and to trademark registration."[866]

The Patent Act of 1952, 35 U.S.C. §§ 1-376, is the federal statute governing
patents.[867] To be patentable, an invention must be novel, useful, and nonobvious.[868]
The statutory test for nonobviousness is whether "the subject matter as a whole
would have been obvious at the time the invention was made to a person having
ordinary skill in the art to which said subject matter pertains."[869]

Three primary classes of patents are granted under the Patent Act: (1) utility
patents, (2) design patents, and (3) plant patents.[870] The general anatomy of a
patent application includes an abstract, summary of the invention, detailed
description, claim set, and selected drawings. The patent claim(s) define the scope

---

[865] 35 U.S.C. § 101.

[866] 35 U.S.C. § 1 (2000).

[867] "Whoever invents or discovers any new and useful process, machine, manufacture, or composition of matter, or any new and useful improvement thereof, may obtain a patent therefore, subject
to the conditions and requirements of this title." 35 U.S.C. § 101 (1999).

[868] 35 U.S.C. §§ 101-103, 112 (2000). *See also* James E. Landis, Amazon.com: A Look at Patenting Computer Implemented Business Methods Following State Street, 2 N.C. J.L. & Tech. 1, 10
(2001) (describing Amazon.com litigation). "The practical utility requirement goes hand in hand
with the description and enablement requirements of 35 U.S.C. § 112." *Id.* The novelty condition of
35 U.S.C. § 102 requires that an invention be new and not "something already introduced." *Id.* at 10.
Landis points out that novelty has been a particular issue in the patenting of computer programs
because "mere automation of a known process should be considered lacking in novelty." *Id.* To be
anticipated by the prior art, a high standard must be met wherein identical elements found in an identical situation and related in the same way must be found within a single prior art reference. The
requirement that an invention not be obvious is defined in 35 U.S.C. § 103. That is, "if the differences between the subject matter . . . and the prior art are such that the subject matter as a whole
would have been obvious at the time the invention was made to a person having ordinary skill in the
art." *Id.* at 10-11.

[869] 35 U.S.C. § 103 (2000).

[870] *Id.* §§ 101, 102.

of an invention. The specification contains a written description of the invention, which enables the use of the invention.

[B]   The Patent and Trademark Office Procedure

[1]   Patentability and Patent Examiners

A USPTO examiner carefully assesses a patent application to ensure that it meets the conditions necessary for patentability. The examiner must, for example, be satisfied that a business methods patent meets the statutory requirements of utility, novelty, and nonobviousness. The subject matter of a patent application is assessed for overlap with any prior art. If prior art references anticipate the claim of a patent, the claim is not valid. The prospective patentee has an affirmative duty to disclose relevant prior art to an examiner, and the examiner must search for prior art. The differences between the prior art references and the patent claim must be significant.

Patent examiners are "persons of legal knowledge and scientific ability" who determine the patentability of inventions.[871] A patent claim consists of the elements that constitute the invention. A threshold question in every patent examination is, "[w]hat, if anything, is it that the applicant 'invented or discovered?'"[872] Certain categories of subject matter, such as "laws of nature, natural phenomena and abstract ideas,"[873] are not entitled to patent protection. A patent examiner may reject a claim because it fails to pass muster as proper subject matter. The patent examiner also compares a patent claim to the prior art, applying the obviousness test of *Graham v. John Deere Co.*[874] If the claimed elements exist in the prior art, there are grounds to reject the claim.[875] The examiner makes an assessment of the prior art by examining four factors: "(1) Determining the scope and content of the prior art; (2) Ascertaining the differences between the prior art and the claims in issue; (3) Resolving the level of ordinary skill in the pertinent art; and (4) Evaluating any objective evidence of nonobviousness (i.e. so-called 'secondary considerations')."[876] The *Deere* court stated only that secondary considerations may be considered in determining obviousness, but subsequent federal circuit decisions make it clear that secondary considerations, when available, should always be considered.[877]

---

[871] *Id.* § 7.

[872] In re Alappat, 33 F.3d 1526 (Fed. Cir. 1994) (dissenting opinion by C.J. Archer, citations omitted).

[873] Diamond v. Diehr, 450 U.S. 175, 185 (1981).

[874] 383 U.S. 1 (1996).

[875] USPTO, Formulating and Communicating Rejections Under 35 U.S.C. § 103 for Applications Directed to Computer-Implemented Business Method Inventions (visited May 9, 2001), http//www.uspto.gov/web/menu/busmethp/busmeth103rej.htm [hereinafter Business Method Rejections].

[876] *Id.*

[877] Sash Controls v. Talon, 1999 U.S. App. LEXIS 994 (Fed. Cir. 1999) (explaining that the district court erred in not allowing evidence of secondary considerations of nonobviousness); Semmler

The examiner of an e-commerce patent application will frequently find it difficult to determine the scope and content of prior art in assessing business method applications, especially because there is no comprehensive database of prior art for Internet-related business method inventions.[878] The examiner must interpret the language of the claimed invention with the prior art reference as a whole and then assess the "level of ordinary skill in the art."[879] The multifactor test for what constitutes ordinary skill in the art includes an analysis of the "(1) educational level of the inventor; (2) type of problems encountered in the art; (3) prior art solutions to those problems; (4) rapidity with which innovations are made; (5) sophistication of the technology; and (6) educational level of active workers in the field."[880]

An examiner may also reject a patent claim on the grounds of nonobviousness. In *Amazon.com, Inc. v. Barnesandnoble.com, Inc.*[881] the district court found "key differences between each of the prior art references and the method and system described in the claims of the '411 patent" claimed by the online book seller.[882] Furthermore, there was "insufficient evidence in the record regarding a teaching, suggestion, or motivation in the prior art that would lead one of ordinary skill in the art of e-commerce to combine the references."[883] Because it can be difficult to find "elusive prior art . . . that will invalidate . . . patents,"[884] some companies pay bounties for information on prior art.

---

v. Honda Motor Co., 1998 U.S. App. LEXIS 28581 (Fed. Cir. 1998) (stating that "inquiries include determining the scope and content of the prior art, the differences between the prior art and claims at issue and the level of ordinary skill in the pertinent art; secondary considerations such as commercial success, long felt but unsolved needs, and the failure of others should also be considered"); *see also* Altech Controls Corp. v. EIL Instruments, Inc., 2001 U.S. App. LEXIS 8089 (Fed. Cir. 2001) (reviewing case in which substantial evidence of secondary considerations was presented).

[878] See Lando, *supra* note 852, at 2-4 and accompanying text (noting efforts to improve prior art searches).

[879] Business Method Rejections, *supra* note 875.

[880] *Id.* (citation omitted).

[881] 73 F. Supp. 2d 1228, 1231-41 (W.D. Wash. 1999). Amazon.com requested preliminary injunctive relief enjoining Barnesandnoble.com from using the patented "one-click" purchasing process. *Id.* at 1231-32. The "one-click" patent described "[a] method and system for placing an order to purchase an item via the Internet" using a streamlined ordering process. *Id.* at 1241. *See generally* Landis, *supra* note 868.

[882] : 73 F. Supp. 2d at 1231-41.

[883] *Id.* at 1240.

[884] Robert L. Kovelman, Companies Offering "Prior Art" Bounties with Hopes of Invalidating Others,' 17 E-Commerce 5 (Nov. 2000) (reporting that patent bounty hunting is supported by Jeff Bezos, CEO of Amazon.com); *see also* Lando, *supra* note 852, at 412-13 (describing market response to business method patents). In response to growing frustration with the issuance of "poor quality" business method patents, Jeff Bezos, Tom O'Reilly, and others created a business out of providing prior art to invalidate business method patents. *Id.* "The business model allows interested parties to post a 'bounty,' usually around $10,000, for prior art that may be used at a later time by bounty posters to invalidate those patents." *Id.* at 413.

[2]   Patent Prosecution

The Board of Patent Appeals and Interference considers appeals for adverse decisions of patent examiners or other issues of priority and patentability.[885] Such petitions are "heard by at least three members of the Board of Patent Appeals and Interference."[886] An applicant for a patent twice rejected by a primary examiner may appeal to the Board of Patent Appeals.[887] An applicant dissatisfied with the Board's decision can further appeal an adverse decision to the United States Court of Appeals for the Federal Circuit.[888]

Patent counsel will work with the company in filing patent applications with the USPTO. Challenging the validity of patents is a strategic defense for claims of infringement. In the 1970s, only one-third of patents reviewed by courts were upheld as valid.[889]

[C]   Anatomy of a Patent

A patent grants the patent holder the right to exclude others from making, using, or commercially exploiting an invention. The public policy underlying patent law is to "confer on its holder a legal monopoly, for a limited period to commercially exploit an invention."[890] In return, the inventor must disclose his or her invention and allow its use after the expiration of the patent term.[891] E-commerce patents place a regulatory burden on Internet companies. This section provides an overview of how patents work, patenting procedures, enforcement of patent rights, and avoiding infringement actions in an online setting.

Patent protection is available for the invention of "any new and useful process, machine, manufacture, or composition of matter, or any new and useful improvement thereof."[892] Patents are not granted where "the differences between the subject matter sought to be patented and the prior art are such that the subject matter as a whole would have been obvious at the time the invention was made to a person having ordinary skill in the art to which the said subject matter pertains."[893]

---

[885] 35 U.S.C. § 7 (2000).

[886] *Id.*

[887] *Id.* § 134.

[888] *Id.* § 141.

[889] Ramos and Berlin, *supra* note 864.

[890] United Kingdom Patent Office, Should Patents Be Granted for Computer Software or Ways of Doing Business (visited May 1, 2001), http://www.patent.gov.uk/about/consultations/conclusions.htm.

[891] *Id.*

[892] 35 U.S.C. § 101 (2000).

[893] *Id.* § 103.

[1] Specifications

A patent application will typically include (1) a specification, (2) a drawing, and (3) an oath by the applicant.[894] Every patent begins with a short title of the invention. The specifications are a "written description of the invention, and of the manner and process of making and using it, in such full, clear, concise, and exact terms . . . to make and use the same."[895] The specification concludes with "one or more claims particularly pointing out and distinctly claiming the subject matter, which the applicant regards as his invention."[896] Claims may be drafted as independent claims, dependent claims, and multiple dependent claims. With a dependent form, reference is made to a claim previously described. "A claim in dependent form shall be construed to incorporate by reference all the limitations of the claim to which it refers."[897] Multiple dependent claims "shall be construed to incorporate by reference all the limitations of the particular claim in relation to which it is being considered."[898]

[2] Drawings of Inventions

An applicant for a patent may include a drawing "where necessary for the understanding of the subject matter sought to be patented."[899] A patent examiner may require a drawing where the "subject matter admits of illustration by a drawing and the applicant has not furnished such a drawing."[900] The USPTO Commissioner may require a patent applicant to "furnish a model of convenient size to exhibit advantageously the several parts of his invention."[901]

[3] Oath

A patent applicant makes an oath attesting that he or she is the original and first inventor of the process, machine, manufacture, composition of matter, or improvement of matter.[902] Joint inventors must each make the required oath.[903]

[4] Examination of Application

Patent examiners study the application and determine whether the applicant is entitled to protection under the law. The patent claims define the matter and

---

[894] *Id.* § 111.

[895] *Id.* § 113.

[896] *Id.*; *see also id.* § 112. The specification must "particularly [point] out and distinctly [claim] the subject matter which the applicant regards as his invention." *Id.*

[897] *Id.* § 111.

[898] *Id.*

[899] *Id.* § 113.

[900] *Id.*

[901] *Id.* § 114.

[902] *Id.* § 115 (covering Oath of Applicant).

[903] *Id.* § 116.

scope of the invention. "The specification shall conclude with one or more claims particularly pointing out and distinctly claiming the subject matter which the applicant regards as his invention."[904]

The Commissioner's patent examiners study the application and compare it to prior art. If a claim for a patent is rejected or some other objection is made, the Commissioner notifies the applicant with the reasons for the rejection or objection.[905] An applicant's failure to prosecute the application within six months after any action by the USPTO is regarded as "abandonment of the application."[906]

Two dates are critical for validity and term of a patent: (1) the date of the filing of the patent application and (2) the date of the granting of a patent.[907] The term for a utility or plant patent filed on or after June 8, 1995, is 20 years from the date the application is filed with the USPTO.[908] Patent prosecution begins with the filing of an application. The patent term for utility or plant applications filed before 1995 is 17 years from the issuance of the patent or 20 years from the filing, whichever is greater. The term for design patents is 14 years from the date the patent issues.

[D]   Software Patents

During the 1980s, the patentability of software-related inventions was an unsettled question. Software may encompass long-distance communications networks and voice, video, and data communication as well as Internet-related business methods. Software and hardware patents are also essential to broadband distribution technologies, telephone-based access services, and other advanced digital services. IBM, Oracle, Novell, and Microsoft are owners of many of the patents important to e-commerce. Software patents are growing exponentially

---

[904] *Id.*

[905] *Id.* §§ 131, 132.

[906] *Id.* § 135.

[907] Kenneth J. Burchfiel, Biotechnology and the Federal Circuit Supplement 77 (1997) (detailing consequences and focus on 20-year patent term). The end of patent term is a critical event for several reasons. *Id.* Under 35 U.S.C. § 286, the "expiration of a patent eliminates the possibility of infringement, and starts the final 6-year period of enforceability after expiration during which an action for damages from infringement during the patent term may be maintained." *Id.*

[908] Oppedahl and Larson LLP, General Information About Patents (visited Apr. 28, 2002), http://www.patents.com/patents.sht (detailing general patent rights and features). The term of a utility patent "filed prior to June 8, 1995 is the later of (1) 17 years from the date of issuance of the patent, or (2) 20 years from the first United States filing date for the patent." *Id. See also* Pub. L. No. 103-465.tit. V, 108 Stat. 4982 (enacted on Dec. 8, 1994) (altering patent term); Burchfiel, *supra* note 907, at 75. "The Uruguay Round Agreements Act replaced the former patent term of 17 years from the date of grant, with a maximum term of 20 years measured from the date of filing a US patent application." *Id.* "The statute requires that the total period of prosecution and enforceability of a U.S. patent is limited to a maximum term of 20 years." *Id.* Under the revised law, the period of prosecution is subtracted from the 20-year maximum term. There is no longer a statutory guarantee of a minimum period of 17 years of enforceability for an issued patent.

because of the greater competence of the USPTO and the formulation of Examination Guidelines for Computer-Related Inventions.[909] In addition, the USPTO has made a concerted effort to recruit and train examiners trained to use the guidelines. Patents have been awarded for software to administer programs, sharpen images, store data, build status indicator, edit graphical resources, facilitate database access, allocate data, organize user interface objects, customize programs, control access point tracking, optimize multidatabase systems, and manage distributed databases.[910]

[E] Patent Infringement

Patent infringement occurs when a person or entity without authority "offers to sell or sells any patented invention, within the United States or imports into the United States any patented invention during the term of the invention."[911] Infringement is a widespread problem in the information economy. One of the problems with software patents is that they provide an exclusive monopoly that may make it difficult for hardware and software producers to avoid infringement.[912] IBM, for example, patented "the software to automatically return the cursor to the start of the next line on a computer screen."[913] Policing a large patent estate can be a difficult, expensive, and time-consuming task.

The statutory presumption of validity applies to e-commerce patents. This presumption operates at every stage of litigation, including a motion for preliminary injunction. The chief defense in a patent infringement case is frequently the claim that a patent is invalid. A party may defend otherwise infringing behavior by showing that a patent is invalid for obviousness or that it was anticipated by prior art.[914] In a patent infringement suit, claim construction determines the scope of a patent claim and is a question of law for a judge to determine.[915] On the other hand,

---

[909] USPTO, Examination Guidelines for Computer-Related Invention, 1184 U.S. Pat. & Trademark Off. Official Gazette 87 (1996).

[910] Robert Greene Sterne, Software Patent Law 1997—Strong Rights Coming of Age (listing software patents granted in 1996 and 1997).

[911] 35 U.S.C. § 271 (2000).

[912] Legal Analysis and Commentary, Big Blue Is Out to Collar Software Scofflaws, Bus. Wk., Mar. 17, 1997, at 29 ("It's hard to be in the computing business—hardware or software—and not infringe on a couple of dozen IBM patents.").

[913] Id.

[914] See, e.g., Amazon.com, Inc. v. Barnesandnoble. com, Inc., 73 F. Supp. 2d 1228. 1240 (W.D. Wash. 1999) (noting that anticipation is a question of fact and only a defense if "all of the same elements are found in exactly the same situation and united in the same way") (citation omitted).

[915] Markman v. Westview Instruments, Inc., 116 S. Ct. 1384, 38 U.S.P.Q.2d 1461 (1996) (defining judicial approach to claim construction). The U.S. Supreme Court held that construction of a patent claim, including interpretation of words of art on which expert testimony is admitted, is a matter reserved entirely for the judge's discretion. Id.

whether the properly construed claims encompass the accused method or composition is a question of fact for the jury to decide.[916] In the typical patent infringement case, the litigation centers on whether prior art references anticipate the
claim(s) of the patent(s).[917] In a patent litigation suit involving a business method,
the issue would likely focus on whether a person skilled in e-commerce would
combine the prior art.[918] To enjoin a competitor's use of an invention, the plaintiff
must demonstrate a reasonable likelihood of success on the merits at trial. The
court must find that the plaintiff's patent is valid and that the defendant's use of
the invention infringes a patent in order to prove irreparable harm.[919]

Infringement may take place in three ways. A direct infringer is a person or
entity who does not have a license or other authority to use an invention but who
nevertheless "uses, offers to sell or sells any patented invention within the United
States" during the patent term.[920] An indirect infringer is a person or entity that
actively encourages another person or entity to infringe a patented invention. Contributory infringement is knowingly selling or supplying a part of a patented invention unless there is a substantial noninfringing use.[921]

The remedies for infringement include (1) injunctive relief against the
infringer, (2) damages or monetary relief against an infringer,[922] (3) treble damages awarded by the fact finder in appropriate circumstances,[923] and (4) reasonable
attorneys' fees to the prevailing party in "exceptional cases."[924] Defenses in
infringement suits include "(1) Noninfringement, absence of liability for infringement or unenforceability; (2) Invalidity of the patent or any claim in suit; and (3)
Any other fact or act made a defense" by the Patent Act.[925]

[F] Patents in Cyberspace

[1] Patents for Push Technologies

One of the strategic decisions that our hypothetical Internet Company, SPC,
will need to make is how it can quickly gain a positive online identity. Many web

---

[916] Burchfiel, *supra* note 907, at 64. The determination of infringement is a "two-step process,
requiring claim construction as a matter of law, followed by comparison of the accused process or
product with the properly construed claims." *Id.*

[917] *Id.* at 1235.

[918] *Id.*

[919] *Id.* at 1246.

[920] Legal Analysis and Commentary, *supra* note 912.

[921] 35 U.S.C. § 271[c] (2000).

[922] *Id.* § 284 (noting that damages award must be "adequate to compensate for the infringement,
but in no event less than a reasonable royalty for the use made of the invention by the infringer,
together with interest and costs as fixed by the court").

[923] The ordinary measure of damages is reasonable royalties, *id.* § 285.

[924] "The court in exceptional cases may award reasonable attorney fees to the prevailing party."
Id.

[925] *Id.* § 282.

sites are content with a "pull method" of attracting visitors and potential customers to the web site. With a pull method, visitors type in the URL or use a standard search engine such as Lycos or Alta Vista to find SPC's web site. The user employs search engines to "pull" information or content about SPC's products and services from the web site. With "pull technologies" the user requests information, in contrast to "push technologies," which target potential customers and web site users.

SPC may soon join the growing number of companies using "push technologies" to transmit knowledge to customers; that is, SPC may decide to "push" content to customers and potential customers. If SPC makes a business decision to use "push" techniques to reach out to potential customers, it will likely need to enter license agreements with the vendors owning the patents or having rights in "push technologies."

[2] Internet-Related Patents*

[a] *Roundup of Internet-Related Patents*

The USPTO recently completed a customer satisfaction survey.[926] Many patent applicants expressed dissatisfaction with the quality of prior art searches and the service provided by the USPTO in response to their problems and complaints.[927] This general sentiment mirrored the frustrations expressed in the area of business method patents.[928] In March 2000, the USPTO announced an action plan for business method patents that included greater training for examiners, revised examination guidelines for computer-related inventions, and expanded search activities.[929] The Manual of Patent Examination Procedures guidelines for computer-related inventions was updated to reflect the *State Street Bank* and *AT&T v. Excel* decisions.[930] A second-level review is now required for all patent applications in Class 705.[931]

The USPTO has recently issued many Internet-related patents that affect Internet sales and services. ChequeMARK Patent Inc., for example, received U.S.

---

* This section was originally written by Peter Stecher, who holds a B.S. in electrical engineering from Massachusetts Institute of Technology and who entered Suffolk University Law School in September 2000. He has also earned approval as a patent agent. This section was revised by James F. Ewing, Ph.D., who serves as a technology specialist for Mintz Levin Ferris Cohn Glovsky and Popeo, P.C. in Boston.

[926] Wynn Coggins, USPTO, Technology Center 2100, The Evolution of the Business Method Patent and Update on the Business Method Action Plan 8, 13 (2000) (summarizing PTO customer survey results).

[927] *Id.*

[928] Lando, *supra* note 852, at 408. Many people criticized the PTO for procedures leading to issuance of "controversial" business method patents. *Id.*

[929] USPTO Office of the Solicitor, Business Method Patent Initiative: An Action Plan (2000) (visited Apr. 28, 2002), http://www.uspto.gov/web/offices/as/ahrpa/opa/ptotoday/mar2001.pdf (detailing Business Method Patents Initiative).

[930] Lando, *supra* note 852.

[931] *Id.*

Patent Number 5,484,988, "Checkwriting Point of Sale Systems," for a "new patent [that] covers Internet purchases where payments from checking accounts are authorized electronically."[932] Furthermore, stockbrokers trading on the Internet can use a patented business method to analyze risk online in real time.[933] The Securities Trading patent allows "value-at-risk" analysis for "real-time" securities transactions.[934] Online brokerage houses will likely need to obtain a license to compete in electronic data trading after the issuance of the "value at risk" patent.

A new patent permitting online loan applications and approvals will likely affect financial services and home mortgage insurers. This "online loan approval" patent constitutes a method and apparatus for closed loop, automatic processing of a loan covering (1) application, (2) underwriting, and (3) the transfer of funds to the successful applicant. The real-time loan patent permits intelligent electronic agents to interact with and obtain necessary information from the loan applicant. This computer application collects all of the information needed to process a loan and contains computer-based decision rules for determining approval of the loan. The application can even trigger electronic fund transfers to the applicant's deposit account and arrange for automatic withdrawals to repay the loan.[935]

---

[932] LML Enters e-Commerce Arena with New Patent Protecting Authorization of Payments from Checking Accounts Made Over the Internet, Excite (visited April 28, 2002), http://news.excite.com/news/pr/000327/bc-lml-enters-e-comm.

[933] Mark B. Garman, U.S. Patent No. 5,819,237 System and method for determination of incremental value at risk for securities trading (1998), http://www.uspto.gov/patft/index.html. The patent discloses a system, method, and product that determine the incremental impact of any number of candidate trades on the value at risk (VaR) measure of a trading portfolio within a trading interval, without requiring that the VaR measure be redetermined individually with respect to each candidate trade. The system includes the software product along with databases storing the trading portfolio(s). In addition, the method and product allow each candidate trade to be normalized with respect to selected criteria, so that a number of individual candidate trades may be ranked with respect to their incremental impact on the VaR measure to determine the candidate trade that best reduces the VaR measure.

[934] Robert Sachs, Method Madness, Patenting Financial Inventions After *State Street Bank,* Daily J., 1999 (visited Feb. 25, 2000), *available at* http://www.fenwick.com/pub/ip_pubs/method%20madness/method%20madness.htm

[935] Jeffrey A. Norris, U.S. Patent No. 5,870,721 System and method for real-time loan approval (1999), http://www.uspto.gov/patft/index.html. The patent discloses a method and apparatus for closed loop, automatic processing of a loan, including completion of the application, underwriting, and transferring funds. It includes use of a programmed computer to interface with an applicant, obtain the information needed to process the loan, determine whether to approve the loan, and effect electronic fund transfers to the applicant's deposit account and arrange for automatic withdrawals to repay the loan. Information is received from the applicant preferably by using voice recognition technology but alternatively by entering alphanumeric information using a personal computer keyboard or the buttons on a telephone. The loan approval determination is made using a neural network with input obtained in part from the applicant and in part from databases accessed by the computer, such as a credit bureau to obtain a credit report. The loan agreement is transmitted by facsimile to and from the applicant when the applicant has access to a facsimile machine or via data file to be printed, or to an agent who delivers the agreement to the applicant when the applicant does not have access. In a preferred embodiment, the applicant accesses the computer from a kiosk where the complete transaction can take place as the applicant waits.

The "reverse auction" patent reflects the rapid growth of Internet-based auctions that permit prospective buyers of goods and services to communicate a binding purchase offer globally to potential sellers.[936] The "reverse auction" patent permits sellers to locate relevant buyers in an efficient manner. This business application software permits the purchasing of offers and a method for binding the buyer to a contract based on the buyer's purchase offer.[937]

Amazon.com owns a highly contested patent for a "single-click method of shopping" ("the 411 Patent") that permits web sites to solve the problem of web site customers abandoning online shopping because of the difficulty with placing an order.[938] The 411 Patent is for a business method that allows a consumer to complete a purchase order for goods or services with a single click of the mouse, making use of information the retailer has saved about the user's address and credit card.[939] The patented process simplifies placing of an order to purchase an item via the Internet, potentially resulting in more online sales and services.[940]

Web site scheduling will likely be improved by a patent issued to eCal, which allows scheduling of events between end users of a system.[941] Double Click is the owner of U.S. Patent 5948061 (1999), which permits the management of advertising over the web.[942] A patentee can enter preventive law license agreements to minimize infringement actions.

---

[936] Jay S. Walker et al., U.S. Patent No. 5,794,207 Method and apparatus for a cryptographically assisted commercial network system designed to facilitate buyer-driven conditional purchase offers (1998), http://www.uspto.gov/patft/index.html. The patent discloses a method and apparatus for effectuating bilateral buyer-driven commerce. The invention allows prospective buyers of goods and services to communicate a binding purchase offer globally to potential sellers, for sellers conveniently to search for relevant buyer purchase offers, and for sellers potentially to bind a buyer to a contract based on the buyer's purchase offer. In a preferred embodiment, the apparatus of the invention includes a controller that receives binding purchase offers from prospective buyers. The controller makes purchase offers available globally to potential sellers. Potential sellers then have the option to accept a purchase offer and thus bind the corresponding buyer to a contract. The method and apparatus of the invention have applications on the Internet as well as conventional communications systems such as voice telephony.

[937] Brian Logest, Brian Logest's Software Patent News: Patent Software Inventions, Oct./Nov. 1999 (visited Apr. 28, 2002), http://www.softwarepatentnews.com.

[938] "Industry studies show that between sixty and sixty-five percent of shopping baskets are abandoned before they are checked out." Ralph Libshon, Madness in the Method: Will 'Method of Doing Business' Patents Undermine the Web?, Netcommerce Mag., Mar. 2000, at 7.

[939] Amazon.com v. Barnesandnoble.com, Inc., 1999 U.S. Dist. LEXIS 18660 (W.D. Wash., Dec. 1, 1999), *vacated and remanded*, 2001 WL 123818 (Fed. Cir., Feb. 14, 2001).

[940] *Id.*

[941] *Id.*

[942] Merriman et al., U.S. Patent 5,948,061 Method of delivery, targeting, and measuring advertising over networks (1999), http://www.uspto.gov/patft/index.html. The patent discloses methods and apparatuses for targeting the delivery of advertisements over a network such as the Internet. Briefly, statistics are compiled on individual users and networks and the use of the advertisements is tracked to permit targeting for the advertisements to individual users. In response to requests from affiliated sites, an advertising server transmits to people accessing the page of a site an appropriate advertisement based on profiling of users and networks.

In August 1998, Netdelivery received a patent for a "method of receiving information over the Internet via an URL."[943] Netdelivery is licensing its new technologies to Microsoft, Netscape, and other "push" vendors.[944] The USPTO recently issued Internet patents that facilitate electronic online commerce. Amazon.com received a software patent to "secure credit card processing of book orders."[945]

[b]   The Impact of State Street

Prior to 1998, methods for doing business were thought to be unpatentable.[946] This argument was predicated upon the well-established principle that mathematical algorithms were not patentable.[947] The USPTO, however, has been increasingly more receptive to the idea, to the point of patenting several software business methods. In 1989, the USPTO issued patents for cash management accounts and

---

[943] Albert Panq, E-Commerce Breakthrough? Netdelivery Gains Patent for Invited Pull, ZDTV (visited Apr. 27, 2002), http://www.zdnet.com/zdnn/st..nn_smgraph_display/0,341,2129869,00.html.

[944] *Id.* (describing how U.S. patent 5,790,793 will be useful to diverse electronic-commerce applications); Higley T., U.S. Patent 5,790,793 Method and system to create, transmit, receive and process information, including an address to further information (1998), http://www.uspto.gov/patft/index.html. This patent discloses a method and system for sending and receiving Uniform Resource Locators (URLs) in electronic mail over the Internet. An electronic mail document containing a URL may have several different types. If the message type indicates a URL, when the received URL type document is read or browsed using a multimedia Internet browser, the URL is looked up so that the information corresponding to the URL is displayed without necessarily displaying any portion of the received message. If the received document is of the Hypertext Markup Language (HTML) type, the document may be displayed and a user may "click" on the URL to look up the information corresponding to the URL. If the received document is of the text type, the text may be converted to the HTML format and the HTML format document displayed so that a user may "click" on the URL to look up the information corresponding to the URL without the need to type in the URL address.

[945] Panq, *supra* note 943.

[946] Landis, *supra* note 868, at 1. Software programming only recently gained official recognition as patentable subject matter. *Id.* "Business methods and mathematical algorithms are not statutorily excluded [subject matter]." *Id.* at 2. Contrary to general perception, the business method exception was presented in dicta almost a century ago. *Id.* at 4 (citing Hotel Security Checking Co. v. Lorraine Co., 160 F. 467 (2d Cir. 1908)); Lando, *supra* note 852, at 407-08. Indeed, financial apparatus and method patents as well as automated financial/management business data processing method patents did not suddenly "spring into being in the late 1990s." *Id.*; *see also* State Street, 149 F.3d at 1375 (citing Rinaldo Del Gallo III, Are "Methods of Doing Business" Finally Out of Business as a Statutory Rejection?, 38 IDEA 403, 435 (1998)). "The business method exception has never been invoked by this court, or [its predecessor], to deem an invention unpatentable." *Id.*

[947] Panq, *supra* note 943; Landis, *supra* note 868, at 3-4. "The mathematical algorithm exception has a clear but twisted path and cannot be attributed to misrepresentation and summarily dismissed." *Id.* at 3. "In relation to e-business software, the complexity and functionality prevents application of the mathematical algorithm exception." *Id.* at 4.

refund anticipation loans.[948] For many decades, the courts and legal scholars were skeptical of the claim that software business methods were patentable.[949]

No single development in case law has spurred the growth of software patents more than the decision in *State Street Bank & Trust Co. v. Signature Financial Group, Inc.*[950] In *State Street*, Signature appealed the decision of a federal court in Massachusetts that granted summary judgment in favor of State Street, holding that the "hub and spoke" financial method was a business method not patentable. Signature owned U.S. Patent No. 5,193,056 (the 056 patent), which discloses a business method to manage and coordinate mutual funds.[951] The hub facilitates a structure, whereas the spokes pool their investment portfolio in a hub that is organized as a partnership. State Street negotiated with Signature for a license to use the multitiered partnership financial service business method. When negotiations broke down, State Street sought a declaratory judgment that the patent was invalid and unenforceable.

The federal district court for Massachusetts granted State Street's motion for partial summary judgment, finding the 056 patent invalid because it was based on

---

[948] Musmanno T., U.S. Patent 4,346,442 Securities brokerage-cash management system (1982), http://www.uspto.gov/patft/index.html. The patent discloses data processing for an improved securities brokerage/cash management system supervises, implements and coordinates a margin securities brokerage account, enables participation in one or more short-term money market or comparable funds, and allows subscriber-initiated use of electronically responsive subscriber identity credit/debit media and/or checking systems. *Id.*; *see also* Longfield RN. U.S. Patent 4,890,228 Electronic income tax refund early payment system (1989), http://www.uspto.gov/patft/index.html. Disclosed is an electronic data processing system for preparation of electronically filed tax returns and authorization and payment of refunds based on the data supplied in

[949] Seth Shulman, Patents Tangle the Web, Tech. Rev., Mar./Apr. 2000, at 71.

[950] State Street Bank & Trust Co. v. Signature Financial Group, Inc., 149 F.3d 1368, *cert. denied*, 199 S. Ct. 851 (Fed. Cir. July 23, 1998); *see also* Lando, *supra* note 852, at 404. The *State Street* decision "put the world on notice that 'methods of doing business' . . . were patentable subject matter in the United States." *Id.* "The State Street pronouncements in its AT&T Corp. v. Excel Communications, Inc. . . . expanded the understanding of patentable subject matter by erasing any distinction between processes and machines for determining compliance" with 35 U.S.C. § 101. *Id.*; *see also* AT&T Corp. v. Excel Communications, Inc., 172 F.3d 1352, 50 U.S.P.Q.2d (BNA) 2d 1447 (Fed. Cir. 1999). *See generally supra* note 852 and accompanying text.

[951] Boes TR, US Patent 5,193,056 Data processing system for hub and spoke financial services configuration (1992), http://www.uspto.gov/patft/index.htm. The "056 patent" discloses a data processing system to monitor and record the information flow and data and make all calculations necessary for maintaining a partnership portfolio and partner fund (hub and spoke) financial services configuration. In particular, the data processing system makes daily allocation of assets of two or more funds (spokes) that are invested in a portfolio (hub). The data processing system determines the percentage share (allocation ratio) that each fund has in the portfolio, while taking into consideration daily changes both in the value of the portfolio's investment securities and in the amount of each fund's assets. The system also calculates each fund's total investments based on the concept of a book capital account, which enables determination of a true asset value of each fund and accurate calculation of allocation ratios between funds. The data processing system also tracks all the relevant data, determined on a daily basis for the portfolio and each fund, so that aggregate year-end data can be determined for accounting and for tax purposes for the portfolio and for each fund.

mathematical algorithms and was therefore an unpatentable business method. The federal district court found that the 056 patent merely input numbers and made calculations and, therefore, did not constitute a patentable invention because the subject matter was not encompassed by 35 U.S.C. § 101.[952]

The Federal Circuit reversed and remanded, concluding that the patent for computing interest on mutual funds, the "hub and spoke" method, was directed to statutory subject matter.[953] The Federal Circuit effectively eliminated the business method exception.[954] The Court of Appeals for the Federal Circuit stated that "the transformation of data, representing discrete dollar amounts, by a machine through a series of mathematical calculations into a final share price, constitutes a practical application of a mathematical algorithm, formula, or calculation, because it produces 'useful, concrete, and tangible results' — a final share price momentarily fixed for recording and reporting purposes."[955]

The *State Street* court narrowed legal doctrine that mathematical formulas were unpatentable subject matter and limited the prohibition against the patenting of mathematical algorithms in the abstract.[956] The decision will continue to have a profound impact on the Internet economy. There is strong empirical evidence that *State Street* represents a paradigm shift for the new information economy.[957] Since the June 1998 decision by the federal circuit court, the filing of "business method patents" has skyrocketed.[958]

The courts will play a significant role in establishing the reach of e-business method patents. Only 23 days after the "One-Click" patent was issued, for example, Amazon.com filed a complaint against Barnesandnoble.com, alleging that the "Express Lane" method used by Barnesandnoble.com infringed Amazon.com's One-Click patent.[959] Barnesandnoble.com's chief defense was that Amazon.com's patent was obvious and therefore invalid. The Express Lane stored information on prior customers, permitting "registered customers to bypass the Shopping Cart and purchase a book with a single mouse click."[960] A Washington court granted a pre-

---

[952] State Street Bank v. Signature Financial Group, 927 F. Supp. 502, 515 (D. Mass 1996).

[953] *State Street Bank,* 149 F.3d 1368.

[954] *Id.*

[955] *Id.*

[956] Diamond v. Diehr, 450 U.S. 175 (1981); *see also* Landis, *supra* note 868, at 9 (noting that *State Street* court follows the USPTO's 1996 Guidelines for Computer-Related Inventions). "Both decisively limit the mathematical algorithm exception as developed by Freeman-Walter-Abele to those claims falling outside of the Alappat functionality output test, . . . while State Street points out that in most or even all cases, the inquiry is altogether unnecessary." *Id.*

[957] John T. Aquino, Patently Permissive: USPTO Filings Up After Ruling Expands Protection for Business and Net Software, A.B.A. J., May 1999, at 30.

[958] *Id.*

[958] Brian Logest, Brian Logest's Software Patent News: Patent Software Inventions (Oct./Nov. 1999), http://www.softwarepatentnews.com. *See generally* Landis, *supra* note 868 (analyzing and detailing Amazon.com case); Matthew G. Wells, Internet Business Method Patent Policy, 87 Va. L. Rev. 729, 731 (2001) (discussing paradigm shift with Amazon.com suit). "Amazon's enforcement of its patent against B&N signaled a shift from competition based on innovation in the marketplace to competition based on raising barriers to entry." *Id.*

[960] Libshon, *supra* note 938.

liminary injunction enjoining Barnesandnoble.com from using the patent and ordering it to remove the Express Lane feature from its web site.[961]

On appeal, the Federal Circuit vacated the preliminary injunction and remanded the case to the district court for further proceedings.[962] The court stated that although Amazon.com demonstrated the likelihood of literal infringement, Barnsandnoble.com raised substantial questions as to the validity of the 411 patent, given the prior art available at the time of the invention.[963] The panel found that Barnes and Noble mounted a substantial challenge to the patent on grounds of obviousness and anticipation. On February 14, 2001, the court ruled that Amazon.com was not entitled to preliminary injunctive relief and remanded the case for further proceedings regarding the validity of the patent.[964]

Internet-related patents will shape the future of e-commerce because the patent gives the holder control of the use of the technology. The level and extent of the control varies depending on the business model of the inventor. A patent holder may obtain a patent for a defensive purpose to discourage competitors. An inventor may realize value from its invention by selling the patent, assigning it, licensing it, or doing nothing with it. The USPTO issues the patent but does not dictate the business model. Patent portfolios are key to market differentiation and control.[965]

Our hypothetical Internet company, SPC, needs to conduct a thorough comparative analysis of risks and utilities before seeking patent protection. The cost-benefit equation is the cost of securing the patent balanced against the potential revenue stream. Internet-related e-commerce patents have a high potential for revenue if they cover critical infrastructure, such as one-stop shopping.[966]

E-commerce patent litigation is a war of attrition: an uneven battlefield where a simple patent dispute may result in expenses of $1.2 million.[967] A small or medium-sized competitor may be unable or unwilling to expend resources to challenge the validity of a patent. Assuming SPC determines that an e-commerce "business" product is useful, concrete, and produces tangible results, the company should retain a registered patent counsel to assist in the steps necessary to file a patent application.[968]

The USPTO announced that it was instituting new policies for the examination of e-commerce patent applications. The revised policy will result in second

---

[961] 73 F.Supp. 2d 1228 (W.D. Wash. 1999).

[962] Amazon.com v. Barnesandnoble.com, 239 F.3d 1343, 1366 (Fed. Cir. 2001).

[963] *Id.*.

[964] *Id.*.

[965] Michael B. Einschlag, Simplifying Patent Portfolio Evaluation by Using Product Differentiators, Spring 1997 (visited Feb. 25, 2000), www.geocities.com/ResearchTriangle/Facility/3078/einsch1.html.

[966] *Id.*

[967] Shulman, *supra* note 949, at 72.

[968] Only counsel who have passed the patent examination of the USPTO and are members of the patent bar can prosecute a patent claim. Specialized knowledge and experience is necessary to draft software patents or Internet-related business model claims.

reviews of applications and "better searches of previous inventions and industry practices."[969] The USPTO plans to immediately "double the sample size of computer-business method patents that get a final quality check."[970] The revised policy will require examiners to search databases to look for prior art to determine whether business methods are widely used or in the public domain.

[c] Licensing E-Commerce Patents

Patent licenses are a major source of revenue for dot-com companies holding e-commerce patents. An *exclusive license*, as its name suggests, prevents the licensor from licensing its technology to more than one party[971] and "bars the licensor from practicing the invention unless he has specifically reserved the right to do so."[972]

SPC may wish to reserve the right to use its own e-commerce patents because an exclusive license would allow only the sole exclusive licensee to practice the invention.[973] An alternative is that SPC expressly reserve the right to use its own technology in its patent license agreements. SPC can warrant that it will not issue other licenses to other competitors.[974] In the absence of a specific reservation of the right to use its own invention, SPC may not enter agreements with other licensees to use the patented technology.[975]

A nonexclusive license allows SPC to practice its inventions and to grant that same right to others. In addition, SPC "may freely license others, or may tolerate infringers; and, in either case, no right of the license is violated."[976] SPC is in a position to file an action against possible infringers if it has entered a nonexclusive patent license.[977] The nonexclusive licensee, however, has no standing to sue for infringement.[978] Nonexclusive licenses are a "waiver of infringement under the licensed invention."[979] Depending on SPC's business objectives, a nonexclusive license may be an optimum solution in that it permits royalty streams while maintaining control over the invention.

The patent license agreement sets the term of the license and conditions of the licensee's use for patented technology.[980] The nonexclusive license permits SPC to use its own technology and to license it to any number of other licensees

---

[969] U.S. to Revise Net Patent Process, C/Net News (visited Apr. 28, 2002), http://www.news.cnet.com/news/0-1007-200-1596357.html.

[970] *Id.*

[971] Shulman, *supra* note 949, at 71.

[972] *Id.*

[973] Cutter Labs., Inc. v. Lyophile-Cryochem Corp., 179 F.2d 80 (9th Cir. 1949).

[974] Harold Einhorn, Patent Licensing Transactions § 1.01 (1997).

[975] *Id.*

[976] Ackerman v. Hook, 183 F.2d 11 (3d Cir. 1950).

[977] Einhorn, *supra* note 975.

[978] Ortho Pharm. v. Genetics Inst., 52 F.3d 1026, 34 U.S.P.Q. 2d 1444 (Fed. Cir. 1995).

[979] *Id.*

[980] *See, e.g.*, L.L. Brown Paper Co. v. Hydroloid, Inc., 32 F. Supp. 857, 44 U.S.P.Q. 655 (S.D.N.Y. 1939).

in the global marketplace. It is the exclusive licensee's responsibility to file an infringement claim. The "field of use" exception permits an exclusive licensor to be named as an unwilling party in an infringement action. The disadvantage, however, is that SPC will need to initiate and pay for the considerable costs of an infringement lawsuit. SPC should choose the form of its licensing agreements based on its business goals. If the goal is to maximize royalties, SPC may wish to enter an exclusive license or to sell its patent.

SPC needs a strategy to manage its patent portfolio for the purposes of commercialization of its invention. Antitrust issues often go hand in hand with licensing.[981] SPC faces the possibility of violating antitrust laws if it is too aggressive in its pursuit of market control. Courts look at the following factors in determining whether a company has too much market power: "(1) when the government has granted the seller a patent or similar monopoly over a product; (2) when the seller's share of the market is high; and (3) when the seller offers a unique product that competitors are not able to offer."[982]

SPC seeks to balance antitrust concerns against market dominance in managing its e-business patents.[983] SPC's legal audit should take into consideration the advantages such as "goodwill, skilled personnel, well established distribution channels, access to raw materials and economies of scale."[984] SPC will use its patent licensing audit as a basis for "developing and prototyping, and securing broad patent coverage, and marketing to qualified licensees."[985]

§ 4.06 GLOBALIZATION OF INTELLECTUAL PROPERTY RIGHTS

E-businesses must be concerned with international protection of intellectual property. Country-specific regimes only have jurisdiction over acts committed in the individual nation-state. French courts, for example, apply French trademark law in resolving domain name disputes.[986] Intellectual property rights are obtained separately in every nation state where protection is desired. In the "brick and mortar" world, corporations must obtain trademarks for overseas operations. McDonald's invests an average of $900 million each year in promoting its 14,000 restaurants in more than 70 countries.[987]

---

[981] Fariba Rad, The New Role of MBA in Licensing, Intell. Prop. Today (1999).

[982] *Tominga*, 682 F. Supp. at 1493; *Mozart Co.*, 833 F.2d at 1345-46.

[983] Rad, *supra* note 981.

[984] Thomas G. Field, Jr., Seeking Cost-Effective Patents, Franklin Pierce Law Center (visited Feb. 28, 2000), www.fplc.edu/TFIELD/sEeking.htm.

[985] Frederic P. Zotos, Unlocking the Potential of Innovations, Intell. Prop. Today (July 1997).

[986] Andre Bertrand, Recent Developments in French Cyberspace Litigation, 3 Cyber. Law 12 (Jan. 1999) (discussing French cases such as Saint Tropez v. Eurovirtuel, TGI de Draguignan 21 Aout 1997, PIBD, 1997, Ill., 588, Les Petites Affiches 9 mars 1998 n [degrees] 29 anote Drefus-Weill (holding that web page www.saint.tropez infringed the name of the city of Saint-Tropez).

[987] Anthony D'Amato & Doris Estelle Long, International Intellectual Property Law 348 (1999).

McDonald's trademarks and logos are registered in the individual countries where it desires protection.[988] Internet companies need to protect their marks against local companies in essential countries. Since there is no single international agency, the owner of intellectual property must seek protection in each country.

Chapter 10 on Global E-Business Issues will cover the internationalization of intellectual property rights in greater depth. This brief section is intended to sensitize U.S. companies that their intellectual property rights acquired in the United States may not apply in many of the countries connected to the Internet. Amazon.com recently learned that its business methods patent validated in the famous *State Street Bank* case by the federal circuit was denied by Japan's Patent Office.[989] The Ministry of Economy, Trade, and Industry notified Amazon.com that its applications for business model patents will be declined because they are "not unique enough."[990] The online company needs to take into account national differences in intellectual property rights to protect rights and avoid liability in cyberspace.

[A]   World Intellectual Property Organization (WIPO)

The World Intellectual Property Organization (WIPO) is an agency of the United Nations "dedicated to helping to ensure that the rights of creators and owners of intellectual property are protected worldwide."[991] With the rise of the Internet, WIPO is increasingly important in protecting intellectual property rights. The globalization of trade that occurs with the rise of e-commerce has made harmonization of intellectual property rights more critical. There are 171 member-states of WIPO, representing 90 percent of the countries of the world.[992] WIPO has succeeded in helping to harmonize diverse intellectual property regimes.

WIPO entered a cooperative agreement with the World Trade Organization (WTO) in 1996[993] and is also the sponsoring agency behind the influential Madrid

---

[988] McDonald's sought protection for its trademarks in South Africa, for example. In the lower court, McDonald's Corporation lost its claim to its well-known trademarks because McDonald's marks were already registered by lesser known local South African companies. A South African Appellate Court reversed the lower court, holding that McDonald's Corporation could introduce survey research to establish that its marks were well known in many sectors of South Africa. *Id.* at 344-348.

[989] Amazon, Signature Financial Denied Business Model Patents, Japan Times Online (May 15, 2001) (visited Apr. 22, 2002), http://www.japantimes.co.jp/cgi-bin/getarticle.pl5?nb20010515a6.htm.

[990] *Id.*

[991] World Intellectual Property Organization, An Organization for the Future (visited Apr. 28, 2002), http://www.wipo.org/eng/infbroch/infbro99.htm#P23_2347.

[992] *Id.*

[993] The United States is a World Trade Organization (WTO) member and a signatory to the Berne Convention.

Agreement.[994] As e-commerce expands, WIPO will play an even more significant role in harmonizing Internet-related intellectual property rules.

WIPO presently has 171 member states and is responsible for administering 21 treaties. WIPO's general polices are to harmonize national intellectual property legislation and procedures, and to facilitate trade and the exchange of intellectual property information. WIPO seeks to provide legal and technical assistance to developing and other countries in the following ways:[995]

- Harmonize national intellectual property legislation and procedures.

- Provide services for international applications for industrial property rights.

- Exchange intellectual property information.

- Provide legal and technical assistance to developing and other countries.

- Facilitate the resolution of private intellectual property disputes.

- Marshall information technology as a tool for storing, accessing, and using valuable intellectual property information.[996]

[B] Copyright and National Origin of the Work

Copyright protection is available for all unpublished works, regardless of the nationality or domicile of the author. Foreign published works are eligible for copyright protection in the United States if *any* of the following conditions is met:

1. On the date of first publication, one or more of the authors is a national or domiciliary of the United States, or is a national, domiciliary, or sovereign authority of a treaty party, or is a stateless person wherever that person may be.
2. The work is first published in the United States or in a foreign nation, that, on the date of first publication, is a treaty party. For purposes of this condition, a work that is published in the United States or a treaty party within 30 days after publication in a foreign nation that is not a treaty party shall be considered to be first published in the United States or such treaty party, as the case may be; or
3. The work is a sound recording that was first fixed in a treaty party; or

---

[994] The Madrid Agreement concerning the international registration of marks and the protocol relating to that agreement is not in effect in 52 countries. *See* World Intellectual Property Organization, International Protection of Industrial Property Introduction (visited Apr. 28, 2002), http://www.wipo.int/eng/general/ipip/intro.htm.

[995] WIPO critics assert that the agency is superimposing the cultural and legal values of the United States and other countries on less developed countries.

[996] World Intellectual Property Organization, WIPO Today (visited Apr. 28, 2002), http://www.wipo.org/eng/infbroch/infbro99.htm#P52_8261.

4. The work is a pictorial, graphic, or sculptural work that is incorporated in a building or other structure, or an architectural work that is embodied in a building and the building or structure is located in the United States or a treaty party; or

5. The work is first published by the United Nations or any of its specialized agencies, or by the Organization of American States; or

6. The work is a foreign work that was in the public domain in the United States before 1996 and its copyright was restored under the Uruguay Round Agreements Act (URAA). Request *Circular 38b,* "Highlights of Copyright Amendments Contained in the Uruguay Round Agreements Act (URAA-GATT)," for further information.

Title I of the Digital Millennium Copyright Act of 1998 (DMCA) amends the 1976 Copyright Act so that the United States complies with the World Intellectual Property Organization (WIPO) Copyright Treaty agreed to in December 1996. The DMCA also contains conforming amendments so that United States copyright law is harmonized with the WIPO Performances and Phonograms Treaty enacted on the same day as the copyright treaty.[997]

---

[997] The "Geneva Phonograms Convention" is the Convention for the Protection of Producers of Phonograms Against Unauthorized Duplication of Their Phonograms, concluded at Geneva, Switzerland, on October 29, 1971.

CHAPTER FIVE

CIVIL LIABILITY ON THE INTERNET

§ 5.01   Overview

§ 5.02   General Principles of Tort Law
    [A]   The Three Branches of Tort Law
        [1]   Intentional Torts
        [2]   Negligence
           [a]   Duty and Breach
           [b]   Proximate Cause and Damages
        [3]   Strict Liability
           [a]   Strict Products Liability
              [i]   Manufacturing defect
              [ii]   Design defect
              [iii]   Failure to warn
              [iv]   Availability in Internet-related cases
           [b]   Economic Loss Doctrine and Computer Law
    [B]   Bases for a Company's Liability for an Employee's Wrongdoing
        [1]   Direct Liability
           [a]   Agent's Actual Authority to Act
           [b]   Apparent Authority
        [2]   Vicarious or Imputed Liability
           [a]   ISP's Imputed Liability
           [b]   Imputed Liability and Independent Contractors
        [3]   Joint Tortfeasors

§ 5.03   Intentional Torts in Cyberspace
    [A]   Assault and Battery
    [B]   Intentional Infliction of Emotional Distress
    [C]   Title VII Claims
    [D]   Trespass to Cyberchattels
    [E]   Spamming as Cyberspace Trespass

§ 5.04   Business Torts in Cyberspace
    [A]   Fraud and Misrepresentation
    [B]   Misappropriation and Unfair Competition
    [C]   Interference with Business Contracts

[D]   Breach of Fiduciary Duty
[E]   Business Defamation

§ 5.05   Internet Torts
[A]   Identity Theft
[B]   Computer Viruses
[C]   Cyberstalking

§ 5.06   Publishing Torts in Cyberspace
[A]   Defamation in Cyberspace
[1]   Parties to a Defamation Action
[a]   Plaintiffs in General
[b]   Public Officials and Public Figures
[c]   Online Service Providers
[2]   Retraction Statutes
[3]   Defenses to Defamation
[B]   Internet Publicity

§ 5.07   Privacy in Cyberspace
[A]   The Internet as a Transparent Society
[B]   Privacy Torts
[1]   Unreasonable Intrusion upon Seclusion
[2]   Tort of Misappropriation
[3]   Right of Publicity
[4]   False Light
[C]   Statutory Regulation of Privacy
[D]   EU Directive on Protection of Personal Data

§ 5.08   Negligence in Cyberspace
[A]   Introduction
[B]   Setting the Standard of Care
[1]   Industry Standard-Setting
[2]   Statutory Standard of Care
[3]   Professional Standard of Care
[C]   Premises Liability
[D]   Defenses Against Negligence in Cyberspace
[1]   Contributory Negligence
[2]   Comparative Negligence
[3]   Assumption of Risk
[4]   ISP Immunity for Negligence

§ 5.09   Strict Liability in Cyberspace
[A]   Strict Products Liability
[B]   Computer Malpractice

§ 5.10   Immunities and Privileges
[A]   Immunities
[B]   Privileges

§ 5.11   Regulation of Cyberspace
    [A]   FTC's Internet-Related Activities
        [1]   Information Policy
        [2]   Online Profiling
        [3]   Obligations Under Gramm-Leach-Bliley Act
        [4]   HIPAA's Privacy Rules for Online Transactions
        [5]   FTC's Consumer Protection Powers
            [a]   FTC's Tools to Combat Cyberfraud
                [i]   FTC subpoena power
                [ii]   Civil investigation demands
                [iii]   Section 6 of the FTCA
                [iv]   Adjudication
                [v]   Rulemaking
                [vi]   Enforcement activity
    [B]   False and Deceptive Advertising in Cyberspace
        [1]   Regulation of Internet Advertising
            [a]   Federal Trade Commission Regulation
                [i]   Section 5(a) of the FTCA
                [ii]   False Internet advertising claims
            [b]   State Enforcement Against Unfair or Deceptive Internet Ads
            [c]   Regulation of Online Spam
            [d]   International Regulation of Internet Advertising
        [2]   Private Attorney General Tort-Based Enforcement
        [3]   Private Common Law Tort Actions
            [a]   Unfair Competition
            [b]   Trade Libel or Disparagement
            [c]   Conversion of Cyberchattels
    [C]   State Enforcement of Online Gambling
    [D]   Telecommuting and Negligence
    [E]   Successor Liability for Online Companies
    [F]   Securities Regulation in Cyberspace
        [1]   Structure and Function of the SEC
        [2]   Federal Securities Law
            [a]   Securities Act of 1933
            [b]   Securities Act of 1934
            [c]   Other Federal Securities Laws
            [d]   NASD Online Regulation
            [e]   Online Securities Litigation
    [G]   FCC Regulation

§ 5.12   Preventive Law Pointers and Supplemental Checklists Aimed at Avoiding Cyberspace Liability
    [A]   Adopt a Communications Policy
    [B]   Preventing the Misuse of the Internet

[C]   Preventing Computer Viruses
[D]   Pleading and Proof of Defamation
[E]   Cookie Warnings
[F]   Employee Handbook and E-Mail Policy
[G]   Online Privacy Policies
[H]   Principles of Privacy
[I]   Insuring Advertising Injuries
[J]   Tips for Reducing the Risks of Telecommuting
[K]   Supplemental Checklists Aimed at Minimizing Cyberspace Liability
    [1]   Jurisdictional Risks in Cyberspace
    [2]   Internet Advertisements
    [3]   Minimizing Exposure for Intentional Torts
    [4]   Publication-Based Tort Liability
    [5]   Employment-Related Torts
    [6]   Torts and Customers
    [7]   Avoiding Liability for Privacy-Based Torts
    [8]   Privacy Concerns
    [9]   Other Terms, Conditions, and Concerns
    [10] Parties' Choice of Law and Forum Agreements
    [11] Chief Privacy Officer
    [12] E-Discovery

§ 5.01   OVERVIEW

Torts are civil actions to recover for wrongs that arise from breaches of duty. Torts may be distinguished from contracts in that a contract arises from the parties' agreement, whereas a tort is a duty fixed by law.[1] Tort rights and remedies are rapidly evolving to confront information age wrongs such as online defamation, the spread of computer viruses, online stalkers, e-mail spammers, identity thieves, online invasion of privacy, and fraudulent Internet marketing schemes. New torts are on the horizon that have the potential for deterring corporate wrongdoers from the destruction of e-documents. Because e-documents may be easily altered, manipulated, or morphed to conceal or disguise wrongdoing, new remedies are required. New computer software has been developed that automatically destroys records containing e-mail messages. The signature crimes of Internet wrongdoers include the use of pseudonyms, false identities, forged e-mail addresses, and encryption to conceal wrongdoing. The tort of spoliation of evidence is currently recognized in only a few jurisdictions but is adaptable to cyberspace to deter the destruction or alteration of smoking gun e-documents.

Since the last edition, old torts have been updated and new regulatory initiatives have been launched by state and federal agencies to extend civil liability on the Internet. The states continue to expand Internet-related enforcement over spam, cybercrime, online gambling, and the distribution of pornography, and state regulation is frequently challenged on Commerce Clause grounds. In one recent case, for example, a court ruled that a North Carolina statute preventing out-of-state wineries from shipping wine to its residents preferred local wineries and constituted a violation of the Commerce Clause of the U.S. Constitution.[2]

State efforts to control unsolicited commercial e-mail, or spam, have generally withstood constitutional challenges; California's Anti-Spamming Act, which imposes criminal and civil liability on spammers, is the most recent example. A growing number of states have updated computer crime statutes to provide litigants with a private cause of action. An Internet company alleged that a web-hosting company's inadequate security permitted a third party to commit a denial-of-service attack on its system.[3] A trial judge issued a temporary restraining order "shutting down three of the Web servers involved in the attack until the companies could prove the vulnerabilities had been fixed."[4] Negligent security claims may be predicated upon a duty to implement reasonable security to prevent hackers from launching attacks. Computer malpractice claims against software consultants, engineers, or designers for negligent security have yet to be recognized by courts.

---

[1] James A. Ballentine, Ballentine's Law Dictionary 1284 (3d ed. 1969) (defining tort action).

[2] Santa Fe Natural Tobacco Co. v. Spitzer, U.S. Dist. LEXIS 5384 (S.D.N.Y. Mar. 29, 2002) (awarding attorneys' fees and costs to tobacco companies after successful Commerce Clause challenge to Internet regulation of tobacco products).

[3] Information Security: See You in Court, CIO Magazine (Nov. 1, 2001), http://www.cio.com/archive/110101/court_content.html.

[4] Id.

Plaintiffs continue to bring defamation claims relating to online postings. In August 2001, an Australian court asserted jurisdiction over Dow Jones & Co., based on allegedly defamatory comments made about a Melbourne businessman. The Australian court found that jurisdiction based on the company's Internet web site and presence was sufficient to litigate a defamation claim.[5]

In the wake of the dot-bomb shakeout, there have been a large number of business tort lawsuits filed by competitors, customers, and investors. In *Stone Castle Financial, Inc., v. Friedman,*[6] a company secured the services of the firm to assist with the acquisition of a software design company. The software company provided confidential information that was to be protected by a confidentiality agreement; it later brought suit claiming that the consultants never intended to abide by the terms of the agreement and almost instantly violated the agreement, benefiting one of the company's competitors. The court ruled that the plaintiff sufficiently pleaded a claim for tortious interference with business advantage because it was reasonably certain that the defendant knew of an anticipated acquisition and shared that information with a rival firm.[7] In *Intel Corp. v. Hamidi,*[8] a California court of appeals upheld a trial court's permanent injunction enjoining a disgruntled ex-employee from sending the company's employees unsolicited e-mails under a trespass to chattels theory

Multimillion-dollar judgments for cyberspace torts are on the rise. A court levied a $65 million judgment against an online defendant who fraudulently pirated the sex.com domain name.[9] A University of North Dakota physics professor won a slander suit against a former student who accused him in online postings of being a pedophile and having odd sexual habits.[10]

Plaintiffs in business libel cases are increasingly using John Doe subpoenas to unveil anonymous web site posters that defame a company. Increasingly, trade libel cases arising out of anonymous web site postings raise First Amendment issues where the postings concern issues of public concern.

The FTC has asked to increase its budget for 2003 and initiated a major anti-spam e-mail initiative; the Commission is also studying the marketing of e-mail lists and patrolling bulk e-mail-sending software[11] and fraudulent online auction practices. It also has enacted regulations implementing the Children's Online Privacy Protection Act (COPPA).

---

[5] All the World's a Forum, Nat'l L.J., Feb. 11, 2002, at B13.

[6] 2002 U.S. Dist. LEXIS 3764 (E.D. Va. Mar. 2, 2002).

[7] *Id.*

[8] 94 Cal. App. 4th 325 (Cal. Ct. App. 2001) (finding that electronic signals generated and sent by computer were sufficiently tangible to support a trespass cause of action in case where ex-employee flooded his company's computer system with mass e-mails).

[9] Laurie Flynn, Cybersquatting Draws Heavy Penalty, N.Y. Times, Apr. 6, 2001, at C6.

[10] Scott Carlson, North Dakota Professor Sues Former Student and a Web Site Over Allegations in an Article, Chron. Higher Ed., Jan. 19, 2001, at A33.

[11] FTC Examining Spam Lists and E-Mail Sending Programs, Wash. Internet Daily 1, Mar. 28, 2002, at 1.

In *In re DoubleClick Privacy Litigation,*[12] the plaintiffs sought damages for an invasion of their privacy, a trespass to their personal property, and the misappropriation of confidential data for DoubleClick's use of cookies to track their online activity, arguing that the use of cookies constituted an unauthorized access of their computers. The federal district court concluded that the Electronic Communications Privacy Act only protects electronic communications stored " 'for a limited time' in the 'middle' of a transmission, i.e. when an electronic communication service temporarily stores a communication while waiting to deliver it,"[13] and granted the defendant's motion to dismiss the plaintiffs' federal claims. In March 2002, a federal court approved a settlement of all state and federal claims against DoubleClick.

This chapter is meant to serve as a road map addressing civil liability on the Internet. Section 5.02 begins with the general principles of tort law. Sections 5.03 through 5.07 explore the various types of tort claims for Internet activities, ranging from assault and battery to identity theft. Sections 5.08 through 5.10 address negligence, strict liability, and immunities and privileges. Section 5.11 discusses the regulation of the Internet with a focus on the FTC. Finally, Section 5.12 provides guidance through sample preventative law pointers and checklists on how to avoid civil liability on the Internet.

§ 5.02 GENERAL PRINCIPLES OF TORT LAW

[A] The Three Branches of Tort Law

A tort is "a private or civil wrong or injury, including an action for bad-faith breach of contract, for which the court will provide a remedy in the form of an action for damages."[14] The word *tort* is "derived from the Latin 'tortus' or twisted."[15] William Prosser begins his classic treatise on torts with the statement that "[a] really satisfactory definition of tort has yet to be found."[16]

An actor is civilly liable for tort damages if his conduct "(a) was intended to cause harm; (b) was negligent; or (c) created extra-hazardous risks to others."[17] Tort damages may be broadly divided into three categories: economic,[18] noneconomic (nonpecuniary or pain and suffering damages),[19] and punitive (exemplary

---

[12] 154 F. Supp. 2d 497, 511-13 (S.D. N.Y. 2001).

[13] *Id.* at 512 (quoting dictionary definitions of *temporary* and *intermediate*).

[14] Black's Law Dictionary 1489 (St. Paul: West, 6th ed. 1991).

[15] William E. Nelson, From Fairness to Efficiency: The Transformation of Tort Law in New York, 1920-1980, 47 Buffalo L. Rev. 117 (1999).

[16] William L. Prosser, Handbook of the Law of Torts 1 (3d ed. 1964).

[17] Fowler Vincent Harper, A Treatise on the Law of Torts: A Preliminary Treatise on Civil Liability for Harms to Legally Protected Interests 12 (1st ed. 1933).

[18] *Economic damages* will typically include medical expenses, loss of past earnings, loss of future earnings, and out-of-pocket expenses attributable to a civil wrong.

[19] *Noneconomic damages,* often referred to as "pain and suffering" damages, are considered to be a form of compensatory damages. *Pain and suffering damages* include compensation for disfigurement, infertility, and the suffering caused by an injury.

damages).[20] In addition, nominal damages may be awarded where there is a technical tort but no actual damages.[21] The purpose of tort damages is "to make the plaintiff 'whole,' i.e., place him in the position he would have been in if he had not been the victim of the tort."[22]

Every state has a wrongful death statute or otherwise recognizes recovery from one whose intentional act, neglect, or default results in the death of another person.[23] At common law, tort actions were extinguished by the death of either the tortfeasor or the victim, but modern survival statutes "provide for the survival of a cause of action notwithstanding the death of a party."[24] Survival statutes vary by jurisdiction, but many economic torts arising out of e-commerce are likely to be excluded. Many survival statutes expressly exclude actions for "libel, slander, malicious prosecution and the like," permitting these largely economic losses or dignitary torts "to abate at death."[25]

American tort law imposes joint liability if two or more tortfeasors are responsible for the plaintiff's injury. If one of the co-defendants pays the plaintiff's compensatory damages, it may seek "contribution or indemnity from another tortfeasor or tortfeasors."[26] Most states do not permit contribution or indemnity for punitive damages.[27]

Individuals injured in personal injury actions will typically enter into a fee arrangement known as the contingent fee contract. Under a contingency fee contract, the attorney is paid a stipulated percentage or portion of the recovery in the event of a successful lawsuit.[28] Online companies will typically engage an attorney to vindicate their tort rights through a retainer or retainer agreement. A retainer is a preliminary fee given to an attorney to secure his services.[29] The advantage of a retainer for the online company is that it obligates the "attorney to represent the client as well as preventing him from taking a fee on the other side."[30]

The three branches of tort law include (1) intentional torts, (2) negligence, and (3) strict liability. Whether a plaintiff's complaint seeks monetary damages or

---

[20] *Punitive damages,* sometimes referred to as *vindictive* or *exemplary damages,* are awarded above and beyond compensatory damages to punish and deter the defendant from engaging in socially harmful or risky activities. *See generally* Thomas H. Koenig and Michael L. Rustad, In Defense of Tort Law (2002).

[21] Jerry J. Phillips, et al., Tort Law: Cases, Materials, Problems 1187 (2d ed. 1997).

[22] *Id.*

[23] James A. Ballentine, Ballentine's Law Dictionary 1187 (3d ed. 1969) (William S. Anderson ed).

[24] *Id.* at 1246.

[25] Dan B. Dobbs, The Law of Torts 807 (2000).

[26] Ballentine, *supra* note 22, at 1287.

[27] *Id.* at 1288.

[28] 1 Stuart M. Speiser, Attorney's Fees, § 2:1 at 82 (1973).

[29] *Id.* at 3.

[30] *Id.* at 7.

injunctive relief, torts based on negligence contain four elements: duty, breach of duty, damages, and causation.[31]

This chapter examines the online company's potential for tort liability by reviewing recent case law developments and applying traditional tort law principles. Tort law is readily adaptable to Internet and web site injury cases. Torts may be committed in chat rooms, videoconferences, news groups,[32] listservs,[33] bulletin boards,[34] or in information or data transfers.[35]

Table 5.1 lists some illustrative examples of each of the three branches of tort law: intentional torts, negligence, and strict liability, which potentially apply to cyberspace.

[1] Intentional Torts

Intentional torts are injuries committed with the purpose to bring about a desired result or a substantial certainty to bring about desired consequences.[36] The Restatement of Torts[37] sets the general standard of liability: "One who intentionally causes injury to another is subject to liability to the other for that injury, if his

---

[31] *Proximate cause* means that cause which, in a natural and continuous sequence, produces an event, and without which cause such event would not have occurred. To be a proximate cause, the act or omission complained of must be such that a person using ordinary care would have foreseen that the event might occur. Proximate cause "has little to do with physical causation, emphasizing instead the continuity of the sequences that produces an event." Bryan A. Garner, A Dictionary of Modern Legal Usage 211 (2d ed. 1995).

[32] A *news group* is an "electronic discussion group, serving as a bulletin board for users to post universally accessible messages, and to read and reply to those from others." Michael Scott, Internet and Technology Desk Reference 339 (1999) (quoting Religious Tech. Ctr. v. F.A.C.T.Net, Inc., 901 F. Supp. 1519, 1524 n.4 (D. Colo. 1995)).

[33] A *listserv* is "an automatic mailing list services . . . that allow communications about particular subjects of interest to a group of people." American Civil Liberties Union v. Reno, 929 F. Supp. 824, 834 (E.D. Pa. 1996), *aff'd*, 521 U.S. 844 (1997).

[34] A *bulletin board system* (BBS) is "an electronic forum for exchanging electronic mail, reading notices and features, carrying on unstructured multilogs and copying programs stored on the host computer. Bulletin boards are videotext systems that provide quick access to information held in databanks. They can be used to transmit information back and forth. They can be used to provide information to a closed group or an open group. Bulletin-board services are sometimes provided as a free service, but may be subject to a charge. They function as electronic notice boards and as electronic mail services." Michael Scott, Internet and Technology Law Reference 51 (1999) (quoting *In re* Application by International Computers Ltd., 5 I.P.R. 263 (Austl. Pat. Off.)).

[35] *See, e.g.*, Martin C. Loesch, Surveying Cyberspace: A Guide to Insurance Defense and Coverage in the Age of Technology, ch. 2, 1998 DRI 1-5, observing that "[d]efamatory statements may be published over private e-mail systems or distributed through the Internet [and] Service provider discussion lists, roundtables, real-time conferences, news groups, listserves and bulletin boards."

[36] Edward J. Kionka, Torts in a Nutshell 146 (1999).

[37] The Restatements of the Law are projects of the American Law Institute (ALI), which seeks to bring uniformity to the common law. The Restatement (Second) of Torts is an influential source of tort law in virtually every state. The Restatements are cited by courts or adopted by state legislatures. Nearly every state, for example, adopted Restatement (Second) of Torts § 402A on strict products liability.

TABLE 5.1
Branches of Tort Law

Intentional Torts	*Negligence*	*Strict Liability*
Intentional Interference with the Person: Battery, assault, imprisonment, intentional infliction of emotional distress, invasion of privacy, defamation	**Actions for Corporate Negligence:** Corporate negligence, negligence per se for violation of privacy statutes, negligent marketing of encrypted software used by third-party criminals, fiduciary duties, liability as government contractors, negligent product design, warning and manufacturing defects, liability for commercial distributors, negligent interference with contract or economic interest, negligent misrepresentation, negligent breach of confidentiality duties, computer malpractice	**Strict Liability— Personal Injury:** Strict liability for abnormal dangers, abnormally dangerous activities, strict products liability: manufacturing, design, and failure to warn
Intentional Interference with Online Business Interests: Trade libel, defamation of corporations, intentional interference with contract and other economic opportunities, unfair and deceptive trade practices, intentional interference with contract, intentional interference with economic opportunity, intentional interference with noncommercial opportunities, wrongful discharge from employment, unfair competition, interference with rights in personality and publicity, fraudulent misrepresentation, breach of fiduciary duties, tortious use of legal process, bad faith breach of contract, and the malicious prosecution	**Imputed Corporate Negligence:** Vicarious liability, *respondeat superior,* special liabilities for partners, co-venturers, special liability of multiple defendants, vicarious liability for telecommuting employees, vicarious liability for independent contractors if nondelegable duties, employers' duty of protection, borrowed servants, imputed negligence	**Enterprise Liability and Corporate Liability:** Vicarious liability for torts of co-venturers, liability of directors and officers for cyberspace torts, Title VII liability, civil rights torts

TABLE 5.1
Branches of Tort Law (Continued)

Intentional Torts	*Negligence*	*Strict Liability*
Intentional Interference with Real and Personal Property: Trespass to land, trespass to chattels, conversion, and nuisance	**Negligence-Based Economic Injuries:** Negligent entrustment, negligent security of Internet web site, premises liability, e-business duty to protect customers, common law duties of lessors, nuisance, computer errors or information torts	**Corporate Liability— Intellectual Property Offenses:** Infringement of intellectual property rights: product design, trademark infringement, trade secret misappropriation, copyright infringement, patent infringement, and rights of publicity

conduct is reasonably culpable and not justifiable."[38] Battery, assault, false imprisonment, intentional infliction of emotional distress, conversion,[39] trespass to land, and trespass to chattels[40] are examples of intentional torts.

Online companies face significant cyberliabilities in the workplace and marketplace. The tort of outrage, for example, may apply where an employee intentionally or recklessly sends harassing e-mail messages to a co-employee. A business competitor that floods a company's computer with spurious messages may interrupt its business and constitute an interference with contract or prospective economic relationships. Similarly, the deliberate introduction of a computer virus into a company's computer system that causes destruction of computer files may be the basis for a conversion lawsuit. A company may be liable for trespass to chattels for sending e-mail spam to subscribers of online services without permission.[41]

EBay, a leading online auction house, sued a competitor for trespassing on its web site with robotic agents.[42] The software agents allegedly searched and copied files on bidding activity from eBay's web site. This is an example of how creative lawyers use traditional torts to punish unlawful access and copying from web sites.

---

[38] Restatement (Second) of Torts § 870 (1979).

[39] *Conversion* is the unlawful exercise of dominion or control over the personal property of another.

[40] *Trespass to chattels* is an interference with the personal property of another. Conversion differs from trespass to chattels only in the measure of damages. With conversion, the remedy is for a forced sale of the personal property, whereas the damages for trespass to chattels is the diminution in the value due to the defendant's interference.

[41] *See, e.g.,* America Online, Inc. v. IMS, No. 98-0011-A (E.D. Va., Oct. 29, 1998) (holding defendant liable for trespass to chattels for the unauthorized mailing of unsolicited bulk e-mail to millions of AOL subscribers).

[42] eBay, Inc. v. Bidder's Edge, Inc., 2000 U.S. Dist. LEXIS 13326 (N.D. Cal. July 21, 2000) (denying motion to dismiss defendant's counterclaims and ruling that some of plaintiff's anticompetitive conduct, such as tortious interference with advertising contract, was unrelated to activity protected under the Noerr-Pennington doctrine).

Online chats may seem relaxed, but a conversation in a chat room, news-group, or web site may become the basis of a defamation lawsuit.[43] A company may be liable for defamation for repeating false rumors about individuals or enti-ties. Messages on the Internet may be retransmitted and posted to newsgroups by anonymous individuals, leading to costly lawsuits.[44]

Anonymous posters may use the Internet to tarnish the reputation of a com-pany by posting false information to an electronic bulletin board.[45] An anonymous false posting to an Internet web site, for example, led to one individual receiving thousands of angry telephone calls, e-mails, and threatening letters.[46]

A University of North Dakota physics professor filed a libel lawsuit against a former students who posted an article about him which accused him of being "a pedophile and having odd sexual habits."[47] The professor won a previous slander suit against his former student.[48] Several professors from San Francisco City Col-lege filed a libel suit against a web site that posted evaluations of their classes.[49] A doctor won a $675,000 libel award for falsely charging him with accepting kick-backs on a Yahoo! message board.[50]

In another case, a Florida appeals court ordered America Online to reveal the names of "individuals who posted [allegedly defamatory statements] under pseu-donyms on their message boards."[51] Anonymous wrongdoers may be unmasked by John Doe subpoenas.[52] However, recently courts have begun to deny issuances of John Doe subpoenas in Internet-related cases.[53]

---

[43] Denis Kelleher, Blaming the Messenger, The Irish Times (May 3, 1999), at 18.

[44] *Id.*

[45] A nonresident who posted allegedly defamatory statements about Virginia residents on a Usenet server was held to have sufficient contact with the forum under the state's long-arm statute to support the exercise of personal jurisdiction. Bochan v. LaFontaine, No. 1:98-CV-1749 (E.D. Va., May 26, 1999).

[46] Zeran v. America Online, Inc., 129 F.3d 327, 330 (4th Cir. 1997) (false posting stated that the plain-tiff was selling offensive T-shirts celebrating the bombing of the federal court house in Oklahoma City).

[47] Scott Carlson, North Dakota Professor Sues Former Student and a Web Site Over Allegations in an Article, The Chronicle of Higher Education (Jan. 19, 2001) at A33.

[48] *Id.*

[49] Katie Dean, Do "Dissed" Teachers Have Case? Wired News (June 12, 2000) (visited Apr. 15, 2002), http://www.wired.com/news/culture/0,1284,36720,00.html.

[50] Margaret Cronin Fisk, Net Libel Verdict Is Upheld, Nat'l L.J. (Dec. 25, 2000) at A 19; *see also* Judge Awards Doctor in Anonymous Net Libel Case, BNA's Internet Law News (Dec. 11, 2000) (citing cnet.com story about first Internet libel case involving anonymous Internet messages).

[51] Steven Bonisteel, Appeals Court: Anonymous Posters Can't Hide," Newsbytes (Oct. 16, 2000) (visited Apr. 15, 2002), htp://www.newsbytes.com/pubNews/00/156753.html.

[52] Grant P. Fondo & Robert Shore, Public Property in Cyberspace, 5 Cyberspace Lawyer 2 (June 2000), citing Compaq Computer Corp v. John Does 1-4 No. CV785143 (Santa Clara Cty. Super. Ct., Oct. 8, 1999); *see generally* John N. Walker, Can You Stop That Anonymous Spammer?, 4 Cyber-space Law. 6 (May 1999) (discussing John Doe subpoenas); *see also* SiliconValley.com, Lawsuits Challenge Anonymous Speech Online (visited Apr. 15, 2002), http://www.siliconvalley.com/cgi-bin/printpage.

[53] America Online, Inc. v. Anonymous Publicly Traded Co., 261 Va. 350, 542 S.E.2d 377 (Sup. Ct. 2001) (refusing to grant access to five unknown defendants in another state alleging it had been

A disgruntled ex-employee of Smith Barney was charged with sending phony e-mails to the company's top executives charging the company with questionable ethics and morals.[54] The ex-employee was an impostor who pretended to be the chief executive officer of the parent company of Salomon Smith Barney.[55] The ex-employee was charged with eight counts of harassment.[56]

In another case, a Washington law firm was accused of launching a "cyber war" against the Internet site Dig Dirt.[57] The company charged the law firm with posting defamatory messages about company officials on a usenet and covering up its activities with a false e-identity.[58]

A company may also be charged with knowledge of its employees' business torts committed within the scope of their employment. What constitutes guilty knowledge of the principal depends on the circumstances of the case.[59] Business torts may be committed face-to-face or by e-mail messages or postings to electronic bulletin boards[60] or newsgroups.[61] A company may also be a plaintiff in a lawsuit where a competitor is unfairly competing with the company, interfering

---

defamed and had confidential information about it revealed on the Internet); Melvin v. John Doe, No. 21942 (Cir. Ct., Loudoun Cty., Va., 1999) (quashing of subpoena against unknown individual on jurisdictional grounds); *see* Dendrite Int'l v. John Does, No. MRS-C-129-00 (Sup. Ct. N.J., Chancery Div., Nov. 28, 2000); *see generally* Virginia Court's Decision in Online "John Doe" Case Hailed by Free-Speech Advocates, N.Y. Times, Mar. 16, 2001 (discussing America Online v. Anonymous Publicly Traded Company); Brief Amicus Curiae of America Online, Inc. in Melvin v. John Doe, Appeal from Order Dated Nov. 15, 2000, by the Ct. of Common Pleas of Allegheny County, Pennsylvania, Civil Division No. GD99-10264) (arguing that proliferation of "John Doe" lawsuits threaten to chill free and protected online speech and that courts should require plaintiffs to demonstrate viable claims before compelling disclosure of identity information); Lyrissa Barnett Lidsky, Silencing John Doe: Defamation & Discourse in Cyberspace, 49 Duke L.J. 855 (2000).

[54] Reuters, Charge Over Smith Barney E-Mail, CNETNEWS.COM (visited Apr. 14, 2002), http://news.cnet.com/news/0-1005-200-332432.html.

[55] *Trolling* is the practice of posting a message on the Internet as an impostor. Meeka Jun, "Trolling" on Internet: Win for On-Line Services, N.Y.L.J. (Nov. 21, 1997), at 5.

[56] *Id.*

[57] The law firm of Steptoe and Johnson, LLP, was accused of cracking into Dig Dirt's web site 750 times and posting defamatory statements using a stolen e-identity. Craig Bicknell, Strange Corporate Hacking Saga, Wired News (Nov. 12, 1999) (visited Nov. 29, 1999), http://www.wired.com/news/politics/0,1283,32488,00.html.

[58] *Id.*

[59] *Id.*

[60] *Usenet* is a term that refers to the "worldwide community of electronic BBS that is closely associated with the Internet and the Internet community. The messages in Usenet are organized into thousands of topical groups, or 'Newsgroups.'" Michael D. Scott, Internet and Technology Desk Reference 523 (1999) (quoting Religious Tech. Ctr. v. Netcom On-Line Comm. Servs., Inc., 907 F. Supp. 1361, 1365 (N.D. Cal. 1995)).

[61] *Usenets* are postings on various subjects on servers on the worldwide Internet. A *newsgroup* is a collection of posted topics on a given subject. A group of law professors, teaching Internet Law, for example, might subscribe to a newsgroup on the topic of cyberspace law. Netscape and Microsoft browsers "provide user support and access to any newsgroup on the Internet. What Is.com, Usenet (A Definition) (visited Nov. 22, 1999), http://www.whatis.com/usenet.htm.

with prospective advantage, or committing torts such as disparagement. These intentional business torts will be discussed in detail in § 5.02.

Other intentional torts, such as battery, assault, and false imprisonment, cannot be used by online companies, as these torts involve the infliction of bodily harm, the apprehension of harm, or confinement, all situations without obvious parallels in cyberspace.

Intentional torts play a key role in punishing emergent forms of wrongdoing because criminal sanctions typically lag behind technological changes. Federal, state, and local enforcement agencies lack the financial, technical, and scientific expertise to punish many Internet-related harms. Many intentional torts are also classifiable as crimes. Recently, the Federal Bureau of Investigation "charged 90 individuals and companies with Internet fraud."[62] Many of the successful prosecutions began with consumer complaints to the FBI's Internet Fraud Complaint Center (IFCC).[63] The online fraudulent schemes included "online auction fraud, credit card fraud, bank fraud, investment fraud, multilevel marketing and pyramid schemes."[64] Each of these Internet crimes could also be the basis for a tortious fraud claim.

[2] Negligence

Negligence is conduct that departs from the reasonable standard of care imposed by law for the protection of others. The elements of a negligence cause of action are (1) duty of care, (2) breach of a duty of care, (3) proximate cause between the breach of the duty of care and the plaintiff's injury, and (4) damages. Negligence is an act or omission where there is a failure to use ordinary care; it is the failure to do that which a person of ordinary prudence would have done under the same or similar circumstances.[65] Ordinary care means that degree of care that would be used by a person of ordinary prudence under the same or similar circumstances.

Courts have had little difficulty adapting negligence principles to the online world. A company's exposure to negligence stems from its web site, its online communications, inadequate security, or retention of unfit employees. In *Benning v. Wit Capital Group, Inc.*,[66] customers of an Internet brokerage firm alleged that the firm owed a duty of reasonable care to maintain the facilities and support systems necessary to provide the services offered its members. The plaintiffs argued that the online brokerage house "failed to use reasonable care in managing customer orders in a fair, consistent, and reasonable manner as required by professional standards."[67] The court dismissed the claim because under Delaware law

---

[62] FBI Cracks Down on Internet Fraud, National Investigation Nets Series of Charges, Pike & Fischer Internet Law and Regulation (May 25, 2001), at 1.

[63] *Id.*

[64] *Id.* at 2.

[65] Restatement (Second) of Torts § 282 (1965).

[66] 2001 Del. Super. LEXIS 7 (Super. Ct. Del., Jan. 10, 2001).

[67] *Id* at *20.

purely economic losses are not recoverable by way of a tort claim.[68] A negligence claim as well as other causes of action were dismissed against America Online in a class action based upon the release of version 5.0 of its software.[69] The court dismissed all claims that AOL version 5.0 caused unauthorized changes to the configuration of computers based upon product liability, negligence, and negligent misrepresentation.[70] In *Yu v. IBM*,[71] the court dismissed claims of consumer fraud, breach of warranty, and negligence because no actual damages were alleged in a Y2K defective software case.

A company may potentially be liable for computer malpractice for its engineers' failure to design hardware or software consistent with high professional standards. A company may also be liable for negligent information security if its firewall or other security technologies fail to protect electronic communications. Courts have been reluctant to recognize the tort of computer malpractice for negligent design of hardware or software. A company has exposure for negligent statements made on its web site as well as for employment-based torts such as the negligent retention of unfit employees. Negligence-based cybertorts are discussed in detail in § 5.08.

[a] Duty and Breach

Negligence is conduct that falls below a standard of care for the protection of others in society. A person is not liable for injuries unless there is a duty of care. The general standard of care is based upon the reasonable person standard. In the case of corporate negligence, the duty of care is that of the reasonable company acting under the circumstances. Violation of a statute, industry standard, or customary usage of trade often establishes corporate negligence.

The definition of a duty of care by one member of society to another is a legal question determined by the court.[72] "In the usual run of cases, a general duty to avoid negligence is assumed, and there is no need for the court to undertake detailed analysis of precedent and policy."[73] The duties owed to a plaintiff by an online company may arise from private duties, such as contract, or public duties, based on a statute or an ordinance. A duty of care may also arise in a company's failure to anticipate tortious or criminal acts of others, although "courts are reluctant to impose a duty to anticipate the criminal or tortious conduct of third parties."[74]

---

[68] *Id.* at *21.

[69] *In re* America Online Version 5.0 Software Litig., 2001 U.S. Dist. LEXIS 6595 (S.D. Fla., Apr. 19, 2001); *see also* Williams v. America Online, Inc., 2001 Mass. Super. LEXIS 11 (Feb. 8, 2001) (refusing to dismiss claim and enforce choice-of-forum clause in lawsuit based upon claim that computers were damaged by America Online version 5.0).

[70] *Id* at *6.

[71] 314 Ill. App. 3d 892, 732 N.E.2d 1173 (2000).

[72] Hamilton v. ACCU-TEK, 62 F. Supp. 2d 818 (E.D.N.Y., June 3, 1999).

[73] *Id.* (citing Restatement (Third) of Torts: General Principles § 6) (Discussion Draft, Apr. 5, 1999) (finding of no duty rare).

[74] *Id.*

The question of whether a defendant owes a duty to a member of society is a question of law often decided on public policy grounds. A company, for example, could be potentially liable for negligently permitting third parties to hack into its web site and steal data or proprietary information owned by others, where that inadequate security results in injuries to third parties.

The concept of duty is based on considerations of public policy, which articulates whether particular classes of plaintiffs are entitled to protection, preventing defendants from being liable "[for] an indeterminate amount for an indeterminate time to an indeterminate class."[75] In a cyberspace context, defendants will argue that they have no duty to third parties for the installation and maintenance of Internet security and that the actions of third parties such as hackers constitute a superseding cause, cutting off any liability of computer consultants or software vendors. Plaintiffs will argue that an online company has a duty to customers or web site visitors since injuries suffered by these parties are reasonably foreseeable. The issue of what is foreseeable is measured by what a reasonable company would take into account in implementing and maintaining Internet security.

A court is likely to find "no duty" for a cyberspace injury if it finds that a cyberspace injury inflicted by a third party such as a hacker was unforeseeable or there was some other superseding causation. Courts have been reluctant to impose tort liabilities in cases dealing with musical lyrics, film, or the content of digital information. It is likely that courts will be disinclined to find tort liability for negligent transmission of information because it conflicts with First Amendment or other public policies.[76] Similarly, courts are disinclined to enforce foreign judgments that are antithetical to First Amendment countervailing policy.[77]

---

[75] Ultramares Corp. v. Touche, Niven & Co., 174 N.E. 441, 444 (N.Y. 1931); *see also* Palsgraf v. Long Island R.R. Co., 162 N.E. 99 (N.Y. 1928) (observing that there was no such thing as "negligence in the air" and the defendant railroad owed no duty of care to an unforeseeable plaintiff).

[76] See, e.g., Sanders v. Acclaim Entm't, Inc., 2002 U.S. Dist. LEXIS 3997 (D. Colo. Mar. 4, 2002) (dismissing claims against makers of violent movies and video games that were allegedly a cause of the Columbine school shootings; court held that the defendants owed no duty to plaintiff, examining factors such as foreseeability, social utility, and First Amendment issues); Davidson v. Time Warner, 1997 U.S. Dist. LEXIS 21559 (S.D. Tex. Mar. 31, 1997) (holding that neither the distributors nor the singer could reasonably foresee that distributing the music would lead to violence; also that music was not a product for purposes of products liability theory); McCollum v. CBS, Inc., 249 Cal. Rptr. 187 (Cal. Ct. App. 1988) (dismissing wrongful death case, finding no reasonably foreseeable risk that a young man's suicide was a consequence of music and lyrics); *cf.* Rice v. Palladin Enters.,128 F.3d 323 (4th Cir. 1997) (finding aiding and abetting liability for distributing manual of detailed factual instructions on how to murder and to become a professional killer).

[77] *See* Yahoo! v. La Ligue Contre Le Racisme et L'Antisemisme, 169 F. Supp. 2d 1181 (N.D. Ca. 2001) (refusing to enforce French order to eliminate Nazi material from online auction site on First Amendment grounds).

[b] Proximate Cause and Damages

The plaintiff must also meet the proximate cause requirement[78] by proving that the breach of duty had a causal connection to the plaintiff's injury. A plaintiff must prove that the defendant's negligence was the "cause in fact" (or a substantial factor bringing about the plaintiff's injury) and demonstrate that "there is no rule of law relieving the actor from liability because of the manner in which his negligence has resulted in the harm."[79] The concept of proximate cause, like legal duty, is used as a liability-limiting tool.[80] In general, a defendant is liable for harm only if an act or omission is a reasonably foreseeable risk of harm to others within the range of reasonable apprehension of that risk. An online company's liability hinges on its general duty to prevent harm that is reasonably preventable.

[3] Strict Liability

The third branch of tort law is strict liability, which imposes liability without a showing of fault or negligence. Strict liability is based on a public-policy decision that certain risky activities should bear the cost of wrongdoing, irrespective of the amount of care taken by the defendant. At common law, for example, a landowner who harbored wild animals on his land was strictly liable for the consequences if the animal escaped. Similarly, a nuclear processing plant is strictly liable for the escape of plutonium, even if it complied with federal nuclear regulatory regulations. It is no defense to strict liability that the defendant followed statutory or industry standards of care.

In the common law of torts, an online company may be strictly liable for computer errors or defects in computer systems under a products liability action.[81] Strict liability may also be based on vicarious liability as in the case of copyright or trademark infringement. An online publisher or web site may be classifiable as a publisher that can be held liable for statements contained in its works even absent proof that it had specific knowledge of the statement's inclusion.[82] In the Columbine school shootings, the shooters were allegedly influenced by violent video games and other electronic media; however, a Colorado federal court dismissed a strict liability claim against the movie and video game for the content of violent video games.[83] The court found that the intangible thoughts, ideas, images,

---

[78] Id.

[79] Restatement (Second) of Torts § 431 (2000).

[80] Dobbs, *supra* note 25, at 445.

[81] Richard D. Williams and Bruce T. Smyth, Computer and Internet Liability: Strategies, Claims and Defenses 7-53 (2002).

[82] W. Page Keeton et al., Prosser and Keeton on the Law of Torts § 113, at 810 (5th ed. 1984).

[83] *Sanders*, 2002 U.S. Dist. LEXIS 3997 (dismissing strict liability and negligence actions against electronic media defendants in case arising out of Columbine school shootings).

and messages contained in the movie and video games were not products within the scope of strict products liability. The court also found that even if the defendants owed a duty to the plaintiffs, the movie and video game defendants were not the legal cause of the plaintiffs' injuries, because the two Columbine students' intentional criminal acts constituted a superseding cause.

[a]   Strict Products Liability

Products liability is a hybrid of both warranty and tort law. In the early 1960s, American courts began to recognize that a commercial seller of any product having a manufacturing defect should be liable in tort for harm caused by the defect regardless of the plaintiff's ability to maintain a traditional negligence or warranty action.[84] The Supreme Court of California was the first court to apply strict liability to a dangerously defective product in *Greenman v. Yuba Power Products, Inc.*[85] In *Greenman,* the plaintiff was severely injured when a malfunctioning lathe, called the "Shopsmith," suddenly released a piece of wood, turning the wood into a missile that injured him. Justice Roger Traynor applied the law of strict product liability, rejecting sales law defense:

> Under these circumstances, it should not be controlling whether plaintiff selected the machine because of the statements in the brochure, or because of the machine's own appearance of excellence that belied the defect lurking beneath the surface, or because he merely assumed it would safely do the job it was built to do. . . . To establish the manufacturer's liability it was sufficient that the plaintiff proved that he was injured while using the [lathe] in a way it was intended to be used and as a result of a defect in design and manufacture, of which plaintiff was not aware that made the [lathe] unsafe for its intended use.[86]

Strict products liability swept the country after the American Law Institute adopted Section 402A, allowing strict liability for all product liability defendants.[87] Section 19 of the Restatement Third defines a "product" as "tangible personal property."[88] If software is classified as a product, a vendor may be liable for products liability.

Strict products liability focuses on whether a dangerous defect in a product causes physical harm to the ultimate consumer. In a products liability action, a plaintiff must prove that (1) a product is defectively designed, (2) the manufacturer failed to warn of a known hazard, or (3) there was a manufacturing defect. A seller is strictly liable for placing a defective product into the stream of commerce that causes physical injuries to the plaintiff.

The Restatement (Third) of the Law of Torts: Products Liability, approved by the American Law Institute in 1997, adopts new, more restrictive products liabil-

---

[84] Restatement (Third) of Torts (Products Liability) § 1, at 6 (1998).
[85] 377 P.2d 897 (Cal. 1963).
[86] 377 P.2d at 901.
[87] Restatement (Second) of Torts § 402A (1965).
[88] Restatement (Third) of Torts (Product Liability) § 19 (1998).

ity rules applicable to commercial sellers and distributors of products. The new rules largely replace strict liability with negligence-based standards in design and failure to warn cases. The Restatement (Third) is increasingly being cited by state courts and is an influential source of the evolving law of products liability.

Section 1 of the Restatement (Third) makes each seller in the chain of distribution liable if there is proof that the product was sold with a defect.

[i] Manufacturing defect. A seller is strictly liable for a manufacturing flaw that constitutes a departure or deviation from a product's intended design. It is no defense in "deviation from intended design" cases that the manufacturer exercised the utmost care. In the Internet context, a manufacturing flaw case would be rare. If an individual software diskette had a manufacturing defect, there would be strict liability. If a manufacturer's quality control resulted in defective software being distributed, a plaintiff will have a strict liability action.

[ii] Design defect. Section 2 of the Restatement defines a design defect as occurring when the foreseeable risks of harm posed by the product could have been reduced or avoided by the adoption of a reasonable alternative design. The Restatement (Third)'s formulation of the design defect replaces § 402A's "consumer expectation" test with a more defense-oriented risk/utility test.[89] The test is whether a reasonable alternative design at a reasonable cost would have reduced the foreseeable risk of harm posed by the product. The risk/utility test of the Restatement (Third) compares the product that caused the injury with the alternative design that arguably would have averted the injury. Courts will examine the effects of the alternative design on the cost of the product, production costs, and effects on product longevity, repair, and esthetics. If the reasonable alternative design approach is adopted for Internet-related cases, a claimant will need to show comparative advantages and disadvantages of different Internet security solutions. The risk/utility test is more akin to negligence than strict products liability. The Restatement (Third) approach to risk/utility is more restrictive than that of states permitting plaintiffs to prove design defect through either the consumer expectation test or risk/utility tests.

[iii] Failure to warn. Similarly, the Restatement (Third) injects negligence-like standards in failure to warn cases. Under § 2(c) of the Restatement (Third), a product is defective if "the foreseeable risks of harm posed by the product could have been reduced or avoided by the provision of reasonable instructions or warnings by the seller."[90]

---

[89] "The consumer expectations test holds a manufacturer strictly liable for any condition not contemplated by the ultimate consumer that will be unreasonably dangerous to him or her." In contrast, the risk-utility analysis weighs a product's risks against its benefits. Consumer expectations are no longer the test for defect, but a single factor that may be considered when assessing design.

[90] Restatement (Third) of Torts: Products Liability § 2(c). *See generally* Marshall Shapo, In Search of the Law of Products Liability: The ALI Restatement Project, 48 Vanderbilt L. Rev. 631

In general, there is no duty to warn of obvious and generally known risks. Most consumer users are aware of the generally known risks of computer hackers, viruses, and the interception of e-mail. A software vendor would have no liability for failing to warn or instruct regarding risks and risk-avoidance measures obvious to the ordinary consumer user. Still, a vendor needs to give reasonable instructions or warnings about such issues as password control or the need to update computer virus software.

[iv] Availability in Internet-related cases. Courts may extend design defect liability to Internet-related wrongdoing. The reasonable alternative design requirement "would add a challenging element to the strict liability action."[91.] Courts have been slow to impose products liability standards on the manufacturing and distribution of software. Courts are far more inclined to apply strict products liability standards to computer hardware where there are injuries in addition to the commercial losses from the defective components. Courts have yet to evaluate the reasonableness of software design alternatives for preventing computer intrusions, denial of service attacks, or the spread of viruses under a products liability theory. Assuming that the economic loss rule may be sidestepped, the plaintiff would need to show that some alternative Internet security software would have reduced or prevented the harm suffered by the plaintiff. A defendant could argue that a software solution would have introduced other dangers of equal or greater magnitude. In the context of the mass market, the plaintiff would need to show that alternative software solutions were available to lower risk and at comparable cost. As the magnitude and probability of foreseeable harm increases, courts may be more inclined to extend products liability theories to cyberspace.

[b] *Economic Loss Doctrine and Computer Law*

The economic loss rule (ELR) bars recovery in products liability actions where the loss is purely economic, that is, direct economic loss to the product itself caused by the defect and consequential damages flowing from the defect, such as lost profits.[92] The rule applies where the harm is to the product itself as opposed to personal injury or other property damages. The ELR "provides that where a purchaser's expectations in a sale are frustrated because the product he bought is not working properly, his remedy is said to be in contract alone, for he has suffered only economic losses."[93]

(VII) (G) (1995); Frank J. Vandall, The Restatement (Third) of Torts: Products Liability Section 2 (b): The Reasonable Alternative Design Requirement, 61 Tenn. L. Rev. 1407 (1994).

[91] *See, e.g.*, Vandall,, *supra* note 90, at 1418 (commenting on draft Restatement (Third)).

[92] Mt. Lebanon Pers. Care Home, Inc. v. Hoover Universal, Inc., 276 F.3d 845 (6th Cir. 2002) (holding that economic loss rule barred recovery of damages to the product purchased, which was a nursing home building); East River Steamship Corp. v. Transamerica Delaval, Inc., 476 U.S. 858 (1986) (delineating border between contract and tort law so that "contract law [will not] drown in a sea of tort").

[93] Imaging Fin. Servs. v. Lettergraphics Detroit, Inc., 1999 U.S. App. LEXIS 2405 (6th Cir. Feb. 9, 1999).

Economic losses such as lost earning capacity or earnings are classified as harms to the person which are recoverable under tort law.[94] However, other categories of economic loss, such as harm to the product itself, are not recoverable. Courts restrict recovery for pure economic loss to the remedies provided by Article 2 of the Uniform Commercial Code.[95] If defective software, for example, causes the shutdown of a business, the remedy would be restricted to the contractually based UCC rather than under products liability law.[96] Computer systems were historically sold as turnkey computer systems. The "hardware and software [was] a complete package such that a purchaser could utilize it for his business as a working system without having to perform any additional programming or system work."[97] Beginning in the 1980s, computer hardware and software began to be sold separately. An online company's computer hardware, if sold separately, is clearly a product, but software is classified as an intangible.

A company can be liable for manufacturing defects in its computers. If a company's computer hardware deviates from its intended design, it would be liable even if it proved that it exercised all possible care. If a plaintiff can establish that the foreseeable risks of harm posed by computer hardware could have been avoided by a reasonable alternative design, the manufacturer may be liable for products liability under a theory of design defect. Finally, if the foreseeable risks of harm posed by a computer could have been reduced or avoided by reasonable instructions or warnings, it would be liable for inadequate instructions or warnings. Section 5.09 examines strict liability causes of action in cyberspace.

Few courts have considered the extension of strict liability to defective computer hardware or software, "but the potential liability is enormous."[98] There is authority for considering computer software a product for purposes of strict products liability.[99] Mass-market software is typically regarded as a good despite its intangible character.[100] One of the reasons why there have been so few strict products liability cases in the field of computer law is the "economic loss rule." It bears noting that strict product liability does not apply to purely economic losses caused by defective hardware or software. Courts could, however, find a manufacturer liable for defective hardware or software where there is loss of life or serious injury caused by bad software. Software failure, for example, was the probable

---

[94] Restatement (Third) of Torts (Products Liability) § 21, cmt. b (1998).

[95] Id. at cmt. d.

[96] Id. (citing example of a defective product destroying a commercial business establishment as an illustration of the economic loss doctrine).

[97] Michael D. Scott, Internet and Technology Law Desk Reference 512 (1999) (citing Management Consultants Ltd. v. Data General Corp., 8 Comp. L. Serv. Rep. 66 (E.D. Va. 1980)).

[98] Lessons to Learn Regarding the Restatement of Products Liability, 15 Comp. Law Strat. 5 (Oct. 1998).

[99] Restatement (Third) of Torts (Products Liability) § 19, cmt. (a) (1998).

[100] Id. (citing Systems Design v. Kansas City Post Office, 788 P.2d 878 (Kan. Ct. App. 1990); Advent Systs. Ltd. v. Unisys Corp., 925 F.2d 670 (3d Cir. 1991); RRX Indus., Inc. v. Lab-Con, Inc., 772 F.2d 543 (9th Cir. 1985)).

cause of the crash of a Boeing 757 that killed 70 persons in Peru.[101] Courts may be receptive to permitting plaintiffs to bring strict liability actions where defective software causes physical injury.[102]

The failures of computer systems have been the proximate cause of "chemical leaks or explosions at chemical or nuclear plants, truck, train or plane collisions; physical injury or death where the systems have involved medical applications; and improper architectural/stress analysis."[103] There is some case law on treating defective information as a "product." A California court imposed liability on the seller of an inaccurate instrument approach chart.[104]

[B] Bases for a Company's Liability for an Employee's Wrongdoing

There are two bases of a company's liability for an employee's torts: direct liability and vicarious liability. (*See* Table 5.2.) An employer is not liable for torts of an employee where it does not know or have reason to know of an unreasonable risk to others.

[1] Direct Liability

Direct liability is based on agency principles. The agency relationship always involves a principal, an agent, and a third party harmed by the agent's wrongdoing. An agency is a "fiduciary relationship that arises when one person (the 'principal') manifests consent to another person (the 'agent') that the agent shall act on the principal's behalf and subject to the principal's control."[105] The common law of agency follows the principle of vicarious liability or *respondeat superior.* The concept of *respondeat superior* embodies the common law maxim "let the principal answer."[106] Under agency principles, online companies will be liable for contracts made by their employees as well as their employees' tortious activities on company computers.

---

[101] Robert Cortijo, Computer Failure & Peru Airplane Crash, Agence-France-Presse (Oct. 4, 1996) at 1.

[102] *See generally* Patrick J. Miyaki, Computer Software Defects: Should Computer Software Manufacturers Be Held Strictly Liable for Computer Software Defects? 8 Santa Clara Comp. & High Tech. L.J. 121 (1992).

[103] Diane Savage, Avoiding Tort Claims for Defective Hardware and Software Strategies for Dealing with Potential Liability Woes, 15 Comp. Law Strat. 1 (Oct. 1998).

[104] Flour Corp. v. Jeppesen & Co., 216 Cal. Rptr. 68, 71 (Ct. App. 1985) (stating that "a sheet of paper might not be dangerous, per se, it would be difficult indeed to conceive of a salable commodity with more inherent lethal potential than an aid to aircraft navigation that, contrary to its own design standards, fails to list the highest land mass immediately surrounding a landing site"); Saloomey v. Jeppesen & Co., 707 F.2d 671 (2d Cir. 1983) (applying Colorado law). *See also* Brocklesby v. United States, 767 F.2d 1288, 1298 (9th Cir. 1985).

[105] Restatement (Third) of the Law of Agency § 1.01 (American Law Institute Council Draft No. 1, Nov. 18, 1999).

[106] Bryan Garner, A Dictionary of Modern Legal Usage 766 (2d ed. 1995) (noting that "under the ordinary rules of *respondeat superior*, the shipowner is responsible for his actions").

TABLE 5.2
Liability for Employee's Torts

Direct Liability for Employee's Torts	Vicarious Liability for Employee's Torts	No Liability for Employee's Torts
Standard: Employee's high rank makes him or her a company's alter ego; imputed liability; high-level employee is acting as the company. The company may have intended the consequences of the employee's actions by ordering the high-level employee to commit wrongdoing. **Exceptions:** Does not apply to acts actually not apparently authorized. A company official is liable for misappropriating a competitor's trade secrets.	**Standard:** Doctrine of *respondeat superior* makes the company liable for the legal consequences of its employee's actions. Company is liable for torts (intentional, negligence, or strict liability) committed within the scope of employment. **Exceptions:** Doctrine does not apply where employee, with apparent authority, defrauded company with third party; does not apply to independent contractors where there is no right to control actions.	**Standard:** Not liable for torts of employee where it does not know or have reason to know of an unreasonable risk to others. **Exceptions:** May be liable in limited circumstance where the duty is nondelegable. May also be liable for "frolic and detour" of errant employee where there is a foreseeable risk of harm.
Typical Example: Inadequate security for computer system leading to loss of confidential information; failure to protect the privacy of the customer information.	**Typical Example:** Company is most likely liable for employee's negligence resulting in physical injury to a person or property. Manager sexually harasses co-worker or third party using e-mail system; employee misappropriates trade secrets of a competitor; imputed tort liability. A company official is liable for misappropriating a competitor's trade secrets.	**Typical Example:** Company is not liable for employee's conduct outside scope of employment and where it does not realize unreasonable danger to others; company is not liable for its employees' hate speech using company computer absent knowledge.

[a] Agent's Actual Authority to Act

Actual authority is when the principal consents to having an agent act on its behalf. A company has direct liability or legal responsibility when the employer authorizes actions taken by an employee. A CEO, for example, may consent to have a high-level manager negotiate a contract on the company's behalf. A company may draft a power of attorney authorizing its subsidiary to sell a piece of real estate. The idea of actual authority requires some writing or other record of the principal's agreement to give the agent authority to act on its behalf. The Restatement

(Third) of Agency draft defines actual authority as when "the agent reasonably believes, in accordance with the principal's manifestations to the agent, that the principal wishes the agent so to act."[107]

A company may create actual authority in a diverse set of circumstances in its Internet activities. A company, may, for example, give a high-ranking agent written authority to negotiate an online contract on its behalf. A senior officer may negotiate for the design of a web site. The term *implied authority* is "often used to mean actual authority either to do what is necessary, usual or proper to accomplish the agent's express responsibilities."[108]

[b] Apparent Authority

Apparent authority is the situation where a third party has a "reasonable belief that the actor has authority to do actions consistent with the position."[109] An agent has the apparent authority for acts necessary or incidental to achieving the principal's objectives.[110] The underlying idea behind apparent authority is the appearance of authority conferred by a company. An agent who appears to a third party to be authorized, but who lacks actual authority, may nevertheless bind the company.

[2] Vicarious or Imputed Liability

Vicarious liability is technically a form of strict liability because the doctrine imposes liability where there is no direct fault on the part of the company. General agency principles make an employer subject to liability for the torts of its employees committed while acting in the scope of employment. An employer, however, can also be vicariously liable for torts committed by an employee.

Vicarious liability evolved out of the medieval law, covering the relationship of master and servant in feudal societies, and the Restatement of Agency (First) continued to use the feudal concepts of master and servant. A "master is a principal who employs an agent to perform service in his affairs and who controls or has the right to control the physical conduct of the other in the performance of the service."[111] A servant is an agent employed by a master to perform services that the master controls or the master has "a right to control."[112]

The Restatement further defined the master/servant relationship as follows:

> A master is under a duty to exercise reasonable care so to control his servant while acting outside the scope of his employment as to prevent him from

---

[107] American Law Institute, Restatement (Third) of the Law of Agency § 2.01 (Council Draft No. 1, Nov. 18, 1999).

[108] *Id.* at § 2.01, cmt.

[109] *Id.* at § 2.03.

[110] *Id.* at § 2.02(1).

[111] Restatement (Second) Agency § 2(1) (1958).

[112] *Id.* at § 2(2).

intentionally harming others or from so conducting himself as to create an unreasonable risk of bodily harm to them, if: (a) the servant is upon premises in possession of the master . . . and (b) the master knows or has reason to know of the necessity and opportunity (ii) that he has the ability to control his servant, and (ii) knows or should know of the necessity and opportunity for such control.[113]

The black letter law was that a "master is subject to liability for the torts of his servants committed while acting in the scope of their employment."[114] In contrast, "a master is not subject to liability for the torts of his servants acting outside of the scope of employment if the master intended the conduct or the consequences, was negligent or reckless or the conduct violated a non-delegable duty."[115]

The doctrine of *respondeat superior* makes an employer liable for torts committed within the scope of the employee's job duties.[116] In contrast, an employer is not liable for activities outside the scope of employment. The test of whether an employee's actions are within the scope of employment turns on issues such as foreseeability and fairness of including the loss as a cost of the employer's business. Courts focus on whether the employee was doing something in furtherance of the duties he or she owes the employer and where the employer exercises control, direct or indirect, over the employee's activities. The practice of telecommuting raises challenging *respondeat superior* issues.

An online employer is generally liable for torts by its employees committed within the scope of their duties. The black letter law is that an employer is not liable for torts committed for personal motives unrelated to the furtherance of the employer's business. In considering whether a particular act falls within an employee's scope of employment, courts examine five factors: (1) the connection between the time, place, and occasion of the act; (2) the history of the relationship between employer and employee as spelled out in actual practice; (3) whether the act is one commonly done by such an employee; (4) the extent of departure from normal methods of performance; and (5) whether the specific act was one that the employer could reasonably have anticipated.[117]

An employer who is negligent in hiring or retaining an ex-hacker or other at-risk individual would be directly liable in negligence in addition to the vicarious liability. In these cases, the employer may have a right of contribution against its co-defendant. The amount of contribution will be determined on a pro rata basis or by the percentage of responsibility that a fact finder assigns each co-defendant. In the context of vicarious liability or *respondeat superior,* there may be a right of indemnification. The practical reality is that contribution or indemnification can

---

[113] Restatement (Second) of Torts § 317 (1965).

[114] Restatement (Second) of Agency § 219(1) (1958).

[115] *Id.* at § 219(2)(a)-(c).

[116] *See, e.g.*, Lundberg v. State, 255 N.E.2d 177 (N.Y. 1969). *Respondeat superior* means "Let the employer respond for the wrongs of the employees." Juline E. Hu et al., Cyberslacking! A Liability Issue for Wired Workplaces, 42 Cornell Hotel & Restaurant Admin. Q. 34 (Oct. 1, 2001).

[117] Haybeck v. Prodigy Servs. Co., 944 F. Supp. 326 (S.D.N.Y. 1996).

only be used to reallocate the cost of wrongdoing where the co-defendant is solvent.

Even where an employee does not act within the scope of his or her employment, an employer may be required to answer in damages for the tort of an employee against a third party when the employer has either hired or retained the employee with knowledge of the employee's propensity for the sort of behavior that caused the injured party's harm.[118] Negligent hiring or retention claims make the employer answerable for an employee's torts because he or she was hired or retained with knowledge of the employee's propensity for the sort of behavior that caused the injured party's harm. Many of the tort claims brought against the Catholic Church arising out of the sexual abuse of children by priests are filed under negligent retention theories.

[a] ISP's Imputed Liability

The Communications Decency Act of 1996 was originally enacted to protect the "infant industry" of online service providers such as America Online, Compuserve, and Prodigy, which faced an unpredictable legal environment.[119] Publishers are traditionally held liable for defamatory statements contained in their works even if they had no prior knowledge of a statement's objectionable content. In contrast, distributors were not held liable for defamatory statements contained in their materials unless it was proven that they had actual knowledge of the defamatory statements.[120] It was unclear before the passage of this act whether courts would classify service providers as publishers liable for defamation or as distributors and therefore largely immune from such liability.[121]

Prior to 1996, courts were sharply divided on whether service providers could be liable for information torts committed by their subscribers or third parties. Section 230 of the CDA immunizes Internet Service Providers for torts committed by subscribers and third parties.[122] The long-term consequence of § 230 is to provide blanket immunity for many torts in cyberspace.

---

[118] *Id.* (holding that company was not responsible to litigant who became infected with AIDS spread by employee who had sex with customers he met online because the employee's sexual intercourse with the litigant fell outside the scope of his employment).

[119] 47 U.S.C. § 230 (c)(1) (2001) (stating that "[n]o provider . . . of an interactive computer service shall be treated as the publisher or speaker of any information provided by another information content provider").

[120] Keeton et al., *supra* note 82, at § 113.

[121] *Id.* at 811.

[122] The case that led Congress to enact § 230 (c)(1) was *Oakmont, Inc. v. Prodigy Servs. Co.,* 23 Media Law Rep. (BNA) 1794 (N.Y. Sup. Ct. 1995) (denying Prodigy's motion to dismiss a defamation action made by a subscriber in a Prodigy newsgroup). Prior to the enactment of the CDA, the Southern District of New York addressed, in *Cubby, Inc. v. CompuServe, Inc.,* 776 F. Supp. 135 (S.D. N.Y. 1991), whether a provider could be liable for defamatory statements made on an online forum. In short, the court was persuaded that CompuServe was a mere distributor. The CDA expressly overruled the *Stratton Oakmont* case, granting service providers a broad immunity for defamatory materials and other tortuous activities committed by third parties on their service.

By its plain language, § 230 creates a federal immunity to any tort cause of action that would make service providers liable for information originating with a third party. It would have been prohibitively expensive, if not impossible, for providers to monitor and censor all postings made on their services. Congress essentially deferred to industry standards, preferring self-regulation to government control.

One of the unintended consequences of § 230 is that it immunizes unfair, deceptive, and predatory practices in cyberspace. In *Ben Ezra, Weinstein, & Co. v. America Online, Inc.*,[123] the plaintiff was a publicly owned company that designed and manufactured corporate finance computer software. In March 1997, the software company filed an action in New Mexico state court against America Online (AOL), asserting state law claims for defamation and negligence. AOL provides its subscribers with updated stock information, which includes data about the market price for specific stocks and the volume of shares traded in the current or previous trading day. Two independent third parties provided inaccurate information on the computer software firm's stock price and volume. The software company claimed that AOL defamed it by publishing the inaccurate information and also alleged that AOL failed to exercise reasonable care in the manipulation, alteration, and change of the stock information. A lower court found that AOL was exempt from these lawsuits under § 230 of the Communications Decency Act (CDA). The Tenth Circuit upheld the lower court, ruling that AOL was an "interactive computer service provider" and therefore immunized from tort liability for publishing inaccurate stock information.

The courts have expanded § 230 beyond defamation to a wide variety of cyberspace torts affecting individuals.[124] *John Does v. Franco Productions*[125] was a class action on behalf of a group of Illinois State University athletes who were videotaped in "various states of undress by hidden cameras and microphones in restrooms, locker rooms, and showers" without their consent. The videotapes were sold on a number of web sites that transmitted still images of nude or partially clothed young male athletes on the Internet. The athletes' cause of action against the Illinois State University for failing to notify the athletes of the existence of the tapes was dismissed on grounds of qualified immunity. The athletes' case against the web sites was immunized by § 230(c) of the Communications Decency Act.

---

[123] 206 F.3d 980 (10th Cir. 2000).

[124] *See, e.g.*, Blumenthal v. Drudge, 992 F. Supp. 44, 49 (D.D.C. 1998) (dismissing defamation case on § 230 grounds); Zeran v. America Online, Inc., 958 F. Supp. 1124, 1131-37 (E.D. Va. 1997) (dismissing cases involving defamatory online postings); Jane Doe One v. Oliver, 775 A.2d 1000 (Jud. Dist. Waterbury, Conn., Mar. 7, 2000) (holding provider immune on claim that would have made it liable for improper e-mail message sent to plaintiff mother's employer).

[125] 2000 WL 816779 (N.D. Ill. June 21, 2000) (holding that Internet Service Providers were immunized from tort lawsuits even where they participated in web hosting and web design activities); *see also* Does v. Franco Prods., 2001 U.S. Dist. LEXIS 8397 (N.D. Ill. June 20, 2001) (certifying class for purposes of injunctive but monetary relief); Does v. Franco Prods., 2000 U.S. Dist. LEXIS 9848 (N.D. Ill. July 12, 2000) (granting motion to dismiss university on grounds of qualified immunity and find that plaintiffs did not show violation of clearly established right when Illinois State University officials failed to inform them of videotapes made without their consent).

In *PatentWizard, Inc. v. Kinko's, Inc.*,[126] Kinko's was classified as a service provider, thus qualifying for CDA immunity. Kinko's rents computers that can be readily connected to the Internet but does not record the identity of persons renting its equipment. In *PatentWizard*, an anonymous Internet user made disparaging remarks about a software package developed by a North Dakota patent lawyer to assist inventors in obtaining patents. The patent lawyer hosted a "chat room" session about software that had been recently released by PatentWizard. "One of several participants in that chat room was a user with the screen name 'Jimmy' who allegedly logged on from a Kinko's computer. During the session, Jimmy made numerous disparaging statements about PatentWizard and its developer which plaintiffs claim defamed them and interfered with their prospective business relationships."[127]

The plaintiff was unable to determine the identity of the person making the remarks since the provider did not record the identities of persons who rented its computers. The plaintiff contended that, due to the configuration of the Kinko's computer network, they have been unable to locate and pursue legal remedies against the anonymous computer user. The plaintiff filed suit against Kinko's alleging (1) negligent failure to monitor its computer network, (2) negligent failure to maintain proper and adequate records, (3) negligent spoliation of evidence, (4) intentional spoliation of evidence, (5) aiding and abetting defamation, and (6) aiding and abetting interference with prospective business relationships.[128] Kinko's moved to dismiss all of these claims, arguing that they are preempted and barred by federal law, and that they are unavailable under state common law. The court ruled that § 230 created "a federal immunity to any cause of action that would make service providers liable for information originating with a third-party user of the service" that and the federal immunity extended to all claims in the plaintiffs' case.[129]

In *Doe v. America Online*,[130] the Florida Supreme Court upheld a lower court's dismissal of a negligence action against an Internet Service Provider (ISP) based on § 230. In *Doe*, the mother of a young boy victimized by a sexual predator filed a tort action, claiming that an AOL user had used an AOL "chat room" to market obscene photographs and videotapes of her minor son.[131] She sought to recover noneconomic damages against the pedophile and against America Online, which hosted the chat room. The claim against AOL alleged that the provider was

---

[126] 163 F. Supp. 2d 1069 (D.S.D. 2001).

[127] *Id.* at 1070.

[128] *Id.* at 1071.

[129] *Id.* at 1071-72. (stating that "the court held that the provider could not be held liable for the alleged defamation, since 47 U.S.C. § 230 provided federal immunity to any cause of action that would make the Internet service provider liable for information originating with a third-party user of the provider's service").

[130] Doe v. America Online, Inc. 783 So. 2d 1010 (Fla. 2001) (upholding trial court's dismissal of state tort actions of negligence and defamation action against ISP with notice of defamatory posting. In October 2001, the U.S. Supreme Court refused to grant a writ of certiorari in Doe v. America Online, Inc., 122 S. Ct. 208 (2001)).

[131] 783 So. 2d at 1012.

negligent per se in its violation of a criminal statute by permitting the distribution of pornography on its service. The plaintiff alleged that AOL aided and abetted the offering of "a visual depiction of sexual conduct involving [John Doe]" and by allowing the user "to sell or arrange to sell child pornography" in its chat rooms.[132] The plaintiff also alleged that AOL was negligent in that "AOL knew or should have known that Russell and others like him used the service to market and distribute child pornography; that it should have used reasonable care in its operation; that it breached its duty; and that the damages to John Doe were reasonably foreseeable as a result of AOL's breach."[133]

The trial court dismissed the plaintiff's complaint against America Online in its entirety, ruling that § 230 of the Communication's Decency Act barred all causes of action. The Florida appellate court certified the question of whether state law tort claims based on distributor liability of an Internet Service Provider were preempted.[134] The appeals court held that America Online could not be liable under Florida state tort law for emotional injuries suffered by the plaintiff as the result of a pedophile's use of chat rooms to market obscene images that depicted the young boy in sexual activities. The court held that AOL was entitled to the § 230 immunity Congress provided for interactive computer services, which applied to the petitioner's claims.[135]

[b] Imputed Liability and Independent Contractors

A company is generally not liable for the torts of independent contractors under traditional principles of the law of agency. An "independent contractor is a person who contracts with another to do something for him but who is not controlled by the other nor is subject to the other's right to control with respect to his physical conduct in the performance of the undertaking."[136] A company, however, may be liable for an independent contractor's conduct if the duty is nondelegable.

In *Seidl v. Greentree Mortgage Co.*,[137] a mortgage company was found not to be vicariously liable for the spam e-mail marketing campaign done on its behalf by an independent contractor. The mortgage company sought summary judgment in an action by a computer science student against it alleging negligence, deceptive trade practices, trespass, and invasion of privacy for e-mail replies to the defendant's advertisements. The court granted summary judgment in favor of the mortgage company, holding that the marketer who sent the spam e-mail advertisements was an independent contractor and not an agent of the mortgage company. The federal district court applied a six-factor test in its determination that the e-mail marketer was an independent contractor rather than an employee. The court

---

[132] *Id.*

[133] *Id.*

[134] *Id.*

[135] *Id.*

[136] *Id.* at § 3.

[137] 230 F. Supp. 2d 1292 (D. Colo. 1998).

observed that whether an individual is an employee or an independent contractor depends on multiple factors in the nature of the service rendered. The traditional test for economic dependence examines six factors: (1) the degree of control exercised by the employer over the work, (2) the worker's opportunity for profit or loss, (3) the worker's investment in the business, (4) the permanence of the business relationship, (5) the degree of skill the work calls for, and (6) the extent to which the work is integral to the employer's business.

A company may have a nondelegable duty to protect the personal information of customers that is not disclaimable. The company's counsel should seek indemnity from third parties for torts that may arise out of nondelegable duties. Suppose a company hires an independent contractor to design its web site. A company, for example, may be vicariously liable for the designer's copyright or trademark infringement for incorporating text, music, video, or logos without the owner's permission as well as an employee may be held liable for improper use of e-mail or the Internet.

[3] Joint Tortfeasors

A company may seek damages from more than one defendant. Assume that networks of hackers are seeking to deny service to a company's web site. The hackers, who are acting in concert, may be sued separately or together for economic injuries caused by the attack.

Joint and several liability makes each co-defendant liable for the entire harm. The plaintiff may sue each defendant separately or together. If a co-defendant is insolvent or unavailable, the plaintiff may seek the entire judgment from the solvent and available defendant. If a co-defendant pays the entire judgment, it may seek contribution from its joint tortfeasor. The right of contribution is a co-defendant's right to seek reimbursement where it has paid more than its share of harm. Indemnity is a closely related tort doctrine, which means roughly that a person promises to make good for incurred losses.

At early common law, joint liability was narrowly conceived of as referring to "vicarious liability for concerted action."[138] The doctrine of joint and several liability makes each joint tortfeasor liable to the plaintiff for an entire loss. Joint and several liability permits a plaintiff to join co-defendants in a single action or recover a judgment in its entirety from any one of them. In addition, an online company may be able to seek indemnity (full payment of the judgment) from another co-venturer in certain situations. The online company may be able to reallocate losses in joint ventures through "hold harmless" and indemnification agreements to shift losses. Joint and several liability has been limited in thirty-five states as a result of tort reform. The abolition of joint liability reallocates the risk that a co-defendant will be unable to pay its share of the damages to the plaintiff.

The issue of multiple defendants in an online tort case will frequently raise difficult issues as to the apportionment of liability. The Restatement (Third) of the

---

[138] William L. Prosser, Handbook of the Law of Torts 291 (4th ed. 1971).

Law of Torts: Apportionment of Liability has formulated new rules for comparative responsibility where there are multiple tortfeasors.

In jurisdictions that recognize joint and several liability, an employer or employee may be jointly and severally liable to an injured person. In joint and several jurisdictions, the injured person may sue for and recover the full amount of damages from any jointly and severally liable person. The law of agency makes a principal vicariously liable for the torts of its agent. An online company paying a judgment based on an employee's actionable negligence may seek indemnity.

In jurisdictions that have abolished joint liability, an injured plaintiff may recover only the severally liable person's share of responsibility. Section 12 of the Restatement on Apportionment notes that in intentional tort cases, the rule is joint and several liability for indivisible injuries committed by multiple tortfeasors. Section 15 makes multiple co-defendants jointly and severally liable when acting in concert. Multiple tortfeasor apportionment may arise in an Internet setting where co-venturers conspire to commit a business tort. A court may be asked to apportion liability between a computer engineer and consultant when security fails on a web site. Apportionment problems occur frequently in the employment relationship. In *America Online Inc. v. National Health Care Discount, Inc.,*[139] a federal district court denied an Internet Service Provider's motion for summary judgment seeking to hold a spam e-mail defendant liable for violations of the Computer Fraud and Abuse Act, the Virginia Computer Crimes Act, and common law trespass to chattels. The defendant transmitted unsolicited bulk e-mail advertising the defendant's products to AOL customers. The court declined to enter a summary judgment order, stating that it could not determine whether the parties who sent the e-mail in question were defendant's agents, acting under its control, or independent contractors.

If two or more computer consultants were liable for negligent security permitting a distributed denial of service attack, there may be a right of contribution if one of the co-defendants pays a settlement.

§ 5.03   INTENTIONAL TORTS IN CYBERSPACE

Intentional torts are divided into torts that interfere with the person and those that interfere with property. Intentional torts against the person include assault, battery, false imprisonment, and the intentional infliction of emotional distress.[140]

---

[139] 121 F. Supp. 2d 1255 (N.D. Iowa 2000).

[140] The elements of intentional infliction of emotional distress are set forth in § 46 of the Restatement (Second) of Torts (1965). Section 46 requires that the plaintiff prove that the defendant by extreme and outrageous conducts intentionally or recklessly caused severe emotional distress. The Restatement requires that the plaintiff prove actual damages, which may be in the form of physical injury, costs for medical care, or other damages. Sams v. Doug Hannon Internet Waterworld, Inc., The Blue Sheet of Northeast Texas (No. 58, 995, Hunt County (Tex.), Apr. 19, 1999). A computer consultant and minority shareholder filed a lawsuit against a nationally known bass fishing expert and his company claiming that they stalked and defamed him and his family over the Internet. The plaintiff received a $510,000 damage award, which consisted of compensation for his share in the company.

Torts such as trespass to land, trespass to chattels, and conversion arise out of the intentional interference with property interests. A trespass to chattel is committed when the defendant intermeddles with the personal property of another.[141] Conversion is the intentional exercise of dominion or control over the personal property of another, which seriously interferes with the plaintiff's right to control it.[142] To state a claim for conversion, the plaintiff must allege that the defendant is responsible for the "deprivation of another's right of property, or use or possession of a chattel . . . without the owner's consent and without legal justification."[143] The defendant must cause the consequences of its act of depriving the owner of property or believe that the consequences are substantially certain to follow from its actions.

The legal definition of intent does not mean that the defendant must act maliciously or with an evil motive. Intent requires that the actor desire to cause the consequences of his act or that he believes that the consequences are "substantially certain." *Specific intent* exists if the defendant desires that its conduct will cause the resulting consequences. The defendant has the requisite *general intent* if it acts, knowing with substantial certainty that its conduct will cause the resulting consequences. Torts in cyberspace are often untraceable, being committed with the help of anonymous remailers, forged e-mail addresses, or computer servers located in distant lands.[144]

One possible source of expanded tort liability for cyberspace is greater use of actions for an innominate or prima facie tort. The concept of innominate torts was first identified by Holmes and Pollock in their "theory of torts, what came to be called the theory of prima facie tort, which holds that any intentional infliction of harm is tortious unless the defendant can justify his action on policy or ethical grounds."[145] Section 870 of the Restatement (Second) of Torts proposed tort liability for defendants who intentionally injured another and could show no justification or excuse, sometimes called the innominate or prima facie tort.[146] The

---

[141] *Chattels* are defined as personal property as opposed to real property. The *trespass to chattels* is an interference with property other than land.

[142] The difference between trespass to chattels and conversion is in the seriousness of the interference. Where the extent and duration of exercise of dominion or control is great, the defendant is liable for the full value of the chattel. In contrast, the trespass to chattels defendant is only responsible for the harm done to the personal property of another.

[143] Universal Premium Acceptance Corp. v. York Bank & Trust Co., 69 F.3d 695, 704 (3d Cir. 1995).

[144] An *anonymous remailer* is an Internet term describing how "identifying information on the original message is removed, and the message is then forwarded anonymously to its intended destination." Michael D. Scott, Internet and Technology Desk Reference 19 (2001).

[145] Mark P. Gergen, Tortious Interference: How It Is Engulfing Commercial Law, Why This Is Not Entirely Bad, and a Prudential Response, 38 Ariz. L. Rev. 1175, 1179 (1996) (discussing the prima facie tort as a concept originating in the correspondence of Oliver Wendell Holmes Jr. and English legal historian Frederic Pollock).

[146] Richard Wright, Once More into the Bramble Bush: Duty, Causal Contribution, and the Extent of Legal Responsibility, 54 Vand. L. Rev. 1071 (2001) (citing Restatement (Second) of Torts § 870 cmt. 1 (1979) ("One who intentionally causes injury to another is subject to liability to the other for that injury, if his conduct is generally culpable and not justifiable under the circumstances.")).

advantage of the innominate tort is that it is a flexible device where the elements of more established tort actions are not present. The innominate tort does not apply to negligence-based or strict liability torts and has not been recognized in many jurisdictions.

[A] Assault and Battery

Torts in cyberspace are rarely committed face-to-face and are often committed anonymously by the use of devices such as anonymous remailers or servers located in distant forums. An unauthorized or unconsented touching of one person by another is a *battery*. An *assault* "is an act which arouses in the plaintiff a reasonable apprehension of an imminent battery."[147] Some physical contact or touching is necessary for there to be a battery.[148] Battery cannot be committed over the Internet because there can be no unwarranted physical contact. For a defendant to be liable for an assault, however, he must place the other person in apprehension of an "imminent contact."[149] Assault is almost impossible to prove in an Internet transmission or e-mail because the recipient is generally not in apprehension of an imminent contact. It is theoretically possible for the recipient of an e-mail message to believe that contact is imminent if a co-employee whose workstation is nearby sends the message. An e-mail message threatening unwanted contact in the future is not an assault. An e-mail message alone "does not make the actor liable for assault unless together with other acts or circumstances they put the other in reasonable apprehension of an imminent harmful or offensive contact with this person."[150]

E-mail threats may constitute a crime as well as a tort. An Oregon teenager received computer messages threatening a school shooting from an unknown individual using the online name "RHS Shooting."[151] Teenagers, for example, have been prosecuted for making threats in Internet chat rooms. A 15-year-old in California was held in juvenile detention for e-mail and chat room threats to kill classmates.[152] An 18-year-old Oregon man could spend a year in jail if convicted of posting a chat room message warning that there would be "a lot of bodies around" a suburban New York high school.[153] Proposed legislation would strengthen the federal criminal sanctions for e-mail threats.[154]

---

[147] Edward J. Kionka, Torts in a Nutshell 151 (1999).

[148] Unprivileged and unconsented physical contact, as in Garratt v. Dailey, 279 P.2d 1091 (Wash. 1955), where a court found a child liable for battery for deliberately pulling a lawn chair out from under his elderly neighbor, which caused her to break a hip. The court found the intent of the defendant may be based upon conduct that is substantially certain to injure the plaintiff.

[149] Section 29(1) of the Restatement states that "[t]o make the actor liable for an assault he must put the other in apprehension of an imminent contact." Restatement (Second) of Torts § 29(1) (1965).

[150] Restatement (Second) of Torts § 31 (1965) (definite elements of assault).

[151] Police Blanket Reynolds Campus, Oregonian, Mar. 8, 2000.

[152] Marjie Lundstrom, Schools Forced into Airport-Security Mode, Apr. 5, 2001; *see also* Good Morning America Broadcast, Mar. 27, 2001 (available on LEXIS, News Group File, All).

[153] *Id.*

[154] Sen. Orrin Hatch (R-UT), News Conference Regarding the Violence Against Women Act, Oct. 11, 2000 (describing proposed legislation that would classify interstate cyberstalking as a federal crime).

Cyberstalking refers to the use of the Internet, e-mail, or other electronic means to repeatedly threaten, follow, or harass another person. Online stalking does not fit neatly into the traditional tort of assault because it lacks the element of imminence. Internet wrongdoers have harmed women by maliciously posting personal information on sadomasochistic web sites and by using new morphing technologies to superimpose their victims' faces onto pornographic pictures. Tort remedies may be the only defense women have against cyberstalking or threatening e-mail transmissions from angry ex-husbands, spurned boyfriends, or strangers. A plaintiff must demonstrate that she was placed in apprehension of an imminent batter to recovery for assault against an online stalker. Electronic stalking that involves harassing e-mail may create a crime or tort of outrage, even if the defendant lacks the present ability to carry out a threat. A company may be vicariously liable for failing to warn third parties if it has prior knowledge of a stalker using company computer systems. California defines stalking as a pattern of conduct the "intent of which was to follow, alarm or harass the plaintiff."[155] California prosecuted a former security guard who used the Internet to impersonate a woman posting Internet messages of her fantasies of being raped.[156] Objectionable messages, however, do not make the sender liable for assault, because the defendant does not typically place his victim in apprehension of an imminent contact.

Electronic stalking that involves harassing e-mail may create a crime or tort of outrage, even if the defendant lacks the present ability to carry out a threat. It is black letter law that mere "words, unaccompanied by some act apparently intended to carry the threat into execution, do not put the other in apprehension of an imminent body contact, and so cannot make the actor liable for an assault. . . ."[157] *Flaming* is the functional equivalent of a "verbal lashing in public."[158] Flaming is a term that refers to "terse, angry, or insulting thoughts communicated via e-mail between employees in a company or published on computer bulletin boards."[159] Messages printed in all capital letters are considered to be flaming.[160] E-mail or online "flaming" may result in fright or humiliation, but still it lacks the imminence requirement. Abusive or insulting e-mail messages, mail-

---

[155] Cal. Civ. Code § 1708.7 (Deering 1999).

[156] "On at least six occasions, sometimes in the middle of the night, men knocked on the woman's door saying they wanted to rape her. The former security guard pleaded guilty in April 1999 to one count of stalking and three counts of solicitation of sexual assault." U.S. Attorney General, 1999 Report on Cyberstalking: A New Challenge for Law Enforcement and Industry 5 (Aug., 1999).

[157] Restatement (Second) of Torts § 31, cmt. (a) (1965) ("For this reason it is commonly said in the decision that mere words do not constitute an assault, or that some overt act is required.").

[158] Whatis.com, What Is . . . Flaming (a Definition) (visited Nov. 14, 1999), http://www.whatis.com/flaming.htm.

[159] Frah Farouque, E-Mail Chatter Could Lead to a Cybersuit, The Age (Melbourne, Australia, June 3, 1995) (quoting Robert Todd of the Sydney, Australia, law firm of Blake Dawson and Waldron).

[160] Michael D. Scott, Internet and Technology Law Desk Reference 210 (1999).

bombs, and flaming do not constitute assault because they are typically threats to inflict bodily harm in the future and are, therefore, not imminent threats.[161]

Flaming, though it probably does not satisfy the imminence requirement of assault, may constitute defamation. One of the first online defamation cases arose out of a dispute between two Australian anthropologists who waged a "flame" war on the Internet attacking each other's professional reputations.[162] Damages for libel were based upon messages posted to an anthropology computer bulletin board. The objectionable statements accused the plaintiff anthropologist of sexual misconduct, racism against Australian aboriginal peoples, and academic incompetence. The court found that the anthropologist was defamed and awarded $40,000 to compensate him for harm to his personal and professional reputation. The tort of defamation will be discussed in detail later in this chapter.

[B]   Intentional Infliction of Emotional Distress

The Restatement (Second) of Torts sets forth the basic elements of the tort of intentional infliction of emotional distress as one who "by extreme and outrageous conduct intentionally or recklessly causes severe emotional distress to another" and states further that such person is "subject to liability for such emotional distress."[163] The elements of a prima facie case of intentional infliction of emotional distress are (1) outrageous conduct by the defendant; (2) the defendant's intention of causing, or reckless disregard of the probability of causing, emotional distress; (3) the plaintiff's suffering severe or extreme emotional distress; and (4) actual and proximate causation of the emotional distress by the defendant's outrageous conduct.[164] States vary in requiring physical injury or manifestation as a required element for a claim of intentional infliction of emotional distress.[165] Some jurisdictions permit a plaintiff to recover for the negligent infliction of emotional distress, but in that case the plaintiff must prove evidence of physical injury or emotional distress.[166]

The tort of *intentional infliction of emotional distress,* often called the tort of *outrage,* allows recovery if a defendant intentionally subjects the plaintiff to serious mental distress. The key question is whether the defendant acted in a manner that may be characterized as extreme or outrageous. "Mere insults, indignities, threats, inconsiderations or petty oppressions or other trivialities do not rise to the

---

[161] Self-help may be useful in preventing harassing e-mails. A kill file, for example, may be used to automatically delete files with certain phrases or words. A kill file may block e-mail messages coming from objectionable persons or dealing with objectionable topics.

[162] Rindos v. Hardwick, No. 1994 of 1993 (W. Austl. Sup. Ct., Mar. 31, 1994).

[163] Restatement (Second) of Torts § 46 (1965).

[164] *Id.*

[165] Curtis v. Firth, 123 Idaho 598, 850 P.2d 749 (Ct. App. 1993) (stating that evidence of physical harm may bear on the severity of emotional harm).

[166] Thomas Moffatt, Tort and Insurance Deskbook: Tort Law, "Recovery of Damages for Emotional Distress" (visited Nov. 13, 1999), http://www.moffatt.com/deskbook/desk1009.html.

level of the outrageous conduct essential to the plaintiff's right of recovery."[167] Some states require a physical manifestation of mental distress or medical evidence to prove emotional distress. In *Zwebner v. John Does Anonymous Foundation, Inc.*,[168] the defendant operated an Internet bulletin board web site called "JohnDoes.org" that posted information from users. JohnDoes.org was a lawsuit based upon the the intentional infliction of emotional distress, defamation, and false light invasion of privacy for a posting by InternetZorro.[169] The court denied a motion to set aside a default order and granted the defendant's motion to amend his answer.[170] In *Van Buskirk v. New York Times Co.*,[171] the court dismissed an action for intentional infliction of emotional distress and defamation based upon a newspaper article and Internet letter on a possible war crimes prosecution. The court found that the statements could not constitute the intentional infliction of emotional distress or defamation.[172] In *Bochan v. La Fontaine*,[173] the court denied a defendant's motion to dismiss for lack of jurisdiction in an intentional infliction of emotional distress and defamation case stemming from posted messages on an Internet newsgroup accusing the plaintiff of being a pedophile. In *Matos v. AFSCME Council 4*,[174] the plaintiff was a public official who charged a local union with publishing defamatory statements on the Internet that harmed his reputation, invaded his privacy, and constituted an intentional infliction of emotional distress. The union published an article on the Internet that said it was investigating the commissioner for using money from a nonprofit organization to bond out an accused sex offender. The web site article "troubled the plaintiff as he was concerned that it could have prevented him from being re-appointed to his position" and that the posting impugned his credibility and integrity.[175] The article also attacked the commissioner's racial and cultural heritage. The article did not identify the commissioner by name, but the court found that it provided sufficient information to allow him to be immediately identified. The court concluded that the online postings were statements made with actual malice and were defamatory. In addition, the computer messages constituted extreme and outrageous conduct, causing the plaintiff to suffer severe emotional stress.

---

[167] Restatement (Second) of Torts § 46, cmt. (1965) (stating that the tort requires outrageous conduct of the magnitude that arouses the resentment of the "average member of the community . . . and lead him to exclaim, 'Outrageous!'").

[168] 2001 U.S. Dist. LEXIS 3298 (D. Ore., Feb. 28, 2001).

[169] *Id* at *3.

[170] *Id* at *2.

[171] 2000 U.S. Dist. LEXIS 12150 (S.D.N.Y., Aug. 24, 2000).

[172] *Id.*

[173] 68 F. Supp. 2d 692 (E.D. Va. 1999); *see also* Revell v. Lidov, 2001 U.S. Dist. LEXIS 3133 (N.D. Tex., Dallas Div., Mar. 21, 2001) (dismissing lawsuit based upon intentional infliction of emotional distress, conspiracy, and breach of duty with regard to an article published on university web site on grounds of lack of personal jurisdiction).

[174] 2001 Conn. Super. LEXIS 2419 (Super. Ct. of Hartford, Aug. 21, 2001) (dismissing department of corrections commissioner defamation claims for Internet postings that allegedly constituted the publication of false and defamatory information regarding a public official).

[175] *Id.* at *15.

Cyberstalking or the sending of threatening or harassing electronic communications may constitute a crime as well as a tort if transmitted in interstate commerce by e-mail or the Internet. Employees of a Massachusetts high-technology company, for example, filed an action for the intentional infliction of emotional distress after being fired for sending disparaging e-mail messages about their chief executive officer. In that case, the employees were not told that their e-mail messages were stored and monitored.[176] The court did not find the actions of the company's president went "beyond all possible bounds of decency and . . . [were] utterly intolerable in a civilized community."[177] An ISP will not be held responsible for e-mail messages causing intentional infliction of emotional distress unless it knew of the contents of the message, "a circumstance that will rarely, if ever, be proved."[178]

[C] Title VII Claims

Title VII of the Civil Rights Act of 1964 provides that it is unlawful to discriminate against an individual with respect to the terms of employment because of sex or race.[179] Plaintiffs filing sexual harassment claims may have tort actions for the "intentional infliction of emotional distress."[180] In addition, Title VII provides tortlike remedies for individuals who are discriminated against in the workplace. Sexual or racial harassment claims are generally based upon discrimination in the conditions of employment.[181] In addition, courts impose vicarious liability principles in hostile workplace claims. An employer may be charged with maintaining a "hostile environment" in violation of federal law.[182]

Courts have determined that employees may establish a "hostile workplace" claim if (1) the conduct in question was unwelcome, (2) the harassment was sex or race-linked, (3) the sexual or racial harassment was severe, and (4) there was a causal connection to the employer.[183] E-mail or Internet communications may be the basis of a hostile workplace claim. An employer may minimize its exposure to

---

[176] Restuccia v. Burk Technology Inc., No. 95-2125 (Mass. Super. Ct., Middlesex County, Dec. 13, 1999).

[177] Id. (quoting Restatement (Second) of Torts § 46).

[178] Lunney v. Prodigy Servs. Co., 250 A.D.2d 230, 237 683 N.Y.S.2d 557, 562 (1998) (entering summary judgment in favor of ISP who was held not liable for the transmission of offensive electronic messages sent in the 15-year-old plaintiff's name to his Boy Scout leader).

[179] Hateful e-mail messages may also be a violation of federal civil rights law. In *United States v. Machado*, No. SACR 96-142-AHS (S.D. Cal. 1998), a University of California-Irvine student was convicted of a federal civil rights violation for sending e-mail messages on a university computer signed "Asian Hater" and threatening Asian students.

[180] Anne Saker, The Law on Sexual Harassment, The News Observer (Aug. 20, 1996).

[181] A government employer may be subject to restrictions in prohibiting state employees from accessing sexually explicit materials online. In Urofsky v. Allen, 1998 U.S. Dist. LEXIS 2139, 1998 WL 86587 (E.D. Va. 1998), a court held a Virginia statute forbidding state employees from accessing sexually explicit materials to be violative of the First Amendment. The court observed that there were legitimate purposes of researching sexually explicit topics that potentially could benefit the public.

[182] *See generally* 29 C.F.R. § 1604.11(a) (1999).

[183] *See, e.g.*, Spicer v. Virginia Dep't of Corrections, 66 F.3d 705, 709-10 (4th Cir. 1995) (*en banc*).

hostile workplace claims by enforcing its e-mail and Internet usage policy. In addition, the employer must promptly investigate claims of sexual harassment. In one recent case the transmission of racially insensitive jokes led to a hostile workplace claim.[184] In another case, a racial discrimination claim was based upon jokes containing "racial undertones" sent on a company's e-mail system.[185] The employer needs to inform its employees of its e-mail policy and to train employees not to send jokes that may be offensive via e-mail.[186] In *Hufford v. McEnaney*,[187] a federal court held that an Idaho fire department violated a firefighter's First Amendment rights when they discharged him for reporting that fellow firefighters had downloaded a large cache of hard-core pornographic files on the fire station's computers. The Ninth Circuit upheld the lower court's decision denying qualified immunity to the defendants because they should have been aware that discharging the plaintiff in retaliation for his truthful whistleblowing violated his constitutionally protected right to free speech.

Employees may base a hostile workplace claim upon a co-employee's abuse of company computer systems. Continental Express Airlines was found responsible for sexual harassment in a hostile workplace claim filed by a female pilot.[188] In that case, a male pilot used computer equipment to superimpose his female co-worker's face onto other female bodies, depicted in pornographic poses. The humiliating pictures were shown to other Continental pilots and transmitted over the Internet.[189] In that case, Continental was found liable under the theories of hostile work environment, ratification of sexual harassment, and negligent retention, training, and supervision. The plaintiff was awarded compensatory damages for the intentional infliction of emotional distress, defamation, and invasion of privacy, as well as punitive damages.

In another case, a group of women who worked as models for an online adult entertainment service filed an intentional infliction of emotional distress and gender discrimination claim against their employer in a sexual harassment case.[190] The online models claimed that their employer encouraged a sexually hostile work environment. The online models alleged that the employer allowed "other employees to view the models' performances." They objected to the videotaping of their

---

[184] Curtis v. DiMaio, 465 F. Supp. 2d 226 (E.D.N.Y. 1999) (rejecting employee's claim that the transmission of two racially sensitive jokes over the company's e-mail system created a hostile work environment).

[185] Daniels v. WorldCom Corp., No. Civ. A 3:97-CV-0721-P, 1998 WL 91261 (N.D. Tex., Feb. 23, 1998) (rejecting plaintiffs' Title VII and 1981 and 1983 of the Civil Rights Act of 1964 claims based upon jokes sent on company computer system).

[186] In *Daniels,* the employer was found not liable because of its prompt remedial measures after learning of the offending messages. In that case, the employees sending the jokes were given oral and written reprimands. *Id.*

[187] 249 F.3d 1142 (9th Cir. 2001).

[188] Butler v. Krebs & Continental Express, Inc., 100 F. Supp. 2d 1058 (N.D. Cal. 2000).

[189] *Id.*

[190] Nude Models Sue Online Service Over Working Conditions, Comp. & Online Indus. Litig. R. (Dec. 2, 1997), at 10.

sexual acts and the distribution of the tapes to fellow employees and customers without their consent.

[D]   Trespass to Cyberchattels

Trespass is a broad "form of action that, at common law, provided for a wide spectrum of injuries, from personal injuries caused by negligence to business torts and nuisances."[191] A trespass to enter upon another's land without consent is actionable. In contrast, "trespass to chattels . . . occurs when one party intentionally uses or intermeddles with personal property in rightful possession of another without authorization."[192] Trespass to chattels is an interference with personal property that includes "tangible goods or intangible rights, as in patents, stocks or shares."[193] Trespass to chattels is only actionable if the defendant dispossesses chattels belonging to another and the chattel is impaired as to its condition, quality, or value. This tort is triggered when the possessor is deprived of the use of the chattel for a substantial period of time. If harm is caused to some person or thing in which the possessor has a legally protected interest, there may also be a trespass to chattels. The plaintiff in a trespass to chattels action will be awarded for injuries to personal property.

In *eBay, Inc. v. Bidder's Edge*,[194] eBay, an Internet auction site, filed suit against Bidder's Edge, an aggregation site for auctions that used electronic robots to gather and aggregate data from a large number of auction web sites. Software robots searched, copied, and retrieved information on auction listings and bids on items. Users of the eBay web site are required to agree to a user agreement by clicking an "I accept" button at the end of the agreement. The eBay site employed "robot exclusion headers," which Bidder's Edge bypassed. In early 1998, eBay granted Bidder's Edge permission to include information on eBay-hosted auctions. The dispute was over Bidder Edge's method for searching the eBay database. Ebay sought to require Bidder's Edge to conduct a search only when a Bidder's Edge user queried the system. Bidder's Edge sought to crawl the eBay system to compile its own auction database. The court granted an injunction finding it likely that Bidder's Edge violated eBay's terms of service agreement and therefore was liable for unauthorized use of the site under a trespass to chattels theory.[195] In February 2001, Bidder's Edge terminated its business, which ended its "virtual trespass" litigation with eBay.[196] In *Ticketmaster Corp. v. Tickets.com, Inc.*,[197] the court denied the plaintiff's application to enjoin the defendant from

---

[191] Bryan A. Garner, A Dictionary of Modern Legal Usage 995 (2d ed. 1995).

[192] Restatement (Second) of Torts § 217(b) (1965).

[193] *Id.* at 149.

[194] F. Supp. 2d 1058 (N.D. Cal. 2000).

[195] *Id.* at 1069-70.

[196] Michael Geist, Bidder's Edge is Going, Going, Gone, BNA's Internet Law News (Feb. 16, 2001) (citing http://www.newsbytes.com/news/01/162050.html).

[197] 2000 U.S. Dist. LEXIS 4553 (C.D. Cal. Mar. 27, 2000).

using spiders to copy factual information contained on the plaintiff's web site. The court rejected the plaintiff's claim that the defendant's use of spiders to collect information constituted an improper trespass of chattel on the plaintiff's computers. The court found that spiders did not cause harm or interfere with the use of the plaintiff's computers and therefore did not constitute a trespass to chattels.

In *Register.com v. Verio, Inc.*,[198] a federal court enjoined Verio, Inc. from using a search robot to extract information from Register.com's WHOIS database of domain names. Register.com contracts with second-level domain name (SLD) holders and collects registration data. It offers its customers web site hosting, domain name hosting, and real-time domain name management.[199] Register.com obtained an injunction to bar Verio, a competitor, from using automated software to access and collect registrant contact information and using that information for mass-marketing purposes. Verio is one of the largest operators of web sites for businesses and provides comprehensive Internet services.[200]

Register.com sued Verio under Section 43(a) of the Lanham Act and the Computer Fraud and Abuse Act of 1986, but amended its complaint to include counts for trespass to chattels and breach of contract.[201] Verio's defense was that the WHOIS database was the functional equivalent of a public utility. However, the court found that the primary purpose of the WHOIS database was to "provide necessary information in the event of domain name disputes, such as those arising from cybersquatting or trademark infringement."[202] Verio accessed the WHOIS database to collect information on customers who registered a domain name to send spam e-mail.[203] The court found Verio's spam e-mail violated Register's terms of use agreement.[204] Verio conceded that it violated Register's posted terms of service agreement by its entry into the WHOIS database.[205] The court rejected Verio's defense that it did not assent to the terms of service and that it was privileged to access the database under Register's agreement with ICANN.[206] Register.com was entitled to injunctive relief because it demonstrated a likelihood of success on the merits and irreparable harm based on Verio's use of its data for marketing, its trespass to chattels claim, and claims for violation of the computer fraud and trademark laws.[207]

In *Internet Doorway, Inc. v. Parks*,[208] Internet Doorway, an ISP, brought an action against a defendant for sending unsolicited mass e-mail advertising for a pornographic web site. The defendant falsified the "from" header to convey the

---

[198] 126 F. Supp. 2d 238 (S.D.N.Y. 2000).

[199] *Id.* at 241.

[200] *Id.*

[201] *Id.*

[202] *Id.* at 242.

[203] *Id.*

[204] *Id.* at 246.

[205] *Id.*

[206] *Id.*

[207] *Id.* at 247.

[208] 121 F. Supp. 2d 1255 (N.D. Iowa 2000).

impression that the e-mail was sent from the ISP.[209] The ISP argued that the defendant's falsified e-mailings constituted a violation of the federal Lanham Act and the state law tort of trespass to chattels.[210]

In *Intel Corp. v. Hamidi*,[211] a California court of appeals extended the tort of trespass to chattels. Hamidi, a former employee of Intel Corp., obtained the company's e-mail address list and repeatedly sent electronic messages to as many as 29,000 company employees. The messages informed their recipients that, upon request, Hamidi would remove a recipient from his mailing list, an offer to which only 450 Intel employees responded. Intel requested repeatedly that Hamidi stop his mass e-mails and was unsuccessful in filtering these messages out. Intel filed suit based upon, among other things, the theory of trespass to chattels. The trial court enjoined Hamidi from sending unsolicited e-mail to addresses on Intel's computer systems. The Court of Appeals of California affirmed, finding that Intel demonstrated a sufficient harm to be entitled to nominal damages for disrupting its business and was entitled to injunctive relief on a theory of trespass to chattels.

To constitute a trespass to chattel, (1) there must be a disturbance of the plaintiff's possession and (2) the disturbance may be by an actual taking, a physical seizing or taking hold of the goods, removing them from their owner, or by exercising a control or authority over them inconsistent with their owner's possession. The appeals court rejected Hamidi's argument that that there was no physical taking in transmitting mass e-mails and ruled that electronic signals generated and sent by computer were sufficiently physically tangible to support a trespass cause.

The court also rejected Hamidi's argument that the injunction violated the First Amendment, reasoning that, as a private property owner, Intel was not required to exercise its rights in a "content neutral" fashion. The California Supreme Court has accepted Hamidi's petition to review the appellate court's decision.

[E] Spamming as Cyberspace Trespass

Spamming is the practice of sending unsolicited or unwanted e-mail in an indiscriminate fashion. The number of junk e-mails has been estimated at 25,000,000 messages per day.[212] The sending of spam e-mail, which can take up a substantial amount of a company's computer resources, is arguably a trespass to chattels.

Spammers abuse accounts created at AOL, Hotmail, Prodigy, or other e-mail systems to facilitate their spamming activities. Spammers create particular problems for ISPs by setting up accounts to facilitate the transmittal of bulk e-mails to

---

[209] *Id.* at 1257.

[210] *Id* at 1259.

[211] 94 Cal. App. 4th 325 (Cal. Ct. App. 2001), *reh'g granted*, 2002 Cal. LEXIS 1883 (Cal. Mar. 27, 2002).

[212] James W. Butler, The Death of Spam and The Rise of DEM: A Bill to Ban It Could Backfire, The Internet Newsletter: Legal & Bus. Aspects (Sept. 1998), at 3.

all ISP subscribers. The e-mail accounts are used to collect responses to the spammer's e-mails and "bounced back" messages.

Spam e-mailers frequently use false return e-mails in their message headings to deflect complaints from recipients.[213] To combat this practice, California's antispam statute requires senders of unsolicited e-mail to supply a valid e-mail address or toll-free number to allow recipients to refuse further messages.[214]

Hotmail, a Silicon Valley company that provides free electronic mail on the World Wide Web, filed a trespass to chattels action against a spammer who sent thousands of unsolicited e-mails to its subscribers advertising pornographic materials and get-rich financial schemes.[215] In one case, a court found that the spammers trespassed on Hotmail's computer space by causing tens of thousands of misdirected and unauthorized e-mail messages to occupy company computer resources.

In a similar case, AOL filed a lawsuit against a spammer for sending large numbers of unauthorized and unsolicited bulk e-mail advertisements to its members.[216] AOL's complaint alleged false designation of origin and the dilution of interest in a service mark under the Lanham Act;[217] exceeding the scope of its subscription agreement, therefore exceeding authorized access in violation of the Computer Fraud and Abuse Act; impairing its computer facilities in violation of same Act; violating Virginia's Computer Crimes Act; and trespass to chattels and violations of both federal and state computer crime statutes.[218] In each case, the court found in favor of AOL.

Spammers have filed antitrust claims against providers as counterclaims to antispam lawsuits. AOL was charged with monopolization[219] by a bulk e-mailer, a claim rejected by a federal court.[220] In that case, the spammer charged AOL with blocking all of their bulk e-mailings.

The Internet industry is currently developing standards governing spamming, which include the use of false headers and other fraudulent or misleading mailings. AOL has filed scores of lawsuits in many states to deter spammers. In *AOL,*

---

[213] David Sorkin, Technical and Legal Approach to Unsolicited Electronic Mail, 35 U.S.F.L. Rev. 325 (2001).

[214] Cal. Bus. & Prof. Code § 17538.4 (2002).

[215] *Id.*

[216] AOL, Inc., v. LCGM, Inc., 46 F. Supp. 2d 441 (E.D. Va., 1998).

[217] To state a claim of trademark infringement under the federal Lanham Act, the plaintiff must allege that (1) the mark is valid and legally entitled to protection, (2) the plaintiff owns it, and (3) defendant's use of the mark is likely to confuse consumers. Chapter 3 provides a detailed analysis of trademarks arising out of online activities.

[218] *See also* AOL, Inc. v. Prime Data Sys., Inc., 1998 U.S. Dist. LEXIS 20226 (E.D. Va., Nov. 20, 1998) (entering a default judgment against defendant spammers for violating state and federal computer law, the Lanham Act, tort law, and common law conspiracy to commit trespass to chattels).

[219] In order to prevail on a monopolization claim, a party must show "(1) possession of monopoly power in a relevant marked; (2) willful acquisition or maintenance of that power in an exclusionary manner; and (3) causal antitrust injury." AOL Inc. v. GreatDeals.Net, reported in 16 Comp. & Online Litig. R. 3 (June 15, 1998).

[220] America Online Inc. v. GreatDeals, Net, No.99-62-A (E.D. Va., May 4, 1999).

Inc. v. LCGM, Inc.,[221] AOL sued spammers who sent unsolicited bulk e-mails to AOL subscribers.[222] The spammers used false "aol.com" addresses in their spam headers. AOL's complaint included charges of trespass to chattels, false designation, and dilution by tarnishment. The federal district court ruled in favor of AOL, finding that the defendants violated the Lanham Act's false designation of origin and dilution, breached its terms of services, and violated the Computer Fraud and Abuse Act. The Virginia federal court imposed punitive damages, treble damages, and attorneys' fees against the spammer, who had sent more than 60,000,000 pieces of unauthorized bulk e-mail to AOL subscribers.[223] The U.S. House of Representatives is considering H.R. 718, the "Unsolicited Commercial Electronic Mail Act," which would make it illegal to continue sending spam e-mail after being requested to stop.[224] The proposed statute would penalize spammers $500 per message for violating the policy.

A number of states have enacted similar antispam laws and have been challenged on constitutional grounds. Washington's antispam statute, which prohibits e-mail senders from sending messages to state residents using misleading subject lines, transmission paths, or third-party domain names without permission, survived a constitutional challenge.[225] The Washington Supreme Court rejected the defendant's challenge that the antispam statute unduly burdening interstate commerce.[226]

California's antispam statute requires any person or entity sending unsolicited e-mail to its residents to (1) establish a toll-free telephone number or valid sender-operated return e-mail address that recipients may use to notify the sender not to e-mail further unsolicited documents, (2) include as the first text in the e-mailed document a statement informing the recipient of the toll-free number or return address that may be used to notify the sender not to e-mail any further unsolicited material, (3) not send any further unsolicited advertising material to anyone who has requested that such material not be sent, and (4) include in the subject line of each e-mail message "ADV:" as the first four characters or "ADV:ADLT" if the advertisement pertains to adult material.[227]

---

[221] 46 F. Supp. 2d 441 (E.D. Va. 1998).

[222] *Accord* Seidl v. Greentree Mortgage Co., 30 F. Supp. 2d 1292 (D. Colo. 1998) (the owner of an Internet domain name sued a mortgage company, which had conducted a bulk e-mail advertising campaign, claiming that the mortgage company used his domain name as an e-mail identifier. The plaintiff alleged that Greentree violated Colorado's Deceptive Trade Practices Act and the Junk Fax Statute. He also alleged the commission of common law torts, including trespass to chattels, negligence, violation of right of publicity, and false light invasion of privacy).

[223] America Online v. IMS, 1998 U.S. Dist. LEXIS 20448 (E.D. Va., Nov. 20, 1998) (noting magistrate judge finding that defendants sent at least 60,000,000 unsolicited pieces of e-mail).

[224] Brian Krebs, House Commerce Committee to Consider Anti-Spam Legislation (Mar. 23, 2001) (reporting vote by House Commerce Committee).

[225] State of Wash. v. Heckel, 24 P.3d 404 (Wash. 2001).

[226] *Id.*

[227] Cal. Bus. & Prof. Code § 17538.4 (2002).

In *Ferguson v. Friendfinders, Inc.*,[228] a California appeals court upheld the California statute, holding that the statute did not regulate commerce occurring wholly outside the state. The court reasoned that the antispam statute applied only when an unsolicited commercial e-mail (UCE) was sent to a state citizen by an advertiser who had equipment in the state. Further, the online advertiser had the technological tools and ability to determine which of the recipients of the UCE lived in the state in order to comply with the statute. Although UCEs were of little cost to the advertisers, they imposed an economic burden on the recipients in both time and money. The court held that protecting a state's citizens from the economic damage caused by deceptive UCEs constituted a legitimate local purpose. Finally, the statute did not violate the Commerce Clause, as it served a legitimate local public interest and the burden it imposed on interstate commerce was not excessive when viewed in light of its local benefits.

Twenty-six states introduced antispam statutes in 2001 alone, and it is likely that they will be upheld provided they do not overly burden interstate commerce.[229]

§ 5.04 BUSINESS TORTS IN CYBERSPACE

Business torts are becoming a serious risk for the online company in an increasingly competitive Internet marketplace. In *Bailey v. Turbine Design, Inc.*,[230] an aircraft conversion company sued a competitor for libel, slander, tortious interference with contractual relations, conspiracy, interference with prospective business advantage, and invasion of privacy. The court granted the defendant's motion to dismiss because the defamatory statements were made on the defendant's passive web site.[231]

Punitive damages are increasingly being sought in online business tort lawsuits. A federal court awarded $65 million to the original owner of the sex.com domain name in a business torts case involving fraud and forgery.[232] A punitive damages lawsuit has been filed against a web site that posted autopsy photographs of racecar driver Dale Earnhardt on the Internet.[233] Lucent Technologies is suing an Italian telescope maker for $20 million in punitive damages to protect its trade secrets.[234] An U.S. jury awarded a Russian immigrant banker $30 million in punitive damages against a Russian newspaper that published a series of defamatory

---

[228] 115 Cal. Rptr. 2d 258 (Cal. Ct. App. 2002) (upholding Cal. Bus. & Prof. Code § 17538.4 ruling that it did not regulate commerce and served a legitimate local purpose).

[229] Spam: State Legislators Taking It On, BNA's Elec. Com. & L. Rep. (visited Mar. 22, 2002), http://pubs.bna.com/ip/BNA/eip.nsf/id/a0a5g9t3c4_.

[230] Bailey v. Turbine Design, Inc., 86 F. Supp. 2d 790 (W.D. Tenn. 2000) (dismissing for lack of personal jurisdiction because defamatory statements were posted on passive web site and there were no other contacts with forum state).

[231] Id. at 796 (noting that defamatory statements were not "expressly aimed" at Tennessee).

[232] Kristen Andelman, $65 Million Awarded in Sex.Com Dispute, The Recorder (Apr. 4, 2001), at 3.

[233] Autopsy Photos Bring On Suit, Wash. Times (May 25, 2001), at B5.

[234] Joseph R. Perone, Lucent Sues Italian Telescope Maker Over Light-Based Web Access, Star-Ledger (Mar. 18, 2001), at 1.

articles claiming that the plaintiff was a swindler, bigamist, and fugitive from justice.[235] A jury found Internet America and several of its principles committed common law and statutory fraud against a plaintiff, awarding $6 million in a case concerning stock options.[236]

[A] Fraud and Misrepresentation

Fraud and *misrepresentation* are torts for willfully deceiving another with intent to cause injury. To prove fraud, the plaintiff must establish that the defendant essentially (1) made a false representation of material fact, (2) knew it was false (or made it with reckless disregard of its truth or falsity), (3) intended that plaintiff rely upon it, and (4) the plaintiff must be injured by reasonably relying on the false representation. A plaintiff claiming fraud must show injury proximately caused by its reasonable reliance on a misrepresentation. Fraud may be based upon making a statement without reasonable grounds for believing it to be true or by suppressing a fact where there is a duty of disclosure.

A *prima facie* case for the tort of misrepresentation occurs when the defendant (1) makes a misrepresentation (2) of material fact (3) for the purpose of inducing the other to act or to refrain from acting in reliance upon it and (4) causes pecuniary loss, (5) even though it is not made fraudulently or negligently.[237] The measure of damages for misrepresentation is the "difference between the value of what the [victim] has parted with and the value of what he has received in the transaction."[238]

Fraud or misrepresentation can also be based on making a promise without any intention of performance, which in turn causes injury or loss to the plaintiff. Misrepresentation, or the common law tort of deceit, occurs when a plaintiff is injured by another's false representations. Liability for fraud or misrepresentation may be actionable under the common law, or state or federal consumer protection statutes.

The reliance element is different for commercial transactions than for consumer transactions. Commercial parties are held to the standard of "justifiable reliance" or "reasonable reliance" standards.[239] The policy justification for the reliance requirement is to encourage recipients of statements to be skeptical about statements that are patently false.[240] The "reasonable reliance" standard determines "the issue of reliance based on all of the circumstances surrounding a transaction, including the mental capacity, educational background, relative sophistication, and bargaining power of the parties."[241] The question of whether

---

[235] Alexander Konanykhine v. Isvestia Newspaper, No. 97-1139 (Arlington Cty., Va., Dec. 13, 1999), reported in Metro Verdicts Monthly.

[236] Cindy Carradine v. Internet Am., Inc., No. 99-08893-H (Dallas Cty. Dist. Ct. Tex., Mar. 26, 2001), reported in The Blue Sheet of Northeast Texas.

[237] Restatement (Second) of Torts §§ 525, 552 (1977).

[238] *Id.* at § 552(c).

[239] The standards are objective based on what is reasonable in the industry or in the usage of trade.

[240] Hickox v. Stover, 551 So. 2d 259 (Ala. 1989).

[241] Foremost Insurance Co. v. Parham, 692 So. 2d 409, 418 (Ala. 1997).

the plaintiff's reliance on the representation is justifiable is a factual determination.[242]

A company may be liable for the tort of deceit for products and services it sells online. Fraudulently representing goods or services on the Internet subjects the seller to liability for the pecuniary losses of those who relied on the misrepresentations.[243] A person selling a baseball bat autographed by Ted Williams or golf clubs purportedly used by President Kennedy, for example, is liable for any misrepresentations made about goods sold in an online auction. Misrepresentation in an online transaction may occur with the sale, licensing, lease, exchange of goods, or the rendering of services.

A company may be found liable for the tort of misrepresentation if it suppresses facts or conceals information material to a consumer's decision to purchase its computers or software. The elements of a suppression claim are (1) a duty to disclose the facts, (2) concealment or nondisclosure of material facts by the defendant, (3) inducement of the plaintiff to act, and (4) action by the plaintiff causing injury.[244] Silence is not fraud unless the company has an obligation to communicate material facts about its computer systems.

In the wake of the World Trade Center bombing, a host of fraudulent web sites sprang up to gather donations under the pretense of collecting money for the victims and survivors. Within an hour of the disaster, numerous bulk e-mail campaigns began promoting "bogus relief efforts."[245]

[B] Misappropriation and Unfair Competition

Unfair competition refers to the torts that punish and deter economic-based deceptive and unfair practices. Unfair competition is subdivided into two parts: (1) consumer confusion as to the source of products and (2) unfair trade practices (a residual category of all other unfair competition laws).[246] The tort of misappropriation prohibits the unauthorized interference by one party with another party's valuable and time-sensitive information.[247] This common law tort was historically considered "a subspecies of the class of torts known as tortious interference with business or contractual relations."[248] The tort of misappropriation was first articulated in a 1918 case between two news services, *International News Service v. The Associated Press*.[249] In *International News*, the plaintiff, Associated Press (AP),

---

[242] AT&T Information Sys., Inc. v. Cobb Pontiac-Cadillac, Inc., 553 So. 2d 529, 532 (Ala. 1989).

[243] Restatement (Second) of Torts § 531 (1976).

[244] *See, e.g.,* Wilson v. Brown, 496 So. 2d 756 (Ala. 1986).

[245] Brian Krebs, Spammers Raise Money for Bogus Victims & Survivor Fund, Newsbytes (Sept. 13, 2001), http://www.infowar.com/law/01/law_091401a_j.shtml.

[246] Legal Information Institute, Unfair Competition Law Materials (visited July 1, 1999), http://www.law.cornell.edu/topics/unfair_competition.html.

[247] Mark Sableman, Link Law Revisited: Internet Linking Law at Five Years, 16 Berkeley Tech. L.J. 1273 (2001).

[248] Prosser, *supra* note 138, at 956.

[249] 248 U.S. 215 (1918).

and the defendant, International News Service (INS), each had news wires that sold subscription services to individual newspapers. The defendant would copy AP stories and dispatch them to their subscribers. The Court recognized that the news service's copying of Associated Press stories constituted unfair competition.[250] Eggheadsucks.com was sued by Egghead for misappropriation of trade secrets, negligent interference with contract, and unfair competition.[251] The court dismissed the claim against the anti-Egghead site.[252]

In *KNB Enterprises v. Matthews*,[253] the California Court of Appeals held that the federal Copyright Act does not preempt right of publicity claims under state law. In that case, the copyright owner of erotic photographs, which had been displayed without authorization and for profit on an Internet web site, brought suit against the web site's operator, asserting a misappropriation claim under California law. The court rejected the defendant's argument that the Copyright Act preempted the state misappropriation claim because human likenesses are not copyrightable.

In *Downing v. Abercrombie & Fitch*,[254] the plaintiffs filed an action against Abercrombie & Fitch for publishing a photograph of them surfing, along with identification of their names in a catalog. The plaintiffs alleged that Abercrombie misappropriated their names and likenesses in violation of California's statutory and common law protections against commercial misappropriation. In addition, they claimed that the publication of the photograph in the catalog violated the Lanham Act and constituted the torts of negligence and defamation.[255] The trial court ruled that Abercrombie's use of the photograph containing the plaintiffs' names and likenesses was proper because it constituted expression protected under the First Amendment.[256] The Ninth Circuit found that the defendant's publication of the photographs was not protected by the First Amendment and that the plaintiffs' claims were not preempted by the U.S. Copyright Act.

The Second Circuit in *National Basketball Association v. Motorola, Inc.*[257] determined that the following elements were necessary to approve misappropriation of news or information: "(i) a plaintiff generates or gathers information at a

---

[250] The court found that the defendant "in appropriating [the news] and selling it as its own is endeavoring to reap where it has not sown, and by disposing of it to newspapers that are competitors of complainant's members is appropriating to itself the harvest of those who have sown." *Id.* at 239-40.

[251] Greg Sandoval, Complaint Site Wins Court Victory (Feb. 9, 2001) (visited Apr. 1, 2001), http://news.cnet.com/news/0-1007-202-4771995.htm.

[252] *Id.*

[253] 78 Cal. App. 4th 362, 364-65 (Ct. App. 2000) (holding that California's tort for publicity claims is not preempted by the U.S. Copyright Act).

[254] 265 F.3d 994 (9th Cir. 2001) (holding that clothing company was not entitled to the nominative fair use defense because there was a genuine issue as to whether the company's use of the surfers' names and pictures in advertising suggested sponsorship or endorsement).

[255] *Id.* at 1001.

[256] *Id.*

[257] 105 F.3d 841, 847 (2d Cir. 1997). *Cf.* Raymond T. Nimmer, Information Law ¶ 3-16 at 3-77 (1996) (arguing "that the general doctrine of misappropriation divorced of any breach of confidence, trademark, goodwill, or similar elements, is not universally accepted").

cost; (ii) the information is time-sensitive; (iii) a defendant's use of the information constitutes free-riding on the plaintiff's efforts; (iv) the defendant is in direct competition with a product or service offered by the plaintiffs; (v) the ability of other parties to free-ride on the effort of the plaintiff or others would so reduce the incentive to produce the product or service that its existence or quality would be substantially threatened."[258]

An action for unfair competition encompasses state[259] and federal deceptive trade practices acts as well as the Lanham Act. Unfair competition encompasses state and federal deceptive trade practices acts as well as misappropriations of trade secrets. A California jury awarded $19,000,000 in a case in which a business partner misappropriated valuable proprietary information and trade secrets.[260]

Misappropriation is the use of another's name for one's benefit, as, for example, in advertising services on the Internet. Commercial web sites have found advertising is the chief source of revenue. Advertisers pay to be seen by users of free web sites. News organizations such as the *Washington Post, Life, Fortune,* and *Entertainment Weekly* sell advertising, which is their primary source of revenue from their web sites. TotalNews, Inc. designed a web site featuring the content of major publishers by inserting a "frame on the computer screen that includes the totalnews.com logos and URL as well as the defendants' advertising."[261]

The *Washington Post* and a number of other news organizations sued Total-News for creating a frame around their content. The plaintiffs contended that Total-News was a "parasitic web site" designed to pocket advertising revenue. The national publications argued that they expended "substantial resources to gather and display the news and information found on their web sites."[262] The defendants caused "each of plaintiffs' web sites to appear within a window on defendants' site . . . misappropriat[ing] valuable commercial property."[263] The plaintiffs further argued that TotalNews promoted their web site to advertisers on the basis of featuring plaintiffs' content. The plaintiffs argued that framing constituted misappropriation and unfair competition because it takes "the entire commercial value of the news reported at each of the plaintiffs' respective [news] sites and literally sells it to others for defendants' own profit."[264] Misappropriation claims occur in a wide variety of web site activities where the defendant is seeking to divert business to its site.

The Restatement (Third) of Unfair Competition treats the appropriation of another company's "intangible assets" as a form of unfair competition. In *Felsher*

---

[258] *Id.* at 845 (cited in Wehrenberg v. Moviefone, Inc., 1999 U.S. Dist. LEXIS 17574 (E.D. Mo., Nov. 1, 1999)).

[259] The misappropriation is a form of state common law unfair competition. Wehrenberg v. Moviefone, Inc., 1999 U.S. Dist. LEXIS 17574 (E.D. Mo., Nov. 1, 1999).

[260] Zachariades v. Smith, No. 336, 999 (San Mateo, Cal., 1993) (reported in Cal. Jury Verdicts & Settl. Rep.) (available on LEXIS, JRVRDCT; ALLVER file).

[261] Complaint of Washington Post Co. v. TotalNews, Inc. (S.D.N.Y., filed Feb. 20, 1997).

[262] *Id.*

[263] *Id.*

[264] *Id.*

v. University of Evansville,[265] an ex-professor terminated by the university six years earlier created Internet web sites and electronic mail accounts containing portions of the names of university officials and a common abbreviation for the university. The Indiana Supreme Court classified the professor's actions as falling into the "copycat" category of cyberpredators. The trial court enjoined the defendant's creation and use of the web sites and e-mail accounts, reasoning that the defendant's sole purpose was harming the reputation of the University of Evansville and its officials. The Indiana Supreme Court upheld the injunction, ruling that the university, as a corporation, did not have a right of privacy, that it might be entitled to relief on a number of legal bases, but that the existing record didn't support such relief.[266] The court found that the individual plaintiffs had stated a claim for the unauthorized misappropriation of their names, reputations, and likenesses and suffered irreparable injury that justified injunctive relief.

[C] Interference with Business Contracts

To establish a claim for tortious interference with prospective business relations, an online business must prove that a competitor's intentional and improper interference prevented the formation of a contract, either by inducing or causing a third party not to enter into or continue relations or by preventing the plaintiff from acquiring or continuing the relations.[267] Many states also recognize actions for tortious interference with prospective economic advantage, which requires a plaintiff to allege and show that the defendant's actions were aimed at injuring the plaintiff's business.

In *Eurotech Inc. v. Cosmos Travel Aktiegnes*,[268] which involved a domain name dispute between an information company and its subsidiary and a travel agency, a Virginia federal court dismissed a claim for tortious interference with prospective economic advantage. The defendant travel agency had previously won the right to use a domain name in a World Intellectual Property Organization (WIPO) UDRP proceeding. The plaintiff claimed that the agency's WIPO claim prevented the company from establishing business relationships with third parties. The court found the plaintiff's claim inadequate to prove that intentional conduct interfered with a business relationship or expectancy, resulting in damage.

Intentional interference with contract and economic opportunity may also occur in a wide variety of Internet activities. This tort involves three parties: "the

---

[265] 755 N.E.2d 589 (Ind. 2001).

[266] A corporation may not claim an invasion of privacy based on the professor's web site and other actions. Among the most recent of these is the court ruling that because "[a] corporation is not an 'individual' with traits of a 'highly personal or intimate nature,'" its privacy law did not extend protection to the corporation. *Id.* at 595.

[267] Seidl v. Greentree Mortgage Co., 30 F. Supp. 2d 1292, 1303 (D. Colo. 1998) (noting that the protected relationship must exist if there is a reasonable probability, not a faint hope, that a contract would result).

[268] 2002 U.S. Dist. LEXIS 3984 (E.D. Va. Mar. 6, 2002).

plaintiff, a person with whom he has a valuable economic relationship, and the person who disrupts that relationship."[269] A company could have an action for economic harm if an online competitor interfered with would-be customers or buyers by planting false rumors about its financial solvency.

The factual circumstances for actionable interference are broad. The *prima facie* case must, however, show "(1) the existence of a contract (or economic opportunity) involving the plaintiff and another; (2) the defendant's knowledge of it; (3) the defendant's malicious, improper, or intentional interference with it; (4) breach of the contract or other legally cognizable disruption of economic opportunity; and (5) resulting damage to the plaintiff."[270]

Tortious interference with contract may be divided into two separate causes of action, one for interfering with contract and one for inducing breach of contract. The Restatement (Second) of Torts divides interference torts into first, those concerning existing contractual rights and, second, those for inducing prospective contractual relations.[271] The second branch of interference of contract, interference with prospective contractual relations, requires (1) a prospective contractual relation, (2) the purpose or intent to harm the plaintiff by preventing the relation from occurring, (3) the absence of privilege or justification on the part of the defendant, and (4) actual damage resulting from the defendant's interference with contract.[272]

The Restatement (Second) of Torts § 768 provides the factors to determine whether a business competitor's interference with a prospective business relationship is proper or improper. The section provides as follows:

> (1) One who intentionally causes a third person not to enter into a prospective contractual relation with another who is his competitor . . . does not interfere improperly with the other's relation if:
>
>   (a) the relation concerns a matter involved in the competition between the actor and the other and
>   (b) the actor does not employ wrongful means and
>   (c) his action does not create or continue an unlawful restraint of trade and
>   (d) his purpose is at least in part to advance his interest in competing with the other.[273]

The Seventh Circuit upheld a ruling of a lower court that a consultant was liable for inducing a breach of contract in *JD Edwards & Co. v. Podany*.[274] The plaintiff company had hired the defendant consultant to review the computer system. The consultant expressed a derogatory opinion about the software without having a basis of knowledge about its functions.[275] The consultant advised the

---

[269] Dan B. Dobbs, The Law of Torts 1257 (2000).
[270] *Id.* at 1260.
[271] Restatement (Second) of Torts § 766 (1979).
[272] *Id.*
[273] Restatement (Second) of Torts § 768 (1979).
[274] 168 F.3d 1020 (7th Cir. 1999).
[275] *Id.*

company to stop installing the software and to stop payment on the check to the licensor.[276] The court found that a reasonable trier of fact could reject the defense of consultant's privilege if asserted by the defendant.

A company employee, consultant, or other person may have privilege to disclose proprietary information or trade secrets and be immune from business torts in limited circumstances. The Restatement (Third) of Unfair Competition permits disclosures relevant to public health or safety, commission of crime or tort, or other matters of substantial public concern.[277]

[D] Breach of Fiduciary Duty

A *fiduciary duty* arises out of a relationship between two parties "when one of them is under a duty to act for or to give advice for the benefit of another upon matters within the scope of the relation."[278] The breach of fiduciary duty depends first on whether a "fiduciary relationship exist[s] at the time of the alleged misconduct."[279] The concept of a fiduciary relationship arises out of the law of trust, and fiduciary duties may be imputed to a wide variety of corporate actors. A breach of fiduciary duty cause of action may be brought against directors, officers, employers, business partners, or joint venturers. The breach of fiduciary duty may also arise when key employees set up a competing business or work for a competitor.[280]

Breach of fiduciary duty is a cause of action that may arise in many different situations arising out of online activities. If a company owes a fiduciary duty to a trade partner, it must conduct its online businesses in good faith and in the spirit of fair dealing. An online company that places its own interest ahead of a party to which it owes a fiduciary duty may be assessed punitive damages for ill-gotten gains.[281]

[E] Business Defamation

Business defamation occurs when a false and defamatory statement is communicated which "prejudice[s] [the plaintiff] in the conduct of its business and

---

[276] *Id.*

[277] Restatement (Third) of Unfair Competition § 40 cmt. c (1995).

[278] Restatement (Second) of Torts § 874, cmt. a (1979).

[279] Robert A. Kutcher and Benjamin W. Bronston, Breach of Fiduciary Duties, Chapter 1 in George F. McGunnigle, Jr., Business Torts Litigation 1 (1992).

[280] Dobbs, *supra* note 269.

[281] *See, e.g.*, DeRance, Inc. v. PaineWebber, Inc., 872 F.2d 1312 (7th Cir. 1989) (court upholding a $7 million punitive damages award against broker who intentionally misled his client, filing reports underreporting losses and acting in opposition to express agreement of trading practices between the client and broker).

deter[s] other from dealing with it."[282] Business defamation is similar to an ordinary defamation case in that a defendant has published a false and derogatory statement about the plaintiff. The test for business defamation is "whether in the circumstances, the writing discredits the plaintiff in the minds of any considerable and respectable class of the community."[283]

In contrast to individuals, who may suffer noneconomic damages from defamation, businesses suffer from pecuniary harm from trade libel. Business defamation claims "are the most common form of content-based liability, but the content of a site can render a Web site operator liable for copyright and trademark infringement, for business torts, and even for securities law violations. Web-based businesses like America Online, Yahoo! and eBay are the most vulnerable to such liability."[284] In *Amway Corp. v. P&G*,[285] Amway filed a complaint against a defendant who published defamatory statements about Amway, its officers, its business practices, and its products on a web site. A Michigan federal court denied the defendant's motion to dismiss, finding that the defendant's Internet site created sufficient contacts with the forum state for the court to exercise personal jurisdiction. The court found that Amway made a *prima facie* showing that the defendant's web site was aimed at the forum state, and that those actions caused harm.

Defamatory commercial speech cases frequently raise a conflict between tort law and the First Amendment, especially when Internet postings address issues of public concern. A telecommunications company filed a defamation case against defendants who posted negative messages about the company on an Internet bulletin board. The defendants argued that the trade libel lawsuit was a transparent effort to intimidate individuals critical of the company's financial performance. The California court granted the motion to dismiss because California's anti-SLAPP (Strategic Litigation Against Public Participation) provisions applied and the defendants' postings were opinions that constituted an exercise of free speech in connection with a public issue.[286] In *Media3 Technologies, LLC v. Mail Abuse Prevention Systems, LLC*,[287] a web-hosting company alleged that its reputation had been injured by being placed on an Internet Service Provider's "blackhole list." The plaintiff argued that the provider's acts constituted defamation, intentional interference with existing advantageous business relations, intentional interference with prospective advantageous business relations, and a violation of Massachusetts' unfair and deceptive trade practices act. The court dismissed all actions, finding no likelihood of success. The court found that the allegedly defamatory statement that the plaintiff's web site was "spam friendly" was an accurate statement. Truth is an absolute defense to trade libel claims.

---

[282] A.F.M. Corp. v. Corporate Aircraft Mgmt., 626 F. Supp. 1533 (D. Mass. 1985).

[283] *See* Smith v. Suburban Rests., Inc., 374 Mass. 528, 529, 373 N.E.2d 215, 217 (1978).

[284] Robert Juman and Marc Greenwald, Beware of Liability for Web Site Postings, N.Y.L.J., Feb. 4, 2002, at S8.

[285] 2000 U.S. Dist. LEXIS 372 (W.D. Mich. Jan. 6, 2000).

[286] Global Telemedia Int'l, Inc. v. Doe 1, 132 F. Supp. 2d 1261 (C.D. Cal. 2001).

[287] 2001 U.S. Dist. LEXIS 1310 (D. Mass. Jan. 2, 2001).

§ 5.05 INTERNET TORTS

[A] Identity Theft

A company's employees may be victimized by "identity fraud" on the Internet. Any anonymous user can claim to have a given occupation or a given expertise.[288] The Internet makes it easy for impostors to assume false identities, and it is therefore a haven for identity theft. In *Andrews v. Trans Union Corp.*,[289] for example, an impostor used a plaintiff's Social Security number to apply for credit. The California federal court held that the plaintiff had a valid claim against the credit-reporting agency. The plaintiff had the burden of proving that it used reasonable procedures for assuring maximum accuracy.[290]

In another case, the court upheld regulations by certain federal agencies under the Gramm-Leach-Bliley Act that addressed responsibilities of financial institutions to protect the privacy of the personal financial information of their customers.[291] The district court held that the regulations did not violate a credit reporting agency's right to free speech under the First Amendment, the regulations did not violate a credit reporting agency's right to due process, and the regulations did not violate a credit reporting agency's right to equal protection under the Fifth Amendment.[292]

A company needs reliable means for identifying and for authorizing potential customers in order to develop reliable e-commerce. Otherwise, it may be subject to tort liability if it permits impostors to gain access to sensitive financial or proprietary information belonging to third persons. New technologies, such as digital certificates, are being developed to combat identity theft.[293]

[B] Computer Viruses

Electronic viruses are virulent codes that may end up destroying the hard drive of a company computer and altering or destroying data or information. These malicious programs infect "executable files or the system areas of hard and floppy disks and then make copies of [themselves]."[294] A computer virus threat is a serious concern for companies, which may lose money, time, and key information assets as a malicious code is unleashed in their systems. The term "virus" was first defined in 1983. In 1982, Apple virus versions 1, 2, and 3 forced multiple computer networks to shut down.[295] In 1988, the Internet worm spread by a graduate

---

[288] David L. Wilson, Your Passport Please: Helping to Ferret Out the Fakes and the Frauds on the Web, Buff. News (Jan. 13, 1998), at 7D.

[289] 7 F. Supp. 2d 1056 (C.D. Cal. 1998).

[290] *Id.* at 1076.

[291] Individual Ref. Servs. Group, Inc. v. FTC, 145 F. Supp. 2d 6 (D.D.C. 2001).

[292] *Id.*

[293] Wilson, *supra* note 288.

[294] Computer Virus FAQ for New Users (visited July 19, 1999), http://www.faqs.org/faqs/computer-virus/new-uers.

[295] As West Nile Virus Threatens, PC Viruses Live On, TechWeb News (Aug. 29, 2000), at 1.

student infected 6,000 computers.[296] In 1990, polymorphic or multipartite viruses were first discovered.[297] Recent viruses have proven to be even more sophisticated. In 1999 the Melissa virus, for example, was designed to infect Word documents and e-mail itself to everyone in the user's Outlook address book, which infected thousands of computers worldwide.[298] Again, in May 1999, computers throughout the world were infected with the CIH virus. Another alarming virus in 1999 was the e-mail virus called "Bubble Boy"[299] that infected computers simply by being viewed in the preview pane of an e-mail program, such as Microsoft's Outlook.[300] It is arguable that it is negligence not to employ standard antiviral software or other measures to detect computer viruses. However, there is little authority for negligence causes of action for carelessly infecting computers with viruses.[301] The widespread presence of viruses from the Internet creates an increased duty of care to prevent the spread of viruses. The duty of care likely includes the mandatory use of state-of-the-art antivirus scans. Reasonable care would also include the routine use of updated products and PC diagnostics.

Deliberately introducing a virus into a computer system can constitute criminal as well as tortious trespass, and it violates criminal state and federal laws. A company that knowingly distributed computer software with viruses would be theoretically liable for fraud or misrepresentation. The introduction of a computer virus could, theoretically, constitute conversion or trespass to chattels as well.[302]

[C]   Cyberstalking

Cyberstalking refers to the use of the Internet, e-mail, or other electronic communications to stalk another person. A large number of companies sell personal information, making it easy to electronically track victims, and cyberstalkers are often difficult to detect because of the use of anonymous remailers. Cyberstalking taking the form of repeated e-mails may constitute a crime or a tort if there is a credible threat. A Department of Justice report suggests that cyberstalking incidents are on the increase.[303] Cyberstalking by an employee may result

---

[296] *Id.*

[297] *Id.*

[298] John D. Penn, Beyond the Quill: Big Brother Really Is Watching: Following Computers' Trails, 1999 ABI JNL. LEXIS 75 (June, 1999).

[299] The virus is named after a famous episode of the "Seinfeld" television show called the Bubble Boy episode.

[300] Robert Schoenberger, Bubble Boy E-Mail Virus Lurks, Gannett News Service (Nov. 11, 1999), at ARC.

[301] *See, e.g.,* George C. Smith & Co. v. Dosco, Inc., 1994 Ohio App. LEXIS 2947 (June 30, 1994) (upholding trial court's failure to award damages as a result of plaintiff's negligence in infecting defendant's computer with the Jerusalem virus).

[302] Robin A. Brooks, Deterring the Spread of Viruses Online: Can Tort Law Tighten the 'Net? 17 Rev. Litig. 343, 365 (1998) (discussing tort remedies for spreading computer viruses).

[303] U.S. Dep't of Justice, Cyberstalking: A New Challenge for Law Enforcement and Industry (1999).

in tort liability for a company under principles of vicarious liability or, if the target is another employee, direct liability for sexual harassment under a hostile workplace theory. Apparent authority may arise in these cases if the agent appears to be acting in the ordinary course of the business.

A tort action can be brought based on cyberstalking by e-mail or the Internet. In *Hitchcock v. Woodside Literary Agency (WLA)*,[304] Jayne Hitchcock, a University of Maryland teaching assistant and writer, answered a web site advertisement soliciting writing samples from "published and unpublished authors."[305] Mrs. Hitchcock received a letter from WLA that praised her writing and solicited her to forward a full manuscript to the agency, along with a $75 "reading and market evaluation fee."[306] Ms. Hitchcock sent a different sample of her writing to WLA using her maiden name, to which WLA responded by sending her a letter that was virtually identical to the letter sent in response to the first writing sample, save for the soliciting of a $150 "reading and market evaluation fee."[307] Ms. Hitchcock concluded that WLA was nothing more than a scam for soliciting bogus fees from aspiring writers. She then posted various notices on Internet bulletin boards denouncing WLA and noting that "legitimate literary agencies did not charge reading fees."[308]

The company responded to Hitchcock's actions by launching a campaign of harassment against her on the Internet. The harassment took many forms, including the posting of messages that falsely claimed that the plaintiff was the author of hard-core pornography. Hitchcock was also sent crude messages, which threatened her with sexual assault. The defendant flooded her e-mail accounts and posted offensive messages to third parties in such a manner as to make it appear she had authored them. Postings, in her name, were made on electronic bulletin boards for beer lovers that called the members "drunks and morons."[309] The online literary agency even went so far as to transmit crank messages, posing as the plaintiff, to insult her co-workers.

The victim filed a lawsuit charging that the agency deliberately placed her in danger of imminent sexual assault by posting Internet messages in her name containing crude sexual propositions. The plaintiff sought to recover damages for personal and professional injury, including the cost of therapy. The federal court dismissed the plaintiff's complaint in its entirety for failure to state a claim.[310] The plaintiff had no alternative for the e-harassment but to close her e-mail account. The online agency was discovered to be the harasser when "it slipped up and left

---

[304] 15 F. Supp. 2d 246 (E.D.N.Y. 1998).

[305] *Id.* at 248.

[306] *Id.* at 249.

[307] *Id.*

[308] *Id.*

[309] *Id.*

[310] The plaintiff's dismissal was partially attributable to defective pleading. The plaintiff stated claims under New York rather than Maryland law, resulting in dismissal of the state claims. The plaintiff, in addition, failed to plead that WLA was a distinct enterprise, which is a requirement of the Racketeer Influenced and Corruption Organizations Act (RICO). All claims were dismissed, and the plaintiff's motion to amend her pleadings was denied. *Id.*

her name and e-mail address in one of the literary agency's Internet ads."[311] Despite this smoking gun, the federal court granted the defendant's motion to dismiss the plaintiffs' RICO claim for failure to state a claim upon which relief could be granted. In the end, there was no remedy available for e-mail harassment and the "e-mail bombs" that shut her e-mail account down. Despite the outcome of this case, companies should not engage in such activities, because other courts could find such behavior illegal and punishable by law.

Vicarious liability would make a company liable for torts that its employees commit while acting within the scope of their employment. The rationale underlying vicarious liability is that the "principal chooses the agent and has the opportunity to train and instruct the agent, as well as the opportunity to install safeguards against predictable forms of misconduct."[312] A company must therefore institute procedures to prevent its employees from using the computer to stalk co-employees or third parties, otherwise it risks being exposed to the possibility of vicarious liability. An employer may be liable for failing to warn others of the dangerous propensities of ex-employees.[313]

§ 5.06   PUBLISHING TORTS IN CYBERSPACE

[A]   Defamation in Cyberspace

The development of new information technologies poses new challenges to the law of defamation. The elements of a defamation action require the plaintiff to prove that the statement (1) is defamatory, (2) is about the plaintiff, (3) was published by the defendant, (4) was made maliciously, and (5) resulted in damages to the plaintiff.[314] The Restatement of Torts defines *defamation* as

> a false and defamatory statement concerning another; an unprivileged publication to a third-party; fault amounting to at least negligence on the part of the publisher, and either actionability of the statement irrespective of special harm or the existence of special harm caused by the publication.[315]

Defamation is a communication "which tends to hold the plaintiff up to hatred, contempt, or ridicule, or to cause him to be shunned or avoided."[316]

---

[311] *Id.*

[312] American Law Institute, Restatement of the Law of Agency § 2.04 (Preliminary Draft No. 3, June 11, 1999).

[313] An employer faces a dilemma in providing information on ex-employees for reference checks. On the one hand, employers may be subject to defamatory statements about their employees. On the other hand, employers may be held liable for failing to warn others of known *propensities of ex-employees to commit crimes. See, e.g.,* Randi W. v. Murrc Joint Unified School Dist., 14 Cal. 4th 1066, 60 Cal. Rptr. 263 (1997) (ex-employer of school molested 13-year-old student; liability for failing to warn new school district that teacher had been dismissed for molesting students).

[314] 3 Restatement (Second) of Torts (1997).

[315] *Id.* at § 558.

[316] W. Page Keeton et al., Prosser and Keeton on The Law of Torts 773 (5th ed. 1984).

Whether a communication is defamatory is judged from the viewpoint of the reasonable person. The test for defamatory meaning is whether the communication "lowers the person's reputation in the community or deters third persons from associating or dealing with him."[317] A statement may be defamatory on its face or defamatory because of context or by innuendo.[318] "A defamatory communication is made concerning the person to whom its recipient correctly, or mistakenly but reasonably, understands that it was intended to refer."[319] Whether words are reasonably construed as defamatory is a preliminary question of law determined by the court.[320]

The U.S. Supreme Court in *New York Times v. Sullivan*[321] reshaped the law of defamation, concluding that it must recognize the "profound national commitment to the principle that debate of public issues should be uninhibited, robust, and wide-open." In *Sullivan,* a city commissioner of Montgomery, Alabama, sued the *New York Times* for an advertisement published in the newspaper to raise money for a legal defense fund for Dr. Martin Luther King, Jr.[322] The plaintiff contended that the *New York Times* advertisement, placed by four black civil rights leaders, defamed him. An Alabama jury agreed, assessing damages of $500,000 against both the civil rights leaders, and the newspaper. The U.S. Supreme Court reversed, holding that in public official cases, the plaintiff must prove with "convincing clarity" that the defamatory statements were made with actual malice.[323]

Defamatory statements may be classified into statements that are defamation "*per se*" or statements that have a defamatory statement due to "extrinsic facts." Slander, on the other hand, is traditionally divided into slander *per se* and slander *per quod.* Slanderous *per se* statements are presumed defamatory, and no special damages must be proven. Showing that the statements refer to a plaintiff and that the plaintiff suffered special damages must be proven for slander *per quod* claims. A growing number of states have codified the law of defamation. The Oklahoma statute, for example, states that "[s]lander is a false and unprivileged publication which (1) charges a person with a crime; (2) accuses him of having an infectious, contagious or loathsome disease or being impotent or promiscuous; (3) maligns him with respect to his office, profession, trade or business; or (4) causes actual damages by its natural consequences."[324]

Written defamation is classified as libel, whereas oral defamation is slander. Courts traditionally will not permit an action for slander absent proof of special damages.[325] It is uncertain whether it is slander if the defendant makes an allegedly

---

[317] *Id.* at 774.

[318] *Id.* at 780.

[319] *Id.* at 783.

[320] *Id.* at 781.

[321] 376 U.S. 254 (1964).

[322] *Id.*

[323] *Id.* at 285-86.

[324] Okla. Stat. tit. 12, § 1442 (1991).

[325] The specific exceptions to the special damage rule for slander are statements that impute a crime, a loathsome disease, or constitute trade libel, which "affect the plaintiff in his business, trade, profession, office, or calling." W. Page Keeton, Prosser and Keeton on The Law of Torts § 111 at 788 (1984).

defamatory statement about the plaintiff in a "chat room." An e-mail message may be printed out and is therefore likely to be libel.

The Internet makes it possible to falsify return e-mail addresses to defame individuals as well as business entities. It is quite common for Internet users to "flame" fellow users on the Internet. Flaming is not only a breach of neti-quette,[326] but it may be the basis for a defamation lawsuit against a company and its employees.[327]

One of the known e-business risks is that anonymous individuals can post false information on online forums that will defame other sellers or interfere with contracts. The eBay system of posting comments on participants appears to func-tion as part of the course of dealing and usage of trade in the electronic auction place.[328] The online auction recently changed the process and form for posting rep-utation comments. A person's rebuttal now appears immediately after the com-ments submitted by other users.

Recently, negative feedback by a purchaser on eBay led to a defamation law-suit in Maryland.[329] The customer purchased a "Color Magic" Barbie doll from a collector using the eBay site. The customer later posted a disparaging comment about purchasing a "Balding Barbie" from the plaintiff.[330] The seller filed a defamation lawsuit, arguing that the disparaging comments thwarted attempts to bid on other items. eBay argued that it builds trust by soliciting positive and neg-ative feedback from customers.[331]

White House aide Sidney Blumenthal and his wife brought a defamation action against the Internet gossip columnist, Matt Drudge, for his false allegation that Mr. Blumenthal was a chronic wife-beater.[332] The plaintiffs also sued AOL, an interactive computer service provider that was the publisher of the electronic ver-sion of the Drudge Report. AOL was dismissed from the case, as it was an ISP

---

[326] *Netiquette* is an "abbreviation for 'Internet etiquette.' Netiquette also refers to the informal norms and rules that develop in the use of the Internet." Michael D. Scott, Internet and Technology Desk Reference 336 (1999).

[327] Flaming may occur in a Usenet newsgroup, web forum, or e-mail to a distribution list. "Cer-tain issues tend to provoke emphatically stated responses, but flaming is often directed at a self-appointed expert rather than at the issues or information itself and is sometimes directed at unwitting but opinionated newbies (new Internet users) who appear in a newsgroup." Whatis.com, What Is . . . Flaming (A Definition) (visited Nov. 14, 1999), http://www.whatis.com/flaming.htm.

[328] Section 1-205 of the Uniform Commercial Code defines a *usage of trade* as "any practice or method of dealing having such regularity of observance in a place, vocation or trade as to justify an expectation that it will be observed with respect to the transaction in question. The existence and scope of such a usage are to be proved as facts. If it is established that such a usage is embodied in a written trade code or similar writing the interpretation of the writing is for the court." U.C.C. § 1-205 (1995).

[329] Zena Olijnyk, Balding Barbie Lawsuit Typifies Peril of E-Commerce, The National Post (Apr. 16, 1999), at CO1.

[330] *Id.*

[331] "E-Bay feedback is the post-transaction commentary that builds trust for customers in on-line auctions." Troy Wolverton, E-Bay User Subject of Auctioneer's Libel Suit, CNET NEWS.COM (visited June 18, 1999), http://www.news.com/News/Items/0,4,35814,00.html.

[332] Drudge v. Blumenthal, 992 F. Supp. 44 (D.D.C. 1998).

immunized by § 230(C) of the CDA. The District of Columbia court found that Drudge's interactive web site specifically focused on D.C. political gossip and that the columnist regularly distributed his writings to D.C. residents. The court, therefore, refused to dismiss the defamation action based upon the defendant's purposeful activity in gathering, soliciting, and receiving D.C. gossip.

In a case of first impression, a corporation anonymously sought to bring a suit against AOL to disclose the identities of John Doe defendants who allegedly defamed the corporation and published confidential material and insider information in Internet chat rooms.[333] The court held that if a party can show that its need for anonymity outweighs public interest in its identity and prejudice to the opposing party, a trial court has discretion to allow the party to proceed anonymously.[334]

Many users of e-mail or those who post to Internet news groups feel free to express opinions they would not make in a business letter or in person.[335] Postings to Internet news groups may result in defamation lawsuits. An AOL subscriber, for example, was sued for libel based on its online criticism of a Caribbean resort and its diving instructor in an anonymous posting.[336]

Libel or slander must be communicated or published to a third person to constitute defamation. The concept of publication "does not mean that the defamatory statement was committed to paper; it means that the statement was conveyed to someone besides the person defamed."[337] Publication may be difficult to establish in an online environment. The statute of limitations for Internet communications is likely to be the date of posting on a web site or the time of transmission in the case of an e-mail message.[338]

[1] Parties to a Defamation Action

[a] Plaintiffs in General

The plaintiff in a defamation action is a living person or entity, although a few states "have made defamation of the dead a crime."[339] The Fourth Circuit upheld a trial court's dismissal of an online defamation lawsuit against an investment advisor for its statement that the plaintiff's magazine was an unpaid promoter on a web site.[340] In *Media3 Technologies, LLC v. Mail Abuse Prevention*

---

[333] America Online, Inc. v. Anonymous Publicly Traded Co., 542 S.E.2d 377 (Va. 2001).

[334] *Id.*

[335] Simon Halberstam, Closing the Portals on Defamation, New Media Age (Oct. 14, 1999), at 25.

[336] Horizon Hotels d/b/a/ Caribbean Inn v. AOL (filed Nov. 1995, Cook County, Ill.) (no published opinion), reported in Perkins Coie LLP: Internet Case Digest (visited June 18, 1999), http://www.perkinscoie.com/resource/ecomm/netcase/Cases-06.htm.

[337] George B. Delta and Jeffrey H. Matsurra, Law of the Internet § 7.02[A] at 7-7 (1998).

[338] John Caher, Tort Rules Applies to Internet Libel Case; Statute of Limitations Begins on Date of Posting, 223 N.Y.L.J. 1 (Mar. 23, 2000).

[339] Keeton, Prosser and Keeton on Torts § 111, at 778-79.

[340] Agora, Inc. v. Axxess, Inc., 2001 U.S. App. LEXIS 6057 (4th Cir., Apr. 9, 2001) (dismissing action concluding that the rating of plaintiff's magazine as unpaid promoter was not actionable as it constituted an expression of opinion based on disclosed or readily available facts).

Systems, LLC,[341] a web hosting company sued an ISP, arguing that it lost business as the result of defamatory remarks related to plaintiff placed in certain files on the provider's web site, as well as by the provider's recommendation to other businesses on its blackhole list not to allow access to web sites hosted by the plaintiff. The court found that the acts of the provider did not constitute defamation since the defendant's assertion that the plaintiff was "spam-friendly" was accurate.[342] In *Bihari v. Gross*,[343] the plaintiff filed a cybersquatting, trademark infringement, and defamation action against a defendant who criticized the plaintiff on its web site.

Corporations or other entities cannot be defamed in the same personal sense as can a living person.[344] A company in Washington, D.C., filed a lawsuit against Specialty Car Sales of Miami, alleging that the owners and employees of Specialty posted two defamatory messages about a FedTrust employee through the eBay feedback system. The negative comments warned potential buyers about the employee, noting that he was "dishonest about the origin of his cars" and potential buyers should "stay away."[345] The online auction house argued that it was protected from defamation lawsuits by the Good Samaritan provision of the CDA.

In a New Hampshire federal case, a defendant posted false information about the plaintiff's company on the Internet to drive down stock prices.[346] Presstek, Inc., the plaintiff, was a New Hampshire developer of digital imaging technology. Presstek sued three individuals for posting defamatory comments to an online chat room to drive down the price of the high-technology company's stock.[347] The defendants were "short sellers," who sell borrowed stock and profit when a company's stock price declines.[348] In a related case, the First Circuit affirmed the dismissal of a defamation and legal malpractice case filed by the principals of Presstek.[349] The objectionable statements alleged organized crime links between the short sellers and the defendants in a federal securities case accused of stock manipulation.

A Seattle financial education company filed a slander lawsuit against 10 users of Yahoo! message boards.[350] The plaintiff named 10 "John Doe" defendants

---

[341] Media3 Technologies, Inc. v. Mail Abuse Prevention Sys., LLC, 2001 U.S. Dist. LEXIS 1310 (D. Mass., Jan. 2, 2001) (denying injunction because it failed to show a likelihood of success on theories of business defamation and other business torts).

[342] *Id.*

[343] 2000 U.S. Dist. LEXIS 14180 (S.D.N.Y., Sept. 28, 2000) (holding that use of metatags incorporating plaintiff's trademark did not violate the Anticybersquatting Consumer Protection Act and finding no infringement or defamation).

[344] *Id.* at 806.

[345] *Id.*

[346] Presstek, Inc. v. Lustig, No. 97463-M (D.N.H., filed Sept. 17, 1997) (claiming that defendants posted false statements to an Internet chat room, to manipulate price of company's stock).

[347] "Once Again an ISP Is Open to Liability for Defamation," 14 Computer Law Strategist 6 (Sept. 1997).

[348] *Id.*

[349] Hugel v. Milberg, Weiss, Bershad, Hynes & Lerach, LLP, 175 F.3d 14 (1st Cir. 1999).

[350] Reuters, Slander Suit Served against Yahoo! Users, Special to CNET NEWS.COM (Mar. 9, 1999) (visited June 18, 1999), http://www.news.com/News/Item-0, 4,33503,00.htm/st.ne.fd.mdh.

and sought to subpoena Yahoo! for their identities. One of the posting defendants claimed that one of the financial company's founders "had been arrested for accepting kickbacks."[351]

A plaintiff received a libel award to compensate him for having been called a liar on a posting to an Internet discussion group. The dispute arose out of an exchange of e-mail followed by an argument. The litigants then "posted electronic 'he-said-she-said' accounts about how the phone call ended" on an Internet discussion group.[352] The objectionable message was the defendant's posting a message entitled "Ken McCarthy is a liar—be warned." The plaintiff filed a defamation lawsuit and received a $5,000 award, which was later overturned on appeal.[353]

A Utah federal court ordered that a web site be removed from the Internet for a short time for allegedly defaming a business.[354] The judge lifted the preliminary injunction in February 1999. In another case, a California court set aside a default motion in a defamation case against a woman who charged a California Highway Patrol officer with sexual harassment on her web site.[355] A British court ordered a Canadian to pay "damages for libeling English physicist Laurence Godfrey during an Internet discussion forum."[356] In *Dendrite International Inc. v. Doe No. 3,*[357] a corporation filed a complaint to prevent the actions of a number of fictitiously named defendants who were posting defamatory messages on the Internet. The trial court denied the company's application for expedited discovery to disclose the identity of the Internet posters.

[b] Public Officials and Public Figures

The law of defamation merges with the First Amendment when the plaintiffs are public officials and public figures. For public officials and public figures, defamatory statements must be proven, by clear and convincing evidence, to have been made with knowledge of their falsity or with reckless indifference to the truth.[358] The preponderance of the evidence is simply the "greater weight of the evidence," which "means the more persuasive force and effect of the entire evidence in the case."[359] In contrast, clear and convincing evidence is a heightened

---

[351] *Id.*

[352] Diana Walsh, Woman Cleared of Net Libel for Calling Man Liar, S.F. Examiner (Apr. 3, 1998), at A-11.

[353] *Id.*

[354] *Id.* at 87.

[355] *Id.* at 88.

[356] *Id.* at 95.

[357] 775 A.2d 756 (N.J. 2001).

[358] Keeton, Prosser and Keeton on Torts § 113, at 806-07.

[359] Florida Supreme Court, Amendments to Standard Jury Instructions—Civil Cases No. SC00-185 (Mar. 2001) at 9 (stating standard jury instruction for Defamation: Public Official or Public Figure Claimant, MI 4.1); *see also* Peterson v. The New York Times, No. 2:99 CV 242, 13 Rocky Mountain Verdicts & Settlements, Inc. (Sept. 2000) (reporting summary judgment for defense in case in which the former Majority Leader of the Utah State Senate had his picture published in the

burden that differs from the preponderance test in requiring evidence that is even more compelling and persuasive. "Clear and convincing evidence" is evidence that is precise, explicit, lacking in confusion, and of such weight that it produces a firm belief or conviction, without hesitation, about the matter in issue."[360] There is no defamation for matters in a person's life that relate to the public interest.[361] Public officials are "those who are commonly classified as public officers, but also public employees who exercise any substantial governmental power."[362]

The public figure doctrine was first articulated by the Supreme Court in *Gertz v. Robert Welch, Inc.*[363] There are two kinds of public figures: general and limited. The general public figure is a public figure for all purposes, whereas a limited public figure is a "public figure only because they have voluntarily injected themselves into the resolution of particular controversies or issues of importance to the general public."[364] The following are the three factors determining whether a plaintiff is a limited purpose public figure: (1) Does a public controversy exist? (2) What is the nature and extent of the plaintiff's participation in the controversy? (3) Is the alleged defamation germane to the plaintiff's participation in the controversy?[365] To qualify as a limited purpose public figure, a public controversy must have existed prior to the electronic transmittal of a message concerning the plaintiff. The actual malice standard would apply to a defamation case brought against a member of the mass media where the publication concerns a matter of legitimate public interest.

In *Curtis Publishing Co. v. Butts*,[366] the Supreme Court extended the requirement of "actual malice" from public officials to public figures.[367] Recently, a New York trial court dismissed an online defamation case arising out of a story published on a web site charging a bank president with ties to drug traffickers. The court ruled that the First Amendment applied to any journalistic web site.[368]

Commentators argue that individuals who engage in discussions of topics on Internet news groups may be "limited purpose public figures" for purposes of defamation law.[369] Whether a plaintiff is a limited public figure will depend, however, on whether a topic discussed on news groups is deemed to be a public con-

---

New York Times and Internet sites in a story relating to the Salt Lake Olympic Bid Committee scandal; basing dismissal on grounds that plaintiff was a public official and public figure).

[360] *Id.* at 9-10.

[361] *Id.*

[362] W. Page Keeton, Prosser and Keeton on Torts §113, at 106.

[363] 418 U.S. 323 (1974).

[364] W. Page Keeton, Prosser and Keeton on Torts §113, at 806.

[365] Waldbaum v. Fairchild Publications, Inc., 627 F.2d 1287, 1296-98 (D.C. Cir. 1980).

[366] 388 U.S. 130, 133 (1967).

[367] *Id.*

[368] Tom Regan, Court Extends Print and Media Protection Online, Christian Science Monitor, Dec. 20, 2001.

[369] Martin C. Loesch et al., Chapter 2, Defamation, in Surveying Cyberspace: A Guide to Insurance Defense and Coverage in the Age of Technology, 1998 DRI 1-5.

troversy, the extent and nature of the controversy, and the extent and nature of the plaintiff's postings to a newsgroup.

[c]   Online Service Providers

Publishers under traditional defamation law are liable for defamatory statements contained in their works even if they had no knowledge of the statement's objectionable content.[370] In contrast, distributors are not liable for defamatory statements contained in their materials unless it is proven that they have actual knowledge of the defamatory statements.[371] Publishers are liable for any defamatory statements they publish, whereas distributors are liable only if they knew or had reason to know that the statements were defamatory.[372]

Courts were divided on how to apply defamation law to ISPs for the libelous postings of third parties. The CDA immunized providers for a wide variety of torts committed by third parties. The role of the ISP resembles a pipe for transmitting data, more like a telephone carrier than a newspaper or distributor.[373]

Prior to the enactment of the CDA, the Southern District of New York addressed, in *Cubby, Inc. v. CompuServe, Inc.*,[374] whether an ISP could be liable for defamatory statements posted on one of its news groups or online forums. CompuServe's bulletin board had an electronic newsletter called Rumorville. The plaintiff began publishing a competing publication he called "Skuttlebutt." A subscriber on CompuServe's bulletin board labeled the Skuttlebutt publication "a start-up scam." The plaintiff brought a defamation action against Rumorville as well as CompuServe, on the legal theory that it was a republisher.[375] The court found that CompuServe exercised no editorial control over materials made available to its subscribers and was therefore a distributor and not a publisher for purposes of the law of defamation. The legal consequence of being defined as a mere conduit or distributor was that CompuServe was not liable for defamatory statements on Rumorville. In short, the court was persuaded that CompuServe was a distributor because it did not review the content and therefore had the same status under defamation law as a public library, bookstore, or newsstand.

In another case decided prior to the CDA, a New York court found Prodigy to be a publisher rather than a distributor, potentially liable for defamatory content made in its newsgroups. The New York court denied Prodigy's motion to dismiss

---

[370] W. Page Keeton et al., Prosser and Keeton on Torts § 113, at 810 (5th ed. 1984).

[371] *Id.* at 811.

[372] Jeffrey P. Cunard, Internet Legal Developments, in Communications 1998, G4-64036 (PLI, 1998).

[373] Traditionally, telephone companies, telegraph operators, and other communication carriers were not liable for defamation. The rise of commercial ISPs, such as AOL, CompuServe, Prodigy, and Delphi, raises novel issues as to whether the provider should be held liable for the torts of its subscribers.

[374] 776 F. Supp. 135 (S.D.N.Y. 1991).

[375] *Id.* at 139.

a defamation action made by a subscriber in a Prodigy newsgroup, in *Stratton Oakmont, Inc. v. Prodigy Services Co.*[376] Prodigy was a family-oriented ISP that advertised that it screened its content, unlike many other providers. Prodigy used software that detected objectionable words and automatically notified the user that their message would be censored.[377] After a message accusing Stratton Oakmont, Inc., of fraudulent securities offerings appeared on Prodigy's electronic bulletin board, Stratton Oakmont filed a defamation lawsuit demanding $100 million in punitive damages from Prodigy.[378] Prodigy's defense was that it was a mere conduit of information and not a publisher.[379]

The court in *Stratton Oakmont* held that the provider could be liable for defamatory statements since it was exercising control over the content of materials available on its services. The court was of the opinion that by reviewing and deleting notes from its bulletin boards on the basis of offensiveness, Prodigy was making decisions as to content and exercising editorial control. On October 24, 1995, the case was settled while the appeal was pending.[380] In an unusual procedural move, Stratton Oakmont agreed to drop its demand for $100 million in damages for defamation in exchange for Prodigy's apology.[381] Stratton Oakmont also agreed not to contest Prodigy's motion to ask the court to reverse or set aside its prior ruling on Prodigy's status as a publisher.[382] The *Stratton Oakmont* case was troubling for ISPs because of the vast potential liability for torts such as defamation, misappropriation, or invasion of privacy.

If ISPs can be held liable for infringing material on their services, there is little reason why the ISP should not be liable for infringing material uploaded by its customers to web sites resident on its server computer. The Clinton Administration's Working Group on Intellectual Property and the National Information Infrastructure favored that tort law for copyright-infringing materials governs ISPs uploaded to their systems.[383] It is hardly surprising that injured

---

[376] 23 Media Law Rep. (BNA) 1794 (N.Y. Sup. Ct. 1995).

[377] Rex S. Heinke and Heather D. Rafter, Rough Justice in Cyberspace: Liability on the Electronic Frontier, Comp. Law. (July 1994), at 1.

[378] Stratton Oakmont, Inc. v. Prodigy Servs. Co., 1995 WL 323710 (S.D.N.Y., May 26, 1995) (unpublished decision).

[379] *Id.* The *Prodigy* case was criticized by many legal academics and in electronic discussion groups on the Internet. Professor I. Trotter Hardy found "sentiment running in favor of Prodigy and for unfettered expression on computer bulletin boards." Matthew Goldstein, Prodigy Case May Solve Troubling Liability Puzzle, Nat'l L.J. (Dec. 19, 1994), at B1 (quoting William & Mary law professor I. Trotter Hardy).

[380] Peter H. Lewis, After Apology from Prodigy, Company Drops Suit, N.Y. Times (Oct. 25, 1995), at D1.

[381] *Id.*

[382] Prodigy Plaintiff Reach Agreement in Libel Case, Deal May Let Online Firms Off the Hook, Chi. Trib. (Oct. 25, 1995), at 3.

[383] U.S. Patent and Trademark Office, Information Infrastructure Task Force, Intellectual Property and the National Information Infrastructure: The Report of the Working Group in Intellectual Property Rights 114 (Sept. 5, 1995).

plaintiffs will seek to hold the ISP vicariously liable for online injuries. Individual online defendants can avoid repercussions for their actions by simply disguising their messages and postings.[384]

The CDA expressly overruled the *Stratton Oakmont* case, granting ISPs a broad immunity for defamatory materials and other tortious activities occurring on their service. Section 509 of the CDA provides that "[n]o provider or user of an interactive computer service shall be treated as the publisher of any information provided by another information content provider."[385] Section 230(c)(1) provides that "no provider or user of an interactive computer service shall be held liable on account of . . . any action voluntarily taken in good faith to restrict access to or availability of material that the provider or user considers to be obscene, lewd, lascivious, filthy, excessively violent, harassing, or otherwise objectionable, whether or not such material is constitutionally protected."[386]

The clear trend in the law is to expand ISP immunity of the CDA to cover a broad range of torts. An Illinois federal court dismissed an invasion of privacy action filed by plaintiffs who were college athletes who were secretly videotaped in various states of undress by hidden cameras in restrooms, locker rooms, or showers.[387] The court granted the ISP's motion to dismiss because they were protected by immunity under Section 230 of the CDA.[388] The court found that the ISP was entitled to the immunity and that it was not vitiated because of the ISP's web hosting activities.[389] In *Ben Ezra Weinstein & Co. v. America Online, Inc.*,[390] the court dismissed a defamation claim because the plaintiff failed to produce evidence that the Internet access provider created information. The court held that absent proof that the provider created the content, it was entitled to immunity for providing access to offending information.

In *Gucci Am. v. Hall & Assocs.*,[391] the plaintiff sued an ISP for trademark infringement, unfair competition, false designation of origin, and breach of prior settlement agreement. The defendant was an ISP that provided web page hosting services to a defendant, who sold jewelry, apparel, and other services on a web site. The plaintiff notified the ISP on two occasions that its customer was violating

---

[384] *See generally* Anne Wells Branscomb, Anonymity, Autonomy, and Accountability: Challenges to the First Amendment in Cyberspace, 104 Yale L.J. 1639, 1641 (1995) (arguing that anonymity and accountability are conflicting values for Internet users).

[385] 47 U.S.C. § 230(c)(1).

[386] *Id.*

[387] John Does v. Franco Productions, 2000 U.S. Dist. LEXIS 8645 (N.D. Ill., June 22, 2000) (dismissing action for intrusion into plaintiff's seclusion against ISP). *See also* Marczeski v. Law, 122 F. Supp. 315 (D. Conn. 2000) (granting defendant's motion to dismiss on grounds of CDA immunity for plaintiff's claim of defamation, harassment, fraud, and ruined reputation on the Internet).

[388] *Id.* at *2.

[389] *Id.* at *3.

[390] 206 F.3d 980 (10th Cir. 2000); *see also* Zeran v. America Online, 129 F.3d 327 (4th Cir. 1998) (holding that AOL was immunized from defamation claim posted by columnist Matt Drudge even when content was paid for and commissioned by provider).

[391] 135 F. Supp. 2d 409 (S.D.N.Y. 2001).

its trademark in its advertising of jewelry on the web site. The court refused to dismiss the plaintiff's trademark infringement lawsuit, holding that the CDA did not immunize the ISP from contributory infringement for information posted on the web site.[392] Chapter Four provides a discussion of the role of the Digital Millennium Copyright Act's safe harbor for copyright infringement claims filed against ISPs.[393] In *Zeran v. America Online*,[394] the court found that AOL was a publisher entitled to immunity for defamatory statements posted on its service. The *Zeran* court observed that "if computer service providers were subject to distributor liability, they would face potential liability each time they receive notice of a potentially defamatory statement—from any party, concerning any message."[395] The plaintiff in *Zeran* argued that the ISP was negligent in permitting an anonymous poster (content provider) to defame him by making a false posting on a computer bulletin board that romanticized the Oklahoma City bombing. The false posting stated that Zeran was selling offensive T-shirts celebrating the Oklahoma City bombing. The plaintiff received hundreds of threatening telephone calls and flaming e-mails as the result of the anonymous third party's actions.

The court held that § 230(c)(1) immunized AOL from "distributor liability" for postings made by content providers.[396] In another case, a Florida court found that AOL was shielded by the CDA's immunity shield for liability for subscriber's use of a chat room to advertise pornographic images of a child.[397] AOL was also shielded from liability for allegedly defamatory statements made by Matt Drudge on the online version of the Drudge Report published on AOL's service.[398] In May 2001, the Blumenthals settled their online defamation lawsuit with Matt Drudge for the paltry sum of $2,000.[399]

In a 1997 case, an anonymous user of an ISP posted false messages that the plaintiffs were performing satanic rituals on children. The plaintiff sued the provider for negligence and the intentional infliction of emotional distress. The court held that the actions were barred by the safe harbor provision of the CDA.[400]

---

[392] Columbia Ins. Co. v. Seescandy.com, 185 F.R.D. 573, 578 (N.D. Cal. 1999) (refusing preliminary injunction against web site based upon trademark infringement stating: "[S]uing the ISP in these cases is most often not productive, either because the ISP lacks the knowledge requisite to be held liable for contributory infringement, or is immune pursuant to section 230(c) of the Communications Decency Act").

[393] *See* Digital Millennium Copyright Act, 17 U.S.C. § 512(c) (2000).

[394] 129 F.3d 327 (4th Cir. 1997).

[395] *Id.* at 333.

[396] *Id.*

[397] Doe v. America Online, Inc., 718 So. 2d 385 (Fla. 4th Dist. Ct. of App. 1998), *aff'd* 2001 Fla. LEXIS 449, 26 Fla. L. Wkly. S. 141 (Sup. Ct. Fla., Mar. 8, 2001) (holding that computer service provider with notice of a defamatory third-party posting is entitled to immunity under § 230 of the CDA).

[398] Blumenthal v. Drudge, 992 F. Supp. 44 (D.D.C. 1998).

[399] Clinton Aide Settles with Matt Drudge, N.Y. Times (May 4, 2001), at A14.

[400] Aquino v. Electriciti, Inc., 26 Media L. Rep. (BNA) 1032 (Cal. Super. Ct. 1997).

In *Immunomedics, Inc. v. Doe*,[401] the court held that a bio-pharmaceutical company could subpoena the records of an ISP to learn the identity of an anonymous Internet poster who had revealed confidential information about the company on a message board maintained by the ISP. The company provided evidence that the anonymous poster was an employee and had breached the employer's confidentiality agreement.[402] The court held that although anonymous speech on the Internet is protected, the First Amendment cannot be used as a shield to protect identity and avoid punishment.[403] In another case, the court held that anonymous members of "dissident" groups can claim privilege to quash subpoenas for their e-mail addresses and online account information under the First Amendment right of association.[404]

Section 230 of the CDA provides immunity from lawsuits for ISPs that fail to screen messages that allegedly constitute defamation, fraud, or other torts.[405] ISPs have been dismissed from lawsuits based on content supplied by third-party content suppliers. A New York court dismissed another action against Prodigy for failing to screen out defamatory e-mail and bulletin board messages that constituted libel, negligence, harassment, and the intentional infliction of emotional distress. The court held that the provider "was not liable because it had no 'participatory function' in disseminating the messages."[406]

The global trend in the law is that the ISP is not liable for third-party content. A French appellate court, however, upheld a $70,000 verdict against a French ISP for hosting anonymously posted nude photos of model Estelle Halliday.[407] The court held that the ISP had a duty to protect the rights of third parties.[408] There is cross-national variation in the potential liability of the ISP for torts or crimes committed online.

[2] Retraction Statutes

Most states have "retraction" statutes that require libel plaintiffs to seek a retraction from the defendant before filing a lawsuit. A Wisconsin appellate court held that libel on an online discussion group was not subject to the retraction requirement because the online libel was not classifiable as a "publication" for purposes of that state's retraction statute.[409] Retraction may be easier on the Internet than with print media.

---

[401] 775 A.2d 773 (N.J. Super. A.D. 2001)

[402] *Id.*

[403] *Id.*; *see also* Dendrite Int'l, Inc. v. Doe No.3, 775 A.2d 756 (N.J. Super. Ct. App. Div. 2001).

[404] Anderson v. Hale, 7 ILR (P&F) 3104 (N.D. Ill. 2001).

[405] 47 U.S.C. § 230.

[406] Microsoft Law & Corporate Affairs, Summary of Global Internet Legal Developments (for the period Jan.-Mar. 1999) 162 (Apr. 1999).

[407] *Id.* at 163.

[408] *Id.*

[409] It's in the Cards, Inc. v. Fuschetto, 535 N.W.2d 11 (Wis. Ct. App. 1995).

[3]   Defenses to Defamation

The two chief common law defenses to defamation are truth and privilege. There is no defamation unless that publication is both defamatory and false.[410] If a "defendant publishes a defamatory statement on a constitutionally privileged occasion, he can either prove truth or require the plaintiff to prove fault."[411] There is absolute immunity from defamation actions for judicial proceedings,[412] legislative proceedings,[413] executive communications,[414] communications between husband and wife,[415] for political broadcasts,[416] and where the plaintiff has given his or her consent.[417] There are a large number of other situations where there is a qualified privilege.[418] Statements that are fair comment on matters of public concern are conditionally privileged,[419] as are communications to one who may act in the public interest.[420]

A media defendant may have a "fair report" privilege to publish defamatory statements. "To ameliorate the chilling effect on the reporting of newsworthy events occasioned by the combined effect of the republication rule and truth defense, the law has long recognized a privilege for the press to publish accounts of official proceedings or reports even when these contain defamatory statements."[421] The trial court determines whether the publication of an allegedly defamatory report is privileged. Assuming a privilege is found, it is for the jury to determine whether the privilege is abused.[422] Federal courts apply a "gist" or "sting" test that defines the accuracy of a statement as being "substantially accurate if its 'gist' or 'sting' is true, that is, if it produces the same effect on the mind of the recipient which the precise truth would have produced."[423]

[B]   Internet Publicity

A company's use of the Internet to tout products and services may lead to legal liability for information that constitutes investor relations. The Securities and

---

[410] W. Page Keeton, Prosser and Keeton on Torts 839 (5th Ed. 1984); Restatement (Second) of Torts § 613, cmt. J.

[411] *Id.* at 840.

[412] *Id.* at 817.

[413] *Id.* at 820.

[414] *Id.* at 821.

[415] *Id.* at 824.

[416] *Id.*

[417] *Id.*

[418] *Id.* at 825.

[419] *Id.* at 831.

[420] *Id.* at 830.

[421] Wilson v. Slatalla, 970 F. Supp. 405, 419 (E.D. Pa. 1998).

[422] *Id.* (stating that "the trial court must then determine whether the occasion upon which the defendant published the defamatory matter gives rise to a privilege" and citing Restatement (Second) of Torts § 619(1)).

[423] *Id.*

Exchange Commission's "staff currently examines an issuer's Web site to insure that the company is complying with the prohibitions against conditioning the market."[424] An e-business needs to audit all publicity, including "routine press releases or ordinary business developments could be deemed to be 'gun-jumping' and, hence, impermissible."[425]

Negative Internet publicity campaigns by ex-employees, customers, competitors, or third parties also raise difficult legal and strategic issues. Courts will be reluctant to order expedited discovery to unveil anonymous posters because of First Amendment issues. Companies frequently claim that anonymous postings cause "irreparable injury" to their businesses.[426] Claims against web sites for knowingly or negligently encouraging or facilitating anonymous libelous postings have been unavailing.[427] Three elements are required for 47 U.S.C.S. § 230 immunity: (1) The defendant must be a provider or user of an interactive computer service, (2) the asserted claims must treat the defendant as a publisher or speaker of information, and (3) the information must be provided by another information content provider.[428] Amazon.com Inc. was found to be immune from liability for allegedly defamatory comments about an author posted by third parties on Amazon's web site.[429]

§ 5.07 PRIVACY IN CYBERSPACE

[A] The Internet as a Transparent Society

Privacy issues are critical for e-businesses, and this section discusses how the common law of privacy is being accommodated to the Internet. Most states recognize some but not necessarily all of the traditional categories of privacy.[430] Internet technologies raise new concerns about tracking individuals' activities on web sites. Increasingly, web sites and marketers use "'web bugs' to track an individual's activity on a web site and when opening, reading and forwarding an

---

[424] Jeffrey E. Lewis and Ajay K. Mehrotra, Investor Relations in the New Economy, Commerce L. Rep., Aug. 2000, at 15.

[425] Id.

[426] Jonathan Bick, Countering Bad E-Publicity Claiming Breach of Contract or Violation of Trade Secrets Can Be More Effective Than Allegations of Libel, N.J.L.J., Jan. 28, 2002.

[427] Sabbato v. Hardy, 2000 Ohio App. LEXIS 6154 (Ohio Ct. C.P. 2000) (dismissing defamation action for distributor liability under CDA § 230); Zeran v. America Online, Inc. 958 F. Supp. 1124, aff'd, 129 F.3d 327 (1997) (same).

[428] Schneider v. Amazon.com, 31 P.3d 37 (Wash. 2001) (dismissing defamation action brought by author of book for negative reviews on Amazon.com's web site).

[429] Id.

[430] Dobbs, supra note 25, at 1197.

e-mail."[431] Web bugs are programmed to collect and analyze data about visitors to sites.[432] Although there is no case law on point, it is arguable that web bugs violate the common law right of privacy of users. Internet users may be unable to pursue invasion of seclusion claims because the Internet is a public place. "With regard to databases, much information collection and use occurs in public, and indeed, many parts of cyberspace may well be considered public places."[433]

Under the common law, "[o]ne who intentionally intrudes, physically or otherwise, upon the solitude or seclusion of another or his private affairs or concerns, is subject to liability to the other for invasion of his privacy, if the intrusion would be highly offensive to a reasonable person."[434] The essence of privacy was first defined as "right to be left alone."[435] Four kinds of interests are protected by a person's right to privacy: (1) unreasonable intrusions upon the seclusion of another; (2) appropriation of the other's name or likeness; (3) unreasonable publicity given to the other's private life; or (4) publicity that unreasonably places the other in a false light before the public.[436]

Tort law is traditionally state law, and therefore online activities may trigger privacy-based torts in any one of 50-plus jurisdictions. Whether an individual state constitutional right to privacy has been violated depends on whether the individual had a reasonable expectation of privacy.[437] The reasonable expectation of pri-

---

[431] Marc S. Roth and Kathleen Fay, Playing "Hide and Seek" with Web Bugs, 10 e-Commerce 6 (Feb. 2001).

[432] "A 'web bug' is typically a text file or graphic embedded in a web page or in an e-mail's HTML code. Also known in the industry as 'invisible GIFs,' 'clear GIFs' or '1-by-1 pixels,' web bugs are efficient to use because they take up little space and are virtually invisible. Web bugs typically use JavaScript, a programming language embedded in the HTML text, to collect information. Among the types of information typically collected by web bugs are the IP address of the computer that the web bug is being sent to, the URL of the page the web bug comes from, and the time it was viewed. Similarly, a web bug embedded in an HTML e-mail enables the text to be secretly returned to its original sender every time the e-mail (containing the bug) is forwarded to other recipients." *Id.*

[433] Daniel J. Sololove, Privacy and Power: Computer Databases and Metaphors for Information Privacy, 53 Stanford L. Rev.1393 (2001).

[434] Restatement (Second) of Torts, § 652B. Samuel D. Warren and Louis D. Brandeis first articulated the tort of invasion of privacy in an 1890 Harvard Law Review article. Samuel D. Warren & Louis D. Brandeis, The Right to Privacy, 4 Harv. L. Rev. 193 (1890).

[435] Judge Thomas Cooley coined the phrase "the right to be left alone." W. Page Keeton et al., Prosser and Keeton on Torts § 117, at 849 (5th ed. 1984).

[436] Restatement (Second) of Torts § 652A (1965) (stating that the right of privacy is invaded by (a) unreasonable intrusion upon the seclusion of another . . . (b) or appropriation of another's name or likeness; or (c) unreasonable publicity given to the other's private life . . . or (d) publicity that unreasonably places the other in a false light before the public").

[437] Alarcon v. Murphy, 201 Cal. App. 3d 1 (1988); *see also* Champion v. State of Georgia, 7 ILR (P&F) 613 (Ga. Super. Ct. 2001) (holding that publishing attorneys' disciplinary actions on a web site does not constitute a violation of privacy rights, due process, or equal protection where the information is part of the public record); Mack v. State Bar of Cal., 112 Cal. Rptr. 2d 341 (Cal. App. Ct. 2001) (same).

vacy varies depending on the setting.[438] In the absence of a reasonable expectation of privacy, there is no cause of action for either the common law invasion of privacy or the constitutional right to privacy.[439]

States vary in their law of privacy. Virginia law, for example, does not recognize the tort of invasion of privacy, in any form, whether intrusion upon seclusion or disclosure of private facts.[440] A Washington state appellate court ruled that the nature of e-mail and ICQ chatting implies consent to recording messages, and therefore such acts of recording do not violate privacy laws.[441] The majority of the states, however, follow the Restatement (Second) of Torts approach to invasion of privacy.

Selling, transferring, retransmitting, and manipulating data is the life-blood of e-commerce. Cookies, for instance, are text files saved "in Netscape Communicator or Microsoft Internet Explorer (the major browsers) directory or folder and stored in RAM while your browser is running."[442] Cookies permit companies to trace online activity of any online visitor, as well as of its customers. The latest device for tracking computer users without their knowledge is the use of "web bugs."[443] Computer users who are able to block cookies do not have the same ability to disable web bugs.[444]

Privacy torts protect dignitary interests as well as property rights.[445] The FTC generally endorses a self-regulation approach to online privacy. The FTC's rules implementing the Children's Online Privacy Protection Act (COPPA) largely defer to industry standards. Courts will sometimes defer to privacy standards developed by industry groups such as the Internet Alliance Privacy Guidelines. Another source of guidance for self-regulatory guidelines is the Better Business Bureau's Sample Privacy Notice and the Direct Marketing Association's "Marketing Online Privacy Principles and Guidance." The privacy policies of America Online, eBay, and CompuServe posted on their respective web sites are another source of information on how the industry protects personal information.

---

[438] Private employees, for example, have no reasonable expectation of privacy in company-owned computer systems. *See, e.g.,* Smyth v. Pillsbury Co., 914 F. Supp. 97 (E.D. Pa. 1996) (holding that an employee has no reasonable expectation of privacy in internal e-mail). A military officer, however, was held to have a reasonable expectation of privacy in his private AOL account. United States v. Maxwell, 45 M.J. 406, 1996 C.A.A.F. 116 (1996).

[439] Bourke v. Nissan Motor Co., No. B068705 (Cal. Ct. App. July 26, 1993) (holding that an employee had no reasonable expectation of privacy because of Nissan's monitoring of e-mail messages).

[440] Jessup-Morgan v. AOL, Inc., 20 F. Supp. 2d 1105 (E.D. Mich. 1998) (citing Brown v. American Broad. Co., Inc., 704 F.2d 1296, 1302-03 (4th Cir. 1983)).

[441] State of Wash. v. Townsend, 7 ILR (P&F) 3058 (Wash. Ct. App. 2001).

[442] Arent Fox Alert, FTC Enforces Made in USA Standard Against Six Major Corporations (visited Aug. 31, 1999), http://www.arentfox.com/alerts/ftc_made_in_usa_2-4-1999.html.

[443] *See supra* note 432.

[444] Arent Fox Alert, FTC Enforces Made in USA Standard Against Six Major Corporations (visited Aug. 31, 1999), http://www.arentfox.com/alerts/ftc_made_in_usa_2-4-1999.html.

[445] Dobbs, *surpra* note 25, at 1198.

[B] Privacy Torts

[1] Unreasonable Intrusion upon Seclusion

There are two elements to an unreasonable intrusion upon seclusion action: (1) an intentional intrusion, physically or otherwise, on another's solitude, seclusion, or private affairs or concerns, which (2) would be highly offensive to a reasonable person.[446] The rise of the Internet and of e-mail threatens privacy today just as the invention of the telephone and of photography did at the beginning of the twentieth century. A company may be liable for the tort of intrusion on a plaintiff's seclusion or solitude into private affairs if it misuses information collected on corporate web sites. The Ninth Circuit recently commented on the new forms of electronic surveillance that have evolved:

> Something as commonplace as furnishing our credit card number or bank account number puts each of us at risk. Moreover, when we employ electronic methods of communication, we often leave electronic "fingerprints" that can be traced back to us. Whether we are surveilled by our government, by criminals or by our neighbors, it is fair to say never has our ability to shield our affairs from prying eyes been at such low ebb.[447]

Corporate employees have no reasonable expectation of privacy against their employers' monitoring of their e-mails.[448] The courts have ruled that e-mail systems are company-owned and that employees will not have a reasonable expectation of privacy as to stored messages.[449] In *McClaren v. Microsoft*,[450] an employee of Microsoft was suspended pending an investigation of sexual harassment. McClaren was terminated, and he then filed suit against the company, alleging invasion of privacy. The plaintiff argued that Microsoft had invaded his privacy by "breaking into" some of his personal folders maintained on his office computer. The court held that the e-mail messages contained on the company computer were not McClaren's personal property, "but were merely an inherent part of the office environment."[451]

The *McClaren* court held that the plaintiff had no reasonable expectation of privacy in the content of the e-mail messages. Even if he had some reasonable expectation of privacy, Microsoft's accessing of his e-mail messages was relevant

---

[446] Valenzuela v. Aquino, 853 S.W.2d 512, 513 (Tex. 1993).

[447] Bernstein v. Justice Dept., No. 97-16686, LEXIS 4214, 4242 (9th Cir., May 6, 1999).

[448] Chapter Nine discusses the issue of workplace privacy in detail. Corporate monitoring of e-mail has been upheld by numerous cases. *See, e.g.*, Bourke v. Nissan Motor Co., No. YC003979 (Cal. Sup. Ct., Los Angeles Cty. 1991) (upholding right of company's systems administrator to read employees' e-mail and to terminate employees based on the contents of e-mails that criticized supervisor); Shoars v. Epson Am., Inc., No. YC003979 (Cal. Sup. Ct., Los Angeles Cty., 1989).

[449] *See, e.g.*, "Privacy Claim Rejected in Employer Access to E-Mail Files," 16 Comp. & Online Litig. Rep. 9 (June 15, 1999).

[450] No. 05-97-00824-CV (Ct. App., 5th Dist. Tex., May 28, 1999).

[451] *Id.*

to its sexual harassment investigation. The court held that the company's interest in preventing inappropriate and unprofessional comments outweighed the plaintiff's claimed privacy interest in those communications.[452]

Independent contractors and other agents are not automatically given privacy rights. In *Fraser v. Nationwide Mutual Insurance Co.,*[453] the court found that where a message was stored after the recipient had read it and the transmission was complete, there was no violation of the Storage Communications Act or the Wiretap Act, which both prohibit unauthorized access to electronic communication in the process of transmission. In this case the plaintiff argued that he was not an employee but an independent contractor and therefore that defendant wrongfully retrieved the contents of an e-mail he had sent to another agent that gave the company cause to terminate his contract.[454]

[2] Tort of Misappropriation

The tort of misappropriation is the taking of another's name or likeness; this was the first form of invasion of privacy recognized by courts.[455] There have been several cases where plaintiffs have sued for misappropriation based on their likenesses appearing on the Internet.

A New York court rejected claims for misappropriation and invasion of privacy[456] where the defendant published a photograph of Howard Stern's bare buttocks on a computer bulletin board. Howard Stern was then running as a candidate for governor of New York. Stern claimed that the use of his name and photograph was a commercial misappropriation. The court rejected this claim, finding the online network to be analogous to a bookstore rather than to a publisher. The court found that the defendant's use of Stern's photograph was incident to a publication that concerned the public interest. The court held that the photograph and likeness of Stern was sufficiently newsworthy and refused to enjoin its publication.

In *NBA v. Motorola,*[457] the National Basketball Association (NBA) sued Motorola, charging the company with misappropriation for offering a pager connected to a web site that would continuously update sports scores as NBA games were being played. Although the court held that copyright law did not preempt the tort of misappropriation claim, it found that reporting scores on Motorola's web site did not constitute the tort of misappropriation.[458]

---

[452] The court cited Smyth v. Pillsbury Co., 914 F. Supp. 97, 101 (E.D. Pa. 1996) in support of its holding that the plaintiff had no reasonable expectation of privacy in e-mail messages stored on a company computer.

[453] 135 F Supp. 2d 623 (E.D. Pa. 2001).

[454] *Id.*

[455] W. Page Keeton, Prosser and Keeton on Torts, at 863.

[456] Stern v. Delphi Internet Servs. Corp., 626 N.Y.S.2d 694 (Sup. Ct. 1995).

[457] 105 F.3d 841 (2d Cir. 1997).

[458] *Id.*

[3] Right of Publicity

The private life of another is invaded if the matter "(1) would be highly offensive to a reasonable person and (2) not of legitimate concern to the public."[459] The *right of publicity* gives a person a right to enjoin an unauthorized use of his or her name or likeness. A federal court reduced a punitive damages award from $850,000 to $350,000 in a right of publicity case against a tabloid for the unauthorized use of a photograph in its print magazine.[460] A celebrity has a property right to "control the exploitation of his or her persona."[461] An online company that uses photographs of any famous entertainment figure needs to obtain rights to use the images or risk exposure to a tort lawsuit. Actress Pamela Anderson Lee and musician Brett Michaels successfully enjoined an adult entertainment web site from displaying images of them engaged in sexual intercourse on the grounds that the publication of the tape invaded their right of publicity under California law.[462]

Summary judgment and an injunction were entered against the operators of a web site containing images of the comedy team The Three Stooges.[463] The web site violated the right of publicity held by the estate of the actors who had played The Three Stooges.

[4] False Light

The fourth privacy-based tort is "publicity which places the plaintiff in a false light in the public eye." The false light in which the other is placed must be highly offensive to a reasonable person. False light is not a strict liability tort, and the actor must have knowledge of or have acted in reckless disregard as to the falsity of the publicized matter and the false light in which the plaintiff was placed.[464]

"The essence of a false light privacy claim is that the matter published concerning the plaintiff (1) is not true . . . and (2) is such a major misrepresentation of his character, history, activities or beliefs that serious offense may reasonably be expected to be taken by a reasonable man in his position."[465] The Restatement (Second) of Torts § 652E (1977) provides:

---

[459] Restatement (Second) of Torts § 652(d) (1979).

[460] Mitchell v. Globe International Publications Co., 817 F. Supp. 72 (E.D. Ark. 1993) (applying Arkansas law).

[461] Michael Scott, Internet and Technology Law Desk Reference 403 (1999).

[462] Michaels v. Internet Entertainment Groups, Inc., 5 F. Supp. 2d 823, 841-842 (C.D. Cal. 1998) (ruling that broadcast of videotape recording of sexual relations between famous actress and rock star not a matter of legitimate public concern).

[463] Comedy III Productions, Inc., v. Class Publications, Inc., 95 Civ. 5552 (SS), 1996 U.S. Dist. LEXIS 5710 (S.D.N.Y. Apr. 30, 1996).

[464] *See, e.g.,* McCormick v. Oklahoma Pub. Co., 613 P.2d 737, 740 (Okla. 1980).

[465] Matos v. American Fed'n of State, 2001 Conn. Super. LEXIS 2419 (Conn. Super. Ct. Aug. 13, 2001).

One who gives publicity to a matter concerning another that places the other before the public in a false light is subject to liability to the other for invasion of his privacy, if

(a) the false light in which the other was placed would be highly offensive to a reasonable person, and

(b) the actor had knowledge of or acted in reckless disregard as to the falsity of the publicized matter and the false light in which the other would be placed.[466]

Zeran v. Diamond Broadcasting, Inc.,[467] arose from a radio station's broadcast in the immediate aftermath of the bombing of the Alfred P. Murrah Federal Building in downtown Oklahoma City. Soon after the bombing, a false posting appeared on an Internet bulletin board announcing the availability for sale of "Naughty Oklahoma T-Shirts" bearing offensive slogans. The posting was made by someone using the screen name "Ken ZZ03" and indicated that the shirts could be ordered by telephone.[468] The number provided was the plaintiff Kenneth Zeran's business.[469] A radio station disc jockey "then went on air, discussing the posting, reading the slogans, and reading Plaintiff's telephone number, and encouraging listeners to call,"[470] as a result of which Zeran "received approximately 80 angry, obscenity-laced calls from the Oklahoma City area, including death threats."[471] The plaintiff filed suit against the station, including a claim of false light invasion of privacy.[472] The Tenth Circuit affirmed summary judgment for the station on all claims, finding that Zeran failed to prove that the radio station employees "either knew the postings were fictitious or acted recklessly, as that term is defined by the controlling authorities"[473] and agreeing with the district court that the radio station employees' reading of the e-mail hoax on air "did not satisfy the level of culpability necessary to impose liability" for false light privacy.[474]

[C] Statutory Regulation of Privacy

The U.S. Constitution does not explicitly grant a right to privacy. "What a person knowingly exposes to the public, even in his own home or office, is not a

---

[466] Restatement (Second) Torts, § 652E (1965).

[467] 203 F.3d 714 (10th Cir. 2000).

[468] *Id.*

[469] *Id.*

[470] *Id.* at 718.

[471] *Id.*

[472] *Id.*

[473] *Id.* at 719.

[474] *Id.* (opining that the radio station was "extremely negligent and violated standards of professional conduct when hosting the Shannon and Spinozi Show on May 1, 1995," but did not manifest the recklessness necessary to impose liability for false light privacy).

subject of Fourth Amendment protection."[475] The United States Supreme Court has, instead, recognized zones of privacy.[476] Public employees may sometimes enjoy a reasonable expectation of privacy in the workplace from searches by an employer.[477] The constitutional right to privacy protects against intrusions by the government, however, not by private corporations.[478] Corporations that transmit information about a person's identity may face liability for the common law tort of invasion of privacy.

[D]   EU Directive on Protection of Personal Data

Chapter Eight on Global E-Business Legal Issues has a more complete discussion of strategic planning issues from the EU Directive on Protection of Personal Data. The European Union Directive on Protection of Personal Data, adopted on October 24, 1995, imposes restrictions on the transfer of "personal data."[479] A "profile" is "a hierarchical collection of personal profile information . . . describing an end user."[480] The concept of informed consent is drawn from the law of medical malpractice, where a patient must consent to undergoing a procedure after receiving information on risks and alternative procedures. "A party requesting an end user's profile must receive the informed consent of the source(s) before collecting and using their information in any manner."[481] Electronic agents may manage the end user profile as well as manage profiles.

European Union Member States were required to harmonize their domestic laws with the Directive by October 23, 1998. The EU Directive was formally adopted by European Commission's Council of Ministers "to guarantee free movement of personal data."[482] Article 25 prohibits the transfer of "personal data" from EU member states to a country lacking "an adequate level of protection" for such data.[483] Article 26 provides exceptions to Article 25 that would allow the transfer to countries lacking an adequate level of protection in delimited circum-

---

[475] Katz v. United States, 389 U.S. 347, 351 (1967).

[476] *See, e.g.,* Roe v. Wade, 410 U.S. 113, 152-53 (1973) (recognizing privacy right in decision to seek an abortion); Griswold v. Connecticut, 381 U.S. 479, 485-86 (1965) (recognizing privacy right in seeking information on contraception).

[477] O'Connor v. Ortega, 480 U.S. 709 (1987).

[478] Katz v. United States, 389 U.S. 347, 360 (1967) (stating that "[t]he Fourth Amendment cannot be translated into a general constitutional right to privacy. That Amendment protects individual privacy concerns against certain kinds of governmental intrusion, but its protections go further, and often have nothing to do with privacy at all.").

[479] The European Union Directive of 95/46/EC on the protection of individuals with regard to the processing of personal data and the free movement of such data, 1995 O.J. (L. 28(1)) 31.

[480] *Id.*

[481] *Id.*

[482] European Commission Press Release: IP/95/822, July 25, 1995, "Council Definitively Adopts Directive on Protection of Personal Data" (visited June 18, 1999), http://www.privacy.org/pli/intl_ors/ec/dp_EC_press_release.txt.

[483] *Id.,* art. 25, 1995 O.J. (L28(1)) at 45-46.

stances.[484] The free movement of data is important to the banking, insurance, and financial services industries.

The aim of the EU Directive is to afford any person whose personal information is transmitted an equivalent level of protection irrespective of the member state transmitting or processing the data. The EU Directive employs general standards, such as "fundamental fairness," rather than bright-line rules in determining compliance. Companies can sell advertising based on the content of sites without notice or disclosure to consumers. The use of electronic identifiers that enhance the ability of web sites to collect information and track users may violate the European Commission Directive on Protection of Personal Data (EU Directive).[485]

At minimum, web site visitors must be given the option of providing personal information or not. The EU Directive consists of legal grounds for processing personal data. The Directive seeks a "balance between the legitimate interests of the people controlling the data and the people on whom data is held" or data subjects.[486] Sensitive data "on an individual's ethnic or racial origin, political or religious beliefs, trade union membership or data concerning health or sexual life" may only be processed with the individual's consent.[487]

European Union Member States "endorse appropriate exemptions and derogation . . . which strike a balance between guaranteeing freedom of expression while protecting the individual's right to privacy."[488] New technologies, such as the World Wide Web Consortium's Platform for Privacy Preferences (P3P), may provide technical fixes for the problem of user profiling. In the interim, a company should give complete disclosure as to what information is collected and what is done with that information. Many web site policies give individual users an opportunity to visit a site without collecting personal information. Industry groups are in the process of developing industry standards for the exchange of profile information. One proposal is to develop industry standards for profile exchanges and a mechanism for service provider control of the profiling of web site visitors.[489]

The core guiding principle for open profiling is "control by source, informed consent, and value exchange."[490] The EU Directive applies to the sale or other transfer of data from country to country, whereas the FTC may "prosecute any inquiry necessary to its duties in any part of the United States."[491] The FTC is the agency that scrutinizes the business practices that impact the exchange of personal

---

[484] The Directive permits data transfers that lack "adequate protection" where the private individual consents to the transfer. *Id.,* art. 26(2), 1995 O.J. (L28(1)) at 46.

[485] Most information technology companies are opposed to the European privacy directive. *See, e.g.,* Benjamin Thorner, Privacy on the Internet (visited July 20, 1999), http://www.brobeck.com/docs/98featurs/0498.htm.

[486] *Id.*

[487] *Id.*

[488] *Id.*

[489] Proposal for an Open Profiling Standard Document Version 1.0 (June 2, 1997) (visited June 18, 1999), http://developr.netscape.com/ops/proposal.html.

[490] *Id.*

[491] 15 U.S.C. § 43 (1995).

data. A company will need to comply with FTC regulations and will need to follow the EU Directive if it handles data from member countries.[492]

In July 2000, the European Parliament rejected the "safe harbor" provisions approved by the United States Department of Commerce and the European Commission. The United States and the European Union completed negotiations over what steps the United States must take to protect personal data originating in European Union countries. The finalized safe harbor provision creates a presumption that the online company adequately protects data privacy. In the absence of a safe harbor, there is a possibility that online companies will have disruptions in transborder data flows to and from European Union countries. The key terms in the safe harbor provision are "notice, choice, onward transfer, security, data integrity, access, and enforcement."[493] The negotiated safe harbor is based on industry self-management where companies will "self-certify their adherence to the privacy principles."[494] The safe harbor makes companies's self-certification practices subject to FTC regulation.[495]

§ 5.08 NEGLIGENCE IN CYBERSPACE

[A] Introduction

Online businesses face a host of new risks for negligent causes of action. "What happens if an employee accidentally transmits a computer virus to a customer and the customer sues you for compensation?"[496] Negligence is conduct where there is an unreasonable risk or danger of injury. The Restatement (Second) of Torts takes the view that any invasion of a legally protected interest, whether based in negligence, strict liability, or intentional misconduct, can be punished under tort law. Torts arising out of the misuse of computer systems are likely to be based on intentional torts rather than negligence. *Negligence* is defined as a departure from the conduct expected of a reasonably prudent person under like circumstances. Companies may create an "unreasonable risk of harm" in cyberspace by engaging in conduct that does not meet industry standards or the standard of exercising reasonable care in the circumstances.

---

[492] TRUSTe Press Release, Survey Reveals Consumer Fear of Privacy Infringement Inhibits Growth of Electronic Commerce (visited July 17, 1999), http://www.truste.org/press/article003.html.

[493] Department of Commerce, Department of Commerce Requests Comments on Data Privacy Principles (Apr. 27, 1999).

[494] The United States Mission to the European Union, Brussels, Belgium, Joint Report on Data Protection Dialogue to the EU/US Summit, July 21, 1999 (visited Feb. 27, 2000), http://www.useu.be/SUMMIT/dataprotect0699.html. *See also* Walter F. Kitchenman, European Privacy Setback May Be Opportunity, ABA Banking J. Sept. 2000 at 127 (describing European Parliament's rejection of U.S. safe harbor for personal data).

[495] *Id.*

[496] Tony Blyfield, "British Expert Offers Advice on How to Guard Against Legal Risks," Daily Mail (Nov. 5, 2000), at 1.

A company's duty to consumers and others may stem from its online business activities. An online company may, for example, be found negligent for failing to screen or train key personnel. A company with outdated or inadequate computer security may be liable for damages caused by a virus, hacker, or third-party criminal.[497] Third parties may pursue a negligence action against a company that fails to protect confidential information, such as trade secrets. Negligence claims against financial institutions may be based upon the claim that a financial institution does not comply with the "five basic security requirements: identification and authentication; privacy and confidentiality; information integrity; system availability, reliability, and performance; and non-repudiation."[498] Another possible cause of action is a web site's duty of system availability, reliability, and performance.[499]

Negligence will frequently depend on the particular cyber risks faced by the online business and the available measures to reduce the radius of the risk. It is possible that a high-profile web site shut down by a distributed denial of service (DDOS) attack could have an action against a computer consultant or computer seller whose inadequate security permitted hackers to launch the attacks. In addition, there is potential liability for a DDOS attack by the owners of the computer systems (zombies) whose negligent security permitted hackers to use it as an instrumentality for a coordinated attack.[500] An online bank may have a duty to develop an infrastructure that is available, reliable, and performs adequately.[501] A financial institution's duty of care will be based on its compliance with industry standard technology solutions to meet its duty to maintain a secure web site.[502] Chapter Three on Internet Security discussed a number of vulnerabilities which could be the basis of a negligence claim. Financial institutions likely have a duty to remediate known organizational vulnerabilities based upon problems associated with weak passwords, backups misconfiguration, and social engineering to gain another's trust.[503]

In addition, financial institutions face heightened cyber risks of internal corruption, illegal money laundering, hackers, and the attempts of Internet competitor to steal confidential information.[504] Financial institutions also face the known risks of identity theft, impostor web sites, viruses, data destruction, and the invasion of privacy.[505] In *James v. Meow Media, Inc.,*[506] the plaintiffs sued a defendant

---

[497] Mark Stefik and Alex Silverman, The Bit and the Pendulum: Balancing the Interests of Stakeholders in Digital Publishing 16 Computer Law. 1 (Jan. 1999).

[498] Glenda Barnes, Cyber Risks and Financial Institutions, in American Bar Association et al., Fidelity Coverage in the Age of E-Commerce (Jan. 26, 2001), at 1.

[499] *Id.* at 2.

[500] Michael R. Overly, Downstream Liability, Info. Security, Sept. 2001, at 49.

[501] *Id.*

[502] *Id.* (discussing eight types of technology to meet security requirements: encryption, public and secret key, digital signatures, certificates and certificate authorities, certificate revocation lists, Kerebros, biometrics, and account-based digital signatures (ABDS)).

[503] Barnes, *supra* note 498 at 8-9.

[504] *Id.*

[505] *Id.* at 10-11.

[506] 90 F. Supp. 2d 798 (W.D. Ky. 2000) (dismissing actions based on negligence, strict liability, and RICO violations).

for producing a movie, video, and Internet materials that allegedly played a role in causing a classmate to murder his classmates in a highly publicized Kentucky school shooting.[507] The court dismissed the negligence claim on the grounds that the defendants owed no legal duty of care since the killer's actions were unforeseeable. The court also ruled that the killer's intervening acts constituted a superseding cause absolving defendants of liability.[508]

A company may have a duty of special responsibility to safeguard the confidential or proprietary data on its computer system. A hospital has a duty not to disclose treatment records and will be liable if it does not prevent patient information from being disclosed to third parties. A company has a duty to use reasonable care in protecting the confidential information of trading partners, customers, and web site visitors.[509] A company is negligently engaging in conduct if the company does not exercise reasonable care under all the circumstances.

Industry standards as required by state statutes or federal laws may set the standard of care. It is customary to set the standard of care based on the burden of precaution measured against the radius of the risk. Judge Learned Hand's algebraic formulation of the concept of reasonable care was articulated in *United States v. Carroll Towing Co.*[510] Judge Hand's risk/utility formula of whether the burden of precaution was less than the probability and extent of damages (B < P × L) was applied to a case regarding a breakaway barge:

> Since there are occasions when every vessel will break from her moorings, and since, if she does, she becomes a menace to those about her, the owner's duty, as in other similar situations, to provide against resulting injuries is a function of three variables: (1) the probability that she will break away; (2) the gravity of the resulting injury, if she does; and (3) the burden of adequate precautions. Possibly it serves to bring this notion into relief to state it in algebraic terms: if the probability be called P; the injury, L; and the burden, B; liability depends upon whether B is less than L multiplied by P: i.e. whether $B < PL$.[511]

Learned Hand's formula is applicable to negligence in Internet transactions as well. Generally, a corporation will be held negligent in Internet transactions where its failure to use due care results in a foreseeable security breach. A company that has a duty to protect the confidentiality of personal information may be negligent under Judge Hand's risk/utility formula. The key question is whether the cost of

---

[507] *Id.* at 800.

[508] *Id.* at 809.

[509] *See* Holtz v. J.J.B. Hilliard W.L. Lyons, Inc., 185 F.3d 732, 744 (7th Cir. 1999) (holding that where there is a special relationship between the parties, each party has a duty to act in reasonable manner).

[510] United States v. Carroll Towing Co., 159 F.2d 169 (2d Cir. 1947).

[511] *Id.* at 171.

precaution is warranted, that is, whether the cost is less than the probability of harm multiplied by the gravity of the resulting injuries.[512]

The Learned Hand test excuses a corporation from taking precautionary measures when the costs of such measures are greater than the potential loss. Accident avoidance on the Internet may also be evaluated by comparing the radius of the risk to the cost of prevention.[513] The Learned Hand formula may be difficult to apply in cyberspace, where there is little empirical data on the potential for injury. No reliable data exists on basic facts such as the number of attacks by hackers or financial losses due to the misappropriation of trade secrets. Similarly, there is little available data on the probability of harm, severity of harm, or the cost of instituting precautions to protect the integrity of online commercial transactions. Efficiency, however, is the starting point for establishing what "ought to be done" by the prudent company in cyberspace. An employer will likely be found negligent where it does not implement reasonable information security devices to protect its information assets.

[B] Setting the Standard of Care

Customary or industry standards are frequently used to calibrate reasonable care. A threshold question for setting the standard of care for the Internet is to examine customs or industry practices. Judge Hand held that compliance with an industry standard or custom may set the floor but not the ceiling of due care.[514] There may be circumstances, however, where a defendant is negligent despite adhering to weak or undeveloped industry practices.

Courts vary in determining what legal significance conformity with custom has in determining the standard of care. At a minimum, evidence of a company's conformity to custom is a factor taken into account in determining breach. Compliance with custom sets the floor but not the ceiling of due care.

[1] Industry Standard-Setting

A violation of a well-accepted industry or other safety standard may be a sufficient basis for a finding of negligence. The infrastructure for Internet commerce is based on technical standards governing modems or configured telephone connections. Industry groups formulate new specifications for network access. Multimedia groups of the telecommunications industry are developing a "low-cost gateway device that will pass voice, video, fax, and data traffic between conventional telephone networks and packet-based data networks such as the Internet."[515]

---

[512] Car manufacturers, for example, do not have an obligation to place foam rubber throughout the passenger compartment or run automobiles on tracks, even though such precautions may reduce the cost of avoidable injuries.

[513] See generally Guido Calabresi, The Cost of Accidents (1961).

[514] The T.J. Hooper, 60 F.2d 737 (1932).

[515] Microsoft Law & Corporate Affairs, Summary of Global Internet Legal Developments 136 (Jan. 1999).

The United Kingdom's Federation of the Electronics Industry organized the "Cards UK 98" conference to help formulate standards for smart card technology and electronic commerce.[516] In Denmark, for example, a self-regulating governing body was formed to police abuses, such as domain name cybersquatting, spamming, and fraud in electronic commerce.[517]

A difficult issue to determine is which industry's standard is applicable to cyberspace. The leading producers of cable modems in Europe, for example, observe a different standard for dealing with digital video broadcasting and audio broadcasting than do procedures of the recently adopted U.S. cable modem standards.[518] Industry standards are relatively undeveloped for Internet businesses. It may be premature to turn to industry standards in many areas where there is no consensus as to custom or standard.[519]

When the issue is negligence in conducting online transactions, compliance or lack of compliance with industry standards is often considered to be probative evidence. The plaintiff's violation of an Internet industry standard may be evidence of negligence. The tort doctrine of avoidable consequences denies the recovery of damages that could have been avoided by the plaintiff's reasonable care.[520] The rule of avoidable consequences comes into play in assessing implementation of industry standards. The Direct Marketing Association (DMA), for example, adopted a privacy policy to protect consumers. The Electronic Privacy Information Center (EPIC) found that "only a handful" of the DMA members followed their own industry-set standards.[521]

[2] Statutory Standard of Care

In general, one is held to the standard of the ordinary person in the circumstances. A plaintiff may be able to rely on the violation of a statute or ordinance as evidence of negligence if (1) the duty created by the statute was intended to protect a class of persons including the plaintiff[522] and (2) the violation of the statute was causally connected to the injury. In many cases, statutes are passed without explicitly providing for civil remedies for private litigants. Jurisdictions differ in

---

[516] *Id.* at 106.

[517] *Id.* at 142.

[518] *Id.* at 138.

[519] "The Internet computer industry is still developing standards for conduct, thus providing the courts little guidance. Software providers, ISPs, and other members of the World Web Consortium and Internet Engineering Task Force have not yet agreed to standards for network security." Robin A. Brooks, Deterring the Spread of Viruses Online: Can Tort Law Tighten the "Net"? 17 Rev. Litig. 343, 357 (1998).

[520] W. Page Keeton, Prosser and Keaton on Torts § 65, at 458.

[521] Marc Rotenberg, Federal Legislation, Strict Enforcement Will Protect People, USA Today (July 7, 1998) at 12A.

[522] Restatement (Second) of Torts § 286 requires proof that the statute protect a class of persons that includes the one whose interest was invaded, protects the particular interest invaded, and protects the interests against the kind of harm that resulted from the violation.

the legal significance given a violation of a statute. In some jurisdictions, the violation of a statute is only some evidence of negligence. In other jurisdictions, an unexcused violation of a statute is negligence *per se* as to the consequences that the statute was designed to prevent. In some jurisdictions, the violation of a criminal statute may be evidence of negligence at least for all consequences that the statute was intended to prevent.[523]

It is quite likely that legislatures will begin to set statutory standards of care for certain Internet activities. A few jurisdictions, for example, require lawyers to encrypt e-mail messages to clients or to obtain the consent of their clients to use unencrypted messages. There are hundreds of examples of legislators setting the standard of care under traditional tort law. When there is a statutory standard of care, plaintiffs may prove negligence by showing (1) that they are members of the class of persons protected by the statute, (2) that the statute protects against the particular interest invaded, and (3) that they suffered the particular harm or hazard envisioned by the statute.[524]

The promulgation of statutory or administrative standards of care might take the form of state standards as to encryption, digital signatures, and other information security devices. In the interests of promoting the development of e-commerce, the federal or state government may adapt commercial-sector standards. The National Computer Security Center of the National Security Agency (NSA) administers the process for the C2 level of computer security certification.[525]

Commercial-sector security standards are modeled after government-published standards. With the rise of statutory standards of care, a wide variance exists on its evidentiary status. Some jurisdictions provide that the violation of a statutory rule is only some evidence of negligence in determining whether a defendant exercised due care in the circumstances. Other jurisdictions provide that an unexcused violation of a statute that results in harm to the class protected by the statute is negligence *per se* as to the consequences that the statute is designed to prevent. The probative value of a statute violation needs to be uniformly treated across states and nations connected to the Internet.

[3] Professional Standard of Care

Professionals such as lawyers, doctors, architects, engineers, and others may have a higher standard of care when it comes to activities on the Internet.[526] It is

---

[523] Falvey v. Hamelburg, 347 Mass. 430 (1964).

[524] Restatement (Second) of Torts § 286 (1965).

[525] *De facto* evaluation of security products vis-à-vis government standards is already occurring. Novell, Inc., formally applied for federal certification for their general-purpose network operating system. According to a research director: "A C2 rating . . . has become a standard for commercial businesses as well as government and military organizations. Customers are using it as a differentiator when making product purchasing decisions." NetWare 4 Enters Final Phase of C2 Evaluation: On Track to Receive First Client-Server Network Rating, PR Newswire (Aug. 28, 1995) (statement of John Pescatore).

[526] *See* Steiner Corp. v. Johnson & Higgins of Cal., 135 F.3d 684, 688 (10th Cir. 1998) (holding that a professional that held himself out as a professional was liable for the negligent performance

quite likely that information security professionals will be held to a higher professional standard of care, similar to those currently imposed on doctors, lawyers, accountants, and so on. Courts, however, have been slow to recognize the concept of computer malpractice.[527] Unlike law or medicine, there is no licensing body or minimal educational requirements for computer technicians. There are only optional certification examinations provided by various vendors that may be useful in setting the standard of care.[528]

Courts have been slow to hold that computer consultants are professionals who, when they violate the standard of care applicable to their profession, are subject to a malpractice action. In *Heidtman Steel Products v. Compuware Corp.*,[529] a Michigan court declined to apply a malpractice standard to computer professionals. The court noted: "Not every worker is a professional for malpractice purposes."[530] The court held that Michigan did not recognize the plaintiff's professional malpractice claim and claim for breach of an implied duty of good faith and fair dealings. The court observed that malpractice is a cause of action reserved for traditional professionals:

> Real estate agencies are no more professions than any other business agencies. A commission merchant or an agent for the sale of any particular kind of personal property acts in an analogous capacity. Anyone can assume and lay down such business at pleasure, and anyone can conduct it in his own way, on such terms and conditions as he sees fit to adopt. There is nothing in our laws which would enable any court to draw a line between such business agencies. They are not classed as professions by popular usage or by law.[531]

[C]   Premises Liability

A property owner who invites the public onto his property for business purposes is potentially liable if those invitees are harmed by negligent or accidental attacks by third parties. Courts will impose liability if the risk of harm to visitors

---

of duties undertaken); *In re* Daisy Sys. Corp, 97 F.3d 1171, 1175 (9th Cir. 1996) (holding that a duty of professional care required the plaintiff to show that the defendant should have used such skill, prudence, and diligence as other members of his or her profession commonly possessed and exercised); *see also* Hospital Computer Sys., Inc. v. The Staten Island Hosp., 788 F. Supp. 1351, 1361 (D.N.J. 1997); Heath v. Swift Wings, Inc., 252 S.E.2d 526, 529 (N.C. Ct. App. 1979).

[527] Thomas G. Wolpert, Product Liability and Software Implicated in Personal Injury, 60 Def. Couns. J. 519, 521 (1993).

[528] Cisco, for example, offers certification courses lasting four or nine weeks for designing and maintaining computer networks. *See* Science, Technology and Medicine, Pittsburgh Post-Gazette, Aug 22, 2001, at W-8. One of the most sought after information technology certifications is the Microsoft Certified Systems Engineer, or MCSE. David Noack, A+ Need Not Pertain Just to Conventional Schooling That's Just One of the Many Certification Degrees for People Looking to Boost Their Tech Skills—and Pay, Investor's Business Daily, Aug. 10, 2001, at 7.

[529] 1999 U.S. Dist. LEXIS 21700 (N.D. Ohio Feb. 19, 2000).

[530] *Id.* at *35.

[530] *Id.*

was reasonably foreseeable.[532] Premises liability lawsuits have traditionally been applied to shopping malls, parking lots, or apartment complexes. The Eleventh Circuit refused to extend local zoning regulations to the broadcast of adult entertainment over the Internet that originated from a residence, in *Voyeur Dorm, L.C. v. City of Tampa*.[533] In *Voyeur Dorm*, the entertainment company argued that it was not an adult use business, and that the code applied to locations or premises wherein adult entertainment was actually offered to the public. It further argued that because the public did not physically attend the location to enjoy adult entertainment, such location did not fall within the purview of the code. The court held that, since the offering occurred when the videotaped images were dispersed over the Internet and into the public eye for consumption, the code could not be applied to a location that did not offer adult entertainment to the public.

Courts have yet to expand premises liability concepts to cyberspace. It is arguable that the owner of a web site, like any other retail establishment, may be liable for dangers associated with third parties that injure customers.[534] Potential and actual liabilities to web site visitors may include torts such as the conversion of credit card numbers, the invasion of privacy, or defamation. Courts may find that an online business has breached an implied contract to provide a secure web site.[535] A web site owner may avoid premises liability by providing reasonable information security and monitoring the web site to reduce the potential for torts or crimes committed against web site visitors or customers.

[D] Defenses Against Negligence in Cyberspace

[1] Contributory Negligence

The defense of contributory negligence bars recovery entirely if the plaintiff's own negligence contributed to the injury. A web site, for example, could

---

[532] Certification exams are provided by Cisco Systems Inc.; "Cisco Certified Internetwork Expert" (CCIE) (visited Apr. 18, 1999), http://www.cisco.com/warp/public/625/ccie; *see also* Microsoft Corp., "Microsoft Certified Professional" (MCP) (visited Apr. 18, 1999), http://www. microsoft.com/mcp; and Novell, Inc., "Certified Novell Engineer" (CNF) (visited Apr. 18, 1999), http://education.novell.com/cnc/cnebroch.htm.

[533] 265 F.3d 1232 (11th Cir. 2001) (refusing to extend local zoning regulations to the broadcast of adult entertainment over the Internet originating from a residence).

[534] Premises liability is based on the notion of prior similar acts that establish the foreseeability of harm. A hospital, for example, was held not liable for a patient's sexual assault where no such assault had occurred previously. *See, e.g.,* K.L. v. Riverside Medical Ctr., 524 N.W.2d 300 (Minn. Ct. App. 1994).

[535] There is no case law on whether an implied contract to provide a secure environment applies to cyberspace. In *K.M.H. v. Lutheran Gen. Hosp.*, 431 N.W.2d 606 (Neb. 1988), the Nebraska Supreme Court held that the hospital entered into an implied contract to provide patients with a secure environment. In *K.M.H.*, a male employee performing a bed check sexually assaulted a patient. A hospital seemingly would owe a higher duty to vulnerable patients than an online business would owe to its customers.

defend against a claim for Internet security on the grounds that plaintiffs contributed to their injuries by losing their passwords. In a contributory negligence jurisdiction, plaintiffs are precluded from any recovery for contributing to the injury. By the early 1980s, only four states continued to adhere to the regressive "all or nothing" rule of contributory negligence: Alabama, Maryland, North Carolina, and Virginia.

In a contributory negligence case, a plaintiff's fault for his own accident precludes recovery. In July 2000, a hacker broke into the University of Washington Medical Center's internal network and downloaded computerized admissions records for 4,000 heart patients.[536] The medical facility would be contributorily negligent if it had permitted this action by failing to implement industry standard security protocols. This troubling security breach raises the question of whether the web site victim of hacker activity may be liable for its contributory or comparative negligence if data about patients or other third parties are intercepted or altered. For example, if a hospital did not have adequate firewalls or encryption, it might be liable for failing to comply with security standards. Under a contributory negligence regime, a plaintiff would be precluded from recovery if it were partially responsible for its own negligence.

[2] Comparative Negligence

As of 1996, 46 states had adopted some form of comparative negligence replacing the harsh "all or nothing" rule of contributory negligence. Four comparative negligence regimes have been adopted by the states: (1) pure, (2) slight/gross, (3) an "equal to" rule or 50/50 rule, and (4) a greater than rule. The pure form of comparative negligence apportions liability in direct proportion to fault. The trend in the law is to adopt a modified form of comparative negligence such as the slight/gross, equal to, or greater than regimes.

[3] Assumption of Risk

If plaintiffs voluntarily assume a known risk, they cannot recover for harm, even if the defendant is at fault. This defense is based on the public policy that one who "knows, appreciates and deliberately exposes himself to a danger assumes the risk."[537] If a web site, for example, warns the user that it does not employ standard security devices, a plaintiff may have voluntarily assumed a known risk.

An e-business will frequently craft exculpatory clauses to limit liability of a potentially culpable party through the express assumption of risk. The assumption of risk is restricted by two requirements: (1) knowledge and appreciation by the plaintiff of the danger it is incurring and (2) voluntary consent to bear that risk.

---

[536] Kevin Poulsen, Hospital Records Hacked Hard (Dec. 7, 2000), http://www.infowar.com/hacker/00hack_120700a_j.shtml.

[537] *Id.* at 103.

The contractual assumption of the risk uses contracts to shift the risks of tort liability. In general, exculpatory clauses are enforced so long as the language is clear and unequivocal and the clause does not violate public policy. For example, a leading case limiting releases invalidated a hospital's release for future negligence.[538] Six factors are used to determine whether an agreement in an exculpatory clause is invalid as contrary to public policy: (1) whether the clauses are used in a business suitable for public regulation, (2) whether the party seeking exculpation is engaged in performing a service of great importance to the public, (3) whether the party holds itself out as willing to perform this service for any member of the public who seeks it, (4) whether the party invoking the clause has greater bargaining power against those seeking services, (5) whether the stronger party uses adhesive contracts with exculpatory clauses, and (6) whether the public is expected to assume the risk of carelessness by the stronger party or its agents.

In addition, courts will not enforce exculpatory clauses purporting to extinguish liability for punitive damages or reckless conduct. Exculpatory clauses are strictly construed and therefore must be explicit in expressing the intent of the parties.[539] The e-business needs to pay particular attention to the validity of releases. Releases exculpating the e-business need to be clear, unambiguous, and explicit.[540]

The same principles that apply to exculpatory clauses apply to indemnification agreements. Indemnification agreements seek to obtain another party's agreement to indemnify or reimburse one from the results of one's own negligence. It is critical that the e-business seeking contractual limits to tort liability "clearly notify the prospective releaser or indemnitor of the effect of signing the agreement."[541]

[4] ISP Immunity for Negligence

The Supreme Court of Florida held that 47 U.S.C. § 230 preempted Florida law as to causes of action based in negligence against an ISP as a distributor of information in violation of Florida criminal statutes proscribing the distribution of obscene literature and computer-generated pornography.[542] In that case, a young boy was lured into engaging in sexual activity in an AOL chat room. The assertion

---

[538] Tunkl v. Regents of Univ. of Cal., 383 P.2d 441 (Cal. 1963) (invalidating clause in hospital admission form).

[539] *See, e.g.*, O'Connell v. Walt Disney World Co., 413 So. 2d 444 (Fla. Ct. App.1982) (denying summary judgment to Walt Disney World because exculpatory clause in release did not clearly release defendant from own negligence).

[540] Keeton, *supra* note 82, § 68, at 484. *See generally* Restatement (Second) of Contracts § 195 (1981) (explaining provisions for valid exculpatory clauses and explaining public policy exceptions).

[541] Ferrell v. Southern Nev. Off-Road Enthusiasts, Ltd., 147 Cal. App.3d 309, 314-15, 317-18 (Cal. Ct. App. 1983).

[542] Doe v. America Online, Inc., 2001 Fla. LEXIS 449, 26 Fla. L. Weekly S. 141 (Sup. Ct. Fla., Mar. 8, 2001) (affirmed and certifying question involving the preemption of state tort law by the CDA's § 230 Good Samaritan immunity provision).

of negligence was based on the argument that AOL knew or should have known that child pornographers were using private chat rooms to market and distribute child pornography.[543] The plaintiff's claim was that AOL did not use reasonable care in the operation of its chat rooms and that the damages to the plaintiff were "reasonably foreseeable as a result of AOL's breach."[544] AOL was dismissed on the grounds that the negligence and other tort claims were barred by 47 U.S.C. § 230.[545] The trial court held that § 230 preempted Florida tort claims based upon negligence "as a distributor of information allegedly in violation of Florida criminal statutes prohibiting the distribution of obscene literature and computer pornography."[546] The Florida Supreme Court held that the tort claims were preempted by § 230(d)(3) because of Congress's policy of "promoting unfettered speech on the Internet."[547] Interactive computer services, such as eBay, are also immunized by the CDA. EBay was immunized from a suit based on negligence and fraud in a case involving the sale of bootlegged music sold on eBay.[548] In addition to the CDA immunity, there is also a common-law qualified privilege that may be asserted in online defamation cases.[549] The statute of defense or repose may also bar an online tort claim.[550]

§ 5.09   STRICT LIABILITY IN CYBERSPACE

[A]   Strict Products Liability

Products liability is the legal liability of manufacturers for injuries caused by the marketing of defective products. *Strict products liability* evolved out of the societal judgment "that people need more protection from dangerous products than is afforded by the law of warranty."[551]

Injured consumers suing under the theory of strict liability need only prove that they were injured by an unreasonably dangerous product. The tort victim need not prove that the manufacturer knew or should have known about the problem or that the company was negligent. The strict liability rule permits consumers to recover as long as their injuries are causally connected to an unreasonably dangerous product. The policy underlying strict products liability is to place respon-

---

[543] *Id.* at 4.

[544] *Id.*

[545] *Id.* at 5-6.

[546] *Id.* at 8.

[547] *Id.* at 22-25.

[548] *Id.*

[549] Lunney v. Prodigy Servs., 94 N.Y.2d 242, 723 N.E.2d 539 (Ct. App. 1999) (applying qualified privilege in favor of ISP in case in which an impostor opened several accounts with provider and posted vulgar and threatening messages on an electronic bulletin board).

[550] Firth v. State, 184 Misc. 2d 105, 706 N.Y.S.2d 835 (Ct. Claims 2000) (granting dismissal of online defamation claim based on the publication of an allegedly defamatory report following an investigation of the state environmental agency).

[551] East River Steamship Corp. v. Transamerica Delval, Inc., 476 U.S. 858 (1986).

sibility for dangerously defective products on corporations rather than on the injured claimant. For further discussion of the general principles of strict liability, see § 5.02[A][3].

In *James v. Meow Media, Inc.*,[552] the parents of the victims of a Kentucky school shooting brought a strict products liability claim against, among others, the sellers of violent movies, video games, and various Internet materials viewed by the shooters. The plaintiffs charged the Internet defendants with distributing certain pornographic and obscene material that caused the killer to act out violence. The court dismissed the strict products liability claim, ruling that the violent movies, video games, and other web site materials were not classifiable as "product[s]."

In *Sanders v. Acclaim Entertainment Inc.*,[553] the victims of the Columbine school shooting filed a similar law suit against the distributor of movies and video games, arguing that these materials influenced the Columbine High School killers. As in *James*, the Colorado court ruled that the movies and video games were not products, holding that intangible thoughts, ideas, and expressive content were not "products" as contemplated by Colorado's strict liability doctrine.

Courts have little difficulty in classifying computer hardware as product for purposes of strict products liability. Statutes of limitations will frequently arise in repetitive stress injury litigation. In a products liability action, the discovery rule mandates that the statute of limitations should not begin to run until the plaintiff knows or through the exercise of due diligence should know of injury, its probable cause, and either manufacturer wrongdoing or product defect. The plaintiff's cause of action is tolled once a plaintiff has implied knowledge of the injury.[554]

Plaintiffs have been largely unsuccessful in strict products liability lawsuits filed against keyboard manufacturers for repetitive stress injuries. In a products liability case arising out of the plaintiff's long-term use of handheld delivery information computers while delivering packages for UPS, for example, the court entered summary judgment in favor of the defendant.[556] In *Naples v. Acer America Corp.*,[555] the plaintiffs sought to recover for injuries sustained from the long-term use of allegedly defective computer keyboards. The federal court granted each defendant's motion for summary judgment on statute of limitations grounds.

[B] Computer Malpractice

Courts have been reluctant to extend products liability as a remedy for defective computer programs.[557] Defective software has the potential to place life and limb in peril. Consider the following, for example:

---

[552] 90 F. Supp. 2d 798 (W.D. Ky. 2000).

[553] 2002 U.S. Dist. LEXIS 3997 (D. Colo. Mar. 4, 2002).

[554] Vass v. Compaq Computer Corp., 953 F. Supp. 114 (D. Md. 1997) (ruling that secretary's repetitive stress cause of action was not time-barred).

[555] Sy v. United Parcel Serv. Gen. Servs. Co., 1999 U.S. Dist. LEXIS 9862 (D. Or. 1999).

[556] 970 F. Supp. 89 (D.R.I. 1997) (dismissing all claims against all defendants).

[557] *See, e.g.,* Chatlos Sys., Inc. v. National Cash Register Corp., 479 F. Supp. 738 (D.N.J. 1979), *aff'd*, 635 F.2d 1081 (3d Cir. 1980).

1. An energy management system in a high school that was programmed to be inoperable until 6:30 a.m. and that prevented an exhaust fan in a chemistry lab from working, thus causing a teacher to inhale chlorine gas.

2. A computer system that generated a warning label for a prescription drug that was inadequate.

3. A computer system used by a pretrial service agency that failed to warn an arraignment judge that an arrestee was out on bond for two previous armed robberies, a circumstance that resulted in the release of the arrestee and grave injuries to a person wounded in another armed robbery attempt.

4. A defective computer and software program that was used to assist physicians in calculating doses of radiation received for patients who were being seeded with radioactive implants to treat cancer of the prostate.[558]

§ 5.10   IMMUNITIES AND PRIVILEGES

[A]   Immunities

Immunity is a term that refers to the special protections that the law accords designated categories of defendants, such as public entities, family members, charities, and other protected groups.[559] The law of torts has historically recognized a number of immunities.

Sovereign immunity was the "principle that the sovereign cannot be sued in his own courts or in any other court without its consent and permission."[560] Judges, for example, are not liable for torts committed in the exercise of their judicial functions.

Section 230 of the Communications Decency Act provides immunity for Internet Services Providers from liability for torts committed by subscribers. For a complete discussion, see § 5.02[B][2][a].

[B]   Privileges

A *privilege* is a rule of law "by which particular circumstances justify conduct which otherwise would be tortious."[561] The two principal intentional tort privileges are (1) consent and (2) "privileges created by law irrespective of consent."[562] Consent may be interposed as a defense to most torts. In addition, a defendant may assert self-defense or defense of others as a privilege.

---

[558] Thomas G. Wolpert, Product Liability and Software Implicated in Personal Injury, 60 Def. Counsel J. 519, 519 (1998).

[559] Dan Dobbs, The Law of Torts 575 (2000).

[560] Ballentine's Law Dictionary 1195 (3d ed. 1969).

[561] Edward J. Kionaka, Torts 178 (1999).

[562] *Id.*

At present, there are few Internet privileges. A law enforcement unit of a cybercrime unit may have a privilege to hack into an online company's web site or to decrypt a message.

§ 5.11 REGULATION OF CYBERSPACE

[A] FTC's Internet-Related Activities

The FTC is the most active agency of the U.S. government in the online world.[563] The FTC web site provides the latest information on its consumer protection. The FTC asserts broad powers to regulate Internet activities under § 5(a) of the FTC Act (FTCA), which prohibits unfair or deceptive acts or practices in or affecting commerce.[564] In addition to its enforcement powers, the FTC is an important policymaker for Internet-related activities. The FTC issued rules for implementing the Children's Online Privacy Protection Act (COPPA) that require online companies to obtain advance consent prior to collecting personal data from children. The FTC staff has also frequently reported to Congress on such cyberspace law issues as harvesting e-mail addresses, online profiling, privacy online, untruthful marketing claims, and fair information practices in the electronic marketplace. The FTC staff has posted all of its Internet-related reports, rules, and interpretations on its excellent web site, *www.ftc.gov.* Online advertisers, for example, should consult guidelines on *Dot Com Disclosures: Information About Online Advertising,* posted on its web site. In addition, the FTC developed regulations implementing COPPA[565] and the Gramm-Leach-Bliley Act (GLBA).[566] The FTC has an active enforcement arm, frequently filing actions against web sites whose Internet business practices are deceptive or unfair.[567] The FTC takes the position that its law enforcement responsibilities apply equally to the "offline and online

---

[563] The Federal Trade Commission was created by 15 U.S.C. §§ 41 et seq. (2000).

[564] 15 U.S.C. § 45(a) (2000).

[565] The Children's Online Privacy Protection Act (COPPA) is codified at 15 U.S.C. §§ 6501 et seq. (2000). COPPA requires operators of web sites directed to children under 13 who knowingly collect personal information to (1) provide parents notice of the site's information practices; (2) obtain prior verifiable parental consent for the collection, use, and disclosure of information; (3) have a mechanism for a parent to review the personal information collected from his or her child; (4) provide a parent with the opportunity to prevent further use of the information; (5) limit collection of personal information as a condition for a child participating in online games; and (6) establish reasonable procedures for protecting the confidentiality, security, and integrity of personal information collected from children. The FTC's COPPA rules became effective on April 21, 2000, and are codified at 16 C.F.R. § 312.

[566] Prepared Statement of Robert Pitofsky, Chairman, The Federal Trade Commission, Before the House Committee on Commerce Subcommittee on Telecommunications, Trade, and Consumer Protection, Recent Developments in Privacy Protections for Consumers, Oct. 11, 2000.

[567] *See, e.g.,* FTC v. ReverseAuction.com, No. 00-0032 (D.D.C., Jan. 6, 2000) (collecting personal identifying information from a competitor's online auction site); FTC v. Rennert, No. CV-S-00-0861-JBR (D. Nev., July 6, 2000) (collecting consumer's personal medical information through online consultations).

worlds."[568] This section focuses exclusively on the FTC's consumer protection powers applicable to Internet-related wrongdoing.[569]

[1] Information Policy

The FTC has been active in investigating and enforcing online privacy in the consumer marketplace since 1995.[570] The FTC's 1998 Report to Congress developed the fair information practice principles: (1) notice, (2) choice, (3) access, and (4) security. The FTC's 1988 Report to Congress reported that almost all web sites in its sample studied were collecting great amounts of personal information from consumers.[571] For example, 92 percent of the web sites studied collected data, yet only 14 percent of sites disclosed how personal information was to be used.[572] The FTC's 2000 survey revealed that 97 percent of its random sample of sites collected personal identifying information.[573] The FTC's 2000 Report showed that 88 percent of the FTC's sample of web sites were giving at least some disclosures. However, only 41 percent of the web sites in the FTC sample were complying with the basic notice and choice standards promulgated in the 1998 FTC Report.[574] The FTC's enforcement activities are having an impact on industry practices. However, there are still too many sites whose practice does not conform to representations made in their posted privacy policies.

[2] Online Profiling

Online profiling is the practice of targeting advertisements to web site visitors based upon an analysis of their online movements.[575] A web site visitor who visits a senior citizen's chat room may soon receive advertisements for funerals, walkers, or Viagra. The Commission held a workshop on online profiling in 1999.

---

[568] Prepared Statement of Robert Pitofsky, Chairman, The Federal Trade Commission, Before the House Committee on Commerce Subcommittee on Telecommunications, Trade, and Consumer Protection, Recent Developments in Privacy Protections for Consumers, Oct. 11, 2000.

[569] The FTC is active on a number of fronts in the field of consumer privacy. On Feb. 1, 2001, the FTC approved a safe-harbor program for compliance with the Children's Online Privacy Protection Act (COPPA). Kathleen Fay, "FTC Approves Safe Harbor for Children's Online Privacy," 17 E-Commerce 7 (Feb. 2001) (describing how guidelines were developed by the Children's Advertising Review Unit (CARU)). *See* the discussion of COPPA in ch. 2 at § 2.05[B][5] and Chapter 6 at § 6.03 [A][2].

[570] *See, e.g.,* Federal Trade Commission, Privacy Online: Fair Information Practices in the Electronic Marketplace: A Federal Trade Commission Report to Congress (May 2000), at i.

[571] *Id.*

[572] *Id.*

[573] *Id.* at ii.

[574] *Id.*

[575] Robert Pitofsky, Testimony on Recent Developments in Privacy Protections for Consumers (Oct. 11, 2000). *See generally* Federal Trade Comm'n, Online Profiling: A Report to Congress pt. 1 (June 13, 2000), http://www.ftc.gov/os/2000/06/onlineprofilingreportjune2000.pdf; and pt. 2 (July 27, 2000), http://www.ftc.gov/os/2000/07/onlineprofiling.htm.

Internet advertisers favored a self-regulatory framework for curbing potential abuses of online profiling.[576] Even though self-control is the best form of control, it is not likely to address the problem of misuse and abuse of profiling by "recalcitrant and bad actors."[577]

[3] Obligations Under Gramm-Leach-Bliley Act

President Clinton signed the Gramm-Leach-Bliley Act (GLBA) on November 12, 1999.[578] Subtitle A of Title V of the GLBA on the "Disclosure of Nonpublic Personal Information" applies to many Internet transactions. The GLBA grants the FTC jurisdiction over financial institutions not subject to regulations by other federal agencies. The GLBA requires financial institutions to disclose to all of their customers the institution's privacy policies and practices with respect to information shared with both affiliated and non-affiliated third parties. The GLBA prohibits financial institutions from disclosing nonpublic personal information about customers to nonaffiliated third parties without adequate disclosure. The GLBA requires financial institutions to have opt-out procedures which give customers the right to opt out of disclosures. The FTC promulgated the GLBA Final Rules governing financial institutions.[579] Subtitle A of Title V of the Gramm-Leach-Bliley Act is entitled "Disclosure of Nonpublic Personal Information (Title V)." Section 505 of the GLBA provides that it is Congress' intent to require "each financial institution" to respect the privacy of its customers and to protect the security and confidentiality of these customers' nonpublic personal information.[580]

SEC's Regulation S-P implements the privacy rules of the Gramm-Leach-Bliley Act. Section 504 of the GLBA requires the SEC and other federal agencies to adopt rules which implement notice requirements and restrictions on sharing a consumer's information.[581] Regulation S-P requires brokers, dealers, investment companies, and investment advisers to provide notice of their privacy policy and to protect the privacy of customer information.[582] The regulation implements § 503 of the GBLA in requiring financial institutions to provide prescribed information on its initial and annual privacy notices. The regulation also specifies the affiliates

---

[576] Pitofsky, Testimony, *supra* note 575.

[577] *Id.*

[578] The Federal Trade Commission issued final rules governing the GLBA on May 24, 2000; *see* Federal Trade Commission, Privacy of Consumer Financial Information; Final Rule, 16 C.F.R. pt. 313 (2000).

[579] *See* Federal Register Notice Requesting Public Comment on Financial Privacy and Bankruptcy, 65 Fed. Reg. 46735 (July 31, 2000).

[580] The Gramm-Leach-Bliley Act, § 504 (2000).

[581] *Id.*

[582] U.S. Securities and Exchange Commission, Final Rule: Privacy of Consumer Financial Information (Regulation S-P), 17 C.F.R. Part 248 (2001) (noting that Regulation S-P "includes requirements for investment advisers registered with the Commission, brokers, dealers, and investment companies"). Section 505 of the Act provides the SEC with enforcement authority with respect to broker-dealers, funds, and registered advisers.

and nonaffiliated third parties to which personal information may be disclosed. Financial institutions must have privacy notices and safeguards in place to protect consumer privacy by July 1, 2001.[583] It was Congress's intent to provide consumers with access to private information about them "maintained by the institutions and the opportunity to correct errors."[584] Regulation S-P dictates that online companies provide customers with a clear and conspicuous notice of their privacy policies and practices. To comply with Reg S-P, companies must not disclose personal information about a consumer to nonaffiliated third parties unless the institution provides certain information to the consumer and the consumer has not opted out of the disclosure. The online company needs to provide annual notices to its customers, post its privacy notice on its web site, and offer its customers the option of opting out of disclosures.

[4] HIPAA's Privacy Rules for Online Transactions

The Health Insurance Portability and Accountability Act of 1996 (HIPAA) applies to health information created or maintained by health care providers who engage in certain electronic transactions, health plans, and health care clearinghouses. The purpose of the HIPAA standards is to provide enhanced protections for individually identifiable health information. The Department of Health and Human Services (DHH) formulated regulations entitled "Standards for Privacy of Individually Identifiable Health Information" for entities covered by HIPAA.[585] HHS's Office for Civil Rights is the HHS Department responsible for enforcing and implementing HIPAA. HIPAA standards are designed "to protect electronic health information from improper access or alteration and to protect against loss of records."[586]

Telemedicine providers are subject to HIPAA as are all health care providers. Health plans, employers, public health authorities, life insurers, clearinghouses, universities, and information systems vendors are all impacted by HIPAA.[587] The HIPAA regulations have three purposes: "(1) to protect and enhance the rights of consumers by providing them access to their health information and controlling the inappropriate use of that information; (2) to improve the quality of health care in the U.S. by restoring trust in the health care system among consumers, health care professionals, and the multitude of organizations and individuals committed to the delivery of care; and (3) to improve the efficiency and effectiveness of health care delivery by creating a national framework for health privacy protection that

---

[583] *Id.*

[584] *Id.* at 4.

[585] Department of Health and Human Services, Office of the Secretary, Standards for Privacy of Individually Identifiable Health Information: Final Rule, 45 C.F.R. Pts. 160-164 (Dec. 28, 2000).

[586] Health and Human Services, HHS Proposes Security Standards for Electronic Health Data, Aug. 11, 1998.

[587] HIPAAdvisory, HIPAA Primer (visited May 26, 2001), http://www.hipaadvisory.com/regs/HIPAAprimer1.htm.

builds on efforts by states, health systems, and individual organization and individuals."[588]

Prior to the passage of HIPAA, states "adopted laws that protect the health information relating to certain health conditions such as mental illness, communicable diseases, cancer, HIV/AIDS, and other stigmatized conditions."[589] HIPAA was enacted as a response to increasing public concern about the loss of privacy coupled with an increasing use of interconnected electronic information systems.[590] Section 160.102 extends HIPAA regulations to "health plans, health care providers who transmit any health information in electronic form."[591] The HIPAA regulation covers health plans, providers, and clearinghouses that transmit individual patient information.[592]

The health care industry invested $10 to 15 billion in information technology, according to a 1996 study by the National Research Council.[593] HIPAA imposes civil and criminal penalties for noncompliance. Providers may use limited patient information without patient authorization. Online businesses will need to comply with information security requirements to comply with HIPAA. Section 501 of HIPAA requires each financial institution to protect the security and confidentiality of personal information. Fines range from $25,000 for multiple violations of the same standard in a calendar year to fines up to $250,000. In addition, individuals may be imprisoned for up to 10 years for knowingly misusing individually health information.[594]

[5] FTC's Consumer Protection Powers

The FTC asserts broad investigative and law enforcement authority to police Internet fraud on the borderless Internet. The FTC has the statutory authority to initiate an enforcement action if it finds "reason to believe" that the FTCA is being violated. The FTC devises regulations, which implement federal consumer protection statutes such as the recent Children's Online Privacy Protection Act of 1998.[595] The FTC has the power to challenge Internet-related "unfair or deceptive acts or practices" by commencing an adjudicatory proceeding under § 5(b) of the FTCA. The FTC has an array of administrative enforcement tools described in the next section.

---

[588] Department of Health and Human Services, Standards for Privacy of Individually Identifiable Health Information, 45 CFR Parts 160-164 (Dec. 28, 2000) at 82463.

[589] Standards for Privacy of Individually Identifiable Health Information; Final Rule, 65 Fed. Reg. 82462, 82463 (Dec. 28, 2000) (publishing regulation to be published in 45 CFR Pts. 160-164).

[590] *Id.* at 82465

[591] HIPPA § 160.102, *id.* at 82475 (citing § 160.102 of HIPPA).

[592] *Id.* at 82477.

[593] *Id.*

[594] *Id.*

[595] Regulations implementing the Children's Online Privacy Protection Act of 1998 were made effective as of April 21, 2000; *see* 16 C.F.R. § 312.1 (2000).

[a] FTC's Tools to Combat Cyberfraud

Section 5(a) of the Federal Trade Commission Act (FTCA) grants the FTC broad enforcement authority to restrain "unfair or deceptive acts or practices in or affecting commerce."[596] The FTC or Commission has broad authority to police antitrust and consumer protection policies. The term *unfair* is defined to mean that the act or practice "causes or is likely to cause substantial injury to consumers which is not reasonably avoidable by consumers themselves and not outweighed by countervailing benefits to consumers or to competition."[597] The FTC moved for preliminary injunctions to restrain the following deceptive practices: (1) a site's deceptive telemarketing enterprise through which the site sold Canadian lottery packages to American consumers,[598] (2) an online pyramid scheme,[599] (3) a fraudulent credit card billing scheme,[600] and (4) deceptive sales practices and false advertising in inducing online subscribers to purchase products supposedly causing weight loss without changes in exercise or diet.[601]

The Commission filed these actions pursuant to its general authority to police "unfair and deceptive practices" under § 5(a) of the FTCA. In addition to § 5(a), the FTC polices a number of specific consumer protection statutes, such as the Magnuson-Moss Consumers Warranty Act, Truth-in-Lending Act, or Fair Credit Reporting Act. Most recently, the FTC enacted regulations implementing the Children's Online Privacy Protection Act of 1998 (COPPA). COPPA "prohibits unfair or deceptive acts or practices in connection with the collection, use, and/or disclosure of personal information from and about children on the Internet."[602] Many of these specific statutes specify what is considered to be an "unfair or deceptive" act or practice under § 5(a) of the FTCA. The Commission enforces the broad mandate of § 5(a) through the dual tools of administrative and judicial processes.[603]

[i] FTC subpoena power. In addition, the FTC may "prosecute any inquiry necessary to its duties in any part of the United States."[604] The FTC, for example, has subpoena power to compel the testimony of witnesses or the production of

---

[596] 15 U.S.C. § 45(a)(1) (2001).

[597] 15 U.S.C. § 45(n) (2001).

[598] FTC v. Growth Plus Int'l Mktg., Inc., 2001 U.S. Dist. LEXIS 1215 (N.D. Ill., Jan. 9, 2001) (issuing injunction to halt online sales of lottery packages).

[599] FTC v. Five-Star Auto Club, Inc., 97 F. Supp. 2d 502 (S.D.N.Y. 2000) (finding site committed unfair or deceptive practices in operating pyramid scheme and ordering reimbursement of consumers and enjoining of future activities).

[600] FTC v. J.K. Publications, Inc., 99 F. Supp. 2d 1176 (C.D. Cal. 2000) (ordering summary judgment on liability of defendants and trial for amount of damages).

[601] FTC v. SlimAmerica, Inc., 77 F. Supp. 2d 1263 (S.D. Fla. 1999).

[602] 16 C.F.R. § 312 (2001).

[603] Federal Trade Commission, A Brief Overview of the Federal Trade Commission's Investigative and Law Enforcement Authority, Apr. 1998 (visited Mar. 12, 2001), http://www.ftc.gov/ogc/brfovrvw.htm.

[604] 15 U.S.C. § 43 (2001) (implementing § 3 of the FTC Act).

documents relating to an investigative matter.[605] An online company subject to a subpoena may challenge the subpoena by filing a petition to quash under FTC Rule 2.7.[606] If a party does not comply with a subpoena, the FTC may seek enforcement in a federal district court.[607]

[ii] Civil investigation demands. While the FTC lacks criminal enforcement authority, it may make a civil investigative demand. The Bureau of Consumer Protection now uses "civil investigative demands" (CID) versus subpoenas which were used prior to the FTC Improvements Act of 1980.[608] A CID has a different scope than that of a subpoena.[609] Both devices are used to elicit documents or oral testimony, but a CID may also require that the recipient "file written reports or answers to questions."[610] A CID may be a more flexible tool for prosecuting Internet fraud than a subpoena because it "provides for service . . . upon entities not found within the territorial jurisdiction of any court of the United States."[611] However, "permissible venue is narrower in a CID enforcement action than in a subpoena enforcement act."[612]

[iii] Section 6 of the FTCA. The FTC may use § 6 of the FTC to require online businesses to provide "annual or special . . . reports or answers in writing to specific questions."[613] The FTC, for example, could conduct a broad study of Internet scams using its § 6(b) authority. Section 6(b) may also be used in an antitrust enforcement investigation.[614] A dot-com company filing a petition to quash may challenge § 6(b) orders.[615] As with subpoenas or CIDs, the FTC may seek federal court enforcement for noncompliance.[616] For example, the FTC could do a study of the industry practices in connection with the collection, use, or disclosure of personal information about children on the Internet using its § 6(b) powers.

[iv] Adjudication. The FTC may file an administrative adjudication to attack an "unfair or deceptive practice" or specific violation of a consumer protection statute, such as the Truth-in-Lending Act or the Magnuson-Moss Act.

The general standard for the FTC filing adjudication is that the Commission has a "reason to believe" that an act or practice violates the law. The FTC has been active in policing deceptive and unfair deceptive trade practices with adult-content

---

[605] 15 U.S.C. § 49 (2001) (implementing § 9 of the FTC Act).

[606] 16 C.F.R. § 2.7 (2001) (noting that a party may raise objections to a subpoena in filing its petition to quash).

[607] 15 U.S.C. § 49 (2001).

[608] FTC, A Brief Overview, *id.* at 2.

[609] *Id.*

[610] 15 U.S.C. § 57b-1(c)(1).

[611] FTC, A Brief Overview, *id.* (describing § 20 CID enforcement action).

[612] *Id.*

[613] 15 U.S.C. § 46 (2000) (implementing § 6(b) of the FTC Act).

[614] FTC, A Brief Overview, *id.*

[615] *Id.*

[616] *Id.*

Internet services.[617] A complaint was filed on October 27, 2000, against Ty Anderson.com, cartoonporn.com, and alienporn.com for unauthorized billing for Internet Services.[618] The federal district court issued a preliminary injunction against these dot-com companies on November 9, 2000.[619]

The FTC is also vigilant in monitoring deceptive and unfair billing practices in other settings. Recently, a complaint was issued against WEBTV Networks, Inc. for its marketing of Internet services.[620] The FTC had "reason to believe" that WEBTV's marketing of its Internet access was unfair and deceptive and issued a complaint setting forth its charges. The parties settled the FTC complaint by entering into a consent agreement. The FTC may also use adjudication to challenge "unfair methods of competition" where there is a violation of the Clayton Act.[621]

[v] Rulemaking. The FTC may enact rules to regulate "unfair or deceptive acts or practices" under § 18 of the FTCA.[622] In 1975, § 18 became the sole and exclusive rulemaking provision in consumer protection cases.[623] To date, the FTC has not exercised its § 18 rulemaking powers.[624]

[vi] Enforcement activity. The FTC has used adverse publicity to drive online con artists out of business. The victims of "dot cons" are uncovered by the FTC's enforcement division, which frequently searches the Internet for questionable practices. FTC's web-surfing enforcers have identified the top 10 dot cons: (1) Internet Auctions, (2) Internet Access Services, (3) Credit Card Fraud; (4) International Modem Dialing, (5) Web Cramming, (6) Multilevel Marketing Plans/Pyramids, (7) Travel and Vacation, (8) Business Opportunities, (9) Investments, and (10) Health Care Products/Services.[625] The FTC has a toll-free number to report online scams, 1-877-382-4357, as well as an online complaint form. The Commission's enforcement authority arises under the FTCA.[626] The FTC has broad authority to prevent fraudulent, deceptive, and unfair business practices in the online marketplace.[627] The FTC "e-cops" search the Internet for unfair or

---

[617] *See, e.g.,* FTC v. Automated Transaction Corp., No. 00-7599-CIV.Hurley (S.D. Fla., Oct. 25, 2000) (issuing TRO with asset freeze and receivership).

[618] FTC v. Anderson, No. C 00-1843P (W.D. Wash., Oct. 27, 2000).

[619] FTC, Summary of Cases (visited Mar. 12, 2001), http://www.ftc.gov/ogc/status/injunct2.htm.

[620] *In re* WEBTV Networks, Inc., File No. 9723162, Agreement, Consent Order.

[621] FTC, Brief Overview, *id.* at 7 (noting that "the Commission proceeds under Section 11 of the Clayton Act, 15 U.S.C. § 21," which parallels § 5(b) of the FTCA).

[622] FTC, Brief Overview, *id.* at 7.

[623] *Id.*

[624] *Id.*

[625] Federal Trade Commission, Dot Cons (Oct. 2000) (visited Mar. 12, 2001), http://www.ftc.gov/bcp/conline/pubs/online/dotcons.htm.

[626] Federal Trade Commission (visited Mar. 12, 2001), http://www.ftc.gov.

[627] *See, e.g.,* 15 U.S.C. § 53(b) (granting the FTC the power to sue to enjoin a practice "[whenever] the Commission has reason to believe . . . that any person, partnership, or corporation is violating or is about to violate, any provision of law enforced by the Federal Trade Commission").

deceptive practices. The FTC's proactive investigative techniques rely upon consumer complaints as well as the patrolling of questionable web sites.

A sampling of recent administrative and court proceedings confirms that the FTC is the most proactive regulatory agency on the Internet. The FTC brought an administrative enforcement action against GeoCities in 1999 for misrepresenting the purposes for which it was collecting information from consumers.[628] The FTC frequently uses its administrative powers to compel web site owners to change their advertising and marketing practices. The FTC settlement agreement with GeoCities requires the site to post a clear and conspicuous privacy notice to consumers about what information is collected and for what purpose. GeoCities is also required by the consent agreement to explain how consumers can access and remove personal information, restricting disclosure to third parties.[629] Finally, the FTC required GeoCities to institute a comprehensive "information practices training program" for its employees and affiliates.[630]

In 2001, the FTC sued Toysmart.com, contesting the potential sale of Toysmart's customer list in the distribution of its bankruptcy estate.[631] Toysmart collected the personal customer information of web site visitors, including "consumers' names, addresses, billing information, shopping preferences and family profile information."[632] Toysmart.com's privacy policy announced that it did not share "personal information voluntarily submitted by visitors to their site"[633] Toysmart ceased operation in May of 2000 and retained the services of a consultant to sell its business and assets. Toysmart solicited bids for the purchase of its assets, including its customer list containing personal information on thousands of consumers.[634] Toysmart's creditors filed a motion for involuntary bankruptcy in June of 2000.[635]

The FTC argued that Toysmart's proposed sale of customer lists and profiles was an "unfair or deceptive act" under § 5(a) of the FTCA.[636] In addition, the FTC argued that the proposed sale violated the Children's Online Privacy Protection Act.[637] The FTC noted that Toysmart represented that it would "never" disclose, sell, or offer for sale customers' personal information. Prior to the ruling of the

---

[628] *In re* GeoCities, Federal Trade Commission, Docket No. C-3849 (Feb. 12, 1999).

[629] *Id.*

[630] *Id.*

[631] *In re* Toysmart.Com, LLC, No. 00-13995-CJK (D. Mass., Jan. 26, 2001) (ruling that the customer instruction may be destroyed in return for the debtor receiving a payment of $50,000).

[632] Federal Trade Commission, First Amended Complaint for Permanent Injunction and Other Equitable Relief, FTC v. Toysmart.com, LLC, Civil Action No. 00-11341-RGS (D. Mass. 2000).

[633] *Id.*

[634] *Id.*

[635] *Id.*

[636] *See* Count 1 of complaint, *In re* GeoCities, Federal Trade Commission Docket No. C-3849 (Feb. 12, 1999).

[637] Count II, *id.*

bankruptcy court, Toysmart entered into a settlement agreement with the FTC to protect the privacy of its customer list.[638]

The Southern District of New York enjoined a "free tour" pornographic web site from its deceptive practice of billing subscribers for visits to its site. The web site offered a free tour as long as the visitor entered credit card information.[639] The adult entertainment site offered "free tours" but at some point began billing the visitor's credit card. The court found the borderline between the free tour and the paid areas of the site to be inconspicuous. The court enjoined the web site, finding that the billing practices likely violated § 5(a) of the FTCA, as well as New York state law. As part of the injunctive relief, the federal court required the site to adopt new billing procedures which gave subscribers conspicuous notice of fees as well as the remedy of canceling a bill, unless they had personally authorized payment.

In another case, the FTC ruled that two companies selling HIV test kits to consumers on the Internet violated §§ 5(a) and 12 of the FTCA.[640] The firms were charged with misrepresenting the accuracy of unapproved HIV tests.[641] The Internet advertisements for the test systems were deemed to constitute false advertising. The promotional materials claimed that the HIV test kits were accurate and economical, which were claims that were deceptive and inaccurate.[642]

[B] False and Deceptive Advertising in Cyberspace

[1] Regulation of Internet Advertising

This section provides a brief overview of three matters: (1) public regulation of Internet advertisements, (2) private tort-based regulation of Internet advertisements, and (3) tort liability for Internet advertisements. Internet torts governing Internet advertisements include trade libel or commercial disparagement, personal defamation, interference with prospective or existing contractual relations, and unfair competition. In addition to advertising torts, there is liability for regulatory actions.

[a] *Federal Trade Commission Regulation*

[i] Section 5(a) of the FTCA. The Federal Trade Commission (FTC) chiefly regulates advertising in the United States, but other federal agencies may

---

[638] Toysmart Given Green Light to Destroy Customer List, 2 Mealey's Cyber Tech Litig. Rep. 1 (Feb. 2001) (reporting that the FTC complaint also charged Toysmart with violation of the Children's Online Privacy Protection Act).

[639] Federal Trade Commission v. Verity Int'l, Ltd., 2000 U.S. Dist. LEXIS 17946 (S.D.N.Y., Dec. 14, 2000).

[640] FTC Settles Trade Claims With Two HIV Test Kit Makers, 14 AIDS Litig. Rptr. 5 (Feb. 12, 2001).

[641] *Id.*

[642] *Id.*

regulate the advertising of specific products.[643] The FTC has the authority to police false advertising[644] that is considered to be "unfair methods of competition in or affecting commerce and unfair or deceptive acts or practices in or affecting commerce."[645] The FTC filed an action against an Internet company for the deceptive practice of "mouse trapping" web site visitors. Mouse trapping involves the redirecting of users to the desired site and then disabling back arrow controls. The user can leave the web site only by shutting down the machine. The laws of advertising and advertising regulations are general in scope and extend to Internet commercial transactions.[646] False and deceptive advertising will subject the online company to regulatory actions by the Federal Trade Commission.

Online companies that use unfair methods of competition or unfair or deceptive advertising, such as false claims about products or services, may be challenged by FTC enforcement. The FTC's enforcement arm has devoted attention to eliminating advertising practices considered to be "deceptive." Section 5 of the Act declared "[u]nfair methods of competition in commerce, and unfair or deceptive acts or practices in or affecting commerce" unlawful.[647]

In *Federal Trade Commission v. Sperry & Hutchinson Co.*,[648] the Court held for the first time that consumers as well as competitors were to be protected from unfair or deceptive acts. The *Sperry* case armed the FTC with authority for its so-called unfairness doctrine. The unfairness doctrine was the FTC interpretation that § 5(a) of the Act allowed it to determine what was "unfair" to consumers, rather than the more limited jurisdiction of determining which trade practices were deceptive. The FTC jurisdiction extends to advertisements that have the capacity to deceive consumers[649] and to materially affect their purchasing decisions.[650] The test for Internet advertisements considers as well whether advertisements will materially affect the purchasing decisions of online customers.

Online advertisements may be outright fraudulent or misleading because of inaccurate claims about products or services. Misleading statements about software or hardware performance that would deceive the consumer acting reasonably under the circumstances would expose an online company to potential enforcement action. A company found to be engaging in unfair or deceptive acts is subject to "cease and desist" orders as well as monetary penalties.

---

[643] "Advertising is regulated in the United States at the federal level by the Federal Trade Commission ('FTC'), the Food and Drug Administration ('FDA') and the Bureau of Alcohol, Tobacco and Firearms ('ATF')." Thomas J. Smedinghof, Introduction to Electronic Commerce: A Road Map to the Legal Issues, American Bar Association, Science and Technology Committee Presentation, adapted from Thomas J. Smedinghof, ed., Online Law (1996).

[644] 15 U.S.C. § 52 (2001).

[645] 15 U.S.C. § 45 (2001).

[646] *Id.* at 14.

[647] 15 U.S.C. § 45(a)(1) (1995).

[648] 405 U.S. 233 (1972).

[649] The "capacity to deceive" is closely related to the "likelihood of confusion" test employed in § 43(a) unfair competition actions under the federal Lanham Act.

[650] Charles McManus, The Law of Unfair Practices 350 (1983).

[ii] False Internet advertising claims. Internet advertisements may be found to be "deceptive" by the FTC if the online advertiser makes false claims about goods or services. As with Article 2 of the UCC, courts distinguish between actionable deceptive advertisements and mere puffery. Puffery is unenforceable seller's talk and refers to "opinion claims about goods that do not constitute the basis of the bargain."[651] The adjective *delicious* in an advertisement would be a puff and not an enforceable warranty. In contrast, a warranty of quality is a statement of fact about goods that goes to the "basis of the bargain."

To constitute the "basis of the bargain, the seller's statement must: (1) relate to the goods and (2) become the basis of the bargain."[652] The primary issue for either an express warranty or an FTC enforcement is whether a seller's statement about goods creates an enforceable warranty or constitutes unenforceable puffery or "seller's talk." The FTC has long presumed that a seller's mere expression of opinion or seller's talk is not calculated to deceive.[653] The greater the specificity, the more likely a seller's statement will be deemed an express warranty.

The FTC filed a complaint against Toysmart.com LLC, an Internet toy seller. Toysmart collected personal customer information submitted by children. In May 2000, the company ceased operations. Among the individual assets offered for sale were customer lists and other personal data. Toysmart certified its privacy policy and represented that it would not transfer data to third parties. Toysmart entered into a consent agreement agreeing not to transfer the data. COPPA requires advertisers who collect online personal information from children under the age of 13 to obtain advance parental consent.[654]

The FTC has the authority to police unfair or deceptive advertising in diverse fact-settings, including e-mail, web sites, or other Internet-related communications channels.[655] An Internet advertisement may be deceptive not only because of a company's misrepresentations, but also by its omissions likely to "mislead consumers . . . and affect consumers' behavior or decisions about the product or service."[656] An act or practice is unfair if the injury caused or likely to be caused, is "substantial . . . not outweighed by other benefits . . . and not reasonably avoidable."[657]

The FTC requires that Internet advertisers, like all advertisers, have a reasonable basis for substantiating advertising claims made about products and ser-

---

[651] Ivan L. Preston, Dimensions at the FTC in Identifying Consumer Response to Advertisements, Washington Regulatory Reporting Association, FTC Watch (June 1996).

[652] U.C.C. § 2-313 (1995).

[653] Carlay Co. v. FTC, 153 F.2d 493, 496 (7th Cir. 1946) (holding representation that a car could go an "amazing distance" without oil to be "nothing more than a form of 'puffing' not calculated to deceive").

[654] 15 U.S.C. § 6501 (2001).

[655] Federal Trade Commission, Advertising and Marketing on the Internet: The Rules of the Road (visited Nov. 27, 1999), http://www.ftc.gov/bcp/conline/pubs/buspubs/ruleroad.htm.

[656] *Id.*

[657] *Id.*

vices.[658] The FTC first articulated the "reasonable basis for substantiation" test in a case involving advertising claims made for Unburn sunburn lotion. The Commission held that it was an unfair trade practice to make an affirmative comparative product claim that a lotion instantly solved the effects of sunburn without a reasonable basis for making the claim.[659] The FTC has the jurisdiction to file enforcement actions against sellers, advertising agencies, web site designers, and any one who disseminates deceptive representations on a web site, in e-mail communications, or in other Internet transmissions.

[b]   State Enforcement Against Unfair or Deceptive Internet Ads

Advertising is regulated by individual states under little FTC acts. These statutes are called "little FTC acts" because they are modeled on § 5(a) of the FTCA. Many states have adopted a version of the Uniform Deceptive Trade Practices Act (UDTPA).[660] Deceptive or misleading advertisements may be deemed deceptive trade practices in states adopting the UDTPA.

The state of Washington's attorney general filed actions against online companies for violating its statute governing unfair and deceptive trade practices. It is likely that state laws governing online sales violate the Commerce Clause of the U.S. Constitution.

[c]   Regulation of Online Spam

A number of states have enacted antispam statutes punishing companies for sending unsolicited e-mail.[661] The common law as well as specific state statutes punish and deter spam e-mail.[662] AOL uses many different causes of action in

---

[658] The FTC gives strict scrutiny to claims about health, safety, or performance. If an Internet advertisement specifies a given level of support for a claim—"tests show X"—the company must be able to substantiate the claim. *Id.*

[659] *In re* Pfizer, Inc., Trade Reg. Rep. (CCH) ¶ 20,056 (FTC 1972) (articulating the test as two steps: (1) What substantiating evidence constitutes a reasonable basis for making a product claim? and (2) Did the respondent in the case produce such evidence?).

[660] A number of states have adopted statutes modeled on the Uniform Deceptive Trade Practices Act. *See, e.g.,* Fla. Stat. §§ 501.201 to 501.213 (1998); Ga. Code Ann. §§ 10-1-370 to 375 (Harrison 1995); 390-407 (Harrison 1993); Haw. Rev. Code § 481A (1995); Idaho Stat. § 49-1629 (1995); Ill. Ann. Code § 815 ILCS 510/1 *et seq.* (Smith-Hurd 1995); Kan. Stat. Ann. §§ 50-623 to 50-643 (1998); La. Stat. 51:1401 to 1418 (West 1995); Maine Stat. tit. 10 §§ 1211 to 1216; tit. 5 §§ 206 to 214 (West 1995); Mass. Gen. Laws Ann. Ch. 93A; Minn. Stat. Ann. § 325D.43-48; Miss. Rev. Stat. § 63-7-203 (1995); Mont. Code Ann. § 61-607 (1995); Nev. Rev. Stat. § 484.6062 (Michie 1995); N.H. Rev. Stat. § 358A (1995); N.M. Rev. Stat. §§ 57-12-1, *et seq.* (Michie 1995); Ohio Rev. Code Ann. §§ 4549.24, 46, 49 (Anderson 1995); Okla. Stat. Ann. tit. 15 §§ 751 to 765 (1995); Ore. Rev. Stat. §§ 646.605 to 656 (1998); Wyo. Stat. §§ 40-12-101 to 112 (1998).

[661] *See, e.g.,* Cal. Bus. & Prof. Code §§ 7538 et al. (Deering Supp. 2001), Illinois Electronic Mail Act, 815 Ill. Comp. Stat. Ann. 511.5 (West Supp. 2001); Wash. Rev. Code Ann. § 19.190.010(2) (West Supp. 2001). *See generally* David E. Sorkin, Technical & Legal Approaches to Unsolicited Electronic Mail, 35 U.S.F. L. Rev. 325, 379 n.13 (2001) (citing antispam state statutes).

[662] *See generally* Sorkin, *supra* note 661.

deterring those sending spam e-mail to individuals using AOL e-mail accounts. In one case, AOL alleged that a defendant's transmission of spam to AOL subscribers violated the Lanham Act, the Computer Fraud and Abuse Act, and the Virginia Computer Crimes Act. In addition to these statutory claims, AOL alleged that the defendant was liable for trespass to chattels and conspiracy.[663]

Washington passed an antispam law that permits the recipients of unsolicited commercial bulk e-mail to recover damages if the e-mail conceals the true identity or location of the sender or contains a misleading subject line.

The Washington State Attorney General filed a statutory action against an Oregon company that sent spam to millions of state residents advertising its new book on how to profit from the Internet. In a related case, a Washington ISP is suing a mortgage company for sending "4,800 unsolicited commercial messages with phony return addresses."[664] Washington's antispam statutes has been declared unconstitutional as unduly restrictive and burdensome, violating the Interstate Commerce Clause of the U.S. Constitution.[665] Virginia makes unsolicited spam e-mail a criminal offense and awards successful litigants with attorneys' fees.[666]

[d] International Regulation of Internet Advertising

The Internet, by its very nature, is subject to international regulations. The European Commission, for example, adopted a proposal for a Directive to regulate distance selling of financial services in 1998.[667] Many European countries have limitations on comparative advertising that would not be objectionable in the United States.

[2] Private Attorney General Tort-Based Enforcement

One of the distinctive features of advertising law is enforcement by private attorneys general.[668] The Lanham Act gives commercial parties standing to sue defendants for unfair and deceptive acts in federal courts. Section 43(a) provides private litigants with private tortlike consumer remedies against unfair practices. Section 43(a) of the Lanham Act provides:

> Any person who shall . . . use in . . . tending falsely to describe or represent the same, and shall cause such goods or services to enter into commerce . . .

---

[663] America Online, Inc., v. CN Prods, 2002 U.S. Dist. LEXIS 1607 (E.D. Va. Jan. 31, 2002).

[664] ISP See No Gift in Spam 'GIFT' Message, 4 The Internet Newsletter: Legal & Business Aspects 14 (May 1999) (noting that the subject line of the message was "A gift for you," a deceptive and illegal message for which a $1,000 penalty may be assessed for each message).

[665] New Anti-Spam Law Unconstitutional, Nat'l L.J. (Apr. 17, 2000), at A6.

[666] Va. Code Ann. §§ 18-2-152.1 et seq. (Michie 1998).

[667] Microsoft Law & Corporate Affairs, Summary of Global Internet Legal Developments (for the period Oct.-Dec. 1998) 93 (Jan. 1999).

[668] *Private attorneys general* are plaintiffs who bring legal actions on behalf of themselves as well as the larger society.

shall be liable to a civil action by . . . any person who believes that he is or is likely to be damaged. . . .[669]

Courts have long interpreted § 43(a) to create a federal statutory tort action providing relief for a broad class of injured or likely to be injured plaintiffs.[670] Two types of advertising are actionable under § 43(a): "false designation or origin" and "false descriptions or representations." Five elements are necessary to state a *prima facie* claim for false advertising in this section: (1) the defendant made false statements about its *own product or services* by the use of misleading statements, partially correct statements, or the failure to disclose material facts; (2) that the advertisements actually deceived or have the tendency to deceive a substantial segment of their audience; (3) that the deception is material; (4) that defendant caused its falsely advertised goods to enter interstate commerce; and (5) that the plaintiff has been or is likely to be injured by false advertising.[671]

A false and misleading advertisement on the Internet must meet the five elements of the *Skil* test to be actionable. An Internet advertisement will be regarded as a "false designation of origin" if it is "likely to cause confusion or to deceive purchasers concerning the source of the goods."[672] The key legal test in a "false designation action" is the creation of "likelihood of confusion by the consuming public as to the source of goods."[673] Section 43(a) prohibits "false descriptions or representations" that apply to Internet advertisements. To prevail on a § 43(a) claim, the plaintiff must prove by a preponderance of the evidence that the Internet advertisement it challenges is false or deceptive.[674] An Internet advertisement must make false statements about its own products or services under § 43(a). It is not actionable under § 43(a) to disparage a competitor's product.[675] The standing to sue under § 43(a) provides remedies to "commercial parties only" who have been sued or are likely to be damaged by falsehoods in advertisements.[676] The standard for preliminary injunctive relief under § 43(a) is "irreparable harm" flowing from the alleged infringement and either "(a) a likelihood of success on the merits or (b) sufficiently serious questions going to the merits to make them a fair

---

[669] 15 U.S.C. § 1125(a) (1999).

[670] *See, e.g.,* L'Aiglon Apparel v. Lana Lobell, Inc., 214 F.2d 649 (3d Cir. 1954).

[671] Skil Corp. v. Rockwell Int'l Corp., 375 F. Supp. 777, 783 (N.D. Ill. 1974).

[672] Salomon/North Am. v. AMF Inc., 484 F. Supp. 846 (D. Mass. 1980).

[673] Pignon S.A. DeMecanique v. Polaroid Corp., 657 F.2d 482, 486-87 (1st Cir. 1981).

[674] Courts will likely apply the analysis in American Home Products Corp. v. Johnson & Johnson, 436 F. Supp. 785 (S.D.N.Y. 1977), *aff'd,* 577 F.2d 160 (2d Cir. 1978) to Internet advertisements.

[675] *See, e.g.,* Bernard Food Indus., Inc. v. Dietene Co., 415 F.2d 1279 (7th Cir. 1969) (holding that false statements must be made about defendant's own product to be actionable under § 43(a) of the Lanham Act). *See also* Skil Corp. v. Rockwell Int'l Corp., 375 F. Supp. 777 (N.D. Ill. 1974) (holding that the plaintiff's advertisement misrepresented its own product as well as impugning a competitor's product).

[676] *See, e.g.,* Johnson & Johnson v. Carter-Wallace, Inc., 631 F.2d 186, 189 (2d Cir. 1980) (restricting standing to commercial parties injured by false advertisements).

ground for litigation" and a balance of hardships tipping decidedly in favor of the moving party.[677]

State little FTC acts modeled on UDTPA provide for private tortlike enforcement as well as public enforcement actions. Chapter 93A of the Massachusetts General Law, for example, authorizes lawsuits by the attorney general,[678] individual consumers,[679] or business competitors.[680] Chapter 93A provides for monetary damages and equitable relief for consumers "injured" as the result of an unfair or deceptive trade practice. While there is no case law on whether false and deceptive Internet advertisements violate Chapter 93A or other UDTPA-inspired acts, it is quite likely that courts would extend these state-based causes of action in the proper case. Section 11 of Chapter 93A provides for punitive damages, such as multiple damages for "willful or knowing violations."[681] Attorneys' fees may be recoverable along with injunctive relief, monetary damages, and treble damages. Relief under Chapter 93A supplements and is in addition to traditional tort remedies as well as relief under the Lanham Act.[682]

[3] Private Common Law Tort Actions

In addition to federal and state statutory causes of action for false advertising, plaintiffs may recover for damages under traditional tort law. False and deceptive advertisements may be the basis for diverse business torts, including unfair competition, disparagement, trade libel, and common law fraud. Comparative advertisements, which disparage competitor's products and services, may constitute possible trade libel or disparagement.

Civil RICO may also be pleaded in Internet-related actions. To sufficiently state a RICO claim, the plaintiffs must plead (1) conduct, (2) of an enterprise, (3) through a pattern (4) of racketeering activity. In addition, the plaintiffs must plead injury to business or property as a result of the RICO violation. To adequately plead a pattern of racketeering activity under 18 U.S.C.S. § 1962(c), a plaintiff must allege that a defendant committed two or more predicate acts of racketeering activity.

[a] Unfair Competition

Unfair competition includes "false advertising, 'bait and switch' selling tactics, use of confidential information by former employee to solicit customers, theft of trade secrets, breach of a restrictive covenant, trade libel, and false representation of products or services."[683] Unfair competition is primarily a matter of state

---

[677] *See, e.g.,* Frisch's Restaurants, Inc. v. Elby's Big Boy of Steubenville, Inc., 670 F.2d 642, 646 (6th Cir. 1982).

[678] M.G.L.A. ch. 93A, § 4.

[679] *Id.* at § 9.

[680] *Id.* at § 11.

[681] *Id.*

[682] Linthicum v. Archambault, 379 Mass. 381, 383 (1979).

[683] *Id.*

law.[684] *Unfair competition* is a common law cause of action generally defined "as the passing off by a defendant of his goods or services as those of another, by virtue of substantial similarity between the two, leading to confusion on the part of potential customers, or the misrepresentation by a defendant of the qualities, origin or contents of his products or services."[685]

[b]   Trade Libel or Disparagement

Trade libel[686] or commercial disparagement is a common law tort action to redress derogatory statements made about a competitor's products. Modern commercial disparagement cases are relatively rare and often pleaded as pendent claims to Lanham § 43(a) actions.

[c]   Conversion of Cyberchattels

Conversion is the unlawful exercise of dominion or control over the personal property of another.[687] At common law, only tangible property could be converted, not intangibles such as software or data. Software and other intangible assets cannot be possessed and may not be literally dispossessed or converted. Modern courts have expanded the tort of conversion to include intangible property.[688] An "employee's destruction of a WordPerfect directory" was held to be conversion.[689] In that case, a former secretary deleted the directory on her last day of work, supposedly to free up computer space. The court found that deleting the directory without a review of the contents was not a standard practice and therefore constituted conversion.[690]

The Restatement (Second) of Torts distinguishes conversion from the lesser offense of trespass to chattels based upon the seriousness of the interference. Trespass to chattels is a diminution in value, whereas conversion is a serious interference with property rights. The doctrinal difference between conversion and

---

[684] *Id.*

[685] Resnick v. Angel Manfredy, 1999 U.S. Dist. LEXIS 5877 *18 (E.D. Pa., Apr. 26, 1999).

[686] *Trade libel* is defined as "an intentional disparagement of the quality of property, which results in pecuniary damage." Aetna Casualty & Surety Co. v. Centennial Ins. Co., 838 F.2d 346, 351 (9th Cir. 1988).

[687] *Conversion* is an intentional tort where the "defendant must intend to exercise substantial dominion over the chattel." Dan B. Dobbs and Paul T. Hayden, Torts and Compensation: Personal Accountability and Social Responsibility for Injury 54 (1997). The measure of damages is for the defendant to pay the full value of the chattel, if the interference is serious enough to justify imposing such liability and if a number of factors were important, including (1) extent and duration of control, (2) the defendant's intent to assert a right to the property, (3) the defendant's good faith, (4) the harm done, and (5) the expense or inconvenience caused. *Id.* (citing Restatement (Second) of Torts § 222A (1965)).

[688] *Id.*

[689] Richard A. Raysman and Peter Brown, Conversion, Trespass and Other New Litigation Issues, 221 N.Y. Law J. 1 (May 11, 1999) (discussing Mundy v. Decker, 1999 Neb. App. LEXIS 3 (Neb. Ct. App., Jan. 5, 1999)).

[690] *Id.*

trespass to chattels is the measure of damages. Less serious incidents of interference are classified as the trespass to chattels. In Prosser's words, "[t]respass to chattels survives today, in other words, largely as a little brother of conversion."[691] Trespass to chattels may result where a licensor exceeds the scope of its license agreement and thereby trespasses on a computer system.[692]

With the evolution of the information-based economy, there is an argument for expanding conversion to intangibles.[693] Conversion is such a pervasive interference with chattels that the tortfeasor "may justly be required to pay the other the full value of the chattel." Trespass to chattels originally required asportation[694] and did not include mere unauthorized use or access to documents that were not destroyed or even modified.[695]

[C] State Enforcement of Online Gambling

The Kansas and Minnesota attorneys general have issued warnings to the online gaming industry about targeting their residents. At least 450 web sites offer Internet gambling: Online casinos and sportsbooks offer traditional wagering and straight-line betting operations.[696] Internet gambling web sites are available to residents located in states where gambling is illegal.[697] Minnesota's attorney general places a warning to Internet users and providers that they are subject to enforcement for illegal activities on the Internet.[698] In particular, the Minnesota attorney general states: "Persons outside of Minnesota who transmit information via the Internet are subject to jurisdiction in Minnesota courts for violations of state criminal and civil laws."[699]

The Minnesota attorney general has targeted Internet gambling that offers Minnesota residents the opportunity to place bets, purchase lottery tickets, or participate in casino-type games.[700] In 1995, the Minnesota attorney general filed a consumer protection lawsuit against Granite Gate Resorts, doing business as On

---

[691] W. Page Keeton, Prosser and Keeton on Torts § 14, at 85-86 (5th ed. 1984).

[692] Hotmail Corp. v. Van Money Pie, Inc., 1998 U.S. Dist. LEXIS 10729 (D.N.D. Cal., Apr. 16, 1998).

[693] *Id.* at 92.

[694] *Asportation* means the "act of carrying away." Asportation is the taking of absolute control of the property. Ballentine's Dictionary 97 (3d ed. 1969).

[695] CompuServe, Inc. v. Cyber Promotions, Inc., 962 F. Supp. 1015, 1020 (S.D. Ohio 1997).

[696] *See, e.g.,* http://dir.yahoo.com/Business_and_Economy/Shopping_and_Services/Gambling/Web_Site_Gambling (visited Aug. 14, 2000).

[697] *See, e.g.,* SportBet.com, Winners Internet Network, and World Sports Exchange.

[698] A large number of Internet gambling web sites advertise services to residents of jurisdictions where gambling is illegal. Some online casinos employ nude hostesses as part of their online casino and sportsbook. *See* Winners Internet Network (visited Mar. 15, 2002), http://www.winr.net/english/benefits.asp.

[699] Statement of Minnesota AG on Internet Jurisdiction, reprinted at Lewis Rose, Advertising Law, Arent Fox law firm web site (visited Nov. 28, 1999), http://www.webcom.com/lewrose/article/minn.html.

[700] *Id.*

Ramp Internet Computer Services, and its officers.[701] The Minnesota attorney general alleged deceptive trade practices, false advertising, and consumer fraud, filing for injunctive and declaratory relief. The attorney general argued that the defendants' online casino reached thousands of Minnesota citizens whose computers enter the Internet web site. The Minnesota district court found sufficient jurisdiction, finding that the defendant purposefully availed of itself of jurisdiction by crossing Minnesota borders through Internet advertisements and by soliciting business for its gaming venture.[702]

In 1997, Missouri's attorney general sued an Idaho Indian tribe, contending that the tribe's online lottery violated Missouri law, "offering betting services to state citizens."[703] A number of federal bills have attempted to regulate the advertising of Internet gambling web sites.[704] The United States Department of Justice charged offshore gambling sites with violation of the Interstate Wire Act.[705] Many of the online casinos are located offshore, making enforcement difficult.[706] In *United States v. Cohen*,[707] the defendant was charged with violating 18 U.S.C. § 1084, which prohibits the use of wire communication facilities to transmit wagers in interstate or foreign commerce. The court held that the defendant violated this statute by using both the Internet and telephones to transmit calls from bettors in New York, where gambling is illegal, to World Sports Exchange in Antigua, where gambling is legal, during which transmissions bets were placed.[708] In litigation involving MasterCard and Visa,[709] the court dismissed claims citing RICO violations, holding that the plaintiffs failed to allege that the defendants committed the pattern of racketeering activity required to establish a RICO violation, given that they had alleged neither a violation of a state statute nor a violation of one of the federal statutes that can serve as the basis of a RICO claim.

---

[701] Complaint of State of Minnesota v. Granite Gate Resorts, Inc., No. C6-95-7227 (Minn. Dist. Ct., Ramsey Cty., July 18, 1995).

[702] State of Minnesota v. Granite Gate Resorts, Inc., No. C6-95-7227 (Minn. D. Ct., Ramsey Cty., Dec. 1996) (order finding jurisdiction over online gambling defendants).

[703] Tim Ito and Sharisa Staples, The Odds on Prohibiting Web Webs, Washingtonpost.com (visited Jan. 25, 1999), http://www.washingtonpost.com/wp-s.../longterm/intgambling/overview.htm.

[704] Section 1085 of S.474, The Internet Gambling Prohibition Act of 1997, would have made it unlawful for a person "engaged in the business of betting or wagering to engage in that business through the Internet or through any other interactive computer service in any State." That bill died in committee, as did a 1996 bill filed in the House of Representatives, H.R. 3526, "to amend title 18, United States Code, with Respect to Transmission of Wagering Information."

[705] Tim Ito and Sharisa Staples, *supra* note 703.

[706] The Gaming Commission of Antigua and Barbuda, for example, regulates World Sports Exchange. SportBet.com has an online link to Australia's largest sports and racing bookmaker. Internet Gaming & Communications Corp. is a publicly traded company that accepts wagers phoned to Antigua. *See* Cynthia R. Janower, Gambling on the Internet (visited Jan. 25, 1999), http://www.ascusc.org/jcmc/vol2/issue2/janower.html.

[707] United States v. Cohen, Docket No. 00-1574 (2d Cir. July 31, 2001), *available at* http://www.tourolaw.edu/2ndCircuit/July01/00-1574.html.

[708] *Id.*

[709] In re MasterCard Int'l Inc., Internet Gambling Litig., Civ. Act. MDL Nos. 1321 and 1322 2001 WL 197834 (E.D. La. Feb. 23, 2001).

The Interactive Gaming Council (IGC) is a standards-setting organization developing a Code of Conduct for online casinos.[710] The government of Antigua and Barbuda formed an alliance with the IGC to establish consumer protection for cybergaming.[711] It is a federal crime to conduct illegal gambling businesses or use wire communications in interstate commerce.

Internet gambling and other activities that may be deemed fraudulent or deceptive are subject to consumer protection regulation. Many states have enacted the Uniform Deceptive Trade Practices Act (UDTPA). The UDTPA varies from state to state, but generally permits actions by the attorney general as well as by private parties. In many states, injunctive relief, double or treble damages, attorneys' fees, and costs are recoverable.[712] Many states that have not adopted the UDTPA have criminal statutes governing false advertising.[713] Internet advertisers may also be subject to enforcement actions brought by the National Advertising Division of the Council of Better Business Bureaus.[714]

[D] Telecommuting and Negligence

Millions of American workers telecommute to work from home with the help of virtual private networks, the Internet, e-mail, and other new technologies. *Telecommuting* is defined as an employer permitting performance of work to occur on a regular basis in a location, usually the employee's home or a telecenter, other than a principal office. For 2000, the number of telecommuters was expected to grow to 25,000,000, up from the 11,000,000 workers who telecommuted in some fashion in 1997.[715] President Clinton identified telecommuting as a means of fostering a family-friendly work environment.[716]

The National Performance Review recommended that federal agencies promote flexiplace and telecommuting.[717] In Japan, one telecommuting center combines telecommuting with a resort setting.[718] Sweden invented the "office train," where managers work for half-pay during an 80-minute train ride in and out of

---

[710] Interactive Gaming Council, IGC, Press Release: Antigua Gambling (visited Jan. 25, 1999), http://www.igcouncil.org.

[711] *Id.*

[712] *See, e.g.*, Mass. Gen. Laws Ann. Ch. 93A.

[713] *See, e.g.*, Alaska Stat. § 45.50.471; 18 (1998); Cal. Civ. Code § 17500 (Deering 1995); Colo. Rev. Stat. § 42-6-206 (1998); Fla. Stat. Ann. §§ 501.201 (West 1999); Kan. Stat. Ann. § 50-626 (1999); Ky. Rev. Stat. § 367.170 (Baldwin 1998); N.D. Cent. Code §§ 51-12-01; 15-1208 (1998).

[714] Mark Sableman, Business Liabilities on the Internet, 16 SPG Comm. Law. 3 (1996).

[715] Beverly W. Garofalo, Telecommuting: Interaction of Employment Law and Tech Change: Employers Are Well Advised to Draw Up Agreements for At-Home Workers, 15 Comp. L. Strat. 1 (Apr. 1999).

[716] Interagency Telecommuting Program, Overview of Telecommuting Today (visited May 29, 1999), http://www.gsa.gov/pbs/owi/overview.htm.

[717] *Id.*

[718] *Id.*

Stockholm.[719] The first teleservice center in the United States was established by Pacific Bell in 1985. IBM, AT&T, Ernst & Young, and a number of other companies are furnishing employees with furniture, equipment, workstations, and other accommodations for telecommuting.[720]

Although it may be difficult to show an employer's vicarious liability for injuries on the physical property of the telecommuter, this may not be the case for direct liability for injuries suffered via the telecommuter's cyberspace. While the use of the telecommuter's property is primarily residential, the Internet connection provided by the employer to the telecommuter is predominately commercial. Millions of Internet telecommuters today work from home and connect to their employer's internal network over the Internet.[721] Telecommuting creates a new security risk because of the possibility that careless telecommuting employees may place an employer's otherwise formidable Internet security systems at risk.

If telecommuters do not comply with information security policies, all confidential and trade secret information to which the telecommuter has access is at risk. Employers could also be liable to third parties for the negligent actions of telecommuters. An employer may protect itself from these lawsuits by following the highest standards of information security. A basic tunnel providing encryption that does not prevent a hacker's access may be viewed as a failure of due care. The heightened standard of an advanced tunnel providing both encryption and access prevention would likely be an adequate standard of care.[722]

[E] Successor Liability for Online Companies[723]

In 1998, there was a record $1.7 trillion in domestic mergers and acquisition activities in a single year.[724] The surge of spin-offs, mergers, takeovers, and other acquisitions among Internet and media companies is gaining momentum. The American Online/Netscape, TCI/AT&T, Adelphia/Century Communications, MCI/WorldCom, and Intel/Dialog mergers are just a few examples. In addition, parent companies are merging with wholly owned subsidiaries, as with Intel's merger with and into Dialogic Corporation. Dialogic Corporation became a wholly owned subsidiary of Intel in July 1999.[725]

---

[719] Interagency Telecommuting Program, Overview of Telecommuting Today (visited Apr. 22, 2002), http://www.gsa.gov/pbs/owi/overview.htm.

[720] *Id.*

[721] Mark Maier, The Law and Technology of Internet Telecommuting, 6 SMU Computer L. Rev. & Tech. J. 22 (1999).

[722] *Id.*

[723] Amy Wilson, Class of 1995, Suffolk University Law School, completed the research for this section.

[724] Thomas J. Dougherty, "Takeovers," Securities Litigation: Planning and Strategies, American Law Institute-American Bar Association Continuing Legal Education, SD79 ALI/ABA 567 (1999).

[725] Intel, Intel Completes Merger with Dialogic, Intel Press Release (visited Apr. 15, 2002), http://intel.com/pressroom/archive/releases/Cn71399.htm.

Successor corporations need to do a due diligence to determine whether they have assumed the tort liabilities of predecessor corporations in the online environment. Although there is no case law pertaining to the successor liability of online companies, traditional principles will easily be extended. The traditional rule of successor liability "provides that a corporation that acquires all, or part, of the assets of another corporation does not thereby assume the liabilities and debts of the predecessor."[726] The general rule is that a corporation that purchases the assets of another corporation is not liable for the liabilities and debts of the predecessor corporation.[727] The four exceptions to the "no liability" for successor corporations are (1) when the successor corporation either expressly or impliedly assumes the liabilities, (2) when the sale is essentially a consolidation or merger of the two corporations, (3) when the successor corporation is merely a continuation of the predecessor corporation, or (4) when the transaction is entered into fraudulently for the purpose of escaping the predecessor.[728]

The first exception is when the purchaser either expressly or impliedly agrees to assume the seller's liabilities.[729] The second exception occurs when a successor corporation is a continuation of the predecessor corporation and there is a continuity of ownership or corporate structure. Successor liability is transferred from the predecessor to the continuing successor corporation. The "mere continuation" exception is not satisfied unless the predecessor is extinguished.[730] The third exception is where a court finds a *de facto* merger instead of an assets purchase.[731] The continuity doctrine requires a number of other findings, including (1) that there be no remedy against the predecessor and (2) that a transfer of the corporate assets must have occurred.[732] The fourth exception is that tort liabilities will be assumed by the successor in the event that the merger or acquisition was a fraudulent transaction, intended to evade liability on debts.[733]

In the field of products liability, a product line exception also holds a successor corporation liable if it continues to market and produce the same product line as the predecessor corporation. A successor products liability manufacturer

---

[726] Annotation, Successor Products Liability: Form of Business Organization of Successor or Predecessor as Affecting Successor Liability, 32 AL.R.4th 196 (1999).

[727] Araserv, Inc. v. Bay State Harness Horse Racing & Breeding Assoc., Inc., 437 F. Supp. 1083 (D. Mass. 1977).

[728] Dayton v. Peck, Stow & Wilcox Co., 739 F.2d 690 (1st Cir. 1984); Schumacher v. Richard Shear Co., 59 N.Y.2d 239, 464 N.Y.S.2d 437 (1983).

[729] *See, e.g.*, Polius v. Clark Equip. Co., 802 F.2d 75 (3d Cir. 1986).

[730] Liability of Successor Corporation, 86 N.Y. Jur. Prods. Liab. § 9 (1998).

[731] *See, e.g.*, McCarthy v. Litton Indus., Inc., 410 Mass. 15, 570 N.E.2d 1008 (1991); Cargill, Inc. v. Beaver Coal & Oil Co., 424 Mass. 356 (1997) (holding that a corporation was liable for obligations of predecessor corporation under the *de facto* merger doctrine).

[732] Diaz v. South Bend Lathe, Inc., 707 F. Supp. 97 (E.D.N.Y. 1989) (noting that a *de facto* merger had occurred based on evidence of assumption of liabilities, continuity of management and personnel, and the dissolution of the predecessor corporation).

[733] Raytech Corp. v. White, 54 F.3d 187 (3d Cir. 1995).

"steps into the shoes" of its predecessor if the successor produces the same product. In *Sheppard v. A.C. & S. Co.*,[734] an asbestos company argued that it was only a successor corporation. The court disagreed, holding that uncertainty existed as to whether the successor continued producing the same harm-causing product line, subjecting it to possible punitive damages.[735]

Assuming one of the four exceptions to the "no liability" rule applies, punitive damages are recoverable against the successor corporation for the torts of its predecessor corporation.[736] Successor liability for the torts of a predecessor is a significant risk for the online company for claims arising out of product liability,[737] environmental issues,[738] and labor and employment relations. An online successor may also be liable for the predecessor corporation's employment law obligations, including collective bargaining agreements and responsibility for unfair labor practices.[739]

[F]   Securities Regulation in Cyberspace

[1]   Structure and Function of the SEC

The Securities and Exchange Commission (SEC) was the federal agency created to protect the integrity of the stock market after the Great Stock Market Crash of 1929. The purpose of the SEC was to restore public confidence in the securities industry and capital markets.[740] The SEC is composed of five Commissioners appointed by the President whose terms last five years. The SEC Chairman is the head of the Commission and also appointed by the President. The SEC Commission has the task of proposing new rules to address market imperfections and enforcing existing rules and laws.[741] The SEC's Division of Corporate Finance

---

[734] 484 A.2d 521 (Del. Super. Ct. 1984).

[735] An online company that merges with another company needs also to consider the risk of assuming environmental cleanup costs. Successor liability is especially important in situations where environmental problems can arise, as the cost for cleanups can be substantial. Under CERCLA (Comprehensive Environmental Response, Compensation and Liability Act), individuals or corporations who own or operate contaminated sites are liable for any cleanup costs. Environmental cases have found that where a successor acts as "a mere continuation" of a predecessor, it will inherit environmental liabilities despite explicit contractual provisions to the contrary. Blackstone Valley Elec. Co. v. Stone & Webster, Inc., 867 F. Supp. 73 (D. Mass. 1994).

[736] Annotation, Liability of Successor Corporation for Punitive Damages for Injury Caused by Predecessor's Product, 55 AL.R.4th 166 (1999).

[737] *See, e.g.,* Holzman v. Proctor, Cook & Co., 528 F. Supp. 9 (D. Mass. 1981); Billy v. Consolidated Machine Tool Corp., 51 N.Y.2d 152, 412 N.E.2d 934 (1989).

[738] *In re* Acushnet River & New Bedford Harbor Proceedings re: Alleged PCB Pollution, 712 F. Supp. 1010 (D. Mass. 1989).

[739] *See, e.g.,* Dealing with Labor and Employment Law Issues in Mergers & Acquisitions, ALI/ABA (July 1998 Course of Study). *See generally* Mark J. Roe, Mergers, Acquisitions and Tort: A Comment on the Problem of Successor Corporation Liability, 70 Va. L. Rev. 1559 (1984).

[740] U.S. Securities and Exchange Commission, Creation of the SEC (visited Apr. 15, 2002), http://www.sec.gov/about/whatwedo.shtml.

[741] U.S. Securities and Exchange Commission, How the SEC Protects Investors, Maintains Market Integrity (visited Apr. 23, 2002), http://www.sec.gov/about/wahtwedo.shtml.

oversees regulations on disclosure documents for publicly traded companies. Each publicly held company is required to file (1) registration statements for newly offered securities, (2) annual and quarterly filings (Forms 10-K and 10-Q), (3) proxy materials sent to shareholders before an annual meetings, (4) annual reports to shareholders, (5) documents concerning tender offers, and (6) filings related to mergers and acquisitions.[742] The SEC web site now includes the EDGAR database of disclosure documents.

[2]   Federal Securities Laws

The federal securities law that may apply to Internet-related transactions include the (1) Securities Act of 1933, (2) Securities Exchange Act of 1934, (3) Public Utility Holding Company Act of 1935, (4) Trust Indenture Act of 1939, (5) Investment Company Act of 1940, and (6) Investment Advisers Act of 1940. In addition, criminal complaints may be available for false online postings about securities.[743]

The SEC staff has published several reports and interpretations on topics such as broker-dealers offering online trading, Internet fraud, online trading, online investing, the use of electronic media by broker-dealers, and the use of Internet web sites to offer securities. The SEC's 2002 report on electronic signatures in global and national commerce reexamines the obligations of issuers to maintain certain records under the Securities Act, the Exchange Act, and Regulation S-T.[744] The SEC's interpretation was that no new standards were required to protect investors and that the obligation "is met by retaining an electronic record of the information in the contract or other record if the electronic record"[745] is accurate and is accessible to the requisite parties for the required period. The SEC reserved the right to impose new standards for electronic retention if questions arise as to the accuracy, integrity, or accessibility of e-records concerning securities. In 1999, California enacted special digital signature acts governing online brokerage.

[a]   *Securities Act of 1933*

The Securities Act of 1933 requires the disclosure of financial information through the registration of securities. Registration statements are made public after filing with the SEC. The 1933 Act also "prohibits deceit, misrepresentations, and

---

[742] U.S. Securities and Exchange Commission, "Division of Corporate Finance" (visited Apr. 23, 2002), http://www.sec.gov/about/whatwedo.shtml.

[743] See, e.g., Michael Geist, Phoney Posting Has Company on the Go, BNA's Internet Law News, Feb. 16, 2001 (citing http://www.newsbytes.com/news/01/162053.html).

[744] Securities and Exchange Comm'n Interpretation, Application of the Electronic Signatures in Global and National Commerce Act to Record Retention Requirements Pertaining to Issuers under the Securities Act of 1933, Securities Exchange Act of 1934 and Regulation S-T (visited Apr. 15, 2002), http://www.sec.gov/rules/interp/33-7985.htm#P35_2474.

[745] *Id.*

other fraud in the sale of securities."[746] The EDGAR database publishes all registration statements and prospectuses and is accessible at the SEC web site. The SEC exempts delimited classes from the registration requirement: (a) private offerings to a limited number of persons or entities; (b) offerings of limited size; (c) intrastate offerings; and (d) securities of municipal, state, and federal governments. The policy behind exempting small offerings is to "reduce the cost of offering securities to the public."[747]

The SEC issued an interpretation that made it clear that issuers, investment companies, broker-dealers, exchanges, and investment advisers who use the Internet to disseminate information about securities may be subject to federal securities laws.[748] The basic principle is that an issuer or other actor is subject to U.S. federal securities law unless it takes steps to disavow targeting persons in the United States. Offerors, for example, need to "implement adequate measures to prevent U.S. persons from participating in an offshore Internet offer"; the SEC "would not view the offer as targeted at the United States and thus would not treat it as occurring in the United States for registration purposes."[749]

The standard of adequate measures turns on what is reasonable given the circumstances. The SEC interpretation provides principles for a safe harbor that an offer is not being targeted to the United States:

- The web site includes a prominent disclaimer making it clear that the offer is directed only to countries other than the United States. For example, the web site could state that the securities or services are not being offered in the United States or to U.S. persons, or it could specify those jurisdictions (other than the United States) in which the offer is being made; and

- The web site offeror implements procedures that are reasonably designed to guard against sales to U.S. persons in the offshore offering. For example, the offeror could ascertain the purchaser's residence by obtaining such information as mailing addresses or telephone numbers (or area code) prior to the sale. This measure will allow the offeror to avoid sending or delivering securities, offering materials, services, or products to a person at a U.S. address or telephone number.[750]

---

[746] U.S. Securities and Exchange Commission, Securities Act of 1933 (visited Apr. 23, 2002), http://www.sec.gov/about/laws.shtml.

[747] *Id.*

[748] Securities and Exchange Comm'n Interpretation, Use of Internet Web Sites to Offer Securities, Solicit Securities Transactions, or Advertise Investment Services Offshore (visited Apr. 15, 2002), http://www.sec.gov/rules/interp/33-7985.htm#P35_2474.

[749] Issuers "increasingly use Web sites to solicit offshore securities transactions and clients without the securities or investment company being registered with the Commission under the Securities Act of 1933 or the Investment Company Act of 1940, or without the investment service provider registering under the Investment Advisers Act of 1940, or the broker-dealer or exchange registering under the broker-dealer and exchange registration provisions under the Securities Exchange Act of 1934." *Id.*

[750] *Id.*

The SEC's interpretation is that if a U.S. person purchases securities or investment services "notwithstanding adequate procedures reasonably designed to prevent the purchase," the Commission would not view this as an offer targeted to the United States.

[b] Securities Act of 1934

The Securities Exchange Act of 1934 created the Commission, which is the chief regulatory agency of the securities industry. The 1934 Act gave the SEC the power to require periodic reports. Companies with more than $10 million in assets whose securities are held by more than 500 owners must file annual or other periodic reports to comply with the 1934 Act. The SEC also governs disclosures in proxy solicitations. A proxy solicitation is designed "to solicit shareholders' votes in annual or special meetings."[751] The 1934 Act also mandates required disclosures for tender offers. The Act requires disclosure from anyone seeking "to acquire more than 5 percent of a company's securities by direct purchase or tender offer."[752] Insider trading is illegal as are "fraudulent activities of any kind in connection with the offer, purchase or sale of securities."[753] Insider trading occurs when a person trades securities as a result of nonpublic information in violation of a duty to "withhold the information or refrain from trading."[754]

The 1934 Act also granted the commission "the power to register, regulate and oversee brokerage firms, transfer agents and clearing agencies as well as the nation's securities self regulatory organizations (SROs)."[755] The New York Stock Exchange and NASDAQ are examples of SROs regulated by the Commission. The 1934 Act requires market participants to register with the commission. SROs are required to have mechanisms for disciplining members for improper conduct and SRO proposed rules, must be published for comment before SEC approval.[756]

Internet stock fraud has been a prime target of the SEC enforcement division. The SEC has filed numerous actions against individuals who used the Internet to pass insider information in violation of Rule 10b-5 of the Securities Act of 1934. To state a cause of action under § 10(b) of the Securities Exchange Act of 1934 and S.E.C. Rule 10b-5, a plaintiff must plead that the defendant made a false statement or omitted a material fact, with scienter, and that the plaintiff's reliance on the defendant's action caused the plaintiff injury. "In the context of S.E.C. Rule 10b-5, predictions are not facts in and of themselves but they contain the factual assertions that the speaker genuinely believes the statement is accurate, that there is a reasonable basis for that belief, and that the speaker is unaware of any undisclosed facts that would tend to seriously undermine the accuracy of the statement.

---

[751] *Id.*

[752] *Id.*

[753] *Id.*

[754] *Id.*

[755] *Id.*

[756] Registration of Exchanges, Association, and Others, *id.*

The materiality of such unstated factual assertion is directly related to prediction or statement made."[757] Section 78u-4(b)(2) of the Private Securities Litigation Reform Act requires a securities fraud complaint to state with particularity facts giving rise to a strong inference that the defendant acted with the required state of mind.[758] To state a *prima facie* case pursuant to § 18(a) of the Securities Exchange Act of 1934, plaintiffs must plead that they purchased or sold a security in actual reliance on a specifically identified document filed with the Securities and Exchange Commission. Section 18(a) also requires that the statement be made in a document filed pursuant to the applicable rules and regulations.[759]

[c]   Other Federal Securities Laws

The SEC has taken a number of affirmative steps to punish and deter Internet fraud. The SEC has been active in enforcing antifraud provisions of the federal securities law in cyberspace. Internet securities fraud involves old investment scams using new information technologies. The SEC and its counterparts in the International Organization of Securities Commissions (IOSCO) conduct an "International Internet Surf Day."[760] The Surf Day conducted on March 28, 2000, involved 220 staff members from 21 IOSCO regulatory authorities.[761] The IOSCO surfers identified over 1,000 questionable sites for follow-up study; 250 sites involved cross-border activity.[762] Many of the questionable sites involved "unregistered offerings, pyramid schemes, unlicensed investment advice and high-yield investments."[763]

The SEC's regulator framework is based upon a model of full disclosure: "all investors, whether large institutions or private individuals, should have access to certain basic facts about an investment prior to buying it."[764] The SEC's Internet fraud enforcement focuses on assuring the accuracy of information about securities promoted on the Internet. The SEC will bring 400 to 500 civil enforcement actions against individuals and companies each year.[765] SEC enforcement may be brought for "insider trading, accounting fraud, and providing false or misleading information about securities and the companies that issue them."[766]

---

[757] Cyber Media Group v. Island Mortgage Network, Inc., 183 F. Supp. 2d 559 (E.D.N.Y. 2002).

[758] 15 U.S.C.S. § 78u-4(b)(2) (2001) (stating that a strong inference of fraud arises where the complaint alleges that defendants (1) benefited in a concrete and personal way from the purported fraud, (2) engaged in deliberately illegal behavior, (3) knew facts or had access to information suggesting that their public statements were not accurate, or (4) failed to check information they had a duty to monitor).

[759] *Id.* § 78r(a).

[760] U.S. Securities and Exchange Commission, SEC and Regulators from Around the World Conduct an International Surf Day to Help Combat Internet Fraud, Press Release 2000-64, Apr. 5, 2000 (visited Apr. 23, 2002), http://www.sec.gov/news/press/2000-44.txt.

[761] *Id.*

[762] *Id.*

[763] *Id.*

[764] U.S. Securities and Exchange Commission, About the SEC, Introduction: The SEC: Who We Are, What We Do (visited Apr. 23, 2002), http://www.sec.gov/about/whatwedo.shtml.

[765] *Id.* at 2.

[766] *Id.*

[d] NASD Online Regulation

NASD Regulations, Inc. is a securities-industry self-regulatory group and is a parent organization of the National Association of Securities Dealers, Inc. (NASD) and the American Stock Exchange, LLC. NASD issued a policy statement on online activities and communications in an NASD Notice to Members.[767] NASD's position is that online communications can qualify as "recommendations" for purposes of the suitability rule.[768] NASD's "suitability rule" provides "that in recommending to a customer the purchase, sale, or exchange of any security, a member shall have reasonable grounds for believing that the recommendation is suitable for such customer."[769] NASD's policy statement addressed the transmittal of information through "broker/dealers' web sites, e-mail, Web phones, personal digital assistants and hand-held pagers."[770]

[e] Online Securities Litigation

The online brokerage business of $415 billion in 2002 is expected to increase seven times by 2003. In 2001, the $9.7 billion in online accounts tripled from 1997.[771] Online trading now accounts for nearly 16 percent of all trades. The number of online trades increased from 100,000 per day to a half million from 1997 to 1999. Yahoo!, AOL, and Microsoft have entered into co-branding arrangements with brokers in which these popular portals receive a flat fee for orders.[772] The potential for fraud in online trading is enormous. The SEC's rules for brokers and financial advisers apply equally to cyberspace. Depersonalized online contacts with customers may make it necessary to determine the customer's needs to fulfill the SEC's suitability rule recommending that investments be tailored to the customer.[773] The use of the Internet to mine data affects broker rules such as the execution obligation, which is the duty to seek out the most advantageous terms for a customer's transactions.[774] The data mining of customers' personal information collected online is a growing concern, and the SEC is charged with developing privacy regulations to comply with the Gramm-Leach-Bliley Act.

The SEC's Office of Internet Enforcement (OIE) administers the Enforcement Division's Internet program. The OIE has the function of detecting and prosecuting online swindles affecting the investing public. Its responsibilites are to

---

[767] NASD Regulation, Inc., NASD Regulation Policy Statement to Brokerage Firms Regarding Suitability in Online Activities and Communications (Mar. 20, 2001).

[768] Id.

[769] NASD Regulations, Inc., NASD Notice to Members 01-23 (Apr. 2001), at 2.

[770] Id.

[771] Securities and Exchange Comm'n, On- Line Brokerage: Keeping Apace of Cyberspace (visited Apr. 12, 2002), http://www.sec.gov/pdf/cybrtrnd.pdf.

[772] Id.

[773] Id.

[774] Id.

- Identify areas of surveillance;

- Formulate investigative procedures;

- Provide strategic and legal guidance to enforcement staff nationwide;

- Conduct Internet investigations and prosecutions (a task it shares with the entire enforcement staff);

- Perform training for Commission staff and outside agencies; and

- Serve as a resource on Internet matters for the entire Commission.[775]

The OIE coordinates a "cyberforce" of SEC attorneys, accountants, and investigators who do Internet surveillance to detect Internet misconduct. The online world is an ideal venue for fraud. In March 2001, the SEC was pursuing well over 200 fraud cases involving Internet securities. Each year the OIE supervises an Internet "sweep," which has yielded hundreds of cases. The SEC filed more than 180 Internet-related cases against companies for fraud for manipulating micro cap stocks in 2001. The OIE has also used sweeps to halt unregistered online offers or so-called free stock. The SEC has also prosecuted online mortgage brokers who used false accounting practices to cover fraudulent operating expenses. The SEC settled an enforcement action against an Internet stock picker known as Tokyo Joe and the company he controlled in March 2001. Tokyo Joe and his company are enjoined permanently "from violating the antifraud and other provisions of the federal securities laws and [he must] pay a large fine for ill-gotten gains and civil penalties."[776]

The SEC is actively prosecuting Internet fraud cases. The SEC has been monitoring online investment newsletters, statements made on bulletin boards, and bogus e-mail investment schemes.[777] Online newsletters may "spread false information or promote worthless stocks."[778] In addition, they sometimes "scalp" the stocks they hype, driving up the price of the stock with their baseless recommendations and then selling their own holdings at high prices and high profits.[779] Another technique of online fraudsters is to use bulletin boards as a way of pumping up a company. Other securities fraudsters pretend to reveal "inside" information about upcoming announcements, new products, or lucrative contracts. Junk e-mail permits contacts with millions of potential investors. The SEC warns online investors of the use of old scams on the new medium of the Internet. Internet

---

[775] Securities and Exchange Comm'n, Internet Enforcement Program, About the Office of Internet Enforcement (visited Apr. 12, 2002), http://www.sec.gov/divisions/enforce/internetenforce.htm (noting that the cyberforce of the OIE may be contacted at enforcement@sec.gov).

[776] Securities and Exchange Comm'n, Internet Enforcement Program, Press Release, SEC Settles Securities Fraud Action Against "Tokyo Joe" (visited Apr. 12, 2002), http://www.sec.gov/news/press/2001-26.txt (reporting that Internet stock picker was required to disgorge all illegal profits and pay a penalty of more than $400,000 and consent to a permanent antifraud injunction).

[777] U.S. Securities and Exchange Commission, Internet Fraud: How to Avoid Internet Investment Scams (visited May 27, 2001), http://www.sec.gov/investor/pubs/cyberfraud.htm.

[778] Id.

[779] Id.

frauds generally fall into the following categories: (1) the "pump and dump" scam, (2) the pyramid, (3) the "risk-free" fraud, and (4) offshore frauds.[780] The SEC has prosecuted cases involving bogus web sites, fake "prime bank" securities, and soliciting investors with whopping returns. The SEC charged 33 companies and individuals with a widespread "pump and dump" stock scheme.[781] An online cross-trading scheme resulted in charges being filed against a New York stock trader.[782]

A large number of private securities actions have been filed in Internet-related cases. In *In re CDNOW Secs. Litig.,*[783] a court granted the defendant's motion to dismiss a putative class action for Internet securities fraud. The plaintiffs in that case failed to plead the necessary element of scienter, material omissions, or misleading statements. In *Benning v. Wit Capital Group, Inc.,*[784] the customers of an Internet brokerage firm sued for fraud and misrepresentation relating to customers' access to initial public offerings. The court denied class certification because fraud and negligent misrepresentation could not be the basis of a class action claim under Delaware law. In addition, the Delaware Consumer Fraud Act could not be pleaded since the conduct did not occur in Delaware. The court also found that the other causes of action failed to satisfy Delaware's Rule 23(a) prerequisites for class certification. The basis of the claim was that the customers were not given the opportunity to purchase initial public offers (IPOs) as defendant advertised.[785]

[G]   FCC Regulation

The Federal Communications Commission (FCC) determines policies for broadband access, ISP access charges, Internet telephony, and unbundling rules for exchange markets. Under the Federal Communications Act,[786] the FCC is vested with the responsibility of proscribing just and reasonable charges, practice, classifications, and regulations regarding wire and radio services. The Telecommunications Act of 1996 articulated a public policy of preserving a free market as to the Internet and interactive computer services. Under the Act, communications services are classified in one of three ways: information service, telecommunication service, or cable service.[787] Cable companies began offering high-speed Internet service, as well as traditional cable television, over their wires even before the

---

[780] *Id.*

[781] James Niccolai, SEC Charges 33 with Net Fraud, InfoWorld Media Group Inc. (Sept. 6, 2000).

[782] N.Y. Stock Trader Settles Charges over Alleged Online Cross-Trading Scheme, Pike & Fischer Internet L. & Regulation, Jan. 9, 2001.

[783] 2001 U.S. Dist. LEXIS 4311 (E.D. Pa., Apr. 10, 2001).

[784] 2001 Del. Super. LEXIS 7 (Super. Ct. of Del., New Castle, Jan. 10, 2001) (denying motion for class certification).

[785] *Id.* at *3.

[786] 47 U.S.C.S. § 151 et seq. (2001); *see also* 47 C.F.R. § 54.500-.519); FCC Staff Report, Broadband Today, Oct. 1999 (visited Apr. 13, 2002), http://www.fcc.gov.

[787] GTE.NET, L.L.C. v. Cox Communications, Inc., 2002 U.S. Dist. LEXIS 2872 (S.D. Cal. Jan. 22, 2002).

Act. The FCC had interpreted the Act to cover pole attachments for these commingled services, and its interpretation had been approved by the Court of Appeals for the District of Columbia Circuit.

In *National Cable & Telecommunications Association v. Gulf Power Co.*,[788] the U.S. Supreme Court held that commingled service and wireless service providers were entitled under the Act to reasonable rates as determined by the FCC. The Court acknowledged that the Act prescribed rate formulas only for attachments by cable television systems solely to provide cable service, and for attachments by telecommunications carriers to provide telecommunications services. However, the Court reasoned that the inclusion of the rate formulas in the Act did not indicate that such rates were exclusive. Thus far, the FCC has not subjected cable broadband to any regulations, although it has broad jurisdiction to prevent discrimination and protect consumers and the public interest.[789] In general, the FCC has had a hands-off philosophy regarding Internet technologies, although it has made policy decisions on issues such as ISP telephone payments.

§ 5.12 PREVENTIVE LAW POINTERS AND SUPPLEMENTAL CHECKLISTS AIMED AT AVOIDING CYBERSPACE LIABILITY

[A] Adopt a Communications Policy

An online company needs to adopt an electronic mail and Internet usage policy to minimize tort liability. Chapter Nine provides detailed policy guidelines on how to develop an e-mail or Internet usage policy. Employers need to train employees on the potential tort liability in postings to discussion groups or e-mail messages. The case law discussed in Chapter Ten illustrates the diverse circumstances in which an online employer as well as an employee may be held liable for improper use of electronic communications.

[B] Preventing the Misuse of the Internet

Sexual and racial harassment should also be included in the company's e-mail and Internet policies.[790] A company may prevent some forms of harassment by restricting or forbidding access to the Internet. Software is available to block access to objectionable sites. The culture of a company is critical to reducing the risk of many online torts. A company should have a contact person so those employees have a method for reporting cyberharassment or other misuses of e-mail or the Internet. Co-employees should also be encouraged to report misuses

---

[788] 122 S. Ct. 782 (2002)

[789] GTE.NET, L.L.C v. Cox Communications, Inc., 2002 U.S. Dist. LEXIS 2872 (S.D. Cal., Jan. 29, 2002).

[790] *See, e.g.,* Rudas v. Nationwide Mut. Ins. Co., 1997 WL 11302 (E.D. Pa., Jan. 10, 1997) (lawsuit based upon sexual harassment by co-worker in the form of graphic e-mail messages). *See* ch. 10 *infra.*

and abuses of e-mail and the Internet.[791] A company may consider dismissing employees for distributing pornography on the Internet. The dean of Harvard's Divinity School was forced to resign after pornography was discovered on his computer.[792] A company must designate a contact person to whom misuses and abuses of company computer systems can be reported in order to detect and deal with warning signs of legal trouble.

[C] Preventing Computer Viruses

The risk of introducing malicious codes into computer systems needs to be managed by prevention rather than legal remedies.[793] Employees need to be educated on how to avoid catching viruses. Topics should include (1) an overview of the types of virus, including PC viruses,[794] Mac viruses,[795] UNIX viruses,[796] macro viruses,[797] Trojan horses,[798] worms,[799] logic bombs,[800] and other viruses; (2) the

---

[791] The Internet usage policy should provide the e-mail and telephone numbers of contact persons to report misuses and abuses of information technologies.

[792] Margie Wylie, Fix and Tell? Since There Is No Code of Ethics, Computer Technicians Who Find Sensitive Personal Files Usually Wonder What to Do, The Times-Picayune (July 15, 1999), at E1 (reporting that Harvard University's computer support technicians found pornographic images stored on Ronald Theimann's Harvard-owned computer, which was kept at home).

[793] In the summer of 1998, my home and school computers were infected with the Anti-Exec virus, which probably originated in a diskette transmitted from Suffolk's Computer Resource Center. At the time, I thought that all floppy disks had been scanned for viruses. While writing this chapter, I found this was not the case when Anti-Exec again infected my personal computer. The host for the virus was an old diskette that apparently had not been scanned. Without an infected diskette or other host, a virus cannot spread. Viruses cannot be eradicated unless all infected objects are replaced with clean backups.

[794] *PC* stands for *personal computer.* A *PC virus* is a term referring to viruses that infect personal computers.

[795] A MAC virus attaches itself to Macintosh computer systems.

[796] *UNIX* is "a software program that controls the operation of computer hardware and the interaction of software applications on that software." Michael D. Scott, Internet and Technology Desk Reference 519 (1999).

[797] A *macro* is a "single instruction that initiates a sequence of operations or module interactions within the program." Scott, *supra* note 796, at 305 (quoting Computer Assoc. Int'l v. Altai, Inc., 982 F.2d 693, 698 (2d Cir. 1992)).

[798] A *Trojan horse* is a computer program that conceals malicious code. "Typically, a Trojan horse masquerades as a useful program that users would want or need to execute. It performs, or appears to perform, as expected, but also does surreptitious harm." Scott, *supra* note 796, at 510.

[799] *Worm* is an acronym for "write once, read many." A worm is a "self-contained program containing malicious code that copy versions of themselves across electronically connected nodes." Scott, *id.* at 550.

[800] "A desirable program which performs some useful function such as logic but which contains a parasite or viral infection within its logic which is undetectable upon casual review. [M]ore properly called a 'time bomb' or 'logic bomb.'" Scott, *supra* note 796, at 303 (citation omitted). There is no "bullet-proof" antiviral program. One expert recommends comparing products at the following web sites: Virus Test Center (UNI-Hamburg), http://agn-www.iformatik.uni-hamburg.de/vtc/naeng.htm; Virus Research Unit (Uni-Tampere), http://www.uta.fi/laitokset/virus; *Virus Bulletin* (industry periodical), http://www.virusbtn.com (visited Apr. 15, 2002), http://members.tripod.com/~k_+wismer/common.htm.

harm viruses can do; (3) how viruses spread; (4) technologies and workplace practices that will reduce the radius of the risk of viruses; (5) antivirus software used by the company; and (6) the name of a contact person who checks on virus alerts and is responsible for preventing or mitigating losses due to viruses.

Employees need to be prepared to implement prompt remedial measures once they discover that the company's computer system is infected. A company's systems administrator needs to know how to promptly mitigate the consequences of malicious codes. Companies may need to initiate data recovery and emergency preparedness measures, such as checking off-site storage networks for viruses. Once a virus, such as Anti-Exec, is detected, it is important to act quickly to prevent the infecting of other computers. The user will need to run scan programs on all floppy disks, as well as computer systems. Antivirus programs such as Norton Utilities or McAfee should be used to scan all computer drives as well as diskettes.[801]

It is important to remember that a virus cannot be transmitted unless a program is executed. A program is executed by "running an application program (like a text editor or game), booting from a disk with an infected DOS boot sector or master boot record, or launching an infected document in one of the components of MS-Office (i.e., Word, Excel, Access, etc)."[802] Simply browsing web sites, for example, does not expose the computer system to viruses; the downloading of unknown databases, however, does pose a risk of transmitting viruses. Viruses strike software, not hardware, and experts agree that no known virus has ever damaged computer hardware.

It is arguable that a disabling routine built into the software is also a virus, unless the license agreement gives notice that the licensor reserves the right to use disabling software, such as time bombs. An active restraint affects the licensee's ability to access its own information, whereas a passive restraint prevents unauthorized use but does not lock the user out of his own computer. Installing an active disabling routine into software may subject a software vendor to intentional tort liability for spreading a computer virus.

[D] Pleading and Proof of Defamation

Counsel must consider whether a publication is protected by the First Amendment or is constitutionally protected speech. They must also consider state variations in the law of defamation. It is always the trial court's province to determine initially whether statements are capable of having a defamatory meaning.[803] A plaintiff may file for a temporary restraining order or injunction against use of the Internet to transmit untrue factual accusations. The defendant may be enjoined from transmitting defamatory statements via the Internet or discussion groups.[804] Before filing a claim, plaintiffs must determine the elements to be pleaded and proven in the jurisdiction. To plead a cause of action for a defamatory publication

---

[801] 15 F. Supp. 2d 246 (E.D.N.Y. 1998).

[802] *Id.*

[803] Resnick v. Angel Manfredy, 1999 U.S. Dist. LEXIS 5877 (E.D. Pa., Apr. 26, 1999).

[804] *See, e.g.*, Internet Am., Inc. v. Massey, No. 96-10955C (Tex. Dallas Cty. Dist. Ct., Oct. 14, 1996).

in Pennsylvania, for instance, a plaintiff must prove (1) the defamatory character of the communication, (2) its publication by the defendant, (3) its application to the plaintiff, (4) the understanding by the recipient of the defamatory meaning, (5) that the defamatory statement's intent is to be applied to the plaintiff, (6) special harm resulting to the plaintiff from its publication, and (7) abuse of a conditionally privileged occasion.[805]

[E] Cookie Warnings

If an online company uses cookies or text files stored in visitors' computers, it should make a full disclosure as to its use of cookies. Web site visitors may object to the storage of cookies in their computer's RAM.

[F] Employee Handbook and E-Mail Policy

Corporate counsel should include a conspicuous statement in the employee handbook that employees have no expectation of privacy in e-mail communications. In its e-mail and Internet usage policies, the employer should specifically warn employees that their e-mail messages are considered company records.

[G] Online Privacy Policies[806]

All corporate web sites should conspicuously display their online privacy policy. The policy should describe the type of information collected about users browsing the web site. If a web site sells goods online, an exception in the privacy policy should be made for its carriers, such as Federal Express, United Parcel Service, or other companies that deliver the product to the purchaser. The privacy policy should give notice that customer information is given to third parties for the purposes of delivery only. In *In re Doubleclick Inc. Privacy Litigation,*[807] the court dismissed claims advanced by the plaintiff class under the Electronic Communications Privacy Act, the Computer Fraud and Abuse Act, and the Wiretap Act arising out of Doubleclick's use and placement of "cookies" on plaintiffs' computers. Doubleclick uses such "cookies" to gather information about the users' use of Doubleclick client web sites. Because Doubleclick's clients consented to such information gathering, the court held that Doubleclick's activities did not violate either the Electronic Communications Privacy Act or the Wiretap Act.

Commercially reasonable methods, facilities, and systems to protect information from unauthorized access should augment the online privacy policy.

---

[805] Furillo v. Dana Corp. Parish Div., 866 F. Supp. 824, 847 (E.D. Pa. 1994) (applying Pennsylvania law).

[806] *See* § 2.07 *supra* for a Sample Privacy Policy Statement.

[807] 00 Civ. 0641 (S.D.N.Y. Mar. 28, 2001), available at http://www.nysd.uscourts.gov/courtweb/pdf/D02NYSC/01-03797.PDF.

Employees and contractors should be required to sign confidentiality agreements not to disclose information without authorization. In the case of children, non-public information should not be transmitted without parental consent.[808]

An online company that sells consumers' personal data to another company operating computer databases is subject to FTC enforcement actions, tort law suits, and unwanted publicity. A number of major newspapers, including *USA Today* and *The Washington Post,* have given widespread negative publicity to companies that sell consumers' personal data collected on the Internet without the users' permission.[809] Even if the FTC does not file an enforcement action against the nonconsensual sale and usage of consumers' personal data, the negative publicity can tarnish a company's reputation. The integrity of an online company's trade and brand names is a key information asset that must be protected.

The Internet connects hundreds of different countries, many of which have different views of privacy. There is no regulatory framework to guarantee the privacy of personal data transmitted on the Internet.[810] Even though some Internet providers have millions of subscribers, companies such as AOL, EarthLink, or CompuServe are private actors, and their activities will typically not qualify as state action. The Internet has diminished privacy more than any other technological innovation. Specially designed software has been developed to sniff data packets, intercept e-mail, and conduct electronic espionage—all without a trace.

The prohibition in the Fourth Amendment of the United States Constitution against unreasonable searches and seizures by government entities does not apply to the private workplace. If the employer is the government, an employee is protected from unreasonable searches and seizures. Employees in private workplaces, however, do not enjoy similar protection from their employer.[811] Private businesses are free to secretly monitor their employees' Internet usage and e-mails, even if they have assured their employees that their use of the computer system is private.[812]

In a Massachusetts case, a CEO spent eight hours reading his employees' e-mail messages and then fired those workers who had made disparaging, but accurate, comments about his sexual liaison with a co-worker. The court rejected

---

[808] These principles were adopted as Individual Reference Services Industry Principles following the Federal Trade Commission's workshop on information privacy issues. EPLR: Commercial Database Vendors' Privacy Principles (visited Nov. 25, 1999), http://www.bna.com/e-law/docs/dbguides.html.

[809] October 8, 1996, letter to Hon. Robert Pitofsky, Chairman Federal Trade Commission from Senators Bryan, Hollings, and Pressler (visited Nov. 25, 1999), http://www.bna.com/e-law/docs/bryan.html.

[810] Neal J. Friedman, The Legal Challenge of the Global Information Infrastructure, Cyberspace Lawyer (Jan. 1998).

[811] O'Connor v. Ortega, 480 U.S. 709 (1987).

[812] Smyth v. Pillsbury Co., 914 F. Supp. 97 (E.D. Pa. 1996).

the employees' claim that the secret monitoring violated the wiretap statute or the common law right of privacy.[813] The courts have uniformly held that computer systems are the property of the employer, and, therefore, the employee has no reasonable expectation of privacy in e-mail communications.

[H] Principles of Privacy

Companies may reduce exposure to privacy actions by adopting privacy policies. If a company has a web site, it should keep potential customers or subscribers informed as to what is done with any personal information collected. Internally, a company should require every employee to understand and follow its privacy policy. Mindless data mining may lead to needless litigation. A growing number of corporate web sites subscribe to the requirements of TRUSTe or Better Web. The TRUSTe certification serves as a warranty that the web site adheres to privacy guidelines followed by the industry.[814] Companies are increasingly mining personal data from their web sites without sufficient protection for that personal data.

An employer should require every employee to follow its privacy policy. The privacy policy should be published on the company's web site and incorporated into employee training. All employees may be required to acknowledge that they understand and will comply with the privacy policy. The FTC published the following privacy policy for its web site, which may also be used as a template for private industry:

> This is how we will handle information we learn about you from your visit to our web site. The information we receive depends upon what you do when visiting our site. If you visit our site to read or download information, such as consumer brochures or press releases:
>
> We collect and store only the following information about you: the name of the domain from which you access the Internet (for example, aol.com, if you are connecting from an AOL account, or princeton.edu if you are connecting from Princeton University's domain); the date and time you access our site; and the Internet address of the web site from which you linked directly to our site.
>
> We use the information we collect to measure the number of visitors to the different sections of our site, and to help us make our site more useful to visitors.
>
> If you identify yourself by sending an e-mail: You also may decide to send us personally identifying information, for example, in an electronic mail message containing a complaint. We use personally identifying information from consumers in various ways to further our consumer protection and competition activities. Visit or talk to us to learn what can happen to the information you provide us when you send us e-mail.

---

[813] Restuccia v. Burk Tcomm, Civil Action No. 95-2125 (Mass. Super. Ct., Middlesex Cty., Dec. 31, 1996).

[814] *See* TRUSTe, Building a Web You Can Believe In (visited July 20, 1999), http://www.truste.org.

We want to be very clear: We will not obtain personally identifying information about you when you visit our site, unless you choose to provide such information to us.[815]

One effective method of transmitting the privacy policy would be through pop-up screens or initial screens that appear when employees log on to their computers or are asked to give their passwords. Employees must be told that they owe a duty to potential customers, co-employees, and other parties to abide by the privacy policy. A company should also require its independent contractors, consultants, and trade partners to abide by the company's privacy policy. Legal counsel should regularly review the company's privacy policy to ensure that it complies with fast-moving national and international developments.

[I] Insuring Advertising Injuries[816]

An online company needs to have liability insurance policies that cover lawsuits based on advertising on the Internet. Advertising injury must be defined under the policies as injuries occurring in the course of Internet activities. A Nationwide insurance policy defined *advertising injury* as injury arising out of one or more of the following offenses:

1. Oral or written publication of material that slanders or libels a person or organization or disparages a person's or organization's goods, products, or services;
2. Oral or written publication of material that violates a person's right to privacy;
3. Misappropriation of advertising ideas or style of doing business; or
4. Infringement of copyright, title, or slogan.[817]

E-business executives should review their insurance binders and speak with carriers to determine what Internet-related claims are covered.[818] Traditional property and casualty insurance may not cover a wide range of cyberrisks. Companies should consider third-party coverage for Internet media "liability risks, privacy violations, security liability risks, and cyber-extortion—all arising out of named perils such as Denial of Service, virus or worm, attack." A company may consider first-party coverage for damage to data and business interruption caused by hackers or cyberextortionists.[819] Legal audits should consider whether risks might be

---

[815] Federal Trade Commission, Privacy Policy for FTC Web Site (last updated June 16, 1999) (visited July 20, 1999), http://www.ftc.gov/ftc/privacy1.htm.

[816] Please refer to Chapter Eight for a general discussion about acquiring insurance for your Internet-related activities.

[817] Micotec Research, Inc. v. Nationwide Mut. Ins. Co., 40 F.3d 968 (9th Cir. 1994).

[818] Wayne Mattus et al., Now More Than Ever, Cybersecurity Audits Are Key, Nat'l L.J., Mar. 11, 2002, at C8.

[819] *See, e.g.*, Internet Security Systems and Marsh Introduce Joint Program to Simplify and Expedite Qualifications for Cyber Risk Insurance, PR Newswire, Mar. 4, 2002.

shifted or insured. The three largest cyberrisks are in the fields of intellectual property, privacy, and network security.[820]

[J] Tips for Reducing the Risk of Telecommuting[821]

"Multitiered firewalls," "demilitarized zones," and "reverse DNS lookup" are Internet security products that do an acceptable job at protecting an employer's internal networks. But what if an attack circumvents all these precautions by coming from a computer that the security system classifies as a trusted machine? Online companies face new risks from telecommuting employees remotely accessing the company's system. Today, millions of Internet telecommuters work from home and connect to their employers' internal networks over the Internet by tunneling through the security systems. The inherent risk is that a hacker could backdoor the security by first compromising a telecommuter's computer and then using its trusted connection to access the employer's internal network. In this way, a hacker would appear to be the trusted telecommuter and would circumvent even the strongest firewall security. This consequently puts at risk all the trade secret and confidential information to which the telecommuter has access.

Although these are dire results, an employer's use of appropriate security precautions reduces the radius of the risk. First, it is critical that telecommuting employees follow the security guidelines of the company's information technology department. While these precautions may add a slight delay in performance, this is more than compensated for in the level of protection they provide.

A second type of critical security tool, and one that is fairly common, is a product to prevent front-door attack on the network. One such security product is encryption technology known as Pretty Good Privacy (PGP). Encryption products protect information by scrambling it; without the correct deencryption key, the information remains scrambled and of little value. Another precaution is to prevent access to an employer's internal network by the use of firewalls. These products, such as Cisco's PIX Firewall, are placed between the Internet and the employer's internal network and interrogate every piece of data that attempts to access the network. If the particular source address or data type is not approved, the firewall discards the packet.

A third common security measure is antivirus products, such as Norton AntiVirus from Symantec, that protect the system in the event a virus gains access to a computer. Here, the antivirus product scans everything that enters the computer and takes appropriate action if a virus is detected.

---

[820] St. Paul Companies Executive Discusses Importance of Identifying and Minimizing E-Risk at Insurance Industry Conference, Bus. Wire, Jan. 2002.

[821] Mark Maier, Esq. wrote this section. He is an associate at Mayer, Brown and Platt in Washington, D.C. He received his B.S. in Electrical Engineering from the Pennsylvania State University in 1987. His J.D. in 2000 is from Suffolk University Law School, where he was graduated in the top 5 percent of his class and with high honors from the Intellectual Property Law Concentration.

In addition to the above security measures, telecommuters should be protected by tunnel products.[822] *Basic tunnels* protect many Internet telecommuters by encrypting the information to which they have access. Basic tunnels, available from Microsoft and AltaVista, for example, create an encrypted path between the telecommuter and the employer's network, which goes over the Internet and through the firewall. *Advanced tunnels,* available from Altiga and 3Com, to name but two products, prevent access with firewall-like features, as well as protect information with encryption. While these advanced tunnels are more costly, they also provide the additional feature of access prevention.

A larger question for employers is how much security is appropriate for any given telecommuter. Although a separate risk-utility analysis should be performed for any given situation, some industry standards are emergent. Take, for example, a typical U.S. corporation with 1,000 or more telecommuters. The cost to implement basic tunnel protection is approximately $5,000, while the cost to implement more secured advanced tunnels is $55,000.[823] Each company will weigh the cost of information security technologies against the value of the information at risk. If one of these telecommuters has access to information worth $50,000 or less, it is not cost-efficient to implement tunnel protection.[824] If the information is valued between $50,000 and $1,000,000, there is likely a need for basic tunnel protection. If the information is worth millions of dollars, advanced tunnel protection should be implemented. The cost of security precautions weighed against the value of the information will also be important in determining whether the company is exercising due care.

[K]   Supplemental Checklists Aimed at Minimizing Cyberspace Liability

An online company needs to complete a self-audit of its web site to minimize tort liability. The legal audit should include the company's web site, e-mail communications, and other Internet channels. The activities of predecessor corporations, trading partners, consultants, telecommuters, and employees using Internet channels should also be included. The legal audit should address the following questions. See also the more extensive checklists in Chapter Eight.

[1]   Jurisdictional Risks in Cyberspace

• Is the web site a passive web site or an active web site subject to personal jurisdiction in many states under applicable long-arm statutes?[825]

---

[822] *Tunnels* are known as Virtual Private Networks (VPNs). *See* Microsoft Corp., Virtual Private Networking: An Overview (May 29, 1998) (visited Apr. 14, 1999), http://msd.microsoft.com/workshop/server/feature/vpnovw.asp.

[823] Mark Maier, The Law and Technology of Internet Telecommuting, 6 SMU Computer L. Rev. & Tech. J. 22 (1999).

[824] *See id.* (contending that for risk-utility analyses of when basic tunnels providing encryption but not preventing access are sufficient protection, as well as when a heightened standard of advanced tunnels providing both encryption and access prevention are mandated).

[825] A web site that is purely informational is likely to be deemed a *passive web site,* in contrast to an *active web site* where goods and services are sold. The greater the commercial activity, the more likely

- Does the company have a "choice of law" notice?

- Does the web site disclaim all consequential damages from the company? From its suppliers or any third parties? In particular, does the web site specifically disclaim incidental and consequential damages, lost profits, and damages from lost data or business interruption? Does the web site specifically mention that the company and its affiliates are not liable, whether based on contract, tort, or any other legal theory? Does the disclaimer make it clear that the web site owes no duty to the web site visitor? Web site visitors should be advised that they use the company's web site at their own risk. The company should make it clear that in delivering the service it is not liable to the web site visitor or to anyone else for losses or injuries. In addition, the company should retain the sole discretion to add, modify, or delete materials on the web site.

- Has the company considered the impact of global Internet access and the possibility that a web site may subject the company to liability in foreign jurisdictions?

- If the company does not desire to accede to laws or regulations of given foreign jurisdictions, does it have limited exposure to liability in these nation states?[826]

[2]   Internet Advertisements

- Does the web site comply with federal, state, international, and industry regulations governing (1) prior substantiation, (2) objective claims for products or services, and (3) comparative advertisements?

- Does the web site meet the Guidelines on Marketing and Advertising on the Internet formulated by the International Chamber of Commerce? Does the company provide adequate self-identification? Fair information practices? Special rules for online advertising to children? Opt-out options to avoid unsolicited advertisements? Does it respect cultural and national norms and sensitivities?

- Does the web site comply with the regulations of government agencies, including the Federal Trade Commission, Food and Drug Administration, and state attorneys general?

- Does the web site contain representations, omissions, or practices that may be deemed to mislead consumers, exposing the company to regulatory action or tort liability?

---

a web site activity will subject a company to jurisdiction in the United States and in foreign countries.

[826] A gambling web site, for example, should post a notice that it is not intended for use in the specifically named states where online casinos are illegal.

- If the web site collects information from children, does the web site comply with FTC regulations regulating contact with children?[827] (The FTC charged a web site covering money and investing issues and directed to children and teens with misrepresenting that personal information collected from the young visitors would be maintained anonymously.[828]) Does the web site comply with the Children's Online Privacy Protection Act of 1998?[829]

- Does the web site adhere to industry guidelines, such as the Children's Advertising Review Unit (CARU) of the Council of Better Business Bureaus, Inc.?[830] CARU guidelines require advertisers to children who collect identifiable information to secure parental permission. Children are also to be told "when they are being targeted for the sale of a product or service."[831]

[3] Minimizing Exposure for Intentional Torts

- Train employees to avoid defamatory statements in e-mail messages, messages posted to listservs, Usenet groups, and online discussion groups.

- Obtain licenses or authorization for photographs and other images for which an individual may have a right to publicity.

- Avoid disparaging comments about competitors in online advertisements, e-mail messages, and other Internet channels of communications.

- Provide adequate information or computer security to protect electronic information.

- Train employees to avoid "flaming" and other misuses of e-mail that may be construed as online harassment.

- Incorporate e-mail and Internet modules in sexual and racial harassment training materials.

- Train employees in the legal consequences of harassment in the form of e-mail messages or Internet-transmitted messages.

- If the company monitors e-mail messages, give notice of monitoring.

- Perform a due diligence to determine whether information posted on web sites violates the right of privacy.

---

[827] The FTC has proposed implementing regulations for the Children's Online Privacy Protection Act of 1998.

[828] Federal Trade Commission, Young Investor Website Settles FTC Charges (May 6, 1999) Press Release (visited June 18, 1999), http://www.ftc.gov/opa/1999/9905/younginvestor.htm.

[829] Parental consent is required to collect personal information on children under the age of 13.

[830] The Better Business Bureau, CARU Gains Support from AOL and Microsoft for Child Privacy Standards (visited Nov. 29, 1999), http://www.bbb.org/advertising/carujoi.html.

[831] *Id.* (The web site should offer a "click here to order" button or instructions that clearly and prominently state that a child must get a parent's permission to order.)

[4]   Publication-Based Tort Liability

- Is the company's e-mail system used in connection with surveys, contests, pyramid schemes, chain letters, junk e-mail, spamming, or other unsolicited messages that may make the company vicariously liable?

- Are employees educated in the proper use of the company's e-mail system? Does this training include modules on defamation, stalking, harassing, right of privacy, and intentional infliction of emotional distress, as well as other torts that may occur if the computer system is misused or abused?

- Are employees advised that they must not distribute or disseminate profane or obscene material that may subject the company to vicarious liability for sexual or racial harassment?

- Are information security measures in place to protect the privacy of web site visitors and of third parties, such as employees, customers, patients, and others, to whom the online company may owe a legal duty?

- Are employees instructed on how to avoid transmitting viruses, Trojan horses, worms, time bombs, and other destructive code?

- Are sufficient information security technologies in place to prevent unauthorized access?

- Are employees advised of the dangers of Internet identity theft and on how to avoid losses due to password mining and other harmful practices?

- Does your company comply with the Children's Online Protection Act, 47 U.S.C. § 231 (2001), which restricts access to obscene materials by persons under age 17?

[5]   Employment-Related Torts

- Are measures in place to prevent liabilities due to telecommuting employees?

- Are proper information security devices, such as tunnels, in place to prevent data loss from negligent telecommuters?

- Is an Internet usage and e-mail policy formulated and enforced? Is the policy updated to meet changing technologies and emerging problems? Are employees warned about possible sanctions for sending inappropriate e-mail messages? Are employees informed that e-mail should be used only for business purposes?

- Are e-mail messages monitored? Are employees warned that e-mail messages and Internet usage are subject to monitoring by the company? Are employees trained that e-mail messages are business documents discoverable and admissible in lawsuits?

- Are employees warned about sending racially or sexually charged jokes or other objectionable e-mail messages?[832]

- Has the company obtained indemnification agreements to hold the company (parent corporation, subsidiaries, affiliates, officers, and employees) harmless for the torts of consultants,[833] web site designers, and online partners?

- If an employee has committed an online tort or crime, has the employer taken appropriate disciplinary action? Is the method of discipline progressive? Is the e-mail and Internet usage policy part of continual training?

[6] Torts and Customers

- Is the company's current privacy policy available on its web site? What is the company's policy about selling the web site user's name, address, e-mail address, or personal information to third parties? Does the web site obtain information before transmitting information about customers? If an ISP hosts the company's web site, does the web site comply with the provider's privacy policy?[834]

- Does the company require web site visitors to enter into webwrap agreements regarding the use of software, documents, and services available on the web site?[835]

- Does the webwrap agreement disclaim all warranties of any kind, including all implied warranties of merchantability, fitness for a particular purpose, title, and noninfringement?

---

[832] *See, e.g.,* Owens v. Morgan Stanley & Co., 1997 WL 403454, at *1 (S.D.N.Y., July 17, 1997) (lawsuit filed because of "smoking gun" racist e-mail messages).

[833] Internet consulting service is projected to grow to "$78.5 billion by 2003, 10 times the $7.89 billion for 1998." Diane Anderson, The Young and the Restless, The Industry Standard (Nov. 8, 1999) at 95.

[834] America Online requires its AOL Certified Merchants to comply with AOL's privacy policies. In general, an ISP will provide that a web site will not share personal information without the user's consent.

[835] Yahoo! for example, structures its webwrap agreements as Terms of Service (TOS). Yahoo! offers its service subject to the visitor agreeing to the TOS. A company's TOS agreement should note that the terms might be updated from time to time without notice. *See, e.g.,* Yahoo! Terms of Service (visited Sept. 7, 1999), http://docs.yahoo.com/info/terms. The terms of service for Yahoo! are divided into clauses covering the following points: (1) acceptance of terms; (2) description of service; (3) registration obligations; (4) Yahoo! privacy policy; (5) member account, password, and security; (6) member conduct; (7) special admonitions for international use; (8) public content posted to Yahoo! (9) indemnity; (10) no resale of service; (11) general practices regarding use and storage; (12) modifications to service; (13) termination; (14) dealings with advertisers; (15) links; (16) Yahoo!'s proprietary rights; (17) disclaimer of warranties; (18) limitation of liability; (19) exclusions and limitations; (20) special admonition for services relating to financial matters; (21) notice; (22) trademark information; (23) copyrights and copyright agents; (24) general information; and (25) violations.

- Does the webwrap agreement warn users that the company is not responsible for special, indirect, or consequential damages from losses due to relying upon web site information? Is the web site offered on an "as is" basis, without warranties of any kind?

- Does the company's web site have a legal page and disclaimers? Does the web site disclaim liability for actions whether based upon contract, intentional tort, strict liability, or negligence arising out of use of the web site?[836]

- What other types of contracts are required to shift or allocate the risk of liability? Does the company have sufficient contract protection for indemnification, warranties, or insurance coverage for cybertorts?

- Does the web site use the latest technology to protect credit card information? Does the web site use SSL encryption for telephoning, faxing, or e-mailing credit card information?

- Does the web site have all proper legal notices as to copyright, trademarks, patents as well as disclaimers for any errors or omissions relating to information on the web site?

[7] Avoiding Liability for Privacy-Based Torts

- Does the web site disclose what personally identifiable data, such as names, addresses, or e-mail addresses, will be collected and for what purposes? If the company plans only to use this data for internal purposes, it should say so. Such a statement, however, is a warranty that personally identifiable data will not be sold or transferred to third parties.

- Does the company's web site comply generally with the European Union Data Protection Directive, which came into effect in October 1998? Does the web site disclose what types of personal information are collected and for what purpose? Do web site visitors have an opportunity to opt out of giving personal information that will be shared or collected?

[8] Privacy Concerns

- Does the web site meet the privacy principles of the Direct Marketing Association (DMA)?[837]

- Does the web site have the certification of TRUSTe?[838] Is the TRUSTe "trust-mark" prominently displayed? The TRUSTe is a "licensing program [that

---

[836] Courts will not enforce disclaimers of tort liability where there is personal injury, but they may enforce such agreements where losses are purely economic.

[837] The DMA, for example, requires its members to post their online privacy policies.

[838] Thomas Dabney, Mastering Consumer Contracting on the Internet, Third Annual High Technology Law Conference, Suffolk University Law School, Boston, Massachusetts (Mar. 1999).

requires] participating Web sites to disclose their online information gathering and dissemination practices."[839] The TRUSTe "trustmark" gives visitors assurance that the web site complies with privacy principles, oversight, and resolution processes.[840] Each TRUSTe certified web site must post a privacy statement disclosing the following: (1) What is being gathered? (2) Who is the gatherer? (3) Uses of the information. (4) How will the information be shared? (5) Choices for collection, use, and distribution. (6) Security procedures to protect personal information. (7) Mechanism for updating and reporting inaccuracies.[841]

- Does the web site comply with international comparative advertising laws?

- Does the web site comply with the requirement that advertisements be in a specific language?[842]

- Does the web site employ online promotions, sweepstakes, or contests that may subject the company to enforcement by state, federal, or international law enforcement?

- Does the web site comply with any industry regulations governing online promotions?[843]

- Do products or services sold on the web site comply with "Made in USA" claims in product advertising, labeling, and packaging?

- Does the web site harvest or otherwise collect information about others, including e-mail addresses, without the user's consent?

- Does the web site have reasonable security to protect the integrity of personally identifiable information?

[9]   Other Terms, Conditions, and Concerns

- Does the web site disclaim endorsements for specific products, processes, or services by trade name or trademark?

- If the company is defined as a service provider, it must designate an agent to receive complaints regarding copyright violations under § 512(c)(2) of the

---

[839] *Id.*

[840] *Id.*

[841] *Id.*

[842] The province of Quebec, for example, requires advertisements to be in French as well as English. There are similar language requirements for advertisements directed to French citizens in France. As an alternative, the web site may have a notice that the advertisements are not directed to citizens of Quebec, France, etc.

[843] Promotions, sweepstakes, and contests "should expressly state [of] which countries entrants must be residents. Such a disclosure should be clearly and prominently placed in all advertising for the promotion." Lewis Rose and John P. Feldman, Internet Marketing: Practical Suggestions for International Advertising and Promotions, Arent Fox (visited Sept. 7, 1999), http://www.webcom.com/lewrose/article/intl.html.

Digital Millennium Copyright Act. Has the company designated an agent or contact person to receive complaints for copyright infringement in connection with the web site?

[10]   Parties' Choice of Law and Forum Agreements

The parties may agree in advance to settle disputes according to the laws of a given jurisdiction. The parties' choice of law clause should be included in all license agreements. The choice of law clause will be enforced provided it has a reasonable relation to the forum. The choice of law clause is a contractual agreement that all disputes be litigated in a specified forum under the principles of law of the specified jurisdiction. License agreements, for example, will typically have a clause governing disputes arising under a contract. In addition, the clause will frequently require the licensee to accept service of process by e-mail or regular mail and waive any jurisdictional or venue defenses that may be available,

EXAMPLE OF PARTIES' CHOICE OF LAW CLAUSE

This license agreement between Suffolk Personal Computers (SPC) [licensor] and _____ [licensee] shall be governed in accordance with the laws of Massachusetts [specify jurisdiction]. All disputes under this license agreement shall be resolved by litigation in the courts of the Commonwealth of Massachusetts including the federal district court of Massachusetts. The licensee consents to jurisdiction of Massachusetts's courts and hereby agrees to accept service of process by e-mail or regular mail. Finally, the licensee agrees to waive any jurisdictional or venue defenses that may be available.

One of the limitations of the parties' choice of law clause is that many torts or civil actions arise out of activities between parties are not in any contractual relationship. Cyberdefamation, virus production, or negligent publication cases will rarely arise out of contractual relations. Similarly, unfair competition in cyberspace or international e-commerce torts will seldom involve parties to a contract. Choice of law clauses may reduce the radius of risk in cybermedicine, spam e-mail, and other torts arising out of contract.

[11]   Chief Privacy Officer

The chief privacy officer (CPO) is "one of the fastest-growing positions in corporate management" with an estimated 350 appointments in the past two years alone.[844] The CPO's duties vary widely depending on the industry. The responsi-

---

[844] Neil Roiter, Newcomers to the Executive Suite, Chief Privacy Officers Decide the Fate of Corporate and Personal Information, Info. Security, Nov. 2001, at 74.

bilities of the CPO may include network and information security as well.[845] The CPO is primarily responsible for compliance with state, federal, and international privacy policies and procedures. The vast majority of web sites have privacy policies, but relatively few have regular audits of the privacy policy in action.

The failure to implement defensible consumer privacy policies may lead to costly regulatory actions or litigation. GeoCities, RealNetwork, and Doubleclick have all been charged with consumer privacy violations leading to costly litigation. The Federal Trade Commission (FTC) has an active enforcement arm to determine whether companies are complying with their posted privacy policies. GeoCities was charged with violating its own privacy policy by secretly collecting customer data and selling the information to third parties.[846] A CPO is a corporate decision-maker as well as a compliance officer to avoid costly public relations disasters such as the following:

(1) The University of Minnesota accidentally identified more than 400 organ donors to the recipients.
(2) Eli Lilly sent e-mail "to more than 600 Prozac users, inadvertently distributing the name and e-mail address of every recipient in the message."
(3) An ex-employee "at telecommunications firm Global Crossing post[ed] names, Social Security numbers and birth dates of company employees on his Web site."[847]

Companies in the field of financial service will need a plan to comply with Gramm-Leach-Bliley. The Royal Bank of Canada hired a CPO who is responsible for privacy-related issues in a wide range of services including "free encrypted cell phones for wireless transactions"[848]

Firms dealing with personal data related to health care must comply with the Health Insurance Portability and Accountability Act (HIPAA). HIPAA has graduated fines for offenses such as the harvesting of medical information.[849]

The CPO needs to answer the following questions to begin a corporate privacy audit:

- For what general purposes do we collect data?

- What data do we currently collect?

- How are they collected?

- Where are they kept?

- How are they kept?

---

[845] *Id.* (noting that "titles for the position vary, including chief information security officer, chief risk officer, and VP of security").

[846] Deborah Radcliff, Privacy: The Liability Link, Computer World, Aug. 27, 2001, at 36.

[847] Maryfran Johnson, Follow the (Privacy) Money, Computerworld, Feb. 25, 2002, at 24.

[848] *Id.*

[849] Radcliff, *supra* note 846.

- How are they secured?

- What risks do collecting and keeping data create?

- Who has access to the data, and for what purpose?

- What data needs do we anticipate moving forward?

- What happens if the data are fraudulently exposed?[850]

The growth of the CPO is in response to lawsuits that have been filed against businesses in diverse sectors: "financial services, Internet e-commerce, pharmaceutical companies, credit bureaus, information brokers and general consumer products firms."[851] The CPO will be chiefly responsible for developing and implementing a privacy program. Privacy programs must consider what personal information is collected (IP number, time of connection, payment information, shipping data, and other collection streams), the uses of information, statements of use, disclosures, and security.[852]

[12] E-Discovery

Electronic smoking guns have been key in famous trials involving Oliver North and Bill Gates and will be critical in the Enron litigation. Software is available to recover deleted or altered e-mail. In a mass products liability case, an e-mail from one company employee to another discussed the side effects of the fen-phen drug, which led to a multimillion-dollar settlement. The smoking gun e-mail message read: "Do I have to look forward to spending my waning years writing checks to fat people worried about a silly lung problem?"[853] Companies are routinely being asked to produce e-mail, backup tapes, or other electronic databases. There are products that can move all electronic documents into a searchable database.[854] An electronic database can only organize what has not yet been destroyed.[855] A company destroys or alters electronic documents at its peril.

The destruction of evidence poses the risk of Rule 26 discovery sanctions, adverse inferences, federal criminal sanctions, and possible tort liability for the spoliation of evidence. The new information technologies make it easy to destroy or alter evidence with a click of the mouse. Fraudulent concealment of evidence

---

[850] Consumers Opt for Financial Privacy, Bank Marketing Int'l, Jan. 21, 2002, at 12 (citing Meridien research report).

[851] Roiter, *supra* note 844.

[852] *See* Kevin J. Connolly, Law of Internet Security and Privacy 172-77 (2002) (providing detailed checklist for privacy policy preparation).

[853] Kristin M. Nimsger, Same Game, New Rules: E-Discovery Adds Complexity to Protecting Clients and Disadvantaging Opponents, Legal Times, Mar. 25, 2002.

[854] Asby Jones, Discovery Becomes Electric, N.Y.L. J., Mar. 11, 2002, at T3 (describing services of companies like "Seattle's Applied Discovery Inc., Portland, Ore.'s Fios Inc., Seattle's Electronic Evidence Discovery Inc. (EED) and Eden Prairie, Minn.'s On Track Data International Inc.").

[855] *Id.*

may constitute an aggravating circumstance leading to punitive damages. The alteration of electronic "smoking guns" relating to existing or pending litigation has led to the prosecution of Arthur Andersen, the accounting firm. A few jurisdictions recognize the tort of the spoliation of evidence for the deliberate destruction of, or the failure to preserve, essential evidence.[856] An insurer's failure to preserve key documents in a class action suit led to a sanction of $1 million.[857] Discovery will frequently extend to e-mail, backup tapes, archived tapes, and even deleted tapes.

If an e-business is involved in pending litigation, it must take preventive law steps to preserve electronic evidence. A company that has a document retention policy will be in a better position than a company that begins to shred documents anticipating litigation. To prevent civil and criminal liability, a company must "halt all electronic document-handling policies that result in the recycling of tapes or other e-data destruction that may destroy potentially relevant files. Data destruction must cease at all locations of both parties."[858] It is risky to "discontinue automatic e-document destruction policies, improperly collecting and imaging electronic data, and modifying Web sites."[859]

The best defense against electronic discovery is that a specific request is intrusive and burdensome. In *Stallings-Daniel v. Northern Trust Co.*,[860] the plaintiff in an employment discrimination case filed a motion for an expert to conduct so-called electronic discovery of her employer's e-mail system.[861] The plaintiff claimed that the employer had altered some of its e-mail documentation before producing it. The employer had, in fact, redacted several documents produced to the Equal Employment Opportunity Commission and did not identify them as redacted. The employee argued that there were "suspicious" e-mails likely altered before production. The court refused to grant the order, finding the employee's fears to be speculative and groundless. The same evidentiary record may persuade other courts to order an independent investigation of an e-mail system.

Electronic discovery is frequently burdensome and costly. In a civil fraud case against a physician, the defense counsel was compelled to review "84,000 pages of written discovery and 15 gigabytes of electronic discovery."[862] In a class action against an e-business, the scope of electronic discovery will be even broader and more costly.

---

[856] Rosenblatt v. Zimmerman, 766 A.2d 749 (N.J. 2001) (discussing distinction between tort actions for spoliation of evidence and fraudulent concealment).

[857] In re Prudential Ins. Co. Sales Practices Litig., 169 F.R.D. 598 (D.N.J. 1997).

[858] Nimsger, *supra* note 853.

[859] *Id.*

[860] Stallings-Daniel v. Northern Trust Co., 2002 U.S. Dist. LEXIS 4024 (N.D. Ill. Mar. 12, 2002).

[861] United States v. Sriram, 2002 U.S. Dist. LEXIS 2928 (N.D. Ill. Feb. 22, 2002).

[862] Nimsger, *supra* note 853 (noting that an attorney has an affirmative duty to locate all data in the client's possession under Rule 26, including data "located on individual desktops and laptops, network hard disks, removable media (e.g., floppy disks, tapes, and CDs) and, increasingly, personal digital assistants (e.g., Palm Pilots) or data in the possession of third parties (Internet Service Providers)").

Rule 26(a) of the Federal Rules of Civil Procedure "requires the disclosure of 'data compilations' (e.g., electronic files, databases, e-mails) following a full investigation of the case."[863] More than 90 percent of business documents are now created electronically, and the vast majority of them are never printed.[864] Companies need a plan to preserve and manage these documents to avoid civil and criminal liability. Companies need to plan handling discovery requests while preserving privileged data.

The failure to embark on a legal audit of documents may lead to dire consequences. A court may use its equitable powers to appoint its own forensics expert to determine whether a party has altered documents. In a Massachusetts case, a court's forensics expert determined that a plaintiff fabricated an e-mail to prove that his case was not barred by the statute of limitations.[865] The electronic smoking gun resulted in the dismissal of the plaintiff's cause of action and an order to pay the expert's fees. Courts will increasingly apply their equitable powers as well as the rules of discovery to impose sanctions on companies that alter, destroy, or fail to preserve evidence.

---

[863] *Id.*

[864] *Id.*

[865] Munshani v. Signal Lake Venture Fund II, 2001 Mass. Super. LEXIS 496 (Mass. Super. Ct. Oct. 9, 2001) (dismissing plaintiff's action and ordering payment of expert's fee).

CHAPTER SIX

THE LAW OF E-COMMERCE TRANSACTIONS

§ 6.01   Overview

§ 6.02   E-Business Models
    [A]   Business-to-Business
        [1]   Electronic Data Interchange
        [2]   Industry Standards for EDI
    [B]   Business-to-Consumer
    [C]   Business-to-Government
    [D]   Consumer-to-Consumer
    [E]   Government-to-Consumer

§ 6.03   Sources of E-Commerce Law
    [A]   Federal Trade Commission
        [1]   Magnuson-Moss Act
        [2]   Children's Online Privacy Protection Rule
        [3]   Telemarketing Sales Rule
    [B]   The Role of Industry Standards
        [1]   OECD Guidelines
        [2]   International Chamber of Commerce
    [C]   Revised UCC Article 2
    [D]   Digital Signatures
    [E]   Electronic Signatures in Global and National Commerce Act of 2000
        [1]   Purpose and Meaning of Digital Signatures
            [a]   Authentication
            [b]   Ceremony
            [c]   Approval
            [d]   Efficiency and Logistics
        [2]   Digital Signature Statutes
            [a]   Prescriptive Model
            [b]   Criteria-Based Model
            [c]   Signature-Enabling Approach
        [3]   Certificate Authorities
        [4]   Technology
        [5]   Attribution Procedures
        [6]   Other Initiatives
    [F]   Privacy in Information Contracts

[G]   Procedural Law of E-Commerce; Choice of Law
    [1]   Uniform Commercial Code
    [2]   Revised UCC Article 1
    [3]   Uniform Computer Information Transactions Act
[H]   Choice of Forum Clauses

§ 6.04   Electronic Contracting Rules
[A]   Electronic Contract Formation
    [1]   Electronic Data Interchange
    [2]   Mass-Market Licenses
        [a]   Shrinkwrap Agreements
        [b]   Content and Interactive Service Agreements
        [c]   Clickwrap Agreements
[B]   Offer and Acceptance
    [1]   E-Mailbox Rule
    [2]   Electronic Contract Formation Rules
[C]   Legal Proof Issues
    [1]   Electronic Authentication
    [2]   Digital Signatures
[D]   Uniform Electronic Transactions Act
    [1]   Purpose
    [2]   Scope
    [3]   Validation of Electronic Signatures
    [4]   Electronic Records
    [5]   Effect of Change or Error
    [6]   Retention of Records
    [7]   Admissibility in Evidence
    [8]   Automated Transactions
    [9]   Receipt of Electronic Records

§ 6.05   Software and Internet-Related Licenses under the Uniform
Computer Information Transactions Act
[A]   Overview
[B]   Structure and Function
[C]   Scope
    [1]   Computer Information Transactions
    [2]   Hybrid or Mixed Transactions
    [3]   Key Definitions
    [4]   Choice of Law and Forum
        [a]   Choice of Law
        [b]   Choice of Forum
        [c]   Venue
[D]   UCITA's Licensing Rules
[E]   Policing Mass-Market Licenses
    [1]   Procedural Protection for Licensees
    [2]   Policing Unconscionable License Agreements

           [3]   Failure of Essential Purpose
    [F] Electronic Contracting Rules
           [1]   Statute of Frauds in Cyberspace
    [G] Warranties
           [1]   Express and Implied
           [2]   Warranties of Quality
               [a]   Express Warranties
               [b]   Implied Warranty of Merchantability
               [c]   Implied Warranty of System Integration
               [d]   Warranties for Information Content
               [e]   Disclaiming and Limiting Liability
               [f]   Specialized Computer Warranty Rules
    [H] UCITA's Canons of Contract Construction
    [I] Transfer of Interests and Rights
    [J] Performance Standards
    [K] Tender, Acceptance, Rejection, and Revocation
    [L] Remedies
           [1]   UCITA's Validation of Freedom of Contract
           [2]   Duties upon Cancellation
           [3]   Material Breach
           [4]   Exclusive and Limited Remedy
           [5]   Fundamental Public Policies
           [6]   Liquidated Damages
           [7]   Disabling Device
           [8]   Statute of Limitations and Repose

§ 6.06   License Agreements
    [A] Granting Clause
    [B] Term for Payment
    [C] Scope of Licensing Agreement; Number of Users
    [D] Different Media
    [E] Licensee's Right to Updates
    [F] Termination Clause
    [G] Disabling Devices
    [H] Warranties, Disclaimers, and Limitations
    [I] Indemnification
    [J] Assignment and Anti-Assignment
    [K] Licensee's Rights
    [L] Confidentiality and Nondisclosure
    [M] Export Restrictions
    [N] Integration or Merger Clause
    [O] Access Contracts: Terms and Conditions of Access

§ 6.07   Internet Taxation
    [A] Introduction
    [B] Challenges Introduced by Electronic Commerce

    [C]   Internet Taxation: The U.S. Perspective
         [1]   The Internet Tax Freedom Act
         [2]   Federal Taxation
    [D]   State Taxation of Electronic Commerce
         [1]   Sales and Use Tax
         [2]   Nexus—Taxable Level of Business Activity
         [3]   Sales and Use Tax on Internet Access
         [4]   Sales Tax Treatment of Online Content
         [5]   Sales Tax Treatment of Computer Software
    [E]   Products versus Services: The Characterization of Revenue
    [F]   Cash versus Accrual
    [G]   International Withholding Tax
    [H]   Other Sources of Taxes and Duties
    [I]   International Taxation of E-Commerce
         [1]   Value-Added Taxes
         [2]   Web Servers and Tax Issues
    [J]   Limiting Tax Liability

§ 6.08   Internet Payment Systems
    [A]   Payment Instruments
         [1]   Credit Cards
         [2]   Debit Cards
         [3]   Electronic Negotiable Instruments
             [a]   UCC Articles 3 and 4
             [b]   Article 4A Wire Transfers
    [B]   Internet Banking
    [C]   E-Cash Payment Systems
    [D]   Electronic Check Developments

§ 6.09   Preventive Law Pointers
    [A]   Complying with the Magnuson-Moss Act
    [B]   Mandatory Arbitration Clauses
    [C]   Webwrap or Clickwrap License Agreements
    [D]   Determining UCITA's Reach
    [E]   Choice of Law and Forum
    [F]   Negotiating Points
    [G]   Draft Your Own Excuse Sections
    [H]   Term and Termination Clauses in License Agreements
    [I]   Web Sites and Credit Cards
    [J]   Clickthrough Agreements
    [K]   FTC Guidelines for Web Advertisements

§ 6.01 OVERVIEW

The growth of electronic commerce raises a number of electronic contracting issues, that are the subject of this chapter. The issues that are addressed in this chapter include the range of electronic contract issues including the enforceability of clickwrap, shrinkwrap, or webwrap terms of service agreements. The digital economy is based upon "assuring shoppers their communications are secure, their personal data is protected, and they will get what they paid for, and the underlying infrastructure is stable no matter where they shop on the Internet."[1] The dot-com frenzy gave way to the rise of e-commerce in 2002.[2] E-commerce is broadly defined as the "buying and selling of goods and services on the Internet, especially the World Wide Web."[3] It's no longer about startups and pure virtual dot-coms. E-businesses are increasingly "looking to find ways to improve [their] IT and back-office operations to take advantage of the opportunities on the Web."[4] Companies that survived the dot-com shakeout are marketing new suites of services and products,[5] including, since September 11, 2001, software and services to ensure cybersecurity and deter cyberattacks.

A new consumer market is extending new products to protect computers for personal, family, and household use. Although the principal priority of corporate security is to protect business data, with increased home use of the Internet, consumers are seeking protection of their privacy and defense of their home computers from hackers, viruses, or other forms of information age crimes.

In general, Internet law updates and adapts common law principles to the Internet. In *Kids Universe v. In2Labs*,[6] the plaintiffs were founders of a retailer of toys, educational products, and computer training services for children. They filed suit seeking lost profits on the theory that the defendants negligently caused a flood in their retail store and prevented them from launching a Web site for the sale of toys. The California Appeals Court upheld the trial court, finding that the plaintiffs have the burden of proving lost profits with certainty.

Online e-contracting at the state level is evolving rapidly, with many states having enacted or considering legislation governing digital signatures, the e-filing of documents, and online licensing. The majority of states have enacted or are considering e-commerce related legislation.[7] New model laws relating to e-commerce

---

[1] Vice President Albert Gore, Towards Digital Equality: The U.S. Government Working Group on Electronic Commerce 1 (2d ed., 1999).

[2] Keith Regan, Dot-Com Job Cuts Near Two-Year Law, E-Commerce Times, Mar. 4, 2002.

[3] Whatis.techtarget.com (visited Jan. 30, 2002), http://whatis.techtarget.com/WhatIsDefinitionPage/0,4152,212029,00.html.

[4] Regan, *supra* note 2.

[5] *See, e.g.*, PR Newswire, Jan. 4, 2002, Financial News, describing Bank Eyes Only, a new credit card protection system that Ezstreetwireless.com introduced to its customers who use credit card payment method; PR Newswire, Nov. 12, 2001, Financial News, discussing Freestar Technologies, Ins. and SSP Solutions software that allowed customers to use their ATM and debit cards for shopping transactions on the Internet in a way similar to traditional credit cards.

[6] Kids' Universe v. In2Labs, 95 Cal. App. 4th 870, 116 Cal. Rptr. 2d 158 (2002).

[7] *See, e.g.*, Conn. Gen. Stat. §§ 19a-25a (1997) (adopting electronic signatures for medical records).

are an important part of this movement. This chapter provides extensive coverage of the Uniform Computer Information Transactions Act (UCITA), approved by the National Conference of Commissioners on Uniform State Laws (NCCUSL) in July 1999.[8] UCITA "represents the first comprehensive uniform computer information licensing law" and adapts traditional contract law to the Internet.[9] UCITA applies to a wide range of Internet-related contracts and is the single most comprehensive body of contract law dealing with cyberspace. UCITA has recently been adopted in Maryland and Virginia and has been introduced in legislatures in Delaware, the District of Columbia, Hawaii, Illinois, Louisiana, New Jersey, and Oklahoma.

In July 1999, NCCUSL also approved the Uniform Electronic Transaction Act (UETA) for enactment in the states. UETA treats electronic records and signatures as the functional and legal equivalent of paper and pencil writings and of manually signed signatures.[10] UETA supports the use of electronic contracts, digital evidence, electronic filing, electronic records, and computer-generated signatures. UETA has already been adopted in 36 states.[11]

The Electronic Signatures in Global and National Commerce Act (E-Sign), which validates electronic signatures and records, went into effect October 1, 2000.[12] E-Sign would normally supplant UETA under the Supremacy Clause of the U.S. Constitution. However, Congress expressly allows UETA to preempt the federal law.[13] The Uniform Commercial Code is being entirely revamped to take into account Internet-related transactions. Revised Article 2 of the UCC provides

---

[8] UCITA is a statute sponsored by the National Conference of Commissioners on Uniform State Laws (NCCUSL). NCCUSL proposes model statutes "on subjects where uniformity is desirable and practicable, and work toward their enactment in legislatures." *See* National Conference of Commissioners on Uniform State Laws (NCCUSL) (visited Apr. 25, 2002), http://www.nccussl.org. UCITA is a successor to Article 2B, which was a proposal of NCCUSL and The American Law Institute (ALI) to make computer information a separate article of the Uniform Commercial Code. ALI withdrew from the Article 2B draft proposal which led NCCUSL to propose UCITA (Article 2B's successor) as a stand-alone statute. As of Apr. 25, 2002, UCITA has been enacted in Maryland and Virginia and introduced in legislatures in Arizona, District of Columbia, Illinois, Maine, New Hampshire, New Jersey, Oregon, and Texas. Carol Kunze, UCITA Online (visited Apr. 25, 2002), http://www.ucitaonline.com/whathap.html.

[9] NCCUSL, A Few Facts About . . . Uniform Computer Information Transactions Act (May 9, 2000), http://www.nccusl.org/uniformact_factsheets/uniformacts-fs-ucita.htm.

[10] *Id.*

[11] The states adopting UETA are Alabama, Arizona, Arkansas, California, Delaware, District of Columbia, Florida, Hawaii, Idaho, Indiana, Iowa, Kansas, Kentucky, Louisiana, Maine, Maryland, Michigan, Minnesota, Mississippi, Montana, Nebraska, Nevada, New Hampshire, New Mexico, North Carolina, North Dakota, Ohio, Oklahoma, Pennsylvania, Rhode Island, South Dakota, Tennessee, Utah, Virginia, and Wyoming. As of April 6, 2001, UETA has been introduced in Connecticut, Illinois, Massachusetts, Missouri, New Jersey, Oregon, Texas, U.S. Virgin Islands, Vermont, and West Virginia. In addition, California introduced a bill repealing nonuniform amendments to UETA and enacting a conforming version. Carol Kunze, UETA Online, What's Happening to UETA in the States, updated Apr. 6, 2001 (visited Apr. 22, 2002), http://www.uetaonline.com/hapstate.html.

[12] The Electronic Signatures in Global and National Commerce Act, 15 U.S.C. § 7001 (2000).

[13] *Id.* § 102; 15 U.S.C. § 7002.

for new electronic contracting rules but does not address whether computer information qualifies as goods.[14] Revised Article 9 of the UCC updates the law of secured transactions for the online economy; for example, a security agreement or financing statement may now be authenticated through electronic means.[15] Revised Article 9 also contains special rules for perfecting security interests in software, electronic, or Internet-related assets,[16] and the 2000 revisions provide rules for perfecting security interests in "electronic chattel paper."[17]

To help put the issues in perspective, case law and statutory developments will be applied to the activities of our hypothetical company, SPC. Before SPC launches its web site, it must consider a wide range of contracting issues to protect its rights. SPC strives to become a dot-com with access to customers in a global Internet marketplace through a virtual online kiosk that will be open for business 24 hours a day, 7 days a week. Are shrinkwrap agreements enforceable? Are warranties disclaimable in software licenses? May clauses in license agreement be struck on grounds of unconscionability or the violation of public policy? What are the limits on choice of forum clauses? Do consumer protections apply to webwrap agreements? Do digital signatures have the same validity as paper-and-pencil signatures? These questions will be answered in the ensuing sections.

SPC permits its customers to download software from its web site. For tangible products, however, SPC must also have contractual arrangements with Federal Express or other shipping services.[18] SPC's virtual store, for example, permits it to merge its software and hardware offerings with those of other individual retailers in electronic catalogs. These transactions may be governed by a patchwork of laws. Revised Article 2 of the UCC applies to goods with embedded computer software or chips, whereas UCITA applies to the transfer of intangibles such as software or data.

This chapter will explore many e-contracting questions by providing an analysis of typical contract issues faced by SPC and other online businesses. More specifically, § 6.02 provides a brief introduction to the most common e-business models. Section 6.03 describes the sources of e-commerce contract law. Section 6.04 examines the evolving legal framework for electronic contracting. Section 6.05 follows with an analysis of the Uniform Computer Information Transactions Act (UCITA), while § 6.06 covers the specifics of licensing agreements. UCITA

---

[14] National Conference of Commissioners on Uniform State Laws, Revision of Uniform Commercial Code, Article 2-Sales (2000 Annual Meeting Draft, July 28, Aug. 4, 2000) (hereinafter Revised Article 2).

[15] UCC § 9-102 (7) (2000 Revisions).

[16] UCC § 9-102 (75) (2000 Revisions) defines software for the first time in Article 9. Electronic records are defined in § 9-102(69) (2000 Revisions), including amendments dating from May 20, 1999, to Mar. 3, 2000.

[17] UCC § 9-105 (Revised Final Draft, 2000); *see also* The American Law Institute, Uniform Commercial Code [New] Revised Article 2A Leases (Council Draft No. 1, Oct. 5, 2000) (updating Article 2A to include electronic agents, records, and signatures).

[18] Michele Midgette, Two Shipping Giants Boost Productivity and Lower Costs Online, Net Com. Mag. (Mar. 1999) at 8.

governs software, web site, and Internet-related contract issues. Section 6.07 provides a multijurisdictional survey of Internet taxation. Section 6.08 provides a brief discussion of Internet payment systems. The chapter concludes with § 6.09, which provides preventive law pointers.

§ 6.02   E-BUSINESS MODELS

This section explores the dynamics of e-business models that sets the stage for an analysis of e-contract issues. IBM describes e-business as a process by which companies meld "the standards, simplicity and connectivity of the Internet with the core processes that are the foundation of business."[19] The e-business uses e-commerce technologies such as web-enabled interfaces, electronic catalogues, web-based electronic data interchange, customer service interfaces, and online ordering and billing systems.[20] SPC's e-business will evolve through stages of development, beginning with its web site, established as an interface through which to improve customer service. SPC's e-business plan is to redesign its business process to cut costs, increase revenues, create new channels of distribution, improve customer service, and offer global support for its medley of hardware and software products.

E-commerce may be broadly divided into four types: business-to-business (B2B), business-to-consumer (B2C), business-to-government (B2G), and consumer-to-consumer (C2C). E-commerce also encompasses diverse commercial practices in which the parties interact over electronic networks rather than by traditional human-to-human exchanges.[21] Additionally, a growing number of federal and state agencies permit government-to-consumer transactions (G2C). SPC is likely to conduct extensive B2B commercial transactions as well as B2C sales from its web site. In addition, SPC will electronically transact B2G business with state and federal agencies.

[A]   Business-to-Business

The B2B marketplace brings businesses together with other businesses to exchange goods, materials, supplies, and services. B2B involves electronic contracts that permit companies to lower costs "via point-and-click comparison shopping or electronically auctioning contracts."[22] E-businesses are devising new e-finance solutions with suppliers and partners. B2B supply networks have been established in the steel, aeronautics, automobile, retail, farming, consumer products, paper, and medical products industries to permit entire industries to buy and sell online.[23]

---

[19] IBM.com, What Is E-business? (visited Apr. 25, 2002), http://www.ibm.com/e-business/info.

[20] Craig Fellenstein and Ron Wood, Exploring E-Commerce, Global E-Business and E-Society 10 (1999).

[21] ISPO, Electronic Commerce and the European Union (visited Jan. 20, 2002), http://www.ispo.cec.be/Ecommerce/answers/introduction.html (defining electronic commerce).

[22] John Witty, Tech's Best Stock Play, Bloomberg B2B Business to Business 53, 55 (June 2000).

[23] Clare Ansberry, Let's Build an Online Supply Network! Wall St. J. (Apr. 17, 2000) at B1.

A B2B model may take the form of a "virtual mall" or electronic catalogs "for purchases between companies [that] allow corporate buyers to search for products based on features and price."[24] B2B is also used in "just in time" strategies for e-procurement, streamlining administrative tasks, and bill presentment and payment.

B2B transactions account for many times more revenues than do B2C retail transactions that get all of the press. In the beginning of 2002, Yahoo's revenues from B2C transactions dropped 40 percent compared to the same quarter a year before and resulted in a quarterly loss of $8.7 million.[25] A Forrester Research study found that the number of companies that used the Internet to purchase supplies went up from 28 percent in the third quarter of 2001 to 45 percent in the fourth quarter of 2001.[26]

[1]   Electronic Data Interchange

Electronic data interchange (EDI) refers to the process by which goods are ordered, shipped, and tracked computer-to-computer using standardized protocol.[27] An estimated "120,000 of the 2 million U.S. companies are EDI trading partners."[28] EDI permits the "electronic settlement and reconciliation of the flow of goods and services between companies and consumers;"[29] financial EDI permits electronic payment and remittance over an automated clearinghouse (ACH).[30] EDI saves money because the computer, and not an office staff, submits and processes orders, claims, and other routine tasks. It represents a significant advance over snail mail in transmitting business information. In one version, business forms may be e-mailed to a trading partner who then "re-keys the data into another business application."[31] Under a more efficient approach, computer-to-computer transactions solve the problem of "poor response time" in the supply chain and reduce

---

[24] Steffano Korper and Juanita Ellis, The E-Commerce Book: Building the E-Empire 8 (2000).

[25] Matthew Guarente, Yahoo! Needs Mojo to Work (visited Jan. 27, 2002), http://www.ecommercetimes.com/perl/story/15972.html; *see also* Nuala Moran, Fallout Is Far from Over in Electronic Marketplace, Financial Times (London) Mar. 13, 2001, at 13 (describing difficulties of the B2B marketplace).

[26] Guarente, *supra* note 25; Keith Regan, Report: B2B E-Commerce Gaining Strength (visited Jan. 27, 2002), http://www.ecommercetimes.com/perl/story/15847.html.

[27] *See* George B. Delta and Jeffrey H. Matsuura, Law of the Internet § 9.02[A] (1998) (stating *EDI* is the transmission, in standard syntax, of unambiguous information between computers of two or more independent organizations).

[28] Craig Fellenstein & Ron Wood, Exploring E-Commerce, Global E-Business and E-Society 26 (2000).

[29] Robert Teitelman and Stephen Davis, How the Cash Flows, Institutional Investor 58 (Aug. 1996).

[30] Federal Reserve Bank of Boston, Fed Flash (June 2, 1998) (visited Apr. 25, 2002), http://www.bos.frb.org.

[31] National Institute of Standards, EDI Tutorial: The Problem Addressed by EDI (May 7, 2000), (visited April 28, 2002) http://www.nist.gov/itl/div896/ipsg/eval_guide/subsection3_5_1.html.

the rate of errors in filling orders because of the greater reliability of computer-to-computer messaging.[32]

EDI began in the 1960s as a computer-to-computer means of managing inventory, bill presentment, shipment, orders, product specifications, and payment.[33] EDI in a nutshell structures business data and message transactions, sometimes in value-added networks (VANs).[34] EDI is made possible because trading partners enter into master agreements to employ electronic messaging permitting computer-to-computer transfers of information and validating computer-to-computer contracts.[35] In the early days of EDI, companies developed their own proprietary format for interchanging data messages. Consequently, the lack of universal standards made it difficult for companies to communicate with many of their trading partners.[36] Generally speaking, North American companies tend to use ANSI X12 protocol while their European counterparts prefer EDIFACT.[37] In addition, there are industry-specific protocol such as the drug and pharmaceutical industry's UCS standard.[38] Since the development of the ANSI X12 protocol, described below in § 6.02[A][2], master trading agreements generally specify the use of the ANSI X12 protocol. Nevertheless, Internet-based B2B commerce evolved out of the EDI that took hold in the 1960s and allowed corporations to transfer purchase orders, invoices, and other business documents electronically.[39]

Today EDI is a well-established B2B means of transmitting information from one computer to another. In 1998, total B2B e-commerce was $671 billion, comprising $92 billion in Internet-based transactions and $579 billion in transactions using EDI over private networks.[40] Visa Canada predicts that e-commerce B2B selling will increase by 22 percent by 2005, "introducing significant new challenges for B2B sales professionals."[41] Physicians employ EDI to make electronic insurance claims, saving $1.50 per claim over paper filings.[42] EDI is used to access commercial, dental, Medicare, Medicaid, and Blue Cross/Blue Shield payers.[43] Electronic trading communities connect health care providers, insurers, and other players in the health care industry. Corporate buying online has been

---

[32] *Id.*

[33] David Kosiur, Understanding Electronic Commerce 1 (1997).

[34] Peter Keen: Electronic Commerce: Relationship; Trust by Design 133 (2000) (discussing nature of EDI and value-added networks).

[35] Electronic Messaging Services Task Force, The Commercial Use of Electronic Data Interchange: A Report and Model Trading Partner Agreement, 45 Bus. Law. 1645 (1990).

[36] National Institute of Standards, EDI Tutorial: History of EDI (visited Apr. 25, 2002), http://www.nist.gov/itl/div896/ipsg/eval_guide/subsection3_5_2.html.

[37] *Id.* at 136.

[38] *Id.* at 133.

[39] *See generally* Benjamin Wright and Jane K. Winn, The Law of Electronic Commerce (3d ed., 1998) (describing a wide variety of e-commerce and e-commerce issues).

[40] Boston Consulting Group, New BCG Study, *id.*

[41] Kristin Doucet, B2B Commerce Growing Slowly, CMA Mgmt., Mar. 1, 2002.

[42] *Id.*

[43] *Id.*

extended to established firms like "Pratt & Whitney (aero-engines), Otis (lifts), and Sikorsky (helicopters)."[44] Despite such activities and migration by companies, online ordering by businesses is more complex than consumer transactions: "For instance, many products are made to detailed specification, not bought off the peg; they are purchased by teams, not individuals, so that the decision to go ahead occurs at a different time and place from the actual transaction; and they are generally bought under long-term contracts, specifying all sorts of quality, price and delivery characteristics."[45]

[2] Industry Standards for EDI

To resolve the difficulties resulting from the lack of universal EDI standards, the American National Standards Institute (ANSI) developed X12 for the electronic exchange of information. ANSI is the clearinghouse for all industry standards in the United States; once ANSI standards are approved, they are widely adopted by the respective industry. The ANSI X12 standard encompasses nearly 200 transaction sets for diverse activities including "communications and controls, product data, finance, government, materials management, transportation, purchasing, industry standards transaction, distribution, warehousing, and insurance."[46] ANSI transaction sets are divided into data segments representing elements of business forms. Each segment within a set is in turn divided into data elements.

Trading partners thus have a standard protocol for specifying price, product code, or other attributes in B2B or B2G transactions. The federal government's adoption of ANSI X12 is covered in Federal Information Processing Standards Publication 161 (FIPS 161-1), available at the U.S. Government Printing Office.[47] The National Institute of Standards and Technology (NIST) administers the federal government's EDI activities.[48] The Department of Defense's Electronic Commerce Acquisition-Program Management Office (ECA-PMO) has published the transaction sets and documents for doing business with the military.[49] The goal is to develop a single set of EDI standards with universally understood protocol.[50]

---

[44] New Life in the Buying Department, E-Management Survey, The Economist (Nov. 11, 2000), at 27.

[45] Id.

[46] U.S. Small Business Administration, Standards Governing EC/EDI (visited Apr. 25, 2002), http://www.sba.gov.

[47] Id.

[48] National Institution of Standards and Technology, EDI Implementation Conventions (May 7, 2000), http://www.nist.gov/itl/div896/ipsg/eval_guide/subsection3_5_4.html.

[49] Supra note 36.

[50] Id.

Other entities promote different standards. The European Community has implemented the Guidelines on Trade Data Interchange (GTD) as its standard syntax.[51] The United Nations is the sponsor of a standard titled EDI for Administration, Commerce, and Transport (EDIFACT).[52] EDIFACT represents a "syntax adopted by the International Organization for Standards (ISO) in 1987." EDIFACT is primarily used in Europe and Asia, not in North America. The EDIFACT standard draws upon both the GTD and the ANSI X12 standards. To attain a worldwide standard for the Internet, ANSI X12 and EDIFACT must be harmonized into a single standard.[53]

[B]   Business-to-Consumer

Business-to-consumer (B2C) commerce is still dominated by "e-tailers" such as Amazon.com and Orbitz.com, a successful B2C venture involving five airlines. E*Trade, a popular online trading platform, is expanding its financial services offerings. Sotheby's, the world's oldest fine arts auctioneer, and eBay Inc., the world's online marketplace, formed a strategic alliance that will result in fine art being sold in live Internet auctions. Consumers will soon be able to make online bids for fine and decorative art, antiques, rare books, jewelry, and collectibles at eBay. "By 2005, 10 percent of the $227 billion in U.S. B2C sales will occur via mobile devices and TVs instead of PCs."[54] B2C sales revenue increased to $47.6 billion in 2001 from $42.4 billion in 2000.[55] The B2C model has become so popular that even prescription medication can be purchased online.

In addition to sales of tangible goods, B2C activities range from online banking and brokerage services to enrollment in distance learning courses and/or downloading of music or software from B2C sites. Hundreds of thousands of eMarketplaces target consumers, ranging from Motley Fool™ for financial information to Quake™ for sports. Online casino games, adventure games, and gaming sites are also popular with consumers, as are sites providing cash incentives or sweepstakes. Adult entertainment, including streaming video, is a highly profitable business that attracts hundreds of millions of consumer dollars.

The prescribing and selling of Viagra online by an unlicensed physician without a physical examination was not a violation of a state law prohibiting unconscionable practices in consumer transactions.[56] Customers located around the world may pursue online shopping through web shopping malls, purchasing things as varied as wine, glass and crystal, pet products, and countless other goods.

---

[51] *Id.*

[52] *Id.*

[53] ANSI has agreed to align the X12 standard with EDIFACT, but this alignment is still in its early stages. *Id.*

[54] Gale Group, B2C Sales Will Occur Via Mobile Devices and TVs Instead of PCs, 5 Intelligent Enterprise 1 (Feb. 1, 2002).

[55] Neiman Marcus Sales Report, WWD, Jan. 31, 2002, at 2.

[56] State of Kan. v. ConfiMed.com, 9 ILR (P&F) 3099 (Kan. Sup. Ct., 2002).

Online shoppers have an unparalleled opportunity to do comparison shopping. Auto-by-Tel™, for example, specializes in the sale or lease of new and used cars, car loans, and car insurance.[57]

People around the world vary in their acceptance of online shopping. In Germany, for example, online shoppers remain concerned about Internet security, uncertain legal rights, high telephone costs for Internet use, poor web site design, long downloading times, and "the lack of a shopping atmosphere."[58] German respondents complained that online stores were often late in delivering goods. Respondents also report frequent lapses of security due to the failure of online sellers or suppliers to encrypt orders.[59] Until recently, the retail online market was predominately a U.S. market. Online sellers will need to adapt their virtual stores to local languages, cultural sensitivities, and legal systems as they expand into European and Asian eMarketplaces.

[C] Business-to-Government

Particularly in the areas of procurement and contracts, various levels of government have begun to use EDI and other electronic commerce methods for business-to-government (B2G) transactions. Governmental agencies cut costs and bring more efficient methods to the procurement process by using e-commerce to transact business. State governments are combining resources to improve their negotiating position with vendors through B2G online malls. A growing number of federal and state agencies use electronic requests for proposals (RFPs) and catalogs. Federal agencies use B2G online transactions to improve supply chain management. State governments, too, are using B2G for procurement and the solicitation of government bids. Governments spend over $50 billion a year, which makes them potentially lucrative customers to traditional businesses. Recognizing their buying power, governments are increasingly inviting online bidding by potential suppliers.[60]

A number of dot-com companies are partnering with cities or government agencies in "electronic payments for taxes, permits, utility bills and other transactions."[61] Vendors contracting with state government agencies in Massachusetts, for example, are encouraged to use B2G ordering, billing, and accounting systems. StateGovCenter.com customizes state-specific e-commerce sites using a variety of

---

[57] *See* http://www.autobytel.com.

[58] Alex McCallum, German Consumers Remain Cautious about E-Commerce, 2 Global E-Commerce: Law and Business Report 1 (Jan. 2000).

[59] *Id.; see also* Forrester Research, Europe: The Sleeping Giant Awakens (visited Oct. 10, 2000), http://www.forrester.com (reporting Europe has the potential to reach $1.6 trillion in online trade by 2004).

[60] Craig Fellenstein & Ron Wood, Exploring E-Commerce, Global E-Business and E-Society 109 (2000).

[61] Glenn R. Simpson, The Web's Final Frontier: City Hall, Wall St. J. (May 17, 2000), at B1.

methods for coping with purchasing goods and services, requests for quotes (RFQs), and open market purchasing.[62]

Government agencies vary in their web site designs and user friendliness in bidding or procurement. SPC will have transaction costs associated with learning how to use government web sites, which may be poorly or inefficiently designed.

[D] Consumer-to-Consumer

A consumer-to-consumer (C2C) model facilitates both transactions between consumers who might otherwise face high transaction costs in finding buyers or sellers and transactions in goods not commonly available through retailers. Online auctions such as eBay™ are a popular C2C model, linking up consumer sellers with consumer buyers interested in auction jewelry, pens, collectibles, electronic equipment, artwork, books, and hundreds of thousands of other consumer goods.[63]

Online trading posts may also be specialized to niche products such as Pokemon™ cards, kitchen products, jewelry, sporting goods, or Hollywood memorabilia. GoAuction.com specializes in art, antiques, collectibles, and sports memorabilia, whereas SkyAuction.com™ is an Internet travel auction site. Stampfair Online Auctions specializes in packets of collectible postage stamps. The BidMore™ online auction permits bidders to purchase foreign stamps in a global auction marketplace.

Auctions may take the form of a traditional auction in which purchasers bid against each one another or of a reverse auction in which purchasers name their price. A growing number of web sites use "reverse auctions"; Priceline.com™ permitted a consumer to place a bid for a flight to Copenhagen, at a price no greater than $500 one-way. In essence, reverse auctions permit buyers to post their needs, and suppliers bid on the opportunity to fulfill them. With reverse auctions, prices move in a downward direction.[64] The reverse bidder specifies departure and return dates, departure and arrival airports, flight times, number of tickets, passenger names, maximum number of connections, airlines, offer price, and the manner of delivery. If the airline accepts the offer price, the purchase is automatically charged to the visitor's credit card.[65] Users must have typed their initials in an icon box "to indicate that they have reviewed the terms and agree to abide by priceline.com's terms and conditions."[66] Bid 4 Vacations uses a similar methodology for vacation and travel packages. Other sites, such as Bid.com™, Bidder's Edge™,

---

[62] Beth Cox, Digital Commerce Launches B2G Marketplace (visited Apr. 28, 2002), http://ecommerce.internet.com/news/news/article/0%2C3371%2C5061_321201%2C00.html.

[63] The auction model developed by eBay and other online auctions for a C2C market extends to B2B markets as well. *See, e.g.,* Harbinger.com, Harbinger Named to Information Week's E-Business 100 List (visited Apr. 27, 2002), http://www.harbinger.com/news/1999/121319999a.html.

[64] Ravi Kalakota, E-Business 2.0: Roadmap for Success 93 (2d ed. 2001).

[65] Priceline.com, Airline Tickets (visited May 9, 2000), http://www.tickets.priceline.com; *see also* Ronna Abrahamson, Airlines Get Cheap, The Industry Standard, Oct. 2, 2000, at 96 (reporting Priceline has two new online airline ticket competitors, savvio.com and Hotwire).

[66] *Id.*

BidFind™, BidNow™, and Bidstream™, use auction search engines to conduct meta-searches of popular auction web sites. A consumer can locate the lowest price on the Internet for any consumer product and use that price as a basis for bargaining at a brick-and-mortar business, such as a car dealership.[67]

Another variation of the online auction has customers band together in groups to increase their purchasing power. The greater the number of interested buyers seeking a particular item, the lower the price per purchaser.[68] Consumer sites providing information have also evolved. Sites like ancestry.com permit visitors to perform genealogical searches, using the site's message boards, classified by family surname. This site also has a location at which consumers can post their family data along with that of other users, thus creating an evolving family tree for that surname.

Online auctions evolved four decades after the rules for sale by auction were drafted in Article 2 of the Uniform Commercial Code (UCC).[69] The Article 2 rules for auctions were drafted to apply to human auctioneers selling goods in lots. The auctioneer's "falling of the hammer" constituted acceptance of the bidder's offer. This symbolic act has no close parallel in Internet auctions, although judges may extend Article 2 rules by analogy to the online auction house.

Under the UCC rules, a court will look to the "usage of trade"[70] to clarify the contracting parties' intent in light of the industry's established practices. The "usage of trade" for auctions generally takes the form of an auction "with reserve" or "without reserve." The traditional auction is "with reserve," meaning that the auctioneer has the discretion to reject the highest bid if it is too low; a sale is "with reserve" unless the goods are explicitly sold "without reserve."[71]

In an online auction, no "fall of the hammer" can signify acceptance, so the operators of virtual or online auctions are developing their own customary practices for listing goods, documenting bid histories, communicating bidding guidelines, and dealing with liability. Online auction sellers frequently set minimum prices and sell their goods explicitly "with reserve" or "without reserve." As in the real world, a virtual auction "with reserve" permits the seller to withdraw the goods at any time. Unlike the real world, however, no auctioneer announces the completion of the sale.[72] An auction "without reserve" means that the auctioneer cannot withdraw the goods unless no bid is made within a reasonable time. In either case, a bidder may retract his bid until the auctioneer announces the end of

---

[67] Some auction brokers offer business applications for online auction sources. Auctionshare.com, for example, sells custom auction sites for various products and services.

[68] *See, e.g.,* http://www.mercata.com.

[69] UCC § 2-328 (2000).

[70] UCC § 1-205(2) provides that a "usage of trade is any practice or method of dealing having such regularity of observance in a place, vocation or trade as to justify an expectation that it will be observed with respect to the transaction in question." UCC § 1-205 (2000).

[71] UCC § 2-328 (2000); *see also* The American Law Institute, Uniform Commercial Code [New] Revised Article 2, Sales § 238 (Council Draft No. 1, Oct. 5, 2000) (updating the concept of "hammer falling" with the "process of completing the auction sale").

[72] UCC § 2-328 (3) (2000).

the bidding period. The existing rules for virtual auctions must be accommodated to evolving online auction practices.

Online auctions use consumer measures of a seller's reputation to build trust in C2C transactions. Consumers give online ratings of their satisfaction with their course of dealing with a given vendor. In a face-to-face auction, the buyer can inspect the lots of goods being auctioned. Many online auction sellers provide photographs of objects being sold, but a photo of an item for sale is hardly the same thing as a hands-on inspection. State and federal regulators are increasingly scrutinizing online fraud at Internet auction sites. It is unclear whether courts will enforce disclaimers of liability by the virtual auction host. An online auction web site that collects personal data along with financial data is subject to the Gramm-Leach-Bliley Act (GLB). Moreover, a web site "that grades and appraises collectibles, such as sports cards or antiques, is also probably subject to GLB. However, a web site that merely sells collectibles, such as an online auction house, or allows an individual to calculate a recommended budget, is probably not subject to GLB."[73]

[E]   Government-to-Consumer

Finally, the Internet allows government-to-consumer (G2C) business transactions. Soon drivers will be able to pay parking tickets online. Most federal agencies already have web sites that provide citizens with government services. The Small Business Administration, for example, offers online courses on implementing business plans.[74] State auditors and attorneys general have sites at which whistleblowers can report unethical or illegal transactions. Federal agencies, such as the Department of Defense, Justice Department, and the USPTO, provide consumers with extensive resources relevant to their services. Citizens can now apply for passports online or, in many jurisdictions, file their tax returns. Millions of American consumers accessed the online version of the Starr Report on President Clinton.

Lawyers as well as ordinary Americans can read online versions of cases before they are published in the law reporters.[75] Recently, the FTC won a federal court order against a London-based operation that earned $1 million selling American consumers unusable "patriotic" web site addresses. The FTC began a new enforcement initiative on e-mail marketers in early 2002. The FTC takes the position that e-marketers that misuse and abuse e-mailing lists may be charged with unfair and deceptive trade practices.

The FTC settled a recent case in which the defendants used pretexting as a means of collecting confidential financial information; "[p]retexting—gathering personal financial data without consumers' knowledge or consent—was outlawed by the 2000 Gramm-Leach-Bliley Act. Since then, the FTC has taken the position

---

[73] Reece Hirsch and Andrew Mar, Gramm-Leach-Bliley Consumer Financial Privacy Rules Apply to Many Web Sites, 6 Cyberspace Law. (Sept. 2001).

[74] Small Business Administration, Business Plan (visited June 7, 2000), http://www.sba.gov.

[75] L. Marshall Smith & Andrew R. Desmond, The More Things Change, 17 Internet Research: New Tools, Same Methods 6 (Sept. 1999).

that pretexting is also unfair and deceptive, and therefore governed by the FTC Act."[76]

§ 6.03   SOURCES OF E-COMMERCE LAW

The substantive law of e-commerce law consists largely of commercial and contract law. Article 2 of the Uniform Commercial Code (UCC), the chief source of law for the sale of online goods, governs online offers, acceptance, consideration, warranties, risk of loss, performance, and remedies for tangible goods. The Convention for the International Sale of Goods (CISG) applies to online sales of goods between merchants in different signatory countries. It is unclear how traditional substantive contract law applies to software downloadable from a web site. In the absence of new substantive rules, courts will stretch traditional principles to apply to web site contracts. The parties may develop their own rules governing web site contracts. Courts will generally enforce contracts entered into by commercial parties in the absence of fraud or a violation of public policy. Increasingly, regulatory agencies are policing unfair or oppressive contract provisions such as choice of law, choice of forum, or limitations of liability. Unfair or deceptive trade practices may be policed by courts, or by state or federal regulatory agencies.

[A]   Federal Trade Commission

The Federal Trade Commission (FTC) is the chief federal agency governing online sales and services. The FTC has promulgated rules to implement the Magnuson-Moss Act, which applies to the sale of consumer goods on the Internet, and it has recently issued the Children's Online Privacy Protection Rule, which governs commercial practices of sites directed to children under the age of 13. The FTC is considering amending its Telemarketing Sales Rule to govern abusive or deceptive web site sales acts or practices. The FTC is considering regulations to ensure that consumers receive adequate information when purchasing computer information products and services.

[1]   Magnuson-Moss Act

The Magnuson-Moss Warranty Federal Trade Commission Improvement Act (Magnuson-Moss Act) applies to consumer products on the Internet with the same force it does to products in the offline world. The Magnuson-Moss Act applies to written warranties "made in connection with the sale of a consumer product by a supplier to a buyer which relates to the material or workmanship."[77] This broad language applies to written warranties for consumer products sold over the Internet. The term *consumer products* means "any tangible personal property which is

---

[76] FTC v. TLD Network Ltd., 9 ILR (P&F) 3158 (N.D. Ill. 2002).
[77] Disclosure of Written Consumer Product Warranty Terms and Conditions, 16 C.F.R. § 701(c)(1) (2000).

distributed in commerce and which is normally used for personal, family, or household purposes."[78]

The threshold for applying the Magnuson-Moss Act is whether a transaction involves consumer products "distributed in commerce" costing more than $15.[79] Courts will have little difficulty holding that Internet sales constitute "use in commerce." It is unclear whether the Magnuson-Moss Act applies to computer software transactions or information products, since software is an intangible rather than a movable good. Courts will apply the Magnuson-Moss Act to hybrid transactions in which computer hardware is the substantial part or predominant purpose.

The Magnuson-Moss Act requires all written warranties to be conspicuously designated as either "full" or "limited." The label *full warranty* signifies that the seller provides all federal warranties, such as a right to a refund if a seller is unable to correct defects. In contrast, the concept of *limited warranty* means that the seller is offering a limited remedy. Few sellers have offered a "full warranty" in the history of the Magnuson-Moss Act. The Magnuson-Moss Act does not apply to merchant-to-merchant sales (B2B) and is chiefly a consumer protection statute governing B2C transactions.[80]

One of the unsettled issues is whether consumer protection laws enacted for a durable goods economy extend to software and other information products. Consumer advocates favor the extension of the Magnuson-Moss Warranty Act to software or other information transactions. One of the key features of the Act is that it does not permit the implied warranty of merchantability to be disclaimed completely for consumer transactions. A prominent NCCUSL commissioner is of the opinion that the Magnuson-Moss Act does not apply to software and other computer information because the Act applies only to "tangible" personal property that is acquired by a "buyer."[81]

Under the Magnuson-Moss Act, the implied warranty of merchantability is not completely disclaimable.[82] The Magnuson-Moss Act provides that a supplier may not disclaim or modify any implied warranty to a consumer if (1) the supplier makes any written warranty to the consumer or (2) at the time of the sale, or within 90 days thereafter, the supplier enters into a service contract with the consumer relative to the consumer product.[83] If a seller gives only a limited warranty, the

---

[78] *Id.* at § 701(b) (2000).

[79] 15 U.S.C. § 2301(13) (2000).

[80] The Magnuson-Moss Act applies "to written warranties on tangible personal property which is normally used for personal, family, or household purposes." 16 C.F.R. § 700.1 (2001): "Nothing in the Act provides that a consumer product be warranted or that a product be warranted for any specific length of time. If however, a written warranty is offered, full disclosure is required, and the warranty information must be made available to consumers before the product is sold."

[81] James C. McKay, UCITA and the Consumer: A Response to Professor Braucher, 5 Cyberspace Law. 9 (Nov. 2000).

[82] The implied warranty of merchantability is not disclaimable if goods are used for personal, household, or family purposes. For further discussion of warranties, *see* § 6.05[G].

[83] 15 U.S.C. § 2308(a)(1) (2) (2000).

implied warranty of merchantability may be limited for the duration of a limited written warranty. The limited duration period must, however, be conscionable and explained in clear and unmistakable language.[84]

If a manufacturer of computer hardware has not corrected or cured problems in its computer system after a reasonable number of attempts, the consumer must receive a refund or replacement without charge, plus reasonable expenses. The Magnuson-Moss Act would provide a remedy to consumers in cases where there are repeated failures to pass acceptance tests as well as failure to provide deliverables, such as source codes, which caused the licensee to withhold payment. If the Magnuson-Moss Act were extended to Internet-related licenses, the implied warranty of merchantability would be nondisclaimable in consumer transactions.

[2] Children's Online Privacy Protection Rule

By 1998, "almost 10 million U.S. children had online access, with over 4 million using the Internet from school and 5.7 million from home. Children are also avid consumers and represent a large and powerful segment of the marketplace."[85] The FTC regulates unfair or deceptive acts or practices in connection with the collection, use, or disclosure of personal information harvested from children at web sites in B2C transactions.[86] Commercial web sites will need to comply with the FTC's Children's Online Privacy Protection Rule, which implements the Children's Online Privacy Protection Act (COPPA).[87] COPPA's regulations must be complied with by operators of web sites that target online advertisements, promotions, and games to children under the age of 13.[88] COPPA applies to any site that (1) "requests that children submit personal information online"; (2) "enables children to make personal information publicly available through a chat room, message board, or other means"; or (3) "uses cookies or other identifying codes to track children's activity on the Internet."[89]

The web site operator must make a threshold determination of whether the web site or online service is directed to children under 13. A web site that sells children's products such as games, books, or other entertainment products needs to comply with COPPA's safe harbor provisions. Web sites directed to children or that collect information from children must post a notice before collecting, using, or disclosing information about a child. However, "consent is not required when a site is collecting an e-mail address of a child for the sole purpose of respond[ing] to a one-time request from the child."[90]

---

[84] *Id.* § 2308.

[85] Joshua Marmund, Can COPPA Work? An Analysis of the Parental Consent Measure in the Children's Online Privacy Act, 11 Fordham I.P., Media & Ent. L.J. 189, 190 (2000).

[86] Children's Online Privacy Protection Rule, 16 C.F.R. § 312 (2002).

[87] 15 U.S.C. § 6501-6506 (2002).

[88] *Id.* § 312.2.

[89] *Id.* § 312.2(a)(b)(c).

[90] *Id.* Federal Trade Commission, How to Protect Kids' Privacy Online (Feb. 2000) (visited Feb. 22, 2002), http://www.ftc.gov/bcp/conline/edcams/kidzprivacy/index.html.

The FTC considers a number of factors in determining whether a given web site targets children. The most important factors include "the subject matter (visual or audio content)," the age of models on the site, "the age of the actual or intended audience, and whether a site uses animated characters or other child-oriented features."[91] The FTC considers an entity an "operator" depending on who owns, controls, and pays for the collection of information.[92] COPPA applies to "individually identifiable information about a child that is collected online, such as full name, home address, e-mail address, telephone number" or other means of identifying or contacting a child.[93] If COPPA applies, the operator must "link to a notice of its information practices on the home page of the web site or online service and at each area where it collects personal information from children."[94] "The FTC informed Congress of the need for parents to better understand the risks to their children's privacy on-line, as well as the need for parental consent concerning the collection and disclosure of their children's personal information."[95] The FTC requires the link to be "clear and prominent."[96]

Personal information is defined to include "(a) [an individuals'] first and last name; (b) home or other physical address; (c) an e-mail address or other online contact information; (d) a telephone number; (e) a Social Security number; (f) a persistent identifier, such as a code; and (g) any other information concerning the child or the parents of that child that the operator collects online from the child."[97] Personal information may be collected directly from a child or passively through devices such as cookies.[98] The FTC suggested the following methods for obtaining consent: operators could "(1) provide a consent form to be signed by the parent and returned to the operator by postal mail or facsimile; (2) require a parent to use a credit card in connection with a transaction; (3) have a parent call a toll-free telephone number; or (4) accept an e-mail accompanied by a valid digital signature."[99]

The FTC requires the site to obtain parental consent and to give conspicuous notice of their information practices.[100] A site must obtain verifiable parental consent *before* collecting a child's personal data. Parents have a right to review personal information provided by a child and to delete the information or to have it deleted.[101] A web site may not condition a child's participation in the web site on

---

[91] *Id.*

[92] *Id.*

[93] *Id.*

[94] *Id.*

[95] Joshua Warmund, Can COPPA Work? An Analysis of the Parental Consent Measure in the Children's Online Privacy Act? 11 Fordham I.P., Media & Ent. L.J. 189, 194 (2000).

[96] *Id.*

[97] 16 C.F.R. § 312.2(a)-(g) (2001).

[98] Federal Trade Commission, How to Comply with the Children's Online Privacy Protection Rule (visited Apr. 22, 2002), http://www.ftc.gov/bcp/conline/pubs/buspubs/coppa.htm.

[99] 11 Fordham I.P., Media & Ent. L.J. 189, 204 (2000).

[100] 16 C.F.R. §§ 312.4, 312.5 (2000).

[101] *Id.* § 312.6.

the collection of personal information.[102] A child's parents must be given the opportunity to restrain further use or collection of information.[103]

A web site must have reasonable security to protect the confidentiality, security, and integrity of personal information collected from children.[104] The FTC COPPA Rule provides a safe harbor for sites as long as they comply with approved self-regulatory guidelines formulated by marketing or online industries.[105] At a minimum, the self-regulatory guidelines must subject operators to the same or greater protections for children as those contained in §§ 312.2 through 312.9 of the FTC's COPPA Rule.[106]

A web site is not entitled to the safe harbor unless it requires operators to comply with the guidelines. The site is required to conduct "periodic reviews of subject operators' information practices."[107] The FTC may be requested to approve self-regulatory guidelines.[108] Industry groups that seek safe harbor must maintain records on compliance for a period of not less than three years.[109] The FTC plans to implement a sliding scale approach to parental consent by April 2002.[110] The method of consent will vary depending on how the web site operator intends to use information. If the use of the information is purely internal, a less stringent method of consent will apply. If the operator is harvesting data for others, however, a more rigorous consent will be required.

The FTC announced a number of initiatives it has taken to enhance compliance with COPPA:

- A settlement with the operators of the Etch-A-Sketch web site resolving alleged violations of COPPA and requiring a $35,000 civil penalty.

- Release of an FTC COPPA compliance survey, and a business education initiative to help children's web site operators draft COPPA-compliant privacy policies.

- Announcement of warning letters to more than 50 children's sites alerting them to the notice provisions of COPPA and the requirement that they comply with these provisions, and the extension of COPPA's sliding scale mechanism for obtaining verifiable parental consent for a three-year period. "Under the sliding scale, a web site collecting personal information solely for its internal use, and not disclosing the information to the public or third parties, may obtain parental consent through the use of an e-mail message from the parent,

---

[102] Id. § 312.7.

[103] Id. § 312.5.

[104] Id. § 312.8.

[105] Id. § 312.10(a).

[106] Id. § 312.10(b)(1).

[107] Id. § 312.10(b)(I).

[108] Id. § 312.10(c).

[109] Id. § 312.10(d).

[110] Federal Trade Commission, How to Comply with the Children's Online Privacy Protection Rule (Nov. 1999) (visited June 8, 2000), http://www.ftc.gov/bcp/conline/pubs/buspubs/coppa.htm.

coupled with additional steps to provide assurance that it is the parent providing the consent. If the web site is going to disclose the personal information to
the public or third parties, the Rule requires that the web site use more reliable
methods."[111] The FTC extended its sliding scale rule until 2005. The FTC will
hold a public notice and comment in connection with the statutorily mandated
review of the sliding scale rule in 2005.

[3] Telemarketing Sales Rule

The FTC's Telemarketing Sales Rule, which prohibits "deceptive telemarketing acts or practices,"[112] has yet to be expanded to telemarketing over the Internet. On February 23, 2000, however, the FTC announced a five-year review of the
rule. Under the rule, telemarketers are required to make material disclosures *prior*
to a customer's payment for goods or services. The customer must be provided
with the total costs to purchase, receive, or use any goods or services.[113] Further,
telemarketers must make specific disclosure about any material limitations or condition to the purchase of goods or services.[114] A telemarketer must disclose its policy for "refunds, cancellations, exchanges or repurchases."[115]

The FTC filed a civil action against Cross Media Marketing Corp. in April
2002 for alleged violations of the FTC's Telemarketing Sales Rule by the firm's
magazine unit.[116] The cable industry is seeking to be exempted from FTC's
national "Do Not Call" list. Cable operators want the ability to sell subscribers
new services "not just for premium channels or more expensive cable packages,
but for new services with which customers might be unfamiliar, such as high-
speed Internet access, video-on-demand or interactive television."[117] The FTC
filed suit against "fraudulent 'inbound telemarketing' offers, in which consumers
allegedly were prompted by classified ads, Internet banners, and other solicitations
to call companies. The FTC actions target five companies that profited from
allegedly bogus work-at-home medical-billing scams, and four companies that
offered so-called advance-fee loan programs."[118]

In any prize promotion, the telemarketer must give the odds of winning a
prize and the factors used in calculating the odds, as well as any costs of or conditions for receiving or redeeming a prize.[119] A telemarketer is liable for deceptive

---

[111] Federal Trade Commission, COPPA Anniversary (visited Apr. 28, 2002), http://www.ftc.gov/
opa/2002/04/coppaanniv.htm.

[112] Telemarketing Sales Rule, 16 C.F.R. § 310.3 (2001).

[113] *Id.* § 310.3(a)(1)(I).

[114] *Id.* § 310.3(a)(1)(ii).

[115] *Id.* § 310.3(a)(1)(iii).

[116] Direct Newsline, Primedia (May 1, 2002).

[117] Monica Hogan, Cable Seeks "Do Not Call" Exemption, Multichannel News, Apr. 22, 2002,
at 18.

[118] Telecom Week in Review, Newsbytes, Apr. 19, 2002.

[119] *Id.* § 310.3(a)(1)(iv).

telemarketing acts for misrepresenting information on costs, limitations, or conditions to purchase or use goods or services.[120] The FTC's telemarketing regulations prescribe rules for a merchant's payment system. A customer's express verifiable authorization is required for payment by check or other negotiable instruments.[121] False or misleading statements or assisting others in deceptive telemarketing schemes is strictly prohibited by the FTC.[122]

The Federal Trade Commission also governs abusive telemarketing acts or practices. The FTC considers it an "abusive telemarketing act or practice" for the telemarketer to use threats, intimidation, or obscene language in requesting or receiving payment.[123] A telemarketer may not request or receive payment for removing derogatory information from a person's credit history, record, or rating.[124] Telemarketers may not repeatedly cause any telephone to ring continuously "with intent to annoy, abuse or harass any person at the called number."[125] Every online company needs to institute written procedures and to train its personnel to comply with telephone calling restrictions, which may extend to its online sales and collection practices.[126] A web site should also voluntarily comply with best practices of industry standards in its online sales practices.

Some states have established laws regarding unsolicited e-mails. Recently, California enacted a law that required senders of unsolicited e-mail messages to establish a toll free number or valid return e-mail address that recipients may use to refuse further unsolicited documents, to include a statement informing the recipient of the toll free number or return e-mail address as the first text in the e-mailed document, to stop sending unsolicited advertising material to anyone who has requested that such material not be sent, and to include "ADV" in the subject line of the e-mail if it pertains to adult material. A California court found that the antispam statute did not unconstitutionally burden interstate commerce and upheld it.[127]

[B]   The Role of Industry Standards

The usage of trade and evolving business practices are explicitly incorporated into the UCC.[128] The UCC's underlying public policy is to "simplify, clarify and modernize the law governing commercial transactions."[129] Karl Llewellyn, Reporter of the UCC, conceptualized the UCC as a semipermanent statute that

---

[120] *Id.* § 310.3(a)(2)(i)-(ii).

[121] *Id.* § 310.3(a)(3).

[122] *Id.* § 310.3(4)(b).

[123] *Id.* § 310.4(a)(1)(2).

[124] *Id.* § 310.4(2).

[125] *Id.* § 310.4(b)(1)(I).

[126] *Id.* § 310.4(b)(1)(ii)(iii).

[127] Ferguson v. Friendfinders, 94 Cal. App. 4th 1255, 115 Cal. Rptr. 2d 258 (2002).

[128] *See* UCC § 1-205(5) (noting that the concept "applicable usage of trade" is used to interpret all UCC agreements).

[129] *Id.* § 1-102(2)(a).

would continually be updated "to permit the continued expansion of commercial practices through custom, usage and agreement of the parties."[130] The goal of the comprehensive commercial statute was a permanent modernity project that would continually be updated to reflect technological and social change.

The UCC was designed to be updated periodically to accommodate new technologies and business practices. UCITA expands the concepts of the UCC to cyberspace commercial transactions, and follows the example of the UCC by anticipating that its rules will evolve as the Internet unfolds.[131] As a result, UCITA, like the UCC, will continually expand through customs, usage of trade, and industry standard.[132] Increasingly, the law of e-commerce is found in industry standards such as those formulated by the International Standards Organization (ISO) and other entities.

[1] OECD Guidelines

The 28 countries of the Organization for Economic Cooperation and Development (OECD) have agreed to new consumer protection guidelines for the electronic marketplace. The guidelines emphasize the importance of providing "truthful, accurate and complete information to consumers" and of avoiding deceptive, misleading, or unfair claims, to "build consumer confidence in the global electronic marketplace."[133] Under the OECD guidelines, an e-business should do the following:

a. use fair business, advertising, and marketing practices;
b. provide accurate, clear, and easily accessible information about the company and the goods or services it offers;
c. disclose full information about the terms, conditions, and costs of the transaction;
d. ensure that consumers know they are making a commitment to buy before closing the deal;
e. provide an easy-to-use and secure method for online payment;
f. protect consumers during electronic commerce transactions;
g. address consumer complaints and difficulties;
h. adopt fair, effective, and easy to understand self-regulatory policies and procedures; and
i. help educate consumers about electronic commerce.[134]

---

[130] UCC § 1-102(2)(b).

[131] UCITA § 113 (2000).

[132] *Id.*

[133] Federal Trade Commission, Electronic Commerce: Selling Internationally, A Guide for Business (Mar. 2000), http://www.ftc.gov/bcp/conline/pubs/alerts/ecombalrt.htm.

[134] *Id.*

[2] International Chamber of Commerce

The International Chamber of Commerce (ICC) formulates guidelines, codes, and rules for advertising and marketing on the Internet.[135] The ICC also proposes ethics for online advertising which take the form of voluntary guidelines.[136] The ICC's voluntary guidelines on interactive marketing advertising cover issues such as online privacy, the protection of personal data, advertising directed at children, and "the varied sensitivities of global audiences."[137] The ICC guidelines require marketers to clearly disclose their identities when posting messages and to not use false headers.[138] The ICC has formed guidelines giving online users the right to control personal information.

An online advertiser is required to state its reasons for collecting information and must safeguard the security of data.[139] The ICC ethical guidelines update the ICC's International Code of Advertising Practices to apply to Internet-related advertising, marketing, and distribution.[140] The ICC also requires online advertisers and marketers to comply with advertising law in the country where the advertising message originates.[141]

[C] Revised UCC Article 2

Article 2 of the UCC applies to online sales of goods just as it would apply in the "brick-and-mortar world." Written long before the rise of e-commerce, Article 2 is being revised to update sales law for Internet commercial transactions such as online sales contracts or Internet sales transactions.[142] Revised Article 2 has electronic contracting provisions that are consistent with the Computer Information Transactions Act and the Electronic Signatures in Global and National Commerce Act of 2000.[143] Presently, for example, Article 2 requires a signed writing for sales of goods valued at $500 or greater. Revised Article 2 raises the statutory minimum to $5,000 and permits the parties to substitute an electronic record for a

---

[135] International Chamber of Commerce, ICC Guidelines on Advertising and Marketing on the Internet, 2 Apr. 1998 (visited May 17, 2000), http://www.iccwbo.org/home/menu_advert_marketing.asp.

[136] International Chamber of Commerce, New International Code Covers Ethics of On-Line Advertising (visited Apr. 27, 2002), http://www.iccwbo.org/home/news_archives/1998/new_international_code_covers.asp.

[137] Id.

[138] Id.

[139] Id.

[140] Id.

[141] Id.

[142] The American Law Institute, Uniform Commercial Code: [New] Revised Article 2—Sales (Council Draft No. 1, Oct. 5, 2000) (hereinafter cited as UCC § R2).

[143] UCC § R2-102 (19) (defining *electronic messages* as "an electronic record or display stored, generated, or transmitted by electronic means for purposes of communication to another").

paper-based writing.[144] Currently the UCC defines a signature or the term *signed* as "any symbol executed or adopted with the present intent to authenticate a writing."[145] Revised Article 2 defines *authenticate* broadly to encompass any encrypted signature or other electronic records.[146]

Article 2 is being revamped to validate the use of software or electronic agents for the formation of sales contracts such as contracts of procurement, orders, and confirmations.[147] Trading partner agreements specify the rules in advance for structured protocols for the computer-to-computer ordering of goods and services. The revision of Article 2 is in large part a modernization project to update the UCC for the information economy. Revised Article 2 expands the concept of a writing to encompass e-records. In addition, the term *signed* will include signatures by authentication.[148] Revised Article 1 also forges new online contracting definitions useful for commercial transactions in cyberspace.[149] Revised Article 1 updates the concept of *conspicuousness* to take into account e-records.[150] The Revised Article defines a *record* to mean "information that is inscribed on a tangible medium or that is stored in an electronic or other medium and is retrievable in perceivable form."[151] The term *send* is updated to include e-records as well as writings.[152]

Revised Article 2 also updates writings to include records and includes electronic authentication as a method for "signing" a sales contract.[153] In October 2000, the federal Electronic Signatures in Global and National Commerce Act (E-Sign) became effective. E-Sign applies to a wide variety of Article 2 transactions and preempts provisions of current Article 2 that do not validate e-signatures

---

[144] UCC § R2-201 (Proposed Final Draft, May 1, 1999).

[145] UCC § 1-201 (39) (2000).

[146] UCC § R2-102(a)(1) (defining *authenticate* as to sign or "to execute or otherwise adopt a symbol, or encrypt or similarly process a record in whole or in part, with present intent of the authenticating person to identify the person or to adopt or accept a record or term").

[147] *See generally* Wright and Winn, *supra* note 39 (describing a wide variety of e-commerce and e-commerce issues); *see also* Carol Kunze, UCC Article 2 (visited Dec. 20, 2001), http://ucitaonline.com/whatsnu.html (stating that NCCUSL did not take a final vote on whether to exclude software from revised Article 2 at its July 2001 annual meeting and that action by the ALI is pending).

[148] The American Law Institute, Uniform Commercial Code, Proposed Amendments to Article 2, Sales (Apr. 16, 2001) (Submitted to the Council to the Members The American Law Institute for Discussion at the Seventy-Eighth Annual Meeting, on May 14-17 of 2001) at prefatory note (hereinafter Revised Article 2).

[149] The American Law Institute, Uniform Commercial Code, Proposed Amendments to Article 1, General Provisions (April 16, 2001) (Submitted to the Council to the Members The American Law Institute for Discussion at the Seventy-Eighth Annual Meeting, on May 14-17 of 2001) at prefatory note (hereinafter Revised Article 1).

[150] Revised § 1-201 (10) (defining *conspicuousness* to include language in the body of an [electronic] record).

[151] Revised § 1-201(33)(a) (ALI Draft, May 2001) (defining record).

[152] Revised § 1-301(38) (ALI Draft, May 2001) (noting that the definition of *send* encompasses "any other way to be received any record or notice within the time it would have arrived if properly sent").

[153] Revised Article 2, *id.*, at Prefatory Note.

and e-records. In addition, E-Sign would likely preempt Revised Article 2 to the extent that there are inconsistent provisions. However, "E-Sign permits the states some latitude to modify its provisions, and Section 2-104(4) of the draft takes advantage of that opportunity except to the extent E-Sign provides protection to consumers."[154] Terms such as *electronic record, information processing system, receipt,* and *record* are assimilated from the Uniform Electronic Transactions Act (UETA).[155]

Revised Article 2 defines *authenticate* to mean "i) to sign a record; or (ii) to attach to or logically associate with a record an electronic sound, symbol, or process, with the intent to sign the record."[156] The concept of authentication is critical to the use of digital signatures. In addition, Revised § 1-201(3) recognizes "electronic signatures" and is harmonized with the definition of signature in E-Sign.[157]

Revised Article 2's definition of *conspicuousness* is updated to include electronic records.[158] There is a "special rule for situations where the sender of an electronic record intends to evoke a response from an electronic agent; the presentation of the term must be capable of evoking a response from a reasonably configured electronic agent."[159] The Article 2 drafters base the "electronic contracting provisions, including the definition of 'electronic,' 'electronic agent,' 'record,' 'electronic processing system,' and electronic aspects of' receive on the Uniform Electronic Transactions Act and are consistent with the federal Electronic Signatures in Global and National Commerce Act."[160]

Electronic events, such as the transmittal of data messages, may be attributed to a person if they were "the act of the person or the person's electronic agent."[161] Revised §§ 2-211 is entitled "Legal Recognition of Electronic Contracts, Records and Authentication."[162] Revised §§ 2-211(1) and (2) are based upon § 7(a) and (b) of UETA.[163] Section 2-201(3) is derived from § 5(b) of UETA.[164] Section 2-211(4) is derived from the Uniform Computer Information Transactions Act (UCITA).[165] The legal significance of § 2-211 taken as a whole is that the electronic medium does not affect its legal significance.[166] Section 2-211(1) borrows from UETA and

---

[154] *Id.*

[155] *Id.*

[156] Revised § 2-103(1)(a) (ALI Draft, May 2001).

[157] Revised § 2-103(1)(a) Prelim. Cmt. (ALI Draft, May 2001) (stating that the concept of authentication is "broad enough to cover any record that is 'signed' within the meaning of present Article 1" . . . and consistent with § 2(8) of UETA as well as E-Sign).

[158] Revised Article 2-103(1)(c) defines *conspicuousness in records* as "intended to evoke a response by e-agents." Revised § 2-103(1)(c) (ALI Draft, May 2001).

[159] Revised § 2-103(1)(c), Prelim. Cmt. (ALI Draft, May 2001).

[160] *Id.,* at Prelim. Cmt. to § 2-103(1)(g) (defining "'[e]lectronic' means relating to technology having electrical, digital, magnetic, wireless, optical, electromagnetic, or similar capabilities").

[161] UCC § R2-212 (2000).

[162] Revised § 2-211 (ALI Draft, May 2001).

[163] Revised § 2-211, Prelim. Cmt. (ALI Draft, May 2001).

[164] *Id.*

[165] *Id.*

[166] *Id.*

E-Sign in stating that "[a] record or authentication may not be denied legal effect or enforceability solely because it is in electronic form."[167] Similarly, a "contract may not be denied legal effect or enforceability solely because an electronic record was used in its formation."[168] Article 2, like UETA and E-Sign, does not require contracts to be formed by electronic means.[169]

Revised 2-212 is entitled "authentication" and states that "[a]n electronic record or electronic authentication is attributed to a person if the record was created by or the authentication was the act of the person or the person's electronic agent or the person is otherwise bound by the act under the law."[170] If a web site user types her name on an e-mail order, it would be considered to be an electronic record and electronic authentication.[171] An employer would be bound by an employee's typing of the company's name on an e-mail purchase order.[172] A computer-to-computer order would be authenticated if a computer was programmed to order goods "upon receipt of inventory information within particular parameters."[173] The principles of agency apply equally well whether a paper-based or electronic medium is used to authenticate an action.[174]

Section 2-213 is entitled "Electronic Communication" and, like § 2-212, is entirely new to Article 2.[175] Section 2-213, like 2-212, borrows from UETA in its rules about electronic communications.[176] Section 2-213 mandates a "duty to read" electronic communications which have a legal effect "though no individual is aware of its receipt."[177] Subsection 2 accords legal certainty as to when a notice or electronic record has been received.[178] Subsection 2 does not address the quality of the content of a record but only the question of receipt.[179] Section 2-204(4)(a) permits contracts to be formed by interacting electronic agents.[180] Electronic or computer-to-computer contracts may be formed "even if no individual was aware of or reviewed the electronic agents' actions or the resulting terms and agreements."[181]

Similarly, a contract may be formed between interaction of a computer and an individual.[182] Contract formation occurs if the individual "is free to refuse to take or makes a statement that the individual has reason to know will: (i) cause the

---

[167] *Id.*

[168] Revised § 2-201(2) (ALI Draft, May 2001).

[169] Revised § 2-201(3) (ALI Draft, May 2001).

[170] Revised § 2-212 (ALI Draft, May 2001).

[171] Revised § 2-212 Prelim. Cmt. (ALI Draft May 2001) (citing example).

[172] *Id.*

[173] *Id.*

[174] *Id.*

[175] Revised § 2-213 (ALI Draft, May 2001).

[176] Revised § 2-213, Prelim. Cmt. (ALI Draft, May 2001).

[177] Revised § 2-213(1) (ALI Draft, May 2001).

[178] Revised § 2-213(2) (ALI Draft, May 2001).

[179] Revised § 2-213, Prelim. Cmt. (ALI Draft, May 2001).

[180] Revised § 2-204(4)(a) (ALI Draft, May 2001).

[181] *Id.*

[182] Revised § 2-204(4)(b) (ALI Draft, May 2001).

electronic agent to complete the transaction or performance or (ii) indicate acceptance of an offer, regardless of other expressions or actions by the individual to which the electronic agent cannot react."[183] Revised Article 2 validates click-through contracts formed on a web site.[184] Contractual intent is based upon programming and uses of computer systems.[185] The sale of goods is increasingly taking place over the Internet. Section 2-204(4)(b) validates a broad range of Internet-related contracts that are based upon "click-through" transactions.[186] Revised Article 2 proposed liberal formation rules when it comes to electronic records. Section 2-206(3) rejects the mirror image rule. Revised 2-206(3) states that a definite and seasonable expression of acceptance in a record operates as an acceptance even if it contains terms additional to or different from the offer.[187] Contracts by electronic agents or "bots" may be formed with or without human review.[188] Electronic agents may be used to purchase tangible goods or computer information.

[D] Digital Signatures

Thirty-six states have either already enacted or are proposing electronic signature acts, according to a survey by the Internet Law and Policy Forum (ILPF).[189] Forty-seven states have considered or enacted electronic authentication legislation, and 13 states have formed task forces to examine the need for digital signatures and other legal infrastructure for electronic contracting.[190] The ILPF survey distinguished between electronic and digital signatures. An *electronic signature* means

> any identifiers such as letters, characters, or symbols manifested by electronic or similar means, executed or adopted by a party to a transaction with intent to authenticate writing. A writing, therefore, is deemed to be electronically signed if an electronic signature is logically associated with such writing.[191]

Digital signatures use a branch of mathematics called *cryptography* to transform writings into unintelligible code that is subsequently translated back into its original form.[192] The attributes of a digital signature are that (1) it is unique to the user,

---

[183] Revised § 2-204(4)(b)(i)(ii) (ALI Draft, May 2000).

[184] Revised § 2-204, Prelim. Cmt. 5 (ALI Draft, May 2000).

[185] *Id.*

[186] *Id.*

[187] Revised § 2-206(3) (ALI Draft, May 2000).

[188] Whatis.com glossary, Definition of Bots (visited Apr. 24, 2002) http://www.whatis.com. (defining a *bot* as an abbreviation for *robot* and referring to programs, such as spiders or web crawlers that simulate human actions).

[189] Internet Law and Policy Forum, Update: Survey of State Electronic and Digital Signature Legislative Initiatives (survey completed by the Seattle law firm of Perkins Coie) (visited Apr. 22, 2002), http://www.ilpf.org/digsig/update.htm.

[190] *Id.*

[191] *Supra* note 189.

[192] *Id.*

(2) it is capable of verification, and (3) it is under the control of the user. Digital signatures use algorithms that are "encrypted and decrypted using public and private keys."[193]

The trend in the law is to accord legal validity to digital signatures and electronic records. Revised Article 2 shares common ground with UCITA in its validation of electronic contracting as a business model.[194] Revised Article 2 gives legal recognition to the concept of the electronic record, which is the functional equivalent of a signed writing.[195] The American Bar Association's Science and Technology Committee has proposed Digital Signature Guidelines, which have been models for statutes adopted by a number of states.

[E] Electronic Signatures in Global and National Commerce Act of 2000

President Clinton signed the federal Electronic Signatures in Global and National Commerce Act (E-Sign) on July 1, 2000, "to promote the use of electronic records and authentication methods in interstate commerce."[196] Section 101 of E-Sign validates electronic records and signatures.[197] "[A] signature, contract or other record relating to such transaction may not be denied legal effect, validity or enforceability solely because it is in electronic form."[198] "[A] contract relating to such transactions may not be denied legal effect, validity or enforceability solely because an electronic signature or electronic record was used in its formation."[199] The E-Sign does nothing to require "any person to agree to use or accept electronic records or electronic signatures, other than a governmental agency with respect to a record other than a contract to which it is a party."[200] An online company should consider employing a public key infrastructure (PKI) or other method to make it difficult to repudiate online contracts.[201]

Section 101 (c) is a consent rule that requires that consumers affirmatively consent prior to receiving electronic communications in lieu of writings. The consent rule gives consumers a prescribed method for withdrawing consent. Consumers may also obtain a paper copy of a record.[202] Consumer disclosures are required if an electronic record is substituted for a paper-based record.[203] The

---

[193] Technology and the Internet, Digital Signatures, Security Tutorial (visited Apr. 22, 2002), http://www.privacyexchange.org/tsi/digitalsig.htm.

[194] *See* UCC § R2-201(a), § R2-203(e) (Proposed Final Draft, May 1, 1999).

[195] UCC § R2-102(18) (Council Draft No. 1, Oct. 5, 2000).

[196] Electronic Signatures in Global and National Commerce Act (E-Sign) Pub. L. No. 106-229, 114 Stat. 464 (2000) (codified at 15 U.S.C. §§ 7001 et seq. (2002)).

[197] *Id.,* § 101.

[198] *Id.,* § 101(a)(1).

[199] *Id.,* § 101(a)(2).

[200] *Id.,* § 101(b)(2).

[201] Sean Doherty, The E-Signature Act Makes Online Transactions Legally Binding, Network Computing, Dec. 10, 2001, at 83.

[202] E-Sign, § 101(c).

[203] *Id.,* § 101(c)(1)(A)(D).

E-Sign prescribes the following disclosures which constitute affirmative consent for consumers: (1) the consumers must have affirmatively consented to use of e-records and not withdrawn consent;[204] and (2) the consumer, prior to consenting, must have been given a "clear and conspicuous statement informing the consumer of any right or option of the consumer to have the record provided or made available on paper or in non-electronic form."[205] Consumers must also be informed of their right to withdraw consent to electronic records.[206] Consumers also have a right to information on how to obtain paper copies of an electronic record and "whether any fee will be charged for such copy."[207]

If special software or hardware is required to access or retain electronic records, the consumer is entitled to a statement of the system requirements.[208] If software or hardware requirements are revised after consumer consent, the consumer is entitled to a statement of how to access and retain records.[209] Consumers have a right to withdraw consent without the imposition of fees or other conditions.[210] The E-Sign Act does nothing to diminish protections for "consumers under any statute, regulation, or other rule of law."[211] Electronic consent or confirmation may not be required to enforce a consumer contract.[212] Contracts made by electronic agents "may not be denied legal effect, validity or enforceability . . . so long as the action of any such electronic agent is legally attributable to the person to be bound."[213]

E-Sign preempts state law except for exceptions set forth in § 102.[214] E-Sign defers to the NCCUSL statute, the Uniform Electronic Transaction Act (UETA).[215] The E-Sign Act preempts state law unless it is an "enactment or adoption of the Uniform Electronic Transactions Act."[216] E-Sign also does not preempt "administrative procedures or requirements for the use or acceptance of electronic records or electronic signatures to establish the legal effect, validity or enforceability of contracts or other records" as long as the procedures or requirements are consistent with the Act.[217] The alternative procedures or requirement must not "accord greater legal status or effect to, the implementation or application of a specific technology or technical specification for performing the functions of creating, storing, generating, receiving, communication or authenticating electronic records or electronic signatures."[218]

---

[204] *Id.*, § 101(c)(1)(B).
[205] *Id.*, § 101(c)(1)(B)(i)(II).
[206] *Id.*, § 101(c)(1)(B)(iii).
[207] *Id.*, § 101(c)(1)(B)(iv).
[208] *Id.*, § 101(c)(1)(C).
[209] *Id.*, § 101(c)(1)(D).
[210] *Id.*, § 101(c)(1)(D)(1).
[211] *Id.*, § 101(c)(1)(D)(2).
[212] *Id.*, § 101(c)(1)(D)(2)(B)(3).
[213] *Id.*, § 101(c)(1)(D)(2)(B)(h).
[214] *Id.*, § 102.
[215] *Id.*, § 102(a)(1).
[216] *Id.*
[217] *Id.*, § 102(a)(2).
[218] *Id.*, § 102(a)(2)(A)(2).

E-Sign exempts a number of substantive areas of the law covered by well-established bodies of law. Specific exceptions are made for contracts, agreements, or records that apply to "the creation and execution of wills, codicils, or testamentary trusts."[219] There is a specific exception against the application of E-Sign for state statutes, regulations, or other rules of law governing adoption, divorce, or other matters of family law matters."[220] E-Sign does not preempt the provisions of the Uniform Commercial Code, other than § 107 and § 1-206 and Article 2 (Sales of Goods) and Article 2A (Leases of Goods).[221] There are additional exceptions for "court orders, notices, or official court documents required to be executed in connection with court proceedings."[222]

E-notice of the cancellations of utility services such as water, heat, and power are not validated by E-Sign.[223] Similarly, notices of "default, repossession, foreclosure, or eviction or the right to a cure, under a credit agreement secured by, or a rental agreement for, a primary residence of an individual" are outside the scope of E-Sign.[224] Product manufacturers may not use e-recall notices of defective products "that risk endangering health or safety."[225] E-Sign is not appropriate for documents accompanying the "transportation or handling of hazardous materials."[226]

Section 104 requires federal and state agencies to devise the standards for the e-filing of records.[227] Federal and state agencies must develop rules, regulations, and orders consistent with the statutory purposes of E-Sign.[228] There must be a "substantial justification for the regulation, order or guidance."[229] Methods must be functionally equivalent "to the requirements imposed on records that are not electronic records; and will not impose unreasonable costs on the acceptance and use of electronic records."[230] E-Sign is not a prescriptive digital signature statute and does not specify a specific technology or technological specification for electronic records. E-Sign requires a study of electronic consent by the Federal Trade Commission.[231] The effective date of the statute is October 1, 2000.[232] E-Sign is pro-consumer in contrast to UETA, a consumer-neutral statute.[233]

---

[219] *Id.*, § 103(a)(1).

[220] *Id.*, § 103(a)(2).

[221] *Id.*, § 103(a)(3).

[222] *Id.*, § 103(b)(2)(A).

[223] *Id.*, § 103(b)(A).

[224] *Id.*, § 103(b)(B).

[225] *Id.*, § 103(b)(C).

[226] *Id.*, § 103(b)(D).

[227] *Id.*, § 104(a).

[228] *Id.*, § 104(b).

[229] *Id.*, § 104(b)(B)(2)(C)(i).

[230] *Id.*, § 104(b)(B)(2)(C) (ii) (I)(II).

[231] *Id.*, § 105(b).

[232] *Id.*, § 107.

[233] Gail Hillebrand and Margot Saunders, E-Sign and UETA: What Should States Do Now?, Part 2, 5 Cyber Lawyer 8 (Feb. 2001) (comparing E-Sign and UETA on consumer consent, preconsent disclosures, notice, and exemptions).

[1] Purpose and Meaning of Digital Signatures

[a] Authentication

A *digital signature* is an electronic identifier, created by encryption technology, intended by the party to have the same effect as a paper-based signature. Traditionally, paper-and-pen signatures are critical to a large number of statutes. In the field of wills and trusts, for example, the signature is evidence that the document is authentic. Under current UCC Article 2, contracts for sales of goods of $500 or more must be evidenced by a writing signed by the party against which enforcement is sought.[234] Negotiable instruments in order form are endorsed by the signature of the payee on the back of the instrument. An "endorsement" means a signature, other than that of a signer as maker, drawer, or acceptor . . . made on the instrument."[235]

In our information age, "a signature authenticates a writing by identifying the signer with the signed document."[236] As electronic mail becomes more established, the need has grown for legislation to establish the validity of e-mail signatures. Courts will increasingly consider the extent to which an e-mail message is a "writing" or statements that an electronic message has been "signed" by the maker in various contexts.[237]

[b] Ceremony

Signatures play a symbolic role in memorializing legal agreements. "The act of signing a document calls to the signer's attention the legal significance of the signer's act, and thereby helps prevent inconsiderate engagements."[238] The ceremonial role may be found in the last testament and will of a testator. A signed writing plays a ceremonial role in the enactment of legislation. A signature must accompany contracts for the sale of land interests. Relatively little case law exists on how the ceremonial role of signatures might be adapted to the Internet

[c] Approval

The ABA's Digital Signature Guidelines state that signatures are used for approval in a wide variety of laws and customs.[239] "Paper-and-pen" signatures have played multiple roles in Anglo-American contracts for many centuries. A

---

[234] UCC § 2-201 (2000).

[235] UCC § 3-204 (2000).

[236] Information Security Committee, Section of Science and Technology, American Bar Association, Digital Signature Guidelines 5 (Aug. 1, 1996) (Digital Signatures Tutorial).

[237] *See, e.g.,* Doherty v. Registry of Motor Vehicles, No. 97CV0050 (Suffolk Dist. Ct. 1997) (visited Apr. 17, 2002), http://www.loundy.com/CASES/Doherty_v_RMV.html (upholding an administrative license suspension initiated by the Massachusetts State Police where the police officer's report of the arrest for driving under the influence was transmitted by e-mail to the Registry of Motor Vehicles without his handwritten signature).

[238] Digital Signature Guidelines, *supra* note 236.

[239] *Id.*

person is not liable on a negotiable instrument, such as a check or promissory note, unless "the person signed the instrument."[240] The signature of the party against whom enforcement is sought frequently proves the acceptance of a contract. A payor bank, for example, certifies a check by placing its signature on the back of the check. A signature also indicates certification of a check, which indicates that the bank intends to honor the check. A payee endorses a check or promissory note by her or his signature. The ABA Information Security Committee observes, "In certain contexts defined by law or custom, a signature expresses the signer's approval or authorization of the writing or the signer's intention that it have legal effect."[241] In the law of agencies, writings are used to prove that the agent is authorized to act on behalf of the principal. The ABA Guidelines develop principles covering the following key issues: "(1) ensuring the identity of the holder of a private key; (2) appropriate responsibility of those engaged in electronic commerce; (3) the concept of a Trusted Third-Party (or "certificate authority"); (4) the link between the public key and the holder of the private key; (5) authentication of dates and times of transactions; (6) authentication of dates and times of transactions; and (7) publication of reports for private keys that are no longer valid/reliable (or 'certificate revocation lists')."[242]

[d] Efficiency and Logistics

Signatures on writings "often impart a sense of clarity and finality to the transaction and may lessen the subsequent need to inquire beyond the face of a document."[243] The ABA Information Security Committee cites the example of a negotiable instrument in which the holder may rely upon the four corners of the instrument to determine the terms of the agreement. A negotiable instrument is a signed writing, which takes a prescribed form.[244] The signature of a drawer of a negotiable draft is evidence of a contract on a negotiable instrument.[245] Electronic commerce requires technologies to allow negotiable instruments to be electronically "signed" by digital signatures.

---

[240] UCC § 3-401 (2000).

[241] Digital Signature Guidelines, *supra* note 236.

[242] State of Texas, Digital Signatures and PKI Service Providers, Standards Review and Recommendation Publication SRRPUB13 (visited May 29, 2001), http://www.state.tx.us/Standards/srrpub13.htm (summarizing the principles of the ABA "Digital Signature Guidelines" developed by the Information Security Committee of the ABA Science and Technology Section); *see also* ABA Information Security Committee of the ABA Science and Technology Section, Digital Signature Guidelines (visited Feb. 28, 2001), http://www.abanet.org/sciteh/ec/isc/dsgfree.htm (publishing electronic version of the ABA Digital Guidelines).

[243] *Id.*

[244] *See* UCC § 3-104 (2000).

[245] *Id.* § 3-401.

[2]   Digital Signature Statutes

Within the past three years, two dozen states have enacted "digital signature laws," with Utah the first to do so.[246] Utah's statute designates a government agency as the certification authority (CA). The role of the CA is to confirm that the subscriber is the person listed in the digital signature, that the information in the certificate is accurate, and that the subscriber is a rightful holder of the private key which corresponds to the public key designated in the certificate.[247] The trend in the law is to treat the digital signature as the functional equivalent of a manual signature. The concept of a digital signature is the electronic equivalent of a signed writing.

Electronic signature and digital signature laws fall into "three categories: prescriptive, criteria-based, and signature enabling."[248] The Internet Law and Policy Forum (ILPF) concluded, "[t]here is still no uniformity among the states' approaches to electronic authentication."[249] One of the difficult issues is whether states should enter into a "cross-border recognition of electronic or digital signatures."[250] The Internet not only crosses state law boundaries but foreign boundaries. To date, none of the state digital signature laws address the international validity of electronic signatures and writings. Electronic commerce is conducted in an evolving legal framework with problems of "regulatory fragmentation and the lack of national and international harmonization of policies."[251] The uncertainty as to the validity of electronic signatures and writings is a trade barrier that can be dismantled only with an international initiative.[252]

[a]   Prescriptive Model

The *prescriptive approach* is a comprehensive and specific regulatory framework, such as the Utah Digital Signature Act,[253] that generally "prescribes" particular detailed technologies rather than standards. The Utah Digital Signature Act provides for a statewide licensing of certification authorities (CAs). A CA has been compared to an Internet passport office, because it is a trusted third party that establishes the identity of transacting parties.[254] The CA establishes the identity of an organization and issues "a certificate that contains the organization's public key

---

[246] Department of Commerce, Public Forum on Certificate Authorities and Digital Signatures: Enhancing Global Electronic Commerce, EPLR: Department of Commerce Notice on Digital Signature Forums (visited Apr. 12, 2002), http://www.bna.com/e-law/docs/digisigcom.html.

[247] Utah Digital Signature Act, Utah Code Ann. §§ 46-3-104 (2001).

[248] Internet Law and Policy Forum, *supra* note 189.

[249] *Id.*

[250] *Id.*

[251] *Id.*

[252] *Id.*

[253] Utah Code §§ 46-3-101 et seq. (2000).

[254] VeriSign, About Secure Server Ids: Frequently Asked Questions (visited Apr. 12, 2002), http://digitalid.verisign.com/server/about/aboutFAQ.htm.

and signs it with the CA's private key."[255] A certificate authority issues security certificates used in Secure Socket Layer (SSL) connections.[256] Utah is the only state to have adopted a digital signature law that is classified as purely prescriptive. Minnesota and Washington have enacted statutes that borrow some of the features of Utah's digital signature statute.[257]

[b]   Criteria-Based Model

The Internet Law and Policy Forum Survey classifies California's act as the exemplar statute for criteria-based authentication statutes characterized by flexibility and broad standards. The California *criteria-based model* has been enacted in 10 states.[258] California does not prescribe any particular technology but incorporates an evidentiary standard into its definition. California treats electronic signatures as legally effective if the signature is

1.   Unique to the person using it.
2.   Capable of verification.
3.   Under the sole control of the person using it.
4.   Linked to the data in such a manner that if the data is changed the signature is invalidated.
5.   In conformity with regulations adopted by the appropriate state agency, usually the Secretary of State.[259]

The digital signature statutes that follow the criteria-based approach, in turn, can be divided into "limited" and "general" statutes. A *limited statute* applies to a given substantive field, such as online contracts, whereas a *general statute* legitimates electronic records in all substantive fields of law. Georgia, Kansas, New Hampshire, and Virginia have enacted general statutes based on California's model.[260]

[c]   Signature-Enabling Approach

Signature-enabling statutes are defined as minimalist because they are standards-based and do not prescribe specific technologies, such as biometrics, for authentication or criteria for validating signatures. The ILPF cites Florida's Electronic Signature Act of 1996 as an example of a statute that accords the digital and electronic signature the same status as a physical writing.[261] Therefore, the Florida statute gives legal recognition to electronic writings and signatures. The statute

---

[255] *Id.*

[256] Matisse's Glossary of Internet Terms (Apr. 22, 2002), http://www.matisse.net/files/glossary.html.

[257] Internet Law and Policy Forum, *supra* note 189.

[258] *Id.* at 6.

[259] *Id.* at 6 (citing Cal. Gov't Code § 16.5 (a) (1995)).

[260] *Id.*

[261] *Id.* at 7.

defines a "writing" to include information "stored in any electronic medium and retrievable in a perceivable form."[262] An electronic signature "means any letters, characters, or symbols, manifested by electronic or similar means, executed or adopted by a party with an intent to authenticate a writing. . . . An electronic signature may be used to sign a writing and shall have the same force and effect as a written signature."[263] The Electronic Signatures in Global and National Commerce Act of 2000 follows the Massachusetts report in not prescribing a particular electronic signature technology. The law legitimates digital signatures without prescribing a particular technology. This approach is sensible where information technologies are rapidly evolving, and today's state-of-the-art authentication may soon become a legal fossil.

The Division of Information Technology of the Commonwealth of Massachusetts, for example, proposed a minimalist statute for writing and signature requirements.[264] The concept of a record for electronic writings and signatures was drawn from the Model Law on Electronic Commerce put out by the United Nations Commission on International Trade Law (UNCITRAL). The Massachusetts minimalist model has proven influential in the recent model statutes of the National Conference of Commissioners on Uniform State Laws. NCCUSL, in turn, has incorporated the concept of the "record" in its Uniform Computer Information Transaction Act and the Uniform Electronic Transactions Acts.

[3] Certificate Authorities

Certificate authorities are "the digital world's equivalent of passport offices, issue digital certificates, and validate the holder's identity and authority."[265] Certificate authorities verify the identity of individuals, issue digital certificates, and manage databases.[266] Leading certificate authorities include VeriSign, Arcanvs, Inc., ID Certify, Inc., and Digital Signature Trust Company. The public key infrastructure (PKI) incorporates certificates that are identified by the certificate authority. VeriSign's certificate authorities "embed an individual's or an organization's public key along with other identifying information into each digital certificate and then cryptographically 'sign' it as a tamper-proof seal, verifying the integrity of the data within it and validating its use."[267] PKIs use certificate hierarchies that have "root keys" linked to all certificates issued by the hierarchy and identified by the certificate authority.[268] The PKI approach includes digital certificates recognized in "popular email packages, Netscape and Microsoft web

---

[262] *Id.* (citing Florida Electronic Signature Act of 1996, Fla. Stat. § 1.01 (1996 Fla. H.B. 942)).

[263] *Id.*

[264] *Id.*

[265] VeriSign, Certificate Authorities (visited Apr. 22, 2002), http://VeriSign.netscape.com/security/pki/cerauth.html.

[266] Robert C. Elsenpeter and Toby J. Velte, eBusiness: A Beginner's Guide 384 (2001).

[267] VeriSign, *id.*

[268] *Id.*

browsers, and more than 40 vendors' web servers."[269] Certificate authorities are also licensed by states and foreign governments.[270] Private certificate infrastructures may be created by a business that is an alternative to the more open infrastructure based upon PKIs.[271] There is little case law on legal issues involved with certificate authorities. The federal government and many states as well as the European Commission have recently recognized the legal validity of digital signatures and electronic records.[272] Contract law principles likely apply between purchasers of digital certificates and certificate authorities.[273] In contrast, tort principles may apply between certificate authorities and merchants who receive certificates from consumers.[274] One theory is that the tort of negligent misrepresentation governs the certificate authority's liability to merchants.[275] The standard of reasonableness will likely govern a certificate authority's liability for losses due to digital certificates.[276] Parties may be able to disclaim contractual liabilities, but it is questionable whether the consequences of unreasonable conduct may be disclaimed.[277]

"CyberNotaries" have been proposed to deal with the problem of authenticating and certifying electronic documents in international Internet commercial transactions. The Science and Technology Committee of the American Bar Association has a CyberNotary Committee to study the role of trusted third parties in electronic commerce.[278] The CyberNotary Committee is exploring the possibility of setting global certification standards for electronic notaries that would be mod-

---

[269] Id.

[270] The Utah Digital Signature Act, Washington State's Electronic Authentication Act, Oregon's Electronic Signature Act, North Carolina's Electronic Commerce Act, California's Digital Signature Regulations, Nebraska's Digital Signatures Act, and the Texas Digital Signature Rule are examples of states licensing certificate authorities. *See* The PKI Page, updated May 23, 2001 (visited Feb. 22, 2002), http://www.pki-page.org. Washington State's Electronic Authentication Act, for example, licenses ID Certify, Inc., VeriSign, Inc., Arcanvs, Inc., and the Digital Signature Trust Company, *id.* The German Signature Act or Signaturegesetz is an example of a foreign government that licenses certificate authorities. *Id.* The German Digital Signature act licenses the following authorities: Deutsche Telekom, Deutsche Post eBusinn, Bundesnotarkammer, DATEV eG, Medizon AG, and Steuerberaterkammer Nurnberg. *Id.* The European Commission has issued a European Directive for Electronic Signatures. The European Telecommunications Standards Institute (ETSI) is developing new standards for Electronic Signatures and Certificate Authorities. *Id.*

[271] Id.

[272] ILPF, The Role of Certification Authorities in Consumer Transactions (visited Apr. 22, 2002), http://www.ilpf.org/work/ca/exec.htm; *see also* State of Texas, Standards Review and Recommendation Publication, Version 2.5 200000729, revised Apr. 24, 2001, Digital Signatures & Public Key Infrastructure (PKI) Guidelines (visited May 29, 2001), http://www.state.tx.us/Standard/srrpub13.htm (providing rules for digital signatures in consultation with a number of Texas state agencies).

[273] Id.

[274] Id.

[275] Id.

[276] Id.

[277] Id.

[278] American Bar Association, Science and Technology Committee, CyberNotary Committee, CyberNotary Committee Home Page (visited Apr. 22, 2002), http://www.abanet.org/scitech/ec/cn/home.html.

eled after international notarial practice.[279] The CyberNotary concept has yet to be adopted in any state or federal law for authenticating electronic documents on the Internet.

[4] Technology

Digital signatures are based upon cryptographic algorithms, also called ciphers, that permit encryption and decryption.[280] The recipient of the message will turn the ciphertext back into "plaintext," a process called *decryption.*[281]

Public key cryptography "is a method for securely exchanging messages, based on assigning two complementary keys (one public, one private) to the individuals involved in a transaction."[282] The public key is publicly available, but only the "signer" knows the private key. A message hash may be used to encrypt a document. The message is encrypted with a private key obtained from a private-public key authority. As a result, the encrypted hash becomes the digital signature of the message that will be different every time a new message is sent.[283]

Single key cryptography is used to help the parties keep a restrictive algorithm secret.[284] The single private key is never published, unlike the public key, which is widely available in books similar to telephone directories. It is not practical for parties in distant locations on the Internet to share a restricted key. Public key cryptography or asymmetric cryptosystems use a public key to encrypt a message and a private key to decrypt it.

[5] Attribution Procedures

The International Chamber of Commerce proposed a broad self-regulatory program governing online contracts, including guidelines for secure and trustworthy digital transactions over the Internet.[285] Trustworthy e-commerce depends on attribution procedures that verify the integrity of transactions and the authenticity of electronic messages. An attribution procedure may be used to detect changes or errors in information. UCITA's Reporter notes that attribution procedures may use "algorithms or other codes, identifying words or numbers, encryption, callback or other acknowledgments, or other procedures reasonable under the circumstances."[286]

---

[279] *Id.* In the United States, the qualifications of a notary are rather minimal, compared to those in other countries.

[280] Bruce Schneier, Applied Cryptography: Protocols, Algorithms, and Source Code in C (2d ed., 1996), at 2.

[281] *Id.* at 1.

[282] VeriSign, Inc., About Secure Server Ids (visited Apr. 22, 2002), http://digitalid.verisign.com/server/about/aboutFAQ.htm.

[283] searchSecurity.com, Digital Signature (visited Feb. 11, 2002), http://searchsecurity.techtarget.com/sDefinition/0,,sid14_gci211953,00.html.

[284] *Id.*

[285] *Id.* at 85.

[286] UCITA § 102(5) (2000).

[6]   Other Initiatives

A number of electronic authentication initiatives have been proposed by private standards-setting organizations:[287]

- In May 2000, the European Commission released a Model Directive on Electronic Commerce.

- The Organization for Economic Cooperation and Development (OECD) has proposed Cryptography Guidelines.

- The International Chamber of Commerce (ICC) has proposed General Usage for Digitally Ensured Commerce (GUIDEC).

- The World Trade Organization (WTO) has formulated comprehensive rules for online contracting, in addition to digital signature rules.

- The United Nations Commission on International Trade Law (UNCITRAL) has promulgated a Model Law on Electronic Commerce.

Article 7 of UNCITRAL's Model Law defines a legal requirement for the signature of a person if (1) a method is used to identify that person and to indicate that person's approval of the information contained in the data message and (2) that method is as reliable as was appropriate for the purpose for which the data message was generated or communicated, in the light of all the circumstances, including any relevant agreement.[288] UNCITRAL is preparing uniform rules for electronic signatures and certificate authorities.[289] The American Bar Association's Science and Technology Committee has developed Digital Signature Guidelines which are also in line with UCITA's e-commerce concepts of attribution and authentication.

[F]   Privacy in Information Contracts

Online contracts are increasingly subject to regulation by the FTC, the chief federal agency formulating principles of fair information practices, which include "consumer awareness, choice, appropriate levels of security, data integrity and consumer access to their personally identifiable data."[290]

The FTC is increasingly policing how web sites collect, compile, sell, and use consumers' personal information.[291] If a corporate web site compiles or col-

---

[287] *See* United States Council for International Business (USCIB), Electronic Commerce (May 13, 2000), http://www.uscib.org/trade/eleccomm.htm.

[288] UNCITRAL Model Law on Electronic Commerce, Article 7 (1999).

[289] Microsoft Law and Corporate Affairs, Summary of Global Internet Legal Developments (Jan. 1999) at 88.

[290] Department of Commerce, Elements of Effective Self-Regulation for the Protection of Privacy and Questions Related to Online Privacy, 63 FR 30729 (June 5, 1998).

[291] Notice Requesting Industry Guidelines and Principles Regarding Online Information Practices, 63 FR 10916 (Mar. 5, 1998).

lects data about users who are children, for example, the company needs to comply with industry guidelines.[292] Web sites should also allow visitors to opt out of allowing the company to share their personal information with other companies.[293] In a landmark multidistrict consolidated class action case, *In re DoubleClick, Inc. Privacy Actions,*[294] the court held that DoubleClick's use of cookies to gather information about Internet users was not a violation of their privacy.

[G] Procedural Law of E-Commerce; Choice of Law

Subject to certain qualifications, parties to a contract may choose which state's law will govern interpretation of the contract. The parties' choice of law is subject to the statutory directives of each state.[295] It is advisable to include a choice of law clause in license agreements because states vary significantly in their law of contracts, tort remedies, and commercial law. The UCC is supplemented by common law and equity principles, as well as by state consumer protection acts, which vary from state to state. In addition, states have adopted many nonuniform UCC amendments and have significantly different tort regimes. Colorado, for example, requires punitive damages to be proven beyond a reasonable doubt, while its neighbor, Nebraska, does not recognize punitive damages at all. Many companies choose the law and forum in the state where they have their chief place of business. "The use of contractual choice of forum clauses has expanded as judicial hostility to them has failed."[296] Most countries will enforce parties' choice of law clauses, but they may not enforce provisions inimical to consumer welfare.

[1] Uniform Commercial Code

The current version of Article 1 of the UCC permits parties to choose the law provided it bears a "reasonable relation" to the commercial contract.[297] Revised

---

[292] *Id.*

[293] The FTC is studying the tactical decision of companies in making "opt out" an arduous process. Companies have a perverse incentive to discourage opt-outs because revenue is dependent on harvesting personal data. Companies, therefore, because their web sites earn revenues from data collection, have an incentive to make it difficult to "opt out" by convincing the consumer not to stop the information flow.

[294] 2001 U.S. Dist. LEXIS 3498 (S.D.N.Y., Mar. 29, 2001). *Cf.* Intuit Privacy Litig., 138 F. Supp. 2d 1272 (C.D. Cal. 2001) (granting motion to dismiss privacy-based claim arising out of cookies on one claim but denying motion to dismiss based on 18 U.S.C. § 270).

[295] Restatement (Second) of Conflicts § 6(1) (1971).

[296] UCC § R1-301, cmt. (Revised Article 1 Members Consultative Group Draft, Feb. 28, 2000).

[297] UCC § 1-105.

§ 1-103 of the UCC eliminates the "reasonable relation" to the choice of law rule in business-to-business transactions.[298] The UCC contains relatively few statutorily mandated provisions.[299] An online company would easily satisfy the "reasonable relation" test if it chose to interpret its license agreements under the law of its state of incorporation. A web site may find it advantageous to choose the law where rights and remedies are favorable. The reasonable relation test would not permit a site to apply the law of Bermuda, for example, unless a reasonable relation existed between Bermuda and the parties to the license agreement.

[2] Revised UCC Article 1

Article 1 of the UCC is being updated "for electronic commerce and communications."[300] The Drafting Committee for Uniform Commerce Code is recommending changes to choice of law to update the rules for electronic commerce and communications. Revised UCC § 1-301 changes the substantive rules currently found in § 1-105. Section 1-105 currently permits the parties to choose the jurisdiction whose law applies, providing the transaction bears a "reasonable relation" to the jurisdiction. Section 1-301 provides that if one of the parties to a UCC transaction is a consumer, an agreement to choose the applicable law is not effective unless certain conditions are satisfied.[301]

Revised UCC § 1-301(b) provides that, in the absence of agreement, the court should apply the forum's choice of law principles. Revised 1-301(b) would enforce choice of law clauses for consumers only if the jurisdiction designated is the "[s]tate or country in which the consumer resides at the time the transaction becomes enforceable or within 30 days thereafter."[302] An agreement may also be effective if the chosen state or country is the place where "the goods, services or other consideration flowing to the consumer are to be used by the consumer" or her or his designee.[303] A consumer is "an individual who enters into a transaction primarily for personal, fam-

---

[298] The American Law Institute, Uniform Commercial Code, Article 1, General Provisions (ALI May 2001 Draft).

[299] The UCC carves out exceptions to the parties' choice of law. The parties, for example, are not permitted to bypass the place of filing for financing statements under § 9-402. Third parties would not be able to determine whether a security interest has been perfected unless filing conforms to the proper place of filing. Multistate transactions under § 9-103 also constrain freedom of choice of law.

[300] Neil B. Cohen, Reporter, and H. Kathleen Patchell, Associate Reporter, Memorandum to Members Consultative Group for Uniform Commercial Code Article 1: Key Issues to Consider (Feb. 28, 2000).

[301] Uniform Commercial Code: Revised Article 1: General Provisions, § 1-301 (Members Consultative Group Draft, Feb. 28, 2000).

[302] *Id.* § 1-301(b)(1).

[303] *Id.* § 1-301(b)(2).

ily, or household purposes" as opposed to professional or commercial purposes.[304]

In business-to-business transactions, the parties have even greater autonomy to choose the applicable law. In nonconsumer transactions, the parties have even greater discretion to choose the applicable law in Revised § 1-301, which does not require that the chosen jurisdiction bear a "reasonable relation" to the transaction.[305] Section 1-301 will not, however, enforce agreements to choose the applicable law if they contravene "a fundamental policy of the State or country whose law would otherwise govern."[306]

[3] Uniform Computer Information Transactions Act

UCITA permits the parties to choose the applicable law for computer information transactions.[307] The parties to a computer information transaction may not, however, use the choice of law to bypass a consumer protection rule.[308] The jurisdiction where the licensor is located when an access contract is entered into applies in the absence of an agreement.[309] In the absence of an agreement, for example, UCITA will apply to millions of AOL access contracts because UCITA has recently been enacted in Virginia.

In a consumer contract that includes delivery of a diskette, CD-ROM, or other tangible medium, the law of the jurisdiction applies where "the copy is or should have been delivered to the consumer."[310] In all other computer information transactions, "the law of the jurisdiction having the most significant relationship to the transaction" applies.[311] SPC will use choice of law clauses so that it may apply a familiar body of law to disputes. Forum selection clauses are presumptively enforceable.[312] Parties are free to choose a forum in advance, and these clauses are enforceable unless shown to be unreasonable.[313] SPC will use choice of law clauses so that it may apply a familiar body of law to disputes.

---

[304] *Id.* § 1-301(f).

[305] *Id.* § 1-301(a).

[306] *Id.* § 1-301(c).

[307] UCITA § 109(a) (2002).

[308] *Id.*

[309] § 109(b)(1).

[310] § 109(b)(2).

[311] § 109(b)(3).

[312] Harris v. Razei Bar Indus., Ltd., 37 F. Supp. 2d 186, 189 (E.D.N.Y. 1998) (citing New Moon Shipping Co. v. MAN B&W Diesel AG, 121 F.3d 24, 29 (2d Cir. 1997)).

[313] See Bremen v. Zapata Off-Shore Co., 407 U.S. 1, 10 (1972); DiRienzo v. Philip Servs. Corp., 2002 U.S. App. LEXIS 5622 (2d Cir. Apr. 1, 2002) ("Ordinarily a strong favorable presumption is applied to that choice. Unless the balance is strongly in favor of the defendant, the plaintiff's choice of forum should rarely be disturbed."); *see also* Lifschitz & Schram, P.C. v. Hazard, 24 F. Supp. 2d 66, 71 (D.D.C. 1998) (noting that if the particular controversy has meaningful ties to the forum, and the plaintiff is a resident of that forum, the plaintiff's choice of forum is given substantial deference).

[H]   Choice of Forum Clauses

The trend in the law is to enforce choice of forum clauses in mass-market licenses. In *Williams v. America Online,*[314] the Massachusetts Superior Court refused to enforce America Online's standard clickwrap terms of service agreement which had a forum selection clause. The *Williams* court held that the forum selection clause was unenforceable. The court found AOL's method of manifesting consent to the terms of service agreement to be defective. In *Jacobson v. Mailboxes, etc., U.S.A.,*[315] the Massachusetts Supreme Court held that forum selection clauses were generally enforceable. However, the Superior Court in *Williams* felt that AOL's method of manifesting assent to be unreasonable. The court also took issue with the reasonableness of the forum selection clause, which would require plaintiffs litigating small claims to travel to Virginia to seek redress from AOL. Finally, the court struck down the forum selection clause on public policy grounds. The court reasoned that Massachusetts consumers should not have to pursue their case in Virginia when a few hundred dollars in damages are at stake. The *Williams* case is one of the first cases in which a court has refused to enforce a forum selection clause in a mass-market license agreement.

The parties to online contracts will be free to choose an exclusive judicial forum and it is likely that forum selection clause will be enforced. The U.S. Supreme Court in *Carnival Cruise Lines, Inc. v. Shute*[316] enforced a forum selection clause on a cruise contract even though it specified that all disputes be litigated in Florida, a forum distant from the consumer's residence. Choice of forum clauses are generally enforceable unless "unreasonable and unjust."[317] Choice of forum clauses are also limited by the doctrine of unconscionability and also may not be enforced on public policy grounds.

§ 6.04   ELECTRONIC CONTRACTING RULES

Every net-based business, large or small, must enter into a large number of contracts in the online world. A *contract* is simply defined as "an agreement upon consideration to do or refrain from doing, a particular lawful thing."[318] The UCC defines the contract as "the total legal obligation which results from the parties'

---

[314] Williams v. America Online, Inc., No. 00-0962 (Mass Super., Feb. 8, 2001), *reported in* 29 Mass. Law. Wkly. 1426 (Feb. 26, 2001); *see also* Groff v. America Online, Inc., 1998 WL 307001 (R.I. 1998) (holding that user was bound by forum selection clause in online license); DiLorenzo v. AOL, 2 ILR (P&F) 596 (N.Y. Sup. Ct. 1999) (enforcing AOL choice of forum clause); Compuserve Inc. v. Patterson, 89 F.3d 1257 (6th Cir. 1996) (validating choice of forum terms in online license).

[315] 419 Mass. 572 (1995); *see also* Harris v. Rzei Bar Indus., Ltd. 37 F. Supp. 2d 186, 189 (E.D.N.Y. 1998) (stating that forum selection clauses are presumably enforceable).

[316] 499 U.S. 585 (1991).

[317] Bremen v. Zapata Off-Shore Co., 407 U.S. 1 (1972); UCITA § 110 (stating that parties may choose an exclusive judicial forum unless the choice is unreasonable and unjust).

[318] Ballentine's Law Dictionary 263 (3d ed., 1969).

agreement."[319] In Revised Article 1 of the UCC, the obligation of good faith is imposed in the performance and enforcement of every commercial transaction.[320]

Section 2-201 requires contracts for the sale of goods of $500 or greater to be memorialized in a writing. Online companies need to have settled expectations of whether an electronic record is the functional equivalent of a writing. The trend in the law is to treat electronic records as functionally equivalent to writings and digital signatures with the same validity as pen-and-paper signatures. "Contracts can be formed through an exchange of e-mail or by accepting an online order, such as when you shop online with a user name and password linked to directory and credit information."[321] There is a growing body of law that treats the online contract as functionally equivalent to the paper-based contract.

[A]   Electronic Contract Formation

Modern contract law makes it possible to make agreements by any reasonable method, including the exchange of electronic records. Article 2 of the UCC notes that "[a] contract for sale of goods may be made in any manner sufficient to show agreement, including conduct by both parties which recognizes the existence of such a contract."[322] At common law, an offer is a manifestation of the offeror's intent to enter into an agreement.[323] The offer may be communicated by the offeror to the offeree orally or in writing. At common law, the offeror was master of the offer and could specify the manner of acceptance. The *mirror image rule* required that an offeree accept the offer in the precise manner called for in the offer.

An advertisement placed in a newspaper or magazine is generally regarded as an invitation to entertain offers rather than an enforceable offer.[324] SPC needs to decide whether it is inviting offers or making definite offers in its web advertisements. If SPC only wishes to entertain invitations of offers and not to make definite offers, it needs to make adequate disclosures "to ensure that any promotional material placed on the Web is not capable of being construed as an offer."[325] On the other hand, SPC may have a business goal of securing online orders and will

---

[319] UCC § 1-201 (11) (2000); *see also* UCITA, § 102(17) (2000) (defining *contract* as "the total legal obligation resulting from the party's agreement").

[320] American Law Institute, Uniform Commercial Code: Revised Article 1: General Provisions, § 1-304 (Members Consultative Group Draft, Feb. 28, 2000).

[321] Sean Doherty, The E-Signature Act Makes Online Transactions Legally Binding, Network Computing, Dec. 10, 2001, at 83.

[322] UCC § 2-204 (2000).

[323] Contracts are generally governed by state law, either the common law for service contracts or the UCC for sales of goods. In contrast, e-commerce typically involves online contracts that "span multiple jurisdictions and may be regulated by the laws of more than one country." J. Fraser Mann and Alan M. Gahtan, Overview of the Legal Framework for Electronic Commerce, in Law of International Online Business: A Global Perspective (Dennis Campbell, ed., 1998).

[324] *Id.* at 40.

[325] *Id.*

therefore need to structure its electronic catalog to constitute definite offers rather than mere advertisements to make offers.

[1]   Electronic Data Interchange

One theoretical difficulty of online contracting is that computers do not "manifest assent" or make offers.[326] E-commerce requires a legal framework that permits computers to make and accept offers. Electronic data interchange (EDI) is one well-established contracting practice for building an electronic trading community; brick-and-mortar companies use electronic networks to communicate with warehouses, distributors, and suppliers all over the world.[327] One United Kingdom supermarket uses EDI trading links to communicate with "customers as far apart as Thailand, Zimbabwe and Guatemala."[328] EDI fraud is a risk in Latin America.

The difficulty of the EDI model, however, is that it requires trading partners to agree in advance to accept the validity of electronic contracts. Trading partner agreements set the ground rules for permitting the ordering of goods or services through computer-to-computer communications, such as given transaction sets that provide for electronic offers and acceptance. Parties to an e-commerce transaction are unlikely to have a contractual relationship predating the transaction.

[2]   Mass-Market Licenses

[a]   Shrinkwrap Agreements

A *shrinkwrap* or *mass-market license* is an "unsigned software license agreement used in consumer and commercial transactions."[329] The trend in the law is to enforce mass-market license agreements if there is an opportunity to review terms and there is assent to the information.[330] Mass-market licenses accompany software modules and may even be printed on the outside of the box. The first paragraph of a typical shrinkwrap license usually provides that the opening of the

---

[326] Contract law focuses on whether a manifestation of assent exists between humans. One advantage of computer-to-computer contract will be a decrease in cases asserting that offers were made insincerely or in jest. *See* Lucy v. Zehmer, 196 Va. 493, 84 S.E.2d 516 (1934) (annulling marriage because it was entered into in jest). Electronic agents will not lack capacity to contract due to drunkenness, mental illness, infancy, or other human infirmities. However, computer software may malfunction due to viruses, defects, or programmer error.

[327] Kewill-Xetal EDI Services, Case Study: Saphir Produce Ltd., Communicating with Supermarkets (visited Apr. 27, 2002), http://www.Xetal.co.uk/case2.htm.

[328] *Id.*

[329] Celeste L. Tito, The Servicewrap: "Shrinkwrap" for Mass-Marketed Software Services, 13 Computer Lawyer 19 (May 1996).

[330] *See* M.A. Mortenson Co., Inc. v. Timberline Software Corp., 998 P.2d 305 (Wash. 2000) (citing UCITA in its opinion validating a limitation on consequential damages enclosed in a "shrinkwrap license" accompanying computer software); *see also* cases discussed *infra* in this section.

package indicates acceptance of the license terms.[331] Servicewrap licenses may be used to distribute software support services just as shrinkwrap is used to transfer software licenses.

The shrinkwrap license conditions access to and use of a company's software on acceptance of its terms and conditions.[332] The licensor's purpose is to create a "reverse unilateral contract,"[333] which is structured so that the customer who opens the plastic wrap and uses the software is bound to the one-sided terms of the shrinkwrap license.[334] Clickwrap and web site terms of service agreements take a similar form. Adobe Systems, for example, provides that the customer's downloading of software from its site signifies agreement to its terms and conditions.[335]

Shrinkwrap license agreements were developed "to avoid the federal copyright law first sale doctrine."[336] The first sale doctrine of copyright law gives the owner of the lawfully made copy the power to "sell or otherwise dispose of the possession of that copy without the copyright holder's consent."[337] Without this doctrine, the purchaser of the first sale of a copy of the software could copy the software and distribute it for himself with impunity. Software is licensed to avoid the first sale doctrine.

Suppose the shrinkwrap license states, "Opening the envelope containing the diskette will constitute your agreement to the license which is contained on the outside of the envelope." The theory is that the license becomes effective when the licensee breaks the shrinkwrap. Courts have refused to enforce shrinkwrap licenses on various grounds. In *Step-Saver Data Systems v. Wise Technology,*[338] the Third Circuit held that the terms of a shrinkwrap license agreement were not enforceable against a reseller. In that case, Step-Saver was a value-added retailer for IBM products. Step-Saver's business was to combine hardware and software to meet the data needs for professionals such as lawyers and doctors.[339] Step-Saver provided a box-top license with all software which disclaimed all warranties. Almost immediately after installing the software on its systems, Step-Saver began receiving complaints from its customers.[340] Step-Saver referred the complaints to the licensor, who was unable to solve the problems. The court refused enforcement of the box-top license, finding that it was a proposed addition to an already existing contract never accepted by the licensee. The court found that the trial court

---

[331] This example is drawn from Morgan Laboratories, Inc. v. Micro Data Base Systems, Inc., 41 U.S.P.Q.2d 1850 (N.D. Cal. 1997); *see* Celeste L. Tito, The Servicewrap Shrinkwrap, *id.*

[332] James Gleick, Click OK to Agree (visited Apr. 22, 2002), http:// www.around.com/agree.html.

[333] Mark A. Lemley, Intellectual Property and Shrinkwrap Licenses, 68 S. Cal. L. Rev. 1239, 1241 (2000).

[334] *Id.* at 1241.

[335] Adobe, CustomerFirst Support (visited Apr. 22, 2002), http://www.adobe.com/supportservice/ custsupport.

[336] Step-Saver Data Systems v. Wyse Technology, 939 F.2d 91, 96 n.7 (3d Cir. 1991).

[337] *Id.* at 96 n.7 (quoting Bobbs-Merrill Co. v. Strauss, 210 U.S. 339 (1908)).

[338] 939 F.2d 91 (3d Cir. 1991).

[339] *Id.* at 93.

[340] 847 F.2d 255 (9th Cir. 1988).

erred and dismissed the licensee's warranty claims since the disclaimers found in the box-top license were not enforceable.

A California court held that the sale of Adobe software was the sale of a good and not a license despite the fact that Adobe sold the software accompanied by an End User License Agreement. The End User License Agreement was also electronically recorded on the computer disk. When purchasers tried to install the software, they were asked to accept the terms of the license to proceed. The court held invalid Adobe's attempt to circumvent the first sale doctrine by compelling a distributor to relinquish rights received under the copyright law. In reaching its decision, the court noted that the distributors paid full value for the merchandise and accept the risk that the software may be damaged or lost; the distributors also accept the risk that they will be unable to resell the product. The secondary market—the consumer—also pays full value for the product and accepts the risk that the product may be lost or damaged. The court found this process to constitute a transfer of title in the good, which constituted a sale and not a license to use.[341]

The Fifth Circuit in *Vault Corp. v. Quaid Software, Ltd.*[342] affirmed a district court's finding that a shrinkwrap license was an unenforceable contract of adhesion. A *contract of adhesion* derives its name from the fact that the weaker party must adhere to the terms of the stronger party. The court refused to enforce a contractual term that prohibited reverse engineering.[343] The court also concluded that federal copyright law preempted Louisiana's Software License Enforcement Act.

Prior to the mid-1990s, U.S. courts were reluctant to enforce shrinkwrap agreements. The recent trend in the law, however, is to enforce shrinkwrap, clickthrough, webwrap, and other mass-market license agreements. In *ProCD v. Zeidenberg*,[344] the Seventh Circuit upheld the enforceability of a shrinkwrap license located inside the packaging of the computer program.[345] The *ProCD* case involved a shrinkwrap agreement that could only be characterized as "pay now"

---

[341] Softman Prods. Co. v. Adobe Sys. Inc., 171 F. Supp. 2d 1075 (C.D. Cal., 2001); *see also* DeLise v. Gahrenheit Entm't, Inc., 9 ILR (P&F) 3139 (Cal. 2002) (holding that an entertainment company's sale of sound recordings in a format that could not be played anonymously violated California's consumer protection statute).

[342] 847 F.2d 255 (5th Cir. 1991); *see also* Specht v. Netscape Communications Corp., 150 F. Supp. 2d 585 (S.D.N.Y. 2001) (ruling that the terms of a license agreement are not binding if a link to such terms appears on, but below, that portion of the web page that appears on the user's screen when such downloading is accomplished); Ticketmaster Corp. v. Tickets.com, 2000 U.S. Dist. LEXIS 4553 (C.D. Cal. Mar. 27, 2000) (holding that a contract could not be created by mere use of a web site on which the plaintiff posted terms and conditions providing that such use would constitute the user's assent to be bound by these terms and provisions).

[343] Reverse engineering is a process by which a computer or software engineer works backward to determine how the software works. The Supreme Court defined *reverse engineering* broadly as "starting with the known product and working backwards to divine the process which aided in its development or manufacture." Kewanee Oil Co. v. Bicron Corp., 416 U.S. 470, 476 (1974). Software reverse engineering is a social good because it enables programmers to develop software that is interoperable with established platforms, such as the Microsoft Office products.

[344] 86 F.3d 1447 (7th Cir. 1996).

[345] *Id.*

and "you'll see the terms later after you pay." The plaintiff compiled a computer database called SelectPhone consisting of more than 3,000 telephone directories.[346] ProCD however, sought to limit the use of the database through a software licensing agreement. The defendant, Matthew Zeidenberg, purchased a copy of Select-Phone in Madison, Wisconsin, but chose to ignore the terms of the agreement.[347] Zeidenberg formed a company to resell the information in ProCD's database.[348]

Zeidenberg charged its customers for access to the information in SelectPhone and made the information available over the World Wide Web.[349] ProCD filed a lawsuit seeking an injunction "against further dissemination that exceeds the rights specified in the license."[350] The federal district court held that ProCD's license agreements were ineffective, since the terms did not appear on the outside of the package and that a customer could not be "bound by terms that were secret at the time of purchase."[351]

The Seventh Circuit reversed, upholding the shrinkwrap agreement. The court applied Article 2 to the license agreement, noting that the UCC permits contracts to be formed in "any manner sufficient to show agreement."[352] The *ProCD* court found that the licensor invited acceptance by silence. The court found that the licensee accepted the software "after having an opportunity to read the license at leisure."[353] In this case, ProCD "extended an opportunity to reject if a buyer should find the license terms unsatisfactory."[354] The court rejected the defendant's argument that he had no choice but to adhere to ProCD's terms once he opened the package.[355]

The court also rejected the defendant's argument that shrinkwrap license agreements must be conspicuous to be enforced.[356] The Seventh Circuit in *ProCD* also rejected the argument that the Copyright Act preempts software licenses.[357] The court did not find the rights created by the license agreement to be within any of the exclusive rights of the Copyright Act.[358] The court noted that strong policy arguments favored the validation of shrinkwrap. "Licenses may have other benefits for consumers: many licenses permit users to make extra copies, to use the

---

[346] *Id.* The U.S. Supreme Court in Feist Publications, Inc. v. Rural Telephone Serv. Co., Inc., 499 U.S. 340 (1991), held that a database of telephone numbers lacked the "originality" necessary for protection under the Copyright Act. The United States does not otherwise provide copyright protection for mere compilations. In contrast, European Union countries provide *sui generis* protection as well as copyright protection for databases. That would not qualify for copyright protection in the U.S.

[347] 86 F.3d at 1449.

[348] *Id.*

[349] *Id.*

[350] *Id.* at 1450.

[351] *Id.* (citing 908 F. Supp. at 654).

[352] *Id.* (citing UCC § 2-204(1)).

[353] *Id.*

[354] *Id.* at 1452.

[355] *Id.*

[356] *Id.*

[357] *Id.*

[358] *Id.* at 1453.

software on multiple computers, even to incorporate the software into the user's products."[359]

In *Hill v. Gateway 2000*,[360] the Seventh Circuit relied on *ProCD* in upholding an arbitration clause in Gateway's software license agreement. Gateway's practice was to mail its computer system with a software license agreement inside the box mailed to the customer. The Seventh Circuit observed that the "terms inside Gateway's box stand or fall together."[361] The court found that the license agreement was enforceable because of the consumer's decision to retain the Gateway system beyond the 30-day period specified in the agreement. The court reasoned that there was acceptance by silence and that the entire mass-market agreement was binding, including the arbitration clause.

The Court of Appeals of Washington recently upheld a standard software license agreement in *M.A. Mortenson Co. v. Timberline Software Corp.*[362] Mortenson, the plaintiff, used a software program to prepare a construction bid and discovered that the bid was $1.95 million less than it should have been because of the malfunctioning of the software. Timberline moved for summary judgment, arguing that the limitation on consequential damages in the licensing agreement barred the plaintiff's recovery. The lower court ruled that the license terms were part of the contract and entered summary judgment in favor of the defendant. The Washington Supreme Court upheld the judgment, ruling that the terms of Timberline's licensing agreement were enforceable and adopting the approach of the *ProCD, Hill,* and *Brower* courts.[363] However, a court held that an Internet service provider providing a new "unlimited use" service plan to subscribers with the caveat that increased traffic could cause "traffic congestion problems" did not breach its terms of service when plaintiffs experienced access and connection problems because,

---

[359] *Id.* at 1455.

[360] 105 F.3d 1147 (7th Cir. 1997).

[361] *Id.* at 1148.

[362] 970 P.2d 803 (Wash. 2000); *see also* Groff v. America Online, 1998 Westlaw 307001 (R.I. Super. Ct., May 27, 1998) (affirming validity of clickwrap agreement because AOL gave the customer the opportunity to read the agreement and signify acceptance); Kaczmorek v. Microsoft Corp., 39 F. Supp. 2d 974 (N.D. Ill. 1999) (upholding mass-market licenses).

[363] ProCD, Inc. v. Zeidenberg, 86 F.3d 1447 (7th Cir. 1996) (enforcing license agreement limiting use of database of telephone numbers); Hill v. Gateway, 2000 Inc., 105 F.3d 1147 (7th Cir. 1997) (enforcing arbitration clause in standard license agreement); and Brower v. Gateway 2000, Inc., 676 N.Y.S.2d 569 (N.Y. A.D. 1998) (enforcing license agreement but finding arbitration clause unconscionable); *see also* Management Computer Controls, Inc. v. Charles Perry Constr., Inc., 743 So. 2d 627 (Fla. App. 1999) (enforcing forum selection clause in shrinkwrap license); Rinaldi v. Iomega Corp., 1999 WL 1442014 (Del. Super. 1999) (holding that conspicuousness was unaffected by delivery in shrinkwrap form); Westendorf v. Gateway 2000, 2000 WL 307369 (Del. Ch. 2000), *aff'd*, 2000 Del. LEXIS 418 (Oct. 12, 2000) (enforcing form contract against donee of computer system); *In re* RealNetworks, Inc. Privacy Litigation, No. 00 C 1366, 5 ILR (Pike & Fisher) 3049 (N.D. Ill. 2000) (holding that clickwrap agreement satisfied a writing for purposes of the UCC); *see also* Caspi v. The Microsoft Network, L.L.C., 323 N.J. Super. 118, 732 A.2d 528 (A.D. 1999) (enforcing clickwrap agreement and choice of exclusive forum); Hotmail Corp. v. Van$ Money Pie, Inc., 47 U.S.P.Q.2d 1020 (N.D. Cal. 1998) (enforcing terms of service agreement on web site).

by clicking on a button to read the ISP's terms of service, the plaintiffs "acknowledged that services would be provided on an availability basis."[364]

Despite this recent trend in favor of enforceability, a climate of uncertainty persists. Consumer groups and legal academics are critical of the *ProCD* court's validation of "silence by acceptance" for adhesive contracts. The next generation of software litigation will center on Internet mass-market licenses. The trend in the law is to permit the enforcement of layered, standard-form license agreements as long as the terms are conspicuously displayed. A licensor needs to explicitly reference the fact that the software is licensed and to explain the legal consequences of licensing. In the *Mortenson* case, the licensor included the terms of the license agreement in every copy of the software and manuals and noted that the software was licensed on the introductory screen display each time the software was used.

[b] Content and Interactive Service Agreements

ISPs such as AOL and MSN enter into two main types of contracts. First, they contract with subscribers to provide Internet access and, often, proprietary content. Second, they enter into license agreements to obtain content from magazines, reports, newsletters, television, radio, and other media so that they can offer subscribers additional value.

When licensing content, an ISP ideally will obtain an international license for all media, including an explicit license to cache a linked web site.[365] If a provider distributes content on ancillary platforms, such as CD-ROM, the license agreement should address this right.[366]

ISPs should give their subscribers notice that the ISPs may be forced to reveal the identities of subscribers in John Doe lawsuits.[367] A number of companies have filed lawsuits to uncover the identities of users who posted "anonymous defamatory opinions . . . on the Internet."[368] Subpoenas resulting from the suits have forced ISPs to reveal the names of individuals who posted the messages using screen names. Providers typically "clickstream" contracts to bind customers.

[c] Clickwrap Agreements

A *clickwrap* or *webwrap agreement* permits a consumer to assent to the terms of an online agreement by his or her conduct. Clickthrough, clickfree, and browsewrap agreements are frequently used to manifest assent in Internet-related

---

[364] Mathias v. America Online, Inc., 2002 Ohio App. LEXIS 876 (Feb. 2002).

[365] *See* Adam H. Lehman, Negotiating Content and Interactive Services Agreements, American Bar Association: Section of Business Law, Committee on Law of Commerce in Cyberspace, Aug. 5, 1996, 1996 ABA Annual Meeting, Orlando, Florida.

[366] *Id.*

[367] John Doe subpoenas are generally addressed to Providers to uncover the identity of customers committing torts or crimes. Mark Gibbs, Responsible Anonymity and John Doe, Network World (June 28, 1999) at 82.

[368] *Id.*

contracts. With a clickthrough agreement, the Internet seller "sets up a proposed electronic form agreement to which another party may assent by clicking an icon or a button or by typing in a set of specified words."[369] An ABA Working Group distinguishes clickthrough agreements "from 'click-free agreements' (also known as 'browse-wrap agreements'), in which the User does not manifest unambiguous assent to the posted terms."[370]

Clickfree agreements are commonly used for web site terms of use and contract-based privacy terms, where the user's action of using the web site is said to constitute assent to the terms without clicking a box or icon saying "I agree," "I consent," or the like.[371] Courts will generally enforce all of these mass-market licenses provided the licensee has an opportunity to review the terms and is able to manifest assent by clicking an icon or underlined text.

With a clickwrap license, the subscriber signifies acceptance or rejection by clicking the mouse on the highlighted "I accept" or "I decline" text. Netscape Navigator, for example, is distributed with the following end-user clickwrap license:

> [B]y clicking on the "accept" button, you are consenting to be bound by and are becoming a party to this agreement. if you do not agree to all of the terms of this agreement, click the "do not accept" button and the installation process will not continue.

Clickwrap agreements are either express contracts or implied-in-fact contracts. Certain elements of the contract are implied from the act of clicking the "I accept" highlighted area. If consumers do not accept the terms of the agreement, they may not use the web site or complete the transactions.

Microsoft Network requires prospective subscribers to enter into clickwrap agreements with exclusive forum clauses. In *Caspi v. The Microsoft Network*,[372] a New Jersey court upheld Microsoft's clickwrap agreement enforcing a forum selection clause.

The federal court in *Specht v. Netscape Communications Corp.*[373] refused to enforce a license agreement that did not make the user aware that he was entering into a contract. The court reasoned that the licensor's failure to require a user to indicate assent to the vendor's license as a precondition to downloading and using its software was fatal to its argument that a contract was formed. The court ruled that downloading the freely offered software was not made conditional upon accepting the terms of the license agreement.

The court found that the software allowed a user to download and use it without taking any action that plainly manifested assent to the terms of the associated

---

[369] Christina Kunz et al., Click-Through Agreements; Strategies for Avoiding Disputes on Validity of Assent, 57 Bus. Law. 401 (2001).

[370] *Id.*

[371] *Id.*

[372] 732 A.2d 528 (N.J. Sup. Ct., App. Div., 1999).

[373] 2001 WL 755396 (S.D.N.Y. July 5, 2001); *cf.* i.Lan Sys., Inc. v. NetScout Serv. Level Corp., 183 F. Supp. 2d 328 (D. Mass. 2002).

license or indicated an understanding that a contract was being formed. The mere act of downloading was not an indication of assent. The court ruled that the primary purpose of downloading was to obtain a product, not to assent to an agreement. The court ruled that the person downloading the software was not bound by the agreement and was therefore not bound by an arbitration clause contained in the license. The trend in the law is for clickwrap contracts to be held valid and enforceable.[374]

In *Hotmail v. Van$ Money Pie, Inc.,*[375] the court upheld an injunction against a Hotmail subscriber who violated the terms of the Hotmail's Terms of Service agreement by sending unsolicited e-mail messages, or spam. The clickwrap agreement at the top of the Hotmail Terms of Service (HTS) had a single button reading "I accept" but no button reading "I decline." The subscriber was advised that "BY COMPLETING THE REGISTRATION PROCESS AND BY CLICKING THE 'I ACCEPT' BUTTON, YOU ARE INDICATING YOUR AGREEMENT TO BE BOUND BY ALL OF THE TERMS AND CONDITIONS OF THE HTS." The consideration for the Hotmail agreement is the member's providing current, complete, and accurate information in the registration. Hotmail, which requires its subscribers to give their name, mailing address, e-mail address, and account and phone number, agrees not to disclose this information unless required to do so by law or legal process. The *Hotmail* court found that the HTS agreement was enforceable, even though there was no "I decline" button.

[B] Offer and Acceptance

An *offer* is a definite statement or conduct manifesting a willingness to enter into a contract. The person making an offer is the *offeror*. The person to whom an offer is made is the *offeree*. It is the offeree who accepts an offer by manifesting assent to the terms of the offer. An exchange of consideration must occur for there to be an enforceable contract.[376] *Consideration* generally takes the form either of a promise or of some performance by the offeree in response to an offer. A *bilateral contract* is a promise for a promise; a *unilateral contract* is a promise in exchange for a requested act. Online contracts, like traditional contracts, require

---

[374] *See, e.g.,* In re RealNetworks, Inc. Privacy Litig., 2000 U.S. Dist. LEXIS 6584 (N.D. Ill. May 8, 2000); Hotmail Corp. v. Van$ Money Pie, Inc., 1998 U.S. Dist. LEXIS 10729 (N.D. Cal. Apr. 16, 1998).

[375] No. C98-20064 (N.D. Cal., Apr. 16, 1998) (upholding clickstream contract and restraining defendant from spam-related activities); i.Lan Sys., Inc. v. Netscout Serv. Level Corp., Civ Act. No. 00-11489-WGY (D. Mass. Jan. 2, 2002) (upholding the validity of a clickwrap agreement despite the fact that the plaintiff purchased the software through a purchase order that did not contain the clickwrap agreement; reasoning that the contract was valid under UCC § 2-204 because the conduct of both parties recognized the existence of such a contract; viewing clickwrap agreement as an additional term permitted by the UCC § 2-207 "so long as that came as no surprise to, and caused no hardship for, the plaintiff"); *cf.* Register.com, Inc, v. Verio, Inc. (S.D.N.Y. Dec. 12, 2000) (holding that although defendant was not expressly required to click an "I Agree" button, the defendant's actions were likely to constitute a breach of terms of use in using plaintiff's Whois database for mass unsolicited advertisement).

[376] The UCC does not define offer, acceptance, and consideration, incorporating concepts of the common law.

an offer, acceptance, and consideration, whether under the common law or under Article 2.

Traditional contract law does not permit silence or inaction to constitute acceptance. Acceptance requires that an offeree communicate her or his assent to the terms of the offer. Acceptance may be manifested by acts such as "speaking or sending a letter, a telegram, or other explicit or implicit communication to the offeror."[377] The mere receipt of an e-mail message may constitute acceptance.

[1]   E-Mailbox Rule

Under the traditional *mailbox rule,* an offeree's acceptance was effective when the offeree dispatched a letter out of his or her control. Delivery of an offer occurs when it is placed in the mail. It is questionable whether the traditional mailbox rule should apply to electronic or Internet-related offers. The ABA Model Trading Partner Agreement declined to follow the mailbox rule.[378] The mailbox rule could be updated to make "acceptance effective from the time it leaves the acceptor's control" if it can be shown that the offer contemplated acceptance by a nonimmediate form of communication.[379] The e-mailbox rule has been updated so that an offer is only effective upon actual receipt. The e-mailbox rule is possible because technology exists for determining when an offeree has received an e-mail.

[2]   Electronic Contract Formation Rules

The UCC presents liberal contracting rules that may be accommodated to electronic contracting. The common law required a "meeting of the minds" of the offeror and offeree for the result to be a contract. In contrast, sales contracts may be formed in any manner sufficient to indicate agreement, including conduct.[380] Article 2 sales contracts do not fail for indefiniteness as long as (1) the parties intend to form a sales contract and (2) a reasonably certain basis exists for giving an appropriate remedy.[381]

The UCC assimilates common law concepts of offer, acceptance, and consideration. The UCC permits the offeror to demand a particular mode of acceptance. If an offer does not invite a specific means of acceptance, however, the offeree may accept by any reasonable manner or medium.[382]

---

[377] Len Young Smith, Essentials of Business Law and the Legal Environment 171 (4th ed., 1989).

[378] Jeffrey B. Ritter and Judith Y. Gliniecki, Symposium: Electronic Communications and Legal Change: International Electronic Commerce and Administrative Law: The Need for Harmonized National Reforms, 6 Harv. J. Law & Tech. 263 (1993).

[379] Andrew D. Murray, Entering into Contracts Electronically: The Real WWW, *in* Lillian Edward and Charlotte Waelde, Law and the Internet: A Framework for Electronic Commerce 22 (2000).

[380] UCC § 2-204 (2000).

[381] *Id.* § 2-204(3).

[382] *Id.* § 2-206(1)(a).

Great uncertainty persists as to whether mass-market license agreements are enforceable. At common law, an offer could be revoked until acceptance since the promise was not yet supported by consideration. Option contracts were an exception to the general rule because an option supported by consideration was irrevocable for the period stated. Section 2-205, Article 2's "firm offer" rule, is also an exception to the common law rule of revocability of offers. Unlike common law option contracts, company offers by merchants need not be supported by consideration. If a merchant makes a signed written company offer, it is irrevocable for a reasonable period not to exceed three months.

UCITA validates shrinkwrap, clickwrap, webwrap, and other mass-market license agreements as long as the licensor gives the prospective licensee an opportunity to review the terms and to manifest assent. In general, UCITA creates, defines, and governs computer information transactions. UCITA provides the ground rules not only for electronic contracts but also for Internet-related licenses. For a complete discussion of UCITA, see § 6.05.

The model statute provides elaborate rules for online contracting, software licensing, electronic warranties, and remedies. UCITA's scope is wide ranging and applies to webwrap agreements, software licenses, access contracts, and a host of Internet-related contracts. An ABA working group completed a content analysis of three recent mass-market license cases, an attorney general settlement, and some FTC guidelines and found "that a click-through agreement may be vulnerable to attack when the User is not required to at least view the terms of the proposed agreement before assenting to them."[383]

[C] Legal Proof Issues

[1] Electronic Authentication

The question of whether data messages are admissible on the same terms as handwritten signatures is an important issue encompassing many substantive fields of law. The common law of contract evolved in an age of "pen-and-pencil." Parties in EDI transactions exchange information in an agreed-upon electronic format from computer to computer. Parties to other online transactions may have no prior agreement, and, in the event of a dispute, authentication may become contentious.

---

[383] *See* Christina Kunz et al., Click-Through Agreements; Strategies for Avoiding Disputes on Validity of Assent, 57 Bus. Law. 401 (2001) (citing cases on enforceability of mass-market licenses); *see, e.g.,* Ticketmaster Corp. v. Tickets. Com, Inc., 2000 WL 525390 (C.D. Cal. Mar. 27, 2000) (holding that user was not bound by terms of use agreement because of difficulty of locating and viewing terms); Williams v. America Online, Inc., 2001 WL 135825 (Mass. Super. Ct. Feb. 8, 2001) (refusing to grant provider's motion to dismiss partially on grounds that it was difficult to view the agreement); *cf.* Caspi v. Microsoft Network, L.L.C., 732 A.2d 528 (N.J. Super. Ct. App. Div. 1999) (enforcing agreement even though the user could assent without scrolling to the bottom of the agreement by clicking the "I agree" icon on the screen).

The procedural rules for online contracting concern legal proof issues and the rules for enforcing substantive rules.[384] One procedural issue is whether an electronic record or a display generated by electronic means by an electronic agent is admissible in court. Many of the states have extended traditional writing and signature requirements to include electronic writings and signatures; in fact, 40 states have enacted or are considering electronic authentication laws.[385]

[2] Digital Signatures

For e-commerce to flourish, electronic records must be validated under rules of evidence and procedure. The procedural question of whether documents may be filed electronically has not been settled in many jurisdictions. The majority of states have enacted digital signature statutes, which are chiefly procedural statutes that validate the admissibility of attribution procedures and digital signatures. Digital signature statutes are chiefly procedural statutes that treat an electronic signature as equivalent to a handwritten signature. For a full discussion, see § 6.03[D].

[D] Uniform Electronic Transactions Act

UETA is the most comprehensive statute yet enacted governing procedural rules for contracting. UETA validates electronic records or electronic signatures, in any transaction, except transactions governed by the UCC.[386] UETA "applies to any electronic record or electronic signature created, generated, sent, communicated, received, or stored on or after the effective date" of the Act.[387] UETA does not apply to any articles of the Uniform Commercial Code, to wills or trusts, to UCITA, or to other state laws.[388] In a conflict between Article 2 and UETA, Article 2 governs.[389] The Electronic Signatures in Global and National Commerce Act of 2000 permits UETA to preempt the federal act.

[1] Purpose

The purpose of UETA is to facilitate e-commerce, "to be consistent with reasonable practices concerning electronic transactions," and to make uniform law.[390]

---

[384] Smith, *supra* note 377, at 5 (defining the distinction between procedural and substantive law).

[385] *Supra* note 189 (Apr. 10, 2000).

[386] UETA has been adopted as of April 28, 2002, in Alabama, Arizona, Arkansas, California, Delaware, District of Columbia, Florida, Hawaii, Idaho, Indiana, Iowa, Kansas, Kentucky, Louisiana, Maine, Maryland, Michigan, Minnesota, Mississippi, Montana, Nebraska, Nevada, New Hampshire, New Mexico, North Carolina, North Dakota, Ohio, Oklahoma, Oregon, Pennsylvania, Rhode Island, Tennessee, Utah, Virginia, West Virginia, and Wyoming.

[387] *Id.* § 4; *see* NCCUSL, Why States Should Adopt the Uniform Electronic Transactions Act (visited Oct. 13, 2000), http://www.nccusl.org/uniformact_why/uniformacts_why_UETA.htm.

[388] *Id.* § 3(b)(c)(d).

[389] American Law Institute, Uniform Commercial Code [New], Revised Article 2 (Members Consultative Group Draft, March 1, 2000).

[390] UETA § 6.

UETA treats electronic signatures as the functional equivalent of "paper-and-pen" writings and manually signed signatures. UETA defines the *electronic signature* as "an electronic sound, symbol, or process attached to or logically associated with a record, and executed or adopted by a person with the intent to sign the record."[391] UETA eliminates barriers to electronic commerce and governmental transactions that use electronic records and signatures. The model statute, if widely enacted by the states, will promote the development of a legal infrastructure for electronic commerce and governmental transactions.

The case for adopting UETA is that it will advance the following commercially reasonable policy goals:

a. To facilitate and promote commerce and governmental transactions by validating and authorizing the use of electronic records and electronic signatures;

b. To eliminate barriers in electronic commerce and governmental transactions resulting from uncertainties relating to writing and signature requirements;

c. To simply, clarify, and modernize the law governing commerce and governmental transactions through the use of electronic means;

d. To permit the continued expansion of commercial and governmental electronic practices through custom, usage, and agreement of the parties;

e. To promote uniformity of the law among the states (and worldwide) relating to the use of electronic and similar technological means of affecting and performing commercial and governmental transactions;

f. To promote public confidence in the validity, integrity, and reliability of electronic commerce and governmental transactions; and

g. To promote the development of the legal and business infrastructure necessary to implement electronic commerce and governmental transactions.[392]

[2] Scope

UETA applies to transactions related to business, commercial, and governmental matters.[393] Wills, codicils, and testamentary trusts are removed from UETA as are the Articles of the UCC. For states enacting it, UETA "applies to any electronic record or electronic signature created, generated, sent, communicated, received, or stored on or after the effective date."[394]

---

[391] *Id.* § 2(8).

[392] C. Robert Beattie, Draft Uniform Electronic Transactions Act, Presentation at 1998 Annual Meeting of the American Bar Association, July 31-Aug. 4, 1998.

[393] UETA § 3, cmt. 1.

[394] *Id.* § 4

[3]   Validation of Electronic Signatures

UETA does not *require* any party to use electronic signatures or records and was intended to remove barriers to e-commerce.[395] UETA applies "only to transactions between parties, each of which has agreed to conduct transactions by electronic means."[396] The single most important impact of UETA is to validate electronic records, electronic signatures, and electronic contracts. Section 7 of UETA provides that "[a] record or signature may not be denied legal effect or enforceability solely because it is in electronic form."[397] UETA legitimizes the concept of electronic contract, providing that "[a] contract may not be denied legal effect or enforceability solely because an electronic record was used in its formation."[398] Electronic records and digital signatures satisfy the legal requirements for writings and signatures.

[4]   Electronic Records

UETA provides the minimum requirements for what constitutes an electronic record. Electronic records must minimally be "capable of retention at the time of receipt."[399] An online communication that "inhibits the ability of the recipient to print or store the electronic record"[400] does not have the status of a retained record. UETA does not supplant other law that may require that a record be posted or displayed in a certain manner.[401] For electronic contracts to be viable, some mechanism of attribution must exist. An "electronic record or electronic signature is attributable to a person if it was the act of the person."[402] Security procedures are frequently employed to establish attribution.

UETA is technology-neutral, and § 9(a) permits electronic records to be "shown in any manner, including a showing of the efficacy of any security procedure applied to determine the person to which the electronic record or electronic signature was attributable." In many states, the parties are free to agree upon a commercially reasonable security procedure used in their business dealings.

Security procedures are useful in protecting the authenticity and integrity of online contracts, verifying that a signature or record is that of the contracting party. A security procedure may also include encryption technology to detect changes or errors in the content of a record or contract. An electronic record or signature is also determined "from the context and surrounding circumstances at the time of its creation, execution or adoption, including the parties' agreement, if any, and otherwise as provided by law."[403]

---

[395] *Id.* § 5(a).
[396] *Id.* § 5(b).
[397] *Id.* § 7.
[398] *Id.* § 7(b).
[399] *Id.* § 8(a).
[400] *Id.*
[401] *Id.* § 8(b).
[402] *Id.* § 9.
[403] *Id.* § 9(b).

[5]   Effect of Change or Error

UETA has a methodology for allocating the risk of errors in electronic records that occur during a transmission between parties. The model statute places the risk of loss due to a transmission error on the party that failed to use an agreed-upon security procedure like Article 4A of the UCC.[404] If both parties fail to use an agreed-upon security procedure, the rule does not apply. The party that follows reasonable security procedures "may avoid the effect of the changed or erroneous electronic record only if the other party deviates upon the agreed-upon procedure."[405] It is reasonable that the party that cuts corners on reasonable security is allocated the risk of a security transmission error.

In an automated transaction, an individual must be given the opportunity for the prevention or correction of errors.[406] An individual seeking to avoid the effect of an electronic record must promptly notify the other person of the error.[407] The person erroneously receiving an electronic record must "return it to the other person" or "destroy the consideration received."[408] The person "must not have used or received any benefit or value from the consideration" received from an erroneous message.[409]

[6]   Retention of Records

"If a law requires a signature or record to be notarized, acknowledged, verified, or made under oath," an electronic signature of the person authorized to perform those acts of verification satisfies the requirement.[410] If the law requires a record to be retained, the retention of electronic records satisfies this requirement.[411] To satisfy the retention requirement, the electronic record must fulfill two separate requirements: (1) It must accurately reflect the information in the record after it is in final form and (2) it must remain accessible for later reference.[412]

[7]   Admissibility in Evidence

The digitization of electronic records is becoming increasingly important in litigation. Courts increasingly require parties in litigation to produce electronic records. Computerized files are discoverable, and courts will order discovery of computerized files.[413] The Illinois Supreme Court Rule 201 defines documents to

---

[404] *Id.* § 10.
[405] *Id.* § 10(1).
[406] *Id.* § 10(2).
[407] *Id.* § 10(2)(A).
[408] *Id.* § 10(2)(B).
[409] *Id.* § 10(2)(C).
[410] *Id.* § 11.
[411] *Id.* § 12.
[412] *Id.*
[413] *See, e.g.,* Gates Rubber Co. v. Bando Chemical Indus., Ltd., 167 F.R.D. 90, 112 (D. Colo. 1996).

include "all retrievable information in computer storage."[414] Section 13 of UETA states that "in a proceeding, evidence of a record or signature may not be excluded solely because it is in electronic form."[415] Computer records have frequently been "smoking guns" in corporate litigation.[416] For a full discussion of smoking guns and e-mail retention, see § 10.03[C] in Chapter Ten. UETA validates the discoverability and admissibility of electronic data and records.

[8] Automated Transactions

UETA provides a legal infrastructure for automated transactions using intelligent electronic agents. Section 14(1) validates contracts formed by electronic agents, even without human review of the terms and agreements.[417] Contracts may be formed by the interaction of an electronic agent and an individual. UETA is a procedural statute, and thus "the terms of the contract are determined by the substantive law applicable to it."[418]

[9] Receipt of Electronic Records

UETA provides that the parties may determine when an electronic record is sent or received. Unless the parties otherwise provide:

> [a]n electronic record is received when it enters an information processing system that the recipient has designated or uses for the purpose of receiving electronic records or information of the type sent and from which the recipient is able to retrieve the electronic record which is under the control of the recipient.[419]

§ 6.05 SOFTWARE AND INTERNET-RELATED LICENSES UNDER THE UNIFORM COMPUTER INFORMATION TRANSACTIONS ACT

[A] Overview

UCITA is the world's first comprehensive code for computer information, including Internet licenses.[420] *Computer information* means information in electronic form.[421] By the mid-1980s, the American Bar Association's Business Law

---

[414] Illinois Supreme Court Rule 20.

[415] UETA § 13.

[416] *See, e.g.*, Knox v. State of Indiana, 93 F.3d 1327 (7th Cir. 1996) (finding e-mail messages in which a supervisor asked employee for sex as evidence in sexual harassment lawsuit); Wesley College v. Pitts, 974 F. Supp. 375 (D. Del. 1997) (admitting e-mail messages in employment case for termination of professor).

[417] UETA § 14.

[418] *Id.* § 14(3).

[419] *Id.* § 15(b)(1)(2).

[420] The UCITA text and official comments are available at http://www.ucitaonline.com.

[421] UCITA § 102(10).

Section had begun investigating the possibility that Article 2 of the UCC could be expanded to cover computer contracts.[422]

In the early 1990s, the National Conference of Commissioners on Uniform State Laws (NCCUSL) and the American Law Institute (ALI) agreed to update the UCC to include software-licensing agreements. Although initially proposed as Article 2B, a new article of the UCC, the model statute proved too controversial to secure the required support of the ALI.[423] Thus, as finally approved by NCCUSL, UCITA is a stand-alone statute that will not be part of the UCC.[424] UCITA governs computer information transactions in Virginia and Maryland. Maryland's UCITA statute has an effective date of October 1, 2000.[425] Maryland created "A Joint Technology Oversight Committee" to oversee the implementation of UCITA and provide recommendations for amendments each year in December until June 30, 2005.[426] Virginia's version of UCITA had an effective date of July 1, 2001.[427] UCITA was introduced in Arizona, District of Columbia, Illinois, Maine, New Hampshire, New Jersey, Oregon, and Texas,[428] but is in effect only in Maryland and Virginia.

UCITA is broadly applicable to a wide variety of software-related contracts. UCITA applies to "computer information transactions,"[429] which include "agreements that deal with the creation, modification, access to, licensing or distribution of computer information."[430] UCITA applies chiefly to the licensing of software and other information. UCITA defines a license as "a contract that authorizes access to, or use, distribution, performance, modification, or reproduction of,

---

[422] Business Law Section, American Bar Association, Ad Hoc Committee on Computer Contracts (1987).

[423] The scores of drafts of Article 2B, which preceded UCITA, were hotly debated by industry, consumer, and bar association groups. In March 1995, NCCUSL approved a "hub-and-spoke" model that treated Article 2B as a separate spoke sharing hub provisions with Articles 2 and 2A. The "hub-and-spoke" model sought to harmonize Articles 2, 2A, and 2B by forging general principles common to each article. The "hub-and-spoke" model envisioned a common hub and separate spokes for Articles 2, 2A, and 2B corresponding to sales, leases, and licenses, respectively.

The "hub-and-spoke" model was opposed by a wide variety of stakeholders, such as the Software Publishers Association. NCCUSL eliminated the "hub-and-spoke" concept but retained Raymond Nimmer as the Article 2B reporter. In addition to Professor Nimmer (Article 2B's technology reporter), the key players for the Article 2B project were the American Bar Association, NCCUSL, and the ALI. Approval by both the ALI and the NCCUSL was necessary before a completed draft could be introduced in the state legislatures.

[424] Thomas Weidlich, Commission Plans New UCC Article, Nat'l L.J. (Aug. 28, 1995) at B1 (noting that NCCUSL appointed Houston law professor Raymond T. Nimmer as technology reporter for the new UCC Article 2B); *see also* Raymond T. Nimmer, Intangibles Contracts: Thoughts of Hubs, Spokes and Reinvigorating Article 2, 35 Wm. & Mary L. Rev. 1337 (1994).

[425] Carol Kunze, UCITA Online, What's Happening to UCITA in the States, updated Apr. 6, 2001 (visited May 28, 2001), http://ucitaonline.com/whathap.html.

[426] *Id.*

[427] *Id.*

[428] Carol Kunze, What's Happening to UCITA in the State (visited Apr. 14, 2002), http://www.ucitaonline.com/whathap.html.

[429] UCITA § 102(11) (2002).

[430] *Id.*

information or informational rights, but expressly limits the access or uses authorized or expressly grants fewer than all rights in the information, whether or not the transferee has title to a licensed copy."[431] UCITA's definition of license includes an access contract such as those for WESTLAW, LEXIS, or AOL as well as a consignment of a copy.[432] It proposes a set of uniform rules and a more certain legal environment for a wide variety of Internet-related mass-market licenses,[433] including software contracts,[434] contracts to download software,[435] access contracts,[436] clickwrap agreements,[437] webwrap agreements, electronic data interchange (EDI),[438] and a host of other Information Age contracts. UCITA also validates shrinkwrap agreements that accompany boxed software.[439] Licensing is

---

[431] UCITA § 102(41).

[432] *Id.*

[433] It is particularly critical for the software industry to know with certainty that mass-market licenses, such as shrinkwrap or clickwrap agreements (*see supra* § 6.04[A][2]), will be enforced. Shrinkwrap and clickwrap agreements are classifiable as mass-market licenses, that is, a standard form used in a mass-market transaction, UCITA § 102(44). *Mass-market transaction*

> means a transaction that is: (A) a consumer contract; or (B) any other transaction with an end-user licensee if: (i) the transaction is for information or informational rights directed to the general public as a whole, including consumers, under substantially the same terms for the same information; (ii) the licensee acquires the information or informational rights in a retail transaction under terms and in a quantity consistent with an ordinary transaction in a retail market; and (iii) the transaction is not: (I) a contract for redistribution or for public performance or public display of a copyrighted work; (II) a transaction in which the information is customized or otherwise specially prepared by the licensor for the licensee, other than minor customization using a capability of the information intended for that purpose; (III) a site license; or (IV) an access contract.

Id. § 1-201(45).
UCITA sharply differentiates between mass-market and non-mass-market transactions, otherwise known as customized or negotiated agreements, which encompass license agreements to develop specialty software and are typically negotiated. Mass-market licenses are offered on a "take it or leave it" basis with standard terms.

[434] Uniform Computer Information Transactions Act (UCITA) Prefatory Note (2001 Amended Statute Approved by NCCUSL) (noting that UCITA is the first statute to govern software contracts and the licensing of computer information).

[435] Uniform Computer Information Transactions Act, Prefatory Note, *Id.*

[436] An *access contract* "means a contract to obtain by electronic means access to, or information from, an information processing system of another person, or the equivalent of such access." UCITA § 102(a)(1) (2000). WESTLAW, LEXIS, Microsoft Network, America Online, and the online version of the Wall Street Journal are subscription services classifiable as "access contracts." An access contract is generally in the form of a license, which "means a contract that authorizes access to, or use, distribution, performance, modification, or reproduction of, information or informational rights, but expressly limits the access or uses authorized or expressly grants fewer than all rights in the information, whether or not the transferee has title to a licensed copy. The term includes an access contract, a lease of a computer program, and a consignment of a copy." UCITA § 102(a)(41) (2001).

[437] *See supra* § 6.04[A][2] (defining clickwrap and webwrap agreements).

[438] *See supra* § 6.02[A][1] (defining EDI).

[439] *See supra* § 6.04[A][2][a] (discussing shrinkwrap agreements).

one way in which computer information is tailored to the information marketplace. Courts have enforced contract terms that, among other things:

- preclude commercial use
- preclude making copies
- grant access
- allow use throughout a site
- preclude distribution of copies for a fee
- preclude modification
- allow distribution only in specific way

- permit commercial use
- permit making multiple copies
- limit access
- limit use to a specific computer
- allow distribution of copies
- allow modification
- limit use to internal operations[440]

The statutory purposes of UCITA are (1) to facilitate computer or information transactions in cyberspace, (2) to clarify the law governing computer information transactions, (3) to enable expanding commercial practice in computer information transactions by commercial usage and agreement of the parties, and (4) to make the law uniform among the various jurisdictions.[441]

UCITA provides substantive rules for e-commerce not found in any other state or federal statute. UCITA, for example, defines and validates the use of electronic agents[442] to form online contracts. UCITA defines *attribution procedure* to mean "a procedure to verify that an electronic authentication, display, message, record, or performance is that of a particular person or to detect changes or errors in information. The term includes a procedure that requires the use of algorithms or other codes, identifying words or numbers, encryption, or callback or other acknowledgment."[443] *Authenticate* means "to sign" or "with the intent to sign a record, otherwise to execute or adopt an electronic symbol, sound, message, or process referring to, attached to, included in, or logically associated or linked with, that record."[444] UCITA follows the methodology of Article 2 in drawing distinctions between substantive rules for "merchants" and "nonmerchants."[445]

---

[440] UCITA, Prefatory Note (2001 Amended Statute Approved by NCCUSL), at 3.

[441] *Id.*

[442] *Id.* § 1-201(27) (defining *electronic agent* to mean "a computer program, or electronic or other automated means, used independently to initiate an action, or to respond to electronic messages or performances, on the person's behalf without review or action by an individual at the time of the action or response to the message or performance").

[443] *Id.* § 1-201(6).

[444] *Id.*

[445] UCITA defines a *merchant* as "a person: (A) that deals in information or informational rights of the kind involved in the transaction; (B) that by the person's occupation holds itself out as having knowledge or skill peculiar to the relevant aspect of the business practices or information involved in the transaction; or (C) to which the knowledge or skill peculiar to the practices or information involved in the transaction may be attributed by the person's employment of an agent or broker or other intermediary that by its occupation holds itself out as having the knowledge or skill."

In the absence of a comprehensive statute for computer transactions in cyber-space, judges and practitioners employ legal fictions cornering and cribbing Article 2 to fit software licensing transactions. The UCITA Reporter argues that a specialized statute is needed for the licensing of information:

> Contracts for computer information are not equivalent to transactions in goods, whether the issues focus on development, commercial exchange, or mass marketing. Computer information contracts emphasize different issues and bring into play a different policy structure on issues ranging from allocation of liability risk to questions about how the right to use the informational subject matter is determined. One (goods) focuses on rights to a tangible item, while the other (computer information) focuses on intangibles and rights in intangibles. The contexts entail different contractual, transaction, property, and underlying social policies issues.[446]

UCITA § 1-201(46). UCITA has a large number of special rules directed to professionals in business. For example, "a licensor of information that is a merchant regularly dealing in information of the kind warrants that the information will be delivered free of the rightful claim of any third person." UCITA § 401. There is a special merchant rules for contracts with varying terms: "An additional nonmaterial term in the acceptance is a proposal for an additional term. Between merchants, the proposed additional term becomes part of the contract unless the offeror gives notice of objection before, or within a reasonable time after, it receives the proposed terms." UCITA, § 201. The idea underlying the merchant is that the experienced or professional in business should be held to a higher standard than a casual seller. Special merchant rules for the UCC include the following: § 2-201(2), the Statute of Frauds; § 2-205, the merchants' only "company offer" rule; § 2-207, the merchants' confirmatory memoranda rule for "battle of the forms"; § 2-209, the merchants' sales contract modification rule; § 2-312, the merchant rule for warranty against infringement; § 2-314, implied warranty of merchantability; § 2-316(2), special merchant rule for disclaiming warranties; § 2-103(1)(b), special merchant rule for good faith; § 2-327(1)(c), the merchants' rule for following reasonable instructions in "Sale on Approval" or "Sale or Return" contracts; § 2-603, special duties for merchant buyers in dealing with rejected goods; § 2-605, the merchants' special rule for waiver of buyer's objection by failure to particularize defects; § 2-509(3), special merchants' rule for risk of loss in the absence of breach; § 2-402(2), the merchants' rule for rights of sellers' creditors; § 2-403(2) the merchants' entrusting rule and power to transfer goods to buyers in the ordinary course of business; and § 2-609, the merchants' right to adequate assurance of performance. UCITA essentially adapts the methodology of Article 2 in having separate rules for merchants and nonmerchants in computer transactions. UCITA defines the *merchant* as a person that "deals in information or informational rights of the kind involved in the transaction" or that otherwise "by the person's occupation holds itself out as having knowledge or skill peculiar to . . . the practices or information involved in the transaction" or a person to which such knowledge or skill "may be attributed by the person's employment of an agent or broker or other intermediary that by its occupation holds itself out as having the knowledge or skill." UCITA § 102(46) (2000). As with Article 2, UCITA has a special Statute of Frauds rule for merchants. *Id.* § 201(d) (stating that where both parties are merchants there is an exception to the writing requirement where notice of objection is not given within 10 days after the confirming record is received). *See id.* § 204(d)(2) ("Between merchants, the proposed additional term becomes part of the contract unless the offeror gives notice of objection before, or within a reasonable time after, it receives the proposed terms"). As with Article 2, UCITA has a large number of special merchant rules.

[446] UCITA Prefatory Note (NCCUSL Annual Draft, July 2000).

[B] Structure and Function

The UCC's purpose is "to clarify the law about business transactions rather than to change the habits of the business community."[447] UCITA, like the UCC, permits the parties to vary statutory provisions. As with the UCC, UCITA incorporates default terms as gap-fillers for missing terms "unless the parties otherwise agree." UCITA's underlying jurisprudence is freedom of contract. As with the UCC, the parties may not disclaim the obligations of good faith, diligence, reasonableness, and due care nor certain consumer protections.

UCITA closely parallels Article 2 of the UCC in structure and function. Article 2 is divided into seven parts with hundreds of sections and subsections. UCITA is divided into nine parts: (1) Definitions, (Subpart A: Short Title and Definitions) (Subpart B: General Scope and Terms); (2) Formation and Terms (Subpart A: Formation of Contracts); (3) Construction (Subpart A: General) (Subpart B: Interpretation); (4) Warranties; (5) Transfer of Interests (Subpart A: Ownership and Transfers) (Subpart B: Financing Arrangement); (6) Performance (Subpart A: General) (Subpart B: Performance in Delivery of Copies) (Subpart C: Special Types of Contracts) (Subpart D: Loss and Impossibility) (Subpart E: Termination); (7) Breach of Contract (Subpart A: General) (Subpart B: Defective Copies) (Subpart C: Repudiation and Assurances); (8) Remedies (Subpart A: General) (Subpart B: Damages) (Subpart C: Remedies Related to Performance); and (9) Miscellaneous Provisions. UCITA is shaped by the software licensing paradigm as well as by the trade practices of the information-based industries. UCITA § 103 sets the scope of the proposed statute as "computer information transactions" with a series of "carve-outs" or exclusions. Section 114 follows the UCC in permitting supplemental principles of law and equity to apply to contracts governed by UCITA.[448] Like Article 2 agreements, a UCITA contract consists of the parties' agreement, course of dealing, course of performance, and usage of trade. UCITA does not supplant fundamental public policies or consumer protections at either the state or federal level.

[C] Scope

[1] Computer Information Transactions

The scope of UCITA is to provide the ground rules for "computer information transactions."[449] UCITA excludes newspapers, motion pictures, and printed information that is in a nondigital format. The UCITA methodology consists of a broad definition of computer transactions with numerous exceptions. Core banking and payment and financial services are outside the scope of the proposed

---

[447] Grant Gilmore, On the Difficulties of Codifying Commercial Law, 57 Yale L.J. 1341 (1948).

[448] UCITA § 114. UCITA also contemplates that the statute will be supplemented by the usage of trade. *See, e.g.,* UCITA §§ 210(a), 302(b).

[449] UCITA § 103(a)(2000).

statute.[450] Insurance services are governed by well-established legal principles and thus are outside the scope of UCITA.[451] The entertainment industry is largely outside the scope of UCITA, although movies, television, radio, and mass media may be classifiable as computer information, as would MP3. If a transaction involves the "rights to create computer information and a motion picture," UCITA does not apply if the "dominant character of the agreement is to create or obtain rights to create a motion picture."[452] Motion pictures and audio or visual programming are not governed by UCITA.[453] Sound recordings, musical works, and phonorecords are also outside of UCITA.[454] UCITA specifically excludes the distribution of music and entertainment, which already have well-established rules for contract formation and the distribution of visual programming or similar products.

UCITA does not govern broadcast, satellite, or cable programming governed by the Federal Communications Act.[455] The licensing of motion pictures, sound recordings, musical works, and phonograph records is also carved out of the proposed UCITA.[456] UCITA excludes "traditional core businesses" such as "information in print form,"[457] such as a newspaper or magazine. The exclusion of the mass media and of the entertainment industry has narrowed the scope of UCITA.[458] UCITA's ill-fated predecessor, Article 2B, was originally drafted to include all information transfers.

In addition, compulsory licenses are excluded from the scope of UCITA.[459] A *compulsory license* is a license granted by the government to use patents, copyrighted materials, or other types of intellectual property.[460] The U.S. government's authority to issue compulsory licenses stems from antitrust and eminent domain laws.[461] A number of federal statutes provide for compulsory licenses; the Clean Air Act, for example, "provides for compulsory licensing of patents related to air pollution."[462] The policy underlying compulsory licenses is "to broaden access to technologies and information in order to achieve a number of public purposes."[463] The compulsory licenses recognized by legal treaties, such as GATT, NAFTA, and TRIPS, are outside the scope of UCITA.[464]

---

[450] *Id.* § 103(d)(1).

[451] UCITA § 103(d)(2)(200).

[452] UCITA § 103(b)(1)(B)(2).

[453] UCITA § 103(d)(3)(A).

[454] UCITA § 103(d)(3)(B).

[455] *Id.* § 103(d)(3).

[456] *Id.* § 103(d)(3)(A)(B).

[457] *Id.* § 103, cmt. 3.

[458] UCITA does not apply to "audio or visual programming . . . provided by broadcast, satellite, or cable, as defined or used in the Communications Act of 1935." *Id.* § 103(f)(1); *see also* § 103(d)(3)(A)(B) (excluding core entertainment, cable, and broadcast from UCITA).

[459] *Id.* § 103(d)(4).

[460] Frequently Asked Questions About Compulsory Licenses (visited Apr. 27, 2002), http://www.cptech.org/ip/health/cl/faq.html.

[461] *Id.*

[462] *Id.*

[463] *Id.*

[464] *Id.*

UCITA does not cover "contracts of employment of an individual other than as an independent contractor,"[465] nor does it apply to service contracts. Law other than UCITA would govern any contract for personal services. UCITA does not cover the licensing of intellectual property, such as patents, copyrights, trade dress, or other intellectual property rights. Revised Article 2 provides, if UCITA is adopted in a state, that Article 2 should defer to UCITA's scope section.[466] Revised Article 2 adapts to sales law many of the provisions of the Uniform Electronic Transaction Act.[467] In a nutshell, UCITA creates a statutory presumption that software purchases are a license, rather than a sale of goods.[468]

[2] Hybrid or Mixed Transactions

Computer transactions may be broadly classified into "four primary categories: sales of goods, licenses of technology, lease agreements and service."[469] Typically sold in a bundled transaction, a computer system consists of hardware[470] and software. Hardware may itself include software components.[471] Purchasing a computer system may also involve services such as initial installation or continuing technical support.

The sale of a computer system may potentially be governed by Articles 2, 2A, and UCITA. Article 2 applies to the sale of hardware, Article 2A to the leasing of computer equipment, and UCITA to software loaded into the computer system. UCITA applies to the entire transaction as long as the "computer information . . . is the primary subject matter."[472] The primary subject matter test is a hybrid between the predominant purpose test and the gravaman of the action tests developed under sales law.

---

[465] UCITA § 103(d)(5).

[466] UCC § R2-103(f).

[467] *Id.*

[468] Amid Criticism, Virginia Delegates Pass Amendment to Controversial Software Law 2001, Electronic Commerce & Law Report (BNA) 151 (Feb. 16, 2001).

[469] Raymond T. Nimmer, The Law of Computer Technology: Rights, Licenses and Liabilities (2d ed., 1992) ¶ 6.01, at 6-3.

[470] *Computer hardware* generally includes the central processing unit (CPU); printed circuit boards, chips, and electronic circuitry; color monitor; keyboard; disk drives, including an internal hard disk, floppy disk, and CD-ROM drives; network card or modem; power source; and ports to connect the computer to outside devices. Hardware also includes peripheral devices, such as a printer, faxphone, scanner, and external disk drives. The CPU is the "brain" of the computer, the logic and control section that executes the binary instructions encoded in software that controls the other parts of the computer. The term *CPU* is often used more generally to refer to the box that contains the CPU, circuit boards, internal drives, and ports.

[471] "Much 'hardware' today is often made up of both hardware and software components. A hard drive most likely contains a microprocessor with some 'firmware' code in it." Robert F. Bodi, Patent Nonsense—Firmware, Software, Hardware, Nowhere, posting to CYBERIA-l@LISTSERV.AOL. COM (Law and Policy of Computer Communication), June 13, 2000.

[472] UCITA § 103(b)(2).

The predominant factor test will examine whether an underlying transaction is primarily a computer information transaction or a common law service. If the underlying transaction is predominantly the sale of goods, Article 2 applies. If the service aspect predominates, the common law applies. The question of whether UCITA applies focuses on whether computer information (that is, software) or goods (that is, hardware) predominate in a mixed or hybrid contract.[473]

In a mixed transaction, in which both goods and computer information are transferred, UCITA applies to computer information. If you purchase a computer with a Pentium III processor from Gateway, Dell, or Compaq, it will be loaded with software such as Windows 2000. A computer system may consist of hundreds of operating systems on the hard drive; the same operating system may run different languages on one personal computer. The software application programs will be covered by UCITA. While computer hardware purchases are covered by Article 2, leased hardware is covered by Article 2A. In addition, state and federal consumer protection laws as well as common law and equitable principles supplement a computer information contract. The gravamen test in mixed or hybrid transactions focuses on the source of a complaint. In a computer contract, it is the source of the problem—hardware or software. If the hardware is defective, Article 2 or Article 2A applies, depending on whether it is sold or leased. In contrast, if the software is defective or fails to perform to specifications, UCITA applies.

[3] Key Definitions

Part I of UCITA deals with definitions and preliminary concerns. Section 102 defines key terms such as access contracts, attribution procedures, authentication, computer information, electronic agents, electronic events, electronic messages, mass-market licenses, receipt, and record. An electronic agent includes a computer program but is not limited to that technology. To qualify as an electronic agent, the automated system must have been selected, programmed, or otherwise used in a way that binds the parties. In automated transactions, an individual does not deal with another individual but with one or more electronic agents that represent both parties. The legal relationship between the person and the automated agent is not fully equivalent to common law agency, but takes into account that the "agent" is not a human actor.[474] Parties who employ electronic agents are ordinarily bound by the results of their operations.[475]

---

[473] *Id.* § 103(b)(2); cf. UCITA § 103, cmt. 4(b)(2) (describing UCITA's approach to mixed transactions as a "gravamen test").

[474] *Id.* §§ 206, 215; *see also* § 102(27).

[475] "Electronic agent means a computer program or electronic or other automated means, used independently to initiate an action or to respond to electronic messages or performances, on the person's behalf without review or action by an individual at the time of the action or response to the message or performance." *Id.* § 102(27).

[4] Choice of Law and Forum

[a] *Choice of Law*

UCITA adopts a choice of law rule similar to the "most significant relationship" test of the Restatement (Second) of Conflicts of Law.[476] Courts will apply the law of the jurisdiction that has the most points of contact with the contractual relationship. The parties may choose the applicable law rather than leave the matter to the courts.[477] For license agreements with consumers, UCITA limits choice of law to avoid an inconvenient forum. A choice of law is unenforceable "to the extent it would vary a rule that may not be varied by agreement under the law of the jurisdiction whose law would apply."[478] UCITA places limits on choice of law for consumer contracts in § 109, unlike the UCC, which has no special consumer limitations.

[b] *Choice of Forum*

The rise of the Internet raises difficult issues as to whether foreign judgments should be enforced where the parties have chosen the forum. Courts will often defer to foreign judgments under the doctrine of comity, ruling that final judgment between the parties in a foreign state will be given full faith and credit unless the judgment violates U.S. law or public policy. However, the comity doctrine may be trumped if a foreign judgment contradicts laws and policies of the United States. A California federal court, for instance, refused to enforce a French court's order restraining Yahoo! because the foreign judgment contravened the First Amendment.[479]

American companies should include clauses in their contracts to preordain choice of law and forum in the event of a dispute. In the absence of an agreement, the court, rather than the parties, determines the applicable law and forum. Courts vary significantly in their choice of law, and foreign countries frequently have very different rules. New York's choice-of-law rule for contracts evaluates the "center of gravity" or "grouping of contacts," with the purpose of establishing which state has the most significant relationship to the transaction and the parties.[480]

In *Williams v. America Online, Inc.*,[481] a Massachusetts federal court refused to enforce the forum selection clause included in AOL's Terms of Service (TOS) agreement. The plaintiffs, who had installed AOL version 5.0 software on their computers, alleged that the installation caused unauthorized changes in the configuration of their computers, making it impossible to access non-AOL Internet

---

[476] *Id.* § 109, cmt. 4.

[477] *Id.* § 109(a) (noting that UCITA enforces agreed choice of law).

[478] *Id.*

[479] *See, e.g.*, Yahoo, Inc. v. La Ligue Contre Le Racisme et L'Antisemitisme, 169 F. Supp. 2d 1181 (N.D. Cal. 2001) (finding that the freedom of speech clause of the First Amendment of the U.S. Constitution would preclude the court's enforcing the French court's order and imposing penalties associated therewith).

[480] Specht v. Netscape Communications Corp., 150 F. Supp. 2d 585 (S.D.N.Y. 2001).

[481] 2001 WL 135825 (Mass. Super. Ct. Feb. 8, 2001).

service. The court found that the alleged injury occurred prior to the plaintiff's being bound to AOL's TOS; consequently, the plaintiffs' claim was not subject to the choice-of-forum clause. The court observed that there were public policy reasons for not requiring Massachusetts consumers to litigate their claim in AOL's forum in Virginia.

In *Westendorf v. Gateway 2000, Inc.*,[482] a Delaware court held that the plaintiff was bound to a shrinkwrap agreement and was bound in her contract with Gateway by retaining the computer for 30 days. The agreement, which shipped with the computer, stated that the user would be bound by the terms of the agreement by not objecting or taking action within a certain time period. The court held that even though the plaintiff, having received the computer as a gift, was a third-party beneficiary, she was bound by Gateway's choice-of-forum clause that specified that disputes were decided by arbitration. A Kansas court refused to enforce an identical shrinkwrap agreement in *Klocek v. Gateway, Inc.*[483]

Choice of forum agreements may be found in a variety of online contracts, including license agreements, trading partner agreements, or web site development agreements. The UCITA Reporter notes that by 1999 more than 100 decisions dealt with Internet personal jurisdiction:

> The decisions reveal an uncertainty about when doing business on the Internet exposes a party to jurisdiction in all States and all countries. The uncertainty affects both large and small enterprises, but [it] has greater impact on small enterprises that are and will continue to be the lifeblood of electronic commerce. Choice of forum terms allow parties to control this issue and the risk or costs it creates. This section allows the agreement to govern, but adds restrictions based on fundamental public policy considerations.[484]

UCITA provides default rules if the parties do not specify choice-of-law governing their license agreements. Similarly, the parties have the discretion to specify an exclusive judicial forum under § 110 of UCITA. Choice of forum clauses are generally enforceable.[485] In addition, an agreement must specify that the forum is "exclusive" to be enforceable.[486]

---

[482] 2000 Del. Ch. LEXIS 54 (Del. Ch. Ct. Mar. 16, 2000).

[483] U.S. Dist. LEXIS 9896 (D. Kan. June 16, 2000) (holding that Gateway's shrinkwrap agreement sent inside the packaging of a computer purchased by the plaintiff did not create a binding contract under Kansas or Missouri law).

[484] *Id.*

[485] Section 110(a) of UCITA enforces choice of forum clauses unless "unreasonable and unjust." Section 110(a) refers to judicial forums rather than arbitration. Arbitration clauses in mass-market licenses are generally enforced. *See, e.g.,* Lieschke v. RealNetworks, Inc., 2000 U.S. Dist. LEXIS 1683 (N.D. Ill. 2000) (finding that clause in a licensing agreement bound the parties to settle their disputes through arbitration); Westendorf v. Gateway 2000, Inc., 2000 Del. Ch. LEXIS 54 (Del. Ch. Ct., March 16, 2000); Levy v. Gateway 2000, Inc., 1997 WL 823611 (N.Y. Sup. Ct., Aug. 12, 1997). *Cf.* Klocek v. Gateway, Inc., 104 F. Supp. 2d 1332 (D. Kan. 2000) (holding that computer manufacturer did not provide sufficient evidence to support finding that plaintiff agreed to arbitration clause contained in its standard terms mailed inside the computer box).

[486] *Id.*

[c] Venue

Because posting something on a web site allows anyone in the world to read it, e-commerce companies run the risk of global exposure to jurisdiction if they are regarded as purposely availing themselves of the benefits of doing business in another place.

Facing the dilemma of broad jurisdictional exposure of e-commerce companies and the constitutional requirement of minimum contacts to subject a company to personal jurisdiction in a particular state, courts created a so-called sliding scale test. Under this test, if the company created a passive, informational web site that is merely accessible from the plaintiff's jurisdiction, courts usually find that the company is not subject to personal jurisdiction.[487] On the other hand, if the company's web site is more than passive, courts have to analyze the nature and extent of the company's activities with the focus on whether the company purposely directed, targeted, or availed itself of the forum in which jurisdiction is sought.[488] If the company clearly conducts business in a foreign jurisdiction using its web site, courts are likely to find a broad jurisdictional exposure.[489]

[D] UCITA's Licensing Rules

Software licensing evolved in the 1980s with the rise of the software industry. By 1992, sales of software were expanding at a rate of two to three times that

---

[487] Business & Tech. Group, Piper Marbury Rudnick & Wolfe LLP, E-Commerce: The Future Is Now 4 (2000); *see, e.g.*, Pheasant Run, Inc. v. Geoff Moyse, 1999 U.S. Dist. LEXIS 1087 (N.D. Ill. 1999) (no personal jurisdiction when web site contained defendant's address and phone number but did not enable Internet browsers to communicate directly with defendant); Wildfire Communications, Inc., v. Grapevine, Inc., 2001 U.S. Dist. LEXIS 18238 (D. Mass. 2001) (three web pages accessible from Massachusetts, a contract for the sale of a domain name with a Massachusetts company governed by Massachusetts law but not containing a forum-selection clause, and an unsuccessful solicitation of a Massachusetts company for an Internet advertisement were insufficient for personal jurisdiction in Massachusetts). *Accord* Blackburn v. Walker Oriental Rug Galleries, 999 F. Supp. 636 (D. Pa. 1998) (improper venue where web site merely contained defendant's advertisement); Amazon.com, Inc. v. Kalaydjian, 2001 U.S. Dist. LEXIS 4924 (W. D. Wash. 2001) (improper venue when defendant's web site was not sufficiently interactive to subject him to personal jurisdiction); Shapiro v. Santa Fe Gaming Corp., 1998 U.S. Dist. LEXIS 2488 (N.D. Ill. Feb. 26, 1998) (800 number and "passively informational" web site insufficient to establish "transacting business" in forum state).

[488] *See, e.g.*, TY Inc. v. Clark, 2000 U.S. Dist. LEXIS 383 (N.D. Ill. 2000) (holding that although defendants' web site was interactive, it simply allowed consumers to exchange information but did not clearly do business over the web site).

[489] *Id. See* Sulton v. Ashley, 2002 U.S. Dist. LEXIS 1270 (S.D.N.Y. 2002) (finding that operation of a web site in a forum state is sufficient to support personal jurisdiction); Inset Sys., Inc. v. Instruction Set, Inc., 937 F. Supp. 161 (D. Conn. 1996) (holding that by continuous advertisement through the operation of a web site in the state, defendant availed itself of the privilege of conducting business in this state and was therefore subject to personal jurisdiction).

of sales of hardware.[490] Licensing is a contract to use computer software or other copyrighted information. Software is licensed, not sold, to circumvent the Copyright Act's "first sale" doctrine, which permits the owner of a particular copy to sell or otherwise dispose of that copy.

If a software developer sold the first copy of its software, it would, in many cases, be unable to realize its investment. The price of a single copy of mass-market software will not begin to reflect the thousands of hours of programming or software engineering and the other expenses of producing the first copy. When software is copied, it is not used up in the same sense as are tangible goods, such as tons of iron ore, bushels of grain, or yards of lumber. Copies of software may be made for negligible or no cost, as is the case for information products downloaded from a web site. The ease of copying or downloading software is the principal difference between transfers of information and sales of goods.

Software contracts, access contacts, multimedia contracts, and a multitude of other online contracts are structured as license agreements rather than as sales to avoid the first sale doctrine. A license is permission to use information under restricted conditions, such as the software, in only one single-user computer. A sale, in contrast, involves the passage of title to goods for a price. A license may be based on the number of copies licensed, the method of distribution, the type of end user, or the form of a license agreement. Mass-market license agreements, for example, will state: "opening this package indicates your acceptance of these terms and conditions."

Customized software, in contrast, is tailored to the user and the terms are generally negotiated. A software developer will typically restrict use through site or time limitations. License agreements place restrictions on use not typically found in the sale or lease of goods. A license, in contrast, is frequently personal, nontransferable, and nonassignable; such restrictions are generally not made on sold or leased goods. A LexisNexis™ license, for example, is a license to electronically display, print, and download copyrighted materials from its databases. Many license agreements, including those used by WESTLAW and LexisNexis™, provide that the agreement may not be transferred or used by more than one person and that it is subject to a number of terms.

Licensing is the primary legal tool for transferring value and information in a dot-com business. SPC's expansion of licensing from its web site has the potential of driving its Internet-based business. Gateway, for example, in selling systems, states in its license: "By keeping your Gateway 2000 computer system beyond five (5) days after the date of delivery, you accept these Terms and Conditions."[491] With Article 2, title to goods passes when the buyer accepts and pays in

---

[490] Carolyn Van Brussel, Mobile PCs "'90s Their Decade," Speaker Claims, Computing Canada 14 (June 22, 1992).

[491] Software contracts, access contacts, multimedia contracts, and a host of online contracts are structured as licenses rather than as sales to avoid the "first sale" doctrine of Copyright Law. A license is permission to use software, databases, intellectual property, or other information. A license may be based on the number of copies licensed, the method of distribution, the type of end user, or

accordance with the contract. No title passes with the licensing of software. Location and use restrictions are necessary if software developers are to realize their investment in developing intangible information assets.[492]

Choice of law is a critically important factor in structuring mass-market license agreements in the Internet economy. A number of state courts have refused to enforce one-sided software licenses.[493] In the early 1990s, a number of state courts ruled that mass-market licenses shipped with computer software were not enforceable because they were not part of the parties' agreement.[494] The Seventh Circuit has broadly enforced mass-market licenses even when the terms were presented after the licensee paid for the software.[495] The Seventh Circuit has also enforced arbitration clauses in mass-market licenses.[496] Maryland and Virginia have enacted UCITA, which broadly legitimates mass-market licenses. Licensors will find it desirable to apply the law of a jurisdiction that has enacted UCITA.

[E] Policing Mass-Market Licenses

UCITA provides a legal infrastructure for mass-market licenses, including access contracts, terms of service agreements, clickwrap agreements, shrinkwrap agreements, and web site user agreements. UCITA's contracting rules apply to the entire transaction if information is the predominant purpose of the transaction. UCITA favors a general freedom of contract, which is moderated by doctrines such as unconscionability, failure of essential purpose, and supplemental consumer protection. UCITA makes it clear that adopting states are free to impose mandatory terms protecting consumers.[497] Adopting states may extend consumer protections applicable to the sale of goods to retail software licenses.

---

the form of a license agreement. Klocek v. Gateway, Inc., 104 F. Supp. 2d 1332, 1335 (D. Kan. 2000). Gateway appears to have shortened the period for acceptance. *See* § 6.03[G][1].

[492] A contract for the sale of goods is one in which a seller agrees to transfer goods that conform to the contract in exchange for valuable consideration. UCC § 2-301 (1999).

[493] *See, e.g.,* Klocek v. Gateway, Inc., 104 F. Supp. 2d 1332 (D. Kan. 2000) (finding issue of fact as to whether mass-market licensee agreed to arbitration clause in adhesive agreement); i.Lan Sys., Inc. v. Netscout Serv. Level Corp., Civ. Act. No. 00-11489-WGY (D. Mass. 2002) (upholding the validity of a license agreement on the ground that the plaintiff explicitly consented to the terms of the agreement by clicking on the "I Agree" button. The court concluded that although the plaintiff had purchased the software before he clicked on the "I Agree" button, he implicitly consented to recognize the existence of the contract under UCC § 2-204.).

[494] *See, e.g.,* Arizona Retail Systems, Inc., v. Software Link, Inc., 831 F. Supp. 759 (D. Ariz. 1993) (ruling that shrinkwrap license agreement shipped with computer software was not part of the agreement); Specht v. Netscape Communications Corp., 150 F. Supp. 2d 585 (S.D.N.Y. 2001) (holding that by downloading software the plaintiff did not agree to be bound by the terms of license agreement, where a link to such terms was on the portion of the web page that appeared on the user's screen when the downloading was complete).

[495] ProCD v. Zeidenberg, 86 F.3d 1447 (7th Cir. 1996).

[496] Hill v. Gateway, Inc., 105 F.3d 1147 (7th Cir. 1997).

[497] UCITA § 104(1).

[1] **Procedural Protection for Licensees**

UCITA broadly validates mass-market licenses as long as "the party agrees to the license, such as by manifesting assent, before or during the party's initial performance or use of or access to the information."[498] The concept of manifesting assent is based on an objective standard rather than a subjective "meeting of the minds." A minimally adequate objective manifestation of assent is an opportunity to review the record, coupled with an affirmative act that indicates assent. Nevertheless, mass-market licenses are a useful legal invention. The alternative to mass-market licensing would be to retain an attorney to negotiate the terms. Negotiated mass-market license agreements are not cost-efficient. One of the difficult policy issues a company must decide is what affirmative conduct constitutes assent. In a paper-based contract, a signature establishes the manifestation of assent.

UCITA permits the manifestation of assent to be fulfilled by an affirmative act such as clicking a display button labeled "I accept the terms of this agreement" or something similar. A licensor must give the licensee a right to a refund if the licensee has not had an opportunity to review the terms and to manifest assent prior to a requirement to pay.[499]

UCITA rejects the doctrine of acceptance by silence for standard-form licenses. Section 112, for example, binds a licensee to the terms of a shrinkwrap or clickwrap agreement as long as the party manifests assent to the terms. Mass-market contracts are enforced if two conditions are met: (1) the user has an opportunity to review the terms of the license and (2) the user manifests assent after having an opportunity to review the terms. UCITA also validates clickwrap agreements requiring that the party had an opportunity to review terms before assenting. The licensor can create a "safe harbor" proving manifestation of assent with a built-in double click requiring the user to reaffirm assent.

Simply clicking an "I accept" text or icon may accomplish the manifestation of assent. A growing number of web site vendors use a "double click" method, which asks customers whether they are certain that they accept the terms of the license. It is quite likely that the reasonable visitor will click through these icons without reading the license agreement prior to payment. UCITA provides mass-market licensees with a right to return if they have no opportunity to review a mass-market license or a copy of it before becoming obligated to pay.[500] A party adopts the terms of a shrinkwrap or clickwrap license if the customer has an opportunity to review the terms and to manifest assent by some affirmative act. Software licenses typically limit all damages and provide an exclusive remedy. Some software licenses prohibit reverse engineering or limit permissible uses.

---

[498] *Id.* § 209.

[499] *Id.* § 209(b).

[500] *Id.* § 209(c).

[2] Policing Unconscionable License Agreements

UCITA adopts the concept of unconscionability from Article 2 that gives courts the power to strike down unconscionable contracts or terms. A software license with inconspicuous terms or a hidden webwrap agreement may be found unconscionable if coupled with unfair or onerous terms.[501] The basic test is whether the license agreement or term should be invalidated because it is "so one-sided as to be unconscionable under the circumstances existing at the time of the making of the contract."[502] The court, in its discretion, will also consider whether the licensee is a consumer and whether deception occurred through surprising terms.

A court has a wide arsenal of remedies when finding evidence of an unfair bargaining process and unfair terms. "A court, in its discretion, may refuse to enforce the contract as a whole if it is permeated by the unconscionability, or it may strike any single term or group of terms" in an online contract or license agreement.[503] A court has the power to police "to enforce the contract, enforce the remainder of the contract without the unconscionable term, or it may so limit the application of any unconscionable term as to avoid any unconscionable result."[504]

[3] Failure of Essential Purpose

An online business is entitled to limit warranties as well as remedies. Licensors should have a minimum adequate remedy if the exclusive remedy fails of its essential purpose, resulting in a right without a remedy. "Section 2-719(2) raises two essential questions: (1) When does an exclusive or limited remedy fail of its essential purpose? and (2) When a remedy fails, what remedies are available to the buyer?"[505] Courts will not enforce a remedy for an adhesive software license that "fails of its essential purpose." If a court finds a remedy has failed of its essential purpose, aggrieved consumers have the full panoply of UCITA remedies at their disposal.

---

[501] The issue of unconscionability is a question of law and must be decided by the trial judge rather than by the jury.

[502] Maxwell v. Fidelity Fin. Serv., Inc., 184 Ariz. 82, 88, 907 P.2d 51, 57 (1995).

[503] Defendants are given an opportunity to present evidence of the circumstances existing at the time of the making of the license agreement or other online contract:

> If it is claimed or appears to the court that a contract or any term thereof may be unconscionable, the parties must be afforded a reasonable opportunity to present evidence as to its commercial setting, purpose, and effect to aid the court in making the determination.

UCITA § 111(b).

[504] UCITA § 111. See Brower v. Gateway 2000, Inc., 1998 N.Y. App. Div. LEXIS 8872 (1st Dept. N.Y. 1998) (finding unconscionable a clause in the contract that required the consumer to pay $4,000 fee, of which $2,000 was nonrefundable, even if the consumer prevailed).

[505] UCC § 2-719.

White and Summers observe that "it is hard to find any provision in Article 2 that has been more successfully used by aggrieved buyers in the last 25 years than Section 2-719(2)."[506] Official Comment 1 to 2-719 states that the statutory purpose of the failure of essential purpose doctrine:

> [I]t is of the very essence of a sales contract that at least minimum adequate remedies be available. If the parties intend to conclude a contract for sale within this Article they must accept the legal consequence that that there be at least a fair quantum of remedy for breach of the obligations or duties outlined in the contract.[507]

Revised Article 2 also retains the doctrine of "failure of essential purpose."[508] Section 803 provides that if an exclusive or limited remedy "fails of its essential purpose, the aggrieved party may pursue other remedies under [UCITA]."[509] The commercial reality is that mass-market license agreements are adhesive contracts offered on a "take it or leave it" basis.

UCITA's adoption of the failure of essential purpose doctrine moderates the harsh effects of the licensor who attempts to offer only a sole and exclusive remedy disclaiming all remedies. Article 2 divides remedies into buyer's and seller's remedies, whereas UCITA does not differentiate remedies for licensors and licensees. UCITA's adoption of the failure of essential purpose doctrine of Article 2 moderates the harsh effects of licensors who offer a worthless remedy.[510] If circumstances cause an exclusive or limited remedy to fail of its essential purpose, a licensee has access to all UCITA warranties and remedies.[511]

When electronic agents do unexpected things, a possibility arises that "common law concepts of mistake may supplement UCITA §§ 206 and 217. In addition, the unconscionability doctrine may invalidate a term caused by breakdowns in the automated contracting processes."[512] The Official Comment to § 2-719 explains that the purpose of the failure of the essential purpose rule is to guarantee buyers a minimum adequate remedy if the sole or exclusive remedy fails.

---

[506] James J. White and Robert S. Summers, Uniform Commercial Code § 12-10, at 449 (5th ed., 1999).

[507] UCC § 2-719, cmt. 1.

[508] Early drafts of UCITA did not incorporate Article 2's doctrine of "failure of essential purpose." Revised Article 2 adopts the rule that the buyer has a minimum adequate remedy if the sole or exclusive remedy fails. *See* UCC Revised Article 2: Sales § 2-719, at 107 (Reporter's Interim Draft, Nov. 1999). Section 2-719(b) of Revised Article 2 provides:

> (b) Where circumstances cause an exclusive or limited remedy to fail of its essential purpose in a contract other than a consumer contract, remedy may be had as provided in this Act. However, an agreement expressly providing that consequential damages are excluded is enforceable to the extent permitted under subsection d.

[509] UCITA § 803(b).

[510] UCC § 2-719(2).

[511] UCITA § 804.

[512] UCITA § 111, cmt. 3.

Section 105(c) of UCITA states that a term of a contract is displaced by consumer protection statutes or administrative rules designed to protect consumers. However, consumer advocates argue that states have not yet extended consumer protection to "licenses in computer information."[513] States may explicitly extend consumer protection to encompass software licenses, as Virginia did when it enacted UCITA in 1999.[514]

[F]   Electronic Contracting Rules

UCITA provides contracting rules that will permit the further expansion of electronic commerce. UCITA's approach is to favor open standards for e-commerce that are technologically neutral: The advent of the Internet as a commercial information resource has highlighted the importance of "electronic commerce," including electronic contracting issues. UCITA has been one source of principles for development of state law rules on contract aspects of electronic commerce. These rules are coordinated with the Uniform Electronic Transactions Act (UETA). However, they go beyond the purely procedural rules in that Act and provide a general contract law framework for electronic transactions involving computer information, where a contract can be formed and performed electronically.[515]

UCITA, like Article 2, does not specifically define offer, acceptance, or consideration, but instead incorporates common law definitions. It provides legal rules for the use of electronic agents in making and performing contracts and also validates "automated transactions," which are contracts formed or performed by electronic messaging.[516]

Almost one-half of all U.S. states have already adopted legislation authorizing electronic equivalents to writing requirements. UCITA, along with UETA and proposed revisions of Article 2 and Article 2A, establishes a uniform state law principle that allows electronic "authentication" as a form of signature and recognizes the equivalence of electronic "records" and paper writings. The second issue deals with how one establishes the terms of an electronic contract. UETA does not generally deal with this issue; UCITA builds on two concepts to set out a framework for contracting and establishing contract terms.

Electronic contracts, by their very nature, are dynamic and often multilayered transactions. With a layered contract, agreement to a contract may not occur at a single point in time. Under webwrap contracts, a party will manifest assent to different terms at different points in time. Section 112 provides that a manifestation of assent creates a binding contract if the party had reason to know that its acts

---

[513] William Denney, Letter to the Editor, UCITA and Consumers, Computerworld, Dec. 3, 2001, at 25.

[514] *Id.*

[515] UCITA Prefatory Note (NCCUSL Annual Meeting Draft, July 2000).

[516] *Id.* §§ 201(c)(1), 201(c)(2), 201(d).

constituted assent.[517] An opportunity to review is a predicate for manifesting assent.

UCITA § 202 follows Article 2 of the UCC in providing liberal contract formation rules for cyberspace transactions and other computer information contracts. *Signed* is defined to mean a mark made with the intent to authenticate, which may be broad enough to include clickwrap agreements. The general rules for "offer and acceptance" are covered by § 203 of UCITA. Section 204 governs the problem of acceptance with varying terms. Conditional offer or acceptance is covered by § 205. The use of electronic agents for offer and acceptance is governed by § 206.

UCITA adapts the concept of manifestation of assent to contract terms to apply to Internet or online contracts.[518] UCITA provides the legal infrastructure for a wide range of electronic contracts. As with Articles 2 and 2A, an Internet or online contract may be enforced, despite having open terms.

[1]   Statute of Frauds in Cyberspace

The Statute of Frauds is a statutory requirement that certain classes of contracts be evidenced by a writing to be enforceable. Originally enacted in England in 1677, the statute was intended to reduce the risks of fraud and false testimony.[519] In this country, "virtually all states have enacted their own version of the statute,"[520] and a less restrictive version of the statute has been incorporated in the Uniform Commercial Code.[521] The United States stands alone in adopting the Statute of Frauds for sales, leasing, and licensing transactions of a threshold amount.[522]

UCITA updates the Statute of Frauds for online contracts by treating a "record" as a functional equivalent of "pen-and-paper" signatures. A *record* "means information that is inscribed on a tangible medium or that is stored in an electronic or other medium and is retrievable in perceivable form."[523]

UCITA is consistent with the Federal E-Signature Act in its treatment of the electronic record as the functional equivalent of writing.[524] UCITA provides essential legal infrastructure for many different forms of electronic contracts. Section 201 of UCITA requires an authenticated record for enforcing license agreements

---

[517] *Id.* § 112.

[518] UCITA's Reporter adapted the concept of manifestation of assent from the Restatement (Second) of Contracts.

[519] E. Allan Farnsworth, Contracts § 6.1 (2d ed., 1990).

[520] *Id.*

[521] *See, e.g.,* UCC § 2-201 ("a contract for the sale of goods for the price of $500 or more is not enforceable by way of action or defense unless there is some writing sufficient to indicate that a contract for sale has been made between the parties and signed by the party against whom enforcement is sought").

[522] *See* UCC §§ 2-201, 2A-201; UCITA § 201.

[523] UCITA § 102(55).

[524] Section 107(d) binds a person who uses electronic agents, "even if no individual was aware of or reviewed the agent's operations or the results of the operation." *Id.* § 107(d); *see* Electronic Signatures in Global and National Commerce Act (effective Oct. 1, 2000).

that are $5,000 or greater and the license is for more than a year.[525] As with Articles 2 and 2A, several exceptions apply to the writing requirement: for example, a license agreement is enforceable after completed or partial performance, an admission in court that a contract exists, or a merchant licensor's failure to answer a confirming record from another merchant.[526]

[G]   Warranties

UCITA adopts the concepts and methods of warranties of authority and quality from Articles 2 and 2A of the UCC. UCITA warranties are updated to adapt to the online contracting world. Warranties of quality consist of express and implied warranties. UCITA divides warranties into two broad categories: warranties of noninfringement and warranties of performance, which parallels the approach to warranties in Article 2 and 2A.

[1]   Express and Implied

UCITA permits licensors to contractually exclude all implied warranties provided that the language is clear, unambiguous, and conspicuous; the limitations are not unconscionable; and the license agreement does not violate fundamental public policies. UCITA divides warranties into two types: warranties of authority (or noninfringement) and performance-based warranties of quality.

Section 401 is the chief warranty that the licensor delivered free of infringing computer information. Merchant licensors warrant that information is delivered free of claims of intellectual property infringement but does not apply to patent licenses. The warranty of noninfringement is functionally equivalent to the warranty of title in Article 2.[527] As with Article 2, there are special merchant rules imposing a higher duty on professional licensors.[528] A merchant licensor warrants that information is delivered free of claims of infringement or misappropriation.[529] Section 401(b)(2) notes that exclusive license agreements are limited by fair use, compulsory licenses, and other recognized limits to exclusivity.[530]

UCITA adapts to information transfers the warranty of quiet possession, which originated in transactions in real property followed in Article 2A, but not Article 2, of the UCC. The essence of the quiet enjoyment warranty is the right of a licensee to exercise contractual rights for the duration of the license without interference by a licensor or a third party. The quiet enjoyment warranty applies only to interference caused by acts or omissions of the licensors. The quiet enjoyment

---

[525] *Id.* § 201(a).

[526] *Id.* §§ 201(c)(1), 201(c)(2), 201(c)(2)(d).

[527] UCC § 2-312's warranty of title is adapted to licensing where title does not pass to the licensee. Special rules are devised for exclusive licenses and the interference warranty not found in Article 2.

[528] *Merchant/licensors* are those who "regularly deal in information of the kind." UCITA § 401(a) (2000).

[529] *Id.*

[530] *Id.* § 401(b)(2)(B).

warranty that the licensor will not interfere with licensee's enjoyment of its interest lasts for the duration of the license agreement.[531] Licensees receive "peace of mind" that they are not purchasing an intellectual property lawsuit along with software. UCITA's noninfringement authority imposes a strict liability standard if the software infringes title or intellectual property rights of others.

[2]   Warranties of Quality

[a]   *Express Warranties*

UCITA's express warranty provisions for computer information transactions are substantially similar to those of UCC § 2-313. Affirmations of fact made by the licensor about computer software or information are express warranties to the extent that they form the "basis of the bargain." Express warranties under UCITA are created by licensors in banner advertisements, sales literature, and advertisements.[532] Web site promotional materials, product descriptions, samples, or advertisements may create e-commerce warranties.

In its 2001 Report, the UCITA Standby Committee proposed to amend § 402(a)(3) requiring that any sample that was part of a final product that was made a part of the bargain would create an express warranty that the performance of the information conformed to the performance of the sample.[533] The Committee deleted the requirement of the original text of UCITA that the final product would "reasonably" conform to the performance of the sample as redundant.[534]

1. How are express warranties created?	"Affirmation of fact" made by the licensor to its licensee in any manner including online brochures, advertising, and sales literature posted on a web site.[535]
2. What is the test for an express warranty?	Does the affirmation of fact relate to information and become "basis of the bargain" or is it merely seller's talk?[536]
3. What words are critical to creating express warranties?	"It is not necessary to use formal words, such as 'warrant' or 'guarantee' or state a specific intention to make a warranty."[537]
4. What web site activity creates express warranties?	(1) Description of information in virtual catalogs; (2) samples, models, or demonstration of software or other products; (3) any banner advertisement, description, sample, or demonstration if it goes to the basis of the bargain. Technical specifications of computer systems.

---

[531] *Id.* § 401(b)(1).

[532] *Id.* § 402.

[533] UCITA Standby Committee Report § 402(a)(3) (Dec. 17, 2001).

[534] *Id.*

[535] UCITA § 402(a)(1).

[536] *Id.* § 402(a)(2).

[537] *Id.* § 402(b).

| 5. What is the difference between express warranties and puffery? | *Puffery* is a mere statement of opinion that does not form an express warranty. Express warranties are actionable representations.[538] |

[b] Implied Warranty of Merchantability

Implied warranties of quality for computer information extend the concept of the implied warranty of merchantability of UCC Article 2 to computer information transactions. UCITA § 403 extends Article 2's merchantability warranty to cyberspace. Computer programs must be fit for their ordinary purpose. UCITA's implied warranty is that "the computer program is fit for the ordinary purposes for which such computer programs are used."[539] A computer program need not be the most efficient, but it must meet general industry standards for performance. A distributor also receives the warranty that information is adequately packaged and labeled and that the copies are "of even kind, quality, and quantity within each unit."[540]

Standard	*Description*
1. Is the computer software fit for its ordinary purpose?	A computer program is fit for the ordinary purpose for which such computer programs are used.[541]
2. Is the program adequately packaged and labeled?	The redistribution warranty is that "the program is adequately packaged and labeled as the agreement requires."[542]
3. Are the copies of computer software within the variations permitted in the agreement?	"[I]n the case of multiple copies, the copies are within the variations permitted by the agreement, of even kind, quality, and quantity, within each unit and among all units involved."[543]
4. Do computer programs conform to labels or descriptions?	"[T]he program conforms to the promises or affirmations of fact made on the container or label."[544]
5. Are there any implied warranties from the parties' course of dealing or from the software industry?	"Unless disclaimed or modified, other implied warranties may arise from course of dealing or usage of trade."[545]
6. Are there any informational content warranties?	Section 403 does not create informational content warranties as to information content such as aesthetics, market appeal, accuracy, or subjective quality.[546]

---

[538] *Id.* § 402, cmt. 6.

[539] *Id.* § 403(a)(1).

[540] *Id.* § 403(a)(2) (B).

[541] *Id.* § 403(a)(1).

[542] *Id.* § 403(a)(2)(A).

[543] *Id.* § 403(a)(2)(B).

[544] *Id.* § 403(a)(3).

[545] *Id.* § 403(b).

[546] *Id.* § 403(c).

[c] Implied Warranty of System Integration

UCITA's implied warranty of system integration is the functional equivalent of the warranty in UCC § 2-312 of "fitness for a particular purpose." The systems integration warranty applies where the customer relies on the software licensor's expertise to make computer information suitable for a particular computer system.[547] SPC, for example could be making a systems integration warranty if a sales representative told a customer that its software would perform with a Windows 2000 platform. The licensor must know of "any particular purpose for which the computer information is required and that the licensee is relying on the licensor's skill or judgment to select, develop, or furnish suitable information."[548] If the transaction resembles a services contract, the warranty does not guarantee results.[549] The systems integration warranty is that the computer components will function as a system, but not necessarily as an optimal system.

[d] Warranties for Information Content

UCITA, unlike Article 2, devises an implied warranty for informational inaccuracies caused by a merchant's negligence.[550] This special warranty applies to merchant licensors or to transfers of information not performed with reasonable care. The warranty for informational content does not arise for published content or when the licensor is merely acting as an information transfer conduit without providing editorial services.[551] Section 404 is based on reasonable care, and this warranty may be disclaimed despite UCITA's general prohibition against disclaiming reasonableness and care.[552]

[e] Disclaiming and Limiting Liability

Just as does Article 2, UCITA permits the parties to disclaim or modify all implied warranties by words or conduct.[553] UCITA validates the universal practice of the software industry in offering software or other computer information on an "as is" basis, without warranties. The software industry universally disclaims all implied warranties. Microsoft, for example, disclaims all express or implied warranties for its software products. Microsoft expressly disclaims any warranty by using the following clause:

> THE SOFTWARE PRODUCT AND ANY RELATED DOCUMENTATION IS PROVIDED "AS IS" WITHOUT WARRANTY OF ANY KIND, EITHER EXPRESS OR IMPLIED, INCLUDING,

---

[547] *Id.* § 405.
[548] *Id.* § 405(a).
[549] *Id.* § 405(a)(2).
[550] *Id.* § 404.
[551] *Id.* § 404(b)(1)(2).
[552] *Id.* § 404(c).
[553] *Id.* § 406.

WITHOUT LIMITATION, THE IMPLIED WARRANTIES OF MERCHANTABILITY, FITNESS FOR A PARTICULAR PURPOSE, OR NON-INFRINGEMENT. THE ENTIRE RISK ARISING OUT OF USE OR PERFORMANCE OF THE SOFTWARE PRODUCT REMAINS WITH YOU.[554]

Content providers typically do not make warranties as to the adequacy or accuracy of information. LexisNexis™, a leading legal information company, and Read-Elsevier, its owner, make the following limited warranty:

NEITHER READ-ELSEVIER [NOR LEXISNEXIS™ OR ITS SOURCES] MAKE ANY WAR-RANTY, EXPRESS OR IMPLIED, AS TO ACCURACY, ADEQUACY, OR COMPLETENESS OF INFORMATION CONTAINED IN THE MATERIALS, WHICH ARE PROVIDED "AS-IS," WITHOUT WARRANTY AS TO MERCHANTABILITY, FITNESS FOR A PARTICULAR PUR-POSE OR USE, OR RESULTS. NEITHER READ-ELSEVIER NOR ANY SOURCES SHALL BE LIABLE FOR ANY ERRORS OR OMISSIONS NOR SHALL THEY BE LIABLE FOR ANY DAMAGES, WHETHER DIRECT OR INDIRECT, SPECIAL OR CONSEQUENTIAL, INCLUD-ING LOSS OF PROFITS, EVEN IF ADVISED OF THE POSSIBILITY. IN NO EVENT SHALL THE CUMULATIVE LIABILITY OF READ-ELSEVIER FOR ALL ACTIONS EXCEED THE AVERAGE MONTHLY FEE PAID BY SUBSCRIBER FOR ACCESS TO THE MATERIALS.[555]

The disclaimers in the above online contracts follow a methodology that closely parallels those of Article 2 and Article 2A of the UCC. As with Article 2, a written disclaimer of the implied warranty of merchantability must mention "'merchantability' or 'quality' or use words of similar import."[556] To disclaim the warranty of fitness, the exclusion must be by a written and conspicuous state-ment.[557] Disclaimers or limitations of liability under UCITA must be conspicu-ously displayed in a record. Although no particular form of language is necessary to disclaim UCITA warranties,[558] to disclaim or modify the warranty of accuracy the record "must mention accuracy or use words of similar import."[559]

UCITA disclaimers and liability limitations are subject to state and federal consumer law and common law and equitable doctrines such as the covenant of good faith and fair dealing and unconscionability. Many web sites will place a notice that they seek disclaimers "to the full extent permissible by applicable law."[560] Web site disclaimers may not alter consumer protection statutes, which

---

[554] Microsoft, Inc., End-User License Agreement for Microsoft Software, clause 8 (stating "limi-tation of liability").

[555] *See* LexisNexis, Terms of Service (visited Feb. 24, 2002), http://www.lexisnexis.com/terms/.

[556] UCITA § 406(b)(1)(A).

[557] *Id.* § 406(b)(1)(2).

[558] Language in the record should disclaim each warranty or use a phrase such as this "program is provided with all faults and the entire risk as to satisfactory quality, performance, accuracy, and effort is with the user." *Id.* § 406(b)(1)(3). *See also* UCC § 2-316(2) (noting that "language must mention merchantability and in case of a writing must be conspicuous, and to exclude or modify an implied warranty of a warranty of fitness the exclusion must be by a writing and conspicuous").

[559] UCITA § 406(b)(1)(B).

[560] In some states implied warranties are not disclaimable for consumer goods, which are defined as goods used for personal, household, or family purposes.

may preclude the disclaiming of implied warranties in consumer transactions.[561]

A UCITA contract may disclaim all liabilities with language such as that the information "is provided with all faults, and the entire risk as to satisfactory quality, performance, accuracy, and effort is with the user" or similar words.[562] Amazon.com, for example, follows UCITA's methodology in disclaiming damages of all kinds:

> THIS SITE IS PROVIDED BY AMAZON.COM ON AN "AS IS" BASIS. AMAZON.COM MAKES NO REPRESENTATIONS OR WARRANTIES OF ANY KIND, EXPRESS OR IMPLIED, AS TO THE OPERATION OF THE SITE OR THE INFORMATION, CONTENT, MATERIALS, OR PRODUCTS INCLUDED ON THIS SITE.
>
> TO THE FULL EXTENT PERMISSIBLE BY APPLICABLE LAW, AMAZON.COM DISCLAIMS ALL WARRANTIES, EXPRESS OR IMPLIED, INCLUDING, BUT NOT LIMITED TO, IMPLIED WARRANTIES OF MERCHANTABILITY AND FITNESS FOR A PARTICULAR PURPOSE. AMAZON.COM DOES NOT WARRANT THAT THIS SITE, ITS SERVERS, OR E-MAIL SENT FROM AMAZON.COM ARE FREE OF VIRUSES OR OTHER HARMFUL COMPONENTS. AMAZON.COM WILL NOT BE LIABLE FOR ANY DAMAGES OF ANY KIND ARISING FROM THE USE OF THIS SITE, INCLUDING, BUT NOT LIMITED TO DIRECT, INDIRECT, INCIDENTAL, PUNITIVE, AND CONSEQUENTIAL DAMAGES.[563]

[f]   *Specialized Computer Warranty Rules*

UCITA forges special rules for computer information warranties where the licensee reprograms or modifies computer software. Essentially, no warranties cover programs that the licensee modifies or alters.[564] Warranties "must be construed as consistent with each other."[565] Exact or technical specifications for computer information displace or supplant "general language of description."[566]

Samples displace general language of description and express warranties trump inconsistent implied warranties other than system integration warranties.[567] UCITA sets the rules for third-party beneficiaries of information-based warranties.[568] Warranties, in general, extend to end-users or those who will exercise information or informational rights. UCITA extends third-party beneficiary concepts to extend warranties to the licensee's immediate family or household.

---

[561] *See, e.g.*, Mass. Gen. Laws Ann. ch. 106, § 2-316A (2000) (prohibiting sellers from disclaiming the implied warranty of merchantability in consumer transactions including sales and services).

[562] UCITA § 406(b)(1)(3) (2000).

[563] *See* http://www.amazon.com/tg/browse/_/508088/107-7376736-2557358 (visited Apr. 21, 2002).

[564] *Id.* UCITA § 407.

[565] *Id.* § 408.

[566] *Id.* § 408(1).

[567] *Id.* § 408(2)-(3).

[568] *Id.* § 409.

[H] UCITA's Canons of Contract Construction

UCITA considers a license agreement to consist of the writing plus supplemental terms. Every UCITA contract consists of (1) express terms of the license agreement, (2) course of performance, (3) course of dealing, and (4) custom or usage of trade.[569] If the parties to a license agreement reduce the final expression of their agreement to a computer record, the parol evidence rule will exclude prior or contemporaneous agreements. UCITA's parol evidence rule substitutes the term *record* for a writing but is otherwise parallel to UCC § 2-202. Like Article 2, UCITA permits integrated writings to be supplemented by course of performance, course of dealing, and usage of trade.

Courts may also receive evidence of consistent additional terms, unless the record states that it is "a complete and exclusive statement of the terms of the agreement."[570] UCITA permits background terms—course of performance, course of dealing, and usage of trade—to supplement a final and exclusive record. The policy underlying UCITA's parol evidence rule is that it is the preservation of the integrity of a computer record that is a final expression of agreement between the parties.[571] Section 302 establishes a hierarchy of contract terms.[572]

As with § 2-209, UCITA contracts may be modified without "consideration." UCITA also provides a methodology for precluding modification or rescission except by an authenticated record.[573] Many license agreements are structured as rolling contracts. Section 304 provides that terms of a contract with successive performances apply to the whole.[574] Access contracts, for example, may change terms of performance by giving notice to the other party. UCITA follows the liberal philosophy of the UCC in permitting contracts to be formed even though the particulars of performance are open.[575]

Standardized gap-fillers play a key role in commercial law because Article 2 permits parties to form an enforceable sales contract even where open terms are present. The UCC provides a number of gap-filler provisions for sales contracts. UCITA follows the UCC in permitting performance with open terms. The default terms in UCITA are those that "are reasonable in light of the commercial circumstances existing at the time of agreement."[576] Article 2 forges specific gap-fillers for price, delivery in single or multiple lots, place of delivery, time provisions, and

---

[569] *Id.* § 301(1).

[570] *Id.* § 301(2).

[571] *Id.*

[572] Express terms supplant course of performance, course of dealing, and usage of trade. Course of performance supplants course of dealing and usage of trade. Course of dealing prevails over usage of trade, which is at the bottom of the hierarchy of terms. *Id.* § 302(a)(1)(2)(3).

[573] *Id.* § 303(b).

[574] *Id.* § 304(a).

[575] *Id.* § 305.

[576] *Id.* § 306.

other terms not settled by the parties.[577] UCITA provides gap-fillers for determining what rights are transferred by granting clauses,[578] the duration of a license,[579] and the default term for performing a contract to another's satisfaction.[580]

The 2001 Report of the UCITA Standby Committee proposes to delete the § 308 default rule concerning the duration of a contract.[581] Currently, § 308 is a gap-filler that addresses the problem when the parties do not specify a duration term. The Standby Committee recommends using the common law by using intellectual property as the template for determining the duration of licenses rather than § 308. This proposed reform will harmonize rules for transferring interests between federal intellectual property law and UCITA.

[I] Transfer of Interests and Rights

Part V of UCITA deemphasizes the role of title, because title does not pass in the typical license agreement.[582] Software is licensed, not sold: Transfer of a copy of software does not transfer informational rights because the licensor retains title and grants only a right to use information.[583]

UCITA supports the free assignability of licenses of information. A purchaser of software may sell or otherwise assign or transfer the rights to use the software unless the agreement otherwise provides. Software or other computer information may be freely assigned unless it "materially increases the burden or risk imposed on the other party" or otherwise materially affects performance.[584] UCITA permits licensors to inject anti-assignment clauses where a licensee cannot voluntarily or involuntarily assign its rights absent the licensor's consent. Part V of UCITA also sets forth the complex rules for financing arrangements for software.[585] UCITA validates contractual restrictions on transfer.

---

[577] Many of the UCC gap-fillers in § 2-305 to § 2-311 boil down to reasonable business practices, which is the same underlying philosophy as that of UCITA. UCITA, like Article 2, uses gap-fillers to fill in open terms. UCITA's gap-fillers provide general terms based upon reasonable business practices. UCITA §§ 306 to 308 apply unless the parties otherwise agree. Section 306, for example, provides a general interpretation rule for issues not covered by the license agreement. The general default rule is that the term be "reasonable in light of the commercial circumstances existing at the time of the agreement." *See* UCITA § 306.

[578] *Id.* § 307.

[579] *Id.* § 308.

[580] *Id.* § 309.

[581] *See* UCITA Standby Committee Report § 308 (Dec. 17, 2001).

[582] *Id.* § 502.

[583] *Id.* § 501.

[584] *Id.* § 503(1)(B).

[585] *Id.* §§ 507-511.

[J] Performance Standards

The performance of a sale contract usually begins with the seller's tender of conforming goods. Part VI of UCITA deals with the performance of computer information contracts and adopts the Article 2 concept of tender for cyberspace contracts. In Article 2, tender refers to the duty of the seller to make goods available to the buyer that conform to the contract specifications. In a sales contract, the buyer has the right to reject goods "if the goods or the tender of delivery fail in any respect to conform to the contract."[586] Article 2 follows a "perfect tender" rule that permits a buyer to reject goods if they fail to conform in any respect to the contract.[587] UCITA's concept of tender is that of a licensor transmitting a copy of software or otherwise enabling use or access to software, databases, or other information.[588] An online store may give a licensee access to downloadable software, which will constitute "tender." WESTLAW® or another online access provider will tender delivery by giving the subscriber an ID to enable use of databases. In contrast, the seller of goods tenders goods that conform to the agreement is entitled to payment; the buyer must accept and pay the contract price if the goods conform to the contract.[589]

UCITA adopts a "material breach" standard for nonmass market transactions departing from the perfect tender rule. An information contract may be cancelled if the licensor is unable to cure a material breach.[590] UCITA performance standards are concurrent: Substantial performance of one party is conditional on the substantial performance by the other party. UCITA defines acceptance as (1) express acceptance, (2) failure to reject, or (3) obtaining a substantial benefit from a copy, (4) comingling copies, or (5) acts inconsistent with the licensor's ownership of information.[591]

A buyer of goods has the right to inspect goods before payment or acceptance. A party receiving a copy of computer information has a similar right to inspect copies to ensure that they conform to the license agreement.[592] Under UCITA, a licensee must accept goods provided they conform to the agreement. Once a licensee accepts a tender of a copy, the licensor has a right to the contract price.[593] UCITA has special performance standards for access contracts, support agreements, and contracts involving publishers, dealers, and end users.[594]

---

[586] UCC § 2-601.

[587] *Id.*

[588] UCITA § 602 (describing enabling use as the electronic equivalent of tendering goods.

[589] UCC §§ 2-507, 2-511. *See also id.* § 2-301.

[590] UCITA's concept of "material breach" parallels the "fundamental breach" standard of Article 25 of the Convention on the International Sale of Goods and the "material breach" standard of the Restatement (Second) of Contracts § 241. Section 704(b) of UCITA retains the perfect tender rule for single delivery mass-market transactions. Cf. § 601(b)(1) (describing material breach standard of performance).

[591] UCITA § 609(a)(5).

[592] *Cf.* UCC § 2-513 and UCITA § 608.

[593] UCITA § 610.

[594] *See id.* §§ 611-613.

The risk of loss provision of Article 2 covers situations where neither party is responsible for the loss, destruction, or theft of goods.[595] UCITA adopts rules for risk of loss and excuses for nonperformance from Article 2. The risk of loss to a copy of information passes to the licensee upon receipt.[596] UCITA's risk of loss rules address the problem of copies lost or destroyed. UCITA shares the heritage of the UCC in rules for shipment and destination contracts. For shipment contracts, "the risk of loss passes to the licensee when the copy is duly delivered to the carrier."[597]

Destination contracts for information require a copy to be tendered at that destination.[598] UCITA adopts the excuse concepts of Article 2 to cyberspace, including impracticability.[599] UCITA adopts the common law doctrine of "frustration of purpose" to cyberspace and other online contracts. A license agreement is excused if there is an "occurrence of a contingency nonoccurrence of which was a basic assumption on which the contract was made."[600] UCITA has ground rules for the termination of a contract that pertain to use restrictions in license agreements.[601] Termination has the legal effect of ending the contract and discharging executory obligations for both parties.

[K] Tender, Acceptance, Rejection, and Revocation

Part VII of UCITA set forth the basic rules for tender, acceptance, rejection, revocation, and repudiation of computer information transactions. Even if a licensor tenders software with a substantial defect, it will have an opportunity to cure, which is borrowed from UCC § 2-508.[602] A licensee that accepts software or other computer information must notify the licensor of any breach. The failure to notify the other party of a breach has the legal consequence of waiver of all remedies for the breach.[603] The purpose of the notice requirement (as in UCC § 2-607(3)) is to give the licensor an opportunity to cure any defective performance.[604]

A licensee may refuse a defective tender of software, but the seller must have an opportunity to cure any problems. UCITA assumes that if the computer software or other information does not measure up to contract specifications, a right exists to refuse performance.[605] Even if a licensee rightfully rejects performance, it is still bound by contractual restrictions on the use of software.[606] A licensee may revoke acceptance if the nonconformity in software or other computer information

---

[595] UCC §§ 2-509, 2-510.

[596] UCITA § 614(a).

[597] *Id.* § 614(b)(1).

[598] *Id.* § 614(b)(2).

[599] UCC § 2-615 to § 2-616 has its parallel in UCITA § 615.

[600] UCITA § 615.

[601] *Id.* §§ 616-617 (stating rules for termination and notice of termination).

[602] *Compare* UCC § 2-508 with UCITA § 701.

[603] UCITA § 702(b).

[604] *Id.* § 703.

[605] *Id.* § 704.

[606] *Id.* § 706(4).

constitutes a material breach.[607] UCITA's methodology requires revocation to occur within a reasonable time after the licensee discovers material defects in software or other information.

The licensee must notify the licensor promptly of the breach in revocation just as with rejection. The consequence of failure of notice is that all remedies are waived. Revocation, as with Article 2, places the party in the same position it would have been in for rejection or refusal. UCITA § 708 also adopts the doctrine of adequate assurance of performance from UCC § 2-609. The concept of an adequate assurance of performance protects the parties' "peace of mind" that a license agreement will be performed.[608] An anticipatory repudiation is intent to breach a contract whose performance is not yet due. A party may seek adequate assurance of performance and suspend performance.

Anticipatory repudiation occurs where a party to a license agreement advises the other that performance will not be forthcoming. Section 709 permits the aggrieved party to await performance or to treat the license agreement as pre-emptively breached, immediately giving the nonbreaching party the full array of UCITA remedies.[609] UCITA's retraction of anticipatory repudiation provision is identical to § 2-611. A repudiation may be retracted unless the aggrieved party has cancelled the contract or changed its position.[610] UCITA follows the "avoidable consequences" rule of the common law and expects parties to take steps to mitigate loss.

[L]   Remedies

[1]   UCITA's Validation of Freedom of Contract

UCITA does not permit an aggrieved party to "recover more than once for the same loss."[611] UCITA gives the parties freedom to devise their own remedies. Remedies for breach of a license agreement "are determined by the [license] agreement."[612] The parties in an online agreement may bypass or contract around UCITA's rights and remedies. UCITA remedies are default gap-fillers that apply in the absence of a specific agreement between the parties. The other party must be placed in breach before UCITA's remedies apply. UCITA rejects the doctrine of election of remedies and grants the power to modify default terms, including all remedies. UCITA remedies are recoverable if the breach is material or nonmaterial.[613]

---

[607] *Id.* § 707(a).
[608] *Id.* § 708.
[609] *Id.* § 709.
[610] *Id.* § 710.
[611] *Id.* § 801.
[612] *Id.* § 701(a).
[613] *Id.*

[2] Duties upon Cancellation

A licensee who violates a use restriction in a license agreement or repudiates a contract is in breach. A license agreement may not be cancelled unless a breach of contract is material. A licensee will have the duty to return software to the licensor at the end of the term. In addition, a licensee may have a continuing duty of confidentiality.

[3] Material Breach

UCITA § 701(b) defines the uncured *material breach* as a substantial failure to perform a term that is an essential element of the agreement, a standard paralleling CISG's fundamental breach standard in Article 25.[614] The parties may define what constitutes a material breach in the license agreement. An events of default clause may define specifically what a "substantial failure to perform" or fundamental breach means.[615] Once a license agreement is cancelled, permission to use software or computer information is also cancelled.

UCITA adopts a substantial performance, or material breach, standard that differs from the perfect tender rule for performance in Article 2, which is not the standard in any country outside the United States. A material breach is a "substantial failure to perform an agreed term that is an essential element of the agreement."[616]

A substantial breach is one that "deprives the aggrieved party of a significant benefit it reasonably expected under the contract."[617] In contrast, Article 2 of the UCC permits a buyer to obtain substitute goods if the goods fail "in any respect to conform to the contract."[618] The perfect tender rule is an unrealistic standard for the software industry: Software may be composed of millions of lines of code. A licensee should not be able to cancel a software contract because of a minor bug or errant line of code.

Under a fundamental breach standard, a question exits as to what level of performance deficit in the software would warrant rejection. The vast majority of fundamental breaches occur when software has bugs that prevent it from performing important contract criteria.

A study of software vendors concluded that the principal types of performance problems with software were (1) form of reports, (2) processing speeds, (3) amount of data that could be handled, and (4) number of multiple users or peripherals that could be used with a computer system.[619] The case law reflects that fun-

---

[614] Cf. 701(b) and Convention on Contracts for the International Sale of Goods (CISG), art. 25.

[615] UCITA § 701(b).

[616] *Id.* § 701(b)(2).

[617] *Id.* § 701(b)-(3)(B).

[618] UCC §§ 2-601, 2-712.

[619] Cynthia Anthony and Michael Rustad, Breach and Adaptation of Computer Software Contracts: A Report to the ABA Software Licensing Subcommittee (June 15, 1993) (surveying industries that produced software for mass-market design applications, student loans, accounting activities, health care insurance claims, and telecommunications services).

damental breach in bad software cases centers on the failure of acceptance testing,[620] deviation from functional specifications,[621] late delivery of computer software and products,[622] the failure of compatibility,[623] and failure to process data at a specified processing speed.[624]

UCITA requires the nonbreaching party to comply with contractual restrictions on the use of computer software or other information, despite the other party's breach.[625] Cancellation is a remedy available to the nonbreaching party only if the breach is material and uncured by the other party.[626] The rightfully rejecting seller has duties as to rejected goods. Merchant-buyers may also have a duty to resell rejected goods.[627] Under UCITA, a licensee in possession of licensed information must follow the instructions of the licensor after cancellation.[628]

[4] Exclusive and Limited Remedy

UCITA permits the parties to substitute an exclusive and limited remedy for the default remedies of the statute.[629] Section 803 permits the aggrieved party to have access to all UCITA remedies if the exclusive or limited remedy "fail[s] of its essential purpose."[630] Similarly, if an exclusive remedy is found to be unconscionable, the aggrieved party may seek any of the statutory remedies of UCITA.[631] UCITA permits the licensor to limit consequential and incidental damages "unless the exclusion or limitation is unconscionable."[632]

---

[620] See, e.g., Whittaker Corp. v. Calspan Corp., 810 F. Supp. 457 (W.D.N.Y. 1992) (finding that "the actual variances from the contract specifications raise a material question of fact as to the value of the delivered system").

[621] See, e.g., Photo Copy, Inc. v. Software, Inc., 510 So. 2d 1337 (La. Ct. App. 1987) (holding that rejection of a computer system was warranted because the software program could not perform a key cross-reference function and observing that the disappointed buyer's "principal motive or cause" in busying the system was to obtain a cross-referencing function).

[622] See, e.g., Cash Management Services, Inc. v. Banctec, Inc., 1988 U.S. Dist. LEXIS 10768 (D. Mass., Sept. 21, 1988) (finding that the late delivery of equipment prevented the vendee from making proper acceptance testing; failure to make prompt delivery within a reasonable time or the time specified in the contract may be deemed a fundamental breach).

[623] See, e.g., Foundation Software v. Digital Equipment Corp., 807 F. Supp. 1195 (D. Md. 1992) (upholding breach of warranty action in case where vendor promised that software would run on the customer's system).

[624] See, e.g., Midland Mgmt. Corp. v. Computer Consoles, Inc., 1992 U.S. Dist. LEXIS 537 (N.D. Ill., Jan. 21, 1992) (finding that the computer system could not support more than 16 concurrent users and that the 32-user capability warranty did not exist).

[625] UCITA § 801(b).

[626] Id. § 802(a).

[627] UCC § 2-603.

[628] UCITA § 802(c).

[629] Id. § 803(b).

[630] UCC § 2-719(2).

[631] UCITA § 803(d).

[632] Id.

[5] Fundamental Public Policies

A court may refuse to enforce an online contract that violates fundamental public policies.[633] Little case law exists on what contract terms a court may find to be contrary to a fundamental public policy. A court would likely find it a violation of public policy to sell hard core pornography or human embryos on a web site. A few software licensors prohibit licensees from publicly criticizing software. Such a draconian term has a chilling effect on free expression and may be invalidated as a violation of public policy. It is unclear whether courts will use the "fundamental public policy" doctrine to invalidate unfair, oppressive, or surprising terms in mass-market agreements. European courts would find a licensor's strict prohibition against reverse engineering likely to violate a public policy in favor of interoperability of computer systems.[634] UCITA seems to give the courts wide discretion to "avoid a result contrary to public policy," although the case law has yet to evolve.[635]

[6] Liquidated Damages

Section 804 parallels UCC § 2-718 validating the use of liquidated damages for online contracts. UCITA provides that damages "may be liquidated by agreement in any amount that is reasonable in light of (1) the loss anticipated at the time of contracting; (2) the actual loss or the actual or (3) anticipated difficulties of proving loss in the event of breach."[636] UCITA, like § 2-718, will enforce liquidated damages clauses as long as the amount is not "unreasonably large."

[7] Disabling Device

Technologies have long been available for licensors to disable computer software or restrict access to databases. Electronic self-help is a UCITA remedy available to licensors as long as they follow the procedural protections UCITA gives licensees. A licensor must follow the procedural rules in § 815(b), however, or be accountable to the licensee for damages. This means that if the conditions of 815(b) are not followed, no electronic self-help is available. The electronic self-help rule follows Part 5 of UCC Article 9, which governs secured transactions. Just as with Article 9, no repossession can take place where a breach of the peace would result. UCITA does not want to grant licensors the unbridled right to use electronic self-help or disabling devices that will cause harm to computer systems

---

[633] *Id.* § 105.

[634] Reverse engineering is necessary to attain interoperability of computer systems. The European Community recognizes a right to reverse engineering to prevent unfair competition, or what we refer to as antitrust.

[635] UCITA § 105(b).

[636] *Id.* § 804(a).

or other foreseeable damage to persons or property other than the licensed information.

The Reporter's Notes to UCITA § 816 state that "there can be no electronic self-help where a breach of peace would result or where there is a threat of foreseeable damage of personal injury or significant physical damamge to property other than the licensed information."[637] The Notes cite an example in which "licensed software is integral to the funds transfer or payment systems of a banking institution, where it pertains to national security systems,"[638] and observe that "[i]n such cases, the remedy of electronic self-help threatens disruption that far exceeds the benefits of allowing its use."[639]

If self-help is unavailable, the licensor may seek injunctive or monetary relief to enforce its rights.[640] UCITA envisions an expedited review of whether a license agreement is justifiably cancelled and electronic disablement permitted. A wrongful repossession of software or information entitles the injured parties to damages. A licensee who suffers a wrongful electronic repossession may seek consequential, incidental, and direct damages. The procedural rights and obligations for electronic repossession are not disclaimable and may not be "waived by agreement."[641]

The use of disabling devices is a very controversial practice in the software industry. Even though UCITA is not yet law in most jurisdictions, it is risky to include disabling devices for self-help repossession without notice to the licensee. An online company, such as SPC, should not use disabling devices unless notice is given to the licensee prior to entering into the license agreement. The disabling device must not be triggered without notice to the licensee.

The self-help electronic repossession remedy of UCITA has been castigated as too restrictive by licensors and as too permissive by licensees. The electronic self-help remedy is available in some cases but cannot be used in mass-market transactions, including consumer transactions.[642] UCITA imposes procedural protections, such as notice and prior consent, on use of electronic self-help as a matter of state contract law. The 2001 UCITA Standby Committee proposes to eliminate electronic repossession or similar self-help in information transactions, proposing instead a right of expedited relief for licensors along with attorneys' fees should they succeed in obtaining preliminary relief.

[8] Statute of Limitations and Repose

UCITA adopts a complicated statute of limitations that combines a discovery rule with a rule of repose. Section 805 imposes a four-year statute of limitations accruing one year after the breach was or should have been discovered. The

---

[637] *Id.* § 816, cmt. 3.
[638] *Id.*
[639] *Id.*
[640] *Id.*
[641] *Id.*
[642] UCITA Standby Committee, Report § 816 (Dec. 17, 2001).

absolute limit to file an action, however, is "five years after the right of action accrues."[643] The parties may agree to reduce the period of limitations to not less than one year after the cause of action accrues.[644] Different statutes of limitation and repose exist for third-party warranty claims.

§ 6.06   LICENSE AGREEMENTS

License agreements come in an almost infinite variety of flavors. They may be exclusive or nonexclusive, mass-market or tailored, developmental or customized; they may apply for a single use or for perpetuity. An exclusive licensee, as the name connotes, is the only party who may use licensed software, data, or intellectual property. Territory, time period, or other factors may restrict license agreements. In November 2001, the UCITA Standby Committee met with representatives of the ABA to discuss possible amendments to UCITA. There are significant policy differences on issues such as "[how] license agreements are formed, mass market licensing, exceptions for libraries and the open source software community; consumer protections, reverse engineering, restrictions on electronic self-help, warranties and the validity of contractual prohibitions against public criticism."[645]

All forms of intellectual property are licensed. Copyrights, for example, are frequently licensed. A record company may license a copyrighted song for the soundtrack of a film. A photographer may license a copyrighted photograph for use in a web advertisement. It is possible, for example, to enter into a license agreement to use digitized MIDI music files that may be downloaded on a corporate web site. An artist may offer the use of one song for $50 for a 12-month period. A corporate multimedia web site may need to obtain licensed text, music, photographs, software, and streaming video and audio. MIDI files are subject to compulsory licenses when not accompanying a motion picture or other audiovisual work.

Rights in patents, trademarks, trade secrets, and software are also licensed. A license may be structured as exclusive, semiexclusive, or nonexclusive. Mass-market license agreements, such as the use of Microsoft's Windows 2000, are nonexclusive because the value is realized by marketing end-user agreements to millions of users. A software program custom designed to control missile warheads is certain to be exclusive, because the customized program is tailored for a single user, the Department of Defense. Software license agreements may provide for code that disables an application if timely royalties are not paid.

Another common form of web site licensing is the terms of use agreement. A web site agreement is a limited license to use materials on a corporate or other web site. A growing number of web sites condition access on payments. A web

---

[643] *Id.* § 805(a).

[644] *Id.* § 805(b).

[645] UCITA Summit Held in D.C., The National Conference of Commissioners on Uniform Laws (NCCUSL), Nov. 21, 2001.

site term of use agreement will give the user notice that the documents, data, software, or other information on the web site are copyrighted. There should typically be notices of trademarks as well. A typical agreement will state that software is made available for specific purposes. The last clause in a web site agreement generally will state, "All rights not specifically granted are reserved." The terms of service agreement may be used to restrain the use of spiders to extract data.[646]

SPC structures its mass-market computer software contracts as shrinkwrap or click-through agreements. SPC's mass-market license agreements will likely not be enforced unless consumers are given an opportunity to review and read the terms prior to paying for or receiving software. SPC's licenses should be structured so that the user is required to take some affirmative act to manifest assent after having the opportunity to review the license terms. The web site customer will be asked to click "I accept" or "I reject" after being given the opportunity to read the terms of SPC's license agreements.

[A] Granting Clause

The *granting clause* is the most legally significant clause in a license agreement because it specifies what rights are being transferred. The granting clause will specify whether a license is exclusive or nonexclusive. A broad granting clause in a license agreement is "of all possible rights and media including all rights then existing or created by the law in the future."[647] A licensee receives all rights described in the licensing agreement. The granting clause will typically reference the terms and conditions of the license agreement. License agreements may be country-by-country or worldwide, exclusive or nonexclusive, or restricted by territory, site, or time period. The granting clause must also address the question of whether the licensee has a right to sublicense software or other information.

A sale of goods is forever, whereas a license agreement may be nonperpetual or perpetual. A nonperpetual license agreement may be structured as a single use agreement or for a fixed period, such as 30 days or a year. The license agreement should spell out whether the licensed technology is worldwide or restricted to a given country or continent. If a licensee is a multinational corporation, it is possible to negotiate a license agreement that will permit worldwide use of the license.

[B] Term for Payment

License agreements may structure payment in many different forms. A software developer may demand a large upfront fee. Alternatively, the licensee may structure upfront fees to correspond to milestones. Royalties in web site agreements may be structured on net sales from a web site or the number of web site

---

[646] Use of Web Spider to Extract WHOIS Data Held Actionable as Breach of Terms of Use, Internet L. & Reg. (Pike & Fischer), Dec. 19, 2000.

[647] UCC § 2B-307(1).

visitors. Subscribers to Books24X7, for example, an online business that places information technology books on the web, pay $399 for an annual subscription and lower costs for multiple-user agreements.[648] The site has a search engine so a user can search through hundreds of books for desired content.[649]

[C] Scope of Licensing Agreement; Number of Users

The license agreement should clearly spell out who is the authorized user. A license agreement should specify that use is for one user only or for multiple users. A license agreement with a multinational corporation should specify whether a foreign subsidiary may use the licensed information. If independent contractors are routinely used, the agreement should specify under what conditions they may use the licensed information. A licensor needs to calibrate the royalties or payments based on the number of users. If the license agreement does not specify the number of users allowed at a given time, the industry standard limits use of software or other information products to a single user. A clause might limit use of software to a single central processing unit. A detailed shrinkwrap license may state that the "software may not be rented, sold, or transferred." The agreement must be clear as to what access is given in the case of an access contract and whether simultaneous use is permitted.

[D] Different Media

A copyright, trademark, trade secret, or patent holder will have the exclusive rights to reproduce and distribute works. The license agreement, for example, will typically specify the type of media for which rights are granted. A license agreement to distribute content on the *New York Times* web site may not cover CD-ROMs. A license to distribute a motion picture may not extend to broadcasting on the Internet. The licensee of software or other information products may negotiate for the rights to obtain updates.

A licensee will need to negotiate specifically for electronic distribution rights. In the software industry, a licensee does not automatically receive updates of a program. In *Playboy Enterprises v. Chuckleberry Publishing,*[650] the defendant used the trade name in a 1979 magazine it called *Playmen,* a name substantially similar to that of *Playboy.* Fifteen years later the defendant established a web site for Playmen. The court held that the injunction also applied to the Internet, even though the medium was different, since the trade name was substantially similar to *Playboy*'s trade name.[651]

---

[648] Gavin McCormick, Books24x7 Puts IT Books on the Web, Mass High Tech (Aug. 16-22, 1999) at 18.

[649] *Id.* at 1.

[650] 939 F. Supp. 1032 (S.D.N.Y. 1996).

[651] *Id.*

The licensee needs to be certain that the license agreement applies to Internet publishing as well as to other media. A number of writers sued the *New York Times* and the Time-Warner magazine group, claiming that the publishers were infringing their rights by distributing articles they wrote on the Internet without permission, even though they had paid for the print versions of these newspaper and magazine articles.[652]

[E] Licensee's Right to Updates

A licensor may take the position that a licensee is not entitled to updates or new versions of software. A licensee may also wish to be informed of improvements or new releases of software. In the case of access contracts, the licensee will want to have the latest updates to a database. In the absence of an agreement, a licensee will not automatically receive new releases or updates. A licensee of mass-market software, such as Windows 2000, will generally pay an additional fee for improved versions of the software.

[F] Termination Clause

A license will generally define the terms of the license agreement. The term of an agreement will begin as of the "Effective Date." A term may begin when software is installed and continue for the life of the license. Licenses may be for perpetuity or for a fixed period, such as a month, year, or other term. The sine qua non of a license agreement is that the title to the program and copies remain the property of the licensor. License agreements will have a termination clause for breach or default. The license agreement should specify the events of default. Events of default will include nonpayment of licensing fees, repudiation, or rejection of conforming software.

[G] Disabling Devices

Disabling devices allow the "software vendor" an effective, practical means to limit the term of a license agreement or to establish conditions under which the license ceases. For example, a licensee may purchase software that contains a disabling routine designed to permit use of the software only until a given date. The licensor might offer a perpetual license of the same software at a higher cost.

A computer lawyer who frequently drafts and reviews license agreements agreed with the proposition that "the vendor should be free to limit the term of a license agreement through time-bombs and other disabling routines."[653] It is likely

---

[652] Nicolas Baran, Inside the Information Superhighway Revolution 143 (2000).

[653] This judgment emerged during an interview with a computer lawyer with 15 years' involvement with software and extensive experience advising licensors or licensees of customized software.

that courts would not require a conspicuous warning or label, leaving it to the licensor to communicate the limitation of the software license.

[H]   Warranties, Disclaimers, and Limitations

Warranty exclusion and remedy limitation provisions are a usage of trade in mass-market software licensing agreements. The Uniform Commercial Code permits parties to exclude implied warranties as long as the language is clear, unambiguous, and conspicuous and not unconscionable.[654] Courts apply Article 2 of the Uniform Commercial Code to software licensing agreements in the absence of a specialized body of law governing computer transactions.[655] For a discussion of warranties under UCITA, see § 6.05[G].

[I]   Indemnification

License agreements will frequently contain indemnification or *hold harmless* clauses. A "hold harmless" clause is an essential term in contracts with third parties who supply content to the web site. Developmental software contracts should contain cross-indemnities in which each party agrees to indemnify the other for third-party claims.

[J]   Assignment and Anti-Assignment

A licensee may want to sublicense content to a third party. A licensor may require the licensee to sign an anti-assignment agreement. The following is an example of an anti-assignment clause: "SPC grants the licensee a nonexclusive, nontransferable, personal license to use the object code version of SPC's XYZ Software on a single central processing unit at the original site where initially installed."

The software license agreement will govern the user's right to assign or resell software. The agreement will govern whether a user moves the physical location of software. A licensor may have objections, for example, if software is assigned to an outsourcing vendor.

---

[654] *See, e.g.,* NMP Corp. v. Parametric Technology Corp., 958 F. Supp. 1536 (N.D. Okla. 1997) (enforcing warranty exclusion and remedy limitation provisions contained in software licensing agreement).

[655] *See, e.g.,* Vmark Software v. EMC Corp., 37 Mass. App. Ct. 610, 642 N.E.2d 587 (1994) (applying Article 2 of the UCC to a software licensing agreement and holding that the licensee met its burden of proof regarding allegations of misrepresentation by the licensor of a software program). *See generally* Andrew Beckerman-Rodau, Computer Software: Does Article 2 of the Uniform Commercial Code Apply? 35 Emory L.J. 853 (1986) (arguing that software licensing agreements should be treated as Article 2 transactions).

[K] Licensee's Rights

An end user should minimally have the right to load and execute software on a single computer. A licensee probably has an implied right to reverse engineer the software to determine and exploit the underlying noncopyrightable ideas. A multinational company will need to negotiate the right to load software on a network file server or to make it available in other ways to multiple users.

[L] Confidentiality and Nondisclosure

A licensor or licensee may be concerned with confidentiality of licensed data or information. Some intellectual property lawyers argue that confidentiality agreements are unnecessary in license agreements. Trade secret or confidentiality agreements impose conditions on the disclosure of confidential or proprietary information.

[M] Export Restrictions

Software agreements may contain a provision by which the licensee agrees not to export or reexport the software product to any country, person, entity, or end user subject to U.S. export restrictions.[656] Microsoft also asks its licensees to warrant that they have not had their export privileges suspended, revoked, or denied.[657] Software licensors are liable if they permit technology to be exported, downloaded, or even reexported to restricted countries. Software, for example, must not be exported to Cuba, Iran, Iraq, North Korea, Sudan, or Syria.[658] Netscape Navigator distributes end-user licenses with the following export control term:

> NONE OF THE SOFTWARE OR UNDERLYING INFORMATION OR TECHNOLOGY MAY BE DOWNLOADED OR OTHERWISE EXPORTED OR RE-EXPORTED (I) INTO (OR TO A NATIONAL OR RESIDENT OF) CUBA, IRAQ, LIBYA, YUGOSLAVIA, NORTH KOREA, IRAN, SYRIA OR ANY OTHER COUNTRY TO WHICH THE U.S. HAS EMBARGOED GOODS; OR (II) TO ANYONE ON THE U.S. TREASURY DEPARTMENT'S LIST OF SPECIALLY DESIGNATED NATIONALS OR THE U.S. COMMERCE DEPARTMENT'S TABLE OF DENY ORDERS. BY DOWNLOADING OR USING THE SOFTWARE, YOU ARE AGREEING TO THE FOREGOING AND YOU ARE REPRESENTING AND WARRANTING THAT YOU

---

[656] The United States Department of Commerce's Bureau of Export Administration (BXA) administers the export license program for encryption products subject to the Export Administration Regulations (EAR). A company must determine its licensing requirements under EAR by comparing its products against the Commerce Control List, which is available online. *See generally* U.S. Department of Commerce, Bureau of Export Administration, Fact Sheet: How Do I Know If I Need to Get a License from the Department of Commerce? (visited Apr. 22, 2002), http://www.bxa.doc.gov/factsheets/facts1.htm.

[657] Microsoft, Inc., End-User License Agreement for Microsoft Software, clause 6 (stating export restrictions).

[658] *Id.*

ARE NOT LOCATED IN, UNDER THE CONTROL OF OR A NATIONAL OR RESIDENT OF,
ANY SUCH COUNTRY OR ON ANY SUCH LIST.[659]

[N] Integration or Merger Clause

An integration clause states that the contract represents the parties' complete
and final agreement. The purpose of the clause is to merge all prior oral and written agreements into the final agreement. An example of a merger clause is "This
Agreement constitutes the entire understanding of the parties with respect to the
subject matter." It is critical that merger clauses be included in all license agreements, including the web site agreement.

[O] Access Contracts: Terms and Conditions of Access

The typical access contract is formed by acceptance of terms through use.
America Online, for example, provides "By using this site, you signify your agreement to all terms, conditions, and notices contained or referenced herein (the
'Terms of Use'). If you do not agree to these Terms of Use please do not use this
site."[660] AOL reserves the right to update or revise the Terms of Use and places the
burden of checking for modified terms on the user. AOL states: "Your continued
use of this site following the posting of any changes to the Terms of Use constitutes acceptance of those changes."[661]

Section 102(1) of UCITA defines an *access contract* as a contract to obtain
electronic access to the information-processing system of another person or the
equivalent of such access. An access to services contract includes online services
for remote data processing, e-mail, or databases. An access contract is an agreement that a subscriber may have electronic access to a company's databases.
America Online, for example, is an access provider because it gives its
38,000,000 subscribers electronic access to or information from its databases.
WESTLAW® and LexisNexis™ afford their subscribers remote access to hundreds of thousands of specialized legal or law-related databases. The Lexis-
Nexis™ or WESTLAW® subscriber is presented with a "take it or leave it" access
contract.

Access providers develop standard-form contracts which they offer to their
customers on a "take it or leave it" basis. The subscriber agrees to the terms and
conditions of use and to the price schedule; these represent the entire agreement,
and without the subscriber's acceptance, no contract exists. Access providers signify acceptance of the access agreement by issuing an identification number that

---

[659] Netscape Communications Corporation, Netscape Navigator End User License Agreement
(1996).

[660] AOL.Anywhere, Terms and Conditions of Use (visited Apr. 27, 2002), http://www.aol.com/
copyright.html.

[661] *Id.*

permits access to the services. Access agreements typically impose restrictions on the licenses. An access agreement will typically be nontransferable and limited to use by one person at a time.

Access contracts may include "contracts for remote data processing, third party e-mail systems, and contracts allowing automatic updating from a remote facility to a database held by the licensee."[662] The *New York Times*, for example, enters into access contracts with subscribers for its online publication. The term *access contract* does not include contracts that grant a right to enter a building or other physical locale.

§ 6.07   INTERNET TAXATION

[A]   Introduction

Governments have the right to impose taxes within their jurisdictions. Each government is generally free to design its own system of taxation, forcing global businesses to comply with literally hundreds of thousands of possible taxing jurisdictions.[663] Within the United States there are currently more than 7,600 state and local tax jurisdictions, which average 500 tax law changes per year.[664] E-commerce creates enormous challenges both for governments as they seek to protect their tax base and for businesses as they seek to comply with the dazzling diversity in tax systems and to avoid double taxation.

A government's ability to tax is limited by the mobility of people and property. American colonists and modern-day tennis stars have each responded to taxes by leaving the jurisdiction. Multinational corporations have further reduced the relative power of governments to impose taxes by shifting activities to jurisdictions that offer the best resources and infrastructure at the lowest tax cost. Governments, in turn, have responded to the increased mobility of business by lowering tax rates, negotiating directly with other taxing jurisdictions to modify existing treaties, and negotiating indirectly through international organizations. The Organization for Economic Cooperation and Development (OECD) plays a leading role in helping governments tackle the economic, social, and governance challenges of a globalized economy, and has played a leading role in defining the impact e-commerce will have on global tax systems. Governments and businesses

---

[662] UCITA § 102(a)(1).

[663] The Framework Communication, A European Initiative in Electronic Commerce, noted that "by its very nature, electronic commerce is transnational and encourages cross-border ordering and delivery of goods and services in the Single Market, that it directly stimulates European growth and competitiveness, and that it represents 'a potentially vital factor for cohesion and integration in Europe.'" Communication by the Commission to the Council of Ministers, the European Parliament, and the Economic and Social Committee, COM (96) 328 Final.

[664] *See, e.g.*, National Tax Ass'n, Communications and Elec. Commerce Tax Project: Final Report i-ii (visited June 15, 2002), http://www.ntanet.org.

share the same objective of expanded global economic development. This requires an environment in which e-commerce is allowed to connect markets with an infrastructure of consistent tax laws, applied on a uniform basis to minimize administrative costs, and avoid the twin terrors of wholesale tax avoidance and double taxation.

The diversity of tax systems creates an administrative nightmare for multinational businesses. Inconsistencies among these systems create numerous risks of two or more jurisdictions taxing the same transaction. Fortunately, the global system of taxation has evolved to provide a significant measure of consistency. Most governments generate the vast majority of tax revenue through the following two tax structures:

- **Direct taxes** are imposed on the income of individuals and entities. The United States imposes taxes on the global income of its citizens and residents. It also taxes foreigners to the extent that they have a "substantial presence" in the country and earn income effectively connected with a U.S. trade or business. To avoid double taxation, the United States gives a foreign tax credit for taxes paid on income that is more properly taxed in another jurisdiction.

  A foreign taxpayer may avoid U.S. tax if it does not have a substantial presence in the United States, interpreted to require at least some minimal physical presence.[665] Since "substantial presence" sets a very low threshold for taxation, the United States has entered into income tax treaties with many other countries. In these treaties, each country agrees to raise the minimum contacts required to impose tax on the other country's residents from "substantial presence" to a "permanent establishment," usually defined to require a fixed place of business in taxing jurisdiction. This higher threshold for taxation enables the United States and its treaty partner to collect more tax for their own residents and encourages greater bilateral trade.

  On December 22, 2000, the OECD issued a report on the impact of e-commerce on the tax concept of a permanent establishment.[666] The report concludes that a web site, by itself, should not be a permanent establishment since it is merely software hosted on one or more servers. Similar to the American standard, the OECD suggests that some minimal physical presence is required to create a permanent establishment. The report notes that physical servers that host a web site might rise to the level of a permanent establishment if their location is fixed and they can complete commercial transactions.

---

[665] In *Piedras Negras Broadcasting Co. v. Commissioner,* 43 B.T.A. 297 (1941), *aff'd* 127 F. 2d. 260 (5th Cir. 1942), a Mexican radio station broadcast its signal across the border. The station broadcast in English and had a majority of American listeners and advertisers. Despite this exploitation of the American market, the station did not have any substantial physical presence in the United States and as a result was determined to be exempt from U.S. taxation.

[666] *See* OECD Committee on Fiscal Affairs, Clarification on the Application of the Permanent Establishment Definition in E-Commerce: Changes to the Commentary on the Model Tax Convention on Article 5 (Dec. 22, 2000).

India has taken a position in marked contrast to most other tax authorities. In September 2001, a commission comprising government and industry officials suggested that electronic commerce may force governments to abandon the concept of permanent establishment and its physical presence test.[667]

Within the United States, state taxation is governed by concepts similar to the "substantial presence" test, called taxable nexus.[668] If a taxpayer does not have any physical presence within a state, the state lacks a nexus or connection upon which to impose tax. Recent decisions have suggested that even substantial numbers of computer servers and other equipment within a state may not be sufficient physical presence to create a taxable nexus.[669]

- **Indirect taxes** are imposed on transactions in property or services. Throughout most of the world, value added tax (VAT)[670] is imposed on a broad range of transactions (tangible property, intangible property, and services) at rates ranging from 15 to 25 percent of the sales price. Businesses receive a credit for "input VAT," equal to the VAT they were charged on their own purchases. This credit avoids double taxation and taxes the value added at each stage of production.

  EXAMPLE: Alpha produces electronic components in France. Alpha sells the components to Beta for Euro30, charging VAT at its local rate. Beta includes these components in a radio, which it sells to Consumer for $100. Beta charges VAT on the full $100 but receives a credit for its "input VAT" on $30. Alpha pays VAT on the value it added ($30), while Beta pays VAT on the value it added ($70).

In the United States, an elaborate system of sales and use taxes (SUT)[671] imposes indirect tax on a narrow base of tangible personal property. Sales of services and intangible property are generally exempt from tax. Rather than taxing all transactions based on value added, the American system only imposes tax on the sale to the "ultimate consumer." The American system relies on an elaborate system of "resale certificates" to exempt sales between businesses.

  EXAMPLE: Alpha produces electronic components in California. Alpha sells the components to Beta for $30. Since Beta has a resale certificate, no SUT is collected. Beta includes these components in a radio, which it sells to Consumer for $100. Beta charges SUT on the full $100.

---

[667] *See* Report on High Powered Committee on Electronic Commerce and Taxation, Sept. 2001.

[668] In *Quill Corp. v. North Dakota,* 112 S. Ct. 1904 (1992), the Supreme Court held that a state cannot tax an out-of-state mail-order seller if the seller does not have any significant physical presence in the state.

[669] *See* America Online, Inc. v. Johnson, No. 97-3786 (Tenn. Ch. Ct. Mar. Mar. 13, 2001).

[670] *See* § 6.07[I](1).

[671] *See* § 6.07[D](1).

[B] Challenges Introduced by Electronic Commerce

Although each tax system is extraordinarily complex, in essence tax is simply a function of value. Sales tax is imposed on gross value, VAT is imposed on net value, and income tax is imposed on growth in value. Each tax system defines *who* is subject to tax, *where* a transaction will be subject to tax, and *what* type of transaction has occurred. E-commerce presents severe challenges for each of these tax criteria:

- **Who is the taxpayer?** Unlike traditional "brick-and-mortar" retail stores, a web site is not clearly tied to any person or organization. The potential anonymity of Internet commerce applies to both buyers and sellers.

- **Where does the transaction occur?** The location of a physical sale is easily determined, but electronic commerce, particularly communications and sales of digital content, has no clear ties to any physical place. Two parties buying and selling on eBay are unlikely to know where the other party is located.

- **What is the nature of the transaction?** Tax systems apply different rules to sales of tangible property, intangible property, and services. E-commerce enables value to be transformed in novel ways. For example, a newspaper is tangible property, whereas an online subscription to the same content provides intangible information. An application service provider (ASP) integrates the value of information into a service for its subscribers.

For e-commerce to achieve its potential, established principles of taxation need to be applied to e-commerce transactions. Great difficulty arises in applying tax rules that are based on territorial concepts to the people and transactions of cyberspace.

Internet taxation continues to be a major issue in political debates within the United States. In 1998 Congress passed the Internet Tax Freedom Act (ITFA), which imposed a three-year moratorium on taxation of Internet-related transactions. On November 28, 2001, President Bush extended the ITFA moratorium on new state or federal taxes until at least November 1, 2003. ITFA also created a commission called the Advisory Commission on Electronic Commerce (ACEC), composed of representatives from both government and industry. The ACEC spent 18 months holding public hearings but was unable to reach the two-thirds majority required by ITFA. In April 2000, the ACEC issued a final report that generally opposes expanded taxation of electronic commerce but does not provide a solid foundation for further legislation regarding the taxation of electronic commerce.

Congress created the ACEC because of the many different constituencies advocating for or against expanded taxation of e-commerce. The number of interested parties alone was sufficient to assure ACEC's failure. First, there are the brick-and-mortar associations that have a pro-tax stance, such as E-Fairness Coalition, National Retail Federation, and the International Council of Shopping Centers.[672] These groups want a sales tax on Internet transactions because without one, they argue, brick-and-mortar companies are at a disadvantage because their products, which include sales taxes, cost more to the consumer than those of their dot-com counterparts. Second, there are the different state governors, who cannot agree among themselves on whether there should be a sales tax on Internet transactions, because the tax will have substantially different effects on different states. Some states legitimately fear major losses in their tax base if taxes are not levied on Internet commercial activities. Third, there are the online companies that want to continue to sell their products free of sales taxes, taking into account the current nexus rules. Fourth, there are lobbyists and antitax organizations like Americans for Tax Reform that want to ensure that their interests and needs are understood and not hindered by the ultimate political stance.[673] Finally, there are the members of Congress who are concerned about public reaction to a new sales tax or other related taxes that may be devised and applied to their online purchases.

Despite the various interest groups and viewpoints involved, there seem to be primarily three pervasive themes. First, eliminate and prohibit any taxes that would stifle the growth of e-commerce. Second, simplify the application of taxes and standardize the tax methodologies applied to both brick-and-mortar and dot-com companies. Finally, develop new levels of tax applications suitable for federal, state, local, and international jurisdictions and applications without overcomplicating current tax law(s). Although it is easy to argue for one position, in practice it is difficult to effectively implement any position without practical challenges. For example, one clouded issue is whether a downloadable software program is classifiable as a good, a service, or neither because it is to be classified as an intangible information asset.[674] The European Union takes the position that web site services should be classified as services.[675] The Commission notes that "VAT legislation makes a basic distinction between the supply of goods and the

---

[672] Other pro-tax organizations are National Governors Association (http://www.nga.org), National League of Cities (http://www.nlc.org), National Conference of State Legislatures (http://ncsl.org), the National Association of Counties (http://www.naco.org), the U.S. Conference of Mayors (http://www.usmayors.org), the Council of State Governments (http://statenews.org), the Multi-Tax Commission (http://www.mtc.org), and the Center for Budget and Policy Priorities (http://www.cbpp.org).

[673] Other antitax organizations are Netfairness (http://www.netfariness.org), E-Freedom.com (http://www.e-freedom.com), Citizens for a Sound Economy (http://www.cse.org), and Cato Institute's Center for Trade Policy Studies (http://www.freetrade.org).

[674] The Council of Ministers of the European Parliament argues that the "consequences of taxation should be the same for transactions in goods and services, regardless of the mode of commerce used or whether delivery is effected Online or off-line." Communication by the Commission to the Council of Ministers, the European Parliament, and the Economic and Social Committee, COM (96) 328 Final. Ideally, the consequences of taxation should be neutral and nondiscriminatory, whether purchased "from within or from outside the EU." *Id.*

[675] *Id.*

supply of services. All types of electronic transmissions and all intangible products delivered by such means are deemed, for the purposes of EU VAT, to be services."[676] This example illustrates that the existing laws governing state and local, federal, and international taxation are being challenged in ways that no one anticipated. If Internet taxation is to become a reality, various issues arise, such as (1) how to develop a system that will be painless yet fair to all parties, (2) how various jurisdictions can enforce compliance, and (3) whether compliance will stifle e-commerce growth and economic prosperity. These questions raise practical questions as to whether parity can be had between brick-and-mortar and dot-com companies. The ultimate question may be, can laws be implemented that can keep pace with the fast-paced and evolving technologies?

[C]   Internet Taxation: The U.S. Perspective

As discussed in the first two chapters, the Internet and the advent of e-business have empowered companies to change the way they do business—buy and sell products and services, interact with suppliers and customers, and hire and interact with employees—in a global economy. Although e-business is, in many cases, clearly a more appealing way of doing business, its means of silently crossing the borders of states and countries complicates the issues of assessing and collecting taxes.

A hypothetical company such as SPC can now sell computer antivirus software programs either by mailing the software on a disk to a customer or by allowing the customer to download the software directly from the SPC web site. Mailing the antivirus software to a customer could take several days, costs more money to distribute, and increases SPC's operating costs, whereas the download procedure is instantaneous, accurate, and reduces distribution and operating costs. The downloading option is clearly more appealing. This convenience, however, complicates the process of assessing and collecting taxes. It is unclear whether a downloadable software program delivered from SPC's web site is a good, a service, or, being an information asset, neither. These characterizations have different tax implications, based in part on how value is created. "E-business has the potential to transform dramatically tax effects by enabling us to control where value is created."[677]

Decades ago, tax laws and regulations were established all over the world and have since served as a means for local governments to generate revenue. None of these tax laws and regulations contemplated the possibility that new technologies would so thoroughly complicate how a given transaction was taxed. Today great uncertainty exists in the global marketplace over taxation and tax processes

---

[676] *Id.* The Commission notes that the application of VAT to e-commerce is consistent with the position taken by the EU and its member states at the World Trade Organization (WTO).

[677] E-Business Tax: A Strategic Weapon in the Digital Age 5 (PricewaterhouseCoopers LLP, 2000).

and the extent to which "sales, value added or similar taxes apply to transactions in the International online services industry."[678]

One of the many problems presented by e-business is the possibility that numerous jurisdictions may claim authority over the same transactions, subjecting a given e-commerce transaction to state, federal, and international taxation. To prevent double taxation and to facilitate continued growth in e-commerce, the United States enacted the Internet Tax Freedom Act.[679]

[1] The Internet Tax Freedom Act

The Internet Tax Freedom Act (ITFA) was introduced in March 1997 by Representative Christopher Cox and Senator Ron Wyden and was enacted into law October 21, 1998.[680] Two of the fundamental purposes of ITFA were to ensure the continued growth of the Internet as well as to prevent multiple or discriminatory taxes which could potentially stifle the growth of e-commerce. In other words, "[t]he ITFA . . . call[ed] on the Clinton Administration to demand that foreign governments keep the Internet free of all taxes and tariffs."[681] Jurisdictions are free to impose taxes on all "e-business sales provided that the tax rate is the same as that which would have been imposed had the transactions been conducted in a traditional manner, such as by mail-order."[682] States may impose taxes on sales of "tangible personal property over the Internet, just as if those sales were conducted" in person.[683] Companies will enjoy a respite from federal taxes until October 21, 2001. On November 28, 2001, President Bush extended the ITFA moratorium on new state and federal taxes until November 1, 2003.[684]

The highlights of ITFA include the following:

- *No federal taxes.* Congress believed it was imperative that no federal taxes be imposed on Internet access or e-commerce for several years.

- *Declaration that the Internet should be a tariff-free zone.* Congress did not want foreign tariffs to hinder the ability of U.S. businesses to compete in e-commerce activities abroad.[685]

- *Establishment of an advisory commission.* Congress set up a high-profile commission to make recommendations for the future taxation of e-commerce. The

---

[678] *See generally* Arthur J. Cockfield, Designing Tax Policy for the Digital Biosphere: How the Internet Is Changing Tax Law, 34 Conn. L. Rev. 333 (2002).

[679] Internet Tax Freedom Act, Pub. L. 105-277, § 1101(a) (Oct. 21, 1998).

[680] *Id.*

[681] Sidney Silham, "If It Ain't Broke Don't Fix It: An Argument for the Codification of the Quill Standard for Taxing Internet Commerce," Symposium on the Second Amendment: Fresh Looks, 76 Chi.-Kent L. Rev. 671, 687 (2000).

[682] *Id.* at 686

[683] *Id.*

[684] Brian Krebs, Bush Signs Two-Year Internet Tax Ban Extension, Newsbytes, Nov. 28, 2001.

[685] *See* Robert Guy Matthews, Tariffs Impede Trade via Web on Global Scale, Wall St. J. (Apr. 17, 2000) at B1.

Advisory Commission on Electronic Commerce consisted of eight business executives, three federal government leaders, and eight state and local government officials.[686] The Commission presented formal recommendations to Congress in April 2000.

- *Three-year moratorium on multiple or discriminatory taxes on e-commerce.* ITFA prohibits multiple and discriminatory taxes on e-commerce.

- *Three-year moratorium on new taxes on Internet access fees.* ITFA prohibits state and local governments from imposing taxes on Internet access fees if such a tax was not in place as of October 21, 1998.[687]

The enactment of ITFA was a preventive measure to ensure the continued growth of the Internet over the next several years. Arguably, the most significant part of ITFA was the establishment of the Advisory Commission on Economic Commerce (ACEC).[688] The ACED consisted of 19 members. These members included six business leaders, eight representatives of the government at different levels, and five other distinguished representatives that included high-ranking leaders of various business like AOL, AT&T, and Time Warner.[689] The ACEC studied, among other things, state and local taxation of Internet access; e-commerce with other countries; sales and use taxes within the United States; and consumption taxes, such as value-added taxes (VAT). Many scholars believed the ACEC's recommendations would bring about dramatic changes in existing tax laws that could result in uniform statewide tax rates, consolidated state tax returns, limitations on tax rate changes, and uniform definitions of which products and services may be subject to tax.[690] However, the members of the ACEC struggled with reaching any type of uniform conclusions.

The Commission was given until April 2000 to submit its final findings to Congress. The ACEC was unable to attain the supermajority consensus mandated by Congress that a recommendation be supported by 13 of the 19 voting members. Although the ACEC did not have enough votes to make a formal recommendation, the ACEC was able to obtain a majority to approve a report with the support of 11 of the 19 voting members, which was meant to provide Congress with some guidance. The recommendation of the ACEC to Congress included the following:

- Repealing the 3 percent federal excise tax on telecommunications services.

- Permanently barring states and local tax jurisdictions from taxing Internet access fees.

- Encouraging states to find a more simplified states sales and use taxation system.

---

[686] http://www.ecommercecommission.org/about.htm (visited June 15, 2002).

[687] *See* § 6.07[D][3], note 732 and accompanying text.

[688] http://www.ecommercecommission.org (visited June 15, 2002).

[689] The Internet Tax Freedom Act, Pub. L. No. 105-277, 1102, 112 Stat. 2681 (1988).

[690] *See generally* Wendy Trahan, The Future of Sales and Use Tax on Electronic Commerce: Promoting Uniformity After Quill, 21 Va. Tax Rev. 101, 106 (Summer 2001).

- Extending the moratorium on multiple and discriminatory taxes until 2006.

- Halting international tariffs on Internet transactions.[691]

The Clinton administration was unhappy with the ACEC's report because its opinions were not balanced. Critics of the ACEC claim that it was pro-business biased and even its government representatives exhibited such a bias, especially Governors James Gilmore and Paul Harris.[692] In the report, the business leaders on the ACEC were able to advocate keeping the Internet a tax-free zone. This position on Internet taxation garnered support from both Democrats and Republicans, including Christopher Cox, Ron Wyden, and Dick Gephardt. However, proponents of Internet taxation were disappointed that the report did not address the concerns of the brick-and-mortar companies. Although the direction of American tax policy is unclear, ultimate tax policy should contemplate three principles. First, a fair tax regime must be instituted for both brick-and-mortar and dot-com companies. This would mean that mail-order, dot-com, and brick-and-mortar companies are all taxed equally.[693] Second, taxation should not unduly distort business or state revenue streams. For example, California accounts for 15 percent of America's business but may only receive a share of tax consistent with Vermont. Third, the state taxing regime should not impose undue burdens of uncertainty on dot-com companies. More specifically, such taxes should be manageable for lawmakers and easy for business to institute and be technologically neutral.[694]

[2] Federal Taxation

On July 1, 1997, the White House issued a "White Paper"[695] that declared, "[T]he United States believes that no new taxes should be imposed on Internet commerce."[696] The White House took the position in the White Paper that "the same broad principles applicable to international taxation . . . should be applied to sub-federal taxation. No new taxes should be applied to electronic commerce, and states should coordinate their allocation of income derived from electronic commerce."[697] The enactment of ITFA ensured that no federal taxes would be placed on Internet access or e-commerce for three years, and, further, restricted individual states from enacting new taxes on e-commerce.

---

[691] Advisory Comm'n on Elec. Commerce, Report to Congress 13-15, 17-18 (Apr. 2000), http://www.ecommercecommission.org/library.html.

[692] *See, e.g.,* David Johnston, Advisory Panel on the Internet Taxes Unlikely to Reach Consensus, N.Y. Times (Mar. 30, 2000) at C1.

[693] *See* 112 Stat. at 2681-723.

[694] *Id.*

[695] White House, A Framework for Global Electronic Commerce (1997), *reprinted in* Daily Tax Rep. (BNA) (July 2, 1997) at L-13.

[696] *Id.* at L-15.

[697] *Id.* at L-16.

[D]   State Taxation of Electronic Commerce

The Commerce Clause of the U.S. Constitution prevents states from imposing taxes that would unduly burden interstate commerce. The fundamental issue is whether or not a company subject to tax has sufficient nexus with the taxing authority. More specifically, our hypothetical company, SPC, could potentially be subject to state taxation anywhere within the United States, as long as nexus is established. The challenge becomes how states can monitor this. E-commerce transactions occur instantaneously, which makes it difficult to determine who the buyer and seller are and where they are respectively located. In short, SPC, a Massachusetts company, could sell a downloadable computer antivirus software program on the Internet to a resident of Batesville, Indiana, without ever knowing the name and address of the end customer. Hence, without knowing the name and physical location of the buyer and seller, it is impossible for states to determine what the applicable jurisdiction is for sales tax purposes. The numerous tax issues that can stem from e-commerce Internet transactions include:

- Who is the customer?[698]

- Where does the customer live?[699]

- Did the transaction constitute a sale of tangible property, the performance of a service, or the transfer of intangible property?

- Which jurisdiction has the authority to tax the sale?

- What online activities constitute sales for sales tax purposes?

- When may a state impose a sales or use tax on online activities?

- What constitutes a sufficient nexus[700] within a taxing jurisdiction?

---

[698] When a customer orders a computer from SPC's catalog, the name of the customer placing the order is recorded, which in turn reveals the identity of the customer. The true identity of a customer is not necessarily known when the product is delivered electronically to an Internet address. The customer could be ordering the product from someone else's computer or under an alias name (the assumption of which is often called *spoofing*).

[699] When a customer orders a computer from SPC's catalog, the product is physically delivered to the customer, which in turn reveals the taxing jurisdiction. The physical location is not necessarily known when the product is delivered electronically to an Internet address.

[700] In the United States, if a taxpayer has sufficient nexus with a state under the Commerce Clause and the Due Process Clause, a state may impose a tax on the interstate transaction. The Supreme Court in *Complete Auto Transit v. Brady* articulated a four-prong test that enables a state to tax interstate transactions under the Commerce Clause. A state tax is legal if (1) it applies to an activity with a substantial nexus with the taxing state, (2) it is fairly apportioned, (3) it does not discriminate against interstate commerce, and (4) it is fairly related to the services provided by the state. Complete Auto Transit v. Brady, 430 U.S. 724 (1976). Whereas, under the Due Process Clause, nexus is satisfied when a minimum connection exists between the state and the person, property, or transaction subject to tax.

- Can states compel buyers to pay self-assessed "use" tax?

- Can states or the federal government institute a means whereby they force all e-commerce related transactions to adhere to set processes whereby all transactions go through an electronic toll booth, enabling them to monitor all activities?

- What kind of record retention requirements are necessary for tax purposes?[701]

State legislatures must resolve many of the above Internet tax issues subject to the federal limitations imposed by Congress. Until comprehensive new legislation governing the taxation of electronic commerce is enacted, traditional tax rules must be used to address these complex issues.

[1] Sales and Use Tax

The concept of the sales and use tax was introduced and enacted in the 1930s.[702] State governments use sales and use taxes to generate revenue within their states.[703] Sales and use taxes constitute an estimated 35 percent of states' total revenue collection opportunities.[704] Sales and use taxes were aimed at generating revenues for states from an industrial economy where the manufacturing and sales of goods were the mainstays of the economy.[705] Now that the world economy has shifted away from an industrial to an information base, the erosion of territorial boundaries threatens to disrupt what has been a significant source of taxation income for many states.

Forty-six states and the District of Columbia impose sales and use taxes on various business transactions.[706] These states impose a *sales tax* on the purchase or lease of tangible personal property, certain services, and intangible properties[707] used within their state boundaries. Most states, excluding Alaska, Delaware, Montana, New Hampshire, and Oregon, tax the sale of products, while several states, such as Hawaii,[708] New Jersey, New Mexico,[709] South Dakota,[710] Texas, and Washington, tax services. Ignoring the distinction between products and services, consumers are required to pay the sales tax, while the seller, as an agent for the state

---

[701] *See generally* Wright and Winn, *supra* note 39, 10-1 to 10-17.

[702] *See* Adam L. Schwartz, Note, Nexus or Not, Orvis v. New York, SFA Folio v. Tracy and the Persistent Confusion Over Quill, 29 Conn. L . Rev. 485, 520 n.28 (citing Richard Pomp & Oliver Oldman, State & Local Tax'n 775 (1996)).

[703] Stewart A. Baker, Beware, the Taxman Cometh to Cyberspace, L.A. Times (Oct. 5, 1995) at 9.

[704] R. Scott Grierson, Legal Potholes Along the Information Superhighway, 16 Loy. L.A. Ent. L.J. 541, 573 (1996).

[705] *See generally* Delta and Matsuura, *supra* note 27.

[706] Four states (Delaware, Montana, New Hampshire, and Oregon) do not assess sales tax. By comparison, nine states (Alaska, Florida, Nevada, New Hampshire, South Dakota, Tennessee, Texas, Washington, and Wyoming) have little or no income tax. These states must rely on sales or property tax for their revenues.

[707] Intangible properties can include intellectual property rights.

[708] Hawaii taxes 155 different services.

[709] New Mexico taxes 155 different services.

[710] South Dakota taxes 130 different services.

government, collects and remits the tax.[711] Table 6.1 outlines the taxation policies of those states imposing a tax on the sale of goods over the Internet.

A *use tax* is a corollary tax aimed at taxing the use, consumption, or storage of tangible property at a rate similar to that of a sales tax.[712] The use tax is collected from the seller when the consumer is domiciled in another state.[713] Assessing the use tax was meant to put local retailers at a competitive parity with out-of-state retailers exempt from sales tax.[714] The problem with use tax lies in enforcement. If U.S. citizens were accustomed to declaring and paying use tax for mail and catalog orders, then perhaps there would not be an issue with how to tax Internet-related transactions. The State of Michigan introduced on its 2000 state tax form a line item that allowed Michigan residents to declare the use tax that they owed for the likes of Internet-related transactions and mail orders. While the state of Michigan attempted to rely on its citizens' self assessment, it is doubtful too many residents will declare anything substantial. The only way for Michigan and other states to get citizens to comply is to enforce self-assessment with civil and criminal penalties to ensure payment of taxes occurs on e-commerce-related transactions.

[2]   Nexus—Taxable Level of Business Activity

One threshold question that must be answered when determining whether sales or use tax is imposed is whether or not nexus[715] actually exists. Sellers are required to collect sales and use tax and submit it to the appropriate state if the seller has a physical presence, also known as nexus, in the consumer's state. *Nexus* has been described as the "degree of business activity that must be present before a taxing jurisdiction has the right to impose a tax, or an obligation to collect a tax, on an entity."[716] A seller can have nexus in a jurisdiction if it has a store, office, warehouse, distribution facility, sales force, agent, or representative to take orders. The question becomes, with Internet transactions, does a server in and of itself constitute nexus? If so, what happens, if in an attempt to avoid nexus, companies relocate their server(s) to tax havens and avoid establishing any physical presence in the forum state?

The Due Process Clause and the Commerce Clause of the U.S. Constitution address the concept of nexus in relation to states imposing a tax on interstate transactions. The Due Process Clause provides that: "No person shall . . . be deprived

---

[711] Robert J. Fields, Understanding and Managing Sales and Use Tax 205 (3d. ed., 1994).

[712] *Id.*

[713] *See* White Oak Corp. v. Department of Rev. Servs. 503 A.2d 582, 585 (Conn. 1986).

[714] National Geographic Soc. v. California Bd. of Educ., 430 U.S. 551, 555 (1977).

[715] For a comprehensive discussion of nexus, *see* Julie M. Buechler, Note Virtual Reality: Quill's "Physical Presence" Requirements Obsolete When Cogitating Use Tax Collection in Cyberspace, 74 N. Dak. L. Rev. 479 (1998).

[716] Karl A. Frieden and Michael E. Porter, State Taxation of Cyberspace, The Tax Adviser (Nov. 1, 1996).

TABLE 6.1
Taxation of Internet Transactions*

State	Sales of Goods over the Internet	Access to the Internet	Download Information/Software
Alabama	Taxable	Exempt	Taxable
Alaska	No sales tax	No sales tax	No sales tax
Arizona	Taxable	Exempt	Taxable
Arkansas	Taxable	Exempt	Exempt
California	Taxable	Exempt	Exempt
Colorado	Taxable	Exempt	Taxable
Connecticut	Taxable	Taxable	Taxable
Delaware	No sales tax	No sales tax	No sales tax
District of Columbia	Taxable	Taxable	Taxable
Florida	Taxable	Exempt	Exempt
Georgia	Taxable	Exempt	Exempt
Hawaii	Taxable	Taxable	Taxable
Idaho	Taxable	Exempt	Taxable
Illinois	Taxable	Exempt	Exempt/taxable
Indiana	Taxable	Exempt	Exempt/taxable
Iowa	Taxable	Exempt	Exempt
Kansas	Taxable	Exempt	Exempt/taxable
Kentucky	Taxable	Exempt	Exempt
Louisiana	Taxable	Exempt	Taxable
Maine	Taxable	Exempt	Taxable
Maryland	Taxable	Exempt	Exempt
Massachusetts	Taxable	Exempt	Exempt
Michigan	Taxable: use tax	Exempt	Exempt/taxable
Minnesota	Taxable	Exempt	Exempt/taxable
Mississippi	Taxable	Exempt	Taxable
Missouri	Taxable	Exempt	Exempt

See generally http://www.vertexinc.com (visited Sept. 20, 2001).

TABLE 6.1 Taxation of Internet Transactions (Continued)

State	Sales of Goods over the Internet	Access to the Internet	Download Information/Software
Montana	No sales tax	No sales tax	No sales tax
Nebraska	Taxable	Exempt and/or taxable	Exempt/taxable
Nevada	Taxable	Exempt	Exempt
New Hampshire	No sales tax	No sales tax	No sales tax
New Jersey	Taxable	Exempt	Exempt
New Mexico	Taxable	Taxable	Taxable
New York	Taxable	Exempt	Taxable
North Carolina	Taxable	Exempt	Exempt
North Dakota	Taxable	Taxable	Taxable
Ohio	Taxable	Taxable: commercial use only	Taxable: commercial use only
Oklahoma	Taxable	Exempt	Exempt and/or taxable
Oregon	No sales tax	No sales tax	No sales tax
Pennsylvania	Taxable	Exempt	Exempt/taxable
Rhode Island	Taxable	Exempt	Exempt
South Carolina	Taxable	Exempt	Exempt
South Dakota	Taxable	Taxable	Taxable
Tennessee	Taxable	Taxable	Exempt/taxable
Texas	Taxable	Exempt up to $25,000	Taxable
Utah	Taxable	Exempt	Taxable
Vermont	Taxable	Exempt	Exempt
Virginia	Taxable	Exempt	Exempt
Washington	Taxable	Exempt	Taxable
West Virginia	Taxable	Exempt	Taxable
Wisconsin	Taxable	Taxable	Exempt/taxable
Wyoming	Taxable	Exempt	Exempt/taxable

of life, liberty, or property, without the due process of law,"[717] "nor shall any State deprive any person of life, liberty, or property without due process of law."[718] The Due Process Clause of the U.S. Constitution requires "traditional notions of fair play and substantive justice"[719] and "requires some definitive link, some minimum connection between a state and the person, property, or transaction it seeks to tax."[720]

The Commerce Clause provides that "[t]he Congress shall have the power . . . to regulate commerce with foreign Nations, and among several States, and with the Indian Tribes."[721] Although this phrase does not literally address state taxation, under the guise of Congress's dormant commerce clause power it has been interpreted as prohibiting state taxes that would impede interstate commerce.[722] The U.S. Supreme Court in *Complete Auto Transit v. Brady*[723] developed a four-prong test that permits states to tax interstate transactions under the Commerce Clause. The high court held a state tax is constitutional if (1) it applies to an activity with a substantial nexus with the taxing state, (2) it is fairly apportioned, (3) it does not discriminate against interstate commerce, and (4) it is fairly related to the services provided by the state.[724]

E-commerce companies have been compared to mail-order companies because they do not always have a physical presence in the states in which they do business. This is relevant because the U.S. Supreme Court addressed the nexus issue when it ruled in *Quill Corp. v. North Dakota*[725] that Quill's mail-order business did not constitute a physical presence in the state. The conclusion reached by the 1992 *Quill* case also affirmed the 1967 *National Bellas Hess*[726] decision in which the Supreme Court ruled that a state could collect sales and use taxes if the company had a physical presence in that state. However, some level of *de minimis* physical presence in the state will not create a taxable nexus.[727] Consequently, Quill was not required to collect sales and use taxes from customers located within the state. The Court did not address the question of whether *Quill* would have been decided differently had the tax issue involving online sales. Arguably, sales over the Internet involve even less physical contact with a state than do catalogs sent through the U.S. mail. Although *Quill* upheld the physical nexus requirement for

---

[717] U.S. Const. amend. V.

[718] *Id.* amend. XIV.

[719] Milliken v. Myer, 311 U.S. 457, 463 (1940).

[720] Quill Corp. v. North Dakota, 504 U.S. 298, 306 (1992) (quoting Miller Bros. Co. v. Maryland, 347 U.S. 340, 344-45 (1954)).

[721] U.S. Const. art I, 8.

[722] *See* Jerome R. Hellerstein and Walter Hellerstein, State and Local Taxation 188-305 (2d ed., 1997).

[723] Complete Auto Transit v. Brady, 430 U.S. 274 (1977).

[724] *Id.*

[725] *Quill*, 504 U.S. at 312. The Supreme Court ruled that Quill's mail-order business did not constitute a physical presence within the state. Therefore, Quill did not have substantial nexus with the taxing state. *Id.*

[726] National Bellas Hess, Inc. v. Department of Rev., 386 U.S. 753 (1967).

[727] Quill, 504 U.S. at 315.

mail-order sales, the Court made it clear that it was within Congressional discretion to introduce legislation resolving the problem of remote sellers. Justice John Paul Stevens wrote, "This aspect of our decision is made easier by the fact that the underlying issue is not only one that Congress may be better qualified to resolve, but also one that Congress has the ultimate power to resolve. No matter how we evaluate the burdens that use taxes impose on interstate commerce, Congress remains free to disagree with our conclusion."

Once ground rules are established by Congress, then states can begin to equitably assess sales tax to dot-com companies and brick-and-mortar companies. This would also level the playing field between mail-order and brick-and-mortar companies. In some cases, companies with a brick-and-mortar presence in a state have not been collecting sales taxes for orders processed online or through mail orders. The California Senate recently passed a bill that would require companies with a presence in the state to collect taxes in online transactions.[728] Companies like Wal-Mart, Kmart, and Barnes & Noble have strategically attempted to find ways around their nexus problems for their own online sales. These companies have created separate companies specifically for their Internet-related business and now collect sales tax in those states where their dot-com companies have nexus.

An e-business strategy allows organizations a wide variety of choices as to where to locate, what employees to hire, and how to buy and sell goods and services. E-businesses should understand that opening new facilities or entering a partnering relationship can trigger significant tax issues, and they should enter into those arrangements after serious deliberations, including knowledge of the tax implications. Having a single telecommuting employee in a foreign jurisdiction can greatly increase an organization's tax exposure. Strategic planning on these issues, including where to locate brick-and-mortar facilities and employees, can help limit an organization's tax exposure. Companies should consult with professional tax advisors or with the members of their corporate tax departments for guidance in these complex matters.

[3]   Sales and Use Tax on Internet Access

Free Internet access is now available from companies such as AltaVista, but most users gain access to the Internet through an Internet Service Provider (ISP) or Online Service Provider (OSP). Accessing an ISP or OSP occurs by dialing a local access number through a local or national telecommunications company. An ISP, such as AOL, charges users a monthly fee (currently $23.95 per month) for unlimited Internet access.[729] This monthly fee bundles access to the Internet with AOL's own online content. Bundling these services makes it difficult to determine

---

[728] *See* Megan Holohan, California Ponders Internet Tax (visited June 15, 2002), http://www.infoworld.com/articles/hn/xml/00/08/31/000831hncaltax.xml?0901frap (discussing A.B. 2412).

[729] AOL's monthly access fee charge is published on its web site, at http://www.aol.com/info/pricing.html (visited June 15, 2002).

how much of the fee goes toward access versus content. Estimates made even as early as 1995 placed ISP and OSP revenues between $1.6 billion and $2.2 billion.[730] This revenue stream was a result of fees charged for Internet access, online services, and advertising.[731]

Needless to say, states view Internet access fees as a lucrative source of state revenue. How states will ultimately tax Internet access is yet to be determined. The enactment of the ITFA prohibits state and local governments from imposing taxes on Internet access fees if such a tax was not in place as of October 21, 1998.[732] This restriction will be effective until October 21, 2001.[733] Table 6.1 (on pages 6-113–6-114) is a state-by-state survey of tax rules for Internet access.

For those states that tax Internet access, some tax it as if Internet access were a telecommunication service.[734] The Telecommunications Act defines *telecommunication* as "the transmission between or among points specified by the user, of information of the user's choosing, without change in the content of the information as sent and received."[735] What constitutes transmission is subject to debate.[736] Internet access, e-mail, and bulletin board services are arguably analogous to cellular or regular telephone calls, which are subject to sales tax.[737] Internet access and e-mail involve additional enhanced services, however, such as the ability to store messages on computer servers, that raise questions as to whether they should, in fact, be subject to sales tax.

[4] Sales Tax Treatment of Online Content

E-commerce offers many new products and services for global customers. One of the most lucrative e-commerce opportunities is online content,[738] including computer software programs, digitized books, digitized magazines, digitized newspapers, digitized pictures, movies, music, video games, and much more.[739] In the United States, online content delivered via e-commerce threatens to compete with the likes of the video (annual revenues in excess of $12 billion), music ($12 billion), movie ($6.5 billion), and print publishing industries ($44 billion).[740]

---

[730] Charles E. McLure, Jr., Taxation of Electronic Commerce: Economic Objectives, Technological Constraints, and Tax Laws, 52 Tax L. Rev. 269, 311 (1997).

[731] *Id.*

[732] A grandfather clause enables certain states to tax access fees. The states include Connecticut, Iowa, New Mexico, North Dakota, Ohio, South Carolina, South Dakota, Tennessee, Texas, and Wisconsin.

[733] *Id.*

[734] Karl Frieden and Michael Porter, The Taxation of Cyberspace: State Tax Issues Related to the Internet and Electronic Commerce, 1996 St. Tax Notes 221-257 (Nov. 14, 1996).

[735] Telecommunications Act of 1996, Pub. L. No. 104-104, 110 Stat. 56, codified as 47 U.S.C. § 153(43).

[736] Delta and Matsuura, *supra* note 27.

[737] *Id.*

[738] McLure, *supra* note 730.

[739] *Id.*

[740] *Id.* at 304.

Given the revenue potential of online content, it is not surprising to find that more than a third of the states currently impose sales and use taxes on online content activities. These states include Connecticut, the District of Columbia, Hawaii, New Mexico, New York, Ohio, Pennsylvania, South Dakota, and Texas.[741] These states tax a variety of electronic services, including some of the following: e-mail, data processing, computer bulletin boards, news and weather reports, credit reports, airline reservations, cable television, software downloads, fax services, "900" telephone number services, and the like.[742] Although a tax may be levied, each state varies as to whether it taxes online sales transactions as an extension of the sales tax imposed on tangible personal property or as a separate category of taxable services.[743]

These jurisdictions also differ as to whether they tax all or just certain aspects of online content. A particular state's approach may be crucial for interpreting ambiguities or challenging possible overreaching of state tax rules. Moreover, the majority of states, including California, Georgia, Maryland, Massachusetts, Michigan, and Missouri, do not tax the electronic transmission of information or other online content-related transactions. Generally, the states that currently do not impose sales taxes on electronic services are those with a narrower sales tax base that encompasses tangible personal property and only a few enumerated services.

For instance, New Jersey has determined that information transferred electronically is not subject to sales tax because no tangible property is involved in the transaction. Other states, such as California, that have issued regulations or rulings on this issue have also generally relied on the fact that the content transferred electronically is nontaxable intangible property, not taxable tangible property.

The position each state is taking on the taxation of online transactions is based on the perceived tax revenue impacts on that given state. Many states are concerned about the loss of state revenue from the nontaxation of online taxations and are working together on a standardized way to collect sales and use tax from Internet transactions, called the Streamlined Sales Tax System (SSTS) for the 21st Century.[744] SSTS was formed in an attempt to persuade Congress to give the states the authority to tax Internet transactions, to stop the billions of dollars in state tax revenue that could be lost each year, and as of April 2002, 28 states had enacted enabling legislation supporting SSTS.[745] Some states, like California and Virginia, oppose assessing sales and use tax on Internet transactions because they fear that an Internet tax will hurt the technology sector in their respective state and will cost

---

[741] Delta and Matsuura, *supra* note 27.

[742] *Id.*

[743] *Id.*

[744] The Streamlined Sales Tax System has been embraced by many states. These states include Alabama, Arkansas, Illinois, Indiana, Iowa, Kansas, Kentucky, Louisiana,, Maryland, Massachusetts, Michigan, Minnesota, Missouri, Nebraska, Nevada, North Carolina, North Dakota, Oklahoma, Pennsylvania, South Dakota, Texas, Utah, Vermont, Washington, Wisconsin, and Wyoming. For a complete state list and the bill status, *see* http://www.cob.sjsu.edu/facstaff/nellen_a/e-links.html. (visited June 15, 2002).

[745] States, Wash. Internet Daily, Apr. 11, 2002, vol. 3, no. 70.

them more in state tax revenue generated from the technology sector than the incremental gain(s) from sales and use tax on e-commerce related transactions. Some states are also concerned that taxation on online sales will create additional nexus for domestic companies in their state, thus forcing that state to share its state tax revenue. For example, Massachusetts Revenue Commissioner Frederick Laskey stated, "A lot of people who are interested in streamlined tax code would like to exert nexus over our companies. We're a booming high-tech area, and there's a lot of states that don't have that."[746] Table 6.2 is a chart from the General Accounting Office which estimates the potential tax revenue losses anticipated from Internet sales in 2003.[747]

[5] Sales Tax Treatment of Computer Software

States are eager to collect "the income from legally owed taxes they currently cannot collect."[748] One common online transaction is the sale of computer software. Neither the Internal Revenue Code (IRC) nor state regulations have provided much guidance as to whether computer software is considered to be tangible or intangible property for sales and use tax purposes. Some states impose a sales tax on software as if it were a tangible personal property while other states tax computer software as if it were the sale of a computer or electronic service.[749] Some states also will not assess a sales tax on computer software sold over the Internet, even if they would tax the same software sold in retail stores.[750]

Court cases that address this issue have also been split. In *South Central Bell Telephone Co. v. Barthelemy*,[751] the court found that computer program master source codes were tangible property. In *Ronnen v. Commissioner*,[752] however, the court came to an opposite conclusion and ruled that software codes were intangible property. Some cases have determined that computer services can be treated as taxable and nontaxable services.[753]

Whether software is considered tangible or intangible appears to be determined on a case-by-case basis and varies from state to state. Table 6.1 on pages 6-113–6-114 lists the tax treatment in each state for computer software and downloads from the Internet.

The Advisory Commission failed to reach any conclusions on this. As a result, e-businesses distributing software over the Internet should be aware of the

---

[746] Andrew Caffrey, Regional Report: States at Odds Over Web Taxes—Holdouts May Hurt Efforts to Simply Tax Codes and Win Taxing Rights, Wall Street Journal (Mar. 7, 2001) at B3.

[747] *Id.*

[748] McCain Urges Swift Action on Moratorium, Pledges Action on E-Commerce Consensus, 2001, Electronic Commerce & Law Report (BNA) 292 (2001).

[749] *Id.* at 10-27.

[750] *Id.* These states include California, Maryland, Massachusetts, Missouri, South Carolina, and Utah.

[751] 643 So. 2d 1240 (La. 1994).

[752] 90 T.C. 74 (1988).

[753] *See, e.g.*, Creasy Sys. Consultant v. Olsen, 716 S.W.2d 35 (Tenn. 1986).

TABLE 6.2
Potential Tax Revenue Losses from Year 2003 Internet Sales

State	Low Estimate (in millions)	High Estimate (in millions)
California	$86	$1,720
Florida	48	595
Michigan	39	415
Massachusetts	25	274
North Carolina	25	279
Tennessee	22	282
Colorado	18	181
All States	$1 billion	$12.4 billion

ongoing uncertainty in characterizing transactions for tax purposes, especially as the digital download of software from the Internet increases.

[E] Products versus Services: The Characterization of Revenue

How a company characterizes its revenue is critical in terms of the ultimate tax treatment. Traditionally, revenue streams for companies are derived from the sale of a product, use of property (rents and royalties), or the provision of a service. With the creation of the Internet, and particularly of e-commerce, the line between a service and a product often becomes blurred. Many e-commerce companies have multiple revenue streams, which may include a combination of product sales, uses of property, and sales of services. For tax purposes, identifying whether an e-business is a provider of products or a provider of services may be difficult, but is an important decision to make, as products and services are taxed differently in different jurisdictions. Services are not subject to sales and use taxes in the United States, for example, whereas in Europe they are subject to VAT.

A restaurant bill serves to illustrate the confusion between a product and a service. Most people characterize restaurants as service-oriented businesses. But the bill that customers pay encompasses the cost of the meal as well as the cost of the planning, purchasing, cooking, serving, and other services provided. Since the meal is the significant income-producing factor, however, under tax law restaurants are considered providers of products rather than of services.

As the restaurant example illustrates, distinguishing products from services can be surprisingly difficult, especially when the service provided includes a tangible good. Many Internet companies can be viewed as selling both products and services. Take, for example, Amazon.com, which offers books, CD-ROMs, videos, and other products. Once a customer places an order, Amazon.com typically notifies a distributor of the order, who in turn ships the products to Amazon.com. Amazon.com then delivers the product to its customer. Clearly this chain of events indicates that Amazon.com is engaged in the sale of products. Amazon.com also engages in service activities, however, such as banner advertising and holding auctions. This analogy can be applied to a multitude of e-commerce companies, such as Barnes & Noble, Beyond.com, and eBay.

Many services that e-businesses provide to customers revolve around either the sale or the use of products. Consequently, it is becoming more difficult for e-businesses to be treated solely as service providers for tax purposes. One possible method of achieving a more favorable tax status would be to separately invoice the sale of products and the provision of services. Pursuant to § 446(d) of the IRC, a taxpayer may gain the tax advantages associated with using a different accounting method for each line of business.

[F] Cash versus Accrual

Another major issue regarding the distinction between a provider of products and a provider of services is the accounting method used for tax purposes. IRC § 471 states that, to reflect income correctly, inventories must be taken at the beginning and end of each taxable year in every case in which the production, purchase, or sale of merchandise is an income-producing factor.[754] Businesses operating with inventory must use the accrual method of accounting. Therefore, providers of products typically use the accrual method of accounting, while service providers utilize the cash method.

In reality, however, it is difficult to identify a business as being clearly either a service provider or a product provider. Two cases illustrate this point: *Knight-Ridder Newspapers, Inc. v. United States*[755] and *Galedrige Constr. Inc. v. Commissioner of Internal Revenue.*[756] Although both cases have similar fact patterns, the courts reached different results. Knight-Ridder Newspapers claimed that newspapers were a service and that the newspapers themselves were insubstantial inventory, since a day-old newspaper was useless; the court, however, required Knight-Ridder to use the accrual method. Similarly, Galedrige's molten asphalt merchandise became useless five hours after it was picked up from the supplier, but the court permitted Galderidge to use the cash method. In both cases, the inventory in question was a significant income-producing factor and a significant cost of total receipts. Neither service could be rendered without the requisite inventory.

---

[754] IRC § 471 (1999).

[755] 743 F.2d 781 (11th Cir. 1984).

[756] 1996 U.S. App. LEXIS 1792 (1996) (unpublished opinion). The court overruled the Commissioner and ruled that asphalt was not considered merchandise held for sale due to its short five-hour life cycle. Galedrige Construction, therefore, could continue to use the cash method for its paving business. *Id.*

The conflicting decisions in these two court cases blur the distinction between a product provider and a service provider.

SPC is an example of an e-business whose tax classification could vary. One of SPC's corporate missions is to sell software online. SPC delivers the software through a distributor to its customer or allows customers to download the software digitally. Consequently, SPC holds little physical inventory and conducts all transactions on a per-order basis. Generally speaking, SPC could be characterized as a company that sells products and should use the accrual method. Without taking title of the software it sells, however, SPC could also be considered a service that delivers software. Consequently, it is unclear whether SPC should utilize the cash or the accrual method.

The main difference between utilizing the cash or the accrual method lies in the timing of tax payments. Under Rev. Proc. 71-21, accrual basis taxpayers may defer to include in their income payments received in one taxable year for services to be performed in the next succeeding taxable year.[757] If SPC is classified as a service company, it cannot defer the advance payment of services, since only accrual-basis taxpayers can defer such advance payment. According to this Rev. Proc., it would be more advantageous for SPC to use the accrual method of accounting, since SPC could prepay for products and thus lower its taxable income.

Under the accrual method, companies with inventory need to record their expected revenue for taxable income. When using the cash method, companies do not have to account for expected revenue, thereby delaying the time when they will have to pay taxes on the anticipated income. Companies using the cash method have the benefit of not having to pay taxes for income that has not actually been received. Another benefit of the cash method is in regard to inventory. Under the accrual method, companies must capitalize related costs to inventory. These expenses will not be deductible until the inventory is sold, thus increasing the company's taxable income and taxes.

Generally speaking, it is more advantageous for companies to be classified as service providers in terms of the cash and accrual methods of accounting, but it has become more difficult for companies to do so. Prior to 1986, the cash versus accrual distinction was important. Service businesses could stay on the cash method if they chose, while businesses that sold property were forced to use the accrual method. After 1996, IRC § 448, which basically forces large corporations (both service and product) to use the overall accrual method of accounting for tax purposes, has applied.[758] The only professions excluded from IRC § 448 are lawyers, accountants, and other large professional service corporations, as defined in IRC § 448(d)(2)(A).[759] The choice of whether to use the cash or the accrual method requires some strategic tax planning. Companies should consult with professional tax advisors or with the members of their corporate tax departments.

---

[757] Rev. Proc. 71-21 (1999).

[758] IRC § 448 (1999).

[759] IRC § 448(d)(2)(A) (1999).

[G] International Withholding Tax

The number of Internet users is predicted to exceed 1 billion by the year 2010.[760] The ability to reach so many potential customers has encouraged businesses around the world to go online. By connecting the entire world to the Internet, traditional territorial boundaries become invisible and "blur . . . the source and character of income."[761] This, in turn, threatens the stability and viability of source-based taxation,[762] the permanent establishment concept,[763] and the meaning of U.S. trade or business as set forth in the Internal Revenue Code.[764]

To deal with impending international tax issues, several countries around the world have set up special commissions to study tax issues resulting from e-commerce.[765] Without changes to existing tax laws, the possibility exists that numerous countries may claim taxing jurisdiction over the same transaction, which could result in double taxation.[766] To avoid this problem and provide consistent treatment on various e-commerce transactions, worldwide rules and policies must be adopted.[767]

Taking a lead in this effort, the U.S. Treasury Department in 1996 published a Discussion Paper entitled *Selected Tax Policy Implications of Global Electronic Commerce.*[768] One of the messages in the Discussion Paper was that the Treasury was prepared to work with taxpayers, tax advisors, technology specialists, academics, foreign tax policy makers, and administrators to better understand the emerging technologies and to formulate rational and enforceable global tax rules.[769]

Coming up with a uniform approach to earnings from online transactions and international taxation issues will be critical to the continued growth and success of e-commerce. As it stands now, each country connected to the Internet has different tax rules on service, product, and royalty income, all of which may have to be

---

[760] *See* For the Record, Wash. Post (July 31, 1998), at A24 (reprinting testimony of William Daley, Secretary of Commerce, before the House Commerce Committee).

[761] *See* David R. Tillinghast, Tax Treaty Issues, 50 U. Miami L. Rev. 455, 456 (1996).

[762] The concept of *source-based taxation* (sometimes referred to as a *territorial approach*) entitles the "source" country to tax the income of nonresidents earned within its borders. Restatement (Third) of the Foreign Relations Law of the United States, § 412(1)(b)-(c) (1986).

[763] *Id.*

[764] Office of Tax Policy, U.S. Dep't of the Treasury, Selected Tax Policy Implications of Global Electronic Commerce 2.4 (1996), *reprinted in* 1996 Daily Tax Rep. (BNA) 226 (Nov. 22, 1996).

[765] Elusive Nature of Commerce on Internet Requires Uniform Rules, Tax Experts Agree, 1998 Daily Tax Rep. (BNA) 36 (Feb. 24).

[766] James D. Ciglar and Susan E. Stinnett, Treasury Seeks Cybertax Answers with Electronic Commerce, Discussion Paper, 8 J. Int'l Tax'n 56, 58 (Feb. 1997).

[767] *Id.*

[768] Office of Tax Policy, *supra* note 764.

[769] *Id.*

modified to bring uniformity to international tax issues. Companies should consult with professional tax advisors or with the members of their corporate tax departments when addressing international tax-planning issues.[770]

[H]   Other Sources of Taxes and Duties

Tax treaties seek to alleviate double taxation and to provide certainty in the marketplace.[771] The United States has a large number of bilateral tax treaties with its trading partners. Customs and duties can be a significant expense and may be overlooked when making sourcing decisions. NAFTA and WTO rules will affect these tax rates and should be considered. Companies should also consider how easily customers in Brazil, for example, can purchase items: Shipping, customs, and duty fees must be calculated and charged correctly to ensure that items move smoothly to customers.

[I]   International Taxation of E-Commerce

Under most international tax treaties, companies that sell goods or services in foreign jurisdictions may be assessed international taxes if a company maintains a permanent establishment[772] within the foreign jurisdiction and the profits are attributable to this permanent establishment.[773] The permanent establishment must have some tangible physical presence within a country, and the presence cannot be temporary. If permanent establishment exists, then the company may be subject to international tax considerations including sales, use, franchise, income, customs, corporation, and value-added taxes. In addition, currency limitations and export issues may apply to Internet transactions that cross international borders. The U.S. Treasury Department believes that the existing international tax rules and principles are sufficient to address the emerging issues relating to e-commerce-related

---

[770] *See generally* Reuven S. Avi-Yonah, International Taxation of Electronic Commerce, 52 N.Y. L. Rev. (1999); John Sweet, Comment: Formulating International Tax Laws in the Age of Electronic Commerce: The Possible Ascendancy of Residence-Based Taxation in an Era of Eroding Traditional Income Tax Principles, 146 U. Pa. L. Rev. 1949 (1998); James D. Ciglar and Susan E. Stinnett, Treasury Seeks Cybertax Answers with Electronic Commerce Discussion Paper, 8 J. Int'l Tax'n 56, 58 (Feb. 1997); Peter A. Glicklich, Stanford H. Goldberg, and Howard J. Levine, Internet Sales Pose International Tax Challenges, 84 J. Tax'n 325 (1996); James D. Cigler, Douglas E. Morgan, and James R. Shanahan, Taxation of Electronic Commerce Puts International Issues in New Light, 1 High Technology Industry 37 (1997); James D. Cigler, Harry C. Burritt, and Susan E. Stinnett, Cyberspace: The Final Frontier for International Tax Concepts? 7 J. Int'l Tax'n 340 (1996); Reuven S. Avi-Yonah, The Structure of International Taxation: A Proposal for Simplification, 74 Tex. L. Rev. 1301 (1996).

[771] Sanjeev Doss, Tax Presence Implications for Doing E-business with the U.S. 17 (May 2000) (on file with co-author Cyrus Daftary).

[772] A permanent establishment is defined within each tax treaty and generally encompasses a fixed place of business such as a branch, office, or factory. OECD, Committee on Fiscal Affairs, Model Tax Convention on Income and Capital, art. 5 (1997).

[773] *See, e.g.,* IRC § 901 (CCH 2001).

transactions.[774] However, just as within the United States, there are practical challenges to establishing a uniform tax system that works for every country, which include:

- Who is the customer?

- Where does the customer live?

- How do you measure the physical presence of e-commerce transactions to decide if the permanent establishment requirement has been met?

- Can a server satisfy the permanent establishment requirement?

- Did the e-commerce transaction constitute a sale of tangible property, the performance of a service, or the transfer of intangible property? If so, what type of tax should be applied?

- Which jurisdiction has the authority to tax the sale?

- When may a country impose a tax on the e-commerce transactions?

- What kind of record retention requirements are necessary for tax purposes for e-commerce transactions?

- Is it possible for businesses to selectively reduce their international tax liability by claiming to have permanent establishments within tax havens that have a lower VAT rate than other countries?

- Can a taxes be levied on an international level without insurmountable tax compliance and administration issues?

These challenges will appear in varying degrees when applying traditional international tax principles that seek to treat brick-and-mortar and dot-com companies equitably. Besides the aforementioned compliance issues, practical issues arise for the international community in administering the compliance effort in the online environment, such as the management of tax returns and calculating the amount of taxes owed. Online companies may be subject to filing tax returns in multiple jurisdictions. One concern is the possible tax implications of using electronic agents or servers in another country that may be deemed sufficient to establish a permanent establishment, giving rise to taxation. Internet-initiated value transfers raise thorny regulatory and tax issues. Coverage of the nuances of international tax issues is beyond the scope of this chapter. The International Chamber of Commerce, however, has identified the following broad categories of significant Internet tax issues:

1. Reliance on existing principles: utilization of internationally accepted tax rules;

---

[774] *See* U.S. Department of the Treasury, Office of Tax Policy, Selected Tax Policy Implications of Global Electronic Commerce (1996), http://www.fedworld.gov/pub/tel/internet.txt (last visited Apr. 12, 2001).

2. Bases for taxation: global taxation for residents versus source taxation for nonresidents;

3. Role of tax treaties: unlimited taxation for residence countries versus limited taxation for nonresidents;

4. Permanent establishment: establishing a taxable nexus for foreign taxpayers in a treaty country;

5. Characterization of income: tax treatment of digital information;

6. Services income: source rule for services income;

7. Residence: test for corporation residence;

8. Transfer pricing: allocation of income for electronic transactions;

9. Administration and compliance: providing for nonburdensome audits of tax returns for e-commerce related income;

10. Indirect taxation: VAT taxation in the country of consumption.[775]

The ICC favors an Internet tax policy based on the assumption that income earned through e-commerce should be treated neutrally by applying traditional tax principles to the Internet to the greatest extent possible rather than formulating a completely new tax regime.[776] The ICC takes the position that the Internet should be "source based."[777] Taking a *source-based approach* means that "service income is only subject to host country income tax if the services are physically performed in the country."[778] The ICC does not recommend replacing a "place of use" test with the source income test.[779] The ICC report argues that the "mind and management" test for corporate residence should apply to the Internet.[780] This corporate residency test focuses on where the management functions of corporations are performed.[781] The ICC favors a tax regime that guards against double taxation for consumption taxes. The ICC opposes the imposition of value-added taxes (VAT) on electronic commerce.[782] The ICC report concludes that no new taxes should be assessed on e-commerce transactions.[783]

[1] Value-Added Taxes

The European Commission's report entitled "A European Initiative in Electronic Commerce" contended that "in order to allow electronic commerce to

---

[775] International Chamber of Commerce, Policy Statement: Tax Issues and Ramifications of Electronic Commerce (Prepared by the ICC Commission on Taxation Jointly with the Business and Industry Advisory Committee to the OECD (BIAC) Dec. 15, 1999) (visited Apr. 22, 2002), http://www.iccwbo.org/home/state.../tax_issues_and_ramifications_of_electronic_commerce.as.

[776] *Id.*

[777] *Id.*

[778] *Id.*

[779] *Id.*

[780] *Id.*

[781] *Id.*

[782] *Id.*

[783] *Id.*

develop, certainty (so that tax obligations are clear, transparent and predictable) and tax neutrality" are necessary.[784] The European Commission, like the U.S. government, supports the principle of "no new taxes" on electronic commerce.[785] Unlike the United States, however, the Commission favors international taxation of e-commerce based on the value-added tax.[786] The Commission notes that e-commerce is "developing, in the area both of 'indirect' electronic commerce (electronic ordering of tangible goods), and 'direct' electronic commerce (electronic ordering and delivery of products and services online over the networks)."[787]

On May 7, 2002, the Commission adopted Directive IP/02/673, which seeks to create a level playing field, subjecting all goods and services sold to European consumers via the Internet subject to the existing VAT, irrespective of country of origin. Under the Directive, online services delivered to private consumers in the EU will be subject to VAT whether supplied by EU or non-EU suppliers. This rule takes effect July 1, 2003, and will impose a dramatic new set of administrative burdens and costs on American companies selling digital goods and services over the Internet. Fortunately, the Commission exempted sales to business customers located in the EU who have themselves registered for VAT, since the VAT charged on such sales would be ultimately offset by future input VAT credits when the EU business resells to its customers. Conversely, sales of digital content by EU businesses to private consumers outside the EU will be exempt from tax under the new directive.

The intent of the Directive is to ensure that services provided for consumption within the EU, including digital goods, are taxed within the EU, regardless of origin. Similar services supplied by Europerators for consumption outside the EU are not subject to VAT in the EU, but VAT on related inputs is elegible for deduction.[788]

A Technical Advisory Group (TAG) of the OECD issued a report titled "Tax Treaty Characterization Issues Arising from E-Commerce" that made recommendations on the character of e-commerce transactions.[789] If adopted by the OECD,

---

[784] COM (97) I57.

[785] E-Commerce and Indirect Taxation, Communication by the Commission to the Council of Ministers, the European Parliament, and the Economic and Social Committee, COM (96)328 Final.

[786] VAT is designed as a general consumption tax that, in principle, applies to all supplies of goods and services. In all cases transactions taking place within the EU, using the medium of electronic commerce and resulting in consumption within the EU, are subject to EU VAT under existing provisions. However, that is not always the case where supplies from non-EU countries are concerned. In the case of goods supplied from a non-EU country to an EU recipient, normal import procedures ensure that VAT is applied regardless of the means used to conduct the transaction. Similarly, certain descriptions of services received by EU businesses from non-EU countries are subject to VAT. However, it should be noted that with few exceptions, services received by EU private persons are not, under existing provisions, subject to VAT (the volumes of such supplies are at present very small). *Id.*

[787] *Id.*

[788] *Id.*

[789] Tax Treaty Characterization Issues Arising from E-Commerce, Report to Working Party No. 1 of the OECD Committee on Fiscal Affairs. Prepared by the Technical Advisory Group on Treaty Characterization of Electronic Commerce Payments (Feb. 1, 2001).

the recommendations will be used to interpret the OECD Model Tax Convention. The most controversial issue the TAG addressed was the characterization of e-commerce as either business profits or royalties.[790] Generally, when two tax treaty countries are involved, business profits are taxable in a country if the profits are associated with a permanent establishment in that country. Royalties are taxable in a country regardless of a permanent establishment. TAG found that most e-commerce transactions did not result in royalties.[791] This is because most of the transactions did not involve the use or exploitation of intellectual property. Hence, further agreement is required by the OECD and other groups to determine the appropriate application and characterization of VAT.

[2] Web Servers and Tax Issues

Another area of uncertainty is whether companies such as SPC are liable for income tax if their web servers are located in another country. The trend in international law is not to base taxes, jurisdiction, or other status on the location of the web server. OECD proposes a tax treaty under which a company is not liable for income tax on business profits merely because it has a web server in another country.[792] The Electronic Commerce Tax Study Group of the OECD felt that assessing a tax based on the location of a server would "present insurmountable tax compliance and administration issues," especially in light of the fact that transactions can happen instantaneously and servers can be moved or web traffic can be rerouted with little effort.[793] The OECD is exploring four international income tax issues: "(1) the effect of a web server in a country, (2) the effect of in-country web site hosting services, (3) the character of transactions involving digital products, and (4) transfer pricing in global e-commerce."[794]

[J] Limiting Tax Liability

Tax consequences are key to deciding what entity to form for an online business. Choosing the right entity to do business is one way to limit tax liability. An online company can be formed as a partnership. Partnerships do not themselves pay federal income tax. Instead, the partners are liable for federal income tax on their share of partnership income. Alternatively, an online company could be formed as a corporation, which pays tax separate from its owners. The owners are

---

[790] David Hardesty, Character of E-Commerce Transactions Part 1, EcommerceTax.com (May 13, 2001) (visited June 15, 2002), http:/ecommercetax.com/doc/051301.htm.

[791] *Id.*

[792] Ecommercetax.com, International Taxation of E-Commerce (Oct. 20, 1999) (visited June 15, 2002), http://www.ecommercetax.com/InternationalTax.htm.

[793] Carol A. Dunahoo, E-Commerce Tax Study Group Responds to OECD Request, 2000 Worldwide Tax Daily 11-18.

[794] Ecommercetax.com, International Income Tax Update (July 9, 1999) (visited June 15, 2002), http://www.ecommercetax.com/International/Tax.htm.

subject to a second tax upon receipt of a dividend or upon the sale or liquidation of their shares. Although the single tax treatment accorded partnerships appears much more favorable than the double taxation of corporate income, partnership income may cause partners to pay tax in many jurisdictions, since each partner is deemed to have earned a share of all the business income of the partnership. The administrative burden of filing U.S. tax returns leads many foreign investors to invest through corporations.

In choosing a form of entity for an online business, tax factors must be weighed against other issues such as control and liability. An online company could be formed as a professional or for-profit corporation to limit personal liability for debts. A growing number of online companies are formed as limited liability companies (LLC) for tax purposes.[795] The LLC gives its members the same limited liability protection accorded to shareholders of corporations.[796] However, "all nonrecourse debt . . . will be allocated to the tax basis of the members' interests accordingly."[797] A company should consult its state's version of the Uniform Limited Liability Act of 1996 to determine rules applicable to forming an LLC in that state. In general, an LLC applies to the secretary of state for authorization.[798] The phrase "limited liability company" or "limited company" or the abbreviations "L.L.C.," "LLC," "L.C.," or "LC" must be included in the entity.[799] To qualify to do business in a state as an LLC, the name must be "distinguishable from names of any corporation, limited partnership or company incorporated."[800] Section 201 of the Uniform Limited Liability Company Act provides the key attribution of the LLC: "A limited liability company is a legal entity distinct from its members."[801] The legal significance of being a distinct legal entity is that "its members are not normally liable for the debts, obligations, and liabilities of the company."[802]

The Uniform Partnership Act, which revised the Uniform Partnership Act of 1914, updates partnership law to provide partners with the possibility of choosing "the registered limited liability partnership form."[803] The objective of the revisions

---

[795] *See generally* Carter G. Bishop and Daniel S. Kleinberger, Chapter 2, Tax Classification of Unincorporated Business Organizations, Limited Liability Companies: Tax and Business Law (2000).

[796] *Id.*

[797] *Id.*

[798] Uniform Limited Liability Company Act § 105 (1997).

[799] *Id.* § 105(a)

[800] *Id.* § 105(b).

[801] *Id.* § 201.

[802] *Id.* § 201, comment.

[803] *See* Uniform Partnership Act (UPA) art. 10 & cmts. (1997). The following states or territories have adopted the UPA with the 1997 amendments: Alabama, Arizona, Arkansas, California, Colorado, Delaware, the District of Columbia, Hawaii, Idaho, Iowa, Kansas, Maryland, Minnesota, Montana, Nebraska, New Mexico, North Dakota, Oklahoma, Oregon, Puerto Rico, the U.S. Virgin Islands, Vermont, Virginia, and Washington. Connecticut, Florida, West Virginia, and Wyoming have adopted the 1994 version of the Act. National Conf. of Commr's on Unif. State Laws, A Few Facts About the Uniform Partnership Act (1994), http://www.nccusl.org/uniformact_factsheets/uniformacts-fs-upa9497.htm (visited Aug. 18, 2000).

is to give new businesses, including online business, an option to form limited liability partnerships.[804]

§ 6.08 INTERNET PAYMENT SYSTEMS

[A] Payment Instruments

[1] Credit Cards

Retail payments are made with diverse instruments, including "cash, checks, credit and debit cards, and the electronic funds transfer system known as the automated clearing house (ACH)."[805] Cash is used for 75 percent of retail transactions in the offline world.[806] Large funds transfers constitute "about 90 percent of the value of noncash transactions made every day."[807]

Credit cards are the dominant means of Internet payment for consumer sales. The law of credit cards is governed by the Truth in Lending Act (TILA) and Regulation Z, enacted by the Federal Reserve Board. TILA, for example, gave consumers the right to dispute billing errors and a methodology for protecting themselves against unauthorized charges. The three leading credit card issuers are Barclays, Visa, and MasterCard. BarclayCard has 13 million affiliate merchants and 650 million customers worldwide, making it the credit card of choice for consumers on the Internet.[808]

Cardholders have $50 total cap on liability for the unauthorized use of a credit card. Cardholders are not even liable for $50 unless the credit card is classified as an "accepted credit card." An accepted credit card means simply that it was issued in response to a consumer's request and that the consumer signed it. Cardholders may assert claims or defenses against the issuer of the credit card.[809] Cardholders are entitled to withhold payment from merchants for claims or defenses that cannot be resolved.[810]

Regulation Z requires that a consumer make "a good faith attempt to resolve the dispute with the person honoring the credit card."[811] Another limitation is that the "disputed transaction occur in the same state as the cardholder's current designated address or, if not within the same state, within 100 miles from that address." Most credit card companies, however, are willing to waive the 100-mile rule, permitting consumers to contest credit card transactions.[812] It is quite unclear

---

[804] See UPA, addendum to prefatory note (1997).

[805] Alice M. Rivlin, Chair, Committee on the Federal Reserve in the Payments Mechanism 1 (Jan. 1998).

[806] Id.

[807] Id. at 6.

[808] Mark Norris & Steve West, eBusiness Essentials 60 (2d ed. 2001).

[809] 12 C.F.R. § 226.12(c).

[810] Id. § 226.12(c)(1).

[811] Id. § 226.12(c)(3).

[812] Wright and Winn, supra note 39, § 20.02[A].

how the 100-mile or same state rule applies to web site transactions. Does the rule depend on the location of the server, the place of incorporation of the online company, or the location of the consumer?[813]

When many customers have disputes with online merchants, the charge back rate grows unacceptably high. Charge back occurs when a cardholder contests a charge. Cardholders must contest charges within 60 days from the date of the issuance of the credit card statement.[814] Online companies must strive to keep their charge back rate low. Web sites that sell adult entertainment services have a high rate of disputes leading to charge backs.

Visa USA considers computer network and information services as well as computer programming, data processing, and integrated systems design to have a high rate of charge backs.[815] Visa USA and MasterCard have recently developed guidelines targeting online businesses considered high risk.[816] Online companies are required to keep charge back rates to a maximum of "1 percent of transactions or 2.5 percent of monthly revenue."[817] Merchants will generally not have a direct relationship with the bank issuing the credit card.[818] Instead, a written agreement between the merchant and merchant bank will be executed.[819] The merchant bank has the job of "collecting receipts from the merchant and transferring them to the issuing bank for credit on its own account at that bank."[820] The merchant bank accepts deposit of credit slips and credits the merchant's account and charges for this service.[821]

[2] Debit Cards

Debit cards have developed more recently than credit cards. They are virtually indistinguishable in appearance. A *debit card,* also known as an *automated teller machine* (ATM) or *banking card,* is simply a vehicle for drawing upon funds already in a checking account.[822] Barclays Bank in London installed the first ATM in 1967.[823] Debit cards are governed by the federal Electronic Funds Transfer Act (EFTA). EFTA applies to transactions in which an electronic debit is made from the customer's account and a credit for the same amount is made to the merchant's account through a point-of-sale (POS) terminal.[824]

---

[813] *Id.*

[814] Henry H. Perritt, Jr., Legal and Technological Infrastructures for Electronic Payment Systems, 22 Rutgers Computer & Tech. L.J. 1, 28 (1996).

[815] Randy Barrett, Newsfront: E'Tailers Caught in Card, Interactive Week (Apr. 10, 2000), at 10.

[816] *Id.*

[817] *Id.*

[818] Perritt, *supra* note 814, at 18.

[819] *Id.*

[820] *Id.*

[821] *Id.* at 22.

[822] Lynn LoPucki, Commercial Transactions: A Systems Approach (1998), 384.

[823] Teitelman and Davis, *supra* note 29.

[824] Lewis Mandell, The Credit Card Industry: A History, xxiii (1990).

Use of debit cards became widespread in the late 1970s and early 1980s. EFTA and Regulation E issued by the Federal Reserve Board require the issuer of debit cards to make mandatory disclosure requirements about the terms for use of the card. Regulation E, for example, requires that the bank's debit card rules be written in simple English. Regulation E provides rules for resolving disputes over erroneous transactions, unauthorized or false authorizations, and other problems.[825]

[3] Electronic Negotiable Instruments

[a] UCC Articles 3 and 4

The Uniform Commercial Code (UCC) was designed to modernize and bring uniformity to the commercial law. Article 3 of the UCC governing negotiable instruments and Article 4 governing bank deposits and collections were last revised in 1990, prior to the widespread use of the Internet for payment. Revised Article 3 provides ground rules for transferring negotiable instruments. Payment by checks, drafts, promissory notes, and other negotiable instruments is covered by Article 3 of the UCC.

The warranties, liabilities, and rules for allocating payment risks are also covered by Article 3. Revised Article 4 authorized the electronic presentment of items as well as validated the practice of truncation. The purpose of the 1990 revisions to Article 4 was to improve the functioning of check collection.[826] Revised Article 4 was designed to permit the presentment of checks to payor banks by electronic transmission of information.[827] An automated clearinghouse (ACH) is designed to facilitate the exchange by banks of checks involving interbank payments.[828]

[b] Article 4A Wire Transfers

Wire transfers governed by Article 4A of the Uniform Commercial Code transfer trillions of dollars.[829] In contrast, point-of-sale and other consumer transactions are covered by the Electronic Fund Transfer Act (EFTA). The two principal systems for wire transfers are the Federal Reserve wire transfer network (FEDWIRE) and the New York ClearingHouse Interbank Payments Systems (CHIPS).

Each payment order contains information, such as the identity of the account from which funds are to be withdrawn, the amount to be transferred, the name and account number of the person to receive payment (the beneficiary), and the name

---

[825] Consumer Credit Protection Act, 15 U.S.C. §§ 1693-1693r (2000).

[826] UCC § 4-101, official cmt. 2 (2000).

[827] *Id.*

[828] Teitelman and Davis, *supra* note 29.

[829] LoPucki, *supra* note 822, at 400.

and location of the beneficiary bank. A fund transfer agreement will also contain definitions, funds transfer services, fees, use of communications, customer identity, limitation of liability, choice of law, authority, and other general terms.[830]

International funds transfers are frequently made through the Society for Worldwide Interbank Financial Telecommunications (SWIFT). SWIFT is a "bank-owned utility for exchanging, payment, and settlement of messages."[831] SWIFT is used to send hundreds of millions of messages each year. SWIFT connects 5,300 member financial institutions in 137 countries and is the primary large-value payment system (LVPS).[832]

Assume Big Company wants to pay an obligation owed to SPC. One option is for Big Company to send SPC a check or a promissory note. Another possibility would be for Big Company to use a credit card to purchase software from SPC's site. By giving its credit card number, Big Company enables SPC to obtain payment from the bank backing the credit card. If Big Company is located in the continental United States, it may also use FEDWIRE to transmit funds. An Article 4A funds transfer is another system of payment.

Funds transfers are typically used for large payment transactions. Suppose Big Company purchased one of SPC's subsidiaries for $500 million. The wire transfer will be a quicker payment option than would using the check collection system. A credit card transaction would be impractical for such a large sum. A wire transfer is an efficient payment system that permits the transfer of millions of dollars for a few dollars.[833]

Funds transfers may occur instantaneously and in a single day where a complex network of intermediary banks exists.[834] Article 4A, unlike other UCC articles, is governed by unique rules not found in Articles 3 and 4.[835] Article 4A sought to balance the interests of banks with those of other commercial and financial organizations.[836] Article 4A employs a specialized vocabulary with key definitions being "payment order," "beneficiary's bank," "receiving bank," and "sender."[837]

[B] Internet Banking

Security First Network Bank became the first fully transactional Internet bank federally insured by the FDIC.[838] The Security First Network Bank uses

---

[830] See Committee on the Law of Commerce in Cyberspace, American Bar Association Section of Business Law, Model Fund Transfer Services Agreement and Commentary, by the Working Group on Electronic Financial Services of the Subcommittee on Electronic Commercial Practices (1994).

[831] Teitelman and Davis, *supra* note 29.

[832] *Id.*

[833] UCC Article 4A: Funds Transfer, Prefatory Note (1989).

[834] *Id.*

[835] UCC § 4A-102, O.C. (2000).

[836] *Id.*

[837] *Id.* § 4A-103 (2000).

[838] Security First Bank, Security First Network Bank, About Security First Network Bank (May 12, 2000), http://www.sfnb.com/infodesk/about.html. SFNB is now owned by RBC Ventura.

state-of-the-art information security "including a secure operating system, data encryption firewalls and routers."[839] Security First reimburses customers "100% for unauthorized transactions or misdirected payments."[840] A customer accesses account data using mouse clicks.[841] A large number of banks have web sites which permit customers to review balances, transfer funds, and pay bills.[842] Stand-alone Internet banks have lost ground "to integrated 'clicks 'n bricks' strategies by traditional banks."[843] For example, Internet bank Dublin's Bank One was acquired by Spain's BBVA.[844] Internet banks have faltered because customers do not have the same sense of security as with traditional banks.[845] Internet banks are also viewed as inconvenient because of slow connections and crashes of computer servers.[846] An estimated "37 percent of all national banks offered transactional online banking at the beginning of 2001, compared with about half that percentage 15 months earlier."[847]

[C] E-Cash Payment Systems

Consumers have been slow to adopt smart cards and e-money methods of payment. CyberCash Inc. was founded in August 1994 to develop a global payments system with secure payment using encryption technology.[848] CyberCash sought "to provide secure, convenient systems for secure credit cards, cash, checks, coins or micropayments."[849] CyberCash sought to promote three payments systems: (1) secure card transport, (2) CyberCash or money messaging, and (3) micropayments to replace coins.[850] CyberCash has a platform that permits merchants to accept payments over the Internet with any merchant bank.[851]

CyberCash was the first vendor to develop "electronic purse cards," which is the Internet equivalent of "walk around money."[852] Micropayments are kept in the virtual equivalent of a coin purse and are used to pay for small-scale Internet goods and services (such as an article downloaded from a news service).[853] Cyber-

---

[839] *Id.*

[840] *Id.*

[841] *Id.*

[842] U.S. Department of Commerce, The Emerging Digital Economy, ch. 4 (April 1998).

[843] Finance and Economics: The Hollow Promise of Internet Banking, The Economist (Nov. 11, 2000) at 91.

[844] *Id.*

[845] *Id.*

[846] *Id.*

[847] Hawke Says Internet Banking Is Growing But Not in Ways Many Have Anticipated 2001, Electronic Commerce & Law Report (BNA) 216 (2001).

[848] CyberCash Plans Software Facility in India, Financial Express (Dec. 21, 1995).

[849] CyberCash as a Virtual Smart Card, Electronic Payments Int'l 9 (Aug. 1, 1995).

[850] *Id.*

[851] CyberCash, CyberCash Products (visited June 9, 2000), http://www.cybercash.com/producdts/index.html.

[852] *Id.* (describing smart cards for virtual "net around" money).

[853] *Id.*

cash is a smart plastic card with an embedded chip that transmits payment much like a prepaid telephone cards.[854] A smart card is a plastic card about the size of a credit card, with an embedded microchip that can be loaded with data, used for telephone calling, electronic cash payments, and other applications, and then periodically refreshed for additional use.[855]

[D] Electronic Check Developments

The Federal Reserve, the central bank of the United States, is studying ways of accepting checks electronically. A recent speech by a member of the Board of Governors of the Federal Reserve System reports the Federal Reserve's interest in check truncation and electronic check presentment.[856] The Federal Reserve Staff is working with the financial service industry in developing means of facilitating electronic presentment and acceptance of instruments.[857] The proposed "Check Truncation Act" proposes to create substitute checks to substitute for original checks.[858] The substitute check would be treated as functionally and legally equivalent to the original check, thus permitting electronic acceptance.[859] Substitute checks would allow depository banks to truncate checks at a point of deposit such as an ATM or a remote branch.[860] Today, electronic check presentment is hamstrung by reliance on "electronic receipt of payment data contained in the MICR line of a check."[861]

Private companies are also examining ways of simulating real checks in online transactions. The USPTO issued a patent for eChecks on Oct. 14, 1997.[862] The patent claim includes "the notion of digital signed payment authorization, including the concept of a digital signature that remains valid even if sub-documents are removed."[863] Clareon Corporation and Xign Corporation are licensees of the core eCheck technology and are marketing Internet checking services.[864] The *eCheck* is an all-electronic transaction that permits electronic presentment and payment.[865] The issuer of an eCheck uses electronic devices to transmit the payment instrument to the payee electronically.[866] The payee

---

[854] *Id.*

[855] www.whatis.com.

[856] The Federal Reserve Board, Remarks by Vice Chairman Roger W. Ferguson, Jr., Before the Independent Community Bankers of America, Washington, D.C. (May 21, 2001) (visited May 28, 2001), http://www.federalreserve.gov/boarddocs/speeches/2001/20010521/default.htm.

[857] *Id.* at 4.

[858] *Id.*

[859] *Id.* at 5.

[860] *Id.*

[861] *Id.* at 6.

[862] eCheck Home Page, Patents Issued (visited May 28, 2001), http://www.echeck.org.

[863] *Id.*

[864] *Id.*

[865] eCheck Home Page, What Is eCheck? (visited May 28, 2001), http://www.echeck.org/overview/what.html.

[866] *Id.* at 2.

"deposits" the electronic check, receives credit, and the payee's bank "clears" the eCheck to the paying bank.[867] Finally, the paying bank validates the eCheck and then "charges" the check writer's account for the check."[868]

§ 6.09 PREVENTIVE LAW POINTERS

[A] Complying with the Magnuson-Moss Act

SPC must comply with the Magnuson-Moss Act warranty provisions for any online sales to consumers. It is unclear whether the Magnuson-Moss Act would apply to licenses related solely to software. The Magnuson-Moss Act creates a federal private cause of action for consumers damaged by the failure of a warrantor "to comply with any obligation under . . . a written warranty."[869] Although the Magnuson-Moss Act does not require SPC to extend a warranty with its computer product, any written warranty offered with a computer product sold to consumers is subject to the requirements of the Act. A Magnuson-Moss written warranty is defined as any affirmation of fact that becomes part of the "basis of the bargain."[870]

Section 103 of the Act provides that warrantors must either conspicuously designate written warranties as "full" or "limited."[871] The term *full warranty* means that the warrantor is promising all of the federal remedies in the Magnuson-Moss Act. In contrast, the term *limited warranty* means that the written warranty does not meet the federal minimum standards. SPC may limit the duration of an implied warranty "to the duration of a written warranty of reasonable duration."[872] To comply with the Magnuson-Moss Act, SPC should prominently label its written warranties as "limited." SPC must clearly and conspicuously limit the duration of implied warranties. SPC can accomplish this by using "clear and unmistakable language and prominently displaying the limitations on its web site."[873]

The Federal Trade Commission also monitors disclaimers and disclosures to ensure that they are clear and conspicuous. A FTC guideline states that "consumers must be able to notice, read, or hear and understand the information."[874] Offers and claims for all online products and services must not be unfair or deceptive. Section 5 of the Federal Trade Commission Act gives the Commission the power to prevent deceptive and unfair acts or practices.[875]

---

[867] *Id.*

[868] *Id.*

[869] 15 U.S.C. § 2310(d)(1) (2000).

[870] *Id.* § 2301(6).

[871] *Id.* § 2303.

[872] *Id.* § 2308.

[873] *Id.* § 2308(b).

[874] Federal Trade Commission, Advertising and Marketing on the Internet: Rules of the Road, Sept. 2000 (visited June 1, 2001), http://www.ftc.gov/bcp/conline/pubs/buspubs/ruleroad.htm. Federal Trade Commission, Advertising and Marketing on the Internet: The Rules of the Road, Apr. 1998 (visited June 8, 2000), http://www.ftc.gov/bcp/conline/pubs/buspubs/ruleroad.htm.

[875] *Id.*

[B] Mandatory Arbitration Clauses

In *Brower v. Gateway 2000*,[876] a New York court upheld a click-through agreement that required any dispute arising out of the plaintiff's purchase of a computer and software to be resolved by arbitration. Gateway shipped its personal computers in a box containing a printed warning stating, "This document contains Gateway 2000's Standard Terms and Conditions."[877] The license agreement also stated, "By keeping your Gateway 2000 computer system beyond thirty (30) days after the date of delivery, you accept these Terms and Conditions."[878] One of the clauses of the contract mandated that all controversies arising out of the computer contract were to be arbitrated in Chicago, Illinois, applying the "Rule of Conciliation and Arbitration of the International Chamber of Commerce."[879]

The court upheld the arbitration clause, holding it did not render the contract an unenforceable adhesion contract. The court stated that because "the consumer has affirmatively retained the merchandise for more than 30 days—within which the consumer has presumably examined and even used the product(s) and read the agreement . . . the contract has been effectuated."[880] The court, however, did find that the $4,000 fee to arbitrate a dispute was unconscionable and excessive "and surely serves to deter the individual consumer from invoking the process," leaving consumers "with no forum at all in which to resolve a dispute."[881] The fee to arbitrate the dispute far exceeded the price of the software, depriving the consumer of any effective remedy. The court remanded the case to the trial court with instructions to appoint an arbitrator who would not charge excessive fees.[882]

It may be advisable to choose a nonlitigation forum, such as arbitration, in standard online contracts. An example of such a clause follows:

> Any Unresolved Dispute shall be settled at the election of either party, by final and binding independent arbitration conducted before the American Arbitration Association (AAA) in New York, New York, U.S.A., and shall be conducted under the rules of the Commercial Arbitration Rules of the AAA then in effect.

> Any party intending to initiate an arbitration of an Unresolved Dispute shall give fifteen (15) days' prior written notice to the other party of its intention to commence an arbitration proceeding. The arbitrator shall interpret the Agreement and any dispute arising from performance or breach governed by the

---

[876] 676 N.Y.S.2d 569 (N.Y. App. Div. 1998); *see also* Westendorf v. Gateway 2000 Inc., No. 17913 (Del. Ch., Mar. 16, 2000), reported in 13 Software L. Bull. 95 (May/June 2000) (upholding mandatory arbitration clause in computer contract even though service contract made no reference to arbitration).

[877] *Id.* at 570.

[878] *Id.*

[879] *Id.*

[880] *Id.* at 573.

[881] *Id.* at 574.

[882] *Id.* at 574-575.

laws of the state of New York. New York's conflicts of law principles are not applicable.

The benefits of arbitration are cost, speed, and the greater probability that the case will be tried before a tribunal with some understanding of the business context.

The Drafting Committee of the Proposed Revision of the Uniform Arbitration Act (RUAA) found that unconscionability and adhesion issues arise frequently with arbitration clauses.[883] The plaintiffs in the class action against Gateway 2000 argued that the mandatory arbitration clause was unconscionable as well as invalid under the "battle of the forms provision in § 2-207" of Article 2.[884] The battle of the forms will rarely occur in mass-market license agreements, since only the vendor supplies a form. Arbitration clauses may be challenged, however, if a court finds procedural and substantive unconscionability. The RUAA Reporter noted that unequal bargaining claims arise frequently in "arbitration provisions involving employers and employees, sellers and consumers, health maintenance organizations and patients, franchisors and franchisees, and others."[885] Web sites that require consumer visitors to submit to arbitration will be embroiled in similar litigation. The plaintiffs in the class action against Gateway 2000 argued that the mandatory arbitration clause was unconscionable as well as invalid under the "battle of the forms" provision in § 2-207 of Article 2.[886]

Courts consider the following factors in deciding whether to enforce arbitration clauses: (1) unequal bargaining power, (2) whether the weaker party may opt out of arbitration, (3) the clarity with which the arbitration clause is drafted, (4) whether the stronger party enjoys an unfair home-court advantage, (5) whether the weaker party had a meaningful opportunity to accept the arbitration agreement, and (6) whether the stronger party used deceptive tactics.[887] Courts have generally "been reluctant to find arbitration agreements to be unconscionable."[888]

At minimum, an arbitration clause must be prominently displayed and clearly written so those visitors understand that they are waiving their jury right and the right to a full trial on the merits. One-sided webwrap agreements that take away many substantive rights without giving consumers meaningful remedies are legally risky. If an exclusive arbitration clause is struck by a court, a web site visitor will have the full array of rights and remedies available under the UCC or common law. The trend in the law is for courts to enforce post-sale license agreements incorporating arbitration clauses provided an opportunity is offered to man-

---

[883] Tim Heinsz, Reporter, Proposed Revision of the Uniform Arbitration Act (RUAA), Memorandum to RUAA Drafting Committee Members, Liaisons, and Academic Advisors, Contracts of Adhesion and Unconscionability (Sept. 28, 1998) (visited Dec. 6, 1999), http://www.law.upenn.edu/bll/ulc/uarba/arb1098m.txt.

[884] Brower v. Gateway 2000, 676 N.Y.S.2d at 573-75.

[885] Heinsz, *supra* note 883.

[886] Brower v. Gateway 2000, 676 N.Y.S.2d at 573-75.

[887] *Id.*

[888] *Id.* (citing authorities).

ifest assent.[889] UCITA defines the manifestation of assent as when "a person, acting with knowledge of, or after having an opportunity to review the record or term or a copy of it: (1) authenticates the record or term with intent to adopt or accept it; or (2) intentionally engages in conduct or makes statements with reason to know that the other party or its electronic agent may infer from the conduct or statement that the person assents to the record or term."[890]

[C] Webwrap or Clickwrap License Agreements

The *clickwrap license agreement,* sometimes called a *webwrap,* is a limited license structured as Terms and Conditions of Use (TOC). Web site user agreements are generally structured as licenses to use information. E*Trade, an online brokerage house, requires users to agree to a "user agreement" governing online tax filing and active trader services.[891] E*Trade's user agreement states that by accessing other web sites through links provided by E*Trade, the user agrees to the terms and conditions dictated by the online broker.[892] Most web site user agreements parallel software license agreements in that they give no express or implied warranties with respect to information. Amazon.com gives notices that content "such as text, graphics, logos, button icons, images, audio clips and software is the property of Amazon.com."[893] Web sites that offer services to users should require users to agree to Terms of Service (TOS) as a condition of use.

The webwrap agreement requires users to agree to the terms of use or to leave the site. The "webwrap" agreement for Ben and Jerry's Homemade, Inc., provides that the use of the site or downloading of material signifies the user's agreement with the company's "terms of use." It gives users notice of restrictions on the use of materials: "No information, software or other material (collectively referred to as 'Materials') from this Site may be copied, modified, reproduced, republished, uploaded, posted, transmitted or distributed in any way."[894] Another term of use is that the user is given no rights under the law of trademarks or copyrights.[895]

The web site use agreement should have a prominent notice that use is subject to compliance with the TOC agreement. Visitors should be required to click assent to the TOC or be transported automatically off the site. Visitors should be

---

[889] Baker and McKenzie, IT/Communications Law Alert, Arbitration Clauses and Shrinkwrap Licenses (visited Dec. 6, 1999), http://www.bakerinfo.com/publications/documents/720_al.htm.

[890] UCITA § 112(a)(1)(2) (1999).

[891] E*Trade, Securities, Inc., User Agreement (visited Feb. 8, 1999), http://www.etrade.com/cgi-bin/gx.cgi/AppLogic%2bHome.

[892] *Id.*

[893] Amazon.com, Inc., Copyright and Disclaimer Page (visited Feb. 8, 1999), http:www.amazon.com/exec/obidos/subst/misc/copyright.html/.

[894] Ben & Jerry's Homemade Ice Cream, Inc., Term of Service (visited Oct. 23, 2001), http://www.benjerry.com/legal.html.

[895] *Id.*

given an opportunity to review the terms and, if a subscriber is required to pay for using the site, to manifest assent.

The online company should reserve the right to change TOC rules and regulations from time to time at its sole discretion. The TOC agreement should be structured as a clickwrap or webwrap agreement, even if no payment is required to access the site or use its services. Many webwrap agreements take the form of a license agreement. Lycos licenses its services for the limited use of online viewing, permitting "no further reproduction or distribution of the Services."[896] The webwrap agreement will generally have a term such as: "By using this site, you agree to these terms of use. If you do not agree to these terms, you may not use this site."[897] The web site "terms of use" agreement will set forth the terms and conditions for use of the site. The site should note that the user is expected to comply with all applicable federal, state, and local laws governing access. The company's site should state that the company owns its trademarks, logos, and service marks, as displayed on the web site. The site should post a general disclaimer that it is not warranting the accuracy of information on its web site or rendering personal services. The site should assume no responsibility for the accuracy of the information. The online company must reserve the right to change programs or products mentioned at any time without notice. The following is a general disclaimer that may be adapted to a particular company's webwrap or clickwrap agreement.

> ALL INFORMATION PROVIDED ON SPC'S WEB SITE IS PROVIDED "AS IS," WITH ALL FAULTS OR WITHOUT WARRANTIES OF ANY KIND EITHER EXPRESS OR IMPLIED. SPC AND ITS SUPPLIERS DISCLAIM ALL WARRANTIES, EXPRESS AND IMPLIED, INCLUDING, WITHOUT LIMITATION, THOSE OF MERCHANTABILITY, FITNESS FOR A PARTICULAR PURPOSE, AND NONINFRINGEMENT OR THOSE WARRANTIES ARISING FROM COURSE OF PERFORMANCE, COURSE OF DEALING, OR USAGE OF TRADE. SPC AND ITS SUPPLIERS SHALL NOT BE LIABLE FOR ANY INDIRECT, SPECIAL, CONSEQUENTIAL, INCIDENTAL, OR PUNITIVE DAMAGES, INCLUDING, WITHOUT LIMITATION, LOST PROFITS OR REVENUES, COSTS OF REPLACEMENT OF GOODS, LOSS OR DAMAGE TO DATA ARISING OUT OF THE USE OR INABILITY TO USE THE SPC WEB SITE OR ANY SPC PRODUCT OR DAMAGE RESULTING FROM USE OF OR RELIANCE ON THE INFORMATION PRESENT, EVEN IF SPC OR ITS SUPPLIERS HAVE BEEN ADVISED OF THE POSSIBILITY OF SUCH DAMAGES.[898]

The TOC agreement should specify that it limits remedies as well as warranties. If goods are sold or software licensed for a price, the site should provide a minimum adequate remedy, or the company risks having its limitation of remedy clause struck under the doctrine of "failure of essential purpose."

---

[896] Lycos, Inc., Legal Services, http://www.lycos.com/.

[897] eToys, Terms of Use (visited Dec. 19, 1998), http://www.etoys.com/html/e_etoysterms.html.

[898] This disclaimer is based on Cisco Systems, Important Notices (visited May 9, 2000), http://www.cisco.com/public/copyright.html.

[D] Determining UCITA's Reach

A large number of information age contracts will be covered by UCITA. Software licenses, unlike the sale of goods, place restrictions on use. Licenses are limiting and may preclude the commercial use of a database, as in a web site. Many web site license agreements limit the downloading of documents for non-commercial use. Licenses may limit the right to access information. LexisNexis™ and WESTLAW®, for example, place limits on access to their databases. A faculty member of a law school has a limited right to access these materials for academic purposes but may not use the services for a private law practice. License agreements may restrict the use of software to a single computer versus a network computer or outsourcer.

What is included under UCITA?

- Licensing of computer information including software, online licenses.

- Internet-related licenses and web site contracts.

- Contracts to develop, modify, or create software.

- Data transfers, access contracts, and data processing contracts.

- Commercial transactions where primary or predominant part is computer information.

What is outside UCITA?

- Financial service transactions, insurance services transactions.

- Audio or visual programming defined by the Communication Act of 1934.

- Broadcast, satellite, or cable programming.

- Motion pictures, musical works, sound recordings, or phonograph records.

- Compulsory licenses.

- Contracts of employment of individuals (other than independent contractor creating or modifying computer information).

- Entertainment services, musical works, or phonorecords.

- Professional services involving performance.

- Licensing of patents, trademarks, copyrights, trade dress, or other intellectual property governed by state or federal law.

- Subject matter covered by Article 3, 4, 4A, 5, 6, 7, 8, or 9 of the Uniform Commercial Code.

- Sales or leases of a computer program not developed particularly for the transaction, sales on leases of goods.

- Computer programs embedded in goods, e.g., a Mr. Coffee™ machine or an airplane navigation system.

- Payment, banking, or financial services.

- Print media, including books, magazines, or newspapers.

- Telecommunication products or services.

[E]   Choice of Law and Forum

Choice of law is a contractual provision that predetermines the law that applies for any dispute involving the contract. SPC should draft a clause that states that the web site is created and controlled by SPC, in the Commonwealth of Massachusetts, USA. As such, the laws of Massachusetts will govern this agreement, including disclaimers, terms, and conditions, without giving effect to any principles of conflict of law.

SPC should include a choice of law clause in every agreement because it may have customers in any state and hundreds of foreign countries. SPC needs a choice of law clause to be assured that Massachusetts' law applies, versus that of another state or foreign jurisdiction. SPC may find Massachusetts law to be favorable because that state does not recognize the common law remedy of punitive damages. Massachusetts' Article 2 is far more consumer-oriented than are the sales laws of all other jurisdictions. SPC's counsel may nevertheless choose Massachusetts because of the company's greater familiarity with the state's consumer protection statutes.

Suppose there is an online transaction between a Massachusetts business and a New York bank. If New York law applies, punitive damages may be recoverable, but not if Massachusetts law applies. SPC may wish to restrict offers in countries that have radically different contracting practices or where the governments might object to the subject matter of the contract. The following "choice of law" clause may be included in paper-based license agreements, nondisclosure agreements, and other Internet-related contracts: "This Agreement shall be governed by the laws of the Commonwealth of Massachusetts."

As with any other Internet-related contract, an integration or merger clause should be included:

> This Agreement states the entire agreement and supersedes all prior agreements, written or verbal, between the parties with respect to the subject matter of this agreement. This agreement may not be amended except by a writing signed by a duly authorized representative of both parties.

Choice of forum is a contractual provision that predetermines the judicial or arbitral forum in the event of a dispute arising out of the web site agreement. If the parties do not otherwise agree to choice of law, the court will make the decision as to the applicable law based upon the following factors:

1. The needs of the interstate and international systems;
2. The relevant policies of the forum;
3. The relevant policies of other interested states and the relative interests of those states in the determination of the particular issue;
4. The protection of justified expectations;
5. The basic policies underlying the particular field of law;
6. The certainty, predictability, and uniformity of result; and
7. The ease in the determination and application of the law to be applied.[899]

If a court does reach the question of a state's interest, "it should concern itself with the question whether the courts of that state would have applied the rule in the decision of the case."[900]

Courts may also consider the following factors in determining the choice of law:

1. The place of contracting;
2. The place of negotiation of the contract;
3. The place of performance;
4. The location of the subject matter of the contract; and
5. The domicile, residence, nationality, place of incorporation, and place of business of the parties.[901]

To avoid uncertainty as to choice of law, SPC should include a choice of law clause in its terms of service, end-user license agreements, and other contracts. SPC should require shoppers to adhere to the following choice of law clause: This site is created and controlled by Suffolk Personal Computers (SPC) in the state of Massachusetts. As such, the laws of the Commonwealth of Massachusetts govern these disclaimers, terms, and conditions, without giving effect to any principles of conflicts of laws. We reserve the right to make changes to our site and to these disclaimers, terms, and conditions at any time.[902]

Courts are predisposed to uphold choice of law clauses given a reasonable relation to the transaction. Occasionally, a court will find that the question of choice of law is covered neither by statute nor by a parties' "choice of law" clause. SPC may also specify arbitration as an exclusive forum for resolving disputes arising under license agreements.

[F]   Negotiating Points

Extensive license negotiations are common in customized or other non-mass market license agreements. Corporate or outside counsel needs to know about the

---

[899] Restatement (Second) of Conflicts § 6.

[900] *Id.* § 186 cmt.

[901] *Id.* § 188.

[902] This form is adapted from Amazon.com, Inc. Copyright and Disclaimer Page (visited Feb. 8, 1999), http:www.amazon.com/exec/obidos/subst/misc/copyright.html/.

technical needs of their clients in order to serve their clients' business objectives. Lawyers with a strong technical background will be in a strong negotiating position. First and foremost, the negotiating lawyer must understand what rights are to be protected: copyright, patents, trade secrets, databases, or proprietary information.

Software or web site development agreements are relational contracts in which it is common to change specifications or to make adjustments to adapt to a rapidly changing online environment. The negotiating terms will vary depending on whether counsel is representing a licensor or licensee. The need may also arise for negotiating with third parties over intellectual property rights. The negotiation of a development contract should not be an exercise of mechanical jurisprudence. Counsel should be cautious about blindly using templates without tailoring these standard forms to the company's unique problems. Software licensing agreements should not be spun out of formbooks used like legal vending machines. Licensing agreements need to be customized if they are to meet the company's business objectives.

[G] Draft Your Own Excuse Sections

Under Article 2, a disclaimer occurs when a seller of goods uses language or conduct to negate or limit implied warranties.[903] UCITA's methodology for disclaiming warranties parallels those of the provisions in Article 2. UCITA allows vendors to disclaim implied warranties, to limit their liability, and to restrict a licensee's remedies within the broad parameters of good faith, commercial reasonableness, and conscionability. A web site needs to limit liability for late delivery due to sales that tax the capacity of the delivery system. SPC should limit its liability in the event of the failure of a third party or of commercial impracticability. Courts will not excuse late delivery even if the demand was unprecedented or shortfalls occurred in the supply chain. Toysrus.com, for example, was the target of several class action lawsuits for the late delivery of 1999 Christmas gifts.[904]

Our analysis of the decided cases under §§ 2-613 through 2-615 reveals that courts are unsympathetic to seller's excuses.[905] The doctrine of commercial impracticality in § 2-615 is almost never successfully invoked in the event of shortfalls in the supply chain or unprecedented price hikes. Similarly, UCITA excuse sections are unlikely to provide licensors with relief in similar circumstances.

Courts take the position that the parties could have protected themselves by contract terms with floors and ceilings on the price. A clause that conditions availability on supply is also likely to be enforceable in a commercial setting. Do not rely on the UCC defaults to "excuse" performance. Draft your own *force majeure*

---

[903] UCC § 2-316 provides the methodology for disclaiming and limiting warranties.

[904] Class actions were filed against toysrus.com in Alabama, Washington, and other states for late delivery of 1999 Christmas gifts. *See* Theresa Forsman, Toysrus.com Sued Again Over Deliveries (visited Feb. 1, 2000), http://www.beren.com/biz/toys19200001193.htm.

[905] The UCC Reporting Service published by Callaghan reprints all decided cases under a given section of the Code.

clauses. The courts expect that commercial sellers are in the best position to devise their own excuse section.

[H]   Term and Termination Clauses in License Agreements

Prior to writing an effective clause, one must consider three important questions: (1) How is the license agreement to be terminated? (2) What are the events of default giving the parties the right to cancel the license agreements? and (3) Are there any obligations, such as confidentiality, which survive termination? Depending on the answer(s), one might draft the clause as follows:

> TERM OF THE AGREEMENT: THE TERM OF THIS AGREEMENT SHALL BEGIN AS OF THE EFFECTIVE DATE, AND SHALL CONTINUE IN FULL FORCE AND EFFECT FOR _____ YEARS UNTIL TERMINATED BY EITHER PARTY UPON AT LEAST NINETY DAYS' PRIOR WRITTEN NOTICE TO THE OTHER OR UPON THE BREACH OF THIS AGREEMENT BY EITHER PARTY.
>
> TERMINATION FOR BREACH OR DEFAULT: EITHER PARTY TO THIS AGREEMENT MAY TERMINATE THIS AGREEMENT IN THE EVENT THE OTHER PARTY SHALL HAVE MATERIALLY BREACHED OR DEFAULTED IN THE PERFORMANCE OF ANY OF ITS MATERIAL OBLIGATIONS, AND SUCH DEFAULT SHALL HAVE CONTINUED FOR _____ (DAYS) AFTER WRITTEN NOTICE WAS PROVIDED TO THE BREACHING PARTY BY THE NON-BREACHING PARTY.

[I]   Web Sites and Credit Cards

The typical payment mechanism for the Internet is authorization through the web site visitor's credit card. Priceline.com™, for example, allows consumers to use a variety of credit cards to make payment for airline tickets and other goods or services. The payment system for airline tickets requires the consumer to give a credit card number and authorization to bill the card if an airline is willing to release seats at the visitor's price. Once the web site visitor clicks "Submit My Request," Priceline will search for a major airline willing to accept the offer. If an airline accepts the visitor's offer price, Priceline immediately locks in the price and charges the visitor's tickets to the credit card number provided.

Visitors give Priceline the authority to charge the price named as well as tax, fees, and shipping charges. The credit card is not charged if the visitor's price is not accepted by an airline. Priceline also permits visitors to store credit card information for future visits. The authorization to charge a credit card is granted by the bank that issued the credit card.

The online merchant designs its web site to prompt customers to enter their credit card numbers and to transmit the information from the Internet to a gateway. The gateway is a server that converts the information entered by consumers into a format that can be read by banks. The gateway transmits the information to the merchant's bank, which uses a "switch" to transmit it to the credit card network, such as American Express, Visa, or Diner's Club. A switch is a server operated by or on behalf of financial institutions. The card network determines the identity of the issuing bank and sends the information to the bank for authorization.

If the credit card transaction is authorized, the authorization is communicated back up the chain to the merchant. The issuing bank reserves the amount of the purchase to the credit card. The entire transaction takes only five to ten seconds.[906] If the credit card authorization is granted, the merchant may ship merchandise or grant the consumer access to services.

The merchant is paid after the goods or services have been shipped. Sending authorizations to the issuing bank pays the online merchant. Specialized methods to allow secure credit card payment combine encryption with existing banking methods for payment authorization.[907] SPC will need to have online relationships with Visa USA and MasterCard International.

[J]   Clickthrough Agreements

A working group of the American Bar Association's Electronic Commerce Subcommittee of the Cyberspace Law Committee of the Business Law Section compiled the following principles for enforceable clickthrough agreements:

> [1] Viewing of Terms Before Assent: The User should not have the option of manifesting assent without having been presented with the terms of the proposed agreement, which should either appear automatically or appear when the User clicks on an icon or hyperlink that is clearly labeled and easily found. Place the means of assent at the end of the agreement terms, requiring the User at least to navigate past the terms before assenting.
>
> [2] Assent Before Access to Governed Item: The User should not be able to gain access to or rights in the website, software, information, property, or services governed by the proposed agreement without first assenting to the terms of the agreement.
>
> [3] Ease of Viewing Terms: The program operating the click-through agreement should give the User sufficient opportunity to review the proposed agreement terms before proceeding. The User should be able to read the terms at his or her own pace; if the terms occupy more than one computer screen, the User should be able to navigate forwards and backwards within the terms by scrolling or changing pages.
>
> [4] Continued Ability to View Terms: Once the User views the terms, the User should be able to review the terms throughout the assent process.
>
> [5] Format and Content: The format and content of the terms must comply with applicable laws as to notice, disclosure language, conspicuousness,

---

[906] This summary of how the credit card payment system works is drawn from First ECOM.COM, Inc., 10A00 Filing (Dec. 10, 1999), Securities and Exchange Commission, Washington, D.C. (visited May 30, 2000), http://www.sec.gov.

[907] VISA and MasterCard use a Secure Electronic Transaction (SET) protocol. The SET user encrypts purchase information so that only the bank will be able read it. The merchant encrypts part of the purchase information, ensuring that the buyer cannot repudiate the transaction.

and other format requirements. The terms should be clear and readable, in legible font. If the law requires specific assent to a particular type of term, the format of the assent process should comply with that requirement.

[6] Consistency with Information Elsewhere: Information provided to the User elsewhere should not contradict the agreement terms or render the agreement ambiguous.

[7] Choice Between Assent and Rejection: The User should be given a clear choice between assenting to the terms or rejecting them. That choice should occur at the end of the process when the User's assent is requested.

[8] Clear Words of Assent or Rejection: The User's words of assent or rejection should be clear and unambiguous.

(a) Examples of clear words of assent include "Yes" (in response to a question about User's assent), "I agree," "I accept," "I consent," or "I assent." Do not use vague or ambiguous phrases such as "Process my order," "Continue," "Next page," "Submit," or "Enter."

(b) Examples of clear words of rejection include "No" (in response to question about User's assent), "I disagree," "I do not agree," "Not agreed," or "I decline."

[9] Clear Method of Assent or Rejection: The User's method of signifying assent or rejection should be clear and unambiguous. Examples include clicking a button or icon containing the words of assent or rejection, or typing in the specified words of assent or rejection.

[10] Consequences of Assent or Rejection: If the User rejects the proposed agreement terms, that action should have the consequence of preventing the User from getting whatever the click-through agreement is granting the User. The User should not be able to complete the transaction without agreeing to the terms. For example, if the click-through agreement would grant the User use of a website, software, or particular data, the consequence of the User's rejection of the proposed terms should be to bar the User from that use. Likewise, if the click-through agreement would give the User rights to goods or services, the consequence of the User's rejection of the proposed terms should be to eject the User out of the ordering process. On the other hand, if the User assents to the proposed agreement terms, the User should be granted access to whatever is promised in the agreement without having to assent to additional terms (aside from those that the User specifies in the ordering process).

[11] Notice of Consequences of Assent or Rejection: Immediately preceding the place where the User signifies assent or rejection, a statement should draw the User's attention to the consequences of assent and rejection. Examples of notice of assent consequences include: "By clicking 'Yes' below you acknowledge that you have read, understand, and agree to be bound by the terms above" or "These terms are a legal contract that will bind both of us as soon as you click the following assent button." Examples of notice of rejection consequences include: "If you reject the proposed terms above, you will be denied access to the [Web site, software, product, services] that we are offering to you."

[12] Correction Process: The assent process should provide a reasonable method to avoid, or to detect and correct, errors likely to be made by the

User in the assent process. A summary of an online order preceding assent is one such means.

[13] Accurate Records: Maintain accurate records of the content and format of the electronic agreement process, documenting what steps the User had to take in order to gain access to particular items and what version of the agreement was in effect at the time. If necessary, for proof of performance, link the User's identity to his or her assent by maintaining accurate records of the User's identifying information, the User's electronic assent to the terms, and the version of the terms to which the User assented. Be sure to comply with applicable privacy laws.

[14] Retention and Enforceability: To meet any legal requirement that a record of the agreement be provided, sent, or delivered, the sender must ensure that any electronic record is capable of retention by the recipient. In addition, for an electronic record to be enforceable against the recipient, the sender cannot inhibit the recipient's ability to print or store the electronic record.

[15] Accuracy and Accessibility After the Assent Process: If applicable law requires retention of a record of information relating to the transaction, ensure that the electronic record accurately reflects the information and, if required, remains accessible to all persons entitled to access by rule of law for the period required by the rule of law in a form capable of accurate reproduction for later reference.[908]

[K]   FTC Guidelines for Web Advertisements

The FTC is the most active federal agency in "enforcing its consumer protection laws online to ensure that products and services are described truthfully in online ads and that consumers get what they pay for."[909] These activities benefit consumers as well as sellers, who expect and deserve a fair marketplace. The FTC takes the position that the general principles of advertising law apply well to web-vertisements. To make a disclosure clear and conspicuous, online advertisers should

- Place disclosures near, and when possible, on the same screen as the triggering claim.

- Use text or visual cues to encourage consumers to scroll down a web page when it is necessary to view a disclosure.

- When using hyperlinks to lead to disclosures,

  - make the link obvious;

---

[908] Christina Kunz et al., Click-Through Agreements; Strategies for Avoiding Disputes on Validity of Assent, 57 Bus. Law. 401 (2001) .

[909] Federal Trade Commission, Dot Com Disclosures (visited Apr. 28, 2002), http://www.ftc.gov/bcp/conline/pubs/buspubs/dotcom/index.html.

- label the hyperlink appropriately to convey the importance, nature, and relevance of the information it leads to;

- use hyperlink styles consistently so that consumers know when a link is available;

- place the hyperlink near relevant information and make it noticeable;

- take consumers directly to the disclosure on the clickthrough page; and

- assess the effectiveness of the hyperlink by monitoring clickthrough rates and make changes accordingly.

- Recognize and respond to any technological limitations or unique characteristics of high-tech methods of making disclosures, such as frames or pop-ups.

- Display disclosures prior to purchase, but recognize that placement limited only to the order page may not always work.

- Creatively incorporate disclosures in banner ads or disclose them clearly and conspicuously on the page the banner ad links to.

- Prominently display disclosures so they are noticeable to consumers and evaluate the size, color, and graphic treatment of the disclosure in relation to other parts of the web page.

- Review the entire ad to ensure that other elements—text, graphics, hyperlinks, or sound—do not distract consumers' attention from the disclosure.

- Repeat disclosures, as needed, on lengthy web sites and in connection with repeated claims.

- Use audio disclosures when making audio claims and present them in a volume and cadence so that consumers can hear and understand them.

- Display visual disclosures for a duration sufficient for consumers to notice, read, and understand them.

Use clear language and syntax so that consumers understand the disclosures.[910]

---

[910] *Id.*

CHAPTER SEVEN

EXPOSURE TO LAWSUITS IN DISTANT FORUMS: JURISDICTION

§ 7.01 Overiew
    [A] Subject Matter Jurisdiction
        [1] Federal Courts
        [2] State Courts
        [3] Forum Selection and Choice of Law Clauses
    [B] Personal Jurisdiction
        [1] Introduction to Personal Jurisdiction
        [2] Challenging Personal Jurisdiction
    [C] The Minimum Contacts Test

§ 7.02 Two Paradigms of Personal Jurisdiction
    [A] General Jurisdiction
    [B] Specific Jurisdiction
        [1] *International Shoe* in Cyberspace
    [C] Conflict of Laws and Choice of Law
    [D] *In rem* Jurisdiction
    [E] Long-Arm Statutes

§ 7.03 Cyber-Jurisdiction Cases
    [A] Purposeful Availment
    [B] Contracts and Purposeful Availment
    [C] Tortious Activities and Purposeful Availment
        [1] Relatedness Test
    [D] Effects Test
    [E] The Sliding Scale of Jurisdiction
        [1] Reasonableness Test
    [F] International Jurisdictional Issues
        [1] European Union
        [2] ABA's Cyberspace Jurisdictional Report
    [G] Obtaining Redress in International Internet Disputes
    [H] International Conventions Governing Jurisdiction
        [1] Brussels Convention on Jurisdiction and Judgments
        [2] Lugano Convention on Jurisdiction and Judgments
        [3] Brussels Regulation
        [4] Hague Convention on Jurisdiction and Judgments
    [I] Minimizing Jurisdictional Exposure

[J]   Obtaining Redress in Domestic Internet Disputes

[K]   Choice of Law in a Global Digital Network

§ 7.04   Preventive Law Pointers and Internet Jurisdiction Guides

[A]   Personal Jurisdiction

[B]   *In rem* Jurisdiction

[C]   *Forum Non Conveniens* in Cyberspace

[D]   Determining the Identity of Visitors

[E]   Minimum Contacts in Cyberspace

[F]   Choice of Law and Forum Clauses

[G]   Factual Circumstances Affecting Internet Jurisdiction Checklists

    [1]   Overview

    [2]   Web Page Advertisements

        [a]   Finding Jurisdiction

        [b]   Declining Jurisdiction

    [3]   Torts or Tort-Like Misconduct

        [a]   Finding Jurisdiction

        [b]   Declining Jurisdiction

    [4]   Online Contracts

        [a]   Finding Jurisdiction

        [b]   Declining Jurisdiction

    [5]   Crimes and Regulatory Activity

        [a]   Finding Jurisdiction

        [b]   Declining Jurisdiction

    [6]   Intellectual Property

        [a]   Finding Jurisdiction

        [b]   Declining Jurisdiction

    [7]   *In rem* Jurisdiction Under the ACPA

        [a]   Finding Jurisdiction

        [b]   Declining Jurisdiction

§ 7.01   OVERVIEW

SPC is about to enter the global electronic marketplace by developing content on its web site to attract potential customers. It has recently expanded its web site to include a free service offering online help for its personal computer customers. The software division offers online assistance and tips for persons with hardware and software problems. The software services division represents the first time that SPC has marketed a product independently of its personal computers division. SPC also manages its software services through fax, e-mail, and Internet chat sessions. Digital messages at the company are transmitted or received by consultants through cell phones, the telephone, e-mail, and real-time instant messages over the Internet.

Within a few months of offering this service, SPC received a demand letter from an attorney in California. In the letter, the plaintiff's attorney claimed that his client used a technical tip from SPC's web site to repair a computer and suffered a personal injury in the process. The defendant has charged SPC with professional negligence and the tort of computer malpractice, which is not yet a recognized cause of action in Massachusetts. SPC has received a motion seeking a preliminary injunction restraining future Internet services from its sites. The California plaintiff must show (1) that it will suffer irreparable harm and (2) either (a) a likelihood of success on the merits of its product liability claim or (b) sufficiently serious questions going to the merits to make them a fair ground for litigation and a balance of hardships tipping decidedly in the plaintiff's favor.

The letter also contained a summons requesting that SPC make a personal appearance in a California court and noted that the defendant was demanding a jury trial. The issue that concerns SPC's counsel is whether a federal court sitting in California may assert personal jurisdiction over SPC, a nonresident, in an action arising from services from SPC's site. The Internet recognizes no boundaries, and now SPC must defend a computer malpractice case in a distant forum.

This chapter examines jurisdictional issues that arise in the operation of a web site. Currently, over 200 million people have access to the Internet worldwide, and thousands of new users are logging on every day.[1] This chapter also explores the constitutional requirements for jurisdiction in cyberspace. In most cyberspace jurisdiction cases, the defendant files a motion to dismiss. However, it is the plaintiff that bears the burden of establishing that jurisdiction exists. To establish that personal jurisdiction over a foreign defendant is proper, the plaintiff must show that (1) the state long-arm statute confers personal jurisdiction over the defendant and (2) the exercise of jurisdiction comports with the constitutional principles of due process.[2] The Internet raises jurisdictional issues that cut across national boundaries. Yet no special tribunal decides cases arising out of Internet activities,

---

[1] Sherman Fridman, Audio Browser Connects Any Telephone To Internet, Newsbytes (Feb. 7, 2000), available in LEXIS, News Library, Curnws file.

[2] Rio Props, Inc. v. Rio Int'l Interlink, 2002 U.S. App. LEXIS 4392 (9th Cir. Mar. 20, 2002).

nor is there a specific jurisdiction known as cyberspace.[3] No international treaty specifically governs Internet jurisdiction. Since no exclusive subject matter jurisdiction exists for cyberspace, courts must apply traditional principles to a new setting.

American courts have applied the traditional minimum contact framework of due process to consider the constitutionality of personal jurisdiction in cyberspace.[4] Courts are likely to apply traditional principles such as foreseeability, minimum contacts, and purposeful availment to Internet-related jurisdiction issues. There is little question that the Internet's worldwide interconnected computer networks challenge territorial-based concepts of personal jurisdiction.[5] Transborder disputes involving difficult questions of jurisdiction may arise in U.S. courts, foreign courts, or international forums.

ICANN's dispute providers handle hundreds of disputes involving parties from different nation states each month. The Uniform Dispute Resolution Procedure (UDRP) of ICANN does not require "minimum contacts" and is available despite the fact that a domain name registrant could be in any of hundreds of countries. "The UDRP is limited to domain names with gTLDs within ICANN's jurisdiction. If the registrant is foreign, the trademark owner may find that the decision will be made by a foreign arbitrator who has an entirely different perspective on trademark issues."[6] ICANN's providers resolve disputes where the complainant and respondent are from any one of a hundred nation states.

Internet-related cross-border disputes may also be resolved in national courts where jurisdiction may be obtained over non-residents. A Swiss court granted an injunction restraining an ex-British Secret Service officer from posting names of secret agents on his web site.[7] A British Columbia Court refused to enforce a judgment of a Texas court, holding that the court had no jurisdiction in a lawsuit

---

[3] Natural Origins Resources v. Kotler, 133 F. Supp. 2d 1232 (D.N.M. 2001); *see also* Weber v. Jolly Hotels, 977 F. Supp. 327, 333 (D.N.J. 1997) (stating that "[a]lthough the Internet is a new medium that raises new issues for the courts, district courts have successfully applied the principles established by *International Shoe* and its progeny to cases involving the Internet"); Mike Hedge, Gutnick Court Case Hears Publication a Centuries Old Question, AAP (June, 2000) (noting that Dow Jones, an American financial publication, was recently the defendant in a defamation suit brought by "a Melbourne entrepreneur, sporting and religious identity" based upon an article published on the Internet about questionable financial dealings).

[4] American Civil Liberties Union v. Reno, 929 F. Supp. 825, 830-32 (E.D. Pa. 1996).

[5] *See, e.g.,* Maritz, Inc. v. Cybergold, Inc., 947 F. Supp. 1328, 1332 (E.D. Mo. 1996) (stating that "[t]he Internet, a new and rapidly developing means of mass communication and information exchange, raises difficult questions regarding the scope of a court's personal jurisdiction in the context of due process jurisprudence").

[6] James D. Kote, Trademark Dispute Resolution Mechanisms for Handling Conflicts in Connection with the New GLTDs, 6 Internet Newsletter 1 (Apr. 2001) (discussing alternative forums such as the UDRP and federal courts for the resolution of domain name disputes).

[7] Perkins Coie LLP: Internet Case Digest, Case Name Unknown (visited May 14, 2001), http://www.perkinscoie.com/casedigest/icd_results.cfm?keyword1+internatonal&topic+Intern (reporting granting of injunction restraining former British Secret Intelligence officer from posting names of secret agents on web site).

brought by a B.C. company for allegedly defamatory comments in an Internet chat room. The court found no link to the forum state and therefore no jurisdiction.[8] A federal court held that personal jurisdiction was lacking over a Canadian defendant in *Mattel, Inc. v. Securenet Information Servs. & 2857111 Can., Inc.*[9] In *Mattel*, the Canadian defendant did not target advertising in New York and had no other contacts with the forum. The court rejected the argument that the Canadian site was doing business in the United States because it accepted U.S. currency. This factor alone did not prove "substantial" revenue from international commerce. In *Cuccioli v. Jekyll & Hyde Neue Metropol*,[10] a New York federal court found that the mere existence of an instate hyperlink to a foreign web site was insufficient to exert jurisdiction over a German company.

The rules for transnational jurisdiction in Internet disputes are unsettled. The American Law Institute and UNIDROIT have formulated a draft proposal for Principles and Rules of Transnational Civil Procedure.[11] The ALI/UNIDROIT proposes four bases for jurisdiction: (1) designation by mutual agreement of the parties; (2) in which a defendant is subject to the compulsory judicial authority of that state, as determined by principles governing personal jurisdiction or by international convention to which the state is a party; or (3) where fixed property is located . . . ; or (4) in aid of the jurisdiction of another forum in which a Transnational Civil Proceeding is pending.[12] The ALI/UNIDROIT Reporter states that these "rules of jurisdiction are recognized in virtually all legal systems."[13] One of the default rules would be to apply "domestic law of the forum concerning exercise of personal jurisdiction."[14]

There is a strong consensus among U.S. courts that a *web site* alone is not a proper basis for personal jurisdiction.[15] Courts have devised a web site plus rule for evaluating jurisdiction-creating contacts in Internet cases. "Such analysis avoids the unjustifiable extreme of universal jurisdiction while at the same time subjecting defendants to suit wherever they have purposely directed their activities."[16]

---

[8] *Id.* (*citing* Braintech v. Kostiuk, CA 024459 (British Columbia Court of Appeals, Mar. 18, 1999)).

[9] 2001 U.S. Dist. LEXIS 6288 (S.D.N.Y., May 15, 2001).

[10] 150 F. Supp. 2d 566 (S.D.N.Y. 2001)

[11] American Law Institute, ALI/UNIDROIT Principles and Rules of Transnational Civil Procedure (Discussion Draft No. 2, Apr. 12, 2001) (draft circulated by ALI Council for discussion and comment).

[12] *Id.* at 34.

[13] *Id.* at 71 (citing 4.1, cmt.).

[14] *Id.* at 72 (noting that provision could apply to organizations, such as corporations, as well as to individuals but may be superseded by international conventions such as the Brussels and Lugano Conventions).

[15] *See* Mink Dev. v. AAAA Dev. LLC, 190 F.3d 333 (5th Cir. 1999); Zippo Mfg. Co. v. Zippo Dot Com, Inc., 952 F. Supp. 1119, 1124 (W.D. Pa. 1997); Geissmann v. Stephens, 2001 Tex. App. LEXIS 332 (Apr. 26, 2001) (stating that a web site alone is not a sufficient basis for jurisdiction); Enterprise Rent-A-Car Co. v. Stowell, 137 F. Supp. 2d 1141 (E.D. Mo. 2001) (granting defendant's motion to dismiss); Dawson v. Pepin, 2001 U.S. Dist. Lexis 10074 (S.D. Mich. Mar. 29, 2001).

[16] Digital Control Inc. v. Boretronics Inc., 161 F. Supp. 2d 1183, 1186 (W.D. Wash. 2001).

United States courts are examining the limits of prescriptive jurisdiction stemming from attempts by individual nation states to regulate the Internet. Yahoo! obtained a declaratory judgment in a California court that a French court's ruling purporting to restrain its activities in the United States was unenforceable because of a chilling effect on its First Amendment rights. The French ruling purported to restrain Yahoo! from selling materials on its site which violated French regulations on anti-hate speech.[17] Yahoo! end-users are able to post Nazi-related propaganda and memorabilia that are illegal in France.[18] The French subsidiary of Yahoo! does not permit such materials to be posted.[19] However, Yahoo!'s U.S.-based site (.com) does not impose such a restriction because it violates the First Amendment.[20] The court order in France requires Yahoo! to "render impossible access by persons in France to objectionable content on servers based in the United States."[21] Another unsettled issue is the right of consumers to litigate Internet-related disputes in their home court. The Hague Conference has also proposed a Convention on Jurisdiction and Foreign Judgments in Civil and Criminal Matters and proposed a pro-consumer rule that will be discussed in Chapter Eight.

Defending a suit in a distant state or country is time-consuming, burdensome, and expensive. Doing business over the Internet may expose a company to unfamiliar substantive law and procedural rules in a foreign jurisdiction.[22] Simply posting information on an electronic bulletin board accessible in a foreign jurisdiction may subject the online company to liability. States generally extend jurisdiction beyond their borders by a long-arm statute, which provides for service of process on nonresidents. At one time, a defendant could flee the jurisdiction, leaving the plaintiff without a remedy. A more mobile, modern society led the legislatures to enact long-arm statutes. The first long-arm statutes were enacted to provide "constructive or substituted service of process on a nonresident motorist" involved in an accident within the jurisdiction.[23]

Today's more modern long-arm statutes permit process to be served on nonresidents for a wide variety of torts and other causes of action. In considering the issue of personal jurisdiction over a nonresident, a court must first apply the forum state's long-arm statute and then determine if the requirements of the long-arm statute are met.[24]

---

[17] Yahoo!, Inc. v. La Ligue Contre Racisme, 169 F. Supp. 2d 1181 (N.D. Ca. 2001) (granting summary judgment in favor of Yahoo! and entering declaratory judgment precluding enforcement of a French court's ruling restraining Yahoo! within the United States; finding no basis for abstention and that comity was outweighed by its obligation to uphold the First Amendment).

[18] *Id.*

[19] *Id.*

[20] *Id.*

[21] *Id.* at 1.

[22] *Foreign jurisdiction* refers to any out-of-state jurisdiction, whether in the same or another country.

[23] James A. Ballentine, Ballentine's Law Dictionary 754 (3d ed. 1969).

[24] Cello Holdings LLC v. Lawrence-Dahl Co., 89 F. Supp. 2d 464, 470 (S.D.N.Y. 2000).

"Personal jurisdiction cannot be sustained unless a defendant has sufficient contact with a forum so as not to offend traditional notions of fair play and substantial justice."[25] The issue of John Doe lawsuits seeking to unveil online identities raises troubling issues about fair play. In recent years, there has been a plethora of John Doe lawsuits targeting anonymous online speakers. AOL reported that it received approximately 475 civil subpoenas seeking identity information about AOL subscribers.[26] "On average, AOL was being asked to unmask the identity of a subscriber more than once a day in 2000."[27] Yahoo! is being asked to unveil online identities an average of once or twice a week in Santa Clara County, California.[28] AOL argues that the use of John Doe subpoenas and lawsuits "threatens to have a chilling effect on protected speech and the growth of the online medium."[29]

Foreign jurisdictions have functionally similar devices, and the number of cases of online companies litigating in foreign jurisdictions is growing. The key question addressed here is what Internet-related activity subjects SPC to jurisdiction in another state or country. The plaintiff has the burden of demonstrating that a defendant web site has sufficient contacts with the forum state to satisfy due process.

This chapter provides a road map for understanding the jurisdictional issues presented by the online world. Section 7.01 begins with an overview of the jurisdictional issues and framework. Section 7.02 discusses in greater detail personal jurisdiction issues. Section 7.03 focuses on explores the criminal and tort-like jurisdictional challenges. Finally, Section 7.04 provides sample preventive law pointers to assist you with your implementation efforts as well as some jurisdictional guidelines to consider when dealing with various online activities.

[A] Subject Matter Jurisdiction

Jurisdiction is defined as the scope of the court's power to adjudicate a controversy.[30] *Subject matter jurisdiction* is a legal concept that refers broadly to the

---

[25] Natural Origins Resources, Inc. v. Kotler, 133 F. Supp. 2d 1232 (D.N.M. 2001).

[26] Brief *Amicus Curiae* of America Online, Inc. in Melvin v. John Does, Nos. 2115 WDA 2000 & 2116 WDA 2000 (Superior Court of Pa., Pittsburgh, Pa., Appeal from Order Dated Nov. 15, 2000); *see also In re* Subpoena Duces Tecum to America Online, Inc., 2000 WL 1210372 at *6 (Va. Cir. Ct., 2000) ("To fail to recognize that the First Amendment rights to speak anonymously should be extended to communications on the Internet would require this court to ignore either United States Supreme Court precedent or the realities of speech in the twenty-first century.").

[27] *Id*. at 11.

[28] *Id*. (citing Blake A. Bell, Dealing with the "Cybersmear," N.Y.L.J. (Apr. 19, 1999) at T3).

[29] *Id*. at 12.

[30] *See* Mary Kay Kane, Civil Procedure in a Nutshell 6 (1985) (discussing subject matter jurisdiction).

power of a court to hear a case. "It is part of a broader universal requirement that a court possess adjudicatory jurisdiction, which encompasses subject matter jurisdiction as well."[31] In *In re Doubleclick Privacy Litigation,*[32] the court granted the defendant's motion to dismiss the plaintiff's federal privacy claims in a case about the use of "cookies" collecting personal information. When the federal claims were dismissed, the court could have retained state law claims under supplemental jurisdiction but chose to dismiss the complaint with prejudice.

[1] Federal Courts

Federal district courts have limited subject matter jurisdiction and may only hear cases involving federal questions or diversity of citizenship cases involving state claims of a value greater than $75,000.[33] The federal question jurisdiction statute states that "the district courts shall have original jurisdiction of all civil actions arising under the Constitution, laws, or treaties of the United States."[34] *Diversity of citizenship* means that the parties are from different states. Diversity jurisdiction was originally conferred on the federal courts to prevent a "home court" advantage. The theory was that a federal court would be a more neutral forum than would the plaintiff's state court. In addition, federal courts have exclusive jurisdiction over patent, trademark, and copyright cases and other statutorily designated categories of disputes. Consequently, the federal district courts have been a forum for a myriad of domain name, online patent infringement, and other Internet-related cases.

A federal district court applies the substantive law that would be applied by the state court in the district where the federal court sits. If SPC filed a lawsuit in the federal district court of Massachusetts, the court would apply Massachusetts law. In addition, the Massachusetts federal court would apply Massachusetts's conflict of law rules. SPC will include a choice of law and forum clause in its web site, shrinkwrap, mass market, and negotiated contracts. The freedom to choose the law and forum is the greatest for commercial transactions. Courts are unlikely to enforce one-sided choice of law or forum clauses for consumer transactions. A web site order form may be devised to screen out consumer sales, if the risk of jurisdiction seems to be too great. Contractual choice of law, forum, and venue

---

[31] American Bar Ass'n, ABA Jurisdiction in Cyberspace, Achieving Legal and Business Order in Cyberspace: A Report on Global Jurisdiction Issues Created by the Internet (July 2000).

[32] 154 F. Supp. 2d 497 (S.D.N.Y. 2001) (granting motion of defendants to dismiss plaintiffs' amended complaint in case over the use of cookies collecting personal information such as names, addresses, home and business addresses, telephone numbers, and searches performed on the Internet, including sites visited). In June of 2001, a California court refused to dismiss a lawsuit against Doubleclick arising out of the same practices. Newsbytes, Doubleclick Privacy Class Action Given Go Ahead, Newsbytes (June 7, 2001) (visited June 7, 2001), http://www.newsbytes.com/news/01/166608.html (reporting California court's refusal to dismiss lawsuit based on misuse of cookies in tracking Internet users).

[33] Congress limits the scope of actions that U.S. federal courts can decide.

[34] 28 U.S.C. § 1331 (2001).

will be enforced in the commercial context, as long as no fundamental public polices are violated.[35]

In *Sallen v. Corinthians Licenciamentos LTDA*,[36] a federal court granted a defendant's motion to dismiss for lack of subject matter in a case involving the conflict between the Anticybersquatting Consumer Protection Act (ACPA) and the Uniform Domain Name Dispute Resolution Policy. The defendant had lost an administrative dispute resolution under the Uniform Domain Name Dispute Resolution Policy to defendant trademark holder and was seeking a declaration that he was not liable under the ACPA. Jurisdiction depends on the facts as they existed when the complaint was brought.

If parties to an online or other mass-market license agreement choose a particular state law to apply to their contract, the courts will uphold this choice of law absent a fundamental public policy that mitigates against enforcement. The Uniform Commercial Code, for example, states affirmatively the "right of the parties to a multi-state transaction or a transaction involving foreign trade to choose their own law."[37] Section 1-105 grants the parties power to choose applicable law as long as the "transaction bears a reasonable relation to this state."[38]

[2] State Courts

Most tort or contract disputes are typically adjudicated in the state courts, the law of torts being largely a matter of state law, as are the fields of contract law, property law, and family or probate law. The state courts also have the residual powers to decide cases not allocated to the federal courts under the U.S. Constitution. An Internet-related action originally brought in state court may be removed to federal court.[39] A federal court exercising jurisdiction in a lawsuit may resolve state causes of action that are also part of the suit under the doctrine of pendent jurisdiction. State courts have been the traditional province of the law of corporations, commercial law, trusts and estates, and countless other substantive fields. The typical procedural devices for challenging jurisdictions are (1) a motion challenging the sufficiency of jurisdiction, (2) a summary judgment motion, or (3) a request for a hearing on jurisdiction.

[3] Forum Selection and Choice of Law Clauses

Parties to transactions can specify a particular forum or choice of law, reducing some degree of uncertainty in the event of a dispute. For example, SPC will

---

[35] The choice of law, forum, and venue, for example, must bear a "reasonable relationship" to the commercial contract. *See* UCC § 1-105 (2000).

[36] 2000 U.S. Dist. LEXIS 19976 (D. Mass. 2000), *rev'd*, 2001 U.S. App. LEXIS 25965 (1st Cir. Dec. 5, 2001) (holding that the federal court had subject matter jurisdiction could show that he was in compliance with the ACPA after having lost UDRP proceeding).

[37] U.C.C. § 1-105, O.C. #1 (2000).

[38] U.C.C. § 1-105 (2000).

[39] The court must agree that 28 U.S.C. § 1441(a) is satisfied.

include a choice of law and forum clause on its web site, shrinkwrap, mass market, and negotiated contracts. The freedom to choose the law and forum is the greatest for commercial transactions. Courts will generally enforce a parties' agreement to adjudicate a dispute in a particular forum applying an agreed upon body of law. The parties to international sales contracts also have the discretion to choose the applicable law.[40] The Convention on Contracts for International Sale of Goods (CISG) applies to sale of goods between parties whose places of business are in different signatory states.[41] Many private international agreements agree to adjudicate disputes in an exclusive forum, such as arbitration.

There are limits to the parties' ability to choose the applicable law or forum. For example, courts are unlikely to enforce one-sided choice of law or forum clauses for consumer transactions. A web site order form may be devised to screen out consumer sales, if the risk of jurisdiction seems to be too great. However, in many European countries, mass-market or shrinkwrap license agreements are not enforceable. Many countries have mandatory consumer protection for distance contracts, which include Internet sales. The parties cannot agree to submit their dispute to the federal courts, as Congress confers jurisdiction to the federal courts.[42]

[B]   Personal Jurisdiction

[1]   Introduction to Personal Jurisdiction

A defendant haled into court in a distant forum may want to avoid the potential expense and unpredictability of going to court in another state by challenging personal jurisdiction. The exercise of personal jurisdiction is reasonable if it comports with traditional notions of fair play and substantial justice. In determining reasonableness, seven factors are considered: (1) the extent of a defendant's purposeful interjection, (2) the burden on the defendant in defending in the forum, (3) the extent of conflict with the sovereignty of the defendant's state, (4) the forum state's interest in adjudicating the dispute, (5) the most efficient judicial resolution of the controversy, (6) the importance of the forum to the plaintiff's interest in convenient and effective relief, and (7) the existence of an alternative forum. As no single factor is dispositive, a court must balance all seven.[43]

A successful challenge of personal jurisdiction will often result in the plaintiff filing the lawsuit in a forum that is more appropriate and convenient for the defendant. A plaintiff must adduce specific facts that support jurisdiction whether in state or federal court. In federal courts, a plaintiff has the burden of showing a

---

[40] Article 6 of the Convention on Contracts for the International Sale of Goods states that "[t]he parties may exclude the application of this Convention or, subject to Article 12, derogate from or vary the effect of any of its provisions." *See* CISG art. 6 (2000).

[41] CISG art. 1 (2000).

[42] ErieNet, Inc. v. VelocityNet, Inc., 156 F.3d 513 (3d Cir. 1998).

[43] Rio Props, Inc. v. Rio Int'l Interlink, 2002 U.S. App. LEXIS 4392 (9th Cir. Mar. 20, 2002).

basis for asserting jurisdiction under Fed. R. Civ. P. 12 (b)(2).[44] For a court to resolve a dispute, it must be able to exercise personal jurisdiction over a defendant, which requires first that the defendant have minimum contacts with the forum state. The purpose of the minimum contact analysis is to protect defendants from having to defend lawsuits in distant forums where they have no meaningful contacts "and therefore may be unfamiliar with the substance and procedural law."[45] Businesses with an online presence may not be summoned to a distant forum unless personal jurisdiction is satisfied. If SPC has minimum contacts with a forum state, a court will move to the next step of the due process analysis and determine whether the exercise of personal jurisdiction over SPC offends "traditional notions of fair play and substantial justice."[46]

In an online dispute, the jurisdictional dispute focuses on the connection between the web site and the state where jurisdiction is asserted. Commercial transactions in the form of online sales are often sufficient to satisfy personal jurisdiction. A plaintiff may not rely solely on bare pleadings to withstand a defendant's motion to dismiss for lack of *in personam* jurisdiction. Finally, personal jurisdiction is acquired by satisfying the requirements of the forum state's long-arm statute.

Service of process must also be calculated to give notice to foreign defendants. The Ninth Circuit U.S. Court of Appeals held that e-mail service upon a foreign Internet gambling business was appropriate alternative service, that advertising Internet business in the forum state provided personal jurisdiction, and that multiple transgressions warranted sanction of default judgment.[47] A plaintiff has the burden of establishing the district court's personal jurisdiction over an out of state defendant. Where a district court did not conduct an evidentiary hearing on the issue of personal jurisdiction in considering a defendant's motion to dismiss pursuant to Fed. R. Civ. P. 12(b)(2), the plaintiff need only make a prima facie showing of jurisdiction. A plaintiff can meet that burden by establishing with reasonable particularity sufficient contacts between the defendant and the forum state to support jurisdiction. Under those circumstances, a court will not consider facts proffered by the defendant that conflict with those offered by the plaintiff and will construe the facts in the light most favorable to the nonmoving party in reviewing a dismissal pursuant to Rule 12(b)(2).[48]

[2] Challenging Personal Jurisdiction

A defendant challenging personal jurisdiction in federal court will file a motion to dismiss.[49] A defendant may challenge personal jurisdiction with an

---

[44] Dagesse v. Plant Hotel NV, 113 F. Supp. 2d 211 (D.N.H. 2000).

[45] Natural Origins Resources, Inc. v. Kotler, 133 F. Supp. 2d 1232, 1235 (D.N.M. 2001).

[46] Soma Medical Int'l v. Standard Chartered Bank, 196 F.3d 1292, 1299 (10th Cir. 1999) (quoting Asahi Metal Industry Co., 480 U.S. 102, 113).

[47] *Rio Props*, 2002 U.S. App. LEXIS 4392.

[48] Neogen Corp. v. Neo Gen Screening, Inc., 2002 U.S. App. LEXIS 3478 (6th Cir. Mar. 6, 2002).

[49] Andrew E. Costa, Comment, Minimum Contacts in Cyberspace: A Taxonomy of the Case Law, 35 Hous. L. Rev. 453 (1998).

interlocutory appeal.[50] A court may permit the defendant to conduct discovery for the purpose of challenging a defendant's motion to dismiss. Courts may also allow the filing of briefs on a motion to dismiss.[51] A United States Court of Appeals applies a *de novo* standard of review to a lower court's decision on whether the exercise of personal jurisdiction complies with due process.[52] The lack of personal jurisdiction is a waivable defense in federal courts, whereas subject matter may not be waived.[53]

If a defendant challenges jurisdiction, the burden shifts to the plaintiff to come forward with sufficient facts to establish personal jurisdiction.[54] The plaintiffs meet this burden by making a prima facie showing of "sufficient contacts between the defendant and the forum state."[55] The plaintiff can typically meet this burden by establishing jurisdictional facts through affidavits or other sworn evidence demonstrating the interconnections between the defendant, the forum, and the litigation. The "minimum contacts" aspect of the due process analysis for exercising jurisdiction can be established through contacts that give rise to specific personal jurisdiction or those that give rise to general personal jurisdiction.[56]

[C] The Minimum Contacts Test

Contemporary jurisdictional analysis in the United States emerged in 1945, long before the Internet was conceived. The Supreme Court in *International Shoe Co. v. Washington*[57] held that a court could maintain jurisdiction over an out-of-state defendant only if the defendant had sufficient "minimum contacts" with the forum state. The public policy underlying the "minimum contacts" test is fairness and justice.[58] Thus, a court may assert jurisdiction over an out-of-state defendant who is doing business in the forum state. Foreign courts also recognize the doctrine of personal jurisdiction, though they may use different terminology. Canada, for example requires a "real and substantial" connection between the dispute and the forum province.[59] The United States Supreme Court noted, in *Hanson v.*

---

[50] Most state courts have enacted state rules of civil procedure that parallel the Federal Rules of Civil Procedure.

[51] GTE New Media Servs., Inc. v. Bellsouth Corp., 199 F.3d 1343 (D.C. Cir. 2000) (noting that an interlocutory appeal may be brought pursuant to 28 U.S.C. § 1292(b) to determine whether the quality and nature of the web site meets the due process standard of minimum contacts).

[52] The court in American Eyewear, Inc. v. Peeper's Sunglasses, 106 F. Supp. 2d 895 (N.D. Tex. 2000), allowed discovery and briefing on the issue of personal jurisdiction.

[53] Mink v. AAAA Dev. LLC, 190 F.3d 333 (5th Cir. 1999).

[54] Fed. R. Civ. P. 12 (h)(1).

[55] Zippo Mfg. Co. v. Zippo Dot Com, Inc., 952 F. Supp. 1119, 1121 (W.D. Pa. 1997).

[56] Mink v. AAAA Dev. LLC, 190 F.3d 333, 335 (5th Cir. 1999) (quoting Latshaw v. Johnston, 167 F.3d 208, 211 (5th Cir. 1999)).

[57] 326 U.S. 310, 319-20 (1945).

[58] *Id.* at 316.

[59] David Woolford, Electronic Commerce: It's All A Matter of Trust: Industry Trend or Event, Comput. Canada (May 7, 1999) at 13.

Denckla,[60] how "[t]echnological progress has increased the flow of commerce between States," resulting in an increase in jurisdiction.[61]

The key question is whether the defendant purposefully availed himself of the benefits of doing business in the forum state. The Supreme Court in *Worldwide Volkswagen Corp. v. Woodson*[62] ruled that a car dealer selling a car in one state is not subjected to jurisdiction in a distant court merely because the buyer has a car accident in the forum state. In product liability cases, a defendant's conduct must be purposefully directed to the forum state. The basis for personal jurisdiction may not be derived entirely from the manufacturer's act of placing a defective product in the stream of commerce.[63] Within the Internet context, the important question is whether the defendant reached out and originated contacts with residents in the forum state.[64] The amount of revenue that the defendant derived from interstate or international commerce is a key factor in determining personal jurisdiction.[65] Courts must determine whether it is proper to exercise specific jurisdiction over a nonresident defendant solely on the basis of that nonresident defendant's Internet contacts with the forum. Some courts attempt to apply traditional principles of personal jurisdiction, while others advocate an entirely new set of standards be created for the Internet.[66]

The flow of e-commerce between countries on the Internet creates the need for predictable and accessible jurisdiction between litigants across the globe. The law of the Internet is rapidly evolving without international treaties addressing cyberspace jurisdiction. Courts seek the closest parallel from the offline world adapted to the commercial realities of cyberspace. Courts often struggle in deciding whether a web site is closest to a publisher, television station, bookstore, or baby-Bell telecom. This chapter explains some of the basic issues of civil procedure that arise in the online world.

§ 7.02 TWO PARADIGMS OF PERSONAL JURISDICTION

Cyberspace places a new twist on the concept of jurisdiction. Is creating a web site purposefully directed to all potential Internet users worldwide or is it similar to placing a product in the stream of commerce? Courts have taken different approaches when faced with relatively identical facts.[67] Since it is unlikely that

---

[60] 357 U.S. 235 (1958).

[61] *Id.* at 250-251.

[62] 444 U.S. 286 (1980).

[63] Asahi Metal Indus. Co. v. Superior Court, 480 U.S. 102 (1987).

[64] Cello Holdings, LLC v. Lawrence-Dahl Co., 89 F. Supp. 2d 464, 470 (S.D.N.Y. 2000).

[65] *Id.*

[66] Joseph Schmitt & Peter Nikolai, Application of Personal Jurisdiction Principles to Electronic Commerce: A User's Guide, 27 Wm. Mitchell L. Rev. 1571 (2001) (examining the development of jurisdiction cases and analyzing current court trends).

[67] *See* Todd D. Leitstein, A Solution for Personal Jurisdiction on the Internet, 59 La. L. Rev. 565, 566 n.2 (1999) (contrasting court opinions in Internet jurisdiction cases).

courts will reach a consensus soon, anyone with a web presence faces the remote possibility that they might have to defend themselves in a distant legal forum.[68]

As the World Wide Web evolved, most web sites were strictly informational and not interactive. An Internet presence was the equivalent of an electronic brochure, available for anyone who stumbled across the links. Consequently, early jurisdiction cases usually involved a controversy independent of the Internet. The web presence was used to try to prove that the defendant had contacts with the forum state.

Many courts found that an informational site was insufficient for jurisdiction without some additional contact with the forum state.[69] Courts have generally inquired as to whether the Internet content provider could have reasonably anticipated defending himself or herself in the distant jurisdiction.[70]

The courts have carved out two generic types of personal jurisdiction: specific jurisdiction and general jurisdiction.[71] The "minimum contacts" test of *International Shoe* may be satisfied by the exercise of general and specific jurisdiction. General jurisdiction exists when the plaintiff's cause of action arises from the defendant's nonforum-related activities. The quantity and quality of an online company's contacts with a forum determine general jurisdiction.

General jurisdiction is properly exercised even if causes of action do not originate in the forum, provided the defendant has "continuous and systematic contacts with the forum."[72] *Specific jurisdiction* is found when the plaintiff's cause

---

[68] *See* Martin H. Redish, Of New Wine and Old Bottles: Personal Jurisdiction, The Internet, and the Nature of Constitutional Evolution, 38 Jurimetrics J. 575, 578 (1998) (analyzing Internet jurisdiction issues and potential roadblocks to commerce). The Minnesota attorney general posted a warning to all Internet users and providers that they are subject to Minnesota jurisdiction for any information that will be disseminated in the state via the Internet. T.J. Thurston, Tackling Conflicts of Law Issues on the Internet, Internet Newsletter: Bus. & Law Aspects (Mar. 1997) at 8.

[69] *Cf.* Hearts v. Goldberger, 1997 U.S. Dist. LEXIS 2065 at *2 (S.D.N.Y., Feb. 26, 1997) (observing nationwide jurisdiction on basis of Internet presence violates traditional case law and policy) and Pres-Kap v. System One, 636 So. 2d 1351, 1353 (Fla. App. 1994) (noting jurisdiction based on online contacts alone would dangerously broaden state courts' reach) with Telco Communications v. An Apple A Day, 977 F. Supp. 404, 407 (E.D. Va. 1997) (asserting jurisdiction based on Internet advertising) and Inset Sys., Inc. v. Instruction Set, Inc., 937 F. Supp. 161, 165 (D. Conn. 1996) (holding Internet advertisement and a toll-free number were sufficient to establish jurisdiction). Enterprise Rent-A-Car v. Stowell, 137 F. Supp. 2d 1151 (E.D. Mo. 2001) (holding there were insufficient minimum contacts to exercise personal jurisdiction over a defendant whose auto web site was accessible to Missouri users, but where users could not purchase cars via the site or exchange information with the defendant.

[70] *See* Matthew Oetker, Personal Jurisdiction and the Internet, 47 Drake L. Rev. 613, 626 (1999) (exploring traditional and Internet-based requirements for jurisdiction).

[71] Helicopteros Nacionales de Colombia, S.A. v. Hall, 466 U.S. 408 (1984).

[72] *See, e.g.,* National Paintball Supply, Inc. v. Cossio, 996 F. Supp. 459, 461 (E.D. Pa. 1998) (applying Pennsylvania law).

of action arises out of a defendant's forum-related activities. Therefore, the cause of action is the same as the basis for jurisdiction.

[A] General Jurisdiction

General jurisdiction exists over a nonresident defendant only if contacts with the forum are so extensive that "it is possible to overlook the fact the cause of action arose elsewhere."[73] "General jurisdiction, which is of less immediate importance in Internet transactions, involves a nonresident defendant whose contacts with the forum state are unrelated to the particular dispute in issue."[74] In contrast, "Specific jurisdiction exists if (1) the defendant has performed some act or consummated some transaction within the forum or otherwise purposefully availed himself of the privileges of conducting activities in the forum, (2) the claim arises out of or results from the defendant's forum-related activities, and (3) the exercise of jurisdiction is reasonable."[75] The test for general jurisdiction is whether the defendant has engaged in "systematic and continuous" activities in the forum state.[76] Another court described the test for general jurisdiction as contacts that are "extensive and persuasive."[77] General jurisdiction permits courts to exercise jurisdiction on nonresidents for all purposes because of the defendant's extensive activities directed at the state. The difference between general and specific jurisdiction is a matter of degree.

Suppose a Massachusetts company launched a web site entitled "Vermont.com" directed exclusively to Vermont Internet users. Assume further that the company's online sales are made exclusively to Vermont residents. If the Massachusetts company had an extensive network of representatives in Vermont, a court would likely hold that the contact is so great as to confer general jurisdiction. Courts seldom find that there is a sufficient basis for general jurisdiction because it "requires far more extensive contact between the forum and the defendant than does specific jurisdiction."[78]

The doctrine of general jurisdiction is useful when there is little or no causal connection between the defendant's wrongdoing and the forum. If a plaintiff cannot establish specific jurisdiction, a court may exercise general jurisdiction over the defendant, provided that the defendant's contacts are "continuous and systematic" with the forum state.[79] Like the Internet, the definition of what level of activity constitutes general jurisdiction online is still evolving.

---

[73] Gene R. Shreve and Peter Raven-Hansen, Understanding Civil Procedure 73 (1989).

[74] Denis T. Rice, Offering Securities on the Internet—2001, 18 Computer & Internet Law. 19 (May 2001).

[75] Bancroft & Masters, Inc. v. Augusta National, Inc., 223 F.3d 1082, 1086 (9th Cir. 2000).

[76] Id. See also Brand v. Menlove Dodge, 796 F. 2d 1070, 1073 (9th Cir. 1996) (noting that standard for general jurisdiction is "fairly high").

[77] Reliance Steel Prods. v. Watson, Ess., Marshall, 675 F.2d 587, 589 (3d Cir. 1982).

[78] Gene R. Shreve and Peter Raven-Hansen, Understanding Civil Procedure 67 (1989).

[79] Helikopteros Nacionales de Colombia, S.A. v. Hall, 466 U.S. 408 (1984).

[B] Specific Jurisdiction

If contacts are not so substantial or continuous as to qualify for general juris-diction, a court may still exercise specific jurisdiction for forum-related acts.[80] Specific jurisdiction exists if (1) an online defendant availed himself of the privi-leges of doing business, (2) the claim arose out of forum-related activities, and (3) the exercise of jurisdiction is reasonable.[81]

Consequently, SPC may be exposed to the product liability jurisdiction of any state where it sells the computers. Internet activities that may give rise to spe-cific jurisdiction include defamation, copyright or trademark infringement, false advertising, and breach of contract.[82] For example, SPC's online product liabilities for placing dangerously defective computers in the stream of commerce may be the basis of specific jurisdiction if the computer was ordered by a state resident who visited SPC's site.

[1] *International Shoe* in Cyberspace

A court must determine whether a nonresident web site is subject to juris-diction under the law of the state as well as due process. The test the Supreme Court articulated in *International Shoe Co. v. Washington*[83] focuses upon whether the nonresident has minimum contacts with the forum state so as to satisfy "tradi-tional notions of fair play and substantial justice under the Due Process Clause of the Fourteenth Amendment."[84] A web site that sells goods or licenses software is entitled to due process. An online company should not be forced to defend claims where the exercise of jurisdiction offends "traditional notions of fair play and sub-stantial justice."[85]

The minimum contacts test may be established by contacts to support spe-cific jurisdiction or contacts that support general jurisdiction when a company's activities are "systematic and continuous." For the minimum contacts test for spe-cific jurisdiction to be satisfied, "(1) the contacts must be related to the plaintiff's cause of action; (2) the contacts must involve some act by which the defendant purposefully avails itself of the privilege of conducting activities within the forum;

---

[80] Burger King v. Rudzewics, 471 U.S. 462, 475 (1985); Bancroft & Masters Inc., 233 F.3d 1082 (9th Cir. 2000).

[81] Cybersell, Inc. v. Cybersell, Inc., 130 F.3d 414, 416 (9th Cir. 1997).

[82] Carl W. Chamberlin, To the Millennium: Emerging Issues for the Year 2000 and Cyberspace, 13 Notre Dame J.L. Ethics & Pub. Pol'y 131, 150 (1999). Additionally, specific jurisdiction was proper in a patent infringement case wherein the defendant infringed the plaintiff's patent online coupon system. Coolsavings.com, Inc. v. I.Q. Commerce Corp., 53 F. Supp. 2d 1000 (N.D. Ill. 1999).

[83] 326 U.S. 310 (1945).

[84] People Solutions, Inc. v. People Solutions, Inc., 2000 U.S. Dist. LEXIS 10444 (N.D. Tex., July 25, 2000) (discussing Constitutional limits of minimum contacts).

[85] Burger King Corp. v. Rudzewicz, 471 U.S. 462, 476 (1985) (quoting International Shoe Co. v. Washington, 326 U.S. 310, 320 (1945)).

and (3) the forum must be such that the defendant should reasonably anticipate being haled into court there."[86]

SPC's aspirations in becoming an e-business may result in a finding that it "purposefully established contacts with the forum state."[87] If SPC is found to have purposely availed itself of the forum by web site sales or other extensive commercial activity, it is likely that a court will find that the exercise of jurisdiction meets the standard of fair play. It is questionable whether a single sale of a computer from SPC's web site would constitute an act of purposeful availment.[88]

A court must determine what law should be applied to claims in an Internet-related case. Federal courts asserting supplemental jurisdiction over state law claims in a federal question lawsuit must follow the choice-of-law rules of the forum state.[89] The majority of jurisdictions follow the "most significant relationship" test in § 145 of the Restatement (Second) Conflict of Laws.[90] Section 145 determines the law of torts according to the local law of the state that has the "most significant relationship to the occurrence and the parties."[91] In the case of contracts, the applicable issues are "(a) the place where the injury occurred, (b) the place where the conduct causing the injury occurred, (c) the domicile, residence, nationality, place of incorporation and place of business of the parties, and (d) the place where the relationship, if any, between the parties is centered."[92]

In the typical e-commerce case, the online company will not be targeting consumers in any one jurisdiction. The closest parallel is a national television or print advertisement not directed at any one state.[93] Courts frequently focus on whether a web site is being used for e-commerce activities rather than merely posting information about the company. Similarly, a Pennsylvania court granted a defendant's motion to dismiss for lack of personal jurisdiction in an antitrust action.[94] The court found that the defendant's passive web page was a mere conduit for corporate information where no business was transacted and therefore no basis existed for exercising general jurisdiction. In another case, the court granted a motion to dismiss for lack of personal jurisdiction where an online company's

---

[86] Kim v. Keenan, 71 F. Supp. 2d 1228, 1235 (M.D. Fla. 1999) (quotation omitted).

[87] *Id.*

[88] *Id.*

[89] America Online, Inc. v. National Health Care Discount, Inc., 121 F. Supp. 2d 1255, 1268 (N.D. Iowa 2000) (denying defendant's motions for summary judgment in Spam e-mail case with federal and state claims).

[90] *Id.* (citing Restatement (Second) Conflict of Laws, § 145).

[91] *Id.* at 1269.

[92] *Id.*

[93] A federal court found that a defendant's web site was not directed at Connecticut any more than any other state declining jurisdiction. The courts observed that the defendant's web site was functionally equivalent to an advertisement in a national magazine or web site. Edberg v. Neogen Corp., 17 F. Supp. 2d 104 (D. Conn. 1998).

[94] Santana Prods., Inc. v. Bobrick Washroom Equip., 14 F. Supp. 2d 710 (M.D. Pa., July 24, 1998).

web site was used for advertising, for providing customer services, and for soliciting new employees. The court held that the web site was passive in nature
because the company did not sell products or engage in other conduct classifiable
as activity for profit on the Internet.[95]

A court may find general jurisdiction even if the controversy does not
arise out of the defendant's activities in the state. Jurisdiction over a London
hotel by a New York resident who was injured in London was proper in New
York, for example, because the hotel maintained a reservation agent in New
York.[96]

In a more contemporary example, an Internet presence alone was insufficient
to support jurisdiction over an out-of-state defendant in a wrongful death action.[97]
In another case, a nonresident defendant in a defamation action did not have sufficient minimum contacts with the forum state required to establish personal jurisdiction under the due process clause because he did not have an office located in
the forum state, did not have employees or sales representatives in the forum state,
did not solicit business in the forum state, and did not derive any income from customers in the forum state.[98] Systematic advertising and business contacts, however,
in addition to an interactive web presence making online sales, may be sufficient
to support general jurisdiction if the server or computer system is also located
within state borders.[99]

A court dismissed the defamation action against a defendant who allegedly
posted defamatory statements about a manufacturer on electronic bulletin boards,
despite a clause that the agreement between the parties was governed by California law.[100] Although the court held that specific jurisdiction could be based on the
fact that the defendant derived benefit from California by having an account with
Yahoo!, a California-based Internet company, the court concluded that "it would
not comport with traditional notions of fair play and substantial justice to do so."
The plaintiff was not a California resident, the defendant's messages did not have
a particular California impact, the messages posted to the bulletin board were disseminated worldwide, and they were not California-directed. That the portal
employees who maintained the electronic bulletin board were located in California was incidental; the bulletin board was part of a worldwide communications
network that was accessible to any Internet user. Defendant was an individual, he
resided in Colorado and did not conduct any commercial activities in California,
and he owned no property in California.

---

[95] Als Scan v. Wilkins, 142 F. Supp. 2d 703 (D. Md. 2001).

[96] Frummer v. Hilton Hotels Int'l, Inc., 19 N.Y.2d 533 (1967). *But see* Romero v. Holiday Inn,
Utrecht, 1998 U.S. Dist. LEXIS 19997 (E.D. Pa., Dec. 15, 1998) (denying jurisdiction on the basis
of defendant's Internet reservation service).

[97] Grutowski v. Steamboat Lake Guides and Outfitters, Inc., 1998 U.S. Dist. LEXIS 20255 (E.D.
Pa., Dec. 21, 1998).

[98] Lofton v. Turbine Design, Inc., 100 F. Supp. 2d 404, (N.D. Miss., Mar. 29, 2000).

[99] Mieczkowski v. Masco Corp., 997 F. Supp. 782 (E.D. Tex. 1998).

[100] Nam Tai Elec. v. Titzer, 93 Cal. App. 4th 1301 (Cal. Ct. App. 2001).

[C] Conflict of Laws and Choice of Law

Three concepts are critical to understanding the question of which law applies to an Internet dispute where the parties are in different states or countries: conflict of laws, choice of law, and contracts where there is a choice of law clause. Conflict of laws is a branch of law that evolved out of private international law, the body of law that applies in international trade. Questions of conflict of laws arise in cases "in which some relevant fact has a connection with another system of law on either territorial or personal grounds, and may, on that account, raise a question as to the application of one's own or the appropriate alternative (usually foreign) law to the determination of the issue."[101]

For example, in an e-commerce patent case, personal jurisdiction will be governed by federal circuit court decisions, not the law of a local U.S. court of appeals.[102] The federal district court will consider both statutory and constitutional issues in deciding challenges to personal jurisdiction. "Determining whether jurisdiction exists over an out-of-state defendant involves two inquiries: whether a forum state's long-arm statute permits service of process and whether assertion of personal jurisdiction violates due process."[103] The due process analysis is the same whether a case arises under federal question jurisdiction or diversity.[104] "A federal diversity court's jurisdictional power over a nonresident defendant may not exceed the limits allowed under state law."[105]

The choice of law occurs in an online setting when a court must choose whether to apply the differing substantive laws of the parties. Choice of law is "a subset of conflict of laws, concerns the necessity of the courts to choose between differing substantive laws of interested states."[106] Conflict of law is when the court determines the applicable law. Where the parties do not make a choice of law, it is the court's duty to determine the applicable law. In limited circumstances, the courts where the parties' choice is contrary to a public policy will not enforce the parties' choice of law.

The Internet is an information technology that permits a simultaneous transmission that challenges strictly territoriality-based concepts. Courts may apply a country of transmission or country of reception approach to Internet communications, borrowing from the developing choice of law rules for satellite transmissions. One approach would be to "apply cumulatively the laws of both the country from where the broadcast originated and the country of reception." Under a second theory, "communication theory," a cross-border transmission would implicate

---

[101] Bryan A. Garner, A Dictionary of Modern Legal Usage 200 (4th ed. 1995) (quoting R.H. Graveson, Conflict of Law 3 (7th ed. 1974)).

[102] *See, e.g.,* Viam Corp. v. Iowa Export-Import Trading Co., 84 F.3d 424, 427 (Fed. Cir. 1996).

[103] Nutrition Physiology Corp. v. Enviros Ltd., 87 F. Supp. 2d 648, 650 (N.D. Tex. 2000).

[104] *Id.* at 651, n.1.

[105] Butler v. Beer Across America, 83 F. Supp. 2d 1261 (N.D. Ala. 2000) (holding that personal jurisdiction could not be asserted by a federal court sitting in diversity in Alabama over a nonresident Illinois defendant in an action arising from a single online sale of beer from the defendant's web site).

[106] Robert A. Leflar, The Nature of Conflicts Law, 81 Colum. L. Rev. 1080 (1981).

the copyright laws of the countries where the program audience was located, and a broadcaster would therefore be required to acquire rights for those jurisdictions."[107]

[D] *In rem* Jurisdiction

The application of the concept of *in rem jurisdiction,* jurisdiction over property rather than persons, to cyberspace activities seems anomalous. Yet *in rem* actions exist for Internet domain names, which are a form of intellectual property. Under United States law, *in rem* jurisdiction affects the rights of all persons in a designated property, whereas *"quasi-in-rem* affects the interests of particular persons in designated property."[108] Internet transactions occur in an international legal environment where the concept of *in rem* jurisdiction may be different. *In rem* jurisdiction in the United Kingdom, for example, refers only to admiralty cases.[109] The law for *in rem* jurisdiction for web servers is relatively undeveloped. The only significant *in rem* action has been in domain name litigation. The Anticybersquatting Consumer Protection Act (ACPA) allows an "owner of a mark" to bring an *in rem* action where a domain name allegedly violates the owner's right in a trademark.[110] The Act allows for *in rem* proceedings by the owner of a mark against a domain name in the judicial district in which the domain name registry is located.[111] Section 1125(d)(2)(A) of the Lanham Act provides as follows:

> The owner of a mark may file an *in rem* civil action against a domain name in the judicial district in which the domain name registrar, domain name registry, or other domain name authority that registered or assigned the domain name is located if:
>
> (i) the domain name violates any right of the owner of a mark registered in the Patent and Trademark Office, or protected under subsection (a) or (c); and
>
> (ii) the court finds that the owner—
>
> (I) is not able to obtain *in personam* jurisdiction over a person who would have been a defendant in a civil action under paragraph (1); or
>
> (II) through due diligence was not able to find a person who would have been a defendant in a civil action under paragraph (1) by—

---

[107] Andreas P. Reindl, Choosing Law in Cyberspace: Copyright Conflicts on Global Networks, 19 Mich. J. Int'l L. 799 (1998).

[108] Hanson v. Denckla, 357 U.S. 235, 246 n.12 (1958).

[109] Kazunori Ihiguro, Traditional Legal Concepts: Basics from Three Experts, Remarks, ILPF 1999 Annual Conference, Jurisdiction: Building Confidence in a Borderless Medium, Montreal, Canada (July 26, 1999).

[110] 15 U.S.C. § 1125(d) (2000).

[111] Caesars World, Inc. v. Caesars-Palace.com, 112 F. Supp. 2d 505 (E.D. Va. 2000).

(aa) sending a notice of the alleged violation and intent to proceed under this paragraph to the registrant of the domain name at the postal and email address provided by the registrant to the registrar; and

(bb) publishing notice of the action as the court may direct promptly after filing the action.[112]

The plaintiff in an *in rem* action under the ACPA is the owner of a trademark. Potential defendants include the owner of the infringing domain name or its assignee. The *in rem* action may be filed if the domain name violates the rights of an owner of a registered mark or protected mark and the court finds that the owner either could not obtain personal jurisdiction over the defendant or through due diligence was unable to locate the defendant.[113] In *Mattel, Inc. v. Barbie-Club*,[114] the plaintiff filed an *in rem* action under the Anticybersquatting Consumer Protection Act of 1999 to enforce its Barbie® trademarks against the registration and use of certain second-level Internet domain names. The parties agreed that captainbarbie.com was registered with Bulkregister.com in Baltimore, Maryland, and there was no *in rem* jurisdiction in New York. However, Mattel argued "that in addition to the registrar's location, an *in rem* action can also be filed pursuant to Section 1125(d)(2)(c)(ii) in any district where the plaintiff deposits with the court documents establishing control over the registration and use of the domain name."[115] The court disagreed, following the analysis of *Fleetboston Financial Corp. v. Fleetbostonfinancial.com.*[116] In *Fleetboston,* the court held that the ACPA did not provide for *in rem* jurisdiction except in the judicial district in which the domain name registry, registrar, or other domain names authority was located.[117]

In *Alitalia-Linee Aeree Italiane S.P.A. v. Casinoalitalia.com,*[118] the plaintiff could not pursue *in rem* relief under the ACPA against a foreign defendant absent a showing that it exercised due diligence in locating the defendant and seeking *in*

---

[112] 15 U.S.C. § 1125(d)(2)(A) (2000).

[113] *Id.*

[114] 58 U.S.P.Q.3d (BNA) 1798 (S.D.N.Y. 2001).

[115] *Id.* at * 4.

[116] 2001 U.S. Dist. LEXIS 4797 (D. Mass., Mar. 27, 2001) (holding that "ACPA does not provide for *in rem* jurisdiction except in the judicial district in which the domain name registry, registrar, or other domain name authority is located, as provided in 15 U.S.C. § 1125(d)(2)(A)").

[117] 138 F. Supp. 2d 121 (D. Mass. 2001). *See* Caesars World, Inc. v. Caesars-Palace.Com, 112 F. Supp. 2d 505, 509 (E.D. Va. 2000) (noting that "*in personam* jurisdiction cannot be based merely on an appearance in an *in rem* action"); Harrods Ltd. v. Sixty Internet Domain Names, 110 F. Supp. 2d 420, 421-23 (E.D. Va. 2000) (holding that "no personal jurisdiction over the owner of the res is acquired by bringing . . . [an *in rem*] action" under the ACPA, and a plaintiff "cannot pursue any cause of action with the potential to impose personal liability" simply by virtue of filing an . . .).

[118] Alitalia-Linee Aeree Italiane S.P.A. v. Casinoalitalia.com, 128 F. Supp. 2d 340 (E.D. Va. 2001).

personam jurisdiction. Similarly, in *Lucent Technologies, Inc. v. Lucentsuck.com*,[119] the plaintiff's *in rem* action was dismissed because the identity and the registrant of the domain name had been found, making personal jurisdiction possible. In *Heathmount A.E. Corp. v. Technnodome.com*,[120] a court ruled that *in rem* jurisdiction to claims against property did not apply to an *in rem* suit to protect trademarks from cyberspiracy under the ACPA. Courts have interpreted the ACPA *in rem* remedy narrowly, which is consistent with the settled principle that *in rem* jurisdiction is an alternative basis for jurisdiction where *in personam* jurisdiction is not available.[121]

Remedies for the *in rem* action include forfeiture or cancellation of the domain name or transfer of the domain name to the trademark owner.[122] The federal district court held that the *in rem* provisions of the federal act did not violate the defendant's due process rights.[123] In *Caesars World, Inc. v. Caesars-Palace.com*,[124] a defendant challenged the constitutionality of the *in rem* jurisdiction procedures of the federal anticybersquatting act. The defendant also argued that the court lacked personal jurisdiction over the defendants. The court found that registration with Network Solutions, Inc. of Virginia satisfied *in rem* jurisdiction.[125]

Harrods Department Store of London filed an *in rem* action under the ACPA to obtain 60 Internet domain names containing its trademarks. The ACPA *in rem* action was dismissed because the plaintiff failed to plead bad faith, an essential element.[126] Another ACPA *in rem* action failed when a Rhode Island financial institution attempted to sue a Brazilian defendant in a Massachusetts court. The court found that there was not adequate contact between the parties and the state.[127] Process may be served to a party in the state where the court is located.

---

[119] Lucent Techs., Inc. v. Lucentsucks.com, 95 F. Supp. 2d 528 (E.D. Va. 2000).

[120] 60 U.S.P.Q.3d (BNA) 2018 (E.D. Va. 2000); *see also* Mitchell, Inc. v. Charleston Library Soc'y, 2000 U.S. Dist. LEXIS 15524 (S.D.N.Y., Oct. 18, 2000) (denying motion to dismiss for lack of personal jurisdiction which was not a relevant concern in an *in rem* action).

[121] Alitalia-Linee Aeree Italiane S.P.A. v. Casinoalitalia.com, 128 F. Supp. 2d 340 (E.D. Va. 2001) (citing 4 Charles A. Wright and Arthur R. Miller, Federal Practice and Procedure § 1070 (2d ed. 1987)) ("Jurisdiction based on property most typically is invoked when one or more defendants or persons with potential claims to the property are nonresidents or jurisdiction over the person cannot be secured. In this sense the *in rem* or *quasi-in*-rem jurisdiction represents an alternative to *in personam* jurisdiction.").

[122] 15 U.S.C. § 1125(6)(2)(D) (2000).

[123] *Id.*

[124] 112 F. Supp. 2d 505 (E.D. Va. 2000).

[125] The court cited Shaffer v. Heitner, 433 U.S. 186 (1977), which held that *in rem* jurisdiction is constitutional providing that the *res* or property in dispute has minimum contacts with the forum state. In the online world, minimum contacts are satisfied when a domain name is registered in the forum state.

[126] Harrods Limited v. Sixty Internet Domain Names, 110 F. Supp. 2d 420 (E.D. Va. 2000); *see also* Porsche Cars N. Am. v. Allporsche.com, 55 U.S.P.Q.3d (BNA) 1158 (4th Cir. 2000) (reinstating trademark dilution claim because of the possible applicability of the *in rem* remedy of the ACPA); Lucent Techs., Inc. v. Lucentsucks.com, 95 F. Supp. 2d 528 (E.D. Va. 2000) (dismissing *in rem* action against defendant domain name because the identity of the registrants was possible).

[127] Internet Domain Name—In Rem Action, Massachusetts Lawyers Weekly (Apr. 16, 2001) at 17.

Absent a specific statutory remedy, such as the ACPA, it is likely that a court will not permit service of process on a *res* without a showing of minimum contacts.

[E] Long-Arm Statutes

A long-arm statute is a means of effecting service of process on a nonresident defendant. Every state has enacted long-arm statutes as the tool for exercising jurisdiction over a defendant located outside of the forum. One of the difficulties of extending the long-arm of state law to the Internet, however, is that every state then becomes the regulator of the Internet.[128] Additionally, state regulation of the Internet may also violate the Commerce Clause of the U.S. Constitution and invade the sovereignty of hundreds of other countries.[129]

There are due process limits to the exercise of personal jurisdiction under the U.S. Constitution. Hundreds of decided U.S. cases exist covering Internet jurisdiction, but few international ones exist. To establish personal jurisdiction, the plaintiffs must satisfy a two-step test. First, the plaintiff must establish personal jurisdiction pursuant to the long-arm statute. Second, they must establish that jurisdiction comports with due process.[130] A federal court sitting in diversity must first determine whether the relevant state long-arm statute permits the exercise of personal jurisdiction. Every state has enacted a long-arm statute permitting constructive service of process on a nonresident. The issue of personal jurisdiction comes before a court on a "Defendants' Motion to Dismiss for Lack of Personal Jurisdiction. States' long arm statutes are construed as extending jurisdiction to the limit of federal due process."[131]

The long arm of the law permits state courts, for example, to acquire jurisdiction over a nonresident motorist who flees the jurisdiction before any action may be commenced against him. Physical presence within the forum is not required to obtain personal jurisdiction over a nonresident defendant. Long-arm statutes are divided into two broad types: (1) statutes that assert jurisdiction over the person to the limits allowed by the Fourteenth Amendment to the U.S. Constitution and (2) statutes that limit the assertion of jurisdiction. A federal court sitting in diversity undertakes a two-step test: "First the court applies the relevant state long-arm statute to see if it permits the exercise of personal jurisdiction, then the court must apply the precepts of the Due Process Clause of the Constitution."[132] Long-arm statutes vary in what activities may trigger the exercise of jurisdiction. In a recent Pennsylvania case, a plaintiff sued Canadian and Barbados defendants for cybersquatting on the domain name "sweetsuccess.com." The court held that

---

[128] This point was made by Thomas P. Vartanian, Whose Internet Is it Anyway? George Mason University, 2000 Global Internet Summit, Vienna, Virginia (Mar. 13-14, 2000).

[129] *Id.*

[130] Noonan v. Winston Co., 135 F.3d 85, 89 (1st Cir. 1998).

[131] Digital Control Inc. v. Boretronics, 161 F. Supp. 2d 1183, 1185 (E.D. Wash. 2001) (quoting Shute v. Carnival Cruise Lines, 783 P.2d 78 (Wash. 1989)).

[132] IMO Indus., Inc. v. Kiekert AG, 155 F.3d 254 (3d Cir. 1998).

defendant's actions of e-mails and telephone calls directed to plaintiff in Pennsylvania to offer to sell the "sweetsuccess.com" domain name were sufficient to confer specific jurisdiction because the sweetsuccess.com site was not merely passive.[133] In a similar Mississippi case, the defendant cybersquatter's alleged use of trademarks to extort money from resident was sufficient contact with the state to satisfy both the Mississippi long-arm statute and federal due process.[134] A Mississippi federal court ruled that it had specific personal jurisdiction over a nonresident sender of e-mail advertising pornographic web sites that had been made to appear as if it had been sent from one of a local ISP's accounts.[135]

Pennsylvania's long-arm statute, for example, extends jurisdiction to the "fullest extent allowed under the Constitution of the United States and may be based on the most minimum contacts with this Commonwealth allowed under the Constitution of the United States."[136] Similarly, New Jersey's long-arm statute provides for personal jurisdiction as far as it is permitted by the Due Process Clause.[137]

Massachusetts is another example of a jurisdiction with an expansive long-arm statute.[138] A Massachusetts court may employ the long-arm statute to obtain jurisdiction on any defendant who commits a tort in the Commonwealth, provided the defendant does business in the state or derives substantial revenues from goods or services. These statutory grounds are spelled out in the long-arm statute. For example, a firm entering into a license agreement with a Massachusetts corporation to offer web site services would be transacting business and thus would be subject to jurisdiction.

A California court held that California courts have jurisdiction over an out-of-state computer programmer who posted technology for decrypting copyrighted digital video disc (DVD) movies on the Internet in a lawsuit alleging he misappropriated trade secrets. California's long-arm statute reaches owners, operators, and publishers of web sites that violate California law by making available for copying or distribution trade secrets or copyrighted material of California companies. By posting a program for decrypting copyrighted DVDs on the Internet, petitioner, a Texas resident, knew or should have known that his conduct was injuring the motion picture and computer industries in California.[139]

A tort such as misrepresentation or fraud communicated on a web site may also be a basis for jurisdiction. Delaware's long-arm statute was not broad enough to encompass the activities of a defendant who posted allegedly defamatory statements on his Internet site.[140] The Delaware long-arm statute provided coverage

---

[133] Lofton v. Turbine Design, Inc., 100 F. Supp. 2d 404 (N.D. Miss. 2000).

[134] McRae's, Inc. v. Hussain, 105 F. Supp. 2d 594 (S.D. Miss. 2000).

[135] Internet Doorway, Inc v. Parks, 138 F. Supp. 2d 773 (S.D. Miss. 2001).

[136] GTE New Media Servs., Inc. v. BellSouth Corp., 199 F.3d 1343 (D.C. 2000) (citing D.C. Code Ann. § 13-423(a) (1981)).

[137] *See* N.J. Ct. R. 4:4-4 (1999).

[138] Mass. Gen. Law Ann. ch. 223A, § 3 (1999).

[139] Pavlovich v. Superior Court, 109 Cal. Rptr. 2d 909 (Cal. App. 6 Dist., 2001).

[140] Clayton v. Farb, 1998 Del. Super. LEXIS 175 (Del., April 23, 1998), reported in Perkins Coie Internet Law Digest (visited Aug. 25, 1999), http://www.perkinscoie.com/resource/ecomm/netcase/Cases-15.htm.

only if the defendant committed a tort and was regularly conducting business in the state. A state's long-arm statute may limit jurisdiction where there is only a passive web site. The District of Columbia's long-arm statute provides:

> A District of Columbia court may exercise personal jurisdiction over a person, who acts directly or by an agent, as to a claim for relief arising from the person's—
> (1) transacting any business in the District of Columbia;
> . . . (4) causing tortious injury in the District of Columbia by an act or omission outside the District of Columbia if he [i] regularly does or solicits business, [ii] engages in any other persistent course of conduct, or [iii] derives substantial revenue from goods used or consumed, or services rendered, in the District of Columbia.[141]

Courts addressing the issue of personal jurisdiction focus on "the nature and quality of commercial activity that an entity conducts over the Internet."[142] The courts have identified three types of commercial activity to help determine the existence of personal jurisdiction: (1) the web site is clearly doing business over the Internet and personal jurisdiction is proper,[143] (2) visitors to a web site can interact with the host computer and exchange information,[144] and (3) the web site is a passive repository of information or advertisements.[145] In a Fifth Circuit case, the jurisdictional contacts were found to be in the "middle ground" of the *Zippo* contacts spectrum. Although the defendant had the potential to interact with, sell products to, and contract with Texas residents on its web site, the evidence presented at trial did not support a finding that this level of activity took place. The court dismissed the case because of lack of personal jurisdiction over the defendant.[146] To establish personal jurisdiction over a nonresident, a court must engage in a two-part inquiry: a court must first examine whether jurisdiction is applicable under the state's long-arm statute and then determine whether a finding of jurisdiction satisfies the constitutional requirements of due process.[147] The greater the interactivity and commercial activity, the more likely it is that a state can use its long arm to exercise personal jurisdiction. Web sites that are passive and noninteractive are not likely to have the continuous and substantial contacts that satisfy the due process requirements for personal jurisdiction.

---

[141] GTE New Media Servs. v. BellSouth Corp., 199 F.3d 1343 (D.C. Cir. 2000).

[142] Zippo Mfg. Co. v. Zippo Dot Com, Inc., 952 F. Supp. 1119, 1124 (W.D. Pa. 1997).

[143] *Id.* at 1124.

[144] Maritz, Inc. v. Cybergold, Inc., 947 F. Supp. 1328 (E.D. Mo. 1996).

[145] An example is Bensuasan Restaurant Corp. v. King, 937 F. Supp. 295 (S.D.N.Y. 1996) (finding no jurisdiction over Columbia, Missouri's Blue Note Cafe jazz club allegedly violating the trademark of the famous New York Blue Note Cafe).

[146] People Solutions, Inc. v. People Solutions, Inc, No. 3:99-CV-2339-L, 2000 U.S. Dist. LEXIS 10444 (N.D. Tex., July 26, 2000).

[147] *See* United States v. Ferrara, 54 F.3d 825, 828 (D.C. Cir. 1995).

§ 7.03   CYBER-JURISDICTION CASES

At least 218 cases have applied purposeful availment analysis to issues of personal jurisdiction in cyberspace.[148] The purposeful availment prong of the personal jurisdiction analysis is met if a defendant's intentional conduct in a foreign state is calculated to cause injury to the plaintiff in the forum state.[149] One of the difficult issues in Internet jurisdictional disputes arises when the only evidence is pleadings and accompanying affidavits.[150] It may be difficult to know whether a defendant targeted a forum state from such scant evidence. Personal jurisdiction may not be based upon the mere fact that a web site is accessible in the forum. As the D.C. Circuit stated: "[t]his theory simply cannot hold water. Indeed, under this view, personal jurisdiction in Internet-related cases would almost always be found in any forum in the country."[151] Since *Hanson v. Denckla*,[152] the concept of purposeful availment means that a defendant has done some act with the forum by which he purposefully avails himself of the privilege of doing business in the forum. "Personal jurisdiction surely cannot be based solely on the ability . . . to access web sites" in the forum.[153]

A number of United States courts have predicated personal jurisdiction upon minimum contacts in cyberspace.[154] In August 2000, there were 228 state and federal cases that dealt with the question of personal jurisdiction in cyberspace. By July 21, 2002, there were 713 cases.[155] The D.C. Circuit observed that the "Internet should [not] vitiate long-held and inviolate principles of federal court jurisdiction."[156] Courts agree that a web site presence alone is not an adequate basis for

---

[148] A July 20, 2002, LEXIS search of the Combined State and Federal Caselaw Database uncovered 218 cases in which courts discussed the term "purposeful availment and Internet." *See generally* Michael S. Rothman, It's a Small World After All: Personal Jurisdiction, The Internet, and the Global Marketplace, 23 Md. J. Int'l L. & Trade 127 (1999).

[149] Sierra Pac. Airlines v. Dallas Aerospace, 2001 U.S. App. LEXIS 4335 (9th Cir., Mar. 12, 2001) (holding that the record did not demonstrate a compelling case that the exercise of specific personal jurisdiction in the forum state would have been unreasonable in cases involving fraud, negligence, and breach of implied warranties).

[150] Meyers v. Bennett Law Offices, 238 F.3d 1068, 1071 (9th Cir. 2001) (holding that plaintiff need only make a *prima facie* showing of jurisdictional facts under purposeful availment prong).

[151] GTE New Media Servs. v. BellSouth Corp., 199 F.3d 1343, 1350 (D.C. Cir. 2000) (holding that personal jurisdiction over defendants was not proper where sole contact was the operation of an Internet web site accessible to persons in the district).

[152] 357 U.S. 235, 253 (1958).

[153] GTE New Media Servs. v. BellSouth Corp., 199 F.3d 1343, 1349 (D.C. Cir. 2000).

[154] *See, e.g.,* Digital Equip. Corp. v. AltaVista Tech., Inc., 960 F. Supp. 456 (D. Mass 1997) (upheld jurisdiction on theory that trademark infringed purposefully availed itself of the forum state by soliciting Massachusetts residents to visit the AltaVista web site); Zippo Mfg. Co. v. Zippo Dot Com, Inc., 952 F. Supp. 1119 (W.D. Pa. 1997) (dividing Internet jurisdiction cases into interactive web sites doing substantial business versus being passive web sites).

[155] LEXIS searches were conducted July 21, 2002, December 21, 2001, June 1, 2001, and August 8, 2000; Combined Federal and State Caselaw, LexisNexis™.

[156] GTE New Media Servs. v. BellSouth Corp., 199 F.3d 1343 (D.C. Cir. 2000) (reversing district court and finding insufficient evidence for personal jurisdiction though permitting additional discovery on the issue).

specific jurisdiction. For there to be personal jurisdiction, SPC's e-business activity must be pervasive, interactive, and permit online sales and service. Plaintiffs will typically use several tests to argue that Internet contacts satisfy due process. Modern courts update the "minimum contacts" test with the purposeful availment test. Purposeful availment correlates positively with the nature and quality of commercial activity on a site. The "purposeful availment" test focuses on whether the Internet or dot-com company sought out business from web site visitors.

[A] Purposeful Availment

The United States Supreme Court first articulated the purposeful availment test in *Burger King Corp. v. Rudzewicz*.[157] The test focuses on whether the defendant sought contacts in or should have reasonably anticipated "being haled into court" in the forum state.[158] The reasonableness test of Burger King requires the consideration of several specific factors: "(1) the extent of the defendants' purposeful interjection into the forum state, (2) the burden on the defendant in defending the forum, (3) the extent of the conflict with the sovereignty of the defendant's state, (4) the forum state's interest in adjudicating the dispute, (5) the most efficient judicial resolution of the controversy, (6) the importance of the forum to the plaintiff's interest in convenient and effective relief, and (7) the existence of an alternative forum."[159] Courts have updated the purposeful availment test in torts and contracts arising out of cyberspace activities. Courts focus on whether Internet advertisements are directed to residents. For example, a court found that a web site that permitted Arizona residents to make hotel reservations at the web site did provide a sufficient basis for personal jurisdiction.[160] Further, a California court held that solicitation of advertisements from California businesses directed toward California consumers and the negotiation for their placement on the Celebrity 1000 web site did not amount to purposeful availment where the ads ran for a few days each during a limited period of time.[161] In contrast, another California court found that Internet advertising, like print advertising in a national magazine, did not constitute purposeful availment of a forum.[162] In another online contract case, a Massachusetts federal district court dismissed the complaint for lack of personal jurisdiction in a breach of contract case involving an Illinois company. The court found that the Illinois company had (1) three web pages accessible from Massachusetts; (2) a contract with a Massachusetts company for the sale of a domain name, governed by Massachusetts law but not containing a forum-selection clause; and (3) a one-time, unsuccessful solicitation of a Massachusetts company

---

[157] 471 U.S. 462 (1985).

[158] World-Wide Volkswagen Corp. v. Woodson, 444 U.S. 286 (1980).

[159] Sierra Pac. Airlines v. Dallas Aerospace, 2001 U.S. App. LEXIS 4335 (9th Cir., Mar. 12, 2001).

[160] Park Inns Int'l, Inc. v. Pacific Plaza Hotels, Inc., 5 F. Supp. 2d 762 (D. Ariz. 1998).

[161] Northern Light Tech., Inc. v. Northern Lights Club, 236 F.3d 57 (1st Cir. 2000).

[162] Osteotech, Inc. v. GenSci Regeneration Sciences, Inc., 6 F. Supp. 2d 349 (D.N.J. 1998).

for an Internet advertisement. The court found no evidence that the Illinois company had Massachusetts customers or even solicited business in that state. The Illinois company was confined to offering Internet service to customers in an Illinois area code. While Massachusetts residents could theoretically purchase the Illinois company's services from a web site or utilize free services, the existence of the pages alone, without any evidence of actual purchases by Massachusetts customers or direct solicitation of Massachusetts customers, did not constitute sufficient minimum contacts for personal jurisdiction.[163] State courts do not agree on the question of whether Internet advertisements confer jurisdiction.

In *State of Minnesota v. Granite Gate Resorts, Inc.,*[164] the court found sufficient contacts to constitute jurisdiction over a nonresident defendant who operated a gambling site on the Internet through a server located in Belize. The court found that the web site actively solicited Minnesota subscribers and violated state advertising and gambling laws. In *Thompson v. Handa-Lopez, Inc.,*[165] jurisdiction was predicated upon the defendant's operation of a casino-type arcade game through its web site in which players entered into contracts to play a game of chance.[166] The application of the purposeful availment test differs depending on whether the underlying claim is a tort or contract claim.

The test of purposeful availment varies depending upon whether the gravamen of the plaintiff's lawsuit is in contract or torts. In contract, purposeful availment focuses on whether a defendant has created a contractual connection to the forum or chose to do business in the forum. Courts frequently focus on the interactivity of the web site in making a determination of contractually based purposeful availment.[167] In a torts case, purposeful availment is satisfied by the effects test. The test focuses on whether the defendant injected a product into the stream of commerce or committed a tort that was likely to have effects in the forum state.[168]

[B] Contracts and Purposeful Availment

Purposeful availment for Internet contracts is based on the level of web site activity in the forum state. Companies that sell goods or render services over the

---

[163] Wildfire Comm., Inc. v. Grapevine, Inc., 2001 U.S. Dist. LEXIS 18238 (D. Mass. Sept. 28, 2001).

[164] 568 N.W.2d 715 (Minn. App. 1997).

[165] 998 F. Supp. 738 (W.D. Tex. 1998).

[166] *Id.*

[167] The leading case is Zippo Mfg. Co. v. Zippo Dot Com, Inc., 952 F. Supp. 1119, 1124 (W.D. Pa. 1997) (articulating a sliding scale of interactivity to identify Internet activity that constitutes purposeful availment); *see also* Neogen Corp. v. Neo Gen Screening, Inc., 2002 U.S. App. LEXIS 3478 (6th Cir. Mar. 6, 2002); Rainy Day Books, Inc. v. Rainy Day Books & Café, L.L.C. 2002 U.S. Dist. LEXIS 2043 (D. Kan. Feb. 5, 2002) (stating that it is the quality rather than merely the quantity of contracts that is critical to a finding of purposeful availment in cyberspace service mark litigation).

[168] *See, e.g.,* Assad v. Pioneer Balloons, Inc., 2001 U.S. App. LEXIS 11944 (9th Cir. June 5, 2001) (finding that cyberspace defamation defendant purposefully availed itself of the forum state's courts by deliberately spreading false information on the Internet). *See generally* Nam Tai Elec., Inc. v. Titzer, 93 Cal. App. 4th 1301 (Cal. Ct. App. 2001) (arguing that purposeful availment in a tort test is satisfied by the effects test).

Internet will likely be considered to have purposefully availed themselves of the forum by ongoing business transactions and online contracts with the plaintiff.[169]

The purposeful availment test in an online contract case focuses on whether the defendant performed some affirmative conduct that allowed or promoted the transaction of business within the forum state.[170] For example, if SPC solicits business in the forum, it is likely that purposeful availment would be found. In contrast, the mere existence of a contract with a forum resident is not enough to pass the purposeful availment hurdle. In a New Jersey case, the plaintiff copyright owner sued an Internet domain name owner for infringement of the use of "west-sidestory.com." The court dismissed the case, holding lack of personal jurisdiction because the defendants' only tie to New Jersey under the traditional personal jurisdiction analysis was a contract, which was not substantial enough to constitute minimum contacts. The court found the web site was passive advertising because it did not sell or offer for sale any of defendants' products.[171] In *JB Oxford Holdings v. Net Trade, Inc.*[172] the federal court granted a defendant web site's motion to dismiss for lack of personal jurisdiction, holding that the defendant had not purposefully availed itself of the privilege of doing business in Florida. The court stated that it found the *Zippo Mfg. Co. v. Zippo Dot Com, Inc.*[173] line of cases persuasive.[174] The court stated that "these cases require more than mere maintenance of a web site accessible in the forum state; they require contacts that illustrate purposeful availment of the privilege of conducting commercial activity in the forum—contacts that tie the defendant to a particular state, not those that merely link with equal strength the defendant to all states."[175] In that case, the defendant used the infringing mark "Net Trade" on web sites that could be used in Florida.[176]

Net Trade's web sites were quite "interactive," permitting viewers to e-mail questions and receive free information about day trading.[177] The court acknowledged the interactivity of the site, but noted that the quality of the contact between the hypothetical viewer in Florida and Net Trade's interactive sites was quite low.[178] The court found that Net Trade's contacts with Florida were insubstantial and were "substantially noncommercial" with "no offices, employees, property or customers in Florida . . . at least to date."[179] Another factor driving the court's decision was the plaintiff's alternative of filing the action in other forums where Net Trade has a commercial presence.[180]

---

[169] *See, e.g.,* CompuServe v. Patterson, 89 F.3d 1257 (6th Cir. 1996).

[170] Assad v. Pioneer Balloon, 2001 U.S. App. LEXIS 11944 (9th Cir. June 5, 2001).

[171] Amberson Holdings LLC v. Westside Story Newspaper, 110 F. Supp. 2d 332 (D.N.J. 2000).

[172] 76 F. Supp. 2d 1363 (S.D. Fla. 1999).

[173] 925 F. Supp. 1119 (W.D. Pa. 1997).

[174] *Id.* at 1367.

[175] *Id.*

[176] *Id.*

[177] *Id.*

[178] *Id.* at 1368.

[179] *Id.*

[180] *Id.*

In the trademark infringement case *American Information Corporation v. American Informetrics, Inc.,*[181] the plaintiff was based in Maryland. The defendant was headquartered in Modesto, California, and sold Internet access and services to individuals and corporations and maintained a web site identified as *ainet.com,* that could be viewed by anyone with access to the World Wide Web, whether the viewer is located in Maryland or elsewhere. American Information Corporation argued for specific personal jurisdiction based on both the "sliding scale" of Internet-based jurisdiction and the effects test. The court ruled that an entirely passive web site cannot create jurisdiction in Maryland simply because it is theoretically available to web users in Maryland and everywhere else. The court reasoned that even a passive web site that uses someone else's trademark as an address does not necessarily generate jurisdiction.

Even though the web site allowed some user interaction, a visitor could not enter into a contract, purchase goods or services, or transact business on the site. The defendant's president affirmed among other things that the company never had a place of business, customers, licenses, or certification in Maryland.

The court held that although not completely passive, the defendant's site, without more, did not subject a company to jurisdiction: "American Information Corporation has made no showing that American Infometrics deliberately targeted its mark, business, or customers."[182] The court reasoned that cases finding personal jurisdiction based on harm involve some form of deliberate targeting of the plaintiff by the defendant, for instance, through defamation.[18.3] The court stated that a California company cannot be haled into court "simply because it established a Web site that uses a protected mark and that accepts inquiries from would-be customers."[184]

Personal jurisdiction was properly exercised in the Internet-based case of *CompuServe, Inc. v. Patterson.*[185] In *Patterson,* a Texas resident advertised his product on an Internet computer system maintained by CompuServe, which was based in Ohio. The Sixth Circuit found that Patterson took direct actions that created a connection with Ohio.[186] Personal jurisdiction was based on the defendant's license agreement with CompuServe and his loading software onto the CompuServe system for others to use, as well as on his web site advertisements.[187]

An Oregon federal court dismissed a trademark infringement and unfair competition action against a retail music seller in *Millennium Enterprises, Inc. v. Millennium Music, LP.*[188] In *Millennium Music,* a retail music seller located in Oregon brought an action against a retail music seller located in South Carolina for trademark infringement and unfair competition. The defendant operated a retail

---

[181] American Infor. Corp. v. American Infometrics, Inc., 139 F. Supp. 2d 696 (D. Md., 2001).

[182] *Id.* at 702.

[183] *Id.*

[184] *Id.* at 703.

[185] *CompuServe,* 89 F.3d at 1368.

[186] *Id.* at 1264.

[187] *Id.*

[188] 33 F. Supp. 2d 907 (D. Or. 1999).

music store in South Carolina under the name "Millennium Music." The defendants sold products through the Internet site as well as in retail outlets. Internet sales totaled only $225 as compared to over $2,000,000 in retail sales from their music stores.

The plaintiff was an Oregon resident who had operated a retail outlet under "Music Millennium" since 1969. The plaintiff purchased a compact disc (CD) from Millennium Music through its web site. The plaintiff objected to the defendants' use of the name, "Millennium Music," arguing that consumers would be confused as to the source or origin of the defendants' CDs. The plaintiff sought damages and injunctive relief under the Lanham Act and common law claims for unlawful trade practices. The defendant moved to dismiss for lack of personal jurisdiction. The court found that the sale of a single CD and sporadic purchases lacked the "continuous and systematic" contacts to satisfy general jurisdiction.

The *Millennium* court also found that a single sale did not constitute purposeful availment.[189] Likewise, the defendants' occasional purchases from an Oregon firm did not satisfy the minimum contacts test.[190] The court also found that the effects of the defendant's infringing activities were not sufficient to satisfy the "effects test."[191] Finally, the court found that the defendants' Internet web site did not constitute a sufficient fair warning so that they would reasonably anticipate being "haled" into court in Oregon.[192] The court held that (1) defendant was not subject to general or personal jurisdiction based on sales of one compact disc to an Oregon resident and purchases from a supplier in Oregon and (2) maintenance of an Internet web site did not subject the defendant to personal jurisdiction in Oregon.[193]

[C]   Tortious Activities and Purposeful Availment

A purposeful availment analysis requires first a preliminary determination as to whether the plaintiff's claim is related to the defendant's contacts with the forum state. Assuming that the claim is related to the contracts, the court next considers whether the defendant purposefully availed itself of the privilege of doing business in the forum. The test asks whether a defendant could have foreseen being haled into a court in the forum. The purposeful availment inquiry "ensures that a defendant will not be haled into a jurisdiction solely as the result of random, fortuitous, or attenuated contacts."[194]

Courts are predisposed to finding that due process is satisfied by Internet-related activities. The New Jersey Superior Court, however, uncovered "only two

---

[189] *Id.* at 910.

[190] *Id.* at 911.

[191] *Id.*

[192] *Id.* at 920.

[193] *Id.*

[194] Mario Valente Collezioni, Ltd. v. Confezioni Semeraro Paol., 174 F. Supp. 2d 170 (S.D.N.Y 2001).

cases in which a court has declined jurisdiction of a non-resident individual or corporate defendant who has used the Internet, e-mail, and computer bulletin boards or forums to make defamatory statements."[195]

It is reasonable to presume that our common law will adapt to the challenges posed by the Internet. With a click of the mouse, reputations may be ruined. "The commission of crimes or civil wrongs via the Internet can be subtler and more damaging than the same acts committed in traditional fashion."[196] Courts have found purposeful availment when the claim involves an intentional tort allegedly committed over the Internet along with evidence that the defendant intentionally directed its tortious activities at the forum state.

In *Jewish Defense Organization v. Superior Court*,[197] a plaintiff filed a defamation action against the Jewish Defense Organization and its leader Mordechai Levi based upon allegedly defamatory statements posted on a World Wide Web page. The allegedly defamatory statement characterized the plaintiff as a "snitch, a dangerous psychopath, anti-Semite and other derogatory statements."[198] The defendants filed motions to quash service of summons. The plaintiff argued that the defendants had continuous and systematic contacts with California through the Jewish Defense Organization web site.

The *Jewish Defense* court, reversing the lower court, found no general jurisdiction as a matter of law.[199] The court also found insufficient evidence to support specific jurisdiction.[200] The court found that the fact that although the defendants "may have foreseen the allegedly defamatory statements might be published in California, that alone is not enough to subject them to personal jurisdiction in this state."[201] The court concluded that there was insufficient evidence "to establish that it was foreseeable that a risk of injury by defamation would arise in California."[202] The court compared the defendant's activities to that of the defendant in *Panavision v. Toeppen*.[203]

In *Toeppen*, the court found the tort-like activity of cyberpirating domain names to be a sufficient basis for jurisdiction because the defendant knew his actions would cause plaintiff harm in the forum state. Unlike Dennis Toeppen, the individual defendant in *Jewish Defense Organization* was not a full-time resident of California, nor did he have clients in California. The defendant had no knowledge that the defamatory statements posted on its web site would "impact a busi-

---

[195] *Id.*

[196] James Garrity and Eoghan Casey, Internet Misuse in the Workplace: A Lawyer's Primer, 72 Fla. Bar J. 22 (Nov. 1998).

[197] 85 Cal. Rptr. 2d 611 (Cal. Ct. of App. 1999).

[198] *Id.* at 614.

[199] *Id.* at 617.

[200] *Id.* at 619.

[201] *Id.* (citation omitted).

[202] *Id.* at 619.

[203] 141 F.3d 1316 (9th Cir. 1998).

ness interest or reputation in California."[204] The court also found the defendant's web site to be passive and not purposefully directed toward the forum state.[205]

In *Drudge v. Blumenthal*,[206] White House employee Sidney Blumenthal and his spouse filed a defamation action against the electronically published gossip columnist Matt Drudge for reporting that Mr. Blumenthal was a spouse abuser. The plaintiffs also sued America Online, an interactive computer service provider that published an electronic version of the Drudge Report. AOL moved for summary judgment, and the columnist moved to dismiss or transfer for lack of personal jurisdiction.

The *Blumenthal* court held that AOL was not liable, as an ISP, for making the gossip column available to its subscribers, but that Drudge had engaged in a persistent course of conduct in the District of Columbia (D.C.), which warranted the exercise of personal jurisdiction. The court found that the columnist's interactive web site specifically focused on D.C. political gossip and that the columnist regularly distributed his electronic column to D.C. residents, solicited and received contributions from D.C. residents, and contacted D.C. residents to gather information for the column. Jurisdiction may be based on tortious activity even if made on a passive web site.[207]

A New Jersey court summarized the case law and found no prior decision where a court had found "personal jurisdiction over a non-resident defendant for allegedly defamatory remarks communicated electronically when the plaintiff did not reside in the forum state, the plaintiff's employment was not based in the forum state, and the defendant's electronically transmitted remarks were not specifically targeted at the forum state."[208]

[1] Relatedness Test

The relatedness test for specific jurisdiction examines the causal connection between the defendant's contacts and the plaintiff's cause of action;[209] it examines the relationship between forum-state activities and the underlying litigation. In an Internet case, the question posed is whether the litigation arose directly from a defendant's online activities or web site. In *Panavision v. Toeppen*,[210] a California-based corporation that specialized in providing film equipment to the movie industry filed suit against Dennis Toeppen, an Illinois resident. The lawsuit grew out of Toeppen's hoarding of Internet domain names identical to Panavision's trademarked names and his attempt to extract a princely sum to pay him to release those names. Toeppen expended $10,000 in his domain name business.

---

[204] *Jewish Defense Organization, id.* at 620.

[205] *Id.* at 620 (citations omitted).

[206] 992 F. Supp. 44 (D.D.C. 1998).

[207] Telco Communications v. An Apple A Day, 977 F. Supp. 404 (E.D. Va. 1997) (basing jurisdiction upon defamatory press releases made on a passive web site).

[208] Blakey v. Continental Airlines, Inc., 1999 WL 402897 *8 (N.J. Super. A.D., June 9, 1999).

[209] Ticketmaster-New York, Inc. v. Alioto, 26 F.3d 201, 206 (1st Cir. 1994).

[210] 141 F.3d 1316 (9th Cir. 1997).

Toeppen's domain name business activities are alternatively described as "domain name hijacking" or cyberpiracy.[211] The *Panavision* court found domain name hijacking to constitute "something more" and sufficiently related to Toeppen's web site to warrant the exercise of jurisdiction. The Ninth Circuit held that (1) Toeppen was subject to specific jurisdiction in California, (2) his registration of plaintiff's marks in his Internet domain names was a "commercial use" under dilution statutes, and (3) his registration of Panavision's mark diluted it. A New York federal district court, however, recently declined to follow *Panavision*'s expansive view of personal jurisdiction on web sites.[212] The *Panavision* court is the high-water mark for the kind of minimum contacts that satisfies due process.[213]

[D]   Effects Test

The "effects tests" for determining personal jurisdiction was first articulated by the U.S. Supreme Court in *Calder v. Jones*.[214] In that case, actress Shirley Jones sued the *National Enquirer* over an article written and edited in Florida and published nationwide.[215] The court found jurisdiction in California, finding that Jones was a California resident and that the story would have its greatest impact in California. The Court held that California had personal jurisdiction over the author and editor because the "effects" of their Florida conduct were chiefly felt in California, the state in which plaintiff lived and worked. The Court emphasized that the alleged tort was not "mere untargeted negligence" but rather "intentional, and allegedly tortious, actions . . . expressly aimed at [the forum state]."[216]

A plaintiff must prove three elements to prove that it is not unfair to find personal jurisdiction against a defendant: "(1) The defendant committed an intentional tort, (2) The plaintiff felt the brunt of the harm in the forum such that the forum can be said to be the focal point of the harm suffered by the plaintiff as a result of that tort; and (3) the defendant expressly aimed his tortious conduct at the forum."[217] In *Remick v. Manfredy*, an attorney specializing in sports and entertainment law licensed to practice in the Commonwealth of Pennsylvania filed suit in a Pennsylvania state court against Manfredy and associates alleging breach of contract, tortious interference with contract, misappropriation of image and likeness, civil conspiracy, and defamation. The case was removed to federal court, where

---

[211] Domain hijacking or cyberpiracy occurs when an individual registers the domain names of famous trademarks and then demands those corporations pay a ransom to release the registered domain names.

[212] K.C.P.L., Inc. v. Nash, 1998 WL 823657 (S.D.N.Y., Nov. 23, 1998).

[213] *See also* Indianapolis Colts, Inc. v. Metropolitan Baltimore Football Club, 34 F.3d 410 (7th Cir. 1994) (holding that the Baltimore Colts team was subject to personal jurisdiction in Indiana even though its only activity was broadcasts of its games on nationwide cable television).

[214] 465 U.S. 783 (1984).

[215] *Id.* at 789.

[216] *Id.*

[217] Remick v. Manfredy, 238 F.3d 248 (3d Cir. 2001) (reversing trial court decision dismissing actions against individuals for lack of personal jurisdiction).

the trial court dismissed because it ruled that it did not have specific personal jurisdiction over the individual defendants. The Third Circuit reversed, finding that the district court did not conduct a claim-specific analysis except as to the breach of contract claim.[218] The Third Circuit based jurisdiction on the contract claim on repeated "informational communications" during the course of the contractual relationship between the parties.[219]

The effects test focuses on the nonresident's committing a tort knowing it will cause harm to the plaintiff in the forum state. The Indiana Court of Appeals held that the use of a company's trademark on a web site, without more, was an insufficient basis for personal jurisdiction.[220] The court rejected the "effects test" of *Calder v. Jones*[221] as inapplicable to a commercial web site. The court found the "effects test" to be inappropriate for cyberspace because the web site activities of corporations were not typically localized in the forum state. The effects test says that a defendant purposely avails itself of the jurisdiction of the forum when its intentional conduct causes harm and the defendant knows that harm will occur in the forum or targeted state. Courts will frequently apply an "effects" test in intentional tort cases to determine whether the defendant's conduct was aimed at the forum state.[222]

Personal jurisdiction can be based upon "(1) intentional actions (2) expressly aimed at the forum state (3) causing harm, the brunt of which is suffered and which the defendant knows is likely to be suffered in the forum state."[223] A Massachusetts federal district found that a California defendant's marketing of cigar humidors on its web site was one of the key factors in establishing jurisdiction over the defendant.[224] The court noted that jurisdiction was proper because the defendant actively chose to market his goods in Massachusetts, and the claim arose out of sales in the forum state. The minimum contacts analysis "has no place in determining whether a state may assert criminal personal jurisdiction over a foreign defendant."[225]

Courts frequently apply the "sliding-scale" analysis articulated by the United States District Court for the Eastern District of Pennsylvania in *Zippo Manufacturing Co. v. Zippo Dot Com, Inc.*[226] in determining whether minimum contacts are

---

[218] *Id.* at 256.

[219] *Id.* at 257.

[220] Conseco, Inc. v. Hickerson, 698 N.E.2d 816 (Ind. Ct. App. 1998); Panavision Int'l v. Toeppen, 141 F.3d 1316 at 1321 (9th Cir 1998) (applying effects test to trademark infringement case: "Jurisdiction may attach if the defendant's conduct is aimed at or has an effect in the forum state."); *see also* Meyers v. Bennett Law Offices, 238 F.3d 1068, 1071 (9th Cir. 2001) (discussing burden necessary for purposeful availment).

[221] 465 U.S. 783 (1984).

[222] Ziegler v. Indian River Cty., 64 F.3d 470, 473 (9th Cir.1995) (applying effects test).

[223] Core-Vent Corp. v. Nobel Indus. AB, 11 F.3d 1482, 1486 (9th Cir. 1993).

[224] Gary Scott Int'l v. Baroudi, 981 F. Supp. 714 (D. Mass. 1997).

[225] State v. Amorosa, 975 F.2d 505, 508 (Ct. App. Utah 1999).

[226] 952 F. Supp. 1119 (W.D. Pa. 1997).

satisfied in Internet-related cases. The *Zippo* "sliding scale" analysis is followed by a number of federal courts of appeal.[227] In *On-Line Techs. v. Perkin Elmer Corp.*,[228] the plaintiff filed suit against the defendants over a dispute over ownership of trade secrets in gas analysis technology. The court granted a motion to dismiss in part because there was no long-arm jurisdiction over a German defendant that had a passive Internet site that did not permit contracts or purchases.

The *Zippo* continuum classifies all Internet-related jurisdiction cases into three types: "At one end of the continuum lies businesses or persons who clearly conduct business over the Internet and have repeated contacts with the forum state such that the exercise of *in personam* jurisdiction is proper."[229] "At the other end of the continuum are defendants who have done nothing more than post information or advertising on a web site that is accessible to users in the forum jurisdiction."[230] The middle ground is the borderline between passive and active sites.[231] "The middle ground is occupied by interactive Web sites where a user can exchange information with the host computer."[232] The Internet has now evolved so that few commercial web sites are purely passive sites. Few cases may now be resolved on the mere interactivity of the site. Recently, courts are looking at the other contacts that the defendant has with the forum state in addition to the *Zippo* analysis. Courts are beginning to look beyond the *Zippo* analysis to the intent or focus of the defendant's activity in addition to the question of interactivity.[233] A web site may be interactive but actual sales in the forum may be sporadic or non-

---

[227] 141 F. Supp. 2d 246 (D. Conn. 2001); Search Force v. Dataforce Int'l, 112 F. Supp. 2d 771 (S.D. Ind. 2000) (noting that the Fifth, Ninth, and Tenth Circuits relied upon the *Zippo Mfg.* sliding scale in exercising jurisdiction based on Internet activity); *see also* Alitalia-Linee Aeree Italiane S.P.A. v. Casinoalitalia.com, 128 F. Supp. 2d 340 (E.D. Va. 2001) (noting that "[a] majority of courts that have addressed the issue have examined "the nature and quality of activity that a defendant conducts over the Internet," and "have applied the analytical 'sliding scale' formulated" in *Zippo*); *see also* Millennium Enters., Inc. v. Millennium Music, LP, 33 F. Supp. 2d 907, 916 (D. Or. 1999) (collecting cases); Starmedia Network, Inc. v. Star Media, Inc., 2001 U.S. Dist. LEXIS 4870 (S.D.N.Y., Apr. 23, 2001) (ruling that the court had personal jurisdiction because the site could be accessed by potential clients in the forum state); ALS Scan, Inc. v. Wilkins, 2001 U.S. Dist. LEXIS 6605 (D. Md., May 18, 2001) (finding no jurisdiction against defendant who had not engaged in any continuous and systematic contacts with the forum).

[228] 141 F. Supp. 2d 246 (D. Conn. 2001) (dismissing German defendants for lack of personal jurisdiction).

[229] Alitalia-Linee Aeree Italiane S.P.A. v. Casinoalitalia.com, 128 F. Supp. 2d 340, 349 (E.D. Va. 2001).

[230] *Id.*

[231] *Id.*

[232] Keelshield, Inc. v. Megaware Keel-Guard, Inc., 2001 U.S. Dist. LEXIS 7012 (C.D. Ill., May 11, 2001) (denying motions to dismiss on lack of personal jurisdiction in case of trademark infringement); *see also* People Solutions, Inc. v. People Solutions, Inc., 2000 U.S. Dist. LEXIS 10444 at *9 (N.D. Tex., July 25, 2000) (stating that "[p]assive *web sites*, on their own, do not provide personal jurisdiction over the owner of the site").

[233] *Id.*

existent.[234] The "economic realities" test will focus on actual sales in the forum as opposed to the interactivity of the site.[235] A prominent Internet law scholar recently argued that the *Zippo* test no longer fits the realities of web sites.[236] The exercise of personal jurisdiction depends upon the nature and quality of commercial activity that the defendant conducts over the Internet.[237]

[E]   The Sliding Scale of Jurisdiction

As e-commerce has expanded, so has the long arm of jurisdiction. Courts have carved out differenct categories of web sites: those with substantial business or e-commerce sites and those that are passive conduits.[238] The degree of interactivity is an important factor in dictating the willingness of a court to exercise jurisdiction over a web site.[239] Passive informational web sites are the least likely to subject a defendant to out-of-state jurisdictions.[240] In one case, an Arizona corporation brought suit against a Florida corporation of the same name.[241] The court affirmed the dismissal of the lawsuit on personal jurisdiction, discussing the distinction between "passive" and "interactive" web sites.[242] The amount of online commercial activity directed to the forum state was a factor. The Florida corporation's web site invited companies interested in Internet advertising to e-mail

---

[234] Ty, Inc. v. Baby Me, Inc., 2001 U.S. Dist. LEXIS 5761 (N.D. Ill., Apr. 25, 2001) (contending that sporadic Internet sales of allegedly infringing toys in forum state were insufficient to confer personal jurisdiction); *see also* World-Wide Volkswagen Corp. v. Woodson, 444 U.S. 286, 287 (1980) (describing the requirement of purposeful availment as "giving a degree of predictability to the legal system that allows potential defendants to structure their primary conduct with some minimum assurance as to whether that conduct will and will not render them liable to suit").

[235] Euromarket Designs, Inc. v. Crate & Barrel Ltd., 96 F. Supp. 2d 824, 833 (N.D. Ill. 2001) (basing jurisdiction upon sale of products over the web site to forum residents and applying *Zippo* test and "effects test" of *Calder*).

[236] Michael Geist, Relatively Recent Jurisdiction Decisions Said to Be Falling Behind Web Technologies, Pike & Fischer Internet Law and Regulation (June 5, 2001) (arguing that "it is often difficult to determine whether a site is active or passive and that courts are moving away from the *Zippo* standard toward a more target-based approach to jurisdiction").

[237] V'Soske, Inc. v. Vsoske.com, 2001 U.S. Dist. LEXIS 6675 (S.D.N.Y., May 23, 2001) (granting motion for a judgment on the pleadings).

[238] Zippo Mfg. Co. v. Zippo Dot Com, Inc., 952 F. Supp. 1119, 1123-1125 (W.D. Pa. 1997).

[239] *See* Maura I. McInerney and Edward G. Biester III, I.P. Claims Based on Internet Contacts, Legal Intell. (June 3, 1999) at 7 (analyzing Internet jurisdiction controversies); Jeremy Gilman, Personal Jurisdiction and the Internet: Traditional Jurisprudence for a New Medium, 56 Bus. Law. 395 (November 2000) (survey of recent Internet-related jurisdictional cases).

[240] *See* Pheasant Run, Inc. v. Moyse, No. 98 C 4202, 1999 U.S. Dist. LEXIS 1087 (N.D. Ill. E.D., Feb. 3, 1999) (finding no jurisdiction arising out of small Internet advertisement); Grutowski v. Steamboat Lake Guides and Outfitters, Inc., 1998 U.S. Dist. LEXIS 20255 (E.D. Pa., Dec., 1998) (denying jurisdiction in a wrongful death action based on passive web advertisement); Cybersell, Inc. v. Cybersell, Inc., 130 F.3d 414, 418 (9th Cir. 1997) (denying jurisdiction because merely creating Internet site did not purposefully direct action towards forum state).

[241] Cybersell, Inc. v. Cybersell, Inc., 130 F.3d 414, 416 (9th Cir. 1997).

[242] *Id.* at 417-418.

them.[243] A New Jersey court recently held that a defendant whose only source of income was generated by a "click-through" option that linked users to other sites lacked contacts that established specific jurisdiction. Even though the defendant made monetary gain by linking visitors to other pages, his site did not sell or offer for sale any of defendant's products. The court classified the defendant's web site as passive advertisement that was not grounds for the exercise of personal jurisdiction.[244]

Web sites that operate as passive advertisements, with company, product, and contact information (telephone and fax number), are usually insufficient for general jurisdiction.[245] While most courts have followed this standard, some jurisdictions disagree and have found that a passive commercial web site must have resulted in some business transactions, exposing the defendant to jurisdiction.[246]

The passive site may still subject a defendant to specific jurisdiction if the web site is the focus of the controversy. A passive web site may contain a defamatory remark, trademark infringement, or disclosure of trade secrets, for example, subjecting the web site operator to potential liability anywhere the plaintiff may be found.[247] In general, a passive web site without "something more" is insufficient for personal jurisdiction.[248]

Courts are likely to find personal jurisdiction where there is an "interactive web site."[249] Recently, courts are looking beyond the "interactivity test" and emphasize the defendant web site's other activities, including the use of the site.[250] Internet advertising alone is not enough to establish jurisdiction even though the Internet is worldwide. If a mere advertisement on the Internet was sufficient, any company advertising its goods and services on the Internet would be subject to

---

[243] *Id.* at 416.

[244] Amberson Holdings LLC v. Westside Story Newspaper, 110 F. Supp. 2d 332 (D.N.J., Aug. 22, 2000).

[245] Atlantech Distrib. Inc. v. Credit General Ins. Co., 30 F. Supp. 2d 534, 1998 U.S. Dist. LEXIS 19950 (D. Md., Nov. 11, 1998).

[246] *See* SuperGuide Corp. v. Kegan, Civ. No. 4:97CV181 (W.D.N.C., Oct. 8, 1997) (asserting jurisdiction over a trademark dispute where trademark was used on defendant's web site).

[247] *See, e.g.,* Naxos Resources (U.S.A.) Ltd. v. Southam, Inc. 1996 U.S. Dist. LEXIS 21757, 21759 (S.D. Cal., Aug. 16, 1996) (observing defamatory Internet article intended for distribution in forum state may be sufficient for jurisdiction); Edias Software Int'l v. Basis Int'l, 947 F. Supp. 413 (D. Ariz. 1996) (finding combined activities of defamatory e-mails, critical web page, and chat room postings conferred jurisdiction).

[248] Cybersell, Inc. v. Cybersell, Inc. 130 F.3d 414, 418 (9th Cir. 1997); *see also* Lofton v. Turbine Design, Inc., 100 F. Supp. 2d 404 (N.D. Miss. 2000) (holding that nonresident defendant in a defamation action did not have sufficient minimum contacts with forum state because he did not have an office within the forum state, did not have employees or sales representatives in the forum state, did not solicit business in the forum state, and did not derive any income from customers in the forum state); Bailey v. Turbine Design, Inc., 86 F. Supp. 2d 790 (W.D. Tenn. 2000) (declining jurisdiction as defamatory postings were not aimed at plaintiff in the forum).

[249] Zippo Mfg. Co. v. Zippo Dot Com, Inc., 952 F. Supp. 1119, 1124 (W.D. Pa. 1997).

[250] Coastal Video Communications Corp. v. Staywell Corp., 59 F. Supp. 2d 562, 571-72 (E.D. Va. 1999) (examining factors beyond interactivity in determining personal jurisdiction of a web site defendant).

Internet jurisdiction in every state and many nations.[251] "Advertising on the Internet has been held to fall under the same rubric as advertising in a national magazine and it is well settled law in this Circuit that advertising in a national publication does not constitute the 'continuous and substantial contacts with the forum state' required to give rise to a finding of general jurisdiction."[252] The greater the interactivity and more commercial the site, the greater the likelihood of jurisdiction. Moving up the scale of potential jurisdiction, a passive site with a customer e-mail response feature may not be sufficient to establish general jurisdiction.[253] A recent court found that defendant's action of e-mailing and telephone calls to offer to sell a domain name to the plaintiff was sufficient to confer specific jurisdiction.[254] The web site with e-mail response approaches the subjective threshold as to what is defined as interactive and sufficient for jurisdiction. A passive site with a customer e-mail contact feature and an event listing, including some events in the forum state, for example, conferred general jurisdiction.[255] Further along the jurisdiction spectrum, a hotel's web site from which residents of the forum state made online reservations was sufficiently interactive for jurisdiction.[256]

Internet sites that permit visitors to download software are considered sufficiently interactive for jurisdiction.[257] An interactive commercial web site featuring a business telephone directory was sufficiently interactive for a court to obtain jurisdiction over a nonresident defendant.[258] Interactivity is not always the death knell to an online exposure to jurisdiction. Some courts have looked beyond interactivity and now assess the degree of commercial activity that the defendant conducts in the forum state.[259] Interactivity, without proof of Internet sales, does not satisfy the minimum contacts test, despite the fact that a web site permits interactivity. An Oregon court, for example, found that an interactive web site that sold products and provided franchise and discount club information was not subject to Oregon jurisdiction since it did not have systematic and continuous contacts in the

---

[251] Origins Natural Resources, Inc. v. Kotler, 133 F. Supp. 2d 1232 (D.N.M. 2001) (finding no personal jurisdiction and criticizing analogy of advertising to radio or TV because "any company advertising on it would be subject to every law of virtually every jurisdiction in the world" based upon Internet advertising).

[252] Remick v. Manfredy, 52 F. Supp. 2d 452, 456 (E.D. Pa. 1999), *reversed on other grounds,* Remick v. Manfredy, 238 F.3d 248 (3d Cir. 2000).

[253] Grutowski v. Steamboat Lake Guides & Outfitters, Inc., 1998 U.S. Dist. LEXIS 20255 (E.D. Pa., Dec. 21, 1998). *See also* Origin Instruments Corp. v. Adaptive Computer Sys., Inc., 1999 U.S. Dist. LEXIS 1451 (N.D. Tex., Feb. 3, 1999) (determining web site with e-mail feature was interactive, but insufficient for general jurisdiction).

[254] Nutrisystem.com, Inc. v. Easthaven, Ltd., 2000 WL 1781924 (E.D. Pa., Nov. 16, 2000).

[255] Vitullo v. Velocity Powerboats, Inc., 1998 U.S. Dist. LEXIS 7120 (N.D. Ill., Apr. 24, 1998).

[256] Park Inns Int'l., Inc. v. Pacific Plaza Hotels, Inc., 5 F. Supp. 2d 762 (D. Ariz. 1998).

[257] *See* 3DO Co. v. Poptop Software, Inc. 49 U.S.P.Q.2d (BNA) 1469 (N.D. Cal., Oct. 27, 1998) (permitting jurisdiction in copyright and trade secret action since defendant's activities were targeted at forum state).

[258] GTE New Media Services, Inc. v. Ameritech Corp., 21 F. Supp. 2d 27 (D.D.C., Sept., 1998).

[259] *See* ESAB Group, Inc. v. Centricut, L.L.C., 34 F. Supp. 2d 323, 330-331 (D.S.C. 1999) (applying commercial activity test to Internet jurisdiction).

state.[260] California has also reexamined and refined the interactivity scale, ruling that interactivity is irrelevant without proof that anyone from the state actually accessed the web site.[261]

A state may also obtain specific jurisdiction over an out-of-state defendant who regularly engages in business via the web or derives substantial online revenue from the state.[262] Direct solicitation of residents in a state via the Internet can expose a defendant to another state's jurisdiction.[263] Also, any defamatory remarks on a web site directed to a plaintiff in a specific state or country may give rise to jurisdiction.[264]

The court in *Zippo Manufacturing Co. v. Zippo Dot Com, Inc.*[265] developed a continuum for examining the presence of personal jurisdiction based on the activities of the web site. The court found a basis for personal jurisdiction even if the defendant limited its contacts to providing, over the Internet, a news service subscribed to by residents within that state. A growing number of other courts apply the *Zippo* test for interactivity of web sites.[266] The *Zippo* court's continuum test for determining Internet presence has become an influential test for determining whether the defendant's web site activities are sufficient to establish personal jurisdiction.[267]

---

[260] *See* Millennium Enters., Inc. v. Millennium Music, L.P., 33 F. Supp. 2d 907, 921 (D. Or. 1999) (finding insufficient conduct or connections to establish jurisdiction with the forum state). Defendants explicitly disclaimed sales or information to Oregon on the web site after they learned of the dispute. *Id.* at 909. This may have removed the risk of further jurisdictional exposure while the lawsuit progressed.

[261] Richard A. Raysman and Peter Brown, Conversion, Trespass and Other New Litigation Issues, 221 N.Y.L.J. 1 (May 11, 1999) at 3; *see also* Frederick H. Bicknese, Web Sites and Personal Jurisdiction: When Should a Defendant's Internet Selling Activities Subject It to Suit in a Plaintiff-Buyer's State? 73 Temp. L. Rev. 829 (2000) (arguing that courts should apply different jurisdictional principles to cyberspace cases because the facts of online jurisdiction are significantly different than traditional jurisdictional cases).

[262] *See* Quality Solutions, Inc. v. Zupanc, 993 F. Supp. 621, 623 (N.D. Ohio 1997) (finding compelling evidence of local solicitation from out-of-state web site, among other channels).

[263] Telco Communications Group, Inc. v. An Apple a Day, Inc., 977 F. Supp. 404 (E.D. Va. 1997).

[264] Blakey v. Continental Airlines, Inc., 156 N.J.L.J. 1165 (June 21, 1999). A contemporary test in the United States for jurisdiction in a defamation action is the *Calder* effects test. Calder v. Jones, 465 U.S. 783 (1984). In a recent Internet dispute, the court articulated the requirements of the effects test as (1) the defendant intentionally committed a tort which (2) was aimed at the forum state and (3) the plaintiff suffered the majority of the harm in the forum state. Imo Indus., Inc. v. Kiekert AG, 155 F.3d 254, 265-266 (3d Cir. 1998). *See also* Barrett v. Catacombs Press, 44 F. Supp. 2d 717 (E.D. Pa. 1999) (applying effects test to Internet defamation and reviewing Internet cases using effects test). Germany takes a more liberal approach to defamation. John R. Schmertz, Jr., and Mike Meier, German District Court Holds That Defamation Action Based on False Information Published on Internet May be Heard by Court in "Any Place" Where Message Can Be Received, Int'l L. Update (July 1997) available in LEXIS, Intlaw Library, Ilawup File. In a domestic Internet defamation dispute, the court found that jurisdiction is proper anywhere the plaintiff can receive the defamatory message. *Id.* For further exploration of an Internet defamation case in the United States, *see* Michelle J. Kane, Internet Service Provider Liability: Blumenthal v. Drudge, 14 Berkeley Tech. L.J. 483 (1999) (analyzing online defamation and ISP liability).

[265] 952 F. Supp. 1119, 1125-27 (W.D. Pa. 1997).

[266] *See, e.g.,* Park Inns Int'l, Inc. v. Pacific Plaza Hotels, Inc., 5 F. Supp. 2d 762 (D. Ariz. 1998).

[267] Zippo Mfr. Co. v. Zippo Dot Com, Inc., 952 F. Supp. 1119 (W.D. Pa. 1997).

National advertising alone was found not to be sufficient for personal jurisdiction in several cases.[268] In *Bensusan Restaurant Corp.*,[269] the Second Circuit found that the operator of a Missouri jazz club named "The Blue Note" was not subject to personal jurisdiction under New York's long-arm statute. The court held that the "The Blue Note" did not commit tortious acts in New York within the meaning of New York's long-arm statute when he established an Internet web site for his club that contained a hyperlink to the famous New York club. The court found that the Missouri club was not engaging in interstate commerce and could therefore not be reached by New York's long-arm statute.[270]

The *Zippo* court made the point this way:

> This sliding scale is consistent with well-developed personal jurisdiction principles. At one end of the spectrum are situations where a defendant clearly does business over the Internet. At the opposite end are situations where a defendant has simply posted information on an Internet web site, which is accessible to users in foreign jurisdictions. A passive web site that does little more than make information available to those who are interested in it is not grounds for the exercise of personal jurisdiction. . . . The middle ground is occupied by interactive web sites where a user can exchange information with the host computer. In these cases, the exercise of jurisdiction is determined by examining the level of interactivity and commercial nature of the exchange of information that occurs on the web site.[271]

Nationwide advertising alone is an insufficient basis for the exercise of personal jurisdiction. In *Digital Control Inc. v. Boretronics*,[272] the federal court articulated a post-*Zippo* test it dubbed the "web site plus" rule. The court stated: "Given the nature of the Internet and the purpose behind the jurisdictional analysis, the 'web site plus' rule developing in the case law appears to be a good rule of thumb for evaluating jurisdiction-creating contacts in Internet cases. Such an analysis avoids the unjustifiable extreme of universal jurisdiction while at the same time subjecting defendants to suit wherever they have purposely directed their activities. Posting information on a web site tells one very little about the purpose or intent of the advertiser."[273]

[1] Reasonableness Test

The *reasonableness test* is a finding that the plaintiff's claim must arise out of the defendant's forum-related activities once a plaintiff has shown minimum

---

[268] Giangola v. Walt Disney World Co., 753 F. Supp. 148, 156 (D.N.J. 1990) (denying personal jurisdiction even though Disney World placed advertisements in local newspapers read by the plaintiff); Mink v. AAAA Dev. LLC, 190 F.3d 333, 336-37 (5th Cir. 1999) (declining personal jurisdiction where sole basis was a web site accessible in a forum state without interactive activity).

[269] 126 F.3d 25, 29 (2d Cir. 1997).

[270] Bensusan Restaurant Corp. v. King, 937 F. Supp. 295 (S.D.N.Y. 1996) (summarizing facts leading to trademark infringement case against Missouri jazz club).

[271] *Zippo Mfr. Co.*, 952 F. Supp., at 1124.

[272] 161 F. Supp. 2d 1183, 1185 (E.D. Wash. 2001).

[273] *Id.* at 1187.

contacts. The exercise of jurisdiction is reasonable if it does not offend "traditional notions of fair play and substantial justice."[274] The reasonableness test examines the fairness of a particular forum, balancing the burden on the defendant against factors such as "the forum state's interest in adjudicating the dispute; the plaintiff's interest in obtaining convenient and effective relief, at least when that interest is not adequately protected by the plaintiff's right to choose the forum; the interstate judicial system's interest in obtaining the most efficient resolution of controversies; and the shared interest of the several states in furthering fundamental substantive social policies."[275] A defendant must make a compelling case to show why the exercise of jurisdiction is unreasonable.

[F]   International Jurisdictional Issues

Chapter Eight discusses international jurisdictional issues in greater depth. In general, international law places limits on the courts' authority over foreign nonresidents involving the Internet.[276] For a foreign court to decide an online dispute involving foreign nonresidents, there must be three bases for jurisdiction: prescriptive, adjudication, and enforcement.[277] An Internet presence automatically equates to an international presence. The problem facing many companies is that they may be subject to personal or prescriptive jurisdiction in many distant forums. A company's web site may be accessed from New Delhi to São Paulo.[278] E-commerce sales that are legal in one country may run afoul of local laws in another country.[279] For example, a French court ordered United States based Yahoo! to prevent French citizens from accessing Nazi memorabilia at the Yahoo! auction site.[280] While such

---

[274] Theo. H. Davies & Co. v. Republic of the Marshall Islands, 174 F.3d 969 (9th Cir. 1999).

[275] Zippo Mfr. Co. v. Zippo Dot Com, Inc., 952 F. Supp. 1119, 1122 (W.D. Pa. 1997) (quoting World Wide Volkswagen Corp. v. Woodson, 444 U.S. 286, 287 (1980)). *See also* Teracom v. Valley Nat'l Bank, 49 F.3d 555 (4th Cir. 1995) (stating that no single factor is dispositive in determining whether jurisdiction is unreasonable).

[276] Denis T. Rice, Offering Securities on the Internet—2001, 18 Computer & Internet Law. 19 (May 2001).

[277] *Id.* (citing Restatement (3d) of the Foreign Relations Law of the United States, § 401, cmt a (1987)).

[278] *See* Vanessa Marsland and Francois Bloch, Book Review: Drawing Lines in Cyberspace, I.P. Worldwide, Mar.-Apr. 1999, available in LEXIS, News Library, Curnws File (warning little control over who can access a web site or from where).

[279] Wendy R. Leibowitz, E-Litigation: Borders in Net Space, Nat'l L.J., June 14, 1999, at B21. A United States court would enforce an incorrectly posted price and an acknowledgment of sale in the buyer's favor, whereas the United Kingdom allows a price to be corrected even after a contract was formed. *Id. See* German Court Overturns Pornography Ruling Against CompuServe, N.Y. Times (Nov. 18, 1999) at C4 (overturning conviction of ISP manager in Bavarian court for failing to block child pornography sites).

[280] Yahoo! eventually banned Nazi memorabilia from its auctions. Due to technical challenges, Yahoo! claimed that it would have been unable to comply with the judge's ruling of blocking items by geographic area. Yahoo Ends Nazi Auctions and Free Lunch, The Standard (Jan. 12, 2001) http://www.thestandard.com/article/0,1902,21189,00.html.

controversial items are permitted for sale in the United States, they are banned by some European countries. In another international example, a British judge has asserted jurisdiction over the content of American web sites.[281] Despite some inconsistent rulings, when compared with other countries, the United States has the most developed and predictable approach to Internet jurisdiction.[282] However, American-grown principles of due process in personal jurisdiction may not apply in foreign jurisdictions connected to the Internet. Intel is the target of a European Commission (EC) investigation tried under the competition law of the European Community. One issue is whether testimony from a prior U.S. antitrust case should be released to the European authorities and introduced in the EC case.[283]

[1]   European Union

The European Union has recognized that the current legal landscape is one of the biggest challenges to international electronic commerce.[284] Indeed, European Internet content providers are concerned with potential liability in every member state of the European Union.[285] Unlike the United States, however, the European Union hopes to harmonize e-commerce regulations across member states rather than allowing each state the sovereignty to develop conflicting laws.[286] The European Commission has been pushing a controversial regulation that gives jurisdiction to the destination country in an Internet transaction.[287]

---

[281] UK Shows Door for Pornography Made in the USA, Computers Today (July 31, 1999) at 78.

[282] See Robert L. Hoegle and Christopher P. Boam, Nations Uneasily Carve Out Internet Jurisdiction, I.P. Worldwide (July/Aug. 1999) available in LEXIS, News Library, Curnws File (listing worldwide Internet jurisdictional challenges).

[283] Jack Robertson, Will Integraph Suit Come Back to Haunt Intel?, Electronic Buyer News, Oct. 29, 2001, at 6.

[284] Commission Resolution on the Communication from the Commission on Globalization and the Information Society: The Need for Strengthened International Coordination, 1999 O.J. (C 104) 128. An ISP from the United Kingdom removed its server from Germany to avoid liability under Germany's strict antipornography laws. Hoegle and Boam, *supra* note 257.

[285] See Commission Adopts Draft Regulation on Jurisdiction, Recognition, and Enforcement of Judgments in Civil and Commercial Matters, Comm'n of the Eur. Communities, Press Release: IP 991510, RAPID (July 14, 1999) available in LEXIS, News Library, Curnws File (citing challenges in European electronic commerce).

[286] See Electronic Commerce: Commission Proposes Legal Framework, RAPID (Nov. 18, 1998) available in LEXIS, News Library, Curnws File (examining proposed ecommerce harmonization directive); Proposal for a European Parliament and Council Directive on Certain Legal Aspects of Electronic Commerce in the Internal Market, 1999 O.J. (C 30) 4 (proposing framework for assessing jurisdiction within the European Union); *cf.* Cyberspace Regulation and the Discourse of State Sovereignty, 112 Harv. L. Rev. 1680 (discussing the challenges of international Internet jurisdiction and state sovereignty).

[287] Lucy Dixon, EC Ruling on E-Trade Favors Destination, Precision Marketing (July 26, 1999) at 44. European courts have taken the opposite approach in international libel cases by granting jurisdiction where the harm originated. Jan J. Brinkhof, Cross-Border Injunctions: Dead in the EU? I.P. Worldwide (Mar./Apr. 1999) available in LEXIS, News Library, Curnws File.

In April 2000, two antiracism organizations filed suit in the Superior Court of Paris against Yahoo! Inc. and its French subsidiary, Yahoo! France.[288] The purpose of the lawsuit was to require Yahoo! Inc. to prohibit the sale of Nazi memorabilia from its auction site.[289] The French court "ordered Yahoo! Inc. to take all measures necessary to make it impossible to access auction services offering Nazi memorabilia as well as any other site or service offering an apology for Nazism or questioning whether Nazi crimes occurred."[290]

A California U.S. district court issued a declaratory judgment that the legal judgment had no effect. The court noted that the extent to which the United States, or any state, honors the judicial decrees of foreign nations is a matter of choice, governed by the comity of nations.[291] The court noted: "Absent a body of law that establishes international standards with respect to speech on the Internet and an appropriate treaty or legislation addressing enforcement of such standards to speech originating within the United States, the principle of comity is outweighed by the Court's obligation to uphold the First Amendment."[292] The court declined to rule on the factual question of whether Yahoo! possesses the technology to comply with the order.[293]

[2]   ABA's Cyberspace Jurisdictional Report

In July 2000, the ABA Committee on Cyberspace Law's Jurisdictional Project released a report detailing default rules for transnational cyberspace transactions.[294] The subcommittee on international transactions has made the jurisdictional initiative prospectus and several research reports on jurisdiction in cyberspace from the U.S. and European perspective available on the ABA web site.[295]

The ABA's Cyberspace Jurisdiction Report studied the role of the Internet in creating potential "jurisdictional conflicts and their resolution."[296] If an online consumer orders goods or services, the retailer, in effect, is pulled into the jurisdiction of the consumer.[297] Another unsettled issue is where the buyer and seller reside for

---

[288] Margaret Khayat Bratt and Norbert F. Kugele, Information Technology: Who's in Charge? The World May Be Worldwide, But Lawmaking Bodies Are Not, 80 Mich. Bar J. 42, 44 (July 2001).

[289] *Id.* (noting the "objects associated with Nazism, such as coins, medals, and other memorabilia").

[290] *Id.*

[291] Yahoo!, Inc. v. La Ligue Contre Le Racisme et L'Antisemitisme, 169 F. Supp. 2d 1181 (N.D. Calif. 2001).

[292] *Id.*

[293] *Id.*

[294] American Bar Association (ABA) Jurisdiction in Cyberspace Project, Achieving Legal and Business Order in Cyberspace: A Report on Global Jurisdiction Issues Created by the Internet (July 2000, London Meeting Draft).

[295] ABA Business Law, Committee on Cyberspace, ABA Jurisdiction Project (May 31, 2000), http://www.abanet.org/BUSLAW/CYBER/initiatives/jurisdiction.html.

[296] *Id.* at 7.

[297] *Id.* at 8.

purposes of jurisdiction where there are cross-border solicitations, advertisements, and sales transactions.[298] The goal of the Cyberspace Jurisdiction Report was to develop jurisdictional default rules for Internet-related jurisdiction.[299]

The first principle of Internet jurisdiction is that "every Internet party should be subject to personal and prescriptive jurisdiction somewhere."[300] *Personal jurisdiction* is defined as the "authority of a state to insist that a default appear and defend a claim."[301] "Prescriptive or regulatory jurisdiction is the authority of a state to regulate an entity's conduct and to penalize its failure to comply with that regulation, either in an enforcement action brought by the state or through the use of its law by its courts to determine the merits of a private claim."[302] The ABA Cyberspace Jurisdiction Report acknowledges that "more than one state (nation state) may be able to assert both personal and prescriptive jurisdiction in electronic commerce transactions," just as in the bricks and mortar world.[303]

The ABA Cyberspace Jurisdiction Report follows the *Zippo* continuum in maintaining that jurisdiction should be based solely "on the accessibility in the state of a passive web site that does not target the state."[304] Another jurisdictional principle is that "[b]oth personal and prescriptive jurisdiction should be assertable over a web site content provider ('sponsor') in a state, assuming there is no enforceable contractual choice of law and forum."[305] For this principle to apply, the provider or sponsor must be a habitual resident of that state or have a principal place of business in that state.[306] In addition, the sponsor must be targeting the national state and the claim must arise out of content on the site.[307] Another default rule is that if a "dispute arises out of a transaction generated through a web site or service that does not target any specific (nation) state, but is interactive," it will be classified as knowingly engaging in business there.[308]

The ABA Report takes a free market approach to jurisdiction. Providers or sponsors are permitted to control exposure to jurisdiction "through the use of disclosures, disclaimers, software, and other technological blocking or screening mechanisms."[309] Providers may require users or other sellers to "identify with adequate prominence and specificity, the state in which they habitually reside."[310] An online company has no way of determining the jurisdiction of site visitors in the absence of a mechanism for unveiling anonymity. The ABA Report encourages

---

[298] *Id.*

[299] *Id.* at 19 (citing jurisdictional default rule 1.1.1).

[300] *Id.*

[301] *Id.* at n.30, p. 5.

[302] *Id.* at n.31, p. 5.

[303] *Id.* (citing jurisdictional default rule 1.1.1).

[304] *Id.* (citing jurisdictional default rule 1.1.2).

[305] *Id.* (citing jurisdictional default rule 1.1.3).

[306] *Id.* (citing jurisdictional default rule 1.1.3(a)).

[307] *Id.* (citing jurisdictional default rule 1.1.3(b)).

[308] *Id.* (citing jurisdictional default rule 1.1.3(c)).

[309] *Id.* (citing jurisdictional default rule 1.1.4).

[310] *Id.* (citing jurisdictional default rule 1.1.4(a)).

sites to provide disclosures about their jurisdictional targets or require express consent to engage in a given transaction.

The ABA Report has special rules for tax jurisdiction. The Report applies prescriptive jurisdictional principles to jurisdiction for the purpose of requiring assistance in the enforcement of taxes.[311] "Jurisdiction for the purpose of imposing a direct tax burden should not be assumed in all cases to be as broad as tax assistance jurisdiction."[312] The ABA Report favors restraint and comity in the exercise of personal, prescriptive, or tax jurisdiction. Principles of international comity include weighing "the interests of other states in the application of their law and the extent to which laws are in conflict."[313] The Report adopts the "dormant commerce clause" proposed by § 403 of the Restatement (Third) of Foreign Relations Law.[314] The "dormant commerce clause" is a restraint against impeding the free flow of commerce.[315] International abstention and doctrines such as forum non conveniens are to be applied "where the interests of justice or convenience of the parties point to a different place as the most appropriate one for the resolution of a dispute."[316]

The ABA Report embraces a pro-choice view of choice of law and forum for B2B transactions. The Report favors "forum selection and choice of law contract provisions" in B2B transactions in the "absence of fraud or abuse."[317] In B2C contracts, "courts should enforce mandatory, non-binding arbitration clauses, where sponsors have opted to use them," and permit the development of a "law merchant."[318] The "law merchant" tradition refers to the informal norms that have evolved from business practices such as the usage of trade.[319] Nonbinding arbitration is not enforced unless the sponsor is committed to enforcing a final award or judgment or has sufficient assets to satisfy a judgment. Consumer nonbinding

---

[311] ABA Business Law, Committee on Cyberspace, ABA Jurisdiction Project at 20 (jurisdictional default rule 1.1.5(a)).

[312] *Id.* (citing jurisdictional default rule 1.1.5(b)).

[313] *Id.* at 21 (citing jurisdictional default rule 1.1.6).

[314] *Id.* at 21, n.52.

[315] *Id.* at 21 (citing jurisdictional default rule 1.1.6(b)).

[316] *Id.* at 21 (citing jurisdictional default rule 1.1.6(d)).

[317] *Id.* at 21 (citing jurisdictional default rule 1.2.1).

[318] *Id.* at 21 (citing jurisdictional default rule 1.2.2).

[319] The Uniform Commercial Code, for example, incorporates the norms of the law merchant. *See* U.C.C. § 1-103 (2000) (supplementing UCC provisions with principles from the law merchant). The law merchant evolved in the medieval fairs of Europe. Informal law merchant juries determined disputes over the sale of goods and were referred to as the "pie powder" courts. The law merchant is defined as "a body of commercial law embracing the usages of merchants, in different commercial countries, but not resting exclusively on the institutions and local customs of any particular country, consisting of certain principles of equity and usages of trade which general convenience and a common sense of justice have established to regulate the dealings of merchants and mariners in all the commercial countries of the civilized world." Ballentine's Law Dictionary 713 (3d ed. 1964) (citation omitted). The modern law merchant would include e-commerce principles recognized by countries doing business on the Internet. It is quite likely that the use of digital signatures is a widely accepted practice of the Internet "law merchant." The advantage of the law merchant is that it develops legal rules that are consistent with the needs of rapidly evolving e-commerce best practices.

arbitration requires "the user's acceptance of an adequately disclosed choice of forum and choice of law clauses."[320] Another fundamental principle is that jurisdictional choice "should be enforced where the consumer demonstrably bargained with the seller."[321] The ABA Report validates jurisdictional choices made by consumers interacting with electronic agents or bots.[322]

The ABA Report endorses safe harbor agreements such as the European Union approach to privacy protection to resolve jurisdictional conflicts.[323] Finally, the ABA Report proposes that a multinational Global Online Standards Commission be formed to develop global protocol standards.[324] The ABA Report argues that "government entities should be cautious about imposing extra-territorial jurisdictional oversight."[325] The Report endorses technological solutions "such as universal protocol standards, employed by intelligent electronic agents [which may] electronically communicate jurisdiction information and rules" which will enable e-commerce.[326] The private sector, contract-based regime for B2B transactions is consistent with the regime proposed by the Hague Convention that enforces choice of forum and law clauses.[327] The ABA Cyberspace Jurisdiction Report is at odds with Article 7 of the Hague Convention that gives consumers the right to file actions against foreign web sites in their own country.[328] Internet sellers favor the right of the seller to determine the forum and choice of law.

While most Internet conflict of law disputes occur in the United States, it is expected that many more disputes will cross borders as international sales expand.[329] Amazon.com, for example, now has more foreign than U.S. sales. It is quite likely that U.S. companies will be litigating more disputes in foreign countries. A U.S. firm may be exposed to foreign lawsuits for torts that do not yet exist

---

[320] ABA Business Law, Committee on Cyberspace, ABA Jurisdiction Project at 21 (citing jurisdictional default rule 1.2.2(b)).

[321] *Id.* (citing jurisdictional default rule 1.2.3).

[322] *Id.* (citing jurisdictional default rule 1.2.4).

[323] *Id.* at 22 (citing jurisdictional default rule 1.3).

[324] *Id.* at 23 (citing jurisdictional default rule 1.4.1-3).

[325] *Id.* (citing jurisdictional default rule 1.4.1).

[326] *Id.* (citing jurisdictional default rule 1.4.2).

[327] Draft Convention on Jurisdiction and Foreign Judgments in Civil and Commercial Matters proposed by the Hague Conference on Private International Law (May 5, 1992).

[328] *Id.* at Art. 7; *see also* Art. 7 (giving employees a right to sue their employers in the employee's forum).

[329] Samuel Goldstein, Courts Can Track a Case Back to You; Your Web Site May Contain Waivers to Protect You, Computer Dealer News (Apr. 2, 1999) at 19. Other countries find the United States' assertion of international jurisdiction unsettling, and this may backfire when other countries expand their jurisdictional reach. *See, e.g.,* Simon Pollard, et al., Domain Names, A View from the Antipodes, Mondaq Business Briefing (May 25, 1999) available in LEXIS, News Library, Curnws File (expressing concern over U.S. assertion of trademark laws in domain name disputes).

under U.S. law.[330] Plaintiffs already have some capacity to forum-shop.[331] The United Kingdom, for example, affords plaintiffs greater rights and remedies in libel cases. In contrast, the United States is one of a few countries to permit a plaintiff to recover punitive damages in a product liability case. Forum shopping is inimical to traditional principles of international law, which recognize jurisdiction in the country of either the plaintiff or the defendant.[332]

Individuals may strategically forum-shop to avoid enforcement action in online businesses that offer offshore gambling, pornography, or other sales or services that violate local laws. Belize and Antigua are popular offshore gambling sites, judging by the hundreds of online web sites.[333] In Canada, for example, some wrongdoers used the Internet to intentionally place their illegal activities outside of the reach of local authorities.[334] In a more dangerous example, a disgruntled intelligence agent from the United Kingdom published a list of names of intelligence agents online, and the United Kingdom could do little to control the information outside of the country.[335] Thus, the inconsistency in regulations further underscores the need for a prudent legal screening of any corporate web site. Some companies choose additional safety measures, as well, such as maintaining one web site for each country in which they plan to do business.[336]

[G]   Obtaining Redress in International Internet Disputes

When the residents of foreign nations are the subjects of an inquiry concerning jurisdiction, there will be a federal government interest in foreign relations

---

[330] *See* Jean Eaglesham, Laying Down Cyberlaw, Financial Times (London) (June 23, 1999) at 22 (discussing absence of uniform Internet rules).

[331] Compare John R. Schmertz, Jr., and Mike Meier, Applying French Data Protection Laws, Int'l L. Update (Dec. 1998) available in LEXIS, News Library, Curnws File (citing French company's pursuit of antitrust dispute in U.S. on Internet basis against French defendant) with Global Roundtable: Taking On The World: If the Future of Business Is Global, So, Too, Is the Business of Law, American Lawyer (Nov. 1998) at 97 (noting foreign companies' desire to avoid American jurisdiction). For an example of international forum shopping, *see* Filetech S.A. v. France Telecom S.A., 157 F.3d 922, 925 (U.S. App. 2d Cir. 1998) (describing French telecommunication antitrust dispute in U.S. court on basis of Internet presence).

[332] *See* I.P. Worldwide (Mar.-April. 1999) available in LEXIS, News Library, Curnws File (suggesting international law may require modification to accommodate Internet issues). Local and international laws have not progressed at the same speed as communications technology. Lesley Stones, Web Site Content Stays Beyond Official Control, Business Day (South Africa) (May 20, 1999) at 30.

[333] The Minnesota attorney general filed an action against an online gambling operation with a server in Belize in Minnesota v. Granite Gate Resorts, Inc., 576 N.W.2d 747 (Minn. 1998).

[334] Pierre Trudel, Jurisdiction Over the Internet: A Canadian Perspective, Int'l Lawyer (Winter, 1998) 1027, 1061. *But see* Minnesota v. Granite Gate Resorts, 568 N.W.2d 715 (Minn. Ct. App. 1997), *aff'd*, 576 N.W.2d 747 (Minn. 1998) (finding Minnesota jurisdiction proper in Internet gambling case over Nevada corporation with server in Belize).

[335] Stones, *supra* note 332.

[336] Psinet.com, home page (visited May 1, 2000), http://www.psinet.com.

at stake. "In every case, however, those interests, as well as the federal government's interest in its foreign relations policies, will be best served by a careful inquiry into the reasonableness of the assertion of jurisdiction in the particular case."[337] A company that has not been able to satisfactorily resolve an Internet-related dispute stemming from a foreign jurisdiction may find sending a letter from an attorney addressing its complaint to be an effective first step.[338] If the letter is unsuccessful, the company could try contacting the local equivalent of the Better Business Bureau in the jurisdiction, if it is appropriate. These options are preferable to filing suit either in the United States or overseas, since this can be an expensive prospect. Also, foreign jurisdictions may favor local defendants. Companies unable to resolve the dispute without litigation, however, may find some U.S. courts sympathetic to their cases and willing to assert jurisdiction. In an Illinois case, a retailer of housewares and furniture sued an Irish retailer of the same products, alleging infringement of the trademark "Crate&Barrel." The court held that specific personal jurisdiction over the Irish retailer was based upon the defendant's maintenance of an interactive Internet web site and solicitation of vendors in Illinois.[339] Alternatively, a well-funded plaintiff may opt to hire local counsel in the country where the harm occurred.

Keep in mind, however, that traditional strategies for resolving disputes in the United States, such as sending a cease and desist letter, may violate local laws in other countries.[340] Prince Sports, for example, had sent a letter to Prince claiming prior trademark rights to the Internet domain name "prince.com" and threatened to sue for trademark infringement unless the domain name was transferred to Prince Sports.[341] In response, Prince initiated an action in the United Kingdom against Prince Sports for making "groundless threats of infringement proceedings under section 21 of the British Trademarks Act of 1994."[342] Thus, Prince Sports was exposed to a cause of action in the United Kingdom and was prevented from having the domain name suspended during the dispute.[343]

International forum shopping may be to a plaintiff's benefit. An American company, for example, used its English subsidiary to obtain jurisdiction over a German corporation for online trademark infringement.[344] Although companies may be

---

[337] Asahi Metal Indus. Co. v. Superior Court of Cal., 480 U.S. 102, 116 (1987) (finding that there was no basis for jurisdiction given the international context and the heavy burden on the alien and the slight interests of the plaintiff and the forum state in the exercise of jurisdiction).

[338] Samuel Goldstein, Courts Can Track a Case Back to You; Your Web Site May Contain Waivers to Protect You, Computer Dealer News (Apr. 2, 1999) at 19.

[339] Euromarket Designs, Inc. v. Crate & Barrel Ltd., 96 F. Supp. 2d 824 (N.D. Ill., May 16, 2000).

[340] *See* Internet Cease and Desist Letter Backfires, Intell. Prop. Strat. (Nov. 1997) at 1 (recognizing defendant followed what would be standard procedures in United States).

[341] *Id.* The British Trademarks Act of 1994 allows relief from a party threatening proceedings for infringement of a registered trademark unless the defendant can show that the acts constituted infringement. *Id.*

[342] Emmanuel Gouge, Legal Update, Brand Strategy (Sept. 19, 1997) at 21.

[343] *See* Dawn Osborne, The Latest Developments in U.K. Trade Marks Law, Mondaq Bus. Briefing (June 16, 1998) available in LEXIS, News Library, Curnws File (suggesting trademark holders with any ownership doubts avoid U.K. jurisdiction in domain name disputes).

[344] Mecklermedia v. D.C. Congress, Ch 40, 1 All E.R, 148 (1997).

able to assert jurisdiction over a defendant and win a lawsuit in this manner, the additional challenge arises of enforcing the judgment over the defendant.[345]

[H]   International Conventions Governing Jurisdiction

The Internet, by its very definition, involves transborder communications across hundreds of countries at the click of a mouse. The Internet can be characterized as an international network of interconnected computers. It would be unreasonable to expect a business to comply with "the consumer protection, securities, criminal, intellectual property, sales, and other substantive laws of every state, country or confederation of countries every time that it offers a service or product on the Internet."[346] Some law must apply, but whose law will govern international Internet contacts remains uncertain. Most e-commerce sites are subject to jurisdiction everywhere. International treaties, however, may govern some aspects of Internet jurisdiction. The traditional principles underlying jurisdiction have been based upon the "exercise of physical coercive control over that territory by the sovereign."[347] Modern jurisdictional analysis is a "mixture of territorial concepts and interest analysis."[348]

A growing number of U.S. courts are exercising jurisdiction over web site activity occurring outside the country's territorial boundaries. Conversely, U.S. companies are increasingly being sued in foreign venues for activities occurring on web servers located in the United States. Presently, little European case law covers Internet jurisdiction, and no statutory solutions exist to answer the question of Internet jurisdiction.[349] Jurisdiction is frequently based on the company's place of business rather than the location of the server.

Courts will presently decide cross-border jurisdictional issues by applying national law principles.[350] For example, Cornell University and a former graduate student were sued in the United Kingdom for defamatory statements posted by the former graduate student on Cornell's computer.[351] In another case, a district court in Virginia ruled it had personal jurisdiction over Hong Kong defendants in a copyright infringement action filed by Playboy Enterprises.[352] The court expressed

---

[345] John DeAngelis & Melissa Dewey, *Internet Jurisdiction: Policy Issues* (visited July 1, 1999), http://www.unc.edu/~deweyma/policy.html#intjur.

[346] Bratt and Kugele, *supra* note 288, at 44.

[347] Henry Perritt, Traditional Legal Concepts: Basics from Three Experts, ILPF, 1999 Annual Conference, Jurisdiction: Building Confidence in a Borderless Medium, Montreal, Canada (July 26, 1999) (visited May 23, 2000), http://www.ilpf.org/confer/trans99/conf99d1.htm.

[348] *Id.*

[349] Agne Lindberg, Jurisdiction on the Internet—The European Perspective: An Analysis of Conventions, Statutes, and Case Law, ABA Committee on Cyberspace Law (May 24, 2000), http://www.abanet.org/buslaw/cyber/initiatives/eujuris.html.

[350] *Id.*

[351] Raysman and Brown, *supra* note 237 (reporting that the court entered a default judgment against the former Cornell graduate student and the university settled out of court).

[352] Playboy Enters., Inc. v. Asiafocus Int'l Inc., 1998 U.S. Dist. LEXIS 10459 (E.D. Va., Apr. 10, 1998).

doubt that the fact that the Hong Kong defendant registered its domain name in Virginia was a sufficient basis for personal jurisdiction. The Virginia long-arm statute, however, contemplated jurisdiction over a nonresident causing tortious injury in that state provided that they do or solicit business in the forum.[353]

On the other hand, a British Columbia court refused to enforce a judgment of a Texas court, holding that it had no jurisdiction in a lawsuit brought by a British Columbia company against a Vancouver resident for allegedly defamatory comments made in an Internet chat forum. The plaintiff had an office in Texas, but the court held that the defendant would need to establish some link to the forum state, such as residency or doing business, to be subject to jurisdiction.[354] Therefore, even if a company obtains a local judgment against a foreign defendant, the judgment may be unenforceable within the jurisdiction.

Similarly, in another foreign jurisdiction claim the magician David Copperfield sued the *Paris Match* magazine for an allegedly defamatory story about his relationship with model Claudia Shiffer.[355] The federal court found no jurisdiction in California over the French publisher, since the *Paris Match* did not direct the defamation to California.[356] The magazine has only a limited distribution in California, and the publisher's Internet web site was a passive site used primarily for advertising.[357] The court held that the *Paris Match* web site had a presence only where the web site was created or maintained or placed on a host computer.[358]

American courts applying foreign law to Internet disputes apply a two-step analysis: first, does the plaintiff satisfy the jurisdiction's long-arm statute? Second, does the contact with the forum state satisfy due process?[359] For foreign courts applying U.S. laws, personal jurisdiction will frequently take the form of whether the country has an interest in resolving a dispute in addition to the question of fairness to the defendant. In the absence of an international treaty, SPC faces an uncertain risk of being sued in a foreign country.[360]

Some foreign and domestic courts have asserted a broad jurisdictional reach in international disputes. For example, a British court recently shut down the web site of a former spy maintained by an ISP in Lausanne, Switzerland.[361] A New York court granted an injunction barring an online gambling site with a server in

---

[353] *Id.*

[354] Braintech v. Kostiuk, No. CA024459 (B.C. Ct. of App., Mar. 18, 1999), reported in the Perkins Coie Internet Case Digest (visited Aug. 25, 1999), http://www.perskinscoie.com/resource/ecomm/netcase/Cases-15.htm.

[355] Copperfield v. Cogedipresse, 26 Med. L. Rptr. 1185 (C.D. Cal., Nov. 3, 1997).

[356] *Id.*

[357] *Id.*

[358] *Id.*

[359] 15 Comp. L. Strat. 1 (Sept. 1998).

[360] *See generally* Dan Burk, "Jurisdiction in a World Without Borders," 1 Va. J. Tech. 3 (1997).

[361] Polly Sprenger, Britain Shuts Down Spy Sites, Wired News (May 12, 1999) (visited May 17, 2000), http://www.wired.com/news/politics/0,1283,19620,00.html (reporting Swiss injunction against publishing international intelligence information on web site).

Antigua from doing business with New York residents.[362] In 1997, a German court asserted jurisdiction to resolve a domain name dispute case where the owner had registered the name in the United States.[363] The Internet's interconnected system of jurisdiction raises the possibility that SPC may be served process in hundreds of foreign jurisdictions as well as in American courts in any of the 50-plus jurisdictions. Another issue is whether SPC can enforce its rights against defendants in foreign jurisdictions. Again, even if a company prevails in an international dispute, it may not be able to enforce its rights against the defendants in a foreign jurisdiction.

The online company will need to take seriously the possibility that it will be held subject to jurisdiction in a foreign country. Little authority exists on what contacts are sufficient to subject a party to jurisdiction in another country.[364] Many nations are taking action to restrict the flow of information on the Internet. Individual nation states have jurisdiction over their own territory, and international jurisdiction will generally be based upon treaty-making agreements.[365]

[1] Brussels Convention on Jurisdiction and Judgments

The Conventions on Jurisdictions and the Enforcement of Judgments in Civil and Commercial Matters (Brussels Convention) provides for the recognition and enforcement of judgments by contracting states. The Lugano Convention is a carbon copy of the Brussels Convention extended to additional signatory states. The European Union (EU) has enacted a number of directives related to Internet commerce but not Internet jurisdiction. The Brussels and Lugano Conventions apply to the online as well as the offline world.[366] The European Economic Community (EEC) entered into the Brussels Convention on Jurisdiction and the Enforcement of Judgments in Civil and Commercial Matters (the Brussels Convention) on September 27, 1968.[367] The Brussels Convention provided "reciprocal recognition and enforcement of judgments of courts or tribunals" in the EEC.[368] The United States

---

[362] State of New York v. World Interactive Gaming Corp., No. 404428/98 (Sup. Ct. N.Y. Cty., July 22, 1999).

[363] Domain Name Challenge, No. 5 U 659/97, 97 0 193/96 (Langericht Berlin, May 26, 1997), Perkins Coie Internet Case Digest (visited June 18, 1999), http://www.perkinscoie.com/resource/ecomm/netcase/Cases-15.htm.

[364] *See generally* Richard A. Crisone and Richard A. Schwartz, Can You Be Sued in Every State in Which Your Site Can Be Viewed? 3 Internet Newsletter: Law & Bus. Aspects (Feb. 1999).

[365] *See generally* Norman J. Vig and Regina S. Axelrod (eds.), The Global Environment: Institutions, Law and Policy (1999) (exploring the difficulties of developing an international order regulating environmental pollution in a global environment).

[366] Agne Lindberg, Traditional Legal Concepts: Basics from Three Experts, ILPF 1999 Annual Conference, Jurisdiction: Building Confidence in a Borderless Medium, Montreal, Canada (July 26, 1999).

[367] European Economic Community, Convention on Jurisdiction and the Enforcement of Judgments in Civil and Commercial Matters (Brussels, Belgium, Sept. 27, 1968).

[368] *Id.* at Preamble.

is not a contracting party to the Brussels Convention, which applies only to EEC countries.

If SPC has a subsidiary located in an EEC country, the Convention would "apply in civil and commercial matters whatever the nature of the court or tribunal."[369] It would take "specific unusual circumstances," however, to make SPC liable for its subsidiary's conduct.[370] Article 2 of the Brussels Convention states that "persons domiciled in a contracting court may be sued in the courts of that state."[371] Article 5 provides that "in matters resulting in a contract," the court is the "place of performance of the obligation in question."[372]

Article 6 provides rules by which a person domiciled in a "Contracting State may be sued in the courts of another Contracting State."[373] Tort or tort-like actions are tried "in the courts for the place where the harmful event occurred."[374] In the case of a consumer transaction, the plaintiff may bring an action in the courts of the contracting state in which he or she is located or the courts where the defendant is located.[375] The parties may opt out of the Brussels Convention by agreement or a choice of law clause.[376] The Brussels Convention also provides for recognition and enforcement of judgments.[377] Judgments in a Brussels Convention signatory country are recognized by the other contracting states.[378] A judgment is not recognized, however, if it is "contrary to public policy in the State in which recognition is sought."[379]

Article 29 provides that "[u]nder no circumstances may a foreign judgment be reviewed as to its substance."[380] A judgment may be enforced in a contracting state by application of an "interested party."[381] Article 32 specifies which national court in EEC countries has jurisdiction to decide applications of enforcement.[382] Article 33 states that "the application shall be governed by the law of the State in which enforcement is sought."[383]

[2] Lugano Convention on Jurisdiction and Judgments

The European Economic Community Union's Convention on Jurisdiction and the Enforcement of Judgments in Civil and Commercial Matters, agreed to at

---

[369] *Id.* at Art. 1.
[370] Nutrition Physiology Corp. v. Enviros Ltd., 87 F. Supp. 2d 648, 655 (N.D. Tex. 2000).
[371] *Id.*
[372] *Id.* at Art. 5.
[373] *Id.* at Art. 6(1).
[374] *Id.* at Art. 6(3).
[375] *Id.* at Art. 14.
[376] *Id.* at Art. 15.
[377] *Id.* at Art. 25-49.
[378] *Id.* at Art. 26.
[379] *Id.* at Art. 27(1).
[380] *Id.* at Art. 29.
[381] *Id.* at Art. 31.
[382] *Id.* at Art. 32.
[383] *Id.* at Art. 33.

Lugano, Italy (the Lugano Convention) on September 16, 1988, also applies to online transactions between member states.[384] The Lugano Convention extends the same principles of jurisdiction and enforcement of judgments to a larger group of countries, including Austria, Belgium, Denmark, France, Finland, the Federal Republic of Germany, Greece, Iceland, Ireland, Italy, Luxembourg, the Netherlands, Norway, Portugal, Sweden, Switzerland, and the United Kingdom.[385]

The Lugano Convention of 1988 simply extends the number of contracting states to the Brussels Convention, adopting identical rules for jurisdiction and the enforcement of judgments. The Convention applies to "judgments given after the date of entry into force of this Convention."[386] The Brussels and Lugano Conventions provide a possible model for Internet-wide adoption. The Conventions are territorially based, but could be extended to legal proceedings arising out of Internet-related commerce. At present, the Burssels and Lugano Conventions only apply to judgments between domiciliaries in EU contracting states.

[3]   Brussels Regulation

Effective March 2002, the Brussels Regulation replaces the 1968 Brussels Convention[387] for all signatories except Denmark. The Brussels Regulation governs jurisdiction in civil and commercial disputes between litigants and provides for the enforcement of judgments. Council Regulation No 44/2001 of December 22, 2002, revises the Brussels Convention of 1968. Article 2.1 of the Brussels Regulation sets forth the general rule that "persons domiciled in a Contracting State shall whatever their nationality, be sued in the courts of that State."[388]

Article 2.2 of the Brussels Regulation provides that nonnationals of member states in which they are domiciled "shall be governed by the rules of jurisdiction applicable to nationals of that state."[389] Article 5.1 provides that "in matters relating to a contract," jurisdiction is in the place of performance. If, for example, SPC sells goods, the place of performance in a member state is the place "where the goods were delivered or should have been delivered."[390]

The Brussels Regulation gives consumers the right to sue a supplier if it "pursues commercial or professional activities in the member state of the consumer's domicile."[391] Article 15(1)(c) extends the consumer home forum rule to

---

[384] European Economic Community, European Free Trade Association, Convention on Jurisdiction and the Enforcement of Judgments in Civil and Commercial Matters (Lugano, Italy, Sept. 16, 1988).

[385] *Id.* at Art. 3.

[386] *Id.* at Art. 54.

[387] Council Regulation (EC) No 44/2001 of December 22, 2000, on jurisdiction and the recognition and enforcement of judgments in civil and commercial matters.

[388] *Id.* at Art. 2.1

[389] *Id.* at Art. 2.2.

[390] *Id.* at Art. 15.1.

[391] *Id.* at Art. 15.1(c).

entities that direct activities to member states. Article 6.1 of the Brussels Regulation provides that a company may be subject to jurisdiction if a co-defendant is domiciled in one of the member states. Article 30 devises a bright line test for determining whether a court in a member state has jurisdiction. A court is deemed to be *seised* if documents have been filed requiring service of process to the defendant. So long as the party has taken the procedural steps necessary for process, the court has been *"seised."* The European Court of Justice has ruled that the Brussels Convention applied to a Canadian company in a contract action brought in a French court.[392] The European Court of Justice decision has far-reaching implications for e-businesses, especially if they are targeting consumers in member countries. It is therefore likely that the Brussels Regulation will also apply to U.S. businesses doing business in Europe.

[4]   Hague Convention on Jurisdiction and Judgments

The Hague Convention on Jurisdiction and the Recognition and Enforcement of Foreign Judgments would assist the online company in the recognition and enforcement of judgments on a transnational basis. Internet industry stakeholders oppose U.S. ratification of the Hague Convention on the grounds that it will make "Internet service providers and Web site operators vulnerable to legal actions based on different national standards."[393] The Internet industry opposes a Hague Convention provision permitting consumers to file suit in their home forum. "The [q]uestion is whether consumer protection policies of state in which Web site is based should apply in state where consumer is based."[394]

Service of process is defined as the delivery of a summons or complaint to the defendant.[395] Federal Rule of Civil Procedure 4(f) allows service to be made on defendants in foreign countries by three methods: "(1) by any internationally agreed means such as the Hague Convention on the Service Abroad of Judicial and Extrajudicial Documents; (2) if there is not an internationally agreed means, or if the applicable international agreement allows other means of service by a number of ways reasonably calculated to provide notice; or (3) by any other means not prohibited by international agreement, if directed by the court."[396]

---

[392] Eugene Gulland, All the World's a Forum: Businesses That Benefit from the Increased Globalization of Commerce Also Face Increased Risks of Liability Abroad, N.J. L.J. (Apr. 29, 2002) (discussing Group Josi Reinsurance Co. S.A. v. Universal Gen. Ins. Co., 2000 E.C.R. I-5925).

[393] Patrick Thibodeau, Pending Deal Alarms E-Commerce Experts; Hague Convention Would Make It Easier for Countries to File Cross-Border Lawsuits, Computerworld, May 28, 2001 (quoting representative of Washington-based U.S. Internet Industry Association).

[394] New Media, Comm. Daily, Feb. 7, 2000.

[395] Henry Campbell Black, Black's Law Dictionary (5th ed., West 1998) 1227.

[396] Nutrition Physiology Corp. v. Enviros Ltd., 87 F. Supp. 2d 648, 652 (N.D. Tex. 2000); *see also* 1958 New York Convention on International Arbitration, United Nations Convention on the Recognition and Enforcement of Foreign Arbitral Awards (June 10, 1958) 21 U.S. 7 2517, 330 U.N. 7.S.3 (enforcing arbitration awards).

An improperly served summons or complaint can result in procedural delays and additional expense. If SPC or any online company is filing suit against a foreign defendant, it may seek prior approval from the court of its proposed method of effecting service of process. Online companies frequently have complex corporate structures, and it is critical to determine whether there is sufficiency of service. If SPC is a defendant, it may file a motion to dismiss for service of process. Service to one of SPC's subsidiaries, partners, or overseas subsidiaries may be grounds for dismissal.

[I] Minimizing Jurisdictional Exposure

Most case analysis suggests that the primary way to reduce jurisdictional exposure is to limit the amount of commerce and interactivity within a web site.[397] Unfortunately, reducing a web site to a passive advertisement may be contrary to the business objectives of companies looking to do business online. Consumers want more than an online yellow pages advertisement. "[T]he likelihood that personal jurisdiction can be constitutionally exercised is directly proportionate to the nature and quality of commercial activity that an entity conducts over the Internet," however.[398]

An alternative to reducing a web presence to passive advertising is posting a forum selection clause within the web pages. For example, a Nevada hotel avoided New Jersey jurisdiction in a personal injury action by posting a Nevada forum selection clause.[399] The court enforced the clause, even though jurisdiction would have been proper because of the commercial, interactive web site and other advertising.[400] Other jurisdictions, however, may not enforce the online forum selection clauses, so they are not a guaranteed method of avoiding out-of-state litigation.

Web sites may also limit jurisdictional exposure by limiting transactions or access by state. A company looking to keep its business and legal exposure to its resident state may require web site visitors to identify their state before proceeding with a transaction.[401] Alternatively, a disclaimer stating that the site is only intended for access from a specific state or disclaiming access from certain states

---

[397] Todd D. Leitstein, A Solution for Personal Jurisdiction on the Internet, 59 La. L. Rev. 565 (1999); *see also* Joseph Schmitt & Peter Nikolai, Application of Personal Jurisdiction Principles to Electronic Commerce: A User's Guide, 27 Wm. Mitchell L. Rev. 1571 (2001) (listing measures to avoid unintended personal jurisdiction such as reducing the use of automated responses, identifying physical location, and negotiating a forum selection clause).

[398] Soma Medical Int'l v. Standard Chartered Bank, 196 F.3d 1292, 1296 (10th Cir. 1999) (citing Zippo Mfg. Co. v. Zippo Dot Com, Inc., 952 F. Supp. 1119, 1123-24 (W.D. Pa. 1997)).

[399] Decker v. Circus Circus Hotel U.S. Dist. Ct. (D.N.J.) 156 N.J.L.J. 813, May 13, 1999. *See also* Caspi v. Microsoft Network, L.L.C., 323 N.J. Super. 118 (N.J. Sup. Ct. App. Div. 1999) (upholding Washington State forum selection clause in online subscription agreement).

[400] *Id.*

[401] Carl W. Chamberlin, To the Millennium: Emerging Issues for the Year 2000 and Cyberspace, 13 N.D.J.L. Ethics & Pub. Pol'y 131, 155 (1999).

may be a helpful precaution.[402] Sun Microsystems limited its potential international exposure from an online contest by specifically listing which countries were eligible.[403] Irrespective of whether geography is limited, web site operators should monitor where visitors and purchasers come from.[404] Companies should be willing to decline sales to any forum where they cannot defend themselves, unless the other party adheres to a choice of law clause.[405]

Alternatively, maintaining interactivity while limiting online business activity can also help minimize exposure. A Canadian company, for example, maintained a web site that allowed e-mail and file exchanges, yet specifically stated that online visitors could not place orders through the site.[406] Since web site visitors could only place orders by printing an order form and faxing it to the company, the court found that the company was not transacting business online.[407] For companies that depend on an interactive, commercial online presence, insurance may be an ideal method of cushioning the potential expense of international litigation.[408]

[J]   Obtaining Redress in Domestic Internet Disputes

Instead of rushing to the uncertainty of a lawsuit, an easy first step in an Internet-related dispute is to send a letter to the other party stating how a company was harmed and recommending how it would like to resolve the matter. If the initial letter is not well received, a follow-up letter from an attorney may help the other party to understand the harmed party's perspective. Additionally, firms can seek the assistance of the local Better Business Bureau or even of an attorney general to help resolve the dispute. As with international dispute resolution, filing a lawsuit can be expensive and time-consuming.

Although some companies may have the resources and time to litigate the matter, more than likely the defendant will try to have the matter dismissed for lack of jurisdiction. Consequently, much energy and expense will go into establishing jurisdiction. Another potential obstacle is naming the defendant. Prior to

---

[402] *See, e.g.,* Kathleen Parrish, Old Laws Shelter Student; D.A. Says Boy's Web Posting About Teacher Can't be Deemed Threat, Morn. Call (July 28, 1998) at A1. A youth avoided criminal charges stemming from a threatening web site by using a disclaimer excluding the threatened individuals from the site. *Id.*

[403] Jonathan I. Ezor, Representing the New Media Company: Advertising on the Web, Comp. Law. (May, 1998) at 6.

[404] Warren E. Agin, Banks Warned Against Potential Problems Via Internet, Commercial Lending, Litig. News (May 14, 1999) available in LEXIS, News Library, Curnws File.

[405] Robert A. Bourque and Kerry L. Conrad, Avoiding Remote Jurisdiction Based on Internet Web Site, N.Y.L.J. (Dec. 10, 1996), http://ljx.com/internet/1210jurs.html.

[406] Desktop Techs., Inc. v. Colorworks Reproduction & Design, Inc., No 98-5029, 1999 U.S. Dist. LEXIS 1934 at *8, *9 (E.D. Pa., Feb. 25, 1999).

[407] *Id.* at 9.

[408] *See, e.g.,* A Major Insurance Innovation for Information Technology Firms (visited July 15, 1999), http://www.chubb.com/news/pr19970815.html (listing insurance services for technology businesses).

the enactment of the ACPA, Porsche Cars sued several Internet domain names directly because the domains were registered either anonymously or by an entity beyond possible jurisdictional limits.[409] The court found that the domain names themselves were beyond the jurisdiction of the court.[410] In most situations, however, companies will more often than not have direct commercial contact with the other party. Additionally, in limited circumstances, the ACPA permits a plaintiff to file suit directly against a domain name. Consequently, naming the defendant should not be an issue.

Companies that are injured via the Internet and thus require the assistance of local law enforcement agencies need to supplement the investigation independently. Local authorities may lack the resources and expertise to pursue Internet crime.[411] Consequently, some companies hire their own investigators and obtain sufficient evidence for the police to issue a warrant and pursue the case.[412]

[K]   Choice of Law in a Global Digital Network

The traditional choice of law endorsed by the Restatement (First) of the Conflict of Laws is *lex loci delictis,* the law of the place where the wrong occurred. The *lex loci delictis* rule is on the decline, with less than 20 percent of the states following the doctrine. The majority of American jurisdictions follow the "most significant" relationship test.[413] Canada, in contrast, follows a strict *lex loci delictis* rule.[414] Internet torts are frequently committed in multiple jurisdictions, though they may originate on a server in a single jurisdiction. *Lex fori,* or the law of the jurisdiction in which the litigation occurs, has not been adopted widely.[415] Commentators argue that "Article 5(2) of the Berne Convention requires application of the copyright laws of the country where the litigation takes place (lex fori) even if the allegedly infringing acts occurred in another country."[416] "The territoriality-based choice of law rules in multinational copyright infringement cases therefore resemble lex rei sitae rules to some extent."[417] The Berne Convention's choice of law rules have been characterized as "an example of a lex loci delicti rule, as it

---

[409] Porsche Cars v. Porsch.com, 51 F. Supp. 2d 707 (E.D. Va. 1999).

[410] *See Id.* at 10-15 (discussing *in rem* jurisdiction with regards to trademark infringement).

[411] *See* Regina Hong, The Safety Zone, Spotlight: Gray Areas Hinder Web Fraud Probes; Limits on Resources, Time, Jurisdiction Often Leave Investigations in Limbo, L.A. Times (May 10, 1999) at B2.

[412] P.J. Huffstutter, Tech Firms Pay Police Agencies to Fight Cyber Crime, L.A. Times (July 26, 1999) at A1.

[413] Richard H. Acker, Comment, Choice-of-Law Questions in Cyberfraud, 1996 U. Chi. Legal F. 437, 440.

[414] Chris Gosnell, Jurisdiction on the Net: Defining Place in Cyberspace, 29 Canadian Bus. J. 344, 344 (1998).

[415] *Id.* at 447.

[416] Andreas P. Reindl, Choosing Law in Cyberspace: Copyright Conflicts on Global Networks, 19 Mich. J. Int'l 799, 822 (1998).

[417] *Id.* at 806.

relies on the location of the infringing acts to determine the applicable copyright law."[418]

The majority of jurisdictions follow the "most significant relationship" test.[419] The Restatement (Second) of Conflicts presumes that the law of the state where the injury occurs applies unless another state has a more significant relationship.[420] The factors of a "significant relationship" analysis include:

1. The needs of the interstate and international systems;
2. Relevant policies of the forum;
3. Relevant policies of other interested states and the relative interests of those states in the determination of the particular issue;
4. Protection of justified expectations;
5. Basic policies underlying the particular field of law;
6. Certainty, predictability and uniformity of result; and
7. Ease in the determination and application of the law to be applied.[421]

Few courts have applied conflict of law principles to cyberspace. Many firms incorporate choice of law clauses into their standard agreements. Since the rules of Internet jurisdiction are still evolving both domestically and abroad, Internet content providers should endeavor to limit their exposure or to reconcile themselves to the potential risks of doing business on the web. Individuals conducting business online should specify their choice of law in the event of a dispute. Those who are injured in an Internet transaction and require legal intervention may face a winding path before finding a forum willing to hear the case.

Where the parties do not choose the applicable law in Internet transactions, the court will apply a choice of law analysis. First, the court examines whether an actual conflict exists. If a court concludes there is no conflict of law, the forum's law will be applied. If there is a true conflict of law, the court will apply the law of the forum that has the greatest interest in having its law applied. In a torts case, the court will review the connection of each state with the tortious activity. In *CAT Internet Services v. Magazines.com, Inc.,*[422] the plaintiff was a Pennsylvania-based Internet and e-commerce company that owned, licensed, and operated web pages at various domains on the Internet. The plaintiff owned the rights and interest in the domain name *www.magazine.com*, which it purchased in August 1999. Its goal was to sell magazines on its site. Defendant Magazines.com was a Delaware corporation with its principal place of business in Murfreesboro, Tennessee The defendant owned the Internet domain address *www.magazines.com*, through which it sells conventional magazines and magazine subscriptions.

---

[418] *Id.*

[419] *Id.* at 452.

[420] *Id.*

[421] Restatement (Second) of Conflicts § 6 (1971).

[422] 2001 U.S. Dist. LEXIS 8 (E.D. Pa. Jan. 4, 2001).

In December 1999, the plaintiff entered into an agreement with a third party, Magazine Mall, Inc., under which the companies agreed to provide links to Internet domain addresses owned and used by Magazine Mall. The plaintiff discovered that the defendant was utilizing its domain name to redirect Internet traffic to the defendant's web site. Plaintiff Internet company sued defendant magazine seller, alleging tortious interference with actual and prospective contractual relations, abuse of process, and wrongful use of civil proceedings/malicious prosecution. The court conducted a conflict of laws analysis with each cause of action and held that Pennsylvania law applied to the plaintiff's interference with contractual relations and abuse of process claims and that the plaintiff had stated the elements of the claims under Pennsylvania law. In determining the state that has the greater interest in having its law applied, courts may consider such issues as the place where the injury occurred; the place where the conduct causing the injury occurred; the domicile, residence, nationality, place of incorporation, and place of business of the parties; and the place where the relationship, if any, between the parties is centered. The choice of law the court applied favored the plaintiff because Pennsylvania recognized a tort action for interference with prospective contractual relations that was a cause of action not recognized in Tennessee. "Where the law is unsettled, it has been noted that the possibility of conflict is greater."[423]

§ 7.04 PREVENTIVE LAW POINTERS AND INTERNET JURISDICTION GUIDES

[A] Personal Jurisdiction

SPC may file a motion to dismiss for lack of personal jurisdiction if it is summoned into a California or other state court. Courts typically apply a three-pronged test to determine whether sufficient basis exists for specific personal jurisdiction: (1) the defendant must have sufficient "minimum contacts" with the forum state, (2) the claim asserted against the defendant must arise out of those contacts, and (3) the exercise of jurisdiction must be reasonable.[424] These principles apply equally well to cyberspace, although they were formulated in the offline world.

SPC will file a motion to dismiss for lack of personal jurisdiction under Rule 12(b)(2) of the Federal Rules of Civil Procedure if there are insufficient minimum contacts. If SPC challenges personal jurisdiction, the plaintiff will bear the burden of making a prima facie case by alleging facts sufficient to establish jurisdiction over a nonresident defendant. SPC must allege facts contesting jurisdiction as

---

[423] Dostana Enters. LLC v. Federal Express Corp., 2000 U.S. Dist. LEXIS 11726 (S.D.N.Y., Aug. 6, 2000) (quoting Hamilton v. Accu-Tek, 47 F. Supp. 2d 330, 333-34 (E.D.N.Y. 1997)).

[424] Zippo Mfg. Co. v. Zippo Dot Com, Inc., 952 F. Supp. 1119, 1122 (W.D. Pa. 1997) (quoting World Wide Volkswagen Corp. v. Woodson, 444 U.S. 286, 287 (1980)).

"[u]ncontroverted allegations by the plaintiff must be taken as true."[425] If there is a conflict in facts concerning personal jurisdiction, the federal district court must resolve doubts in favor of the plaintiff.[426]

[B]   *In rem* Jurisdiction

SPC must follow the prescribed procedures for filing an *in rem* action under the ACPA. First, SPC must have filed an action against a company or person. Second, SPC must have attempted personal service or have served by publication if personal service was not practical. Third, the ACPA requires SPC to obtain court permission before filing an *in rem* action. SPC has the burden of proving that the domain name violates its trademark rights prior to filing an *in rem* action. The court must grant SPC formal permission prior to filing its lawsuit against the infringing domain name(s). While the ACPA does require the filing of an *in personam* suit first, the court may waive that requirement if the circumstances are such that it "would be fruitless and a waste of resources."[427]

[C]   *Forum Non Conveniens* in Cyberspace

Forum non conveniens is a principle that states, in the ends of justice, that a controversy may be tried in another court and jurisdiction declined. An American court may refuse to decide an Internet-related dispute between nonresidents, which is more appropriately tried in a foreign court. A *forum non conveniens* case is fact-specific with general standards rather than bright-line rules for guidance. A federal court's inherent power to decline to entertain a case over which it has jurisdiction is embodied in the doctrine of *forum non conveniens*. The doctrine serves the ends of justice and the convenience of the parties and their witnesses.[428] Congress enacted 28 U.S.C. § 1404(a), which essentially codified the common law doctrine of *forum non conveniens* in federal courts. "To prevail on a *forum non conveniens* motion to dismiss, the defendant must show as a threshold matter that an adequate alternative forum exists."[429]

In *DiRenzo v. Chodos*,[430] a court reversed the dismissal of an Internet securities fraud case because the trial court gave too little deference to the plaintiffs' choice of forum. The Second Circuit reversed a dismissal of a lawsuit by Nigerian émigrés' under the Alien Tort Claims Act on *forum non conveniens* grounds, holding that the United States was not an inconvenient forum.[431] In *Cable News*

---

[425] Nutrition Physiology Corp. v. Enviros Ltd., 87 F. Supp. 2d 648 (N.D. Tex. 2000) (citing Mink v. AAAA Development LLC, 190 F.3d 335, 335 (5th Cir. 1999)).

[426] *Id.*

[427] Caesars World, Inc. v. Caesars-Palace.com, 112 F. Supp. 2d 502, 50 (E.D. Va. 2000).

[428] DiRenzo v. Chodos, 232 F.3d 49, 56 (2d Cir. 2000).

[429] *See* Peregrine Myanmar Ltd. v. Segal, 89 F.3d 41, 46 (2d Cir. 1996).

[430] 232 F.3d 49 (2d Cir. 2000).

[431] Wiwa v. Royal Dutch Petroluem Co., 226 F.3d 88 (2d Cir. 2000).

Network v. CnnNews.com,[432] CNN filed an *in rem* action under the Anticybersquatting Act against a domain name used by a Chinese web site. The defendant sought to have the case dismissed on *forum non conveniens* grounds because all the defendants were located in China and therefore it would be more convenient to have the trial in China. But the court held that the issue is a domain name and the certificate for the domain name is located within the district. Further, under the ACPA, "the relevant public and private interests favor the forum because it is the situs both of the domain name in issue and of the pertinent registry."[433] The court found little doubt that the CNN trademark was well known throughout Asia, including in China. A defendant's motion to transfer was denied in *About.com, Inc. v. Aptimus, Inc.*[434] in a case which arose out of the failure of the defendant to pay for Internet advertising services. The defendant argued that the contract action should be transferred to Washington to assure that the parties' respective financial means would not affect the outcome of the suit. The court found no evidence for the defendant's assertions concerning the financial well-being of the parties and denied the transfer order.

Venue refers to the locality where a lawsuit may be brought and an action may be dismissed because it is an inconvenient forum.[435] The public policy for having a venue requirement "is to protect defendants from being forced to defend lawsuits in a court remote from their residence or from where the acts underlying the controversy occurred."[436] It is the court's duty to determine whether venue was proper at the time the plaintiff's complaint was filed.[437] SPC may seek transfer of venue if it can demonstrate that the convenience of the parties and interests of justice dictate a transfer under 28 U.S.C. § 1404(a).[438]

SPC may bring a patent infringement lawsuit where the defendant resides or where the defendant has committed acts of infringement and has a regular and established place of business. SPC has a brick-and-mortar place of business in Massachusetts and may be sued in the federal district court of Massachusetts. It may be difficult, however, to determine where acts of infringement occurred when the infringing activity occurs at a defendant's web site. The definition of "where the defendant resides" may be determined by guidelines set out in 28 U.S.C. § 1391(c). In e-commerce patent cases, the special venue statute applies as in any patent infringement lawsuits.

[D] Determining the Identity of Visitors

An online company may limit its jurisdiction by not accepting orders from countries or states where the risk of litigation is too great. In the online order form,

---

[432] 2001 U.S. Dist. LEXIS 21388 (E.D. Va. Dec. 21, 2001).

[433] *Id.*

[434] 2001 U.S. Dist. LEXIS 6102 (S.D.N.Y., May 11, 2001).

[435] Nutrition Physiology Corp. v. Enviros Ltd., 87 F. Supp. 2d 648, 652 (N.D. Tex. 2000).

[436] *Id.*

[437] Hoffman v. Blaski, 363 U.S. 335, 342-344 (1960).

[438] 28 U.S.C. § 1400(b) (2000).

it is important to have visitors designate their country of residence. The web site may use blocking software to automatically reject or disable orders from countries or states presenting unacceptable risks of jurisdiction. Blocking software may also be used to disable orders from countries having an unacceptably high rate of credit card fraud. Software programs also exist that permit the site to choose parameters for targeted sales or services. A company offering online sales of wine or spirits, for example, may not want to take the risk of filling orders in countries or states prohibiting the online sale or importation of liquor. In addition, the web site may post a prominent disclaimer that sales or services are not meant to be targeted for a designated list of countries. It is a cost-benefit analysis for the web site operator to determine which countries or jurisdictions it wishes to block.

[E] Minimum Contacts in Cyberspace

The "minimum contacts" standard for exercise of personal jurisdiction over a nonresident company may be met in two ways: First, a court may assert specific jurisdiction over a nonresident defendant if the defendant has purposefully directed his activities at residents of the forum and the litigation results from alleged injuries that arise out these activities. Second, general jurisdiction may be based on the defendant's overall business contacts. If the contacts are substantial, the court may nonetheless maintain general personal jurisdiction over the defendant based on business contacts with the forum.[439] To obtain jurisdiction over a nonresident company in a federal diversity case, a plaintiff must show both that jurisdiction is proper under the laws of the forum state and that the exercise of jurisdiction does not offend due process.[440] The minimum contacts test has been expanded to cyberspace.

The Due Process Clause of the Fourteenth Amendment permits the exercise of personal jurisdiction over a nonresident defendant "so long as there exists minimum contacts between the defendant and the forum State."[441] To meet the minimum contacts test, an online company must have reasonably anticipated being subject to a court. In addition, a court's exercise of jurisdiction must meet the standards of "fair play and substantial justice." More than 200 cases have been decided on issues of Internet jurisdiction. Section 7.04[G] presents a summary of the factual circumstances where courts found jurisdiction or declined jurisdiction. An increasing number of Internet cases involve multiple factual circumstances. In the first wave of Internet jurisdiction cases, a "sliding scale" applies, in which the greater the commercial activity and interactivity, the more likely that the company is subject to personal jurisdiction.

Courts will seldom find Internet general jurisdiction unless the Internet site specifically directs substantial contacts with the forum. An Internet site directed to

---

[439] Intercon, Inc. v. Bell Atlantic Internet Solutions, Inc. 205 F.3d 1244 (10th Cir. 2000).
[440] *Id.*
[441] World-Wide Volkswagen Corp. v. Woodson, 444 U.S. 286, 291 (1980).

contractors in Massachusetts, for example, would warrant a finding of general juris-diction in Massachusetts. General jurisdiction occurs when the contacts are so sub-stantial and of such a nature as to justify a lawsuit for actions arising from dealing distinct from those activities. In contrast, specific jurisdiction arises when there is a sufficient relationship among the defendant, the cause of action, and the forum.

[F]   Choice of Law and Forum Clauses

Courts will generally uphold choice of law and forum selection clauses.[442] Many companies with an online presence, especially those which license software or service, will want to include a choice of law clause, such as the following:

> _____ grants its customers a nonexclusive, nontransferable license to use the _____ software package. This agreement specifically excludes the United States Convention of Contracts for the International Sale of Goods. All users agree that the laws of the State of _____ govern the agreement, excluding the State of _____ conflict of law rules.

It is also advisable to include a choice of forum clause, because a plaintiff's choice of forum is entitled to substantial deference from the courts.[443] A firm's Internet site can agree to forum selection as well as contain a choice of law clause.

The U.S. Supreme Court validated forum selection clauses in international transactions in _Carnival Cruise Lines v. Shute_.[444] Choice of forum clauses are "_prima facie_ valid."[445] Another court held that there was a rebuttable presumption in favor of the enforcement of forum selection clauses.[446] A New York trial court approved the following Internet Service Provider's forum selection clause in a 1997 case:[447]

---

[442] _See, e.g.,_ Caspi v. Microsoft Network, 732 A.2d 528 (N.J. Super. Ct. App. Div. 1999) (uphold-ing forum-selection clause in Internet service provider agreement).

[443] _See, e.g.,_ Apache Prods. Co. v. Employers Ins. of Wausau, 154 F.R.D. 650, 653 (S.D. Miss. 1994) (listing factors relevant to a change of venue).

[444] 499 U.S. 585, 593-594 (1991) (stating that "[a] clause establishing ex ante the forum for dis-pute resolution has the salutary effect of dispelling any confusion about where suits arising from the contract must be brought and defended, sparing litigants the time and expense of pretrial motions to determine the correct forum and conserving judicial resources that otherwise would be devoted to deciding those motions").

[445] Hirschman v. National Textbook Co., 184 A.D.2d 494, 495 (N.Y. 2d Dept. 1992) (stating that to set aside a forum selection clause a party must show either that enforcement would be unreason-able and unjust or that the clause is invalid because of fraud or overreaching, such that a trial in the forum set in the contract would be so gravely difficult and inconvenient that the challenging party would, for all practical purposes, be deprived of his or her day in court); _see also_ Evolution Online Sys., Inc. v. Koninklijke P77 Nederland, N.V., 145 F.3d 505 (2d Cir. 1998) (noting that forum selec-tion clauses are generally enforced).

[446] TAAC Linhas Aereas de Angela v. TransAmerica, 915 F.2d 1351 (9th Cir. 1990) (validating a forum selection clause that mandated arbitration for disputes arising out of air transportation agreement).

[447] Spera v. AOL, No. 06716/97 (Sup. Ct. N.Y., Dec. 23, 1997) (visited June 30, 1999), http://legal.web.aol.com/decisions/dlother/spera.html.

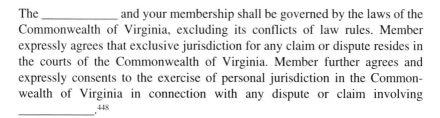

The _____ and your membership shall be governed by the laws of the Commonwealth of Virginia, excluding its conflicts of law rules. Member expressly agrees that exclusive jurisdiction for any claim or dispute resides in the courts of the Commonwealth of Virginia. Member further agrees and expressly consents to the exercise of personal jurisdiction in the Commonwealth of Virginia in connection with any dispute or claim involving _____.[448]

The court found that under the terms of the above forum selection clause, the plaintiff agreed to litigate all claims or disputes between the parties in Virginia. The court rejected a claim that the forum selection clause was an adhesion contract or unconscionable.[449] Litigators will frequently file a motion to dismiss actions in foreign countries on grounds of *forum non conveniens*.

[G]   Factual Circumstances Affecting Internet Jurisdiction Checklists

[1]   Overview

This section is an annotated summary of the key cases on jurisdiction in cyberspace. Minimum contacts in cyberspace frequently centers on whether a defendant has "purposefully availed" itself of the privilege of doing business in the forum. The issue of purposeful availment frequently turns on factual circumstances such as whether the web site targeted residents in the forum state. The first section is a summary of cases that focus on commercial activity based upon web site advertisements. Section two is a summary of cases that touch upon tort and tort-like misconduct. Section three identifies cases that impact online contracts. The last section addresses crimes and regulatory issues.

[2]   Web Page Advertisements

This section is an annotated summary of key cases in which web page advertisements were the key factual circumstance in determining personal jurisdiction in cyberspace. The test for personal jurisdiction is whether a web site advertisement constitutes purposeful availment, thus subjecting the defendant to jurisdiction. Courts frequently focus on whether a given online advertisement is targeting the forum state. The key question is whether the defendant sought out forum residents with advertisements. If the web site advertisement is merely an information source, it is likely to be classified as a passive site. Jurisdiction from a mere web site advertisement without interactive features such as online ordering capacity will be insufficient to confer jurisdiction. The interactivity of the site and the targeting of the advertisement are likely to make the exercise of jurisdiction "reasonable."

---

[448] *Id.*
[449] *Id.*

[a] Finding Jurisdiction

1. A web page advertisement in a local paper soliciting contributions was sufficient to trigger jurisdiction.[450]

2. A web page advertisement and service agreement as well as delivery of software to six New York subscribers was found sufficient for jurisdiction.[451]

3. A mere Internet advertisement and toll-free telephone number for inquiries satisfied jurisdiction.[452]

4. Jurisdiction was found for an out-of-state corporation operating a web site that sold 3,000 passwords to forum state residents, giving them access to newsgroup postings.[453]

5. An interactive web site in conjunction with telephone, e-mail, and personal contacts with a Chicago marketing firm constituted sufficient minimum contacts for jurisdiction in Illinois.[454]

[b] Declining Jurisdiction

1. A passive Internet advertisement alone is an insufficient basis for the exercise of personal jurisdiction.[455]

2. A web site presence alone is insufficient to meet the minimum contacts test.[456]

3. A passive web site that solicited participation in an essay writing contest for children and that posted a toll-free telephone number for contacting the defendant was an insufficient basis for personal jurisdiction.[457]

---

[450] Heroes v. Heroes Found., 958 F. Supp. 1, 4-5 (D.D.C. 1996) (holding that web page and web site advertisement in a local paper soliciting contributions was a sufficient basis for exercise of jurisdiction); Park Inns Int'l, Inc. v. Pacific Plaza Hotels, Inc., 5 F. Supp. 2d 762 (D. Ariz. 1998) (advertising hotel on web site); Shoppers Food Warehouse v. Moreno, 746 A.2d 3120 (D.C. Ct. App. 2000) (basing jurisdiction upon extensive advertising).

[451] American Network, Inc. v. Access America/Connect Atlanta, 975 F. Supp. 494, 498-499 (S.D.N.Y. 1997). *See also* Standard Knitting Ltd. v. Outside Design, Inc., No. 00-288 (E.D. Pa., June 2000) (predicating jurisdiction on interactivity of size and sales in forum of $50,000).

[452] Inset Sys., Inc. v. Instruction Set, Inc., 937 F. Supp. 161, 165 (D. Conn. 1996); Telco Communications v. An Apple A Day, 977 F. Supp. 404, 407 (E.D. Va. 1997) (holding advertisement and solicitation over the Internet via a web site confers jurisdiction).

[453] Zippo Mfg. Co. v. Zippo Dot Com, Inc., 952 F. Supp. 1119 (E.D. Pa. 1997).

[454] Cool Savings.com, Inc. v. IQ Commerce Corp., 53 F. Supp. 2d 2000 (N.D. Ill. 1999).

[455] Cybersell, Inc. v. Cybersell, Inc., 130 F.3d 414, 418-19 (9th Cir. 1997) (holding that an Internet advertisement alone is an insufficient basis for jurisdiction); Ty, Inc. v. Clark, 2000 U.S. Dist. LEXIS 383 (N.D. Ill., Jan. 14, 2000) (declining jurisdiction over Cheshire, England, passive site).

[456] E-Data Corp. v. Micropatent Corp., 1997 WL 805282 (D. Conn. 1997) (finding no jurisdiction based on Internet site alone).

[457] American Homecare Federation, Inc. v. Paragon Scientific Corp., 27 F. Supp. 2d 109 (D. Conn. 1988) (holding out-of-state defendant that sponsored passive web site had insufficient contacts with Connecticut to permit personal jurisdiction).

4. Passive web site advertisement for a Missouri jazz club with the same name as a well-known New York City jazz club was an insufficient basis for jurisdiction.[458]

[3]   Torts or Tort-Like Misconduct

This section focuses on torts or tort-like misconduct in cyberspace. Long-arm statutes were originally enacted to make nonresident motorist accountable for injuries arising out of automobile accidents. Prior to the long-arm statute, the nonresident could cross state borders, avoiding liability. The long-arm statute permitted a court to subject a nonresident motorist to jurisdiction for torts committed in state. In the age of the Internet, torts are committed on web sites that may be accessible by forum residents. The posting of defamatory statements or fraudulent misrepresentations may cause an injury to a resident in the forum. The key issue in torts in cyberspace is when sufficient minimum contacts exist to satisfy the minimum contacts test.

[a]   Finding Jurisdiction

1. Jurisdiction was satisfied in a case involving columnist Matt Drudge, who made an allegedly defamatory statement on his web site about White House aide Sidney Blumenthal.[459]
2. A court found that a web site that permitted Missouri citizens to input their personal information was sufficient to subject a defendant to jurisdiction in a Missouri court.[460]
3. Minimum contacts satisfied due process in an online fraud case where statements about stocks were transmitted via e-mail as well as by telephone.[461]
4. The defendant's posting of a defamatory statement on a web site accessible in Arizona was a sufficient basis for exercising personal jurisdiction.[462]
5. The court held that the tort prong of Mississippi's long-arm statute was satisfied, despite absence of any related sales or other such business activity by defendant in state, because the purpose of defendant's conduct was not to sell goods, but to extort money from owner of mark.[463]

---

[458] Bensusan Restaurant Corp. v. King, 126 F.3d 25 (2d Cir. 1997).

[459] Blumenthal v. Drudge, 992 F. Supp. 44, 54 (D.D.C. 1998). *See also* Blakey v. Continental Airlines, 751 A.2d 538 (N.J. 2000) (holding that employer's knowledge of sexual harassment subjects it to jurisdiction).

[460] Maritz, Inc. v. Cybergold, Inc., 947 F. Supp. 1328 (E.D. Mo. 1996).

[461] Cody v. Ward, 954 F. Supp. 43, 47 (D. Conn. 1997) (holding that fraudulent misrepresentations made via e-mail and telephone messages satisfied minimum contacts test).

[462] Edias Software Int'l, LLC. v. Basis Int'l Ltd., 947 F. Supp. 413 (D. Ariz. 1996).

[463] McRae's, Inc. v. Hussain, 105 F. Supp. 2d 594 (S.D. Miss. June 30, 2000).

6. In *Bochan v. LaFontaine*,[464] a court found that statements made by the defendants on the Internet about an individual known to be a Virginia citizen would satisfy the test of foreseeability. It was foreseeable that the defendant would be haled into court in Virginia for defamatory Internet postings.

7. In another case, the court held that the plaintiff established that the defendant purposefully availed itself of jurisdiction in Louisiana with an allegedly defamatory e-mail.[465]

8. In *Internet Doorway, Inc. v. Parks*,[466] a court denied a defendant's motion to dismiss for lack of personal jurisdiction in an action for falsified e-mail based upon unfair competition and the tort of trespass to chattels. Jurisdiction was based upon the defendant's e-mail solicitation and a tortious injury occurring in the forum state. The court found it reasonably foreseeable that the defendant would be haled into court to answer for the effects of the e-mail solicitation.

9. In an Oregon case,[467] the court refused to set aside a default order in a defamation case on the Internet. The court refused to consider the defenses of failure to state a claim and lack of personal jurisdiction as they were not raised initially or fully briefed.[468]

10. The court in *Gupta v. Rubin*[469] refused to dismiss the plaintiff's case in a tort action based upon the failed financing of an Internet business.

11. The Third Circuit in *Remick v. Manfredy*[470] reversed a district court's order dismissing for lack of jurisdiction in an Internet-related case for breach of contract and tortious interference with contractual relationships.

12. The Ninth Circuit reversed a decision of a lower federal court dismissing its action against a defendant service management company and airplane repair company for lack of specific personal jurisdiction in *Sierra Pacific Airlines v. Dallas Aerospace*.[471] In that case, the defendant made numerous representations about the subject airline engine expressly

---

[464] 68 F. Supp. 2d 692 (E.D. Va. 1999) (finding jurisdiction based upon persistent course of conduct in forum state of Virginia).

[465] Belliono v. Simon, 1999 WL 1059753 (E.D. La. 1999).

[466] 138 F. Supp. 2d 77 (S.D. Miss. 2001) (denying defendant's motion to dismiss for lack of personal jurisdiction ruling that tortious injury occurred in the forum state).

[467] Zwebner v. John Does Anonymous Found., Inc., 2001 U.S. Dist. LEXIS 3298 (D. Or., Feb. 28, 2001) (refusing to set aside a default order in Internet defamation, privacy, and intentional infliction of emotional distress case involving defendant using the name InternetZorro).

[468] *Id.* at *10.

[469] 2001 U.S. Dist. LEXIS 450 (S.D.N.Y., Jan. 25, 2001) (denying defendant's motion to dismiss and granting plaintiff leave to amend complaint).

[470] 238 F.3d 248 (3d Cir. 2001) (reversing dismissal for lack of jurisdiction against defendant boxer; affirming dismissal of claims against other defendants).

[471] 2001 U.S. App. LEXIS 4335 (9th Cir., Mar. 12, 2001) (reversing and remanding case based upon record demonstrating that exercise of specific jurisdiction in the forum would not have been unreasonable).

aimed at the plaintiff in the forum.[472] The court found allegations of intentional conduct and effects expressly aimed at the plaintiff.[473]

13. In *Oasis Corp. v. Judd*,[474] default judgments were entered against defendants who launched a "gripe site" on the Internet under the domain name "boycott-em.com." The default judgments were vacated and the actions rendered moot on the ground that the trademark-based injuries and defamatory remarks were communicated to third persons in Ohio, the forum state.[475] In that case, the defendant established a web site to complain about his insurance company, Oasis. The court found no basis for asserting jurisdiction as the servers were not located in the forum nor was there any meaningful interaction between the web site and the forum state.

14. A federal court dismissed an Internet defamation lawsuit filed by a FBI agent who was blamed for the deaths of passengers on Pan Am Flight 103 on a web site publication.[476]

15. In *Ty, Inc.v.. Baby Me, Inc.*,[477] the maker of Beanie Babies brought an action alleging that the defendant infringed its trademark and trade dress for producing toys confusingly similar to the plaintiff's toys. The defendant moved to dismiss for lack of personal jurisdiction. The court held that, while mere registration of a domain name for a web site by itself was not enough to create personal jurisdiction, the defendant was subject to suit in the forum state based on the defendant's active Internet business, which generated revenue through direct commercial transactions with forum state residents. Despite the defendant's contention that its business was primarily directed toward sales in its resident forum, the defendant chose to and in fact did sell its toys in the forum state. The size of the defendant's business and its significant distance from the forum state were insufficient to render jurisdiction unreasonable or constitute a deprivation of due process.

16. In *Griffs v. Luban*,[478] the defendant repeatedly posted messages in an Internet newsgroup that directly attacked the professional credentials of the respondent and were related to her employment in Alabama. The defendant had challenged the plaintiff's credentials by repeatedly posting defamatory messages online stating that she had received her degree

---

[472] *Id.* at *5.

[473] *Id.* at *6.

[474] 132 F. Supp. 2d 612 (S.D. Ohio 2001) (vacating default judgments and dismissing defamation and trademark infringement lawsuits against gripe-site defendants).

[475] *Id.* at 622.

[476] Revell v. Lidov, 18 Computer & Online Indus. Litig. Rep. 13 (Apr. 13, 2001) (granting motions to dismiss defamation actions on personal jurisdiction grounds).

[477] 2001 U.S. Dist. LEXIS 5761 (N.D. Ill., Apr. 20, 2001).

[478] 633 N.W.2d 548 (Minn. Ct. App. 2001) (reasoning that Minnesota resident defendant should have anticipated that she could be haled into court in Alabama to prove the truth of 100 derogatory messages posted on a chat line between December 1996 and June 1998 about the respondent).

from a "Cracker Jack box." The plaintiff responded in a private e-mail to the appellant, and the University of Alabama posted a message verifying that the respondent had taught noncredit courses in Egyptian history and culture in the university's special studies department since 1980. The plaintiff obtained a judgment against the defendant in Alabama.

The defendant continued to post messages, even after threatened with legal action. The Minnesota court was asked to enforce the default judgment under the Uniform Enforcement of Foreign Judgments Act, which requires a threshold finding of personal jurisdiction. The court found a sufficient basis for jurisdiction because the repeated messages could be, and were, received in Alabama.

17. In *Information Technologies International, Inc. v. ITI of North Florida., Inc.*,[479] the court refused to dismiss an action for lack of personal jurisdiction based on breach of fiduciary duty, breach of contract, and violation of the Illinois Consumer Fraud and Deceptive Business Practices Act. The defendants argued that they were not doing business in the forum state, Illinois, and that the alleged acts of the individuals occurred entirely in Florida. The court found that the individuals directed tortious acts at one company as an Illinois business, because jurisdiction was warranted. The company sufficiently alleged an economic loss attributable to the individuals' actions in redirecting the company's accounts receivable. The individuals reached across state boundaries and into Illinois by hacking into the company's computer system and changing the remittance address to redirect accounts receivable from Illinois to Florida.

[b]   Declining Jurisdiction

1. The operation of a web site available to Indiana residents that allegedly defamed a national corporation and infringed its trademarks was an insufficient basis for personal jurisdiction.[480]

2. A New Jersey court dismissed a female airline pilot's lawsuit for sex discrimination and defamation for statements made on Continental Airline's internal electronic bulletin board. No evidence existed that the pilots targeted their electronic postings for New Jersey, nor was another basis found for personal jurisdiction over the defendant pilots.[481]

---

[479] Info. Techs., Int'l, Inc. v. ITI of N. Fla., Inc., 2001 U.S. Dist. LEXIS 19475 (N.D. Ill. Nov. 26, 2001).

[480] Conseco, Inc. v. Hickerson, No. 29A04-9802-CV-85, 1998 Ind. App. LEXIS 1328 (Ind. Ct. of App., Aug. 14, 1998); *see also* Jewish Org. v. Superior Ct. of L.A. Cty., 72 Cal. App. 4th 1045 (1999).

[481] Blakey v. Continental Airlines, 730 A.2d 854 (N.J. Super. Ct. 1999) (holding that no personal jurisdiction existed for statements made on airline's electronic bulletin board).

3. In *Revell v. Lidov,*[482] the plaintiff sued Columbia University alleging defamation, intentional infliction of emotional distress, conspiracy, and breach of duty arising out of an article published on the Internet posted to the university's web site. The court granted a motion to dismiss, applying the sliding scale test of *Zippo Dot Com.*[483] The court found Columbia's site to be interactive but falling into the passive web site end of the *Zippo* continuum.[484]

4. In *GTE New Media Services v. BellSouth Corp.,*[485] the plaintiff filed a complaint against defendants under the Sherman Antitrust Act arguing that they were engaged in a conspiracy to dominate the Internet business directories' market. The D.C. Circuit reversed the district court, finding no basis for personal jurisdiction where the sole contract was the operation of an Internet web site accessible in the District of Columbia.[486]

5. In *Smith v. Hobby Lobby Stores,*[487] the court declined personal jurisdiction over a Hong Kong manufacturer in a product liability action in which the plaintiff's daughter was killed in a fire caused by a defective artificial Christmas tree. The tree was purchased in an Arkansas store, and the plaintiff sought indemnification from the Hong Kong manufacturer. The court found an insufficient basis for minimum contacts based upon an Internet site where there no Internet sales to Arkansas citizens.

6. In *Black & Decker, Inc. v. Pro-Tech Power, Inc.,*[488] the defendant sold and advertised tools on the Internet. The court found that such a contact was not a purposeful availment of Virginia, the forum state.

7. In *Future Tech. Today, Inc. v. OSF,*[489] a Florida corporation brought an action for breach of contract and conversion against an Illinois corporation. The contract was for the remediation of the plaintiff's computer system to become Y2K ready. The court found no personal jurisdiction because there were no sales over the Internet and all contract negotiations took place by telephone and the defendant never came to Florida.[490]

8. A Missouri court refused to exercise jurisdiction over an out of state casino as a result of an injury suffered from the husband and wife while at the casino.[491] The plaintiffs argued that the casino solicited business in

---

[482] 2001 U.S. Dist. LEXIS 3133 (N.D. Tex., Mar. 21, 2001) (granting motion to dismiss because defendants lacked minimum contacts with the forum state).

[483] *Id.* at *11 (citing Zippo Mfg. Co. v. Zippo Dot Com, Inc., 952 F. Supp. 1119 (W.D. Pa. 1997)).

[484] *Id.* at *12.

[485] GTE New Media Servs. v. BellSouth Corp., 199 F.3d 1343 (D.C. Cir. 2000) (reversing district court on issue of personal jurisdiction but permitting additional discovery on the issue.

[486] *Id.* at 1345.

[487] 968 F. Supp. 1356 (W.D. Ark. 1997).

[488] 26 F. Supp. 2d 834 (E.D. Va. 1998).

[489] 218 F.3d 1247 (11th Cir. 2000).

[490] *Id.* at 1251.

[491] Bell v. Imperial Palace Hotel/Casino, Inc. 2001 U.S. Dist. LEXIS 21450 (E.D. Mo., Oct. 25, 2001).

Missouri based on the casino's maintaining a web site that offered information about it and allowed visitors to the web site to make online hotel reservations. The court held that the nature and quality of the casino's web site did not alone weigh toward an exercise of personal jurisdiction. In that case, there was no contention that the plaintiffs had made arrangements for hotel reservation at the casino via the Internet, nor had they even seen the web site. The court also found that the husband and wife did not show continuous and systematic contacts necessary to make a prima facie case for the exercise of general jurisdiction.

[4] Online Contracts

The next summary of case law focuses on jurisdiction based upon online contracts. In the typical online contract case, the court focuses on contacts between the non-resident and forum resident. For example, where was the contract negotiated? Courts frequently apply the *Zippo* court's continuum in resolving online contract disputes. Was the web site passive or interactive? Did the parties have any contacts such as targeted e-mail advertisements from seller? Where were UCC financing statements filed? For purposes of determining personal jurisdiction in contract actions, an online defendant must have performed some affirmative conduct that allows or promotes the transaction of business within the forum state. Soliciting business in the forum state will generally suffice if it results in contract negotiations or the transaction of business. However, the mere existence of a contract with a forum resident is generally an insufficient basis for jurisdiction.[492]

[a] *Finding Jurisdiction*

1. Jurisdiction was found where Texas citizens entered into contract to gamble on the Internet.[493]
2. A party that made a software contract with an Internet Service Provider in Ohio was subject to jurisdiction to litigate that contract.[494]
3. In *Intercon, Inc. v. Bell Atlantic Internet Solutions, Inc.*,[495] the Tenth Circuit reversed a lower court order dismissing an action against an out-of-state corporation for lack of personal jurisdiction. In that case, a Delaware corporation offered a dial-up Internet service with a similar domain name. The plaintiff's mail server suffered slow-downs due to thousands of unauthorized messages routed through it by defendant.[496]

---

[492] Assad v. Pioneer Balloon, 2001 U.S. App. LEXIS 11944 (9th Cir. June 5, 2001).

[493] Thompson v. Handa-Lopez, Inc., 1998 WL 142300 (W.D. 1998).

[494] Compuserve, Inc. v. Patterson, 89 F.3d 1257 (6th Cir. 1996) (finding jurisdiction based upon contractual relationship and contracts between software provider and marketer).

[495] 205 F.3d 1244 (10th Cir. 2000) (reversing judgment and remanding case because plaintiff made *prima facie* showing of purposeful availment and that personal jurisdiction was reasonable).

[496] *Id.* at 1245-46.

4. A subsidiary was subject to personal jurisdiction after it responded to e-mail inquiries from the forum, issued price quotes on request, discussed the product with a potential partner, purchased parts from the forum, and sent promotional materials to the forum state. The court declined to find jurisdiction against the parent corporations, whose maintenance of web site did not establish personal jurisdiction where all inquiries were forwarded to and handled by the subsidiary.[497]

5. In *Intercon, Inc. v Bell Atlantic Internet Solutions, Inc.*,[498] the defendant's continued use of a server in the forum state, even after it learned that it was not authorized to do so and that the excess use was causing problems for the true owner, supported jurisdiction.

6. In *CoolSavings.Com Inc. v. IQ.Commerce Corp.*,[499] the defendant's interactive coupon web site, coupled with nationwide access to the site, actual use by citizens of the forum state, and additional efforts to create a market in the forum state, justified the exercise of personal jurisdiction);

7. In *Zippo Mfg. Co. v. Zippo Dot Com, Inc.*,[500] a web site that resulted in thousands of contracts with residents of the forum state supported jurisdiction.

[b] Declining Jurisdiction

1. A British bank's passive, informational Internet web site, the filing of Uniform Commercial Code (UCC) financing statements, and filing of five civil cases in Utah to recover monies or foreclose on trust deeds did not constitute substantial and continuous local activity sufficient to subject the bank to general personal jurisdiction under Utah law.[501] In *Barrett v. Lombardi*,[502] the court dismissed a lawsuit against a former co-venturer and corporation arising out of a failed Internet business because of the lack of personal jurisdiction. The First Circuit did not find the corporate defendant's contacts to satisfy a purposeful availment of the privilege of conducting activities in Massachusetts.[503]

---

[497] 3D Sys., Inc. v. Aarotech Labs., Inc., 160 F.3d 1373 (Fed. Cir. 1998).

[498] 205 F.3d 1244 (10th Cir. 2000).

[499] 53 F. Supp. 2d 1000 (N.D. Ill. 1999).

[500] 952 F. Supp. 1119 (W.D. Pa. 1997).

[501] Soma Medical Int'l v. Standard Chartered Bank, 196 F.3d 1292 (10th Cir. 1999) (dismissing action by Utah account-holder against British bank for breach of contract and negligence for disbursing funds upon unauthorized signature). *See also* Bedrejo v. Triple E Canada, Ltd., 984 P.2d 739 (Mont. 1999) (declining jurisdiction over passive web site).

[502] 239 F.3d 23 (1st Cir. 2001) (affirming lower court's dismissal in part for failure to demonstrate personal jurisdiction over corporate defendant).

[503] *Id.* at *7.

2. Jurisdiction was not found because the defendants' only tie to New Jersey under the traditional personal jurisdiction analysis was a contract, which was not substantial enough to constitute minimum contacts.[504]

3. The court affirmed a dismissal against defendants for lack of personal jurisdiction against former co-venturers and corporations alleging contractual claims and torts arising out of failed Internet business in *Barrett v. Lombardi*.[505] The mere acceptance of shares transferred within the forum state does not constitute minimum contacts subjecting a foreign corporation to jurisdiction in the forum state.[506]

[5] Crimes and Regulatory Activity

There have been relatively few cases involving criminal jurisdiction in cyberspace. The earliest criminal jurisdiction case was *United States v. Thomas*,[507] in which a California couple were prosecuted in California for sending pornographic pictures to residents in Tennessee. Courts are more likely to decline jurisdiction in state regulatory cases than in state or federal criminal prosecutions for transmitting pornography on the Internet. The test applied in criminal and regulatory tests is likely to focus on the reasonableness of state prosecution or regulation. Is the state prosecution or regulatory action reasonable to comply with the *International Shoe* "traditional notions of fair play and substantial justice?"

The USA PATRIOT bill, a U.S. antiterrorism statute signed into law on October 26, 2001, expands the types of computer systems that fall under federal jurisdiction to include those belonging to foreigners.[508] The new federal criminal statute permits the United States to charge cybercriminals even if the Internet traffic is merely routed through U.S. computers or routers.[509] An estimated 80 percent of all Internet traffic passes through U.S. computer systems, which means that the United States is asserting jurisdiction over any activity involving "a computer located outside the United States that is used in a manner that affects interstate or foreign commerce or communication of the United States."[510] The PATRIOT bill "expedites telephone taps and e-mail traces, including the power to attach a phone tap or e-mail surveillance order to an individual, as opposed to a device."[511]

---

[504] Amberson Holdings LLC v. Westside Story Newspaper, 110 F. Supp. 2d 332 (D.N.J., Aug. 22, 2000).

[505] 239 F.3d 23 (1st Cir. 2001) (affirming dismissal on grounds of personal jurisdiction).

[506] *Id.* at 27.

[507] 74 F.3d 701 (6th Cir. 1996).

[508] George V. Hulme, Antiterrorism Law Targets Hackers Around the World—Patriot Bill Gives the United States More Power to Prosecute Foreign Cyberhackers, Info. Wk., Dec. 3, 2001.

[509] *Id.* (quoting Mark Rasch, Vice President of Predictive Systems Inc. and former head of the U.S. Department of Justice Computer Crime Unit).

[510] *Id.*

[511] Anti-Terrorist Bills Reach Deep into Cyberspace, Broadband Networking News, Oct. 9, 2001.

[a] Finding Jurisdiction

1. A California couple was convicted of Tennessee obscenity laws based on a Tennessee postal employee's downloading of obscene materials from the defendants' web site.[512]
2. The Minnesota attorney general filed suit against an online gambling site for violating Minnesota's gambling laws.[513] The court found a sufficient basis for jurisdiction, because the site actively solicited subscribers and was accessed by Minnesota residents.
3. A New York court found sufficient personal jurisdiction against a New York defendant's e-mail sales activities on the Internet.[514]

[b] Declining Jurisdiction

1. Court upheld dismissal of criminal charges for Internet sales of beer to out-of-state minors.[515]
2. An Alabama federal court sitting in diversity found no personal jurisdiction where a nonresident defendant made a single sale of beer from its web site.[516] The plaintiff filed a lawsuit against the Illinois corporation for selling beer to her son, asserting a claim under Alabama's Civil Damages Act.[517] The court found an insufficient basis for either general or specific jurisdiction, noting that this was an isolated sale.[518] The court observed that the defendant did not engage in national advertising or otherwise have continuous and systematic contacts with Alabama.[519]
3. A Massachusetts federal court ruled that Massachusetts regulators could not apply Massachusetts cigarette advertising regulations to the Internet.[520]
4. The U.S. Court of Appeals for the District of Columbia found an insufficient basis for jurisdiction in a case involving the Sherman Antitrust

---

[512] United States v. Thomas, 74 F.3d 701 (6th Cir. 1996) (upholding Tennessee criminal convictions against California couple for transmission of obscene materials over Internet). *See also* State v. Cain, 360 Md. 205, 757 A.2d 142 (Md. Ct. App. 2000) (finding jurisdiction in theft by deception case).

[513] State of Minnesota v. Granite Gate Resorts, Inc., 568 N.W.2d 715 (Minn. App. 1997).

[514] Vacco v. Lipsitz, 174 Misc. 2d 571, 663 N.Y.S.2d 468 (Sup. Ct. 1997). *See also* GTE New Media Services Inc. v. Bellsouth Corp., 199 F.3d 1343 (D.C. Cir. 200) (finding jurisdiction in antitrust action); State v. Beer Nuts, Ltd., 29 S.W.3d 828 (Mo. 2000) (finding jurisdiction for soliciting and selling beer in forum).

[515] State v. Amorosa, 975 P.2d 505 (Ct. App. Utah 1999).

[516] Butler v. Beer Across America, 83 F. Supp. 2d 1261 (N.D. Ala. 2000).

[517] The act provides for a civil action by the parent or guardian of a minor against anyone who knowingly and illegally sells or furnishes liquor to the minor. *Id.* at 1262.

[518] *Id.* at 1266.

[519] *Id.* at 1266, n.7.

[520] Lorillard Tobacco Co. v. Reilly, 84 F. Supp. 2d 180 (D. Mass. 2000).

Act where there was only the ability of D.C. residents to access Internet yellow pages.[521]

5. A New York federal court dismissed an antitrust claim against another French company, ruling that it had no jurisdiction to decide the issue.[522]

[6]   Intellectual Property

The final annotations summarize the vast body of case law governing jurisdiction in intellectual property disputes. The majority of the summarized cases concern trademark infringement in cybersquatting cases. The test for personal jurisdiction is frequently whether the defendant purposefully availed himself by harmful acts directed to the plaintiff in the forum. The *Zippo* continuum of whether a web site is interactive or passive has been cited in scores of trademark infringement actions. Recently, there have been a large number of trademark cases under the Federal Trademark Dilution Act and the Anticybersquatting Consumer Protection Act of 1999 (ACPA). The chart summarizes *in personam* actions under the ACPA. Courts determine whether personal jurisdiction applies in Internet cases by examining the level of interactivity and commercial nature of the information found on the web site. The first category includes Internet sites that are highly interactive, allowing users to download, transmit, or exchange information with the defendant via the computer, including online contracts between the defendant and the plaintiff. The second category includes passive web sites that merely provide information. Courts have declined to exercise personal jurisdiction in cases involving merely passive web sites. The third category involves a hybrid of the first two, "involving interactive web sites in which a user can exchange some information with the host computer."[523] In general, courts will not exercise personal jurisdiction where the only contact with the forum is a passive web site. The exercise of personal jurisdiction is far more likely where the forum is interactive and there are only contacts by the nonresident in the forum state. Courts are increasingly looking beyond the *Zippo* continuum to other contacts with the forum state in determining personal jurisdiction.

[a]   *Finding Jurisdiction*

1. A domain name cyberpirate was found liable to a lawsuit in California because his attempt to sell a domain name containing a corporation's famous trademark was deemed sufficient for jurisdiction.[524]

---

[521] GTE New Media Servs., Inc. v. BellSouth, 199 F.3d 1343 (D.C. Cir. 2000).

[522] Filetech v. France Telecom, No. 95 Civ. 1848 (S.D.N.Y., Mar. 22, 2001), reported in 18 Computer & Online Indus. Litig. Rep. 10 (Apr. 24, 2001) (dismissing antitrust claim that France Telecom was engaged in monopolization in violation of the Sherman Act on grounds of Foreign Sovereign Immunity Act, 28 U.S.C. § 1605(a)(2)).

[523] Sunshine Distribution v. The Sports Auth. Mich., Inc, 157 F. Supp. 2d 779, 785 (E.D. Mich. 2001).

[524] Panavision Int'l v. Toeppen, 938 F. Supp. 616 (C.D. Cal. 1996) (finding that the defendant purposefully availed himself by harmful acts directed to the California plaintiff); American Eye-

2. A Colorado company was subject to jurisdiction in Massachusetts because it purposefully directed advertising, an interactive web site, and targeted advertising to Massachusetts customers.[525]

3. A Pennsylvania court found that it had no personal jurisdiction over a nonresident corporation in a trademark infringement lawsuit, given that the company had not transacted business or rendered services in that jurisdiction.[526] A passive site that advertises services is not enough contact with the forum.[527]

4. The act of linking a famous trademark to an adult entertainment site in a trademark infringement case satisfied due process.[528]

5. Federal district court in New York had personal jurisdiction over a California domiciliary in a trademark dilution act under the Federal Trademark Dilution Act and the Anticybersquatting Consumer Protection Act.[529]

6. Specific jurisdiction was proper where the defendant instructed a third-party resident to develop an Internet web site and a home page containing infringing trademarks and using web site to solicit online orders.[530]

7. Specific jurisdiction found in domain name action involving a cybersquatting claim involving famous Barbie trademark.[531]

8. In *Panavision International, L.P. v. Toeppen*,[532] the Ninth Circuit affirmed personal jurisdiction in trademark case filed by owners of the marks PANAVISION® and Panaflex®. In Panavision, Dennis Toeppen registered the domain names panavision.com and panaflex.com, posting pictures of Pan, Illinois, on one web site and the word *hello* on the other.

---

wear, Inc. v. Peeper's Sunglasses & Accessories, 106 F. Supp. 2d 895 (N.D. Tex. 2000) (upholding personal jurisdiction in case involving a cyberpirate who registered domain names with owners' trademarks and offered to sell them back to the rightful owners for a handsome profit).

[525] Hasbro, Inc. v. Clue Computing, Inc., 994 F. Supp. 34 (D. Mass. 1997).

[526] Desktop Technologies, Inc. v. Coloworks Reproduction & Design, Inc., 1999 U.S. Dist LEXIS 1934 (E.D. Pa., Feb. 24, 1999).

[527] *Id.* at *8.

[528] Archdiocese of St. Louis v. Internet Entertainment Group, Inc., 34 F. Supp. 2d 1145 (E.D. Mo., Feb. 12, 1999).

[529] Cello Holdings, LLC v. Dahl, 89 F. Supp. 2d 464 (S.D.N.Y. 2000) (holding that due process was not violated by the exercise of personal jurisdiction in a trademark dilution case brought by the New York holder of the trademark "cello" for use with expensive audio equipment against a California registrant who owned the Internet domain name "cello.com.").

[530] Board of Directors of First Church of Christ the Scientist v. Robinson, 123 F. Supp. 2d 965 (W.D.N.C. 2000) (finding specific personal jurisdiction in contract to develop web site and using site to solicit online orders).

[531] Mattel, Inc. v. Internet Dimensions, Inc., 2000 U.S. Dist. LEXIS 9747 (S.D.N.Y. 2000) (finding sufficient basis for specific personal jurisdiction in case involving trademark infringement, dilution and cybersquatting).

[532] Panavision Int'l, L.P. v. Toeppen, 141 F.3d 1316 (9th Cir. 1998) (affirming exercise of personal jurisdiction over Illinois man for trademark dilution lawsuit in California).

The cybersquatter then attempted to sell the domain names to Panavision. The Ninth Circuit premised jurisdiction on the defendant's intention of doing business in California and tortious attempt to extort money from a California trademark owner. The court upheld jurisdiction, employing the "effects test."

9. In another case, personal specific jurisdiction was found in a declaratory judgment action in a patent infringement case.[533]

10. The court found specific jurisdiction over defendant cybersquatting on the domain name "sweetsuccess.com" The defendant's action of e-mails and telephone calls directed to plaintiff in Pennsylvania to offer to sell the "sweetsuccess.com" domain name was sufficient minimum contacts.[534]

11. Defendant allegedly infringing on trademark "Crate&Barrel" was held to have minimum contacts that established specific personal jurisdiction based upon the defendant's maintenance of interactive Internet web site and solicitation of vendors in Illinois.[535]

12. In *Keelshield, Inc. v. Megaware Keel-Guard, Inc.*,[536] the court refused to dismiss a trademark infringement action on grounds of personal jurisdiction in a cybersquatter case.

13. In *Starmedia Network, Inc. v. Star Media, Inc.*,[537] a federal court refused to dismiss for lack of personal jurisdiction in a case where the defendant registered its domain name and used part of the plaintiff's registered domain name. The court found that the site was commercial and derived substantial income from interstate commerce, including potential sales to New York residents.

14. A court found sufficient minimum contacts to satisfy due process for personal jurisdiction in a case where the owner of a trademark sued a domain name owner alleging infringing its trademark in *Northern Light Technology, Inc. v. Northern Clubs, Inc.*[538]

15. In a trademark dispute over an Internet domain name, the trial court, for lack of personal jurisdiction, dismissed the action over the Georgia defendant.[539] The Ninth Circuit reversed, finding that the defendant engaged in wrongful conduct that individually targeted the plaintiff in California.[540] The court concluded that the plaintiff demonstrated the

---

[533] Stomp, Inc. v. NeatO, LLC, 61 F. Supp. 2d 1074 (C.D. Cal. 1999) (finding jurisdiction in a patent infringement case).

[534] Nutrisystem.com, Inc. v. Easthaven, Ltd., 2000 WL 1781924 (E.D. Pa., Nov. 16, 2000).

[535] Euromarket Designs, Inc. v. Crate & Barrel Ltd., 96 F. Supp. 2d 824 (N.D. Ill., May 16, 2000).

[536] 2001 U.S. Dist. LEXIS 7012 (C.D. Ill., May 11, 2001) (upholding personal jurisdiction in cybersquatting case).

[537] 2001 U.S. Dist. LEXIS 4870 (S.D.N.Y., Apr. 24, 2001).

[538] 97 F. Supp. 2d 96 (D. Mass. 2000).

[539] Bancroft & Masters, Inc. v. Augusta Nat'l, Inc., 223 F.3d 1082 (9th Cir. 2000).

[540] *Id.* at 1088

purposeful availment necessary for an exercise of personal jurisdiction.[541]

16. In *American Bio Medical Corp. v. Peninsula Drug Analysis Co.,*[542] the Delaware court held that a New York plaintiff could file its action against defendants in Delaware for patent infringement and violation of the Lanham Act in the sale of a product called "Rapid Drug Screen." The court found the defendant's activities were aimed at the forum permitting the reasonable exercise of personal jurisdiction. The defendant's forcing the plaintiff to bring suit or lose control of its web site satisfied the effects test.

17. In *Nissan Motor Co., Ltd. v. Nissan Computer Corp.,*[543] the court permitted the exercise of personal jurisdiction over the creator of the web site with the name Nissan used as its domain name. The court found that the defendant directed its activity toward the forum state.

18. A North Carolina court held jurisdiction was proper in a church's trademark infringement claim against a nonresident dissident religious organization and permanently enjoined the dissident organization from displaying infringing marks on a wesite. The court found that the nonresident dissident organization purposefully availed itself of privileges of conducting activities in North Carolina in direct actions to create a connection with North Carolina by downloading the church's web page design onto its domain, located and maintained in North Carolina, "and then consistently sending information, including solicitations for contributions and sales of merchandise."[544] Thus, the North Carolina district court's exercise of specific personal jurisdiction over the dissident organization was constitutionally reasonable.

[b]   Declining Jurisdiction

1. A passive web site that infringes intellectual property rights on the plaintiff's web site alone is an insufficient basis for jurisdiction.[545]

2. A defendant's passive web site was an insufficient basis for a Texas court asserting personal jurisdiction over a Norwegian defendant in a patent infringement lawsuit.[546]

---

[541] *Id.*

[542] 1999 WL 615175 (D. Del. 1999) (holding personal jurisdiction based upon Internet web site and mailings to Delaware).

[543] 89 F. Supp. 2d 1154 (C.D. Cal. 2000).

[544] Christian Science Bd. of Directors of First Church of Christ, Scientist v. Nolan, 259 F.3d 209 (4th Cir. 2001).

[545] Hearst Corp. v. Goldberger, 1997 WL 97097 (S.D.N.Y. 1997) (holding that an infringing site alone did not subject a defendant to New York jurisdiction where there were no sales to New York or any other contact; Mink v. AAAA Dev., L.L.C., 190 F.3d 333 (5th Cir. 1999) (declining jurisdiction in infringement lawsuit because site lacked interactivity).

[546] Agar Corp. v. Multi-Fluid, Inc., 45 U.S.P.Q.2d (BNA 1444) (S.D. Tex. 1997).

3. Personal jurisdiction may not be predicated upon mere availability of an interactive web site to forum residents. The court held that there were insufficient contacts even though the trademark infringement lawsuit arose out of material on the web site.[547]

4. A court granted a defendant web site's motion to dismiss, finding that the court lacked general and specific jurisdiction over the defendant.[548] In *Millennium Enterprises, Inc. v. Millennium Music, Inc.*,[549] a South Carolina defendant sold music in its retail and Internet web sites using the Millennium Music® trademark. The court ruled that there was no purposeful availment based upon sporadic sales in the forum. In that case, the defendants sold only 15 compact discs to nine customers in six states and one foreign country.[550] The only sale in the forum was by a friend of plaintiff's counsel upon his instruction.[551] The court found no purposeful availment upon this "manufactured" contact, dismissing the action.[552]

5. In *America Online v. Chih-Hsien Huang*,[553] a court ruled that a California defendant who registered a domain name that infringed the trademark of the plaintiff was not subject to jurisdiction.

6. In *American Information Corp. v. American Infometrics*,[554] a Maryland federal court dismissed all claims for lack of personal jurisdiction. The defendant in that case was based in California and maintained a web site that could be viewed by anyone with web access. However, a visitor could not enter into a contract or transact business on the site.

7. In *Enterprise Rent-A-Car Co. v. Stowell*,[555] a trademark owner sued a defendant domain name owner for cybersquatting. The motion to dis-

---

[547] Phat Fashions L.L.C. v. Phat Game Athletic Apparel, Inc., 2001 U.S. Dist. LEXIS 113386 (S.D.N.Y., Aug. 13, 2001) (finding personal jurisdiction lacking in absence of business transactions in forum state and that web site and injury in forum state was insufficient); Neogen Corp. v. Neo Gen Screening, Inc., 2000 U.S. Dist. LEXIS 12032 (W.D. Mich., Aug. 21, 2000) (dismissing trademark infringement action for lack of personal jurisdiction); Berthold Types Inc. v. European Mikrograf Corp., 102 F. Supp. 2d 928 (N.D. Ill. 2000) (noting no jurisdiction because of passive site in trademark infringement case).

[548] Millennium Enters., Inc. v. Millennium Music, LP, 33 F. Supp. 2d 907 (D. Or. 1999) (holding that the court lacked general and specific jurisdiction because there was not the requisite minimum contact with the forum).

[549] *Id*. at 909.

[550] *Id*.

[551] *Id*.

[552] *Id*. at 912.

[553] America Online v. Chih-Hsien Huang, 106 F. Supp. 2d 848 (E.D. Va. 2000) (declining to find jurisdiction upon registration of domain name alone).

[554] 2001 U.S. Dist. LEXIS 4534 (D. Md., Apr. 12, 2001) (dismissing action based upon federal trademark and Maryland common law for the defendant's user of plaintiff's service mark and a World Wide Web address; basing decision on *Zippo* test and effects test of *Calder*).

[555] 137 F. Supp. 2d 1141 (E.D. Mo. 2001) (granting defendant's motion to dismiss on grounds of lack of personal jurisdiction in part).

miss was granted on grounds of lack of personal jurisdiction. The defendant's residence was split between another state and the Kingdom. The question was whether mere publication of defendant's *web site* on the Internet was a sufficient contact with the forum. The court found that no forum state visitors to the site purchased classic cars or even contacted the defendant about buying cars. The court transferred the case to the U.S. forum where the defendant resided.

8. A court concluded that it had neither specific nor general jurisdiction in a lawsuit in which the plaintiff claimed that the defendant was publishing its copyrighted photographic images on the Internet without permission.[556]

9. A defendant's motion to dismiss on personal jurisdiction grounds was granted in *Miami Breakers Soccer Club, Inc. v. Women's United Soccer Association*,[557] a trademark infringement and unfair competition case. Minimum contacts was based upon the defendant's participation in a soccer combine and draft, participation in a soccer classic, operation of a web site, defendant's advertising, and planning for a woman's soccer franchise in the forum state.[558]

10. In *Amazon.com, Inc. v. Kalaydjian*,[559] the defendant's motion to dismiss a trademark infringement and dilution lawsuit was granted. In *Amazon.com*, the defendant marketed sun-tanning products in California. The court found no purposeful availment by merely registering a trademark similar to plaintiff's as a domain name and posting a web site on the Internet.[560]

11. In *Rannoch, Inc. v. Rannoch Corp.*,[561] the court held there was not personal jurisdiction over the defendant in a trademark infringement action where the defendant used the plaintiff's registered trademark in its domain name.

12. In *Virtuality v. Bata Limited*,[562] the court did not find specific or general jurisdiction in Maryland based on the defendant's passive web site where the web site provider was located in Canada.

13. The fact that the defendant operates a web site that could be accessed from the forum state was an insufficient basis for finding personal jurisdiction in a Maryland court. The plaintiff sued the foreign publisher defendant for copyright infringement. The negotiations and performance of the contract took place outside of the forum, and the law of another

---

[556] ALS Scan, Inc. v. Wilkins, 2001 U.S. Dist. LEXIS 6605 (D. Md., May 18, 2001).

[557] 2001 U.S. Dist. LEXIS 6392 (S.D. Fla., Apr. 27, 2001).

[558] *Id.* at *4.

[559] 2001 U.S. Dist. LEXIS 4924 (W.D. Wash., Feb. 22, 2001) (granting defendant's motion to dismiss trademark dilution and infringement action).

[560] *Id.* at *16.

[561] 52 F. Supp. 2d 681 (E.D. Va. 1999) (holding that there was no personal jurisdiction over the defendant in trademark infringement action).

[562] 138 F. Supp. 2d 677 (D. Md. 2001).

state governed interpretation of the contract. The web site displayed contact information for the company, including its telephone number and address, along with advertisements and retail prices for the books. In addition, the web site provided at least two ways to order the advertised materials. Visitors could either send an e-mail to the defendant requesting an electronic order form or e-mail a fax number to the defendant so that the order form could be faxed to the potential customer. No orders were ever received through the web site from consumers in Maryland.[563]

14. A court dismissed a trademark infringement case involving an owner of a trademark for cosmetics who sued a clothing manufacturer. The court held that the nonresident owner had no personal contacts with the state, and the manufacturer's sale of the product via the Internet distributor had resulted in insufficient contacts with the state to satisfy due process.[564]

15. A court held personal jurisdiction was not proper in a case where a Washington company brought trademark infringement and dilution claims against a New York company. The defendant's allegedly false assurances that it would not infringe the plaintiff's mark and the allegation that the plaintiff acted with knowledge of the defendant's existence were insufficient to establish personal jurisdiction.[565]

16. A web site that contains a link to an infringing web site is not sufficient to subject it to personal jurisdiction.[566]

17. In *Maynard v. Philadelphia Cervical Collar Co.*,[567] the court held there was no personal jurisdiction over a patent infringement defendant based on a single sale by a third-party distributor to the plaintiff, a single letter to the plaintiff, and a passive web site.

[7] *In Rem* Jurisdiction Under the ACPA

The ACPA makes clear that *in rem* actions may be brought under the ACPA only if *in personam* jurisdiction over the domain name registrant does not exist. However, if *in personam* jurisdiction over the registrant does not exist, then the registrant cannot constitutionally be joined as a necessary party. Service of process under the *in rem* provision of the ACPA is governed by 15 U.S.C.S. § 1125(d)(2)(B), which provides that the actions under 15 U.S.C.S. § 1125(d)(2)(A)(ii) shall constitute service of process.

Section 1125(d)(2)(A)(ii) imposes two requirements for proper service of process: (1) sending a notice of the alleged violation and intent to proceed under this paragraph to the registrant of the domain name at the postal and e-mail address

---

[563] Ottenheimer Publishers, Inc. v. Playmore, Inc., 158 F. Supp. 2d 649 (D. Md. 2001).

[564] Origins Natural Resources, Inc. v. Kotler, 133 F. Supp. 2d 1232 (D.N.M. 2001).

[565] Cognigen Networks, Inc. v. Cognigen Corp., 174 F. Supp. 2d 1134 (W.D. Wash. 2001).

[566] Perry v. Boston Capital Ventures, 2001 U.S. Dist. LEXIS 18789 (W.D.N.Y. Oct. 29, 2001).

[567] 2001 U.S. App. LEXIS 18834 (Fed. Cir. Aug. 15, 2001).

provided by the registrant to the registrar and (2) publishing notice of the action as the court may direct promptly after filing the action.

[a] Finding Jurisdiction

1. In *CNN L.P. v. cnnews.com*,[568] the court found that the plaintiff satisfied the criteria for an *in rem* action under the Anticybersquatting Consumer Protection Act (ACPA). The court ruled that an owner of a mark may maintain an *in rem* action against an infringing domain name (1) if the action is brought in the jurisdiction where the registrar or registry of the infringing domain name is located and (2) if *in personam* jurisdiction over the registrant does not exist.

2. In the *National Collegiate Athletic Association v. NCAABasketballodds.com*,[569] plaintiff NCAA contended that the defendant's registration of a domain name containing the mark NCAA with two domain name registrars violated its rights. The NCAA contended that the defendant's domain names constituted "cyberpiracy" or "cybersquatting" in violation of the ACPA, falsely suggesting an affiliation with, or sponsorship by, the NCAA, thereby confusing and frustrating consumers when they attempt to access official NCAA Internet web sites. The defendant was found to have violated the NCAA's trademark rights under the ACPA, and the NCAA was entitled to the transfer of the defendant domain names.

3. In *Harrods Ltd. v. Sixty Internet Domain Names*,[570] the famous British department store sued the defendants, 60 Internet domain names registered by an Argentinian company, in an *in rem* civil action under the ACPA. The court found *in rem* jurisdiction because *in personam* jurisdiction was lacking over the registrants and entered judgment in favor of the department store, finding that the company that registered the names acted with bad faith intent to profit by the similarity between the names.

[b] Declining Jurisdiction

1. In *Mattel, Inc. v. Barbie-Club*,[571] the court ruled that it lacked subject matter jurisdiction over the claim against the challenging defendant and against any other defendant whose domain name registrar was not located in New York.

2. In *Fleetboston Financial Corp. v. Fleetbostonfinancial.com*,[572] the court held that "ACPA does not provide for in rem jurisdiction except in the

---

[568] CNN L.P. v. CNNNEWS.COM, 162 F. Supp. 2d 484 (E.D. Va. 2001).

[569] 2001 U.S. Dist. LEXIS 20796 (E.D. Va. Jul. 17, 2001).

[570] 157 F. Supp. 2d 658 (E.D. Va. 2001).

[571] 2001 U.S. Dist. LEXIS 5262 (S.D.N.Y. May 1, 2001).

[572] 138 F. Supp. 2d 121 (D. Mass 2001).

judicial district in which the domain name registry, registrar, or other domain name authority is located."

3. In *Shri Ram Chandra Mission v. Sahajmarg*,[573] a domain name registrant and its president were dismissed from the action because of lack of personal jurisdiction. The plaintiff then filed this suit *in rem* against the domain name in question seeking the transfer of the domain name from the current registrant to the plaintiff. The court dismissed the *in rem* action, finding that the ACPA required publication and that a plaintiff in an *in rem* action must have sent a notice by postal mail and e-mail and must have published notice of the action as the court may have directed promptly after filing the action.

4. In *Hartog & Co. v. SWIX.COMF*,[574] the plaintiff sought transfer of the Internet domain names pursuant to the ACPA. The court found that the plaintiff was not entitled to *in rem* relief and entered judgment to that effect. The court found that the domain names were confusingly similar to the plaintiff's mark, but there was no proof of the defendant's bad faith. Among relevant factors, the defendant had properly registered Swiss trademarks rights to the relevant mark for a bona fide business, the defendant's company had used the domain names in the Swiss market in Internet sites accessible under those names since 1996, the defendant's Internet services business was entirely different from the plaintiff's ski products business, and the defendant never intended to divert the plaintiff's customers from plaintiff's own web site. The court also found that the plaintiff had not established dilution by blurring, and dilution through tarnishing did not exist in this case.

---

[573] 139 F. Supp. 2d 721 (E.D. Va. 2001).
[574] 136 F. Supp. 2d 531 (E.D. Va. 2001).

CHAPTER EIGHT

GLOBAL E-BUSINESS LEGAL ISSUES

§ 8.01   Introduction: The Global Legal Marketplace
    [A]   Overview of Global Legal Issues
    [B]   The Internet as a Global Legal System
        [1]   Classical World System Theory
        [2]   The Internet as a Modern World System
        [3]   Core Countries of the Internet
        [4]   Semi-Periphery Internet Countries
        [5]   Countries of the Internet Periphery
        [6]   Global Internet Legal Audits

§ 8.02   International E-Business Legal Audit
    [A]   European Competition Concerns
        [1]   European Union Regulations
        [2]   Licensing Practices and Dominance
    [B]   Intellectual Property Concerns
        [1]   Extraterritoriality
        [2]   National Treatment
        [3]   Most Favored National Status
        [4]   Protecting International Intellectual Property Rights
            [a]   Global Copyright Issues
            [b]   Global Internet Trademark Issues
            [c]   International Domain Name Issues
            [d]   E-Commerce Patents
        [5]   Trade Secrets
        [6]   Web Site Linking
        [7]   Database Protection
        [8]   Moral Rights of Authors
    [C]   International Jurisdiction Issues
        [1]   The Hague Convention on Jurisdiction and Foreign
            Judgments
        [2]   Service of Process Abroad
        [3]   Brussels Regulation
        [4]   ABA Report on Cyberspace Jurisdiction
    [D]   Internet Privacy
    [E]   Third-Party Content
    [F]   Torts, *Delicts,* and Civil Wrongs
    [G]   Internet Advertising
        [1]   European Advertising Standards
        [2]   International Chamber of Commerce Guidelines

[H] Internet Taxation
[I] Online Contract Formation
    [1] UNCITRAL Model Law on Electronic Commerce
    [2] EU Electronic Signature Directive
    [3] EU Distance Selling Directive
    [4] Electronic Commerce Directive
    [5] International Sales of Goods
[J] International Products Liability
[K] Internet Payment Systems
[L] Internet Employment Issues
[M] Internet Regulatory Issues
[N] Global Cybercrime Law Enforcement
    [1] Economic Espionage Act
    [2] The Federal Wiretap Statute
    [3] International Cybercrime Statutes
    [4] Barriers to Internet Criminal Law Enforcement
[O] Consumer Protection
[P] Online Financial Services
[Q] International Standards

§ 8.03 International Business Issues
[A] International Orders for Goods and Services
[B] Exports and Re-Export Licenses
[C] Insuring Against Cyber Risks
[D] Linguistic and Cultural Customization of Global Web Sites

§ 8.04 Resolving International Disputes and Preventive Law Pointers
[A] Conflict of Law, Choice of Law, and Choice of Forum
[B] International Arbitration
[C] Preventive Law Pointers
    [1] Step-by-Step Guide to European Community
         Trademark Applications
    [2] Global Internet Domain Name
    [3] Patent Cooperation Treaty
    [4] Distance Contracts
    [5] International Sales Contracts
    [6] Software Licensing Agreements
    [7] Internet Regulation
    [8] Import and Export Regulation
    [9] Localizing Web Sites
    [10] Minimizing the Risk of Jurisdiction
    [11] Complying with EU Competition Law
        [a] Article 81 of the EC Treaty
        [a] Article 82 of the EC Treaty
    [12] Data Protection Directive

[13] **Enforceability of Forum Selection Clauses**
    [a]   **Introduction**
    [b]   **Explicit Forum Selection Clause**
    [c]   **No Forum Selection Clause**
    [d]   **Probable Unenforceability of a Foreign Judgment**

§ 8.01   INTRODUCTION: THE GLOBAL LEGAL MARKETPLACE

The number of Internet users worldwide passed 530 million in 2001, up from fewer than 200 million users at the end of 1998. By the end of 2005, the number of worldwide Internet users is expected to double to 1.12 billion.[1] The Global Internet Trends report on Internet access and penetration found that 498 million people now have Internet access from home. "In the fourth quarter of 2001, 24 million people gained Internet access at home. The rate of growth of the global Internet population was in the fourth quarter was nearly double the third quarter's 15 million new at-home users."[2]

With this global rise of the Internet, a common Internet vocabulary is rapidly evolving and understood in many countries. The Oxford English Dictionary's online version is including a large number of words from Internet culture: "FAQ, HTTP, HTML, homepage, information superhighway, MP3, search engine, Spam, smiley face, snail mail, WAP, and Y2K."[3] Net speakers share a common vocabulary, but increasingly come from radically different cultures and legal traditions. Quebec, for example, has a requirement that the French language be used on signs and in businesses. A Quebec court ruled that the French language requirement applies equally well to the Internet, acknowledging that the Internet is borderless.[4] The e-Business selling goods or rendering services in foreign countries must comply with different cultural norms as well as statutes, directives, or conventions of supranational organizations as well as different countries.[5] However, the great

---

[1] Computer Industry Almanac, Inc., Internet Users Will Top 1 Billion in 2005; Wireless Internet Users Will Reach 48% in 2005 (visited Apr. 21, 2002), http://www.c-i-a.com/pr032102.htm.

[2] Michael Pastore, At-Home Internet Users Approaching Half Billion (visited Apr. 22, 2002), http://cyberatlas.internet.com/big_picture/geographics/article/0,,5911_986431,00.html.

[3] Kieren McCarthy, More Net-Speak Enters Oxford English Dictionary (June 15, 2001) The Register (visited June 18, 2001), http://www.theregister.co.uk/content/6/19724.html.

[4] Procureur Gen. du Quebec v. Hyperinfo Can., Inc., No.: 550-61-000887-014, Province de Quebec, District de Hull (Can. 2001), http://aix1.uottawa.ca/~geist/hyperinfo.htm, *reported in* Perkins Coie LLP, Internet Case Digest, http://www.perkinscoie.com/casedigest/.

[5] Directives are designed to harmonize European Union member states' laws governing the treatment of various legal rights and remedies. The Data Protection Directive of the European Union, for example, provides a general framework (of individual rights and information practices respecting the processing of personal data, which the Directive applies as any information relating to an identified or identifiable natural person. "The Directive establishes a floor upon which member states may build enhanced information privacy protections. It requires that member states enact national legislation implementing its provisions. . . . The Directive requires generally that, subject to limited exceptions, personal data may be processed only if the data subject has unambiguously given his consent. . . . The Directive gives individuals a right of access to personal data that is subject to processing by the controller of that data, as well as the ability to correct inaccuracies or to erase or block personal data that is processed in a manner inconsistent with the Directive's standards. Under the Directive, the data subject has the right to object to the processing of personal data about him. Finally, the Directive requires member states to provide individuals with judicial remedies and a right to compensation for violations of their rights under the Directive. Federal Trade Commission, European Union Data Protection Directive (visited June 19, 2001), http://www.ftc.gov/reports/privacy/APPENDIXb.htm.

variety, variability, and rapidly changing e-business legal environment in different countries requires web site localization. Web sites need to be customized for languages, currencies, or other national or cultural characteristics.[6] Any e-business transmitting data from any of 15 member states of the European Union (EU) must be aware of each country's data protection law implementing the Data Protection Directive that went into effect in October 1998.[7]

The European Parliament, for example, approved a Directive on Electronic Commerce to apply to the Eurozone.[8] The EU's Data Protection Directive prohibits EU entities from transmitting personal information to the United States and other countries with weak privacy laws.[9] The Eurozone represented by the EU "has common laws, a shared moral vision . . . a single currency and a real political identity."[10] The licensing of software to the Eurozone and other countries raises a host of international issues, including differences in copyright protection, patent protection, trademark protection, trade secret protection, international payment issues, and differences in language and culture.[11]

Europe is ahead of the United States in its development of the wireless Internet.[12] The wireless Internet applications use Wireless Application Protocols. "Conventional Web pages are written in Hypertext Markup Language; WAP sites are written in Wireless Markup Language."[13] Researcher IDC estimates that worldwide wired Internet subscribers will number more than 540 million by the year 2003.[14] The e-Business must take into account differences in legal systems as well as differences in economic development in countries such as Albania, Bulgaria, Barbados, Bulgaria, Cameroon, Great Britain, Herzegovina, Iran, Japan, Kenzy, Norway, Oman, Philippines, St. Helena, Seychelles, and Turkmenistan. Another difference in procedural system is the difference between common-law and civil-law systems. "The common-law systems all derive from England and include

---

[6] Europa, Trading and Marketing on the Internet and in Similar Communication Systems: The Nordic Consumer Ombudsmen's Position Paper (visited Apr. 22, 2002), http://europa.eu.int/comm/internal_market/comcom/newsletter/edition18/page20_en.htm.

[7] The 15 members of the European Union are Austria, Belgium, Denmark, France, Finland, Germany, Greece, Ireland, Italy, Luxembourg, Netherlands, Portugal, Spain, Sweden, and the United Kingdom.

[8] Europa, Adopted by Parliament on May 4, 2000 (visited Apr. 22, 2002), http://europa.eu.int/ISPO/ecommerce/legal/legal.html.

[9] Online Privacy: U.S. About to Come in From the Cold? Wired (Feb. 2001) at 4.

[10] Misha Glenny, How Europe Can Stop Worrying and Learn to Love the Future: Science and Technology Are at the Heart of a New Culture War—Pitting America's Exuberance Against Continental Conservatism, Can We Talk? Wired (Feb. 2001) at 102, 112.

[11] Lisa W. Wannamaker and E. Gail Gunnelis, What to Look for in International Software License Agreements, Gigalaw.com. (visited June 9, 2001), http://www.gigalaw.com/articles/gunnells-2000-05-pl.html.

[12] GSM Europe is the European interest group of the GSM Association, the premier global body behind the world's leading wireless communications standard.

[13] Patricia Daukantis, Feds Wary Over Wireless: Industry Trend or Event, 11 Gov't Computer News 1 (May 21, 2001).

[14] Kim M. Bayne, Wireless Devices: The New Marketing Frontier 10 (Dec. 2000).

Canada, Australia, New Zealand, South Africa, India, and the United States, as well as Israel, Singapore, and Bermuda."[15]

Counsel for an e-business must also have some understanding of civil law traditions in places as diverse as France, Germany, Italy, Spain, and the countries of Latin America. Japan, and China.[16] Countries connected to the global Internet may not embrace U.S. legal norms. China, for example, recently ordered ISPs to monitor private e-mail and impose legal sanctions for illegal postings appearing on web sites they host.[17] The Ministry of Information Industry posted new regulations representing Beijing's latest efforts to tighten its grip on the only major medium in China not requiring that foreign software vendors "guarantee in writing that their products do not contain hidden programs that would allow spying or hacking into Chinese computers."[18] Chinese citizens are not permitted to install foreign-made software into their computer systems, to prevent the Internet from being an instrumentality for political opposition.[19] The civil-law systems originated on the European continent and include those derived from Roman law and canon law.[20] To complicate matters, an e-business may have its core activities in one country and subsidiaries or suppliers in other countries. The e-business must take into account the roles of the EU, United Nations, and the World Trade Organization, as well as the civil and criminal codes of hundreds of countries. The e-Business may be configured "to deflect regulatory, anti-trust or tax laws; others may have emerged from financial maneuvers such as leveraged buyouts; and still others may have been defined in terms of product, function or geography."[21] If an e-Business is involved in sales and services to other countries, it is necessary to follow international and national developments in Internet law.

The e-business shipping goods or rendering service across borders will need to comply with customs and export regimes in each country where it does business. An August 2000 Report by Forrester concluded that approximately half of surveyed companies involved in global trade had difficulties in calculating landed cost and handling regulatory compliance issues.[22] The Internet enables Suffolk Personal Computers (SPC) to market its sales and services to hundreds of countries around the world. As SPC develops the content portion of its web site, it will need to compy not only with national and international laws but also local customs, currencies, and codes. Increasingly, online companies are exporting services

---

[15] The American Law Institute, ALI/UNIDROIT: Principles and Rules of Transnational Civil Procedure (Discussion Draft No. 2, Apr. 12, 2001) at 6.

[16] *Id.*

[17] China Orders Internet Providers to Screen E-mail, Use Less Foreign Software, Siliconvalley.com (visited Jan. 20, 2001), http://siliconvalley.com/docs/news/tech/004019.htm.

[18] *Id.*

[19] *Id.*

[20] *Id.*

[21] Harry W. Arthurs, The Hollowing Out of Corporate Canada, Chapter One in Jane Jenson & Boaventura de Sousa Santos, Globalizing Institutions: Case Studies in Regulation and Innovation 30-31 (2000).

[22] Statistics on Global Trade, Reprinted from Forrester, Delivering the Global Goods (Aug. 2000) (visited May 30, 2001), http://www.tariffic.com/Docs/Newsroom/mediakit1.htm.

as well as sales of goods. With the export of services such as computer consulting, there are no export licenses, import certifications, or export declarations.[23]

This chapter examines emerging e-business and legal issues that cross international borders. The latter portion of this section sets the stage for the international issues that may arise for those dot-com companies that intend to solicit customers outside the United States. Section 8.02 provides a brief overview of the substantive international legal issues. Section 8.03 explores some practical international business issues, and section 8.04 assists with resolving global Internet disputes and provides guidance through preventive law pointers.

[A]   Overview of Global Legal Issues

The shrinking of national boundaries creates new problems in compliance with legal norms and standards. A systematic analysis of international issues is beyond the scope of this section. However, online companies or Internet portals such as Yahoo! that cross national borders must be prepared to comply with international law, foreign laws, and transnational industry standards as well as EU Directives.[24] The basic principles governing online contracts, intellectual property, jurisdiction, choice of law, conflicts of law, and civil and criminal liability apply equally well on the Internet.

American lawyers tend to approach e-commerce with a myopic view, concerned with how U.S. law applies in an international legal environment. However, the correct method of analysis is to examine how key foreign law applies to the U.S. e-business's activities that cross international borders.[25] Localized legal audits must be conducted in countries where sales and services are likely to occur.[26]

---

[23] United States Department of Commerce (Vol. 2) Export America: The Federal Source for Your Global Business Needs 3 (Apr. 2001) (noting that "[t]here is no Shippers Export Declaration, no export licensing, or import certification filed with a service export").

[24] The European Union has a large number of directives on everything from lifts to telecommunications terminals. European Union, The New Approach Directives (visited June 18, 2001), http://www.newapproach.org/directiveList.asp.

[25] We are indebted to Professor Hans Hendrik Lidgard of the University of Lund in Sweden for helping us understand this perspective. Professor Lidgard taught this perspective in his International Business Transactions course as a visiting professor at Suffolk University Law School in the Spring of 2001.

[26] The concept of the legal audit shares much common ground with the methods of financial audits, but the focus is different. The purpose of a legal audit is to prevent legal liabilities and protect rights. Legal auditors will need to learn about how the Internet works as well as business models. This chapter focuses on the international legal issues legal audits of web sites seeking to do business in the global marketplace. Legal auditors will need to understand many of the same factors as financial auditors. The legal audit also needs to understand the "volume, velocity and nature of transactions, taxation, legal and regulatory requirements and accounting policies implemented." Watchdog Tells Auditors to Improve Web Skills, Accountancy Age (Apr. 26, 2001) at 3 (citing findings from Auditing Practice Board of the United Kingdom).

This chapter is a monitoring system for early warning of problems of the global marketplace.[27] The early warning system examines a wide variety of new legal developments and directives, such as regulation of content, contract law, intellectual property law, data protection, and international jurisdiction and the enforcement of judgments.

[B] The Internet as a Global Legal System

If you advise an e-business, you will need to track foreign and international developments to protect rights and avoid infringing the rights of others. The Internet is a global marketplace that potentially includes the home pages for every nation in the world and all territories. One prominent analyst projects that there will be 673 million Internet users worldwide at the end of 2002 and over one billion users by 2005. The slogan is that with the Internet, you can "buy anything, anywhere, anytime."[28] The reality is quite different. Forrester Research found that only a minority of companies are prepared to handle international orders. Most countries willing to accept international orders confine shipping to a few target countries in Europe and Asia.[29] North America is expected to have only a 30 percent share of the world Internet economy by 2005.[30] The Internet global economy is in a process of transformation. Sweden, Norway, and Denmark have the highest percentage of citizens using broadband Internet, which permits information to be received at 10 megabits, which is two hundred times faster than Internet access through a modem.[31] In Western Europe, consumers are unwilling to pay a premium for broadband Internet access and it is predicted that only "10 percent of the households in France, Germany and Britain will have broadband access by 2006."[32]

In the next section, we apply Immanuel Wallerstein's World System Theory to the global Internet marketplace. Wallerstein notes that capitalism has been around since the Sixteenth Century as a basic system originating in Western Europe and expanding to become a global world-economy.[33] In the new millennium, there is a rapidly evolving world system based upon the Internet, software licensing, and transfers of information.

---

[27] Tim Tongson, Turning Risk into Reward: Good Enterprise Risk Management Includes A E-Business's Vision, Strategic Plans, Financial Objectives and Tolerance for Risk, Best's Review (Dec. 2000) at 45, 56 (noting that every organization needs to develop monitoring systems for early warning "to understand emerging experience and sources of profit to achieve long-term success").

[28] Commission Junction (visited Apr. 1, 2002), http://www.cj.com/buyanytime.

[29] Delaney, IBM Signs Outsourcing Contracts, id. at 6.

[30] Ric Duques & Garen K. Staglin, Payment Revisited: Circa 2000 (Payment DNA: A White Paper) (visited June 9, 2001), http://www.eoneglobal.com/whtpaper.html.

[31] BBC News Report, Broadband Access in Sweden (June 21, 2001).

[32] Michael Pastore, Broadband Lacks a European Audience (visited Apr. 19, 2002), http://cyberatlas.internet.com/markets/broadband/article/0,,10099_968611,00.html.

[33] Interview with Immanuel Wallerstein by Linda Skates, Radio New Zealand, Transcribed by Bruce Dyer (visited June 13, 2001), http://www.geocities.com/Athens/Academy/1223/rf20-crisis.html.

[1]   Classical World System Theory

Immanuel Wallerstein sought to explain why the world system evolved in Europe versus another hemisphere.[34] Wallerstein was interested in the emergence of a capitalist world economy from 1300-1450. He divided the world system into (1) core, (2) periphery, and (3) semi-periphery countries.[35] The first core nations to develop were England, France, and Holland in northwestern Europe.[36] The core countries controlled investment as well as production, exploiting the labor forces of periphery countries. The core states of Western Europe "developed strong central governments, extensive bureaucracies and large mercenary armies."[37] The countries of the periphery were at the opposite end of the economic development continuum. During early capitalism, the less-developed regions were Eastern Europe and Latin America.[38] Wallerstein argued that the core countries "expropriated much of the capital surplus generated by the periphery through unequal trade relations."[39]

The semi-periphery regions were in the borderland between core and periphery countries in terms of stages of development. The semi-periphery consisted of countries in decline or peripheral countries "attempting to improve their relative position in the world economic system."[40] Wallerstein classified Portugal and Spain as examples of declining core nations. "Other semi-peripheries at the time were Italy, southern Germany and southern France."[41] The semi-periphery served as "buffer between core and periphery."[42] Wallerstein's world system developed through four stages of growth: (1) the birth of the world system (1300-1450), (2) the consolidation of the states within the new world system (1450-1670), (3) the rise of industrial capitalism (eighteenth century and beyond), and (4) the shift to manufacturing economy in the first decades of the twentieth century.[43]

[2]   The Internet as a Modern World System

If Immanuel Wallerstein's theory was updated to explain the rise of the Internet as a dynamic system, he would classify the United States as the core hegemonic power of the information age world economy. The Internet got its start in

---

[34] "History, in illuminating the past, illuminates the present, and in illuminating the present, illuminates the future." Benjamin N. Cardozo, Nature of the Judicial Process 53 (1921).

[35] Immanuel Wallerstein, The Modern World System I: Capitalist Agriculture and the Origins of the European World Economy in the Sixteenth Century (1974).

[36] Modern History Sourcebook: Summary of Wallerstein on World System Theory (June 13, 2001), http://www.fordham.edu/halsall/mod/wallerstein.html.

[37] *Id.* at 2.

[38] *Id.*

[39] *Id.*

[40] *Id.* at 3.

[41] *Id.*

[42] Bert N. Adams & R.A. Sydie, Sociological Theory 458 (2001) (discussing Wallerstein's world system theory).

[43] Modern History Sourcebook, Summary of Wallerstein on World System Theory, *id.* at 4-5.

the United States as a project of the U.S. government. "The Internet is a global network of networks enabling computers of all kinds to directly and transparently communicate and share services throughout much of the world."[44] The global e-Business universe may be divided into core, periphery, and semi-periphery countries based upon the level of business activity. The Computer Industry Almanac reports that "by the year 2001, 490 million people around the world will have Internet access. Only 15 countries account for nearly 82 percent of worldwide users."[45] Today's world system is based upon transborder information flow on the Internet rather than traditional trade routes.[46] The worldwide trade framework of the World Trade Organization[47] consists of 135 members including China, Russia, former Soviet republics, Taiwan, and Saudi Arabia has spearheaded the development of a world system.[48]

[3] Core Countries of the Internet

The core nations of the Internet are those of North America and Western Europe, and Japan, South Korea, Australia, and New Zealand, which have large numbers of Internet users, Internet hosts, and a high proportion of citizens owning personal computers.[49] "Europe, Japan, and a host of other countries represent large, sophisticated markets for all types of e-commerce activities."[50] As a practical matter, selected core countries will likely be the targets for most e-business

---

[44] Internet Society (ISOC): All About the Internet (visited Apr. 12, 2002), http://www.isocdot.org/internet.

[45] Cyber Atlas, The World's Online Populations (visited Mar. 12, 2001), http://cyberatlas.internet.com.

[46] Peter Keen et. al., Electronic Commerce Relationships: Trust by Design 81 (2000) (discussing transborder information flow as basis of e-commerce).

[47] The World Trade Organization is an international organization devoted to developing rules for world trade and lowering trade barriers. "Decisions in the WTO are typically taken by consensus among all member countries and they are ratified by members' parliaments. Trade friction is channeled into the WTO's dispute settlement process where the focus is on interpreting agreements and commitments, and how to ensure those countries' trade policies conform to them. That way, the risk of disputes spilling over into political or military conflict is reduced." World Trade Organization, The WTO in Brief (visited June 15, 2001), http://www.wtodot.org/english/thewto_e/whatis_e/inbrief_e/inbr00_e.htm. The WTO describes its role in lowering trade barriers as breaking "other barriers between peoples and nations." *Id.*

[48] Henry T. King, The WTO: What It Does and Doesn't Do, How it Affects U.S. Business, 22 Middle East Executive Rep. 8 (Oct. 1999).

[49] The top 15 core countries in descending order of share of Internet users are (1) United States (36.2%); (2) Japan (7.18%); (3) Germany (5.10%); (4) U.K. (4.77%) (5) China (4.20%); (6) Canada (4.05%); (7) South Korea (3.95%); (8) Italy (3.08%); (9) Brazil (2.84%); (10) France (2.39%); (11) Australia (2.16%); (12) Russia (1.77%); (13) Taiwan (1.73%); (14) Netherlands (1.45%); and (15) Spain (1.39%). The U.S. has 33% Share of Internet Users Worldwide Year-End 2000 According to the Computer Industry Almanac (quoting Egil Juliussen) (visited Mar. 12, 2001), http://www.cla.com/200103iu.htm.

[50] Gregory J. Kirsch, Strategies for the Use of Patents by Start-up Internet Companies, Gigalaw.com (visited June 9, 2001), htp://www.gigalaw.com/articles/kirsch-2000-07-p5.html.

activities. The Internet economy grew up in a span of less than 10 years in contrast to the capitalist world economy that evolved over centuries. The Information Age economy was built on the interconnected network of computers that originated in the United States and expanded to core developed countries. The Internet was pre-figured in a 1973 project of the U.S. Defense Advanced Research Projects Agency (DARPA).[51] The purpose of the Internet was "develop communication protocols which would allow networked computers to communicate transparently across multiple, linked packet networks."[52]

In the mid-1980s, the U.S. National Science Foundation (NSF) developed the major backbone communication service for the Internet which was based on packet switching.[53] The United States' primary trading partners are Canada, Mexico, and the Eurozone countries as well as Japan and a few other Asian countries.[54] When Amazon.com was founded in 1995, it did business in 45 countries and all U.S. states within a month's time.[55] Core countries sometimes join forces with semi-periphery countries, as was the case with the North American Free Trade Agreement (NAFTA) that joined the United States, Canada, and Mexico. Mexico is making the transition from semi-periphery to core, and soon all NAFTA members will be classified as core nations. Mexican businesses earned 20 percent of their total sales from Internet-related sales in 2001.[56] The core countries of Europe belong to the EU,[57] whereas the Asian nations are members of ASEAN.[58]

The southern "cone of South America formed a regional trade framework called Mercosur whereas the Andean Pact countries have joined forces."[59] The United States is by far the most important core nation in the Internet economy, accounting for more than a third of world users (36.2 percent of 135.7 million). The United States also is core of the top domains in the new economy. For example, the most popular web sites visited by United Kingdom Internet users were predominately American sites: (1) Yahoo; (2) Freeserve; (3) MSN; (4) Microsoft; (5) AOL; (6) GeoCities; (7) Demon; (8) Amazon; (9) Excite; and (10) BBC.[60] The

---

[51] Internet Society (ISOC), A Brief History of the Internet and Related Networks (visited June 13, 2001), http://www.isocdot.org/internet/history/cerf.html.

[52] Id.

[53] Id. at 1.

[54] Helen Marano, World Trade on Tour, 2 Export Am. 17 (Apr. 2001).

[55] Elsenpeter and Velte, note 3, at 10.

[56] Clair Saliba, Study: Global Slice for Online Sales To Double in 2001, E-Commerce Times (May 31, 2001) (citing IDC study) (visited May 30, 2001), http://www.ecommercetimes.com/perl/story/10141.html.

[57] The European Union accounts for "376 million people who happen to speak 11 languages and use 14 currencies." Frank Ros, Meet Your New Advisory Board, Wired (Apr. 2001) at 194, 196.

[58] Henry T. King, The WTO: What It Does and Doesn't Do, How It Affects U.S. Businesses, 22 Middle East Executive Rep. 8 (1999).

[59] Id. The Andean Pact countries include Colombia, Ecuador, Peru, and Bolivia, Joanna Ramey, Firms Urge Andean Pact Action: Andean Trade Preference Act, WWD, Oct. 9, 2001 (available on LEXIS).

[60] Cyberatlas, Geographics: European Internet Audience Data (visited Apr. 18, 2002), http://cyberatlas.internet.com.

EU members, Canada, Australia, New Zealand, and Japan would also be classifiable as core countries.[61] The Eurozone is a critical center for a "burgeoning Internet Culture . . . where Internet usage within the EU surged from 18 to 28 percent in 2000."[62] The relatively developed economies of Asia, Africa, and South America account for most of the semi-periphery zones. Brazil is one of the few Latin American countries in the core. China has an estimated 16.9 million Internet users out of a population of 1.3 billion.[63]

[4] Semi-Periphery Internet Countries

The semi-periphery countries lie in the borderline between the most developed core countries and the least developed periphery countries. Semi-periphery countries of the new economy are typically found in Asia, Latin America, and Eastern Europe. Malaysia has recently proposed the creation of an Internet Code of Conduct that would make sites accountable for their content.[64] The less-developed nations of the semi-periphery do not have the seamless distribution networks for delivering or storing goods that are taken for granted in core countries. Many online businesses refuse to fill orders in semi-periphery and periphery countries because they do not have local warehouses or are unable to compute price, delivery, taxes, and tariffs accurately.[65] Core countries have policies that facilitate electronic commerce. The United States presently has a moratorium on Internet taxes and on new, multiple, and discriminatory taxes on e-commerce.[66] E-businesses are frequently reluctant to fill international orders in general because of the inability to "accurately measure the total cost of fulfillment."[67] The semi-periphery countries are rapidly revamping their laws to protect intellectual property rights.

Semi-periphery countries have a lower percentage of Internet users and a relatively low level of e-commerce in contrast to the core countries. East Asia contains a number of semi-periphery countries, including China, Indonesia, Malaysia,

---

[61] Canada, for example, trades chiefly with other core countries such as the United States, the United Kingdom, and Eurozone countries. The foreign investors, in Canada, also tend to be foreign investors from core countries. Sixty-three percent of the foreign investors originate in the United States, versus 23 percent from European Union Countries. Japan investors constitute 4 percent of foreign investors in Canada. Harry W. Arthurs, "The Hollowing Out of Corporate Canada?" Chapter One in Jane Jenson & Boaventura de Sousa Santos, Globalizing Institutions: Case Studies in Regulation and Innovation (2000).

[62] Misha Glenny, Howe Europe Can Stop Worrying and Learn to Love the Future, id. at 112.

[63] Jiang-yu Wang, The Internet and E-Commerce in China: Regulations, Judicial Views, and Government Policies, 18 The Computer & Internet Lawyer 12 (Jan. 2001) (reporting that "China's Internet user population and its infrastructure capacity will double each year").

[64] Michael Geist, BNA's Internet Law News (May 30, 2001) (reporting Internet news story at http://technology.scmp.com/ZZZJ287W5NC.html).

[65] Forrester Report, Mastering Commerce Logistics (Aug. 1999), reprinted as Tariff Product Fact Sheet (visited May 30, 2001), http://tariffic.com/Docs/Newsroom/mediakit1.htm.

[66] Dorgan Says Business Activity Nexus Issues Slowing Progress on Internet Tax Legislation, Pike & Fischer Internet Law & Regulation (May 18, 2001) at 1.

[67] Id. at 6.

Philippines, and Thailand. "Microsoft India has played a key role in the development of India as a semi-periphery state supplying core states with programming and other infrastructure for the software industry."[68] India is considered to be a "pocket of excellence" in the Internet economy.[69] In contrast, Turkey is a country whose government seeks to control its citizens' contacts with the Internet.[70] Turkey's Parliament enacted a statute that imposed similar restrictions on Internet publishing as are currently imposed for print media. The statute enacted by the Turkish Parliament did not include the requirement that government approval be secured prior to setting up a web site.[71]

Brazil is the largest and most important influential semi-periphery country in South America and will likely soon achieve core nation status.[72] India is likely to become a key player in e-commerce, but only "2.5 percent of the Indian population is online" accounting for "less than one per cent of India's retail sales."[73] Semi-periphery countries able to make the transition from semi-periphery to core tend to promote Internet policies that are less local or parochial.[74] "The leading Latin American markets today are Brazil, Mexico, Argentina, and Chile,"[75] which are semi-periphery countries in the process of transition. However other countries of the semi-periphery have slipped from core status or are unable to make the transition to the new information economy. Semi-periphery countries need to revamp telecommunications laws to make the transition to core status. The key barriers to developing e-commerce are "telecommunications services, non-competitive transportation and delivery services, weak or non-existent electronic payment systems infrastructures and onerous merchandising restrictions."[76]

---

[68] Local Software Industry Gains Useful Experience, Saigon Times (Apr. 17, 2001).

[69] *See generally* Osama Manzar, et. al, The Internet Economy of India (2001); *see* Madanmohan Rao, Emerging Markets, Pockets of Excellence, India in a Global Internet Economy (visited Apr. 18, 2002), http://www.isoc.org/oti/articles/0401/rao2.html (describing India as a "pocket of excellence" in the Global Internet economy).

[70] Turkish Draft Law Sparks Outcry in E-Media Sector, reported in, Michael Geist's BNA's Internet Law News (June 1, 20001) (reporting draft Turkish media law, which would require the country's Internet Web site operators to submit their pages to a prosecutor before publication in http://www.siliconvalley.com/docs/news/reuters_wire/1237085l.htm)).

[71] Turkey Passes Law Restricting Internet Publishing, Gigalaw.com (June 8, 2001) (citing article published in The Wall Street Journal).

[72] Brazil has an economy which is ranked eighth in the world, larger than those of Mexico, Argentina, and Chile combined, RIO 2001, 2 Export Am. 25 (Apr. 2001).

[73] Daksha Baxi, IFA Asia Regional Conference on E-Commerce and International Taxation, 3 Tax Planning Int'l E-Commerce 15 (Jan. 2001).

[74] *Id.*

[75] Madanmohan Rao, Emerging Markets, Pockets of Excellence: India in a Global Internet Economy (visited June 18, 2001), htp://www.isoc.org/oti/articles/0401/rao2.html.

[76] Third Annual Report, U.S. Government Working Group on Electronic Commerce, Leadership for the New Millennium: Delivering on Digital Progress and Prosperity 52 (2000).

[5] Countries of the Internet Periphery

Periphery countries are defined here as nations having a low level of Internet usage and relatively few computer servers. One key measure of whether a country is in the periphery is a population with an Internet usage rate of 10 percent or less. Another key indicator of periphery status is a low number of host servers. The periphery countries would consist of nations with low percentages of Internet users, personal computer owners, or with few host servers. Nepal is an example of a country where the telecommunications infrastructure is weak.[77] Some countries of Southeast Asia (Vietnam, Thailand, Myanmar, and Cambodia) "only recently opened [their] gates to the Internet."[78] Peripheral countries would include the least developed countries of Africa: Chad, Cameroon, Central African Republic, and Rwanda. African countries that are likely to develop their Internet market are South Africa, Dubai, and Tunisia.[79] Dubai, for example, launched a "tax-free Internet City."[80] The periphery would also include less developed countries (LDCs) in Latin America, such as Haiti and the Dominican Republic. The countries of the periphery and semi-periphery argue that new global standards disproportionately benefit core counties. The United States has been lobbying LDCs to ratify WIPO[81] treaties on minimum intellectual property protection.[82] The Organization for Economic Cooperation and Development (OECD) has been attacked as "threatening the fiscal sovereignty of jurisdiction of small states."[83]

---

[77] Larry Press, Electronic Commerce in Nepal, On the Internet (visited June 18, 2001), http://www.isoc.org/oti/articles/0401/press.html (reporting initial connectivity to the Internet in 1994 and only 9,000 ISPs).

[78] Madanmohan, Rao, The Internet in Laos: A Rough Guide (visited June 18, 2001), http://www.isoc.org/oti/articles/0401/rao3.html.

[79] Rao, Pockets of Excellence, *id.*

[80] *Id.*

[81] "The World Intellectual Property Organization (WIPO) is an international organization dedicated to promoting the use and protection of works of the human spirit. These works—intellectual property—are expanding the bounds of science and technology and enriching the world of the arts. Through its work, WIPO plays an important role in enhancing the quality and enjoyment of life, as well as creating real wealth for nations. With headquarters in Geneva, Switzerland, WIPO is one of the 16 specialized agencies of the United Nations system of organizations. It administers 21 international treaties dealing with different aspects of intellectual property protection. WIPO counts 175 nations as member states. Please visit the links below for more information—both general and specific—on WIPO." World Intellectual Property Organization, About WIPO (visited Apr. 16, 2002), http://wipodot.org/about-wipo/en.

[82] The WIPO and the United States Patent & Trademark Office cosponsored a conference for African states on the need to protect intellectual property rights in Kenya in 1999 and Senegal in 2000. The U.S. Department of Commerce has held similar seminars on protecting intellectual property rights in Lagos, Nigeria, Gaborone, Botswana, and Windhoek, Namibia. Third Annual Report, U.S. Government Working Group; Madanmohan Rao, Emerging Markets, Pockets of Excellence: India in a Global Internet Economy (visited Apr. 18, 2002), http://www.isoc.org/oti/articles/0401/rao2.htmlp on Electronic Commerce, Leadership for the New Millennium: Delivering on Digital Progress and Prosperity 53 (2000).

[83] Jeffrey Owens, OECD, Paris, Promoting Fair Tax Competition, 3 Tax Planning International E-Commerce 17 (Jan. 2001).

The Internet is just one of the major factors stimulating economic globalization. The seamless Internet has linked the core nations with the periphery and semi-periphery. Economic globalization has three principal causes: (1) liberalized international trade and the movement of capital, (2) accelerating technological progress and the rise of the Internet, and (3) deregulation.[84]

[6] Global Internet Legal Audits

An e-business will need to decide where to focus its international business transactions. An e-business is a transnational corporation that is increasingly being regulated worldwide. The managerial culture of the e-business must reconfigure its business processes to comply with diverse legal norms and standards. A transnational e-business must theoretically take into account the national legislation of any country where technology is transferred or sales and services rendered.

This chapter discusses the importance of restructuring and reconfiguring legal audits to globalize the e-business. A legal audit will need to take into account the European Commission's rules on competition as well as national legislation. Directive 95/46/EC on the Protection of Individuals with Regard to the Processing of Personal Data and on the Free Movement of Such Data applies to the Internet just as it applies to the brick-and-mortar world.[85] American companies need to comply with U.S. privacy protections as well as the privacy protections in other countries when doing business on the Internet.

E-businesses need to comply with privacy protections, intellectual property protections, competition law, and international private law rules. The Internet counselor will identify global legal vulnerabilities and offer advice for the drafting of remedial plans, compliance guidelines, legal forms, and employee training. If the e-business retains outside counsel, the results of the audit may be protected by attorney-client privilege. With the results of the audit in hand, and in consultation with outside counsel, the potential hazards or violations should be ranked, from those posing great danger to those with negligible risk. The greatest risks in the Internet world economy will be in core countries where SPC's computers are sold and software is licensed. A Business-to-Business (B2B) exchange between SPC and a European trading partner may involve the exchange of sensitive customer data subject to the European Union Directive on Data Protection. If an e-business seeks to do business in the semi-periphery or periphery countries, it must also take into account the less-developed legal infrastructure to protect intellectual property.

---

[84] European Parliament, Glossary: Economic Globalization (visited Apr. 22, 2002) http://www.europa.eu.int/scadplus/leg/en/cig/g4000g.htm#g2 (explaining economic globalization as a function of "the liberalisation of international trade and capital movements; accelerating technological progress and the advent of the information society").

[85] Directive 95/46/EC on the Protection of Individuals with Regard to the Processing of Personal Data and on the Free Movement of Such Data (visited Apr. 15, 2002), http://www.cdtdot.org/privacy/eudirective/EU-Directive_.html.

It is crucial that e-businesses balance the costs and benefits of risky Internet business policies and practices. Nevertheless, conducting periodic self-audits will protect the corporate name and assets while avoiding costly litigation or possible fines and reducing legal bills. A legal audit must also take into account the allocation of risk for cargo theft in transnational sales. The next section is a legal audit for global self-audits of international issues. Preventive measures must be implemented before an e-business launches its web site. In addition to the Internet legal audit, the e-business should seek out other ways to protect its interests, such as indemnification or insurance. The chapter concludes with a review of e-commerce insurance coverage and providers as well as alternative dispute resolution options. The legal audit needs to track national and international regulation with an emphasis on the core countries that may affect the e-business.

§ 8.02   INTERNATIONAL E-BUSINESS LEGAL AUDIT

The following sections provide brief overviews of each substantive field of global Internet law. First, we look at how European competition rules compare to the U.S. antitrust law. Next come intellectual property concerns, which include copyright, trademark, domain name issues, linking, framing, e-commerce patents, and trade secrets. Also covered are issues that many online businesses may not have considered, such as jurisdiction, privacy issues, third-party content, tort liability, advertising, and taxation.

[A]   European Competition Concerns

The e-business executive needs some broad understanding of the major legal institutions of the European Community. The *European Council* refers to meetings of the heads of state of the 15 European Union member states. The *Council of the Union* is the European Union's main decision-making institution. It consists of the ministers of the 15 member states responsible for the matters on the agenda: foreign affairs, farming, industry, transport, or emergent issues.

The *European Commission* "is a body with powers of initiative, implementation, management and control . . . composed of twenty independent members (two each from France, Germany, Italy, Spain and the United Kingdom and one each from all the other countries)."[86] The *European Parliament* is the elected body representing the 370 million EU citizens and consists of 626 directly elected representatives of member states. The European Parliament "considers the Commission's proposals and is associated with the Council in the legislative process, in some cases as co-legislator, by means of various procedures (codecision procedure, cooperation procedure, assent, and advisory opinions among other activities)."[87]

---

[86] European Parliament, Glossary: Institutions, Policies & Enlargement of the European Union (visited Apr. 19, 2002), http://www.europa.eu.int/scadplus/leg/en/cig/g4000e.htm#e18.

[87] *Id.*

The European Union's key Internet-related directives encompass e-commerce, electronic signatures, distance selling, data protection, databases, copyrights/patents, encryption, conditional access, e-money, telecoms/electronic communications, and cybercrimes.[88]

[1] European Union Regulations

This section briefly examines European Competition Regulations that share common ground with U.S. antitrust law. E-businesses accepting orders for goods are involved in international business transactions. The e-business needs to comply with the competition rules of the EU Commission as well as national authorities.

The European Commission is the chief legal institution responsible for applying the legal framework for ensuring free competition in the Single Market. The EC Competition Rules are found in Articles 81 and 82 of the Treaty of Rome.[89] European competition law consists of national legislation in individual member states as well as regulations applying across the EU. The overarching purpose of European competition law is to eliminate barriers to trade. The Treaty of Rome created the European Community in 1957 to promote the free movement of goods and prevent anti-competitive practices.[90] The Treaty of Rome Articles 30 to 37 called for eliminating quantitative restrictions on trade between Member States to facilitate the free movement of goods.[91] Article 36 requires the protection of industrial and commercial property and the elimination of arbitrary discrimination or restrictions on trade.[92]

The European Commission has challenged a number of high-profile mergers. The online company must weigh the risk of anticompetitive effects against the potential efficiencies of the merger. Have you weighed this risk against potential efficiencies of the merger? Mergers or potential takeovers must be audited for their anticompetitive effects.

The European telecommunications industry tends to be dominated by state monopolies or a single quasi-government entity in many countries. In less developed countries, consumers must deal with high prices and long waits for hookups. Telecommunications regulatory reform is a high priority throughout much of Europe. Bottlenecks in telecommunications are a chief obstacle to the growth of

---

[88] Clifford Chance, EU Legislation (visited Apr. 22, 2002), http://www.cliffordchance.com/uk/practice-areas/e-commerce/leg-pol/eu/ (summarizing Directive 20000/31/EC (2000) (Electronic Commerce); Directive 1999/93/EC (2000) (Electronic Signatures); Directive 97/7/EC (1997) (Distance Selling); Directive 95/46/EC (1995) (Data Protection); Directive 96/9/EC (1996) (Database); Directive 2001/29/EC (2001) (Copyrights/Patents); Council Regulation no 3381/94 (1994) (Encryption); Directive 98/84/EC (1998) (Conditional Access); Directive 2000/46/EC (2000) (E-Money); and Convention on Cybercrime).

[89] UK Department of Trade & Industry, European Community Competition Law (visited Apr. 17, 2001), http://www.dti.gov.uk/cacp/cp/eurocom.htm.

[90] *See generally* Terrence Prime, European Intellectual Property Law 1 (2000).

[91] *Id.* at 5.

[92] *Id.*

e-commerce in many countries.[93] Monopoly telecommunications providers in Europe and other regions have abused their dominant position and thwarted competition for Internet Services.[94] Competition in telecommunications is a critical priority for the Eurozone.

[2] Licensing Practices and Dominance

The licensing of online information must comply with U.S. antitrust law as well as European competition law.[95] The e-business needs to do a careful study of its licensing practices to determine whether it complies with European competition law.

Many of the licensing terms routinely included in software distribution agreements may be challenged as anticompetitive. For example, pricing terms in software license agreements may be found to be anticompetitive under EU standards that differ from U.S. antitrust law. Another questionable clause is one that restricts distribution by geographic areas. Licensing agreements considered unobjectionable in the United States may be the subject of a European competition investigation. It is questionable to include rebates for loyalty by an e-business considered to be in a dominant position.[96]

Microsoft has been investigated since the mid-1990s for its licensing practices in the distribution of software. Microsoft, for example, has been charged with anticompetitive conduct in its licensing practices in the United States and Europe. Microsoft's release of Windows 95 led to the antitrust suit in *Caldera, Inc. v. Microsoft Corp.*[97] In *Caldera*, the plaintiff claimed that Microsoft's licensing practices were designed to eliminate the threat of DOS as a competitor.

EU competition law does not permit the restriction of passive sales. The block exemption on vertical restraints only applies to "active sales into a territory" providing "that they are designed to protect an exclusive territory or customer group allocated to a distributor."[98] The concepts of "active" and "passive" sales are difficult to apply to the Internet.[99] One of the difficult issues in assessing competition law is to extend the concept of vertical guidelines to the Internet. The EU's Competition Commissioners are investigating the distinction between "active" and "passive" sales on the Internet:

---

[93] Daksha Baxi, IFA Asia Regional Conference on E-Commerce and International Taxation, 3 Tax Planning International E-Commerce 14, 15 (Jan. 2001).

[94] *Id.* at 48.

[95] The European legal community generally refers to antitrust as competition law. *See* Slaughter and May, An Outline Guide to Takeovers in the United Kingdom (2001) (describing UK Competition Legislation, EU Competition Rules and UK Competition Referral and EC Compassion Proceedings).

[96] *Id.*

[97] 72 F. Supp. 2d 1259 (D. Utah 1999).

[98] *Id.*

[99] *Id.*

The solution we have adopted in our vertical guidelines considers that using a web-site to distribute products is in general considered a form of passive selling and that every distributor must be free to use the Internet to advertise and sell products. Clauses preventing a distributor from selling online would only be permissible if a certain specific use of the Internet amounted to active sales. In addition, the approach adopted distinguishes between taking steps to help customers find an Internet Site (active sales) and taking steps to facilitate sales to customers who have already found the site (passive sites).[100]

[B] Intellectual Property Concerns

An e-business must protect its intellectual property in the global marketplace of the Internet.[101] The online business must make certain that it does not lose its intellectual property in the fast-paced digital environment.[102]

Most companies lack the resources to protect intellectual property rights in every country connected to the Internet. The first step is to do an intellectual property audit, i.e., to inventory the intellectual property owned by the e-business and determine what steps should be taken to protect rights and avoid liability. The 1994 agreement on Trade-Related Aspects of Intellectual Property (TRIPS) provides a minimum floor for intellectual property on the Internet.[103] Under the TRIPS agreement, the term of a protection for works, other than photographic works or works of applied art, shall be no less than 50 years from the point of publication.[104] TRIPs provide copyright protection for data compilations in machine-readable form.[105] Copyright protection "shall not extend to the data or material itself. . . ."[106]

An e-business selling goods and services in continental Europe must also take into account moral rights not recognized under U.S. law. The e-business needs to acquire moral rights or seek permission to alter materials on a web site. Content license agreements, for example, need to include terms covering moral rights that may not be recognized under U.S. copyright law whereas trademark, copyright, and patent rights enforceable in the United States do not apply to the borderless Internet.

---

[100] *Id.*

[101] "The new digital environment which sustains the emergence of the Information Society dramatically changes the economics of content. The Internet is one gigantic copying machine. All copyrighted works can now be digitized and, once put on the Net or on any particular off-line medium, copying tends to be effortless, costless, widespread and immediate." European Union, Intellectual Property Rights (IRP) (visited Apr. 17, 2002), http://europa.eu.int/ISPO/ecommerce/issues/ipr.html.

[102] *Id.* "Controlling the distribution and the usage of IPR protected digital material has become a major concern to the emergence of electronic commerce applications dealing with immaterial goods." *Id.*

[103] The members of the World Trade Organization that developed TRIPS had 134 members on Feb. 10, 1999. Paul Goldstein, Cases and Materials on International Intellectual Property 36 (2000).

[104] TRIPS Agreement, *id.* at Art. 12 (stating Term of Protection).

[105] *Id.* at 10(2).

[106] *Id.*

[1] Extraterritoriality

In general, intellectual property rights are left to each nation to enforce.[107] A copyright infringement claim may not be brought in the United States for conduct committed entirely outside the territorial boundaries of the United States.[108] Copyright law has no extraterritorial effect, and infringing actions that take place entirely outside the United States are not actionable.[109] However, the territoriality doctrine means that an e-business must take steps to protect its intellectual property outside the United States. Intellectual property on the Internet presents a challenge to the principle of territoriality because "intellectual property rights in a single object can simultaneously exist, and be exploited, in dozens of countries."[110]

Courts will have jurisdiction "to apply the Lanham Act to allegedly infringing conduct occurring outside the United States when necessary to prevent harm to United States commerce."[111] In determining whether the Lanham Act is given extraterritorial effect, courts consider the following three factors: (1) whether the defendant is a United States citizen; (2) whether a conflict exists between the defendant's trademark rights under foreign law and the plaintiff's rights under domestic law; and (3) whether the defendant's conduct has a substantial effect on United States commerce.[112] Extraterritorial application of intellectual property may not be available for conduct occurring outside the United States.[113]

Extraterritoriality may be found where a U.S. citizen is the controlling force behind a corporation which is placing orders for allegedly infringing goods.[114] A key factor in applying the extraterritoriality doctrine is whether a foreign infringer's activity has a substantial effect on U.S. commerce that will cause consumer confusion.[115] In a trademark infringement case involving imports, the "defendants' reliance on foreign imports to further their alleged infringing scheme, defendants' orchestration of their foreign activities from the United States, and the high probability of consumer confusion both in the U.S. and abroad clearly established a substantial effect on U.S. commerce warranting extraterritoriality to be applied."[116]

---

[107] "United States courts have generally been reluctant to accept cases involving extraterritorial infringement." Mark A. Lemley et al., Software and Internet Law 766 (2000) (discussing doctrine of extraterritoriality).

[108] Subafilms, Ltd. v. MGM-Pathe Communications Co., 24 F.3d 1088 (9th Cir. 1994) (en banc).

[109] Id.

[110] Paul Goldstein, Cases and Materials on International Intellectual Property, id. at 18.

[111] A.V. by Versace v. Gianni Versace, 126 F. Supp. 2d 328 (S.D.N.Y. 2001) (holding that injunction barring infringing actions taking place outside of United States could be given extraterritorial effect, given the circumstances of the case).

[112] Id. at 336 (discussing Vanity Fair Mills, Inc. v. T. Eaton Co. 234 F.2d 633 (2d Cir. 1956)).

[113] The leading case on extraterritorial application of the Lanham Act is Steele v. Bulova Watch Co., 344 U.S. 280 (1952) (affirming injunction prohibiting sale of ersatz Bulova watches in Mexico because sales adversely affected Bulova's reputation in the United States and abroad).

[114] Id. at 338.

[115] Id. at 339

[116] A.V. by Versace v. Gianni Versace, 126 F. Supp. 2d 328, 341 (S.D.N.Y. 2001).

[2] National Treatment

The overarching purpose of the WTO has been to create a rule of law to govern world trade.[117] All of the core countries are part of the WTO, and it has a disproportionate influence on the Ministerial Conference.[118] The WTO is devising global Internet rules in its new multilateral Trade Round. The United States has actively lobbied the WTO to make the Internet a tariff-free zone.[119] Seventy-nine countries are signatories to the WTO Agreement on Basic Telecommunications, and 71 countries "have agreed to adopt pro-competitive regulatory principles."[120]

The movement to protect intellectual property in the international arena began with two late nineteenth-century treaties, the 1883 Paris Convention and the 1889 Berne Convention.[121] Victor Hugo founded the Association Literaire et Artistique Internationale (ALAI) in Paris in 1878 to develop "an international convention for the protection of literary and artistic property."[122] The Berne Convention of Literary and Artistic Works grants worldwide copyright protection in member states including the United States.[123] The Berne Convention recognizes the concept of national treatment. Article 5(1) of the Berne Convention, 1971 Paris Text, provides that authors shall enjoy in protecting countries "the rights which their respective laws do now or may hereafter grant to their nationals, as well as the rights specifically granted by the Convention."[124] The Berne Convention was effective only after March 1, 1989, and is not retroactive.[125] "The Berne Convention does not give copyright protection to works produced without copyright notices prior to March 1, 1989."[126]

National treatment is a bedrock principle of multi-lateral and regional trade agreements. For example, the "GATT-Uruguay Round . . . set intellectual property on the path of globalization by creating universal minimum standards."[127] National treatment is also embodied in Article 3 of the Agreement on Trade-Related

---

[117] Mario Monti, EU Competition, *id.*

[118] *Id.*

[119] Global Information Infrastructure Commission, Electronic Commerce: A Comparison of U.S., EU, MITI, and GIIC Reports on Electronic Commerce (Mar. 27, 1998) (visited June 3, 2001), http://www.giicdot.org/focus/ecommerce/eccompares.html.

[120] Third Annual Report, U.S. Government Working Group on Electronic Commerce, Leadership for the New Millennium: Delivering on Digital Progress and Prosperity 46 (2000).

[121] Samuel K. Murumba, Intellectual Property in the Global Marketplace, N.Y. L.J. 2 (May 23, 2000).

[122] Jennifer L. Shotz, Intellectual Property at Columbia Law School, Columbia Law Report 5 (Spr. 2001) (describing how Columbia Law School houses the headquarters of the United States branch of the ALAI).

[123] The Berne Convention had 140 member state signatories as of July 15, 1999. Paul Goldstein, International Legal Materials on Intellectual Property 148 (2000).

[124] Paul Goldstein, Cases and Materials, *id.* at 20.

[125] Edward F. Langs, Software Licensing Agreements 53 (1994).

[126] *Id.*

[127] Murumba, Intellectual Property in the Global Marketplace, *id.*

Aspects of Intellectual Property Rights (TRIPS Agreement).[128] Article 3 of the TRIPS Agreement states that "[e]ach Member shall accord to the nationals of other Members treatment no less favorable than that it accords to its own nationals with regard to the protection of intellectual property."[129]

[3] Most Favored Nation Status

The concept of the Most Favored Nation (MFN) treatment is basic to the World Trade Organization that includes General Agreement on Tariffs and Trade (GATT) (goods), General Agreement on Trade in Services (GATS) (services), and Trade-Related Intellectual Property (TRIPS) (intellectual property).[130] Article 4 of the TRIPS agreement gives most-favored national treatment to all other signatories.[131] National treatment is fundamental to the entire WTO framework that applies equally well to world e-commerce. The WTO encompasses the GATT and the GATS as well as TRIPS.[132] MFN status grants trade preferences to countries that give similar preferences to the United States.[133] MFN status allows businesses that import foreign goods into the United States to benefit from lower tariffs on exported goods.

[4] Protecting International Intellectual Property Rights

[a] *Global Copyright Issues*

Copyright persists in works of authorship meeting the requirements of originality and fixation. Copyright protects software as well as "HTML code and design features" of web sites.[134] Materials posted on a web site must satisfy the originality requirement as well as the fixation requirements to receive copyright protection. As noted in Chapter Four, it is advisable that a copyright notice be

---

[128] Testimony of Andrew Pincus, General Counsel, House Commerce Telecommunications, Trade and Consumer Protection, Copyright Protection of Information on the Internet, FDCH Congressional Testimony (June 19, 1999).

[129] Agreement on Trade-Related Aspects of Intellectual Property Rights, Including Trade in Counterfeit Goods, *id.* at Art. 3.

[130] Henry T. King Jr., The WTO: What It Does and Doesn't Do, How It Affects U.S. Businesses, 22 Middle East Executive Reports 8 (Oct. 1999).

[131] Article 4 states: "With regard to the protection of intellectual property, any advantage, favor, privilege or immunity granted by a Member to the nationals of any other country shall be accorded immediately and unconditionally to the nationals of all other Members." Agreement on Trade-Related Aspects of Intellectual Property Rights, Including Trade in Counterfeit Goods (1994) at Art. 6.

[132] *Id.*

[133] Fair Trade Watch, What Is Most Favored Nation Status? (visited Apr. 14, 2002), http://www.fairtradewatchdot.org/MFNwhatis.html.

[134] Ron N. Dreben & Johanna L. Werbach, Top 10 Things to Consider in Developing an Electronic Commerce Web Site, 16 The Computer Lawyer 17 (May 1999).

affixed to materials on web sites. As of March 1, 1989, no notice is required.[135] Copyright notices are advisable to put infringers on notice worldwide that material on a web site is protected by copyright. Even though a copyright notice is not required by the Berne Convention, "[n]otice defeats any claim by an 'innocent' infringer."[136] The web site and material posted must have been registered with the U.S. Copyright Office. Copyright registration is required to file an action in U.S. federal court for infringement.[137] An online company with headquarters in the United States is likely to obtain initial copyright registration in the U.S. Copyright Office. Registration does not generally apply to foreign plaintiffs.[138] Many countries connected to the Internet belong to multilateral or regional treaties that provide copyright protection to U.S. citizens.

The online company must also avoid infringing the copyrights of third parties connected to the Internet. It is considered a prima facie case of copyright infringement to post or download copyrighted information without permission. In the United States, the burden of proof for copyright infringement requires the plaintiff to demonstrate ownership of a valid copyright, and the defendant's unauthorized copying is not protected by fair use or other defenses.[139] An e-business may have exposure to claims based upon vicarious or contributory infringement if it permits or discourages illegal copying of software, music, or other data from its web site. In the United States, simple linking is likely not going to lead to a claim of copyright infringement against an e-business. However, linking may result in copyright infringement claims in other nation states.[140]

Copyright issues frequently interrelate with employment law when it comes to web sites. An e-business needs to prevent employees or independent contractors from exploiting web site copyrighted materials or a copyrighted web site. If a target country follows the work-for-hire doctrine, there should also be employment agreements assigning web site copyrights to the company. If the U.S.-based e-business contracts with a foreign web site consultant or designer, it is possible that the consultant will own the copyright in the web site content or its design.[141]

---

[135] Berne Convention Implementation Act of 1988, codified at 17 U.S.C. § 405(d) (2002).

[136] Edward Langs, Software Licensing Agreements 53 (1994).

[137] 17 U.S.C. § 411(a) (2002).

[138] *Id.* (noting that "[a]s a general rule, under American law, the prelitigation registration does not apply to foreign (i.e., non-American) authors including persons or companies who initially acquired copyright protection under the Canadian Copyright Act, and by virtue of the international copyright conventions, acquired copyright protection in the United States (unless publication occurred simultaneously in Canada and the United States).").

[139] Playboy Enters., Inc. v. Hardenburgh, 982 F. Supp. 503 (N.D. Ohio 1997).

[140] In France or Germany, it is illegal to link to web sites advocating National Socialism. A French court ordered an ISP to cease linking to a plaintiff's site with infringing materials. *See* Perkins Coie LLP: Internet Case Digest (visited June 2, 2001), http://www.perkinscoie.com/casedigest/icd_results.cfm?keyword1=international&topic=International (reporting Integra v. STI Calvacom, Trib. Com. Nanterre (ord. Ref. June 10, 1996)).

[141] *See* Mark Lemley et. al., Software and Internet Law 649 (2000) (noting that computer programs produced by employees may vest copyright with the employee rather than the employer).

Do the authors of web sites have moral rights that need to be taken into account? Even if a copyright is transferred, the author may still have moral rights, such as the right "to claim authorship in the work and to object to any distortion, mutilation, or modification" of the copyrighted works.[142] A web site developer may claim that the site may not be modified nor have its "look and feel" changed because of his personal moral right. Moral rights need to be assigned to the company to avoid such issues.

Under U.S. law, many databases do not qualify for copyright protection because they do not satisfy the originality requirement. An e-business may have databases that have the requisite creativity to be protected as "original works of authorship."[143] In contrast, the European Union gives a 15-year term of protection, called *sui generis* protection.[144] The term *sui generis* is Latin for "of its own kind."[145] In the context of intellectual property law, *sui generis* protection is special-purpose legislation covering a narrow category of intellectual property. Another example of *sui generis* legislation was the Semiconductor Chip Protection Act of 1984.[146] An intellectual property audit must also determine whether the online company is unfairly extracting data from the databases of third parties. Unfair misappropriation of data may infringe the *sui generis* or database rights and constitute copyright infringement under the European Parliament's Copyright and Rights in Database Regulation (1997).

Another key difference between U.S. law and the law of other countries is the doctrine of fair use. Keep in mind that when U.S. materials are used in Canada, the Canadian doctrine of fair use applies, not the liberal fair use rule of the U.S. Copyright Act of 1976.[147] Another difference is that the First Amendment may permit copying that would otherwise be infringing. Foreign courts may have a different view of copyright infringement on the Internet. A Netherlands appeals court reversed a lower court ruling that music and movie file trading on the Internet violates copyright law.[148]

[i]   Multilateral Copyright Treaties

[A] Berne Convention and TRIPS. The United States is a signatory to the Berne Convention and the Stock Agreement of July 14, 1967, which created a world organization for copyrights and for revision of related treaties as well as the

---

[142] *Id.* at 54.

[143] In *Feist Publications, Inc. v. Rural Telephone Serv., Co.*, 499 U.S. 340 (1991), the Supreme Court held that a mere compilation of facts was not protected under copyright law because it lacks originality.

[144] Database Directive, *id.* at Art. 10

[145] James A. Ballentine, Ballentine's Law Dictionary 1236 (3d ed. 1964).

[146] Mark Lemley, Software and Internet Law 727 (2000).

[147] *Id.*

[148] John Borland, Ruling Bolsters File-Traders' Prospects, C/Net News.com (Mar. 28, 2002), http://news.com.com/2100-1023-870396.html (reporting that the Dutch company distributing file-swapping software used by Grokster and Sharman networks was not liable for copyright infringements and other illegal actions by people using their software).

TRIPS Agreement. The Berne Convention treats computer programs—whether in source or object code—as literary works.[149] The United States is also a member of the TRIPS Agreement. Each of these treaties provides the United States with MFN treatment. Members of TRIPS agree to comply with the 1971 Berne Convention. Under the terms of the Berne Convention, copyright protection extends to expression but not ideas.[150] Computer software—whether source or object code—is protected as a literary work under the Berne Convention.[151]

Citizens of the United States enjoy copyright protection in any member country of TRIPS so long as registration is properly executed in the U.S. Copyright Office. The U.S. law of copyright protects *works of authorship*, which are defined by statute to include such creations as literary works, musical works, dramatic works, pantomimes, and pictorial works, motion pictures, and multimedia works such as streaming video.[152] As described in Chapter Four, copyright protection is accorded to original works fixed in a tangible medium of expression.[153]

[B] WIPO copyright treaties. The United States is a member of a number of bilateral, regional, and multilateral treaties. Many of the global intellectual property treaties are administered by the World Intellectual Property Organization (WIPO).[154] The United States is a member of global intellectual property treaties administered by WIPO, which is a specialized agency of the United Nations. The purpose of WIPO is to protect intellectual property rights worldwide. WIPO was

---

[149] Peter Maggs et al., Internet and Computer Law: Cases, Comments & Questions 267 (2001) (excerpting International Business Machines, Technical Board of Appeal of the European Patent Office, 1999, Case No. T 0935/97-3.5.1).

[150] TRIPS Agreement, *id.* at Art. 9(2).

[151] *Id.* at Art. 10.

[152] 17 U.S.C. § 102(a) (2000).

[153] *Id.*

[154] WIPO classifies intellectual property into three groups. The first group is for intellectual property protection in each nation state. "The second general group, known as the global protection system treaties, ensures that one international registration or filing will have effect in any of the relevant signatory States. The services provided by WIPO under these treaties simplify and reduce the cost of making individual applications or filings in all the countries in which protection is sought for a given intellectual property right. The third and final general group is the classification treaties, which create classification systems that organize information concerning inventions, trademarks and industrial designs." World Intellectual Property Organization, Treaties and Contracting Parties (visited June 16, 2001), http://wipo.org/treaties/index.html. The Patent Law Treaty, Trademark Law Treaty, and Berne Convention for the Protection of Literary and Artistic Works are examples of the first group for intellectual property protection in a given nation state. The Patent Cooperation Treaty and the Madrid Agreement Concerning the International Protection of Trademarks are examples of global protection system treaties. These treaties make it easier for signatory states to file centrally to avoid local filings. Classification treaties have a narrower role of making it easier to organize trademarks, inventions, and designs. The Locano Agreement covering industrial designs is a classification treaty, as is the Nice Agreement for the Registration of Marks. *Id.*

formed by a Convention signed at Stockholm, Sweden, on July 14, 1967. One of the WIPO's most important roles is to administer multilateral treaties dealing with intellectual property law.[155] WIPO's International Bureau of Intellectual Property administers intellectual property-related treaties.[156] WIPO spearheaded two Internet-related copyright treaties on December 20, 1996.[157] The two Internet Treaties were the "WIPO Copyright Treaty (WCT) and the WIPO Performance and Phonograms Treaty (WPPT)."[158] The purpose of the WIPO Copyright Treaty of 1996 was to develop remedies against the "circumvention of effective technological measures" to protect Internet-related copyrights.[159] The WIPO Copyright Treaty provided legal remedies for the illicit removal or alteration of "electronic rights management information."[160]

The United States enacted the Digital Millennium Copyright Act of 1998 (DMCA), which implemented the WIPO copyright treaties. The thrust of the WIPO Copyright Treaty is to require all signatories to give adequate protection and remedies against circumventing technological protection measures.[161] Section 1201 of the DMCA amends Chapter 12 of the U.S. Copyright Act of 1976 to prohibit the circumvention of access control technology and trafficking in devices to circumvent copyright.[162] The WIPO Copyright Treaty and the WIPO Performances and Phonograms Treaty have been ratified by the United States but do not go into force until 30 countries ratify them.

The DMCA limits a service provider's liability for transmitting, routing, providing connections for, or providing intermediate storage of material that infringes a copyright provided certain conditions are met. To qualify for a "safe harbor" from copyright infringement claims, the provider must implement a procedure for terminating repeat violators. The provider also must have no knowledge of or financial benefit from the infringement. The DMCA requires service providers to post information on how to report copyright infringement.[163] The provider must also remove infringing materials once given notice of the infringing activity on its site. The e-business must register an agent with the U.S. Copyright Office to receive complaints about infringement. The e-business must prominently post information how to contact the copyright agent on its web site. Finally, the DMCA

---

[155] Anita Sharma, Esq., was the source for this brief introduction to the World Intellectual Property Organization.

[156] Convention Establishing the World Intellectual Property Organization, signed at Stockholm on July 14, 1967, and as amended on September 28, 1979, Art. 2 (ii).

[157] The WIPO Copyright Treaties are available at http://www.wipodot.org/treaties/ip/wipo-copyright/index.html.

[158] Intellectual Property: WIPO Urges EU to Accelerate Ratification of Internet Treaties, 178 Tech Europe 1 (Dec. 23, 2000).

[159] WIPO Copyright Treaty, *id.* at Art. 11 (WIPO Copyright Treaty adopted by the Diplomatic Conference on Dec. 20, 1996).

[160] *Id.* at Art 12 (1)(i).

[161] *Id.*

[162] Section 1201(a) of the Digital Millennium Copyright Act of 1998.

[163] *See* Chapter Four for an extended discussion of the DMCA.

requires the provider to inform account holders and subscribers of its policy of terminating repeat infringers. Anticircumvention devices are used to protect JPEG images, DVDs, and MP3 music files.

[C] *European Commission Copyright Directive.* The EU's Council of Ministers approved the Directive on Copyright in the Information Society on April 9, 2001.[164] The Directive gives emphasis to " 'new' Information society products and services (both on-line and off line via CDs for example)."[165] The Copyright Directive will enable the EU to ratify the WIPO "Internet" treaties, which were adopted in 1996. EU Member States now have 18 months to implement the Directive.[166] The Directive harmonizes principles such as the anticopying devices and rights management systems with provisions that parallel the DMCA. The Copyright Directive creates a copyright law exception permitting network operators to make temporary copies without violating European copyright law.[167] Service providers, telecommunications operators, and providers will be permitted to make temporary cache copies under the Directive. This exception permits network operators and providers to efficiently transmit copyrighted material over the Internet. The Directive has also created an exception for reproduction or copying for teaching, "where a copyrightholder has in place an anti-copying device."[168] The Directive rules on the circumvention of anticopying devices were the most controversial.[169] The Europeans consider the new Copyright Directive as an essential party of the legal infrastructure for remaining competitive.[170]

[b] Global Internet Trademark Issues

Trademarks evolved with the "growth of machine-made merchandise" in the early eighteenth century.[171] A trademark was traditionally defined as "a word symbol, figure, form, or device . . . used by a manufacturer or vendor of goods, to designate the origin or ownership of his goods, and used by him to distinguish his

---

[164] The European Commission, Europa, Commission Welcomes Adoption of the Directive on Copyright in the Information Society by the Council (visited Apr. 12, 2002), http://europa.eu/comm/ionternal_market/en/intpropp/news/copyright.htm.

[165] European Commission, Commission Welcomes Council Agreement on a Directive on Copyright in the Information Society (visited June 13, 2001), http://europa.eu.int/comm/internal_market/en/intprop/intprop/news/601.htm.

[166] EU Ministers Approve New Digital Copyright Directive, 17 e-Commerce 12 (Apr. 2001).

[167] The European Commission, Commission Welcomes Adoption of the Directive on Copyright in the Information Society, *id.*

[168] *Id.*

[169] European, Commission Welcomes Council Agreement on a Directive on Copyright in the Information Society (visited Apr. 14, 2002), http://europa.eu.int/comm/internal_market/en/intprop/intprop/news/601.htm. "The Directive applies Community exhaustion and not international exhaustion for the distribution right. The exhaustion right is that there is no right to restrict further distribution in the Community." *Id.*

[170] The Directive on Copyright in the Information Society, *id.*

[171] Norman F. Hesseltine, A Digest of the Law of Trade-Marks and Unfair Trade 1 (1906).

good from those manufactured or sold by others."[172] An audit of trademarks used on the global Internet has different concerns not true during the rapid development of trademark law in the nineteenth century. Trademarks on the Internet are arbitrary signs posted on web sites with the intention of designating origin. Trademark issues may occur with the use of materials on a web site as well as metatags. Trademark issues may raise international issues where a trading partner joining a co-branding agreement is located in a foreign country. Third parties, for example, must be authorized to affix or use distinguishing marks on postings to corporate web sites.

Trademark issues may occur when third parties infringe trademarks by posting materials to a web site. Corporations must protect their valuable brand names worldwide and also avoid accidental trademark infringement. The e-business must first determine where trademark protection is sought. Trademark registration in the USPTO does not extend beyond U.S. borders. All trademarks used on the e-business web site must be owned, licensed, or assigned to the e-business. The use of trademarks of others in comparative advertisements permitted under U.S. law may violate the law of European countries. Increasingly, e-businesses have a portfolio of trademarks that are licensed or co-branded to web sites targeted to foreign markets. Under TRIPS, individual member states set the ground rules for the licensing of trademarks.[173]

If trademarks of competitors are used in metatags, there is a potential risk of trademark infringement in foreign countries. In the United States, fair use may protect the use of trademarks in metatags, but the doctrine may be applied differently in other societies. The concept of trademark fair use may not be recognized in the intellectual property regimes of other countries. The forging of e-mail headers may constitute trademark infringement.[174]

Trademark protection will likely be sought in Eurozone core countries as well as core countries in other regions. No e-business has the resources to file for trademark registration in every periphery or semiperiphery country. Trademark protection must be obtained in the countries the e-business is targeting. Local counsel may be retained in European countries as well as other core countries. Under TRIPS, the minimum term of initial registration and renewal is 7 years, in contrast to the 10-year period in the USPTO.[175] The terms of trademark registration vary significantly from one country to another. Special attention must also be made to renewal terms. Trademarks must be used or they are lost. Registration may be cancelled for nonuse. The signatories to TRIPS are permitted to cancel a trademark registration if nonuse is for "an uninterrupted period of at least three years."[176] Member states are permitted to develop their own trademark registration procedures as long as they comply with the basic floor of protection granted by

---

[172] *Id.* at 2 (citation omitted).

[173] TRIPS Agreement, *id.* at Art. 21.

[174] Charlotte Waelde, Forthcoming Internet Trade Mark Disputes? Chapter 8 in Lilian Edwards & Charlotte Waelde, Law & the Internet: A Framework for Electronic Commerce 171, 178 (2000).

[175] TRIPS Agreement, *id.* at Art. 18.

[176] TRIPS Agreement, *id.* at Art. 19.

TRIPS. Many countries require evidence of use or a trademark registration will be cancelled. International trademark law is filled with pitfalls that may be avoided by consulting with local trademark specialists. If there are import restrictions on goods or services protected by a trademark, TRIPS considers it a valid reason for nonuse.[177]

An e-business may seek to file trademark and unfair competition lawsuits in national courts. Procter & Gamble, for example, successfully enjoined a Chinese web site whose dot.com.cn web site violated China's Trademark Law and Law against Unfair Competition. A Shanghai People's Court "found that the web site was registered with intent to misrepresent and that the use of the plaintiff's widely recognized Safeguard trademark caused confusion and unfair competition."[178] Foreign courts may also file lawsuits in U.S. courts vindicating intellectual property rights. In *Harrods Limited v. Sixty Internet Domain Names*,[179] a court considered the conflict between trademarks and domain names in a cross-border setting.

Any individual or entity may file a single application obtaining trademark protection in the EU countries by a filing in the European Community Trademark Office in Alicante, Spain. A member country to the Madrid Agreement provides that "once a national of a member country has registered a trademark in its home country, the trademark may be registered in all member countries by depositing its certificate of registration with the Central Registration Bureau in Berne, Switzerland."[180] "Nationals of countries that are not members of this convention may not obtain such 'international registrations' unless they have a 'real and effective industrial or commercial' presence in a member country through which they can obtain the necessary home country registration."[181] The United States is not yet a party to the Madrid Agreement. The Madrid Agreement signed in Madrid, Spain, on June 28, 1989, concerns the International Registration of Trademarks.[182]

The United States favors domestic and international agreements to harmonize "uniform standards that address trademark infringement and priority of rights . . . as well as uniform standards for registering Internet domain names.[183] The countries agreeing to the Madrid Agreement have a mechanism for international registration of marks.[184] The trademark offices of the country of origin prescribe

---

[177] TRIPS Agreement, *id*. at Art. 19(2).

[178] Perkins Coie LLP: Internet Case Digest, citing Procter & Gamble v. Shanghai Chenxuan Zhingeng Sci. & Technology Dev. Co., Shanghai No.2 Intermediate People's Court (Oct. 9, 2000) (visited May 14, 2001), http://www.perkinscoie.com/casedigest/icd_results.cfm?keyword1+domain%20name&topic+.

[179] 110 F. Supp. 2d 420 (E.D. Va. 2000) (filing *in rem* action under Anticybersquatting Consumer Protection Act of 1999 against 60 domain names containing the word "Harrods").

[180] Paul Supnik, The Madrid Convention (visited Apr. 14, 2002), http://www.softwareprotection.com/softwareprotection2001/main.htm.

[181] *Id*.

[182] See Madrid Agreement, *id*.

[183] Global Information Infrastructure Commission, Electronic Commerce: A Comparison of U.S., EU, MITI, and GIIC Reports on Electronic Commerce (Mar. 27, 1998) (visited Apr. 14, 2002), http://www.giicdot.org/focus/ecommerce/eccompares.html.

[184] *Id*. at Art. 1.

applications for international registration.[185] Applicants for international registration need to specify goods or services using the classification of the Nice Agreement.[186] The date of registration in a contracting country (of the Madrid Agreement) means protection will be in every contracting country.[187] Registration of a mark in the International Bureau is for a 20-year initial term plus the possibility of renewal.[188]

Are there any geographical indications that identify goods as originating in a TRIPS member state? Geographical origin rules are dictated by member states. TRIPS would, for example, prevent a foreign country such as Canada from using the term Vermont Maple Syrup, as a misleading geographic origin.[189] A German online site cannot, for example, use the term Bordeaux Wines in its online sales.[190]

[c]   *International Domain Name Issues*

[i] New Top-Level Domains. The Internet Corporation for Assigned Names and Numbers (ICANN) validated seven new top-level domains (TLDs), depicted in Table 8.1.[191] ICANN describes four proposals (*.biz, .info, .name,* and *.pro*) as designed for relatively large, unsponsored TLDs,[192] while the remaining "three proposals (*.aero, .coop,* and *.museum*) are for smaller "sponsored" TLDs.[193] RegistryPro was accredited by ICANN to register *.pro* domain names.[194] The new professional domain means "only accountants, lawyers and physicians will be permitted to register .pro Internet addresses."[195] In contrast, any individual or organization may register domain names with the .info new TLD.

Restricted TLDs include *.biz* for businesses, *.name* for individuals, *.pro* for professionals, *.museum* for museums, *.aero* for the air travel industry, and *.coop* for nonprofit organizations.[196] WIPO has recently proposed new rules for protecting against "bad faith, abusive, misleading or unfair" registration of domain names

---

[185] *Id.* at Art. 3.

[186] *Id.* at Art. 3(2).

[187] *Id.* at Art. 4.

[188] *Id.* at Art. 5, Art. 7.

[189] TRIPS Agreement, *id.* at Art. 22(2)(a).

[190] TRIPS Agreement, *id.* at Art. 23.

[191] ICANN contracted with the U.S. government to develop the domain name system. The European Parliament recently voted that ICANN be independent from the American government. The European Parliament argued that ICANN should be neutral and not under the control of the U.S. government if it is to achieve its promise as a truly global legal institution. European Union: European Parliament Demands ICANN Be Independent of U.S. Government Control, 2 World Internet L. Rep. 5 (Apr. 2001).

[192] "'TLD' refers to a top-level domain in the DNS." ICANN, The New TLD Program (updated May 30, 2001) (visited June 1, 2001), http://www.icanndot.org/tlds.

[193] ICANN, The New TLD Program (updated May 30, 2001) (visited Apr. 18, 2002), http://www.icanndot.org/tlds.

[194] DotPro Chief Expects to Be Selling Addresses by Nov., News.bytes com (May 30, 2001) (visited Apr. 18, 2002), http://www.newsbytes.com/news/01/166277.html.

[195] *Id.*

[196] Netnames, Press Release (Nov. 19, 2000) (visited May 30, 2001), http://www.netnames.com.

TABLE 8.1
ICANN's Seven New Top-Level Domains

TLD	Purpose
.aero	Air-transport industry
.biz	Businesses
.coop	Cooperatives
.info	Unrestricted use
.museum	Museums
.name	For registration by individuals
.pro	Accountants, lawyers, and physicians

that include personal names, pharmaceutical substance names, names of government entities, and geographical names.[197] The professional registry seeks to enter into agreements "with the world's major professional associations (the American Medical Association, American Bar Association, United Kingdom Law Society, etc.)."[198]

The new TLD for information, *.info,* will be an unrestricted TLD, open to any business or person to register for any purpose,[199] whereas *.biz* will be a restricted TLD open only for commercial or business purposes. The new TLD for *.biz* is not intended for exclusively personal or noncommercial purposes.[200] In the near future, the *.biz* domain will shortly permit the online business "to submit trademark claims before the application process is opened."[201] The fee-based service seeks to notify domain-name applicants "of a trademark owner's claim when they submit an application for a claimed name and, if they decide to go ahead with the registration, the business submitting the claim will be notified of the registration."[202] ICANN's procedures are not finalized and subject to further refinement. The domain name system is an example of a new quasi-government form of a global legal institution.

---

[197] WIPO Consultation Hits Washington, BNA's Electronic Commerce & L. Rep. (May 30, 2001) reported in Michael Geist, BNA's Internet Law News (July 1, 2001) (reporting http://pubs.bna.com/ip/BNA/eip.nsf/id/a0a4f9r5z5).

[198] *Id.*

[199] Vincent Cerf, ICANN Accredits New Top-Level Domains—.biz and. info Registration Process To Begin This Summer, ICANN Announcement (May 15, 2001) (visited Apr. 18, 2002), http://www.icanndot.org/announcements/icann-pr15may01.htm.

[200] *Id.* (stating those registry operators NeuLevel (.biz) and Afilias (. info) were among seven registry operators for new TLDs selected by the ICANN Board of Directors in Nov. 2000 following an open process for submission of proposals).

[201] ICANN Announcement, *id.*

[202] *Id.*

ICANN recently entered into an agreement with VeriSign, Inc. to operate the *.org* registry.[203] The agreement is that VeriSign will operate the *.org* registry until 2002 and *.net* registry until June 30, 2005.[204] Finally, VeriSign will "continue to operate the *.com* registry until at least the expiration date of the current agreement in 2007."[205] The agreement gives the U.S. government access to the registry to determine whether it is providing equal treatment to all domain name registrars, including VeriSign's registrar business. One of the most controversial issues is the selection of ICANN board members and governance.

[ii] Resolving Domain Name Disputes

[A] WIPO Arbitration and Mediation Center. The WIPO Arbitration and Mediation Center was "established in 1994 to offer arbitration and mediation services for the resolution of international disputes between private parties."[206] The WIPO Center has evolved into a dispute resolution service provider for challenges related to the misuses and abuses of Internet domain names. WIPO's center "received 1,841 gTLD cases,"[207] concerning over 3,200 domain names in 2000.[208] WIPO's center accounted for 6 percent of all ICANN cases in 2000.[209] In the latter half of 2000, an average of six domain name disputes was filed each calendar day.[210]

WIPO is the dispute resolution service provider for the *.com, .net,* and *.org* gTLDS as well as a number of country code top-level domains (ccTLD).[211] WIPO cases covered complaints from 46 countries and respondents from 73 countries.[212]

---

[203] ICANN Announcement, ICANN and VeriSign Sign on Dotted Line (May 25, 2001) (visited Apr. 18, 2002), http://www.icanndot.org/announcements/icann-pr25may01.htm.

[204] *Id.*

[205] *Id.*

[206] WIPO, The WIPO Arbitration and Mediation Center (visited June 6, 2001), http://arbiter.wipo.int/center/index.html.

[207] The concept of a gTLD refers to a generic top-level domain name. The *dot.com, dot.org.,* and *dot.pro* are examples of generic top-level domains (gTLDS). In addition, there are "country code TLDS like *.fr* (France) and *.us* (United States. [They] are non-generic because they refer to specific geographic areas." Heather N. Mewes, Memorandum of Understanding on the Generic Top-Level Domain Name Space of the Internet Domain Name System, 13 Berkeley Technology L.J. 235, 236-37 (1998).

[208] WIPO Arbitration and Mediation Center, Domain Name Dispute Resolution Service in 2000 (visited June 6, 2001), http://arbiter.wipo.int/domains/index.html.

[209] *Id.*

[210] *Id.*

[211] A ccTLD is a country code. There are 248 cc TLDS. *See* Karla Lemanski-Valente and Timothy Majka, Domain Names and Trademark Issues in the European Union, Gigalaw.com (visited June 9, 2001), http://www.gigalaw.com/articles/2001/valente-2001-05-p3.html. The following countries are examples of cc TLDs served by WIPO's Center: "Ascension Island, Antigua & Barbuda, American Samoa, Bahamas, Cyprus, Guatemala, Mexico, Namibia, Niue, Philippines, Pitcairn Island, Romania, St. Helena, Trinidad and Tobago, Tuvalu, Venezuela, and Western Somoa." WIPO Arbitration Center, *id.*

[212] WIPO Arbitration Center, *id.*

WIPO panelists are from 37 countries in all regions.[213] United Kingdom respondents are the second leading user of the WIPO Center, accounting for 9.3 percent of complaints (171) and 8.1 percent of respondents (150) in 2000.[214] Nearly half of the domain name complainants (897) using the WIPO center were from the United States, as opposed to 51 percent of the respondents (943).

WIPO's web site at http://www.arbiter.wipo.int/domains provides the full text of decisions as well as case statistics on cases filed and resolved. WIPO's web site also contains model complaints, responses, and online filing forms. Prior to filing a complaint with WIPO, the e-business needs to study the list of panelists and profiles. Finally, the ICANN Policy, Rules, and WIPO Supplemental Rules are available on the WIPO web site. WIPO's center has an e-mail list that sends information on recent developments. ICANN's domain name dispute resolution system has been the venue of a number of transborder disputes. WIPO's Center is working on procedures to resolve disputes involving multilingual domain names in Chinese, Japanese, Korean, and other languages.[215] WIPO's Center is also working on services for new gTLDS (*.aero, .biz, .coop, .info, .museum, .name,* and *.pro*). Complainants in domain name disputes have a choice of whether to file complaints with WIPO's Center, e-- Resolution, CPR Institute, and The National Arbitration Forum.[216]

[B] ICANN's UDRP. ICANN's Uniform Dispute Resolution Procedure uses arbitration panels to resolve domain name and trademark disputes.[217] ICANN has designated four organizations to administer UDRP administrative Proceedings: WIPO, CPR Institute for Dispute Resolution, e-Resolution, and The National Arbitration Forum. The complainant is permitted to forum-shop for the most pro-plaintiff provider. Each provider's prior decisions are available for statistical analysis online.[218] The Provider must follow the UDRP Policy, the UDRP Rules, and Supplemental Rules of the Provider. The National Arbitration Forum of Minneapolis requires the complainant to send the complaint, any attached evidence, the Complaint Transmittal Sheet, and a copy of ICANN's UDRP Policy to its Minneapolis headquarters. Complainants are permitted to send complaints by e-mail.[219]

---

[213] *Id.*

[214] Spanish residents filed 90 complaints (4.9%) in 2000. Five and a half percent of the respondents originated in Spain. Germany accounted for 3.6% of the complaints but only .8% of respondents. India accounted for 2.4% of the complainants and 1.4% of the respondents in 2000. Australia complainants accounted for 2.4% of WIPO complaints in 2000 followed by Japan with 2.3% of the complainants. The domiciles of complainants were scattered among approximately 80 different countries.

[215] *Id.*

[216] ICANN Dispute Resolution Policy (visited Apr. 20, 2002), http://www.icann.org/udrp/approved-providers.htm.

[217] The United States government signed a contract with ICANN to manage the domain name system.

[218] World Intellectual Property Organization, Arbitration and Mediation Center, Decisions (visited June 20, 2001), http://arbiter.wipo.int/domains/decisions/2001/d0000-0199.html.

[219] National Arbitration Forum (visited Apr. 20, 2002), http://www.arbforum.com/domains/domain-filing.asp.

"An Administrative Proceeding can be defined as a process in which two parties present their respective views of a conflict to a neutral and impartial third party, the panel. The panel will hear the parties' claims in conformity with ICANN's Policy, ICANN's Rules, and Supplemental Rules. After both parties have had a fair chance to make their case, the panel, after deliberation, will issue a decision that is binding on the parties."[220] The Uniform Domain Name Resolution Policy (UDRP) is an alternative dispute resolution mechanism, not a court of law. The WIPO Arbitration and Mediation Center issues administrative panel decisions, not legal decisions. The UDRP requires that a complaint be filed. The provider will then verify that the complaint satisfies the formal requirements of the UDRP Policy. The UDRP's principal sanction is to transfer a domain name to the complainant. To prevail in a UDRP proceeding, the plaintiff must prove that (1) the domain name is identical or confusingly similar to a trade mark or service mark in which the complainant has rights; and (2) the respondent has no rights or legitimate interests in respect of the domain name; and (3) the domain name has been registered and is being used in bad faith. Each provider is required to follow ICANN's Policy and Rules.

A UDRP plaintiff needs to allege that the defendant registered a domain name in bad faith. Evidence of registration and use in bad faith is when someone registers a domain name for the purpose of selling or transferring it to the owner of a trademark that is incorporated in the name or confusingly similar to it. It is also considered bad faith to register a trademark to prevent an owner of the trademark or service mark from using it. It is also bad faith to register a domain name for the purpose of disrupting a competitor's business. Finally, it is bad faith to use a domain name incorporating the trademark of another to attract Internet users to your web site.

A sampling of decisions from WIPO's Center reveals that many of the decisions have global dimensions. WIPO, for example awarded the "barcelona.com" domain name to the City Government of Barcelona, finding that the defendant registered the name in bad faith. Country-level domains have also led to disputes being filed with ICANN's dispute resolution panels. There was also a dispute over the .au country-level domain. Australia filed an action with WIPO to wrest control of the .au domain from a university computer programmer.[221] A WIPO panel transferred the "jimihendrix.com" domain name to Experience Hendrix.[222] WIPO is compiling an interim report on the WIPO Internet Domain Name Process. Key issues will be on how to handle the issue of personal names, names of international

---

[220] E-Resolution, Domain Name Administrative Proceeding, http://www.eresolution.ca/services/dnd/arb.htm (visited June 19, 2001) (describing procedures of e-Resolution, one of four ICANN-approved providers of administrative proceedings).

[221] Michael Geist, BNA's Internet Law News (June 6, 2001) (citing http://australianit.news.com.au/common/storyPage/0,3811,2073842%255E442,00.html).

[222] Perkins Coie LLP: Internet Case Digest, citing Experience Hendrix, LLC v. Hammerton, WIPO Case No. D20000-0364 (Aug. 2, 2000) (granting transfer of domain name).

intergovernmental organizations (IGOs), and domain names with geographic references.[223] ICANN is taking a "wait and see" approach to the registration of personal names as domain names. The ICANN procedure proposes that bad faith be shown in the registration of domain names with geographic indications of source.[224] WIPO issued an Interim Report on "certain predatory and parasitical practices in domain name registrations."[225]

WIPO's Interim Report on the Internet Domain Name Process makes some noteworthy recommendations. The Interim Report is directed at what WIPO describes as "certain predatory and parasitical practices" in the registration of non-trademark domain names. Among the recommendations contained in the report are limitations on the ability to register certain non-trademark "identifiers," including names and acronyms of international intergovernmental organizations, such as the United Nations or the WIPO and geographical indications such as the names of countries. The WIPO report proposes to prohibit the registration of International Nonproprietary Names (INNS) for pharmaceutical substances as domain names. The recommendations arising out of the Second WIPO Process must be approved by ICANN as well as by WIPO's member states.[226]

[C] Country level domain name disputes. When entering another country's online market, companies must take into account local infrastructure requirements and cultural preferences, the first and foremost of which is localizing domain names. Domain names fall into one of two Internet classifications: gTLDs that have a worldwide market (i.e., *.com, .net,* and *.org*); and ccTLDs that have a localized market (i.e., *.de* for Germany or *.au* for Australia). While gTLDs—particularly dot-com domains—are the primary choice of U.S.-based companies, ccTLDs are the domain category of choice for foreign companies.[227]

Domain name disputes have been adjudicated in the courts of a large number of countries.[228] A Virginia federal court extended the Anticybersquatting Consumer Protection Act to vindicate the rights of a foreign trademark registrant, the city of Barcelona, Spain. In the city of Barcelona case, the city obtained the right to the domain name *Barcelona.com* in a UDRP proceeding. WIPO's UDRP panel ordered the transfer of transfer of the domain name on the grounds that the defendant's use infringed the city of Barcelona's trademark. The defendant filed a declaratory judgment after the WIPO proceeding seeking a ruling that the city did not lawfully register its name, and the city filed a counterclaim based on the

---

[223] Pike and Fischer, WIPO Officials Come to Washington, Seeking Support for Trademark Law Expansion Online (May 30, 2001).

[224] *Id.*

[225] WIPO Issues Interim Report on the Internet Domain Name Registration System, 18 e-Commerce 9 (May 2001).

[226] *Id.*

[227] Karla Lemanski-Valente and Tim Majka, International Internet Domain Registrations, 17 e-Commerce 1 (Oct. 2000).

[228] Diane Cabell, Foreign Domain Name Disputes 2000, 17 The Computer & Internet Lawyer 5 (Oct. 2000).

ACPA. The federal court ruled that the ACPA applied to foreign trademarks and that the defendant acted in bad faith in registering the domain name.[229]

WIPO has decided a number of cases in which place names, either alone or in combination with other identifying elements, have been held to constitute trademarks or service marks. However, a WIPO tribunal found that the city of Heidelberg, Germany, was not entitled to the German country code domain name, *Heidelberg.de*. Although a regional court in Mannheim had held that the city of Heidelberg was entitled to the name, the WIPO panel ruled that the city failed to prove that "Heidelberg" was either a trademark or a service mark. The city of Heidelberg did not show that it had a legitimate right or interest in the domain name, and its complaint failed under paragraph 4(a)(i) of the UDRP policy. The panel ruled that mere geographical terms or place names did not fall within the policy.[230]

Individual nations have their own rules on domain name registrations for country codes. Sweden, for example, has a prior assessment scheme that only permits corporations with a presence in the country to register a domain name. An e-business will seek to register its domain names with cc-TLDs.[231] "Other parties are also free to use the exact same name in a different TLD, leading to rights holders trying to register in as many TLDs as possible in order to obtain the greatest protection of their trademarks and other intellectual property rights."[232]

Companies seek to own a ccTLD to localize marketing, to increase search engine capability, to have uniform global branding, and to have greater intellectual property protection.[233] The United States has a "first come, first-served" method of registration. Diane Cabell of Harvard's Berkman Center surveyed domain names in the judicial systems of various nations. Her conclusion was that "[m]any have not yet heard a domain name case."[234] She also found wide variance in rules for registration:

> Unlike the United States, most nations require prior registration of a trademark to attain protection, so ignorance of a prior claim is not an excuse. Some national registries, like Norway, limit domain registrations to an e-Business's official trade name (e.g. Ford), prohibiting registration under product names (e.g. Bronco). Sweden only issues domains to domestic commercial entities.

---

[229] Barcelona.com Inc. v. Excelentisimo Ayuntamiento de Barcelona, No. 00-1412-A (E.D. Va. Feb. 22, 2002), 19 Computer & Online Ind. Litig. Rep., Mar. 12, 2002, at 4.

[230] Stadt Heidelberg v. Media Factory, WIPO Case No. D2001-1500 (2001), http://arbiter. wipo.int/domains/decisions/html/2001/d2001-1500.html (citing many prior decisions ruling that geographic place names alone are outside the UDRP policy, including Brisbane City Council v. Joyce Russ Advertising Pty Ltd., WIPO Case D2001-0069; Brisbane City Council v. Warren Bolton Consulting Pty Ltd., WIPO Case D2001-0047; and Chambre de Commerce et d'Industrie de Rouen v. Marcel Stenzel, WIPO Case D2001-0348).

[231] Protecting the Good Name of the On-Line Sports Brand, Sports Marketing (Feb. 13, 2001) at 4 (noting complexity of having 240 ccTLDs and myriad registration rules).

[232] *Id.*

[233] Lemanski-Valente and Timothy Majka, Domain Names and Trade Issues in the European Union, *id.* at 1.

[234] Cabell, Foreign Domain Name Disputes 2000, *id.*

Brazil cancels the domain if it isn't used within six months; Finland has a limit of one domain per e-Business.[235]

In Hong Kong, the prior assessment method required three things of domain name registrants: "(1) a local presence in Hong Kong (i.e., an e-business/business registered with the Companies Registry, or a school registered with the Education Department, etc.); (2) payment of a fee of $200HK (Hong Kong dollars); and (3) the applicant should not own any other 'dot.hk' domain names."[236] The Hong Kong domain name system was changed to a "first come, first-served" system without the need for prior assessment.[237] UDRP panels are drawn from diverse legal and cultural traditions that may not share the American view of free expression. In one recent case, a WIPO panel ordered that the domain name *vivendiuniversalsucks.com*, which had been registered by a critic of the French firm, Vivendi Universal be transferred to the corporation. The respondent argued that he registered the disputed domain name to create a site for the free expression of criticism of the company's business practices. The panel acknowledged a split of opinion about the "sucks" cases in its ruling: "By the same reasoning, being satisfied that certain members of the public in general and 'Internauts' in particular, not being English speakers and/or aware of the meaning of the word 'sucks' in the Internet world, would be likely to understand 'sucks' as a banal and obscure addition to the reasonably well-known mark VIVENDI UNIVERSAL." The panel ruled that *vivendiuniversalsucks.com* refers to goods or services and met the requirements of paragraph 4(a)(i) of the UDRP Policy.[238]

[d] E-Commerce Patents

[i] Patent Cooperation Treaty. Patents must be filed in every country where patent protection is sought. An e-business registered in the United States must be aware that different rules apply to obtaining patent protection in the global marketplace. For example, the United States awards patents to the first person to invent, whereas the rest of the world awards patents to the "first to file" the patent application.[239] To date, WIPO has been unable to negotiate a treaty to harmonize patent law.[240] Patent protection in almost every country is based upon first to invent versus first to file a patent application. The United States is a member of the Patent

---

[235] *Id.*

[236] Garbriela Kennedy, Asian Developments: Domains of the Day: Proposals for the Overhaul of the Administration and Assignment of Domain Names in Hong Kong, 5 Cyber. Law. 33 (Sept. 2000).

[237] *Id.*

[238] Vivendi Universal v. Sallen, WIPO Case No. D2001-1121(2001) (ordering transfer of domain name), http://arbiter.wipo.int/domains/decisions/html/2001/d2001-1121.html.

[239] International Chamber of Commerce, Current and Emerging Issues Relating to Specific Intellectual Property Rights (visited Apr. 14, 2002), http://www.iccwbodot.org/home/intellectual_property/current-emerging/roadmap.asp. (hereinafter, "ICC, Intellectual Property Rights").

[240] *Id.*

Cooperation Treaty (PCT) that permits the filing of a single international patent application. The PCT application is helpful when seeking patents in the PCT contracting states. "The PCT allows individuals and companies within member countries or regional patent systems to file a patent application in one member country, and then file a second patent application in a second member country within one year of the first filing," and have the benefit of priority.[241] Another advantage of the PCT is it allows the International Application to be filed within a one-year period.[242] "The international application can be used to extend the time period up to 30 months before which a second patent application needs to be filed in a second country or regional patent office."

In 1998, there were 67,007 international applications under the PCT system.[243] After the PCT application report is sent to the applicant, patent claims are made in the countries where protection is sought. The concept of the European patent is still in its infancy but promises to offer advantages of cost savings and efficiency in that a single application would apply to all countries in the EU. Historically, an applicant has had to obtain patent protection in each country versus a centralized filing. The PCT provides the filing of one patent application rather than numerous filings in national or regional patent applications.[244]

[ii] European Patent Convention. The European system of patents not only has national patents, but a relatively new European patent that is granted by the European Patent Office in Munich. The European Community Patent System was established under Article 235 of the EC Treaty.[245] A 1997 Green Paper asked whether the Community patent system or intergovernmental conventions like the Luxembourg Convention on the Community Patent of 1975 would be used.[246] The United States Patent and Trademark Office has taken a much broader view of the patentability of e-commerce business methods and software.[247] The European Patent Convention (EPC) provides protection in member states for a term of 20 years from filing. Article 63 of the EPC requires all member states to harmonize their patent term to 20 years.[248] Article 69 of the EPC states that "[t]he extent of protection conferred by a European patent or a European patent application shall be determined by the terms of the claims."[249] The European Patent system "would

---

[241] Gregory J. Kirsch, Strategies for the Use of Patents by Start-Up Internet Companies, Gigalaw.com (visited June 9, 2001), http://www.gigalaw.com/articles/kirsch-2000-07-p5.html.

[242] Id.

[243] World Intellectual Property Organization, Patent Cooperation Treaty (visited Apr. 14, 2002), http://www.wipodot.org/eng/general/ipip/pct.htm.

[244] Id.

[245] The European Commission, Internal Market, Patents-Commission Approves Green Paper (June 25, 1997) (visited Apr. 14, 2002), http://europa.eu.int/comm/internal_market/en/intprop/indprop/558.ht.

[246] The European Commission, Internal Market, Patents-Commission Approves Green Paper, id.

[247] International Chamber of Commerce, Current and Emerging Issues, id.

[248] European Patent Convention, EPC, id. at Art. 63.

[249] European Patent Convention, EPC, id. at Art. 69.

coexist with patents issued by national offices and the European Patent Office (created by the 1973 Munich Convention)."[250] The preliminary application filed during the international phase will automatically defer national processing and give the applicant a better basis and more time to decide where to file patent applications.[251]

Business methods patents have yet to become accepted in Europe. Software patents have yet to become recognized and a proposed Directive would "harmonise the conditions for the patentability of inventions related to computer programs."[252] Europeans are also tuned into the role of patents in restraining competition. The European Commission is studying the role of "employees' inventions to determine whether clauses in employment contracts can constitute an obstacle to innovation."[253] Restrictive covenants in employment contracts may have a chilling impact on competition if they are too broad.

The online business needs to protect its patents and restrain patent infringement. In the United States, literal infringement means the accused invention literally infringes each element of a patent claim. Courts outside the United States may not recognize the doctrine of equivalents.[254] The *equivalents doctrine* broadens the definition of infringement to cover an accused device if it essentially adopted the claim even though the literal wording of the claim was sidestepped. The courts employ a functional or result test that asks whether the different element in the accused device works the same way to reach the same result as the element in the patent claim.[255] Patent terms may be harmonized but patent litigation varies in the Member States.[256] Cultural differences often play a determinative role in patent litigation.

[iii] European Patent Law. Ladas and Perry's Guide to European Patent Office Practice notes that the approach to patents in France and England is "the theory that a patent represents a contract between society and the inventor."[257] In contrast, the German view tends to be paternalistic and "[p]atents are granted

---

[250] European Commission, Patents: Commission Outlines Ambitious Series of Measures (visited June 6, 2001), http://europa.eu.int/comm/internal_market/en/intprop/indprop/99.htm.

[251] World Intellectual Property Organization, What Is the PCT? (visited Apr. 14, 2002), http://www.wipodot.org/pct/guide/en/gdvol1-01.htm

[252] *Id.*

[253] *Id.*

[254] The United States Supreme Court vacated and remanded a federal circuit court decision that essentially abolished the doctrine of equivalents in Festo Corp. v. Shoketsu Kinzoku Kogyo Kabushiki Co., 122 S. Ct. 1831 (2002). The U.S. Supreme Court reaffirmed the doctrine of equivalents in its holding that patent claims protect not only the literal claims but also insubstantial changes and substitutions that add nothing but a transparent attempt to take the copied matter outside the claim.

[255] Professor Andrew Beckerman-Rodau, a patent law teacher in Suffolk University Law School's High Technology Law Program, provided this explanation of the doctrine of equivalents.

[256] Ladas & Perry, Ladas and Parry Guide to European Patent Office Practice, Post-Grant Issues (visited Mar. 16, 2001), http://www.ladas.com/GUIDES/PATENT/EPOPractice/EPOPractGuide-8.html.

[257] *Id.*

because the state has decided, in its wisdom, and as part of the exercise of its power as *parens patriae*."[258] Procedure in patent trials also varies significantly.

In Germany there is no discovery, but in "France and Italy the Court can order inspection of premises."[259] The Europeans have been slow to recognize e-commerce and software patents. E-commerce and software patents have evolved rapidly in the United States since the federal circuit court's decision in *State Street Bank and Trust Co. v. Signature Financial Group, Inc.*[260] E-commerce patents have yet to develop outside the United States. In fact, there is no strong consensus that software is patentable among European countries. E-commerce or ways of doing business patents are not recognized in most countries. The United Kingdom's Patent Office recently issued a report rejecting patent protection for computer software and ways of doing business.[261]

[iv] Barriers to E-Commerce Patents. The United Kingdom Patent Office invited views "on how far computer software and ways of doing business should be protected by patents."[262] The UK Patent Office observed that a "vast amount of innovative software development [is] taking place without patent protection at present (though like all software, it is protected by copyright against direct copying)."[263] The UK Patent Office Report concluded that extending patentability to software developers would "divert time and effort into making sure they are not infringing patents and seeking and enforcing them, would impose a major burden."[264] The UK Patent Office Report argued that the case had not been made that extending "patentability would increase innovation in this field . . . [but it may have the] opposite effect."[265] The Report also rejected the argument that the "Open Source" software movement was threatening innovation, observing that software has flourished during the last decade of Open Source software.[266] The UK Patent Office found that virtually all respondents "opposed patents for business methods where no computer was involved" and "[t]he great majority also opposed patents for computer-implemented business methods if there is no technological innovation."[267]

The UK Patent Office was also concerned that business methods had the potential of affecting "all the sectors in which that sales method might be useful."[268] The Report acknowledged that some new e-business methods did involve

---

[258] *Id.*

[259] *Id.*

[260] 149 F.3d 1368 (Fed. Cir. 1998) (ruling that mathematical algorithm used in mutual fund hub and spoke business method was patentable as long as it produced "a useful, concrete and tangible result").

[261] The UK Patent Office, Should Patents Be Granted for Computer Software or Ways of Doing Business: The Government's Conclusions (visited Mar. 13, 2001), http://www.patent.gov.uk/about/consultations/conclusions.htm.

[262] *Id.* at ¶ 1.

[263] *Id.* at ¶ 15.

[264] *Id.*

[265] *Id.*

[266] *Id.* at ¶ 16.

[267] *Id.* at ¶ 21.

[268] *Id.*

"considerable R&D cost to realize."[269] Japan's Patent Office notified Amazon.com that it was rejecting its one-click-ordering patent legitimized in the United States.[270] The Patent Office of Japan's Ministry of Economy also rejected the business model patent that was the subject of the famous *State Street Bank* case that launched the business model patent revolution in the United States.[271]

In February 2002, the Commission of the European Communities proposed the Directive on the Patentability of Computer-Implemented Inventions. The Directive, intended to harmonize patent law among the member sates, would extend patent protection "to software applications of a 'technical nature' but not to patents for business methods per se."[272] The proposed Patent Directive stated: "[Although] computer programs 'as such' are excluded from patentability by Member States' patent laws and the European Patent Convention (EPC) . . . thousands of patents for computer-implemented inventions have been granted by the European Patent Office (EPO) and by national patent offices. The EPO alone accounts for more than 20,000 of them."[273] Although European patent protection for software or methods of doing business is not well-established as in the United States, it appears that the paths of patent law are beginning to converge.[274]

[5] Trade Secrets

A *trade secret* is information that is valuable to a company because the information is secret. Customer lists, business plans, and other proprietary information may be protected as trade secrets. While trade secrets may impart a competitive edge to an e-business's intellectual property arsenal, they are vulnerable to mass dissemination over the Internet. Many countries connected to the Internet do not share the U.S. level or style of protection of trade secrets, and some do not have any statute or case law addressing trade secrets. The TRIPS Agreement requires "WTO Member States to provide adequate protection for undisclosed information."[275] The North American Free Trade Agreement (NAFTA) "has a more explicit and detailed set of provisions binding its members to protect trade secrets.[276] Certain business methods that may not qualify for patent protection may

---

[269] *Id.*

[270] Amazon, Signature Financial Denied Business Model Patents, Japan Times (May 15, 2001) (visited May 22, 2001), http://www.japantimes.co.jp/cgi-bin/getarticle.pl5?nb20010515a6.htm.

[271] *Id.*

[272] Richard Gervase and Robert Clarida, Patents Securing Protection for Software Inventions in Europe, 18 E-Commerce Law & Strategy 1 (Mar. 2002).

[273] *Id.*

[274] *Id.* (stating that "[t]he difference between the U.S. and Europe and between the U.S. and Japan is that in Europe there has to be a technical contribution provided by the invention").

[275] Mark Lemley et al., Software and Internet Law 654 (2000) (citing Article 39(2) of TRIPS, which requires members to prevent "information lawfully within their control from being disclosed to, acquired by or used by others without their consent in a manner contrary to honest commercial practices").

[276] *Id.* at 655 (citing 1711(1) of NAFTA governing trade secrets as well as Article 1711(2)).

nonetheless be trade secrets and intellectual property assets critical to the e-Business's online strategy.

Unlike patents, trademarks, or copyrights, a trade secret instantly loses its value when it is revealed to the public. Companies must take steps to keep their trade secrets intact and away from broad online publication. E-mail and Internet usage policies should give employees notice of their duty to protect trade secrets or other confidential information. Employment agreements need to be customized to take into account different legal regulations and different views on covenants against competition. Nonsolicitation covenants may not be enforceable in Western European countries. Nondisclosure and confidentiality agreements are critically important to protecting an e-Business's trade secrets.

In the United States, employers have a wide discretion in monitoring e-mail or Internet usage to prevent trade secret theft. E-mail or Internet usage monitoring may not be permitted in continental European workplaces. If monitoring is not permitted, other steps must be taken to protect trade secrets. Certainly, confidential documents must be encrypted or otherwise protected with access controls.

[6]   Web Site Linking

As discussed in Chapter Four, simply linking to another web site is unlikely to violate copyright law. However, it is possible that linking could constitute unfair competition if a deep link bypasses the web site's advertising. It is also possible that linking could constitute a form of unfair competition if done in a misleading way. Links pose even greater risks in a number of European countries. Raising capital to develop and operate a site poses different concerns in an international setting. European competition law restricts licensing clauses that are widespread practices in the United States. There is a built-in conflict between the rights of intellectual property owners and erecting unfair barriers to trade or anticompetitive methods of licensing.[277] In some countries, there may be copyright infringement exposure for linking to an affiliate with infringing content. Similarly, there may be a risk factor if advertisements on linked sites fail to take into account cultural and national differences.

[7]   Database Protection

The European Union's 1996 Directive on the legal protection of databases provides for copyright protection for original databases as well as a *sui generis* protection for nonoriginal databases.[278] The purpose of the Database Directive is

---

[277] *See generally* Terrence Prime, European Intellectual Property Law (2000). Call centers, which do not offer customer service to different cultures and language groups, are likely to lose customers. A number of sites are opening call centers in Asia. SpeechWorks International, Inc. is a leading conversational speech recognition provider. Kirk Laughlin, A Reborn Asia Opens for Business, TeleProfessional 39, 40 (May 2000).

[278] 96/9/EC of the European Parliament and of the Council of March 1996 on the legal protection of databases; Official Journal L 077 of 27/03/96 (396L0009) (Database Directive).

to improve protection for databases in EU Member States and to eliminate differences in the legal protection of software. Copyright protection applies if the "selection and arrangement of the data or contents" qualifies as an "original intellectual creation."[279] The Database Directive "concerns the legal protection of databases in any form."[280] The Directive applies to *databases,* which are defined as meaning "a collection of independent works, data or other materials arranged in a systematic or methodical way and individually accessible by electronic or other means."[281]

The Database Directive applies to "the legal protection of computer programs" as well as "the term of protection of copyright and certain related rights."[282] The Directive requires member states to provide a *sui generis* right for the maker of a database that provides remedies for the "substantial investment in either obtaining, verification or presentation of the contents to prevent *extraction* and/or re-utilization of the whole, or a substantial part" of a database.[283] Extraction is a form of misappropriation of a database. The Directive defines extraction as meaning "the permanent or temporary transfer of all or a substantial part of the content of a database."[284] The Database Directive recognizes an exception to the *sui generis* protection for data used in teaching or scientific research.[285]

The purpose of the *sui generis* right is to protect the authors of databases from wholesale extraction or appropriation of substantial portions. Article 6 of the Directive provides for a copyright protection for databases in contrast to Article 9 that is the *sui generis* provision. The *sui generis* right covers substantial copying from databases but not unsubstantial copying. The European Union Directive requires the member states to amend their statutes to comply with the Directive.[286] Austria's Parliament, for example implemented the Database Directive in 1997 amendments to its copyright code.[287]Austria's copyright law already protected databases with the minimum modicum of originality. In addition, Austria now affords nonoriginal databases "*sui generis*" right of protection. The European Community grants a 70-year copyright term for original databases qualifying for copyright protection. In addition, the European Community recognizes a 15-year *sui generis* protection for databases.

---

[279] Canadian Government, Database Protection and Canadian Laws—The European Database Directive (visited June 13, 2001), http://strategis.ic.gc.ca/SSG/ip01059e.html.

[280] Database Directive, Directive 96/9EC of the European Parliament and of the Council of 11 March 1996 on the legal protection of databases, at Art. 2.

[281] *Id.* at Art. 1(1).

[282] *Id.* at Art. 2.

[283] *Id.* at Art. 7

[284] *Id.* at Art. 7(2)(a).

[285] *Id.* at Art. 9.

[286] Directive on the Legal Protection of Databases of 11 March 1996 (Official J.L. 77/20 of 27 Mar. 1996).

[287] Austria was implementing the Database Directive, Directive 96/9/EC of the European Parliament and of the Council of 11 March 1996 on the legal protection of databases.

The European Union Database Directive endorses a "sweat of the brow" or the author's investment of energy and resources in compiling databases.[288] In the United States, there is no copyright protection or *sui generis* statute protecting databases. The United States does not accord copyright protection to mere compilations that lack originality. Many databases lack originality and therefore do not qualify for copyright protection. In the meantime, the information industry is pressing for a federal law to protect databases from misappropriation.[289] The supporters of the Digital Millennium Copyright Act introduced a provision for database protection dropped in the Conference Report.[290]

[8] Moral Rights of Authors

Moral rights "are the author's right to be identified as the author of the work and that the author's reputation will not be diminished by the way the work is used."[291] Moral rights protections are not recognized under American copyright law. In *Gilliam v. American Broadcasting Co.*,[292] the creators of the television series "Monty Python's Flying Circus" argued that the rebroadcast series that shortened the programs and edited them greatly violated their moral rights.[293] The court defined the concept of *droit moral* or moral right as "including the right of the artist to have his work attributed to him in the form in which he created it."[294] The Second Circuit stated that "American copyright law, as presently written does not recognize moral rights or provide a cause of action for their violation, since the law seeks to vindicate the economic rather than the personal rights of authors."[295] Moral rights protect an author's personal, noneconomic interests.[296] The American law of copyright has long recognized the economic value or utility of the work rather than the author's creative *sui generis* right.[297] Rights of attribution or integrity arise out of rights of artists or other web site designers.[298] The

---

[288] Canadian Government, The European Database Directive (visited June 13, 2001), http://strategis.ic.gc.ca/SSG/ip01059e.html (noting that Article 7 vests the *sui generis* right on makers of the database that is based upon the "sweat of the brow" or industrious collection of data).

[289] Mark A. Lemley, Software and Internet Law 412 (2000).

[290] Jonathan Band, Digital Millennium Copyright Act (visited Apr. 19, 2002), http://www.drfcdot.org/issues/graphic/2281/JB-Index/JB-Memo/jb-memo.html.

[291] David Canton, Contract Law Determine Site Ownership, The London Free Press (May 19, 2000).

[292] 538 F.2d 14 (2d Cir. 1976).

[293] *Id.* at 25.

[294] *Id.* (citing Melville Nimmer on Copyright).

[295] *Id.* at 25-26.

[296] Leicester v. Warner Bros., 232 F.3d 1212 (9th Cir. 2000).

[297] The U.S. Supreme Court in Wheaton v. Peters, 33 U.S. 591, 672 (1834) (discussing literary property as "founded upon the same principles of general utility to society, which is the basis of all other moral rights and obligations").

[298] Carter v. Helmsley-Spear, Inc. 71 F.3d 77, 81 (2d Cir. 1995) (citing Ralph E. Lerner & Judith Bresler, Art Law 417 (1989)).

Gilliam court did find that the Lanham Act protected the creators from the excessive mutilation or altered versions of their comedic television series.[299]

In *Johnson v. Tuff-N-Rumble Management, Inc.*,[300] a federal court noted that American courts "generally do not recognize moral rights, unlike foreign jurisdictions."[301] The first explicit moral rights protection in the United States was the Visual Artists Rights Act of 1990.[302] Congress' limited recognition of moral rights for visual artists[303] has been described as "creeping into American copyright law."[304] Moral rights are undeveloped in American copyright law, and a "licensor has no 'moral right' to control the quality of licensed depictions."[305]

Foreign authors, creators, and performing artists have moral rights in the integrity of their works not recognized in the United States.[306] For example, an Australian architect argued that radical alterations to the National Gallery destroyed the integrity of his design and violated moral rights.[307] Victor Hugo's descendants filed an action based on moral rights against a French journalist who wrote and published a sequel to Hugo's *Les Miserables*.[308] Likewise, the great-grandson of Victor Hugo also argued that Disney's cartoon film *The Hunchback of Notre Dame* violated the integrity of the author's work.[309]

An Internet search uncovered a number of web sites that were charging a fee to download ringing tones from themes from famous performers such as Madonna or the theme from "Mission Impossible."[310] The practice of copying melodies in ringing tones may constitute an infringement of copyright not protected by the defense of fair use in the United States and other countries. "The moral rights of the writer may also be infringed through the derogatory treatment of their work, having a beautiful melody reduced to a ringing tone."[311] In 1997, Hong Kong

---

[299] *Id*. at 26.

[300] 2000 U.S. Dist. LEXIS 18299 (E.D. La., Dec. 8, 2000).

[301] *Id*. at *10.

[302] Quality King Distributors, Inc., v. L'Anza Research Int'l, Inc., 523 U.S. 135, 150 (1998) (discussing Congress' enactment of the Visual Artists Right Act of 1990 to protect the moral rights of certain visual artists); *see* Carter v. Helmsley-Spear, Inc., 71 F.3d 77 (2d Cir. 1995) (reversing lower court's order enjoining removal of a work of visual art installed in a commercial building in a Visual Artists Right Act action).

[303] *Id*. at 149 (quoting 2 P. Goldstein, Copyright § 5.12 (2d ed. 1996)).

[304] Ty, Inc. v. GMA Accessories, 132 F.3d 1167, 1173 (7th Cir. 1997); *see also* Seshadri v. Kasraian, 130 F.3d 798 (7th Cir. 1997) (collecting cases on moral rights).

[305] Rey v. Lafferty, 990 F.2d 1379 (1st Cir. 1993) (holding that licensed use of the character "Curious George" did not trigger a moral right to control the quality of depiction).

[306] Jonathan Band, Millennium Copyright Act, *id*.

[307] NGA Original Architect Consulted on Changes, AAP Newsfeed (June 6, 2001).

[308] Stuart Jeffires, Hugo's Heirs Hate "Miserable" Sequel: Publisher Who Dared to Produce a Follow-Up to a Great Man's Classic Work Is Sued for £410,000, The Observer (London) (June 3, 2001) at 26.

[309] *Id*.

[310] Robert Uhlig, Mobile Phone Tones "Rob Musicians of Royalties," The Daily Telegraph (London) (Apr. 25, 2001) at 13.

[311] *Id*. (citing Clare Griffiths, an Intellectual Property lawyer).

enacted a copyright bill that "recognized moral rights of integrity: the right to be identified as an author and the right to object to derogatory treatment of one's work."[312]

[C]   International Jurisdiction Issues

The American "due process" model of personal jurisdiction is not followed by other legal regimes. However, the general standard of reasonableness underlies other legal systems. The global law governing jurisdiction in cyberspace includes EU Directives as well as national approaches. One of the most difficult issues is to determine which jurisdiction should apply to cyberspace. With borderless transactions, it is unclear how sovereign countries can control cyberspace. In fact, the Internet, which is interconnected and transnational, challenges traditional jurisdiction based upon geography and "the effects of actions are immediately felt throughout the world regardless of location."[313] Consumer advocates oppose the draft convention on the grounds that it will dilute the doctrine of fair use and have potentially anticompetitive outcomes despite its provision that consumers may sue in their home court forum.[314]

The Consumer Affairs Council of Ministers favors a special rule for consumer contracts, which would designate the choice of law and jurisdiction as the consumer's country of residence.[315] In international jurisdiction cases, there are three types of jurisdiction: (1) jurisdiction to prescribe, (2) jurisdiction to adjudicate, and (3) jurisdiction to enforce.[316] *Prescriptive jurisdiction* means that a forum nation "has jurisdiction to prescribe law with respect to (1) conduct that, wholly or in substantial part, takes place within its territory; (2) the status of persons, or interests in things, present within its territory; (3) conduct outside its territory."[317] An e-business is concerned with rules of conflict of jurisdiction chiefly in civil and commercial matters. The U.S. e-business should be aware that jurisdiction rules vary significantly from the American minimum contacts-based framework.

An e-business is also concerned with judicial cooperation in the enforcement of judgments in Internet-related litigation. American courts will not recognize judgments in foreign countries that do not comply with due process of law.[318] There is likelihood that "U.S. courts cannot enforce a foreign judgment rendered

---

[312] Shirley Kowk, Hong Kong Constructs New IP Regime, IP Worldwide (Mar./Apr. 1997).

[313] Aron Mefford, Lex Informatica: Foundations of Law on the Internet, 5 Ind. J. Global Leg. Stud. 211, 216 (1997).

[314] Participants Debate IP Simplications at Roundtable on Draft Hague Convention, Pike & Fischer, Internet Law & Regulation (May 17, 2001) at 1 (quoting James Love of the Consumer Project on Technology, who argues that "the whole treaty should be disposed of").

[315] *Id.*

[316] Denis T. Rice, Offering Securities on the Internet—2001, 18 The Computer & Internet Lawyer 19 (May 2001) (citing Restatement (3d) of the Foreign Relations Law of the U.S. § 401, comment (a) (1987)).

[317] *Id.*

[318] Restatement (Third) of the Foreign Relations Law of the United States (1987).

without sufficient contacts or purposeful availment to justify jurisdiction."[319] As detailed in Chapter Seven, a passive web site without additional contacts is insufficient to satisfy minimum contacts. Sporadic sales or other contacts will likely be insufficient to satisfy due process, thus making foreign judgments unenforceable in the United States.

In contrast, interactive web sites with other contacts with a foreign forum will likely satisfy due process requirements, making foreign judgments enforceable. Another factor that must be taken into account is that "U.S. courts will not enforce foreign libel judgments inconsistent with the First Amendment."[320]

Another problem that may arise with Internet jurisdiction is the issue of parallel proceedings. It is theoretically possible for an e-business to be sued in hundreds of forums for the same course of conduct. An e-business "has three possible responses to parallel proceedings: (1) stay or dismiss the domestic action, (2) enjoin the parties from proceeding in the foreign forum (referred to as an antisuit injunction), or (3) allow both suits to proceed simultaneously."[321] Another possibility is to file an antisuit injunction in a foreign court.[322]

[1] The Hague Convention on Jurisdiction and Foreign Judgments

The proposed Hague Convention on Jurisdiction and Foreign Judgments in Civil and Commercial Matters[323] is "a global regime to address potential conflicts of jurisdiction and the recognition and enforcement of judgments with greater legal certainty."[324] The Hague Convention will apply to most civil and commercial judgments, but not disputes over revenue, customs, or administrative matters.[325] In addition, the Hague Convention will not apply to wills, marriage, insolvency, arbitration, admiralty, Social Security, child support, and other family law exceptions.[326] The Convention will not exclude actions by governments, a government agency, or any other person acting on behalf of a country.[327] The Hague Conven-

---

[319] Kurt A. Wimmer and Joshua A. Berman, United States Jurisdiction to Enforce Foreign Internet Libel Judgments (visited May 20, 2001), http://www.pf.com.

[320] Id.

[321] Daniel G. Murphy et. al., International Legal Developments in Review: 1999: Business Transactions and Disputes, The International Lawyer, 34 Int'l Law 545 (2000). See, e.g., Posner v. Essex Insur. Co., 178 F.3d 1209, 1222-24 (11th Cir. 1999) (dismissing claim against Bermuda insurer on international abstention grounds).

[322] See Daniel G. Murphy, International Lawyer 1999 Developments, id. (citing Credit Suisse First Boston (Europe) Ltd v. MLC (Bermuda) Ltd, [1999] 1 Lloyd's Rep. 767 (Q.B. 1998)).

[323] The Hague Conference on Private International Law, Preliminary Draft Convention on Jurisdiction and Foreign Judgments in Civil and Commercial Matters, amended version, adopted by the Special Commission on Oct. 30, 1999 (visited June 12, 2001), http://www.hcch.net/e/conventions/draft36e.html.

[324] Civil Law, RAPID: Commission of The European Communities, Doc: 00/33 (Dec. 20, 2000).

[325] Id. at Art. 2.

[326] Id. at Art. 1(2)(a(-(h)

[327] Id. at Art. 1(3).

tion does not apply "unless all the parties are habitually resident in that State."[328] The test for habitual residence for a corporation or other entity is where (1) it has a statutory seat, (2) it was incorporated, (3) it has central administration; or (4) it has its principal place of business.[329] The proposed Hague Convention on Jurisdiction and Enforcement of Foreign Judgments will greatly enhance SPC's ability to enforce civil judgments across borders.[330] In particular, the question of whether a court can exercise jurisdiction to deal with the case under its own law is known as the law of the forum or *lex fori*.[331] Another question is which law a court should apply to resolve a dispute.[332] American precedents on personal jurisdiction are not followed by the proposed Convention.

The Hague Convention provides that if the court has jurisdiction, it has exclusive jurisdictions because of a policy-based decision to avoid parallel proceedings.[333] A court is expected to exercise international comity[334] or abstention if another court has jurisdiction.[335] Commercial parties have the right to choose an exclusive forum. If the exclusive forum is in a noncontracting state, courts in contracting states should decline jurisdiction or suspend proceedings "unless the court or courts chosen have themselves declined jurisdiction."[336] Choices of forum clauses are enforceable if entered into or confirmed in writing or by "by other means of communication which renders information accessible."[337]

The Hague Convention does not require signatories to enforce judgments considered to be "manifestly incompatible with that country's public policy."[338] The Hague Convention applies to a wide range of substantive fields of law encompassing almost all civil and commercial litigation. The Hague Convention enforces all choice of forum clauses in B2B contracts.[339] The Hague Convention proposes that the consumer determine jurisdiction in B2C contracts. The Hague Convention

---

[328] *Id.* at Art 2.

[329] *Id.* at Art. 3(2)(a)-(d); Elizabeth Longsworth, The Possibilities for Cyberspace—Including a New Zealand Perspective, Chapter One in UNESCO, The International Dimensions of Cyberspace Law 1 (2000).

[330] The most recent version of the Hague Convention is found at http://www.hcch.net/e/conventions/draft36e.html.

[331] Longsworth, The Possibilities for Cyberspace, *id.* at 37.

[332] *Id.* at 35.

[333] *Id.* at Art. 4(a)

[334] *International comity* is the comity of or between nations. "It is the extent to which the law of one state or nation is allowed to operate within the dominion of another." James A. Ballentine, Ballentine's Law Dictionary 220 (3d ed. 1964).

[335] *Id.* at Art. 4(1).

[336] *Id.* at Art. 4(1).

[337] *Id.* at Art. 4(a)(b).

[338] The Hague Convention, *id.* at Art. 28(f) (stating public policy exception to enforcement of judgments and jurisdiction).

[339] Professor William Woodward notes that the Rome Convention "restricts the effect of a contractual choice of law to non-mandatory law in domestic contracts and . . . affirmatively gives consumers the mandatory protections of their habitual residence notwithstanding a contrary choice of law." William J. Woodward, Letter to Professor Elizabeth Warren, Leo Gottlieb Professor of Law, Harvard Law School, Member, American Law Institute Council (Nov. 23, 1999).

has far-reaching implications for e-commerce. The principal default of the Convention is that a "defendant may be sued in the courts of the country where they are a 'habitual resident.'"

[2] Service of Process Abroad

An online company attempting to enforce a U.S. judgment abroad will likely need to consult with foreign counsel. The United States is a signatory to two relevant international agreements: the Hague Convention on the Service Abroad of Judicial and Extra-Judicial Documents in Civil or Commercial Matters[340] and the Inter-American Convention on Letters Rogatory.[341] The Federal Rules of Civil Procedure permit service by registered or certified mail and return receipt requested unless prohibited by the law of the foreign country.[342] The U.S. State Department recommends that service of process or subpoena not be made by regular mail.[343] If a country where service is desired is not a Hague Convention signatory, "the most expeditious method may be to retain the services of a local foreign attorney or process server. Rule 4(f)(2)(C) provides for personal service unless prohibited by the laws of the foreign country. The attorney (or agent) can execute an affidavit of service at the nearest American embassy or consulate, or before a local foreign notary which can be authenticated."[344]

The *letter rogatory,* or letter of request, "is a request from a court in the United States to a court in a foreign country requesting international judicial assistance, which is often employed to obtain evidence abroad, but is also utilized in effecting service of process and particularly in those countries which prohibit other methods of service."[345] The U.S. State Department has published useful information on its web site on how to obtain letters rogatory to facilitate the serving of process or subpoenas.[346]

---

[340] The Hague Convention on the Service Abroad of Judicial and Extra-Judicial Documents in Civil or Commercial Matters, 20 U.S.T. 1361, *available at* http://travel.state.gov/hague_service.html.

[341] The signatories are Argentina, Brazil, Chile, Colombia, Ecuador, Guatemala, Mexico, Panama, Panama, Paraguay, Peru, United States, Uruguay, and Venezeula.

[342] Fed. R. Civ. P. 4(f), 4(f)(2)(C)(ii).

[343] "American courts have held that formal objections to service by mail made by countries party to a multilateral treaty or convention on service of process at the time of accession or subsequently in accordance with the treaty are honored as a treaty obligation, and litigants should refrain from using such a method of service." U.S. Department of State, Service of Legal Documents Abroad (visited Dec. 25, 2001), http://travel.state.gov/service_general.html (citing DeJames v. Magnificence Carriers, Inc., 654 F.2d 280 (3d Cir. 1981), *cert. denied,* 454 U.S. 1085; Porsche v. Superior Court, 123 Cal. App. 3d 755 (1981)).

[344] *Id.* (citing Wright and Miller, Federal Practice & Procedure § 1136 (1987) regarding proof of service).

[345] *Id.* (noting that "[i]n some countries service by letters rogatory is the only recognized method of service.")

[346] *Id.* (noting that the procedural requirements for a letter rogatory vary from country to country and providing flyers on "Preparation of Letters Rogatory" via the State Department's automated fax service or home page on the Internet located at http://travel.state.gov/service_general.html).

Service by publication, although well accepted in the United States, may not be valid in a foreign country. Waiver of service may also not be recognized in a foreign country. If a cause of action is against a foreign government, the officers of the Foreign Service may serve a summons, complaint, and notice of suit on a foreign government. Table 8.2 on the next page is a State Department summary of methods of service abroad.

[3]   Brussels Regulation

The Brussels Regulation[347] governs jurisdiction in civil and commercial disputes between litigants and provides for the enforcement of judgments. Effective March 2002, it replaces the 1968 Brussels Convention[348] for all signatories to the convention except Denmark; it does not yet supplant the Lugano Convention of 1988, which extended the 1968 Brussels Convention to new member states joining the EC.

The Brussels Regulation gives consumers the right to sue suppliers in their home court. Article 15 provides that if a business "pursues commercial or professional activities in the Member State of the consumer's domicile,"[349] the consumer may sue in the court where he or she is domiciled. Article 15(1)(c) extends the consumer home forum rule to entities that "direct[] such activities" to the consumer's domicile. The far-reaching consumer provisions apply equally to the e-business targeting European consumers. See § 7.03[H][3] for a more comprehensive discussion of the revised Brussels Regulation.

[4]   ABA Report on Cyberspace Jurisdiction

A Report of the American Bar Association (ABA), titled "Achieving Legal and Business Order in Cyberspace: A Report on Global Jurisdiction Issues Created by the Internet," was released in July of 1999 at the ABA Meetings in London.[350] A key threshold question is whether the Internet should be thought of as a "means of communication, or a technological state of mind."[351] The ABA Report examines several areas: "(1) jurisdictional solutions to puzzles posed by the technology . . . (2) changes in jurisdictional paradigms which support those solutions; and (3) the doctrinal framework that has and is continuing to emerge which, in

---

[347] Council Regulation 44/2001, 2001 O.J. (L 12) 1, http://europa.eu.int/eur-lex/pri/en/oj/dat/2001/l_012/l_01220010116en00010023.pdf [hereinafter Brussels Regulation].

[348] Brussels Convention on Jurisdiction and the Enforcement of Judgments in Civil and Commercial Matters, 1968 O.J. (C 189), *consolidated version available at* http://europa.eu.int/eur-lex/en/archive/1998/c_02719980126en.html.

[349] Brussels Regulation, *supra* note 330.8, art. 15(1).

[350] Report of the American Bar Association (ABA) Jurisdiction in Cyberspace Project, Achieving Legal and Business Order in Cyberspace: A Report on Global Jurisdiction Issues Created by the Internet, 55 Bus. Law. 1801 (Aug. 2000).

[351] *Id.*

TABLE 8.2
U.S. State Department
Summary Chart: Methods of Service Abroad

Method	Pros	Cons
Service treaty/ convention country service by foreign central authority	Service generally guaranteed; no service problems re future enforcement proceedings abroad	Translation usually required; expense; time: 3 months + to serve
Service by international registered or certified mail, return receipt requested	Fast, inexpensive	Possible problems enforcing judgment abroad; problems with proof of service
Service by agent (foreign attorney or process server)	Personal service; timely	Expensive; possible problems enforcing judgment abroad
Service by publication	Timely; inexpensive	Possible problems enforcing judgment abroad
Waiver of service	Timely; inexpensive	Possible problems enforcing judgment abroad
Letters rogatory (letter of request)	No service problems re future enforcement proceedings abroad	Time consuming: 6 months to a year; translation required: expensive

turn, supports the described changes."[352] The ABA Report also proposes to extend a minimum contacts framework to Internet transactions worldwide.

The general requirement of reasonableness is always relevant for the exercise of international jurisdiction.[353] The ABA Report on Cyberspace Jurisdiction notes that "more than one state may be able to assert both personal and prescriptive jurisdiction in electronic transactions."[354] The ABA Report argues that a mere "passive web site" should not be the basis of jurisdiction—personal or prescriptive—in the absence of a proof that the forum state was targeted.[355] The ABA

---

[352] *Id.*

[353] *Id.* (enumerating reasonableness and the general factors in § 403(2) of the Restatement (3rd) of the Foreign Relations Law of the United States).

[354] ABA Report on Jurisdiction in Cyberspace, *id.* at § 1.2.1 (stating "[a]bsent fraud or related abuses, forum selection, and choice of law contract provisions should be enforced in business-to-business electronic commerce transactions").

[355] *Id.* at § 1.1.2.

Report defers to contractual choice of law and forum clauses.[356] If parties have not otherwise agreed, jurisdiction (prescriptive and personal) is assertable where the "sponsor is a habitual resident of that state or has its principal place of business in that state."[357] Jurisdiction is proper for actions that arise out of the content of the site where the forum has been targeted.[358]

[D] Internet Privacy

Web sites need to consider whether they are violating the privacy rights of persons depicted on the Internet. Amazon.com, for example, has been investigated in Europe for violating data protection laws in the collection of personal data on visitors.[359] Belgium, Denmark, Germany, Spain, France, Greece, Italy, Ireland, Luxembourg, The Netherlands, Austria, Austria, Sweden, Finland, and the United Kingdom have enacted statutes implementing the Data Protection Directive.[360]

The United States and the European Commission are in the process of negotiating draft language in transactions involving the transfer of personal data.[361] The U.S. Department of Commerce on July 21, 2000, issued the Safe Harbor Privacy Principles. The Safe Harbor Principles define *personal data* and *personal information* as data about an identified or identifiable individual that are within the scope of the Directive, received by a U.S. organization from European Union countries and recorded in any form.[362] "Notice" is a key feature of the safe harbor. The data transferor must inform individuals the purposes for which it collects and uses information. Individuals must be offered the choice of opting out of sharing of personal information to third parties.

Organizations "may not transfer information unless they apply the Notice and Choice principles."[363] An organization may not disclose information to third

---

[356] *See, e.g., id.* at § 1.1.3.

[357] *Id.* at § 1.1.3(a).

[358] *Id.* at § 1.1.3(b).

[359] Kathleen Fay, Amazon.com Worldwide Operations Under Fire for Revising Privacy Policy, Electronic Commerce Developments of Note, 17 e-Commerce 7 (Dec. 2000) (noting that the United Kingdom is being asked to enjoin Amazon.com's U.K. affiliate for violating UK's data protection act).

[360] European Union, Data Protection: Implementation of Directive 95/46 (visited Apr. 20, 2002), http://europa.eu.int/comm/internal_market/en/media/dataprot/law/impl.htm. The United Kingdom's implementation was by the Data Protection Act of 1998. The Netherlands adopted secondary legislation implementing the data protection directive on September 1, 2001. *Id.*

[361] European Commission Rejects U.S. Request to Rework Model Privacy Contract Provisions, Pike & Fischer, Inc. (May 10, 2001).

[362] U.S. Department of Commerce, Safe Harbor Privacy Principles (visited Apr. 20, 2002), http://www.export.gov/safeharbor/shprinciplesfinal.htm.

[363] *Id.*

parties without ascertaining "that the third party subscribes to the Principles or is subject to the Directive."[364] "Organizations creating, maintaining, using or disseminating personal information must take reasonable precautions to protect it from loss, misuse, and unauthorized access, disclosure, alteration and destruction."[365] The United States' Safe Harbor negotiated with the Department of Commerce also advocates data integrity, which provides "[a]n organization may not process personal information in a way that is incompatible with the purposes for which it has been collected or subsequently authorized by the individual."[366] Individuals must have "access to personal information about them that an organization holds and be able to correct, amend, or delete that information where it is inaccurate, except where the burden or expense of providing access would be disproportionate to the risks to the individual's privacy in the case in question, or whether the rights of persons other than the individual would be violated."[367] Finally, the Safe Harbor requires mechanisms for effective privacy protection.

The American approach to Internet privacy is an industry self-regulatory approach. In July 2000, Internet advertisers adopted fair "Principles for Online Preference Marketing."[368] The United States is also participating in the Platform for Privacy Protection (P3P), which is a standard developed by the World Wide Web Consortium enabling visitors to "express their privacy preferences through their browsers."[369] The U.S. government is also lobbying international organizations in favor of the self-regulation approach.[370] The United States is also a major player in the Global Business Dialogue on Electronic Commerce and the Trans-Atlantic Business Dialogue that seeks to harmonize different privacy regimes.[371] The United States had representatives in the movement to develop a transnational online privacy seal. In May of 2000, BBBOnline and the Japan Information Processing Development Center (JIPDEC) released a transnational seal that can be earned by either the JIPDEC or the BBBOnline privacy seals.[372]

Canada's first case under under its recently enacted Personal Information Protection and Electronic Documents Act (PIPED) ruled that the use of street surveillance cameras in a town in the Northwest Territories was unlawful. The court ruled that "live video pictures and recorded video pictures of individuals qualify as 'personal information' under the Act, and as such, cannot be collected or used

---

[364] *Id.*

[365] *Id.*

[366] *Id.*

[367] *Id.*

[368] Network Advertising Initiative, Principles for Online Preference Marketing (visited May 1, 2001), http://www.ftc.gov/os/2000/07/NAI%207-10%20Final.pdf.

[369] Third Annual Report, U.S. Government Working Group on Electronic Commerce 40 (2000).

[370] The United States government "continues to promote an industry self-regulation approach to privacy protection with groups such as the OECD, the Free Trade Area of the Americas, and the Asia Pacific Economic Cooperation," *id.*

[371] *Id.*

[372] *Id.*

in the context of a commercial activity without the informed consent of the information being taped."[373]

[E] Third-Party Content

A large number of countries are seeking to regulate Internet content. Serbia, for example, enacted a statute prohibiting its citizens from insulting the government on the Internet.[374] China blocked a web site featuring a BBC Mandarin webcast.[375] Saudi Arabia has long blocked Internet materials it classifies as obscene.[376] A South Korean Court fined a defendant for posting nude photographs on the Internet.[377] The Internet may subject the e-business to criminal investigations for illegal Internet content. Content may be illegal for religious, political, gender, or cultural reasons. The First Amendment of the United States Constitution may protect the same content. The online company should be aware that its web site might be blocked if it is selling products considered objectionable in a given country. Make certain that the web site does not insult a culture or political group in a target state. The company may have liability for insults or other objectionable materials posted on message boards by employees or third parties.

ISPs in Europe oppose increased law enforcement surveillance of the Internet as burdensome. "The privacy commissioners are concerned about a proposal known as Enfopol 38, drafted by police authorities in European countries, that calls for telecom and Internet providers to store so-called traffic data. Traffic data—as opposed to the actual communications content—include lists of calls, faxes or e-mail messages a person made, received or missed. Some of this information is stored for billing purposes but is usually deleted after a short time—typically three months."[378]

[F] Torts, *Delicts*, and Civil Wrongs

The global online business needs to consider how to reduce exposure to torts. The law of torts evolved under common law since the middle of the nineteenth century, when it was first recognized as a branch of law and taught in American law schools.[379] The law of torts is based primarily on the common law, which is

---

[373] Elaine Keenan Bengts, Privacy Commissioner of the Northwest Territories, News Release (June 20, 2001), http://www.privcom.gc.ca/media/an/nt_010620_e.asp.

[374] Microsoft Law & Corporate Affairs, Summary of Global Internet Legal Developments for the Period Oct.-Dec. 1998 (Jan. 1999) at 7.

[375] *Id.*

[376] *Id.* at 9.

[377] *Id.*

[378] Boris Grondahl, European ISPs Resist Police Demands for Data, Industry Standard (June 13, 2001) (visited Apr. 12, 2002), http://www.thestandard.com.

[379] *See generally* Thomas H. Koenig and Michael L. Rustad, In Defense of Tort Law (2001) (describing origin of tort law in Chapter One).

state law in the United States. Tort law is made even more complicated by the rise of the Internet. It is clear that the law of torts applies to a multitude of web site activities. Tort law is readily adaptable to the Internet, as we learned in Chapter 5. Torts may be committed in chat rooms, videoconferences, news groups, listervs, and computer bulletin boards. Torts may be committed by e-mail, posting information on web sites, or intercepting data from intended recipients. There is a great deal of uncertainty as to how existing tort law applies to e-commerce. An e-commerce portal could be liable for a host of tort claims for defamation, negligence, fraud, or information torts, and even personal injury for failed software. A Dutch Internet service provider obtained a court order against Abfab for sending unsolicited bulk mail to XS4ALL subscribers. An Amsterdam judge ruled "that XS4ALL has no legal conveyance obligation and can therefore ban third parties from sending spam through its systems."[380]

The three branches of American tort law are (1) intentional torts, (2) negligence, and (3) strict liability. An e-business is subject to liability under all three branches of tort law by citizens of different countries harmed by web site activities. U.S companies may be exposed to the risk of liability for tort-like *delicts* or civil wrongs. *Delicts* are acts "by which one person, by fraud or malignity, causes some damage or tort to some other."[381] The concept of the *delict* is a noncontractual obligation for which there is civil liability. *Delicts* share much common ground with the common law of torts.[382] In civil law countries, torts are frequently classified as *delicts*. In the United Kingdom, choice of law rules apply equally for torts and *delicts*.[383] In England, the term *torts* refers to civil wrongs. In Scotland, the parallel term is the *delict*.[384] One difference between torts and *delicts* is that torts are private law actions whereas *delicts* may be public as well as private.[385] The concept of the quasi-*delict* roughly parallels the Anglo-American remedy of restitution.[386] European civil wrongs are divided into intentional, unintentional, and strict liability *delicts*.[387] A plaintiff generally receives money damages for *delicts*, just as in the law of torts.

In common law countries, there are three broad categories of torts: intentional torts, negligence, and strict liability. To prove negligence, a plaintiff must

---

[380] Abfab Can No Longer Spam XS4ALL Subscribers, XS4ALL News (Mar. 7, 2002), http://www.xs4all.nl/uk/news/overview/spam_e.html.

[381] 'Lectric Law Library's Lexicon, *"Delict"* (visited June 19, 2001), http://www.lectlaw.com/def/d123.htm.

[382] *See generally* Christian Von Bar, The Common European Law of Torts 1, The Core Areas of Tort Law, Its Approximation in Europe, and its Accommodation in the Legal System (1999).

[383] Private International Law (Miscellaneous Provisions) Act 1995 (c. 42) Pt. III: Choice of Law in Tort and *Delict* (visited Apr. 19, 2002), http://www.hmso.gov.uk/acts/acts1995/Ukpga_) 19950042-en-4.htm.

[384] *Id.*

[385] 'Lectric Law Library's Lexicon, Definition of *Delict, id.*

[386] *Id.*

[387] *Id.*

prove by a preponderance of the evidence each element of negligence: duty, breach of duty, proximate causation, and injury. Strict liability is increasingly being followed in product liability actions in other countries. The doctrine of strict liability for abnormally dangerous activities was originally developed in England. Strict product liability, in contrast, was a doctrinal development in the United States in the 1960s. In the United States, there is little case law on whether an online business has a legal duty to take affirmative action to secure a web site.[388] However, it is likely that foreign money judgments are enforceable for such claims under the principles of international comity.[389]

The largest number of international Internet tort cases has been publication torts. One of the main concerns flowing from the growth and globalization of the Internet is the increased amenability of U.S. media companies to bring suit for libel in foreign jurisdictions.[390] A Canadian court recently ordered iPrimis to identify an anonymous e-mailer in a defamation action. In that case, an anonymous e-mail message was sent to employees of a toy e-business criticizing the e-business's president.[391] In May of 2001, a New Zealand court considered a defamation case against an Internet Service Provider in a case in which an allegedly libelous e-mail was transmitted to members of the Internet Society of New Zealand on December 23, 1999.[392] This was the first case in which a New Zealand court was asked to consider an ISP's liability for Internet defamation published by a third party.[393] American courts are unlikely "to enforce foreign libel judgments, based

---

[388] Negligent security or premises liability lawsuits have long been recognized in U.S. law. Section 314A of the Restatement (Second) of Torts provides that a business has a duty to protect business invitees placed in danger on the premises. See Bias v. IPC Int'l Corp., 1997 U.S. App. LEXIS 3913 *7 (4th Cir. 1997). Similarly, the negligent failure to provide adequate security of a web site may result in liability for an e-Business. It is unclear whether an insurance e-Business would have a duty to defend on a negligent security claim brought by a web site visitor. Cf. Liquor Liab. Joint Underwriting Assoc. v. Hermitage Ins. Co., 419 Mass. 316, 644, N.E.2d 964 (1995) (holding that an insurer had a duty to defend a negligent claim brought by a patron of a bar injured by a co-patron). If a web site has been a known high crime area, there is an issue of whether its past experience requires a heightened duty of care. See Restatement (Second) of Torts § 344 (1965). Prior similar occurrences of crimes committed on web sites would indicate that dangerous conditions were readily foreseeable. See Martin v. Wal-Mart Stores, Inc., 1992 U.S. App. LEXIS 1473 (10th Cir., Feb. 6, 1992) (noting that prior similar occurrences were linked to the nature of defendant's business operations; dismissing case because plaintiff produced no evidence of defendant's pertinent operating methods).

[389] Kurt A. Wimmer and Joshua A. Berman, United States Jurisdiction to Enforce Foreign Internet Libel Judgments (visited Apr. 20, 2002), http://www.pf.com/cgi-bin/om-isapi.dll?c.

[390] Id.

[391] Perkins Coie Internet Case Digest (visited Apr. 14, 2002), http://www.perkinscoie.com/casedigest/icd_results.cfm?keyword!=international&international&topic+international (discussing In re iPrimus, Inc., Ontario Superior Ct. (Sept. 6, 2000)).

[392] Michael Foreman, Net Defamation Case Tests Law, New Zealand Herald (Apr. 24, 2001) (visited June 10, 2001), http://www.nzhearld.co.nz/storydisplay.cfm?storyID=184771.

[393] Id.

on statements in non-Internet media, that are inconsistent with the standards of the First Amendment."[394] Countries vary significantly in their attractiveness for plaintiffs in international tort litigation. England, for example, has been described as a "libel magnet" because of its rules that benefit libel plaintiffs.[395]

Fraud claims continue to be a major risk factor for the high-tech business. PricewaterhouseCoopers' 2000 Securities Litigation Study found that "more than half of the 201 shareholder class action lawsuits filed in federal courts last year contained allegations of financial fraud. . . . Fifty-three percent of all cases filed in 2000 contained financial fraud allegations, and PricewaterhouseCoopers expects the number of cases containing this type of allegation to continue at this pace in 2001."[396] Foreign litigants may have standing to file securities fraud lawsuits in federal court based upon electronic road shows or other solicitations transmitted over the Internet. In addition, accountant firms may be liable for Internet-related securities fraud.[397] In the United States, false or misleading statements may be the basis of trespass to chattels action. Foreign countries may prosecute false or misleading statements, such as false e-mail headers, as crimes or civil wrongs.[398] In the United States, there is a right of publicity and remedies for the appropriation of a plaintiff's identity.[399] It is a tort to use a plaintiff's identity in advertising or to use a public figure's "name, likeness, voice or other aspect of identity."[400] The right of publicity is not well developed in most countries connected to the Internet.

European countries primarily follow "*lex loci delicti* or the law of the place where the tort was committed."[401] One difficulty in Internet tort cases is deciding conflict of law disputes. European Union countries have a division of authority "as to whether the place of the act or the place of the harm is used."[402]

[G]   Internet Advertising

Advertising regulation for the Internet may occur under the common law, state law, federal law, and international law. Advertising is an inexpensive method

---

[394] Wimmer and Berman, United States Jurisdiction to Enforce Foreign Internet Libel Judgments, *id.* at 1.

[395] Lilian Edwards, Defamation and the Internet, Chapter 11 in Lilian Edwards & Charlotte Waelde, Law and the Internet: A Framework for Electronic Commerce 258 (2d ed. 2001).

[396] *Id.*

[397] The accounting community argues that it should have limited liability for audits of dot.com companies. "'There were lots of promises made about more money being made available,' he says. 'It is very difficult to put in going concern clauses when astute investors, management teams, directors and venture capitalists who are the closest to the e-Business all believe it has a strong chance of succeeding." In Practice, Dot.com Audits, We Want to Believe, Global News Wire (May 25, 2001).

[398] Australia: Guilty Plea on Misleading Spam Charges, 2 World Internet Law Report 16 (Apr. 2001).

[399] Dan B. Dobbs, The Law of Torts 1198 (2000).

[400] *Id.*

[401] Peter P. Swire, Symposium on Jurisdiction and the Internet: Of Elephants, Mice, and Privacy: International Choice of Law and the Internet, 32 Int'l Law 991 (1998).

[402] *Id.*

of reaching a vast audience of potential customers, but it also poses a risk of subjecting an Internet company to jurisdiction in a distant forum. The web is a worldwide venue, however, and advertising on it may subject an e-business to consumer or other substantive laws in hundreds of countries. Cultural sensitivities may create new risks for the online advertiser. France, for example, prosecuted Georgia Tech University for advertising its overseas program in France in an English-only format.[403] The same rules that apply to other forms of advertising also apply to electronic marketing. In Western Europe wireless application technologies are widely adopted, enabling users to have access to the Internet. "Frost & Sullivan estimates that by 2006, there is the potential for 37 billion wireless advertisements and alerts to be sent in Western Europe. Revenues generated in the Western European wireless banner ads sector will rise from U.S. $51.5 million in 2001 to $464.7 million in 2006."[404]

Advertisements must be culturally customized for different countries as the e-business expands internationally. Advertisements may be the basis for lawsuits alleging trademark dilution and infringement, commercial disparagement, defamation, fraud, and other civil wrongs. Internet advertising may constitute minimum contacts required for specific personal jurisdiction under U.S. law. Personal jurisdiction is frequently asserted over nonresident defendants on the basis of interactive web sites. A U.S. e-business may find that an Internet advertisement subjects itself to jurisdiction in a foreign venue.[405] The Germans do not permit comparative advertising, a rule that does not apply in the United States or the United Kingdom.[406] Online advertisements must not only meet U.S. standards, but international standards. Under U.S. law advertising claims must not be misleading, unfair, or deceptive. Disclaimers must be clear and conspicuous. The disclosures should be prominently displayed on the web site.

[1] European Advertising Standards

Counsel can consult the European Advertising Standards Alliance to learn more about cross-border advertising issues.[407] Since 1992 the Alliance has been coordinating the cross-border complaints system, which has been successful in solving complaints of a cross-border nature. The Alliance issues Euro-Ad alerts

---

[403] Perkins Coie LLP: Internet Case Digest, Defense of the French Language v. Georgia Tech (Apr. 29, 1998) (reporting dismissal of case on procedural grounds a lawsuit against the Metz, France campus of Georgia Tech for maintaining a Web site in English only).

[404] *See* Frost & Sullivan study in M2Press (June 12, 2001) (available on LEXIS News Group File).

[405] *Venue* is a distinct requirement for personal jurisdiction. "Personal jurisdiction focuses on the convenience of the particular jurisdiction for the parties to litigate the suit, particularly the defendant." Kimberly A. Moore, Forum Shopping in Patent Cases: Does Geographic Choice Affect Innovation? 79 N. Car. L. Rev. 889, 895 (2001).

[406] Michael Chisskick, Effective Contracting on the Internet: Outlining the Legal Position for Conducting E-Business in the UK, 1 E-Commerce Law 9, 10 (May 2001).

[407] European Advertising Standards Alliance (visited Apr. 19, 2002), http://www.eala.net/pages/topnavi.htm.

about "genuine sharp or illegal practice, where the advertiser is uncontactable or is moving between several countries."[408] Euro-Ad alerts are "sent to Alliance members, the European Advertising profession, European consumer organizations, the EU Commission and the International Marketing Supervision Network."[409] Most Euro-Ad alerts involve misleading directed mail. A complaint, for example, was made about a mailing from Malta "which led consumers to believe they had won a car, and only had to pay 159 FF in participation costs. When they received the prize, it turned out to be a miniature toy version of the car."[410] Another alert is a warning about Nigerian money transfers.[411] The fraudulent direct mailing offers consumers money in "response for use of his bank account to transfer over-invoiced money to an account outside Nigeria."[412] Advertising considered to be deceptive or unfair by the Federal Trade Commission may also be subject to actions by European regulators.

[2]   International Chamber of Commerce Guidelines

The International Chamber of Commerce (ICC) has promulgated influential standards for advertising and marketing over Electronic Networks. The ICC is the "world's foremost developer of ethical conduct for advertising and marketing practices."[413] The global e-Business should consult the ICC Guidelines that incorporate the ICC's Codes on Advertising Practice, Sales Promotion, Direct Marketing, and other standards.[414] The ICC relies primarily on broad standards rather than bright-line rules. The general ICC standard is that "advertising and marketing should be legal, decent, honest and truthful."[415] The ICC takes a country-of-origin approach to Internet marketing. All advertising and marketing messages "should be legal in their country of origin."[416] If the ICC approach was adopted by a court, U.S. advertisers would be permitted to use comparative advertisements or mention the trademarks of competitors, practices considered unfair in some European countries. However, the ICC also states that advertising and marketing "should be sensitive to issues of social responsibility and should in addition conform to generally accepted principles as regards ethical marketing."[417]

---

[408] *Id.*

[409] *Id.*

[410] *Id.*

[411] One of the authors received this fraudulent solicitation while writing this chapter and forwarded it the appropriate federal law enforcement authorities.

[412] *Id.*

[413] International Chamber of Commerce, ICC Guidelines on Advertising and Marketing on the Internet (Apr. 2, 1998) (visited Apr. 19, 2002), http://www.iccwbo.org/home/statements_rules/rules/1998/internet_guidelines.asp.

[414] *Id.* at Art. 1.

[415] *Id.*

[416] *Id.*

[417] *Id.*

Advertisers on the Internet "who post commercial messages via the Internet should always disclose their own identity and that of the relevant subsidiary, if applicable, in such a way that the user can contact the advertiser or marketer without difficulty."[418] Internet providers need to heed Article 3, which requires that costs associated with electronic sales, and marketing be disclosed. "Advertisers and marketers should clearly inform users of the cost of accessing a message or service where the cost is higher than the basic telecommunications rate."[419] There is a notice requirement that gives users "a reasonable amount of time to disconnect from the service without incurring the charge."[420] Advertisers and marketers are to "respect the role of particular electronic news groups, forums or bulletin boards" and not send Spam e-mail.[421]

Article 5 of the ICC Guidelines sets standards for the collection and use of personal data of web site visitors. Marketers are not to use personal data in a way incompatible with disclosed purposes.[422] Advertisers need to take "reasonable precautions to safeguard the security of their data files."[423] Users should be given the opportunity "to refuse the transfer of data to another advertiser or marketer."[424] Online mechanisms should be given to permit users "to opt-out by electronic means" of data transfers.[425] Advertisers should also have an opportunity to correct data or obtain data relating to him or her.[426] Advertisers or marketers on the Internet need to "post their privacy statement on their online site."[427] Unsolicited commercial messages should not be sent to users who indicate they do not wish to receive them.[428]

Article 6 of the ICC Guidelines provides voluntary standards relevant to advertising to children. Advertising should not exploit children or contain content harmful to children.[429] Advertising should identify material that is intended for only adults.[430] Parents and adults should be encouraged by advertising to supervise their children's online activities.[431] Article 7 asks advertisers to be sensitive to messages that may be "perceived as pornographic, violent, racist, or sexist on the global Internet."[432] The online company should be aware that the ICC regulations are voluntary industry standards, and subordinate to existing national law.[433]

---

[418] Id. at Art. 2

[419] Id. at Art. 3.

[420] Id.

[421] Id. at Art. 4.

[422] Id. at Art. 5(1).

[423] Id. at Art. 5(2)

[424] Id. at Art. 5(3).

[425] Id. at Art. 5(3).

[426] Id. at Art. 5(5).

[427] Id. at Art. 5(6).

[428] Id. at Art. 6.

[429] Id.

[430] Id.

[431] Id.

[432] Id. at Art. 7.

[433] Comment No. 1 to the ICC Guidelines is that "ICC Codes and Guidelines are always subordinate to existing law." Id.

[H]   Internet Taxation

The European Union or Eurozone relies heavily on the value-added tax (VAT) levied by customs. This is not a form of taxation recognized in the United States.[434] The United States, as one of the 135 countries that are parties to the World Trade Organization (WTO), has spearheaded an agreement to promote duty-free and tax-free cyberspace. The Internet has also raised new issues for customs and indirect taxation.[435] In response, the United States has led a worldwide movement to promote Internet commerce by preventing discriminatory taxes in the global environment.[436] The U.S. Department of Treasury is working with The Organization for Economic Cooperation and Development (OECD) to formulate global Internet taxation conditions of "neutrality, efficiency, certainty, simplicity, effectiveness, fairness and flexibility."

The OECD Ministers released a report on how "to eliminate harmful preferential tax regimes and criteria to identify tax havens and other harmful tax practices."[437] The OECD's June 2000 report identified "35 jurisdictions meeting the criteria for being tax havens."[438] When an e-business begins to sell goods or render services to individuals and entities in other countries, it must consider international tax issues. For a U.S. e-business that sells goods to citizens in Europe, the VAT is typically "built into the price that the end consumer pays."[439] The European Commission presented a proposal urging that the United States adopt a value-added tax on online products.[440] The United States opposes any attempt by the European Commission or non-EU members to collect value-added taxes on electronically delivered products.[441]

However, the U.S. exporter would receive a refund if customs officials charged a VAT on goods exported from European countries.[442] The value-added tax system was designed for tangible goods. It is likely that imposing VAT on software and other intangibles would be "more trouble than it is worth, especially if competition pushes the price of such digital goods to very low levels."[443] The

---

[434] *See* Agreement on Trade-Related Aspects of Intellectual Property Rights; *see also* Agreement on Trade-Related Aspects of Intellectual Property Rights (Apr. 15, 1994), Marrakesh Agreement Establishing the World Trade Organization, Annex 1C, 33 I.L.M. 1125, 1197 (1994).

[435] Global Information Infrastructure Commission, Report, *id.* at 4 (noting that "the [European Commission] and the member states have recently decided to start an analysis of the impact and consequences of electronic commerce on customs and indirect taxation" and that the EU Commission as well as the OECD Committee is studying Internet taxation).

[436] *Id.* at 48.

[437] Jeffrey Owens, OECD, Paris, Promotion Fair Tax Competition, 3 Tax Planning International E-Commerce 17 (Jan. 2001).

[438] *Id.* at 17.

[439] Hal R. Varian, Debating the Prospect of E-Commerce Taxation: Taxation of Electronic Commerce, 13 Harv. J. Law & Tech. 639 (2000).

[440] *Id.* at 49.

[441] *Id.* (citing http://www.treas.gov/press/releases/ps80.htm).

[442] *Id.*

[443] *Id.*

European Commission proposed a rule that exempted digitally delivered goods purchased by EU consumers from the VAT. The European Commission proposal to charge the member states rejected VAT on digital products from outside the European Community to consumers within the Community.[444]

The European Commission's value-added tax proposal would have suppliers register with one member state to cover all suppliers.[445] The VAT proposal would have charged a VAT to a broad array of products including "the supply of software, of data processing, of computer services including web hosting, web design and similar services and of information, where any of these are made by electronic means including broadcasting."[446] The biggest political obstacle was the rule that "a non-Community supplier could pick one member state for registration, to cover all supplies to Community consumers."[447] Suppliers would have a built-in incentive to choose a Member State with a low VAT rate that would result in a "competitive advantage over a Community supplier from a high-rate state."[448] Future proposals may require non-Community suppliers to register in every member state where they make sales to consumers.[449] One of the unresolved issues is how remote sellers will collect taxes on international Internet transactions. One solution to this quandary would be to allow "non-Community suppliers to register in only one Member State, but to share out the VAT revenues between all the member states."[450] Proposals to reform the Internet tax system will require a multi-lateral treaty that balances local versus global issues.

[I]   Online Contract Formation

[1]   UNCITRAL Model Law on Electronic Commerce

Internet sales and services are classified as international business transactions. As such, the general principles governing international business contracts may be found in U.S. law, the national law of trading countries, and the Convention on Contracts for the International Sale of Goods (CISG). The purpose of CISG is to adopt uniform rules governing contracts for the international sale of goods. The Internet is a new source of liability for many companies, ranging from the possibility that a dot-com company will be sued in a distant forum for copyright or trademark infringement to defamation in online forums, from breaches of information security and invasion of privacy to online fraud claims or tax liabilities. Risks experienced by a bricks-and-mortar e-business may multiply as an

---

[444] Richard Baron, VAT—Where Next for Europe? 3 Tax Planning International: E-Commerce 10 (Jan. 2001).

[445] *Id.*

[446] *Id.*

[447] *Id.*

[448] *Id.*

[449] *Id.* at 12.

[450] *Id.*

e-business goes online and confronts new dangers, such as vicarious liability for telecommuting employees, negligent information security, or Internet-related business torts. It is unclear whether a court in a foreign jurisdiction would find an e-business negligent for failure to encrypt trade secrets or confidential information.[451]

The United Nations Commission on International Trade Law (UNCITRAL) in 1996 issued the UNCITRAL Model Law on Electronic Commerce.[452] The purpose of the Model Law was "to promote the harmonization and unification of international trade law, so as to remove unnecessary obstacles to international trade caused by inadequacies and divergences in the law affecting trade."[453] The Model Law "applies to any kind of information in the form of a data message used in the context of commercial activities."[454] Article 4 of the Model Law validates the legal recognition of data messages.[455] Electronic data messages are admissible and given the same weight as other evidence.[456] Article 9 sets forth rules on the retention of data messages.[457] Article 13 validates the formation and validity of electronic contracts.[458] The concept of *attribution* is concerned with the identity of

---

[451] Joshua M. Masur, Safety in Numbers: Revisiting the Risks to Client Confidences and Attorney-Client Privilege Posed by Internet Electronic Mail, 14 Berkeley Tech. L.J. 1117, 117 (1999) (noting possibility "that a court will eventually find negligence in the failure to encrypt").

[452] The United Nations Commission on International Trade Law (UNCITRAL) adopted the UNCITRAL Model Law on Legal Aspects of Electronic Data Interchange (EDI) and Related Means of Communications (Model Law) in 1996 in furtherance of its mandate to promote the harmonization and unification of international trade law. Preamble, *id.* "Over the past quarter of a century, UNCITRAL, whose membership consists of States from all regions and of all levels of economic development, has implemented its mandate by formulating international conventions (the United Nations Conventions on Contracts for the International Sale of Goods, on the Limitation Period in the International Sale of Goods, on the Carriage of Goods by Sea, 1978 ('Hamburg Rules'), on the Liability of Operators of Transport Terminals in International Trade, on International Bills of Exchange and International Promissory Notes, and on Independent Guarantees and Stand-by Letters of Credit), model laws (the UNCITRAL Model Laws on International Commercial Arbitration, on International Credit Transfers and on Procurement of Goods, Construction and Services), the UNCITRAL Arbitration Rules, the UNCITRAL Conciliation Rules, and legal guides (on construction contracts, countertrade transactions and electronic funds transfers").

[453] UNCITRAL has produced a large number of model laws to facilitate world trade, including the Conventions on Contracts for the International Sale of Goods, on the Limitation Period in the International Sale of Goods, on the Carriage of Goods by Sea, 1978 ("Hamburg Rules"), on the Liability of Operators of Transport Terminals in International Trade, on International Bills of Exchange and International Promissory Notes, and on Independent Guarantees and Stand-by Letters of Credit), model laws (the UNCITRAL Model Laws on International Commercial Arbitration, on International Credit Transfers and on Procurement of Goods, Construction and Services), the UNCITRAL Arbitration Rules, the UNCITRAL Conciliation Rules, and legal guides (on construction contracts, countertrade transactions and electronic funds transfers).

[454] UNCITRAL Model Law on Electronic Commerce, General Assembly Resolution 51/162 of 16 Dec. 1996 at Art. 1.

[455] UNCITRAL's EDI Model Law, *id.* at Art. 4.

[456] *Id.* at Art. 8.

[457] *Id.* at Art. 9.

[458] *Id.* at Art. 14.

the message sender.[459] A *data message* is defined as "information generated, sent, received or stored by electronic, optical or similar means including but not limited to, electronic data interchange (EDI), electronic mail, telegram, telex, or telecopy."[460] UNCITRAL's model law does not supplant any rule of law designed to protect consumers.[461]

UNCITRAL adopted a general freedom of contract where the provisions of the Model Law may be varied by agreement.[462] UNCITRAL prefigured the E-Sign Act of 2000 validating digital signatures and electronic records.[463] Article 5 of the Model Law gives legal recognition to data messages used in EDI.[464] "Information shall not be denied legal effect, validity, or enforceability solely on the grounds that it is in the form of a data message."[465] A data message is treated with the same validity as a writing.[466] Similarly, where the law requires a signature of a person, the data message serves as a functional equivalent.[467] Data messages may be treated as originals, where "the law requires information to be presented or retained in its original form."[468] The retention of data messages satisfies legal requires for the retention of documents under UNCITRAL's Model Law.[469]

[2]   EU Electronic Signature Directive

The European Union (EU) seeks to develop a legal infrastructure for electronic commerce.[470] The European Union's Directive on Electronic Signature validates electronic signatures and thus eliminates barriers to electronic or online communications.[471] The legal recognition of electronic signature and the accreditation of certification-service providers are needed for e-commerce. "Electronic communication and commerce necessitates electronic signatures and related services allowing data authentication; divergent rules with respect to legal recognition of electronic signatures and the accreditation of certification-service providers in the

---

[459] *Id.* at Art. 11.

[460] *Id.* at Art. 2(a).

[461] *Id.* at Art. 1, cmt.

[462] *Id.* at Art. 4.

[463] President Clinton signed the Electronic Signatures in Global and National Commerce Act (E-Sign) on June 30, 2000. Chapter 6 has an extensive discussion of the role E-Sign will have in validating electronic signatures and records as well as the delivery of legally required notices and disclosures. E-Sign is consistent with the 1996 Model Law on Electronic Commerce issued by the United Nations Commission on International Trade Law (UNCITRAL).

[464] *Id.* at Art. 5.

[465] *Id.*

[466] *Id.* at Art. 6.

[467] *Id.* at Art. 7.

[468] *Id.* at Art. 8.

[469] *Id.* at Art. 10.

[470] European Union, Electronic Commerce in the Internal Market (visited Apr. 12, 2002), http://europa.eu.int/comm/internal_market/comcom/newsletter.

[471] Directive 1999/93/EC of the European Parliament and of the Council of 13 December 1999 on a Community framework for electronic signatures, Official Journal L 013, 19/01/2000 p. 0012-0020.

Member States. . . ."[472] The European approach to digital signatures is technology-neutral in contrast to the prescriptive models of U.S. states such as Utah.[473] The goal of the Directive is to encourage the inoperability of electronic-signature products.[474] It is anticipated that certification services will be used across borders and over open networks.[475] The Directive acknowledges that electronic signatures have a wide variety of circumstances and applications and therefore does not limit electronic signatures to "the issuance and management of certificates."[476] The EU Electronic Signature Directive "does not preclude the establishment of private-sector based supervision system nor does it oblige certification-service providers to apply to be supervised under any applicable accreditation scheme."[477]

At minimum, certification providers issuing qualified certificates must: "(a) demonstrate the reliability necessary for providing certification services; (b) ensure the operation of a prompt and secure directory and a secure and immediate revocation service; (c) ensure that the date and time when a certificate is issued or revoked can be determined precisely; (d) verify, by appropriate means in accordance with national law, the identity and, if applicable, any specific attributes of the person to which a qualified certificate is issued; (e) employ personnel who possess the expert knowledge, experience, and qualifications necessary for the services provided . . . (f) use trustworthy systems and products . . . and ensure the technical cryptographic security of the process supported by them; (g) take measures against forgery of certificates . . . (h) maintain sufficient financial resources . . . to bear the risk of liability for damages; (i) record all relevant information concerning a qualified certificate . . . (j) not store or copy signature-creation data of the person to whom the certification-service-provider provided key management service; (k) before entering into a contractual relationship . . . set out the precise terms and conditions regarding the use of the certificate . . . and (l) use trustworthy systems to store certificates in a verifiable form."[478]

The Directive sets forth the requirements for signature-creation devices.[479] Signature-creation data used for generating signatures may only be used once.[480] Signature-creation data must be protected against forgery with the best available technology.[481] Signature data must be "reliably protected by the legitimate signa-

---

[472] Preamble, *id.* at 8.

[473] Preamble at 8 (stating "[r]apid technological development and the global character of the Internet necessitate an approach which is open to various technologies and services capable of authenticating data electronically").

[474] Preamble, *id.* at 5.

[475] *Id.* at 9-10.

[476] *Id.* at 9.

[477] *Id.* at 13.

[478] *Id.* at Annex II (specifying requirements for certification service providers issuing qualified certificates).

[479] *Id.* at Annex III (specifying requirements for secure signature-creation devices).

[480] *Id.*

[481] *Id.*

tory against the use of others."[482] Secure signature-creation devices "must not alter the data to be signed or prevent such data from being presented to the signatory prior to the signature process."[483] The Directive has several recommendations for secure signature verification.[484] The process should be ensured that "the data used for verifying the signature correspond to the data displayed by the verifier."[485] There must be a method for reliably verifying and displaying signatures.[486] Verifiers should be able to "reliably establish the contents of the signed data."[487] The authenticity and validity of the certificate must be reliably verified.[488] It is important that the signatory's identity be correctly displayed and verified.[489] There must be mechanism for clearly indicating the use of a pseudonym.[490] Security-relevant changes must also be able to be reliably detected.[491]

In general, the Directive validates and legally recognizes electronic signatures but does not mandate a regulatory framework.[492] An *electronic signature* is defined as data in electronic form that is attached to electronic data and serves as a method of authentication.[493] "The Directive contributes to the use and legal recognition of electronic signatures within the Community; a regulatory framework is not needed for electronic signatures exclusively used within systems, which are based on voluntary agreement under private law."[494] Advanced electronic signatures must satisfy the following four conditions to be enforceable: (1) be uniquely linked to the signatory; (2) capable of identifying the signatory; (3) means that the signatory can maintain sole control; and (4) linking to data "which it relates in such a manner that any subsequent change of the data is detectable."[495] A *certification service provider* "means an entity or a legal or natural person who issues certificates or provides other services related to electronic signatures."[496] *Certificates* mean "an electronic attestation which links signature-verification data to a person and confirms the identity of that person."[497]

Member states are not able to make "certification services subject to prior authorization."[498] The Directive adopts a freedom of contract model that gives parties the right to agree to accept electronically signed data.[499] Each member state is

---

[482] *Id.*

[483] *Id.*

[484] *Id.* at Annex IV (specifying recommendations for secure signature verification).

[485] *Id.* at a.

[486] Appendix IV, *id.* at b.

[487] Appendix IV, *id.* at c.

[488] Appendix IV, *id.* at d.

[489] Appendix IV, *id.*

[490] Appendix IV, *id.* at f.

[491] Appendix IV, *id.* at g.

[492] Appendix IV, *id.* at 16.

[493] *Id.* at Art. 2.

[494] *Id.*

[495] *Id.* at Art. 2(a)(d).

[496] *Id.* at Art. 2(11).

[497] *Id.* at Art. 2(9).

[498] *Id.* at Art. 3(1).

[499] *Id.*

responsible for establishing systems for overseeing certification service providers.[500] The member states are to respect "the legal effectiveness of electronic signatures and in such systems and their admissibility as evidence should be recognized."[501] The Directive seeks to balance consumer and business needs.[502] Certification service providers "may not restrict their services to a given member state" and certificates must be "permitted to circulate freely in the internal market."[503] Member States may not deny the legal effectiveness of a signature or record or the admissibility as evidence if it is in electronic form.[504]

Legal validity is based upon an assumption that "advanced electronic signatures which are based on the qualified certificate and which are created by a secure-signature-creation device: (a) satisfy the legal requirements of a signature . . . and (b) are admissible as evidence in legal proceedings."[505] A qualified certificate must contain (1) an indication that the certificate is issued as a qualified certificate; (2) the identification of the certification service provider and the state in which it is established; (3) the name of the signatory or a pseudonym, which shall be identified as such; (4) provision for a specific attribute of the signatory to be included if relevant, depending on the purpose for which the certificate is intended; (5) signature-verification data which correspond to signature-creation data under the control of the signatory; (6) an indication of the beginning and end of the period of validity of the certificate; (7) the identity code of the certificate; (8) the advanced electronic signature of the certification service provider issuing it; (9) limitations the scope of use of the certificate, if applicable; and (10) limits on the value of transaction for which the certificate can be used, if applicable.[506]

One of the unsettled questions is the liability of certificate service providers that are called certificate authorities in the United States. In the United States, providers will typically seek to limit liability for the issuance of certificates. The EC Directive provides that member states shall "ensure that by issuing a certificate as a qualified certificate to the public. . . . the service-provider is liable for damage caused to any entity or legal or natural person who reasonably relies on the certificate."[507] Providers are in effect required to give warranties as to the accuracy of all information on certificates at the time of issuance.[508] Another warranty is that the signatory corresponds to "the signature-verification data given or identified in the certificate."[509] A certificate service provider may be absolved from liability "if he proves that he has not acted negligently."[510] However, all providers

---

[500] *Id.* at Art. 3(3).

[501] *Id.*

[502] *Id.* at 14.

[503] *Id.* at Art. 4 (1)(2).

[504] *Id.* at Art. 5(2).

[505] *Id.* at Art. 5(1).

[506] *Id.* at Annex I, Requirements for Qualified Certificates.

[507] *Id.* at Art. 6(1).

[508] *Id.* at Art. 6(1)(a).

[509] *Id.* at Art. 6(b).

[510] *Id.* at Art. 6 (1) (c).

who issue a certificate are "liable for damage caused to any entity or legal or natural person who reasonably relies on the certificate for failure to register revocation of the certificate."[511]

A certificate service provider may defend this claim on the basis that "he has not acted negligently."[512] Providers may limit "the value of the transaction for which the certificate can be used, provided that the limit is recognizable to third parties."[513] The provider "shall not be liable for damage resulting from this maximum limit being exceeded."[514] The Directive also has rules on cross-border certification services with third-party countries.[515] The Directive asks that the European Council negotiate bilateral and multilateral organization to standardize certification service provider practices.[516] Providers are required to meet data protection laws as "to the processing of personal data and on the free movement of such data."[517]

[3] EU Distance Selling Directive

The European Union Directive on the Protection of Consumers in Respect of Distance Contracts (Distance Selling Directive) places limitations on online contracts directed to consumers in the 15 member states.[518] Each member state has its own statutory regulation addressing the Distance Selling Directive. The United Kingdom Directive addresses "contracts for the supply of services concluded at a distance" between merchants and consumers.[519]

The Distance Selling Directive applies only to B2C,[520] not B2B or B2G transactions. "The distance contract is one where supplier and consumer do not

---

[511] *Id.* at Art. 6(2).

[512] *Id.*

[513] *Id.* at Art. 6(4).

[514] *Id.*

[515] *Id.* at Art. 7.

[516] *Id.* at Art. 7(2).

[517] Article 8 requires providers to meet the requirements of the Data Protection Directive that went into effect in October 1998. *Id.* at Art. 8.

[518] Directive 97/7 of the European Parliament and of the Council of 20 May 1997 on the Protection of Consumers in Respect of Distance Contracts, Official Journal L 144 of 04/06/1997 (Distance Selling Directive); *see also* Financial Services: Amended Proposal for a Directive on Distance Marketing. A Directive Concerns the Distance Marketing of Consumer Financial Services, COM/1999/385.

[519] Department of Trade & Industry (United Kingdom) Distance Selling Directive—Implementation in the U.K. (visited Apr. 14, 2002), http://www.dti.gov.uk/cacp/ca/distance/dist.htm (hereinafter U.K. Distance Selling Directive); *see also* Directive 97/7 of the European Parliament and of the Council of 20 May 1997 on the Protection of Consumers in respect of Distance Contracts, Official Journal L 144 of 04/06/1997 (Distance Selling Directive); Financial Services: Amended Proposal for a Directive on Distance Marketing. A Directive Concerns the Distance Marketing of Consumer Financial Services, COM/1999/385.

[520] B2C is business to consumer in contrast to B2B, which signifies business to business. Finally, B2G is business to government e-Commerce.

come face to face up to and including the moment at which the contract is concluded (i.e. mail order, telephone sales, electronic commerce)."[521] The Directive applies to the rendering of professional services[522] at a distance as well as sales.[523] The Directive does not apply to the marketing of financial services.[524] The Directive does not apply to the sale of real property but may apply to leases and rental agreements.[525] The Directive does not cover telephone services and other telecommunications operations.[526] The Directive requires consumers to be provided with information about the seller in "a clear and comprehensible manner and in good time before the conclusion of any distance contract."[527]

The Distance Selling Directive requires the online seller and other distance supplier to provide the following information prior to conclusion of the contract: (1) name and address of supplier, (2) main characteristics of goods or services, (3) price, (4) arrangements for payment, (5) existence of right of withdrawal where appropriate, and (6) the cost of using the means of distance communication.[528]

Written confirmation in a durable medium must be given to the consumer unless "the information has already been given in writing prior to the conclusion of the contract."[529] The written confirmation must minimally include (1) written information on the conditions for exercising the consumers' right of withdrawal, (2) geographical address to the supplier's place of business, (3) information on any after-sales service and guarantees, and (4) conditions for canceling the contract where it is of unspecified duration or exceeds one year.[530] Article 6 of the Directive "gives consumers the right to withdraw from contracts within seven working days without penalty and without giving any reason."[531] The period of withdrawal begins from the date of receipt or the date of the conclusion of the contract.

The *date of the conclusion* of the contract is when the contract is formed, not performed.[532] If the consumer has not received the written confirmation information required by Article 5, the period of withdrawal is extended to three months.[533]

---

[521] U.K. Distance Selling Directive, *id.* at Art. 2.

[522] The traditional dichotomy is between sales and the rendering of services. Under U.S. law, two tests are used when a contract is a hybrid containing both the sales of goods and services. The first test is the predominant purpose test that asks whether a transaction is predominantly a sale or service. The second test is the gravamen test that looks at whether the sales aspect or the service aspect of a transaction substantially caused an injury. In other words, the gravamen test focuses on the source of the problems. If the rendering of professional services is the source of the complaint, the common law of best efforts applies. If the problem is defective goods, Article 2 of the UCC applies.

[523] U.K. Distance Selling Directive.

[524] *Id.*

[525] *Id.*

[526] *Id.* at Art. 2.3.

[527] *Id.* at Art. 4.

[528] *Id.* at Art. 4.

[529] *Id.* at Art. 5.

[530] *Id.*

[531] *Id.* at Art. 6.

[532] *Id.*

[533] *Id.*

A consumer does not have a right to cancel (1) contracts for service already begun; (2) contracts for goods and services where price is calculated by fluctuations in the financial market; (3) contracts for goods supplied to the consumer's specifications (i.e., a tailored suit); and (4) contracts for supply of video, audio, or computer software where the seal of the shrinkwrap is broken by the consumer.[534] It is unclear whether a consumer would have a right to cancel a contract for software downloaded from a web site where there is no seal to be broken.[535]

A consumer's assent to a click-wrap agreement may be viewed as the functional equivalent of "breaking the seal" of shrinkwrap.[536] The Directive requires the seller to give the consumer a refund for any money paid. The seller may assess the cost of postage for goods returned. The consumer must be reimbursed with 30 days of the consumer giving notice that they are exercising the right of cancellation.[537]

[4]   Electronic Commerce Directive

The European Union Electronic Commerce Directive took effect on January 6, 2002. Directive 2000/31/EC requires member states to recognize electronic contracts. The Directive requires merchants to provide consumers with disclosures such as what steps are required to create a binding contract, the means for correcting errors in orders, and the languages in which the contract terms are presented. The Directive was proposed to promote the free movement of e-commerce services and guarantee access for services throughout the member states. The Directive "will ensure that Information Society services benefit from the Internal Market[538] principles of free movement of services . . . throughout the EU."[539] The Directive establishes rules for online contracting, marketing, advertising, and for the liability of providers. The Directive addresses issues such as rules for the liability of Internet Service Providers, choice of law, electronic contracts, spam e-mail, digital signatures, and e-filing of records. The Directive also seeks to eliminate barriers to an integrated information-based economy.

The European Parliament approved the Electronic Commerce Directive in May of 2000. The Directive validates electronic contracts, establishes the liability of Internet intermediaries, provides for online dispute resolution, and provides for

---

[534] *Id.* at Art. 6.3.

[535] The commentary to the Distance Selling Directive states: "In some cases, this wording is not entirely clear (e.g. computer software may be supplied on-line in which case the term 'unsealed' refers to the user's indicating assent . . ."). Distance Selling Directive, *id.*

[536] *Id.*

[537] *Id.* at Art. 7.

[538] All of the Directives advance the Internal Market between member states. The goal of the European Union has been to form a single market and eliminate market barriers.

[539] European Commission, Electronic Commerce: Commission Welcomes Final Adoptions of Legal Framework Directive (visited June 9, 2000), http//www.europa.eu.int/comm/intrnal_market/en/media/eleccomm/2k-442.htm.

other harmonized e-commerce rules.[540] Electronic signatures are not legally discriminated against in EU member countries. The EU approach is not to mandate a particular technology such as digital signatures, asymmetrical cryptography, or biometrics.[541] The Electronic Signature Directive was enacted by the European Commission to permit someone to send and receive data over electronic networks. The Directive provides legal validity to electronic signatures as long as the signature product meets specific requirements.[542] An electronic signature is considered to be the equivalent of a handwritten signature and may be introduced into evidence.[543] Electronic signatures are "subject to the legislation and control by the country of origin."[544]

[5] International Sales of Goods

As a merchant, SPC is selling computer hardware subject to international sales law, the UN's Convention on Contracts for the International Sale of Goods (CISG).[545] The United Nations approved CISG in 1980, and the United States became a signatory to CISG in 1988. CISG is a hybrid statute borrowing "concepts and methods from the common law system that the United States inherited from the British system and the civil law system of Europe."[546] CISG applies to "contracts of sale of goods" if two requirements are satisfied: (1) the contracting parties must be from countries that have signed the Vienna Convention or CISG and (2) the subject of the sales agreement must be between commercial parties and not for consumer goods, certain obligations to pay money, ships, vessels, hovercraft, or the sale of electricity.[547]

CISG shares much common ground with Article 2 of the Uniform Commercial Code (UCC), but there are important differences. CISG, for example, does not recognize the Statute of Frauds, the parol evidence rule, or the perfect tender rule. CISG remedies are more standards-driven than the formulaic approach to separate buyer and seller's remedies under Article 2 of the UCC. Article 6 of CISG gives the parties to an international sales contract the right to opt out of CISG.[548] The

---

[540] *Id.*

[541] European Commission, Commission Welcomes a New Legal Framework to Guarantee Security of Electronic Signatures (visited June 9, 2000), http://europa.eu.int/comm/intrnal_market/en/media/sign/99-915.htm.

[542] *Id.* (discussing Directive 1999/93/EC of 13 Dec. 1999 on a Community framework for electronic signatures).

[543] Directive 1999/93/EC of 13 Dec. 1999 on a Community framework for electronic signatures.

[544] *Id.*

[545] The United Nations Convention on Contracts for the International Sale of Goods (CISG) was prepared by UNCITRAL and issued for signature in Vienna in 1980. Because CISG is classified as a self-executing treaty, no domestic or federal legislation was necessary.

[546] John E. Murray, Jr., Buying Abroad Invokes International Law Challenge: Contracts Governed Under the United Nations, 123 Purchasing 25 (1997).

[547] CISG, *id.* at Art. 3(2).

[548] *Id.* at Art. 6.

parties to a CISG transaction have the discretion to choose applicable U.S. or foreign law to govern all or parts of a transaction. SPC's counsel needs to make a strategic decision on whether it wants its B2B international contracts determined by CISG, foreign law, the UCC, or some other body of law. SPC's licensing of software may opt out of CISG in favor of the proposed Uniform Computer Information Transactions Act (UCITA).

Filanto v. Chilewich[549] is one of the few U.S. cases interpreting the provisions of CISG. CISG applies automatically to nonconsumer transactions if the seller and buyer have their places of business in different signatory countries. The parties are free to opt out or to choose which provisions of CISG apply to their sales transaction. If the parties choose to opt out, they should state that "the law of [your state] is the governing law and that the Convention for the International Sale of Goods shall not apply."[550]

It is theoretically possible to draft a hybrid Internet contract that incorporates terms based on CISG, UCITA, and UCC. CISG may be applied to the formation rules of the sale of a computer monitor, whereas UCC may apply to the warranties or remedies. UCITA could be applied to the software in a hybrid contract involving goods and intangibles such as software or other information transfers. The recent case law validates mass-market license agreements. Proposed UCITA favors the enforceability of shrinkwrap and other mass-market licenses.[551] SPC's mass-market licenses may not be enforceable in the global marketplace. An empirical study of the laws of 24 countries concluded that there is no clear consensus on the enforceability of shrinkwrap licenses in the global marketplace.[552] Relatively few countries freely enforce shrinkwrap licenses.[553] SPC's counsel must draft its license agreements considering the diverse contracting laws in its target markets. A number of other contracting rules differ in other important respects. The EU has a number of Directives that must be complied with in the Internet global marketplace.

Devising uniform rules for safeguarding commercial transfers of information that would be a familiar template no matter where the parties reside would be a desirable international development. The International Chamber of Commerce (ICC) proposes a broad self-regulatory program governing electronic commerce, including guidelines for secure and trustworthy digital transactions over the Internet.[554] The search for uniform contracting rules as a movement in private international law has evolved rapidly over the past century.[555] Past efforts at creating international commercial law have been spearheaded by the United National Commission for International Trade (UNCITRAL), the International Institute for the

---

[549] 789 F. Supp. 1229 (S.D.N.Y. 1992).

[550] Paul F. McIntosh, Selected Aspects of International Sales Transactions: The United Nations Convention on Contracts for the International Sale of Goods, 103 Bus. Credit 36 (Oct. 1, 2001).

[551] UCITA § 103 (1999).

[552] Mark Lemley, Intellectual Property and Shrink-wrap Licenses, 68 S. Cal. L. Rev. 1239 (2000).

[553] *Id.* at 1252-53.

[554] *Id.* at 85.

[555] Anthony D'Amato and Doris Estelle Long, International Intellectual Property Anthology 3 (1996).

Unification of Private Law (UNIDROIT), the Council on Europe, and the International Chamber of Commerce (ICC). UNCITRAL's Model Law on Electronic Commerce is consistent with UCITA's e-commerce infrastructure. The Model Law, like UCITA, validates the digital signature as the functional equivalent of the "pen and pencil" signature.

[J] International Products Liability

The European Commission is considering rules for rights and liabilities for the producers of defective products.[556] The European Commission originally enacted a directive concerning liability for defective products in 1985 and in 1999 adopted Directive 99/34/EC, which makes the producers of nonprocessed agricultural products liable without fault for damages to health caused by defective products. Product manufacturers already are "obliged to make good any damage to health, safety, and property caused by a defective product" under the 1985 Directive.[557] The Commission's Green Paper on products liability considers the expansion of strict liability principles to all products, including computer systems.

[K] Internet Payment Systems

The United States alone "represents a $115 billion market for financial institutions, technology vendors and third-party service providers" which accounts for approximately half of the total payments market on a global scale.[558] E-payment systems include checks, credit cards, and new forms of currency such as digital cash. Credit cards are the principal payment system for B2C sales. A web site will need a merchant account before it can accept credit card orders. Credit card fraud is 12 times higher on the Internet than in brick-and-mortar businesses.[559] Digital money has not yet gained widespread acceptance as a means of payment. The United States Department of Treasury is "the world's largest issuer of smart cards accounting for 3 million transactions and 375,000 cards."[560] The Department of Treasury is studying e-checks and other Internet-related payment systems, and the European Union recently enacted a Directive on the supervision of electronic money institutions.[561]

---

[556] Product liability is covered by Directive 85-374/EEC, OJ L 210 (25 July 1985) as amended by Directive 99/34/EC, OJ L 141 (4 June 1999).

[557] The European Commission, The Commission Adopts a Green Paper on Producer Liability (visited May 10, 2000), http://europa.eu.int/comm/internal_market/en/update/consumer/99-580.htm.

[558] Ric Duqes and Garen K. Staglin, eONE Global, Payments Revisited: Circa 2000 (Payments DNA: A White Paper) (visited June 9, 2001), http://www.eoneglobal.com/whtpaper.html.

[559] *Id.*

[560] *Id.*

[561] European Union, EU Directive on the pursuit and prudent supervision of the business of electronic money institutions; EU Directive 2000/12/EC.

[L]   Internet Employment Issues

Internet employment law needs to take into account foreign law as well as U.S. law. An e-business having foreign subsidiaries will need to take into account statutes or case law governing wrongful dismissal, layoffs, disciplinary rules, worker self-management rules, as well as special rules for employee compensation and takeovers. An e-business with a branch in Germany will need to comply with regulations concerning employment privacy. A subsidiary located in the United Kingdom will need to comply with the Employment Rights Act of 1996 (ERA), which applies to terms of employment and dismissal of employees.[562] The ERA requires employers to supply employees with a written statement that employment has begun and other particulars such as the "scale or rate of remuneration," intervals at which remuneration is paid, and terms and conditions relating to hours of work.[563] The ERA provides for remedies for wrongful dismissal, such as damages, reinstatement or a lump sum for redundancy.[564] Remedies turn on whether an employer is terminating an employee for wrongful dismissal, unfair dismissal and redundancy.[565]

Chapter Ten on E-Mail and Internet Usage Policies needs to be localized for foreign employment laws that may be triggered by telecommuting employees or employees located in overseas environments. The e-mail and Internet usage policies need to be customized to deal with cultural and legal differences. E-mail monitoring, for example, may not be done without an employee's consent in some nations. E-mail monitoring may not be legal even with consent of employees in other countries. A multinational e-business will need to roll out e-mail and Internet usage policies with careful attention to local legal environments and cultural differences. The policies will need to be tailored for language, cultural, and legal differences. Many European countries have statutes or common law protecting employees when companies are taken over. Domestic law or EU law may, for example, protect pension provisions.[566]

Restraints on employees and former employees in the form of restrictive covenants will also need to be localized. In England, an employee may be placed on "garden leave," which involves withdrawing "an employee from his regular duties [and] requiring him to stay home whilst retaining him as an employee."[567] In the United Kingdom, "garden leave" is also known as "sterilizing an employee."[568] In general, the longer the period of sterilization, the less likely a court is to enforce it.[569] The key issues involving restriction on employment that need to be localized

---

[562] Slaughter and May, The Engagement and Dismissal of Employees (Nov. 1999), submitted by Mark Carsdale, Slaughter & May for Legal & Strategic Issues for New Businesses (March 15-16 2001), Suffolk University Law School, Advanced Legal Studies.

[563] Id.

[564] Id.

[565] Id.

[566] Slaughter and May, Key Employment Issues for Transfers of Undertakings (Dec. 1997).

[567] Slaughter and May, Restraints on Employees and Former Employees (May 1996).

[568] Id.

[569] Id.

for national legal differences are (1) covenants against soliciting customers, (2) nondealing covenants, (3) noncompetition covenants, (4) confidentiality clauses, and (5) the effect of restrictive covenants on termination of employment.[570]

[M]   Internet Regulatory Issues

A number of countries have taken steps to regulate the Internet. In the United States, the FTC and the FCC are the key regulatory agencies. The FTC plays a key role in enforcing antitrust issues in the new economy. In Europe, the Court of First Instance in Luxembourg considers diverse "matters ranging from mega-mergers and intellectual property to staff disputes within the EC."[571] State and federal regulatory agencies police unfair and deceptive trade practices. An American-based e-business needs to comply with regulatory rulings in Europe, as illustrated by the European Commissioner for Competition Policy's "opposition to WorldCom's $138 billion merger with Sprint."[572]

The U.S. Securities and Exchange Commission has released a number of Internet-related SEC Interpretative Releases. The Commission released a statement on the use of the Internet "to Offer Securities, Solicit Securities Transactions, or Advertise Investment Services Offshore."[573] The SEC has also issued a release on Use of Electronic Media for Delivery Purposes.[574] The SEC's Internet Fraud Sweep has uncovered fraudulent schemes involving foreign entities.[575] The SEC's 2000 Internet Fraud sweep involved foreign entities and individuals using the Internet to communicate with potential U.S. investors.[576] A Canadian promoter sold shares for a new e-business without registering a public offering.[577] Two residents of Germany were charged with false statements made on web sites about baseless financial and stock price projections.[578] The e-business needs to study its electronic newsletters, web sites, e-mail messages, and postings on Internet web

---

[570] *Id.*

[571] Michael Learmonth, Europe on My Mind, The Industry Standard (Oct. 30, 2000) at 67.

[572] *Id.*

[573] U.S. Securities and Exchange Commission, Interpretation: Statement of the Commission Regarding Use of Internet Web Sites to Offer Securities, Solicit Securities Transactions, or Advertise Investment Services Offshore, Release No. 33-7516.htm (Mar. 23, 1998).

[574] U.S. Securities and Exchange Commission, Use of Electronic Media for Delivery Purposes; Action: Interpretation: Solicitation of Comment, 17 CFR Pts. 231, 241, and 271, Release No. 33-7233; 34-36345; IC-21399 File No. S7-31-95 (visited Mar. 12, 2001), http://www.sec.gov/divisions/enforce/internetenforce/interpreleases.shtml.

[575] SEC Continues Nationwide Crackdown Against Internet Fraud, Fourth Internet Sweep Brings to More Than 180 the Total Number of Internet Cases Filed (visited March 12, 2001), http://www.sec.gov/news/prss/2000-124.txt.

[576] *Id.*

[577] SEC v. Donald Rutledge and Gregory Skufca, Crackdown Against Internet Fraud, *id.*

[578] *Id.* (noting that baseless recommendations and touting of stocks violated Section 17(b) of the Securities Act of 1933, § 10(b) of the Securities Exchange Act of 1934, and Rule 10b-5 under the Exchange Act).

sites to determine whether it is complying with securities regulations in the United States as well as foreign countries.

A number of nation states connected to the Internet attempt to prevent their citizens from accessing materials available on servers located in other countries. Germany, for example, is considering blocking neo-Nazi content available on sites originated in the United States.[579] A German court refused to prosecute Yahoo! for permitting postings of Nazi memorabilia auction.[580] It is unclear how any individual country may ban hate speech.[581] A German court "ruled that the owner of an Australian Web site denying the Holocaust took place could be jailed for violating a German law against hate speech."[582] The court rejected the defense that the web sites were Australia-based and not subject to German law.[583]

In addition to national regulatory efforts, there is regulation by supranational organizations such as the European Union. The EU's Data Protection Directive went into effect in October of 1998. Member states must ensure personal data transferred to nonmember states is adequately protected.[584] The *European Union Directive* requires that personal information transmitted outside the EU be protected. The U.S. Department of Commerce and the European Commission negotiated a "safe harbor" to comply with the Data Protection Directive.[585] The EU approved the privacy safe harbor on May 30, 2000.[586] Companies obtain a "safe harbor" by binding themselves to data protection principles.[587]

[N] Global Cybercrime Law Enforcement

Hack attacks on Yahoo! ebay, Amazon.com, E*trade, Buy.com, and other well-known web sites were launched in a blitzkrieg by unknown perpetrators.[588] The globalization of criminal use of the Internet has resulted in new institutions of crime control. The United Kingdom's national criminal intelligence service formed a new national high-tech crime unit based in London.[589] Many countries

---

[579] Germans Combat Internet Hate Sites Based in U.S., 33 Nat'l J. 1650 (June 2, 2001).

[580] Perkins Coie LLP, Internet Case Digest (visited Apr. 14, 2002), http://www.perkinscoie.com/casedigest/icd_results.cfm?keyword1+copyright&topic+Copyrigh.

[581] *Id.*

[582] Balint, Cyber-Law's Growing Pains, *id.*

[583] *Id.*

[584] The European Commission, Data Protection: Commission Endorses 'Safe Harbor' Arrangement with U.S. (visited Apr. 7, 2000), http://europa.eu.int/comm/internal_market/en/media/dataprot/news/harbor4.htm.

[585] *Id.*

[586] Michael Geist, EU-U.S. Safe Harbor Deal Inches Closer, BNA's Internet Law News (May 10, 2000) (citing http://www.wired.com/news/politics/0,1283,36235,00.html).

[587] *Id.*

[588] Scott Rosenberg, The Net Scare, Salon.com (Feb. 10, 2000) (visited Apr. 14, 2002), http://www.salon.com/tech/col/rose/2000/01/10/web_attacks.

[589] Jimmy Burns & Jean Eaglesham, Police Unit to Target Cybercrime, Financial Times (Nov. 13, 2000) (visited Apr. 14, 2002), http://news.ft.com/ft/gx.cgi/ftc?pagename+View&c=Article&cid=FT39XPTHIFC&live=true.

connected to the Internet are ill-equipped to detect and prosecute cybercrime. A survey of 52 countries found that only 9 amended their statutes to encompass computer-related crime.[590] The Philippines was unable to prosecute the student who launched the "Love Bug" virus because there was no statute governing computer viruses. In June of 2001, the Philippines brought its first hacking case against ex-employees of a business school who copied training modules without permission.[591]

One in three countries have no specific statutes covering computer crimes on the Internet.[592] There is a growing consensus that international cooperation is required to punish and deter Internet crimes. The goal is to develop "a uniform criminal justice system whereby signatory nations cooperate in the field of investigation, evidence gathering, enforcement and prosecution."[593] The first section below examines United States statutes governing the theft of trade secrets in cyberspace. The Economic Espionage Act is a federal statute governing the theft of trade secrets. Next, international legal solutions for dealing with crimes committed in cyberspace are discussed in detail.

Private law enforcement plays a critically important role in prosecuting Internet Crime. The ICC Commercial Crime Services of the International Chamber of Commerce in Paris formed a cybercrime unit.[594] The ICC Commercial Crime Services provide advice on Internet security and investigate interference of corporate computer networks.[595] The Service recently investigated a bogus web site in the Russian language offering to sell securities similar to a famous British bank. The Service has uncovered a number of "dubious web sites, particularly those set up to closely resemble the sites of large, well-known companies."[596] The ICC Cybercrime unit also plays a role in working with international law enforcement officers about Internet crime.[597]

[1] Economic Espionage Act

The Economic Espionage Act (EEA) provides criminal sanctions and civil actions to enjoin damages for the misappropriation of trade secrets. The EEA was

---

[590] John Leyden, Cybercrime Laws Are Super Weak (July 12, 2000) The Register (visited June 12, 2001), http://www.theregister.co.uk/content/6/15311.html.

[591] Alex F. Villafania, Metropolitan Computer Times, Philippines NBI Clamps Down on Cyberthieves, Newsbytes (June 12, 2001) (visited Apr. 14, 2002), http://www.newsbytes.com/news/01/166778.html.

[592] Id.

[593] Howard L. Steele, Jr., The Web That Binds Us All: The Future Legal Environment of the Internet, 19 Hous. J. Int'l L. 495, 531 (1997) (discussing European Conventions and United Nations Model Treaties for international criminal law enforcement).

[594] International Chamber of Commerce, ICC Cybercrime Unit (visited June 19, 2001), http://www.iccwbo.org/ccs/menu_cybercrime?unit.asp.

[595] Id.

[596] ICC Commercial Crime Services, Cybersleuths Track Down Bogus Web Sites (visited Apr. 14, 2002), http://www.iccwbo.org/ccs/news_archives/2000/cybersleuths.asp.

[597] Id.

enacted "against a backdrop of increasing threats to corporate security and a rising tide of international and domestic economic espionage."[598] The EEA criminalizes "economic espionage"[599] and the "theft of trade secrets."[600] The EEA would treat the theft of trade secrets by ex-employees, business competitors, and foreign powers as federal crimes. The EEA punishes those who misappropriate trade secrets with the intent of benefiting foreign governments, foreign instrumentalities, or agents.[601] A trade secret misappropriated for the benefit of "anyone other than the owner" is punishable by criminal and civil penalties.[602] The EEA permits parallel civil actions to restrain the misappropriation of trade secrets, "including appropriate injunctive relief against any violation" of the statute.[603] An individual whose misappropriation of trade secrets benefits a foreign government, instrumentality, or agent maybe sentenced to a federal prison for up to 15 years and fined up to $500,000.[604] A business competitor or other entity that steals a trade secret benefiting a foreign government can be fined up to $10 million.[605]

The EEA applies to any individual who transmits, receives, or possesses stolen trade secrets.[606] It is questionable whether the EEA would apply to non-utilitarian hackers who deface web sites or countercultural hackers. A defendant must have the *mens rea* needed to commit a crime defined by the EEA.[607] Section 1831 requires that a defendant convert a trade secret "to the economic benefit of anyone other than the owner thereof," including the defendant.[608] In addition, § 1832 requires the defendant have intent or knowledge that its offense will benefit a foreign government, instrumentality, or agent.[609] A foreign hacker who defaces a corporate web site or places a political slogan in a government web site would not be liable under § 1832. The EEA criminalizes stealing or appropriating trade secrets whether by "fraud, artifice or deception."[610] The EEA also criminalizes those who make copies or "duplicate, download, upload, alter, destroys . . . replicates, transmits, delivers, sends, mails, communicates or conveys a trade secret."[611]

The EEA provides tort-like remedies for the electronic misappropriation of trade secrets in addition to criminal sanctions. There have been relatively few criminal prosecutions under the EEA, presumably because of the difficulty of

---

[598] United States v. Hsu, 155 F.3d 189 (3d Cir. 1998).

[599] 18 U.S.C. § 1831 (2000).

[600] 18 U.S.C. § 1832 (2000).

[601] 18 U.S.C. § 1831 (2000).

[602] 18 U.S.C. § 1832 (2000).

[603] 18 U.S.C. § 1836(a) (2000).

[604] 18 U.S.C. § 1831(a)(5) (2000).

[605] 18 U.S.C. § 1831(b) (2000).

[606] 18 U.S.C. § 1832(a)(3) (2000).

[607] 18 U.S.C. § 1831 *et seq.* (2000).

[608] 18 U.S.C. § 1831 (2000).

[609] *Id.*

[610] 18 U.S.C. § 1831(a) (2000).

[611] *Id.*

detecting computer intrusions leading to a trade secret.[612] Private enforcement of the EEA has played some role in most trade secret cases. The corporate victim will typically conduct an internal investigation, turning evidence of wrongdoing over to the authorities. In the trade secrets case, the corporate victim completes its own investigation and turns over smoking gun documents to public authorities. To date, there are few reported prosecutions against international defendants where prosecutors have uncovered the misappropriation of trade secrets from U.S. computer networks.[613]

[2]   The Federal Wiretap Statute

The Federal Wiretap Statute is part of The Omnibus Crime Patrol and Safe Streets Act of 1968. The federal wiretapping statutes cover "wire," "oral," and "electronic" communications. The Federal Wiretap Act distinguishes between the interception of an electronic communication at the time of transmission from the retrieval of such a communication after it has been placed into "electronic storage."[614] "During the transmission phase, any protection against unlawful interception . . . is governed by § 2511."[615] When messages arrive and are in storage, "the same messages are subject to § 2701."[616] The Fifth Circuit held in *Steve Jackson Games, Inc. v. United States Secret Service*[617] that the electronic storage of an electronic communication is by definition not part of the communication. "Section 2511(1)(a) forbids . . . the interception of electronic communications. An *interception* is defined as the 'acquisition of the contents of any . . . electronic . . . communication through the use of any electronic, mechanical or other device.' "[618]

An electronic communication by definition cannot be intercepted when it is in electronic storage. By definition, only communications are capable of being

---

[612] A LEXIS search on Apr. 19, 2001, yielded only 11 cases with the search "Economic Espionage Act." Three of the cases in the search concerned a conspiracy to steal processes, methods, and formulas for an anticancer drug produced by a major pharmaceutical e-Business. *See* Hsu v. United States, 155 F.3d 189 (3d Cir. 1998); United States v. Hsu, 40 F. Supp. 2d 623 (E.D. Pa. 1999); United States v. Hsu, 982 F. Supp. 1022 (E.D. Pa. 1997).

[613] *See, e.g.,* United States v. Martin, 228 F.3d 1 (1st Cir. 2000) (discussing case in which defendant was caught when she inadvertently sent an e-mail attachment containing stolen trade secrets to an e-Business manager); United States v. Yang, 74 F. Supp. 2d 724 (N. D. Ohio 1999) (discussing case in which defendant was caught through joint collaboration of FBI and corporate victim). *Cf.* United States v. Hsu, 40 F. Supp. 2d 623 (E.D. Pa. 1999); Hsu v. United States, 155 F.3d 189 (3d Cir. 1998); and United States v. Hsu, 982 F. Supp. 1022 (E.D. Pa. 1997) (deciding case where investigation was spearheaded by an undercover FBI agent whom the defendant mistakenly believed was a technological information broker).

[614] Interceptions are covered by 18 U.S.C. §§ 2510-22 and access to information in electronic storage by 18 U.S.C. §§ 2701-11 (2000). *See* Bohach v. City of Reno, 932 F. Supp. 1232 (D. Nev. 1996).

[615] *Id.* at 1236.

[616] *Id.*

[617] 36 F.3d 457, 461, 462 (5th Cir. 1994).

[618] *Id.*

intercepted.[619] The Federal Wiretap Act requires law enforcement officers to obtain court orders before intercepting telephone conversations. The Federal Wiretap Act requires the government to limit eavesdropping to voice communications that are connected to the topic under investigation. One of the difficulties prosecutors encounter is that they may lack the information technologies necessary to investigate cybercriminals. Prosecutors lack the adequate technical expertise to track foreign hackers and are also hamstrung by due process restrictions on the interception of data not found in other countries.

[3] International Cybercrime Statutes

At present, there is no uniform treaty addressing cybercriminal law or the procedural aspects of policing Internet related crime. A Norwegian judge who is an expert on computer law stated at a Group of Eight countries meeting: "Computer attacks, unlike murder or robbery, [are] still not universally recognized as a crime."[620] Cybercrime, by its very nature, is international, and requires new forms of creative multilateral law reform. The long arm of criminal law cannot easily reach a hacker living on another continent or operating in an offshore haven.[621] The United Kingdom recently launched a high-tech crime unit to work with police forces on investigating organized crime on the Internet.[622] The Council of Europe's Convention on Cybercrime is the first international instrument dealing with cybercrime.[623] The Cybercrime Convention applies to the member states of the EU and Canada.[624] The aim of the Draft Convention is to adopt "a common criminal policy aimed at the protection of society against cyber-crime . . . by adopting appropriate legislation and fostering international co-operation."[625] The Draft Cybercrime Convention provides uniform guidelines for national legislation for the definition of computer crimes and calls for international standards for transborder search and seizure.[626]

---

[619] Id.

[620] Christine Gregoire, Law Enforcement Challenges in Cyberspace, Prosecutor (Sept./Oct. 2000) (quoting "Stein Schjolberg, a Norwegian judge who tracks computer crime laws around the globe").

[621] The Hague Convention on Jurisdiction and Foreign Judgments will make it easier to obtain jurisdiction and enforcement judgments in the global marketplace. Negotiations on the draft Hague Convention have been ongoing since 1994. The Hague Convention would apply to criminal offenses on the Internet as well as civil and commercial causes of action. See E-Commerce Dominates Talks on More Legal Co-Operation, European Report (Feb. 28, 2001) (available on LEXIS).

[622] Britain Launches Hi-Tech Cybercop Unit (visited Apr. 19, 2001), http://www.theregister.co.uk/content/6/18341.html.

[623] EU-Canada Declaration on the European Security Defense Policy, Key Document DOC: 00/33, Commission of the European Communities, RAPID (Dec. 20, 2000) (available on LEXIS).

[624] EU-Canada Summit-Ottawa, Cybercrime, RAPID (Dec. 20, 2000).

[625] Preamble to Draft Convention on Cybercrime, PC-Cy (2000) Draft No. 19, Council of Europe, Strasbourg (site visited on Apr. 14, 2002), http://www.conventions.coe.int/treaty/en/projets/cybercrime.htm. (Draft Convention on Cybercrime).

[626] Id.

The Convention proposes uniform substantive criminal law to govern the "confidentiality, integrity and availability of computer data and systems."[627] The Convention classifies the illegal interception of wireless communications as a computer crime.[628] Computer viruses and the deliberate destruction of data are classified as the crimes of "data interference"[629] and "system interference."[630] The sale and distribution of anticircumvention devices and other hacker tools are proscribed by the Convention.[631]

Title I of the Cybercrime Convention proposes that each country classify offenses against the confidentiality, integrity, and availability of computer data and systems as crimes.[632] International cooperation is required to detect and punish computer hacking, data theft, and the interference with computer systems through fraud or forgery.[633] Title II of the Cybercrime Convention proposes a number of computer-related offenses for computer-related forgery[634] and computer-related fraud.[635] Titles III and IV cover content-related offences related to child pornography[636] and copyright-related offenses.[637] Title V covers the law of attempts,[638] corporate liability,[639] and proportionate sanctions for computer crimes.[640] In addition, Title II covers criminal procedure for computer crimes.

Article 14 of the Cybercrime Convention requires each signatory state to develop rules for the search and seizure of stored computer data.[641] The rules for discovery are covered for production orders,[642] the preservation of electronic or computer evidence,[643] expedited disclosure of traffic data and other related data by Internet providers,[644] and rules for the interception of data.[645] The Convention asks for legislative and other measures to establish jurisdiction over computer and Internet-related crimes.[646]

Chapter III of the Cybercrime Convention provides for international cooperation for computer crime investigations[647] and treats computer crime as an extra-

---

[627] Draft Convention on Cybercrime, Chapter II, Section 1, Title I, *id.*

[628] Draft Convention on Cybercrime, *id.* at Art. 3, Illegal Interception.

[629] Draft Convention on Cybercrime, *id.* at Art. 4, Data Interference.

[630] Draft Convention on Cybercrime, *id.* at Art. 5.

[631] Draft Convention on Cybercrime, *id.* at Art. 6.

[632] *Id.* at Chapter II, Section 1, Title 1.

[633] *Id.*

[634] Draft Convention on Cybercrme, *id.* at Art. 7.

[635] Draft Convention on Cybercrime, *id.* at Art. 8.

[636] Draft Convention on Cybercrime, *id.* at Art. 9.

[637] Draft Convention on Cybercrime, *id.* at Art. 10.

[638] Draft Convention on Cybercrime, *id.* at Art. 11.

[639] Draft Convention on Cybercrime, *id.* at Art. 12.

[640] Draft Convention on Cybercrime, *id.* at Art. 13.

[641] Draft Convention on Cybercrime, *id.* at Art. 14.

[642] Draft Convention on Cybercrime, *id.* at Art. 15.

[643] Draft Convention on Cybercrime, *id.* at Art. 16.

[644] Draft Convention on Cybercrime, *id.* at Art. 17.

[645] Draft Convention on Cybercrime, *id.* at Art. 18 (still under discussion).

[646] Draft Convention on Cybercrime, *id.* at Art. 19.

[647] Draft Convention on Cybercrime, *id.* at Art. 20.

ditable offense.[648] Many of the other measures in Chapter III concern mutual assistance in the investigation and prosecution of computer crime based upon electronic evidence.[649] Article 23 develops a mechanism for responding to mutual assistance requests for borderless computer crimes.[650] Articles 24 through 29 require signatory states to adopt legislative measures to implement mutual assistance.[651] Article 24, for example, provides mechanisms for obtaining an "expeditious preservation of data" on a computer system or server in another territory.[652] Parties are required to promptly disclose traffic data and may refuse such requests only if it would trigger sovereign immunity, security, the public order, or other essential interests.[653]

The Cybercrime Convention is likely to result in greater international cooperation that is necessary to enforce and prosecute crimes on the borderless electronic frontier. At present, there is limited enforcement of transnational organized crime on the Internet because of the ease of committing crimes offshore or using anonymous e-mailers. Cybercrimes such as hacking require mutual cooperation that has been already instituted for intellectual property offenses, money laundering, child pornography, and illegal drug trafficking. It may be several years or more before the negotiations about the Draft Convention are completed. The Convention "would also make the production, distribution and possession of certain computer programs illegal when the intent is to use them to commit malicious acts."[654]

Few question the need for a convention, but the Convention is opposed by a wide variety of industry and civil liberties groups. Internet Service Providers who seek a minimal global regime preferring a market-based enforcement regime oppose the Draft Convention.[655] The Dutch Association of Internet Service Providers criticized the Draft Convention as being tilted too far in favor of government and law enforcement control of the Internet.[656] The United States Chamber of Commerce opposes the Draft Convention as imposing unworkable and possibly unlawful restraints on e-commerce and U.S. businesses on the Internet.[657] One of the difficulties is how to detect and punish cybercrimes while preserving fundamental rights and freedoms that vary across nation states.[658] At present, there

---

[648] Draft Convention on Cybercrime, *id*. at Art. 21.

[649] See, e.g., Draft Convention on Cybercrime, *id*. at Art. 22.

[650] Draft Convention on Cybercrime, *id*. at Art. 23.

[651] Draft Convention on Cybercrime, *id*. at Arts. 24-29.

[652] Draft Convention on Cybercrime, *id*. at Art. 24.

[653] Draft Convention on Cybercrime, *id*. at Art. 25.

[654] Dorothy E. Denning, Disarming the Black Hats, Information Security (Oct. 2000) at 1.

[655] Reuters, Freedom v. Rules Bring Cybercrime Treaty Clashes (Mar. 6, 2001) (visited Apr. 18, 2002), http://www.cyber-rightsdot.org/cybercrime.

[656] *Id*. (quoting Fred Eisner from the Dutch Association of Internet Providers).

[657] United States Chamber Opposes European Cyber Crime Treaty (Dec. 2000) (visited Apr. 14, 2002), http://www.cyber-rightsdot.org/cybercrime.

[658] Cyberrights & Cyber-Liberties (UK), "Information Related to Cybercrime Policy Making Process within the Council of Europe, European Union, G8, and the United Nations" (visited Apr. 14, 2001), http://www.cyber-rightsdot.org/cybercrime.

is no effective global cybercrime involvement and greater international cooperation is urgently needed.

Law enforcement agencies are better prepared to deal with crime in the streets
versus computer crime, which is perpetrated by white-collar criminals. Most states
have computer crime statutes, though most states do not have any significant law
enforcement presence in cyberspace. Each state, for example, has a computer crime
statute but only a handful of prosecutions.[659] The number of cybercrimes is increasing but appropriating enforcement funds is not a priority at the local level. Most
countries have little or no Internet crime enforcement because they lack resources
and an adequate legal infrastructure to address crime on computer networks.

Internet crimes are seldom detected or prosecuted without the proactive investigative work of corporate investigators. An online corporation will need a skilled
computer investigator to detect and track online wrongdoers. Online forgers or
intruders will typically leave few digital footprints in contrast to a traditional crime
scene. Skilled cybercriminals will be able to easily bypass information security
devices without leaving DNA evidence, fingerprints, or other information found in
law enforcement databases. Computer records are easier to alter than paper and
pencil records. Electronic robbers or forgers typically leave fewer clues than other
white-collar criminals who alter checks or intercept promissory notes. A skilled
forger who adds zeroes to a check will typically leave more clues than a digital thief
will. The use of false e-mail headers, offshore sites, and anonymous remailers
makes it more difficult for law enforcement officers to catch cybercriminals.

Cybercrime is borderless, by its very nature, permitting new methods of concealing wrongdoing.[660] An international cybercriminal group calling themselves
the "Phonemasters" was able to "penetrate computers systems of MCI, SPRINT,
AT&T, Equifax and even the National Crime Information Center."[661] Another network of cybercriminals stole $10 million in funds from "bank accounts in Cali-
fornia, Finland, Germany, the Netherlands, Switzerland and Israel."[662] Foreign
terrorist groups such as Hizbollah, Hamas, and the supporters of Osama bin Laden
use the Internet as a target and a tool "to formulate plans, raise funds, spread propaganda, and to communicate securely."[663] Bin Laden and his supporters were
reported to have used encrypted messages in secure web sites to plan the September 11, 2001, tragedy at the World Trade Center and Pentagon.

---

[659] "Florida and Arizona became the first states to pass specific laws against computer abuse." By
1988, 47 states enacted specific laws against computer crime. Richard C. Hollinger & Lonn Lanza-
Kaduce, The Process of Criminalization: The Case of Computer Crime Laws, 26 Criminology 59
(1988).

[660] Statement of Michael A. Vatis, Director, National Infrastructure Protection Center, Federal
Bureau of Investigation on Cybercrime, "On Cybercrime," Testimony Before the Judiciary Committee, Criminal Justice Oversight Subcommittee and House Judiciary Committee, Crime Subcommittee, Washington, D.C. (Feb. 29, 2000) (visited Apr. 18, 2002), http://www.usdoj.gov/crimnal/
cybercrime/vatis.htm

[661] *Id.*

[662] *Id.*

[663] *Id.*

[4]   Barriers to Internet Criminal Law Enforcement

Internet crimes such as telephone toll fraud or scams may involve small economic losses to many, making it difficult to prosecute. Internet chiseling occurs when a large number of Internet users lose small amounts of money. Internet work at home schemes will typically ask Internet users to send a relatively small amount of money, such as $25 or $35, to get started earning $750 per week at home. Victims who lose small amounts of money are reluctant to report their losses to law enforcement.[664] There may also be snooping-type crimes where there is little by way of economic damages.[665] The victims of corporate espionage may be reluctant to report computer crimes to the authorities because of adverse publicity. E-businesses are reluctant to report cybercrimes to the authorities because of the very real fear that adverse publicity will hurt business.

[O]   Consumer Protection

A large number of initiatives have been taken to protect consumers on the Internet. The European Union has enacted a large number of directives protecting consumers.[666] The European Union has enacted a Directive on unfair terms in consumer contracts.[667] The European Court of Justice ruled that Directive EC/93/13 addressing unfair terms in contracts applied only if a buyer is a consumer. The Court of Justice ruled that Article 2(b) of the Directive meant any natural person who was acting outside his or her trade, business, or profession. The judgment concerned two Italian companies that signed contracts for the supply of automatic drink dispensing machines at their place of business.[668] In addition, there is consumer protection relating to prices of products offered consumers as well as a

---

[664] Corporate victims of network intruders who suffer large losses are also reluctant to report computer crimes. *See* Richard P. Salgado, Working with Victims of Computer Network Hacks USA Bulletin (Mar. 2001, U.S. Department of Justice) (visited Apr. 18, 2002), http://www.usdoj.gov/criminal/cybercrime/usaMar.2001_6.htm (reporting survey by the Computer Security Institute and the FBI finding that only one in four of computer crime victims reported the matter to authorities).

[665] James Johnston, Are Commercial Snoopers in the Same League as Hackers, Legal Times (Jan. 3, 2000) at 17.

[666] "Among other measures, a Directive on the Protection of Consumers in Respect of Distance Contracts (97/7EC), a Directive on the Protection of Individuals with Regard to the Processing of Personal Data and on the Free Movement of Such Data (95/46EC), a Directive on Treatment of Personal Information in the Telesector (97/66EC) and a Directive on Injunctions for the Protection of Consumers' Interests (98/27EC) have been adopted." Each of these Directives applies equally well to the "Internet for trading and marketing." Europa, Commercial Communications Newsletter 18, Trading and Marketing on the Internet and in Similar Communication Systems—The Nordic Consumer Ombudsmen's Position Paper (visited Apr. 20, 2002), http://europa.eu.int/comm/internal_market/comcom/newsletter/edition18/page20_en.htm.

[667] Council Directive 93/13/EEC on Unfair Terms in Consumer Contracts.

[668] Consumer Policy: ECJ Rules on Unfair Clauses Directive, European Rep. (Nov. 28, 2001) (reporting rulings in companion cases involving Italian companies, Cape Snc, Idealservice SRl, and Idealservice MN RE Sas/OMAI Srl).

Directive on misleading advertising.[669] Article 5 of the Data Protection Directive protects the confidentiality of electronic messages for the processing of personal data.[670] Member states "must prohibit any kind of interception or surveillance of electronic messages by others than the senders and receivers."[671] The European Union member states require contractual obligations on the Internet to include all of the consumer rights found in the brick-and-mortar world.[672]

In addition to the European Union, the WTO, OECD, and UNCITRAL have e-commerce standards that protect consumers. The OECD Council, for example, released "Guidelines for Consumer Protection in the Context of Electronic Commerce."[673] The OECD position is that consumer law and practices must protect against the "fraudulent, misleading, and unfair commercial conduct."[674] The OECD standard is similar to the U.S. Federal Trade Commission's jurisdiction in policing unfair and deceptive trade practices.[675] The OECD concern is that fragmented local regulations do not adequately address consumer protection on the Internet.[676]

At present, there is no international framework for consumer protection in the global electronic marketplace. The two basic approaches to consumer protection are the "country-of-destination" jurisdictional system and the "country-of-origin/prescribed-by-seller rule."[677] The business community argues that the country-of-origin approach should be adopted because it provides them with "a predictable regulatory environment and reduced compliance costs."[678] Consumer confidence may be undermined by this approach because it arguably (1) "encourages a 'race to the bottom,' which would reduce consumer protections on a global scale; (2) frustrates the ability of law enforcement to protect its citizens; (3) impedes informed decision-making by consumers; (4) places U.S. companies at a competitive disadvantage; and (5) deprives consumers of meaningful access to judicial recourse."[679]

Voluntary organizations also play a role in protecting consumers in the global Internet. The European Coalition Against Unsolicited Commercial Email has played a key role in documenting the negative impact of junk e-mail.[680] One

---

[669] Directive 98/6/EC concerning consumer protection relating to the indication of prices of products offered to consumers, Directive 84/450 concerning misleading advertising. See Europa, Newsletter 16-17 (visited Apr. 20, 2002), http://europa.eu.int/comm/internal_market/comcom/newsletter/edition16-17/page04-04_en.htm.

[670] *Id.*

[671] *Id.*

[672] *Id.*

[673] Organization for Economic Cooperation and Development, Recommendation of the OECD Council Concerning Guidelines for Consumer Protection in the Context of Electronic Commerce (2000).

[674] *Id.* at 1.

[675] Federal Trade Commission Act, § 5 (2000).

[676] OECD, Guidelines for Consumer Protection, *id.* at 1.

[677] Federal Trade Commission, Bureau of Consumer Protection, Consumer Protection in the Global Electronic Marketplace (Sept. 2000) at iii.

[678] *Id.*

[679] *Id.*

[680] The Coalition Against Unsolicited Email, Unsolicited Commercial Email-Spam (visited June 11, 2001), http://europa.eu.int/ISPO-ecommerce/issues/spam.html.

study shows that junk e-mail costs Internet users $10 billion (Euros) a year world-wide. The European Commission works with consumer associations throughout Europe on consumer protection.[681] The Nordic Consumer Ombudsmen opposed the EU "country-of-origin" approach to Internet consumer transactions. The Ombudsmen argues that "[c]ompanies established in markets that provide a 'high' level of consumer protection will feel disadvantaged and put pressure on their administrations to lower consumer protection to allow them to compete equally."[682] Another risk is that companies will shop around for countries that have the lowest level of consumer protection.[683]

[P] Online Financial Services

The European Commission has proposed a Directive to develop an integrated European financial market.[684] The proposed Directive on Financial Services requires member states to coordinate the supervision of "financial conglomerates" across borders and sectors.[685] The Commission's concern is that the supervision of financial services is largely limited to banking/investment and insurance.[686] The Directive is a response to the tendency to develop conglomerates in the EU financial markets and financial services industry.[687]

[Q] International Standards

Industry standards are incorporated into many substantive fields of the law. The concept of the usage of trade is based upon "regular or established practices in an industry."[688] The Uniform Commercial Code (UCC), for example, supplements the provision of the UCC with industry standards.[689] The usage of trade is an implied term in every commercial transaction. Private international law has always turned to industry standards as an important source of law.[690] William Murray, Lord Mansfield, an eighteenth-century English chief justice, was the father of

---

[681] Europa Newsletter 18, Trading and Marketing on the Internet and in Similar Communications Systems—The Nordic Consumer Ombudsmen's Position Paper (visited Apr. 14, 2002), http://europa.eu.int/comm/internal_market/comcom/newsletter/edition18/page20_en.htm.

[682] Id.

[683] Id.

[684] The European Commission, Europa, Financial Services: Commission Proposes Directive on Prudential Supervision of Financial Conglomerates (visited Apr. 14, 2002), http://europa.eu.int/comm/internal_market/eb/finances/cross-sector/conglomerates2.htm.

[685] Id.

[686] Id.

[687] Id.

[688] Uniform Commercial Code, § 1-205(2) (stating that trade usage gives particular commercial meaning to a given locality or trade).

[689] See Uniform Commercial Code, § 1-103 (2001) (supplemental principles including the law merchant are incorporated in the commercial law); see also Uniform Commercial Code, § 1-205(2) (incorporating the usage of trade as part of every UCC contract).

[690] F.D. MacKinnon, Origins of Commercial Law, CCV L. Q. Rev. 30 (1936).

international commercial law and chief justice of the King's Bench from 1756 to 1788. Lord Mansfield believed that commercial law should be consistent with accepted usages of trade. Lord Mansfield appointed juries of merchants to help resolve commercial disputes. The law of commercial instruments grew out of the law merchant tradition.[691] The law merchant tradition today refers to the customary rules and standards that apply in international trade.[692] Today, the law merchant tradition applies to the Internet. The law merchant in cyberspace refers to the customary rules and industry standards that apply universally in e-commerce.

The United States and the 29 other members of the Organization for Economic Cooperation and Development (OECD) agreed to the Guidelines for Consumer Protection in the Context of Electronic Commerce approved by the OECD Council in December 1999.[693] The OECD standards are designed for effective consumer protection for online business-to-consumer transactions. The aim is to encourage "fair business, advertising and marketing practices; clear information about an online business's identity, the goods or services it offers and the terms and conditions of any transaction; a transparent process for the confirmation of transactions; secure payment mechanisms; fair, timely and affordable dispute resolution and redress; privacy protection; and consumer and business education."[694]

In general, consumers should have the same effective and transparent rights and remedies against deceptive or fraudulent practices as in any other form of commerce. Advertising and marketing should be clearly identifiable from other forms of information in cyberspace. Consumers have a basic right to know the identity of the business marketing goods and services on the Internet. Businesses should be able to substantiate any claims about their online products. It is critical that law enforcement agencies and regulators be able to contact the Internet business. The terms and conditions of products or services need to be available in more than one language if offered to different language groups. Consumers should be offered an itemized list of costs, delivery expenses, or transportation costs associated with the online sale of goods or rendering of services. Clear warnings or instructions should accompany online sales just as in the brick and mortar world. Transactions should be conducted according to the OECD Guidelines Governing the Protection of Privacy and Transborder Flow of Personal Data (1980). Members also endorse the OECD Ministerial Declaration on the Protection of Privacy in Global Networks.

Consumers should have a clear method for reviewing their orders and correcting any errors. Payment mechanisms must be secure and understandable. Online businesses should have a simple and transparent method for consumers to

---

[691] William Averred Britton, Handbook of the Law of Bills and Notes, § 2 at 4 (1943).

[692] *See* Leon Trakman, The Law Merchant: The Evolution of Commercial Law (1983).

[693] OECD Council, Guidelines for Consumer Protection in the Context of Electronic Commerce (Dec. 9. 1999), http://www.oecd.org/pdf/M00000000/M00000363.pdf

[694] OECD, Guidelines for Consumer Protection in the Context of Electronic Commerce (last updated Mar. 26, 2001), http://www.oecd.org/EN/document/0,,EN-document-44-1-no-24-320-44,00.html.

opt out of commercial e-mail. The OECD principles acknowledge the special protections owed children in the online business environment. Each online business should offer consumers a low-cost and easy-to-use alternative dispute resolution mechanism for disputes over the quality of goods and services. The OECD endorses the principle that online consumers have the same rights as in traditional businesses. The OECD endorses a self-regulation approach and principles of technology and media neutrality.[695]

ISO establishes business norms for e-commerce, as does the WTO's promulgation of e-commerce standards to promote a free and fair global trading system.[696] The WTO released draft global trade rules that addressed issues such as the taxation of commerce over the Internet, international payment systems, and privacy.[697] The ISO includes national standards entities such as AFNOR, ANSI, BSI, CSBTS, DIN, and SIS, but coordinates its activities with some 500 international and regional organizations.[698] Lawrence Lessig argues that cyberspace law is regulated by four kinds of restraint: (1) law, (2) social norms, (3) markets, and (4) the architecture of the Internet.[699] Laws are backed up by sanctions, norms are enforced by the community, and markets have the constraint of prices.[700] The architecture of the Internet refers to the constraints imposed by standards.[701] Lessig's argument is that codes and standards constrain behavior and are a form of regulation.[702] The basic Internet protocols are standards that permit the identification of the user, as does the user's IP address.[703] Industry standards are a form of regulation in the field of commercial law and constitute one way of measuring the standard of care in tort law. Professor Lessig cites the importance of the World Wide Web Consortium's P3P protocol that "would enable individuals to select their preferences about the exchange of private information and then enable agents to negotiate the trade of such data when an individual connects to a given site."[704] This section explores the role of international standards and standards-setting organizations in regulating the global Internet.[705]

---

[695] OECD Council, *supra* note 693.

[696] International Standards Organization (ISO), Standards and World Trade (visited May 13, 2000), http://www.iso.ch/wtotbt/wtotbt.htm.

[697] Siliconvalley.com, Global Rules for Web Trade Needed—New WTO Head, http://www.siliconvalley.com/docs/news/tech/026070.htm.

[698] *Id.*

[699] Lawrence Lessig, The Law of the Horse: What Cyberlaw Might Teach, 113 Harv. L. Rev. 501, 507 (1999).

[700] *Id.*

[701] *Id.*

[702] *Id.*

[703] *Id.* at 516.

[704] *Id.* at 521.

[705] Lessig also argues that law regulates code and cites the example of the Digital Millennium Copyright Act's anticircumvention provision as an example of regulating code. "This provision regulates efforts to circumvent technologies designed to protect copyrighted material. If you attempt to evade these technologies, you will have committed a felony. Or analogously, if you try to pick the lock, you will have committed the trespass." *Id.* at 539.

International standards-setting organizations are creating standards that significantly impact e-commerce practices. The WTO Code of Good Practice requires its signatories to "accept and comply with a code of good practice for the preparation, adoption and application of standards."[706] Good practices set the basic rules for food safety, plant health, environmental issues, and standards for trade in services.[707] The WTO seeks transparency and nondiscriminatory trade in services and goods through the use of international standards. SPC will need to comply with the technical specifications or other WTO criteria used in its "materials, products, processes, and services." International standardization is rapidly evolving in the field of e-commerce.[708] ISO standards have been widely adopted worldwide for telephone cards, credit cards, and "smart" cards. A credit card issued by an American bank is of a standard set of specifications that may be read by ATMs around the world. Without standardization in thickness, these payment devices may not be used worldwide.[709] Global standards are necessary for online contracting, authentication, digital signatures, and electronic data interchange for the Internet to fulfill its promise as a worldwide marketplace.

§ 8.03   INTERNATIONAL BUSINESS ISSUES

[A]   International Orders for Goods and Services

International issues occur because an e-business's web site can sell its goods and services in a global marketplace. Shipping will be a big issue for SPC as it expands internationally. SPC's online sales will require it to become familiar with customs, codes, tariffs duties, and foreign currencies.[710] Forrester Research recently found that 46 percent of U.S. companies refuse to accept international orders because of their unfamiliarity with international norms.[711] The U.S. Postal Service published a useful publication on USPS Global Delivery Services.[712] "Global Express Guaranteed is an international expedited shipping option from the U.S. Postal Service and DHL Worldwide Express. It is available in 20,000

---

[706] Federal Trade Commission, Bureau of Consumer Protection, *id.*

[707] *Id.*

[708] European Union, The IST Programme and Electronic Commerce Standardization: Report of the open meeting organized jointly by CEN/ISSS Electronic Commerce Workshop and European Commission DG XIII on 5 March 1999 (visited Apr. 14, 2002), http://europa.eu.int/ISPO/ecommerce/issues/standardization.html.

[709] International Standards Organization, Introduction to ISO (visited Apr. 14, 2002), http://www.iso.ch/infoe/intro.htm.

[710] *See generally* Monique I. Cuvier, Border Crossing: If You Sell Online, Be Prepared to Handle Foreign Currencies and Shipping. Here's How, Emerging Business 122 (Summer 2001).

[711] *Id.* (citing study of Forrester Research)

[712] United States Postal Service, USPS Global Delivery Services (visited June 1, 2001), http: www.uspsglobal.com.

retail locations throughout the United States. Global Express Guaranteed offers you reliable, date-certain shipping to thousands of destinations in more than 200 countries/territories worldwide."[713] The e-business will need to determine duties and taxes imposed by customs.[714] Internet sales are expected to double from 2000 to 2001 with the leaders being "United States, Korea, Japan, and Mexico, whose share of total revenue will increase 10 percent."[715] If the United States e-business wants to expand its share of international revenue, it may consider localizing its web sites directed to individual countries. A recent IDC study found that "posting multiple languages on a web site could expand business, but was not the most important factor in bolstering online sales."[716]

[B]   Export and Re-Export Licenses

The Internet frequently involves importing or exporting issues. A web site visitor purchasing cheese on the Internet may be in violation of import regulations that prohibit the "importation of dairy products from particular countries without a permit."[717] The Internet requires compliance with customs in importing goods purchased over the Internet from foreign countries.[718] In addition, the Internet-related e-business may need to file for export licenses for encrypted software.[719]

---

[713] *Id.*

[714] The United States Postal Service, USPS Global Delivery Services, *id.* (stating "though it is impossible to pre-determine which packages will be subject to duties and taxes and what these amounts may be, please be aware that the recipient is responsible for the payment of such taxes").

[715] Clare Saliba, Study: Global Slice for Online Sales to Double in 2001, E-Commerce Times (May 31, 2001) (visited Apr. 14, 2002), http://www.ecommercetimes.com/perl/story/10141.html.

[716] *Id.* (citing study by IDC of Framingham, Massachusetts).

[717] U.S. Customs, Internet Transactions (visited Apr. 14, 2002), http://www.customs.ustreas.gov/impoexpo/inetrade.htm.

[718] *Id.*

[719] The Department of Commerce has an export portal providing advice for the exporting of software subject to encryption. The Department of Commerce exempts most encryption items, making them eligible for export under a license exception. However, the e-Business needs to "carefully review the encryption policy in Part 740 and 742.15 of the Export Administration Regulations (EAR) before you submit a license application. If your product and/or end-user do not qualify for a license exception or an encryption licensing arrangement, you must request an individual export license for your transaction. These license applications are reviewed on a case-by-case basis. This guidance is designed to help you in applying to export certain encryption items not eligible for a license exception or encryption licensing arrangement and should only be used in conjunction with the relevant portions of the Export Administration Regulations (EAR). Examples are encryption exports that require a license are exports of technology (ECCN 5E002), products that contain an open cryptographic interface, or 'non-retail' products to government end-users located outside the countries listed in Supplement 3 to Part 740. Also, all exports of encryption items to the terrorist-supporting and embargoed countries require an export license." U.S. Department of Commerce, Export Portal (visited June 1, 2001), http://www.export.gov/docFS_Explore.html. Online companies are required to submit the original BXA Form 748P, 748P-A (if applicable), 748P-B (if applicable), and supporting documents, in accordance with Part 748 of the EAR, to the following address:

"An export of technology or source code (except encryption source code) is 'deemed' to take place when it is released to a foreign national within the United States."[720] The Department of Commerce regulations apply equally to software transmitted on the Internet.[721] Software or other information transfers downloaded from the Internet are not subject to customs or duties. Tangible goods, however, are subject to customs regulations. The United States Customs Service is the federal agency responsible "for ensuring that all goods entering and exiting the United States do so in accordance with all applicable U.S. laws and regulations."[722] It is the role of Customs to enforce export regulations for other government agencies, including the Department of Commerce's Export Administration Regulations. Exports may require a Shipper's Export Declaration (SED). A consumer purchasing goods on the Internet from a foreign country is an importer and subject to the same customs rules as any other sale.

[C] Insuring Against Cyber Risks

The policy should also protect the e-business from any of the aforementioned violations, not only within the United States but also worldwide. SPC needs

---

Bureau of Export Administration
U.S. Department of Commerce
14th Street and Pennsylvania Avenue, N.W.
Room 2705,
Washington, D.C. 20444,
Attn: "Application Enclosed"

Recently, the Department of Commerce is accepting electronic filing of documents through systems they have dubbed as SNAP or ELAIN. Please fax the supporting documents to BXA (fax number: 202-501-0784), or send them to the U.S. Department of Commerce, Bureau of Export Administration, Information Technology Controls Division, Room 2625, 14th & Pennsylvania Ave., N.W., Washington, D.C. 20230.

[720] An export of technology or source code (except encryption source code) is "deemed" to take place when it is released to a foreign national within the United States. *See* § 734.2(b)(2)(ii) of the Export Administration Regulations (EAR). For brevity, these questions and answers refer only to "technology" but apply equally to source code. *Id.* "The Export Administration Regulations (EAR) definitions distinguish between software and technology. Software is one of the groups within each of the categories of items listed on the Commerce Control List (CCL). Software which is delineated on the CCL is controlled." *Id.* Licenses are required for technologies including software considered to be U.S. origin technologies. An e-business that develops software in a joint venture with a foreign e-Business may also be subject to re-export controls. *See* § 734.4(c)(3), (d)(3), and (e) of the Export Administration Regulations (EAR).

[721] "Any foreign national is subject to the 'deemed export' rule except a foreign national who (1) is granted permanent residence, as demonstrated by the issuance of a permanent resident visa (i.e., 'Green Card'); or (2) is granted U.S. citizenship; or (3) is granted status as a 'protected person' under 8 U.S.C. § 1324b(a)(3). This includes all persons in the U.S. as tourists, students, businesspeople, scholars, researchers, technical experts, sailors, airline personnel, salespeople, military personnel, diplomats, etc." *Id.*

[722] United States Customs, AES/Export Links (visited June 12, 2001), http://www.customs. ustreas.gov/imp/exp2/export/explicns.htm.

inland marine insurance against the real risk of cargo theft in international transportation. Shipments of video game players, clothes, liquor, and cigarettes are particular targets of cargo theft.[723] Goods in transit are more vulnerable than goods in warehouses which may be more easily guarded.[724] Chapter Nine on Conducting a Legal Audit and Managing Risk discusses insurance for e-Business transactions.

[D] Linguistic and Cultural Customization of Global Web Sites

The globalization of SPC's business needs to be tailored for linguistic and cultural differences.[725] Special attention must be given to the culture and language of core countries of the European Union. The global Internet market will be composed 60 percent of customers living outside the United States, with greater than 40 percent non-English speakers by 2003.[726] Call centers, for example, must be multilingual to develop meaningful customer relationships.[727] Reserving a domain name in a national European registry involves different concerns because foreign registries have different rules. Obtaining a domain name in Sweden is based upon prior assessment, whereas in the United States the prevailing norm is a race to the registry or "first come, first-served." Marketing an Internet web site requires SPC to understand different social norms and cultural traditions. A web site will need to be localized for local time, currency, and cultural preferences. Web site users in the United States prefer more text in contrast to a preference for pictures in Hong Kong and other Asian cultures.[728] However, pictures or models should be Asian models rather than Americans on Asian web sites.[729] The Far East is a huge potential Internet market, but different business practices must be taken into account to attract these customers.[730] Adequate support for multilingual and cross-cultural information access will require consultation with local experts.

---

[723] Sally Whitney, Vanishing Act: Cargo Theft Has Mushroomed in the Last Few Years, Giving Insurers New Headaches and New Opportunities, Best's Review (Dec. 2000) at 59.

[724] *Id.* at 60.

[725] *See generally* Official Journal of the European Communities, Proposal for a Council Decision Adopting a Multiannual Community Program to stimulate the development and use of European digital content on the global networks and to promote linguistic diversity in the Information Society (2000/C 337 E04) (submitted by the Commission on 24 May 2000).

[726] Patricia Resende, When Going Global, Content Is King, but Localization Rules, Mass High Tech (Feb. 5-11, 2001) at 12 (quoting Tim Garrant, author of Writing for Multimedia and the Web).

[727] A recent study of e-commerce sites shows that only 36% of customers were satisfied with their experience in contacting sites. Jennifer Perez, E-Commerce Sites Failing to Satisfy Customers, TeleProfessional 14 (May 2000)

[728] Susan Iszumi, Localizing Web Sites, Presentation at the Tenth International World Wide Web Conference, Hong Kong (May 1-5, 2001).

[729] Patricia Resende, When Going Global, Content Is King, but Localization Rules, *id.*

[730] Kirk Laughlin, Reborn Asia Opens for Business, *id.* at 40.

Web-based multimedia will need to be scalable to different cultures. Cultural differences play a key role in approaches to Internet regulation.[731] Cultural blunders due to lack of sensitivity to localized conditions can also lead to legal troubles.[732] A web site targeting the People's Republic of China may wish to consider avoiding notes in red ink and use of the number 4, which signify death.[733] Models on web sites should not be depicted showing the sole of their shoe or foot to another.[734] E-mail targeted communications to Germans should be careful about using first names which are "reserved for family members and close friends."[735] For example, Michael Rustad would not be referred to as Mike, but as Herr Doktor Professor in Germany. It is common in European countries to use professional titles to address professionals. Web sites need to understand how cultures communicate to sell goods and services effectively.

"What flies in Peoria won't get you where you want to go in Paris, Prague or Pago-Pago."[736] For example, in Asian countries it is important to develop bonds of trust and loyalty through connected intermediaries.[737] Content such as comparative advertisements may be unobjectionable in the United States but strictly prohibited in a number of European countries. Selling advertisements directed at foreign countries inevitably involves localization. Advertising should be localized as what may be a joke in one culture may be a taboo or culturally sensitive in another culture.[738] Internet web sites should be audited for taboos and sensitivities stemming from "politics, religion, ethnicity, geography, gender or humor."[739] Domain names need to be localized for cultural and national differences. "[T]ales of 'cross-cultural conflict—*faux pas* and blunders' abound."[740] American advertisements may not translate well in the global market. Fortune 500 companies have made some legendary cultural blunders. McDonald's recently was criticized for "trying to sell its beef and pork fare in Hindu and Muslim India."[741]

Web sites may need to be localized for cultural differences within the United States. Burger-King was also castigated for using a character with an Islamic name, Rasheed, in a Miami radio advertisement eating a bacon-cheddar burger.[742]

---

[731] *See generally* Mark Norris, eBusiness Essentials: Technical & Network Requirements for the Electronic Marketplace 35 (2000) (discussing cultural differences between Eastern and Western Europe and the United States).

[732] Margaret Kammeyer, The Other Customs Barriers: Cultural Research Avoids Business Blunders, 2 Export America 32 (Apr. 2001).

[733] *Id.* at 32.

[734] *Id.*

[735] *Id.*

[736] Etiquette International, First Get Good (visited Apr. 14, 2002), http://www.etiquetteintl.com/Articles/FirstGetGood.asp.

[737] *Id.*

[738] *Id.*

[739] *Id.*

[740] Max H. Bazerman et. al., Negotiation, Annual Review of Psychology 279 (Jan. 1, 2000).

[741] Robert Preston, Beware a Jingoistic Approach to Global E-Business, Internet Week (Mar. 19, 2001).

[742] Gil Griffin, Public Eye, The San Diego Union-Tribune (Mar. 17, 2000) at E-2.

The Council on American-Islamic Relations argued that the advertisement was deeply offensive because a person "with a Muslim name would be praising a sandwich that contains pork."[743] The Chevrolet Nova was marketed in Latin America without elementary research on the meaning of nova in the Spanish language. Nova means "don't go."[744] Filipino Muslims found the movie *Live Show* deeply offensive against the integrity of women.[745] The cultural ethos and customs of any culture will have an impact on ways of doing business. An e-business selling commodities would have to take into account the European campaign against genetically modified (GM) organisms.[746] Many European countries refuse to import GM foods.[747] German B2B web sites permitting online trading have found it difficult to supplant traditional markets where there are longstanding relationships of trust.[748] A social psychologist "described the process of intercultural negotiation as akin to a dance in which one person does a waltz and another a tango."[749]

Many nation states have sensitivity about languages. "The English language is a very difficult language. The grammar is complicated, the vocabulary huge and pronunciation and spelling are terribly inconsistent."[750] All of these factors pose significant risks of cultural misunderstandings in web site communications. An e-business may be subject to Greek laws that prohibit marketing products to children unless the web site is translated into Greek.[751] A German court ruled that a German hate crime law applies to foreign web sites as long as the content is accessible in Germany.[752] The problem with this decision is that it may impede the "worldwide flow of information and lead to applying one nation's laws to the citizens of other countries.[753] Web sites will need to be localized to take into account language, currency, and general etiquette for different targeted countries.[754] Empirical

---

[743] *Id.*

[744] Patricia Resende, When Going Global, Content Is King, but Localization Rules, *id.*

[745] Churck Salapuddin, What Islam Says About "Live Show," Business World (Mar. 27, 2001) at 5.

[746] Misha Glenny, How Europe Can Stop Worrying and Learn to Love the Future: Science and Technology Are at the Heart of a New Cultural War—Pitting America's Exuberance Against Continental Conservatism, Wired (Feb. 2001) at 102, 106.

[747] *Id.*

[748] Edmund L. Andrews, The Bread's Hot in Germany, the Internet Is Lukewarm, N.Y. Times (Apr. 18, 2001) (visited June 13, 2001), http://www.nytimes.com/2001/04/18/technology/18ANDR.html.

[749] Max H. Bazerman, Negotiation, Annual Review of Psychology 279 (Jan. 1, 2000) (citing Tinsley (1999)).

[750] Nancy Hatch Woodward, Do You Speak Internet? Focus On International HR; 44 HR Magazine S12 (Apr. 1, 1999).

[751] Andy Sullivan, Online Sales Rules Still Not Settled, The Toronto Star (Feb. 26, 2001) at 1 (giving example of Greek language law).

[752] Steve Kettmann, German Hate Law: No Denying It, Wired News (Dec. 15, 2000) (visited Apr. 17, 2002), http://www.wired.com/news/politics/0,1283,40669,00.html.

[753] *Id.*

[754] A number of general web sites are devoted to exploring cultural differences as cited in Margaret Kammeyer, The Other Customs Barrier, 2 Export America 33 (Apr. 2001) (citing www. executivplanet.com; www.etiquetteintl.com; www.worldbiz.com; www.fitadot.org; www.bena. com/ewinters/OnlineTutorial.html; www.culturalsavvycom; www.japan-guide.com/e/e622.html;

studies show that "43 percent of all Web users in 1999 were non-English speakers, with Japanese, Spanish and German the most prevalent non-English languages."[755]

§ 8.04   RESOLVING INTERNATIONAL DISPUTES AND PREVENTIVE LAW POINTERS

[A]   Conflict of Law, Choice of Law, and Choice of Forum

Forum selection clauses may be used in terms-of-service agreements as well as other license agreements. The online business will use choice of law and forum clauses. Click your heels together three times and say, "There's no place like home, there's no place like home."[756] The typical web site contract requires the web site visitor to agree to litigate all lawsuits in the provider's home court. An e-business needs to choose a jurisdiction that is the most favorable to its business mission.[757] The best way to get the home forum advantage is a forum selection clause drafted by the licensor. Network Solutions, Inc., for example, requires that all disputes over the registration of domain names be brought in Virginia.[758] Most U.S. courts will enforce a forum selection clause so long as it is not fundamentally unfair.[759] The U.S. Supreme Court upheld a forum selection clause against a passenger in a non-negotiated contract for a cruise in *Carnival Cruise Lines, Inc. v. Shute.*[760]

In *Williams v. America Online, Inc.,*[761] a Massachusetts court refused to enforce a forum selection clause drafted by AOL that required the users of AOL 5.0 software to "agree that exclusive jurisdiction for any claim or dispute with AOL or relating in any way to your membership or your use of AOL resides in the court of Virginia and you further agree and expressly consent to the exercise of personal jurisdiction in the courts of Virginia in connection with such dispute."[762]

---

www.traderscity.com/abcg/culture.htm; www.cyborlink.com/besite/latiname.htm; and www.users. erols.com/iauinc.

[755] Ric Duques & Garen K. Staglin, eONE Global, Payments Revisited: Circa 2000 (Payments DNA: A White Paper) (visited Apr. 14, 2002), http://www.eoneglobal.com/whtpaper.html.

[756] Kimberly A. Moore, Forum Shopping in Patent Cases: Does Geographic Choice Affect Innovation? 79 N.C. L. Rev. 889 (2001) (quoting *The Wizard of Oz* (Metro-Goldwyn-Mayer 1939)).

[757] Gareth Moran, E-Business Must Beware Legal Pitfalls (June 2, 2001) ZDNetUK.news (visited Apr. 14, 2002), http://wews.zdnet.co.uk/story/0,,s2088115,00.html (quoting English barrister on necessity of choosing a favorable jurisdiction and noting non-uniformity of European e-commerce laws).

[758] Barnett v. Network Solutions, Inc., 38 S.W.3d. 200 (11th Dist. Ct. of App. Tex., 2001) (affirming dismissal of appellant's suit on the grounds the forum named in the parties' forum clause specified Virginia as the choice of forum).

[759] *Id.* (enforcing forum selection clause and finding that it was not fundamentally unfair).

[760] 499 U.S. 585 (1990) (enforcing choice of forum clause on ticket purchased in state of Washington requiring consumer to adjudicate all disputes in the state of Florida).

[761] 00-0962 (Middlesex Cty. Mass., Feb. 2001) (denying AOL's motion to dismiss class action brought against AOL for economic losses caused by AOL Version 5.0; refusing to enforce choice of forum clause).

[762] *Id.* at *2.

In that case, the economic harm caused by AOL 5.0 was alleged to have occurred prior to the consumer's agreement with the terms-of-service agreement (TOS).[763] The plaintiff argued that the AOL customer is asked to agree with terms before having an opportunity to read the TOS.[764] The plaintiff argued that AOL's installation software changed the configuration of his network settings after downloading the software.[765] The court stated that "[p]ublic policy suggests that Massachusetts consumers who individually have damages of only a few hundred dollars should not have to pursue AOL in Virginia."[766] Finally, the court denied AOL's motion to dismiss the plaintiff's complaint on *forum non conveniens* grounds.[767]

American courts will enforce forum clauses in international transactions "so long as it is fair and reasonable to do so."[768] Potential conflict-of-law issues abound in Internet disputes, making alternative dispute resolution ideal for some parties. The International Chamber of Commerce, which handles cases from more than 100 different countries, is developing an online arbitration service. Civil litigation is not an ideal option for Internet-related conflicts. Online contracts should contain an agreement to arbitrate online disputes. Many U.S. companies include an arbitration clause in their standard software license agreements. Gateway, for example, has a dispute resolution clause requiring arbitration. Gateway's dispute resolution clause requires "any dispute or controversy arising out of or relating to this Agreement, its interpretation or any related purchases shall be resolved exclusively and finally by arbitration."[769]

In general, most parties do not specify the choice of law or forum when it comes to torts or *delict*s. In most European countries, the law of the country in which the tort of *delict* occurs is the applicable law.[770] The Internet may involve elements occurring in different countries. In the United Kingdom, for a cause of action resulting in personal injury, the law of the country where the individual sustained the injury is the applicable law.[771] If the tort involves damages to property, the applicable law is the country where the property was damaged.[772] The test that applies to the Internet is "the law of the country in which the most significant element or elements of those events occurred."[773]

---

[763] *Id.*

[764] *Id.*

[765] *Id.*

[766] *Id.* at *3.

[767] *Id.*

[768] Cambridge Biotech Corp. v. Pasteur Sanofi Diagnostics, 433 Mass. 133 (2000) (enforcing freely negotiated contract in international transaction).

[769] Westendorf v. Gateway 2000, Inc., 2000 Del. Ch. LEXIS 54 (Ct. of Chancery of Del., Mar. 16, 2000), *aff'd by* 763 A.2d 92 (Del. Sup. Ct. 2000) (reprinting Gateway 2000's arbitration clause).

[770] Private International Law (Miscellaneous Provisions) Act 1995 (c. 42) Part III: Choice of Law in Tort and *Delict.*

[771] *Id.* at ¶ (2)(a).

[772] *Id.* at ¶ 2(b).

[773] *Id.* at ¶ 2(c).

[B] International Arbitration

Alternative dispute resolution (ADR) such as arbitration or mediation is less expensive and saves more time than lawsuits.[774] The chief international convention on arbitration is the 1958 New York Convention on the Recognition and Enforcement of Foreign Arbitral Awards.[775] The New York Convention addresses the aspects of commencing and enforcing an arbitration action, but does not address the procedures to be employed in an international arbitration.[776] The New York Convention has 120 signatory states and permits for the general enforcement of arbitration awards.[777] The New York Convention requires signatory countries "to recognize arbitration agreements, to refer cases to arbitration pursuant to such agreements, and to generally enforce arbitral awards made within any party state."[778] An order compelling arbitration under the Convention on the Recognition and Enforcement of Foreign Arbitral Awards is not appealable.[779]

The forum selection clause in an Internet-related contract needs to specify the procedures for resolving disputes as well as the forum. The choice of a forum is a strategic decision in the Internet marketplace. Forum selection may consider institutions as "the World Intellectual Property Organization (WIPO), the American Arbitration Association (AAA), the International Chamber of Commerce (ICC) and the London Court of International Arbitration."[780] The ADR clause should not only specify arbitration as the means of resolving dispute but also the forum. The following is an arbitration clause choosing the American Arbitration Association as the forum:

> Any and all disputes, demands, claims, or controversies arising out of or relating to this contract or the breach thereof, shall be settled by binding arbitration pursuant to the Rules of the American Arbitration Association. Judgment upon the award rendered by the arbitrator may be entered into any court or administrative tribunal having jurisdiction thereof. Costs of the arbitration shall be borne equally by the parties and they shall be responsible for their own attorney's fees.[781]

---

[774] W. Chris Harrison, e-Business Troubleshooter: Free Market Justice: How Arbitration and Mediation Can Help You Avoid Litigation Lunacy, Emerging Business (Summer 2001) at 200.

[775] *See* New York Convention on the Recognition and Enforcement of Foreign Arbitral Awards (June 19, 1958), 21 U.S.T. 2517, T.I.A.S. No. 6997, 330 U.N.T.S. 38.

[776] ALI/UNIDROIT, Principles and Rules of Transnational Civil Procedure, *id.* at 3 (citing Geoffrey C. Hazard, Jr. and Michele Taruffo, Transnational Rules of Civil Procedure, 30 Cornell Int'l L.J. 493, 493-94 (1997)).

[777] Raymond Joe & Julian S. Millstein, Practice Tips: Think Arbitration When Drafting Net Contracts, 17 E-Commerce 1 (Mar. 2001) (urging the use of arbitration to resolve Internet disputes).

[778] *Id.*

[779] Filanto v. Chilewich Int'l Corp., 984 F.2d 58 (2d Cir. 1993); McCowan v. Dean Witter Reynolds Inc., 889 F.2d 451, 453 (2d Cir. 1989) (reference of claims to arbitration in embedded proceeding unappealable despite district court's statement that it had granted motion to dismiss).

[780] *Id.*

[781] W. Chris Harrison, e-Business Troubleshooter, Free Market Justice: How Arbitration and Mediation Can Help You Avoid Litigation Lunacy, Emerging Business 200, 203 (Summer 2001) (reprinting sample AAA clause for ADR).

The AAA has recently developed guidelines for resolving e-commerce related disputes. The AAA released "a new B2B eCommerce dispute management protocol. Initial signatories to the protocol include AT&T; BellSouth; Clifford Chance LLP; DaimlerChrysler AG; Debevoise & Plimpton; FedEx Corporation; Freshfields Bruckhaus Deringer LLP; Honeywell; Hughes Hubbard & Reed LLP; Microsoft Corporation; PepsiCo, Inc.; Philips Semiconductors, Inc.; Pitney Bowes, Inc.; Skadden, Arps, Slate, Meagher & Flom LLP; Sullivan & Cromwell; Unisys Corporation; Wells Fargo & E-Business; and Wilson, Sonsini, Goodrich & Rosati."[782]

A party may choose to submit a dispute to the "World Intellectual Property Organization (WIPO), American Arbitration Association (AAA),[783] the International Chamber of Commerce (ICC) and the London Court of International Arbitration."[784] For example, a Japanese toy maker who filed a claim with a WIPO panel won the right to its domain name incorporating its trademark Pochacco.[785] An e-Business may wish to develop a method of ADR to resolve small-value claims. It is impractical for consumers to litigate most online disputes. The FTC argues that ADR is the only "practical way to provide consumers with fast, inexpensive, and effective remedies, and can reduce businesses' exposure to foreign litigation."[786] Private sector programs such as "certification programs, rating systems, codes of conduct, and escrow and insurance programs" will help prevent consumer disputes.[787] An e-business may prefer arbitration in other Internet contracts.[788] It is critically important that the arbitrator have the technical expertise to understand Internet technologies.[789] Companies in the United States may wish to file their anticybersquatting actions in federal court because of the limited scope of remedies under ICANN.[790]

---

[782] American Arbitration Association, American Arbitration Association Announces New Electronic Commerce Protocol Standards Developed for Online Business-to-Business Dispute Management, New York, New York (Jan. 4, 2001).

[783] The American Arbitration Association was founded in 1926 "as a not-for-profit, public service organization dedicated to the resolution of disputes through the use of arbitration, mediation, conciliation, negotiation, democratic elections and other voluntary procedures. In 1999, more than 140,000 cases were filed with the Association in a full range of matters including commercial finance, construction, labor and employment, environmental, health care, insurance, mass claims and technology disputes. Through 37 offices nationwide and cooperative agreements with arbitral institutions in 38 other nations, the AAA provides a forum for the hearing of disputes, rules and procedures and a roster of impartial experts to hear and resolve cases." American Arbitration Association (visited May 30, 2001), http://adrdot.org.

[784] Id.

[785] Nintendo Wins "Pokemon" Domain Name Dispute, Kyodo News International (Nov. 2000) (reporting that the U.S. subsidiary of the Japanese e-Business, Ninetendo, was given a transfer of a domain name by a WIPO panel).

[786] Federal Trade Commission, Bureau of Consumer Protection, Consumer Protection in the Global Electronic Marketplace iii (Sept. 2000).

[787] Id.

[788] Id.

[789] Id.

[790] ICANN panels do not have the power to award damages. A federal court in Pennsylvania awarded $530,000 in damages and attorneys' fees in Electronic Boutique Holding Corp. v. Zuccarini, 2000 U.S. Dist. LEXIS 15719 (E.D. Pa., Oct. 30, 2000) (awarding the largest statutory award

If mass-market license agreements are used, there is a risk that the arbitration clause is unenforceable if the court refuses to enforce a shrinkwrap or click-wrap agreement. Another pitfall is that some countries, notably "Brazil, India, Israel, South Korea and South Africa . . . consider intellectual property disputes as non-commercial and, therefore, not subject to arbitration."[791] Arbitration clauses are likely to be enforced in the B2B transaction. The EU and the United States issued a joint statement on the desirability of private market-driven dispute resolution or arbitration in cross-border transactions.[792]

[C] Preventive Law Pointers

[1] Step-by-Step Guide to European Community Trademark Applications

The European Union community trademark (CTM) provides a great number of advantages for the e-business seeking trademark protection in Europe. One successful CTM application will give a registrant protection in all 15 member states of the European Union: Austria, Belgium, Denmark, Finland, France, Germany, Greece, Ireland, Italy, Luxembourg, the Netherlands, Portugal, Spain, Sweden, and the United Kingdom. What follows is a cradle-to-grave guide to filing a community trademark (CTM) application.

As with U.S. trademark registration, a CTM mark must be distinctive. If a mark is not distinctive enough, it will not be approved. As with U.S. trademark law, secondary meaning may be proven.[793] CMT trademark protection may only be obtained by registration. Four groups may register trademarks in the European Trademark Office in Alicante, Spain: "(1) nationals of a Member State; (2) nations of a state that is a party to the Paris Convention or a member of the World Trade Organization; (3) The applicant is domiciled or has an establishment in a Member State or Paris Convention State; or (4) the applicant is a national of a state that gives reciprocal protection to the Member States and recognizes CTM registration as proof of country of origin."[794]

FILING A CTM

[1] Register your trademarks in the core counties where your site is selling goods or rendering services. Trademark statutes vary significantly from one coun-

---

under the Anticybersquatting Consumer Protection Act of 1999 to date; finding that the defendant's registering of commonly misspelled web sites netted defendant millions of dollars through deceptive use of mousetrapping visitors seeking legitimate sites).

[791] Raymond Joe and Julian S. Millstein, Think Arbitration When Drafting Net Contracts, 17 e-Commerce 1 (Mar. 2001).

[792] ADR Mechanism Promoted in Cross-Border Context, 17 e-Commerce 11 (May 2001).

[793] Peter K. Yu, The Basics of Community Trademarks in the European Union, Gigalaw.com (visited June 9, 2001), http://www.gigalaw.com/articles/yu-2000-11-p2.html.

[794] Id.

try to another but have a unitary community in European Community.[795] The U.S. has a robust method of protecting trademarks in contrast to many other countries.[796]

[2] If you are doing significant business in Europe, apply for a Community Trade Mark (CTM). The CTM has a 10-year initial term and additional 10-year renewal periods.[797] The Commission of the European Communities has established rules for the Community Trade Mark (CMT).[798] A U.S. e-business may file a CMT application because it is a member of the 1883 Paris Convention.[799]

[3] Your company needs to comply with time limits for filing CMT applications. However, a CMT may only claim "Paris Convention priority based on a national application filed no more than six months before, in a country, that is a party to the Paris Convention or to the World Trade Organization."[800]

[4] Prior to seeking international registration, you will frequently need an existing national registration for the same mark in one or more EU countries. This registration permits an "owner to maintain the rights of the previously existing national registration."[801] Once the CMT registration is made, the national registrations in the individual EU member states may be allowed to lapse.[802]

[5] The CTM application is filed in Alicante, Spain, which is the European Community Trademark Office. The CTM examination procedure consists of a two-phase reexamination: (1) inherent registrability; and (2) examination on grounds of refusal.[803]

[6] The CMT application may be filed in 11 official EU languages, including English.[804]

---

[795] E.C. Regulation on the Community Trademark, Council Regulation (EC) No 40/94 of 20 December 1993 on the Community trademark, *id.* at Art. 1 (2) (stating that "[a] Community trade mark shall have a unitary character. It shall have equal effect throughout the Community: it shall not be registered, transferred or surrendered or be the subject of a decision revoking the rights of the proprietor or declaring it invalid, not shall its use be prohibited, save in respect of the whole Community."). *Id.* at Art. 2.

[796] J. Dianne Brinson and Mark F. Radcliffe, Internet Law and Business Handbook 280 (2000) (noting that Germany and Japan have almost no protection for unregistered trademarks, whereas in these countries famous marks are protected without registration).

[797] The European Community Trademark Act (CTM) "allows trademark owners to secure unitary trademark protection throughout the 15 EU countries, by requiring only one application registration fee and renewal fee per mark, and by allowing a trademark owner to maintain trademark rights throughout the EU by using its mark in only one EU country." Internlaw, Ltd., European Union Adopts Community Trademark Act (visited June 9, 2001), http://www.lectlaw.com/filesh/il-3.htm.

[798] Commission Regulation (EC) No 2868/95 (Dec. 13, 1995) (implementing Council Regulation (EC) No 40/94 on the Community Trademark).

[799] *Id.*

[800] *Id.*

[801] *Id.*

[802] *Id.*

[803] *Id.*

[804] *Id.*

[7] The CTM application must pass phases one and two before a registration is granted. The "official registration fee is approximately $1,430 (U.S.) for up to three classes and $260 for each additional class."[805]

[8] Your e-business's CMT application for a European Community trademark must contain a request for registration of the mark as a Community trade mark.[806]

[9] The CMT application must give "[t]he name, address and nationality of the applicant and the State in which he is domiciled or has his seat or an establishment."[807] An U.S. e-business may designate a representative located in an EU member state.

[10] The names of natural persons shall be indicated by the person's family name and given name(s) in the CMT application.[808]

[11] If names of legal entities are used, the CTM application must "state their official designation, which may be abbreviated in a customary manner; furthermore, the law of the State governing them shall be indicated."[809]

[12] The CMT application must contain all the necessary contact information. The telegraphic and Teletype address, telephone as well as fax numbers, and details of other data communications links may be given.[810]

[13] "Only one address shall, in principle, be indicated for each applicant; where several addresses are indicated, only the address mentioned first shall be taken into account, except where the applicant designates one of the addresses as an address for service."[811]

[14] The completed list of the goods and services for which the trademark is to be registered.[812] Is it in accordance with Rule 2 of the CMT?[813]

[15] The date of filing determines the priority of the trademark.[814] Article 33 provides exhibition priority is established by a declaration stating the name of the exhibition and the first display of the goods and services.[815]

[16] "The common classification referred to in Article 1 of the Nice Agreement Concerning the International Classification of Goods and Services for the Purposes of the Registration of Marks of 15 June 1957, as revised and amended, shall be applied to the classification of the goods and services."[816]

---

[805] *Id.*

[806] *Id.* at Rule 1(a).

[807] *Id.* at Rule 1(b).

[808] *Id.* at Rule 1(b).

[809] *Id.* at Rule 1.

[810] *Id.*

[811] *Id.* at Rule 1(e).

[812] This is Rule 2 of Title I of the Application Procedure. Commission Regulation (EC) No 2868/95 (Dec. 13, 1995), implementing Council Regulation (EC) No 40/94 on the Community trade mark (visited June 9, 2001), http://members.tripod.com/~EECO/ctmrules.htm.

[813] *Id.* at Rule 1(c).

[814] *Id.* at Rule (1)(f) (noting that when a priority of a previous application is claimed (Article 30) that "a declaration to that effect, stating the date on which and the country in or for which the previous application was filed").

[815] *Id.* at Rule 1(g).

[816] *Id.* at Rule 2.

[17] The CMT requires that the "list of goods and services shall be worded in such a way as to indicate clearly the nature of the goods and services and to allow each item to be classified in only one class of the Nice Classification."[817]

[18] "The goods and services shall, in principle, be grouped according to the classes of the Nice classification, each group being preceded by the number of the class of that Classification to which that group of goods or services belongs and presented in the order of the classes under that Classification.[818]

[19] The CMT Rules have the following requirements: "(1) If the applicant does not wish to claim any special graphic feature or color, the mark shall be reproduced in normal script, as for example, by typing the letters, numerals and signs in the application. The use of small letters and capital letters shall be permitted and shall be followed accordingly in publications of the mark and in the registration by the Office."[819]

[20] The CMT trademark shall be reproduced on a sheet of paper separate from the sheet on which the text of the application appears. The sheet on which the mark is reproduced shall not exceed DIN A4 size (29.7 cm high, 21 cm wide) and the space used for the reproduction (type-area) shall not be larger than 26.2 cm x 17 cm. A margin of at least 2.5 cm shall be left on the left-hand side. Where it is not obvious, adding the word "top" to each reproduction shall indicate the correct position of the mark.

[21] "The reproduction of the CMT mark shall be of such quality as to enable it to be reduced or enlarged to a size not more than 8 cm wide by 16 cm high for publication in the Community Trade Mark Bulletin. The separate sheet shall also indicate the name and address of the applicant. Four copies of the separate sheet carrying the reproduction shall be filed."[820]

[22] "Where registration of a three-dimensional CMT mark is applied for, the application shall contain an indication to that effect. The representation shall consist of a photographic reproduction or a graphic representation of the mark. The representation may contain up to six different perspectives of the mark."[821]

[23] If colors are used for CMT trademarks, the representation must be in color.[822]

[24] "The application fee for up to three international (CMT) classes, including search fees, is approximately $1,268 (U.S.) plus $260 for each additional class."[823] Trademark owners have the option to renew trademarks for an additional 10 years for $3,250 and $260 for each additional class.[824] Rule 4 defines

---

[817] *Id.*

[818] *Id.* at Rule 2(3).

[819] *Id.* at Rule 3.

[820] *Id.* at Rule 3(2).

[821] *Id.* at Rule 3(4).

[822] *Id.* at Rule 3(5).

[823] Interlaw, Ltd., European Union Adopts Community Trademark Act (visited Apr. 14, 2002), http://www.lectlaw.com/filesh/il-3.htm.

[824] CMT Regulation, *id.* at 3.

the "fee payable for the application as including the basic fee and a class fee for each class exceeding three to which the goods or services belong."[825]

[25] The European Trademark Office issues a receipt including the file number, representation description, or other identification of the mark.[826]

[26] The CMT applicant "shall indicate a file number of the previous application and file a copy of it within three months from the filing date and the copy must be certified."[827]

[27] If priority is claimed, your e-business has a three-month window to submit a copy of the relevant registration. If the registration is in the USPTO, it is advisable to have it certified.[828]

[28] If your e-business is claiming seniority of a registered trademark in a member state, there must be a declaration of seniority. The date of effective trademark registration must be indicated and submitted within a period of two months from the filing of the CTM application.[829]

[29] A CMT application will be rejected if it does not formally request the registration of the mark as a Community trademark.[830] Another formal requirement is complete information identifying the applicant.[831]

[30] If a CMT application does not list its "goods and services, for which the mark is to be registered," it will be rejected.[832] A representation of the mark must also be included as well as the basic fee.[833] If an application is rejected at the first phrase, notice will be given to the applicant at the address given for service.[834] The applicant has an opportunity to correct deficiencies in the application but may lose the right of priority during the period of the cure.[835]

[31] The publication of the application has information such as the applicant's name and address, claim of priority or seniority, and a reproduction of the mark.[836]

[32] An e-business or individual may enter an opposition "on the basis of one or more earlier marks or rights."[837] There is a fee of $455 for an opposition. Oppositions may be based on "a prior CTM registration, national registration, international registration under the Madrid Agreement, or common law mark as in the United Kingdom."[838]

---

[825] *Id.* at Rule 4.

[826] *Id.* at Rule 5(1).

[827] *Id.* at Rule 6(1).

[828] *Id.* at Rule 6(1).

[829] *Id.* at Rule 6(2).

[830] *Id.* at Rule 9(1)(a)(ii).

[831] *Id.* at Rule 9(1)(a)(ii).

[832] *Id.* at Rule 9(1)(a)(iii).

[833] *Id.* at Rule 9(1)(a)(iv) and (b).

[834] *Id.* at Rule 9(2).

[835] *Id.*

[836] *Id.* at Rule 12.

[837] *Id.* at Rule 15.

[838] Interlaw, Ltd., European Union Adopts Community Trademark Act, *id.* at 2.

[33] You must comply with CMT opposition procedures and list the file number of the application against which opposition is entered.[839] The opposition must state whether the earlier mark is a Community Mark or an internationally registered mark.[840] Have all the other requirements for Rule 15 opposition been met? An opposition only applies to the CTM registration, as opposed to individual EU countries.[841]

[34] You must present sufficient facts, evidence, and arguments in support of opposition if you expect to successfully challenge a CMT mark. Your arguments must be accompanied by authenticated documents.[842] The European trademark office will not approve generic marks or marks that violate public policy. In addition, the Office will not approve marks that "deceive the public as to the nature, quality or geographical origin of the goods and services."[843]

[35] The commencement of opposition occurs "two months after receipt of the communication."[844]

[36] The opposing party may have to furnish proof of use or give valid reason for nonuse. The use declarations shall specify "the place, time, extent, and nature of use of the opposing trademark for the goods and services in which respect it is registered and on which the opposition is based."[845] Evidence of use may be in the form "of supporting documents and items such as packages, labels, price lists, catalogues, invoices, photographs, newspaper advertisements, and statements in writing."[846]

[38] An application may "obtain the seniority of one or more earlier registered trade marks."[847]

[39] A trademark owner is given a notice of expiration of a registration.[848] Has the application for renewal contained the necessary information?[849]

[40] There is a procedure for transferring or assigning CMT marks. The provisions for transfer of marks are under Article 17 of the Regulation. Rule 31 requires that the application for registration of a transfer be made.[850] There is a provision for registration of a transfer relating only to some of the goods and services for which a mark is registered. The application must indicate which goods and services have been transferred.[851]

---

[839] Commission Regulation (EC) No 2868/95, *id*. at Rule 15.

[840] *Id*.

[841] Interlaw, Ltd. European Union Adopts Community Trademark Act, *id*.

[842] Commission Regulation (EC) No 2868/95, (EC) No 2868/95, *id*. at Rule 16.

[843] *See generally* Peter K. Yu, The Basics of Community Trademarks in the European Union, *id*.

[844] CMT Regulation, *id*. at Rule 19.

[845] *Id*. at Rule 21.

[846] *Id*. at Rule 21(3).

[847] *Id*. at Rule 28 (noting that the application must cite the registration number of the mark and other information, such as the name and address of the representative).

[848] *Id*. at Rule 29.

[849] *Id*. at Rule 30.

[850] *Id*. at Rule 31.

[851] *Id*. at Rule 32 (specifying the rules for Partial Transfers).

[41] Rule 33 sets forth a registration of grants or transfers of licenses.[852] The registration of license specifies whether the license agreement is exclusive or not.[853] There is a provision for recording semi-exclusive or territorially limited licenses.[854] "A license in respect of a Community trade mark shall be recorded in the Register as a sub-license where it is granted by licensee whose license is recorded in the Register."[855]

[42] Cancellations or modifications in the licenses or other rights may also be registered.[856]

[43] An e-business may apply to revoke or declare a mark to be invalid.[857] The European Trademark Office conducts revocation or invalidity proceedings after an examination of the application.[858]

[44] Collective marks are available for associations or other legal persons qualifying for a collective mark.[859]

[45] There is a Board of Appeals for challenging trademark office actions.[860] However, notice of an appeal must be given within two months of the decision.[861] The rules of evidence and proceedings are found in Title XI of the Rules.[862]

[2] Global Internet Domain Name

The e-business seeking to do business worldwide needs to consider international considerations when protecting domain name rights. Each country has different procedures for registering domain names. Some countries reserve domain names for corporations doing business in their country. Other countries permit a domain name to be filed even if there is no prior corporate presence in the country. The following guidelines are strategic issues in protecting SPC's domain name in the core countries where it is doing business.

[1] Register your domain name in all core countries where you are targeting your business.

[2] Register federal or foreign trademark registration for your domain name if it is distinctive enough to qualify for protection.[863]

---

[852] *Id.* at Rule 33 (specifying the rules for Registration of Licenses and other rights).

[853] *Id.* at Rule 34.

[854] *Id.* at Rule 34(3).

[855] *Id.* at Rule 34(2).

[856] *Id.* at Rule 35.

[857] *Id.* at Rule 37.

[858] *See* Rule 40. The rules for revocation or invalidity proceedings are found in Rules 37-41.

[859] The rules for Community Collective Marks are found in Title VIII of the Rules, Rule 42.

[860] Rules 48 to 51 govern notice of appeals and examination of appeals, *id.* at 48-51.

[861] *Id.* at Rule 52.

[862] *See Id.* at Rules 52-74.

[863] Ron N. Dreben and Johanna L. Werbach, Top 10 Things to Consider in Developing an Electronic Commerce Web, 16 Computer Law. 17 (May 1999)

[3] Conduct a search or hire a service or have a provider conduct a search to determine ownership of domain names. One difficulty of searches of domain names is that there is no single database for assessing domain name ownership.[864]

[4] Localize your domain name registrations for country-level requirements. Sweden, for example, has a system of prior assessment, which requires a presence in the country to file for a domain name. The most popular ccTLDs are in the European Union countries.[865]

[5] Register your ccTLD before your competitors or cybersquatters in "first to file" jurisdictions.

[6] If you discover a cybersquatter, consider filing an arbitration proceeding before an ICANN-approved panel.[866] Do a cost/benefit analysis of using the quicker and cheaper ICANN procedure rather than a lawsuit in federal court. One of the limitations of the anticybersquatting federal statutes is the expense and time consumed in litigation. ICANN is a speedy, inexpensive procedure. However, no money damages are available under ICANN, unlike a federal court proceeding. ICANN panelists can transfer or cancel domain name registrations but not award money damages.

[7] Be sure you read and understand the ICANN Policy[867] prior to filing a complaint with a provider.

[8] Consult the ICANN Rules for the adjudication of a domain name dispute.[868]

[9] If you are a plaintiff in a UDRP action, you will need to decide where to file your complaint.

[10] File your complaint with the most pro-plaintiff provider. Currently, the most pro-plaintiff provider is the WIPO Arbitration and Mediation Center. Do your own analysis of UDRP decisions for recent trends.

[11] Confirm the identity of the Registrar for the contested Domain Name.

[12] Confirm that you have the required contact information for the respondent cybersquatter. If you are seeking federal court relief, you will not have *in rem* remedies unless personal jurisdiction is unavailing. The UDRP procedure requires that you provide contact information. Your best source of information is the Registrar's Whois Database. A domain name registrant who gives false contact information may lose the domain name in a default judgment.

[13] Be certain UDRP complaint is filed in the proper form to avoid early dismissals. Each UDRP complaint must state: (1) the parties' names; (2) domain

---

[864] However, companies such as Thomson and Thomson conduct searches for trademarks that may have priority or seniority and thus conflict with domain names.

[865] Karla Lemanski-Valente and Timothy Majke, Domain Names and Trademark Issues in the European Union, *id.*

[866] *Id.*

[867] ICANN, ICANN Policy (visited Apr. 14, 2002), http://www.icann.org/udrp/udrp-policy-24oct99.htm.

[868] ICANN, ICANN Rules (visited Apr. 14, 2002), http://www.icann.org/udrp/udrp-rules-24oct99.htm.

name and registrar; (3) prior procedural history, such as any e-mail correspondence between the parties, notification of the complaint, and commencement of proceedings; (4) factual background underlying cybersquatting or other bad faith use of domain name; (5) parties' contention (for example, the claim that a domain name used by a cybersquatter is confusingly similar to the complainant's trademark); and (6) facts showing cybersquater (or other wrongdoer) registered a domain name or used it in bad faith.

[14] Be certain that any evidence about your use of trademarks and your competitor's actions are accurately stated. You will need to demonstrate that your competitor's use of a domain name was in bad faith in order to prevail. If a complainant seeks to sell a domain name to you containing your trademark for a large profit, there will be strong evidence of bad faith. A business competitor's registration of a domain name to restrain competition is also evidence of bad faith. To prepare for the panel proceeding, research the panelists' prior UDRP decisions. You may also gain insight into panelists' background and predispositions by doing Internet searches.

[3] Patent Cooperation Treaty

The Patent Cooperation Treaty is a multilateral treaty concluded in Washington, D.C., in 1970, amended in 1979 and modified in 1984.[869] The PCT is open to signatories to the Paris Convention for the Protection of Industrial Property (1883).[870] The PCT is administered by WIPO and has 101 signatories as of April 2001. An e-Business may seek patent protection "for an invention simultaneously in each of a large number of countries by filing an 'international' patent application."[871]

The PCT permits individuals or entities in member countries to file with either the national patent office of a contracting state or with the International Bureau of WIPO in Geneva.[872] Applicants who are nationals or residents of a contracting state and party to one of the European Patent Conventions may file patent applications with the European Patent Office (EPO).[873] The legal impact of an international application in each contracting state is "the same as if a national patent application had been filed with the national patent office of that State."[874] International applications are subject to "international searches" conducted by one of the major patent offices.[875] The advantage for the e-business of filing a PCT

---

[869] World Intellectual Property Organization, International Protection of Industrial Property, Patent Cooperation Treaty (1970) (visited Apr. 14, 2002), http://www.wipodot.org/eng/general/ipip/pct.htm.

[870] *Id.*

[871] WIPO, Patent Cooperation Treaty, *id.*

[872] *Id.*

[873] The United States e-Business will find that the international application "gives the applicant more time and a better basis for deciding whether and in what countries to further pursue the application." WIPO, What Is the PCT? Chapter II, *id.*

[874] *Id.*

[875] The major patent offices include: "The Patent Offices of Australia, Austria, China, Japan, the Russian Federation, Spain, Sweden, the United States, and the European Patent Office," *id.* at n.1.

application is that "the applicant has 18 months more than he has in a procedure outside the PCT to reflect on the desirability of seeking protection in foreign countries, to appoint local patent agents in each foreign country, to prepare the necessary translations, and to pay the national fees."[876] The PCT's provision of filing a single international application is an alternative to filing numerous national or regional patent applications. Another advantage is the information gained in the PCT search process.

The e-business will make the decision where to incur the considerable costs of securing patent protection in individual countries. The international application gives the e-business the necessary time to evaluate the legal environment of countries where the invention is being patented. The publication of the international application places the world on notice about the possible patentability of a claimed invention.[877]

[4] Distance Contracts

If there is a contract with a nonconsumer in a different signatory state, CISG automatically applies unless the parties opt out in favor of another body of law such as the Uniform Commercial Code. Foreign consumer protection statutes will also apply to international sales of goods.

The EU Distance Selling Directive applies to SPC's web site sales just as it would in the brick-and-mortar world. To comply with the Distance Directive, SPC will need to provide the consumer with (1) e-business's name and address, (2) principal characteristics of goods or services, (3) price, (4) arrangement for payment, (5) existence of the right of withdrawal, and (6) cost of using means of distance communications such as telephone service. What is your e-business's return policy? Do you give consumers a right of withdrawal? You must permit consumers to have a cooling off period of at least seven days from the receipt of the customer's order.

[5] International Sales Contracts

Your web site needs a procedure for transmitting offers, accepting orders, and documenting completed sales. If SPC's web site contract is with a non-consumer from a different signatory state, CISG applies. CISG applies to contracts of sale of goods between parties whose place of business are in different states.[878] CISG does not apply to consumer sales, meaning "goods bought for personal, family or household use."[879] CISG governs contracts "in which the preponderant part of the obligations of the party who furnishes the goods consists in the supply

---

[876] Id.
[877] Id. at 2.
[878] Id. Art. 1.
[879] Id. Art. 2.

of labor or other services."[880] Although web site leases of computer equipment are uncommon, these transactions are outside of CISG. SPC may use a choice-of-law clause to make a lease agreement subject to Article 2A of the UCC governing the leases of goods.

An online business may opt out of CISG, excluding application of the Convention or varying its provisions.[881] SPC, for example, could have choice of law, opting out of the CISG in favor of Massachusetts' Article 2 of the UCC. In an international commercial transaction, the sales law of another country may apply. The Sale and Supply of Goods Act applies to sales of goods in the United Kingdom.

The United States is one of the few countries to have a Statute of Frauds. CISG does not require evidence of a writing for a sales contract to be enforceable. It may be unclear as to when an electronic offer becomes effective. In the case of e-mail offers or other Internet-related acknowledgements, it may be desirable to request a return receipt. Article 15 of CISG provides that "[a]n offer becomes effective when it reaches the offeree."[882] In the bricks-and-mortar world, an advertising brochure or circular in a newspaper is an invitation *to make an offer,* as opposed to *an offer.* In the Internet environment, is it reasonable for a web site visitor to rely on SPC's pricing information as irrevocable offers?

Offers and acceptance need to be tailored for CISG in an online sale of goods. Article 16 of CISG states that "it is reasonable for the offeree to rely on the offer as being irrevocable when the offeree has acted in reliance on the offer.[883] SPC may consider structuring its online kiosk or electronic catalogue as merely invitations for offers as opposed to enforceable offers. CISG provides that an "offer may be revoked if the revocation reaches the offeree before he has dispatched an acceptance."[884] SPC should conspicuously give notice that it may revoke offers or amend its electronic catalogue at any time. CISG does not permit the parties the remedy of cancellation of the contract unless there is a "fundamental breach."[885] The standard of performance in a single delivery of goods is the perfect tender rule. If a sales contract fails in any respect, the seller is deemed to be in breach.[886] Another unsettled issue is the enforceability of mass-market licenses such as a clickwrap agreement in Europe.

SPC needs to pay careful attention to warranties it gives for its computer hardware or software. Although the term *warranty* is never used in CISG, the Convention incorporates warranty-like provisions to the sale of goods. Internet international contracts must consider differences in culture, language, and governing law. Choice of law, choice of forum, and conflict of law are important factors in

---

[880] *Id.* Art. 3(2).

[881] *Id.* at Art. 6.

[882] *Id.* at Art. 15(a).

[883] *Id.* at Art. 16(2)(b).

[884] *Id.* at Art. 16(1).

[885] *Id.* at Art. 25.

[886] UCC § 2-601 (1999).

international contracts. The European Community recognizes the validity of electronic signatures. The European Draft Directive 98/297/EC validates electronic signatures.[887] Article 2 of the Uniform Commercial Code governs the sale of goods originating in the United States. Foreign sales law may apply to the consumer sale of goods where CISG is inapplicable.

[6] Software Licensing Agreements

The Uniform Computer Information Transactions Act (UCITA) applies to information licenses, including Internet-related software contracts, in Maryland and Virginia. It is unclear whether foreign courts will enforce the provision of UCITA. It is quite unlikely that European courts will enforce choice-of-law clauses imposing UCITA on cross-border contracts. It is also unlikely that a European court would require a consumer to prosecute a case against an Internet Service Provider in Virginia, Ohio, or other preferred U.S. forums for providers. The provisions of UCITA will likely be a useful model for new methods of software distribution that load software on a single disk or CD rather than the desktop. The newest wave of software licensing is through "application service providers" that give Internet access to software through log on services.[888]

The newest form of license agreement is the service agreement by application service providers (ASPs). ASPs emerged in the late 1990s as a new method of distributing software. The software distribution method is based upon services versus a sale. Microsoft, for example, is "linking programs to distributed services."[889] Distributed service agreements seem tailored to the licensing model, because it is clear that the user does not own the software.[890] A service agreement may be defined by a different legal standard such as "best efforts," as opposed to the fundamental breach standard of Article 25 of the CISG.

[7] Internet Regulation

Many of the Internet restrictions will depend on specific products. If a web site is selling software, there will be export regulations as well as distance selling regulations. National restrictions on advertising or the sale of products apply to Internet sales or services. The regulations for Internet sales vary significantly by product category. The FDA regulations apply to pharmaceuticals or medical products over the Internet. In contrast, there are different regulations for the sale of

---

[887] Yves Poullet, "Some Considerations on Cyberspace Law," Chapter 4 *in* The International Dimensions of Cyberspace Law (UNESCO, 2000).

[888] John Markoff, E-Business Special Section, Software's Next Leap Is Out of the Box, N.Y. Times (June 13, 2001) (visited Apr. 14, 2002), http://www.nytimes.com/2001/06/13/technology/13MARK.html.

[889] *Id.*

[890] *Id.*

securities on the Internet. The sale of medicine on the Internet may trigger regulations in different countries.[891] The United States has a more liberal regime for advertising medicines than in many other countries. For example, in Colombia, the advertising of medicines is "forbidden in all mass media," which includes over the Internet.[892]

Countries vary in their regulations about Internet-related securities issues. In Germany, for example, it is acceptable to notify shareholders by e-mail for invitations to attend shareholder meetings, agendas, and all other matters.[893] Your online business needs to be aware of the following Internet scams identified by the Federal Trade Commission and consumer protection agencies in Australia, Canada, and Europe: (1) Internet Auction Fraud, (2) Internet Service Provider Scams, and (3) Internet Web Site Design/Promotions.[894] Be certain your web site is not the subject of an enforcement action for illegal sweepstakes, contests, or gambling. Recently, New Jersey sued three online casinos originating offshore for violation of that state's Consumer Fraud Act.[895] If sweepstakes or contests are used, there must be a compliance check with foreign jurisdictions as well as state and federal gaming or contest regulations.

[8]   Import and Export Regulation

Check the antiboycott regulations that may apply to any of SPC's software downloaded from the web site. Be certain that your company has the necessary export licenses from the Department of Commerce to export software. Exports and re-exports are subject to the Export Administration Regulations (EAR) administered by the U.S. Department of Commerce's Bureau of Export Administration (BXA).

The BXA licenses software that has a dual use, being commercial software with a military application. The BXA maintains a list of individuals and countries where designated products may not exported or re-exported. The key export questions on restricted exports include: Who will receive it? Is the recipient on the denied person's list? What will the recipient do with it? Remember that licensing is dependent upon the technical specifications, destination, end use, and end user. Determine other activities which the end user of software may be involved in.[896]

---

[891] Each target nation state will have different regulations on the advertising and sale of goods that will differ significantly depending on the product. In Colombia, for example, the restrictions applicable to the sale of medicine and pharmaceuticals have been extended to the advertising and sale of medicines over the Internet; *see* Regulations on Advertising and Sale of Medicines on the Internet, 2 World Internet L. Rep. 4 (Apr. 2001) (reporting ruling of Colombia's equivalent of the FDA).

[892] *Id.*

[893] Roman Banwaldt (Clifford Chance Law firm, Berlin, Germany), Germany, New Registered Shares Act Permits Key Role for E-Media, 2 World Internet L. Rep. 5 (Apr. 2001).

[894] Law Enforcement Officials from Around the World Tackle "Top 10" Online Scams, 18 Computer & Internet Law. 31 (Jan. 2001).

[895] Martin Stone, New Jersey Sues Three Offshore Online Casinos, Newsbytes (June 19, 2001), http://www.newsbytes.com/news/01/166979.html.

[896] U.S. Department of Commerce, The Bureau of Export Administration, Fact Sheet: How Do I Know If I Need to Get a License from the Department of Commerce? (visited Apr. 15, 2002), http://www.bxa.doc.gov/factsheets/facts1.htm.

This standard asks whether the recipient of the exported (or re-exported) software is involved with other questionable activities.

In less than clear-cut cases, SPC may wish to consult with the BXA if it is unsure about the propriety of an export on the Internet. The BXA web site offers online assistance in determining whether SPC or other online companies have obligations under the EAR. Special agents work with the business community in enforcing EAR regulations.[897] The BXA operates an advice line and maintains a list of firms and individuals who have been denied export and re-export privileges.[898]

"Can you trust the seller to provide accurate information about the item being shipped in the Customs section of the shipping documents? Giving misleading or inaccurate information about the nature of the item and its value is illegal. And it is the importer . . . who could face legal action and fines for this violation."[899] The seller must complete an accurate customs declaration. The seller must provide you with the following information which is necessary for a customs declaration: "(1) seller's name and address; (2) quantity of each type of item being shipped; (3) purchase price in U.S. dollars; (4) weight of the item; and (5) country of origin."[900] Another concern is whether any of goods being imported are gray market goods,[901] i.e., whether contractual restrictions on foreign distributors can be used to stop other parties from entering the gray market.[902]

[9] Localizing Web Sites

A cultural sensitivity audit needs to be completed prior to the launching of a web site. An e-business may consider a specific web site targeting a different country or zone of countries. The key issue is how to localize the web site to take into account different norms, laws, and cultural preferences. Cultural anthropologists have long pointed out how cultural insensitivity can lead to misunderstandings. The Internet is a foreign marketplace with diverse cultures and legal regimes that are tailored for local conditions. Ethnocentrism is the tendency to impose one's own cultural norms on a foreign culture. To avoid ethnocentrism, the web site developer needs to take cultural differences into account. At a minimum, a

---

[897] Boston's Export Enforcement Field Office, for example, is located in Room 350, 10 Causeway Street, Boston, MA 02222 (Telephone: 617-565-6030; Fax: 617-565-6039). The BXA has enforcement offices in New York, Washington, Miami, and Chicago. Contact information and web site forms are available at http://www.bxa.doc.gov/factsheets/ExporterAssistance.html. The BXA's Antiboycott Advice Line is 202-482-2381, operating 9 a.m. to 4.p.m. (FAX 202-482-0913).

[898] The file of denied persons is over 300KB and takes 2-3 minutes to download. *Id.*

[899] U.S. Customs, Internet Transactions, Checklist (visited Apr. 14, 2002), http://www.customs.ustreas.gov/impoexpo/inetraade.htm.

[900] *Id.* at 3.

[901] Shubba Ghosh, An Economic Analysis of the Common Control Exception to Gray Market Exclusions, 15 U. Penn. J. Int'l Bus. Law. 373 (1994) (noting that gray markets are outlets not authorized by manufacturers and therefore not permitted).

[902] Robert W. Clarida, Licensing, IP Worldwide (Aug. 1998).

localized web site will need to be in the language(s) of a target nation state. E-business web site developers and operators will need to have some understanding of the target culture. Domain names may be targeted to specific countries in target countries:

> International ccTLDs provide a foundation for localized content (e.g., yahoo.de contains news articles relevant to Germany), local customer service (e.g., consumers prefer a local customer service department in their local tongue and time zone), local inventory (a book store with a .de domain in Germany will be selling books in German), local shipping (overseas shipping is costly and time consuming) and local currency acceptance.[903]

One major cultural difference between the United States and the Eurozone countries is the value of privacy. The use of "cookies" or IP-address harvesting may be unobjectionable in the United States, but violate privacy norms in other countries. Web site content such as advertising must be sensitive to different cultures. Third-party advertising and content must also be included in the audit. One of the greatest cultural differences is in the field of information torts arising out of web site publications. Many defamation cases are arising out of web site publications that reflect different cultural and legal traditions.

Office Depot has launched different web sites tailored to specific countries.[904] An e-business such as SPC will need to consult with local members of the business community to determine the best web site design, a strategy used by Office Depot.[905] Cultural factors have an impact on the use of emoticons in e-mail. "While Westerners take such signals from the mouth (smiley face), the Japanese tend to take them from the eyes."[906] Another difference is that in Japan these face icons "are not embraced by business people for serious conversations."[907] Vendors such as GlobalSight can assist the e-business in localizing its web sites country by country.[908]

Click-wrap agreements may need to be tailored to reflect local laws concerning disclosure, conspicuousness, and other factors. If there is uncertainty as to the enforcement of click-wrap or mass-market licenses, contracting may be augmented by a standard written contract prior to shipping merchandise or rendering services. A web site needs to be localized for export or re-export restrictions. Web sites will need to restrict sales to embargoed countries or countries requiring an export license.

---

[903] Karla Lemanski-Valente and Time Majka, International Internet Domain Name Registrations, 17 e-Commerce 1 (Dec. 2000).

[904] Robert Preston, Beware a Jingoistic Approach to Global E-Business, Internet Week 9 (Mar. 19, 2001).

[905] *Id.*

[906] Miki Tanikawa, "In Japan (*_o_*) Means Happiness, Int'l Herald Trib. 4 (May 8, 2000) (noting that the difference in emoticons varies from each feature the culture emphasizes).

[907] *Id.*

[908] Robert Preston, Beware a Jingoistic Approach, *id.*

[10] Minimizing the Risk of Jurisdiction

The radius of the risk of international jurisdiction may be reduced by clearly targeting consumers in enumerated countries. In the United States, jurisdiction is frequently determined on the issue of whether the site "purposefully avails" itself of the forum. A web site disclaimer that the site is not dealing with given nation states is advisable. One danger is that a web site publisher in America may be posting content viewed in Saudi Arabia which might have dire consequences under Saudi law.[909] It may be advisable to require customers to disclose their residence. In the absence of some form of identification, a site has no way of knowing whether a customer is from a given nation state.[910]

Electronic agents or bots may be programmed to exclude residents of states where an activity or service is restricted. Citizens who are from countries where the liability risk is too great should be blocked from ordering goods or services from your web site. Bots, of course, may be used to prevent exporting software to restricted countries such as Afghanistan, Cuba, or Iraq.

[11] Complying with EU Competition Law*

Unlike the broad standards of U.S. antitrust law, European anticompetitive laws have specific rules or guidelines. In Europe, the major threats to competition are mutual price cooperation, collusion, and the elimination of price uncertainty. Regular price wars between companies are acceptable as long as the purpose does not include driving out the competition or attempting to gain total control of the market. The European Commission (EC) emphasizes nonmarket dividing arrangements because they encourage the free flow of goods between the member states. Competition law policy promotes the overarching concept of a single market throughout the European Union (EU). To achieve the goal of uniformity, EU law has priority over the domestic law of individual national states. When there is a conflict with member state law, EU law governs.

The EU, like antitrust authorities in the United States, finds it difficult to apply antitrust or competition law to the Internet because traditional competition law does not mesh well with rapidly evolving information technologies (IT). Frequently the legal lag between competition law and IT creates an uncertain legal

---

[909] Aron Mefford, Lex Informatica: Foundations of Law on the Internet, 5 Ind. J. Global Leg. Stud. 211, 216 (1997).

[910] "Internet addresses do not correspond to physical locations. . . . Net publishers are also unlikely to consider that their audience is broader than that of persons in their own jurisdiction and will therefore fail to take appropriate precautions." *Id.* at 217.

* This practice pointer was authored by Jessica M. Natale, a 2002 graduate of the Suffolk University Law School and an editor of the *Journal of High Technology Law*. Ms. Natale studied competition law with Professor Hans Henrik Lidgard of the law faculty of the University of Lund, Sweden, in the summer of 2001. Professor Lidgard's ideas are reflected in the arguments presented in this section.

environment. Currently, it is unclear how basic concepts and methods of anticompetitive law apply to the Internet. One difficulty is to determine how IT should be classified and whether it constitutes its own market or is connected to others. Anticompetitive behavior cannot be detected or prohibited if the specific market is unknown or unknowable. In general, the EU Competition Commissioner supports the spirit of technology and does not want anticompetition laws to impede the development of the European e-economy.

The European anticompetitive laws are more specific than the U.S. ones, but there are indications of them becoming more "American" in their approach in the future. The common law approach of creating law around precedent may become more common.[911] In any event, always consult European counsel before entering into international trade agreements.

[a]   Article 81 of the EC Treaty

Article 81 attempts to prevent collusion, price fixing, limiting or control of production, and sharing markets. Any agreement for absolute territorial protection of a product is to be avoided as it is subject to strict scrutiny by the EC. What is key here is whether the anticompetitive behavior has an effect on other member EU states. Pending approval, specific violations of Article 81 are eligible for an exemption by the EC. Typically exemptions are granted for license, research, and vertical agreements.

The following four factors must be shown for Article 81 to apply:

1. *Undertaking:* An entity that is performing commercial activities. The entity does not have to be for profit. The law does not specifically define an undertaking but it has included in past cases towns, governmental agencies, companies, individuals and trade unions.[912]

2. *Agreement:* A decision by associates otherwise known as "gentlemen's agreements" or any concerted or practice activity, for example, a uniform price increase for the same product all over Europe.[913] The EU Treaty's competition rules strictly proscribe cooperation with competitors irrespective of the form or method. An agreement dividing markets is a per se violation but is not enough to be anti competitive without first having some effect on the European market.[914]

3. *Trade Criteria:* Placing the goods or services in commercial usage or trade, that affects the EU member states. Anticompetitive trade acts include, for example, sharing markets and applying dissimilar condi-

---

[911] We are indebted to Professor Lidgard, who made this argument.

[912] Treaty Establishing the European Community, Mar. 25, 1957, art. 81(1) (as amended), *available at* http://www.europa.eu.int/eur-lex/en/treaties/dat/ec_cons_treaty_en.pdf.

[913] *Id.*

[914] *See* Völk v. Vervaecke, 9 July 1969: [1969] ECR 295, [1969] CMLR 273 (holding that an agreement made concerning price fixing for 600 washing machines would have a de minimis impact on the general washing machine market).

tions to equivalent transactions with other parties, thereby placing them at a competitive disadvantage.[915]

4. *Competition Criteria:* Any undertaking that eliminates competition in respect of the products in question.[916]

[b]   Article 82 of the EC Treaty

Article 82 attempts to prevent unilateral activities, such as a group of entities agreeing to price fixing. No exemptions are available for violations of this article. All three of the following criteria must be satisfied to find a violation of Article 82:

1. *Dominant Position:* The anticompetitive entity must have a dominant position in the market. Fifty percent control of a market creates a presumption of dominance. Of course the market itself must be defined in which the dominant position exists. When there is no substitute for a product, it is its own separate market.[917] Being a large company alone does not mean a dominant position.

2. *Trade Criteria:* The trade of the product must have an effect on trade in the European Union.

3. *Abuse of Dominant Position:* an entity abuses its dominant position in the market by driving out others, price fixing, refusing to supply raw goods, and selling a product below variable costs (total costs to make the product), to name a few examples, with its motive being to eliminate competitors.

[12]   Data Protection Directive

The EU's Data Protection Directive requires all personal data transferred to countries outside the Union to benefit from "adequate protection."[918] The European Commission recently approved language for standard contractual clauses regarding personal data transferred from the European Union to the United States and other non-Union countries. Companies employing standard clauses will have a safe harbor in complying with the "adequate protection" requirements of the Directive. As of early 2002, only "Switzerland, Hungary and the US 'Safe Harbor' arrangement have been recognised as providing adequate protection (see IP/00/865)."[919]

The Directive requires that the following general principles be applied:

---

[915] EC Treaty, *supra* note note 912, art. 81(1)(d).

[916] *Id.* art. 81(3).

[917] United Brands Co. v. EC Comm'n, 1978 Rep. of Cases 0207-0315 (Feb. 14, 1978).

[918] Directive 95/46/EC on the Protection of Individuals with Regard to the Processing of Personal Data and on the Free Movement of Such Data, 1995 O.J. (L 281) 31.

[919] European Commission, Data Protection: Commission Approves Standard Contractual Clauses for Data Transfers to non-EU Countries (visited Jan. 19, 2002), http://www.europa.eu.int/comm/internal_market/en/dataprot/news/clauses2.htm.

- Personal data should be collected only for specified, explicit, and legitimate purposes.

- The persons concerned should be informed about such purposes and the identity of the data controller.

- Any person concerned should have a right of access to his/her data and the opportunity to change or delete data that are incorrect; if something goes wrong, appropriate remedies must be available to put things right, including compensation or damages through the competent courts.[920]

"The standard contractual clauses contain a legally enforceable declaration ('warrant') whereby both the 'Data Exporter' and the 'Data Importer' undertake to process the data in accordance with basic data protection rules and agree that individuals may enforce their rights under the contract."[921]

[13]   Enforceability of Forum Selection Clauses*

[a]   *Introduction*

A choice of forum clause is a contractual provision that predetermines the law that applies for any dispute involving the contract. Choice of forum clauses allows parties to control the issue of jurisdiction and all the other interests associated with that choice of forum. U.S. courts generally will enforce forum selection clauses because the plaintiff's choice of forum is "entitled to substantial deference."[922] The forum selection clause governs the choice of jurisdiction in the agreement, but its power is restricted by fundamental public policy considerations, such as unfairness, unequal bargaining power of the parties, and coercion. If the parties do not otherwise agree to choice of law, the court will make the decision as to the applicable law based upon factors such as the parties' needs and relevant policies of the different jurisdictions.[923]

Suppose that two independent companies, the American company SPC, which has its principal place of business in Massachusetts, and the Swedish company Tamarin Enterprises, enter into a license agreement concerning a patent for a business method for computerizing web site advertising revenue. The American licensor accuses the Swedish licensee of breaching the license agreement and

---

[920] *Id.*

[921] *Id.*

* This practice pointer was authored by Jessica M. Natale, a 2002 graduate of the Suffolk University Law School and an editor of the *Journal of High Technology Law*. Ms. Natale studied competition law with Professor Hans Henrik Lidgard of the law faculty of the University of Lund, Sweden, in the summer of 2001. Professor Lidgard's ideas are reflected in the arguments presented in this section.

[922] UCITA § 109(a) (1999).

[923] Restatement (Second) of Conflicts § 6.

claims $80,000 in damages. Depending on whether the parties included a forum selection clause in their agreement, the results may be very different.

[b] Explicit Forum Selection Clause

The forum selection clause in the first scenario states the following:

> All claims and disputes arising under and in relation to this contract will be litigated before the state and federal courts of Suffolk County, Massachusetts, United States of America. The licensor and the licensee agree to proper and adequate notice of process to the licensee or its agent, and accept service of process in advance to appear in a Massachusetts court on the specified date and time.[924]

After the court has reviewed the public policy considerations mentioned above, such as unfairness, unequal bargaining power of the parties, and coercion, the court is likely conclude that the U.S. jurisdiction clause serves the purpose of the agreement itself and does not violate any public policy issues.

A party choosing to litigate in a foreign forum must consider issues such as the cost of the trial and the level of confidence a U.S. court will have in the judgment of a foreign court.[925] In this case, the licensor, after carefully weighing its options, decided to insert a forum selection clause designating a Massachusetts court rather than a Swedish court.

The U.S. intellectual property laws usually have exterritorial effects, except for patent statutes.[926] U.S. courts have, however, granted injunctions against foreign activities that have a sufficient nexus to infringing activity in the United States.[927] Presumably, the licensor knew about this and figured it into its decision to have U.S. jurisdiction in the license's forum selection clause. Therefore the licensor should be rewarded for its well-worded forum selection clause, by having the U.S. court uphold its U.S. jurisdiction clause against the licensee.

Generally choice of forum clauses are enforceable unless they are unreasonable, unjust or violate some fundamental public policy.[928] The Supreme Court has established a strong presumption in favor of the validity of forum selection clauses:[929] "Where the parties have by contract selected a forum, it is incumbent

---

[924] Some other examples of forum selection clauses: "that this Guaranty shall be governed by the laws of the Commonwealth of Massachusetts and each Guaranty consents to the jurisdiction of any court located in the Commonwealth," BVCIBC Funding, LLC v. La Jolla Texaco, 2001 Mass. Super. LEXIS 488, *2; and "[the agreement] is to be construed under and governed by the laws of the State of California," Jacobson v. Mailboxes Etc. U.S.A., Inc., 646 N.E.2d 741, 744 (Mass. 1995).

[925] Philip L. McGarrigle, The Role of Foreign Judgments in Patent Litigation: A Prospective and Strategic Overview, 39 J. L. & Tech. 107, 141 (1998).

[926] Margaret A. Boulware, An Overview of Intellectual Property Rights Abroad, 16 Hous. J. Int'l l 441, 490 (1994).

[927] Id.

[928] Bremen v. Zapata Offshore Co., 407 U.S. 1 (1972).

[929] Id.

upon the party resisting to establish that the choice was unreasonable, unfair or unjust."[930]

The licensee might argue that the forum selection clause is unenforceable because the burden of litigating in the United States is an unreasonable burden. In *Carnival Cruise Lines, Inc. v. Shute*,[931] however, the Supreme Court enforced a forum selection clause on a cruise contract involving international transactions that specified that all disputes be litigated in Florida. By analogy, we could expect that the U.S. forum is not unreasonable for the licensee given that they signed the license containg the U.S. forum selection clause and should reasonably have been on notice about the U.S. forum merely by the fact of the American citizenship of the licensor and probable minimum contacts with the U.S.

In a recent case with similar facts, *International Business Machines Corp. v. Harrysson*,[932] IBM sued a former employee for breaching of an employee compensation agreement containing a noncompete clause. The defendant executed the agreement in exchange for compensation under the company plan. The defendant, a Swedish national, moved to dismiss on grounds of forum non-conveniens, because of his lack of assets in the United States. The court dismissed the defendant's motion because "in each and every such agreement Harrysson agreed to submit to the exclusive jurisdiction and venue of the federal and state courts in New York to resolve any disputes that might arise out of or relate to the agreement (the agreements themselves were governed by New York law)."[933]

A forum selection clause must state clearly the choice of a forum; otherwise it may be interpreted as a choice of law clause.[934] The licensor's forum selection clause leaves no ambiguity as to the preferred American jurisdiction.

[c]   No Forum Selection Clause

The hypothetical case involves two companies, one domiciled in Massachusetts. Assuming the bulk of the transactions occurred there, the most logical and convenient forum is a Massachusetts court, despite the licensor's oversight in omitting a forum selection clause. The licensee, presumably being a sophisticated party and used to dealing with international business transactions, was at least aware of the likelihood of the United States being the forum in which disputes would be settled, by the mere fact that the licensor is an American company with its principal place of business in the United States.[935] Therefore, it was highly

---

[930] Forsythe v. Saudi Arabian Airlines Corp., 885 F.2d 285, 287 (1989) (noting that *Bremen* established the presumption).

[931] 499 U.S. 585 (1991).

[932] 116 F. Supp. 2d 485 (S.D.N.Y. 2000).

[933] *Id.* at 486.

[934] *See, e.g.,* Glovegold Shipping, Ltd., v. Sveriges Angfartyus Assurans Forening, 791 So. 2d (Fla. Ct. App. 2000). In *Glovegold*, the agreement provided, "[this agreement] shall be governed by the Laws of the state of Florida." The court found that this was not a forum selection clause because it was titled "Governing Law" and did not contain the word *forum* or *venue*. *Id.* at 14.

[935] *See, e.g.,* General Elec. Co. v. Siempelkamp GMBH & Co., 29 F. 3d 1095, 1099 (1994).

unlikely that the licensee was exploited or unfairly treated in the patent license agreement and cannot argue that it was ignorant of the possibility of U.S. jurisdiction.

If for some reason a U.S. court found that the Swedish courts had jurisdiction, the Swedish courts would still most probably rule that a U.S. court is the most appropriate forum for this case. Because "[t]he jurisdictional provisions of the Brussels Convention apply only to Community domicilairies and do not always apply to defendants domiciled outside the European Community,"[936] it is very uncertain whether any articles apply to the licensor at all. Article 17 states that an agreement must be in writing or evidenced in writing or in a form that accords with international trade or commerce.[937] Certainly in the first scenario, the licensor's forum selection clause was evidenced in writing and consented to by the licensee. Furthermore, Article 17 was amended in 1978 to permit jurisdiction for an agreement whose clauses do not conform to all of the Article's strict requirements of writing, but nonetheless being "in international trade or commerce, [are] in a form which accords with practices in that trade or commerce of which the parties are or ought to have been aware."[938] Therefore, even if the U.S. patent license agreement did not conform to all of the requirements of Article 17 of the Brussels Convention, it still could be held to be a valid agreement under European law.

[d] Probable Unenforceability of a Foreign Judgment

Even if a Swedish court were to render a judgment stating that Sweden is the appropriate forum, the judgment would not be upheld in U.S. courts. To this day, discretion for recognizing foreign judgments is not based on the Constitution, legislation, or treaties.[939] Instead any such recognition is based on "comity," a doctrine that extends U.S. legal discretionary power to give effect to foreign judgments unpredictably.[940] Comity alone is an unpersuasive argument for the U.S. courts to recognize a Swedish legal judgment in our case.

A court needs to weigh and balance the specific facts of the case to achieve the appropriate result when deciding whether to recognize a foreign judgment.[941] In determining whether to apply the foreign judgment, a U.S. court should consult the Restatement (Third) of Foreign Relations Law, asking questions such as "Did the court provide due process? Did the court have proper jurisdiction?"[942] Most likely, even if the foreign court complies with the guidelines set forth by the

---

[936] Linda J. Silberman, Judicial Jurisdiction in the Conflict of Laws Course: Adding a Comparative Dimension, 28 Vand. J. Transnat'l L. 389, 402 (1995).

[937] Gerald Moloney, The Brussels Convention on Jurisdiction and the Enforcement of Foreign Judgments: Papers and Precedents from the Joint Conference with the Union des Avocats Européens held in Cork, at SEC. 5. (1989), http://www.maths.tcd.ie/pub/IrishLaw/chap_3.htm#Neither party.

[938] Id.

[939] McGarrigle, *supra* note 925, at 3-4

[940] Id.

[941] Id. at 135-36.

[942] Id.

Restatement, the courts will apply federal law if there are federal claims set forth, especially for the exclusive jurisdiction of the Federal Circuit.[943]

The licensee could also raise the argument that the U.S. courts lack subject-matter jurisdiction, on the theory that the U.S. contacts were too small and infrequent with Sweden to satisfy the required minimum contacts element of jurisdiction. The inquiry as to the sufficiency of the minimum contacts is fact-specific and is beyond the scope of this discussion.[944] Therefore, considering the explicit U.S. forum selection clause in the patent license and the low likelihood of success of the enforcement of a foreign judgment, a U.S. court will most likely uphold the licensor and licensee's agreement for U.S. jurisdiction.

---

[943] *Id.* at 133.

[944] AVC Nederland B.V., v. Investment P'ship, 740 F.2d 148, 152 (1984).

CHAPTER NINE

CONDUCTING A LEGAL AUDIT AND MANAGING RISK*

§ 9.01   Overview: Risk Management

§ 9.02   Legal Audit Checklists
    [A]   E-Business Plans
    [B]   Intellectual Property Concerns
        [1]   Copyrights
        [2]   Trademarks
        [3]   Domain Names
        [4]   E-Commerce Patents
        [5]   Trade Secrets
        [6]   Linking
        [7]   Framing
        [8]   Moral Rights of Authors
    [C]   Exposure to Lawsuits in Distant Forums: Jurisdiction
    [D]   Internet Privacy
    [E]   Third-Party Content
    [F]   Torts and Information Security
    [G]   Internet Advertising Overview
        [1]   Internet Advertisement General Checklist
        [2]   Internet Advertisement Checklist for Lawyers
    [H]   Internet Taxation
    [I]   Online Contract Formation
    [J]   Internet Payment Systems
    [K]   Employment Issues
    [L]   Regulatory Issues
    [M]   E-Mail and Internet Usage Checklist
        [1]   General Things to Consider
        [2]   Usage Disclosures
        [3]   Information Security and Usage Procedures
        [4]   Training and Education
        [5]   Disaster Recovery
        [6]   Internal Corporate Investigations

---

* We would like to thank Todd Krieger, Esq., of the Bose Corporation, and Cuan Coulter of PricewaterhouseCoopers for their editorial contributions to this chapter.

        [7]   System Administrators
        [8]   Role of Counsel
  [N]   Information Security Checklist
  [O]   Terms and Conditions of Use
  [P]   UCITA
  [Q]   Web Site Intellectual Property Audit
        [1]   Risk/Exposure Analysis
            [a]   Internet Copyright Issues
            [b]   Trademark Ownership
            [c]   Avoiding Trademark Infringement in Cyberspace
            [d]   Domain Names in Cyberspace
            [e]   Clearance of Publicity Rights
            [f]   Trade Secret Preventive Law
            [g]   Linking or Framing Agreements
            [h]   Indemnification from Content Providers and Third Parties
            [i]   E-Commerce Patents
        [2]   Licensing Intellectual Property
        [3]   Web Site Development
        [4]   Sample Content License Agreement
  [R]   Global E-Business Legal Planning

§ 9.03   Insurance Policies
  [A]   E-Commerce-Related Insurance
  [B]   Acquiring Internet-Related Insurance
  [C]   Director and Officers Liability Insurance
  [D]   Internet Insurance Companies
        [1]   American International Group
        [2]   Chubb Technology Insurance Group
        [3]   INSUREtrust.com
        [4]   Techinsurance.com
  [E]   Commercial General Liability Coverage
  [F]   Internet Insurance Audit

§ 9.04   Online Dispute Resolution
  [A]   Introduction
  [B]   The Case for Online Dispute Resolution
        [1]   Time Is Money
        [2]   Solutions for Consumers
            [a]   Online Product Sales/Auctions
        [3]   International Disputes

§ 9.05   Preventive Law Pointers
  [A]   Suggestions for Handling Copyright and Trademark Infringement
        [1]   Notice of Copyright Infringement

       [2]   Innocent Infringement of Trademarks Accidentally Misused

  [B]   SPC's Proper Use of Its Trademarks

  [C]   Copyright Clearance Center

  [D]   Know Your Insurance Coverage

       [1]   InsureTrust.com

       [2]   Aegis Internet Insurance

       [3]   Net Secure

       [4]   Snaith Insurance

       [5]   Professional Insurance Agents, Ltd.

       [6]   Complete Insurance

       [7]   Insurance Information Institute

       [8]   PTC.i Solutions

       [9]   ClickforCover.com/Ensurancebusiness.com

      [10]   PayAssurance.com

      [11]   Internetins.com

      [12]   eHackerInsurance.com

      [13]   InsuranceSTOP.com

      [14]   TruSecure

§ 9.01 OVERVIEW: RISK MANAGEMENT

Despite the potential economic benefits, the Internet can be a new source of liability for many companies, ranging from the possibility that a dot-com company will be sued in a distant forum for copyright or trademark infringement to defamation in online forums, from breaches of information security and invasion of privacy to online fraud claims or tax liabilities. In addition, e-business losses from cyber criminals or virsuses need to be anticipated. Given these issues, the risks experienced by a bricks-and-mortar company may multiply as a company goes online and confronts new dangers such as vicarious liability for telecommuting employees, negligent information security, or Internet-related business torts. Tort liability may arise out of inadequate computer security or the failure to promptly remediate security breaches.

Online companies have also been targeted in class actions filed by investors. Intel was the target of a class action by consumers arising out of a minor defect in its Pentium chip that caused computational errors in rare circumstances. Intel was involved in another firestorm of activity in its launch of the Pentium III chip, incorporating a digital identification of users.[1] A large number of tort lawsuits have arisen over spam e-mail, online fraud, identity fraud, defamation, business libel, invasion of privacy, unfair competition, misappropriations, and other business torts. These risk factors need to be either prevented or insured against in a comprehensive legal audit.

An e-business faces many new audit risks and exacerbates many traditional audit risks. The speed of change in many companies is not just technologically related. Rather, the changes are driven by business reasons that are powered by new technologies. Irrespective of the rationale for the change, e-businesses have drastically and fundamentally changed the business environment in which everyone operates.

Companies should engage attorneys who understand information technology as well as online-related business models to properly implement a legal audit of e-business risk factors. More specifically, attorneys need to understand their clients' e-business, intellectual property, and employment law; the emerging technologies; and the potential impact on their clients' industry and business, in the event of exposures. A well-trained attorney will identify legal vulnerabilities and offer advice for the drafting of remedial plans, compliance guidelines, legal forms, and employee training. If the company retains outside counsel, the results of the audit may be protected by attorney-client privilege. With the results of the audit in hand, and in consultation with outside counsel, the potential hazards or violations should be ranked, from those posing great danger to those with negligible risk. Not all legal uncertainty should be viewed negatively; some developing legal risks may also prove to be valuable opportunities for improving an organization. In addition

---

[1] Daniel Armor, The E-Business Revolution: Living and Working in an Interconnected World at 128 (2000).

to the e-business backgrounds, it may be beneficial to involve lawyers with experience in industry-specific regulations. Regulations vary significantly by industry, and compliance guidelines vary appropriately.

Without a basic e-business expertise, subtle changes in business structures and contractual arrangements can have drastic effects on the intended results. If the business strategy is not properly understood from the beginning and the implications of the strategy fully considered, it may be very difficult to revert back to the intended result.

It is crucial that companies appreciate the costs and benefits of risky Internet business policies and practices. Some developing profiles of legal risk may not be corrected immediately. Define the strategic objectives and be flexible when implementing the corrective or remedial measures. No matter how many precautions are taken, potential legal liability may still exist. An e-business may consider third-party insurance coverage for consequential damages resulting from computer security intrusions, the transmission of viruses, and hacker attacks.[2] Nevertheless, conducting periodic self-audits will protect the corporate name and assets while avoiding costly litigation or possible fines and reducing legal bills. In addition, periodic audits can facilitate improved operational efficiencies; reduce risk; identify client products/services opportunities and e-business topics that should be discussed with senior management; and provide multiple methods for learning and improving the e-business.

Section 9.02 provides a series of checklists to assist companies in conducting an Internet legal self-audit. Certain activities may raise a red flag, alerting companies that some online practices may expose them to serious legal liability. Preventive measures before entering cyberspace will enhance the long-term health of the online company. In addition to the Internet legal audit, the company should seek other ways to protect its interests, such as indemnification or insurance, which are discussed in § 9.03. Section 9.04 discusses alternative dispute resolution options. The chapter concludes with the preventive law pointers in § 9.05.

§ 9.02   LEGAL AUDIT CHECKLISTS

Generally speaking, the risks resulting from companies engaging in e-business are not conceptually different from traditional business risks; they just surface in different ways. The success of any audit will hinge upon (1) understanding the company's e-business objectives; (2) identifying the risks that affect those objectives; (3) understanding the controls needed to protect against the risks; (4) assessing whether the objectives, risks, and controls are aligned to minimize the company's exposure; and (5) assembling an audit team that has the appropriate expertise to conduct the audit.

The following checklists ask probing questions and offers guidance on issues confronting e-businesses, as well as suggesting legal issues for further research.

---

[2] *See generally* Kurt D. Baer and Carl E. Metz, "Cybersubro" Claims: The Next New Things, 21 E-Bus. Ins. Rep. 7 (2001).

First are listed the key questions for assembling a comprehensive e-business plan. The activities identified in the e-business plan will largely determine what preventive law steps need to be instituted. Next come intellectual property concerns, which include copyright, trademark, domain name issues, linking, framing, e-commerce patents, and trade secrets. Also covered are issues that many online businesses may not have considered, such as jurisdiction, privacy issues, tort liability, advertising, and taxation.

[A] E-Business Plans[3]

SPC needs a comprehensive e-business plan that will attract venture capital.[4] The business plan is critical not only in defining the e-business strategy but also in identifying its legal vulnerabilities. Some online legal liabilities are generally predictable, and, thus, avoidable. Companies aspiring to be e-businesses must develop an acceptable risk management framework. The team conducting a preventive law audit should consult with those persons most familiar with company processes and operations. Self-audits must be continually updated and upgraded to take into account new profiles of risk or danger. E-commerce legal audits should focus on validating strategic objectives that will be acceptable for the online business community.

Some e-business activities require more frequent quality control review than others. Aside from the traditional hands-on audit, access controls, screening software, and programs that examine patterns of e-mail traffic or Internet usage are tools that can help auditors identify developing or emergent risks. The audit process must be an integral part of the corporation's strategic and tactical goals. The e-business plan for SPC is reprinted in Appendix A of this book. SPC's e-business plan will require tailoring, depending upon the company's business mission. If SPC's principal mission is to sell and deliver computers via its web site, it will have a different set of vulnerabilities than will an online bookstore, auction house, or car dealer.

SPC's mission of online computer sales will present challenging Internet-related contracting, advertising law, international jurisdictional, intellectual property, tax, and regulatory issues. The e-business plan is a roadmap to the legal risks that must be considered prior to the launch of the web site. The e-business plan requires first and foremost a detailed description of the company's business. SPC needs to be clear as to what business it is in as well as why investors should be interested in that business. What products or services are offered? Why is SPC in the best position to carry out the business plan?

---

[3] *See* Appendix A for a sample business plan.

[4] IBM was the first to use the term *e-business* to mean a "secure, flexible and integrated approach to delivering differentiated business value by combining the systems and processes that run core business operations with the simplicity and reach made possible by Internet technology." *Id.* (quoting IBM definition of e-business).

E-BUSINESS PLAN CHECKLIST

1. Does your company have a comprehensive e-business plan? Will the e-business plan attract sufficient additional venture capital? Why is the Internet the ideal location for your business? What special features make an e-business plan attractive to investors and customers? What distinguishes it from its competitors? Does the e-business plan appoint the right people to staff operations? Will the team present a credible case for funding? Does your company have a specific product to sell? Have appropriate license agreements been obtained? The more comprehensive the e-business plan, the more likely it will be to obtain adequate funding. How much money does your company have? What funding is minimally needed to serve your customers and operate your web site for a year or more without appreciable revenues? What is your projected cash flow? What is your strategy for achieving income projections? Has the company fully defined a strategy for the tactical execution of all facets of its e-business plan? What factors and risks could adversely affect the e-business's ability to execute the strategic plan? How will management measure, monitor, and control the actual results achieved and ensure the accuracy of the information collected? Relatively few businesses have a strong e-commerce strategy covering business as well as legal concerns.[5]

2. Will the management of the e-business be distinct or autonomous from the core business? Will all e-business-related efforts be under the control of a centralized function? Due to the new risks introduced by being an e-business, will the business require new management skills? Will the dot-com management team have e-business skills, or will they simply be reassigned from roles within the brick-and-mortar organization? What types of monitoring controls need to be put in place? Will these controls be different from those of the brick-and-mortar company?

3. Are all of the elements of a business plan completed? Is there a cover sheet? Executive summary? Statement of purpose? Table of contents? Supporting materials? Does the cover sheet include the online company's name, mailing address, e-mail address, and identifying information about the principals of the company? Are up-to-date biographies of the principals included? Does the executive summary provide clear statements of investment objectives, business strategies, operations and management, schedules, financial projections, and investor returns? Have you made a convincing case as to why your Internet site will be more profitable than those of your competitors? Who are your competitors? Have you researched your competitors' business strategies? Have you conducted online searches of how your competitors do business online? If your competitors are publicly traded companies, have you visited the Securities and Exchange Commission site and searched for 10-Ks, 10-Qs, and other publicly available documents? How

---

[5] TechWeb, Study: Companies Lack Comprehensive E-Business Plan, Information Week, Nov. 29, 1999 (visited June 15, 2002), http://www.informationweek.com/story/IWK19991129S0007 (citing KPMG Benchmarking Partner Study of 48 companies, most with $1 billion or more in revenue).

is your business different from that of dot-com businesses that already have web site presences? What impact will the e-business have on the corporation's brick-and-mortar reputation?

4. Does your business plan describe the opportunities for launching a web site? To what extent will the web site focus on a global network? Whether the company has a global or domestic vision, to be successful as an e-business, speed and time to market are essential. This in turn requires companies to put in place technologies and processes that will increase efficiency and responsiveness while reducing costs. Is your company an e-business leader or follower? Does your business plan emphasize quality, pricing, or other variables that will ensure success? Will your goods and services become known for their quality, reliability, or price, or a combination of these factors? What kind of image do you want to project in the online world? Is your customer base high brow, middlebrow, or low brow? What magazines do your potential customers read? How do you intend to personalize advertising and promotions to reach your customers? Will your web site use real-time customer service to ensure customer loyalty? What features have you incorporated in your site to ensure that your customers will not be one-time customers or "one-shotters"? Do you have a strategy for developing "relational contracts" with your customers? Have you given customers the option of being informed about new products and services? An opt-out feature should be included in all e-mail updates on products and services. Depending on the company's international presence, this may need to be an "opt-in" feature to comply with specific privacy regulations.

5. Is the description of the online business adequate? Is there a description of marketing, competition, operating procedures, personnel, business insurance, and financial data? Are you an established legacy business seeking out a new business channel, or a new venture? How will your site attract new customers? What are your online business objectives? If you are a legacy business, you will need to explain how your operations will be retooled to become an e-business. An e-business must have a plan that has realistic earnings and cash flow. This is the difference between a successful e-commerce business and an "e-showcase."

6. Is there a sufficient description of how services are to be rendered? Is there an overview of online sales and services? What is SPC's principal vision for its Internet business? Does the overview describe the company's customer experience, proposed customer base, projected customer growth, and price? Do you own or have the rights to use your proposed e-business methods? Be sure that your e-business company can really create value for the organization, which is translated into increased shareholder value. The value or benefits of being online could be derived from cost reductions, enhanced brand recognition, partnerships or joint ventures leading to new revenue streams, or accelerated growth due to new distribution channels and an expanded customer base.

7. Is the business development and marketing section of the business plan sufficiently developed? What are you selling? Why should web site visitors buy your products or services? Why will customers benefit from your product or service? In the early days of the dot-com economy, it was sufficient to state the purpose of the web site as entering the global Internet marketplace. Because the Internet economy has developed, investors today want more detailed business development and marketing information. Does your marketing plan define your targeted Internet markets? What are your anticipated product offerings? Are you planning to target foreign sales? How do you intend to increase your market share? What will attract customers to your site?

8. Does the financial data reflect loan applications, capital equipment, a balance sheet, a breakeven analysis, and income projections? What supporting documents are needed to support a detailed three-year analysis of income? What procedures are necessary to monitor the cash flows derived from the online business activities? Is electronic evidence more susceptible to manipulation? Is electronic evidence more difficult to understand and verify its source of origination? Should the e-business plan include quarter-by-quarter projections for the first year's revenue stream? Does the business plan include the tax returns of the principals?

9. Determine your virtual store's principal customer base. Is it the B2B market or the consumer market?[6] Have you identified your customer base by nationality, age, sex, income, educational level, and other demographic variables? Are you personalizing sales and services tailored to demographic variables? What mechanisms do you have for personalizing your advertising for your customer base? Do you provide real-time customer service? What is SPC's plan to attract customers to its site? Do you have a call center that can handle customer service?

10. What is your online marketing plan to promote goods and services? What is the "look and feel" of your web site? Have you developed "style guides" to ensure consistency in the "look and feel"? Check out its components. Do you have a customer loyalty program? How will your advertising reach your target market? Will your advertising be directed to other countries? If so, will foreign language advertising text be tested for nuance, meaning, and legal or regulatory effects? What surveys or other empirical research have you completed to better understand your proposed customer base? Is your web site directed to business-to-business, business-to-government, or business-to-consumer market segments? What is your company's online niche? Have you addressed how your business model differs from the competition? Have you done a comparison of your web site to your most successful rival(s)?

11. Will the company accept orders for goods and services electronically? Who will verify the interfaces (manual or electronic) between the web site (or other form of electronic data capture) and the back-office/fufillment systems since the systems may not transfer data accurately? How will transaction records be managed since most will be electronic and therefore more difficult to check? How will the company manage the risk of pervasive pricing errors? How will the

---

[6] *See* David McGuire, Gartner Predicts Breakneck B2B E-Commerce Growth, Newsbytes, Mar. 13, 2001 (stating that the B2B market is expected to increase to $8.5 trillion by 2005).

company define the contractual relationship between itself and the potential client? What types of new controls will be required to govern how contractual arrangements are adhered to?

12. Will your company accounts be settled online at the time of trans-action (i.e., with a credit card or other electronic currency)? Will new payment mechanisms need to be put in place (e.g., credit card processing, online escrow service agreements, etc.)? Can the business afford credit card chargebacks (e.g., customer disputes) and fraudulent charges? Will the company need to introduce additional security measures to make sure the credit card transactions are secure? Who will bear the credit card fraud risks, the credit card company or the online business?

13. Will the online company outsource its fufillment/distribution of its goods and services? Is it reasonable to place undue reliance on one distributor or delivery company? What controls will be established to ensure that the interfaces between the web site and fulfillment databases facilitate accurate orders being sent out? Will the company face contingent liabilities/redundancy issues if it has significantly reduced or outsourced its entire distribution operation? What happens if the outsourced distribution company is not able to deliver the client goods satisfactorily? Are new contractual terms required to determine the liability attributable to the company and vendor?

14. Do you address how you are different from your competition? Did you do an analysis of your competitor's web site? Will your web site create channel conflict? An online bookstore will need to explain why its product or services are superior to those of Amazon.com. Who are your competitors, direct and indirect? What promotions, advertising, and sales strategies will help your company gain an edge on your competitors? What is your projected customer growth? What pricing is necessary to increase customer growth? Is your pricing strategy based on markup or cost? Is your pricing below that of the competition? Will your pricing cover costs as well as projected profit margins?

15. How does your e-business plan describe business development and marketing? What co-branding or partnership development is necessary to achieve business development? Will your online company partner with (a) virtual shopping centers, (b) Internet publishing companies, (c) application service providers, (d) Internet infrastructure companies, (e) software companies, (f) Internet Service Providers, (g) Web development companies, (h) financial institutions, or (i) portals? What is your company's online branding strategy?

16. Will you maintain your own web site? The management team should review the web site in detail, as this provides valuable insights into how the web site measures up to the business plan. This review should also rate the effectiveness of the web site compared to the strategic objectives.

17. Will the company incur costs to develop or purchase the web site? There are unique and complex accounting issues surrounding web site development and acquisition costs.

18. When is the launch site for your web site? Will password-protected demonstrations be given prior to launch? Do you have an adequate startup and operational budget? Does the operating budget cover the possibility of increased personnel for customer service, web site developers, consulting services, and new capital equipment? How will content be refreshed?

19. Will your company demonstrate its products and services at Internet trade shows? Do sales personnel understand the legal issues in promoting products and advertising? Has counsel reviewed the copy used in advertising and promotional materials? Is the copy in advertising and promotional material accurate as well as attractively packaged? Do press releases about the potential success of product offerings and potential market opportunities comply with SEC requirements in not assuring results? Can all statements made in sales literature be substantiated by facts? Do statements made in online advertisements create enforceable express warranties that are nondisclaimable? The only way to disclaim an express warranty is not to make statements that become part of the "basis of the bargain."

20. What public relations tools will be used to create a buzz about your company's web site? What is your Internet strategy for promoting your site? Are you offering sweepstakes or games of chance that may be illegal in some jurisdictions?

21. Who will perform the e-business legal audit? Has an outside audit system been established to review and document risks? A company may decide to retain a major accounting firm or a law firm experienced in legal and e-business issues. Outside firms need to work closely with corporate counsel and with key personnel who understand the company's e-business plan.

22. What staffing is necessary for operations to create a profitable online business? Who is the president or chief executive officer? Does the president or chief executive officer have the personal qualities, experience, and credentials to succeed in commercializing e-business activities? Who is the vice president of services? Vice president of technology? Vice president of finance and administration? Vice president of marketing?

23. Are the technology positions staffed with the right people?
> Director of Applications Development
> Director of Web Technologies
> Web Operations Manager
> Systems Architect
> Senior Server Engineer
> Director of Operational Development/Risk Management
> Director of Operations
> Manager of Networking Security
> Quality Assurance Manager
> Documentation Manager
> Privacy Officer

24. Who will staff marketing/business development?
> Senior Sales Representatives
> Partner Development Representatives
> Marketing Manager

25. Who will staff management and production?
Director of Account Management
Accounts Manager
Manager of Training
User Interface Designer

26. Who will staff finance and administration?
Controller
Human Resources Manager
Accounts Receivable
Accounts Payable

27. Has the company sought out experienced persons who understand the commercial realities of online marketing?
Online Marketing and Public Relations Manager

28. Will the IT team assume primary responsible for managing the business? The IT management may not have adequate general, industry, or strategic management skills to effectively control the e-business operations.

29. Have you considered giving your employees a stake in the company? Self-management and employee ownership plans create incentives for employees who thereby gain a stake in the company. Is your company structured as a Limited Liability Partnership (LLP), Limited Liability Corporation (LLC), or other entity such as a C or S corporation? Also keep in mind that the accounting for incentive schemes is often highly complex and may require legal and tax review.

30. Who are your online company's management and advisors? Does your plan e-business include a Board of Directors? A management team? Do you have the right people in place to operate your online business? Are they organized into an enterprise-wide team?

31. Will the company post its financial statements on the web site? Local auditing regulations may require companies to include the audit or review opinion.

32. What types of partnerships, joint venturers, or co-branding strategies should be considered to help scale and leverage your business opportunities on the Internet?

33. Have you previously completed an e-business legal audit? If so, how did this audit compare to the last audit?

34. Has the company considered entering into content syndication agreements?

35. Have you fully defined a strategy for the execution of your e-business aims?

36. Will SPC's forward-look statements seeking funding or statements in press releases qualify for the safe harbor provisions of the Private Securities Litigation Reform Act of 1995? SPC should include qualifiers noting that its projections are subject to risks and uncertainties that could cause actual developments to differ materially from those contemplated. If an online company has completed 10-K forms, it should refer potential investors to the Company's Annual Report on Form 10-K filed with the United States Securities and Exchange Commission for specific risks and uncertainties. If SPC is considering a merger or other relationships with other companies, it can study their SEC filings on the World Wide Web at the Securities and Exchange Commission's Edgar database, found at www.sec.gov.

The next section describes the principal legal issues relevant to e-business plans.

[B] Intellectual Property Concerns[7]

Intellectual property is the chief asset of most online companies. Intellectual property must be protected on the Internet just as in the offline world. An audit of intellectual property rights focuses on copyrights, trademarks, patents, and trade secrets. The first step for an intellectual property audit is to inventory the intellectual property owned by the company. A company may not have rights to all intellectual property used for web site content, however, even if it paid for the content. If web site designers are independent contractors, the "work for hire" doctrine does not apply and the designers may retain rights to the content. Licenses or assignments may convey intellectual property rights and remedy the content ownership issue.[8] Software and other intellectual property is licensed rather than sold. A license gives permission to use software, data, or other intellectual property for the term of the license agreement.[9] A license gives the licensee or user permission to access software, data, information, or other intellectual property restricted by the permitted users as well as the term of the license agreements. A license agreement needs to be structured to maximize revenue streams. Nonexclusive licenses permit a licensor to divide up markets in the global Internet economy.

A licensee must not exceed the terms granted in the license agreement or the result will be breach of contract or infringement for copyrighted information. What content do you own? What content must you acquire? You will need to obtain necessary clearances and assignments to use the content of others on your site.

The second step is to determine how to protect each type of intellectual property on the web site. Copyrights protect the online company's software, manuals, artistic works, and content on its web site. Use copyright notice on web site agreements and on the web site home page itself. Trademarks will protect the online company's trade names, slogans, corporate name, and trade dress on its web site and even its domain name. The USPTO permits domain names to be registered as trademarks if distinctive and used in commerce. Your company's business model may also be patentable. An online computer store's special expertise in online selling may constitute a patentable business process.

---

[7] For a complete discussion of intellectual property issues, see Chapter Four.

[8] H. Ward Classen, Fundamentals of Software Licensing, Fourth Annual High Technology Law Conference, Licensing in a Network Environment, Suffolk University Law School (cosponsored with the Boston Patent Law Association), Mar. 10, 2000.

[9] General Talking Pictures, Inc. v. Western Electric Co., 304 U.S. 175, 181 (1938) (defining a patent license as a "mere waiver of the right to sue").

Additionally, some organizations list their trademarks and service marks in their web site agreements so that all users are placed on notice regarding the organization's intellectual property. License agreements, confidentiality agreements, and assignments of rights may be used to protect intellectual property on the Internet. The primary goal is to obtain ownership, assignments, or licenses for all content on your web site to avoid infringing the intellectual property rights of others.

A third step is determining whether other companies are infringing your company's intellectual property rights. The Internet can help you determine whether another company is misusing your trademarks, copyrighted materials, patents, or other intellectual property. Outside search services have software products to monitor your company's trade name, trademarks, patents, or trade secrets in cyberspace. It is a good idea to supplement search services with your own periodic Internet searches for possible misuses and abuses of intellectual property assets.

[1] Copyrights[10]

Copyright issues are a significant part of Internet law, since technology makes duplicating images or sounds relatively easy. The reproduction of images, sound, or text without permission may constitute infringement, exposing the defendant company to civil and criminal liability.[11] All facets of a web site are potentially protected by copyright law: materials, documents, computer programs, pictures, artwork, photographs, images, sounds, video text, articles, designs, HTML code, and JavaScript code, as well as the entire web site itself.[12] The purpose of the audit is to determine what copyright materials are created or developed by the company and what rights need to be acquired. Another critical step is to develop a strategy for protecting the intellectual property owned by the e-business. The exclusive rights of a copyright owner to distribute, display, and transmit works of authorship apply to works on the Internet.[13]

A web site operator should protect the company's copyrighted materials and avoid infringing the copyrights owned by others. A company may be directly liable for copyright infringement for posting unauthorized copyrighted materials on its web site.[14] Clip art or even HTML code may appear to be free for the taking from other web sites. Do not let your corporation discover the hard way that

---

[10] For a full discussion of copyright issues, see § 4.02.

[11] *See* Neils Schaumann, Intellectual Property in an Information Economy: Copyright Infringement and Peer-to-Peer Technology, 28 Wm. Mitchell L. Rev. 1001 (2002).

[12] *See generally* the U.S. Copyright Office, Basics of Copyright (visited May 15, 2000), http://lcweb.loc.gov/copyright/.

[13] *See generally* Jane C. Ginsburg, Copyright and Control Over New Technologies of Dissemination, 101 Colum. L. Rev. 1613 (Nov. 2001).

[14] *See, e.g.,* Playboy Enterprises, Inc. v. Webbworld, Inc., 968 F. Supp. 1171 (N.D. Tex. 1997) (holding an operator of a web site directly liable and the principals vicariously liable for infringement for permitting Playboy's copyrighted materials to be uploaded on its site).

your web site designer made a costly mistake. Your company should seek indemnification and subrogation agreements for infringement claims for content supplied by third parties. The Berne Convention of Literary and Artistic Works grants worldwide copyright protection in member states, which include the United States.[15]

COPYRIGHT CHECKLIST

1. Has your company evaluated the business issues regarding copyrighted materials used on your web site? Does your web site designer seek to use images that require licensing, or does he or she use original images created just for your web site? What will it take to enhance the "look and feel" of your site? Who will create or supply the written content? What will it take to entice and engage customers at your web site? What copyright issues need to be resolved? Is there a process that validates that designers are operating within the style guidelines laid out?

2. Does your company either own, license, or have assigned rights to use all images, including artwork and photographs, on the site? Remember, just because a company has the right to publish copyrighted materials in a print publication does not mean it can automatically extend that right to web site publications. If a company has obtained clearance for publishing images, this permission must explicitly include Internet publication. If a third party supplies images, permissions must be obtained in writing. Make sure that contractors use only cleared images or at least provide you with the sources of the images. Some web sites have specific procedures for copyright infringement claims because of the frequency of claims of infringement.[16] If third parties supply content, do they own or have a license to use all content? Consider requiring content providers to indemnify you for copyright infringement claims.

3. Has your company registered its web site with the U.S. Copyright Office? Have copyright notices been posted in the form "© 2003, Suffolk Personal Computers, All Rights Reserved"? Your company may register printed pages or a disk of your web site with the U.S. Copyright Office.[17] Is there a terms of use notice on your web site that addresses copyrights? The notice should specify authorized uses and whether copying, transmission, or modification of copyrighted materials is allowed. A web site owner should not grant users the right to make derivative works from copyrighted materials. While it is not necessary to register to protect your copyright, registration provides proof of copyright data and makes it possible to receive statutory damages in the event of infringement.[18]

---

[15] Rodney D. Ryder, Intellectual Propery Rights: The Grey Matters, Computers Today, April 15, 2000.

[16] *See* Notice and Procedure for Making Claims of Copyright Infringement (visited May 15, 2002), http://www.msnbc.com/procedurenotice.asp (displaying copyright infringement claim procedure).

[17] *See* Chu Moy, Avoid Copyright Infringement in E-commerce, E-Business Advisor, Dec. 1998, at 12 (explaining copyrightability of web pages).

[18] *See generally* The U.S. Copyright Office (visited May 15, 2002), http://lcweb.loc.gov/copyright.

Databases may be protected as compilations under the U.S. Copyright Act provided that the collection or data or preexisting material qualifies as original expression. A collection of facts alone in alphabetical or other similar organization is unlikely to qualify for copyright protection as an original work of authorship.

4. Do all posted images appear with independent copyright notices? To protect your artwork and photographs from reuse, affix copyright notices to each image.[19] The notice should state "Copyright [your company] 2003, all rights reserved."[20] The notice should be imbedded in the image file and not in text independently placed below the image. Persons seeking to use the images without permission cannot remove the notice without affirmatively modifying the image.

5. Does your site contain document attachments (MS Word, Adobe Acrobat)? If so, are you using technology that prevents the unauthorized reproduction (printing) of these?

6. Are copyrighted images posted on the web site protected with digital watermarks to facilitate tracing unauthorized copying? Digital watermarks are hidden code that can help identify the source of an image.[21] The data is only visible through special software and can contain information about the copyright holder and provide proof of authenticity. Digital signatures may be used to determine the authenticity of electronic documents, and digital watermarks may be useful in assuring the authenticity of audio files.[22] A web site designer should require customers to warrant that they have the right to use trademarks, copyrights, patents, and other intellectual property posted on the site.

7. Does the web site post general copyright notices encompassing all images, text, sound, code, and content? The entire "look and feel" of the web site should be protected with a general copyright notice on each page. SPC's web site, for example, may be copyrighted and labeled "Copyright © 2003, Suffolk Personal Computers, Inc. All rights reserved." A web site owner may wish to reserve rights to reproduce materials or, alternatively, to encourage copying of posted materials. No warranties should be given for the accuracy of copyrighted materials. Forrester Research, which produces proprietary information on Internet trends, for example, permits "members of the press to cite a copy of each graph, slide, or a portion of text less than a paragraph long contained in the Information, provided that all portions of text are identified as 'Source: Forrester Research, Inc.' "[23]

---

[19] *Id.*

[20] *Id.*

[21] *See* Richard Raysman and Peter Brown, The Digital Millennium Copyright Act, N.Y.L.J., Dec. 8, 1998, at 3 (describing technologies to protect copyrighted materials).

[22] State of Washington Office of the Secretary of State, Frequently Asked Questions About Digital Signatures (visited May 15, 2002), http://www.secstate.wa.gov/ea/overview_faq.aspx?m=undefined.

[23] Forrester Research, Inc., Citation Policy (visited May 15, 2002), www.forrester.com/ER/Press/Citation/0,1774,0,FF.html.

8. Does the web site use any clip art or other graphics that may require copyright clearance? Have copyright clearances been verified? If third parties supply clip art or other graphics, have they provided verification of copyright clearances? Clip art may contain use restrictions for electronic media. Check the terms and get clearance in writing.[24] Many web sites borrow clip art from other sites. This approach is inadvisable without prior permission from the web site operator. Some web sites contain copyright waivers. An individual who can enforce the copyright, however, may have originally posted the clipped image.

9. Have copyright notices been embedded within the HTML or other code? Protect your code by placing a copyright notice at the top of the code and within the body of the code. Clearly state your policy in phrasing such as "No part of this document may be reproduced without express written permission of [your company]."

10. Does the company own the rights to use the HTML or other code? Make sure that your programmer did not "borrow" any proprietary content from another site. Obtain written permission if any third-party sources were used. Some sites employ code from many different sources. If you notice anything out of the ordinary within your site, check with your programmer about the source.

11. Has the company retained the rights to the computer code or does the programmer retain these rights? Unless there are written terms to the contrary, the copyright in a work for hire goes to the employer. Make sure any third-party agreements with contractors convey the copyright to the employer. Some programmers may offer favorable prices for creating a web site because they recycle their code. If you have any customized features built into your site that you want to protect, have the programmer agree in writing to convey the copyright to you and not to reuse the code. Let all of your employees know that you retain the rights to all materials produced on behalf of the company and that nothing should be reused externally without the company's express permission. It is much easier early in the process to let employees know that you retain the rights to the code rather than to pursue them after they use the code elsewhere.

12. If the programmer retained the rights, does the company have permission to modify or change the web site? The right to make derivative works is one of the exclusive rights of copyright owners. A web site may change daily or even more frequently, and it is therefore important to obtain the right to make derivative works as well as the original web site. Copyright extends to derivative works. If you did convey the copyright to the programmer, check on the limits to modifications. Successful web sites are constantly changing; do not let your firm be exposed to unnecessary liability because of a poorly worded contract. You may find that you are locked into using the contractor for any further changes. This can create a potentially difficult and expensive situation.

13. Is the web site using music, video, or audio that requires copyright clearance or license agreements? The audio industry has taken a firm stance

---

[24] *See generally* U.S. Copyright Office (visited May 15, 2002), http://lcweb.loc.gov/copyright.

against online infringement. Do not use any popular music without obtaining written permission. If you do not have the resources to license music, consider using original or classic MIDI[25] files that are in the public domain. A web site's copyright issues will turn on the type of activity occurring on a site. A web site inviting visitors to upload and download pirated software would clearly be infringing. Many web site activities are not as clear. The Recording Industry Association of America has pursued several high-profile cases against web sites and online services that facilitated copyright infringement of musical works.[26]

14. Is all the text on the web site original content or, if not, is it attributed to the appropriate third parties? Make sure that any articles from other sources are attributed to the proper author and source. Do not unnecessarily expose your company to a contributory or vicarious infringement lawsuit over copyrighted materials because a content provider you hired used materials owned by a third party. Have a clear attribution and antiplagiarism policy as well as a copyright policy to avoid problems.

15. Have you posted a clearly written "terms and conditions" policy advising visitors of permitted and prohibited uses of materials on the site? Is there a terms of service agreement? Does the terms of service address the visitor's responsibilities? What are the restrictions in the terms of service? A copyright policy may permit visitors to view, download, scan, and copy articles, software, images, or any other items for redistribution. Some sites encourage such borrowing.[27] Make your policy obvious if you want to discourage reuse.[28] Web site development can be expensive, and you should endeavor to protect your intellectual property. Also, the images, text, and sounds in your site may help make it unique. Any reproduction of your original work can diminish the site's value and appeal.

16. Does the online company qualify for a "safe harbor" from copyright infringement? Section 512 of the Digital Millennium Copyright Act (DMCA) limits a service provider's liability for transmitting, routing, providing connections for, or providing intermediate storage of material that infringes a copyright provided certain conditions are met. To qualify for a "safe harbor" from copyright infringement claims, the provider must implement a procedure for terminating

---

[25] The term *MIDI* is short for Musical Instrument Digital Interface files. MIDI files have been subject to compulsory licenses since a 1996 decision by the U.S. Copyright Office. *See* Industry Leaders Hail Copyright Decision, Interactive Daily, Sept. 18, 1996 at 1 (stating that "MIDI is a computer code that enables people to use multimedia computers and electronic musical instruments to create and enjoy music").

[26] Jenny Eliscu, Napster Fights Back: MP3 Site Contests Lawsuit While Users Remain Defiant, Rolling Stone, June 22, 2000, at 29.

[27] *See* Snap-Shot Wallpaper (visited May 15, 2002), http://www.snap-shot.com/ (Snapshot's copyright policy permits visitors to view, download, scan, and copy images from its free desktop and screensaver galleries).

[28] *See,* the Anne Geddes Official Web Site (visited May 15, 2000), http://www.annegeddes.com/indexpages.asp?P=Z.

repeat violators. The provider also must have no knowledge of or financial benefit from the infringement. The DMCA requires service providers to post information on how to report copyright infringement. The provider must also remove infringing materials once given notice of the infringing activity on its site. The company must register an agent with the U.S. Copyright Office to receive complaints about infringement. The company must prominently post information on how to contact the copyright agent on its web site. Finally, the DMCA requires the provider to inform account holders and subscribers of its policy of terminating repeat infringers. Infringing copies of JPEG images and MP3 music files are pirated far more often than text.[29]

[2] Trademarks[30]

"A trademark is often a valuable property of a seller or manufacturer, because it is the symbol of the company's goodwill and of its products and services."[31] Trademarks can represent a significant portion of a corporation's assets. The Internet, however, has opened a new forum for widespread trademark misuse, potentially diminishing the value of that asset. Domain names can be registered as trademarks, assuming that they are sufficiently distinctive. Amazon.com was one of the first Internet companies to register a ".com" trademark.[32]

Trademarks are registered in the U.S. Patent and Trademark Office of the U.S. Department of Commerce. In addition, "[m]any states register trademarks to maintain a public record and allow others to search the record before choosing and using a new trademark."[33] The U.S. Trademark Office will examine a trademark application to determine whether the proposed mark is distinctive enough to qualify for protection. The number of trademarks with ".com" as a suffix has exploded.[34] Trademark rights are acquired by actual use in commerce. The term "use in commerce" means the use of a mark in the ordinary course of trade and not merely a reservation of a right to use marks in conjunction with the sale of goods.[35] Infringers may use trademarks in domain names and metatags and within the web pages themselves.[36]

---

[29] Armor, *supra* note 1. *See also* A&M Records, Inc. v. Napster, Inc., 2000 U.S. Dist. LEXIS (N.D. Cal. Aug. 10, 2000) (enjoining Napster from enabling users to copy digital files of copyrighted music without payment or permission).

[30] For a full discussion of trademark issues, *see* § 4.03.

[31] Small Business Administration, Starting Your Business: Patents, Trademarks and Copyrights (visited June 10, 2002), http://www.sba.gov/starting/indextrademarks.html (contributed by J. Thomas McCarthy).

[32] Dechert, Price, and Rhoads, Annual Report on Trends in Trademarks 2000 (visited May 29, 2000), http://www.dechert.com/news/_byline/may_00.html (citing USPTO trademark applications data).

[33] Small Business Administration, Starting Your Business, *supra* note 31.

[34] Dechert, Price, and Rhoads, *supra* note 32.

[35] Maritz v. Cybergold, Inc., 947 F. Supp. 1328, 1335 (E.D. Mo. 1996).

[36] Linda A. Goldstein, Emerging Issues in Online Advertising and Promotion Law, 570 PLI/Pat 821, 860 (1999); *see also* Playboy Enterprise v. Calvin Designer Label, 985 F. Supp. 1220 (N.D. Cal. 1997).

Corporations must protect their valuable brand names worldwide and also avoid accidental trademark infringement. The U.S. is a signatory to the Trade-Related Aspects of Intellectual Property Rights (TRIPS), administered by WIPO. Each of the 150 signatory countries provides basic trademark protections that member countries must implement.[37] Courts recognize the value of trademarks to both consumers and companies and may offer redress to a company claiming infringement from a "cybersquatter."[38] Online trademark disputes can be time-consuming and expensive; use this checklist to reduce the potential risk of any accidental infringement.

TRADEMARK CHECKLIST

1. Has intellectual property counsel audited the key business issues surrounding trademarks? What trademarks can be protected? How important is your brand name? Do you have a good domain name for differentiating online goods and services? Is your domain name distinctive enough to qualify for trademark protection? As a separate issue, have you also registered domain names that are similar to yours, e.g., Amazen.com, and have you registered similar domain names in international locations? Can the trade dress of your web site be registered as a trademark? Do you expect your brand name to be significant in the future? Are trademarks being used in commerce? If a trademark is registered, the owner must file an affidavit between the fifth and sixth year of registration certifying that the trademarks are being used in commerce.[39] Use must be proven at the time of every ten-year renewal as well, and even an "'incontestable" registration might be attacked on the basis of fraud in the allegations of use or of abandonment if use has been too scant.[40] The online company must use its marks in Internet sales or services or risk a finding of abandonment due to nonuse.

2. Does the company have the rights to use all trademarks or logos within the site? Has your company completed a thorough trademark search or retained a search firm with the expertise to examine state, federal, or international databases?[41] Is the ™ trademark symbol used with trademarks not yet registered with the U.S. Patent and Trademark Office? Is the registered ® symbol used for trademarks or trade names already registered? If you have created a new brand name or product for sale online, check to see that it does not infringe on someone

---

[37] Chu Moy, Protection Your Company's Trademarks for Global E-Commerce, e-Business Advisor, Oct. 1998, at 16.

[38] Avery Dennison Corporation v. Sumpton 1999 WL 635767 (9th Cir. 1999), citing Intermatic Inc. v. Toeppen, 947 F. Supp. 1227, 1239 (N.D. Ill., 1996); *see also* Andrew Baum and Mark Epstein, New Dilution Act Used to Evict "Cybersquatter"; courts have ruled that owners of famous marks are entitled to those marks in domain names, Nat'l L.J., Jan. 27, 1997.

[39] *See generally* Bradley Haas, Trademark Protection and Acquiring the Status of Incontestibility, 12 J. Contemp. Legal Issues 159 (2001).

[40] *Id.*

[41] Thomson and Thomson is the leading trademark search firm. However, online searches may be conducted on LexisNexis or Dialog.

else's name or product.[42] Second, be very cautious if you are using another company's trademarks in comparisons.[43] Make sure that the comparison is valid and supported by testing. Comparative advertising is illegal in a number of European countries.

3. Has your company chosen trademarks that qualify for federal registration? Fanciful or coined marks are the strongest marks, followed by arbitrary, suggestive, and descriptive marks. Trademarks do not protect generic marks. A descriptive mark, which is quite weak, may gain secondary meaning through online advertising or publishing. The U.S. Trademark Office will not register marks that disparage living or deceased persons or marks that are immoral, deceptive, or scandalous.

4. Has your company obtained federal registration for its trade name, logos, slogans, and other trademarks? Federal registration may be renewed for subsequent 20-year terms as long as the trademark continues to be "used in commerce." The symbol ® may be used for federally registered trademarks. An online company needs to apply for trademark registration to help protect its marks. The USPTO trademark examiners determine whether the mark meets the conditions for trademark protection.[44] The USPTO also permits "intent to use" applications as well as applications where the mark has already been "used in commerce." Trademarks must not be "confusingly similar" to other trademarks. With an intent to use application, there is no need to prove "use in commerce" prior to registration. Federal registration provides protection for trademarks in the continental United States. The proposed trademarks are published in the USPTO's *Official Gazette.* Trademarks lacking distinctiveness may be published in the *Supplemental Registry* and eventually obtain protection through acquired meaning. Once registration is approved, the registration is good for an initial term of ten years, which may be extended for additional terms.

5. If any other trademarks are mentioned on your web site, are comparisons protected by the trademark doctrine of "fair use"? Could consumers be confused about the ownership of trademarks mentioned on your site? Do you make any comparisons that may constitute deceptive or unfair advertising? Trademark infringement, like copyright infringement, is a strict liability offense. If your company sells brand-name products from other manufacturers, it must spell out the relationship between your company and the original manufacturers to avoid any confusion. Get written permission from the manufacturer to mention its products by name and include pictures (if appropriate) to use in electronic commerce. If you were an independent distributor of Coca-Cola, for example, the site should state that you are only a distributor, not Coca-Cola. Comparative advertising that

---

[42] *See generally* the United States Patent and Trademark Office web site, specifically Basic Facts About Registering a Trademark (last visited May 15, 2002), http://www.uspto.gov/web/offices/tac/doc/basic/; *see also* Bitlaw, Trademarks on the Internet (last visited May 15, 2002), http://www.bitlaw.com/trademark/index.html.

[43] *See* Lanham Act, 15 U.S.C. §§ 1114, 1125(a) (1998).

[44] Small Business Administration, *supra* note 31 (contributed by Thomas McCarthy).

mentions the trademarks of others must be supported with substantiation by tests, surveys, or other evidence.[45]

6. Has your company obtained necessary clearances to use trademarks owned by others? If SPC sold Macintosh computers, for example, SPC must place a notice on the web site indicating that Macintosh is a registered trademark of Apple Computer, Inc. and not affiliated with SPC. SPC should also require that others provide proper notices of its trademarks, servicemarks, and trade names.

7. Does your web site employ characters or other content that parodies trademarked characters? Parodies are entitled to a degree of First Amendment protection for free speech.[46] L.L. Bean, for example, was unable to enjoin the L.L. Beam sex catalogue parody under a trademark dilution theory because of First Amendment rights.[47] Parody has also been conceptualized by courts as a form of trademark "fair use." Parodies are entitled to a First Amendment protection under U.S. law provided a court agrees that a passage qualifies as a parody. Parodies are protected speech if three conditions are met: (1) Is the object of reference "not readily identifiable without use of the trademark"? (2) Is no more of a mark taken than is reasonably necessary to refer to the object? (3) Does the use of the trademark in no way imply sponsorship or endorsement?[48] A parody may not be entitled to protection outside the United States unless there is a functionally equivalent doctrine. Most countries connected to the Internet have a more restrictive view of speech on the Internet. However, U.S. courts will be disinclined to enforce foreign judgments contrary to the First Amendment or important public policies relevant to free expression.

8. Be sure your metatags do not infringe the trademarks of others, which may lead to a trademark infringement or unfair competition lawsuits. Advise your web site designers to avoid misusing the trademarks of others in metatags that have the effect of diverting traffic from another company's site. Does your company use metatags derived from the trademarks of others in registering its site with search engines? Do keyword monitoring to determine whether your competitors or others are using your trademarks in metatags in ways that might confuse visitors or tarnish your marks. Use trademarks in metatags in a way that you would want others to use them. Metatags may not be used to unfairly divert traffic from your competitor's site. Competitors may not use your trademarks in metatags to divert traffic to their site. Does your competitor's use of metatags tarnish or dilute your trademarks?[49] Begin with a "cease and desist" notice. Have you

---

[45] *See* Ameritech Agrees to Halt Comparative Advertising Against Cellular One, 14 Communic. Daily 4 (Dec. 28, 1994) (reporting Ameritech's agreement to stop comparative advertisement with claims not supported by tests or surveys).

[46] Andrew R. Basile, Chapter 13, Trademark Rights, in Thomas J. Smedinghoff, ed. Online Law; The SPA's Legal Guide to Doing Business on the Internet 221 (1996).

[47] L.L. Bean, Inc. v. Drake Publishers, Inc., 811 F.2d 26 (1st Cir. 1987).

[48] Fish and Richardson, Trademark Parody: The Joke's on Who? (visited Sept. 30, 2000), http://www.fr.com/publis/ththou5.html. (summarizing standards for "fair denominative trademark use").

[49] An adult entertainment or hate speech site using an online company's trademarks in metatags would also tarnish or dilute those marks.

conducted online searches to determine how your trademarks are being used, mis-used, or abused on the Internet? Do not try to generate traffic by exploiting other brands. If you sell other brands on your web site, get written permission to use the names within your metatags. Never use a competitor's name or product names in the metatag.[50]

9. Do you need to employ federal remedies for domain name infringement? Your company may also have remedies under the Anticybersquatting Consumer Protection Act of 1999 (ACPA) if a domain name owner incorporates your company's trademarks. A likely cause of action exists under the federal antidilution act if a cybersquatter registers a famous mark. In addition, the ACPA provides remedies against those attempting to sell domain names for a profit with "bad-faith" intent. An *in rem* remedy may be sought if a trademark owner cannot locate registrants of allegedly infringing domain names.[51]

10. Is the online company's domain name registrable as a trademark? Advertising sales or service on a web site is probably sufficient to meet the Lanham Act's "use in commerce" requirement. It is also possible to file an "intent to use application" for a domain name used as trademark. A domain name, like any other trademark, must be distinctive to qualify for protection.

11. Has your company filed trademark registrations in foreign countries? Has your e-business filed its trademark in the European Community? Trademark registrations in the United States Patent and Trademark Office provide trademark protection only within the boundaries of the United States. SPC, for example, will typically register its trademarks in core countries where it sells goods or renders services. SPC should consider filing a European Community Trademark. Any individual or entity may file a single Community Trademark (CMT) application obtaining trademark protection in the EU countries by a filing in the European Community Trademark Office in Alicante, Spain. Trademark protection may only be obtained by registration. Four groups may register trademarks in the European Trademark Office in Alicante: "(1) nationals of a Member State; (2) nations of a state that is a party to the Paris Convention or a member of the World Trade Organization; (3) the applicant is Community Trademark (CMT) domiciled or has an establishment in a Member State or Paris Convention State; or (4) the applicant is a national of a state that gives reciprocal protection to the Member States and recognizes CTM registration as proof of country of origin." Because the United States is a member of the World Trade Organization and a signatory to the Paris Convention, SPC, which is domiciled in the United States, may file for a CMT. It is likely that the United States will soon become a Madrid Pro-

---

[50] Goldstein, *supra* note 36; *see also* Playboy Enterprises v. Calvin Designer Label, 985 F. Supp. 1220 (N.D. Cal. 1997). *See* Brookfield Communic. v. West Coast Entertainment Corp., 174 F.3d 1036 (9th Cir. 1999) (holding that use of third party's trademark in metatag caused "initial interest confusion"); N.V.E. Pharm., Inc. v. Hoffman-LaRoche, Inc., 1999 U.S. Dist. LEXIS 20204 (D.N.J. Dec. 27, 1999); SNA, Inc. v. Array, 51 F. Supp. 2d 554 (E.D. Pa. 1999).

[51] 15 U.S.C. § 1125(d)(2)(A). *See* Broadbridge Media v. Hypercd.com, 2000 U.S. Dist. LEXIS 9516 (S.D.N.Y. 2000) (holding that bad-faith intent is a predicate of an *in rem* action under the ACPA); Harrods Ltd. v. Sixty Internet Domain Names, 2000 U.S. Dist. LEXIS 11911 (E.D. Va. Aug. 15, 2000).

tocol signatory. SPC should register its marks in those countries in which it is doing business, not every country connected to the Internet.

[3] Domain Names[52]

A domain name represents a company's gateway on the Internet. Memorable domain names can be valuable assets as well as the subject of heated litigation. Multiple companies and speculators are increasingly competing to register the same domain name. Other companies register as many of the most desirable domain names as they can. SPC should police competitors who register domain names that infringe or dilute its trademarks or trade name. SPC should enjoin defendants who intentionally adopt the SPC trademarks as domain names in order to capitalize on its marks. The failure to monitor trademarks may result in an estoppel defense or a loss of rights in the mark.

Registration in the ".com" domain can be obtained online at http://www.net-worksolutions.com. Network Solutions' web site also contains a search engine to check on the availability of a domain name, at *http://rs.internic.net/cgi-bin/whois.*[53] The Internet Corporation for Assigned Names and Numbers (ICANN) manages the Internet domain name system. ICANN has certified hundreds of registries and administers the dispute resolution system formulated by the World Intellectual Property Organization (WIPO). Comparison shopping for pricing and other features of approved registries are recommended.

DOMAIN NAMES CHECKLIST

1. Has your company registered its domain name? Have you searched ICANN registrars' databases to determine the availability of a given domain name?[54] Can your domain name be protected as a trademark? Does your domain name infringe another's trademark? Has your company taken steps to prevent others from using your trademarks as domain names? Has your company's domain name been registered at country-level registries where you desire a presence? Countries vary on whether they register domain names of foreign countries. Some countries follow the "first come, first served" approach. France, for example, follows a prior assessment method requiring a corporate presence prior to accepting country-level protection. After spending thousands of dollars and hundreds of hours attracting traffic to your web site, it would be unfortunate if a dispute resolution tribunal or court ordered your company to "cease and desist" using the name and conveying it to another party. Do a trademark search before you decide on your domain name. Consider registering your domain as a trademark.[55] If you have

---

[52] *See also* § 4.03[L].

[53] Todd Krieger, Internet Domain Names and Trademarks: Strategies for Protecting Brand Names in Cyberspace, 32 Suffolk U. L. Rev. 47 (1998).

[54] ICANN (visited June 15, 2002), http://wwww.icann.org (ICANN has a list of registrars).

[55] *Id.*

already created the site, and it is potentially infringing on someone else's brand name, consult a trademark attorney to assess the relative strength of the other trademark. You may be able to continue to use the domain name if the trademark is abandoned or in another product class.[56] Otherwise, the trademark holder may grant a license for a reasonable fee.

2. Should you register other domain names to protect your trademark and increase traffic? Since domain name registration is relatively inexpensive, consider registering other names to prevent someone else from registering the name in the future.[57] Make it easy for consumers looking for your web site to locate your online address. Register your name in all top-level domains (TLDs). The online company should register the domain name in the ".com," ".org," and ".net" TLDs. SPC should consider a ".biz" registration. Also, in the event your domain name is prone to being misspelled, register the most common or frequent misspellings. Fidelity Investments, for example, has registered "www.fidelitu.com."[58] It may also be advisable to register domain names in foreign countries. Many countries, such as France or Sweden, require a presence in the country in order to file for domain name protection.

3. Have you conducted a trademark search to determine whether your domain name may already be a registered trademark? Have you registered common misspellings of your domain name? Have you registered the .com, .net, and .org versions of your domain name? If a domain name infringes on the trademarks of others, the domain name registration may be cancelled. In addition, the online company is exposed to an unfair competition and trademark infringement lawsuit. Hundreds of lawsuits have been filed against domain name registrants where the domain name incorporates a trademark of another. The Internet Corporation for Assigned Names and Numbers (ICANN) replaced Network Solutions Inc. in administering the management of the domain name system. ICANN has accredited a large number of domain name registrars around the globe to provide competitive registration services for the .com, .net, and .org domains. ICANN adopted a uniform dispute resolution policy to deal with domain name disputes, based on recommendations of the World Intellectual Property Organization (WIPO). Do periodic keyword monitoring to determine whether your trademarks or domain names are being misused or abused. Your company may register its domain name with a national extension, such as .uk for the United Kingdom or .fr from France. Some countries, such as Sweden (.se) and France (.fr), require a local presence (prior assessment) in order to register a domain number, whereas other countries, such as Fiji (.fi) and Tonga (.to), are unrestricted.

4. Does your firm have a cause of action against a domain name registrant under the Anticybersquatting Consumer Protection Act (ACPA)?[59] The ACPA was enacted as an amendment to the Trademark Act to provide remedies for cyberpiracy or cybersquatting. The ACPA provides remedies against parties who

---

[56] Id.

[57] Id.

[58] Id.

[59] 15 U.S.C. § 1125 (2000).

are "registering, trafficking in, or using domain names (Internet addresses) that are identical or confusingly similarly to trademarks with the bad-faith intent to profit from the goodwill of trademarks."[60] A competitor's domain name may blur the distinctive quality of a mark or tarnish your mark.[61] A plaintiff may proceed with an *in rem* action against a user of a domain name if the plaintiff is unable to obtain *in personam* jurisdiction.[62] It may be difficult to obtain personal jurisdiction where the domain name owner uses false addresses or other misleading personal information. An *in rem* action is against the domain itself, whereas *in personam* or personal jurisdiction is against the owner of the domain name. The *in rem* remedy of the ACPA imposes strict procedural requirements before permitting this remedy.

5. Does your company have a cause of action under the Lanham Act against alleged infringers? To have standing for trademark infringement lawsuits, a company must prove that the other party was using a mark in commerce in a way that is likely to cause consumer confusion. Another theory is that the unauthorized user is diluting or tarnishing a company's marks.

[4] E-Commerce Patents[63]

Business method patents have skyrocketed after the federal circuit court's decision in *State Street Bank and Trust Co. v. Signature Financial Group, Inc.*[64] Since 1998, hundreds of patents covering Internet-related business methods have been issued. Amazon.com's "one-click" technology for online shopping, for example, was issued a patent.[65] Soon after, Amazon.com sued Barnesandnoble.com for infringing its "single-click" patent, although the injunction was later overturned.[66] Priceline.com sued Microsoft over a "name your own price" patent.[67] The large number of new e-commerce patents creates a greater risk of exposure to an expensive patent infringement lawsuit.

An online business may consider obtaining patent protection for its own business methods that satisfy the novelty, utility, and nonobvious standards of the U.S. Patent Act. Patents, however, are the most expensive and time-consuming methods of obtaining intellectual property rights. The software patent examiners of the USPTO do not have good databases for establishing "prior art."[68] A finding

---

[60] Lucent Technologies v. Lucentsucks.com, 2000 U.S. Dist. LEXIS 6159 (E.D. Va., 2000) (quoting H.R. Rep. No. 106-412, at 7 (1999)).

[61] *Id.*

[62] 15 U.S.C. § 1125(d)(2)(A).

[63] *See* § 4.05.

[64] 149 F.3d 1368 (Fed. Cir. 1998).

[65] L. Scott Tillett, Patent Office Takes a Fresh Look at The Net, Internet Week, May 15, 2000. *See* Kelly Jackson Higgins, The Other IP—It Exploits Patents to Protect E-Assets, Internet Week, July 17, 2000 (reporting 2,600 e-business patents filed in 1999).

[66] Amazon.com v. BarnesandNoble.com, 239 F.3d 1343 (Fed. Cir. 2001) (reversing a preliminary injunction enjoining one-click ordering for web site sales).

[67] Steve Alexander, Patents in E-Commerce, Computerworld, Apr. 24, 2000, at 58.

[68] *Id.*

of prior art is necessary in making a finding that a proposed patent is unique. This task may be next to impossible "in the digital world [where] software or [information technology] does not necessarily have a prior art."[69] Another complaint about the e-commerce patents is that they are overly broad, having a chilling impact on the development of the Internet.[70]

E-commerce patents for business methods such as online ordering systems may be obtained through a process called patent prosecution. To prosecute its e-commerce patents, your company will need to retain a patent lawyer who is entitled to practice before the USPTO. Next, a company will need to decide whether to license its e-commerce technology, which may be a source of significant revenue. Business method patents are not recognized in the countries of the European Union. Many countries have yet to validate software patents, let alone business method patents.

E-BUSINESS PATENTS CHECKLIST

1. Does your company have any business methods that are covered by patents held by others? The United States Patent and Trademark Office expanded its patent search information site to include 30,000,000 documents.[71] E-commerce business methods grant the patent owner a 20-year period to prevent others from using the business process. As prior art databases improve, it will increasingly be possible to mount successful challenges against Internet-related business method patents.

2. Do any of the web site technologies or business methods infringe on e-commerce patents owned by third parties? Some e-commerce technologies have been patented for routine activities including online coupons and hyperlinks.[72] If your programmer develops any new business method, consult with a member of the patent bar with experience prosecuting these claims. Patent prosecution is expensive and time-consuming, but the right e-commerce patent may result in substantial licensing revenue streams. Business method patents now exceed 10,000, with the greatest expansion in computer and Internet-based patents.[73]

3. Has an audit been conducted of e-commerce business methods used in the online company's virtual store or web site? Priceline.com, for example, is the patent owner of the reverse auction system.[74] Amazon.com owns a patent for

---

[69] *Id.* (quoting Marc Perl, general counsel for Information Technology Association of America).

[70] Steve Alexander, *supra* note 67.

[71] United States Patent and Trademark Office (visited May 20, 2002), http://www.uspto.gov.

[72] CoolSavings.com Inc. v. IQ Commerce Corp., 53 F. Supp. 2d 1000, 1001 (N.D. Ill., June, 1999). Laura Rohde, British Telecom Claims to Have Patent for Hyperlinks, Infoworld, June 26, 2000 (claiming patent for linking).

[73] Joel M. Freed and Thomas F. Reynolds, The New Patent Landscape, 18 Computer & Internet Law. 1 (Dec. 2001).

[74] Priceline.com has filed several patent infringement lawsuits against other online firms using the reverse auction method. *See* Juno Charges Qualcomm, Netzero Violated Patent, Electronic Commerce News, June 19, 2000 (reporting case).

the security of credit card transactions, whereas Cybergold holds a patent for paying web site visitors who view advertising on its site.[75] Netincentives holds a patent for an online frequent buyer program, whereas Open Market owns the electronic shopping cart and real-time payments patent.[76] Patents may be invalidated by demonstrating prior use or that the patent was too broad or lacks novelty, or for nonobviousness.

4. Are any of your trade secrets patentable? Assess the value of your trade secrets and consider whether a patent might be more appropriate to protect your competitive advantage.[77] Keep in mind the expense and length of time required to obtain a patent and also a patent's duration. Trade secrets may last until the secret is disclosed, while patents are limited to 20 years. On the other hand, trade secrets offer no protection against reverse engineering, while patents do.[78] The speed of the Internet revolution, however, no longer rewards those who can warehouse trade secrets; it rewards companies that bring new products quickly to market.[79]

5. Is international protection of patents necessary? European patents are coordinated through the European Patent Convention (EPC), but Europe has yet to achieve a unified patent system.[80] The EPC "specifically excludes patent protection for software in the form of computer programs."[81] The European Directive on the Legal Protection of Computer Software, however, "allows a freedom: opening the door for logic algorithms and programming language—excluded from copyright protection" in Europe.[82] If software patents are in doubt, it is unlikely that most European countries would issue business method patents.

[5]   Trade Secrets[83]

The law of trade secrets is a matter of state law, unlike the other branches of intellectual property law, which are largely defined by federal statutes. The majority of states have adopted the Uniform Trade Secrets Act (UTSA). UTSA defines

---

[75] *See* Thomas E. Anderson, Aces: Emerging Intellectual Property Issues in Cyberspace, 78 MI Bar Jnl 1260 (Nov. 1999).

[76] *Id.*

[77] Peter Toren, Protecting Prevailing Intellectual Property, New York L.J., Mar. 21, 2000, at S8.

[78] *See* Michael Bettinger and Peter Berger, Can Intellectual Property Be Protected on the Internet? Legal Backgrounder, Apr. 14, 2000, available in LEXIS, News Library, Curnws File (listing online intellectual property threats).

[79] Edward Iwata, IBM Revs Up to Internet Speed. Tech Alliances Begin Adjustment to New Economy, USA Today, Mar. 14, 2000, at 3B.

[80] Hans Henrik Lidgard, European Perspective on Licensing in a Network Environment, Keynote Address, European Perspective on Licensing in a Network Environment, Fourth Annual High Technology Law Conference, Licensing in a Network Environment, Suffolk University Law School (co-sponsored with the Boston Patent Law Association), Mar. 10, 2000.

[81] *Id.*

[82] *Id.*

[83] *See* § 4.04.

trade secrets more broadly than jurisdictions following the Restatement of Torts. UTSA requires companies to adopt "reasonable measures" to protect trade secrets. Companies will not be able to obtain damages for the misappropriation of trade secrets if they have not instituted adequate remedies to protect secrecy.

While trade secrets may impart a competitive edge to a company's intellectual property arsenal, they are vulnerable to mass dissemination over the Internet. Certain business methods that may not qualify for patent protection may nonetheless be trade secrets and intellectual property assets critical to the company's online strategy. Unlike patents, trademarks, or copyrights, however, a trade secret instantly loses its value when it is revealed to the public. Once information becomes generally known, it loses its value as a trade secret asset. Companies must take steps to keep their trade secrets intact and away from broad online publication. E-mail and Internet usage policies should give employees notice of their duty to protect trade secrets or other confidential information. Nondisclosure agreements (NDAs) are critical to protecting an e-business's trade secrets. Trade secrets may be lost at a click of the mouse despite NDAs. Ex-employees may also maliciously disclose trade secrets.

TRADE SECRETS CHECKLIST

1. Has your company inventoried its trade secrets? By identifying and cataloguing trade secrets, a company can better assess the risks of having its secrets disclosed. A company that relies heavily on trade secrets should implement a comprehensive policy of trade secret protection. Something as simple as a recipe can be a significant competitive advantage to a food processor. Most companies will have customer lists, business methods, and other proprietary information that has value only if it is kept secret. Unlike patents, a trade secret does not need to be novel and nonobvious—it could be as simple as a minor improvement over existing technology. Step back and examine your products, plans, or processes for any information that has actual or potential value if it is kept secret.

2. Does your company have a systematic policy for protecting trade secrets? What are the requirements for protecting trade secrets in your company's jurisdiction? All relevant documents should be labeled "confidential." Most companies now require all employees and contractors to sign trade secret nondisclosure agreements, giving the companies recourse if the agreements are breached. Educate employees regarding the value and vulnerability of trade secrets. Consider not only single-event education, but ongoing periodic training that reiterates the need for confidentiality. Also, consider requiring employees to periodically reaffirm their nondisclosure agreements.

3. Are your software engineers, web content managers, programmers, or other critical employees familiar with your trade secret policy and the risks of disseminating trade secrets online? Control potential trade secret leaks at the spigot of online publication. A marketing manager wishing to publish a new product announcement online may not realize that the product specifications have economic value if kept secret. Injunctive relief may be required to prevent the future disclosure of trade secrets.

4. Has your company implemented a formal e-mail and Internet usage policy that specifically covers trade secrets? Does your company monitor employee e-mail and Internet usage? Are employees given prior notice that messages are monitored? Employees can easily forward documents within a company and beyond. Confidential data should be labeled and encrypted. Labeling an e-mail "confidential" will put the employee on notice to limit distribution. Any e-mail monitoring policy should also include searching for key words relating to trade secrets. This may provide an early warning system if a secret is forwarded beyond the company's firewall.[84] The Internet usage policy should address the question of downloading files containing viruses. The policy should require that material not be downloaded without first scanning for viruses.[85] No user should download material from the Internet without knowing the source. The policy should state the procedure for reporting virus outbreaks.

5. Does your company encrypt and otherwise protect trade secrets that are transmitted electronically? Sophisticated encryption technology can help protect software or other data distributed over networks. Programmers have also devised methods of creating programs that protect themselves from unauthorized access by self-destructing.[86] John Doe subpoenas may be required to enjoin anonymous Internet posters of trade secrets. Courts will not issue subpoenas requiring providers to unveil anonymous posters unless they can meet a standard of irreparable harm.

6. Do you require your key employees to sign confidentiality agreements as well as covenants not to compete? Do you require your employees to sign confidentiality agreements agreeing to hold trade secrets and other proprietary information secret? Does your confidentiality agreement require employees to return all company documents that have been classified as trade secrets? The confidentiality agreement should spell out the scope of proprietary information that is classified as a trade secret.

7. Do you require your key employees to sign agreements assigning to the company inventions completed with company resources and on company time? Are all assignment of inventions clauses reasonable in terms of breadth and period of time?

8. Are confidentiality clauses included in every license agreement, whether standard form or negotiated? A licensor will require a licensee to take all reasonable measures to maintain the confidentiality of all proprietary information in its possession or control. In fulfilling any developmental software contract, the customer may give a developer confidential information relevant to the project. The agreement should specify the specific use for which information is disclosed

---

[84] For a more detailed examination of e-mail and Internet usage policies, *see* Chapter Ten.

[85] City of Seattle, Internet Use Policy and Virus Protection Policy, Sept. 10, 1995 (visited May 15, 2002), http://www.mrsc.org/infoserv/seattle.htm

[86] Bettinger and Berger, *supra* note 78.

and carefully define acceptable uses. At minimum, the developer should agree to treat all confidential material with the same measures it uses to protect its own confidential information. Source code, for example, is generally regarded as confidential. Online companies should decide whether to limit access to confidential information to the recipient's employees on a "need to know" basis.

9. Is there a confidential information clause in all of your agreements? Are the agreements reasonable in time, scope, and purpose? Does it cover all formulas, patterns, compilations, programs, devices, methods, or processes with actual or potential economic value? In the event of litigation, the attorney for the company must have a protective order to protect trade secrets and other confidential information.

[6] Linking[87]

Linking is one of the main vehicles of navigation through the World Wide Web. Simple linking will rarely present legal problems, since it is widely used and an accepted part of the Internet. Without links, online visitors would have to learn about your web site and get its address from potentially expensive traditional media. Yet the free spirit of Internet linking is diminished when companies are the target of unwanted links or of links that bypass a main web page. Would you want your web page to be linked to an unsavory site? Several trademark infringement lawsuits alleging tarnishment have been filed by plaintiffs objecting to links to unsavory adult entertainment sites.[88]

Alternatively, a visitor to your web page may develop a dispute with a linked destination and sue you for sponsoring the site. Another objectionable practice is *deep linking,* that is, bypassing the home page and advertising of the linked site and thus "cherry-picking the best of a linked site."[89] Linking cases have been litigated under theories of copyright, trademark, and unfair competition law.[90] Ticketmaster, for example, sued Microsoft for unfair competition after Microsoft deep linked to its site.[91] Establishing, posting, and enforcing a linking policy are helpful tools for avoiding linking disputes. Linking agreements are the best preventive law device for avoiding trademark and false endorsement claims. The FTC has guidelines for making hyperlink disclosures clear and conspicuous. The courts have provided little guidance on the limits of linking, so a cautious approach is well warranted. It is likely that U.S. courts will not enforce civil or criminal for-

---

[87] *See* §§ 2.05[C], 4.02[G].

[88] *See generally* Michael Wu, Playboy Enterprises, Inc. v. Netscape Communications Corp. and Excite, Inc.: The Impact of Banner Ad Keying on the Development of E-Commerce, 2001 Minn. Intell. Prop. Rev. 1 (2001).

[89] *See generally* Marc Sableman, Link Law Revisited: Internet Linking Law at Five Years, 16 Berkley Tech. L.J. 1273 (Fall 2001).

[90] *Id.*

[91] Ticketmaster and Microsoft settled their lawsuit after Microsoft agreed to cease the deep linking practice. *See* Ticketmaster Corp. v. Microsoft Corp., No. 97-3055 DDP (C.D. Cal. filed Apr. 28, 1997) (Complaint).

eign judgments based on simple linking because such a ruling would violate public policy in having a seamless Internet. Merchant linking agreements should be used where there is any question that the linked suit might object to a link.

LINKING CHECKLIST

1. Have you evaluated the business benefits and risks associated with external links? Can your company be held liable for dilution of a competitor's trademark or copyright infringement because of linking? A useful page of current, relevant links may bring visitors back to your site and generate traffic. On the other hand, does your organization want to provide a vehicle that leads visitors to other web sites? Additionally, does your company want to dedicate resources to ensuring that the relevant links are updated and/or working properly?

2. Do you have permission to link to all destination sites? Some companies do not want other links to their web pages. If you do not have the resources to obtain written permission from all of your linked sites, check to see if the sites have posted a linking policy. Comply with any requests to remove links; better yet, seek permission first.

3. Does your web page have a linking policy posted on its site? Do your web site designers have clear guidance on the company's rules for linking? Do other web site visitors have guidance on what linking practices are permitted? Your web site designers need to understand your linking policy. Let visitors know your linking policy. You may want to require written permission from anyone who wants to link to your site and reserve your right to revoke permission. Some sites may want to eliminate linking completely. Your linking policy may link to your main web page but not allow deep links to other pages. Many web sites do not have a linking policy; examine your business needs before you decide which approach is appropriate for your company.

4. Do any of your links use logos or stylized text? While text links usually do not raise an eyebrow from the destination sites, logos or stylized text may raise issues of trademark infringement.[92] Unless you have express written permission, use only text links.[93] Do not use a corporate logo, image, or trademark text.[94] Any confusion regarding unauthorized endorsement from another company can expose your company to a trademark infringement or unfair competition lawsuit.[95] Use the same text for all external links.

---

[92] BitLaw, Linking and Liability (last visited May 15, 2002), http://www.bitlaw.com/internet/linking.html.

[93] Id.

[94] Id.

[95] Trademark infringement occurs when a seller uses a mark confusingly similar to a registered trademark. "Any seller who uses a mark so similar to a registered trademark that it is likely to cause customer confusion is an infringer and can be sued in a state or federal court. The court compares the conflicting trademarks as to similarity in sound, sight and meaning." Small Business Administration, Starting Your Business—Patents, Trademarks and Copyrights (visited June 10, 2002), http://www.sba.gov/starting/indextrademarks.html.

5. Have you disclaimed liability from any external links? Let visitors know that the links are placed for their convenience and should not be interpreted as an endorsement. Note that you accept no liability from use of the linked sites.[96] You do not want to be sued because of a dispute between one of your visitors and a linked web site. You may want to enter into a linking agreement that spells out acceptable uses as well as rights to indemnification or subrogation rights.

6. Are visitors clearly notified that they are leaving the site if they click on a link? Does the link imply an endorsement or affiliation with the linked site? Let visitors know that the links will take them to another company's web site. Minimize the possibility that a consumer might confuse the linked site with your site and file suit against your company.

7. If your linking does not violate trademark or copyright law, will other parties nonetheless find it objectionable?[97] The safest policy complies with the law and links only in ways the linked site finds unobjectionable.[98] If a linked site has objections to a link, it could lead to costly litigation, unfavorable publicity, and ultimately undermine your best interest.[99] It is advisable to consider linking agreements to prevent disputes even though simple linking would likely constitute fair use.[100]

8. Does your company have linking agreements with parties who might otherwise object to a link between their site and yours? What is the effective date? What is the policy about attribution? The reciprocal linking agreement should begin by naming the parties, providing their addresses, and stating the purpose of the agreement: "This linking agreement is entered into as of January 1, 2003, between Suffolk Personal Computers, a Massachusetts corporation, and Lund Computers, Inc., located in Lund, Sweden. The purpose of this agreement is to assist SPC in obtaining a market share of the Northern European marketplace."

9. Does your web designer follow the FTC staff's guidelines for the labeling, description, and placement of hyperlinks? The FTC offers specific guidelines for hyperlinking to disclosures, including placement on web pages.[101] If your web site complies with the FTC guidelines for hyperlinking to a disclosure, your company will likely have safe harbor on the issue of conspicuousness. The FTC states that "[D]isclosures that are an integral part of a claim or inseparable from it . . . should be placed on the same page and immediately next to the claim."[102] The FTC notes that the key factors for hyperlinks are "the labeling or description of the hyperlink, the consistency in the use of hyperlink styles, its placement and prominence on the Web page, and the handling of the disclosure on

---

[96] *Id.*

[97] David Mirchin, Can You Be Legally Liable for Hypertext Linking? (visited May 15, 2002), http://www.silverplatter.com/hypertext.html.

[98] *Id.*

[99] *Id.*

[100] *Id.*

[101] Federal Trade Commission, Dot Com Disclosures (visted June 8, 2002), http://www.ftc.gov/bcp/conline/pubs/buspubs/dotcom/index.html.

[102] *Id.*

the click-through page."[103] In addition, the FTC offers the following advice: (a) choose the right label for the hyperlink; (b) make it obvious; (c) label the link to convey the importance, nature, and relevance of the information it leads to; (d) don't be coy; (e) don't be subtle; (f) use hyperlink styles consistently; (g) place links near relevant information and make them noticeable; (h) make it easy to get to the disclosure on the click-through page; (i) get consumers to the message quickly; (j) assess the effectiveness of a hyperlink disclosure; (k) don't ignore data that your hyperlinks are not followed by visitors; (l) don't ignore technological limitations on scrolling; (m) recognize and respond to the characteristics of each technique (that is, pop-up windows or interstitial pages); (n) research consumer behavior to determine the effectiveness of your communication of disclosure information; (o) don't focus only on disclosures for the order page; (p) disclose information required in the banner clearly and conspicuously; (q) incorporate or flag required information creatively; (r) evaluate the size, color, and graphics of the disclosure in relation to other parts of the web site; (s) don't let other parts of an ad get in the way; (t) repeat disclosures on lengthy web sites, as needed; (u) "repeat disclosures with repeated claims, as needed"; (v) "for audio claims, use audio disclosures"; and (w) "display visual disclosures for sufficient duration."[104]

10. Does your company have a process (manual or automated through software tools) of identifying all links on your web site pages? Is this list examined for proprietary links and the like on a periodic basis?

[7] Framing[105]

Framing is an easy way to bring external content to your site without recreating other web pages.[106] Framing is also a controversial web practice, because the frame retains the look, feel, and content of one web site while visitors are actually viewing another.[107] Frames may block or divert advertising or confuse consumers as to the site's origin.[108] If you employ frames beyond your own site, the following checklist should help you to reduce your risk. If you want to avoid unwanted framing, this checklist will provide some assistance.

FRAMING CHECKLIST

1. Have you examined the benefits and risks of framing? Do you want to provide external content within your own web site?

---

[103] *Id.*

[104] These suggestions paraphrase the applicability of FTC law to the use of links in Internet advertising. *Id.*

[105] *See* §§ 2.05[D], 4.02[G][4].

[106] Digital Equipment Corporation v. Altavista Technology, Inc., 960 F. Supp. 456, 461 (D. Mass. 1997) (citing Maura Welch, Framing the News, Boston Globe, Feb. 27, 1997 at D4).

[107] *Id.*

[108] *Id.*

2. Is your framing policy posted on your site? Many companies oppose framing because frames may obscure banner advertising and make your web site appear within another site. On the other hand, your company may take the position that any traffic is likely to increase clickstreams and revenue even if visitors view your content within a frame. Post a clear framing and linking policy conspicuously on your web site. If your company does not want its site framed, there are programming tricks and software tools that prevent unauthorized framing.[109] Also, if you find that your site is the target of frequent, unwanted framing, consider changing the addresses of your internal links so any frames are forced to start at your front page.

3. Have you obtained written permission for any external framing? Get written permission for any external framing. Frames can be very useful because they eliminate the need to recreate content that exists on another site. Framing can, for example, help you make use of the up-to-date technical specifications posted by the manufacturer of goods you resell. If the manufacturer approves your framing, you can reduce some of the time and expenses associated with web site development.

4. Make the frame obvious. Design the frame so that all external frames are clearly distinct from the web site's content. Avoid the possibility that visitors will become confused about whether they are at your site or at the framed destination.[110] Avoid obstructing any critical information on the destination site if you employ framing.

5. Have you disclaimed liability from any framed sites? Do not expose yourself to liability if a visitor to your site is injured by a site that you have framed. Let visitors know that the frame is for their convenience and that you do not endorse the destination site. You will need a different disclosure if you are partnering with the framed site or sharing revenues.

6. Have you entered into agreements to permit framing of your site or for your company to frame the content of others? Does the agreement specify how the frame appears on the page? Have the parties agreed as to how the framed site will appear to the visitor? What are events of termination for the framing agreement? It is advisable that the parties agree to some cost-effective and speedy alternative dispute resolution mechanism to resolve linking or framing disputes.

[8] Moral Rights of Authors[111]

The moral rights of authors originate in the copyright laws of civil law countries, but they have not been recognized under U.S. copyright law.[112] Article 6 of

---

[109] *Id.*

[110] *Id.*

[111] *See* § 4.02[I][1]. *See* I.S. Sees Administrative Nightmare in Copyright of Web Site Proposals, Comm. Daily, Sept. 25, 2000 (commenting on WIPO's copyright proposal governing moral rights for performers).

[112] *See, e.g.,* Vargas v. Esquire, 164 F.2d 522, 527 (7th Cir. 1947) (stating that the concept of moral rights of the author is not a doctrine recognized under U.S. copyright law).

the Berne Convention, however, validates the right of integrity and attribution of works of authorship.[113] The right of integrity maintains, essentially, that a work cannot be distorted in a way that will ruin the reputation of the creator.[114] The right of attribution is the right of the true creator to have his or her name on a work and "non-authors are prevented from having their names attached to the author's work."[115] In addition to the moral rights recognized by the Berne Convention, different moral rights are available under national law.[116]

No court decisions have extended the concept of moral rights to web sites. To be on the safe side, however, web site creators should be required to assign any moral rights to the company. It is possible that a European court could find that a company's redesign of a web site violated a web site designer's moral right of integrity. The moral rights of authors originate in the copyright laws of civil law countries, but they have not been widely recognized under U.S. copyright law.

MORAL RIGHTS CHECKLIST

1. Have you obtained assignments for moral rights, such as the right of integrity, attribution, and distortion, from web site designers? The online company should require that the web site designer assign any moral rights to the company. Assignments of moral rights should be routinely included in any license agreements with content providers even though the probability of a successful lawsuit is remote.

2. Have you obtained assignments for moral rights for all content providers? This includes audiovisual performers, scriptwriters, and other authors.

3. Has your company entered into indemnification and hold harmless clauses with joint venturers?

[C] Exposure to Lawsuits in Distant Forums: Jurisdiction[117]

The moment a web site is launched, the online company is not only subject to local or state law but also potentially to the laws of distant states or countries. Few activities are more time-consuming or expensive than appearing in a distant court to defend your online activities. Many companies enter cyberspace without considering the possibility of becoming subject to lawsuits in distant forums. The rules for jurisdiction, however, are rapidly evolving to accommodate online disputes. Still, a strong element of unpredictability remains, especially where the web site is in the gray zone between passivity and interactivity. Courts may set standards based on their current needs, even if these conflict with precedents in cases

---

[113] Ronald B. Standler, Moral Rights of Authors in the USA (visited June 6, 2002), http://www.rbs2.com/moral.htm.

[114] *Id.*

[115] *Id.*

[116] The French, for example, recognize the right of disclosure, the right to withdraw or retract, and the right to reply to criticism. *Id.*

[117] For a complete discussion of jurisdiction, *see* Chapter Seven.

with similar facts from other jurisdictions; the federal district court's decision in *Zippo Mfr. Co. v. Zippo Dot Com, Inc.,*[118] however, has been an influential precedent in many jurisdictions.

Few in the online business community understand the legal risks of jurisdiction. Personal jurisdiction cannot be established by using a server in the forum or entering into a contract.[119] Personal jurisdiction "is directly proportionate to the nature and quality of commercial activity that an entity conducts over the Internet."[120] The definition of "minimum contacts" is still unclear with regard to Internet business.

Personal jurisdiction is positively correlated with commercial activity; the greater the interactivity and commercial activity, the greater the likelihood a court will find that an online company is subject to personal jurisdiction in a distant forum. Passive web sites that permit neither interactivity nor online sales or services pose a low risk of personal jurisdiction in an out-of-state forum. Few companies are willing to restrict their web site to a mere conduit of information, however. The majority of web sites permit electronic purchasing and sales activity, according to a 1999 study by the American Bar Association.[121] Less than a third of the companies surveyed had web pages that provided only general information.[122]

EXPOSURE TO DISTANT FORUMS CHECKLIST[123]

1. Does your web site clearly state the limits of its geographic scope? Inform web site visitors of the geographic reach of your site and consider excluding orders from high-risk jurisdictions. The threat of being sued in a distant court grows in relation to the geographic scope of your business.[124] Some states and countries may have specific regulations about products or services. You may want to let visitors know that you will not make sales to any states or countries whose restrictions you don't plan to observe.[125] Software is available to "red flag" orders from high-risk jurisdictions with an unacceptably high risk of fraud.

---

[118] 952 F. Supp. 1119 (W.D. Pa. 1997); *see also* Citigroup v. City Holdings Co., 97 F. Supp. 2d 549 (S.D.N.Y. 2000) (holding that a web site alone, even if it offers goods for sale, cannot alone confer jurisdiction); Telebyte v. Kendaco, Inc., 105 F. Supp. 2d 131 (E.D.N.Y. 2000) (same).

[119] Anderson Holdings LLC v. Westside Story Newspaper, 2000 U.S. Dist. LEXIS 12102 (D.N.J. Aug. 22, 2000).

[120] Zippo Manufacturing Company v. Zippo Dot Com, Inc., 952 F. Supp. 1119, 1124 (W.D. Pa. 1997).

[121] American Bar Association, ABA/ACCA Survey of Electronic Commerce Practices, Jan. 17, 1999 (visited June 15, 2002), http//www.abanet.org/scitech/abaacca.html.

[122] Thirty-one percent of respondents did not sell or purchase products or services on web sites. *Id.*

[123] We would like to thank Patrik Lindskough of the University of Lund Law School in Sweden for his editorial contributions to this checklist.

[124] *Supra* note 121.

[125] Decker v. Circus Hotel, 49 F. Supp. 2d 743, 748 (D.N.J., 1999).

2. Have you posted a choice of law/forum selection clause? Do your agreements also include choice of venue clauses? Are nonmandatory dispute resolution mechanisms offered to consumers? No matter what the scope of your business, you should limit your exposure by a choice of law and forum clause in your preferred jurisdiction.[126] Inform visitors that use of your web site is conditioned upon their assent to your forum selection clause.[127] If you are selling products from your web site, reiterate your forum selection clause in the sales transaction page.

3. Does your e-business comply with the trade regulations of the United States and key trading partners? Is the company in compliance with import and export regulations and restrictions on encrypted software? Do your e-mail advertisements comply with foreign or state antispamming laws?[128] Use ethical direct e-mail marketing. Opt-in e-mail marketing is less risky than indiscriminate spamming.[129] The FTC considers rules that apply to writing to be adaptable to e-mail. The FTC considers rules that apply to ads or printed material to apply to e-mail advertisements as well.[130]

4. Can you track the extent of your jurisdictional exposure based on sales and visits? Do you require users to identify the forum of residence? Do you require those who access your site to agree to resolve disputes in your jurisdiction? Are choice of forum, law, and venue class prominently posted on the company's web site? Are visitors to your site required to acknowledge acceptance of these terms? The forum selection clause or choice of law is more likely to be enforced in business-to-business than in business-to-consumer transactions. The sales volume and number of visitors per region may help you to evaluate your jurisdictional exposure.[131] If you can provide adequate data, courts may be reluctant to assert jurisdiction in a state where you have done a minimal percentage of your business.[132] Additionally, some states require registration with the secretary of state if you are conducting sufficient business in the state.

5. Is your company considering entering into agreements with arbitration clauses? A decision should be made as to whether arbitration will be mandatory or not, since arbitration may be more cost-effective than litigation. Some companies avoid arbitration because it may be less predictable than litigation. A sample clause could simply state: "Any controversy or claim rising out of or relating to this web site

---

[126] *Id.*

[127] *Id.*

[128] The Supreme Court of Washington upheld the constitutionality of Washington's commercial electronic mail act in State v. Heckel, 143 Wn. 824, 24 P.3d 404 (2001). The court reversed a lower court judge's ruling that the Act violated the Commerce Clause of the U.S. Constitution.

[129] *See* Whitehat.com, Inc., Best Practices (visited June 8, 2002), http://www.wh5.com/bestpractices.cfm (describing ethical direct e-mail marketing as opt-in marketing).

[130] Federal Trade Commission, Dot.Com Disclosures (visited June 8, 2002), http://www.ftc.gov/bcp/conline/pubs/buspubs/dotcom/index.html.

[131] Zippo Manufacturing Company v. Zippo Dot Com. Inc., 952 F. Supp. 1119, 1124 (W.D. Pa. 1997).

[132] *Id.*

agreement shall be settled by arbitration in Boston, Massachusetts, in accordance with the American Arbitration Association's Commercial Arbitration Rules."

6. Does your company track the states and countries to which its products are shipped or services rendered? You may want screening software that rejects orders or at least red flags orders from jurisdictions likely to cause legal trouble. Your local customers may request shipments to distant addresses. Such transactions may expose you to the laws and courts of the recipient's address. Make sure that any geographic limitations for sales are enforced for shipments as well.

7. Do you have a specific territorial or noncompetition agreement for your key products and services that is updated to apply to information products sold on the company's web site? Do not forget about any territorial restrictions that you might have agreed to long before the Internet became a viable sales channel. If you set North America as your only targeted market, what do you do if you receive an order from Europe? You may be able to amend the agreement to define electronic commerce restrictions or to modify your web site to forward extraterritorial sales to another site. Consider using an attorney to ensure favorable terms in the contract modification.

8. Is a defendant in an online lawsuit amenable to service of process? Service of process must be provided under a United States statute or under a state's long-arm statute. Web site visitors should be required to provide their address and location to reduce the exposure to lawsuits in unfavorable jurisdictions. A defendant is subject to a long-arm statute if it commits a tortious act within the state and the cause of action arises from the act.[133]

9. Is your company's web site interactive, passive, or in the borderland? Having a web site on the Internet is not enough in itself to create jurisdiction, without "something more." Web sites that are highly interactive and permit online orders will likely be found to be subject to specific jurisdiction. Web sites that provide only corporate information will not be found to be engaging in business with the forum.

10. Will the exercise of personal jurisdiction interfere with the sovereignty of another country? The exercise of jurisdiction that does implicate sovereignty concerns is a key factor in declining jurisdiction.

11. Will the exercise of jurisdiction by a court over an online dispute interfere with principles of domestic or international comity? Comity is a concept referring to the deference that a domestic court must pay to the act of a foreign government not otherwise binding on the forum.

12. Does your company need an offshore secure facility for an e-mail server containing sensitive data? Online gambling web sites have chosen havens such as Antigua for their places of business. HavenCo has created a satellite-linked

---

[133] Lucent Technologies, Inc. v. Lucentsucks.com, 2000 U.S. Dist. LEXIS 6159 (E.D. Va., May 3, 2000).

sovereign nation called Sealand.[134] The goal of the Principality of Sealand is to host B2B financial transactions and "e-mail servers as well as sensitive data backups."[135] HavenCo.com's press release notes that it is "offering the world's most secure managed collocation facility based in the world's smallest sovereign territory."[136] Sealand permits companies to "operate any type of business within the limits of our Acceptable Use Policy without officially registering for that type of business."[137] It is unclear whether data sanctuaries will ultimately succeed as safe havens from regulators. Representatives of the Group of Eight (G8) nations are seeking ways to prevent the formation of "digital havens."[138] Governments and business partners will likely have concerns about the anonymous and pseudonymous nature of "data havens."

13. Are there public policy reasons why foreign judgments against American online businesses will not be enforced?

14. Does your company understand the consumer rules of the new Brussels Regulation adopted by the European Union? The Brussels Regulation replaces the 1968 Brussels Convention. The Brussels Regulation applies to all Brussels Convention signatories except Denmark, which has opted out of the new regulations. The new Brussels Regulation governs jurisdiction in civil and commercial disputes between litigants and provides for the enforcement of judgments. The Council Regulation (EC) No 44/2001 of December 22, 2002, revises the Brussels Convention of 1968.

15. Where can your company be sued? Article 2.1 of the Brussels Regulation sets forth the general rule that "persons domiciled in a Contracting State shall whatever their nationality, be sued in the courts of the State." Article 2.2 provides that nonnationals of member states in which they are domiciled "shall be governed by the rules of jurisdiction applicable to nationals of the state." This means that an e-business has its place of business in its central place of administration or principal place of business (Art. 60).

16. Does your company target contracts to EU countries? Article 5.1 provides that "in matters relating to a contract," jurisdiction is in the place of performance. If SPC sells goods, the place of performance in a member state is the place "where the goods were delivered or should have been delivered" (Art. 15.1(b)).

17. Does your e-business render services in EU countries? In services contracts, jurisdiction occurs where the services were provided (Art. 15.1(b)).

18. Does your e-business have exposure to torts, delicts, or civil wrongs that are noncontractual? Article 15(3) provides that in "matters relating to tort, delict, or quasi-delict, jurisdiction is in the Member States for the place where the harmful event occurred or may occur."

19. Does your e-business enter into consumer contracts in member countries of the European Union? Consumers have the right to sue a supplier if

---

[134] Declan McCullagh, A Data Sanctuary Is Born, Wired News, June 8, 2000.

[135] *Id.*

[136] HavenCo., Welcome to HavenCo.com (visited June 8, 2002), http://www.havenco.com.

[137] *Id.*

[138] *Id.*

it "pursues commercial or professional activities in Member State of the consumer's domicile." (Art. 15.1(c)). This means that an e-business that directs its consumer transactions to Europe can be sued in the consumer's home court. Article 15.1(c) extends the consumer home forum rule to entities that direct activities to member states. It is quite likely that a web site in different languages that accepts the Euro as a currency is directing its activities to member states. A web site that does not wish to be subject to the home-court rule for jurisdiction over consumer contracts needs to employ blocking software or other techniques that red flag European consumer transactions.

20. Is your e-business partner a codefendant who directs activities to European consumers? Article 6.1 of the Brussels Regulation provides that a company may be subject to jurisdiction if a codefendant is domiciled in one of the member states.

21. Has a court in a member state been seised of proceedings? Article 30 devises a bright-line test for determining whether a court in a member state has jurisdiction. A court is deemed to be seised if documents have been filed requiring service of process to the defendant. As long as the party has taken the procedural steps necessary for process, the court has been "seised."

22. Has your company done the planning necessary to comply with the Brussels Regulation? The European Court of Justice ruled that the Brussels Convention applied to a Canadian company in a contract action brought in a French Court.[139] It is likely that the Brussels Regulation will also apply to a U.S. company transacting with European buyers.

[D]   Internet Privacy[140]

The personalization of web site visitors or collecting data poses significant risks of tort liability or enforcement actions by the Federal Trade Commission (FTC) or other regulators. If a company invades the privacy of a web site visitor or employee or discloses customer information in a manner inconsistent with its privacy policy or the law, it may be subject to liability for the resulting harm.[141] The American courts traditionally recognized four privacy-based torts: intrusion upon seclusion or solitude, appropriation of name or likeness, publicity given to private life, and publicity placing a person in a false light.[142] Entities that misuse data gathered on their web sites could face claims for breach of contract or even unfair and deceptive trade practices, if the use is beyond the scope of the company's privacy policy.

---

[139] Eugene Gulland, All the World's a Forum: Business That Benefit from the Increased Globalization of Commerce Also Face Increased Risks of Liability Abroad, N.J. L.J. (Apr. 29, 2002) (discussing Group Josi Reinsurance Co. S.A. v. Universal Gen. Ins. Co., 2000 E.C.R. I-5925).

[140] See § 5.07.

[141] Restatement of Torts (2d) § 652A (2000).

[142] The categories of the privacy tort were first articulated in William L. Prosser, Privacy, 48 Cal. L. Rev. 149 (1960).

It has taken several years for consumers to be comfortable enough to do business and transfer personal information online. The European Union has already adopted comprehensive privacy regulations, and the United States is examining legal measures as well. The United States, unlike the EU, lacks comprehensive general privacy legislation,[143] although there are specific requirements for industries that regularly work with sensitive data, such as banking and health care.

The European Union member countries approved a safe harbor, permitting the transfer of data between Europe and the United States, to entities that meet the stringent safe harbor requirements.[144] The Data Protection Directive, which went into effect in October 1998, only permits transfers of personally identifiable data to countries with an adequate standard of privacy protection, which does not include the United States. Several countries in Europe include civil and criminal penalties for the violation of personal data protection laws. Privacy is also a key issue for U.S. regulators, who are concerned with the proliferation of deceptive online privacy practices.[145] The FTC regularly monitors web sites to determine whether a company's stated privacy policy is consistent with its trade practices.

The business community has developed some industry standards for online privacy as an alternative to government regulation.[146] There are, however, several privacy-related regulations in the United States. For example, the Children's Online Privacy Protection Act (COPPA) requires web site operators to provide safeguards for collecting personally identifiable information from children under the age of 13. The following checklist can help you draft a policy that matches your business needs and your data practices.

INTERNET PRIVACY CHECKLIST

1. Does your company collect personal, individually identifiable data? Does it require and perform data collection and maintenance? Does it have a privacy policy? Internet advertisers tout their ability to track visitors as they navigate through the web. Data harvesters make it possible to tailor web site advertisements to the visitor's interests. A growing number of Internet users, however, will not purchase goods or services from sites that do not have privacy policies. Web sites may also collect personal information through cookie files, pixel beacons, usage data, and the harvesting of other personally identifiable information. A web site collecting personal information in the United States may be subject to regulatory action by the Federal Trade Commission.

---

[143] *See generally* Robert M. Gellman, Can Privacy Be Regulated Effectively on a National Level? Thoughts on the Possible Need for International Privacy Rules, 41 Vill. L. Rev. 129 (1996).

[144] FTC Recommends Privacy Legislation, 17 E-Commerce 8 (June 2000).

[145] Children's Online Privacy Protection Act, 15 U.S.C. §§ 6501-06, 16 C.F.R. § 312.1-312.2 (2000).

[146] The Clinton Administration's July 1997 White Paper, A Framework for Global Electronic Commerce, favored a private sector code of conduct to protect privacy.

2. Does your web site provide notice of your company's information collection practices? Are consumers offered a choice about how personally identifiable information is collected and shared with others? Is there an easy method for opting out of data collection or sharing? Does your web site have a privacy policy statement that describes your company's personal information gathering and dissemination practices? To gain trust of visitors, your company must post its privacy policy on its web site. Internet privacy is a critically important step in gaining the trust necessary for sales or services. New self-regulatory initiatives have been devised to build networks of trust.[147] Many companies subscribe to Internet seal programs to help build consumer trust. WebTrust, for example, is a certification program (developed by the American Institute of Certified Public Accountants) that provides a seal of approval assuring visitors that their personal information will not be misused.[148] A subscribing company that does not follow WebTrust's privacy policy may be terminated from its seal programs. In addition, a company misleading the public about its privacy policy may be subject to law enforcement or regulatory action.[149] TRUSTe, PrivaTrust, BBB Online, Web Watchdog, BizRate, and WebTrust.net offer web site certification programs. BBB Online, for example, is a self-regulation tool for fostering consumer trust and confidence on the web.[150] BBB OnLine's "Reliability Seal" is the most widely used certification program on the Internet.[151] An online seal or certification program should include a method of enforcement, such as the AICPA's WebTrust service. If subscribers are not held accountable to high standards, the value of the seal or certification will erode. The best certification programs have third-party audits by accounting firms or other third parties. Each of these self-regulation tools is designed to address Internet consumer protection issues.

3. Has your company adopted and implemented a Personal Data Protection Program?[152] Has the company prominently posted its web site privacy policy? Do consumers have access to the personally identifiable information that is collected? Has the personal data protection policy been made part of a compliance program? Have employees been educated about the data protection program? Use of a third-party enforcement system or "seal system" will make it more likely that visitors will provide personally identifiable information. A growing number of companies refuse to purchase advertisements from web sites that do not have robust privacy policies. The online company may want to build trust by representing the five principles for adequate personal data protection formulated by the Global Business Dialogue (GBDe). The online company needs to first adopt and implement a Personal Data Protection Policy. The policy must be enforced

---

[147] The Network Advertising Initiative (NAI) is an example of a self-regulatory group (visited May 5, 2000), http://www.network.advertising.org.

[148] *Id.*

[149] The audience determines whether an advertisement is misleading. Bates v. Arizona, 433 U.S. 350, 383 n.37 (1977).

[150] BBBOnLine (June 15, 2002), http://www.bbbonline.org/.

[151] *Id.*

[152] Global Business Dialogue on Electronic Commerce, Protection of Personal Data, http://consumerconfidence.gbde.org (recommending adoption of a data protection program).

company-wide in the form of a training and compliance program involving key company executives and employees. Second, a company needs an "opt-out" mechanism if it is collecting personal data from site visitors. Third, the company must only use and distribute personal data in accordance with the purpose for which it was collected. Fourth, the company must give visitors assurance of reliability in the protection of their personal information. Finally, the web site must give visitors a right of access, disclosure, and an opportunity to correct or delete personal information.[153]

4. Does your company's web site subscribe to an online privacy seal program? The TRUSTe "trustmark" or seal is awarded to web sites that follow prescribed privacy principles and comply with verification and consumer resolution processes.[154] The verification feature of the TRUSTe seal permits visitors to click on a "click-to-verify" seal. The visitor is then taken to the TRUSTe site, where he or she can check a list of all licensees who participate in the program.[155]

5. Does your web site collect personal data of visitors? Is there an opt-out mechanism and a specified purpose? A growing number of industry groups endorse an opt-out provision for the collection of personal data.

6. Is your company's use of personal data consistent with its policy to protect the privacy of personally identifiable information in company databases? A web site's privacy policy is an enforceable online contract and must be followed. The FTC sued Internet portal GeoCities for failing to abide by its own posted privacy policy.[156] Make sure that your company's data gathering practices match your policy. The FTC is concerned with four primary areas of privacy: notice, choice, access, and security.[157]

7. Is there a privacy policy posted on the order or sales page or data collection page? Shoppers are more comfortable ordering from a company with a posted policy. If you do make your mailing list available to other companies, disclose that fact, and give buyers an opportunity to opt-out of that mailing list.

8. Does your commercial web site target children under age 13? Does the web site comply with the Federal Trade Commission implementing the Children's Online Privacy Protection Act (COPPA)? If your site targets advertising, promotions, and other information to children under 13, it is subject to 16 C.F.R. § 312.1-312.2 (2000). COPPA requires verifiable parental consent before your site can collect personally identifiable information from children. Your site needs to limit data harvesting to what is necessary for a child's participation in an activity.

---

[153] *Id.*

[154] TRUSTe, TRUSTe for Web Users, Frequently Asked Questions (June 15, 2002), http://www.truste.org/users/consumers_faqs.html.

[155] *Id.*

[156] David Medine and Christine Varney, Enforcement Actions, Nat'l L. J., Aug. 6, 2001, at A23.

[157] *See* Ron N. Dreben and Johanna L. Werbach, Top 10 Things to Consider in Developing an Electronic Commerce Web Site, Computer Lawyer, May 1999, at 17 (highlighting potential online privacy issues). The Online Privacy Alliance sets out three requirements for a privacy policy: what information do you collect, how do you use it, and does the visitor have the option to keep data from being used? Grant Lukenbill, IBM Sends Out a Shout on Privacy, DM News, April 5, 1999, at 1.

The web site's privacy policy must be posted prominently and in clear language. Verifiable parental consent must be obtained prior to collecting, using, or disclosing personally identifiable information from a child. Online sellers should also consult the Children's Advertising Review Unit (CARU) of the Council of Better Business Bureau, which has published guidelines for children's advertising.

9. If your site transmits or receives sensitive information in regulated industries, is it subject to heightened duties of care? A web site dedicated to health care issues may, for example, deal with sensitive medical records. The American Medical Association requires physicians to take the "utmost care and effort in protecting the confidentiality of medical records, including computer records."[158] The unauthorized disclosure of personal medical records may expose your company to federal or state statutory damages as well as common law tort actions.

10. The Fourth Amendment of the U.S. Constitution does not apply to claims of privacy in e-mail or Internet usage for private employees. State statutes may provide more protection for employees. The State of Washington's Privacy Act makes it "unlawful for any individual, partnership, corporation, association of the State of Washington, its agencies and political subdivisions to intercept or record any private communications transmitted by telephone, telegraph, radio or other device between two or more individuals between points within or without the state by any device electronic or otherwise designed to record and/or transmit said communication regardless of how such device is powered or actuated, without first obtaining the consent of all participants in the communication."[159]

11. How does your company use data? Does your company use the data for sales fulfillment and analysis? Is the data ever sent to third parties for any purpose? What do the third parties do with your data? All of these issues must be addressed in the privacy policy.

12. Does your company export personal data from the European Union to the United States or another country? The EU data privacy directive and its local implementation carry stiff penalties for noncompliance. In addition, participants in the U.S. safe harbor program could face substantial fines if they do not follow the regulations. If your company or a subsidiary is exporting any data, either internally or to a third party, ensure that the transfer complies with all relevant privacy regulations.

13. Does your company have insurance for e-business interruption from cybercrime?[160]

[E]   Third-Party Content[161]

A message board or program exchange can be helpful for customers and provide a forum for customer support and feedback. But if your web site allows post-

---

[158] AMA Reg. 5.07.

[159] Revised Code Wash. 9.73.030 (2000) cited in Isabel R. Safora, Municipal Policies on Internet Usage and E-Mail Document Retention (April 1997) (visited June 15, 2002), http://www.mrsc.org/ infoserv/safora.htm.

[160] Joia Shillingford, Insuring Against Cybercrime, Financial Times (London), Sept. 5, 2001, at 1.

[161] *See* §§ 2.05[C][2], 4.02[F].

ing of messages or programs, do not let yourself get involved in a lawsuit because a visitor posts objectionable material on your web site. With a carefully crafted policy and good monitoring, you can make postings an asset and not a liability. Web site posters should be warned of the dangers of defamatory, harassing, offensive, or illegal materials. Posters should be required to indemnify and hold the company harmless for causes of action arising out of chat room postings.[162]

THIRD-PARTY CONTENT CHECKLIST

1. Are third parties permitted to post any materials on your site? While it may be impossible for you to monitor content, check to make sure that items posted to the site match your business objectives. If you find that your server is being abused, assess the business risk of censoring or removing the message board.

2. Do you have a policy limiting the scope of posted material? Warn visitors not to post anything defamatory, infringing, or illegal, and let them know that inappropriate material may be deleted. Regularly audit your site for inappropriate postings. Postings by employees on company stocks, for example, may subject the company to a lawsuit for insider trading. The Securities and Exchange Commission recently charged 19 defendants with the first Internet-based insider trading case for passing tips online.[163]

3. Have you clearly disclaimed any liability from third-party postings for defamation, copyright, trademark, or other infringement? Limit your company's liability for lawsuits from a third party's postings on your web site.

4. Have you reserved any rights to reuse the posted materials? You may want to reprint, for example, reviews, laudatory recommendations, or examples of how a product is being used.

5. Have you reserved the right to transmit or retransmit posted materials?

6. Have you reserved the right to remove posted materials or to terminate the visitor's access for any reason or for no reason?

7. What framework exists to manage and control the third-party content on your site?

[F] Torts and Information Security[164]

The attacks of September 11, 2001 have created new fears about Internet security. An Information Technology Association of America (ITAA) survey

---

[162] The liability for chat room conversations varies from country to country. German courts, for example, have held that there is "criminal responsibility for defamatory statements made during online conversations." Heinder Buenting, The New German Multimedia Law—A Model for the United States? 14 The Computer Lawyer 17 (Sept. 1997).

[163] Michael Geist, Net Insider Trading Action Launched, Internet Law News (March 15, 2000).

[164] *See* Chapter Five.

revealed that nearly three in four Americans worried about the possibility of cyber-attacks against critical infrastructure.[165] Seventy-four percent were concerned that their personal information could be stolen or misused by cyberthieves.[166] According to the results of a KMPG study surveying U.S. and Europe business executives, many companies do not yet have a comprehensive plan of information security.[167] Only 39 percent of respondents viewed "information security as a strategic business issue that requires an integrated organizational solution."[168] The KPMG survey found that nonmanagement employees were significantly behind the upper ranks on being informed about information security matters. In fact, 95 percent said their CEOs were informed, but only 77 percent felt their boards were completely informed, 38 percent said middle management was informed, and just 11 percent said that nonmanagement staff was informed.[169]

In the past five years, more than 150 legal decisions have addressed the question of whether personal jurisdiction is proper in Internet tort cases. A climate of uncertainty persists as to whether tort theories apply to defective software or computer malpractice on the Internet.[170] Online companies are concerned about the possibility of class action lawsuits for defective software, computer viruses, inaccurate information on products, and other problems with Internet contracts.

A tort is a civil injury for which the court will provide a remedy for damages. Torts not only protect against intentional invasion but also against negligent invasions of rights.[171] Torts are not only concerned with personal injury but also with economic injuries. Torts may be committed in chat rooms, message boards, forged web sites, by e-mail, or in conjunction with an online sales or service. Prevention and cost avoidance are the primary aims of tort law.

Dot-com companies need to institute preventive law directed to changing policies and practices that are legally risky. The goal of a self-audit is to seek out any operational problems that need to be corrected before they bankrupt the company or result in a public relations disaster. The next step is to correct those issues and reduce the company's exposure to cyberspace-related lawsuits. Although a self-audit is nothing new for most corporations, a cyber legal audit will apply traditional legal principles to the new venue in which the e-businesses operates. A regular self-audit process that reviews e-business processes and procedures is critical to limiting tort liability. Neglecting legal issues that arise from the self-audit might preclude a company from venturing into a particular market, curb the devel-

---

[165] CyberAtlas Staff, Internet, Computer Security Concerns Americans (visited Dec. 25, 2001), http://www.cyberatlas.internet.com/bigpicture/geographics/article.

[166] *Id.*

[167] Industrial Companies Advancing in Information Security But Major Gaps Exist in Their Preparedness, KPMG Study Reveals, PR Newswire, Nov. 15, 2001.

[168] *Id.*

[169] *Id.*

[170] *See generally* John M. Conley, Tort Theories of Recovery against Vendors of Defective Software, Practicing Law Institute: Patents, Copyrights, Trademarks and Literary Property Course Book, PLI Order No. G4-3855 (Oct. 25-27 1990).

[171] Restatement (Second) of Torts § 1 (2000).

opment of a promising new product or service, and/or even potentially bankrupt the developing dot-com business altogether.

In addition to tort liability, other negative legal consequences can follow from failing to anticipate profiles of danger. The negative legal consequences include (1) a particular activity found to be unlawful; (2) a controversial lawful activity that could result in high compliance costs; (3) a particular activity with an unexpected effect resulting in lost revenues and/or a tarnished reputation; (4) loss of ownership, control, or inability to protect certain assets; and (5) a particular activity exposing the company to new sources of liability.[172]

Extending preventive law to cyberspace can serve as an early warning system against even greater corporate troubles. The remedy of punitive damages may result in even larger damage awards. Punitive damages are awarded where there is some "smoking gun" evidence that an online company concealed, suppressed, or knowingly failed to correct a dangerous computer software defect or fraudulent online practice. While employers do not have a duty to monitor the e-mail and Internet communications of their employees, they have a duty to take "effective measures to stop co-employee harassment when the employer knows or has reason to know of such harassment."[173] An employer may also have an interest in monitoring e-mail or Internet usage for the detection of other illegal conduct.[174] An online employer who knows of online torts by employees but fails to take prompt remedial action may be liable for punitive damages. Punitive damages are awarded to punish and deter the defendant and others from repeating wrongdoing. Aggravating circumstances, such as the destruction of evidence, concealment of fraudulent practices, or many prior similar injuries, are key to the awarding of punitive damages.[175]

An online company that distributes software from its site may be liable for product liability if a defect in the software causes personal injury. Product liability is a field that evolved largely since the 1960s to make sellers or distributors liable for harm to persons or property caused by defective products.[176] Sellers have long been liable for manufacturing defects. It has only been since the 1960s, however, that courts began basing product liability on a strict liability basis in addition to the traditional negligence or warranty actions.[177] Preventive law can result in the design of safer products and services in the online world as well. A host of relevant legal issues should be reviewed. A company with a web site is liable not just for injuries in its store, but also for any injuries incurred online. Online injuries go

---

[172] *See generally* Secure, Defend, and Transform: The Complete E-Business Legal Strategy, PricewaterhouseCoopers, Spring 1999, at 7 (explaining online risks).

[173] Blakey v. Continental Airlines, Inc., No. A-5-99 (New Jersey Supreme Court, June 1, 2000) (visited June 8, 2000), http://lawlibrary.rutgers.edu/courts/supreme/a-5.99.opn.html.

[174] Safora, *supra* note 159.

[175] *See generally* Michael L. Rustad, Unraveling Punitive Damages: Current Data and Further Inquiry, Wisc. L. Rev 14 (1998); Michael L. Rustad, How the Common Good Is Served by the Remedy of Punitive Damages, 64 Tenn. L. Rev. 793 (1997).

[176] Restatement of the Law Third (Torts) Product Liability § 1 (1997).

[177] *Id.* at § 1, Comment a.

beyond the traditional "slip and fall" and encompass harms ranging from web site defamation and online harassment to liability for defective software. Additionally, a company can be held responsible not only for its own torts but also for those of employees or independent contractors.

TORTS AND INFORMATION SECURITY CHECKLIST

1. Does your company have a policy minimizing the risk of online fraud? The tort of misrepresentation or fraud may arise from false statements made on the online company's web site. A company needs a fraud-screening program to avoid being victimized by online fraud. Internet merchants can tailor fraud screens to their business. Screens may be based on risk factors such as expected time of purchase, expected purchase frequency, match between ship-to and bill-to addresses, e-mail/IP host, and orders originating in international locations.[178] It is critical that a fraud screen be able to validate credit cards.[179] Fraudulent credit card activity may account for as much as "39% of total attempted order revenue."[180] Sophisticated fraud detection methods are critical for reducing fraudulent credit card transactions and identity theft. Vendors are using artificial intelligence to screen for fraudulent and nonapproved credit card transactions.[181] State attorneys general have consumer protection divisions that may file criminal or civil actions against companies engaging in consumer fraud.[182] Does your company share information with other companies to punish and deter cybercrime?

2. Has the company minimized its exposure to lawsuits for fraudulent sales or services? An online company must avoid being a defendant in a fraud lawsuit. United States investors sued Corel for misrepresenting its financial results.[183] A fraudulent statement made in an e-mail message or on a listserv may expose the company to a fraud action. An online company may also have tort causes of action for computer fraud. Hackers may use false credit card numbers to order software or hardware from the company. Fraud in cyberspace would cover any fraudulent behavior through which another party made misrepresentations to

---

[178] CyberSource FraudScan™, Internet Fraud Screen (visited June 15, 2002), http://www.cybersource.com/solutions/risk_management. *See also* Brian Fonseca, Keeping Internet-Business Fraud in Check, InfoWorld, March 23, 2000, at 28 (noting high risk of Internet business fraud).

[179] *Id.*

[180] *Id.*

[181] *Id.*

[182] The Massachusetts attorney general formed a cybercrime unit that has charged online businesses with online fraud. New Jersey's attorney general recently filed civil fraud lawsuits against eight online pharmacies for selling regulated drugs without a license in the state. BNA, New Jersey: State Files Consumer Fraud Charges Against Eight Online Pharmacies, 9 BNA's Health Law Reporter (News: Drugs & Devices) (Apr. 6, 2000).

[183] Michael Geist, Corel Sued Over Financial Misrepresentations, Internet Law News (Mar. 15, 2000).

gain a financial advantage.[184] A web site that fraudulently makes a representation of fact about goods or services sold on its site will be liable for fraudulent misrepresentation.[185] A software vendor who licenses software knowing that the performance standards are not as represented in the promotional literature will be liable for misrepresentation.[186] A software licensor may be liable for misrepresentation fraud if he or she "does not have the confidence in the accuracy of his representations that he states or implies."[187] Fraud in online sales may also be found if the seller "knows that he does not have the basis for his representation that he states or implies."[188] An online company may also be liable for negligent misrepresentation if it provides false information in a business deal.[189]

3. If you distribute software, does your company adequately test it? Is there a software quality assurance policy? A company may be exposed to the possibility of strict product liability if defective software causes personal injury or death of a user. Inadequate testing or the defective design of software may expose a company to class action suits as well. An online company may also be exposed to product liability under a theory of negligence if it fails to follow accepted industry standards for assuring software liability.[190] A software company can be found negligent for the failure to test adequately or for defective design. What degree of care would a reasonable software vendor take in testing its software?[191] A software vendor may also be liable for product liability under a theory of breach of implied warranty of merchantability under Article 2 of the UCC. Negligence is a malleable cause of action that may apply to a wide variety of activities. An online software engineer may be liable for negligence for not conforming to professional standards of care in programming software. The standard of negligence may apply to an online company's failure to use due care in preventing computer viruses from infecting the computers of others. Courts have been slow to extend strict liability

---

[184] Restatement (Second) of Torts § 525 (2000) (summarizing the common law of all U.S. jurisdictions).

[185] The plaintiff must prove that she justifiably relied upon the misrepresentation, to her detriment. The representation may concern either an existing or a past fact. Restatement (Second) of Torts § 525, comments d, e (2000).

[186] Restatement (Second) of Torts, § 526 (2000) (explaining state of mind for fraud or misrepresentation).

[187] *Id.* at § 526(b).

[188] *Id.* at § 526(c).

[189] *Id.* at § 552, comment a (stating that liability for negligent misrepresentation is based upon the "failure to exercise reasonable care of competence in supplying correct information").

[190] The standard by which negligence is determined is based upon reasonableness. Negligence is a departure from a standard of conduct demanded by the community for the protection of others against unreasonable risk. Restatement (Second) of Torts § 283, comment c (2000). A company, for example, must conform its practices to those of a reasonable company under like circumstances. Industry standards or best practices are often the best proof for what a reasonable company would do under like circumstances. In general, "an act is negligent if the risk is of such magnitude as to outweigh what the law regards as the utility of the act or of the particular manner in which it is done." Restatement (Second) of Torts § 291 (2000).

[191] Restatement (Second) of Torts § 282 (2000).

to computer software because of the economic loss rule.[192] Most courts limit strict product liability to cases where a defective product causes physical injury to the plaintiff. A producer of software has the potential of designing a software product that causes personal injury to the user or third parties. A producer of a coffee machine with a defective computer chip would face the same product liability as a manufacturer of an automobile with a defective fuel system. Software failure has led to airplane crashes, automobile accidents, chemical leaks, and medical product failure. A company can be exposed to breach of warranty lawsuits as well as strict product liability lawsuits for bad software that causes death or physical injury. Product liability lawsuits may be minimized by greater quality control. The correction of errors or bugs prior to release is key to product liability prevention. Once you learn of problems with hardware or software, take prompt measures to correct bugs or errors. Software license agreements will exclude all warranties and consequential damages.

4. Does your company's web site incorporate a terms and conditions agreement disclaiming warranties and limiting consequential damages? Does it offer an online chat service? Are visitors advised not to use the chat room in a manner inconsistent with netiquette as well as applicable laws and regulations? Are visitors advised about the dangers of defamatory remarks, obscene materials, or misappropriating the rights of others? Are visitors required to specifically agree not to publish, post, or display defamatory, profane, sexually explicit, racially offensive, or illegal materials? The terms and service agreement may also seek indemnity for any losses, costs, or damages arising out of the misuse or abuse of the chat room. Does the company reserve the right to terminate access to the chat room at any time, for any or for no reason? Even though torts may not be limited or disclaimed, you may obtain indemnification for users who cause torts to third parties. A company may limit or disclaim liability for economic losses due to negligent design or operation of the web site. Any web site operator should meet or exceed industry standards for information security for and the design and operation of its web site.

5. Does your company have exposure to business torts? Are your competitors intentionally and improperly competing with your online business? The most common online business torts are fraud or misrepresentation, unfair competition, breach of fiduciary duty, interference with contract, and interference with prospective contractual relation.

6. Does your company have a regularly updated, comprehensive e-mail and Internet usage policy? Are these policies part of an enterprise-wide training program? Employees must be trained in the proper use of e-mail and the Internet. An e-mail and Internet usage policy should be instituted and continually updated. Employers may not have an unfettered right to monitor employees' Internet usage or e-mail in European countries.

---

[192] The "economic loss" rule is a court-constructed doctrine restricting recovery in strict product liability cases to the consequences of defective products that cause personal injury. Strict product liability lawsuits may not be filed where the injury is only to the product itself or consists only of economic losses, such as lost profits.

7. Are Internet security measures tailored to your company's web site? Has your company installed the latest antiviral software and a training program to minimize viruses? Does your company disclaim the warranty for viruses in all software downloadable from your site? The latest antiviral software programs must be updated regularly. Employees must be instructed on the perils of down-loading files from unknown or questionable sources. Do you disclaim or limit consequential damages or warranties for the introduction of viruses that destroy data or information? Train employees to avoid viruses caused by opening unknown e-mail messages. Educate employees on how to remove viruses promptly. Create a data recovery plan to minimize losses due to viruses.

8. Is your company liable to third parties or independent contractors? A company should obtain indemnification and hold harmless agreements from web site developers, consultants, partners, employees, and third parties. The goal is to use contractual means to reduce vicarious liability for torts committed by others. An online company is liable for the torts of its employees but not, in most cases, of independent contractors. You may wish to structure contracts as independent contractor relationships versus employment relationships. A company will be vicariously liable for an independent contractor's torts for nondelegable duties.

9. Monitor incoming spam or unsolicited e-mail. Incorporate screening software if necessary. You may have a cause of action when third parties send unsolicited e-mail to employees. Create a policy against unauthorized and unsolicited bulk e-mail advertisements sent to employees. You may charge the spammer with false designation of origin when false headers are used to reach employees. Also, a company may charge spammers with a variety of other torts stemming from the spammer's impairment of its computer facilities. On the other side, your company may be liable for trespass to chattels for sending unsolicited e-mail advertisements to subscribers of online services.

10. Does your company have and enforce a computer security policy? A company may be found negligent for using outdated security measures that permit a hacker to compromise the data of a third party, especially where there is a heightened duty. Web site operators should monitor their web sites to promptly detect and respond to intrusions or attacks on the computer system. Companies need a strong recordkeeping system to detect and avoid information security breaches that may trigger a negligence action from third parties. Additionally, a close relationship with law enforcement can minimize the consequences of intrusions to a computer system or web site. Prompt investigations and responses will make it more likely that the company can find third parties using anonymous remailers or servers to commit torts against the company. Also, institute password or other information security controls for access. Keep in mind that a company may be liable to third parties for unwittingly disclosing confidential information, such as trade secrets. Have precautions in place to protect the personal data of customers, employees, and third parties. Companies must use reasonable procedures to protect personal data or be subject to economic losses caused by impostors and other wrongdoers. Do your security administrators have continuous contact with information services providing valuable security, hacking, and virus alerts? Can you show diligence in acting on this type of information?

11. Has your company completed a preventive law audit to minimize and assess tort liability? If your company has been sued, has it taken corrective action to promptly mitigate the cost of injury? If the company has prior knowledge of the tortious activities of its employees but takes no action, it may be exposed to tort damages, including punitive damages. A preventive law audit provides some evidence that the company is not recklessly indifferent to the public, thus precluding or mitigating punitive damages exposure. Companies that promptly undertake corrective action have, in effect, an early warning system against tort liability. Delay, neglect, and cover-ups are highly correlated with the imposition of punitive damages.

12. Do your company's business contracts take into account online issues? As in the brick-and-mortar world, most of a company's tort liability will stem from business contracts and torts. Review your business contracts to be sure that you are treating competitors, partners, and others fairly. Do not interfere with the contractual relationships of other parties. If you have an online partnership, you may be held to a higher duty of loyalty. The breach of fiduciary duty is commonly asserted in a wide variety of online activities. Companies must monitor their business contracts to be certain that deceptive or opportunistic conduct does not subject the company to punitive damages in class action lawsuits.

13. Does your Internet usage policy advise employees about the sanctions for posting derogatory messages? An Internet usage or e-mail policy will reduce the radius of the risk of a company being liable for libelous statements made in public forums by company employees. E-mail messages or Internet postings about another company's stock prices or lawsuits or any other derogatory information may expose your company to defamation lawsuits.[193] An online company should regularly monitor anticompany sites, that may be transmitting defamatory, false, or misleading messages. Procter & Gamble, for example, has long been hounded by false rumors about some of its products. A company that is too aggressive in silencing Internet critics, however, may suffer adverse publicity.[194]

Your company should include a prohibition against online harassment in its e-mail or Internet usage policies. Pornographic images left on computer screens may, for example, be evidence of a hostile workplace. Title VII of the Civil Rights Act of 1964 makes it unlawful to discriminate against an individual in an employment setting because of sex or race. The use of e-mail to sexually harass co-

---

[193] CNET.COM, Telco Files Net Defamation Suit, CNET.COM NEWS, May 29, 1999 (visited Feb. 24, 2000), http://news.cnet.com/news/0-1005-200-343372.htm?tag=.

[194] The Internet, by its very nature, makes it relatively easy to mount a protest campaign against a company for overreaching in its pursuit of legal rights. Archie Comics sent a cease and desist letter to the domain name owner of Veronica.com because the domain allegedly infringed the comic book character, Veronica. It turned out that the owner of the Veronica.com domain name had registered it for his infant daughter named Veronica. Archie Comics dropped the infringement claim in the wake of a wave of criticism on Internet listservs.

employees is common in today's online environment. In addition to Title VII, companies may be liable directly for the tort of outrage because of objectionable online conduct. A company's liability for the tort of the intentional infliction of emotional distress may be based on a reckless retention of a known harasser. In addition, a company may be directly liable for negligent hiring or retention where there are prior similar incidents of harassment. The use of the Internet or e-mail to sexually harass co-employees may be minimized by prompt progressive discipline against offenders. A company may make a decision to monitor e-mail or Internet usage, but this step should not be taken unless employees receive notice.

14. Does your company have a system for the retention and destruction of electronic documents? A company may be exposed to liability for the deliberate destruction, alteration, or failure to preserve essential evidence in the event of a lawsuit. Companies risk liability for the spoliation of evidence as well as discovery sanctions or criminal penalties for the deliberate destruction. Do you have a shadow or dark site offline that contains key business information in the event your web site is destroyed or altered by hackers?[195]

15. Has your company received clearance from all living persons depicted in web site images who have a right to publicity or to privacy? Have all depicted persons sign a release form allowing the site to transmit online pictures, photographs, or other images? Obtain a release even if the photograph shows just a portion of a person's face or body.[196] If you are using photographs from third parties, have them provide copies of the release and indemnification.

16. Does the web site potentially infringe celebrities' right to publicity? Do not use celebrity look-alikes without permission.[197] Several celebrities have successfully sued companies for right to publicity for using their depicted characters without permission.[198] Images that bear a remote resemblance to a famous personality may trigger a right to publicity lawsuit. Consult an intellectual property specialist if the web site designer wants to use a celebrity look-alike or parody.

17. Do your e-contracts have a clause that holds vendors responsible for any security breach caused by defects in software? If you are a software vendor, do your contracts disclaim warranties or limit remedies for security breaches?

18. Does your company have adequate disaster recovery and database backups? Do you have software that permits backup data to be utilized and

---

[195] Armor, *supra* note 1 (recommending a dark site containing important business information as a disaster recovery method).

[196] *See* Cohen v. Herbal Concepts, Inc., 63 N.Y.2d 379, 472 N.E. 2d 307, 482 N.Y.S. 2d 457 (1984) (holding image of woman and child's bare backs constituted unauthorized use).

[197] *See generally* Onassis v. Christian Dior-New York, Inc., 1984, 122 Misc. 2d 603, 472 N.Y.S.2d 254, affirmed 110 A.D.2d 1095, 488 N.Y.S.2d 943 (observing model in perfume advertisement had close resemblance to Jackie Onassis); *see also* Hoffman v. Capital Cities ABC, Inc., 33 F. Supp. 2d 867 (C.D. Cal. 1999) (affirming judgment in favor of actor Dustin Hoffman, whose face was used in a computer animation).

[198] *See* Allen v. Men's World Outlet, Inc., 679 F. Supp. 360 (S.D. N.Y. 1988) (finding likelihood of confusion in advertisement using Woody Allen look-alike despite disclaimer).

upgraded? Enterprise-class backups are easier to accomplish because of new backup options. A backup strategy must be calibrated to the type of data.[199]

19. Are you protecting data that are the crown jewels of your e-business? Is your Secure Sockets Layer Server (SSL) using adequate RSA keys? A recent survey of 137,000 SSLs found that 15 percent use RSA keys shorter than 900 bits. Short RSA keys are susceptible to being compromised.[200] Short RSA keys may also subject an e-business to negligent Internet security claims.

20. Has your e-business determined the size of the backup window? Full backups may be done every two hours. A company should determine whether a once-a-week full backup is adequate. Presently, storage technologies account for two-thirds of "an average enterprise's IT budget."[201]

21. Have you tested your systems' ability to restore data? How much downtime is acceptable in your backup plan?[202]

22. Is your company prepared for hacker attacks on routers? The chief router vulnerability is in the Border Gateway Protocol, "which is the routing tables from different vendors' equipment."[203] The hacker uses false tables defining invalid paths to clients to divert traffic to an "Internet wasteland."[204] It may be necessary to add additional layers of authentication on routers using public key infrastructure (PKI) technology.[205]

23. Has your company reviewed the Rome II rules on noncontractual obligations? The concept of noncontractual obligations parallels the American law of torts. Noncontractual obligations would cover damages caused by defective products.

[G] Internet Advertising Overview[206]

Online advertising is an inexpensive method of reaching a vast audience of potential customers. The web is a worldwide venue, however, and advertising on it may subject a company to consumer or other substantive laws in hundreds of countries.[207] Cultural sensitivities may create new risks for the online advertiser. Regulators in France, for example, fined the Italian firm Bennetton for an advertisement "exploiting the suffering of AIDS victims."[208] The same rules that apply

---

[199] Henry Baltazar, Extreme Backup, EWEEK, Apr. 15, 2002, at 43.

[200] Dennis Fisher, SSL Keys Coming Up Short: Netcraft Survey Shows 15 Percent of U.S. Servers Use RSA Keys That Are Shorter Than Maximum, EWEEK, Apr. 15, 2002, at 30.

[201] Anne Chen, Backup Window Shrinks But Not the Cost, EWEEK, Apr. 15, 2002, at 44.

[202] *Id.* at 46.

[203] Rutrell Yasin, Latest Hacker Target: Routers, Internet Wk., Dec. 17, 2001, at 9.

[204] *Id.* at 9 (citing CERT Coordination Center advisory).

[205] *Id.* (noting how BGP routing protocol diverts replies and "inserts bogus BGP table defining invalid path to client").

[206] *See also* § 2.05.

[207] *Id.*

[208] *Id.*

to other forms of advertising apply to electronic marketing.[209] The following checklist can help you identify any issues that could contravene some fundamental areas of advertising law.

[1] Internet Advertisement General Checklist

INTERNET ADVERTISEMENT CHECKLIST

1. Has an audit of legal risks been completed before launching online advertisement campaigns?

2. Disclosures must be made to prevent online advertisements from being misleading, unfair, or deceptive. Disclaimers must be clear and conspicuous. The disclosures should be prominently displayed on the web site.[210]

3. Are your online advertisements clear and conspicuous? The FTC recommends placing disclosures near or on the "same screen as the triggering claim."[211] Use text or cues to encourage consumers to scroll down, when necessary, to view a disclosure. Make links obvious and label them appropriately. Use consistent hyperlink styles. Place hyperlinks near relevant information. Make links noticeable. Monitor click through rates. Make appropriate changes to make disclosures clear and conspicuous. Take into account framing and other limitations when making online disclosures. Display disclosures prior to purchase. Make disclosures clear when working in conjunction with banner advertisements.[212]

4. Have you minimized the possibility that your advertising will be regarded as spamming? Are e-mail advertisements or postings to listservs violating antispam laws or netiquette?[213]

5. Does the online advertiser have the copyright, trademark, right of publicity, and right of privacy clearances on any content incorporated in an online advertisement? If an online advertisement contains photographs, music, stills, video, or other copyrighted material, does the advertiser have the proper intellectual property rights? Will any third party providing content indemnify and hold harmless the web site owner for any third party infringement claims?

---

[209] Federal Trade Commission, Advertising and Marketing on the Internet: The Rules of the Road, Apr. 1998 (visited June 8, 2002), http://www.ftc.gov/bcp/conline/pubs/buspubs/ruleroad.htm.

[210] Federal Trade Commission, Advertising and Marketing on the Internet: The Rules of the Road (visited June 8, 2002), http://www.ftc.gov/bcp/conline/pubs/buspubs/ruleroad.html.

[211] *Id.*

[212] *Id.*

[213] The term *netiquette* refers to the informal norms governing appropriate conduct on a listserv, chat room, or other online forum. Sending unsolicited e-mail advertisements or disseminating advertisements to unrelated listservs will provoke a backlash among Internet users, if not a lawsuit for spamming. Internet service providers such as America Online or CompuServe will frequently enjoin online advertisers for sending unsolicited e-mail to subscribers. The courts reject advertisers' claims that they have a First Amendment right to send unsolicited e-mail. *See, e.g.,* CyberPromotions, Inc. v. America Online, 24 Med. L. Rptr. 2505 (E.D. Pa. 1996).

6. If you list prices, do they match your current price list? Keep all of your information up to date. You do not want to accidentally sell your products at last year's prices or at prices that conflict with your traditional retail strategy. Your pricing must take into account profit margins. Do not charge the customer a higher price than that appearing on your web site. Post your pricing policy, letting consumers know that prices are subject to change without notice and disclaiming liability for typographical errors. If your programmer drops a zero from the price of your product, it could be a costly problem if you did not disclaim liability for the error. Make disclosures noticeable in terms of size, color, and graphics in context with overall web page.[214] Repeat disclosures in lengthy sites.[215] Use audio or video disclosures so the consumer can easily understand them. Use clear language and syntax.[216]

7. Review entire web sites. Are all Internet advertisements nondeceptive and claims backed up by firm substantiation? Internet advertisements must be truthful, not misleading, and not unfair. The Federal Trade Commission (FTC) requires advertising claims be substantiated, especially those concerning health, safety, or performance.[217] The FTC found that Listerine's statements about promising fewer colds was not substantiated.[218] The FTC and other domestic and foreign agencies comb the web for deceptive advertising.[219] Section 5 of the Federal Trade Commission Act gives the FTC the power "to prevent deceptive and unfair acts or practices."[220] The FTC considers a representation, omission, or practice to be deceptive if it is likely to "(1) mislead consumers; and (2) affect consumers' behavior or decisions about the product or service."[221] The FTC considers an act or practice unfair if the injury it causes or is likely to cause is "(1) substantial, (2) not outweighed by other benefits, and (3) not reasonably avoidable."[222] Avoid any deceptive advertising, including unfair comparisons, exaggerations, or other claims that cannot be substantiated by scientific fact.[223] The FTC does regulate advertisements that go to the "basis of the bargain," not seller's talk or "puffery."[224] *Puffery* means an expression of opinion rather than a statement of fact.[225] A company claiming that its computers are compatible with all personal computer peripherals should clarify

---

[214] *Id.*

[215] *Id.*

[216] *Id.*

[217] Federal Trade Commission, *supra* note 210.

[218] Warner Lambert, 86 F.T.C. 1398, (1975), aff'd, 562 F.2d 749 (D.C. Cir. 1977).

[219] Federal Trade Commission *supra* note 210; *see also* In the Matter of DoubleClick, Inc., FTC Complaint (filed Feb. 10, 2000) (reporting FTC action for company's misuse of cookies in creating profiles of users), reported in Perkins Coie L.L.P. Internet Case Digest (visited June 15, 2002), http: www.perkinscoie.com/casedigest.

[220] *Id.*

[221] *Id.*

[222] *Id.*

[223] *Id.*

[224] Section 2-313 of Article 2 of the UCC addresses express warranties defined as statements of facts about goods that go to the basis of the bargain, in contrast to mere seller's talk.

[225] Wilmington Chemical, 69 F.T.C. 828, 865 (1966).

the limits of compatibility, noting, for example, that the products may not work with older computers or with new, unanticipated technologies. Clearly list all potential costs and do not leave out any hidden charges, including shipping, handling, or taxes.[226]

8. Does your company make product comparisons that mention other brands? Are comparisons fair and backed up by substantial evidence? Comparative advertising is a well-established practice in the United States, but it is prohibited in a number of European countries. Avoid listing your competitors' names or brands on your web site.[227] It may be an invitation to a legal dispute. Some countries do not look favorably on product comparisons. A trademark holder may not prevent the use of words necessary to communicate ideas, however.[228] Product comparisons are generally considered fair use under the trademark law.[229]

9. Does scientific testing support all product and service comparisons? If you post product comparisons or claims, make sure that you have the data to back up the claims.[230] It may be helpful to put a link leading to specifics about the tests (for example, date of testing, agency conducting the tests, numeric results, and so on).

10. Demonstrations must depict product performance under conditions of normal use.[231] Do not make questionable claims about performance of software or other products sold online. Stick to performance claims, which are supported by empirical studies or other scientific data.

11. The web site must comply with local, state, federal, and international regulations governing sweepstakes or games of chance. Are online advertising campaigns regarded as lotteries subject to state, federal, or international law? Is the web site designed to screen out visitors from jurisdictions where sweepstakes or games of chance are illegal? Does the web site post notices that sweepstakes or games of chance are not directed to jurisdictions where these activities are illegal?

12. Does your company sell advertising space on your web site to other companies? Have you obtained warranties, indemnification, and hold harmless clauses that advertising content will not lead to third-party claims? A company

---

[226] Id.

[227] See Lanham Act, 15 U.S.C. §§ 1114, 1125(a) (1998); Abbott Laboratories v. Mead Johnson & Co. 971 F.2d 6, 16 (7th Cir. 1992); see also Bitlaw, Trademarks on the Internet (last visited June 15, 2002), http://www.bitlaw.com/trademark/internet.html#discovery.

[228] See New Kids on the Block v. News America Publishing, Inc., 971 F.2d 302, 308 (9th Cir. 1992) (holding that newspaper could print trademarked name of musical band to identify band).

[229] The fair use test consists of three factors: (a) the product must be one not readily identifiable without the use of the trademark; (b) only so much of the mark may be used as is reasonably necessary; and (c) the user must not suggest sponsorship or endorsement. Playboy Enterprises International v. Netscape, 55 F. Supp. 2d 1070, 1084 (C.D. Cal. 1999).

[230] Abbott Laboratories v. Mead Johnson & Co. 971 F.2d 6, 16 (7th Cir. Ind.) (holding that statements technically true may nevertheless be misleading).

[231] Federal Trade Commission, *supra* note 210.

may be liable for reviewing the claims in the advertisements of other parties. The FTC maintains that advertisers or web site designers "are responsible for reviewing the information used to substantiate ad claims [and] may not simply rely on an advertiser's assurance that the claims are substantiated."[232]

13. Has your company purchased advertising space from another web site? Have you obtained indemnification or hold harmless clauses for third party-actions? Is the pricing based on impression rates, clickthrough rates, or actual sales? How will your advertising message be displayed?

14. Does your company comply with state antispam statutes? The typical antispam statute forbids the online advertiser from masquerading as a third party by using false headers. e-mail addresses, or the domain name of a third party without permission.[233]

15. If you have a refund policy, refunds must be made available to dissatisfied online consumers.[234]

16. Your company must have a reasonable basis for stating or implying that your products can be shipped within a certain time. The FTC's Mail or Telephone Order Merchandise Rule states that if you can't ship when promised, you must send customers a notice advising them of the delay and of their right to cancel.[235] It is likely that the FTC Mail or Telephone Order Merchandise Rule applies to Internet sales.

[2]   Internet Advertisement Checklist for Lawyers

INTERNET ADVERTISEMENT CHECKLIST FOR LAWYERS

1. Does your web site comply with your state's ethical requirements? As a matter of practice, your webmaster should understand what the ethical and professional responsibility requirements are for a web site within your jurisdiction. Additionally, certain jurisdictions require that all changes to the web site be saved and stored for a period of time.

2. Does the a visitor know where you or your firm is licensed? Your law firm should indicate which states you are licensed to practice in. This information should be very clearly noted and highly visible. Furthermore, your law firm web site should clearly state that the web site is not intended to give legal advice.

3. Does the person you are communicating with know that you are a lawyer? Always consider how and where you meet someone on the Internet. The context and forum in which you interact with people is very important. For exam-

---

[232] *Id.*

[233] E. Gabriel Perle, et al., Electronic Publishing & Software: Part III, 17 The Computer Lawyer 27 (Mar. 2000).

[234] Federal Trade Commission, *supra* note 210.

[235] *Id.*

ple, if you casually enter a chat room, you should exercise a high degree of discretion in terms of what you are saying. You should make it clear whether you are giving friendly advice or actual legal advice.

4. How do you ensure your conversations are secure? There is always an element of risk that someone can eavesdrop on your conversations. However, lawyers should use good judgment and for all confidential information use private e-mails, virtual private networks, and encryption technology.

5. Do you really know who your client is? The Internet can bring you many potential clients. While this may seem like a blessing, lawyers should always do appropriate background checks on their clients—this includes conflict checks and the like.

6. Are you retaining records of your Internet advertisements and web site in compliance with your state's requirements?

[H] Internet Taxation[236]

President Clinton originally signed the Internet Tax Freedom Act into law on October 21, 1998, and it was extended by President Bush until 2005. The Internet Tax Freedom Act imposes a moratorium on certain state and local taxes associated with Internet or e-commerce sales or services. The Act established an Advisory Commission on Electronic Commerce, which made recommendations on issues such as sales and use taxes on Internet sales. The Commission also made recommendations on international tariffs on electronic transmissions. States are considering new proposals to collect sales taxes.

Contrary to popular opinion, the Internet is not tax-free. "Sales tax for items purchased online works exactly like it does for other mail order purchases."[237] On May 30, 2000, California proposed a statute that clarifies its existing rules governing Internet taxation. The proposed statute "would not tax sales from companies that have no brick and mortar stores or warehouses in the state."[238] California would require book retailers and others with stores or warehouses in the state to collect sales taxes on the Internet.[239]

The rules governing taxation are complex: taxes are generally based, however, on value. A good e-business tax advisor will enable you to control where value is created. Careful consideration of tax issues in the planning stages of your enterprise can yield significant benefits to your company in the form of its e-business structure, distribution plan, and sales model. Careful consideration of tax issues from the beginning will help you avoid problems later.

---

[236] *See* § 6.07.

[237] Ann Kandra, Tax-Free Internet? Don't Count on It? PC World 39 (June 2000).

[238] Reuters News Service, California Assembly Approves Internet Tax Measure, May 30, 2000 (visited June 1, 2000), http://legalnews.findlaw.com/legalnews/s/20000530/economycaliforniainternet.html.

[239] *Id.*

INTERNET TAXATION CHECKLIST

1. What are your tax footprints? Can you easily create a taxable nexus? Remember that a single telecommuting employee can trigger a significant tax liability. Employees, agents, or partners can create a tax footprint, so outsourcing some of the company's work may reduce the tax footprint. Strategic planning in advance will help limit your organization's tax liability. Cisco Systems is a good example of smart planning by an Internet-enabled company. Cisco claims that it transacts 85 percent of its orders and 82 percent of its customer inquiries over the Internet. Cisco can close its books in one day, and, using the Internet, it can manage 37 manufacturing plants around the world, only two of which it owns.

2. Does your organization have inventory? Is that inventory a significant income-producing factor? Remember the restaurant example and check the law. It pays to know the tax law in the jurisdictions in which you conduct business.

3. Do you distinguish the character of your products from that of your services? You could sell your products separately from your services. Sell the computer without the support and charge separately for support services. Selling set-top boxes to allow access to the Internet yields a wholly taxable product sale. Giving away free set-top boxes and assessing a charge for Internet access services is a better tax decision.

4. Where do online sales occur? Many transactions involve service providers in one jurisdiction, consumers in another, billing in a third, and distribution of products in yet a fourth jurisdiction. Could each one of these jurisdictions impose a tax on the transaction for sales and use tax purposes?

5. Who is the customer? Where does the customer live? If a customer's e-mail address is *cdaftary@aol.com,* can AOL's proprietary database be accessed in order to obtain the location of the consumer? What happens if the company does not have a process to identify the different locations of its customers, and this inability results in errors in the amount of sales tax charged?

6. Which jurisdiction has the authority to tax an online commercial or consumer sales or service? Is the authority based on the location of the customer, the jurisdiction that distributes the product or service, the jurisdiction of the server that hosts the web site, or within the jurisdiction that issued the bill?

7. What types of online transactions are acceptable to be subject to sales and use taxes? Is the transaction a sale of tangible property, of services, or of intangible property? Can the sale of tangible property, services, or intangible property be subject to or exempt from tax? Does nexus have to be established before imposing such a tax? Does the presence of a web page located on a server create nexus, or is nexus possibly established in the state in which the vendor has access to the Internet via an ISP or OSP?

8. Is there sufficient documentation detailing the taxable transaction? What records do taxing authorities require? Is there an audit trail? How long should electronic records be retained? Is an off-site storage facility, such as a SAN, necessary for storing duplicate records?

9. Where are your employees, center of manufacturing, and distribution centers? Where is your company's taxable nexus? Can outsourcing be used to limit your company's tax liability?

10. Does your company have inventory? Many dot-com companies have no inventory, which may be a significant income-producing factor.

11. Are you clearly distinguishing sales from services? If you sell a computer without support or charge separately for support services, the transaction is completely taxable. A few companies give away free set-top boxes with a charge for Internet access services, which reduces tax liabilities.

12. Has your company made a decision on how to deliver products or services? Tax liabilities frequently turn on whether a transaction is structured as a sale or a service. Many states also base tax liabilities on whether computer software is classifiable as tangible goods or as an intangible information product. Software downloadable on a web site does not involve the transfer of tangible goods. The value of software sold in a store lies not in the diskette or CD-ROM but in the information embedded on the media. Software downloadable at a web site may have a limited tax footprint. In many jurisdictions, no tax will apply to downloads.

13. Is there a uniform structure or simplified method of complying with sales taxes? The National Governors' Association is calling for the development of a system through which goods or services may be taxed in a uniform and consistent way across state lines.[240] At present, the state tax system is unable to prevent discriminatory or multiple taxation. Another problem for state governments is that no mechanism compels remote Internet sellers to collect state taxes.[241] The National Governors' Association has recently proposed exempting small companies (with annual gross sales between $100,000 and $200,000) from collecting state sales taxes on out-of-state sales.[242] Online companies will need to closely follow state tax liabilities especially where remote sellers are required to collect sales taxes for any state.[243] The Internet Tax Freedom Act established a moratorium on special, multiple, and discriminatory taxes on e-commerce at the federal, state, and local levels.[244]

14. Your web site needs a software program that computes and displays sales taxes online. Many web sites do not display the sales tax, but, rather, compute the sales tax in back-room processing.[245]

15. Are there any ways to sidestep taxes? The use tax can be avoided by downloading software, for example.[246] A growing number of e-commerce companies with "facilities in many states sidestep sales taxes by setting up separate companies

---

[240] National Governors' Association, NGA Policy: Streamlining State Sales Tax Systems Answers the Questions (visited June 15, 2002), http://www.nga.org/nga/salestax/1,1169,,00.html.

[241] *Id.*

[242] *Id.*

[243] *Id.*

[244] Internet Tax Freedom Act, Pub. L. No. 105-277, § 1101(a) (Oct. 21, 1998).

[245] Kandra, *supra* note 237.

[246] *Id.*

to handle e-commerce."[247] An online company may need to be formed as a separate corporation for tax planning purposes.

16. What are the tax implications if there are currency conversion errors?

[I]   Online Contract Formation[248]

UCC Article 2 governs the commercial sale of goods, whereas the Uniform Computer Information Transactions Act (UCITA) was designed to apply to information licenses, including Internet-related software contracts. UCITA's rules closely parallel those of Article 2 because the drafters originally sought to make software licensing part of the Uniform Commercial Code.[249] In July 1999, the National Conference of Uniform State Law Commissioners approved UCITA for introduction into the states as a stand-alone statute. UCITA tailored Article 2 to fit software, multimedia contracts, access contracts, and other online transactions. As of May 2000, Maryland and Virginia were the only states to have enacted UCITA. In states that have not enacted UCITA, courts will apply Article 2 by analogy to software licenses, access contracts, and other Internet-related agreements.

SCOPE OF ONLINE CONTRACTS CHECKLIST

1. How do you identify and authenticate online customers? How does the company ensure that its customer have the capacity to enter into online contracts?

2. What constitutes a contract in an electronic environment? What constitutes reliable documentation/evidence for legal purposes? Can any of the terms be negotiated? Should certain contractual arrangements be precluded from online negotiations?

3. What law applies to online contracts? Article 2 of the Uniform Commercial Code provides a set of default rules for the sale of goods. Article 2 applies to "transactions in goods," which makes it clear that Article 2 may be extended to transactions in which there is no technical transfer of title.[250] The Uniform Computer Information Transactions Act (UCITA) deals with computer information transactions involving the creation, modification, licensing, and distribution of

---

[247] *Id.* (noting that Barnes & Noble's bn.com web site is structured as a separate corporation so that only the residents of the four states in which Barnes & Noble has warehouses or offices will be assessed sales tax for Internet sales).

[248] For a complete discussion of electronic contract issues, *see* Chapter Six.

[249] UCITA is a stand-alone statute that evolved from a project to make Article 2B, dealing with information transactions, part of the Uniform Commercial Code. The proposed Article 2B would have expanded the scope of the code to include software contracts, online contracts, webwrap contracts, access contracts, and other information contracts. UCITA, like its predecessor, applies to computer information transactions.

[250] 1 Ronald A. Anderson, Uniform Commercial Code § 2-102.4 (3d ed. 1981).

computer information.[251] An online contract involving both goods and services is a hybrid transaction that may be subject to more than one branch of law. Article 2 applies if goods are movable at the time of identification.[252]

4. Does UCITA apply to software licenses, clickwrap agreements, or other Internet-related transactions? Is your information protected by disclaimers and limitations of liability that comply with the dictates of Article 2 of the UCC? Counsel representing licensors may want citations to UCITA as a way for courts to adapt Article 2 to cyberspace. Section 1-105 permits the parties to a UCC transaction to choose the applicable law, providing it has a reasonable relationship to the contract. The parties are generally free to choose to apply UCITA, the Convention for the International Sale of Goods (CISG), or some hybrid body of law in place of Article 2. CISG excludes any "contract in which the preponderant part of the obligation . . . consists in the supply of labor or other services."[253] Supplementary principles of law and equity may apply to a commercial transaction.[254] UCITA is a set of default rules for Internet licenses that may be varied by agreement. Do your mass-market license agreements comply with the protections provided licensees in UCITA?

UCITA Contract Formation Checklist

(a) UCITA applies to computer information transactions.[255] Determine whether your transaction is governed by UCITA. UCITA does not apply to financial services, audio, cable, satellite, and entertainment services.[256] Although only Virginia and Maryland have enacted UCITA, courts may apply UCITA by analogy. UCITA does not apply to software embedded in goods such as automobile brakes.

(b) A term of license agreements may not create a result contrary to public policy.[257] Little case law covers what terms might be deemed to violate a fundamental public policy. A clause in a license agreement that prohibits negative reviews of software would likely be unenforceable for public policy reasons.

(c) Online license agreements may not be enforced if they conflict with a consumer protection statute or administrative rule.[258] Online sales of computer hardware that incorporates software must comply with federal

---

[251] UCITA § 103 Official Comment 1 (NCCUSL Draft for Approval, July 1999). *See,* What is UCITA (visited Oct. 2, 2000) http:www.UCITAonline.com.

[252] UCC § 2-105 (2000).

[253] CISG art. 3(2) (2000).

[254] UCC § 103 (2000).

[255] UCITA § 103(a).

[256] The term "computer information transactions" is broad enough to encompass many Internet-related contracts. Section 103(d) provides exclusions or carve-outs for UCITA. *See* UCITA, § 103(d).

[257] UCITA, § 105(b).

[258] *Id.* § 105(c).

warranty laws, such as the Magnuson-Moss Act. It is unclear whether the Magnuson-Moss Act applies to software since the federal warranty act applies to consumer goods, not intangibles.

(d) Incorporate a choice of law and forum selection clause in every computer information license agreement for the transfer of software or other information. In the absence of an agreement, access contracts such as Lexis-Nexis or the law where the licensor is located will govern. Minnesota law, for example, would govern Westlaw, whereas Ohio law would construe Lex-isNexis access contracts.[259]

(e) If a commercial transaction involves both software and goods, UCITA will apply only to the part of the transaction dealing with software.[260] However, if the predominant purpose of a mixed transaction is the licensing of information, UCITA will apply to the whole transaction.

(f) Choice of law may not be enforceable for consumer contracts. A choice of law is not enforceable in a consumer contract to the extent that "it would vary a rule that may not be varied by an agreement."[261] An online "consumer contract that requires delivery of a copy on a tangible medium is governed by the law of the jurisdiction in which the copy is or should have been delivered to the consumer."[262] The parties may opt in or opt out of UCITA except in mass-market transactions, where "opt-outs" must be "conspicuous."

(g) Parties may generally "choose an exclusive judicial forum unless the choice is unreasonable and unjust."[263] The choice of forum clause must explicitly state that the judicial forum is exclusive if it is to be enforced.[264]

(h) Courts will refuse to enforce unconscionable terms in online license agreements.[265] The court must afford parties an opportunity to present evidence of commercial setting, purpose, and effect of allegedly unconscionable clauses.[266] UCITA preserves state and federal consumer protection statutes.

(i) Online contracts should be structured so that a person has an opportunity to review contractual terms before payment.[267] If there is no opportunity to review the terms before a person has an obligation to pay, the person must have the right to a refund.[268] The manifestation of assent may be

---

[259] *See id.* § 109(b)(1).

[260] *Id.* § 103(b)(1).

[261] *Id.* § 109(a).

[262] *Id.* § 109(b)(2).

[263] *Id.* § 110(a). *See* Henry K. Lee, Judge Calls AOL Litigation Terms Unfair, 5 S.F. Chronicle, Sept. 28, 2000 (reporting California court's refusal to order transfer of lawsuit filed by AOL users to Virginia because it would be unfair and unreasonable).

[264] *Id.* § 110(b).

[265] *Id.* § 111.

[266] *Id.* § 111(b).

[267] *Id.* § 112.

[268] *Id.* § 112(e).

achieved through the use of electronic agents. There is no manifestation of assent in the absence of an opportunity to review the record.[269] An electronic record is given the same validity as a writing.

(j) Freedom of contract permits any provision of UCITA to be varied by agreement except the obligations of good faith, diligence, reasonableness, and due care or negligence.[270] In addition, the limits on enforceability imposed by unconscionability or fundamental public policy may not be waived or varied by agreement.[271] UCITA also places limits on agreed choice of law, choice of forum, the requirements for manifesting assent, and the opportunity for review.[272] UCITA's mandatory consumer protection rules may not be disclaimed, including limitations on self-help measures such as disabling the software.[273]

(k) A good faith as well as supplemental principle of law and equity applies to UCITA transactions. In addition, commercial reasonableness and usages of trade permeate every provision of UCITA.[274]

(l) Online contracts with a contract fee of $5,000 or more must be authenticated by a record indicating that the contract has been formed.[275]

(m) Online "contracts may be formed in any manner sufficient to show agreement, including offer and acceptance or conduct of both parties or operations of electronic agents which recognize the existence of a contract."[276] Electronic agents may form contracts, but the court may grant relief from "fraud, electronic mistake or the like."[277] UCITA validates messages coming from electronic agents.

(n) The online site needs to establish the type of authentication or record acceptable to it.[278] A party adopts the terms of a record by manifesting assent to a record.[279] UCITA legally validates electronic records, electronic agents, and electronic authentication.[280]

(o) An online company should adopt a commercially reasonable attribution procedure or one approved by both parties.[281]

(p) In Internet-type transactions, a licensor must "afford an opportunity to review the terms of a standard form contract . . . before becoming

---

[269] *Id.* § 112(a).
[270] *Id.* § 113(a)(1).
[271] *Id.* § 113(a)(2).
[272] *Id.* § 113(3).
[273] *Id.* § 113(3)(A)-(J).
[274] *Id.* § 114.
[275] *Id.* § 201.
[276] *Id.* § 202.
[277] *Id.* § 206.
[278] *Id.* § 107.
[279] *Id.* § 208.
[280] *Id.* § 107.
[281] *Id.* § 108.

obligated to pay."[282] Standard terms "must be displayed prominently and in close proximity to a description of computer information."[283]

(q) Attribution procedures for commercial transactions must be commercially reasonable.[284]

(r) The mail box rule of the common law does not apply to online transactions: "Receipt of an electronic message is effective when received even if no individual is aware of its receipt."[285]

5. Consumer goods costing greater than $15 sold at the web site are subject to the federal Magnuson-Moss Act. The Magnuson-Moss Warranty Act applies to written warranties for goods used for personal, family, or household purposes. The FTC is considering expansion of the Magnuson-Moss Act to apply to mass-market software. The Magnuson-Moss Act applies "to written warranties on tangible personal property which is normally used for personal, family, or household purposes."[286] The Magnuson-Moss Act does not apply to business-to-business transactions. Web site warranties must be clearly and conspicuously differentiated or labeled as either "full warranty" or "limited warranty." Full warranty means that the seller is meeting the federal minimum standards.[287] If a full warranty is given, a warrantor must provide a minimum remedy without charge if the product does not conform to the written warranty.[288] Few, if any, online sellers will be willing to offer a full federal warranty. The full warranty obligates the supplier to correct defects, malfunctions, or nonconforming quality defects without charge. Full warrantors may not exclude or limit consequential damages for breach of warranty nor limit the duration of implied warranties.[289] If a full warranty is not given, the seller must "conspicuously designate it a 'limited warranty.'"[290]

Implied warranties of quality cannot be entirely disclaimed under the Act, but they may be limited in duration so long as the limitation is in "clear and unmistakable language and prominently displayed on the face of the warranty."[291] A seller may limit the duration of an implied warranty covered by the act. The Magnuson-Moss Act requires sellers to make other mandatory disclosures to consumer-buyers.[292] Warranties that violate the Magnuson-Moss Act are ineffective.[293]

6. Does a state's version of the Uniform Deceptive Trade Practices Act (UDTPA) apply to online agreements, clickwrap agreements, and other Inter-

---

[282] *Id.* § 211.

[283] *Id.* § 211(1)(A).

[284] *Id.* § 212.

[285] *Id.* § 215.

[286] 16 U.S.C., § 700.1 (2000).

[287] 15 U.S.C., § 2303 (2000).

[288] *Id.* § 2304.

[289] *Id.*

[290] *Id.* § 2308.

[291] *Id.*

[292] *Id.*

[293] *Id.* § 2308.

net-related web site practices? The UDTPA, unlike the UCC, provides remedies for attorneys' fees, costs, and double or treble damages in selected cases. The UDTPA may apply in cases of fraudulent or deceptive online business practices.

7. Does the United Nations Convention on Contracts for the International Sale of Goods (CISG) apply to nonconsumer sales of goods between parties in different signatory states? The United States signed CISG in 1988, and most industrialized countries are also signatories. CISG applies "to contracts of sale of goods between parties whose places of business are in different [signatory] states."[294] CISG does not apply to product liability actions for personal injury caused by goods.[295] In contrast, UCC Article 2 permits plaintiffs to recover damages for personal injury as a form of consequential damages.[296] The parties can opt-out of CISG or exclude the application of any of its applications.[297]

8. Do any of the Federal Trade Commission (FTC) regulations apply to online sales? Do your online sales and services comply with FTC regulations? The FTC is considering expanding its telemarketing rules to apply to Internet web sites. To be on the safe side, web sites should avoid Internet acts or practices that would be deceptive or unfair if done by a telemarketer. A web site must prominently disclose any material disclosures prior to a customer's payment for goods or services. In an online sale of goods, the customer must be given the total costs to purchase, receive, or use any goods or services.[298] The web site merchant must obtain express verifiable authorization for payment by check or negotiable instruments. FTC rules apply equally to e-commerce, as do state deceptive and unfair trade practices acts.

9. Does the web site comply with the Directive on Distance Selling and the Directive for Contracts for Financial Services? The European Union directives apply to contracts with consumers in European Community countries.[299] Are web site visitors given the right to reflect before concluding a contract with a supplier? The directives give consumers a right of withdrawal after reflection. Are consumers given the right to cancel financial services contracts within 14 days, or 30 days in the case of mortgage loans, life assurance, and operations pertaining to personal pensions?[300] The directives require a consumer's prior consent "for the use of automated distance communications systems without human intervention, such as faxes."[301] Member states "must ensure that adequate and effective complaints and redress procedures to [exist] settle disputes between suppliers and consumers."[302]

---

[294] CISG, art. 1.

[295] CISG, art. 5.

[296] UCC, § 2-715(2)(b) (2000)

[297] CISG, art. 6.

[298] Telemarketing Sales Rule, 16 C.F.R. § 310.3 (2000).

[299] *See, e.g.,* Directive 97/7/EC (prohibiting the supply of services without the consumer's specific and valid consent) (visited June 15, 2002), http://europa.eu.int/comm/internal_market/en/finances/consumer/fspropen.pdf.

[300] *Id.*

[301] *Id.*

[302] *Id.*

10. Are choice of forum clauses included in online contracts to reduce uncertainty about e-commerce jurisdiction? The parties are free to opt in or out of UCITA, subject to protections for mass-market transactions. Choice of law, forum, and venue clauses are used to reduce the uncertainty of doing business on the Internet. Choice of forum permits parties to reduce the probability of litigating in a distant forum. UCITA allows parties to a license agreement to choose an exclusive judicial forum unless it is "unjust." It is critical to state that the forum is exclusive. or courts may not enforce a choice of forum.

11. What contracts are required to launch the company's web site?

(a) Web Design and Hosting Agreement. Web design and hosting agreements are frequently entered into by small and medium companies.[303]

Web Design and Hosting Checklist

❏ Do you have a web design and hosting agreement? Who is bound by the agreement?

❏ Is there a clause creating a binding contract between the web designer and the customer?

❏ Is the description of services adequate? Does the host acquire the domain name on behalf of the customer?

❏ Is disk storage adequate for the web traffic and quantity of graphics, sound, and video files? Are e-mail autoresponders and forwarding included?

❏ Is the web traffic allowance adequate?

❏ Does pricing reflect expected traffic? Penalties may be assessed by your host if you exceed your traffic allowance, unless the parties otherwise agree. Length of service? Service start date? Renewal by client? Refund policy?

❏ Does the web site provide traffic reports?

❏ Is the setup fee reasonable? The monthly service fee? Does the cost reflect allowances for extra traffic? Is a shopping cart feature available? Real Audio support? CGI programming? Database services? What conditions govern web design and hosting?

❏ What warranties are given in the hosting agreement? Is there a waiver of damages as well as warranties? Is the host liable for the loss of data as the result of delays, nondeliveries, or service interruptions?

---

[303] *See, e.g.,* Aramedia.net, Virtual Web Hosting Agreement (visited Jan. 21, 2000), http://www.aramedia.net/agree.htm.

❒ Does the web host offer a domain name service?

❒ What is the payment term? Is there a set-up fee?

❒ Are cross-indemnities and hold harmless clauses included in the agreement?

❒ Has the online company reserved the right to approve changes in the terms of the agreement? Many web host agreements reserve the right to make changes to the terms and conditions of hosting agreements without notice to the company.

❒ Is there a merger clause?

❒ What are the events of termination? What law applies in the event of a dispute? Have both parties provided contact information?[304]

❒ Your web design and hosting agreement needs a contracting clause such as: "This agreement for web design and hosting is made and entered between Web Hosting Inc., located at 41 Temple Street, Boston, Massachusetts 02108-4977 and Suffolk Personal Computers, located at 120 Tremont Street, Boston, Massachusetts 02108-4977.

❒ Does the agreement contain delineation of responsibility for data privacy? In a hosting arrangement, your customers' data will reside on the hosts' equipment and may be accessible to them.

(b) Clickwrap License Agreements. Have clickwrap license agreements been developed for downloading software from the company's web site? A license agreement is a contract to use or access software. A licensor is the person who grants a right to use software, and the licensee is the party acquiring the right to use software for the terms of the license.[305] A clickwrap license is a standard form mass-market license entered into by web site visitors when they download software from a web site. A web site visitor may be asked to accept or decline terms with one click and then be asked to confirm with a second click that they are certain they accept. The "double click" method is designed to prevent a user from disaffirming the act of clicking through screens. Do clickwrap agreements comply with the prescriptions of UCITA in providing an opportunity to review terms as well as manifesting assent? A clickwrap agreement should be structured so that the visitor has an opportunity to review the terms prior to clicking the "I accept" icon or text. A single click on an icon or underlined text would satisfy UCITA's requirement of manifestation of assent. Terms of the license agreement should be available to the licensee prior to purchase. UCITA binds a party to the terms of a shrinkwrap or clickwrap agreement if the party had reason to know that

---

[304] *See, e.g.,* Online Solutions Web Hosting Reseller Agreement, Online Solutions Web Hosting Reseller Agreement (Jan. 21, 2000), http://www.onsol.com/reseller_agree.html.

[305] UCITA, § 102 (2001).

his or her acts would be treated as assent to the terms.[306] Mass-market licenses are adopted "only if the party agrees to the license, such as by manifesting assent, before or during the party's initial performance or use . . . or access to the information."[307] A company must afford a web site visitor "an opportunity to review the terms of a standard form license before the information is delivered or the licensee becomes obligated to pay, whichever comes first."[308]

(c) Webwrap Agreements. If a company does not give a web site visitor opportunity to review a mass-market license before becoming obligated to pay, is there a return policy giving the visitor the right to a refund, along with reasonable expenses? UCITA requires licensors to give licensees a refund along with reasonable expenses if software or information is delivered without giving a licensee an opportunity to review terms of a standard form agreement.[309]

(d) Internet-Related Licenses. Are the terms of Internet license agreements displayed prominently and in close proximity to the description of computer information? A company may also disclose "the availability of the standard terms in a prominent place on the site for which the computer information is offered."[310]

(e) Cross-Border Internet Sales Contracts. The Council of the European Union adopted a Directive on the Protection of Consumers in Respect of Distance Contracts.[311] Member states may determine the language used. If you are doing business with European Union states, consider web sites with different languages. Be sure that disclaimers and limitations of liability are accurately translated. The Distance Contract Directive was originally conceived for communications by telephone, where the consumer could not see the product. Where consumers cannot see the products, a right of withdrawal from the contract should be available.[312] An online business in the United States is subject to the Distance Selling Directive if it has a subsidiary in the consumer's country of residence.[313] The web site, as with any distance seller, "must provide consumers with notice of the provisions of the Directive and of codes of practice that may exist in this field."[314] An online contract qualifies as a "distance contract," which "means any contract concerning goods or services concluded between a supplier and a consumer under an organized sales or service-provision scheme run by the supplier."[315] A supplier "means

---

[306] UCITA, § 112.
[307] UCITA, § 210(a).
[308] UCITA, § 212(1).
[309] *Id.*
[310] UCITA, § 212(1)(b).
[311] EU Directive 97/7/EC, *supra* note 299.
[312] *Id.*
[313] *Id.*
[314] *Id.*
[315] *Id.* at art. 1.

any natural or legal person . . . conducting distance contracts in their professional or commercial capacities."[316] Written confirmation must be given to a consumer prior to conclusion of the contract.[317] At minimum, the confirmation for consumer contracts must contain the right of withdrawal, the geographical address of the supplier, information on services and guarantees, and the means for canceling a contract.[318] The right of withdrawal must exist for a period of at least 7 working days.[319] A supplier must execute an order within a period of 30 days from the time the consumer sends his or her order.[320] Member states are required to provide means for chargebacks and cancellations in the event of fraudulent use of credit cards.[321] Clickwrap or webwrap agreements may not be used to waive consumer rights.[322] In the United States, UCITA preserves state and federal consumer protection.

12. What forms of ongoing online contracts are necessary?

13. What service-level agreements are outlined for each vendor relationship?

Online Contract Checklist

(a) Conduct an audit of all online or Internet-related contracts. Update standard form contracts to fit the realities of online contracting. The first step in an online contracting audit is to do an inventory of all Internet-related agreements. Existing contracts may need tailoring to fit e-commerce transactions. Online companies typically have diverse means of contracting, including Private Virtual Area Networks, Internet e-mail, Internet web sites, direct dial, EDI, and FTP through the Internet or by fax. Of online companies selling goods, 28 percent sold them online; and many consumers have purchased goods online.[323] Parties enter online contracts through e-mail, mass-market, or standard form contracts; Electronic Data Interchange; customer data formats; web catalogs; or secure sockets via web site processing.[324] Many online contracts are never completed on paper forms or reduced to hard copies.

(b) Online offers and acceptance may be formed in any reasonable manner including by e-mail, computer-to-computer, or through webwrap agreements. Offers can invite acceptance by any reasonable manner. Revised

---

[316] *Id.* at art. 3

[317] *Id.* at art. 5(1)

[318] *Id.*

[319] *Id.* at art. 6.

[320] *Id.* at art. 7.

[321] *Id.* at art. 8.

[322] *Id.* at art. 12.

[323] American Bar Association, ABA/ACCA Survey of Electronic Commerce Practices (Jan. 17, 1999), http://abanet.org/scitech/abaacca.html.

[324] *Id.*

Article 2 of the UCC has updated rules validating online contracting, as does UCITA.

(c) Enter into enforceable online contracts. Online contracts may be signed with digital signatures in many jurisdictions. Structure online catalogues as "invitations to offer" rather than as offers. A company may use international certification networks when inviting offers in foreign countries. Vendors such as GlobalSign offer personal digital certificates for assuring the authenticity of electronic signatures.[325]

(d) Where appropriate, create computer-to-computer contracts without human review. Prior to the development of the Internet, Electronic Data Interchange (EDI) permitted orders to be filled computer-to-computer. Revised Article 2 of the UCC and the Uniform Computer Information Transaction Act permit the formation of online contracts. Electronic agents are computer programs that can be used to initiate an action or to respond to electronic records or performances. Electronic agents "with or without review or action may form contracts by an individual."[326] Revised Article 2, the Uniform Computer Transactions Act and the Uniform Electronic Transactions Act validate the concept of online computer-to-computer contracts. To be on the safe side, however, the parties should enter into trading partner agreements validating computer-to-computer contracts. UCITA treats the "record" as the functional equivalent of a signed writing that has the effect of permitting the electronic signatures to satisfy the Statute of Frauds.[327] A "record" updates a writing to include information inscribed or stored in an electronic medium, provided it is retrievable.[328] The concept of the e-signature has been updated to include signing by digital signatures or other encryption processes.[329]

(e) Digital signatures and electronic records in most jurisdictions may satisfy the Statute of Frauds. The validation of electronic signatures and records is evolving rapidly. Use digital signatures to ensure the integrity of data messages. Article 2 of the UCC requires a writing signed by the party against whom enforcement is sought for goods worth $500 or greater.[330] The proposed revisions to Article 2 require a record for the sale of goods for $5,000 or greater.[331] The United States is one of the few countries to require a Statute of Frauds. The Convention for the International Sale of Goods does not have a Statute of Frauds or parol evidence rule, unlike Article 2 of the UCC.

---

[325] GlobalSign, GlobalSign Certificate Center (visited June 15, 2002), http://www.globalsign.net.

[326] Revised Article 2, Sales, § 2-103(17) (American Law Institute Discussion Draft, Apr. 14, 2000).

[327] UCITA, § 201.

[328] UCITA, § 201(a).

[329] UCITA, § 102(a)(6)(A).

[330] UCC, § 2-201 (2000).

[331] Revised Article 2, § 2-201(a) (American Law Institute Discussion Draft, Apr. 14, 2000).

(f) An electronic record is treated with the same legal effect as paper-based writings. A record is the e-commerce equivalent of a writing.

(g) Structure your terms of service, clickwrap, and other standard form contracts as license agreements. What specifically is being licensed? Who are the parties to the license agreements? There must be a granting clause, which gives the licensee the right to use software or other licensed intellectual property for the term of the license agreement. Also necessary is a choice of law, forum, and venue clause for each license agreement to avoid litigating in distant forums with unfamiliar law. The license agreement must clearly specify who is covered by the agreement. Is this a license for a single site? Are subsidiaries covered? What other key terms should be defined? Does the licensee have the right to updates? Is there an effective date for each license agreement? What is the grant of rights? Is the license agreement exclusive, semiexclusive, or nonexclusive? May rights under a license agreement be assigned? What is the payment term? What are the specific deliverables? Is there a period of acceptance testing during which a licensor can work out bugs in software? What is the term of the license? Is there any confidentiality provision? Who owns the intellectual property? If the licensor supplies intellectual property, what warranties are given? Are there cross-indemnities given by the parties? May the license agreement be assigned or delegated? What warranties are given? What are the limitations of warranties and damages? Is there an integration or merger clause? What are the events of termination? What are the remedies and method of dispute resolution? What is the venue and jurisdiction for legal actions?

(h) Do liberal contract formation rules apply to Internet-related contracts? UCITA, for example, validates automated transactions in which contracts are formed by bots or electronic agents.[332] In fact, a party is bound by operation of its bot or electronic agent even if no individual reviewed its actions. UCITA validates computer-to-computer contracts and grants records the same legal effect as a paper and pen writing.

(i) The modification of online contracts requires no consideration.[333] An online company may consider drafting a clause specifying that no modifications are valid unless made in writing.

14. What other online contract terms need to be tailored for the specific commercial transaction in cyberspace?

Online Contract Terms Checklist

(a) Offers and acceptance depend upon the "intent of the parties." Contracts may generally be formed in any manner sufficient to show agreement, including conduct. What is the prescribed method of forming contracts at the

---

[332] Knowbots or intelligent agents, e-mail agents, and shopping agents are increasingly used in Internet transactions. The trend in the law is to permit contracts to be formed by electronic agents.

[333] *See* UCC § 2-209 (2000).

company's web site? Contracts in the online environment may be formed on web sites, e-mail, or computer-to-computer. A clickwrap agreement may be structured so that a web site visitor signifies acceptance by the action of clicking an "I accept" button or icon. Does your web site offer online contracts with an opportunity to review the terms prior to the manifestation of assent?

(b) Is there a merger clause, which is evidence of the parties' final expression of its online contracts? Course of dealing, course of performance, and usage of trade may also supplement a final agreement. Supplemental terms such as industry standards are considered part of the contract unless specifically disclaimed or modified by agreement. Article 2, UCITA, and UNIDROIT's "Principles of International Commercial Contract Law" permit evidence of course of performance, course of dealing, and usage of trade to supplement contracts.[334]

(c) Online contracts must not be blatantly unfair or oppressive. A court may void such contracts as unconscionable. The test of unconscionability is whether the weaker party has a realistic choice in acceding to the terms.[335] The basic test for whether an online contract is unconscionable is whether it is one-sided, oppressive, or has unfair or surprising terms.

(d) Is there a legal framework for conducting electronic commerce in your jurisdiction? The European Parliament validated online contracts and other e-commerce legal infrastructure for the 15 European Union countries in May 2000.

15. What web site and online warranties are required? See Tables 9.1, 9.2.

TABLE 9.1
UCC Warranties for Online Sales of Goods

Types of Article 2 Warranties	Description
§ 2-312	Warranty of title and noninfringement
§ 2-313	Express warranty
§ 2-314	Implied warranty of merchantability
§ 2-314	Fitness for a particular purpose

---

[334] UNIDROIT'S Article 2.17 states that a "contract in writing which contains a clause indicating that the writing completely embodies the terms on which the parties have agreed cannot be contradicted or supplemented by evidence of prior statements or agreements. However, such statements or agreements may be used to interpret the writing."

[335] Courts require that the weaker party prove both procedural unconscionability (unfair bargaining) and substantive unconscionability (unfair, oppressive, or surprising term) in order to obtain relief. The fact that a shrinkwrap or clickwrap agreement is adhesive does not mean that it is unconscionable and unenforceable.

TABLE 9.2
UCITA Warranties for Online Licensing of Software

§ 401	Warranty and obligations concerning noninterference and noninfringement
§ 402	Express warranties
§ 403	Implied warranty: Merchantability of computer program
§ 404	Implied warranty: Information content
§ 405	Implied warranty: Licensee's purpose—System integration
§ 406	Disclaimer or modification of warranty

Internet Warranty Checklist

(a) Are your products and services displayed in an online store at your web site? Any description of the specification of goods in an online catalog creates express warranties under the Uniform Commercial Code. A Gateway™ computer described as having a 15.1 XGA TFT Color Display, for example, is given an express warranty by description. Inclusion of the words "56K modem" creates a warranty about the speed of the modem as does the expression "3.5" diskette drive." An advertisement noting that a computer features the Intel Pentium III processor creates a warranty. It would be a breach of warranty if the processor was, in fact, a Pentium II. An express warranty is any "affirmation of fact or promise made by the seller to the buyer which relates to the goods and becomes part of the basis of the bargain."[336] Express warranties cannot be disclaimed once created.

(b) Does the company demonstrate goods or services through virtual tours on the web site? Express warranties are created by descriptions of goods, which go to the basis of the bargain. Online advertisements, catalogs, and advertisements may give rise to express warranties. Any sample or model, which involves a demonstration of goods, creates express warranties. The words of creation and negation of warranties must be reconcilable. The best way to disclaim express warranties is not to make affirmative statements or to act in any way that goes to the "basis of the bargain."[337] Online advertisements and demonstrations should be reviewed to determine whether they accurately depict the performance of software or other products.

(c) Has your company completed an audit of what warranties it gives in connection with the sale of goods or services from its web site? Article 2 of the UCC is the applicable law for warranties for the sale of goods, unless the parties otherwise agree. The common law will apply to rendering professional services, such as computing consulting services or web site

---

[336] UCC, § 2-313(1)(a).
[337] UCC, § 2-313.

design. UCC Article 2 recognizes the following warranties: (1) implied warranty of title and noninfringement; and (2) warranties of performance: express warranties, implied warranty of merchantability, and implied warranty of fitness for a particular purpose. Do your goods conform to the six minimal standards of merchantability: (i) Do your goods pass without objection in the trade (§ 2-314(2)(a))? (ii) Are your goods of fair, average quality (§ 2-314(2)(b))? (iii) Are the goods fit for their ordinary purpose (§ 2-314(2)(c))? (iv) Are the goods even in quality (§ 2-314(2)(d))? (v) Are the goods adequately contained (§ 2-314(2)(e))? (vi) Do the goods conform to representations on the label (§ 2-314(2)(f))?

(d) Has your company followed the prescribed methodology for disclaiming warranties for the sale of goods? The Uniform Commercial Code prescribes precise rules for disclaiming warranties and limiting liability. General disclaimers are ineffective to disclaim UCC warranties. Specific language must, for example, be used to disclaim the warranty of title or noninfringement. ("Seller makes no warranty of title or noninfringement.") Section 2-316 of the UCC provides the prescribed method for disclaiming warranties of performance. To exclude or modify the implied warranty of merchantability, the disclaimer must mention merchantability. If the disclaimer is in the form of writing, it must be "conspicuous."[338] General disclaimers such as "there are no express or implied warranties" are unenforceable. To disclaim the warranty of merchantability, the seller must mention the word "merchantability" or use phrases such as "with all faults" or "as is."[339] The fitness for a particular purpose is an implied warranty, which operates as a matter of law. To qualify for a fitness warranty, the buyer must prove: (i) the seller has reason to know of any particular purpose for which the goods are required; (ii) the seller has reason to know that the buyer is relying upon the seller's knowledge; and (iii) the buyer must actually be relying on the seller's skill or judgment in selecting goods.[340] When disclaimers are posted on a web site, the writing must be conspicuous. Implied warranties, unlike express warranties, are generally disclaimable.[341] Express warranties are affirmations of fact, which go to the basis of the bargain of the sale of goods.[342] Express warranties are made in sales literature, banner advertisements, and demonstrations of products. The best way "to avoid liability for an express warranty is to not make it in the first place."[343]

(e) The Federal Trade Commission's Rule on Pre-Sale Availability of Written Warranty Terms applies to consumer products costing $15 or

---

[338] UCC, § 2-316.

[339] *Id.*

[340] UCC, § 2-315.

[341] The Magnuson-Moss Act does not generally permit sellers to disclaim implied warranties. 15 U.S.C. § 2308. Even the Magnuson-Moss Act, however, permits sellers to limit the duration of implied warranties.

[342] UCC, § 2-313.

[343] Douglas J. Whaley, Problems and Materials on Commercial Law 103 (5th ed. 1997).

more.[344] The seller must make written warranties available at the point of sale. An online seller must also make warranties from manufacturers available as well as the warranties provided by the retailer.

(f) UCITA Warranties of noninfringement and performance warranties apply unless disclaimed or limited.

UCITA Warranties Checklist

(a) Merchant licensors may warrant that information is delivered free of any claims for intellectual property infringement.[345] The noninfringement warranty continues for the entire term of a license agreement.[346] Software delivered to customers must be free of any claims of infringement. The warranty of noninfringement applies only to rights arising in the United States.[347] A licensee may wish to negotiate for a noninfringement warranty covering the world or specified countries.[348] Merchants may give another merchant the equivalent of a quitclaim warranty with respect to infringement or misappropriation.[349]

(b) Express warranties for license agreements closely parallel those for the sale of goods. An express warranty is created for an "affirmation of fact or promise made by the licensor to its licensee, including by advertising, which relates to the information and becomes part of the basis of the bargain."[350] This means that banner advertisements, online catalog descriptions, demonstrations, or samples may constitute express warranties. An express warranty is created even if there are no words of "warranty" or "guaranty."[351] Seller's talk or puffery, which express merely opinions or commendations, do not qualify as enforceable express warranties.[352]

(c) UCITA updates the implied warranty of merchantability to apply to Internet-related transactions.[353] Merchant licensors warrant that a "computer program is fit for the ordinary purposes for which such computer programs are used."[354] Software must "be adequately packaged and labeled."[355] If there are multiple copies of software or other information, the copies must be of "even kind, quality and quantity."[356] The computer program must conform to

---

[344] Federal Trade Commission, *supra* note 210.
[345] UCITA § 401.
[346] *Id.* § 401(b)(1).
[347] *Id.* § 401(c)(2).
[348] *Id.*
[349] *Id.* § 401(e).
[350] *Id.* § 402(a)(1).
[351] *Id.* § 402(b)(1)(2).
[352] *Id.* § 402(3).
[353] *Id.* § 403.
[354] *Id.*
[355] *Id.* § 403(2)(A).
[356] *Id.* § 403(2)(B).

any "affirmations of fact made on the container or label."[357] Implied warranties may also arise from the course of dealing between the parties and from usages of trade that arise in the computer industry.[358] There is no implied warranty for the accuracy of information.[359]

(d) No implied warranty for informational content is created under UCITA's Implied Warranty for Informational Content.[360] A merchant that "compiles, processes, provides or transmits informational content warrants to [the] licensee that there is no inaccuracy in the informational content caused by the merchant's failure to perform with reasonable care."[361] The license agreement should contain a similar clause.

(e) If a licensor in an Internet-related transaction has reason to know of a particular purpose for software or other information, it may be making a system integration warranty.[362] The system's integration warranty parallels the warranty of fitness for a particular purpose. For there to be an integration warranty, the licensee must prove that the licensor had reason to know of a particular purpose for software or other computer information. The licensee must be relying upon the licensor's skill or judgment in selecting software or other information.[363]

(f) Licensors need to follow UCITA's methodology in disclaiming or modifying warranties.[364] To disclaim the implied warranty of merchantability for a computer program, the language must mention "merchantability," "quality," or similar words.[365] To disclaim an informational accuracy warranty, "the language in a record must mention 'accuracy' or use words of similar import."[366] The language to disclaim the systems integration warranty "must be in a record and be conspicuous."[367] The integration warranty may be disclaimed with a conspicuous disclaimer that states "There is no warranty that this information, our efforts, or the system will fulfill any of your particular purposes or needs" or similar words.[368]

(g) UCITA permits the licensor to disclaim all implied warranties other than the noninfringement warranty with an expression such as "as is" or "with all faults."[369] It is necessary to disclaim the noninfringement warranty with specific language.

---

[357] *Id.* § 403(3).
[358] *Id.* § 403(b).
[359] *Id.* § 403(c).
[360] *Id.* § 404.
[361] *Id.*
[362] *Id.* § 405.
[363] *Id.*
[364] *Id.* § 406.
[365] *Id.* § 406(1)(A).
[366] *Id.* § 406(1)(B).
[367] *Id.* § 406(B)(2).
[368] *Id.*
[369] *Id.* § 406(4)(c).

(h) If software or other information can be examined fully, there "is no implied warranty with respect to defects that an examination ought in the circumstances to have revealed to the licensee."[370]

(i) Implied warranties "may also be disclaimed or modified by course of performance, course of dealing, or usage of trade."[371] It is not recommended to rely upon these implied disclaimers. Use clear language specifically disclaiming implied warranties.

(j) Warranties "must be construed as consistent with each other and as cumulative, [unless] that construction is unreasonable."[372]

16. What performance and remedy clauses are necessary?

Performance and Remedies Checklists

(a) The standard of performance for online contracts is that performance should "perform in a manner that conforms to the contract."[373] A licensor will have a right to a cure if the software does not conform to the contract. An uncured material breach of contract entitles the other party to cancel the contract.[374] UCITA permits cancellation only for material breaches of performance, in contrast to the "perfect tender" rule of UCC Article 2.[375]

(b) Electronic restraints such as software programs or devices may be used to regulate performance. Restraints, for example, may prevent uses inconsistent with a license agreement.[376] It is a good idea to give the licensee notice of electronic restraints on duration or number of uses.

(c) *Force majeure* or excuse clauses should be tailored for the agreement rather than rely upon the default provisions of UCITA.[377]

(d) A party in breach of contract may cure the breach at his own expense.[378]

(e) The seller is entitled to notice of breach or the buyer is precluded from recovery.[379] In non-mass-market license agreements, the licensor must give "seasonable notice of a specific nonconformity and make a demand for cure."[380]

(f) UCITA adopts the tender, acceptance, rejection, and revocation concepts from UCC Article 2.[381] The refusal of tender parallels the concept

---

[370] *Id.* § 406(4)(d).

[371] *Id.* § 406(4)(e).

[372] *Id.* § 408.

[373] *Id.* § 601(a).

[374] *Id.* § 601((b)(2).

[375] *See* UCC, § 2-601 (2000).

[376] UCITA § 605.

[377] *See id.* §§ 614, 615.

[378] *Id.* § 703.

[379] UCC § 2-607(3) (2000).

[380] UCITA § 703(b).

[381] *See id.* Part 6.

of rejection in Article 2. The tender of a copy of software or other information that "is a material breach of contract" permits the nonbreaching party to "(1) refuse the tender; (2) accept the tender; or (3) accept any commercially reasonable units and refuse the rest."[382] A party accepting a nonconforming tender may revoke acceptance if he had a reasonable assumption that the licensor would seasonably cure the nonconformity.[383] UCITA follows UCC Article 2 in recognizing an adequate assurance of performance, anticipatory repudiation, and the retraction of anticipatory repudiation.[384]

(g) UCITA follows UCC Article 2 in not permitting a party to recover more than once for the same loss.[385]

(h) The nonbreaching party may cancel if there is a material breach that has not yet been cured.[386]

(i) Upon cancellation, executory obligations are discharged. The licensee has no further right to use licensed information after cancellation.[387]

(j) If the online advertisement uses phrases such as "satisfaction guaranteed" or "money-back guarantee," the refund policy must be to give a full refund with no questions asked.

(k) Limit remedies as well as warranties. Many online sellers offer a sole and exclusive remedy in lieu of Article remedies. UCITA provides that "a party is in breach of contract" as "determined by the agreement."[388]

(l) Agreements may modify or substitute for the default remedies of UCITA.[389] The remedy offered buyers must be meaningful. "Failure or unconscionability of an agreed exclusive or limited remedy makes a term disclaiming or limiting consequential or incidental damages unenforceable unless the agreement expressly makes the disclaimer or limitation independent of the agreed remedy."[390] Article 2 buyers may challenge an exclusive remedy with § 2-719(2), which states: "Where circumstances cause an exclusive or limited remedy to fail of its essential purpose, remedy may be had as provided in this Act."[391] UCITA adopts the doctrine of failure of essential purpose from UCC Article 2. If an exclusive or limited remedy "causes the remedy to fail of its essential purpose," the parties may pursue any of the UCITA remedies.[392]

(m) The measurement of damages may not include avoidable consequences. The nonbreaching party has a duty to mitigate damages.[393]

---

[382] Id. § 704(a)(1)-(3).
[383] Id. § 707, § (a)(1).
[384] Id. § 708-§ 710.
[385] Id. § 801.
[386] Id. § 802(a).
[387] Id. § 802(c).
[388] Id. § 701.
[389] Id. § 803.
[390] Id. § 803(c).
[391] UCC § 2-719(2).
[392] UCITA § 803(2)(b).
[393] Id. § 807(a).

(n) Consequential damages are not recoverable for "the content of published informational content unless the agreement" expressly provides for such damages.[394]

(o) Damages must not be speculative and must be reduced to the present value as of the date of breach.[395]

(p) A licensor's damages will generally consist of accrued and unpaid contract fees or the market value of other consideration not received.[396] Licensors may obtain consequential and incidental damages, but all damages must be calculated in a reasonable manner.[397]

(q) The licensee's damages are measured by the "market value of the performance that was the subject of the breach plus restitution of any amounts paid for performances not received."[398]

(r) Specific performance may be ordered provided adequate safeguards are maintained to ensure confidentiality of information.[399]

(s) Electronic repossession or self-help is a controversial means of exercising a licensor's rights. Electronic self-help is not permitted unless a licensee separately authorizes electronic self-help.[400]

(t) A licensor must give notice before exercising electronic self-help, even if the licensee has authorized this remedy.[401]

17. Have you complied with European Community (EC) contract law?
The European Community Treaty has created new legal institutions designed to harmonize the law. The purpose of uniform laws throughout Europe is to facilitate commerce and reduce transaction costs in cross-border transactions. The European Union (EU) is increasingly harmonizing its contract law, especially when it comes to consumers; seven directives were issued from 1985 to 1999.[402] Directives are formulated by the European Commission and finalized by the European Parliament. When an EU Directive is approved, each of the 15 member states must enact legislation implementing it.[403] One of the difficulties of complying with European contract law is that each country has its own regime of contract law. The European Commission has adopted a sector-by-sector approach in enacting contract law directives. The Commission has enacted directives affecting cross-border contracts of sale, service contracts, and financial services.[404] In addition to the

---

[394] *Id.* § 807(b)(1).
[395] *Id.* § 807(2)(e).
[396] *Id.* § 808.
[397] *Id.* § 808(C)(D)(2).
[398] *Id.* § 809(a).
[399] *Id.* § 811.
[400] *Id.* § 816(a)(c).
[401] *Id.* § 816(c)(1).
[402] Commission of the European Communities, Communication from the Commission to the Council and the European Parliament on European Contract Law, Brussels, Nov. 7, 2001, COM (2001) 398 final.
[403] Dan Williamson, The Right Side of the Law, Revolution, Mar. 27, 2002.
[404] *Supra* note 402.

directives governing contract law, Europe is in the process of codifying general principles of contract law that parallel the Restatement of Contracts so influential in American contract law. If your e-business sells goods to EU countries, it is critical to review the directives in the relevant sales or service sector. In all B2C sectors, it is critical to comply with Directive 1999/44EC of the European Parliament and of the Council of May 25, 1999, which, for example, applies to SPC's sale of computer systems to consumers in Europe. Similarly, all consumer transactions in Europe must comply with Council Directive 93/13/EEC of April 5, 1993, governing unfair terms in consumer contracts (OJ L 95, 21.4.1993).

European Community Contract Law Checklist[405]

(a) Does your e-business transmit data within countries of the European Union? The Data Protection Directive of October 1995 requires your company to comply with specific rules for processing and transferring data. The data protection directive gives data subjects control over the collection, transmission, or use of personal information. The data subject has the right to be notified of all uses and disclosures about data collection and processing. A company is required to obtain explicit consent as to the collection of data on race/ethnicity, political opinions, union membership, physical/mental health, sex life, and criminal records. The directive requires that personal information be protected by adequate security. Data subjects have the right to obtain copies of information collected as well as the right to correct or delete personal data. It is important that consent be obtained from the data subject prior to entering into the contract (Article 7). Data may not be transferred to other countries without an "adequate level of protection" (Article 25). Article 23 makes a company liable for the unlawful processing of personal data. Damages may be assessed for collection or transmitting information without data subject consent.

(b) Does your e-business contract with consumers in the European Union? If so, it must comply with the new Brussels Convention, which went into effect in March 2002. The new Brussels Regulation was proposed as Council Regulation (EC) No 44/2001 of December 22, 2000. Article 15.1 of the Brussels Regulation provides that a consumer may sue in his domicile if a person " who pursues commercial or professional activities in the Member State of the consumer's domicile or, by any means, directs such activities to that member state . . . and the contract falls within the scope of such activities." A web site that directs advertisements to residents of a member state is subject to the consumer provisions of the Brussels Regulation.

(c) Has your company considered whether the Rome Convention of 1980 applies to its contractual obligation? The Convention on the Law

---

[405] Special thanks to Professor Patrik Lindskough of the University of Lund Law School in Sweden for his assistance in creating this checklist.

Applicable to Contractual Obligations (the Rome Convention), 23 O.J. Eur. Comm. 1, art. 3? Article 3.3 of the Rome Convention provides that parties may not contract around mandatory rules such as the unfair terms provisions. The Rome Convention otherwise adheres to a freedom of contract regime. The e-business contracting with a Rome Convention signatory should consider choice of law and forum clauses. Arbitration clauses are generally enforceable in international contracts under the New York Convention.

(d) If you are an e-tailer, do you comply with the directive on distance sellers? The Distance Selling Directive requires the e-business to provide "postal addresses, full delivery costs, and date and terms of contract via a 'durable medium.' "[406]

(e) Does your e-business comply with the e-commerce directive? This directive requires specific information be provided to consumers; it requires "clear contact details, trade and public registration details, along with full tax or delivery costs." The directive requires commercial communications to be clearly labeled.[407]

(f) Does your business comply with EU directives on consumer goods? Directive 1999/44 EC of the European Parliament and of the Council of May 25, 1999, on certain aspects of the sale of consumer goods and associated guarantees applies equally well to Internet-related consumer transactions. The directive on consumer goods contains provisions similar to Article 2 of the Uniform Commercial Code. However, there are significant differences. Under Article 2 of the UCC, the perfect tender rule gives buyers a right to reject goods if they fail in any respect to conform to the contract. The UCC remedies apply to the time of tender, unlike the directive, which gives consumers a two-year period to exercise rights as to defective products (Article 5(1)). The directive presumes that any nonconformity found in the first six months after delivery existed at tender. Unlike Article 2 buyers, consumers under the directive have a right of repair or replacement without charge or inconvenience (Article 3(2)). The directive also has provisions on product guarantees. As with the Magnuson-Moss Act, there are rules on the content of guarantees. The directive does not permit consumers to waive or limit their rights under it (Article 7(1)).

(g) Do your B2C contracts comply with the directive on unfair terms in consumer contracts? Council Directive 93/13/EEC of April 5, 1993, on unfair terms in consumer contracts applies to Internet-related transactions. The unfair terms directive policies unfair terms where there is an imbalance of power between the company and consumer (Article 1). The directive applies to one-sided (adhesion) contracts where the terms are offered on a

---

[406] Williamson, *supra* note 403 (discussing distance selling directive in Europe).

[407] *Id.* (describing e-mail marketing and spam provisions of the electronic commerce directive).

"take it or leave it" basis. Any ambiguity in a consumer contract is construed against the company in favor of the consumer (Article 5). The central provision of the unfair terms directive is that contractual terms found to be unfair are unenforceable. European courts tend to be pro-welfaristic, as opposed to U.S. courts, which tend to be consumer neutral.

(h) Does your company's web site comply with contracts negotiated away from the premises? Contracts negotiated away from business premises protect consumers under Council Directive 85/577/EEC of December 20, 1985. The distance selling directive gives consumers a right to cancel the contract within seven days. The web site needs to conspicuously inform European consumers of the right to cancel the contract (Article 4).

(i) Does your web site comply with the directive on distance sellers? Directive 97/7/EC of the European Parliament and the Council of May 20, 1997, on the protection of consumers in respect of distance contracts applies to B2C transactions. The directive broadly applies to goods or services between suppliers and consumers. The distance selling directive requires consumers to receive clear and comprehensive information on the identity of the seller, qualities of the goods and services, the address for payment and performance, a right of withdrawal, the period for which the offer remains valid, and the minimum duration of the contract. A web site will be required to send e-mail to confirm the time of performance. Article 5 requires consumers be given a right of withdrawal, a place for consumer complaints, and conditions on service.

(j) Does your web site minimize exposure to liability for defective products under the Council Directive 85/374/EEC of July 25, 1985? The products liability directive essentially develops strict products liability rules for products sold in member states. The directive has a three-year statute of limitations (Article 10).

(k) Does your web site comply with the directive on electronic commerce? Directive 2000/31/EC of the European Parliament and of the Council of June 8, 2000, on certain legal aspects of information society services, in particular electronic commerce, in the internal market, legitimates e-contracting. Member states are required to minimize obstacles to e-commerce and to enact transparent rules. The e-business that accepts electronic communications is required to acknowledge receipt of the recipient's order without undue delay (Article 11(1)). A web site or other provider must give recipients the technical means to correct input errors prior to placing orders (Article 11(2)).

(l) Do your web site's electronic signatures provisions comply with Directive 1999/93/EC of the European Parliament and of the Council of December 13, 1999 on a Community framework for electronic signatures? Compliance with the directive ensures that the e-signature will have the same legal status as a paper and pencil signature. Electronic signatures are admissible as evidence in the same fashion as traditional signatures.

(m) Does your web site comply with consumer credit provisions of the Council Directive? Council Directive 87/102/EEC of December 22, 1986, for the approximation of the laws, regulations, and administrative provisions of the member states concerning consumer credit, as modified by Directives 90/88/EEC and 98/7/EEC, applies to consumer credit, including transactions that permit consumers to delay payment. The consumer credit directive requires the creditor to disclose terms, rate of interest, and charges.

[J] Internet Payment Systems[408]

Credit cards are the principal means for payment for B2C sales. A web site will need a merchant account before it can accept credit card orders. Credit card fraud and charge backs are major problems for web sites. Digital money has not yet gained widespread acceptance as a means of payment.

ONLINE PAYMENTS CHECKLIST

1. What payment systems are required for web site sales and services? What credit card agreements? What new bank/customer relationship is needed? What mechanism does the company use to allocate the risk of lost, stolen, altered, or counterfeit credit cards? A cardholder is not liable for the unauthorized use of her or his credit cards unless it is an "accepted" card. An accepted card is defined as a credit card that the cardholder requested and signed. A cardholder is not liable for unauthorized use in excess of $50.[409] The online seller is liable for fraudulent credit card payments, not the merchant bank.

2. What types of payment methods are used for electronic sales and purchase transactions? Credit card payments are the best-established payment systems for business-to-consumer sales and services. Recently, however, merchants have been exploring alternative payment systems, such as prepaid cash cards. Online companies targeting a broader consumer market are adopting products such as InternetCash.[410] Online music stores, such as Coconuts, Planet Music, and the Wall, use software that permits the use of prepaid cash cards.[411] Online companies use a variety of payment systems, including the use of negotiable instruments, electronic funds transfer,[412] credit card payment at the time of sale,

---

[408] *See* § 6.08.

[409] 12 C.F.R., § 226.12(b)(2).

[410] L. Scott Tillett, Merchants Grapple With Payment Options—Integration Still a Hurdle as Credit-Card Alternatives Emerge, Internet Week, May 22, 2000.

[411] *Id.*

[412] The Electronic Fund Transfer Act ("EFTA") establishes the rights, liabilities, and responsibilities of participants in electronic fund transfer systems. EFTA requires participants to adopt certain practices for dealing with preauthorized transfers, error resolution, and liability limits for unauthorized transfers. *See* Federal Trade Commission, *supra* note 210.

e-checks at the time of sale, electronic fund transfer at the time of sale, subscription accounts, purchase orders, and electronic bill presentment and payment.[413]

3. Does your web site take steps to keep your *chargeback* rate low? The online seller is liable for resolving chargeback problems, not the merchant bank. What steps does the company take in resolving disputes with customers? What is your return or refund policy? Cardholders may assert claims or defenses against the card issuer[414] or withhold payment from merchants for claims or defenses that cannot be resolved.[415] The cardholder "may withhold payment up to the amount of credit outstanding for the property or services that give rise to the dispute and any finance or other charges imposed on that amount."[416] If a "cardholder withholds payment of the amount of credit outstanding for the disputed transaction, the card issuer shall not report that amount as delinquent until the dispute is settled or judgment is rendered."[417] Regulation Z requires the "cardholder to make a good-faith attempt to resolve the dispute with the person honoring the credit card."[418] Another limitation is that the "disputed transaction occur in the same state as the cardholder's current designated address or, if not within the same state, within 100 miles from that address." Most credit card companies waive the 100-mile rule to contest a credit card transaction.[419] It is unclear how the 100-mile or same state rule applies to web site transactions.[420] "It is uncertain whether an Internet transaction will be deemed to have taken place at a consumer's residence, at the site of the e-commerce server, or at the primary place of business of the merchant."[421]

4. Does the online company consider co-branded credit cards as part of a direct mail marketing effort? Sears, Roebuck and Company has a co-branded credit card with MasterCard and Sears logos.[422] Credit card issuers must be careful not to issue credit cards except by special request from consumers.

5. Does your company's virtual store need a Merchant Credit Card Processing Account? A company that sells goods or renders services from a web site needs a credit card processing account. First National Merchants Solution permits web sites to accept Visa, MasterCard, Discover, American Express, Diners Club, and JCB.[423] A web site must be able to accept a wide variety of credit cards. In

---

[413] *Id.*

[414] 12 C.F.R., § 226.12(c).

[415] 12 C.F.R., § 226.12(c)(1).

[416] *Id.*

[417] 12 C.F.R., § 226.12(c)(2).

[418] § 226.12(c)(3).

[419] Benjamin Wright and Jane K. Winn, The Law of Electronic Commerce § 20.02[A] at 20-4 (3rd ed. 1998).

[420] *Id.*

[421] *Id.* § 20.02[A], at 20-4, 20-5.

[422] Sears Debuts Mailing for Co-Branded MasterCard, DM News Daily, June 1, 2000.

[423] First National Merchant Solutions (visited June 15, 2002), http://www.foomp.com/marketing/Marketing?BANKID=MS&LVLNBR=3&NAV_ITM_KEY=MS1001.

addition, the web site may have a toll-free telephone number so customers reluctant to transmit credit card numbers on the Internet can supply credit card information personally. A few online web sites accept checks or permit cash on delivery (COD).

6. The company requires secure sessions with processing or merchant banks for its web site. Does the payment system incorporate a Secure Electronic Transaction (SET) Protocol? Secure online payments may also be achieved by the use of Secure Socket Layers (SSL). Secure protocol is not a payment system but a means for assuring party authentication and the secure transmission of data.[424] The American Bankers Association is the parent company of ABAecom, a subsidiary dedicated to facilitating electronic banking and e-commerce.[425] ABAecom has partnered with Digital Signature Trust Co. to provide a public key infrastructure to ensure privacy, authentication, data integrity, and nonrepudiation for Internet-related financial transactions.[426] ABAecom helps banks build trust through its SiteCertain certification program.[427] The SiteCertain seal gives customers verification that they have reached an authentic Internet bank web site. SiteCertain provides a web site authentication seal and is in the process of developing digital certificates to enable banks and customers to engage in secure communications.

7. The online payment system needs protection against forgery and the alteration of messages. One of the difficulties of online contracting is to determine the authenticity of messages. An online company needs a means for verifying the source of electronic messages received. Web site visitors also seek assurances of a web site's authenticity. Verisign's "click to verify" seal assures web visitors that they are at the correct site. The ABA Survey found that the use of e-mail return addresses was the most common means of authenticating data messages.[428] Relying on e-mail addresses as the sole method of authentication is hazardous, however, since e-mail addresses and headers may be falsified or altered. Of the respondents, 22 percent used PINs or passwords to verify the source of electronic messages, whereas only 12 percent used digital signatures with public key encryption.[429] A digital signature uses private keys to "sign" a message, and the recipient uses the signer's public key to determine whether or not the digital signature is valid. The online merchant will want to install configurable antifraud detection software.

8. Does the company use signature certificates based on public keys to conduct electronic contracts to ensure an environment of authenticity, message integrity, and nonrepudiation? Public key-based digital signatures, digital

---

[424] Veronique Wattiez Larose, Electronic Payments: Perspective from Quebec, ABA ECP Home Page (visited June 15, 2002), http://www.abanet.org/scitech/ec/ecp/veronique.html.

[425] ABAecom, About ABAecom FAQs (visited June 15, 2002), http://www.abaecom.com/abt_faq.htm.

[426] *Id.*

[427] *Id.*

[428] *Id.*

[429] *Id.*

images of signatures, SSL certificates,[430] fax confirmations, and verification through trusted third parties such as banks are commonly used as certification mechanisms for companies engaging in e-commerce.[431] Digital signatures were used by 14 percent of survey respondents in the 1998 ABA Science and Technology survey.[432] Digital signatures, encryption, and SSL certificates use encryption to prevent forgery. The American Bankers Association's ABAecom uses digital certificates, issued and signed by a Certificate Authority (CA), that vouch for the identity of the certificate holder.[433] The CA issues a certificate binding the certificate holder's public key to his or her identity.[434] The use of trusted third parties allows for individuals to securely engage in e-commerce "with assurance of sender and recipient authenticity, privacy, message integrity, and non-repudiation."[435]

9. How does your company determine that a data message it receives has not been altered? An online company needs a systematic procedure for verifying document integrity in order to transmit and receive electronic offers and acceptance. If a funds transfer is altered, the addition of an extra digit may result in a multimillion dollar loss. Repeat back acknowledgments were used by 29 percent of the ABA respondents to verify that the messages they received had not been altered, whereas only 11 percent used digital signatures.[436]

10. Implement electronic bill presentment and payment for B2B transactions. A B2B system may be designed to couple billing data with information delivery.[437]

11. Implement payment fraud software. Companies can install software that "flag[s] suspected transactions with higher-than-normal dollar values or exotic mailing address[es] that don't match with other payment information submitted by the consumer."[438]

12. If you are a creditor who bills online customers for goods or services, you must comply with the Fair Credit Billing Act. The act requires you to acknowledge consumer billing complaints promptly and to investigate reported errors. A creditor must post payments to a consumer's account promptly and refund overpayments.[439]

---

[430] SSL is short for Secure Sockets Layer, which is a technology for verifying the identity of visitors. GlobalSign, GlobalSign Digital Certificate Services, and PKI Solutions (visited May 28, 2000), http://www.globalsign.net.

[431] *Id.*

[432] *Id.*

[433] *Id.*

[434] *Id.*

[435] *Id.*

[436] *Id.*

[437] Tim Wilson, E-Bills Fire Up Exchanges, Internet Week, May 15, 2000, http://www.internetwk.com/story/INW20000511S0002.

[438] Tillett, *supra* note 410.

[439] Federal Trade Commission, *supra* note 210.

[K]   Employment Issues[440]

INTERNET EMPLOYMENT CHECKLIST

1. E-Mail and Internet Usage Policies

(a) Has the online company implemented an e-mail and Internet usage policy? Are the policies included in your training programs? Are the policies updated regularly? Companies should appoint a contact person who can provide advice on compliance. The contact person should be available by e-mail, if not in real time.

(b) Do the policies provide employees with notice that e-mail and Internet access are for business purposes? The policy needs to be realistic and enforceable. A policy strictly prohibiting personal use of e-mail may not be enforceable in many work settings. The policy should notify employees that they have no legitimate expectation of privacy in their Internet use.

(c) Does the policy include notice that e-mail or Internet usage is subject to monitoring and that employees have no reasonable expectation of privacy in using these tools? Does the company advise employees that it intends to cooperate with law enforcement in the event that an employee is charged with violating local, state, or federal law in abusing e-mail or the Internet? Increasingly, American online companies partner with the Federal Bureau of Investigation, Interpol, and other law enforcement agencies to curb software piracy and other crimes.

(d) Are employees given specific training on how to avoid misusing or abusing the Internet? Do employees know the boundaries of acceptable use? Are prohibitions in place against downloading intellectual property without authorization? Are employees given notice of the actions the company intends to take to curb abuses? E-mail training should explain the negative consequences of threatening, obscene, harassing, political, or objectionable online communications. In a June 2000 case, the New Jersey Supreme Court considered whether Continental Airlines had a duty to prevent defamatory statements made by its employees on an online computer "bulletin board."[441] A unanimous court held that an employer who has noticed that its employees are using the Internet to defame and harass a co-employee has a duty to remedy that harassment.[442] An employer who did not promptly correct offensive online work-related behavior may be liable to a lawsuit for discrimination. The New Jersey Supreme Court found that Continental Airlines might be directly liable for the online harassment of its employees[443] and might also

---

[440] *See* Chapter 10.

[441] Blakey v. Continental Airlines, Inc., 164 N.J. 38, 751 A.2d 538 (2000).

[442] *Id.*

[443] *Id.*

be liable for a co-employee's harassment under an agency theory and remanded the case for further fact-finding.[444]

2. What preventive law precautions need to be taken in other areas related to employment and the Internet?

(a) A company must promptly take measures to stop work-related online harassment. An employer has a duty to take effective measures to stop e-mail or other online harassment when the employer knows or has reason to know that such harassment is taking place.[445] The employer should institute a mechanism through which employees can promptly report online harassment, and the employer take effective measures to stop online misuse and abuse. Electronic audios of inbound and outbound files transmission to and from the company may be instituted.

(b) Draft nondisclosure and noncompetition agreements to protect trade secrets. Does your company have nondisclosure and noncompetition agreements? Do the confidentiality agreements extend beyond the period of employment? Are the agreements enforceable by time and geographic limitations? Nondisclosure and noncompetition agreements must be reasonable in scope, territory, activity, and duration.

(c) Employees must be advised of the consequences of misappropriating trade secrets or confidentiality.[446] Do your company's e-mail and Internet policies describe in sufficient detail the specific confidential material that is to be safeguarded?

(d) Nondisclosure and confidentiality agreements are useful in protecting against the disclosure of subject matter that may be patented. Exit interviews should be conducted to remind employees of their continuing duty to maintain the confidentiality of information covered by a nondisclosure agreement.

(e) Determine the legal status of employees, independent contractors, consultants, and partners. A company that takes no effective action to prevent online torts by its employees may be liable directly or under an agency theory such as vicarious liability. Vicarious liability, for example, will frequently turn on whether a person is classified as an employee or an independent contractor. An employer may be liable for its employees' torts committed within the scope of employment, but will generally have no liability for the torts of independent contractors. In the dot-com world, a number of nontraditional employment relationships may exist that present the possibility that an "employee" may be classified by a court as an independent contractor. Conversely, a court may decide that an "independent contractor" should be treated as an employee for tax and

---

[444] *Id.*

[445] *Id.*

[446] *See, e.g.,* DoubleClick Inc. v. Henderson 1997 WL 731413 (N.Y. Misc. 1997) (finding that ex-employee of an online advertising agency violated confidentiality agreement in forming a competing online company).

social security purposes. Courts will compare form to substance when examining a company's employment classifications.

(f) Employment issues may arise with the development of a web site. A web site development and service agreement should classify the designers and other consultants as nonemployees. If web site designers and providers are not employees, the work for hire doctrine does not apply. It will, therefore, be incumbent on a company to obtain assignments of intellectual property rights. Nondisclosure and confidentiality agreements are critical to a wide variety of web services agreements. Web site provider agreements, Internet service provider agreements, web site advertiser agreements, end-user license agreements, and multimedia development agreements should all have specific clauses addressing confidentiality and nondisclosure. A simple nondisclosure agreement binding co-venturers would state: "Neither party shall disclose the existence of or the terms and conditions of this agreement without prior written consent of the other party." In the case of co-venturers, cross-indemnity clauses may be appropriate. Each party should defend, indemnify, and hold the other harmless and pay damages and costs arising out of any claims or actions brought by third parties for infringement of intellectual property rights.

(g) If your company recruits employees online, all recruiting materials must comply with federal and state antidiscrimination laws, just as in the offline world. It is common in cyberspace to have online employment applicants as well as telecommuting employees. Online applications must comply with state and federal employment law. Many online businesses hire a variety of temporary employees. You may minimize negligent screening, hiring, and retention claims by checking the credentials of employment applicants.

3. What steps has your company taken to protect confidential information? The directors, officers, and other key employees owe the online company a fiduciary duty.

4. What steps has your company taken to prevent insider trading under federal securities law? What measures has the company taken to prevent insider trading? SEC Rule 10b-5 prevents company directors, officers, and other insiders from using "inside information" in the sale or trading of securities. Insiders not only have a duty not to trade upon insider information but also not to pass tips on to friends, family members, or associates. An online company may also wish to establish its own policies against securities transactions involving company securities.

[L] Regulatory Issues

State and federal regulatory agencies police unfair and deceptive trade practices. The Federal Trade Commission regulates privacy issues as well as unfair and deceptive trade practices on web sites. Web sites that sell goods or services in regulated industries are subject to regulatory actions. The New Jersey Attorney General's office, for example, targeted web sites selling Viagra and other prescription drugs without a license in the state.[447] State attorneys general in Illinois, Kansas, and Missouri each targeted online pharmacies, alleging violation of state consumer protection statutes.[448] Missouri also prohibits the online "beer of the month" clubs from selling to customers located in the state.[449] Companies that sell regulated products, such as alcohol or tobacco, must be vigilant with their online practices to ensure compliance with state and federal laws.

INTERNET REGULATION CHECKLIST

1. Does your company store records in electronic form that may be required by federal, state, or local regulators? Are there corresponding backup storage facilities for records?

2. What steps does your company take to verify that data messages you receive have not been altered? Do you use electronic authentication tools, such as digital signatures? Are digital signatures treated with the same legal effect as "paper and pen" signatures? Do electronic records have the equivalent legal effect as paper-based records?

3. Does your company do periodic backup of records? Are your confidential records protected by passwords, biometrics, voice verification, or other security tools?

4. Does your company have a systematic document retention policy that includes electronic records? Does your record retention policy follow local, state, and federal rules for record retention?

5. Does your e-mail system have a mechanism for deleting messages after a defined period of time?

6. Does your company provide training in recordkeeping to employees and other authorized users?

7. Does your e-mail or Internet policy treat e-mail as records? Is there a document destruction policy that applies to e-mail?

8. The Division of Enforcement of the U.S. Securities and Exchange Commission (SEC) investigates possible violations of federal securities laws on the Internet.[450] The SEC has jurisdiction for the sale of securities subject to the registration requirements of the Securities Act of 1933. Sale of securities on eBay or other auction sites would be a violation of the Securities Act of 1933. The

---

[447] BNA, New Jersey: State Files Consumer Fraud Charges Against Eight Online Pharmacies, 9 BNA's Health Law Reporter (News: Drugs & Devices), Apr. 6, 2000.

[448] *Id.*

[449] Michael Geist, Internet Beer Distribution Shut Down, Internet Law News (Mar. 15, 2000), (citing http://www.ago.state.mo.us/031400b.htm).

[450] Securities and Exchange Commission, SEC Division of Enforcement Complaint Center (visited June 15, 2002), http://www.sec.gov/complaint.shtml.

SEC polices web sites offering securities, soliciting securities transactions, or advertising investment services offshore.[451]

9. The Federal Trade Commission polices web sites offering online investment opportunities.[452] Off-shore investment opportunities are particularly suspect. The FTC publishes a list of the top ten online scams.[453]

10. The United States, as well as other countries, controls the use of cryptography products. Companies must comply with government regulations of cryptographic security products. The Export Administration Regulations (EAR) of the Bureau of Export Administration of the Department of Commerce requires export licenses for shipment to its list of countries subject to embargoes or other special controls.[454] The Bureau of Export Administration (BXA) has several offices with which to consult when determining licensing requirements.[455] To comply with export controls, commodity classifications must be obtained. For encryption products, a license from the Department of State may be needed. Forms for license applications and commodity classification requests are available online.[456] The Bureau of Export Administration posts a list of firms and individuals denied export and re-export privileges.[457] To avoid a visit from agents or the EAR Office of Enforcement, do not distribute software with these firms or individuals.

11. Online companies need to be sure that they are not subject to export controls. The BXA maintains on its web site a number of forms and services for requesting assistance.[458] This helps the BXA ensure a level playing field. Special agents work with the business community to discover export violations. The BXA Enforcement Hotline is 1-800-424-2980.

12. Export controls do not apply to U.S. citizens with greater than 56-bit encryption installed on a personal laptop. This exception pertains when traveling to countries under embargo or to countries deemed terrorist by the government.[459] In addition, an encrypted product may be exported to a foreign subsidiary of a U.S. company "to protect company proprietary data" under a license

---

[451] Securities and Exchange Commission Interpretive Release, Interpretation, Statements of the Commission Regarding Use of Internet Web Sites to Offer Securities, Solicit Securities Transactions, or Advertise Investment Services Offshore (visited June 15, 2002), http://www.sec.gov/divisions/enforce/internetenforce.htm.

[452] Federal Trade Commission, FTC Consumer Alert! (visited June 15, 2002), http://www.ftc.gov/bcp/menu-internet.htm.

[453] Id.

[454] The Bureau of Export Administration, U.S. Department of Commerce, BXA's Assistance to Exporters (visited June 11, 2000), http://www.bxa.doc.gov/factsheets/ExporterAssistance.html.

[455] Id.

[456] Id.

[457] Id.

[458] Id.

[459] Georgetown computer scientist Dorothy E. Denning and her colleague William E. Baugh have written an Easy Guide to Encryption Export Controls, Sept. 25, 1999 (visited June 11, 2000), htttp://www.cs.georgetown.edu/~denning/crypto/Export/regs.html.

exception.[460] In general, mass-market products using 56-bit DES or RC4 are exportable.[461] The BXA web site should be consulted to determine whether a given country is eligible to receive general-purpose encryption software. The Wassenaar Arrangement was created in July 1996 to restrict control exports.[462] The Wassenaar Secretariat formulated a Dual Control List extending to "c encryption hardware and software cryptography products above 56-bits," including Web browsers, e-mail applications, electronic commerce servers, and telephone scrambling devices.[463] In addition, mass-market products "over 64-bits are subject to controls for two years."[464] The member states of the European Union recognize "the same list of dual-use goods (generally based on the COCOM and Wassenaar lists), destinations and guidelines."[465] If your online company is shipping encryption commodities outside the United States, it has the burden of determining whether such a practice is allowed under the Commerce Department's export licensing jurisdiction.[466]

13. Do your web sites, webcasts, or Internet roadshows comply with SEC regulations?[467]

14. Does your company have a comprehensive policy governing privacy?

15. Should your company consider appointing a chief privacy officer (CPO) to help formulate privacy policies in online industries such as health care, financial services, or marketing, where regulations are stringent?

[M]   E-Mail and Internet Usage Checklist

[1]   General Things to Consider

E-MAIL AND INTERNET USAGE CHECKLIST

1. Does the company have an acceptable usage policy? Does the chief administrator of the Internet and e-mail system monitor employees' use of the company computer systems?

2. Is the monitoring narrowly tailored so that it does not constitute an invasion of the employee's right of privacy under the U.S. Constitution, state

---

[460] *Id.*

[461] *Id.*

[462] Electronic Privacy Information Center, Cryptography and Liberty 1999: An International Survey of Encryption Policy 13 (1999).

[463] *Id.* at 13.

[464] *Id.*

[465] *Id.* at 18.

[466] The Bureau of Export Administration, U.S. Department of Commerce, Frequently Asked Questions (visited June 15, 2002), http://www.bxa.doc.gov/factsheets/ExpFAQ1.html.

[467] Blake A. Bell, The Internet Has Changed the Way (and the Reasons) Plaintiffs and Regulators Sue Business, 5 WallStreetlawyer.com 1 (June 2001).

constitutions, or the common law?[468] Massachusetts, for example, has enacted the Massachusetts Privacy Law, which grants persons "a right against unreasonable, substantial or serious interference with his/her privacy."[469] Massachusetts, as with many other states, attempts "to balance the legitimate business interests of the employer with the privacy rights of the employee."[470]

3. Does the usage policy emphasize that online communications are not private and confidential? A common assumption is that "e-mail is as private and confidential as communication via the U.S. Postal Service. However, most e-mail, voice-mail and computer systems are in fact anything but private and confidential."[471] SPC can reduce employees' expectations of privacy by giving them notice that the system is subject to monitoring.

4. SPC needs to monitor the effectiveness of its usage policies by asking a series of questions. Are the e-mail and Internet usage policies enforced? To whom are misuses reported? Is there a standard protocol for investigating security intrusions or other information security disasters?

5. Are employees consulted appropriately in formulating policies? A multinational corporation with subsidiaries in Germany, France, and other European countries may need to consult with workers' councils or other groups before launching an Internet or e-mail policy.

6. Many e-mail dangers are the direct result of faulty employment practices. As discussed in Chapter 3, it is the "enemy within" the company, not outside hackers, who poses the greatest security threat to an organization. Employees and other knowledgeable insiders who know the computer system's loopholes and know how to avoid getting caught account for most security breaches. In general, it is not the failure of the firewall or other information technology that leads to a security breach, but the failure to detect insiders within the system. No firewall, virtual private network, or other technology can thwart computer attacks by disgruntled employees and other insiders.[472]

"Social engineering" is an information security term describing the use of trickery to gain access to a company computer. A wrongdoer, for example, may pose as a telephone or computer technician to gain access to company computers or may call the computer help desk posing as a trusted insider. Firewalls or other technologies will not detect social engineering faults and other "enemies within."

7. What can users do with SPC's computer systems? Are the foreseeable uses covered by the written policy?

---

[468] Bourke v. Nissan Motor Corp., No. B068705 (Cal. Ct. of App. 2d App. Dist., July 26, 1993).

[469] M.G.L.A. 214, § 1B ("Massachusetts Privacy Law").

[470] C. Forbes Sargent III, Electronic Media and the Workplace: Confidentiality, Privacy and Other Issues, 41 Boston Bar J. 6, 19 (May/June 1997).

[471] *Id.* at 6.

[472] Curtis E. A. Karnow, Computer Network Risks: Security Breaches and Liability Issues: The Judicial System Is Only Starting to Address Related Privacy Matters, 15 Comp. L. Strat. 1 (Feb. 1999).

8. What is the scope of the usage policy? It is important to clearly define the scope of the usage policy to determine how it is to be enforced. Below is a checklist of questions to help determine the scope of the usage policy:

(a) Are there separate policies on e-mail and Internet usage?

(b) Are training modules adapted to SPC's e-business activities and plans?

(c) Does the Internet policy cover postings to listservs or USENET discussion groups?[473]

(d) Does SPC's policy address e-mail exchanges both within and beyond the company?

(e) What persons are covered by SPC's e-mail and Internet usage policy?

(f) Does the policy cover all employees, including those in foreign subsidiaries?

(g) How should the policy be adapted to meet local conditions? An e-mail policy launched in Switzerland will require translation into German, Italian, and French. A policy launched in Canada will require translation into French to comply with Quebec statutes. A web site launched in France will also need to comply with French language requirements.

(h) Does SPC's policy cover consultants?[474]

(i) May the company monitor the electronic communications of consultants, temporary workers, and other employees?[475]

(j) What records are kept of e-mail and Internet usage? Are the records monitored or reviewed? Who reviews them? How long are e-mail messages retained?

(k) What type of analysis (if any) is applied to e-mail and Internet usage records? Does the company develop profiles of risk or danger based on empirical studies of its employees' e-mail or Internet usage?

---

[473] The Internet contains listservs, or mailing list services, that permit communications about particular subjects of interest to groups of people. Subscribers submit messages on the list topic to the listserv; these are then forwarded via e-mail to all subscribers. A corporation may be concerned if employees use the corporate e-mail system to transmit messages on listservs devoted to controversial topics, such as abortion, hate groups, swapping, and many other topics. A policy may prohibit distributing messages on nonwork topics. A listserv can have thousands of participants, and it is possible that a defamatory statement will be attributed to a company, not just one or more of its employees.

[474] Consultants may be the source of considerable liability. The Seventh Circuit recently upheld a lower court ruling in which a corporate consultant was held liable for inducing a breach of contract. The Seventh Circuit stated that the consultant's privilege is a qualified privilege limited to advice within the consultant's engagement. *See* Consultant Liable for Inducing Breach of Contract, 15 Comp. L. Strat. 1 (Mar. 1999) (citing J.D. Edwards & Co. v. Podany, No. 98-2486, 1999 U.S. App. LEXIS 2666 (7th Cir., Feb. 22, 1999)). Uncertainty exists as to what aspects of e-mail policy would apply to a consultant in the absence of a specific agreement with the consultant or a management-consulting company concerning acceptance of the policy.

[475] Andersen Consulting LLP v. UOP and Bicker & Brewer, No. 97 C-5501, 1998 U.S. Dist. LEXIS 1016 (D. Ill., Jan. 23 1998).

(l) Does the company have an emergency preparedness team to investigate promptly discovered misuses or abuses of e-mail and the Internet? Does the company have a prescribed method for investigating abuses and misuses of its e-mail or Internet systems? Employees should not be disciplined or sanctioned without a proper investigation or due process, as described in employee handbooks or other company policies. The general rule should be that a company should make "no sudden moves" in disciplining employees.

(m) Does the online company have a corporate counsel or consult outside law firms about its e-mail and Internet policies? What role does counsel play in investigating and enforcing these policies? Corporate counsel will often play a critical role as point person in an internal investigation.

(n) What procedures have been instituted for an internal investigation? A thorough internal investigation and appropriate discipline of the transgressing employee may mitigate or obviate vicarious liability of the company.

(o) What "spin control" or disclosures should be made if e-mail abuses are reported outside the company? In some cases, the public relations department may need to make a public statement if e-mail messages with company addresses have exposed the company to bad publicity or worse.

(p) Does the systems administrator monitor the Internet for use of company trade names, trademarks, or return e-mail addresses? The posting of e-mail with a company message to a hate group, for example, may tarnish the company's reputation.

(q) Does a company take prompt steps to punish employees who abuse e-mail or computer systems? A company's prompt disavowal of the employee's action and its disciplining of the employee will, for example, preclude a finding that the company ratified the employee's actions.

(r) Does the online company have a contingency plan for recovering from an intrusion or abuse of its e-mail or Internet systems?

(s) Does SPC have a disaster recovery plan? To reduce the radius of the risk, corporate e-mail systems should not be used by employees to conduct extraneous online businesses, romances, solicitations, or political organizing.

9. Has SPC installed blocking software programs to limit employee access to objectionable sites? Have monitoring programs been installed to reduce the radius of the risk of employee misconduct on the Internet? Software is available for monitoring employees' keystrokes and may even capture screen shots revealing illegal or unethical activity.

10. Does filtering and logging software monitor e-mail usage?

11. What methods are used to enforce employee filters? Preventing employees from accessing objectionable sites is less disruptive to company operations than would be the unwanted publicity associated with punishing employees for violating corporate policies.[476]

---

[476] *Id.*

12. Does SPC prohibit workplace access to sites containing porno-graphic materials, hate speech, and political content?

13. Does SPC require its employees to obtain specific authorization to visit paid sites or subscriber sites?

14. If SPC has a formal policy of limiting access to objectionable sites, it will reduce the risk of a "hostile workplace" claim based on its acquiescence in the behavior of workers who openly view pornography or racist materials in the workplace.[477] It is quite common for employees to e-mail sexist and racist jokes to fellow employees. All online companies should implement a procedure for reporting misuses of e-mail and the Internet. A contact person should be in place, as well as procedures for reporting violations of company computer or Internet policies.

14. Does SPC have a policy of forbidding the transmission of off-color or objectionable jokes? A female employee of a California software company filed a sexual harassment lawsuit based on messages she received via the company's electronic bulletin board.[478] E-mail transmissions of offensive jokes may be used as evidence that SPC ratifies employee misconduct. A system of graduated discipline with a continuum of sanctions from warnings to suspensions or dismissals must be enforced.

15. Are SPC's employees advised of the legal troubles that may result for them and the company from misuse or abuse of e-mail or the Internet?

16. Employees should be trained in proper use of e-mail and the Internet. Training may use actual case studies of companies found liable for their employee's misuse or abuse of e-mail. Chevron, for example, agreed to settle for $2.2 million a sexual harassment case brought by four female plaintiffs. The plaintiffs in that case claimed they had been sent offensive e-mail messages, including a joke "listing twenty five reasons why beer is better than women are."[479] If employees are not disciplined for abusing the Internet or e-mail system, SPC's policy may be deemed abandoned or relegated to the ashcan of dead-letter laws or regulations.[480]

17. Does SPC provide regular training on the specific issue of harass-ment in the electronic workplace? E-harassment videos and training sessions should be part of employee education. The e-mail messages that led to litigation in past cases may be used in sociodramas, role-playing, and other training exercises. SPC's training module should describe the problem of misdirected e-mails; e-mails with racist, sexist or offensive jokes; and online stalking.

---

[477] *Id.*

[478] Peter Brown, Policies for Corporate Internet and E-Mail Use, Third Annual Internet Law Institute, 1999, 564 PLI/Pat 637 (June 14-15, 1999) (reporting that the software company entered into a confidential settlement with the plaintiff(s)).

[479] Marcia Stepaneck, When the Devil Is in the E-Mails, Bus. Wk., June 8, 1998, at 78.

[480] UCLA law professor Eugene Volokh notes that "Rules mandating punishment are all well and good but they depend on management's willingness to punish. Many employers might be quite reluctant to formally reprimand people who are accessing pornographic sites. . . . If the punishment is based on central monitoring of the sites the employee accesses, this will be just an unpleasant reminder of the degree to which the employees lack privacy." Eugene Volokh, E-Mail Message to Cyberia-listserv@aol.com (Nov. 11, 1997).

18. Does SPC have limited access systems in place to protect confidential information?

19. Does the password or other limited access system comply with industry standards?

20. Is there an effective hierarchy of access that limits access to key confidential information?

21. Does the access system apply to paper-based documents as well as to computer systems?

22. Does SPC require encryption of important e-mail messages containing confidential information? The policy may also address the problem of employees misusing encryption by stealing company data, encrypting it, and distributing it to competitors or third parties.[481]

23. What is the employee's reasonable expectation of privacy? Does the employee's expectation of privacy accord with corporate policy on e-mail and Internet access? Most states do not recognize a cause of action for invasion of privacy based on an employer's monitoring of e-mail stored on a company computer.[482] Most courts hold that a company-owned computer system is not the personal property of employees, and therefore employees do not have a reasonable expectation of privacy in e-mail messages.[483] A notice to this effect should be displayed each time employees boot up their computers.

24. Does the computer system contain defensive programs, such as EtherPeeker, which monitor and record the addresses of visitors to its web site? The systems administrator or webmaster should conduct audits of log files to determine who is accessing the web site. In some cases, the log files will show evidence of hacking, business espionage, or other online crimes or torts.

25. Have backup power and storage capabilities been implemented? Off-site storage or a SAN are used in the event that a computer system goes down or is compromised.[484] Some electronic data are transitory and should be erased. Other data, however, need to be either preserved in the event of dispute or otherwise erased in compliance with a written document retention policy.[485] E-mail messages deleted pursuant to a retention policy will be defensible in the event of litigation. In contrast, the deletion of e-mail messages in response to a discovery request will result in sanctions or liability for spoliation of evidence.

26. What means of physical security are in place to protect confidential corporate information? Is an effective marking system in place to calibrate documents based on the level of security they require? Are the physical means appropriate to the type of information to be protected? Is access controlled at corporate facilities?

---

[481] James Garrity and Eaghan Casey, Internet Misuse in the Workplace: A Lawyer's Primer, 72 Fl. Bar J. 22 (Nov. 1998).

[482] *Id.*

[483] *Id.*

[484] Committee on Federal Courts, Discovery of Electronic Evidence: Considerations for Practitioners and Clients, 53 The Record 656, 657 (Sept./Oct. 1988).

[485] *Id.*

27. What types of access controls are in place? Does the company have locked areas in which authorization for entry is limited? Are monitoring cameras used in high-security areas? Are physical searches conducted in high-security facilities? Are biometrics used to control access to computer systems?

28. Do the systems administrator and key company personnel understand the necessity of preserving data in case of a dispute? The federal and state rules of discovery create an obligation to produce relevant electronic data. If litigation is pending, a letter should be sent to opposing counsel informing them of their obligation to preserve all electronic evidence. E-mail discovery requests must be broad enough to take into account off-site storage facilities, multiple servers, and other computer systems.

29. Are there adequate human resources to support the company's efforts in the e-business?

[2] Usage Disclosures

Does the company e-mail or Internet policy incorporate the following provisions?

- The employer owns the e-mail system.

- Company e-mail is designated for use for business purposes only (no solicitation or distribution).

- The employee acknowledges that e-mail may be monitored and disclosed by the employer.

- Humor and sarcasm, which are often misinterpreted, should not be used in e-mail.

- The e-mail system is not used for personal matters or comments about others.

- E-mail messages should not be sent in anger.

- All messages are to be deleted 30 days after they are sent, unless archived by the recipient.

- Employees should archive only important or critical messages.

- Employees should organize archived messages by subject and should delete groups of messages when they are no longer needed.

- Archived messages will be subject to review and may be required to be produced in the event of litigation.[486]

---

[486] Peter v. Lacoutre, Presentation at the Rhode Island Bar Association Annual Meeting (June 1996) 45 R.I. Bar J. (1998).

[3] Information Security and Usage Procedures

All online companies will have usage policies that set forth the conditions for computer usage or access. The following is a checklist of access and usage control issues.

INFORMATION SECURITY AND USAGE PROCEDURES CHECKLIST

1. Employees must change their passwords regularly and must use difficult-to-guess passwords, that is, not their first names, the names of family members, or other similar, easily "cracked" passwords. The majority of PC purchasers use the default password that comes with the machine. Many other users utilize easily guessed passwords, such as the user's first name. SPC may install a password-cracking program that identifies easily guessed passwords and may require employees to change their passwords regularly.

2. Does the policy limit employees' access to the Internet? Public employers that use blocking software to limit access to sexually explicit content may be violating the First Amendment.[487] First Amendment challenges for blocking access to objectionable web sites or for locking employees out of their computer systems may be made for public but not private employers. Unanticipated consequences may occur from well-intentioned efforts to block access to objectionable content. A private university or think-tank, for example, may be researching the topic of silicon breast implants. Software that blocks sites mentioning the word "breast" may inadvertently block web sites critical to the research mission.

3. Does the e-mail system use pop-up disclaimers and warnings before users can access the system that provide conspicuous notice of the prevailing e-mail policies? Disclaimers in the form of conspicuous pop-up windows may also be used in corporate web sites before a user is permitted to view and/or download data, images, or other information. A general disclaimer should, essentially, warn web site users that they access the corporate web site at their own risk. It is theoretically possible that users may be injured by posted information, ranging from bomb-making instructions to home remedies. If SPC permits employees and others to post information on a web site listserv, the company should disclaim any responsibility for third-party torts, crimes, or objectionable activities.[488] Pop-up warnings should advise all employees of e-mail policy and should require "click" agreement with the usage policy before they can proceed to log onto company computers.

[4] Training and Education

SPC's training and education module on e-mail and Internet usage is critical to its goal of reducing liability. All employees should be required to sign the e-mail

---

[487] Urofsky v. Gilmore, 216 F.3d 401 (4th Cir. 2000) (holding that the regulation of state employees' access to sexually explicit material did not violate the First Amendment).

[488] *See also* § 5.05.

and Internet usage policies to indicate that they are aware of the content of the policies. Even if SPC's employees misuse the system, this evidence of the employee training or education program may mitigate civil penalties or damages. The following is a checklist for employee education and training issues:

TRAINING AND EDUCATION CHECKLIST

1. What methods are used for training the supervisory staff on the proper uses of the corporate e-mail system? What training is given to new employees or has been given to existing employees? Does the training include an explanation of the purposes for which the e-mail and Internet may be used? Employees may be required to agree to the terms and conditions of the e-mail and Internet policies before being given a password. Pop-up screens may be developed to remind the user that the systems are for business use only.

The pop-up message and policy should explain that all messages are stored and are subject to monitoring and review by the systems administrator. The employee may be asked to consent to the terms and conditions of the e-mail system, including recording and monitoring of messages.[489] Many companies use a statement specifying that the employees' use of the system constitutes their consent to company usage policies.[490] Are training modules updated in response to changes in the corporate or legal environment?

2. Does the training explain the company's policy on the personal use of e-mail? SPC should consider adding disclaimers to personal messages to the effect that the data message is not an official correspondence from the company. Disclaimers may also state that "the sender does not have authority to enter into contracts on behalf of SPC." SPC's training should explain the special hazards of e-mail, such as its instant transmission.

3. What ongoing activities communicate the corporate e-mail and Internet usage policies? Does the company use warning screens when the user logs onto the computer to advise the user about known security vulnerabilities, restricted activities, and other security-related information?

4. The e-mail training and education program should be part of new employee orientation. The training module should explain and illustrate the legitimate and illegitimate uses of company computers. All employees must be instructed about the consequences of violating the Internet usage or e-mail policies. As e-mail and Internet usage policy evolves, a mechanism should be in place for updating the training of existing employees. Changes to the e-mail or Internet usage policy can be explained in a clickwrap agreement.

---

[489] The employee's consent to monitoring is a well-established defense to the Electronic Communication Privacy Act (ECPA). "In order to avoid potentially violating state and federal wire tapping laws, as well as the ECPA, employers may want to include a statement that the employee's use of the e-mail system constitutes their consent to the company's recording and monitoring of the employee's e-mail messages." Sargent, *supra* note 470.

[490] *Id.*

5. Does the e-mail and Internet usage-training module cover the pitfalls of misdirected e-mails? The danger of misdirected e-mail is legendary. Many law companies have notices about the risk of misdirected faxes. A similar warning or disclosure should appear on e-mail messages in the event that they are misdirected. Misdirected faxes and e-mails are a staple of litigation, occurring often when overworked lawyers or paralegals inadvertently include an opponent in an e-mail "cc." A misdirected e-mail became the smoking gun in a Massachusetts trade secrets case.[491] The systems administrator may develop a technical fix to avoid inadvertently sending e-mail messages to competitors or opposing counsel. It is an open question as to whether the inadvertent access of e-mail is an "implied waiver of the attorney-client privilege as it is for misdirected faxes."[492]

6. The e-mail and Internet usage policies should include employee training about the discoverability of electronic information.[493] Is there a training module on electronic smoking guns? What training techniques are used to teach proper e-mail and Internet usage? Does the company use role-playing, video presentations, literature distribution, posters, letters from management, and online information to convey its position on the proper use of the Internet and e-mail? The synopses of cases may be incorporated into training. In a 1994 sex discrimination case, the smoking gun was an e-mail message stating "I want you to get that [redacted] out of here. I don't care what you have to do."[494]

7. Is there a training module on the misuse of e-mail to spread rumors or make derogatory comments about co-employees, supervisors, trade partners, competitors, or other third parties that may result in lawsuits? Does the training program include information on copyright protection accorded web site materials and the legal consequences of unauthorized copying?

8. Is e-mail monitored to determine whether employees are misusing or abusing their computer accounts? A nongovernment employer's search of an employee's computer files will not violate the Fourth Amendment. The court in *United States v. Simons*[495] held that an employer's search of an employee's computer hard drive did not violate the Fourth Amendment of the United States Constitution. The Fourth Amendment "search and seizure" protection applies against government intrusions and is inapplicable to private employers.

If a company conducts its search in cooperation with the local, state, or federal government, the right against unreasonable searches and seizures may be triggered. This was not the case in *Simons*, where the employer was not acting in

---

[491] Baystate v. Bentley Systems, Inc., 946 F. Supp. 1079 (D. Mass. 1996).

[492] Evan R. Shirley, Dilbert, Supermodels, and Confidentiality of E-Mail Under Hawaii Law, 3 Hawaii B.J. 6 (Mar. 1999).

[493] Discovery of Electronic Evidence: Considerations for Practitioners and Clients, 53 The Record 656 (Sept./Oct. 1998).

[494] Marianne Lavelle, Digital Information Boom Worries Corporate Counsel, Nat'l L.J. (May 30, 1994) at B1 (noting that defendant settled the discrimination case for $250,000).

[495] 29 F. Supp. 2d 324 (E.D. Va. 1998).

concert with the government. As with other constitutional rights, the right against government intrusion is balanced against public or social interests.

9. Does the training explain how cultural attitudes toward e-mail, such as its informality, may result in increased liability? Angry diatribes and "battles of emotional e-mail messages" are a formula for legal liability. The training module should use examples of how informal e-mail messages lead to a lawsuit. The training should emphasize that e-mail is discoverable and will be treated by the courts as e-records.

10. Does the training explain that e-mail messages should have the proper emotional tone? An e-mail message should be composed with care, and employees should avoid overly emotional diatribes or "battles of the e-mails."

11. Is there a feedback form to encourage employees to comment on the e-mail and Internet usage policies? The feedback form should identify a contact person who is available to clarify any aspect of SPC's e-mail or Internet usage policy.

12. Does the training module illustrate the risks of transmitting or forwarding jokes or off-color stories on the company's e-mail system? The training module should cite prior cases in which a company was charged with maintaining a hostile work environment because of the transmission of jokes of a sexual nature. Prior similar acts of e-harassment may make a company directly liable as acquiescing or ratifying a hostile workplace.

13. Are employees advised of the hazard of transmitting or forwarding ethnically, racially, or sexually insensitive jokes over the company e-mail system or the Internet?[496] Courts have held that while one or two racial e-mail messages will not in themselves constitute a hostile work environment, they may represent the beginning of a pattern of harassment.[497] Prior similar harassing messages, however, make it possible for a plaintiff to prevail on a claim of a hostile work environment. If a company had knowledge of prior similar incidents and took no action, an argument may be made that it ratifies the misconduct. A company's reprimand of employees guilty of sending offensive e-mail is key to a defense against claims of Title VII, civil rights claims, or hostile work environment claims.[498] Therefore, an e-mail monitoring policy should also note that formal reprimands will follow when any offensive content is reported or discovered.

---

[496] A company will likely prevail in a claim in which an insensitive e-mail joke alone constitutes the evidence of a hostile work environment. The cost of defending against these claims, however, is not insignificant.

[497] Owens v. Morgan Stanley & Co., Inc., 1997 Westlaw 403454 (S.D.N.Y. 1997) ("As a matter of law [the sending of a single racist e-mail message], while entirely reprehensible, cannot form the basis for a claim of hostile work environment"); Curtis v. DiMaio, No. QDS 02760859 (E.D.N.Y., Apr. 23, 1999) (holding that the transmission of two racially insensitive jokes did not constitute a hostile work environment).

[498] Daniels v. WorldCom Corp., No. Civ. A.3:97-CV-0721-P, 1998 WESTLAW 91261 (N.D. Tex., Feb. 23, 1998).

[5] Disaster Recovery

The Computer Emergency Response Team (CERT) at Carnegie-Mellon University was originally started by the Department of Defense following an Internet "worm" attack that crashed computers throughout the country.[499] The CERT Coordination Center provides incident response services to web sites that have been victimized by attacks. CERT also publishes security alerts and research on information security and computer intrusions.

CERT's Coordination Center provides the following tips for disaster recovery, which may be adapted to any misuse or abuse of an e-mail or Internet system. Every company should establish contingency plans to include procedures necessary to maintain the organization's e-commerce presence.

1. Before you get started.
   (a) If you have a security policy, consult your policy;
   (b) If you do not have a security policy:
       i.   Consult with management;
       ii. Consult with your legal counsel;
       iii. Contact law enforcement agencies; and
       iv. Document all of the steps taken to recover from an intrusion.
2. Regain control.
   (a) Disconnect compromised system(s) from the network; and
   (b) Copy an image of the compromised system(s).
3. Analyze the intrusion.
   (a) Look for modifications made to system software and configuration files;
   (b) Look for modifications to data;
   (c) Look for tools and data left behind by the intruder;
   (d) Review log files;
   (e) Look for signs of a network sniffer;
   (f) Check other systems on your network; and
   (g) Check for systems involved or affected at remote sites.
4. Contact CERT/CC and other sites involved.[500]
   (a) Contact the company official charged with incident reporting;
   (b) Contact the CERT Coordination Center; and
   (c) Obtain contact information for other sites involved.
5. Recover from the intrusion.
   (a) Install a clean version of your operating system;
   (b) Disable unnecessary services;
   (c) Install all vendor security patches;

---

[499] *See* Computer Emergency Response Team (CERT) (visited June 15, 2002) www.cert.org/nav/aboutcert.html.

[500] Also contact federal, state, and local law enforcement agencies, if appropriate.

       (d) Consult CERT advisories, summaries, and vendor-initiated bulletins;

       (e) Cautiously use data from backups; and

       (f) Change passwords.

  6. Improve the security of your system and network.

       (a) Review security using the Unix Configuration Guidelines;

       (b) Review the security tools document;

       (c) Install security tools;

       (d) Review the site for single points of failure;

       (e) Conduct volume and stress testing of the architecture;

       (f) Enable maximal logging; and

       (g) Configure firewalls to defend networks.

  7. Reconnect to the Internet and update your security policy.

       (a) Document lessons learned from being [root] compromised;

       (b) Calculate the cost of this incident; and

       (c) Incorporate necessary changes (if any) in your security policy.[501]

[6] Internal Corporate Investigations

INTERNAL CORPORATE INVESTIGATIONS CHECKLIST

1. What circumstances and conditions determine special investigations of employee's e-mail or Internet usage? What kind of action was taken?

2. When is the Internet Service Provider (ISP) contacted? Is there an ISP contact available 24 hours a day, 7 days a week?

3. What records does the ISP keep to document Internet abuses? Does the company permit its employees to use private chat rooms or send Instant Messages? America Online, for example, keeps no records on private chat rooms or its Instant Message feature.

4. What action was taken to punish the employee: verbal warnings, reprimands, suspension, or termination of employment?

5. What type of report is submitted? Does the Internet usage policy require a report? If so, what is its intended audience? Are incident reports used to develop risk profiles?

6. At what point in an investigation is law enforcement contacted?

7. Have SPC's managers been consulted to facilitate internal coordination?

8. Is a legal investigation required? What is the role of corporate counsel? Is there an emergency preparedness team to deal with severe abuses of the Internet or e-mail usage policy?

---

[501] CERT Coordination Center, *Improving Security* (visited June 15, 2002), http://www.cert.org/tech_tips/root_compromise.html.

9. In the case of an attack on SPC's computers or the introduction of malicious code, has law enforcement been consulted? Has the incident been reported to the CERT Coordination Center at Carnegie-Mellon University? Does SPC receive CERT advisories? Does SPC have telephone numbers and contact information for CERT Coordination Center advisors?

10. What steps have been taken to recover from an intrusion? Has SPC's security policy been updated to reflect new security vulnerabilities? Is the computer system secure?

11. What local, state, or federal laws have been violated? At what stage should law enforcement agencies be contacted?

12. What is SPC's legal responsibility to inform third parties about intrusions?

13. Should the local Federal Bureau of Investigation (FBI) field office be contacted?[502] Companies should not hesitate to enlist the expertise of cybercrime units of the FBI, Department of Justice, or state attorneys general.

14. Should the U.S. Secret Service be informed? In general, the U.S. Secret Service should be informed if an intrusion involves the theft or abuse of credit card information, threats to the President of the United States, and impersonation of the President of the United States through forged e-mail.[503] The Secret Service main phone number is (202) 435-7700. The number for the Financial Crimes Division, Electronic Crimes Section, is (202) 435-7607.[504]

15. What is the nature of Internet-related threats? If racist or sexist e-mail messages are transmitted to SPC employees or others, has legal counsel been notified? Many companies have human resources departments or equal opportunity units that handle this type of event.

16. Who else has been notified? SPC may also need to notify others in the organization responsible for investigating discrimination claims. Doing nothing is not an option, because a company may be deemed to ratify or acquiesce in wrongdoing if it takes no remedial steps. The steps a company has taken to investigate e-mail misuse serve as documents in a defense against charges that the company ratified the wrongdoing of its employees.

17. Is the internal investigation conducted in a spirit of good faith and fair dealing? Does it employ procedures specified in the company's usage policies? The investigation of e-mail or Internet misuse must be fair-minded and in accordance with established policy.

18. Have employees been informed of the negative consequences of violating usage policies? Employees must have notice of the consequences of misusing e-mail or the Internet. The use of pop-up warnings on computer screens may be used to reinforce training modules.

---

[502] The web site for the FBI National Computer Crime Squad (NCCS) is http://www.emergency.com/fbi-nccs.htm.

[503] CERT Coordination Center, Improving Security (visited June 15, 2002), http://www.cert.org/tech_tips/root_compromise.html.

[504] *Id.*

19. Is a progressive method used to discipline employees for misuse and abuse of the Internet? Sanctions for misuse of e-mail or the Internet should consist of graduated steps, ranging from informal reprimands to dismissals. Is a system of progressive discipline in place that includes giving notice of violations and calibrating punishment from reprimands to dismissals?

20. If a company does not have a prescribed method for conducting internal investigations, it should develop an enforcement mechanism before launching usage policies.

21. Who is responsible for internal investigations of the misuse and abuse of computer systems? Is that committee or person different from the personnel that installed or designed the computer system?

22. What procedures have been instituted to ensure a fair and orderly investigation? Is corporate counsel consulted prior to launching an investigation? Does the corporate security committee have good contacts with local, state, and federal law enforcement?

23. What technologies have been installed for electronic audits of prohibited URLs and other restricted web sites?

24. What procedure has been instituted for reporting abuses? Abuses of e-mail and the Internet may constitute sexual or racial harassment.

25. Have employees been trained to recognize abusive, unlawful, or inappropriate e-mails? Has the training explained how e-mail abuse can subject the employee to personal liability? Has the training explained how a company may be found vicariously liable for a hostile work environment claim arising out of e-mail or Internet abuse?

26. Have employees been warned about accessing objectionable web sites or employing obscene or pornographic screen savers? Have employees been warned about visiting pornographic commercial or noncommercial web sites? Unlawful pornography is more frequently found on Usenets than on commercial sites. A recent survey of Usenet newsgroups uncovered more than "50 sites whose newsgroup title alone suggests the availability of unlawful content."[505]

27. Has blocking web sites prevented objectionable materials from being transmitted via computer bulletin boards?

28. Has the company given notice that it intends to monitor the e-mail and Internet usage of employees?

[7]   Systems Administrators

Systems administrators must be trained to police the e-mail and Internet in a manner consistent with the desired business model and corporate culture. The sys-

---

[505] Garrity and Casey, *supra* note 481.

tems administrator's e-mail monitoring must balance the privacy interest of the employees against the employer's legitimate interest in preventing misuse and abuse. The systems administrator will normally have the task of monitoring excessive use or abuse of e-mail or Internet access. The checklist below was designed to help companies to develop an effective systems administrator role; SPC, for example, must designate someone within the organization to take ultimate responsibility for overseeing the e-mail system.

In a large multinational corporation, numerous contact people may be needed to coordinate Internet and e-mail usage so employees can report abuses of the computer systems promptly. A company such as SPC should appoint a central administrator or webmaster to assure that its e-mail and Internet systems are used in compliance with company guidelines. In the absence of such an administrator, a systems administrator should receive the specialized training necessary to assure the integrity, availability, and confidentiality of e-mail and Internet usage. SPC should employ a qualified systems administrator or webmaster to monitor its e-mail policy.

The systems administrator may be appointed to monitor the e-mail system, web site, and Internet usage patterns. The e-mail auditor should *not* be the same person as the e-mail or Internet systems designer, who may have a blind eye to its vulnerabilities. It is critical that e-mail usage be audited by an independent professional that does not have a stake in the design of the computer system and can therefore be open to its vulnerabilities.

E-MAIL MONITORING CHECKLIST

1. Does SPC's systems administrator for the e-mail and Internet computer systems understand the hazards, risks, and vulnerabilities associated with the misuse of e-mail?

2. Corporate counsel should meet with the systems administrator to explain legal vulnerabilities and the company's obligation to comply with any electronic discovery ordered by the courts. E-mail messages are considered to be records that may be subject to discovery. A company with millions of e-mail messages originating in a corporate extranet may find it expensive to comply with discovery orders. Courts, for example, may require a company to produce hard copies of e-mail messages.[506] Corporate counsel may want to obtain estimates for the cost of retrieving electronic information, including e-mail, to support motions to share the cost of producing this information.[507]

---

[506] Committee on Federal Courts, Discovery of Electronic Evidence: Consideration for Practitioners and Clients, 53 The Record 656, 663 (Sept./Oct. 1998).

[507] *Id.* at 665.

3. Has the systems administrator been briefed on legal risks and vulnerabilities regarding e-mail and Internet systems? Does the systems administrator have a good understanding of the litigation and other risks attendant on e-mail and Internet access?

4. Does the systems administrator also administer SPC's program of software licensing? Does the software license agreement have established procedures for determining whether software use is in compliance with the company's license agreements?

5. What procedures are in place for training employees in the importance of not downloading unlicensed software? The systems administrator may implement an automatic inventory program to enforce this policy.

6. The systems administrator should give strict scrutiny to questionable hyperlinks to web sites that could expose the company to liability.[508]

7. Does the systems administrator perform regular checks of the e-mail and Internet computer systems? Periodic spot checks must be conducted on a regular basis to investigate known hazards and risks.

8. Does the systems administrator check firewalls and software filters on a regular basis? Does the systems administrator check log files of web site activity at least twice a day?

9. The web site should be periodically checked for applets. "An applet is a program written in the Java™ programming language that can be included in an HTML page, in much the same way an image can be included."[509]

10. Are web site visitors warned about the hazards of applets? Before a visitor is permitted to download an applet, he or she should be warned of their potential dangers. A Java™ technology-enabled browser will cause the applet's code to be transferred to the accessing computer system and executed by its browser.[510] The Java™ Virtual Machine Software may reduce the radius of risk of dangerous applets. The primary risk of applets is that they will infect company computers with malicious codes.

11. Is the systems administrator responsible for updating the e-mail and Internet Usage policies? Are incident reports used to draft modifications to the policies?

12. Do the company's data security standards comply with best industry practices?

13. What policies and procedures have been established to govern the transmittal and receipt of confidential or proprietary data?

---

[508] Employees who link the company name to hard-core pornography, hate speech sites, and other objectionable material will create embarrassment if not liability for the company. Another danger is employee use on company computers of unlicensed versions of popular software. Not only is this against the law, but it subjects the company to potential litigation.

[509] Java, The Source for Java™ Technology, Java.sun.com, Applets (visited June 15, 2002), http://java.sun.com/applets/index.html.

[510] *Id.*

[8] Role of Counsel

ROLE OF COUNSEL CHECKLIST

1. Does corporate counsel review the company e-mail and Internet policy on a regular basis to ensure compliance with new statutes or regulations? Is there a process (automated or manual) that will inform corporate counsel of changes to policies?

2. Do the usage policies comply with state and federal laws, including the Federal Wiretap Act, the Electronic Communications Privacy Act, the right of privacy, and other applicable laws and regulations?

3. What role does outside counsel play in developing or reviewing the e-mail or Internet usage policies? SPC's corporate counsel may seek the assistance of outside counsel for Internet-related legal issues.

4. Does the corporate counsel play a role in determining the hazards of the e-mail and Internet systems and the probability of their occurrence?

5. Does the due diligence include revising policy in light of legal developments or litigation over e-mail or Internet usage?

6. What steps are taken to avoid known e-mail or Internet legal vulnerabilities? Does the company learn from history, or will it be condemned to repeat its mistakes?[511]

7. How are the e-mail and Internet usage policies revised? By whom? Is an audit conducted on a regular basis? Does this result in revisions to revises and updates in the e-mail and Internet usage policy?

8. Does the audit committee evaluate feedback forms from employees regarding the policy?

9. How are the policies kept up to date? With the Internet, "all things change. . . . There is nothing . . . which is permanent. Everything flows forward; all things are brought into being with a changing nature."[512] Internet and e-mail usage policies need to be continually updated, or they will soon become "too vague, outdated, or not actively enforced."[513]

10. Is information learned about the e-mail and Internet policies incorporated into training modules?

11. What procedures are institutionalized to ensure that employees understand and comply with the e-mail policy?

12. What role does corporate counsel have in developing training modules to prevent legal troubles? Is e-mail and Internet usage part of an ongoing program of corporate education?

13. Are the e-mail and Internet usage policies audited for workability, accessibility, and "plain English"? The usage policy must be tailored for the

---

[511] As George Santayana stated, "Those who cannot remember the past are condemned to repeat it."

[512] Shirley, *supra* note 492 (quoting the Roman poet Ovid, 43 B.C.–A.D. 17).

[513] Garrity and Casey, *supra* note 481.

company's size, economic standing, and scope of business (that is, whether it is a national or multinational online corporation). The type of policy must be customized for the particular needs of the company. If most or many employees do not speak English, is the policy translated into their primary language?

14. Does the policy comply with the laws of other countries? In the case of companies with foreign subsidiaries, policies must be tailored for semantic nuances and cultural differences, as well as for foreign regulations and laws. In many European countries, for example, Internet usage policies may be challenged on privacy grounds. If employee consultation is required with worker's councils in a regime of self-management, consultation with employee representatives should take place before, not after, the launch of a policy.

15. Is corporate counsel included in the emergency preparedness team? Does corporate counsel supervise the monitoring of e-mail or Internet usage? Does monitoring balance employees' privacy expectations with the company's "need to know?" The courts have generally upheld the right of employers to monitor and intercept employees' e-mail messages transmitted over the company's computer system.[514]

16. Does the corporate counsel have contacts and readily accessible telephone numbers and e-mail addresses for local, federal, and international law enforcement officials? Does the corporate counsel subscribe to Carnegie-Mellon's CERT Coordination Center advisories?

17. Does the corporate counsel receive a briefing on computer system vulnerabilities? After security breaches, does the counsel receive a briefing on how the computer system has been reconfigured to prevent similar intrusions in the future? CERT found that hackers were able to victimize nationally known companies with denial of service attacks by exploiting already well-known vulnerabilities. SPC may avoid similar attacks by following CERT advisories and incident notes.

18. What role does counsel play in helping the company to recover from an intrusion or attack by an employee or third party?

19. Has counsel consulted with the usage policy developers and enforcers to be sure that proper steps are followed? The first step in recovery is to consult the company's security policy.

20. Has counsel documented all of the steps taken in recovering from attacks and regaining control of the computer system in the event it is compromised?

21. Is the corporate counsel active in looking for Internet hazards, as opposed to reacting to a litigation disaster?

22. Does corporate council have a mechanism for tracking changes to content on the web site? If not, how are they made aware of changes that could affect regulatory or legal compliance?

---

[514] Smyth v. The Pillsbury Co., 914 F. Supp. 97 (E.D. Pa. 1996) (upholding termination of employee based on intercepted e-mail messages, despite giving assurance that there would be no monitoring, because employee has no reasonable expectation of privacy in e-mail messages transmitted on company computers).

[N]   Information Security Checklist

INFORMATION SECURITY CHECKLIST

1. Has the company designated key personnel for auditing its security policy? Have systems administrators, network administrators, and security personnel been trained to recognize signs of intrusion?[515]

2. Has the company completed an audit of its information assets to determine what it needs to protect? What tools have been implemented for auditing information security?

3. Has the appropriate level of network security been established, calibrated to the importance of the material to be protected? Are secret documents available only on a "need to know" basis? Has a scale been established indicating levels of confidentiality (for example, confidential, secret, and top secret)?

4. Have access controls for levels of security been implemented and are they being enforced?

5. What procedures have been instituted to train employees in the organization's policy for e-mail and Internet usage? Does user education include how to respond to security breaches or other suspicious incidents?

6. Does the company web site follow accepted standards for information security to ensure transactional integrity? Is the web site secure for credit card sales? Is the web site certified as meeting high-level accepted industry standards?

7. Are procedures in place to protect the company's computer system from malicious code, such as Trojan horses, network worms, or other computer viruses? Do employees know what to do if they receive a virus?

8. Is there a standard computer incident reporting form?[516]

9. Have tests been run on the web site to check for security holes? Has the company used the equivalent of "flight simulators" to check the security of computer networks?[517]

10. Have servers been reconfigured to block third-party e-mail relays by spammers?[518]

11. Does the company have established procedures for informing employees of the organization's information security policy and of any changes to it?

12. Does the company have a disaster recovery procedure in the event of an information intrusion?

---

[515] Carnegie-Mellon's Software Engineering Institute has a center for responding to computer intrusions. *See* the Carnegie-Mellon Computer Emergency Response Team web site, www.cert.org.

[516] Companies may use the computer incident form devised by the Computer Security Technical Center at the Lawrence Livermore National Laboratory (visited June 15, 2002), http://www.ciac.org/ciac/SecurityTools.html.

[517] *Id.*

[518] *Id.*

[O]   Terms and Conditions of Use

TERMS AND CONDITIONS OF USE CHECKLIST

1. Does the Terms and Conditions of Use (TOC) agreement provide for acceptance of terms through use? Does the TOC agreement provide that the visitor cannot use the site without agreeing to the terms? Does the TOC agreement reserve the company's right to update or revise the terms and conditions of use?

2. Does the TOC agreement give the web site visitor notice that any right not expressly granted is reserved by the owner of the site?

3. Is the web site visitor asked to check the TOC agreement periodically for any changes?

4. Is there a provision for displaying any changes in the terms of use or for e-mailing registered visitors concerning any changes?

5. Is there a disclaimer of any responsibility for links to third-party sites? Does the TOC give notice that the company is not responsible for the content of any linked sites? The TOC should also note that the company is not responsible for accuracy, copyright compliance, legality, decency, or compliance with local cultural and legal norms.

6. Does the TOC state that the company does not endorse any sites to which it is linked and takes no responsibility for content on linked sites? The linking notice should warn users that the linked sites are not under the control of the company.

7. The TOC agreement should state that content and materials available on the web site are protected by trademarks, copyrights, patents, trade secrets, license agreements, or other proprietary rights. Visitors should be required to agree not to sell, license, distribute, or create derivative works from the web site content.[519]

---

[519] AOL.Com has a broad proprietary rights clause:

> You acknowledge and agree that all content and materials available on this site are protected by copyrights, trademarks, service marks, patents, trade secrets, or other proprietary rights and laws. Except as expressly authorized by America Online, you agree not to sell, license, rent, modify, distribute, copy, reproduce, transmit, publicly display, publicly perform, publish, adapt, edit, or create derivative works from such materials or content. Notwithstanding the above, you may print or download one copy of the materials or content on this site on any single computer for your personal, noncommercial use, provided you keep intact all copyright and other proprietary notices. Systematic retrieval of data or other content from this site to create or compile, directly or indirectly, a collection, compilation, database or directory without written permission from America Online is prohibited. In addition, use of the content or materials for any purpose not expressly permitted in these Terms of Use is prohibited.
>
> As noted above, reproduction, copying, or redistribution for commercial purposes of any materials or design elements on this site is strictly prohibited without the express written permission of America Online. Permission is granted only when certain limited criteria are met. For information on requesting such permission, please click **here.**

AOL.com, Terms and Conditions of Use (visited June 15, 2002), http://www.aol.com/copyright.html.

8. Is there a term or condition by which the visitor agrees not to "sell, license, rent, modify, distribute, copy, reproduce, transmit, publicly display, publish, adapt, edit or create derivative works from such materials or content?"[520]

9. What rights of reproduction, copying, or redistribution does the company give users? AOL.com, for example, grants the user the right to make one copy of materials on the web site for personal, noncommercial use.[521]

10. Does the TOC Agreement warn users against removing or altering copyright or trademark notices from any copied material?[522] If copying is permitted, the visitor should be warned to keep intact all copyright notices.

11. Does the TOC require express written permission to create a compilation or database from content on its site?[523]

12. Is written permission from the company required for commercial use of data or intellectual property from its site? Is the name and contact information for seeking permissions posted on the site?

13. Does the TOC agreement grant a limited license agreement for a visitor who submits or posts content to the site? Does the TOC require visitors who submit or post content to warrant that they own or otherwise control all of the rights to the content? AOL, for example, obtains its limited license from visitors with the following terms:

> By posting or submitting content to this site, you:
>
> 1. grant America Online and its affiliates and licensees the right to use, reproduce, display, perform, adapt, modify, distribute, have distributed and promote the content in any form, anywhere and for any purpose; and
>
> 2. warrant and represent that you own or otherwise control all of the rights to the content and that public posting and use of your content by America Online will not infringe or violate the rights of any third party.[524]

14. Does the TOC set forth a procedure for making claims of copyright infringement? A TOC agreement might model its procedure for responding to copyright infringement on that of America Online. The TOC might be structured with a hyperlink to click for obtaining further instructions on making a copyright claim. The Digital Millennium Copyright Act requires that SPC appoint an agent designate to handle copyright claims. SPC's TOC must identify an agent to receive notices of copyright infringement that may occur on its web site. Secondly, SPC must register the agent with U.S. Copyright Office. Finally, SPC's TOC must note the company's policy for dealing with subscribers or users who are repeat infringers. If these safe harbor rules are followed, a site or provider exercising no editorial control will not be liable for infringement by third parties that post content on the site.

---

[520] *Id.*

[521] *Id.*

[522] *Id.*

[523] *Id.*

[524] *Id.*

15. Does the TOC disclaim all warranties for information accuracy on its web site? Does the TOC also disclaim warranties of merchantability, fitness for a particular purpose, and other express or implied warranties, including title or infringement? The TOC should also disclaim any accuracy of information posted on its site, claiming only accuracy to the extent of its best efforts.

16. Are the terms and conditions clearly marked as a link and visible on every page?

[P]   UCITA

Maryland and Virginia have recently adopted UCITA. In those jurisdictions, UCITA applies unless the parties have opted out by choosing another body of law. Licensors may choose to apply Virginia or Maryland law to their transaction. The parties to a UCITA agreement have freedom of contract to opt in or out of various provisions. The parties to a UCITA transaction may agree to incorporate some UCITA provisions but may not contract around duties of good faith, commercial reasonableness, or due care. The parties are not free to opt out of mandatory consumer protection, such as the Magnuson-Moss Act. UCITA cannot be used to cover transactions not otherwise within the scope of the proposed statute. The following is a checklist of issues to consider for all UCITA-related contracts.

UCITA-RELATED CONTRACTS ISSUES CHECKLIST

1. Who are the parties? Who is the licensor or licensee? Does the license agreement use the vocabulary of license versus a sale transferring title? The purpose of licensing is to avoid the "first sale" doctrine of the Copyright Act. A licensor does not "sell" software, but licenses it. A license involves more limited rights than does a sale. If no specific term describes the parties, questions arise as to whether software is licensed on a single- or multiple-user basis.

2. How exclusive is the license agreement? Is it exclusive or nonexclusive? The typical mass-market license is nonexclusive, which means that the software is licensed to the general consuming public. A software license agreement tailored to a single organization may be nonexclusive or semi-exclusive.

3. What is the term of the license agreement? A mass-market license may be perpetual, whereas a tailored agreement may be for a designated term. When does the term of the license agreement begin? One possibility is that the term of a mass-market software license begins at the time of the downloading of the software from the licensor's site. In a development software contract, the term might begin after a period of acceptance testing or with the initial installation of the software.

4. What law is applicable to the license agreement? Have the parties considered the complex factors for opting in or out of UCITA? One reason to opt in is that a company, such as SPC, is engaged in electronic commerce. UCITA validates electronic contracting practices, electronic records, and authentication. UCITA validates contract formation by electronic means, such as "click-through" agreements, as long as minimal procedural standards are met. Are SPC's B2B data messages sent without review by humans? Does SPC have a trading partner agreement supplementing UCITA? Does SPC use electronic agents to initiate or respond to electronic messages without human review?

5. Have the parties chosen a given law and forum? UCITA will enforce choice of law clauses to the extent that it does not diminish consumer protection. Is the contractual choice of forum reasonable and just?

6. Has the licensor implemented an attribution procedure verifying that the digital signature, record, or message is that of the company? Are attribution procedures commercially reasonable, and do they comply with best practices in the industry?

7. If contracts are made by electronic agents, have the parties allocated the risk of a transmission error or error in content? Who is liable if an electronic transmission or information-processing system creates an error? In the case of SPC's transactions, have the parties determined the conditions for attributing electronic messages to SPC? Does the procedure for attribution comply with best practices or computer industry standards?

8. Do mass-market licenses such as clickwrap or webwrap agreements comply with UCITA's rules for validating mass-market licenses? Mass-market licenses are not enforceable unless the licensee manifests assent after an opportunity to review the terms. Does SPC, for example, conspicuously provide users with an opportunity to review the terms prior to requiring the user to "manifest assent" by clicking an icon or button? Does SPC give users an opportunity to review a contract record or terms? Does the "opportunity to review" also give reasonably configured electronic agents an opportunity to react? What mass-market warranties are given?

> a. Quiet enjoyment and noninfringement?
> b. Implied warranty for merchantability of computer program?
> c. Warranties for system integration or fitness for a particular purpose?
> d. Warranty for informational content?
> e. Express warranties such as sales literature, specifications, television advertisements, or banner advertisements?
> f. Disclaimers and limitations on warranties? Does SPC follow UCITA's prescribed methodology in disclaiming or limiting warranties?
> g. Has SPC modified the default remedies of UCITA? What are the events of breach? When do the parties have a right to cancel the contract?
> h. Have the parties agreed to a liquidated damage clause? Are the liquidated damages unreasonably small or large?
> i. Have the parties elected different remedies from UCITA or Article 2?
> j. Have the parties substituted a sole and exclusive remedy for UCITA remedies?

9. Has SPC substituted a repair or replacement remedy for UCITA's remedies? If the parties have a sole and exclusive remedy, what is the backup remedy if the exclusive remedy fails of its essential purpose? Have caps been placed on direct damages? Have consequential damages been disclaimed? Does the backup remedy include a refund? Does the right to refund disclaim consequential, incidental, special, and penal damages?

10. Have the parties reserved the right to disable software or to undertake self-help repossession in the event of default?

11. Has the company correctly configured its agreement?

a. Is the clickwrap structured so that the web site visitor clicks either "I accept" or "I decline"? The form of the clickwrap agreement is acceptance of terms and conditions by use. Is it clear that the visitor signifies agreement to all terms, conditions, and notices? The following is an example of an acceptance of terms through use clause: "By using the SPC site, you signify your agreement to all terms, conditions, and notices contained or referenced by [the Terms of Use]."

b. Does the statement of terms and conditions of use include all applicable terms, such as those included in AOL.com's Terms and Conditions of Use clause? These terms are (1) Acceptance of Terms Through Use; (2) Agreement to Rules of User Conduct; (3) Third-Party Sites; (4) Proprietary Rights; (5) User's Grant of Limited License; (6) Procedure for Making Claims of Copyright Infringement; (7) Disclaimer of Warranties; (8) Limitation of Liability; (9) Indemnification; (10) International Use; (11) Choice of Law and Forum; (12) Severability and Integration; (13) AOL Mail on the Web Registration Agreement; (14) AOL Mail on the Web Billing Notice; and (15) Termination.[525]

[Q]   Web Site Intellectual Property Audit

Before a company—such as our hypothetical SPC—launches a web site, it needs to complete an audit to protect its intellectual property and to avoid infringing the rights of others. A legal audit for intellectual property in cyberspace begins with SPC's survey of what property it owns. SPC needs to view content on its web site as one of the intangible assets that fuel its dot-com business activities. What types of intellectual property are used in SPC's online business? What steps has SPC taken to protect each intellectual property right? SPC's goal is to maximize the value from its intellectual property assets. SPC needs to complete a web site audit of its own intellectual property as well as of its exposure to infringement claims for intellectual property owned by third parties.

Does SPC, for example, own the HTML code that comprises its site? If outside web site consultants and designers have been used, does SPC have assignments or work-for-hire agreements with them? The intellectual property owned by SPC has, potentially, diverse sources. SPC may choose to use software license agreements to protect its software, such as diskettes or CDs. If software is downloaded directly from its web site, SPC will need to enter web wrap or "click

---

[525] *Id.*

through" license agreements. If SPC's site is co-branded with a co-venturer, who owns the content? Does SPC have clearance to use the trademarks and trade name of its co-venturer? Has SPC spelled out the uses that can be made of its own trademarks and trade names? All of these questions must be considered.

Preventive law should be the focus of an intellectual property audit undertaken prior to launching a web site.[526] Preventive law is the fence at the top of the cliff versus the ambulance in the valley below. What are the specific hazards and risks that SPC should consider before engaging in online commercial transactions? SPC could lose millions of dollars from the infringement of a company's literary or artistic works. SPC should also be concerned with the tarnishment, or dilution, of its corporate name and reputation as well as dilution or tarnishment of its trade name, trademarks, or service marks when it becomes a dot-com company.

A legal audit of SPC's intellectual property also "endeavors to identify legal soft spots and [the need for] legal improvements."[527] SPC's legal audit is particularly warranted when trying to avoid legal trouble with intellectual property in cyberspace. The SPC web site may contain pictures of famous movie stars or content belonging to third parties. If this content is in the public domain, however, it may be used without permission.

[1] Risk/Exposure Analysis

SPC's web site exposes it to the risk of trademark infringement, copyright violations, trade secret misappropriation, and related risks. SPC should also use a search service to determine whether others are infringing on its intellectual property. SPC must monitor the use by others of its trademarks, copyrighted materials, patents, and trade secrets.

[a] Internet Copyright Issues

INTERNET COPYRIGHT ISSUES CHECKLIST

1. Are works displayed on SPC's web site protected by copyrights held by third parties? The display of content on a computer screen is in a sufficiently fixed medium of expression to qualify for copyright protection. The existence of any of the following should be noted:

    (a) Music;
    (b) Text;
    (c) Video clips;
    (d) Software code;
    (e) Graphics;
    (f) Photographs;

---

[526] It is an open question whether a web site needs to exist to be sued for trademark infringement.

[527] Louis Brown, Preventive Law, Glossary, Part II, Prevent. L. Rptr. (Sept. 1988) at 19.

(g) Audio; and

(h) Streaming video.

2. Does SPC.com have a "terms and conditions of use" agreement? Does the agreement use a clickwrap or webwrap agreement such as the following?

> By using the SPC web site, you signify your agreement to all terms, conditions, and notices contained or referenced herein (SPC's "Terms of Use"). If you do not agree to SPC's terms of use, please do not use this site. SPC reserves the right to update or revise the SPC Terms of Use. Please check the SPC Terms of Use periodically for changes. Your use of the SPC site following posting of the changes at the Terms of Use page constitutes your acceptance of those changes.

3. Does SPC give notice that copyrights, trademarks, service marks, patents, trade secrets, or other proprietary rights protect all content and materials on its sites?

4. Does SPC give a limited license to use content? SPC should require that visitors warrant or represent that they will not "distribute, copy, reproduce, transmit, publicly display, publicly perform, publish, adapt, edit, or create derivative works from materials or content on SPC's web site."[528]

5. If SPC's web site permits visitors to post or submit content to designated pages on its site, does SPC obtain a limited license to use, reproduce, display, perform, adapt, modify, distribute, have distributed, and promote the content in any form, anywhere, and for any purpose?[529]

6. Does SPC require its web site visitor who posts materials to warrant that the materials do not infringe the copyright or other rights of any third party?

> By posting materials on the [SPC] web site, you warrant and represent that you own or otherwise control all the rights to the content and that public posting and use of your content by America Online will not infringe or violate the rights of any third party.[530]

7. Does SPC disclaim warranties and limit liability for its products, services, and content? Many web sites use UCC Article 2 methods for disclaiming warranties. The "as is" or "without all faults" disclaimer effectively disclaims the implied warranty of merchantability. SPC should, however, specifically exclude warranties of title, merchantability, and fitness for a particular purpose as well as liability for the infringement of third party's intellectual property rights. SPC should give no warranty as to the accuracy of content.

---

[528] This clause is adapted from AOL.com, AOL Anywhere Terms and Conditions of Use (visited June 15, 2002), http://www.aol.com/copyright.html.

[529] *Id.*

[530] *Id.*

SPC [and its subsidiaries, joint venturers, etc.] do not warrant that the content on its web site is accurate, reliable, or correct. SPC makes no warranty that content will be available at a given time or location. SPC also makes no warranty that its content is free of viruses or other harmful components. Your use of SPC content is at your own risk.[531]

8. Does SPC limit its liability for content supplied by others? SPC must also limit the liability of its subsidiaries for incidental, consequential, noneconomic, direct, indirect, special, or other damages resulting from the use of content. It is important for SPC to disclaim consequential damages as well as incidental damages. The limitation should also mention that SPC is not liable for damages under contract (that is, UCC, common law, Convention for the International Sale of Goods), tort, strict liability, or any other cause of action. SPC should also post a notice that some jurisdictions do not allow the exclusion of limitation of incidental or consequential damages.[532]

9. Has SPC sought indemnification from web site visitors that post content to its site? SPC should require web site visitors who post content to indemnify and hold harmless SPC and its subsidiaries (affiliated companies, employees, contractors, officers, directors, and so on) for any liabilities, claims, or expenses that arise from a users' violation of the terms of use or their misuse of the site. SPC should reserve the right to assume the exclusive control of the defense, subject to indemnification. Visitors should guarantee that they will cooperate with SPC in asserting any available defense.[533]

10. Is the content sufficiently original to qualify for copyright protection? Databases may lack the originality necessary to qualify for protection, but they may be protected by license agreements governing access and conditions of use.

11. Who owns the copyrighted material? If SPC employees have produced work, is it within their scope of employment to qualify as a work made for hire? If independent contractors produce web site content, does SPC have permission to use the work?

12. Has work produced by independent contractors been assigned, transferred, or purchased by SPC? SPC needs agreements, assignments, or transfers of the right to use content created by third parties unless covered by the work for hire doctrine.

13. Is SPC a joint author with another entity or person? If SPC produces a web site in partnership with another entity, the site may be classified as a joint work. SPC must enter an agreement setting forth the rights of joint authors.

---

[531] This clause is modeled after AOL.com's disclaimer of warranty in AOL Anywhere Terms and Conditions of Use, *id.*

[532] Massachusetts' version of Article 2 of the Uniform Commercial Code in M.G.L.A. Chapter 106 does not permit sellers to disclaim implied warranties of merchantability in consumer sales. The Magnuson-Moss federal warranty act permits sellers of consumer to limit the duration, but not to disclaim the implied warranty of merchantability entirely.

[533] AOL.com, AOL Anywhere Terms of Use, *supra* note 528.

14. Have all text, images, and other copyrighted materials been cleared for copyright ownership? Does SPC have a license or assignment to use copyrighted materials posted on its web site but belonging to others? If SPC does not own or license content, it must not post content on its web site unless it is in the public domain or protected by fair defense. If content is not owned, licensed, or assigned, it may be displayed if it is in the public domain or covered by the defense of fair use.

15. Is posted content public domain material not protected by the U.S. Copyright Act?[534]

16. Is SPC claiming fair use for materials not covered by its own copyrights? Is SPC's use of the copyrighted materials commercial or noncommercial? What is the nature of the work? What is the amount or substantiality of the portion of the work displayed on SPC's web site? What is the potential effect of SPC's copying on the potential market for the materials?

17. Is there a copyright notice on SPC's web site and on all of its web pages? Notices need to be included for text, graphics, music, video, and all other copyrightable materials. In addition, a notice of copyright should cover the graphics, selection, arrangement, and overall design of the SPC web site.

18. Does SPC have a designated agent and posted contact information, to comply with the ISP safe harbor provisions of the Digital Millennium Copyright Act (DMCA)? Does SPC qualify as a provider for the limitation on liability for caching, storing, or routing copyrighted materials owned by third parties?

19. Does SPC have a linking, framing, and metatag policy posted on its web site? Does SPC freely permit linking, or does it require linkers to meet certain conditions? Is framing or deep linking prohibited in the absence of agreement?

20. Does SPC monitor the Internet for copyright infringement? Does SPC protect itself against copyright infringement by including digital watermarks in its materials or other technological devices to monitor copyright use?

21. Is SPC using likenesses, voices, or images of famous personalities or celebrities? Have rights of publicity been cleared?

22. Do copyrighted photographs depict nonfamous SPC employees or nonemployees? If so, has the right to use these photographs been cleared to avoid invasion of privacy or false light lawsuits?

23. The digitalization of a photograph, for example, arguably modifies an author's moral right against modification. Do agreements to purchase copyright also include waivers of the authors' moral rights? It may be advisable to include an "international use" clause, such as the following, in the terms of use:

> SPC makes no representations that materials in this site are appropriate or
> available for use in locations outside the United States, and accessing them

---

[534] Government reports, such as White Papers produced by the Department of Commerce or Copyright Office, may be published without permission, as they are in the public domain. The Copyright Office, for example, has a list of photographs in the public domain.

from territories where contents are illegal is prohibited. Those visitors who choose to access this site from locations outside the United States do so on their own initiative and are responsible for compliance with local laws.[535]

24. Does the copyrighted material comply with language restrictions? Web sites originating in Quebec or France, for example, must include a French-language translation. If there is no French translation, the international use notice should state that SPC makes no representation that materials from its site are appropriate for or available in Quebec or France.

25. Are databases protected and licensed by a separate license agreement setting forth terms and conditions of use?

26. Does SPC have a choice of law and forum clause that takes into account intellectual property rights? The choice of law and forum clause makes the user's web site activity conditional on agreeing to an exclusive jurisdiction in the event of a claim or action arising out of use of the web site.

27. Does the Uniform Computer Information Transactions Act (UCITA) apply to a terms of services agreement? UCITA limits the licensor's discretion in choice of law and forum for consumer licensees.

28. Has SPC reserved the right to terminate a user's access to the web site or to remove content posted by visitors? SPC should also reserve the complete discretion to cancel access to the site as a self-help remedy. SPC should also warn users that it has the discretion to remove posted material that is potentially infringing or illegal.[536] Yahoo! reserves the right to "terminate the accounts of users who infringe the intellectual property rights of others."[537] SPC's "copyrights and copyright agent" clause, below, is based upon the Yahoo! terms of service agreement.

> If you believe that your work has been copied in a way that constitutes copyright infringement, please provide SPC's Copyright Agent the following information:
>
> 1. An electronic or physical signature of the person authorized to act on behalf of the owner of the copyright interest;
>
> 2. A description of the copyrighted work that you claim or believe has been infringed;
>
> 3. A description of where the material that you claim is infringing is located on the site;
>
> 4. Your address, telephone number, and e-mail address;
>
> 5. A statement by you that you have a good faith belief that the disputed use is not authorized by the copyright owner, its agent, or the law;
>
> 6. A statement by you, made under penalty of perjury, that the above information in your Copyright Infringement Notice is accurate and that you are the copyright owner or are authorized to act on the copyright owner's

---

[535] AOL.com, AOL Anywhere Terms of Use, *supra* note 528.

[536] The Digital Millennium Copyright Act gives the provider a statutory right to remove potentially infringing materials.

[537] Yahoo!, Yahoo! Copyrights and Copyright Agent (visited June 15, 2002), http://docs.yahoo.com/info/copyright/copyright.html.

behalf. SPC's Copyright Agent for Notice of claims of copyright infringement can be reached as follows:

By mail:
Michael L. Rustad
120 Tremont Street
Boston, Massachusetts 02108-4977
By telephone: 617-573-8190
By fax: 617-305-3079
By e-mail: profrustad@aol.com

29. Has SPC obtained permission to post electronic postings for print publications? SPC should update each of its grants-of-copyright agreements to include electronic or Internet-related publishing as well as other media, such as CD-ROMS or technologies yet to be developed. The purpose of this clause is to avoid copyright infringement lawsuits by including print publication in electronic databases.

30. Does the Terms of Service Agreement warn users about posting content that is illegal, infringing, harmful, threatening, abusive, defamatory, obscene, hateful, or otherwise objectionable?

31. Are there any moral rights in copyrighted works created for SPC's web site? Has SPC entered an agreement with the creator to alter or modify works on its web site?

32. Does an infringing web site violate criminal law for criminal copyright infringement?

[b]   Trademark Ownership

TRADEMARK OWNERSHIP CHECKLIST

1. Has SPC registered all of its online trademarks, service marks, or certification marks? Have any of SPC's trademarks been registered at the state level? Are the marks distinctive, or have they acquired secondary meaning?

2. Are the words descriptive of the trademark's goods or services so that they will not qualify for protection? Descriptive terms are not protectable unless invested with secondary meaning acquired by use in commerce.

3. Are these marks distinctive enough to qualify for trademark protection? The domain name http://www.computers.com is inherently generic and therefore can never be registered as a trademark. Can secondary meaning be built up with descriptive marks through online advertising, promotions, or other publicity?

4. Are any of SPC's trademarks confusingly similar to another party's mark? What is the strength of SPC's mark? What is the similarity of the mark to a senior mark used on the Internet? Is there evidence of actual confusion? What is the likelihood of confusion on the Internet?

5. Has SPC conducted a search to determine whether trademarks are available? Has SPC completed an Internet-based search as well as a search of USPTO's database?

6. Has SPC filed trademark applications for each of its marks? SPC may consider applying for trademark protection for its domain name. SPC's applications may be based upon "actual use" or "intent to use."

7. Have SPC's marks been examined by the USPTO? Have SPC's marks been published in the *Trademark Gazette*? Have the trademarks been challenged in the opposition period?

8. Has SPC posted trademark notices for each of its trademarks, service marks, certification marks, or collective marks?

9. Are SPC's trademarks used as key words for banner advertisements in third-party Internet search engines?[538] If so, is this an infringing use of the trademarks?

10. Are third parties using marks identical to or confusingly similar to SPC's trademarks?

11. Are competitors using SPC's marks in a way that blurs the distinctiveness of its marks or tarnishes the mark?

12. Does SPC's mark qualify as a famous mark, so that it may obtain federal antidilution action?

13. If SPC's marks do not qualify for federal antidilution protection, are they protected by state antidilution statutes or the common law?[539]

14. May injunctive relief or damages be recovered under the Federal Trademark Dilution Act of 1995?[540]

15. Is SPC using its trademarks to sell goods or services? Whether an action is for infringement or dilution, a plaintiff must prove that its trademark (1) is used in commerce, (2) is nonfunctional, and (3) is distinctive.[541]

16. Is SPC using the registration symbol, ®, for its online brands? SPC may only use the symbol when its mark has been registered in the USPTO. It is improper to use this symbol at any point before the registration issues.

17. Is the registration symbol, ®, used in SPC's trademark applications? SPC should not use the registration symbol mark in a drawing submitted with an application; the symbol is not considered part of the mark.

18. If the metatags of other parties are critical to SPC's marketing plan, it must enter co-branding or license agreements to use those metatags.

---

[538] P.T. Barnum advised: "Advertise your business. I owe all my success to printer's ink." Banner advertisements are the online functional equivalent of printer's ink.

[539] Most states have antidilution statutes, which protect the distinctive quality of trademarks. California, for example, provides protection against injuries to business reputation, or dilution, even "in the absence of competition between the parties or the absence of confusion as to the source of goods or services." Cal. Bus. & Prof. Code § 14330 (1999).

[540] The federal act requires that the plaintiff prove that "(1) its mark is famous; (2) defendant is making commercial use of the mark in commerce; (3) the defendant's use began after the plaintiff's mark became famous; and (4) the defendant's use presents a likelihood of dilution of the distinctive value of the mark." Panavision Int'l, L.P. v. Toeppen, 141 F.3d 1316, 1324 (9th Cir. 1998) (interpreting 15 U.S.C. § 1125(c)(1)).

[541] I.P. Lund Trading v. Kohler Co., 163 F.3d 27, 36 (1st Cir. 1999).

19. Is SPC granting the right to license its trademarks on another party's web site? What conditions are placed on the other party's use of SPC's trademarks? Does the license include notice of trademarks and service marks?

20. Does SPC monitor the Internet to determine whether its trademarks are properly used? One danger is that distinctive trademarks may be become generic. Aspirin is an example of a once distinctive trademark that has lost its ability to distinguish the source of goods. Are competitors or others using SPC trademarks in a manner that will tarnish or blur its marks? Are competitors copying SPC web site interfaces and the "look and feel" of the site in a way that constitutes trade dress infringement? Is the competitive web site similar to SPC's site in its use of video, graphics, colors, background, and overall web site design?

21. Are competitors using SPC marks in a way that constitutes unfair competition by falsely inferring origin?

22. Has a competitor removed SPC's trademarks from copyrighted material, a practice that may constitute unfair competition as "reverse passing off"?

23. Does SPC have state remedies for dilution or unfair competition, in addition to Lanham Act remedies?

24. Are there any other potential defendants who may be charged with either contributory infringement or vicarious infringement?

25. Are competitors using SPC's marks in a manner that may be defended on the grounds of "fair use"? SPC's trademarks, for example, may be referred to in a comparative advertisement on a competitor's web site. Noncommercial use of SPC marks in online publications is protected by fair use.

[c]   Avoiding Trademark Infringement in Cyberspace

TRADEMARK INFRINGEMENT AVOIDANCE CHECKLIST

1. Is SPC using another entity's trademark, trade name, or trade dress on its web site?

2. Has SPC obtained authorization or licenses to use another's trademark, trade name, or trade dress?

3. Is SPC's use of trademarks, trade names, or trade dress protected by "fair use"?

4. Is SPC's use of trademarks, trade names, or trade dress covered by a license agreement?

[d]   Domain Names in Cyberspace

DOMAIN NAME CHECKLIST

1. Has SPC registered its domain name with an ICANN accredited registry? All registrars in the .com top-level domains follow the Uniform Domain Name Dispute Resolution Policy. Has SPC sought protection in the .bus top-level domain and considered registering other new domains such as .info? Have they registered similar domain names as their original name?

2. If SPC's domain name is being used by a cybersquatter or other abusive registration, will the company submit a complaint to the approved dispute-resolution service provider?

3. Does SPC have a cause of action under the Anticybersquatting Consumer Protection Act of 1999, the Federal Antidilution Act, or under § 43(a) of the Lanham Act?

[e]　Clearance of Publicity Rights

PUBLICITY RIGHTS CLEARANCE CHECKLIST

1. Have releases been obtained for any commercial uses of the right of publicity (name or likeness of individuals) for content on the web site?

2. Have releases been obtained for electronic reproduction rights for any photographs of identifiable persons?

[f]　Trade Secret Preventive Law

TRADE SECRET PREVENTIVE LAW CHECKLIST

1. A trade secret is information that has potential or actual value to SPC's business and must be kept secret. Does SPC have a company-wide trade secret protection program? What steps has SPC taken to avoid the disclosure of trade secrets on the Internet?

2. What limitations have been placed on the time of nondisclosure?

3. Have all employees signed nondisclosure agreements reasonable in duration and scope? Have departing employees been briefed on the continuing duty of confidentiality?

4. Have reasonable security precautions been implemented to encrypt confidential information? Have legends of confidentiality been applied to data and other information considered to be trade secrets?

5. Have reasonable steps been taken to prevent the inadvertent disclosure of trade secrets or patentable technologies disclosed on SPC's web site?

6. Does SPC avoid misappropriating the trade secrets of others or acquiring confidential information by improper means?

7. Do SPC's employee handbook, personnel policies, and training all emphasize the continuing obligation of confidentiality and nondisclosure?

8. Does an instance of theft of trade secrets violate criminal law, such as the Economic Espionage Act of 1996? Have public authorities been contacted?

9. What steps have been taken to prevent the publication of trade secrets on the Internet which publication would make these secrets generally known?[542]

---

[542] Central Point Software v. Nugent, 903 F. Supp. 1057 (E.D. Tex. 1995) (posting of software to computer bulletin board destroyed trade secret).

[g]   Linking or Framing Agreements

LINKING OR FRAMING AGREEMENT CHECKLIST

1. Has SPC monitored links to its site to determine whether any of the links tarnish the company's reputation?

2. Does SPC reserve the right to enter licensing agreements to link or frame third-party sites? Simple linking probably does not require a licensing agreement, but deep linking or framing may be an infringement of a third party's intellectual property rights or a business tort. SPC needs to monitor the Internet to detect unauthorized framing or deep linking.

[h]   Indemnification from Content Providers and Third Parties

INDEMNIFICATION CHECKLIST

1. Does SPC enter indemnification and hold harmless agreements with content providers, joint venturers, web designers, and other parties providing content or developing its site?

2. Is an indemnification clause included on SPC's "terms and services" agreement? If SPC permits outside parties to post information to the web site, is there a notice that the company is not liable for third-party infringement?

3. Has SPC sought indemnification for third parties for any infringement actions arising out of content provided by them?

[i]   E-Commerce Patents

Rights in a business methods patent may be lost in the United States if a patent application for an e-commerce or any other invention is not filed within a year of disclosing, using, or selling goods or services using the invention. Before touting a new invention on a web site, a company should consider the possibility that patent rights may be lost.

E-COMMERCE PATENT CHECKLIST

1. Does SPC's site publish information about its e-business inventions that would cause it to be barred from obtaining a U.S. patent under 35 U.S.C. § 102(b)? Internet publicity about inventions may be construed as prior art, triggering the statutory bar under § 102(b).

2. Has SPC posted materials on its web site that may create a risk of the statutory prepublication bar to obtaining a patent?

3. Has SPC obtained a license to use another's e-commerce business method covered by a patent?

4. Is SPC's use of e-commerce business methods noninfringing?

5. Does SPC have any e-commerce methods which may be patentable? Business methods are patentable if they comply with all other requirements for patentability. Has SPC completed a study of prior art? The "prior art analysis must include any document relevant to the claim including advertisements and demonstrations of e-commerce methods on its web site." Prior art includes any papers or demonstrations given at conferences or trade fairs, such as The Internet Expo.

6. Has SPC retained a person experienced in prosecuting software or e-commerce patents? Only a person who is a member of the patent bar may represent others in patent applications.

7. Is your patent attorney familiar with rapidly evolving rules for software inventions?

8. Does SPC receive copies of correspondence with the PTO concerning e-commerce patents?

9. Has SPC completed a cost-benefit analysis prior to seeking a business method patent?

10. Is the e-commerce patent patentable? Does SPC's proposed invention meet the standards of utility, novelty, and nonobviousness? Nonobviousness is frequently a problem element with e-commerce patents.

11. Has SPC given the patent attorney enough information about its e-commerce business method so that adequate disclosure may be made on the patent application? Adequate disclosure is required by the federal patent statute, 35 U.S.C. § 112 (2000).

12. Has SPC determined how it plans to use the e-commerce invention? Has SPC assisted the patent attorney in reviewing prior art? "Prior art is everything reasonably relating to the subject matter of an invention that exists at the time you file a patent application for that invention."[543] SPC is frequently in a position to provide the patent attorney with publications or other documents relevant to prior art.[544]

13. Have claims for e-commerce patents been carefully constructed to avoid the prior art?[545]

14. Has an analysis been completed of the economic value of the e-commerce patents? Has the claim been constructed as not to be overly broad or too narrow?[546]

15. Are any of SPC's competitors infringing its business method patents? There is no infringement unless SPC's method contains all of the features of a competitor's patent claim.

16. Prior to filing suit, has SPC studied its competitor's web sites, SEC filings, and other information about its business method? A claim of patent infringement requires that each element be supported.

17. Are there alternatives to litigation, such as licensing, cross-licensing, or other agreement between the parties?

---

[543] Thomas A. Turano, Obtaining Patents 2-5 (1997).

[544] SPC is required to disclose to the USPTO all prior art of which it is aware. "A patent is presumed valid over all prior art of record." 35 U.S.C. § 282 (2000).

[545] *Id.*

[546] *Id.* at 2-6.

18. If a business method of a competitor is found to be infringing, what steps have been taken to challenge the infringing use?

19. Patent litigation is expensive and poses a risk that SPC's claim will be invalidated. How likely is it that SPC's business method patent will be invalidated in the event of patent litigation?

20. Is SPC careful to avoid infringing the patents of others?

21. Has SPC received notice that it is infringing an e-commerce or business patent of a competitor? What is the best response to a charge of infringement? Is there prior art which may be used to challenge the patent held by a competitor? What defenses does SPC have to an infringement claim? What alternatives are there to litigation such as licensing, cross-licensing, or joint ventures?

[2] Licensing Intellectual Property

SPC will use licensing agreements as the principal tool with which it protects its intellectual property rights and avoids infringing the rights of third parties. "A license is a contract by which the owner of an intellectual property right (such as a patented invention) conveys to another the right to make, use, and/or sell the intellectual property. In return, the owner receives financial or other consideration, typically a share of the revenues or profits."[547] SPC should consider entering agreements with content providers to share revenue generated through a web site linked to a content area.

INTELLECTUAL PROPERTY LICENSING CHECKLIST

1. Do SPC's license agreements clearly specify what intellectual property rights are granted, the term of the license agreement, geographic restrictions, reverse engineering restrictions, assignability, warranties, remedies, events of default, and method of termination? With multimedia licenses, it is necessary to obtain permission to use video, sound, text, and images.

2. Has SPC determined which party owns the content on its web site? A web site with hundreds of thousands of pages presents the challenge of determining which rights have to be cleared. SPC will typically license content from third parties or enter agreements with parties who will provide content as well as web site design. A traditional print media disseminator may grant the service provider the right to distribute a magazine or newspaper.

[3] Web Site Development

Companies with web sites may decide to outsource the development of the web site, in which case the following questions should be considered.

---

[547] Stites and Harbison, Licensing Your Intellectual Property Rights (visited June 15, 2002), http://www.iplawky.com/wcsb/licensin.htm.

WEB SITE DEVELOPMENT CHECKLIST

1. Who owns the trade dress of the web site? Does this include style guides, custom fonts, colors, etc.?

2. Who owns the information posted on the web site?

3. Is the web site a "work for hire?"

4. What will the developer own?

5. Who is responsible for obtaining license agreements for information posted on the web site?

6. If a company has a license agreement to use information, does the scope of the license cover posting information on a web site?

7. Does a company care that its content is copied from the web site?

8. If a developer provides content, will the developer indemnify the company for any third party infringement lawsuits? If the development entails custom applet creation or the like, are there escrow agreements in place?

[4] Sample Content License Agreement

The following agreement, annotated with comments, is a sample agreement entered into between SPC and a content provider.

SAMPLE AGREEMENT

This agreement ("Agreement") is entered into as of the _____ day of [month, year] ("Effective Date"), by and between SPC, a Massachusetts Corporation, located at 120 Tremont Street, Boston, Massachusetts 02108-4977 ("SPC") and XYZ Content Provider, a _____ [state], located at [address] ("Content Provider").[548]

I. RECITALS[549]

A. SPC maintains a web site on the Internet ("SPC.com"). SPC's site allows its users to search for and access content, an online catalogue, as well as providing other sites on the Internet.

B. Content Provider owns or has the right to distribute certain software content and maintains a related site on the Internet.

C. SPC and Content Provider wish to distribute content provider's software-related content through the SPC web site.

---

[548] It is important to specify the effective date of the agreement. If the beginning and termination dates are available, both dates should be stated. It is also essential to specify who is bound by the agreement.

[549] The recitals are treated as part of the agreement and provide context for interpreting the license. The recitals should state the objectives for the agreement.

II. AGREEMENT[550]

Therefore, the parties agree as follows:

A. Content Provided to SPC

(1) Content provider will provide to SPC the content described in Exhibit A ("software-related content"). The software-related content will comply with the description in Exhibit A. The Content Provider, however, does not warrant that the content is error free, only that the content complies with the description and technical specifications in Exhibit A.

(2) SPC may incorporate the software-related content on its web site.

B. Content Ownership and License Agreement

(1) Content Provider retains all rights, title and interest in and to the software-related content worldwide (including all Intellectual Property rights). Content Provider hereby grants SPC a nonexclusive, worldwide license to use, reproduce, distribute, transmit, and publicly display the Content in accordance with this agreement. Content Provider also grants SPC the nonexclusive right to sublicense Content to its wholly owned subsidiaries and to joint ventures in which SPC participates for the sole purpose of using, reproducing, distributing, transmitting, and publicly displaying the Content in accordance with this Agreement.

(2) SPC will retain all right, title, and interest in and to the SPC web site and all of its pages worldwide (including, but not limited to, ownership of all copyrights, the look and feel of its web site, trademarks, trade names, logos, patents, the right of publicity, and all other intellectual property rights).[551]

C. Trademark Ownership and License

(1) Content Provider will retain all right, title, and interest in and to its trademarks, services marks, and trade names worldwide, including any goodwill associated therewith, subject to the limited license granted to SPC hereunder. Any use of any such trademarks by SPC shall inure to the benefit of Content Provider.

(2) SPC agrees not to take any action inconsistent with Content Provider's trademark ownership.

(3) SPC retains all rights, title and interest in its trademarks, service marks, and trade names worldwide, and in addition, certification marks worldwide, including any good will associated with its rights. Any use of SPC's trademarks

---

[550] The agreement is the heart of the license, which states a present intention to be bound, and the consideration, which may be the form of mutual promises.

[551] It is also advisable to include definitions and rules of construction for the agreement. Definitions of intellectual property rights, enhancements, derivative works, SPC brands, and other properties should be specified.

by Content Provider shall inure to the benefit of SPC. Content Provider agrees not to take any action inconsistent with SPC's trademark ownership.

(4) The parties grant to the other, a nonexclusive, limited license to use its trademarks, service marks, or certification marks only as specifically described in this agreement.

(5) Upon termination of this agreement, SPC and Content Provider agree to cease using the other party's trademarks, service marks, certification marks, and trade names, except as the parties agree in writing.[552]

D. Term and Termination

Initial Term. The initial term of this Agreement will begin on the Effective Date and will end on _____ [date] _____ unless automatically terminated by an Event of Termination.

(1) **Events of Automatic Termination**
   (a) This Agreement will terminate automatically if SPC no longer sells software at its web site or an equivalent web site.
   (b) This Agreement will terminate automatically if SPC no longer supports its web site or an equivalent web site.

(2) **Events of Termination by Material Breach**
   (a) Termination Due to Breach. Either party may terminate this Agreement, effective upon thirty (30) days' written notice, if the other party fails to cure any material breach of its obligations under this Agreement within thirty (30) days following written notice to such party.
   (b) A material breach occurs if there are two or more material errors, failures, or outages of the Content in any thirty (30) day period. SPC may elect to immediately terminate this agreement upon written notice to Content Provider. In addition, SPC may enter into other arrangements for the acquisition of similar content.
   (c) A material breach occurs if SPC fails to pay it licensing fees within 30 days after being billed. If the agreement is terminated, SPC is responsible for any unpaid licensing fees.
   (d) Upon termination of this agreement, SPC agrees to purge Content Provider's software-related content from its web site. SPC must delete or purge all content within 7 days of the termination of this agreement.
   (e) SPC may retain Content in its off-site storage network archive for regulatory or other purposes related to the archiving of information and not for redistribution or use of the content therein.

---

[552] The grant of rights clause should spell out what is granted and what is not granted in a content license agreement. It is important that the parties acknowledge who has the rights, title, and interest in SPC brand features, trademarks, and trade names.

III. REPRESENTATIONS AND WARRANTIES

A. Each party to this Agreement represents and warrants to the other party that: (1) such party has the full corporate right, power, and authority to enter into this Agreement and to perform the acts required of it hereunder; (2) the execution of this Agreement by such party, and the performance by such party of its obligations and duties hereunder, do not and will not violate any agreement to which such party is a party or by which it is otherwise bound; and (3) when executed and delivered by such party, this Agreement will constitute the legal, valid, and binding obligation of such party, enforceable against such party in accordance with its terms.

B. Content Provider warrants that it owns, or has obtained the right to distribute and make available as specified in this Agreement, any and all Content provided to SPC as described in Exhibit A.

C. Except for the Content, SPC warrants that it owns, or has obtained the right to distribute, the material on its web site.

IV. INDEMNIFICATION

Each party will indemnify the other party and its customers and affiliates for, and hold them harmless from, any loss, expense (including reasonable attorneys' fees and court costs), damage or liability arising out of any claim, demand, or suit resulting from (a) a breach of any of its respective covenants or warranties under this Agreement, (b) the failure of such party to have all rights and authority necessary to fulfill or perform its obligations pursuant to this Agreement in compliance with applicable laws; and (c) the infringement of intellectual property rights of any third party or the violation of any law by such parties' contributions and/or performance here under (e.g., in the case of SPC.com and the Content Provider's software-related content described in Exhibit A).

SPC will indemnify, defend and hold harmless Content provider, its affiliates, officers, directors, employees, consultants, and agent from any and all third-party claims, liability, damages, and/or costs (including but not limited to attorneys' fees) arising from:

(i) Its breach of any warranty, representation, or covenant in this agreement;

(ii) or any claim arising from content displayed on SPC.com from any modification made to the content by SPC or by content provider at the direction of SPC.

(iii) Content provider will promptly notify SPC of any and all such claims and will reasonably cooperate with SPC with their defense and/or settlement. The defense and settlement will be controlled by SPC.

Content provider will indemnify, defend, and hold harmless SPC, its affiliates, officers, directors, employees, consultants, and agent from any and all third-party claims, liability, damages, and/or costs (including but not limited to attorneys' fees) arising from:

(iv)   Its breach of any warranty, representation, or covenant in this agreement.

(v)   Alternatively, any claim arising from content provided by Content Provider displayed at the SPC web site.

(vi)   Any claim that the content infringes or violates any third party's copyright, patent, trade secret, trademark, right of publicity, or right of privacy, or contains any defamatory content.

(vii) SPC will promptly notify Content Provider of any and all such claims and will reasonably cooperate with Content Provider with the defense and/or settlement. Content Provider will control its defense and settlement.

(viii) As a condition to indemnification, (a) the indemnified party will promptly inform the indemnifying party in writing of any such claim, demand, or suit, and the indemnifying party will fully cooperate in the defense thereof; and (b) the indemnified party will not agree to the settlement of any such claim, demand, or suit prior to a final judgment thereon without the consent of the indemnifying party.

V. CONFIDENTIAL INFORMATION

A. Definition: "Confidential Information" means all nonpublic confidential and proprietary information which the disclosing party identifies in writing as confidential before or within thirty (30) days after disclosure to the receiving party or which, under the circumstances surrounding disclosure, the receiving party should have understood was delivered in confidence.

B. Nondisclosure. Each party agrees (1) to hold the other party's Confidential Information in strict confidence, (2) not to disclose such Confidential Information to any third party, and (3) not to use the other party's Confidential Information for any purpose other than to further this Agreement. Each party may disclose the other party's Confidential Information to its responsible employees, and, in the case of SPC, the employees of SPC with a bona fide need to know such information and subject to a nondisclosure agreement, but only to the extent necessary to carry out this Agreement.

C. Each party agrees to instruct all such employees not to disclose such Confidential Information to third parties, including consultants, without the prior written permission of the disclosing party.

D. Exceptions. Confidential Information will not include information which (1) is now, or hereafter becomes, through no act or failure to act on the part of the receiving party, generally known or available to the public; (2) was acquired by the receiving party before receiving such information from the disclosing party and without restriction as to use or disclosure; (3) is hereafter rightfully furnished to the receiving party by a third party, without restriction as to use or disclosure; (4) is information which the receiving party can document was independently developed by the receiving party without use of the disclosing party's Confidential Information; (5) is required to be disclosed by law, provided that the receiving party uses reasonable efforts to give the disclosing party reasonable notice of such required disclosure and to limit the scope of material disclosed; (6) is disclosed with the prior written consent of the disclosing party; or (7) is SPC.com content provided by SPC pursuant to this Agreement.

Upon the disclosing party's request, the receiving party will promptly return to the disclosing party all tangible items containing or consisting of the disclosing party's Confidential Information.

E. Injunctive Relief.

EACH PARTY ACKNOWLEDGES THAT ALL OF THE DISCLOSING PARTY'S CONFIDENTIAL INFORMATION IS OWNED SOLELY BY THE DISCLOSING PARTY (OR ITS LICENSORS) AND THAT THE UNAUTHORIZED DISCLOSURE OR USE OF SUCH CONFIDENTIAL INFORMATION WOULD CAUSE IRREPARABLE HARM AND SIGNIFICANT INJURY TO THE DISCLOSING PARTY, THE DEGREE OF WHICH MAY BE DIFFICULT TO ASCERTAIN.

F. General Provisions.

(1) Governing Law and Venue. This Agreement and any disputes arising under, in connection with, or relating to this Agreement will be governed by the laws of the Commonwealth of Massachusetts, excluding its conflicts of law rules. The state and federal courts in Boston, Massachusetts, will have exclusive venue and jurisdiction for such disputes, and the parties hereby submit to personal jurisdiction in such courts. The prevailing party in any such dispute will be entitled to recover costs of suit (including the reasonable fees of attorneys and other professionals).

(2) Notices. All notices or other communications to or upon SPC.com and Content Provider under this Agreement shall be by telecopy or in writing and telecopied, mailed, or delivered to each party at its address set forth in the introductory paragraph of this Agreement or such other address or telecopier number as either party shall notify the other. All such notices and communications, when sent by delivery service, shall be effective on the third business day following the deposit with such service; when mailed, first-class postage prepaid and addressed as aforesaid in the mails, shall be effective upon receipt; when delivered by hand, shall be effective upon delivery; and when telecopied, shall be effective upon confirmation of receipt.

Suffolk Personal Computers By /s/ Cyrus Daftary
Title: Chief Operating Officer, SPC
Content Provider By /s/
Title: Chief Operating Officer, Content Provider

[R]   Global E-Business Legal Planning

The global Internet is a world system potentially useful in selling goods and rendering services in hundreds of countries. The downside of the global Internet is that the e-business or e-tailer must do legal planning to comply with regulations governing the sale of goods on the Internet. Many e-businesses will be targeting

European Union countries, and a number of new directives apply to e-commerce. The European perspective on private international law must be considered as well as supranational directives such as the Electronic Commerce Directive, Directive on the Protection of Consumers in Respect to Distance Selling, the Rome Convention, and the Brussels Regulation. If your company is targetting other core countries, it must consider other national and supranational regulations.

1. Does your company comply with the EC Council Regulation on jurisdiction and the recognition and enforcement of judgments in civil and commercial matters ("Brussels I Regulation")? Brussels I limits the extent to which an e-business can impose choice of law or choice of forum clauses in consumer transactions.

2. What steps have been taken to specify choice of law and forum? Conflict of law principles determine whether the law of some other state or nation will be recognized. The conflict of law consists of principles a court applies in deciding which forum's tort, contract, or other law applies. The e-business needs to take steps to determine what law applies as opposed to letting the court decide. Section 1-105 of the UCC permits parties to choose the law as long as it has a reasonable relation to the contract. Brussels I adapts freedom of contract principles for B2B but not B2C transactions.

3. Does Brussels I affect e-business jurisdiction and enforcement of judgments? Brussels I went into effect on March 1, 2000, and supplants the 1968 Brussels Convention and the 1988 Lugano Convention in most European Union countries.[553] The aim of Brussels I is to facilitate electronic commerce and make jurisdiction and the enforcement of judgments more predictable. Brussels I gives consumers a right to file actions in their home court. One statutory purpose of the regulation is to protect consumers from litigating in distant forums. Brussels I applies to most substantive fields of civil and commercial law, with the exception of matrimonial cases, revenue, customs, administrative, wills, succession, bankruptcy/insolvency, social security, and arbitration cases.

4. Is your e-business domiciled in a member state? Article 60 of Brussels I defines the domicile of a company as its place of incorporation or registered office. The chief jurisdiction rule for B2B transactions is that a defendant company may be sued in its place of domicile. If the defendant is domiciled in one of the member states, it is subject to Brussels I. The signatories to Brussels I include the European Union states plus a few nonmember states who are signatories to the 1968 Brussels Convention and the 1988 Lugano Convention. If the company is not domiciled in one of the member states, it is subject to national rules of the country where it is doing business. In a few cases, a member state may be subject to regulations by the older Lugano or Brussels Conventions. The purpose of Brussels I is to provide for the free movement of judgments as well as avoiding the problem of concurrent judgments (see Article 10).

---

[553] Council Regulation (EC) No 44/200/ of December 22, 2000, on Juridiction and the Recognition and Enforcement of Judgments in Civil and Commercial Matters (hereinafter Brussels I).

5. Is your e-business domiciled in a member state and involved in a contractual dispute? The key organizing principle underlying Brussels I is jurisdictions based on domicile. Article 11 makes jurisdiction as always available for obtaining jurisdiction on a defendant. Subject matter may warrant a diferent basis for jurisdiction in limited circumstances (see Art. 11). In the case of a contractual dispute, the defendant may be sued in the place of performance (see Art. 5(1)). In service contracts, the defendant may be sued where services are rendered (see Art. 5.3). In contracts for the sale of goods that place is stated to be where, under the contract, the goods were delivered, or should have been delivered, in a member state. With the sale of goods, the place where a suit may be brought is the place of delivery. The place of delivery will vary depending on the delivery term. In a shipment contract, the place of delivery is where the goods are placed on a carrier. In contrast, the delivery place is frequently the buyer's business in a destination contract. Brussels I applies to most areas of commercial and civil law.

6. Is your e-business subject to tort liability as a domiciliary? In tort actions, a defendant may be sued where the harm takes place. The European Union approach is similar to the purposeful availment or the effects test used to determine personal jurisdiction in the United States. In general, there must be some act by which the defendant purposefully avails itself of the privilege of conducting business within the forum state. There is little by way of case law or official comments to determine where harm takes place in an Internet setting.

7. Is your e-business targeting consumers in member states? Consumers have the right to sue suppliers in their home state court. Choice of law or forum clauses may not alter this absolute consumer right. A nonresident supplier is subject to the home state rule if it directs commercial activities to the state (see Art. 15). Suppliers do not have the right to bypass the home state rule because the pro-consumer rule is nonwaivable in insurance, consumer, and employement contracts (see Art. 14).

8. Has a judgment been "seized" in a Brussels I member state? The Brussels Convention uses the concept of "seized" to refer to the instituting of proceedings against a defendant. In general, a case has been seized if proceedings have been instituted (see Art. 15). In some cases, a case has not been seized until proceedings have been instituted.

9. Does your e-business comply with the EUs data protection directive? Are data subjects given the choice of unambiguously giving consent to the access of personal data? Do "data subjects" have a right to access to personal data? Does the processing of personal data comply with the directive? Do data subjects have the right to correct inaccuracies or to erase or block personal data?

10. Has your company's web site been localized for different languages, currencies, legal standards, regulations, or national, religious, and cultural characteristics? It is critical that your audit include the legal and regulatory systems of core countries where you are targetting sales or services.

11. Does your company's licensing regime comply with Articles 81 and 82 of the Treaty of Rome?

12. Do your licensing practices comply with European rules regarding anti-competitive practices?

13. Do your licensing agreements include rebates for loyalty that violate the EC directive?

14. Do your licensing agreements violate EC regulations governing the restriction of passive sales?

15. Does your web site comply with distance selling regulations? The Directive on Protection of Consumers in Respect of Distance Selling binds non-member e-businesses targetting EU consumers.

16. In B2B transactions, have choice of forum and law clauses been drafted? Are the name and address of the supplier posted conspicuously? Is the principal corporate address disclosed? Is the pricing information accurate and clearly posted? Have arrangements for payment been disclosed? Have consumers been given a statement of rights in the event of dispute?

17. Does your web site violate the trademarks of companies in other countries? The use of a foreign country's trademark as a metatag may divert traffic looking for the web site. To prove infringement, a trademark owner must prove that the competing use of the mark is capable of generating a likelihood of confusion concerning the source of its product. Most countries have a procedure for registering marks.

18. Has your e-business been victimized by cybersquatting or cyberhijacking? WIPO's Arbitration and Mediation Center under the new Uniform Dispute Resolution Policy is a cost-efficient and speedy way of transferring domain names.

19. Does your company own copyrighted materials that might be deemed public goods? The EU's Digital Copyright Directive (2001/29/EC) requires member states to develop regulations permitting access to copyright protected works for the public good. The public purpose access is broader than under current U.S. law. Another difference between U.S. law and EU law is in the treatment of databases. Under European law, databases may be protected as a compilation, collection, and assembling of materials even if they lack originality. The "sweat of the brow" or the investment in time and effort in compiling databases warrants protection in European countries. Under the European Community's directive there is a 15-year *sui generis* right as well as the 70-year copyright term for qualifying databases. The European Union adopted database protection in a directive that requires individual signatory countries to develop conforming amendments.

20. Does your site's practice of deep linking bypass the first page of another site? Deep linking, or the bypassing of a web site's advertising by drilling deep into the site, may violate European law. Deep linking may expose a company to copyright or trademark infringement action in European countries or other regions.

21. Do your company's linking practices expose it to criminal or civil enforcement by European regulators? Under U.S. law, there is no liability for a defendant linking to a third party's web site for infringing materials on that site.

There may be liability in a foreign country, especially in Western Europe. In Germany, for example, third-party links may create criminal liability if the links are to Nazi hate speech.

22. Does your company comply with the WIPO copyright treaties of 1996? The World Intellectual Property Organization (WIPO) promulgated the December 1996 treaties that led to the DMCA. The WIPO Copyright Treaty of 1996 requires signatory powers to provide remedies against defendants who circumvent technological protection measures and tamper with copyright management information. The DMCA's anticircumvention rules makes it a crime to create or sell technologies to circumvent copyright protection devices. Title I of the DMCA amends the 1976 Copyright Act so that the United States complies with the WIPO Copyright Treaty agreed to in December 1996. The long-term trend in U.S. copyright law is greater convergence with the copyright regimes of many European countries.

23. Does your web site violate the moral rights of European artists? *Droit morals* is a French term that gives authors a right to control the fate or disposition of their works. Moral rights include (1) the right of attribution, (2) integrity, (3) spirit, and (4) personality. The idea underlying moral rights is that the artist has a right to protect the integrity of his work. It is critical that a company obtain assignments of moral rights. Artists' moral rights are protected by the Berne Convention for the Protection of Literary and Artistic Works.

24. What protections has the company taken with respect to confidential information? As under U.S. law, trade secrets may be virtually any form of confidential information, including customer lists, databases, computer software, formulas, product designs, architectural plans, business plans, and algorithms. An e-business should require its employees to sign standard noncompete/nondisclosure agreements as a condition of employment. A company must have made reasonable efforts to maintain the secrecy of information. It may not be enough to have a formal policy regarding confidentiality of documents if there is no mechanism of enforcement. At minimum, documents should be labeled with a confidential and proprietary mark as evidence that they are confidential. In addition, confidential information must be protected on a need-to-know basis to prevent the disclosure of trade secrets. The use of encryption and the other information security tools described in Chapter Three is essential in protecting trade secrets on the Internet.

25. Does your commercial web site contain sexual materials? The sexual abuse of children via the Internet is the subject of international law enforcement initiatives.

26. Does your web site provide consumers with a right to return defective goods for a full refund? The proposed Directive on European Consumer Goods and Guarantees gives consumers a right to repair or replacement of defective goods. If repair or replacement cannot be accomplished within a reasonable time, the consumer is entitled to a full refund.

§ 9.03 INSURANCE POLICIES

[A] E-Commerce-Related Insurance

E-commerce is growing rapidly as corporations throughout the world leverage information technology and venture into the new frontier of cyberspace.[554] E-commerce offers to save companies a tremendous amount of money by reducing costs and adducing timesaving benefits, all while potentially increasing revenues.[555] Yet the Internet can involve significant risks, as well. Internet insurance policies covering e-commerce activities are necessary because traditional coverage may not adequately cover online activities.[556]

In a joint survey by the FBI and the Computer Security Institute, 64 responding corporations revealed that in the preceding 12 months they had experienced computer related security breaches.[557] Other computer related computer risks include copyright or trademark infringement, domain name disputes, slander or defamation, libel claims, e-mail abuse violations, plagiarism, tort liability, and claims of false advertising.[558] When considering the business aspects of e-commerce, often these potential risks are easily overlooked.

[B] Acquiring Internet-Related Insurance

To complicate matters further, it is very easy to be exposed to such risks. Risks come from both inside and outside the company. A disgruntled employee, an outside computer hacker, or a virus program can disrupt vital systems. Depending on the scale and scope of the intrusion, a company could have serious financial exposures. Some policies do not cover cybercrime but only "physical dangers such as floods, fire, and storms."[559] As a practical matter, it is impossible for companies to prevent every possible infraction, especially since some risks are outside their control. Companies should consider, therefore, supplementing their existing insurance policies with policies such as computer network liability, breach of

---

[554] Reliance National, The Choice (1st Quarter, 1999) (visited May 15, 2000), http://www.reliancenational.com/choice/9901/cyberrsk.htm. As of June 2000, Reliance Insurance Company stopped writing virtually all new and renewal property and casualty business. On May 29, 2001, Reliance consented to the entry of an Order of Rehabilitation by the Commonwealth Court of Pennsylvania. On October 3, 2001, the Commonwealth Court of Pennsylvania ordered Reliance Insurance Company into liquidation (visited June 15, 2002), http://www.relianceinsurance.com.

[555] Id.

[556] Id.

[557] Id.

[558] Id.

[559] Joia Shillingford, Insuring Against Cybercrime, Fin. Times (London), Sept. 5, 2001 (quoting insurance broker as stating that most business interruption polices were not designed to address cybercrime or computer crime).

security coverage, crime and intranet insurance,[560] online internet insurance,[561] and errors and omissions policies.[562]

Regardless of what type of coverage is sought, companies should, at a minimum, consider protecting themselves against defamation,[563] viruses,[564] unauthorized access,[565] intellectual property infringement,[566] and failures of their web sites.[567] When purchasing Internet liability insurance for e-mail, Internet, intranet, or e-commerce violations, companies should look for policies that include protection from negligent acts, errors and omissions, breach of duty, infringement of intellectual property rights, breach of confidentiality, unauthorized access, libel and slander.[568] The policy should also protect the company from any of the aforementioned violations not only within the United States but also worldwide.[569]

Since this genre of coverage is normally not inexpensive and the risks covered can be very narrowly defined by entities offering coverage, the decision to transfer risk by insurance (as with any decision to transfer risk) should be made in the context of the overall risk management control framework in place over the entity's e-business operations.

[C] Director and Officers Liability Insurance Policy

The recent dot-com economic slowdown, coupled with corporate management problems experienced by the likes of Enron, WorldCom, Xerox, and Aldephia Communications, has made insurance coverage for officer and director liability insurance significant. As more companies restate their financials and/or face corporate bankruptcies, shareholders and corporations rely on the Internet for important business

---

[560] CNNFN, WISP Insurance Protects Firms from E-Commerce Problems, May 3, 1999 (visited May 15, 2000), http://www.cnnfn.com/digitaljam/newsbytes/130035.html.

[561] *See* Insuranc-e Internet Insurance (visited May 15, 2000), http://www.insuranc-e.com.

[562] Melvin Simensky and Eric C. Osterberg, The Insurance and Management of Intellectual Property Risks, 17 Cardozo Arts & Ent L.J. 321 (1999). E&O policies should be broad enough to cover Internet transactions; for example, the matter covered should be expanded to include numerical, audio, visual, and any other form of expression. *Id.*

[563] A company may be exposed to defamation lawsuits for the actions of their employees in e-mails, listservs, electronic bulletin boards, and other Internet-related channels of communication.

[564] Virus protection should not only protect the company, but should also ward off third-party claims of damage to hardware or software resulting from a virus received via e-mail or off the corporate web site. A company should disclaim all warranties and limit liability for viruses. Visitors should also receive notice that the company gives no warranty regarding viruses, and they should be advised to use up-to-date antivirus software to prevent damage due to viruses.

[565] Unauthorized access should protect against failure of computer security systems, web site vandalism and theft, destruction of electronic data, and other related occurrences.

[566] Intellectual property issues include disputes over domain names, copyrights, trademarks, trade dress, framing, linking, and the like.

[567] Companies need to protect themselves and third parties from financial losses that may result from any online violations.

[568] Chad E. Milton, Insurance for Internet Content and Services, 520 PLI/Pat 437, 440 (1998).

[569] Simensky and Osterberg, *supra* note 562.

functions, and employees or third parties may be forced to bring lawsuits against officers and directors for alleged breach of their fiduciary duties of loyalty[570] and care.[571]

Given the complex business environment, it is difficult to assess whether a particular business strategy employed by officers and directors will be successful. The legal protection afforded directors is the business judgment rule, which has been characterized as a presumption that in making a business decision the directors of a corporation acted on an informed basis, in good faith, and in the honest belief that the action taken was in the best interests of the company.[572] When the business judgment rule is satisfied, it will provide two distinct types of protection.[573] First, it will prevent directors from being personally liable for decisions that later turn out to be misguided or unprofitable. Second, it will also protect the integrity of the decisions made by the corporations' board from challenges by shareholders or third parties.[574] Hence, provided that the decisions can be supported by a rational business purpose and absent an abuse of discretion, the judgment will be respected by the courts.

[D]   Internet Insurance Companies

To date, the insurance industry has not devised boilerplate or standard Internet-related policies; therefore, companies need to do some due diligence before purchasing a policy for online activities. The first Internet-specific insurance policy is InsureTrust, a policy offered by Reliance Insurance Company of Illinois.[575] The InsureTrust policy offers "claims-made and reported coverage for third-party losses with liability limits of up to $10 million."[576] Insurance companies also offer third-party liability policies covering the negligence of a company that installs security products such as software.[577]

The online company should tailor its insurance policies according to its risks. A company that transmits sensitive financial or medical data on the Internet needs a different policy than does a computer company that sells routers worldwide. The consequences of a security breach for a securities firm are different from those of a hospital. A company offering Internet payment services to online stores will need insurance protecting against the theft of credit card numbers. When shopping for Internet insurance, businesses should first evaluate their needs, based on the

---

[570] The duty of loyalty requires directors to act in the best interests of the corporation free from any conflict with their personal financial interests.

[571] The duty of care requires directors to make all decisions on an informed basis.

[572] Aronson v. Lewis, 473 A.2d 805, 812 (Del. 1984).

[573] Robert G Heim, E-Practice: Business Judgment in Turbulent Times, N.Y. L.J., Mar. 23, 2001, at 16.

[574] Id.

[575] Robert D. Chesler and Robyn Ann Valle, Internet Insurance: Old and New Policies Protect E-Commerce, Corp. Couns. (Nov. 1999).

[576] Id.

[577] Kurt D. Baer and Carl Metz, "Cybersubro" Claims the Next Thing, E-Business Ins. Legal Rep., Feb. 7, 2001.

type of business in which they are engaged.[578] Companies that are primarily content providers should have protection against intellectual property risks, including licensing issues and defamation.[579] Service providers should guard against defamation, invasion of privacy, intellectual property, and failure of the software or online service.[580] Those companies that use the Internet for advertising or e-commerce need to be wary about errors and omissions, intellectual property concerns, and computer security breaches.[581]

When considering insurance, first determine your potential risks and the type of assets you have and then determine the type of insurance you need and your financial resources available to purchase a policy.[582] Currently, several insurance companies offer specialized insurance policies specifically addressing liability arising from Internet and computer usage; these include American International Group, Chubb Technology Insurance Group, East West Insurance, INSUREtrust.com, Internet Insure, and Techinsurance.com.

[1] American International Group

American International Group launched an insurance policy covering liability for loss of money or electronic funds for insured Internet transactions.[583] The policy, called InsureSite[SM], also provides coverage for personal injury claims, computer equipment, and business interruption caused by vandalism, viruses, and other perils.[584]

[2] Chubb Technology Insurance Group

Chubb Insurance established a Technology Insurance Group (TIG) in the late 1990s.[585] TIG was to take a global view of insurance needs, tailoring its policies to the electronic industry.[586] TIG offers several policies addressing the insurance needs of technology companies, including Multimedia Liability Insurance.[58] This policy features insurance for copyrighted and trademarked materials; coverage for plagiarism and unauthorized use of titles, slogans, and so on; expanded advertising and personal injury coverage; global coverage; and flexibility.[588] In addition, Chubb offers coverage for errors and omissions, electronic data processing, and machinery breakdowns—all specifically targeted at high-technology companies.[589]

---

[578] Milton, *supra* note 568.

[579] *Id.*

[580] *Id.*

[581] *Id.* at 441.

[582] *Id.*

[583] American International Group (visited June 15, 2002), http://www.aig.com.

[584] *Id.*

[585] Chubb Group of Insurance Companies (visited June 20, 2002), http://www.chubb.com.

[586] *Id.*

[587] *Id.*

[588] *Id.*

[589] *Id.*

[3] INSUREtrust.com

INSUREtrust.com[590] strives to "instill enterprise-wide accountability, responsibility and financial recourse in networked environments."[591] INSUREtrust.com focuses its business not only on providing insurance coverage but also on providing integrated insurance and risk management solutions for e-commerce.[592] INSUREtrust.com offers a variety of insurance policies, including Internet/network computer liability coverage, covering claims from intrusion into a trusted network; digital asset protection, which covers network computer theft, computer viruses, corruption, and business disruption due to network inaccessibility; and network extortion and ransom, which protects against wrongful system takeovers, alteration of passwords, and loss of system control.[593] Additionally, INSUREtrust.com offers public key infrastructure policies for digital certification.[594]

[4] Techinsurance.com

Techinsurance.com offers technology specific insurance plans,[595] including errors and omissions insurance as well as professional and general liability insurance for computer professionals.[596] Some of the key features of these policies include optional coverage for copyright and intellectual property infringement and worldwide coverage.[597] The professional liability policy protects against errors and omissions, intellectual property claims, libel and slander claims, invasion of privacy, and misappropriation.[598] The general liability insurance program allows computer professionals to supplement their policies with electronic equipment and media protection, which protects computer hardware, software, and data, including business interruption expenses.[599]

[E] Commercial General Liability Coverage

Commercial general liability (CGL) policies may cover intellectual property, defamation, or data corruption claims to the extent that they are covered in the advertising or property damage provisions.[600] Courts have construed such language in CGL insurance to provide at least defensive coverage for intellectual

---

[590] INSUREtrust.com (visited June 15, 2002), http://www.INSUREtrust.com.

[591] *Id.*

[592] *Id.*

[593] *Id.*

[594] *Id.*

[595] Techinsurance.com (visited June 15, 2002), http://www.techinsurance.com.

[596] *Id.*

[597] *Id.*

[598] *Id.*

[599] *Id.*

[600] *Id.*

property claims arising from the Internet.[601] In Minnesota, the court of appeals has held twice that CGL carriers "were obligated to defend suits involving loss or erasure of data."[602]

Within CGL insurance policies, certain provisions allow for recovery for transactions on the Internet. One such provision is for advertising injury.[603] This type of provision provides coverage for intellectual property claims and is included in most CGL policies.[604] Advertising injury provisions often cover patent infringement and trademark infringement arising in the course of advertising and should be applicable to Internet advertising.[605] It is unclear, however, if online transactions, such as e-mail or chat room conversations, would be covered under typical advertising provisions.[606] Also at issue are web sites that promote a service or product even though they are set up as question and answer boards that provide information rather than make solicitations.[607]

A personal injury coverage provision may also be afforded under the CGL.[608] Personal injury coverage is relatively uncontroversial; it includes coverage for slander, libel, and invasion of privacy.[609] A conflict may occur, however, if a policy excludes advertising, publishing, or broadcasting.[610] Personal injury provisions will likely cover noncommercial online transactions, such as e-mail, while commercial web sites would be covered under an advertising provision.[611]

[F] Internet Insurance Audit

INTERNET INSURANCE CHECKLIST

1. Does your commercial general liability (CGL) policy cover computer or ISP failure, including loss of valuable data? A CGL policy generally insures against claims for damages from bodily injury, property damage, personal injury, and advertising injury.[612] Whether electronic data constitutes "tangible" property under standard-form CGL insurance policies is a vital point.[613] Many standard-

---

[601] *Id.* at 442.

[602] *Id.* at 443.

[603] Bruce Telles, Insurance Coverage for Online Torts, 584 PLI/Lit 239, 258 (1999).

[604] *Id.*

[605] *Id.* at 261-265.

[606] *Id.* at 266.

[607] *Id.* at 267.

[608] *Id.* at 273.

[609] *Id.*

[610] *Id.* at 274.

[611] *Id.*

[612] David B. Goodwin and Steven O. Weise, Risk Management in Cyberspace, The Risk Report, Nov. 1998, at 8. See the Heller Ehrman White and McAuliffe web site (visited May 15, 2000), http://www.hewm.com/search/art.shtml?id=295&parea=BA.

[613] Lorelie S. Masters, Professionals Online: Advice for Travels on the Information Superhighway, 16 Computer Lawyer 1 (Mar. 1999).

form CGL policies use the term property damage in a narrow sense, meaning only physical injury to tangible property.[614] Thus, you must either prepare for disputes with your insurance company or consider adding statements to the CGL policy to clarify that property damage coverage includes loss from or of computer software, hardware, or services.[615] Courts have upheld coverage for loss or damage to computer data or databases.[616] Consider adding statements to protect against interruption if your server goes down or from viruses or other particular software losses.

2. Does your CGL policy's "advertising injury" clause adequately cover intellectual property claims? The advertising injury clause is the one most likely to cover intellectual property claims; to obtain coverage under it, one must demonstrate a causal connection between the injury and the policyholder's advertising activities.[617] Copyright and trademark infringement can fall under the "advertising injury" clause, but you will only receive coverage if you demonstrate a causal connection between advertising and the alleged infringement. The damage from infringing on a trademark most often occurs in the context of advertising, so the causal connection may be easy to demonstrate.[618]

3. Does your CGL policy's personal injury or advertising injury clause adequately protect against defamation claims? Whether web sites constitute "advertising" or "publishing" could affect insurance coverage for defamation claims. Whether Internet-related activities constitute "advertising" is an issue yet to be fully developed, although courts have rejected narrowing the definition of "advertising."[619] You may wish to purchase media or Internet liability policies to ensure that you have coverage for these risks.[620] A 1998 change to the standard-form CGL policies requires that, to be covered, an "offense must occur in the advertisement itself, rather than (as in previous forms) in the insured's advertising activities."[621] Thus, it is important to review a policy's endorsements to ascertain whether the insurer has excluded coverage for a potential claim.[622] Insurance coverage for emerging technologies is tricky business. Yahoo! purchased a CGL policy and, in a fairly straightforward case of trademark infringement, had to settle the claim and then sue its insurer for coverage.[623]

4. Is your errors and omissions coverage sufficient? This is particularly important if your business sells products created by your business. There may be

---

[614] *Id.*

[615] *Id.*

[616] *Id.*

[617] Goodwin and Weise, *supra* note 612.

[618] *Id.*

[619] Masters, *supra* note 613.

[620] *Id.*

[621] *Id.*

[622] *Id.*

[623] *See* Yahoo! Seeks $2 Million in Suit Against Its Insurer, Computer & Online Industry Litigation Reporter, 5 Aug. 1997, at 24448, discussing Yahoo! Inc. v. Federal Insurance Co. No. CV767426 (Cal. Super. Ct. Santa Clara Cty, complaint filed July 9, 1997), which settled out of court.

liability for failure of software or a computer system to meet a customer's expectations, and traditional errors and omissions ought to apply.[624]

5. Are the special insurance policies available for your company's web sites? As discussed above, many special insurance policies cover Internet activities. Such policies include media and Internet liability insurance; crime and fidelity insurance; and tort liability insurance. Media and Internet liability insurance usually covers only broadcasting, publishing, and advertising against defamation liability, but it may include defamation or torts to businesses that have web sites. Crime and fidelity insurance covers employee and third-party theft claims. Most policies do not cover Internet problems, but some are beginning to cover these claims, such as tort liability for harm from products sold online. Bottom line: To minimize risks, e-commerce will require more than CGL insurance. Seek out insurers who will work with you to cover your business risks properly.

6. Does your company have an officer and director of liability insurance policy? Be sure to have your corporate governance board advise officers and directors of their fiduciary duties of loyalty and care.

§ 9.04   ONLINE DISPUTE RESOLUTION

[A]   Introduction

Civil litigation is not an ideal option for Internet-related conflicts. Some online disputes can lead to years of paralysis as companies become mired in the overburdened, technologically challenged legal system.[625] Plaintiffs could drown in legal fees before they have their day in court.[626] Those with the fortitude and resources to make it to trial may be subjected to an unfair ruling by a judge who does not comprehend the technology. Consumers may be reluctant to shop online because of a lack of an affordable method of recourse against Internet vendors. International parties may face a choice of law nightmare, with courts reluctant to assert jurisdiction.

While insurance policies may be one way to protect Internet transactions, alternative dispute resolution may be ideal for the unique dynamics of conflicts in cyberspace by offering the parties a rapid, cost-effective, predictable, and reasonable solution. Ombuds[627] and the Virtual Magistrate[628] and offer online dispute resolution.

---

[624] Masters, *supra* note 613.

[625] *See, e.g.,* Interstellar Starship Services, Ltd. v. Epix, Inc., 983 F. Supp. 1331, 1336 (D. Or. 1997) (ruling on a two-year domain name dispute).

[626] *See* Mary Allen, Mediators Help Lighten Courts' Load, Capital, Apr. 13, 1998, at A1 (cautioning that parties to litigation will spend thousands of dollars in legal fees).

[627] Ombuds is a dispute resolution site run by Professor Ethan Katsh. Professor Katsh is the co-director of the Center for Information Technology and Dispute Resolution at the University of Massachusetts. *See* http://www.ombuds.org/center/index.html (visited June 15, 2002).

[628] The Virtual Magistrate debuted in 1996 to mediate domain name disputes and ISP subscriber problems. *See* http://www.vmag.org (visited June 15, 2002).

[B] The Case for Online Dispute Resolution

[1] Time Is Money

Online activities are measured in Internet years.[629] A typical calendar year can represent seven Internet years.[630] While Internet time flies by, a company whose name is exploited online may lose thousands of potential customers and countless revenue opportunities to a trademark pirate.[631] The Internet product life cycle is rapidly diminishing compared with traditional outlets.[632] Consequently, competitive threats, coupled with the distraction and costs of a lawsuit, can quickly relegate a company to the boneyard of online failures. A legal system that has evolved over 200 years lags behind the demands of a technology limited only by the speed of the fastest modem.[633]

In some jurisdictions, the average civil litigation conflict may last for three years.[634] After the trial, one or both parties might appeal seeking a retrial, further extending the length of the conflict. One district court has become popular because it only takes seven months from the time of the complaint to get to trial.[635] Such a time-consuming system is completely contrary to the rapidly evolving world of e-commerce.[636] The court system lacks a mechanism for quickly obtaining redress. In some cases, filing a a request for a preliminary injunction with its expedited hearing might suspend the status quo until a full trial on the merits can be held.[637] A preliminary injunction may be ordered when there is irreparable harm and a probability of legal success on the merits of the case. A court will also consider whether sufficient question exists regarding the merits of the case and whether delay will cause additional hardships to the moving party.[638] Meeting the

---

[629] Internet years may be no longer than 47 days. Lisa Greim Everitt, Tech Worker Shortage Tackled, Denver Rocky Mountain News, Sept. 13, 1999, at 1B.

[630] Thomas Vartanian, If You Build It, They Will Come, Am. Banker, Sept. 10, 1999, at 8.

[631] See Mark Williamson, Business Warned of More to Come From Cyber Squatters, Scotland on Sunday, Sept. 19, 1999, at 4 (examining the cost of recovering a pirated domain name).

[632] See Christine Lepera and Jeannie Costello, The Use of Mediation in the New Millennium, N.Y.L.J., May 6, 1999, at 3 (listing advantages of mediation for intellectual property disputes).

[633] As early as 1994, Internet legal analysts recognized the unique dynamics of computer network disputes and the inappropriateness of traditional legal systems for coping with those dynamics. See David R. Johnson, Dispute Resolution in Cyberspace (visited June 15, 2002), http://www.eff.org/pub/Legal/Arbitration/ (proposing a "law of cyberspace" to contend with online disputes).

[634] Jon Schmitz, Where Have All the Judges Gone? Pittsburgh Post-Gazette, Feb. 15, 1998, at A1. This exceeds the American Bar Association's recommendation that 90 percent of civil cases be resolved within one year. Id.

[635] See Scott A. Zebrak, A Step-by-Step Guide to Handling Domain Name Disputes, Computer Lawyer, Apr. 1999, at 21 (suggesting legal strategies for domain name and trademark conflicts).

[636] According to one online dispute resolution service, the average time required by the court system to resolve a civil claim is 30 months. See Phil Borchmann, Web Sites Help End Bad Posturing by Lawyers, Insurance Companies, Chicago Trib., July 19, 1999, at 2 (describing benefits of new online alternative dispute resolution services).

[637] F.R.C.P. § 65(a) (1995).

[638] Coca-Cola v. Tropicana Products, Inc., 690 F.2d 312, 315-316 (2d Cir. 1982).

court's requirements to show hardship to obtain a preliminary injunction may still require more time than a plaintiff can afford. A district court judge, for example, denied Playboy's motion for a preliminary injunction in an online trademark case because Playboy could not show sufficient harm.[639] Playboy had already waited two months from the time of filing the complaint until the case came before the court.[640] While the parties were waging their legal battle, thousands of customers may have been diverted to third-party web sites that took advantage of Playboy's name.

Additionally, the fast-moving nature of online communication can create unique conflicts.[641] Internet cases are still novel to some judges and attorneys. Several plaintiffs, for example, have sued the wrong party in domain name disputes.[642] Since no codified rules cover for online activities, parties to an Internet-related lawsuit might be surprised by the results. Unlike arbitration or mediation, litigation can be uncertain in time and cost.[643]

Internet disputes must be settled quickly. Online dispute resolution promises to radically reduce the time required to settle disputes. Commercial dispute resolution sites like clickNsettle.com[644] and Cyber\$ettle.com[645] claim that they can settle disputes within hours rather than the traditional 12 to 30 months. Other online dispute resolution benefits include the convenience of each party being able to choose the time for meeting and eliminating the expense and inconvenience of travel.[646] Arbitration and the use of private judges may be more appropriate for resolving high-stakes online disputes. Web site development and hosting agreements should have arbitration clauses or agreements for resolving disputes in hearings before private judges.

Mediation is also a viable option to reduce the cost of litigation, and is likely to become an even more popular option over the next few years. Currently, traditional mediation fees in some areas can total \$1,200, whereas online mediators charge approximately \$500.[647] Costs are a major factor in driving consumers and businesses toward commercial online dispute resolution web sites. Commercial sites[648] like Cyber\$ettle.com and Clicknsettle.com offer their customers low fee structures. Cyber\$ettle.com requires insurance companies to pay a \$25 registration

---

[639] Playboy Enterprises v. Netscape Communications, No SA CV 99-320 AHs, 1999 U.S. Dist. LEXIS 9638 at *13-14 (C.D. Cal. S.D. June 24, 1999).

[640] *Id.* at *1-2.

[641] Robert C. Bordone, Electronic Online Dispute Resolution: A Systems Approach—Potential Problems, and a Proposal, 3 Harv. Negot. L. Rev. 175, 180 (Spring, 1998).

[642] Courts have consistently held that the domain name registrar, NSI, was not liable for third-party registration or domain names that infringed trademarks. *See* Zebrak, *supra* note 635.

[643] E. Casey Lide, ADR and Cyberspace: The Role of Alternative Dispute Resolution in Online Commerce, Intellectual Property, and Defamation, 12 Ohio St. J. on Disp. Resol. 193, 199 (1996).

[644] *See* http://www.clicknsettle.com (visited June 15, 2002).

[645] *See* http://www.cybersettle.com (visited June 15, 2002).

[646] William J. Snyder, Online Settlement: The Future Is Now, Metropolitan Corporate Counsel, Aug. 1999, at 26.

[647] Robert L. Sharpe, Jr., Internet Negations Eliminate Egos and Accusations, Legal Intelligencer, Aug. 31, 1999, at 1.

[648] Another commercial site is http://www.settleonline.com (visited June 15, 2002).

fee and a $75 engagement fee, and each side pays a $200 settlement fee, regardless of the settlement amount.[649] Clicknsettle.com requires that a claimant pay a $25 registration fee (a $100 registration fee for a high priority case) a $50 engagement fee, and a settlement fee of $100 for cases that settle for less than $10,000 or of $200 for cases that settle for more than $10,000.[650]

Without the opportunity to engage in low-cost online dispute resolution, many companies might be forced to accept a position or to give up rights. Total-News Corp., for example, settled a framing, linking, and trademark dispute with several well-funded plaintiffs because it could not afford a lengthy appeal.[651] Other defendants may quickly give up a rightfully owned domain name rather than face the expense of defending themselves in court. In short, as online alternative dispute resolution sites become more popular, they will prove to be a cost-effective, efficient alternative to the courts.[652]

Relationships are key in the Internet business. Internet commerce has spawned a new type of business environment wherein competitors work together on some projects and compete on others. The adversarial nature of litigation is inappropriate in this business dynamic. Arbitration and mediation can provide a nonadversarial approach and preserve critical business relationships.[653]

[2]   Solutions for Consumers

Online pyramid salesmen and other electronic con artists quickly recognized the Internet as a medium for consumer fraud. Unfortunately, cybermediation did not provide viable remedies for fraud.[654] Fraud is an impediment to the growth of consumer e-commerce.[655] Online shoppers who fall victim to an unscrupulous cybermerchant may have a difficult time finding help. The United States government has encouraged business to create an internal dispute resolution mechanism to address consumer complaints about online transactions.[656] This would add an additional level of consumer confidence in online transactions.

---

[649] *See* http://www.insurance.com/gen/cybersettle699.html (visited June 15, 2002).

[650] Mathew Goldstein, Mediator Morphs into Web Service, and Finally Gets Wall Street's Notice: New Feature Enables Online Settlement, Crain's New York Business, Aug. 9, 1999, at 12.

[651] 97 Civ. 1190 (PKL) (S.D.N.Y., Feb. 20, 1997).

[652] Department of Energy ADR Policy (visited June 15, 2002), http://www.gc.doe.gov/adr/adr-policy.html.

[653] *See* Raymond L. Ocampo Jr., Mediation: The Preferred Route to Resolving High-Tech Disputes, ABA Bulletin of Law/Science & Technology, July 1999, at 5 (observing software developers competing with operating system licensors).

[654] The often touted Virtual Magistrate project handled only one case during a three-year experiment. Wendy R. Leibowitz, Let's Settle This, Online, Nat'l L.J., July 5, 1999, at 20.

[655] *See, e.g.,* Matt Roush, Web-Certified: CPAs, Better Business Bureau Approve Sites for Consumers, Crain's Detroit Business, July 19, 1999, at 33 (citing consumer hesitation to provide credit card numbers and personal information online).

[656] OECD Looks to Consumer Internet Regulations, Communications Daily, Sept. 9, 1999, available in LEXIS, News Library, Curnws File.

The Better Business Bureau (BBB) views itself as a provider of consumer information and as a referee. This organization has traditionally been a great resource for consumer tips. With the increased popularity of the Internet, however, the BBB has expanded its service offerings. The BBB provides web site certification to give consumers a degree of comfort when shopping on a certified commercial web site.[657] Businesses certified by the BBB are required to commit to the BBB's dispute resolution process.[658] Consumers and businesses can turn to BBB to resolve traditional and online disputes,[659] or the BBB may be used to assist in resolving conflicts over online privacy policy violations.[660]

[a] Online Product Sales/Auctions

The Internet has triggered an explosion in auction opportunities for a myriad of products, ranging from toys to antiques to vacations. Unfortunately, parties are not always happy with the results of their online transactions. A buyer may receive damaged merchandise, for example, or the parties may disagree about the quality of the goods.

Some auction sites offer mediation services to increase customer comfort.[661] Several online auctions have tested online dispute resolution through the Online Ombuds Office, a service of the University of Massachusetts.[662] The Online Ombuds Office was able to resolve more than 50 percent of the disputes that it mediated stemming from transactions at the eBay and Up4sale auction sites.[663] This matches the success rate for online resolution of non-Internet-related disputes.[664] Cases involving fraud or abuse of the auction system are not suited to alternative dispute resolution.

Online mediation for auction sites adds an additional guarantee of quality service by providing a convenient method for resolving disputes.[665] Other commercial sites selling third-party goods should consider adding an online mediation service. Some web sites include a mandatory mediation clause for any Internet contract to guarantee efficient dispute resolution.[666]

---

[657] Matt Roush, Web-Certified: CPAs, Better Business Bureau Approves Sites for Consumers, Crain's Detroit Business, July 19, 1999, at 33.

[658] *Id.*

[659] Bill Lubinger, Better Business Bureau is a Referee, Not Regulator, Plain Dealer, Aug. 23, 1999, at 4C.

[660] BBBOnline Privacy Program (visited June 15, 2002), http://www.bbbonline.org/Privacy.

[661] *See* Stephen Labaton, Can Defendants Cry 'E-Sanctuary' and Escape the Courts? NY Times, Sept. 22, 1999, at G39 (explaining challenges of selling goods online).

[662] Online Ombuds Office (visited June 15, 2002), http://www.ombuds.org/center/index.html.

[663] Wendy R. Leibowitz, Cybermediation: ADR in the Electronic Age, N.J.L.J. July 5, 1999, at 26.

[664] Cyber$ettle claims a 50 percent success rate in 3,000 cases. Phil Borchmann, Web Sites Help End Bad Posturing by Lawyers, Insurance Companies, Chicago Trib., July 19, 1999, at 2.

[665] Leibowitz, *supra* note 663.

[666] *See* Mediation in a Nutshell (visited June 15, 2002), http://www.internetneutral.com/nutshell.htm (explaining online mediation process).

[3]   International Disputes

Potential conflict of law issues abound in Internet disputes, making alternative dispute resolution ideal for some parties.[667] The International Chamber of Commerce, which handles cases from more than 100 different countries, is developing an online arbitration service.[668] Parties may be reluctant to leave themselves vulnerable to a foreign jurisdiction, so an arbitration clause may be an ideal compromise.

§ 9.05   PREVENTIVE LAW POINTERS

[A]   Suggestions for Handling Copyright and Trademark Infringement

While this book is not intended as a substitute for legal advice, the suggestions in this section may help parties resolve some disputes quickly. Sending letters incorporating these guidelines may correct the innocent infringer who has "borrowed" some element of your site. If your intellectual property is infringed by a competitor or you experience some economic damage from another party, seek legal counsel before taking any action.

Taking a nonadversarial stance in letting the other party know of their innocent mistake may lead that party to move quickly to correct the infringement. Before sending the notice of infringement, however, take time to check that you have the rights to the material and that the other web site is using the material without your permission. If you have any doubt, seek the assistance of counsel before sending a request to remove the material. A letter would be appropriate, for example, if a web site made copies of original images appearing on your site. On the other hand, seek counsel if you want to pursue a site using pictures similar but not identical to yours. In the worst-case scenario, your infringement letter could backfire, if your web designer actually borrowed the material from the other site.

Several web sites have posted examples of their infringement notices online. The University of Virginia takes a gentle approach, letting recipients know that they may have violated the Copyright Act and providing information about copyrights.[669] Viacorp's notice of infringement, on the other hand, directly asserts that material on the infringing site was taken from Viacorp's web site without permission.[670]

---

[667] *See* Alejandro E. Almaguer and Roland W. Baggott III, Shaping New Legal Frontiers: Dispute Resolution for the Internet, 13 Ohio St. J. on Disp. Resol. 711 (1998) (listing challenges of resolving online conflicts in traditional legal fora).

[668] International Trade Court Plans Internet Arbitration, Lawyer, Aug. 2, 1999, at 7.

[669] University of Virginia Library, Copyright Policy and Law: Copyright Notice (visited June 15, 2002), http://gopher.lib.virginia.edu/copyright/notice.html.

[670] Infringement Notice from Viacorp (visited June 15, 2002), http://www.viacorp.com/infringe.html.

[1]   Notice of Copyright Infringement

Any notice for copyright infringement should include the following elements:

1. Specific information on what was taken (which image, text, sound, and so on).
2. The full Internet address at which the infringement is taking place, including the paths, that is, *www.suffolkpcs.com/computers/info.htm.*
3. The address of the site (from which the copyrighted material was taken).
4. The action you want the infringer to take: remove the image, provide attribution, and so on. If you want payment, make sure to check with an attorney before sending the letter.
5. How the infringer can contact you with questions.
6. If necessary to clarify the infringing element, a print copy of the web page with the item(s) in question circled.
7. Let the infringer know whether the copyrighted material was registered.

[2]   Innocent Infringement of Trademarks Accidentally Misused

This section covers trademarks accidentally misused within a web site, not in infringing domain names. Domain name and trademark issues are addressed elsewhere in § 8.02[B][3] and in § 4.03[K]. Refer to legal counsel any infringement by anyone exploiting your trademark for profit. Finally, if you want the trademarked name removed, make sure that the web site infringes your exclusive right to the name.[671]

The letter for trademark infringement should mention the following elements:

1. The identity of your trademark. Specify if it is locally or federally registered.
2. The full Internet address at which the infringement is taking place, including the paths: that is, *www.suffolkpcs.com/computers/info.htm.*
3. Your company's name.
4. The actions you want the infringer to take: remove the trademark, provide attribution, and so on. If you want payment, make sure to check with an attorney before sending the letter.
5. How the infringer can contact you with questions.
6. If necessary to clarify the infringing element, a print copy of the web page with the item(s) in question circled.

---

[671] *See* Todd W. Krieger, Internet Domain Names and Trademarks: Strategies for Protecting Brand Names in Cyberspace, 32 Suffolk U. L. Rev. 1, 60 (1998) (addressing limits to trademark rights).

[B] SPC's Proper Use of Its Trademarks[672]

Trademark rights are acquired by the *proper* continuous use of the trademark. Two problems arise when a trademark is used improperly, both of which may result in loss of trademark protection. First, improper use can result in a judicial finding that a trademark has not been used in commerce. Bear in mind that to support a statement of use you must submit examples of the trademark that show the trademark being used properly in commerce. Second, improper use can lead to the trademarked term becoming generic. A trademark becomes generic when the trademark literally enters the language and becomes the common name for the product. The rationale for creating the category of generic marks is that no manufacturer should be given exclusive right to use words that generically identify a product.

Improper use of trademarks can be costly to a company, if not deadly to a product. Success of an online company, such as SPC, and especially of dot-com companies, is often linked to the company's name, its product names, or both. Losing trademark protection because of improper use may result in others using your trademark and profiting off the goodwill associated with your name.

The difference between proper and improper use of a trademark is grammatical. Trademarks are adjectives that describe a specific brand of product. Since trademarks are adjectives, they need to be used with a noun that they modify. SPC, in order to remain diligent in protecting its trademarks, should consider implementing guidelines on trademark usage. SPC's Millennium II, for example, is software. The adjective is *Millennium II,* and the noun it modifies is *software.* It is incorrect to say "when you enter data into the Millennium II, you will see the green light come on." This is incorrect, because in this statement Millennium II is used as a noun. When the term is not used as an adjective—when it does not describe a specific brand of product—it is not being used as a trademark. The correct way to make this statement would be "When you enter data into the Millennium II software, you will see the green light come on."

In addition, it is important to set trademarks apart from the nouns they modify. There are many ways to accomplish this. Capitalizing, italicizing, or boldfacing the trademark will suffice. Alternatively, stylizing the trademark not only sets the trademark apart, but adds strength and character to the trademark.[673] Finally, as previously discussed, adding the appropriate symbol (® or ™) will also set the trademark apart.

---

[672] Timothy Hadley, Technology Licensing Manager, Abbott Laboratories, Bedford, Massachusetts, is the author of this section.

[673] Stylizing means adding a design, whether a shape, color, or other elements, to the trademark. The application for registration of a trademark makes it possible to use codes to inform the USPTO of your design. Keep in mind that the sine qua non of trademark protection is distinctiveness. The strength of a trademark is determined by how distinctive it is. Accordingly, a mark that is fanciful, such as the unique word *Xerox,* or stylized, such as the cursive style of type used by Coca-Cola, is afforded the most protection. At the other end of the trademark spectrum, and receiving less protection, are arbitrary trademarks.

Other rules to keep in mind to use a trademark properly include never using the trademark in the possessive or plural form and never shortening, abbreviating, or creating acronyms out of the trademark. Again, using the possessive form or plural form of Millennium II (for example, "Millennium II's new features" or "Buy two Millennium IIs") turns the trademark into a noun. By abbreviating the trademark or creating acronyms you are not using your trademark, regardless of whether it is used as an adjective or not. Internally, for example, especially in R&D, SPC employees refer to Millennium II as "MII." Using it internally in that fashion does not create a problem for the trademark, but if the abbreviation was used in ad campaigns, those ads would not support a statement of use. The best course of action for SPC, given the likelihood that "MII" will become an alternative name for their product, is to seek trademark registration for the acronym. A prime example of the usefulness of registering acronyms and abbreviations is offered by America Online and its abbreviated counterpart, AOL.

The rules for proper use of a trademark can be summarized as follows:

1. Always use trademarks as proper adjectives.
2. Always set trademarks apart from the nouns they modify.
3. Never use trademarks in the possessive or plural form.
4. Never abbreviate or create acronyms out of the trademarks.
5. Always use appropriate trademark symbols (® or ™).

The rules are not meant to be draconian in their application. If they were, trademarks would lose some of their benefit, because the constant use of symbols and noun descriptors can be costly both financially (especially in software, where each bit is valued) and aesthetically. Accordingly, SPC operates under the following modified guidelines. For each page, noun descriptors are to be used at least 50 percent of the time. In addition, the noun descriptor must be used for the first reference on the page. Trademark symbols must be used at least once per page, either at the first reference or, preferably, where the trademark will be most noticeable.

Administratively, SPC implements its guidelines by having a paralegal review all web pages, advertising material, product packaging, disk labels, and manuals to ensure proper trademark usage. This procedure also facilitates the review of SPC's use of other companies' trademarks in its materials to ensure that they are being used properly and that these companies receive proper attribution. Finally, SPC's paralegal ensures that trademark notice (for example, "Millennium II is a registered trademark in the United States and/or other countries") is given.

It can be said that policing your own use of your trademarks is only half the battle. That is, to be sure that your trademark does not become generic it is also necessary to police the use of your trademarks by others. Third-party use of your trademarks in a noninfringing manner is known as referential use. In the software industry, referential use is critical. In order to sell any software, for example, you must inform the consumer of the disk operating system required to use your software. Combined with plug-ins, drivers, peripherals, and so on, your software package is likely to carry the trademarks of many different companies.

Granting permission for the referential use of your trademarks can be efficiently accomplished by having a dedicated web page that lists all of your trademarks, along with the rules for proper use mentioned above. Examples can be found on the following web sites:

> Sun Microsystems: www.sun.com/policies/trademarks/index.htm
> Corel: www.corel.com/legal/trademarks.htm
> Oracle: www.oracle.com/html/3party.html
> Apple: www.apple.com/legal/guidelinesfor3rdparties.htm
> Microsoft: www.microsoft.com/trademarks
> Netscape: www.netscape.com/legal_notices/trademarks.html
> Adobe: www.adobe.com/misc/trademarks.html
> IBM: www.ibm.com/legal/copytrade.phtml

[C] Copyright Clearance Center[674]

In 1995, Texaco, Inc., settled a ten-year-old copyright infringement lawsuit stemming from Texaco's practices of photocopying articles from scientific journals and distributing the articles to employees without paying royalties to the publishers.[675] To settle this high profile lawsuit, Texaco paid "slightly more than $1 million, plus a retroactive licensing fee to the Copyright Clearance Center."[676]

Texaco's practice of photocopying articles and distributing them to employees is a widespread practice but one not protected by the copyright law doctrine of fair use.[677] Startup online companies also should be aware of the hazards of distributing copyrighted materials without permission. Furthermore, with the ease and rapidity at which electronic media can be duplicated and shared, companies must protect themselves. If a company distributes software or other copyrighted materials beyond the scope of its license agreement, it can be subject to a copyright infringement lawsuit.

One way companies can protect themselves is by subscribing to the Copyright Clearance Center (CCC). The CCC was formed in 1978 to facilitate compliance with U.S. copyright laws by providing licenses for the reproduction and distribution of copyrighted material.[678] Presently, the CCC manages rights relating to more than 1,750,000 works and represents more than 9,600 publishers and hundreds of thousands of authors.

The CCC offers many forms of licenses, from those designed for academic organizations to others used by for-profit organizations. A license for a for-profit organization, known as an Annual Authorization Service, enables all employees in an organization to lawfully make unlimited photocopies for internal use of

---

[674] Timothy Hadley, Technology Licensing Manager, Abbott Laboratories, Bedford, Massachusetts, is the author of this section.

[675] Association of Research Libraries Bimonthly Newsletter, ARL 180, May 1995.

[676] *Id.*

[677] American Geophysical Union v. Texaco, 37 F.3d 882 (2d Cir. 1994).

[678] *See* http://www.copyright.com (last visited June 15, 2002).

excerpts of copyrighted information contained in one of CCC's titles. The single annual fee is determined on the basis of annual photocopying projections by the company using a calculation method based on number of employees and the type of industry in which the company is engaged. By subscribing to CCC, companies do not need to contact individual rightsholders for permission, pay individual royalty fees, or track each photocopy transaction.

[D] Know Your Insurance Coverage[679]

Online companies need to first determine what risks need to be covered and what coverage may be obtained at what price. An insurance audit needs to examine the full array of risks which need to be insured. What follows is a brief review of select Internet insurance companies and the type of coverage that they provide.

[1] InsureTrust.com

URL: http://www.insuretrust.com/

[a] *What Coverage Does It Provide?*

EXPRESStrust has been developed specifically to offer protection for brick-and-mortar companies which currently deploy or have plans to implement e-business initiatives. The insurance policy provides both first-party and third-party insurance coverage, which may be purchased separately or as a package.

EXPRESStrust's first-party protection, EXPRESStrust Digital Asset Protection Insurance, includes coverage for injuries from computer fraud, damage to digital assets, and business income and extra expense. EXPRESStrust Contingent Claims Made Excess Liability Insurance covers third-party liabilities resulting from electronic property damage, personal and advertising injury, and information asset damage.

[b] *What Are the Warranties?*

- Total annual revenues of $25 million or less;

- Fewer than 500 employees;

- Fewer than 500 workstations; and

- The insured must maintain a commercial general liability policy with an admitted carrier with policy limits equal to, or greater than, the limits requested for EXPRESStrust Liability (ineligible classes may apply).

---

[679] This section was written by Jessica M. Natale, 2002 graduate of the Suffolk University School of Law.

[c] How Much Monetary Coverage, Premium Costs?

Premiums start at $2,500 for basic coverage on lower-risk accounts, with $1 million in limits. Premiums will increase as customers seek higher limits, which can be purchased up to $5 million for each coverage part.

[2] Aegis Internet Insurance

URL: www.irastore.com/pl/prod01.htm

[a] What Coverage Does It Provide?

They specialize in errors and omissions insurance and professional and general liability insurance specifically designed to protect web site designers, computer consulting companies, contract programmers, software developers, and Internet Service Providers. Specifically:

- Libel
- Invasion of privacy
- Infliction of emotional distress
- Copyright infringement
- Trademark infringement
- Errors and omissions in cyber content
- Errors and omissions in providing cyber services for others.

[b] What Are the Warranties?

Not stated on the web site.

[c] How Much Monetary Coverage, Premium Costs?

The minimum premium for a limit of $250,000 is $1,000 plus the cost for the policy fee. The actual cost is based upon the scope and size of the business. $10,000,000 policy limit capacity.

[3] Net Secure

URL: http://www.netsecuresite.com/ns/nssite.nsf/Frameset?OpenForm& Query=Main:Home

[a] What Coverage Does It Provide?

Net Secure covers first-party and third-party losses due to programming errors and network and Web site disruptions; theft of electronic information assets, including intellectual property; content injury, such as web-related defamation; copyright infringement and false advertising; and losses associated with breach of privacy and the inadvertent release of personal information.

[b] What Are the Warranties?

To qualify for Net Secure, a proposed insured must undergo a two-step review: the first assesses insurance needs, the second analyzes a company's security risks. The average cost of these reviews is $7,500 to $15,000.

[c] How Much Monetary Coverage, Premium Costs?

In the event of a system crisis such as a security breach or web-site disruption, this coverage provides funds up to $50,000 for the use of security, public-relations, or technical support.

[4] Snaith Insurance

URL: www.iii.org/media/issues/internet_insurance.html

[a] What Coverage Does It Provide?

English company that offers legal protection against worldwide actions for

- Libel
- Malicious falsehood
- False attribution or authorship
- Passing off
- Unintentional infringement of intellectual property
- Unintentional breach of confidentiality
- Negligent statement
- Theft/destruction of data insurance

Offers web site designers professional indemnity:

- Infringement of other's copyright
- Infringement of intellectual property rights, such as those relating to software
- Unauthorized use of systems or programs of others
- Libel and slander
- Breach of client confidentiality

- Fraud and/or dishonesty of employees
- Irrecoverable fees (including amounts contractually owed to your subcontractors) that your client is justifiably refusing to pay due to your negligence.

[b]   What Are the Warranties?

None stated on the web site.

[c]   How Much Monetary Coverage, Premium Costs?

Covers up to £10,000,000 in damages.

[5]   Professional Insurance Agents Ltd.

URL: www.pro-ii.com/commerce.htm

[a]   What Coverage Does It Provide?

This company offers coverage for ISP and e-commerce providers:

- Internet liability insurance
- Professional indemnity insurance and commercial
- Public, employers, and products liability insurance

It covers several areas of Internet liability:

- Infringement of copyright
- Breakdown of service
- Unauthorized access to records, sensitive data
- Negligent acts, errors, and omissions
- Loss of documents (including web sites)
- Libel and slander

[b]   What Are the Warranties?

No explicit warranties are listed on the web site. However, several factors are taken into consideration in the Internet Liability Insurance Proposal Form, such as frequency of checking the web site for viruses, update software, use of encryption, products sent abroad, and traffic.

[c]   How Much Monetary Coverage, Premium Costs?

Monetary coverage: £100,000, £250,000, £500,000, £1,000,000.

[6] Complete Insurance

URL: www.completeinsurance.com/tech-ip/internetliabins.htm

[a] *What Coverage Does It Provide?*

This company offers Internet liability insurance for "companies concerned about security, privacy, credits/customer funds, denial of service, hackers."

The web site poses several advertising pitches:

- Could your customer be sued for a breach of privacy over your network?

- Are your clients concerned about the privacy of data stored on your network?

- Could your customer be sued if your network was shut down and its customers/suppliers could not access it?

- Does your customer use, accept, send, or manage for itself any digital signature or digital certificates?

- Does your customer conduct electronic transactions that, if any of the following occurred, it could be sued?

  - The transaction was accidentally sent with a virus.

  - The transaction was altered before, during, or after the transmission by a hacker.

  - The transaction was tie sensitive and you were unable to deliver or receive it.

  - The transaction required confidentiality, and this was breached.

- Would your customer be able to increase revenues if it were able to tell customers that it was insured for **Breach of Security**, **Denial of Service**, and **Intellectual Property Liability**?

- Would **YOU** be able to **increase revenues** if you were able to tell customers that you were insured against these exposures?

[b] *What Are the Warranties?*

No explicit warranties are listed on the web site.

[c] *How Much Monetary Coverage, Premium Costs?*

Not explicitly listed on the web site.

[7] Insurance Information Institute

URL: www.iii.org/media/issues/internet_insurance.html

[a] What Coverage Does It Provide?

Coverage can include:

- Loss of business income
- Public relations
- Intellectual property
- Difference in conditions
- Interruption of service
- Electronic publishing liability

[b] What Are the Warranties?

No explicit warranties are listed on the web site.

[c] How Much Monetary Coverage, Premium Costs?

In general, companies with revenues of $1 billion or less can expect to pay premiums of about $25,000 to $125,000 for at least $25 million in coverage. Coverage limits can be as high as $200 million.

[8] PTC.i Solutions

URL: www.ptclawyers.com
Entire web site is under construction. No information available at this time.

[9] ClickforCover.com/Esurancebusiness.com

URL: www.clickforcover.com

[a] What Coverage Does It Provide?

ClickforCover.com is an English company that offers Esurance™. This insurance covers the risks associated with daily Internet activities. It offers compensation to UK companies against loss, hackers, viruses, credit card and employee fraud, business interruption, and legal action.

It also offers IT consultants, forensic experts, PR consultants, and lawyers.

[b] What Are the Warranties?

No explicit warranties are listed on the web site.

[c] *How Much Monetary Coverage, Premium Costs?*

Monetary coverage: not stated on the web site.

Premium costs: The cost for this insurance starts at £20 a month and increases depending upon the company.

[10] **PayAssurance.com**

URL: www.diartstudio.com/portfolio/pa2

[a] *What Coverage Does It Provide?*

This company acts as a broker, having several insurance companies in its portfolio that offer e-Commerce fraud insurance, hacker insurance, and web server insurance.

[b] *What Are the Warranties?*

Coverage offered to companies.

[c] *How Much Monetary Coverage, Premium Costs?*

Not stated on the web site.

[11] **internetins.com**

URL: www.internetins.com

[a] *What Coverage Does It Provide?*

This company acts as a broker, having several insurance companies in its portfolio that offer e-commerce fraud insurance, hacker insurance, and web server insurance.

[b] *What Are the Warranties?*

Coverage offered to companies.

[c] *How Much Monetary Coverage, Premium Costs?*

Not stated on the web site.

[12] **eHackerInsurance.com**

URL: www.ewebsiteinsurance.com/coverages.html

[a]   What Coverage Does It Provide?

Coverage available:

- e-business interruption
- Systems costs for restoring lost or corrupted data and software
- Electronic vandalism
- Corruption
- Data loss
- Misappropriation of corporate identity: impersonating company data, forgery online, copyright and trademark infringement
- Employment liability: sexual harassment via computer systems, employee sabotage of computer

[b]   What Are the Warranties?

Not stated on the web site.

[c]   How Much Monetary Coverage, Premium Costs?

Not stated on the web site.

[13]   InsuranceSTOP.com

URL: www.insurancestop.com/internet-general-liability.html

[a]   What Coverage Does It Provide?

The company offers

- Internet insurance
- Multimedia liability insurance
- Electronic commerce
- e-commerce insurance

[b]   What Are the Warranties?

Not stated on the site.

[c]   How Much Monetary Coverage, Premium Costs?

Not stated on the site.

[14]   TruSecure

URL: www.trusecure.com

[a]   *What Coverage Does It Provide?*

TruSecure is a variation of hacker insurance, which will certify a site and pay clients $20,000 regardless of whether there is a loss—for malicious intrusion and data theft from a certified network.

This company also offers Internet liability insurance, which insures against losses arising out of employee dishonesty, check forgery, and third-party computer and fund-transfer fraud. Coverage is aimed at manufacturers, wholesalers, and retailers.

[b]   *What Are the Warranties?*

Not stated on web site.

[c]   *How Much Monetary Coverage, Premium Costs?*

Not stated on web site.

CHAPTER TEN

E-MAIL AND INTERNET USAGE POLICIES*

§ 10.01   Overview

§ 10.02   Risks from E-Mail and Internet Usage
- [A] Risks Posed by E-Mail
  - [1] Hostile Workplace Claims
  - [2] Ex-Employee Access to Systems
  - [3] Inappropriate Use of E-Mail
  - [4] Identity Theft
  - [5] Business Espionage and Trade Secrets
  - [6] Defamation
  - [7] Fraud
  - [8] Intellectual Property Infringement
  - [9] Corporate Liability for Crimes
    - [a] Gambling and Games of Chance
    - [b] Pornography and Obscene Materials; Controversial Web Sites
    - [c] Unlawful Interception of Electronic Communications
    - [d] Computer Fraud and Abuse Act (CFAA)
  - [10] Corporate Liability for Civil Infractions
- [B] Scope of the Risk
  - [1] Overview
  - [2] Employees and Others Outside Company Offices
    - [a] Telecommuters
    - [b] Independent Contractors

§ 10.03   Risk Management
- [A] Reallocating Risks of Loss
  - [1] Indemnification or "Hold Harmless" Clauses
  - [2] Nondisclosure Agreements
- [B] Employee Training and Supervision
- [C] Smoking Guns and Retention of E-Mail Messages
- [D] Electronic Monitoring of Employees

*We would like thank Eric P. Doyle, Esq., of PricewaterhouseCoopers and Beth Brown, a student at Suffolk University Law School for their written, editorial, and strategic contributions to this chapter.

　　　　　　[E]　Information Security
　　　　　　　　　[1]　Enforcing Information Security
　　　　　　　　　[2]　Antivirus Practices
　　　　　　[F]　Reducing Regulatory Enforcement Actions
　　　　　　[G]　Avoiding Privacy Claims
　　　　　　[H]　Insurance

§ 10.04　E-Mail and Internet Usage Policies
　　　　　　[A]　Key Issues
　　　　　　　　　[1]　Legal Audits
　　　　　　　　　[2]　Legal Autopsies and Near Misses
　　　　　　　　　[3]　Web Site Activities and Jurisdiction
　　　　　　[B]　Key Components of Any Policy
　　　　　　　　　[1]　Title
　　　　　　　　　[2]　Table of Contents
　　　　　　　　　[3]　Purpose/Background of Policy
　　　　　　　　　[4]　Scope/Permitted Purposes/Authorized Company
　　　　　　　　　　　　Activities
　　　　　　　　　[5]　Permitted Users
　　　　　　　　　[6]　Copying and Publishing
　　　　　　　　　[7]　Third-Party Rights
　　　　　　　　　[8]　Monitoring E-Mail and Internet Usage/No Expectation
　　　　　　　　　　　　of Privacy
　　　　　　　　　[9]　Telecommuting Employees
　　　　　　　　　[10]　Other Clauses/Mandatory Terms
　　　　　　　　　[11]　Conscious Delay
　　　　　　　　　[12]　Mechanics of Implementation
　　　　　　　　　　　　[a]　Standard Message Signatures
　　　　　　　　　　　　[b]　Message Filters
　　　　　　　　　　　　[c]　Spelling Checks
　　　　　　　　　　　　[d]　Corporate Internet Netiquette
　　　　　　[13]　Contact Person
　　　　　　[14]　Definitions

§ 10.05　Sample E-Mail and Internet Usage Policy

§ 10.06　Launching an E-Mail and Internet Usage Policy
　　　　　　[A]　Risk Assessment and Internet Access
　　　　　　[B]　Authenticating and Monitoring E-Mail Usage
　　　　　　[C]　Employee Education
　　　　　　　　　[1]　Use of Internet and E-Mail During Off-Hours
　　　　　　　　　[2]　Notice of Monitoring
　　　　　　　　　[3]　Cooperation with Law Enforcement Officials
　　　　　　[D]　Enforcement of E-Mail and Usage Policies
　　　　　　[E]　Even-Handed Enforcement of Internet Usage Policy

§ 10.07   Preventive Law Pointers
            [A]   Terminating Ex-Employees' E-Mail
            [B]   Telecommuting Employees
            [C]   Independent Contractor Status
                   [1]   Sample Nondisclosure and Confidentiality Agreement
                          for Independent Contractors
            [D]   Electronic Discovery
            [E]   E-Mail Notice
            [F]   Sample Confidentiality Agreement Encompassing E-Mail
                   and Internet Usage Safeguards

Appendix 10-1:   Department of Commerce Internet Use Policy

§ 10.01   OVERVIEW

E-mail and the Internet have profound implications for employment law, as reflected in the following hypothetical example:

> Suffolk Personal Computers (SPC) encourages its employees to develop through continuing education after work. One employee, Peter Atkins, wants to advance in his career and enrolls in an evening law school program. One of his required courses is constitutional law. Peter decides to do some of his homework after working hours on his work computer, after everyone else has gone home. His third assignment requires him to explore the issues surrounding hate speech. Pete decides that the Internet would be a great way to do his research, and he downloads several articles and prints out the contents of a number of controversial web sites. He forgets, however, to pick up his printouts before leaving.
>
> The next day, another employee notices some of the things that Peter had downloaded from the Internet and accidentally left on the printer. The printout she found included offensive racial slurs denigrating her ethnicity. She immediately brought the documents to Peter's boss. Shortly thereafter, his boss received a telephone call from the systems administrator regarding an e-mail with a controversial subject line heading that Peter had sent to his professor. Peter was terminated for abusing the Internet at work by downloading and e-mailing offensive materials.
>
> SPC had no Internet or e-mail use policy, and Peter has retained counsel to bring wrongful discharge and invasion of privacy claims against SPC.

Like many companies, our hypothetical e-business Suffolk Personal Computers considers its e-mail and intranet to be its digital nervous system, and it expects that these tools may be used predominately for business purposes.[1] SPC already uses its e-mail system to foster greater communication among and within departments by distributing corporate documents such as employee-benefit information, employee handbooks, sexual harassment policies, and expense forms.[2]

As the hypothetical illustrates, however, e-mail is fraught with potential pitfalls for unwary companies. On the one hand, the e-mail system can enhance the risk that an employee will harass or discriminate against co-workers or defame third parties.[3] A minor lapse, such as leaving employees off a distribution list for employment-related information, can provide evidence to support a discrimination

---

[1] *See generally* Bill Gates, From Business @ the Speed of Thought: Using a Digital Nervous System (1998) (explaining that a company's digital nervous system begins with the rule that communications flow through e-mail).

[2] Lori Jorgensen, Connection to Risk? Managing the Exposures of Cyberspace, 45 Risk Mgmt. 14 (Feb. 1, 1998) (noting that Microsoft employees use the company's intranet to access a variety of company databases).

[3] *See, e.g.,* Lian v. Sedgwick James, Inc., 992 F. Supp. 644, 648 (S.D.N.Y. 1998) (describing defamation action where a supervisor sent an allegedly defamatory e-mail about former employee). As Chapter Five explains, SPC may be liable for wrongdoing committed by its employees within the scope of their duties.

claim. On the other hand, a vigilant company that monitors e-mail use to reduce hazards may expose itself to invasion-of-privacy claims.[4]

Companies must achieve a balance between serving business needs and minimizing exposure to potential liability, especially since it is estimated that losses for companies worldwide grew from $4.3 billion in 1999 to $11.6 billion in 2000 because of the Internet and e-mail at work.[5] The volume of e-mail traffic continues to rise rapidly, creating an information flood or glut. An e-business loses money and time from e-mail overloads, and companies may buckle under an e-mail mountain of data. A survey found that "nearly a quarter of staff spent more than an hour sorting through e-mail, of which 34 percent was deemed irrelevant" to any business activity.[6] Monitoring e-mail usage is particularly justified where an employer has reasonable grounds to believe that employees are engaging in illegal conduct or other misconduct that might subject the company to liability.

Similar issues exist with the use of the Internet or intranets. In addition, companies that deploy laptop computers to their employees may unwittingly heighten the potential for Internet abuse. While employees may be more reluctant to violate policies while at work, after hours they may feel less bound by company policy. In the privacy and comfort of their homes, they may be tempted to use their company laptops to surf the Internet or e-mail off-color jokes to friends and family or download hardcore pornography.

The Enron debacle illustrates the role e-mail plays in litigation. A whistle-blower at Enron was fired for violating the company's e-mail and Internet usage policy. In the cases that will stem out of Enron, courts will need to balance a company's right to control use of e-mail and the public's right to know. The employee who leaked private company information onto the Internet helped to unveil a systematic pattern of corporate malfeasance.[7] "The . . . fired employee, according to Enron, was the person who revealed . . . on the Internet that Enron had paid $55 million in retention bonuses to top managers and executives just before it filed for bankruptcy protection and laid off 4,000 workers," and he had also criticized his employer heavily online.[8]

Moreover, "[i]t was not clear how Enron identified the employees behind the postings. People who post messages on Yahoo! often believe that they cannot be

---

[4] Electronic monitoring involves the collection of information about an employee's use of a company's computer, e-mail, or the Internet. *See, e.g.,* McLaren v. Microsoft Corp., 1999 Tex. App. LEXIS 4103 (Ct. of App. Tex., May 28, 1999) (holding that employee's expectation of privacy was outweighed by employer's interest in preventing the inappropriate use of its e-mail system); Bourke v. Nissan Motor Corp., No. B-687-5 (Cal. Ct. of App., July 26, 1993) (holding that employer's review of e-mail did not invade his right of privacy under the California Constitution or common law); United States v. Simons, 206 F.3d 392 (4th Cir. 2000) (holding that FBI's e-mail policy vitiated employer's expectation of privacy).

[5] Cyberklick: You Are Not Alone, Statesman, Mar. 4, 2001.

[6] Technology—Drive Down Your E-Mail Traffic, Network News, July 18, 2001.

[7] Alex Berenson, Enron Fired Workers for Complaining Online, N.Y. Times, Jan. 21, 2002, http://www.nytimes.com/2002/01/21/business/21WORK.html.

[8] *Id.*

traced if they do not use their real names. But many companies have the technical means to track the online activities of employees who use company computers and servers."[9] Even more, this employee stated that "he understood why he was fired. 'I was using their equipment . . . I was in their building, and it was a flagrant violation of company policy to do what I did. I'm not going to litigate it. I don't think it was unfair.' "[10]

Experts expect to recover incriminating documents regarding Enron's operations contained in e-mail smoking guns that will be used to prosecute those individuals and institutions involved in the collapse of Enron.[11] The potentially damning effect of an e-mail was also highlighted in the Arthur Andersen obstruction of justice case, which resulted in Andersen being convicted and having to resign from all audit-related services effective September 2002.[12]

This chapter provides a road map for navigating the most common risks and hazards presented by the online-enabled workplace. Section 10.02 begins with an overview of the legal troubles associated with the misuse and abuse of e-mail and the Internet. Section 10.03 focuses on minimizing e-mail and Internet-related hazards. Section 10.04 presents practical tips for instituting effective e-mail and Internet usage policies. Section 10.05 presents important considerations and sample elements to incorporate in policies. Section 10.06 provides guidance on how to implement an e-mail and Internet usage policy. Finally, Section 10.07 provides sample preventive law pointers to assist you with your implementation efforts.

§ 10.02   RISKS FROM E-MAIL AND INTERNET USAGE

[A]   Risks Posed by E-Mail

The risks associated with e-mail and Internet usage may be placed in two broad categories, internal and external. The internal risks are those that result in litigation, disputes with unions, hostility from employees, and loss, theft, or publication of proprietary or damaging information. The external risks are those that expose the company to negative press and law suits by third parties. For example, the risk encountered by SPC above was an internal risk, one that resulted in litigation between SPC and its employee. Using this basic dichotomy will help in addressing each risk because there are different technology and policy solutions for each type of risk. Internal risks are addressed first in the following sections.

---

[9] *Id.*

[10] *Id.*

[11] Sean Fewster, Hi-Tech Text As Evidence, The Advertiser, Mar. 7, 2002, at 19.

[12] *See generally* Milton Lawson, Andersen Argues Shredding Was Routine, UPI, June 5, 2002; "Nancy Temple, the in-house counsel at Andersen, would have had little sense of the magnitude of events she was triggering when she ordered a few changes in a memo related to the third quarter Enron results on October 16. But it was that single e-mail that finally proved enough for the nine men and three women of the jury to find Andersen guilty of obstruction of justice on Saturday." David Teather, Accountants Figure Out Cost of Andersen's Conviction, *Guardian*, June 18, 2002, at 23.

These risks are difficult to address through technology and typically will be addressed through policy and disciplinary measures, i.e., an e-mail and Internet usage policy as described in §§ 10.04 and 10.05. On the other hand, the external risks, such as the risk that a company employee misappropriates proprietary information, may often be addressed through technology by implementing security measures as described in § 10.03.

[1]   Hostile Workplace Claims

Employers may be subject to Title VII–based sexual harassment claims because of stalking, harassing, or unwanted e-mails. E-mail jokes, even though they may be sent in a spirit of fun, may expose an employer to sexual harassment and sex discrimination lawsuits. Increasingly, courts are validating the actions of employers who terminate employees for online activities. The Supreme Court appears to have tightened its position in regard to hostile workplace claims. In previous decisions the Court found companies that took quick corrective action not liable for workplace sexual harassment, but recently the Court has required companies not only to take corrective measures but also to have preventive measures in place. It may no longer be enough for a company to have an enforceable e-mail use policy. The Court seems inclined to find a corporation liable if it does not make reasonable efforts to implement protective technologies, such as a corporate tracking program, which could prevent harassment in the first place. E-harassment can also exact a high toll on a corporation financially. For example, in 1994 four Chevron employees sued the corporation for sexual harassment after receiving off-color e-mails. Chevron reportedly settled this case for a sum in excess of $2.2 million.

A Pennsylvania court upheld the discharge of an employee for using e-mail to send personal messages and to criticize management.[13] In an Illinois case, an employee stalked a co-worker with repeated unwanted e-mails. The court upheld the denial of benefits to the harasser, determining that "certain conduct intentionally and substantially disregards an employer's interests."[14]

An employee filed a complaint against a state employer, charging quid pro quo and hostile environment sexual harassment, claiming that she was denied the promotion because of a negative reference from her supervisor. The federal district court in Tennessee granted the employer's motion for judgment as a matter of law, finding the agency's antiharassment policy with a zero-tolerance approach to sexual harassment to be a key factor in its decision.[15] An e-business should disseminate its sexual harassment policy by e-mail as well as the traditional means of distribution.

---

[13] Oaster v. Unemployment Comp. Bd., 705 A.2d 507, 508 (Pa. Commw. Ct. 1998).

[14] Caterpillar, Inc. v. Department of Employment Sec., 730 N.E.2d 497, 505 (Ill. App. Ct. 2000).

[15] Idusuyi v. Tennessee Dep't of Children's Servs., 2002 U.S. App. LEXIS 2463 (6th Cir. Feb. 11, 2002).

The misuse of e-mail by employees can subject a company to claims of a hostile work environment or to a retaliatory discharge claim. Sexually charged e-mails may become the basis of a harassment claim.[16] For example, an employee sued the *Chicago Sun-Times* newspaper for sex discrimination that created a hostile workplace based in part on a veteran employee's repeated offers of a ride to another employee.[17] The smoking gun in that case was an e-mail from the supervisor that stated: "I know I'm getting to be a pain [in] the butt with these ride offers. And I apologize. But I can't help myself."[18] In an even more blatant example in *Knox v. Indiana*,[19] a sexual harassment claim was based on an e-mail message from one employee to another asking the plaintiff whether she wanted a "horizontal good time." In another case, *Litman v. George Mason University*,[20] a university student and employee of the university terminated the plaintiff's research position with a professor. The professor sent her an e-mail that stated: "Don't marry someone you live with. Marry someone you can't live without."[21] Although these statements may not be objectionable on their face, they may, nevertheless, serve as evidence of sexual or other harassment.

In a recent court decision in Utah, the court held that even if the company did not warn its employees about sending sexually explicit or offending e-mails while on the job, they will nonetheless be held accountable for their actions.[22] The harassers were found to have violated the employer's policy against transmitting sexually oriented and offensive e-mails multiple times. Although they admitted transmitting the messages, they claimed ignorance that such conduct was against the employer's policy. Utah's Workforce Appeals Board found that although the employees were culpable, they did not have knowledge of the policy and therefore there was not just cause for the termination. The Utah Court of Appeals reversed the board, finding that the employees were fired for just cause and moreover were not eligible for unemployment benefits.[23] The employer argued that "it is 'incomprehensible' for the Board to hold that a worker could be unaware of the dangers of having sexually offensive materials, including videos depicting sexual acts, sent between co-workers in a company's computer network."[24] The court agreed, by holding that "the employee's conduct violated a universal standard of behavior, lack of a specific warning did not preclude a finding that he had 'knowledge of the conduct which the employer expected.'"[25]

---

[16] Comiskey v. Automotive Indus. Action Group, 40 F. Supp. 2d 877 (E.D. Mich. 1999).

[17] Greenslade v. Chicago Sun-Times, Inc., 112 F.3d 853 (7th Cir. 1997) (affirming dismissal of Newspaper Employee's Title VII claim).

[18] *Id.* at 864.

[19] 93 F.3d 1327 (7th Cir. 1996).

[20] 1999 U.S. Dist. LEXIS 261 (Jan. 5, 1999).

[21] *Id.*

[22] Autoliv ASP, Inc. v. Department of Workforce Servs, 29 P.3d 7 (Utah Ct. App. 2001).

[23] *Id.* at 12.

[24] *Id.*

[25] *Id.* at 11.

E-businesses should require employees to sign a statement that they have read and understand the company's e-mail and Internet usage policy to establish the element of the employee's knowledge. In addition, a company needs a clear explanation of what is forbidden conduct in the policy and consistent enforcement of that policy. The rationale for banning sexually explicit and offensive materials is that it exposes the employer to vicarious liability for sexual harassment and sex discrimination lawsuits. It is arguable that sending out a harassing e-mail from a company URL is similar to sending out a fax with a company logo or address.[26]

Sending e-mails with jokes that denigrate minorities creates potential liability for a racial discrimination claim against a company.[27] A New York court held that a single e-mail, even though reprehensible, could not constitute a sufficient basis for a hostile workplace claim.[28] On the other hand, in *Sattar v. Motorola, Inc.,*[29] a supervisor sent an employee hundreds of e-mails that gave the plaintiff dire warnings of the consequences of turning his back on the Islamic religion. The plaintiff in *Sattar* requested 210,000 pages of e-mail messages.[30] Even though the company ultimately won the case, the litigation was expensive, embarrassing, and time-consuming. In another case, a Michigan employee transmitted an e-mail message to African-American female co-workers about a male African-American client of the company's. The e-mail message was sent to a supervisor who found the e-mail message to be offensive and disrespectful, so the employee was subsequently terminated. The ex-employee filed suit against his former employer for reverse discrimination. Even though the company prevailed on a summary judgment motion, the e-mail misuse resulted in costly and time-consuming litigation as well as negative publicity.[31]

Federal acts other than civil rights statutes may provide a basis for a claim. In *United States v. Casciano,*[32] for example, a cyberstalker was convicted of violating the Violence Against Women Act. The evidence included numerous unsolicited e-mail messages. The United States Supreme Court recently upheld a section of the Communications Decency Act (CDA) that prohibits indecent e-mail intended to harass or annoy the recipient.[33] Cyberstalking laws may result in lia-

---

[26] Firms Wake Up to the Pitfalls of Rogue E-Mails from Staff, Scotsman, Oct. 16, 2001.

[27] Curtis v. DiMaio, 2000 U.S. App. LEXIS 902 (2d Cir., Jan. 25, 2000) (affirming dismissal of hostile work place claim based on sending and receipt of racially charged e-mails).

[28] Owens v. Morgan Stanley Co., Inc., 1997 U.S. Dist. LEXIS 10351, 1997 WL 403454 (S.D.N.Y. 1997).

[29] 138 F.3d 1164 (7th Cir. 1998). *See also* Mieritz v. Hartford Fire Ins. Co., 2000 U.S. Dist. LEXIS 4965 (N.D. Tex., Apr. 15, 2000) (granting summary judgment in favor of employer in dismissal of auditor for attaching scripture verses to his e-mails contrary to company's e-mail policy).

[30] The supervisor who sent the hundreds of e-mails was transferred to the United Arab Emirates prior to the plaintiff's termination. The court found that the plaintiff was not terminated as the result of not following the Islamic religion and held for the defendant.

[31] Donley v. Ameritech Servs., Inc., 1992 U.S. Dist. LEXIS 21281 (E.D. Mich. 1992).

[32] 124 F.3d 106, 109 (2d Cir. 1997).

[33] ApolloMedia Corp. v. Reno, 526 U.S. 1061 (1999) (summarily affirming lower court opinion that § 223(a) of the CDA may constitutionally prevent the transmission of obscene communications over the Internet).

bility where the company had knowledge of an employee's wrongdoing and took no remedial steps.

If a company establishes and enforces a formal e-mail use policy, employees who claim to be the victims of harassment by co-employees may not prevail in court. While the policy may not forestall a claim, it may provide important evidence of an environment in which objectionable behavior is not sanctioned or tolerated. Employees from a Texas company, for example, filed suit for racial discrimination based on four jokes with racial overtones sent via internal e-mail.[34] The court rejected the plaintiffs' claims, which were based on Title VII and §§ 1981 and 1983 of the Civil Rights Act of 1964. The company prevailed by showing that it pursued the incident with oral and written reprimands to the employee who had sent the offending e-mail. Further evidence in the company's favor was its appointment of a staff member to advise employees of the policy against using e-mail for nonbusiness purposes.

[2] Ex-Employee Access to Systems

The risk posed by disgruntled ex-employees who continue to have access to the company intranet is far greater than that of industrial espionage. A number of companies have suffered losses because they did not terminate an ex-employee's access to computer systems. Some security breaches are caused by the company's simple failure to prevent ex-employees, consultants, and other insiders from accessing the computer systems. When an employee is terminated, a standard procedure should be in place for reviewing the ex-employee's computer files and e-mail messages. Passwords and authentication devices must be changed to prevent the ex-employee from retaining access to company computers. Some companies allow terminated employees, as part of a severance or layoff plan, to retain access to the company's e-mail system to assist them in finding new jobs. This benefit presents risks if the ex-employee has a grievance against the company or is not acting in good faith.

In one case, a California court held that a former employee of Intel Corporation, who had sent more than 30,000 e-mails critical of the company, committed trespass to chattel, and enjoined him from e-mailing the employees remaining at his former workplace. A California state court enjoined a former Intel employee from sending further e-mails, ruling that his actions were not protected by the First Amendment's Free Speech Clause.[35] Intel successfully argued that the e-mails

---

[34] Daniels v. WorldCom Corp., No. Civ. A.3:97-CV-0721-P, 1998 WESTLAW 91261 (N.D. Tex., Feb. 23, 1998); Curtis v. DiMaio, 2000 U.S. App. LEXIS 902 (2d Cir., Jan. 25, 2000) (affirming finding that sending and receiving racially-charged e-mail messages did not alone create a hostile workplace).

[35] Ex-Employee's E-Mails to Intel Workers Are Not Protected Speech, Judge Rules, 16 Comp. & Online Indus. Litig. Rptr. 8 (May 18, 1999) (reporting that California state court granted Intel's motion for summary judgment, finding that ex-employees transmission of thousands of e-mails to current Intel employees constituted trespass to chattels). This case is being appealed with support from the Society of Harvard Law School and the ACLU. *See* Intel Corp. v. Hamidi, 94 Cal. App. 4th 325, 114 Cal. Rptr. 2d 244 (Cal. Ct. App. 2001) (upholding injunction against former employee of Intel who flooded the company's e-mail system after being terminated; upholds injunction based on

were clogging its corporate e-mail system, and that the corporate computer system was not a public forum for First Amendment purposes.

The ex-employee argued that the e-mails did not harm Intel. The court, however, stated that "any impairment in the value to Intel of its e-mail system is sufficient to show injury."[36] The court observed that Intel was injured due to the loss in productivity from employees wasting time reviewing the thousands of unwanted e-mails they received from the ex-employee. Consequently, Intel also lost time and money in attempting to block the ex-employee's e-mails as well as in responding to employees' concerns about the e-mail messages.[37]

Corporations have been successful in stopping outsiders from sending unwanted e-mails by suing on state law theories of trespass or nuisance. These causes of action are an important and powerful tool when a corporation is faced with a deluge of unwanted messages. Recent claims of this nature have resulted in remedies such as injunctive relief and money damages. More than ever courts have begun to view a corporation's network, software, and online connection as an essential and valuable piece of property. A company may find it difficult to pursue this claim because e-mail transmissions will often be sent across state lines and typically cross international borders. A federal statute, 18 U.S.C. § 875, makes threatening e-mail transmissions actionable under federal law if the transmission of threats is classified as interstate commerce.[38]

[3] Inappropriate Use of E-Mail

E-mail messages tend to be more informal and emotive than business letters. An e-business that transmits e-mail from SPC's URL "has clear implications for the business—effectively it is like sending out a fax on company headed paper."[39] E-mail messages can also be forwarded easily throughout the company and beyond with the click of a mouse. Employees should be warned against a "stream of consciousness" approach: Messages that seem innocuous when dashed off may appear damning during discovery or at trial. Spelling checks, grammar checks, and other measures should be used: E-mail messages should be written with as much care as any business letter, with the assumption that the e-mail will be read by the same audience as a business letter or memo directed to the same person.

In addition, topics that have far-reaching implications are not appropriate for communication through e-mail for the reasons mentioned above. Such communications should be well thought out and the distribution limited. E-mail is typically not the appropriate medium of communication to achieve these goals. Moreover,

---

an action for trespass to chattels and rejecting defense based on free speech); see also Intel Corp. v. Hamidi, 2002 Cal. LEXIS 1883 (Cal. Mar. 27, 2002) (granting petition for review).

[36] *Id.*

[37] *Id.*

[38] *See* United States v. Kammersel, No. 2-97-CR-84C, 1998 U.S. Dist. LEXIS 8719 (D. Utah June 3, 1998) (finding that e-mail messages are actions in interstate commerce).

[39] *Id.* (arguing that the issue of e-mail privacy in the workplace has become contentious).

where corporate counsel is involved, there may be issues involving waiver of the attorney-client privilege that results from communicating via e-mail. The ABA Model Rules and most states' rules provide that use of unencrypted e-mail does not constitute a waiver of confidentiality. However, some courts have held that inadvertently forwarding an e-mail to a third party may result in a waiver of the attorney-client privilege.[40]

[4]   Identity Theft

Identity theft can include obtaining and exploiting an employee's Social Security number for financial gain or access to corporate security clearance. Identity theft can result in criminals using an employee's security clearance to steal trade secrets, money, or computer data. Adequate security of personal information about employees must be instituted to guard against the possibility that a co-worker may sell personal information to unscrupulous third parties. Some organizations require all personal and confidential information be encrypted. Employees should be instructed that e-mail or the Internet should never be used to transmit personal or sensitive information. Furthermore, employees should safeguard their passwords and avoid using the same password for e-mail and accessing secured sites.

[5]   Business Espionage and Trade Secrets

Aside from harassment claims and other torts, some criminal laws can help a company that has been harmed or expose a company to criminal liability for an employee's actions. One of the dangers of the Internet is the possibility that employees or ex-employees will divulge trade secrets online. Malicious employees can make files and records disappear with the push of a button and distribute confidential records worldwide in a matter of minutes.[41] A trade secret includes any information, "including a formula, pattern, compilation, program, device, method, technique or process" that has independent economic value and is subject to reasonable efforts to maintain secrecy.[42] In addition, a trade secret may not be information "that is generally known or ascertainable by proper means."[43] The Restatement of the Law of Unfair Competition defines *trade secrets* broadly to

---

[40] Matthew J. Boettcher, Concerns Over Attorney-Client Communication Through E-Mail: Is the Sky Really Falling?, 2002 Law Rev. of Mich. St. U. Detroit C. of L. 127 (Spring 2002).

[41] *See e.g.*, United States v, Martin, 228 F.3d 1 (1st Cir. 2000) (affirming conviction on finding that defendant conspired via e-mail with veterinary lab technician to steal trade secrets from employees); *See generally*, James Garrity and Eoghan Casey, Internet Misuse in the Workplace: A Lawyer's Primer, 72 Fl. Bar J. 22 (Nov. 1998).

[42] Uniform Trade Secrets Act § 1(4) (defining trade secrets).

[43] *Id. See also* Ford Motor Co. v. Lane, 67 F. Supp. 2d 745 (E.D. Mich. 1999) (holding that in absence of confidentiality agreement or fiduciary duty between the parties, injunction could not enjoin publication of trade secrets on the Internet).

include "any information that can be used in the operation of a business or other enterprise and that is sufficiently valuable and secret to afford an actual or potential economic advantage over others."[44]

Whether a trade secret has been lost on the Internet depends upon the following factors:

> (1) The amount of information that was exposed as compared to the "entire" relevant set of secret data; (2) The amount of time that the information remained exposed; (3) The extent to which the Internet gained actual (as opposed to theoretical) access to the information; (4) Whether the disclosure was referring to a defined group, making notice more practical; (5) The extent to which the information was disclosed to persons who are in a position to understand and use it; (6) Whether the owner took prompt action by giving notice and seeking to correct the situation by self-help and through the courts; and (7) The extent of the *bona fide* reliance by those whom the situation may have be exposed.[45]

Once a trade secret is transmitted on the Internet, the probabilities are that it will no longer be classified as a trade secret. The Uniform Trade Secrets Act requires a company to maintain secrecy and to use reasonable efforts to do so. Access controls must be instituted to prevent employees from posting company secrets to the Internet. This begins with limiting access to trade secrets to those employees who have a genuine business reason. Further, each employee should be bound by a confidentiality agreement. Without such an agreement there is no guarantee that trade secrets are protected.[46] In many cases a message may be displayed on the employee's computer monitor that requires the employee to agree to confidentiality each time he boots the computer.

A company's e-mail system or a company computer connected to the Internet may be the instrument used for a trade secrets crime. Software or other proprietary information may be downloaded and transmitted by cybercriminal employees. The threat of misappropriated information being published online is not hypothetical. A former member of the Church of Scientology, for example, posted confidential church documents on the Internet. A former Gillette employee was sentenced to 27 months in jail for transmitting "600MB or megs of secret data and drawings from the confidential Gillette project onto his laptop computer and [disclosing] the proprietary information by fax and e-mail to Gillette competitors, including Schick, Wilkinson and BIC."[47]

---

[44] Restatement of the Law of Unfair Competition § 39 (1995).

[45] James Pooley, Is Nothing Secret? The Newest Communication Medium Threatens Sensitive Business Information (visited Apr. 6, 1999), http://www.ipmag.com/pooley.html.

[46] Ford Motor Co. v. Lane, 67 F. Supp. 2d 745 (E.D. Mich. 1999).

[47] Mark D. Seltzer and Angela A. Burns, The Criminal Consequences of Trade Secret Misappropriation: Does the Economic Espionage Act Insulate Your Company's Trade Secrets from Theft and Render Civil Remedies Obsolete? 16 Comp. & Online Indus. Lit. Rptr. 13 (Jan. 5, 1999).

The Economic Espionage Act of 1996 criminalizes the theft of trade secrets.[48] The criminal statute requires the government to prove beyond a reasonable doubt that an individual acted with specific intent to steal trade secrets with knowledge that the trade secret was proprietary and knowledge that the theft of trade secrets would injure the victim. Prior to the Economic Espionage Act, prosecutors were powerless to pursue criminals who stole sensitive corporate data and crossed state lines.[49]

A growing number of states statutes criminalize the theft of trade secrets and intangible assets.[50] Criminal liability for trade secret misappropriations may be prosecuted under state criminal or penal codes. In one case, prosecutors filed trade secret charges against two Silicon Valley executives under California's penal law. The smoking gun in the case was deleted e-mail files. Charges were later dropped, though only after a four-year investigation.[51]

The risk of the misappropriation of trade secrets may be correlated with the organizational culture and whether the employment relationship is based solely on collecting a paycheck, or the "cash nexus."[52] Employers tend to "overestimate employee loyalty, or their own skills in detecting computer-based misconduct."[53] On the other hand, if a spirit of good faith and fair dealing pervades the workplace, a higher standard of behavior will usually result.

Self-control is the best form of control in an organization, and it is attained in an online company by recruiting, training, and retaining quality employees. In the information age, the workplace that treats employees like disposable plug-in, plug-out parts is more likely to have problems with the misappropriation of information.

The risk of trade secret theft is greater where executives as well as employees jump from company to company. In fact, the FBI reports that domestic and foreign espionage resulted in the theft of intellectual property in excess of $300 billion in 1997.[54]

---

[48] 18 U.S.C. § 1832 (1997). The Act defines a trade secret as follows: (1) The owner took reasonable measures to keep the information secret commensurate with the value of the trade secret and (2) the information derives actual or potential independent economic value from not being made known to the public. 18 U.S.C. § 1839(3)(A)(B) (1997).

[49] Dan Goodin, Busting Industrial Spies, The Recorder (Sept. 25, 1996) at 1 (noting how "outsiders had downloaded a sensitive business proposal and run off to New Mexico [and that] the U.S. attorney's office declined to go after the culprits since the theft of intangibles was not yet a federal crime").

[50] *Id.* (noting that California criminalizes the transmission of stolen trade secrets); *see also* Ruckelshaus v. Monsanto Co., 467 U.S. 986 (1984) (holding that pesticide manufacturer had protectable trade secrets under the Trade Secrets Act, 18 U.S.C. § 1095, which penalizes any employee of the U.S. government who discloses trade secret information revealed in the course of his duties).

[51] The case was People v. Eubanks, No. S049490 (Ca. Superior Ct., charges dropped Nov. 19, 1996), *reported in* DA Drops Prosecution of Executives; California Supreme Court Might Rule on Appeal, Software L. Bull. 14 (Jan. 1997).

[52] The concept of the cash nexus was prefigured in Karl Marx and Frederick Engels' *Communist Manifesto.* Today, the concept of the cash nexus is widely used by industrial sociologists to describe a workplace in which calculation and self-interest predominate versus moral involvement.

[53] Garrity and Casey, *supra* note 41.

[54] Curtis E. A. Karnow, Computer Network Risks: Security Breaches and Liability Issues: The Judicial System Is Only Starting to Address Related Privacy Matters, 15 Comp. L. Strat. 1 (Feb. 1999) (quoting FBI report).

[6] Defamation

The risk of being subject to a defamation lawsuit is a significant exposure. For example, the web content manager at SPC maintains a grudge against his former employer. Working late one night, he posts his opinion on the SPC site. The next week, the competitor files a defamation suit against SPC. Such online defamation claims may arise out of a wide variety of e-mail or Internet communications: in chat rooms, on web sites, or from forwarded e-mail that defames individuals. In addition, companies may also be subject for trade libel for defamatory statements made about other companies.

Defamation is the communication of an unprivileged false and defamatory statement about a plaintiff, transmitted to a third person, and, as noted in Chapter Five, § 5.05[A], it is traditionally subdivided into oral slander and written and published libel in physical form.[55] The Internet may provide the means for either: a recorded audio clip or wave file downloaded and replayed may constitute either libel or slander. The traditional rule is that publishers are liable for any defamatory content, but mere distributors are not liable unless they know or have reason to know of the defamatory statement.[56]

Free speech and opinions may take a back seat to the threat of litigation online. A psychiatrist who hosted a web site brought a defamation action against the host of a rival web site for defamation in *Barrett v. The Catacombs Press.*[57] The statements by the defendant attacked the plaintiff in his capacity as an advocate against health care fraud and in favor of fluoridation of water sources.[58] The plaintiff was a psychiatrist involved in investigating and dealing with many aspects of health care. His web site, called Quackwatch, provided information about health fraud and quackery. The Quackwatch web site addressed the fluoridation debate with a web page entitled "Fluoridation: Don't Let the Poisonmongers Scare You."

---

[55] Section 230 of the Communications Decency Act immunizes providers for providing access to defamatory information and other torts. *See, e.g.,* Ben Ezra, Weinstein & Co. v. America Online, Inc., 206 F.3d 980 (10th Cir. 2000) (upholding immunity for defamation cause of action); Zeran v. America Online, 129 F.3d 327 (4th Cir. 1997); John Does v. Franco Productions, 2000 U.S. Dist. LEXIS 8645 (N.D. Ill., June 22, 2000) (dismissing action against provider who transmitted images of college athletes filmed by a secret camera); Jane Doe One v. Oliver, 46 Conn. Supp. 406, 755 A.2d 1000 (2000) (striking claims against provider for improper e-mails on immunity grounds). The Good Samaritan Defense of the Communications Decency Act of 1996 gives interactive computer services immunity for defamation and other torts committed on SPC's web site. SPC may be liable for its own defamatory statements made by company officials acting within their scope of duties, however. *See* 47 U.S.C. § 230 (2000), Ben Ezra Weinstein v. America Online, Inc., 206 F.3d 980 (10th Cir. 2000) (upholding § 230 immunity for provider in defamation action); Eric M. D. Zion, Protecting the E-Marketplace of Ideas by Protecting Employers: Immunity for Employers under Section 230 of the Communications Decency Act, 54 Fed. Comm. L.J. (May 2002)

[56] Jeffrey P. Cunard et al., Communications Law 1998: Internet Law Developments, Practicing Law Institute, Patents, Copyrights, Trademarks, and Literary Property Course Handbook Series, PLI Order No. GA-4039 (Nov. 1998).

[57] 44 F. Supp. 2d 717 (E.D. Pa. 1999).

[58] *Id.*

The plaintiff sent the defendant an e-mail threatening a lawsuit after seeing her web site.[59]

Attorneys should be careful when making statements in chat rooms or in online bulletin boards. Although attorneys enjoy an absolute immunity from suit for claims made during a judicial proceeding, there is no similar immunity for statements published online. Chat rooms and bulletin boards can be a useful legal tool but are also fertile grounds for the growth of defamation claims, as they communicate information to the public at large.

[7] Fraud

Companies may be subject to a number of direct liabilities, such as fraud or products liability for knowingly placing defective software on the market, or it may be indirectly liable for fraud committed by hackers who steal its customers' credit card numbers or personal information. Fraud is frequently invoked in trade libel cases redressing injuries to business reputation.[60] Companies may be held liable for online defamation for the statements of an employee made in advertisements, chatrooms, and other Internet-related forums.

In *Lunney v. Prodigy Services Co.,*[61] the New York Appeals Court extended a common law privilege designed for telegraph services to Internet service providers covering defamatory statements made on their forums. In that case, an unknown third party opened a Prodigy account in the name of a 15-year-old Boy Scout. The unknown subscriber transmitted an offensive and threatening e-mail to the boy's local Boy Scout leader. The scout leader reported the matter to the boy's scoutmaster, who confronted the boy and demanded an explanation. In response to the report, Prodigy then closed the boy's account because of a breach of the subscriber's agreement, as pointed out by the scout leader's complaint.

The plaintiff brought suit against Prodigy for libel, negligence, and harassment—all the product of a fraudulent e-mail sent using Prodigy's network. The *Lunney* court dismissed the claims against the online service provider, holding that it was not liable for defamatory materials placed on its system without its knowledge.[62] Other companies, however, may not be as lucky as Prodigy and may be held liable for online defamation if their systems carry derogatory statements about competitors or their products.

---

[59] The court declined to exercise jurisdiction over the defendant because he neither targeted nor solicited Pennsylvania residents and otherwise did not meet the minimum contact tests.

[60] *See, e.g.,* Barrett v. Cazacombs Press, 44 F. Supp. 2d 717 (E.D. Pa. 1999), Seidl v. Greentree Mortg. Co., 30 F. Supp. 2d 1292 (D. Colo. 1998).

[61] 1998 N.Y. App. Div. LEXIS 14047 (Sup. Ct. N.Y. App. Div. 1998); Lunney v. Prodigy Servs. Co., 94 N.Y.2d 242, 723 N.E.2d 539 (Ct. of App. of N.Y. 1999), *cert. denied,* 120 S. Ct. 1832 (2000) (upholding finding that provider was entitled to the common-law qualified privilege accorded telephone companies and thus sheltered from liability).

[62] *Id.*

[8]   Intellectual Property Infringement

E-mail gives the user the capability of sending data files, pictures, and even video, instantaneously.[63] For example, Jeff Uslan, director of information protection at 20th Century Fox in Los Angeles, "oversee[s] the e-mail and Internet usage of over 10,000 employees. [He] must make sure that confidential information about movie scripts, deals, and other Fox business does not leak outside the company's e-walls. 'We look more for the loss of intellectual property and e-mail borne viruses.'"[64] When a user sends material to which someone else holds the copyright, he or she risks infringing the copyright. A company may reduce its own exposure to infringement actions by owning, licensing, or assigning all copyrightable materials on its web site. At minimum, proper notice of copyright must be given for all content supplied by the company and third parties. Due diligence should cover all materials provided by third parties, as well as by the company. Copyrights and trademark clearance must be obtained for any pictures, images, cartoons, photographs, illustrations, streaming video, graphics, text, or other content.

To protect its rights, a company's notices must encompass rights in text, graphics, selection, and arrangement, as well as in the "look and feel" or overall design of its web site.[65] If the web site developer supplies content, the company will need a license agreement to use, modify, update, and maintain materials on the web site. The web site agreement should cover all intellectual property rights, including copyrights, trademarks, trade secrets, patents, and the right of publicity. The company should enter into an agreement with the web site developer to obtain the ownership interest in the web site.

If the company permits web site visitors to post information on chat rooms, listservs, or other pages on its sites, a terms of service agreement should be implemented. The company must make it clear that it is not liable for outside postings by third parties and that it does not endorse individuals or entities posting information.[66]

---

[63] America Online and Kodak are developing a technology for sending pictures directly from photo processing shops to e-mail accounts. Polaroid Corporation has licensed technology from NASA that will enable users to send over the Internet images secured from tampering through the use of special digital cameras and digital signatures.

[64] Sacha Cohen, Thought Cop, InfoWorld, Feb. 26, 2001.

[65] Amazon.com sued a web site in Greece for copyright and trademark infringement. The Greek site registered the domain name "amazon.gr" and replicated "the look and feel" of Amazon.com's web site. Trademarks/RICO, Amazon.com Sues Greek Site for Trademark, Copyright, RICO Violations, Andrews Comp. & Online Indus. Litig. Rep. 3 (Sept. 21, 1999).

[66] To protect its own intellectual property rights, SPC will need to do the following: (1) obtain or register its domain name; (2) seek warranties that intellectual property obtained from others does not infringe the intellectual property rights of others; (3) obtain, register, and protect its trademarks and copyrights; (4) obtain patents or licenses to use e-commerce patents; (5) audit all content on its web site; and (6) use license agreements when obtaining content. Section 8.02[B] provides a systematic discussion of the legal audit for intellectual property rights.

The creation of peer-to-peer network clients has created new risks of intellectual property infringement. Peer-to-peer networks allow Internet users to connect directly to one another's computers and exchange files without regard to copyright or trademark. This type of file exchange became the subject of *A & M Records, Inc. v. Napster, Inc.*[67] Many of these file-swapping, peer-to-peer software clients will operate through a company's firewall, allowing employees to swap copyrighted software, images, and even video clips through the company's network. Although a contributory infringement claim in such circumstances may seem tenuous, the law is still largely unsettled even after *Napster*. Accordingly, companies should consider prohibiting the use of such peer-to-peer software in their Internet usage policies.

[9]   Corporate Liability for Crimes

[a]   *Gambling and Games of Chance*

Business activities on the Internet permissible in the state where a company is based may create a risk of liability in other jurisdictions where the activity is prohibited. An offer of a promotion, sweepstakes, or gambling may be regulated in some states and countries. Companies will need to investigate the laws of multiple jurisdictions before launching an online promotion or sweepstakes. Due diligence will include a notice that the contest or game is void in countries where it is prohibited.[68]

[b]   *Pornography and Obscene Materials; Controversial Web Sites*

Employees' abuse of corporate e-mail systems and Internet access raises serious productivity concerns. It is estimated that "one in four of all e-mail image attachments are pornographic."[69] Nearly two-thirds of responding companies reported that employees "accessed sexually explicit web sites at work. Greater than a quarter of companies took disciplinary action against employees for sex site surfing."[70] Another survey found that "employees at three well-known companies

---

[67] 239 F.3d 1004 (9th Cir. 2001).

[68] In a recent article, it was noted that "[a]s of this writing [published June 2000], the majority of states have laws which could be construed to ban Internet gambling. These states include Alabama, Arizona, California, Colorado, Connecticut, Delaware, Hawaii, Illinois, Kansas, Louisiana, Massachusetts, Minnesota, Missouri, Nebraska, Nevada, North Carolina, Pennsylvania, Texas, and Utah, who have, or arguably have, prohibited the individual act of Internet gambling. California, Hawaii, Indiana, and New York are just a few of the many states that are currently in the process of reforming their laws to explicitly prohibit the individual act of Internet gambling." Computer Crimes and the Respondeat Superior Doctrine: Employers Beware, 6 Boston U. J. of Science and Technology Law 6 (June 1, 2000), Mark Ishman, at 71.

[69] James McNamara, New Weapon in War on E-Porn Launched, Manchester Evening News, July 11, 2001.

[70] Karnow, *supra* note 54.

spent the equivalent of 350 eight-hour workdays accessing the Penthouse Magazine Web site in a single month."[71] Unlimited access to the Internet may allow wayward employees to locate pornography or other objectionable materials from one of the thousands of web sites that provide it.[72] "Live feed" web sites enable employees to view live performances of sexual acts from their desktop, which may expose their companies to potential liability for a hostile workplace claim.[73]

The e-mail and Internet policy must address company concerns about downloading obscene, indecent, and other questionable content. Even if the material is not illegal or objectionable, downloaded video, music, and other publications may overload the corporate computer system and create a distraction that impedes workplace productivity. Employees have no First Amendment right to misuse proprietary computer systems.

In addition to productivity losses, the company may also be exposed to civil liability, criminal liability, or bad publicity. The e-mail system is an efficient means for forwarding documents, including pornographic or obscene messages, and it is a common practice to forward off-color jokes or other objectionable materials to multiple recipients. The simple act of forwarding these jokes may unwittingly expose a company to a discrimination lawsuit under Title VII of the Civil Rights Act of 1964 and state discrimination laws.[74] A company is also potentially subject to a hostile workplace claim when off-color or racist jokes are e-mailed to company employees.[75]

In 1996, the Prodigy corporation was sued by a young woman who had contracted HIV after having sexual intercourse with a Prodigy employee. The young woman claimed that the Prodigy employee was a sexual predator who lured her into the relationship through countless hours of e-mail chat and offers of free company services and gifts. Prodigy was ultimately not liable for the actions of its employee. The case was dismissed because the employee's acts were not within the scope of his employment, but Prodigy was forced to expend resources in the litigation.[76]

In some countries, the mere possession of obscene materials not objectionable in the U.S. may be regarded as a serious offense. The federal Child Online Protection Act, for example, that makes it a crime to "knowingly . . . , by means

---

[71] Thomas P. Klein, Electronic Communications in the Workplace, Legal Issues and Policies, Third Annual Internet Law Institute 1999 (PLI Patents, Copyrights, Trademarks and Literary Property Course Handbook Series, No. G0-005(1)).

[72] Garrity and Casey, *supra* note 41.

[73] General Media, Inc. v. Shooker, 1998 WL 401530 (S.D.N.Y., July 16, 1998) (citing affidavit of A. Guccione, *Penthouse* magazine); *see* Yamagushi v. United States Dep't of Air Force, 109 F.3d 1475 (9th Cir. 1997) (basing hostile workplace claim in part upon offensive e-mail messages).

[74] *See, e.g.,* Rudas v. Nationwide Mut. Ins. Co., 1997 WL 11302 (E.D. Pa., Jan. 10, 1997) (dismissing e-harassment case predicated upon sexually-charged e-mail messages).

[75] A federal court rejected a claim by African-American employees of Morgan Stanley & Co., alleging that a racist e-mail joke transmitted on the company's computer system created a hostile work environment. Owens v. Morgan Stanley & Co., No. 96 Civ. 9747 DLC (S.D.N.Y., July 1997).

[76] Haybeck v. Prodigy Servs. Co., 944 F. Supp. 326 (S.D.N.Y. 1996).

of the World Wide Web, make any communication for commercial purposes that is available to any minor and that includes any material that is harmful to minors."[77] Law enforcement authorities may confiscate company computers involved in distributing child pornography on the Internet.

Many prosecutors take the position that they may prosecute anyone found to have pornographic materials on their computers. A computer specialist working for the U.S. Senate, for example, was arrested for sending pornographic images from his office at the Senate. The dean of the Harvard Divinity School was dismissed for storing large quantities of pornographic images on his university-owned computer.

An employee who downloads pornography may be violating state and federal criminal law. Courts have little difficulty admitting e-mail messages to show a defendant's state of mind while engaging in illegally sanctioned activity. In *United States v. Hall,*[78] the Sixth Circuit omitted e-mail messages as evidence of the defendant's online solicitation of child pornography under the other-bad-act exception to the hearsay rule, which is the exception. It is unlikely that a company such as SPC will be prosecuted for the possession of pornography, but it would lose time and money while cooperating with law enforcement if a police unit seized company computers to prosecute an employee. Even if not liable for downloaded materials, a company will at least suffer adverse publicity, particularly in the case of child pornography. Charges against a high-level employee for possessing pornographic materials would be a public relations disaster. In a worst-case scenario, a company might be found liable for the downloaded materials. Companies should check to be sure that their web sites comply with relevant law regarding obscenity and pornographic materials.

An Internet usage policy must take into account the possibility that employees will download offensive material from the Internet. A company must make it clear that employees are not free to download offensive material from the Internet or to forward offensive e-mails.

Companies may also be exposed to adverse publicity if their employees use company computers to post messages to newsgroups or to visit web sites relating to such controversial topics as abortion, white supremacy, or neo-Nazism. Employees should be warned that it is a misuse of company Internet access to visit or contribute to any controversial site. The general standard to be communicated is that the computer system is to be used primarily for business purposes.

In addition to the usage policy, the company may want to institute technological safeguards, such as filters that restrict access to web sites containing hate speech, pornography, or other objectionable materials. Companies must decide which sites to restrict in order to avoid legal liability. Employees should be

---

[77] United States v. Hall, 2000 WL 32010 (6th Cir., Jan. 4, 2000) (admitting e-mails as evidence of state of mind in child pornography conviction); United States v. Simons, 206 F.3d 392 (4th Cir. 2000) (upholding conviction of employee for storing child pornography on company computer).

[78] *Id.*

instructed to use their own e-mail addresses for personal messages. A "business purposes only" policy might be stated as follows:

> If you wish "to send personal e-mail from the office, use your own e-mail software, e-mail account, and ISP, or use one of the free-e-mail services available on the Web."[79] Personal e-mail messages should be sent and responded to after work hours. Employees should be cautioned that if objectionable materials are transmitted on a company computer, a search and seizure of a company's computer system may result in adverse publicity to the company.[80]

[c] Unlawful Interception of Electronic Communications

A company that intercepts the e-mail or other electronic communications of a business rival or competitor is subject to criminal and civil liability under the Electronic Communications Privacy Act of 1986 (ECPA).[81]

In a recent case, the court upheld the meaning of *intercept* and also confirmed that "the ECPA did not eliminate the during-transmission requirement from the Wiretap Act."[82] The court affirmed that "the common meaning of intercept then requires the electronic communication to be acquired before it reaches its intended destination, *i.e.*, during its transmission."[83] The plaintiff claimed that the defendants acquired the e-mail after the senders sent the e-mail and the intended recipients received it. The court held that "because the acquisition occurred after—not during—transmission, Plaintiff fails to state facts to support a Wiretap-Act violation."[84]

The ECPA states that any person who "intercepts, endeavors to intercept, or procures any other person to intercept or endeavor to intercept electronic communications" is subject to fines and/or imprisonment.[85] Any person who intercepts

---

[79] Mike Elgan, The Dangers of E-Mail: Follow These 15 Rules for Your E-Mail System and Steer Clear of Legal Woes CMPNET (Apr. 12, 1999). The Internet offers at least 700 free e-mail services.

[80] The employee may be subject to criminal liability for transmitting visual images through an online computer system. It is a federal crime to transport obscene materials for the purpose of sale or distribution in interstate or foreign commerce. 18 U.S.C. § 1465 (1997). The Communications Decency Act of 1996 immunizes employers from tort liability "for the obscene or harassing use of electronic telecommunications by their employees 'unless the employee's or agent's conduct is within the scope of his employment or agency and the employer (a) having knowledge of such conduct, authorizes or ratifies such conduct, or (b) recklessly disregards such conduct.'" Peter Brown, Policies for Corporate Internet and E-Mail Use, Third Annual Internet Law Institute, 1999, 564 PLI/Pat 637, 639 (June 14-15, 1999) (quoting Communications Decency Act of 1996).

[81] 18 U.S.C. §§ 2510 et seq. (1998). *See* McVeigh v. Cohen, 983 F. Supp. 215 (D.D.C. 1998) (issuing injunction against Navy from discharging plaintiff for homosexual conduct because of possible violation of the Electronic Communications Privacy Act of 1996, 18 U.S.C. § 2703). *See, e.g.*, Fraser v. Nationwide Mut. Ins. Co., 135 F. Supp. 2d 623 (E.D. Pa. 2001) (finding no violation of federal wiretap and stored communications statutes when insurance company searched agent's stored e-mail and terminated agent).

[82] Eagle Inv. Sys. Corp. v. Tamm, 146 F. Supp. 2d 105, 112 (Mass. 2001).

[83] *Id.*

[84] *Id.*

[85] 18 U.S.C. §§ 2510 et seq. (1998).

electronic communications including e-mail may be subject to civil damages.[86] The ECPA has an exception to liability if the employees or other parties to a communication give prior consent to monitoring and interception. A second exception is that a private communication network may intercept its employees' electronic communications in the course of system maintenance.

The ECPA prohibits employers from intercepting e-mail messages, but the Act does not apply if an employee consents to e-mail monitoring.[87] Some companies may decide to monitor e-mail only if a complaint has been filed against an employee. In a Massachusetts case, an employee was fired supposedly for the excessive personal use of e-mail. The president of the company monitored the company's e-mail system and discovered that the employee was e-mailing messages about an affair the employee was having with another employee. The terminated employee filed a lawsuit against the company and its president, alleging unlawful interception of wire communications, invasion of privacy, the negligent infliction of emotional distress, the intentional infliction of emotional distress, interference with contractual relations, and loss of consortium. The Massachusetts Superior Court entered summary judgment for the defendant on the claims of intentional infliction of emotional distress and tortious interference with contractual relations but not on the claims of wrongful termination, invasion of privacy, negligent infliction of emotional distress, and loss of consortium.[88] The court held that (1) the ex-employer's interception was actually the automatic backup system itself, which was protected interception; (2) the ex-employer's conduct did not exceed all possible bounds of decency in a civilized society; (3) the ex-employee's alleged sleeplessness, stomachaches, and headaches manifested objective symptomatology of physical harm; (4) the ex-employee did not allege an existing or prospective contract with a third party; and (5) there was a genuine issue of fact as to the ex-employee's reasonable expectation of privacy.[89]

In a wrongful termination case, an employee was fired "based on her unsatisfactory work performance, including her use of e-mail for personal matters."[90] After being fired, she threatened to sue them, so in response the employer printed out all her e-mails.[91] Even after "attend[ing] a program that advised employees about their use of electronic communications [and told them] that (i) Spokane County Information Systems Department had the capability of monitoring all e-mail; (ii) not to put anything on e-mail that they would not want on the front page of the newspaper, and (iii) County equipment was not for personal use,"[92] she continued to use her e-mail for personal use. The court found that the employee's

---

[86] *Id.* § 2520.

[87] *Id.* § 2511(2)(d).

[88] Restuccia v. Burk Tech., Inc., 1996 Mass. Super LEXIS 367 (Middlesex Super. Ct. Aug. 22, 1996).

[89] *Id.*

[90] Tiberino v. Spokane County, Officer of the Prosecuting Attorney, 103 Wash. App. 680, 683 (2000).

[91] *Id.* at 684.

[92] *Id.* at 688.

e-mails "contain[ed] information relating to the conduct of a governmental or proprietary function . . . [so] the e-mails are 'public records.' "[93] The court sought to balance the public interest in the e-mails with the personal contents: "Certainly, the public has an interest in seeing that public employees are not spending their time on the public payroll pursuing personal interests. But it is the amount of time spent on personal matters, not the content of personal e-mails or phone calls or conversations, that is of public interest. The fact that [she] sent 467 e-mails over a 40 working-day time frame is of significance in her termination action and the public has a legitimate interest in having that information. But what she said in those e-mails is of no public significance. The public has no legitimate concern requiring release of the e-mails and they should be exempt from disclosure."[94]

Many states have enacted state ECPA wiretap statutes, which parallel the federal statute. Maryland, for example, requires both parties to consent to any tape recording of telephone conversations. Linda Tripp's secret taping of Monica Lewinsky was arguably a violation of Maryland's wiretap statute. "It is a crime in Maryland, for example, for any person to willfully intercept, endeavor to intercept, or procure any other person to intercept or endeavor to intercept, any wire, oral or electronic communication."[95] Maryland's wiretap statute provides heightened fines to punish the unauthorized interception for "commercial advantage, malicious destruction or damage, or private commercial gain."[96]

In another workplace case, a technology coordinator was charged with felony violation of Pennsylvania's ECPA for accessing the e-mail account of his supervisor.[97] The defendant copied e-mail messages from his supervisor's account and distributed them to his supervisor without his authorization. The charges were dismissed because the federal judge found no evidence that the e-mail was accessed simultaneously at the time of transmittal.[98] The judge also found it an issue of material fact as to whether the technology coordinator had the authority to access e-mail messages.[99]

In yet another e-mail workplace case, the court granted summary judgment to a company after it determined that the company had acquired the e-mail from post-transmission storage that is not within the Wiretap Act, because "retrieval of a message from storage after transmission is complete is not 'interception' under the Act."[100] The plaintiff was an independent contractor of the employer who rented computer equipment from the employer.[101] The company made it a standard that

---

[93] *Id.* at 691.

[94] *Id.*

[95] Office of the State Prosecutor v. Judicial Watch, 737 A.2d 592 (Md. Ct. App. 1999) (citing Maryland Wiretap and Electronic Eavesdropping Statute).

[96] *Id.*

[97] Felony Charges Dismissed Against Ex-Employee Who Accessed E-Mail, 16 Comp. & Online Indus. Litig. Rptr. 6 (May 18, 1999).

[98] *Id.*

[99] *Id.*

[100] Richard Fraser v. Nationwide Mut. Ins., Co. 135 F. Supp. 2d 623, 636 (E.D. Pa. 2001).

[101] *Id.* at 628.

anytime someone logged on to the AOL [company] system, a notice appeared on the screen that said:

> Please note: for everyone's mutual protection, AOL SYSTEM use, including electronic e-mail, MAY BE MONITORED to protect against unauthorized use.[102]

The company searched its file server, including the employee's e-mails, because it was looking for proof of a suspected violation of company policy, which the search in fact revealed.[103]

Not only must companies be concerned about liability arising from the actions of their employees, but they must also avoid violating the privacy rights of employees. Obtaining employees' consent to monitoring and reducing employees' reasonable expectation of privacy will reduce the scope of the company's risks. Therefore, an e-mail and Internet usage policy should condition e-mail usage on consent to monitoring. The policy should state the conditions for monitoring. Systems administrators should monitor e-mail only on a "need to know basis."[104]

[d] Computer Fraud and Abuse Act (CFAA)

Gaining unauthorized access to another person or entity's computer system may also constitute a federal or state computer crime. The federal computer crime statute is the Computer Fraud and Abuse Act (CFAA). The federal computer crime statute punishes those who "intentionally access . . . a protected computer without authorization" and cause damage.[105] All actionable under the CFAA are unauthorized access of a computer to obtain information relevant to national security, financial, or credit information; unauthorized interstate or foreign access of a federal government computer; and fraudulent trafficking in stolen passwords. The statutory threshold is that the unauthorized access results in a loss of $1,000 or greater.

In addition, every state except Vermont has enacted "little computer crime statutes."[106] These statutes make it a crime to access computer systems for harmful purposes, but are seldom prosecuted.

[10] Corporate Liability for Civil Infractions

Besides criminal liability, use of e-mail systems creates the risk of civil liability. For example, using an e-mail system to send unsolicited e-mail may have

---

[102] Id.

[103] Id. at 631.

[104] Elgan, supra note 79.

[105] 18 U.S.C. § 1030(a) (1999); United States v. Morris, 928 F.2d 504 (2d Cir. 1991) (imposing criminal liability for unleashing "worm" on the Internet causing computer crashes); see also North Tex. Preventive Imaging v. Eisenberg, 1996 Dist. LEXIS 19990 (C.D. Cal., Aug. 26, 1996) (holding that CFAA applied to "timebomb" inserted in computer system).

[106] Mark D. Rasch, Criminal Law and the Internet, Chapter 11 in Joseph Ruh, ed., The Internet and Business: A Lawyer's Guide to the Emerging Legal Issues (1995).

legal consequences. The European Parliament is attempting to address the issue of unsolicited e-mail by requiring that e-mail recipients opt in.[107] See also Chapter Five for a complete discussion of civil liability.

[B]   Scope of the Risk

[1]   Overview

The key members of an organization must be aware not only of the various risks, but also how far those risks extend in terms of company personnel. E-mail is becoming the preferred method of business communication. In 1999, almost one in ten of all company documents was transmitted by e-mail. In 2001, the London Internet Exchange had "360,000 e-mails being exchanged at any moment through their servers."[108] By 2002, it is anticipated that the number of documents transmitted via e-mail will increase to 14.6 billion.[109] E-mail makes "it so easy to access, transmit and even alter the most sensitive corporate documents that companies have to worry about their own employees' sharing of confidential information with competitors and unauthorized persons."[110] Employees and independent contractors today have access to corporate e-mail and network systems not only through PCs and terminals, but also through personal digital assistants (PDAs), and pagers.[111] Technical and managerial employees are increasingly using e-mail pagers or PDAs to communicate with vendors, customers, potential customers, and information providers. These communication devices can transmit and receive messages around the globe.

The convenience of these devices, combined with traditional concepts of respondeat superior, exponentially increases the scope of risk for an organization.[112] This convenience should be balanced against the risks of their misuse and abuse. In certain circumstances, it is reasonably foreseeable that a company's employees will use the company's e-mail system to commit crimes or torts or to infringe intellectual property rights. For instance, the company may be directly liable for negligently hiring or retaining an employee who has engaged in "prior similar" acts. One employee may send sexually charged messages to another,

---

[107] Euro Parliament (visited June 15, 2002), http://wwwdb.europarl.eu.int/oeil/oeil_ViewDNL. ProcedureView?lang=2&procid=4483 (on spamming, Parliament accepted the Council's common position, thus approving an opt-in system for e-mail, faxes, and automated calling systems, which means that users should give prior permission for receiving unsolicited electronic communications for marketing purposes).

[108] Technology—Drive Down Your E-Mail Traffic, Network News, July 18, 2001.

[109] Gerard Panaro, Elements of a Successful E-Mail Policy, Part I (visited Mar. 26, 2000), http://www.bankinfo.com/hr/e-mailpol.html.

[110] Id.

[111] See generally SkyTel5 (visited July 27, 1999), http://www.skytel.com (describing pager device that permits the user to receive and answer e-mail).

[112] Mark Ishman, Comment: Computer Crimes and the Respondeat Superior Doctrine: Employers Beware, 6 Boston U. J. of Science and Technology Law (June 1, 2000).

exposing the company to a lawsuit alleging a hostile work environment. An employee may abuse Internet privileges by downloading unlicensed software from the Internet, subjecting the company to either a vicarious or contributory copyright infringement claim or a visit from the Software Publishers Association.[113] Employees may hack into a business competitor's e-mail system, triggering charges of criminal liability.[114] In addition, the company may be directly liable for regulatory offenses from stock manipulation or false statements made on web sites. Table 10.1 presents an overview of a company's e-mail and Internet liabilities.

Any e-mail policy must take into account the company's industry and corporate culture and should be tailored to known risks. Although an e-mail policy cannot immunize a business from liability caused by misuse of the company's computer system, the expense of developing a good e-mail policy may be far less than retrofits, lawsuits, and damage to corporate reputations.

[2] Employees and Others Outside Company Offices

[a] Telecommuters

While most companies can enforce and monitor their e-mail policies for employees at their corporate offices, it becomes more difficult for remote offices and telecommuting employees. Home-based telecommuting employees may work anywhere from Burlington, Vermont to Singapore with remote access to the corporate office. Business travelers often create a temporary "virtual office" in their hotel rooms or in temporary office space, using a direct connection to their companies' computer systems. Most companies provide access to their networks through a virtual private network (VPN) that gives users private, secure access to the company's information assets.

Whereas a traditional intranet uses dedicated cables between nodes (desktop computers, switches, etc.) of the network, a VPN uses the public Internet to connect remote users to a company's intranet. The privacy element is provided by the fact that the data streams are encrypted, typically using the security protocol, IP Security, or IPSec. Part of the difficulty in implementing a VPN is distributing the software "client" that enables the remote user access through the VPN. Each user who connects to the company's intranet through VPN uses a dial-up or similar cable modem connection to obtain a connection to the Internet, i.e., an IP address.

---

[113] The Software Publisher's Association (SPA) uses ex-employees and other informers to root out companies that use unlicensed software. The SPA has a private software police force that seeks to stigmatize the wayward corporation by widely publicizing copyright infringement.

[114] Labwerks, Inc. v. Sladekutter, Ltd., No. 99-160 (W.D. Pa., Feb. 17, 1999), *reported in* Hacking into Competitor's E-mail Violates Wiretap Law, Judge Finds, 16 Comp. & Online Indus. Litig. Rptr. 1 (Mar. 16, 1999); United States v. Simons, 206 F.3d 392 (4th Cir. 2000) (upholding conviction of FBI employee for storing child pornography on company computers, ruling that employee had no reasonable expectation of privacy given FBI Internet usage policy).

TABLE 10.1
Examples of E-Mail and Internet-Related Risks

Types of Risk	*Direct Liability*	*Imputed Liability*
Intentional Torts: Fraud or misrepresentation; defamation; trade libel, business torts; trespass to chattels; conversion; and invasion of privacy; intentional infliction of emotional distress; spoliation of evidence for destroying e-mails without justification. Torts may also be claimed in a statutory sexual or racial harassment context as in 42 U.S.C. §§ 1981, 1985 or 1986.	Fraudulent misrepresentation of goods or services sold on web site; defamatory statements about individuals or competitors made by corporate officers; spam or junk e-mail sent to subscribers of online services; introduction of computer viruses; public disclosure of private facts about a plaintiff that are offensive to the reasonable person.	Master/servant; *respondeat superior* (liability for torts committed within scope of employment); joint venturer; partners; joint tortfeasors (harm from tortious acts done in concert with others); joint and several liability (suit against SPC separately or together with other defendants); vicarious liability for defamation (if SPC is deemed to be a publisher).
Negligence: An act or omission that falls below the standard of care established by law for the protection of others; computer malpractice; failure to prevent viruses and maintain information security; failure to protect confidential data of third parties due to a security breach; negligent publications.	Violating duties of care imposed by statute, industry standards, or other standards of care, e.g., a negligent misrepresentation of material fact published on SPC's web site.	Negligent acts committed by employees, servants, joint venturers, or partners may cause company to be liable jointly and severally for negligent concerted action.
Strict Liability: Internet sale of defective computer hardware that leads to personal injury or property damage; imputed liability for acts of employees misusing the Internet.	Corporate liability is imposed for defective products that are unreasonably dangerous. Most jurisdictions impose an "economic loss" rule that will not permit tort recoveries where the loss is purely economic.	Corporation is liable for anyone in the distribution chain that sells defective products. SPC may be able to sue its suppliers for strict product liability or to seek indemnification for defective computer components.
Securities Law: SPC is potentially liable for statements made on its web site, e-mail transmissions and other Internet-related communications; SPC's web postings, Internet road shows, or statements made about	May be imposed for uses and misuses of SPC's web site in conjunction with the Internet or intranet; liability for reaching investing public via web pages. Type of liability: shareholder class action or liability for predictions	Statements that employees, partners, or venturers make about SPC's stock. Company may be jointly and severally liable for underwriters' activities; failure of web site designer to update or correct information about company's

TABLE 10.1 (Continued)

Types of Risk	Direct Liability	Imputed Liability
stocks in chat rooms expose it to federal or state securities enforcement actions. False or misleading web site statements with intent to deceive under SEC Rule 10b-5; online scams; fraudulent sales of stocks; fraudulent sales of securities.	about stock made on web site; failure to follow SEC guidelines with respect to investor communications via e-mail or the Internet; false statements made in prospectuses; failure to comply with federal securities regulations; failure to post disclosures about stock prices.	stock offerings or underwriters' IPO; employees' offering to sell securities or stocks prior to registration; failure to screen sales literature of third parties. No vicarious liability for linking to other's security offerings.
E-Mail or Internet-Related Crimes by Employees: Downloading and transmitting obscene and pornographic material on the SPC web sites; hate speech; computer crimes; child pornography; and theft of trade secrets.	A company will not be prosecuted for criminal acts of its essential employees outside the scope of duty. Company must turn over e-mail records or other computer-resources to law enforcement. The company, at minimum, may suffer public relations problems from crimes committed on company computers; transaction costs in investigating pornography on company computers, for example.	SPC may be liable for an employee's accessing a competitor's computer without authorization or for corporate espionage. SPC will not normally be liable for its employee's knowing release of a virus computer code. SPC will not normally be liable for an employee's downloading of pornography on the company computer. SPC is not liable for online stalking or threats via e-mail unless wrongdoing is authorized or ratified by the company.
Privacy Law: Because SPC is a private company, it is not normally liable for constitutionally based privacy actions; SPC is liable under the Electronic Communications Privacy Act for intercepting e-mail without cause or justification; SPC is also liable for privacy-based torts and country-specific data protection, as well as for observing the European Union Data Protection Directive.	Liability under the Electronic Communications Privacy Act (ECPA) for interception of e-mail or other electronic communications; employee's consent is a defense to an employer's monitoring or interception of stored messages; implied right to review messages in administering the computer system. Liability may also include privacy torts (intrusion upon seclusion, false light, or misappropriation or public	SPC may be liable if one of its employees was authorized to monitor co-employees' e-mail usage; SPC should have a policy limiting employees' reasonable expectation of privacy. Higher risk of a privacy tort in states with a higher level of protection for privacy, such as California; e-mail and Internet usage policy can limit or eliminate reasonable expectation of privacy.

(continued)

TABLE 10.1 (Continued)

Types of Risk	Direct Liability	Imputed Liability
	disclosure of private facts) and state ECPA statutes; European Data Privacy Directive; and privacy statutes of other countries.	
Regulatory Offenses: Federal Trade Commission (FTC) Regulations of Advertising and Business Practices.	False advertisements on its web site; liabilities for unfair or deceptive trade practices.	SPC may be vicariously liable for the false advertisements of partners and co-venturers.
Infringement of Intellectual Property Rights: Copyright Infringement: Using the Internet to download pirated software, using e-mail to infringe the copyrights of others. **Trade Secrets:** Use of e-mail to steal or transmit trade secrets; criminal liability as well for trade secret theft (Economic Espionage Act of 1996). **Trademarks:** Using company's computer to download material protected by trademarks. **Patents:** Infringing Internet-related patents in web site technologies.	Direct infringement: Ownership of a valid copyright in the infringed work and copying by the defendant with access. Operators of SPC web site may be liable for incorporating copyrighted materials on the web site. Posting of copyrighted materials on company web site, bulletin board, or chat room; using another's trademark or a substantially similar trademark when advertising goods or services in a way "likely to cause confusion," blurring, or tarnishing of marks; using another's mark as a domain name; strict liability for direct infringement; dilution in trademarks; criminal penalties for copyright infringement.	Contributory infringement: (1) SPC had knowledge that others were posting infringing materials on its web site; or otherwise (2) materially contributed to copyright infringement; or (3) culpable conduct for secondary liability. Vicarious infringement: Employer may be liable for infringement by employees or joint venturers where there is a right to supervise and a financial interest in the copyrighted materials; third-party liability for online conduct.
Other: Corporate liability for violation of export controls; taxation of e-commerce; failure to provide adequate security on web site; first amendment issues; liability for web site crashes or service outages.	Liability of cross-border data flow of restricted software.	Exporting encryption software to a foreign subsidiary.

Once connected to the Internet, the VPN client application on the remote user's computer is executed, establishing a secure "tunnel" to the company's intranet.

In *TBG Ins. Servs. Corp. v. Superior Court*,[115] an employer provided two computers for an employee's use, one to permit the employee to work at home. The employee signed an electronic and telephone equipment policy statement and agreed in writing that his employer could monitor his computers. The employee was terminated for misuse of his office computer. After the employee sued the employer for wrongful termination, the employer demanded production of the home computer. The employee refused to produce the computer, and the trial court refused to compel production. The appellate court concluded that, given the employee's consent to his employer's monitoring of both computers, the employee had no reasonable expectation of privacy when he used the home computer for personal matters. The trial court erred in denying production.

[b] Independent Contractors

At times, companies may engage independent contractors for their expertise. Depending on the business's needs, these contractors may have access to the corporate e-mail and other computer or Internet resources. If an independent contractor misuses the company's Internet access or e-mail, the company may be found vicariously liable, despite the fact that the misuse was committed by an independent contractor. Hence an organization should not operate under a false impression that it is immune from the e-mail or Internet torts of its independent contractors.[116] Since independent contractors often use their own equipment or store the information of more than one client in their files, these workers often have a higher expectation of privacy from inspection. As such, corporations who wish to monitor e-mail transmissions or Internet use of independent contractors should make dedicated efforts to give notice of any monitoring or planned inspections. Alternatively, companies can provide the independent contractors with company machines.

§ 10.03 RISK MANAGEMENT

[A] Reallocating Risks of Loss

Contracts are the principal device to allocate or reallocate e-mail and Internet-related risks. Companies should enter into contracts with employees and third-party vendors or service providers, to preserve confidential information. Conversely, the typical site developer, if outsourced, will seek to limit all liability, including consequential and punitive damages.

---

[115] 2002 Cal. App. LEXIS 1839 (Cal. Ct. App. Feb. 22, 2002).

[116] *See* Hard Rock Cafe Licensing Corp. v. Concession Serv., Inc., 955 F.2d 1143, 1150 (7th Cir. 1992); Broadcast Music, Inc. v. The Club S. Burlesque Inc., 36 U.S.P.Q.2d (BNA) 1664, 1666 (N.D. Ga. 1995).

[1] Indemnification or "Hold Harmless" Clauses

Indemnification shifts losses from one party to another. Although a company cannot disclaim liability for its own torts, it may seek indemnification for torts committed by third parties. Companies should seek to be indemnified and held harmless for wrongdoing arising out of misuse and abuse of their e-mail system and the Internet. It should require its outside consultants, web site developers, trading partners, and telecommuting employees who have access to its Internet and e-mail systems to indemnify and hold harmless the company from any and all losses, liabilities, expenses, and damages from any claims, demands, actions, or proceedings that may be initiated on the grounds of misuse or abuse of the company's computer system. This indemnification and hold harmless clause applies to claims based on torts, contract, breach of fiduciary duty, and intellectual property infringement actions. Indemnification may also be sought for violations of local, state, federal, and international regulations.

Companies may seek indemnification from consultants, developers, and third parties supplying content to their web sites. An indemnification agreement should include language requiring the trading partner or consultant to "indemnify, defend, and hold harmless the company, its directors, officers, employees, and consultants for its own wrongdoing." The company should require its web site developers to obtain insurance for its web site activities. Where the company uses independent contractors, agreements with the independent contractors should contain indemnification language to ensure that the independent contractors understand that they are responsible for their own actions and any abuses. While the indemnification may be limited to the economic value of the consulting contract, companies should rely primarily upon their own insurance to limit corporate exposure. Further, the web site developer should be required to make good for any losses caused by torts, crimes, infringement, or other defaults. E-commerce related patents are on the rise, and one resulting danger is that a developer's web site architecture may violate one or more Internet-related patents. The company, as the indemnified party, should have peace of mind that the developer is not infringing some third-party's copyrights, trademarks, trade secrets, licenses, or other intellectual property rights.

[2] Nondisclosure Agreements

A company can protect its proprietary information, confidential information, and trade secrets by entering into confidentiality agreements with its employees, consultants, trading partners, subsidiaries, and affiliates to protect confidential information. The agreement should cover confidential and proprietary information that has already been disclosed to the other party. Furthermore, a company's employment agreements should make it clear that confidential and proprietary information and trade secrets are the property of the company. To see a sample nondisclosure agreement, refer to § 10.07[C][1].

[B] Employee Training and Supervision

Employee education is the chief risk management device for e-mail and Internet torts committed by employees. Companies must develop e-mail and Internet usage policies that inform workers about the proper use of its computer system. Despite the dangers, currently only about one in two companies has an e-mail policy in place.[117] E-mail and Internet usage policy must be a part of employee training programs if it is to be effective. A written e-mail and Internet usage policy, combined with training, can be used to mitigate or avoid legal liability. Companies should also provide e-mail and Internet training for both new personnel and existing employees. Internet and e-mail usage is also an issue for departing and ex-employees. An ex-employee should be reminded about these continuing obligations to keep company documents and information confidential. A company's training module should emphasize that employees are subject to tort as well as criminal liability for the theft of trade secrets. During these sessions, employees must be educated on what is considered a trade secret or confidential information.

The training should explain what the company's expectations are for the protection of trade secrets, confidential information, and proprietary information. E-mail may be a means for insiders to accomplish theft, bribery, misrepresentation, or business espionage. In general, the extent of protection of trade secrets depends on what steps the owner takes to protect its confidential information.[118] Including the protection of trade secrets in an Internet or e-mail usage policy is evidence that the trade secret owner is taking reasonable steps to maintain secrecy.

Another reason why employee training and supervision are so important to a company is to prevent accidental disclosure of private information. "Eli Lilly sent regular e-mail messages to people using its Prozac antidepressant. While the mailings were supposed to be sent in a blind carbon copy format, the company accidentally failed to hide recipients' addresses, which revealed them to all of the other users."[119] This resulted in the company's suffering bad publicity because of its inadvertent disclosure. Although Eli Lilly was not required to pay money, it is required to develop its security so that it does not happen again.[120] Such security lapses result in not only potential legal liability but also loss of credibility.

[C] Smoking Guns and Retention of E-Mail Messages

Managing electronic data is very difficult because, unlike paper-based documents, electronic files cannot simply be torn up or incinerated. Oliver North and

---

[117] Marcia Stepanek, When the Devil Is in the E-Mails, Bus. Wk. (June 8, 1998) at 72 (citing Nov. 1997 study in which only 51% of survey respondents reported training workers in the appropriate use of e-mails).

[118] Ruckelshaus v. Monsanto Co., 104 S. Ct. 2862, 2873 (1984).

[119] Robert MacMillon, Eli Lilly Settles Privacy Charges with FTC, Newsbytes, Jan. 18. 2002, http://www.newsbytes.com/news/02/173779.html.

[120] Id.

his secretary, Fawn Hall, thought that he had shredded all paper-copies and deleted all computer files pertaining to the Reagan Administration's involvement in the Iran/Contra affair.[121] North "was confronted with electronic copies of these documents and other information that congressional investigators and forensic experts were able to recover from backup computer tapes."[122] As Iran Contra defendants learned, "the 'delete' key does not obliterate a file . . . files generally remain intact until they are overwritten."[123] Even if files have been deleted, computer forensics experts are frequently able to undelete computer files and recreate erased materials.[124] Online employers need to view e-mail as evidence and to visualize how a top plaintiff's attorney will use e-mail to show a company's motivation or state of mind.

"Investigations of employee e-mail . . . increased an average of thirty percent each year from 1994 to 1996."[125] "Smoking-gun e-mail has become so common in workplace lawsuits that almost 10% (9.4%) of US companies have been ordered by courts to produce employee e-mail, and 8.3% have battled sexual harassment and/or sexual discrimination claims stemming from employee e-mail and/or Internet use."[126] Just like files on a hard drive, it is a myth that deleted e-mail no longer exists for later discovery.[127] E-mail messages "survive long after the supposed deletion and may only be permanently deleted when the computer needs the then available space." Computer experts can easily recover "deleted" information that the computer has not yet overwritten and can even reconstruct partially overwritten data.[128] Whether for an internal investigation or as part of discovery, companies may employ forensic computer analysts who have the expertise to "'bag' the employee's computer by copying the entire hard drive onto a high-density disk."[129] E-mail and other data may be deleted by permanently opening up the hard drive and crushing the magnetically coated platters.

---

[121] "One of the most notorious examples [of e-mail smoking guns] was Oliver North's attempt to cover up arm sales to support the Contras in Nicaragua. North believed that he had deleted e-mail messages but the messages were reconstructed with the help of computer forensics experts." Matthew J. Bester, A Wreck on the Info-Bahn: Electronic Mail and the Destruction of Evidence, 6 Commlaw Conspectus 75 (1998).

[122] James K. Lehman, Litigating in Cyberspace: Discovery of Electronic Information, 8 S. Carolina Lawyer 14, 15 (Mar./Apr. 1997).

[123] Laurie Thomas Lee, Watch Your E-Mail! Employee E-Mail Monitoring and Privacy Law in the Age of the "Electronic Sweatshop," 28 J. Marshall L. Rev. 139 (1994).

[124] Linda Himelstein, The Snitch in the System, Bus. Wk. (Apr. 17, 1995), at 104 (citing case in which a judge awarded $25.5 million in a trade secrets action against a software developer based on recreated deleted computer files showing incriminating memorandum).

[125] Id.

[126] American Mgmt. Assoc., E-Mail Study (visited Jan. 10, 2002), http://www.amanet.org/research/emssurvey.htm.

[127] Charles A. Lovell and Roger W. Holmes, The Dangers of E-Mail: The Need for Electronic Data Retention Policies, 44 R.I. Bar J. (Dec. 1995).

[128] Id.

[129] Alexander I. Rodriquez, All Bark, No Byte: Employee E-Mail Privacy Rights in the Private Sector Workplace, 47 Emory L.J. 1439, 1439 (1998).

One of the difficult decisions employees must make is which e-mail messages constitute business records, what the appropriate retention policy should be, and how long messages should be archived. Hundreds to millions of messages are transmitted daily on the Internet. A large multinational corporation could generate a million or more messages per day. It may be impractical to track down every e-mail message that has been forwarded or retransmitted, but not impossible. Even if a message is deleted from an employee's computer, a copy of the message may have been printed out or stored on a diskette. The forwarded e-mail may, in turn, have been forwarded to many other locations across the world and stored by a recipient. Transmitted, forwarded, or stored e-mail messages from an employee may prove to be the "star witness" in an antitrust, business tort, sexual harassment, discrimination, business contract, or similar case.

E-mails are classified as company documents and should be managed by a document retention and destruction policy. The recent developments involving Enron and Arthur Andersen have illustrated the tension presented by corporate document retention policies.[130] Such a policy is of vital importance. The policy should not have as its goal to destroy potential evidence but rather the retention of records pursuant to a statutory or regulatory requirement or for a specific business purpose.[131] E-mail messages are subject to discovery and are treated as company records.[132] E-mail has no special privilege and is admissible in a court proceeding as evidence.[133] Rule 34 of the Federal Rules of Civil Procedure permits a party to request an inspection and copy of documents, including electronic information.[134] Discovery requests should specifically include all media, including backup copies, which have been outsourced to an off-site storage facility. E-mail messages have proved valuable in a number of recent cases. In *Workers' Compensation Division v. Pampell*,[135] the plaintiff introduced a "a copy of a dated and time stamped e-mail

---

[130] *See supra* note 12. (Arthur Andersen was convicted of obstruction of justice for destroying documents while under an SEC subpoena.)

[131] Once litigation begins, opposing counsel will request a copy of the document retention policy. Any policy that expressly requires the destruction of damaging documents, including e-mail, may in itself be damaging evidence. *See* Todd N. Thompson, The Paper Trail Has Gone Digital: Discovery in the Age of Electronic Information, 71 J. Kan. B.A. 16, Mar. 2002, at 20.

[132] Reuters Ltd. v. Dow Jones Telerate, Inc., 1997 WL 545807 at *2 (N.Y. App. Div., Sept. 4, 1997) (noting that subpoena *duces tecum* gave a nonparty "less than two days to go through 30 years of documents, including e-mail, computer data, etc."). *See also* Falise v. American Tobacco Co., 1999 U.S. Dist. LEXIS 20608 (E.D.N.Y., Dec. 28, 1999) (declaring tobacco litigation documents not privileged because of the widespread availability of the documents).

[133] Wesley College v. Pitts, 1997 WL 557554 (D. Del. Aug. 11, 1997).

[134] E-mail messages were admitted, for example, against a defendant charged with fraud and bribery in United States v. Ferber, 966 F. Supp. 92, 99 (D. Mass 1997).

[135] 1997 WL 576470 at *2 (Tex. Ct. App., Sept. 18, 1997). *See also* Canizales v. Microsoft Corp, NSWIRComm 118 (Sept. 1, 2000) (noting e-mail exchanges in $9 million judgment in termination of employment action decided by New South Wales (Aust.) Industrial Relations Commission); United States v. Poehlman, 217 F.3d 692 (9th Cir. 2000) (reversing conviction as much of the evidence was in the form of breezy, informal e-mails with numerous grammatical, spelling, and syntax errors).

message" as evidence that an appeal was timely. E-mail evidence was also key to establishing a landowner's notice of a security problem in a premises liability case.[136] An e-mail message was a critical piece of evidence in a false advertising claim brought by a publisher of physics journals against competitors challenging a study ranking journals; the court noted "an e-mail message which criticized [one plaintiff's] prices" and "characterized its journals."[137]

E-mail messages have also been essential for establishing liability in a number of recent employment cases.[138] In *Harrow v. Prudential Insurance Co.,*[139] e-mail messages were admitted in a wrongful denial of benefits case. A motion to compel production of e-mail uncovered the e-mail messages. In *Evans v. Toys R Us-Ohio, Inc.,*[140] an e-mail message was used to show a co-employee's predisposition to discriminate against minorities. The smoking-gun message revealed the company's knowledge that the employee in general had a predisposition to be "hard on minorities and men." Kenneth Starr's investigation of Monica Lewinsky's e-mail messages in the President Clinton investigation were regarded as electronic smoking guns.[141] The House Judiciary Committee, as part of the evidence collected by independent counsel, released e-mail excerpts.[142] It is common for the "electronic smoking guns" to be incriminating e-mails carrying racist jokes or other objectionable messages.[143]

A company should list specific content "that should never be discussed in e-mail, such as sensitive personnel issues, company secrets, and personal information" and publish such restrictions in an employee handbook.[144] In the absence

---

[136] Holder v. Mellon Mortgage Co., 1997 WL 461982 at *3 (Tex. Ct. App., Aug. 14, 1997) (noting that e-mail from employee "lodge[d] a formal complaint about the virtually non-existent security for our parking garage" showing that employer had notice of security problem).

[137] Amsterdam BV v. American Inst. of Physics, 1997 WL 528086 at *8 (S.D.N.Y., Aug. 26, 1997).

[138] Samuel A. Thumb and Darrel S. Jackson, E-mail Litigation Puts Companies On Alert: Third-Quarter Review, 3 The Internet News. Legal & Bus. Aspects 10 (Dec. 1998) (noting that "e-mail has become a common type of evidence in civil litigation and periodically plays a role in criminal trials"). *See, e.g.,* Miller v. Alldata Corp., 2001 U.S. App. LEXIS 15684 (6th Cir. July 6, 2001).

[139] 76 F. Supp. 2d 558 (D.N.J. 1999).

[140] 32 F. Supp. 2d 974 (N.D. Ohio 1999).

[141] Roberta Fusarao, Cases Highlight Need for E-Mail Policies, 32 Computerworld 20 (Oct. 5, 1998).

[142] Linda Tripp sent e-mail released by the House Judiciary Committee to Monica Lewinsky on Oct. 27, 1997. Tripp wrote: "From now on, leave me alone. Don't bother me with all your ranting and raving and analyzing of this situation. And don't accuse me of somehow 'skewing' the truth— because the reality is that what I told you is true. I really am finished, Monica. Share this sick situation with one of your other friends, because frankly, I'm past [being] nauseated about the whole thing. LRT." *See* The Clinton/Starr Texts (visited Jun. 15, 2002), http://www.ardemgaz.com/prev/Clinton/e-mail.html.

[143] Beverly W. Garofalo, Technology in the Workplace: Can E-Mail Lead to Liability? What Employers Need to Know to Protect Themselves, 13 Comp. L. Strat. 1 (Apr. 1997) (reporting on lawsuit against Morgan Stanley & Company and Citicorp based on racist jokes transmitted on company's e-mail system).

[144] Elgan, *supra* note 79.

of a written directive, if an employee has any doubt about whether e-mail is an appropriate means by which to transmit sensitive information, that employee should not use e-mail in that case. Companies need retention policies to protect their e-mail messages and systems. E-mail is classifiable as business records critical for "legal, regulatory, tax, contractual and evidentiary purposes."[145] Companies need a full audit plan to determine where e-mail records and documents will be stored. SPC needs an electronic recordkeeping policy to protect itself in litigation as well as in regulatory enforcement actions. Companies must consider state and federal regulations in determining what e-mail records should be retained or purged. Companies should advise all employees that the company will turn over e-mail records in response to a subpoena. The key elements of a record retention policy are "(1) the types and form of records to retain; (2) retention periods; and (3) record destruction."[146]

Such a policy is critical because e-mail messages believed to be deleted may be reincarnated with the assistance of data recovery services. When creating such policies it is essential to characterize the type of information. The policy must delineate what key documents to retain for tax or regulatory purposes and what documents can be purged on a scheduled basis. Federal and state statutes will dictate the minimum periods for which records must be retained. Generally speaking, e-mail messages need not be retained or backed up beyond one year unless a specific duty exists to retain messages beyond that period. Retaining outdated e-mail messages beyond six months exposes the company to unnecessary risks. One danger of retaining e-mail messages beyond a limited period is the expense of complying with discovery orders. Documents deleted in compliance with the company's retention policy should reduce the risk and cost of litigation substantially. Upon implementing a record retention policy, companies must also outline a record destruction policy. Among other things, the policy should outline how to dispose of old and archived e-mail messages.

Since e-mail may be stored in many locations, and this may make it difficult for a company to properly purge all records. E-mail may exist on both the sender(s)' and the recipient(s)' personal computers, the e-mail servers that provide e-mail services, or on offline backup material. While a company can do little to prevent the retention of e-mail on foreign servers, it may implement a Total Security Policy (TSP) to reduce the risk of unwanted e-mail remaining on its own computing equipment. SPC's TSP contains the following provisions:

1. All SPC employees must set their e-mail software to purge or archive e-mail messages after 21 days.
2. All SPC servers will be set to purge e-mail 21 days after receipt unless the e-mail has been archived.
3. All SPC employees will be informed that any message saved for more than 180 days must have management approval.

---

[145] Thomas J. Smedinghoff, Online Law: The SPA's Legal Guide to Doing Business on the Internet, ch. 5 (1996).

[146] *Id.* at 66.

4. All SPC employees will use security software, such as PGP, to do a free-space wipe of their hard drive at end of every week.[147]

5. All SPC servers will use security software to do a free-space wipe at the end of every month.[148]

6. At the end of every quarter, the backup library will be reviewed. All archives more than six months old will be destroyed, unless a business reason exists for retaining the record.

7. All SPC backup media in circulation will be replaced with new media every six months.

8. All SPC employees will be instructed to do a secure delete and purge of any document or e-mail according to its security classification.[149]

9. SPC will create an e-mail and document security classification that includes the following designations:

   (a) Top Secret: Message or document may not be sent by e-mail but only by secure courier. The document or message must be destroyed after recipient reads it, and no copies may be made. No additional distribution will be allowed.

   (b) Secret: Message or document may only be sent by e-mail on internal systems and must be encrypted. The document or message should be destroyed as soon as possible by both the sender and the receiver, and in no case should it be retained after 180 days. No additional distribution will be allowed.

   (c) Confidential: Message or document may only be sent on SPC's internal systems. The document or message should be destroyed by both sender and receiver as soon as possible. No additional distribution will be allowed.

   (d) Sensitive: Message or document should only be sent on SPC's internal systems. It should not be shown to anyone outside the company. It should only be retained with express authority of management.

   (e) Proprietary: Message or document should only be sent to employees with a need to know the information. If sent outside SPC, the message must be encrypted. It should only be retained with express authority of management.

SPC's cost of responding to discovery requests may be overwhelming if all e-mail is kept. Keeping everything will also increase the risk that "spontaneous,

---

[147] Deleting a file does not destroy all traces of the document on the storage medium. The document may still exist on the computer's hard drive, and magnetic traces may exist for an extended period of time. Security software will not only delete the file in the operating system's file management table, it will also write over the space the file occupied with a string of 1s followed by a string of 0s. Successive iterations will enhance the chance that the document will be fully purged. By performing the same operation on a hard disk's free space, it will help ensure that deleted documents remain deleted.

[148] *Id.*

[149] *Id.*

sound-byte communication . . . common in internal e-mail" will be uncovered.[150] In a Massachusetts case, an "internal corporate e-mail message followed an incriminating conversation between the defendant and a co-worker."[151] The trial court admitted the e-mail under the excited utterance exception to the hearsay rule.[152] Electronic files may contain inflammatory information in prior drafts not accessible in hard-copy form. A retention policy can reduce the cost of burdensome discovery requests. A company may take "steps to protect against abusive discovery and to avoid any inappropriate disclosure."[153] The plaintiff became a defendant and the employee was charged with a felony for falsifying an e-mail message.[154]

An ex-employee of Oracle was charged with perjury for deleting portions of an e-mail message. The e-mail message discovered simply stated that the vice president of the company was terminating an employee. Computer forensic experts located an electronic version of the e-mail message proving that the e-mail was actually created by the former employee, not by the executive. A company destroying e-mail messages may be subject to an adverse inference or have a default judgment entered against it.

E-mail and other electronic documents are no less subject to discovery requests than are paper records. Where requests are overly broad or excessive, it may be possible to shift costs from the defendant to the plaintiffs In *Murphy Oil USA, Inc. v. Fluor Daniel, Inc.,*[155] a refinery owner sought to compel the company to produce e-mail responsive to its discovery requests. The company argued that the expense of production outweighed the benefit of discovery. The court concluded that the costs of producing the e-mail should be shifted to the refinery owner because the marginal value of the e-mail was modest at best, the company did not retain backup tapes of its e-mail for any current business purpose, and the e-mail was not relevant to the company's counterclaims. The court reasoned that the company could not have the opportunity to assert that its e-mail was confidential or privileged without bearing the cost of retrieving the e-mail. However, the company was to bear the cost of culling pertinent e-mail from the nonresponsive e-mail and identifying the privileged or confidential e-mail found within the pertinent e-mail.

An e-business may argue that extensive e-discovery requests are unduly burdensome and that the opposing party should pay the costs or cull their interrogatories and other discovery requests. In general, an e-business must bear the expense of complying with discovery requests but may invoke the federal court's discretion under Fed. R. Civ. P. 26(c) to grant orders protecting it from undue burdens or shifting costs. Courts apply a balancing test in considering such factors as

---

[150] *Id.*

[151] Bester, *supra* note 121.

[152] *Id.*

[153] "Rule 34 does not provide for 'roaming' discovery, which may result if a party were granted direct access to a defendant's computer system." *Id.* (citing Belcher v. Bassett Furniture Indus., Inc., 588 F.2d 904, 906-07 (4th Cir. 1978)).

[154] *Id.* at 15.

[155] 2002 U.S. Dist. LEXIS 3196 (E. D. La. Feb. 19, 2002).

(1) the specificity of the discovery requests, (2) the likelihood of discovering critical information, (3) the availability of such information from other sources, (4) the purposes for which the responding party maintains the requested data, (5) the relative benefit to the parties of obtaining the information, (6) the total cost associated with production, (7) the relative ability of each party to control costs and its incentive to do so, and (8) the resources available to each party. Each of these factors is relevant in determining whether discovery costs should be shifted in this case.[156]

[D] Electronic Monitoring of Employees

A growing number of companies are monitoring e-mail and Internet communications to prevent exposure for the online torts and crimes of their employees. One estimate is that more than "20 million employees have their e-mail, computer files, or voice mail searched by employers."[157] In a survey by the American Management Association taken in 2001, "more than three-quarters of major U.S. firms (77.7%) record and review employee communications and activities on the job, including their phone calls, e-mail, Internet connections, and computer files."[158] Even if e-mail is not monitored, it is subject to subpoena. This monitoring can be as unobtrusive as simply logging the amount of traffic generated by an employee, or as intrusive as reading individual e-mails or viewing an employee's computer screen in real time.[159] Software is available that "monitors activity—anything from Web sites visited to keystrokes tapped—and then transmits that information to someplace, or someone, else."[160] Software is available that captures every keystroke that makes it possible to key-log every web site visited. Unscrupulous competitors or foreign spies may also use spyware or other surveillance software to collect business intelligence.[161] The e-business needs to consider incorporating countermeasures to prevent software spies. "For example, Zone Alarm, which is free at *www.zonealarm.com*, displays a dialog box informing you that an

---

[156] *See* Rowe Entm't, Inc. v. William Morris Agency, Inc., 205 F.R.D. 421 (S.D.N.Y. 2002) (granting defendant's motion for a protective order and requiring plaintiffs to bear the cost of discovery of e-mail).

[157] Felhaber, Larson, Fenlon, and Vogt, What's Happening in Employment Law, 9 Minn. Employment L. Letter 4 (1999).

[158] 2001 AMA Survey: Workplace Monitoring & Surveillance, Summary of Key Findings (visited June 15, 2002), http://www.amanet.org/research/pdfs/ems_short2001.pdf (the survey further stated that "[o]ver three-quarters of respondent firms (76.4%) have disciplined employees for misuse or personal use of office telecommunications equipment, and 31% have dismissed individuals for those reasons").

[159] *See* Electronic Privacy: Hearing on H.R. 4908 Before the Subcomm. on the Constitution, Comm. on the Judiciary, 106th Cong. 2000 WL 1257244 (2000) (discussion of various types of e-mail monitoring software).

[160] Rick Klau, Spyware can Pose a Threat to your Data and, by Extenion, that of your Clients: Learn How to Avoid the Snoopers, L. Prac. Mgmt., Mar. 2002, at 14.

[161] *Id.*

application is trying to send data. You then have the option of disabling that application or blocking the communication."[162]

Courts have upheld the employer's right to monitor and police its e-mail system.[163] In the employment context, courts continue to recognize that employers have legitimate interests in policing their e-mail systems. In an early California case, employees filed a class action against Epson America for the company's routine monitoring of e-mail. The Court of Appeals of California dismissed all claims, finding no invasion of privacy and no unlawful wiretap.[164] A company has an obligation to monitor computer systems for improper use.[165] A growing number of companies have been the target of lawsuits for permitting objectionable e-mail messages to be transmitted on their computer systems.[166]

Private employees do not have a general constitutional right to privacy because they do not satisfy the state action requirement.[167] For public employees, the U.S. Supreme Court, in *O'Connor v. Ortega,*[168] held that the test of "reasonableness" applies to searches and seizures conducted by public employers, rather than the usual Fourth Amendment requirement of a warrant supported by "probable cause."[169] In *Leventhal v. Knapek,*[170] an employee's computer was searched as a result of suspected work-related misconduct. The Second Circuit Court of Appeals found on appeal that "[e]ven though Leventhal had some expectation of privacy in the contents of his office computer, the investigatory searches by the DOT did not violate his Fourth Amendment rights."[171] The court stated that "[a]n investigatory search for evidence of suspected work-related employee misfeasance will be constitutionally 'reasonable' if it is 'justified at its inception' and of appropriate scope."[172] Similarly, in *Tiberino v. Spokane,*[173] an employee was terminated

---

[162] *Id.*

[163] *See generally* John Arneo, Note, Pandora's (E-Mail) Box: E-Mail Monitoring in the Workplace, 14 Hofstra Lab. L.J. 339 (1996); *compare* Heather Rowe, UK Developments Monitoring of E-Mails, 4 Cyber. Law. 34 (Nov. 1999) (arguing that monitoring e-mail without guidelines could violate U.K.'s Human Rights Act of 1998).

[164] Flanagan v. Espon America, BC 007036 (1990) (cited in 41 Boston Bar J. 6, 19 (1997)).

[165] C. Forbes Sargent III, Electronic Media and the Workplace: Confidentiality, Privacy and Other Issues, 41 Boston Bar J. 6, 19 (May/June 1997) (arguing that it is an open question whether an employer has a duty to monitor e-mail messages to discover instances of sexual or racial harassment).

[166] *Id.*

[167] *See* Smyth v. Pillsbury Co., 914 F. Supp. 97 (E.D. Pa. 1996) (finding company's interest in preventing inappropriate e-mail activity on its own systems outweighs any employee privacy interest); McLaren v. Microsoft Corp., No. 05-97-00824-CV, slip op. at 5 (Tex. App.-Dallas, May 28, 1999). *See also* Paul M. Schwartz, Beyond Lessig's Code for Internet Privacy: Cyberspace Filters, Privacy Control, and Fair Informational Practices, 2000 Wis. L. Rev. 743 (2000).

[168] 480 U.S. 709 (1987).

[169] *Id.*

[170] 266 F.3d 64 (2d Cir. 2001).

[171] *Id.* at 75.

[172] *Id.*

[173] 13 P.3d 1104 (Wash. App. Div. 2000).

for, among other misconduct, sending excessive personal e-mails. Tiberino filed an action seeking to prevent the release of her e-mails to the media. The court, on appeal, found that although Tiberino's e-mails were public documents, they were protected from disclosure as "personal information"[174]

The federal Electronic Communications Privacy Act (ECPA) prohibits the unauthorized interception and disclosure of electronic communications,[175] but employers will generally require that employees provide consent to monitoring. The monitoring of every e-mail message is not practical or desirable, just as eliminating all personal use of the computer is a policy impossible to enforce. Companies should enact e-mail and Internet policies that are based on common sense, trust, and discretion.[176] The company's ethos should not be that of Big Brother, but companies have a need to know whether their systems are being used in ways that create serious hazards and risks.[177] A company should not monitor its employee's e-mails without notice and a compelling justification. At minimum, the employer that monitors e-mail should give notice to employees that e-mail is subject to review by a systems administrator. Another common problem with Internet access is the tendency of some employees to surf the Internet for online pornography, sports broadcasts, and other sites unrelated to their work; such "goofing" may detract from workplace performance.[178]

Pennsylvania's House of Representatives introduced legislation requiring notice to employees of electronic monitoring by employers.[179] The Pennsylvania bill requires employers who engage in any type of electronic monitoring to give prior written notice of the types of monitoring that may occur.[180] An employer may monitor, without notice, if it has reasonable grounds to believe that a violation of law or other misconduct has occurred or if a message has contributed to a hostile workplace. If an employer fails to provide notice, it is subject to a "maximum civil penalty of five hundred dollars for the first offense, one thousand dollars for the second offense and three thousand dollars for the third and each subsequent offense."[181]

An organization-wide e-mail and Internet usage policy should be designed in part to reduce employees' "reasonable expectation of privacy." Privacy claims aris-

---

[174] *Id.*

[175] 18 U.S.C. §§ 1367, 2232, 2510 et seq., 2701 et seq., 3117, 3121 et seq. (1997).

[176] "A sensible Internet usage policy allows employees a certain amount of trust and latitude. Most companies don't check the destination of each and every telephone call to ensure that calls are work-related. Most companies don't mind if employees use their PCs for personal reasons during off hours. . . . However there are some very good reasons for tracking employee Web usage." Tim Wilson, Monitoring Employee Web Usage Is Desirable and Necessary, Comm. Wk (Aug. 11, 1997).

[177] *Id.*

[178] *Id.*

[179] Pennsylvania House Bill No. 5398 requires notice to employees of electronic monitoring by employers. *See* Substitute House Bill No. 5398, Public Act No. 98-142, An Act Requiring Notice to Employees of Electronic Monitoring by Employees (visited Mar. 26, 2000), http://www.cga.state.ct.us/ps98/act/pa/pa-01242.htm.

[180] *Id.*

[181] *Id.*

ing out of monitoring employees may be defended successfully to "the degree to which the employer has reserved the right to monitor communications, and the reasons it has engaged in monitoring."[182] Invasion of privacy claims based upon an employer's monitoring of e-mail or Internet usage have been largely unsuccessful,[183] but these claims have been expensive and time-consuming.[184] Companies will vary on the extent to which they monitor e-mail or Internet usage. The culture of the workplace as well as the security risk will dictate the degree of monitoring. A company may make a policy decision only to monitor e-mail or Internet usage when it has reason to believe that the employee is not productive, is downloading pornographic materials, or is accessing X-rated sites.[185] A company must give its employees notice that they have no expectation of privacy in their e-mail or Internet usage. Accordingly, SPC's e-mail and Internet policy should reserve the right to monitor its employees and should give conspicuous notice that e-mail and Internet usage is subject to monitoring.

If SPC has overseas subsidiaries, it needs to determine whether workplace monitoring violates foreign law. In December 2001, the New South Wales Law Reform Commission released a report critical of the widespread practice of surveillance.[186] Surveillance is used routinely in Australia for the following purposes:

- law enforcement, as carried out by police, the New South Wales Crime Commission, the Australian Security Intelligence Organisation, and other such agencies;

- private investigation, most commonly in relation to suspected insurance frauds related to motor vehicle accident and workers' compensation claims, but also in family law cases and other matters;

- workplace monitoring by employers;

- media reportage;

- enhancing public safety through traffic and crowd control; and

- protection of private property.[187]

---

[182] Restatement (Second) of Torts § 652(b) (1979).

[183] See, e.g., Bourke v. Nissan Motor Corp., Case No. B-68705 (Cal. App. July 26, 1993) (rejecting privacy claim where employee signed agreement that e-mail would be used for business purposes and where he had knowledge of the employer's practice of monitoring).

[184] See Gregory V. Mersol, Employer/Employee Rights on the Information Highway—Is There a Right of Privacy? 4 Cyber Law 10 (June 1999) (noting that "invasion of privacy claims are, at present, the most significant claims in connection with e-mail communications").

[185] Maura Kelly, Your Boss May Be Monitoring Your E-Mail, Salon.com, Dec. 8, 1999 (noting that the New York Times monitors e-mail if it has a reasonable suspicion of lost productivity due to misuse of the Internet).

[186] New South Wales Law Reform Comm'n, Report 98, Surveillance: An Interim Report (2001) (visited Dec. 19, 2001), http://www.lawlink.nsw.gov.au/lrc.nsf/pages/r98chp01.

[187] Id.

The Privacy and Personal Information Act of 1998 introduced a set of principles that regulate the way public sector agencies should deal with personal information in New South Wales.[188] The Act covers "not only traditional ideas of data storage such as paper files but also such things as electronic records, video recordings, photographs, genetic material and biometric information, like fingerprints."[189] The Law Reform Commission suggested the possibility that common law torts apply to surveillance. "The laws of trespass, nuisance and defamation, while not specifically relating to electronic surveillance, may regulate activities associated with surveillance in certain circumstances and provide the subject of the surveillance with some redress."[190]

[E]   Information Security

E-mail and Internet usage policies need to be coordinated with the company's information security policy, which must be tailored to its business plan and corporate organization. An Internet usage policy must convey the importance of security. A company must complete an Internet Security Audit prior to going online.

Curtis Karnow has identified six fundamental principles of information security that apply to businesses of all sizes:

1.   Authentication: verifying the identity of a participant;
2.   Authorization: determining whether personnel have access to a particular operation;
3.   Assurance: a basis for users to determine whether a system is secure;
4.   Audit: trail or log to detect security breaches and devise responses;
5.   Integrity: a basis for determining whether data is uncorrupted; and
6.   Confidentiality: privacy of communication and whether system is used by authorized user.[191]

Violating any of these principles can result in problems. A company may have liability for lax security if hackers obtain and disclose personal information of employees, customers, trading partners, or other persons.[192] Suppose a hospital permits a hacker with a "previous conviction for child molestation to access computer files to retrieve the phone numbers of young female patients to whom he then made obscene phone calls."[193] The casual use of passwords can result in compromising a company's computer network. In another case, hackers broke into a university computer and retrieved e-mail addresses and encoded passwords and

---

[188] *Id.*

[189] *Id.*

[190] *Id.*

[191] Karnow, *supra* note 54.

[192] John R. Christiansen, Liability for Information Security, 3 The Internet Newsletter: Legal & Bus. Aspects 7 (Jan. 1999).

[193] *Id.*

then sent racist messages to 20,000 e-mail users. The falsely identified "originator" of the messages received death threats, and his reputation was severely harmed.[194]

[1]   Enforcing Information Security

SPC's computer system and data network are as mission critical as its telephone service.[195] Companies need to assure third parties of the security of their web sites. An information security policy is evidence that SPC took reasonable precautions to protect the trade secrets and confidential information supplied by third parties. This evidence is vital to a company. Further, the company should use the latest antihacking technologies to adequately protect confidential information provided by third parties. The company needs filters for smurf or denial of service attacks and other known security intrusions. There must be provisions for the backup of information on a company's web site and an emergency preparedness system to protect its customers in the event that the web site is crashed by outside hackers or other causes. Refer to the Preventive Law Pointer in Chapter Two, § 2.07[C], for a sample security policy.

[2]   Antivirus Practices

The "I Love You" e-mail virus forced Ford Motor Company to shut down its entire e-mail system for four days.[196] Computer viruses downloaded from the Internet pose serious risks to corporate computer systems. Viruses have the potential to delete files, corrupt files, alter data, or lock the user out of his or her computer. Some viruses may crash a computer system or destroy the hard drive.[197] Mandatory virus-checking software should be installed on all computers. Spot-checks should be made to determine whether users have disabled these features. The Internet and e-mail policy should warn employees of the risks of viruses. Additionally, employees who bypass virus-scanning programs should incur consequences. The highly destructive Melissa virus of 1999, for instance, was sent as an innocuous-seeming e-mail attachment.

A company is susceptible to liability if viruses or malicious code is transmitted through its computers and computer software. A virus, for example, may cause the licensee's computer hard drive to crash, resulting in significant economic harm. Companies should disclaim liability for viruses and, if possible, either reallocate the risk of viruses to third parties or insure against such risk. A standard clause should state that the company makes "no warranty as to viruses,

---

[194] *Id.*

[195] Ralph Kisiel, On Guard: Cyberterror Threat Has Auto Industry Beefing Up, Auto. News, Dec. 3, 2001, at 27.

[196] *Id.*

[197] Karnow, *supra* note 54.

and it is the responsibility of the assignee to use antivirus software." The company must be certain that antivirus measures are enforced throughout the company. The systems administrator should perform regular checks for viruses and other destructive code. Antivirus software, such as the McAfee package, should be installed and used on the desktop and at the mail server. Mail servers now have the capacity to detect viruses and "quarantine infected mail." Antiviral programs need to be frequently updated or they foster a false assurance of protection.

Before a user is allowed to download anything from a web site, a pop-up warning (or window) should note the risks involved. Antivirus software must be activated for anything downloaded from a third party's web site. Employees who download material from the Internet may cause the introduction of malicious computer code or viruses that disable or destroy computer files. A company must install the latest antivirus program and instruct employees not to open e-mail attachments without authorization.

[F]   Reducing Regulatory Enforcement Actions

Companies must comply with the regulations affecting Internet advertisements, sale of securities, taxation, unfair and deceptive trade practices, pricing laws, and consumer protection. One notable example is the investigation of Priceline.com.™ The Connecticut Attorney General, after receiving complaints, launched an investigation.[198] Even if the investigation does not lead to legal action, the negative publicity does enormous damage to an organization's credibility. SPC must institute adequate policies, terms of use conditions, and other related safeguards to ensure compliance with state and federal regulation. SPC, for example, sells computers to consumers as well as to businesses, and it must comply with the mandatory written warranty rules of the Magnuson-Moss Act, including labeling written warranties as either "limited" or "full," or it risks exposure to a consumer protection lawsuit.[199]

[G]   Avoiding Privacy Claims

An e-business should conduct a comprehensive privacy audit that examines whether the company is complying with privacy statutes or the common law in the following areas:

*   E-commerce privacy protection;

*   Health records;

*   Children and online privacy;

*   Wireless communications;

---

[198] AG Investigates Priceline, Conn. L. Trib. (Oct. 9, 2000), at 4.
[199] 15 U.S.C. §§ 2301 et seq.

- Privacy in government contracts;

- Information and systems security;

- Financial privacy;

- Corporate privacy policies and industry privacy codes;

- Privacy audits;

- Privacy compliance programs and privacy training;

- Company recruitment of chief privacy officers;

- Web bugs, wiretaps, and electronic surveillance;

- Employee records;

- Biometrics, including facial recognition technology;

- Licensing, outsourcing, and personal information;

- Documents containing personal information on insolvency;

- International data transfer;

- Privacy notices for web sites; and

- Privacy protection for European contracts.[200]

To minimize liability for privacy-related lawsuits, companies must fully disclose their own privacy and data protection practices and give web site visitors an opportunity to "opt out" of any data-mining of personal information.[201] The Federal Trade Commission (FTC) is studying ways to protect personal information held by Internet e-businesses. SPC will need to disclose its privacy policy to web site visitors. In addition, SPC's terms and services agreements must cover privacy and data protection issues. SPC must take steps to protect the confidentiality of any personal information supplied by its trading partners or customers. Finally, SPC should act to minimize its exposure to common law torts of privacy, including claims arising out of false light, intrusion of seclusion, and public disclosure of private facts.

Every company must also comply with applicable comprehensive privacy and data protection laws that have been enacted in most countries connected to the

---

[200] Simon Chester, Privacy Emerges as a Plum Target for New Business—and a Critical Component of Management Agenda, L. Prac. Mgmt., Mar. 2002, at 24.

[201] SPC's privacy policy must be balanced against a need to learn about web site business activity. The e-business economy is based on data-mining to quantify monthly hits, user sessions, hits per day, and consumer information. *See generally* Matthew M. Neumeier, E-Commerce Storefront Development and Hosting (E-Commerce: Strategies for Success in the Digital Economy, Practicing Law Institute: Patents, Copyrights, Trademarks and Literary Property Course Handbook Series (PLI Order No. Go-0090, Aug./Sept. 1999) (arguing that information about web site visitors and customers is "one of the most valuable assets a business garners from its web site").

global Internet.[202] To minimize its liability for violating the privacy of web site visitors, it must comply with the laws of many nations. The European Union Directive on Data Protection requires privacy safeguards where data is transferred to countries that do not provide "adequate protection." The European Directive on Data Privacy became effective on October 25, 1998. The European Commission has negotiated a safe harbor with the United States which must be approved by the European Parliament.

The U.S. must also consider privacy regulations of individual nations. The Swedish Data Protection Act, for example, would prohibit SPC from harvesting names, addresses, and other personal information from its web site without prior consent.[203] Ireland published its data protection rules for privacy on the Internet in November 1998.[204] New Zealand brought its privacy policies up to date to "ensure an adequate level of protection."[205] Companies will need to examine the data protection laws and practices of many countries to ensure that they will not be sued in a distant forum. The United States has yet to be classified as a country with an adequate level of protection under Article 25 of the Directive.

[H]   Insurance

Insurance policies reallocate risk of loss to a third-party insurer. Insurance policies should be reviewed to ensure that they cover any e-mail or Internet-usage related risks possible. "The new economy already has claimants seeking coverage for a range of losses from damaged hardware and software to claims of defamation. Coverage disputes have arisen about whether these losses are covered under traditional commercial general liability policies (CGL) or under newer policies specifically designed for e-commerce risks."[206] For example, risks created by e-mail and Internet usage include invasion of privacy and defamation; intellectual property claims can be covered by existing or expanded commercial general liability policies.[207] For a more detailed discussion of insurance needs and requirements for e-businesses, refer to § 9.03. Be aware, however, that many policies contain exclusions for damages resulting from everything from trademark

---

[202] Global Internet Liberty Campaign (GILC), An International Survey of Privacy Laws and Practice (visited Dec. 25, 1999), http://www.gilc.org/privacy/survey.

[203] Microsoft Law & Corporate Affairs, Summary of Global Internet Legal Developments 65 (Jan. 1999) (summarizing of global Internet legal developments for the period Oct.-Dec. 1998).

[204] *Id.*

[205] *Id.* at 67.

[206] Larry P. Schiffer, Commentary, New Risks for the New Economy—What Does It Mean for Reinsurers?, Mealey's Litig. Rep.: Reinsurance 23 (February 8, 2001).

[207] See Dawn Dinkins, Commentary, Internet Liabilities: A Look at Coverage Under the Traditional Commercial General Liability Policy, Andrews Corp. Officers and Dirs. Liab. Litig. Rep. (January 2, 2001).

infringement to defamation.[208] Accordingly, any new policy under consideration as well as existing policies should be reviewed by experienced counsel.

§ 10.04   E-MAIL AND INTERNET USAGE POLICIES

The last mechanisms for risk management that will be discussed are e-mail and Internet usage policies. These mechanisms are the key to effective preventative maintenance and therefore deserve their own section. Every company needs an e-mail and Internet usage policy to reduce liability resulting from the misuse and abuse of corporate computers. Although the media may portray litigation as random lightning strikes beyond a company's control, many online hazards are preventable and avoidable. A preventive law program for the e-mail and the Internet is a required component of any risk management program, and corporate auditing of e-mail or Internet usage reduces the radius of the risk. Corporate counsel can play a significant role in preventive counseling, whether by drawing up an Internet or e-mail policy or by reviewing policies drafted by others. In the Enron case, review and adherence to such a policy may have prevented the more egregious conduct.[209]

The e-mail and Internet usage policy should be structured as a contract or written agreement. Computer access should be conditioned upon reading and agreeing to the terms of the usage policies. A technology-leading company should not rely upon a template but should undertake a legal audit before devising its policy.

The usage policy should make it clear that the e-mail system and Internet usage is solely for business purposes by stating specifically that: "The company's computer facilities [include all designated computer systems under the policy] are provided to the employee for business uses." The purpose of this disclosure is to eliminate the widely held perception that the company computer belongs to the employee.

The policy should also include a disclosure about the employee's reasonable expectation of privacy. In many organizations in which passwords are issued, employees often believe that their computer use is private; the belief that e-mail is private is even more widespread. The statement may note that "The Company's equipment may be inspected by an authorized employee at any time even though you may have a password, encryption, or other security device in place." If the company monitors employees' e-mail messages, it should describe permitted uses and the consequences of violating the policy.

---

[208] Joshua Gold, Insurance Coverage for Internet and Computer Related Claims, 19 No. 4 Computer and Internet Lawyer 8 (April 2002).

[209] John S. Baker Jr., Asian Wall St. J., June 21, 2002, at A9 (it has been reported that "[u]ltimately jurors did agree that one person, Anderson staff attorney Nancy Temple, acted with corrupt intent" when she instructed David B. Duncan, the lead partner on the Enron account, to delete a passage from an e-mail).

The e-mail policy should be enforced, and enforcement should be nondiscriminatory and even-handed. Monitoring web sites can lead to abuses. Failure to enforce the policy generally may result in the company being unable to invoke the policy in a specific instance.

The policy should incorporate graduated methods of discipline. The U.S. Navy disciplined 500 employees for transmitting sexually explicit e-mail.[210] Less serious offenses may be dealt with informally. More serious offenses may be punished by verbal warnings, written reprimands or warnings, payroll deductions, suspensions, or terminations. In 1999, the New York Times fired 20 employees in a payroll processing center for transmitting "inappropriate and offensive" e-mail.[211]

The basic policy should explain how crimes, torts, and other liabilities accrue from the misuse or abuse of the computer system. The employee should be advised that downloading unlicensed software, installing it from a CD-ROM, or exceeding the permitted number of licensed copies of software may subject the company and the employee to liability.[212] Downloading pornography or transmitting hate speech may likewise result in liability. In addition, employers should warn all employees that their companies will cooperate with local, state, and federal law enforcement authorities investigating any criminal activities by employees, and that in the event of a subpoena, companies may be required to produce e-mail records.

It is important to give employees clear illustrations of what constitutes a misuse or abuse of the Internet or e-mail. Employees should be warned that inappropriate use of the computer may result in sanctions as well as possible criminal or civil liability. Here is an example of such a statement:

> SPC's communication systems are provided for your use in conducting business on behalf of SPC. Prohibited, inappropriate, or unauthorized use of these systems is grounds for disciplinary action. An example of such misuse or abuse includes such acts as sending anonymous messages using company systems to harass or defame an employee, an organization, or other party.

Companies need in-house training to help their employees understand the proper use of the e-mail system and the Internet and the principles of information security. Computer users should be required to change their passwords or user identifications periodically. Computer systems used to download data or software or to store data for another company will raise more issues than systems for only internal use.[213]

---

[210] American Mgmt. Assoc., E-Mail Study (visited Jan. 10, 2002), http://www.amanet.org/research/emssurvey.htm.

[211] *Id.*

[212] Tom Lowry, Software Pirates Risk Sailing into Stormy Seas, Comm. World (Jan. 29, 1999) (noting also that "the use of illegal software opens up an organization to software viruses and to lost productivity because unlicensed software is not eligible for software technical support or upgrades").

[213] It is a common practice to lease storage space for databases to other companies. EMC Corporation, for example, provides a web site where companies such as Toys R' Us lease storage space for its databases.

An e-mail policy needs to take into account the industry and corporate culture and must be tailored to known risks. An e-mail fault tree identifies all of the paths that are correlated with known hazards. An e-mail policy does not immunize a business from liability caused by misuse of the company's computer, but the expense of developing a good e-mail policy may be far less expensive than retrofits, lawsuits, or damage to corporate reputations.

Organizations must bear in mind when drafting these policies that there are federal bodies of law with which the organization must comply. Two of the most important such bodies of law are the National Labor Relations Act (NLRA)[214] and the Electronic Communications Privacy Act of 1986.[215] The critical issue with the National Labor Relations Act is access to employees.[216] In one case, the NLRB held that "By discriminatorily prohibiting bargaining unit employees from using the electronic mail system for distributing union literature and notices, the Company has violated Section 8(a)(1)."[217] Employers must draft e-mail policies so that they do not interfere with employee rights under the National Labor Relations Act. This may be accomplished by including a clause which states:

> Nothing in this e-mail usage policy should be construed to prohibit any employee from using e-mail for communications protected under the National Labor Relations Act.

The second important federal law consideration, the Electronic Communications Privacy Act, governs whether an employer may monitor employees' electronic communications. Fortunately, there is a simple and easy way to comply with this federal statute. The statute provides that "[i]t shall not be unlawful under this chapter . . . to intercept a wire, oral, or electronic communication . . . where one of the parties to the communication has given prior consent to such interception. . . ."[218] Accordingly, every employment agreement should contain a clause that requires the employee to consent to the company monitoring the employee's e-mail. This consent, together with notice in the e-mail usage policy that e-mails will be monitored, will give the company the best protection against privacy claims. In addition, global e-businesses will need to comply with national labor laws requiring consultation with worker's councils prior to launching e-mail and Internet usage policies.

The e-business needs a policy to ensure that the company is complying with the Children's Online Privacy Protection Act (COPPA), which restricts data collection for children under the age of 13. The Federal Trade Commission (FTC) has prescribed guidelines for the collection and use of personally identifiable information about children under the age of 13. Parental consent is a predicate to any

---

[214] 29 U.S.C. §§ 151-169 (2002).

[215] 18 U.S.C. §§ 2510-2522, 2701-2711 (2002).

[216] *See* E.I. du Pont de Nemours & Co., 311 NLRB Dec. (CCH) 893 (May 28, 1993).

[217] *Id.* at 897.

[218] 18 U.S.C. § 2511(2)(d).

data collection effort. To date, the FTC has filed and settled five law enforcement actions relating to COPPA. In April 2001, the FTC announced settlements with three web site operators that failed to comply with COPPA.[219] An online company must make privacy a key part of any web site or workplace legal audit.

[A]   Key Issues

[1]   Legal Audits

Legal audits of Internet usage involve a careful examination of the legally significant facts of employees' use, misuse, and abuse of the company's computer systems. The objectives for a legal audit of computer usage are to promote efficiency, limit liability, and improve productivity. Does the company have a reporting system that allows employees to report violations of the policies? An online company needs to prevent future legal problems through an operations review of e-mail and Internet usage.[220] How can the company improve its use of e-mail and the Internet? For a more detailed discussion of legal audits, refer to § 9.02.

[2]   Legal Autopsies and Near Misses

Corporations need to learn from past mistakes to avoid repeating their mistakes. The goal of corporate counsel is to help companies become "first trial learners," avoiding repetition of their mistakes.[221] Some analysts claim that two kinds of companies do business on the Internet: those who have had e-mail litigation disasters and those who will have them in the future. Prior similar mistakes may be the basis for a claim that the company is ratifying or acquiescing in wrongdoing. Disaster recovery is a part of legal prevention for high-technology companies. Corporate counsel can play a key role by analyzing the misuse or abuse of the e-mail system or the Internet that resulted in litigation or a "near miss."

Legal counsel will determine whether charges should be filed against wayward employees, ex-employees, or others who had misused the company computer system. Legal counsel determines the civil and criminal causes of action that may be at issue. Legal counsel will also decide whether to contact law enforcement to investigate a computer intrusion. Legal autopsies of e-mail or Internet abuse are completed to prevent future incidents. The purpose of the audit is to uncover the reasons for a company's direct or indirect liability from abuse of

---

[219] Orrin S. Shifren, Settlements Reached with Web Site Operators Charged with Violating COPPA, Cyberspace Law., Mar. 2002, at 13.

[220] Edward A. Dauer, Preventive Law Dictates Going to Root Causes to Prevent Claims from Arising, 7 Preventive L. Rep. 12, 13 (Sept. 1988).

[221] A one-trial learner changes its practices in the wake of legal disasters, as opposed to becoming a repeat player litigating the same legal problems over and over.

the Internet or the computer system.[222] A company's team will need to carefully document the steps it takes to recover its computer system after any abuse or intrusion.

[3] Web Site Activities and Jurisdiction

A company may make a strategic decision to limit its web site activities to minimize the possibility of being "haled into a court in a distant forum." A passive web site may be the source of liability in some jurisdictions. The Internet presents a somewhat uncertain legal environment for determining jurisdictional questions. Calls have been made for an international treaty governing Internet jurisdiction. In the absence of a worldwide solution to Internet governance, however, courts have treated jurisdiction as a question of "old wine in new bottles."

The question still lingers of whether a company that establishes an e-mail system and Internet site is exposed to the risks of being sued everywhere. Many companies will use choice of law and forum clauses to reduce the possibility of litigating in a distant or inconvenient forum. The courts, however, continue to apply a minimum contact analysis to determine jurisdiction. It is clear that personal jurisdiction may not be based simply on a web page and an e-mail address.[223] Similarly, the registration of a domain name alone is not enough to establish it, either, because personal jurisdiction is based on commercial activity. A web site and e-mail system may subject a company to personal jurisdiction. The more active the site, the more likely the exercise of personal jurisdiction in a distant forum.

A California court found that a defendant's passive web site, which permitted e-mail and file transfers but not the taking of orders online, did not constitute jurisdiction for a Canadian company in a domain name dispute.[224] The court found that the protocol of the web site, which required customers to print out an order form from the site and then to fax the order to company headquarters in Canada, was evidence that it was a passive site.[225] The court concluded that contacts were insufficient to satisfy the due process requirements of personal jurisdiction.[226] The court compared the site's e-mail capability to electronic response cards, and held that this capability did not alter the site's status as a passive advertisement.[227] For a complete discussion of jurisdiction issues, see Chapter Seven.

---

[222] *Id.* at 15 ("Legal autopsies and litigation audits are techniques that run a film backwards—analyses of the portfolio of legal claims designed, like an epidemiological study, to locate the underlying factual causes of legal ill health. Every legal claim is just a late chapter in a much longer story.").

[223] Cybersell, Inc. v. Cybersell, Inc., 130 F.3d 414 (9th Cir. 1997) (finding a web page and an e-mail address alone to be insufficient basis for personal jurisdiction).

[224] Jurisdiction: Desktop Technologies, Inc. v. ColorWorks Reproduction & Design, Inc. Judge Finds No Jurisdiction Over Canadian Company in Domain Name Case, 16 Comp. & Online Indus. Litig. Rptr. 9 (Mar. 16, 1999).

[225] *Id.*

[226] *Id.*

[227] *Id.*

[B] Key Components of Any Policy

[1] Title

The Internet and e-mail use policy may be divided into separate e-mail and Internet use policies or a combined policy may be used. The policy should be titled appropriately (1) Company Internet Use Policy, (2) Company E-Mail Use Policy, or (3) Company Internet and E-Mail Use Policy. The title of the policy should be conspicuously displayed on a computer screen as well as in printed materials.

[2] Table of Contents

Policies should have indexes of topics covered. Online versions could have a search engine to help employees find topics. Topics will vary depending on the company and industry. Every policy should address key definitions, background, scope, policy, sanctions, risks, rights, and responsibilities.

[3] Purpose/Background of Policy

The document should state the company's purpose for enacting a policy. A policy may simply provide guidance for using information technologies, or it may mandate appropriate uses and define misuses and abuses. The policy should state that the employer owns the e-mail and computer system. Some companies state that they own all e-mail messages as well,[228] but this poses the risk that the company adopts all e-mail messages, even those that might subject them to additional liability.[229] The e-mail policy "does not insulate a business from the effects of employee carelessness or stupidity."[230] The company should incorporate e-mail and Internet horror stories into the training employees receive about the policy.

Policies should have information on why computer use is restricted. A public institution, such as the Commerce Department or a state university, may have Internet legal issues not present in the private economy. The University of North Carolina, for example, enacted the Internet and e-mail policies across all branches of the state college system, based on a model developed by the Computer and Internet Legal Issues Committee.[231]

---

[228] One law company recommends ownership of all data on the company's computers as a means of establishing the right to monitor use. *See* Felhaber, Larson, Fenlon, and Vogt, *supra* note 157.

[229] *See, e.g.,* Stauss v. Microsoft Corp., No. 7433 LEXIS (S.D.N.Y. 1995) (describing sexually explicit e-mail messages in sex discrimination case).

[230] Felhaber, Larson, Fenlon, and Vogt, *supra* note 157.

[231] *See* University E-Mail Retention Policy, The University of North Carolina at Greensboro, Approved by Chancellor Sullivan (May 13, 1998) (visited June 15, 2002), http://www.uncg.edu/apl/POLICIES/iip019.htm.

[4] Scope/Permitted Purposes/Authorized Company Activities

The e-mail and Internet policy must state clearly the policy's scope. The scope section of the policy sets forth the persons to whom policies and guidelines apply. Do guidelines vary depending on departmental unit, or do they apply across-the-board to all corporate units? Are policies applicable to closely-held corporations or foreign subsidiaries? Are consultants and temporary employees bound to follow the policies? Do policies apply only to the use of the Internet at work, or do they also apply to employer-provided computers in employees' private residences? Are telecommuters subject to the Internet or e-mail use policies? The Department of Commerce Internet Use Policy, for example, applies department-wide, including employees using at-home computers provided by the government. Policies should state that they supersede all earlier adopted policies. Providing an effective date of enactment for a policy is also appropriate. It is important to have a clause that e-mail or Internet usage is for business purposes.

Companies should define the permitted purposes or scope of what is acceptable within their usage policy. Most companies define the rationale for such usage and preclude all non-business-related activities.

[5] Permitted Users

It is important to specify who is permitted to use corporate Internet access and/or e-mails. Such a statement can alert an employee that family members or other nonemployees are not permitted users. In addition, if the company's independent contractors have access to the company's e-mail system and Internet access, the contractors should be required, at a minimum, to agree to be subject to the same terms and conditions that regular employees observe. The policy should therefore require that the hiring manager of the contractor obtain such agreement in writing.

[6] Copying and Publishing

Companies need to alert users that they must observe copyright and license agreements that may apply when downloading files, documents, and software. Furthermore, employees must realize that distributing content over the Internet can be deemed a form of publishing and the necessary safeguards should be implemented.

[7] Third-Party Rights

Every policy should outline prohibited activities, including but not limited to abusive or objectionable language, statements that defame or libel others, and statements that infringe on the privacy rights of others, as well as obscene or objectionable materials.

[8] Monitoring E-Mail and Internet Usage/No Expectation of Privacy

Companies should disclose to their employees that they reserve the right to access and reveal the content of all communications and activities, e.g., downloads. Companies that decide to monitor communications should advise their employees that they plan to monitor their e-mail messages. A company must conspicuously give notice that it has the right to monitor and review all e-mail and Internet messages. A company's written e-mail policy must state in unequivocal terms that an employee's use of the company's e-mail system constitutes a consent to supervisor's monitoring of e-mail and Internet usage. A prominent disclosure about the possibility of supervisory monitoring should be included in an online or computer dialogue. Finally, it may be advisable to obtain a paper-and-pen signature of the employee agreeing to being monitored. Each of these procedures disabuses the employee of the expectation that e-mail or Internet usage is private. Companies can reduce their risk of invasion of privacy lawsuits by obtaining employees' prior consent to monitoring and review of e-mail and Internet usage.

A growing number of developers sell software that electronically examines an employee's Internet usage.[232] A company may install a software package to monitor all e-mail and Internet usage or to monitor intermittently. Kill files may block incoming messages from individuals repeatedly e-mailing employees in the company for unauthorized purposes. Microsoft, for example, used an e-mail filtering device that relegated e-mail greeting cards to the spam ashbin.[233] Blocking software may be employed to restrict access to objectionable web sites. Employees may also block e-mail from various individuals and entities to screen out objectionable sites.[234]

A study estimates "that the average worker spends 49 minutes per day dealing with e-mail, up 35% from last year."[235] Another study also "estimates that management-level workers [spent] four hours a day on e-mail" during 2002.[236] Because of excessive time spent on e-mail, filtering out e-mail that is inappropriate for work can help to reduce the time spent.

Surf Control is an example of a software company that develops tools to supervise employee's actions while online to protect the company from any liabilities.[237] Surf Control's e-mail filter is used as a tool to filter all types of e-mail; one type is to "recognize explicit adult image files."[238] This e-mail filter will help

---

[232] *See, e.g.,* WinWhatWhere Corp. (visited June 20, 1999), http://www.winwhatwhere.com.

[233] TRO Stops Microsoft's Blocking of Blue Mountain's E-Mail Greeting Cards, 16 Litig. Rptr. 1 (Jan. 19, 1999) (reporting that California judge issued a temporary restraining order against Microsoft in Hartford House, Ltd. v. Microsoft Corp.).

[234] *See, e.g.,* MIMEsweeper, developed by Content Technologies, which filters junk e-mail, blocks URLs, and can be useful when developing a content security policy.

[235] A Study to Determine the Obvious, Cyberspace Law., July 2001, at 17.

[236] *Id.*

[237] SurfControl Releases Latest Email Filtering Tool and Best Practice Guide on Workplace Email Usage, M2Presswire, Nov. 11, 2001.

[238] *Id.*

to keep employees from being distracted with e-mail unrelated to work since it can filter out e-mails with "attachments that undermine productive work." Such companies as AT&T, Cisco Systems, Hewlett Packard, IBM, and Intel already use Surf Control.[239] Websense Inc. offers a similar approach, but their software may also be configured to allot time intervals when employees will be free to use the Internet for personal use, after which access to the Internet will be limited.[240] More than 14,000 clients use Websense worldwide.[241]

Another detection system, developed by Raytheon, allows

> companies [to] see everything going on their network, even what an individual worker is doing on the Net, without the worker being aware of it. It can see what you're e-mailing, where you are surfing, if you are sending anything to be printed, collaborating with anyone on a Word document, accessing or changing the database—everything you're doing on the network. [It] can detect and analyze Web pages, e-mail, digital video and sound files, spreadsheets, word documents, FTP, instant messages, even passwords. To give an example, it can get all the data on a 250-terminal network in about 20 minutes.

The most advanced system costs $65,000, and the less advanced system costs $25,000, but even though Raytheon has sold 140 copies, no company has yet admitted to using it to monitor its own employees.[242]

Monitoring employees' actions online is important to protect not only the employer from potential liabilities but also company e-mail servers from damage. Increases in e-mail passing through the company's e-mail servers at any time need to be monitored to prevent an overload of e-mails that could prevent the servers from working properly.[243] Adding more servers, as some companies have, will only postpone the problem.[244] Filtering spam—an estimated 25 million spam messages are sent out each day, equaling 10 percent of all Internet e-mail—can also limit the e-mail coming into the server.[245]

E-mail from online retailers could also be filtered. Research suggests that "50% of respondents who have registered with online retailers have used their work e-mail accounts, using up vital network bandwidth and storage on company mail servers."[246] Filtering retail e-mail can reduce time wasted reading during work and wear on the servers, especially during the holidays, when "users are being inundated with [commercial e-mails, many containing] animation and images, so the amount of bandwidth they use is higher than a standard e-mail."[247]

---

[239] *Id.*

[240] Dirty Downloads: Companies More Rigorous Against Internet Smut on the Job, Canadian Press, June 19, 2001.

[241] *Id.*

[242] Cyberklick: You Are Not Alone, Statesman (Mar. 4, 2001).

[243] *Id.*

[244] *Id.*

[245] *Id.*

[246] Neville Rawlings and Ann Fielder, Christmas Can Be Costly for Businesses Too; E-mail in the Workplace Pushes Up Indirect Costs for the Business, M2 PressWire, Dec. 5, 2001, at 1.

[247] *Id.*

The International Data Corporation has estimated "that corporations world-wide spent $62 million on Internet filtering and monitoring software in 1999" and predicts "that the figure will rise to $561 million by 2005."[248] The American Management Association has estimated that "more than three-quarters of U.S. firms now monitor their employees' phone calls, e-mails, Internet activities and computer files."[249] No one is immune from e-mail and Internet monitoring, not even the judges of the Ninth Circuit Court of Appeals, who ordered that the monitoring be disabled, however, after finding out about it.[250] The Judicial Conference's Committee on Automation disagreed with the judges, stating that "federal employees—including judges—should continue to be monitored for Internet misuses[251] and should be blocked from such activities as downloading music."[252]

Whatever technology or policy is adopted, the company must take steps to train employees in the proper use of the corporate computer system. Although software filtering can screen out a lot of objectionable material, it is not fail-safe. It cannot prevent accidental or intentional e-mail from an employee that may create a liability risk. It is best to use multiple methods, such as a filtering system, education, and formal company policies that should include random checks of where employees have visited.[253]

[9] Telecommuting Employees

Companies need to address telecommuting issues in their Internet usage policy or in a separate agreement. The telecommuting policy should also address the issue of whether family members may use the employee's computer or access company computers. The policy should limit the employee's access to confidential company computer files. Attempting to monitor an employee's Internet use from home imposes an additional burden on the company. Suppose, for example, that a family member or another third party sends harassing messages to the president of a competing company. At minimum, a company could be exposed to public scorn, ridicule, and bad publicity, even if it had no knowledge of the telecommuter's wrongdoing. Telecommuting, if unchecked by clear policy directives, can create great potential for liability for companies. At minimum, a telecommuting policy should advise telecommuters that company equipment can be used only for business purposes.

---

[248] *See* Kisiel, *supra* note 195.

[249] American Mgmt. Assoc., E-Mail Study (visited Jan. 10, 2002), http://www.amanet.org/research/emssurvey.htm.

[250] Jerry Crimmins, Even Federal Judges Come Under Surveillance When Online, Chicago Daily L. Bull., Aug. 14, 2001.

[251] David McGuire, More Libraries Filtered in 2001, Newsbytes (Jan. 9 2002), http://www.newsbytes.com/news/02/173523.html.

[252] *Supra* note 250.

[253] SurfControl Releases Latest Email Filtering Tool and Best Practice Guide on Workplace Email Usage, M2Presswire, Nov. 11, 2001.

Finally, the policy statement regarding telecommuting should make clear the company's position that such arrangements cannot be made for all employees. Clear guidelines should be made available to all employees regarding how employees are selected for telecommuting arrangements.[254]

[10] Other Clauses/Mandatory Terms

Usage policies may also address security concerns, firewall concerns, connectivity requirements, and encryption requirements. This section addresses a number of mandatory and optional terms for policies. The Internet and e-mail policies will typically be cross-referenced with Internet security and other usage policies. Policies will vary in their stance toward personal use. The Commerce Department, for example, permits government computers to be used only for authorized purposes, but distinguishes between the types of use permitted during working and nonworking hours on equipment provided by the Department.[255] It treats the use of Internet services like the use of any other government equipment and resources. A company's Internet policy will typically have guidelines for responsible use, including, if needed, a specialized protocol for sensitive or confidential information.

In addition, it is prudent to include direction for individuals regarding retention of e-mail messages consistent with the company's document retention policy. In particular, in the event of investigation by any state or federal body, the policy should require that any individual who has concerns regarding retention of e-mail messages contact general counsel for direction. This will ensure that proper and consistent guidelines are followed by individuals as well as the information systems staff who maintain a backup of e-mail databases.

[11] Conscious Delay

Companies should assess the particular risks attendant to e-mail and Internet usage in their company and take steps to minimize risk. A company should not wait until after a major public relations or legal disaster to formulate an e-mail policy.[256] If electronic documents are requested in discovery, counsel should review them. Counsel may need to advise clients of the importance of preserving the integrity of electronic documents.[257] Electronic data is easier to alter or manipulate

---

[254] Beverly W. Garofalo, Telecommuting: Interaction of Employment Law and Tech Change: Employers Are Well Advised to Draw Up Agreement for At-Home Workers, 15 Comp. L. Strat. 1 (Apr. 1999).

[255] *See* U.S. Department of Commerce Internet Use Policy, Appendix 10-1 to this chapter.

[256] *See generally* Controlling E-mail and Internet Use: Don't Wait Until It's Too Late to Formulate E-mail Policy, 4 Conn. Employ. L. Ltr. 2 (Apr. 1999).

[257] Committee on Federal Courts, Discovery of Electronic Evidence: Considerations for Practitioners and Clients, 53 The Record 656, 663 (Sept./Oct. 1998).

than are paper-based documents. A litigant may require the producing party to trace the chain of custody and to attest to the integrity of electronic information.[258]

[12]   Mechanics of Implementation

[a]   Standard Message Signatures

For official correspondence, create an e-mail signature that is automatically added to the end of the outgoing message stating the sender's name, address, and title or authority. For incidental personal correspondence, the e-mail should have a standard disclaimer that the communication is personal and not to be imputed to the company. Some companies mandate the use of e-mail signatures that make it clear that the employee's message does not speak for the corporation. Companies should minimally post a disclaimer that the company is not responsible for the contents of the message. They may also want to institute digital or automatic signatures in the proper form.

[b]   Message Filters

A corporate e-mail system may provide filters that specify subjects to be filtered out. If some unknown outside party is harassing a company, the messages out from given addresses can be filtered. Software filters may be used to block pornographic or other objectionable web sites.[259]

[c]   Spelling Checks

To avoid online spelling errors, require spell checkers to be used for all official e-mail communications. Often, persons write e-mails in an informal style that can at times approach stream-of-consciousness, and they may disregard spelling or grammatical errors. The use of spell checkers, formal headings, and a formal signature line is critical for e-mail to be treated as company records.

[d]   Corporate Internet Netiquette

Employees should receive training on Internet norms, often referred to as "netiquette." Netiquette boils down to common courtesy and temperate use of e-mail. E-mail messages may descend into personal or emotional attacks that users would rarely allow themselves in a telephone call or formal corporate letter. E-mail training should emphasize the liability associated with inflammatory e-mail statements that use the company's corporate e-mail return address. It should also cover basic style issues such as not typing messages in ALL CAPS, the Internet equivalent of shouting.

---

[258] *Id.* at 663.

[259] Software may also help block junk e-mail and URLs and permit SPC systems administrators to enforce information security policies.

[13]   Contact Person

Every policy should provide a contact person or persons who can provide sure-footed guidance on interpreting the policy. Feedback forms should be directed to the contact person. Feedback forms should be reviewed regularly, and companies should respond to them, where appropriate. The contact person should provide an e-mail address as well as a telephone number. All inquiries about the policies should be promptly answered.

[14]   Definitions

An e-mail and Internet usage policy should have a glossary of definitions written in plain English and other languages where appropriate. Definitions of terms will include basic definitions covering topics such as systems administrator, legal custodian, e-mail messages, flaming, netiquette, firewalls, discovery, electronic smoking guns, listservs, spam, mail headers, Virtual Personal Networks, URLs, domain names, and web sites.

§ 10.05   SAMPLE E-MAIL AND INTERNET USAGE POLICY

INTERNET USAGE POLICY

I. PURPOSE

This document is SPC's Internet policy, which provides the ground rules for the use of the Internet by all employees in all SPC divisions. The policy applies to all employees, partners, consultants, and others having access to SPC's computer system. The goal of the policy is to help you use the computer system while minimizing the possibility of creating legal trouble for you and the company. Another goal is to ensure economical, effective, and efficient management of Internet usage and to encourage collaborative efforts within SPC.

II. TABLE OF CONTENTS

Contact Person for Information and Assistance

Definitions

Background

Illustrations of Use, Misuse, and Abuse of the Internet

Scope of Policy

Policy

Restrictions on Business Use

Responsibilities

III. DEFINITIONS

A. Internet. A global web connecting more than 1,000,000 computers. Currently, the Internet has more than 30,000,000 users worldwide, and that number is growing rapidly. More than 100 countries are linked into exchanges of data, news, and opinions. Unlike online services, which are centrally controlled, the Internet is decentralized by design. Each Internet computer, called a host, is independent. Its operators can choose which Internet services to provide to its local users and which local services to make available to the global Internet community. Remarkably, this anarchy by design works exceedingly well.

B. World Wide Web (WWW or "the Web"). A system of Internet servers that supports specially formatted documents. The documents are formatted in a language called HTML (hypertext markup language) that supports links to other documents, as well as graphics, audio, and video files. This means users can jump from one document to another simply by clicking on hot spots. Not all Internet servers are part of the World Wide Web. Several applications, called web browsers, make it easy to access the World Wide Web; three of the most popular are Mosaic, Netscape Navigator, and Microsoft's Internet Explorer.

C. Suffolk Personal Computers Home Page. The main page of SPC's web site. Typically, the home page serves as an index or table of contents to other documents stored at the site.

D. SPC's Web Site. A web site (location) on the World Wide Web. Each web site contains a home page, which is typically the first document users see when they enter the site. The site may also contain additional documents and files. Each web site is owned and managed by an individual, company, or organization. SPC's web site is owned and managed by our company.

E. Firewall. SPC's employees are responsible for maintaining the security of SPC's firewalls. That is, SPC employees are responsible for maintaining the secrecy of their passwords. A firewall cannot protect SPC's confidential information unless employees do their part by following the information security policy. SPC has a number of information security devices that enforce a boundary between two or more networks. A network firewall, or packet filter, examines traffic at the network protocol level. Application-level firewalls also re-address outgoing traffic so that it appears to have originated from the firewall rather than from the internal host. A firewall is part of SPC's information security policy.

IV. BACKGROUND

The Internet, a public telecommunications service, was established as a cooperative effort to provide worldwide networking services among educational institutions, government agencies, and various commercial and nonprofit organizations. High-speed networking technologies and developments have made the Internet a desirable research tool, a good source for an expanding body of research, and a means for information dissemination and general communication. The Internet has expanded to include government information, educational information systems, archives, and business resources. The Internet also includes functions such as those for electronic mail (e-mail), remote computer networks, file transfers, the World Wide Web (WWW), and wide area information servers.

SPC's access and use of the Internet has grown exponentially since the company made the decision to become an e-business. Online services, such as the WWW, have greatly increased user access to a wider, and more diverse, community of information resources. As SPC has a number of employees in divisions throughout the world, a growing number of SPC employees are telecommuting through the use of tunneling technologies that permit remote access to company computers. This increased access has many benefits for the company, but it also poses new dangers and liabilities. This dramatic increase in communication capabilities makes it necessary to establish policies regarding the proper and efficient use of Internet.

V. SCOPE OF POLICY

SPC considers the Internet a fundamental communications tool for supporting SPC's business model. The policies and guidelines in SPC's Internet policy apply to the management of all Internet services company-wide. The Internet usage policy will be updated from time to time. You will receive e-mail notification of any supplemental policies affecting use of the Internet.

VI. POLICY

SPC encourages its employees to use the Internet to advance the business goals of the company. Use of the Internet, however, requires responsible judgment, supervisory discretion, and compliance with SPC's Internet usage policy. In addition, computer users must comply with SPC's information security policy. This requires the user to be aware of information technology security and other privacy concerns. Users must also be aware of and follow SPC's rules for Internet usage. Your use of SPC's computer system is conditional upon your acceptance of the terms and conditions of this policy. Your use of the e-mail and Internet constitutes your consent to the company's review and monitoring of e-mail messages.[260]

A. Personal Use of E-Mail and the Internet
Internet services provided by SPC are to be used for business purposes. Internet service represents a corporate resource that must be managed in

---

[260] Douglas M. Towns, Legal Issues Involved in Monitoring Employees' Internet and E-Mail Usage, Gigalaw.com (visited Jan. 14, 2002), http://gigalaw.com/articles/2002/towns-2002-01.html (recommending notice and consent language for company's electronic communications systems).

an efficient and cost-effective manner. A user, for example, should not download lengthy video files for personal use. The following list of examples includes some, but not all, improper uses of the Internet.

1. The use of SPC's computer system to pursue private commercial business activities while at work. The use of SPC's computer or web site to conduct a private business venture.

2. The use of SPC's computer system to work for a political party, candidate for partisan political office, or partisan political group.

3. The use of SPC's computer system to participate in nonbusiness chat rooms including religious or political objectives.

4. Accessing web sites for no business purpose that results in additional charges to the company, such as commercial sites.

5. Use of the e-mail system for nonbusiness purposes. You should consider e-mail messages to be the same as any other corporate record, that is, as subject to review by SPC's systems administrator. SPC employees are subject to sanctions, culminating in termination, for unprofessional, threatening, or other abusive behavior on the e-mail or Internet systems. If SPC's systems administrator finds evidence that an employee has used the company's computer system to commit a crime, the company will cooperate with law enforcement in prosecuting the employee. SPC reserves the right to turn over e-mail messages with objectionable content to law enforcement officials.

6. Use of the computer to engage in hate speech or other discriminatory conduct.

7. Downloading, transmitting, or viewing sexually explicit material.

8. Downloading, transmitting, or viewing Internet sites that would embarrass or bring unfavorable publicity to you and the company.

9. Use of the computer system to commit a crime or to violate a statute or regulation.

10. Misuse of the computer system by using it to disrupt the workplace or to violate the trust of the company in any way.

11. Downloading unlicensed software, music, or other material that may infringe the intellectual property rights of others.

B. Duty to Report Offensive, Illegal, or Inappropriate E-Mail
It is your duty not to transmit offensive, illegal, or inappropriate e-mail. It is also your duty to report the receipt of any such material or any such behavior by others of which you become aware.

C. The Use of SPC's Computer(s) and Systems Is Not Private
Your use of SPC's computer system, e-mail system, and Internet access may be monitored. E-mail is not private, and anyone using SPC's computers has no reasonable expectation of privacy in their e-mail communications and Internet usage. SPC reserves the right to monitor and

review all e-mail messages and Internet usage at our sole discretion. Furthermore, you waive any right of privacy in e-mail messages and consent to monitoring and disclosure by the company. Anyone using SPC's equipment consents to such monitoring and is advised that if such monitoring reveals possible evidence of criminal activity or employee misconduct, SPC managers may provide the evidence of such monitoring to law enforcement officials. Individuals are not guaranteed privacy while using SPC's computers and should, therefore, not expect it. To the extent that employees wish that their private activities remain private, they should avoid using SPC's Internet or e-mail for illegal or prohibited activities.

D. Limited Personal Use of E-Mail and the Internet

SPC's general policy is that e-mail and Internet usage is for business purposes and should be used in accordance with company guidelines. In addition, your use of SPC's computer system must be in accordance with other company policies and procedures. Limited personal use of e-mail during working hours is permissible. As a guideline, your personal use of e-mail and the Internet should be similar to your personal use of the telephone. SPC employees should be careful not to create the impression that a personal e-mail has been sent on behalf of the company. At no time may SPC's e-mail addresses be used in a manner that gives the impression that the company authorizes an otherwise personal communication. The privacy of personal e-mail or of Internet communications cannot be guaranteed and is subject to monitoring.

Personal use of e-mail should be occasional and should not be allowed to interfere with your job. You should avoid spending an excessive amount of time on the Internet. Sending more than one or two personal e-mail messages per day should be considered a rough standard of excessive use. You are not authorized to download software, music, or other materials from the Internet without prior authorization. You must avoid filling up the mail boxes of co-employees, as well as your own mail box, with personal messages; this may prevent delivery of business messages.

VII. RESTRICTIONS ON BUSINESS USES

The e-mail or the Internet should not be used to send confidential information, proprietary information, or trade secrets without prior written authorization from your manager. Authorized confidential information should be conspicuously labeled as confidential and should be sent using encryption software provided by SPC. SPC employees should consult with their managers before transmitting highly sensitive information, even if encryption is used. E-mail messages are easily misdirected, and it is the duty of every SPC employee to take care in determining the correct e-mail address.

VIII. RESPONSIBILITIES

A. Each manager is responsible for ensuring that the guidelines in this policy are fulfilled.

B. SPC's systems administrator has responsibility for SPC's e-mail system, Internet activities, and overall network data management. The coordinator is expected to have the following skills and background:

- Method and type of communications access.

- Internet host and domain names.

- TCP/IP addresses.

- Domain name services.

- Internet applications, for example, file transfer protocol (ftp), WWW, and others.

- Network security and data integrity.

I, _____, acknowledge that I have read and agree to the conditions and terms of this Internet usage policy. I acknowledge that SPC does not guarantee the privacy of e-mail communications or Internet usage. I understand that SPC has reserved the right to monitor or review all e-mail and Internet communications and use. I consent to the terms and conditions of this e-mail and Internet usage policy. All prior and contemporaneous agreements are merged into this agreement.

Signature   Effective Date

Further information and assistance on this policy may be obtained from:

Systems Administrator
Building XYZ
1 SPC Street
SUFFOLK PERSONAL COMPUTERS
Boston, Massachusetts 02108-4977
617-573-0000
sysadmin@spc.com

§ 10.06   LAUNCHING AN E-MAIL AND INTERNET USAGE POLICY

The launch of a company-wide policy is a complex undertaking, and it may be difficult to institutionalize when the company has subsidiaries in a number of countries and a complex corporate structure. The company's e-mail and Internet usage policy should be cross-referenced to the company's other human resources policies such as nondiscrimination. Human resources training on a harassment policy should make it clear that e-mail and Internet usage is covered by the company's policy.[261] Multinational corporations may need to consult with unions or other local entities to understand local laws and restrictions. In West Germany, for example, which has a co-determination system of worker control, a company should obtain approval from the worker's council. If a significant number of employees do not speak English, the e-mail or Internet policy will need to be translated into the relevant languages.

[A]   Risk Assessment and Internet Access

Before drafting and implementing a policy, a company's legal team must first perform a legal audit of its computer system to gain a better understanding of the company's specific risks and dangers. The form of the audit will depend on the nature of the company's operating systems, its applications, its backup systems, and its disaster recovery procedures.[262] Policies must be customized to fit business models. Boilerplate forms may identify issues, but every policy should be customized to the organization's specialized needs. An Internet and e-mail policy appropriate for the Defense Department, for example, would not be suitable for Amazon.com or eTrade. Each company needs to determine the appropriate purposes to which its e-mail and Internet access can be put, and then devise its policy accordingly. More specifically, if e-mail is used solely for internal purposes, one set of consequences follow. In contrast, if e-mail is used for advertising, transmitting data, and the conduct of trade or commerce, other consequences will follow.

[B]   Authenticating and Monitoring E-Mail Usage

Routine checks should be conducted on a weekly basis to determine whether subject and personal authorization policies are followed. The greater the need for confidentiality, the higher the security. "Some confidences are so valuable, that the client will want to take extraordinary steps to protect them."[263] Spot checks should

---

[261] *Id.* (recommending that employer's e-mail policy be integrated with the company's harassment and nondiscrimination policies).

[262] A Federal Courts Committee recommends some of the following questions be asked to determine the radius of the security risk: "Where are all of the potential sources of electronic information? Cover the following possibilities with the client: floppy diskettes kept by the client, or the employees, in their offices or at their homes; files on individual computer hard drives in employees' offices, on portable drives that can be attached to a computer, on laptops used by employees off site, or on personal computers used by employees at their homes; files on a network or central system's hard drive and servers, and on and off site backup files. What is the client's retention policy with respect to electronic evidence?" Committee on Federal Courts, Discovery of Electronic Evidence: Considerations for Practitioners and Clients, 53 The Record 656, 658 (Sept./Oct. 1998).

[263] William Freivogel, Internet Communications—Part II, A Larger Perspective, VIII ALAS Loss Prevent. J. 2, 4 (Jan. 1997) (cited in 3 Haw. Bar J. 6).

also be conducted periodically to thwart wrongdoing by those familiar with the timing or patterning of scheduled security audits.

A security policy uses techniques of authentication to determine authorization.[264] *Authentication* means "to sign, or to execute or adopt a symbol or sound, or encrypt a record in whole or in part, with intent to either identify a party or adopt a record."[265] Routine checks should be made as to whether unauthorized modems or other network connection devices, such as routers, bridges or gateways, have been connected to an internal network.[266] The systems administrator or other person should also design a backup system for company computers. Individual desktops should be set to automatically back-up documents every 15 or 30 minutes.

[C] Employee Education

Preventive measures for e-mail and Internet-related hazards can be accomplished with proper employee education. A company's principal e-mail or Internet-related hazard is imputed liability for the torts, crimes, and other bad acts of its employees. A company's primary risk management is in its employment, training, and supervision of its employees. Commentators advising high-tech companies recommend the *Providence Journal* Rule: Employees are instructed not to "write anything in e-mail that you do not want to see on the front page of the *Providence Journal*."[267] Another way of stating this is to caution employees "not to say things in an e-mail that they are not willing to have repeated at the water cooler or in court."[268]

An Internet usage policy should be integrated with new employee training. Additionally, it should be made part of the employment handbook, which may have to be reissued annually. The policy should cover whatever computer systems and electronic information are considered company computer systems and data sources. A contact person should be designated to answer questions employees might have about the policy. In a small or medium-sized corporation, it may be possible to obtain signed acknowledgments from the employees that they have read and understand the terms of an Internet access policy.

Another technique is to ask employees to visualize their e-mail messages in the hands of a plaintiff's attorney or prosecutor attorney. Yet another more realistic visualization is to ask employees to imagine that their e-mail messages are

---

[264] Karnow, *supra* note 54; *see also* People v. Lee No. C38925 (Cal. Super. Ct., Jan. 30, 1997) (visited Oct. 2, 2000), http://www.perkinscoie.com (reporting first criminal conviction from falsifying e-mail to extort settlement from employer in sexual harassment action).

[265] U.C.C. § 2-102(2) (Dec. 1, 1998).

[266] *See* Carnegie-Mellon Computer Emergency Response Team, Security Practices & Evaluations (visited June 15, 2002), http://www.cert.org.

[267] *See* Peter Lacourtune, Discovery and the Use of Computer Based Information in Litigation, 45 R.I. Bar J. 9 (Dec. 1996).

[268] *Id.*

being read to a jury in an employment termination lawsuit. Summaries or synopses of recent e-mail litigation can serve a training purpose by showing how misuse of the computer system can turn into a tort horror story.

[1] Use of Internet and E-Mail During Off-Hours

If a company provides an employee with a laptop, desktop, or other computer system used at home, a clear statement should be made of what constitutes appropriate use during work hours and off-hours. The Commerce Department, for example, permits employees to use computers for nonofficial uses: the general guideline is that the Department "expects employees to conduct themselves professionally while using Department resources and [to] refrain from using Department resources for activities that are disruptive to the workplace or in violation of public trust."[269] Under this policy, however, employees may not use printers or supplies for personal use. Further, the policy prohibits the use of government computers for political or partisan purposes, including direct or indirect lobbying.

Corporate users, like government users, should be warned about using computers for engaging in discriminating conduct, obtaining or viewing sexually explicit materials, or violating state, federal, or international law or a professional code of conduct.[270] An online company, like the government, should not permit users access to subscription or paid Internet sites unless such access serves a business purpose. While it is difficult for companies to monitor every employee at all hours, teaching corporate personnel to use sound business judgment and common sense should go a long way to reducing legal expenses.

[2] Notice of Monitoring

Although some courts have upheld terminating employees on the basis of intercepted messages where no warning of monitoring was given, it is prudent to include a conspicuous notice of monitoring in any e-mail or Internet access policy. The monitoring warning will be useful evidence that the employee did not have a reasonable expectation of privacy. The Commerce Department's monitoring warning states: "Like all other Government computer use, use of Government equipment for personal use of the Internet may be monitored and recorded. Anyone using Government equipment consents to such monitoring."[271]

Many high-tech companies are reluctant to prohibit all personal use of e-mail or the Internet. Such a strict policy would be unenforceable for many Silicon Valley companies. If personal use is permitted, a statement in the policy should caution against personal use that interferes with work. The Commerce Department Internet Use Policy provides the following statement on personal use that may be

---

[269] *See* U.S. Department of Commerce Internet Use Policy, Appendix 10-1 to this chapter.
[270] *Id.*
[271] *Id.*

adapted to the private electronic companies. A Fortune 500 company with foreign subsidiaries will need to adapt its policy to accommodate specific organizational realities. The Commerce Department usage policy provides in relevant part:

> Unless prohibited by the specific policies of the employee's bureau/operating unit, limited personal use of e-mail during duty hours is permissible, as such use will help promote proficiency in electronic communications, including use of the Internet, and provides an alternative method for authorized personal communications, which will promote Government efficiency. At no time may Government e-mail addresses be used in a manner which will give the impression that an otherwise personal communication is authorized by the Department. Personal use of e-mail cannot interfere with the official business of the employee or organization, such as spending an inappropriate amount of time during duty hours (e.g., sending more than four brief messages per day), filling up a mailbox with personal messages so as to prevent official messages from being delivered, or disseminating chain letters.[272]

Companies need a written corporate Internet usage policy that fits with their corporate cultures and business models. The goal of a usage policy is to minimize liability caused by employees or independent contractors using corporate computer networks.

[3]   Cooperation with Law Enforcement Officials

The policy should note that if monitoring reveals telltale evidence of criminal activity or misconduct, the company may provide evidence to local, state, or federal law enforcement officials. A corporation may be the subject of criminal charges for the theft of confidential information from a business rival. An innocent company may face potential liability for the acts of its malicious employees performed within the scope of their duties. Companies also face the risk that employees or unknown third parties will plant false computer evidence.[273] Lost, deleted, or altered e-mail messages may be reconstructed to determine whether a cover-up or attempt to obstruct justice has occurred.

[D]   Enforcement of E-Mail and Usage Policies

An Internet policy may become a dead letter without an enforcement mechanism. An employee may argue that an employer's long-standing custom of not enforcing an Internet usage policy creates an *estoppel* argument; that is, because the employer has enforced the policy arbitrarily or not at all, it is precluded from enforcing the policy against the employee.

---

[272] *Id.*
[273] Garrity and Casey, *supra* note 41.

Each company should designate someone within the organization to be ultimately responsible for overseeing the company's computer system. The SPC systems administrator needs the necessary training and technical background to assure the availability, integrity, and confidentiality of company e-mail and Internet usage. A leading law company warns companies against the danger of adopting draconian policies that will be unenforceable. Many policies state that computer, e-mail, or Internet access is strictly limited to business use and prohibit *any* personal use.[274] An absolutist policy such as this "loses its value for most, if not all, purposes" if not enforced.[275] The company recommends a policy stating that "occasional, careful, nonoffensive personal use is permitted on the employee's own time."[276]

[E] Even-Handed Enforcement of Internet Usage Policy

The reason for an Internet usage policy is to protect the company, which can be accomplished only by enforcement. An employer that selectively enforces the Internet policy may be exposed to lawsuits based on racial or sexual discrimination. An employer that arbitrarily enforces the policy against middle-aged women employees, for example, may be charged with sex and age discrimination. A company that monitors only the e-mail of black women, while not scrutinizing data messages of other groups, may be charged with both sex and race discrimination. Consequently, it would be prudent for companies to consistently apply their policies amongst all employees.

§ 10.07 PREVENTIVE LAW POINTERS

[A] Terminating Ex-Employees' E-Mail

Companies need a well-defined procedure for terminating an employee's e-mail and Internet access at the moment of termination of employment. This can usually be done when the employee has an exit interview and/or is required to hand in all keys and security clearances and computer equipment. Upon receipt of these items, the employee's access to e-mail databases should be terminated.

[B] Telecommuting Employees

If employees are permitted to telecommute, what special safeguards are in place to govern the use of corporate computer systems outside of the office? Telecommuting employees may work from home, remote sites, or satellite offices, using direct access to internal corporate networks. The information accessed by

---

[274] Felhaber, Larson, Fenlon and Vogt, *supra* note 157.
[275] *Id.*
[276] *Id.*

telecommuters can be protected while the employee is in transit by the use of a secure tunnel, that is, over an encrypted path between the telecommuter, via the Internet, to the internal corporate network.[277] Although the implementation of a VPN may be very complicated, including the integration of heterogeneous subsystems, there are vendors that provide end-to-end service. There is a VPN consortium for VPN vendors and users which provides information and links.[278]

[C] Independent Contractor Status

SPC must have the exclusive right to use, create, or modify materials created by consultants. The consultancy agreement will set forth the specific provisions dealing with time of performance. The consultancy arrangement has some drawbacks as compared with regular employment. Employees, for example, are covered by workers' compensation, whereas consultants are not.[279]

The consultancy agreement should also cover the consultant's use of employer's equipment, e-mail, and the Internet; sexual harassment; and the procedure for protecting a company's trade secrets and other proprietary information. E-mail impersonation, eavesdropping, and threats by employees may result in lawsuits against SPC. The following is a sample clause of a consultancy agreement:

> This independent contract or consultant agreement is between Suffolk Personal Computers (SPC), a Massachusetts corporation, and _____.
> _____ is an independent contractor and not a partner, joint venturer, or employee of SPC. _____ shall not represent itself as having any other status or relationship than that of independent contractor. SPC, likewise, agrees not to refer to _____ as anything other than an independent contractor or consultant, unless the parties otherwise agree.

[1] Sample Nondisclosure and Confidentiality Agreement for Independent Contractors

Some companies may choose to have an independent contractor or consult sign a Confidentiality Agreement which would also guard against e-mail and Internet usage abuses. A sample Non-Disclosure Agreement might include:

NONDISCLOSURE AND CONFIDENTIALITY AGREEMENT

In consideration of my employment as an Independent Contractor with SPC (the "Company"), I hereby agree as follows:

---

[277] Mark Maier, Corporate Negligence Arising from Internet Telecommuters (1999) (unpublished High Technology Honors Thesis, Suffolk University Law School) (2000).

[278] *See* http://www.vpnc.org. (last visited June 15, 2002).

[279] One advantage of the employment relationship for SPC is the exclusivity bar of the workers' compensation act. SPC is immunized from workplace-related torts if the employee is covered by workers' compensation.

1. **Proprietary Information.**

(a) I recognize that my relationship with the Company is one of high trust and confidence by reason of my access to and contact with the trade secrets and confidential and proprietary information of the Company. I will not at any time, either during my employment with the Company or thereafter, disclose to others, or use for my own benefit or the benefit of others, (i) any of the Developments or (ii) any confidential, proprietary or secret information owned, possessed or used by the Company including without limitation, trade secrets, processes, data, know-how, marketing plans, forecasts, unpublished financial statements, budgets, licenses, prices, and employee, customer and supplier lists with regard to the product named Alpha (collectively, "Proprietary Information"). I have been informed and I understand that the product known as Alpha, its design, implementation, and function, constitutes Proprietary Information.

(b) My undertakings and obligations under this Section 1 will not apply, however, to any Proprietary Information which: (i) is generally disclosed to third parties by the Company, without restriction on such third parties, or (ii) is approved for release by written authorization of the undersigned, Cyrus Daftary.

(c) Upon termination of my employment with the Company or at any other time upon request of the Company, I will promptly deliver to the Company all notes, memoranda, notebooks, drawings, records, reports, files and other documents (and all copies or reproductions of such materials) in my possession or under my control, whether prepared by me or others, which contain Proprietary Information. I acknowledge that this material is the sole property of the Company.

2. **Other Obligations.**

I acknowledge that the Company from time to time may have agreements with other persons or with the U. S. Government, or agencies thereof, which impose obligations or restrictions on the Company regarding inventions made during the course of work under such agreements or regarding the confidential nature of such work. I agree to be bound by all such obligations and restrictions which are made known to me in writing and to take all action necessary to discharge the obligations of the Company under such agreements.

Furthermore, in the course of my employment as an Independent Contractor, I acknowledge that I will have access to Company e-mail, computer networks, and passwords. As such, I agree to be bound by the Company's E-mail and Internet Use Policy which I have reviewed and signed as a part of the Company's Employee Handbook and shall keep all such information Confidential for a period of two years following the termination of my relationship with the Company.

3. **Miscellaneous.**

(a) The invalidity or unenforceability of any provision of this Agreement shall not affect the validity or enforceability of any other provision of this Agreement.

(b) This Agreement may not be modified, changed, or discharged in whole or in part, except by an agreement in writing signed by all of the undersigned parties. I agree that any change in my duties, salary, or compensation after the signing of this Agreement shall not affect the validity of this Agreement. The provisions of this paragraph (b) shall not supersede the terms of any written employment agreement between me and the Company, and if any such terms contradict or are inconsistent with the provisions hereof, the forms of such written employment agreement shall govern.

(c) This Agreement will be binding upon my heirs, executors, and administrators and will inure to the benefit of the Company and its successors and assigns.

(d) No delay or omission by the Company in exercising any right under this Agreement will operate as a waiver of that or any other right. A waiver or consent given by the Company on any one occasion is effective only in that instance and will not be construed as a bar to or waiver of any right on any other occasion.

(e) I expressly consent to be bound by the provisions of this Agreement for the benefit of the Company or any subsidiary or affiliate thereof to whose employ I may be transferred (subject to any written employment agreement I may have with the Company) without the necessity that this Agreement be re-signed at the time of such transfer.

(f) I understand that this Agreement does not recite any obligation on the Company to continue my employment by it.

(g) As my obligations under this Agreement are special, unique, and extraordinary, breach by me of any term or provision of this Agreement shall be deemed material and shall be deemed to cause irreparable injury not properly compensable by damages in an action at law, and the rights and remedies of the Company hereunder may therefore be enforced at law or in equity, by injunction or otherwise.

(h) This Agreement is governed by and will be construed as a sealed instrument under and in accordance with the internal substantive laws of the Commonwealth of Massachusetts.

I HAVE READ ALL OF THE PROVISIONS OF THIS AGREEMENT, AND I UNDERSTAND AND AGREE TO EACH OF SUCH PROVISIONS.

Date: _____   _____
                               Signature/Printed Name

Date: _____   _____
                               Cyrus Daftary

[D] Electronic Discovery

The typical company's organizational attitude toward e-mail is that it is private and informal. E-mail messages are company documents that are discoverable and the company-wide attitude should be that e-mail messages are corporate records. Rule 34 of the Federal Rules of Civil Procedure provides that data compilations may be discovered. Companies need a comprehensive policy on how long e-mail messages should be retained in addition to a policy delineating what to save. If e-mail messages are deliberately destroyed, the company may face liability for the tort of spoliation of evidence or discovery sanctions.[280] The destruction of e-mail may result in an adverse inference that the destroyed message contained evidence that was unfavorable to a company's litigation posture.[281] E-mail needs to be purged on a regular basis to prevent the company computer from being swamped with irrelevant and outdated information.

E-mail should be purged at scheduled intervals rather than as a response to discovery. Requests for the discoverability of e-mail make it imperative that a company change its cultural attitude toward e-mail. Off-color jokes, racist comments, flaming, and emotive battles-of-e-mails within the company or with company outsiders are to be assiduously avoided because they increase the risk of litigation. To protect the company from charges of spoliation of evidence or discovery sanctions, it needs a written retention policy that is enforced. If e-mail messages are destroyed because of routine housekeeping or scheduled purging of the system, the probability is much lower that a court will draw an adverse inference against the company.

[E] E-Mail Notice

Below is an example of the type of e-mail notice that should be placed on all e-mail messages originating from SPC or any other online company:

> This is e-mail from Suffolk Personal Computers (SPC), a Massachusetts company. The contents of this e-mail (and any attachment) are confidential to the intended recipient at the e-mail address to which it has been addressed. You are not permitted to disclose the information in this e-mail to anyone other than this addressee, nor may it be copied or otherwise be retransmitted. If

---

[280] One of the few spoliation cases involving electronic data was in Applied Telematics, Inc. v. Sprint Communications Co., L.P., No 94-4603, 1996 U.S. Dist. LEXIS 14053 (E.D. Pa., Sept. 17, 1996). In *Applied Telematics*, the plaintiff sought "a default judgment where the defendant failed to prevent relevant data from being overwritten on backup tapes once a week in the normal course of business." The court found the defendant at fault and awarded monetary sanctions for the spoliation of evidence. Committee on Federal Courts, Discovery of Electronic Evidence: Considerations for Practitioners and Clients, 53 The Record 656-666 (Sept./Oct. 1998) (reporting *Applied Telematics* case).

[281] *See, e.g.,* Computer Associates Int'l v. American Fundware, Inc., 133 F.R.D. 166, 170 (D. Colo. 1990) (ordering default judgment for destruction of evidence). *Cf.* State ex rel. Wilson-Simmons v. Lake County Sheriff's Dep't, 82 Ohio St. 3d 377 (Ohio 1998) (holding that racist e-mail messages exchanged between government employees was not a public record under Ohio's public records act because these messages did not document activities of a public office).

received in error, please contact SPC at 617-573-0000 (Massachusetts, USA) and delete the message from your e-mail system. Please note that neither SPC nor the sender accepts any responsibility for viruses, and it is your responsibility to scan attachments (if any). No contracts may be concluded on behalf of SPC or any subsidiary of SPC by means of e-mail communications unless expressly stated by a separate signed written agreement.

[F] Sample Confidentiality Agreement Encompassing E-Mail and Internet Usage Safeguards

CONFIDENTIALITY AGREEMENT

This Agreement is entered into as of the 15th day of December, 2002, by and between Suffolk Personal Computers ("SPC") and Joe Employee ("Employee"), with a principal place of business located at 129 Tremont Street, Boston, MA 02110.

SPC has hired Employee to provide services in furtherance of its business needs. In connection with Employee's performance of the services for SPC, SPC has requested that Employee observe certain Employment Guidelines as noted in SPC's Employment Handbook and E-mail/Internet Usage Policy Handbook ("Handbooks"). Employee agrees to be bound by the terms of the Handbooks, which may be updated as required with or without written notice to the Employee. Furthermore, Employee agrees with the following terms and conditions:

1. **Confidentiality.** Employee acknowledges that it will be provided or come into contact with information that is confidential and/or proprietary information of SPC ("Confidential Information") and Employee agrees:

(a) that it will maintain the Confidential Information in confidence, using such degree of care as is appropriate to avoid unauthorized use or disclosure, but not less than a reasonable degree of care;

(b) that it will not disclose any Confidential Information, except with SPC's prior written consent or as otherwise provided herein;

(c) that upon termination of Employee's employment, or at any time SPC may so request, Employee will promptly deliver to SPC, or, at SPC's option, will destroy all memoranda, e-mail and paper notes, paper and electronic records, reports, media and other physical or electronic documents and materials (and all copies thereof) regarding or including any Confidential Information which Employee may then possess or have under its control; and

(d) Confidential Information is and shall remain the sole property of SPC. Employee shall gain no interest or rights in or to Confidential Information by virtue of its being disclosed to Employee.

2. **Confidential Information.** For purposes of this Agreement, Confidential Information shall include all technology and business information of SPC, including but not limited to:

(a) e-mail, proprietary SPC computer networks, other internal electronic files;

(b) processes, methodologies, data, knowledge, know-how, computer software, source code, object code and documentation;

(c) information relating to planned or existing computer systems and systems archi-tecture, methods of processing and operational methods;

(d) customer lists, sales, profits, organizational restructuring, new business initia-tives, business strategies and financial information;

(e) confidential information of third parties with which a party conducts business; and

(f) other information which is marked "Confidential" and/or "Proprietary."

Notwithstanding the foregoing, Confidential Information shall not include information that (i) is or becomes generally known to the public not as a result of a disclosure by Employee, (ii) is rightfully in the possession of Employee prior to disclosure by SPC, or (iii) is received by Employee in good faith and without restriction from a third party, not under a confidentiality obligation and having the right to make such disclosure.

3. **Permitted Disclosures.** Employee shall be permitted to disclose Confidential Information only as follows:

(a) to officers, directors, employees and agents of Employee ("Personnel") having a need to know such information; and

(b) if disclosure is required by law; however, Employee shall notify SPC in writing in advance of such disclosure, and provide SPC with copies of any related informa-tion so that it may take appropriate action to protect the Confidential Information.

4. **Remedies.** Employee acknowledges that the disclosure of Confidential Informa-tion may cause irreparable injury to SPC and/or its affiliates. SPC may, therefore, be entitled to injunctive relief upon a disclosure or threatened disclosure of any Confi-dential Information, without a posting of a bond by SPC. Without limitation of the foregoing, Employee shall advise SPC immediately in the event that it learns or has reason to believe that any of its Personnel who has had access to Confidential Infor-mation has violated or intends to violate the terms of this Agreement, and will rea-sonably cooperate with SPC in regaining possession of the Confidential Information and seeking injunctive relief. This provision shall not in any way limit such other remedies as may be available to SPC at law or in equity.

5. **Noncompete.** Employee agrees that during the period that it is employed by SPC, and for a period of twenty-four (24) months thereafter, Employee will not develop or market, or have developed for it or any SPC client, products and services which are similar to the products and services being developed or contemplated by SPC.

6. **General.** Unless otherwise set forth in a separate agreement signed by the parties, the failure of SPC to enforce any provision of this Agreement shall not be construed as

a waiver or limitation of its right to subsequently enforce and compel strict compliance with every provision of this Agreement. If any term or provision of this Agreement shall be invalid or unenforceable to any extent, the remainder of this Agreement shall be valid and enforced to the fullest extent permitted by law. This Agreement and performance hereunder shall be governed by the law of the Commonwealth of Massachusetts. This Agreement sets forth the entire agreement of the parties with respect to the subject matter hereof. This Agreement may not be amended or modified except pursuant to a written agreement signed by the parties hereto.

ACKNOWLEDGED AND AGREED:

Employee   Suffolk Personal Computers

By: _____   By:_____

Name: _____   Name: Cyrus Daftary

Title:_____   Title: President

Date: _____   Date: 12/15/02

APPENDIX 10-1
DEPARTMENT OF COMMERCE INTERNET USE POLICY

1. **Purpose**

   This document states the Department's policy and provides guidance for managing the use of the Internet by operating units and other organizational components, and by employees within Commerce.

   The goal is to ensure economical, effective and efficient management of Internet usage and encourage collaborative efforts among the Commerce components to achieve this end.

2. **Contents**

Topic	Paragraph
Information and Assistance	3
Definitions	4
Background	5
Scope	6
Policy	7
Responsibilities	8

3. **Information and Assistance**

   Guidance on this policy may be obtained from:

   Office of Systems & Telecommunications Management (OSTM)
   HCH Building, Room 6086
   202-482-0120

4. **Definitions**

   Internet. A global web connecting more than a million computers. Currently, the Internet has more than 30 million users worldwide, and that number is growing rapidly. More than 100 countries are linked into exchanges of data, news and opinions. Unlike online services, which are centrally controlled, the Internet is decentralized by design. Each Internet computer, called a host, is independent. Its operators can choose which Internet services to provide to its local users and which local services to make available to the global Internet community. Remarkably, this anarchy by design works exceedingly well.

   World Wide Web (WWW or "Web"). A system of Internet servers that supports specially formatted documents. The documents are formatted in a language called HTML (HyperText Markup Language) that supports links to other documents, as well as graphics, audio, and video files. This means you can jump from one document to another simply by clicking on hot spots. Not all Internet servers are part of the World Wide Web.

There are several applications called Web browsers that make it easy to access the World Wide Web, three of the most popular being Mosaic, Netscape Navigator and Microsoft's Internet Explorer.

Home Page. The main page of a Web site. Typically, the home page serves as an index or table of contents to other documents stored at the site.

Site. A site (location) on the World Wide Web. Each Web site contains a home page, which is the first document users see when they enter the site. The site might also contain additional documents and files. Each site is owned and managed by an individual, company or organization.

Firewall. A system or combination of systems that enforce a boundary between two or more networks. A network firewall, or packet filter, examines traffic at the network protocol level. An application-level firewall also readdresses outgoing traffic so it appears to have originated from the firewall rather than the internal host.

5. *Background*

The Internet, a public telecommunications service, was established as a cooperative effort providing worldwide networking services among educational institutions, government agencies and various commercial and non-profit organizations. High speed networking technologies and developments have made the Internet a desirable source for expanding research interest and information dissemination and communications. The Internet has expanded to include government information, educational information systems, archives and business resources. The Internet also includes functions such as those for electronic mail (e-mail), remote computer networks, file transfers, World Wide Web (WWW) and wide area information servers.

The Department's access and use of Internet have grown exponentially. On-line services, such as the WWW, have greatly increased user access to a wider and more diverse user community of information resources. This dramatic increase in communication capabilities makes it necessary to establish policies regarding the proper and efficient use of Internet.

6. *Scope*

The Internet is considered to be a fundamental communications tool that may be used to support the Department's missions and information dissemination requirements. These policies and guidelines apply to the management of Internet services within all organizational units of the Department and may be supplemented by additional guidelines developed by departmental operating units, including the use of Government provided telecommunications resources in employees' private residences. To the extent that existing Department-wide policies and directives relating to e-mail and the Internet are inconsistent with this policy, this policy shall supersede the previous policies or directives. The

Departmental Public Affairs office and other operating unit offices may also issue policy regarding the content and management of Internet data and information.

7. *Policy*

It is the policy of the Department to allow and encourage the use of Internet services to support the accomplishment of the various missions of the Department. Use of the Internet requires responsible judgment, supervisory discretion and compliance with applicable laws and regulations. Users must be aware of information technology security and other privacy concerns. Users must also be aware of and follow management directives for Internet usage.

Internet services provided by the Department, like other Government equipment and resources, are to be used only for authorized purposes. The Department recognizes that it is in the interest of the Government that Department personnel become proficient and maintain proficiency in using the Internet. To this end, the restrictions outlined below regarding Internet use during official working hours and non-working hours should be followed by Department employees using Internet services provided by the Department.

The following specific statements reflect official guidance on Departmental use of the Internet:

a. Internet services provided by the Department during official working hours are to be used for authorized purposes only. This may include using Internet services to train personnel on using the Internet, provided prior approval is obtained from an employee's supervisor.

b. Internet service represents a corporate resource that must be managed in an efficient and cost effective manner. Departmental operating units should establish guidelines for accountability and responsibility for use of the Internet and e-mail by their respective employees.

c. Internet access should be achieved using standard and commonly available tools, unless a specific requirement calls for a unique approach. The Department's Office of Systems and Telecommunications Management should be informed in advance of requirements for unique solutions or approaches.

d. Operating units should ensure that their presence on the Internet fulfills mission requirements in a professional manner. Operating units should also ensure that information that they make available via the Internet is accurate, relevant, up-to-date, and is professionally presented.

e. Operating units and Departmental offices may use the Internet to exchange information with the public and internally as an information technology tool. It is to be considered as one of a number of tools and an alternative commercial communication network that is available to DOC.

f. Information technology security requirements shall be a primary consideration in the decision process leading to the use of the Internet. Operating Units must take adequate precautions when processing data or storing data on computers connected to the Internet and when transmitting data on or through the Internet. Chapter 10 of the Department's Information Technology Management Handbook defines certification and accreditation requirements for all sensitive and classified general purpose and application systems. These certification and accreditation requirements apply to use of the Internet for processing or transmitting sensitive or classified data. For classified data, the Director of the Office of Security is the Department's Principal Accrediting Authority and the Director for Budget, Management and Information and Deputy Chief Information Officer is the Designated Approving Authority.

Chapter 10 of the IT Management Handbook also addresses malicious software concerns. Given the extreme vulnerability to viruses and other malicious software occasioned by use of the Internet, operating units must ensure that processes and procedures to minimize risk from malicious programs are in place. Operating units may require that virus checking software be used in conjunction with Internet use.

g.   Unless prohibited by the specific policies of the employee's bureau/operating unit, the use of Internet services and e-mail provided by the Department during non-working hours is not limited to official purposes only. This policy will assist employees in becoming proficient in using the Internet and will enhance their professional development at de minimis expense to the Government. However, employees may not use government printers or supplies in conjunction with personal Internet and e-mail activities. Activities for which Department Internet and e-mail services may not be used, during working or non-working hours, include the following:

   (1)   the pursuit of private commercial business activities or profit-making ventures (i.e., employees may not operate a business with the use of the Department's computers and Internet resources);

   (2)   matters directed toward the success or failure of a political party, candidate for partisan political office, or partisan political group;

   (3)   prohibited direct or indirect lobbying;

   (4)   use of Internet sites that result in an additional charge to the Government;

   (5)   engaging in prohibited discriminatory conduct;

   (6)   the obtaining or viewing of sexually explicit material;

   (7)   any activity that would bring discredit on the Department; or

   (8)   any violation of statute or regulation.

Of course, the Department expects employees to conduct themselves professionally while using Department resources, and employees must refrain from using Department resources for activities that are disruptive to the work place or in violation of public trust.

Like all other Government computer use, use of Government equipment for personal use of the Internet may be monitored and recorded. Anyone using Government equipment consents to such monitoring and is advised that if such monitoring reveals possible evidence of criminal activity or employee misconduct, system personnel may provide the evidence of such monitoring to Department and law enforcement officials. Individuals are not guaranteed privacy while using government computers and should, therefore, not expect it. To the extent that employees wish that their private activities remain private, they should avoid using the Department's Internet or e-mail for such activities.

h. Unless prohibited by the specific policies of the employee's bureau/operating unit, limited personal use of e-mail during duty hours is permissible, as such use will help promote proficiency in electronic communications, including use of the Internet, and provides an alternative method for authorized personal communications, which will promote Government efficiency.

At no time may Government e-mail addresses be used in a manner which will give the impression that an otherwise personal communication is authorized by the Department.

Personal use of e-mail cannot interfere with the official business of the employee or organization, such as spending an inappropriate amount of time during duty hours (e.g., sending more than four brief messages per day), filling up a mailbox with personal messages so as to prevent official messages from being delivered, or disseminating chain letters.

8. *Responsibilities*

a. ***Operating units and Departmental offices must ensure that employees are aware of these policies and guidelines.*** Ultimately, it is the responsibility of the management official or supervisor who provides the equipment and/or Internet access to carry out this Internet Use Policy. Accordingly, these organizations should:

    (1) Designate a point of contact within each bureau for discussion and coordination of Internet usage and notify OSTM of the representative appointed.

    (2) Assure that use of the Internet by the operating unit and its members is consistent with these policies and guidelines and applicable laws, including the Privacy Act and the Paperwork Reduction Act.

    (3) Coordinate and oversee their organization's Internet activities and network data management.

    (4) Establish their own procedures as necessary to promote Department-wide interoperability and cooperation.

(5)   Provide the necessary technical safeguards for appropriate availability, integrity and confidentiality of operating unit systems and procedures.

(6)   Adhere to established Departmental electronic mail and network address management policies where applicable.

(7)   Participate in the development of Internet information content, usage policy and operating standards with OSTM when requested.

(8)   Assess and validate organizational needs for Internet access using their own established business practices and mission program requirements.

(9)   Determine appropriate management controls and technical safeguards to be used for Internet usage, establishing supplemental Internet use procedures and user guidelines as necessary. Because the connection of existing user networks to the Internet presents security risks, the use of firewall technology between local networks and the Internet should be considered.

(10) Periodically assess the effectiveness of their established management controls for Internet access within their organization.

(11) Provide access mechanisms in accordance with Department policy for Internet connectivity for employees who have an authorized purpose for Internet access from home or on authorized travel.

b.   ***Operating unit and Departmental office users of Commerce network resources must:***

(1)   Coordinate Internet access and Internet services with the appropriate telecommunications, network management, and program management officials. Coordination will include, at a minimum:

 • Method and type of communications access.

 • Internet host and domain names.

 • TCP/IP addresses.

 • Domain Name Services.

 • Internet applications, e.g., file transfer protocol (ftp), WWW, and others.

 • Network security and data integrity.

(2)   Ensure that basic principles of accountability and responsibility apply to electronic data dissemination and the use of the World Wide Web.

c. ***DOC organizational units are encouraged to develop WWW sites that display creativity and mission focus.*** However, operating units should ensure that all Web sites within their organization:

(1) Are subject to appropriate management controls.

(2) Remain official information sources over which the Department retains complete editorial control.

(3) Are not "personal" home pages or contain personal information unrelated to official business (e.g., in no circumstance should Department-supported Web sites include items such as vacation or family photographs, links to an employee's personal interest information, or links to partisan political organizations).

(4) Clearly display the DOC seal or text indicating DOC affiliation.

(5) Clearly display the operating unit's seal, emblem, logo or text indicating the title of the organization.

(6) Contain a uniform resource locator (URL) reference to the Department of Commerce Home Page. (http:www.doc.gov).

(7) Contain appropriate contact information (such as name, phone number, and e-mail address) for technical and content questions.

(8) Include only links to Government sites and to non-government sites that are directly related to the Department's mission or necessary to carry out the Department's business. If links to non-government sites are referenced, operating units should provide a clearly visible statement specifying that the Department of Commerce does not endorse any particular product, company, information provider, or the content of the referenced sites. However, if the link is included as part of legitimate and approved export promotion activities, the statement need not disclaim the companies or products at issue.

(9) Are not used for direct or indirect lobbying, including links to sites which engage in or advocate indirect lobbying.

(10) Adhere to any future directives on DOC Web management.

d. ***Use of Trademarks & Service Mark:*** When using any trademarks or service marks, it is recommended that the ™ or ® symbols be used, as appropriate. By definition, trademarks are used to identify tangible goods, while service marks are used to identify services (including the provision of online databases).

The ™ symbol is used on marks that are considered to be trademarks by the Department but have not yet been registered. The ® symbol is used only where the mark is actually registered with the U.S. Patent & Trademark Office. Use of these symbols is not mandatory, but suggested. Further, repetitive use of these symbols is not necessary if it becomes cumbersome or awkward.

Where appropriate, it is recommended that the phrase "[name of trademark] is a (registered, if so) trademark of the U.S. Department of Commerce [or name of individual agency]." Example: "NTIS® and FedWorld® are registered trademarks and service marks of the National Technical Information Service."

Please call the Office of the Chief Counsel for Technology for guidance in using Departmental trademarks and service marks.

APPROVED: W. Scott Gould /s/ /   8/28/98
                 Signature   Effective Date

THE BUSINESS PLAN: LEGAL AND STRATEGIC GUIDANCE FOR WRITING A BUSINESS PLAN FOR YOUR DOT-COM VENTURE

§ A-1 OVERVIEW

A business plan is your story. The business owner's enthusiasm for the business and dedication to its success should leap off the pages. Potential alliance partners, investors, and even corporate headquarters want to know why they should risk their money, time, and energy to deal with you, your business, and your company's products and services. Tell them. Be clear and concise. Show your audience that you have goals to achieve and have thought through the steps you will take to surmount obstacles and achieve those goals.

Manage the plan, and be sure to update it at least twice a year. While business plans are valuable to management and members of the company as a benchmark of progress and success, the business plan is also an important marketing document that can be used to solicit venture financing, potential joint ventures, and recruit top talent, just to mention a few things.

There is no such thing as the "perfect" business plan. The initial plan is reflective of the founders and their vision of the business. As times change, so do the internal corporate leaders, directives, needs, as well as external forces such as competition and the marketplace. Therefore, any plan must be fluid and capable of adapting to the demands of competitors and consumers. In essence, the business plan is a white paper; it will always be enhanced, updated, and changed just as products mature over time. This Appendix highlights certain points you ought to consider when pulling together your business plan. We have distilled the basic ideas that most people look for in a business plan into a "model" business plan for our hypothetical business, SPC (see page A-9). Please note: This Appendix does not pretend to be exhaustive; rather, it is intended mainly as a springboard for your ideas.

§ A-2 DEFINE YOUR OBJECTIVE(S)

A good business plan should be a critical management tool that serves many purposes. Some of those purposes are to

- Tell a compelling story of the business owner's enthusiasm for the business and expresses his or her dedication to its success.

- Define the company's mission (for example, to be the best player in our niche) and goals (for example, to be a $25M company by year 3).

- Define the current state of the competition and the market appetite for the business.

- Attract financing (venture capital, private financing, angel investors, etc.).

- Attract key potential team members, executives, directors, or employees.

- Facilitate relationships to foster strategic alliances, joint ventures, or manage other key third-party relationships.

- Provide a strategic and tactical guide as a benchmark for success or failure.

§ A-3   THINGS TO CONSIDER

There are many things that people can put into a business plan, especially as the business matures and grows over the years. Some key things to include are a cover page executory nondisclosure agreement; an executive summary of no more than two pages; a confidentiality clause; a description of the business, its products, and its services; a statement of the market for the business and status of your competition; a business development and marketing strategy; the identity of the management team; and financial projections with realistic returns on investment (ROI).

[A]   Confidentiality Agreement

Many business plan provide insights to trade secrets, technologies, or methodologies that are in the process of being patented or registered. However, in the interest of attracting suitable investors and partners it may not be practical or feasible for companies to wait for full registration. To protect confidential information, give your business plan only to those who first sign a Confidentiality or Nondisclosure Agreement.

The purpose of a Confidentiality Agreement is to protect the business by putting readers on notice that the information in the business plan is proprietary, and cannot be copied, shared, disclosed, or otherwise compromised by the reader. If readers are on notice of their limited, proper use of the plan, then a contract is formed that is actionable in case of a breach—say, disclosure—by the reader. The business plan should not be distributed without the Confidentiality Agreement being executed first. Additionally, you ought to exert some control over the number of people to whom you distribute the plan. Many business plans are numbered and recorded, so it is known who has which copy of the plan.

[B]   Executive Summary

[1]   Generally

The executive summary is one of the most important sections of your document. It may be written first as an outline and filled in later, or last as a summary of high points. In either case, the completed executive summary should be at the beginning of your business plan. Executives may give the summary a two-minute read to decide if it is worth their time to read the rest. Therefore, the executive summary should be succinct, articulate, and should entice the reader to turn to the rest of the document.

Depending on the overall format and substance of the business plan, the executive summary should touch on the company's mission; investment objective (if any); business strategy; why this business is a compelling proposition now; its business model; operations and management; financial projections, including return on investment; and perhaps a calendar of major milestones accomplished and to be achieved to meet financial goals.

[2]   Why Us, Why Now?

Describe the reason why your business is compelling now. Is market share moving toward online vendors in your industry? Does your business provide a better, faster, cheaper, easier mousetrap to a rapidly growing segment of the market? Give your business "context" so, for example, your later arguments about the competitive advantage of your latest release of software hit home. Connect the dots for your readers; do not make them guess as to why your products and services are positioned for growth in today's environment.

[C]   Description of Products and Services

Identify and describe the products and services being sold by your company. Then highlight your product/service milestones, or if this is a startup, highlight the benefits your products and services will bring to your customers.

[D]   Business Development and Market Strategy

Excellent products and services do not guarantee market success and dominance. To achieve market success, work toward a marketing strategy. The strategy should outline product and company positioning (marketing) as well as supply and distribution channels (how the company will distribute its product and services in the marketplace). Draw a distinction between sales and marketing—they are two very different functions, but must be approached as a coordinated pair.

Marketing relates to many things. We've listed a few here for your consideration:

1. Establishing a target market: Who is your optimal target customer? How many of them are there? What are their priorities?

2. Getting the word out: How will you launch the products—press releases, discussions with analysts, agreements with search engines, advertising blitz on other media, TV, radio, etc.?

3. Product and company positioning: What is your positioning slant or angle? Will your products be the Rolls Royce or the Civic of its market niche?

4. Branding: What will be your calling card? What will you be known for?

Just placing goods and services in the commerce stream and hoping for the best is not enough—the marketing strategy must show that the company understands the tasks involved and can accomplish them, whether it be through trade shows, joint ventures, mass mailings, print and electronic advertising, or via its direct sales force or telemarketers.

Brand recognition, credibility, value proposition, and pricing all play a role and must be noted in the business plan. These things inevitably require an analysis of risks, competition, market communication, and branding and promotion opportunities.

[E]   Identify the Management Team

The credentials and accomplishments of the management team are critical success factors for any company. Potential investors want to be sure that they are making a sound financial commitment based on a seasoned and experienced management team. The best of ideas and companies have been destroyed by weak management.

The description of the management team should be broken down by the appropriate functional roles and titles. Each functional role should list the education, experience, and unique qualifications of that person, to highlight the strengths each management team member contributes to the company's potential success. If there are certain positions that have not been filled, companies should detail the expected responsibilities of the individuals who will fill them.

[F]   Financial Projections and Return on Investments

Financial projections should provide a three-year forecast. Most plans typically try to project five years out, in an effort to show positive return on investment. When developing your projections, provide any assumptions that were made when creating the forecast. Venture capitalists have stated that in funding decisions, they believe the assumptions made by business owners are much more important than the financial projections, which can be conjecture. Assumptions used in your business plan give those who read it a way to see if your assumptions about market trends match their's. Companies generally make assumptions about cost of sales, product development, sales, revenue recognition, and other investment costs. This way potential investors are fully informed and can make decisions based on the business plan and your stated assumptions.

When asking for an investment, it is important to determine how much funding is really required. The more money needed, the more control one is likely to give up to get the funds. This trade-off becomes disruptive when investors do not see a quick return on their investment, which can result in changes in the management team or a company's business objectives.

§ A-4 PREVENTIVE LAW POINTERS: MUTUAL NONDISCLOSURE AGREEMENT

When looking for potential business partners to outsource certain business processes or functions, it may be necessary to execute mutual nondisclosure agreements to protect the interests of both parties. The following is an example of a mutual nondisclosure agreement with relevant terms.

MUTUAL NONDISCLOSURE AGREEMENT

Dated: March 1, 2002

Parties:

> Suffolk Personal Computers (*"SPC"*)
> 120 Tremont Street
> Boston, MA 02108
>
> and
>
> Potential Partner (*"PP"*)
> 123 Anywhere Street
> Philadelphia, PA 19954

This Agreement relates to discussions between the parties identified above regarding a potential business relationship. In connection with such discussions, either party hereto or such party's affiliates or representatives (when referenced in such capacity, the *"Owner"*) may disclose to the other party, or such other party's affiliates or representatives (when referenced in such capacity, the *"Disclosee"*) certain information of a trade secret or confidential nature. Among such disclosures may be a disclosure by SPC to PP of certain technical and business information relating to SPC's portal applications (referred to herein as the *"Disclosure"*), and the disclosure by the PP to SPC of information relating to its service offering application and related requirements in such regard (referred to herein as the *"Requirements"*). In consideration of having the opportunity of such a business relationship, it is understood and agreed that the Disclosure and the Requirements and certain other matter and information as specified below that may be disclosed by one party to the other shall be treated as "Confidential Information" in accordance with this Agreement.

1. ***Subject Matter.*** Information to be deemed *"Confidential Information"* for purposes of this Agreement shall include any information communicated to Disclosee by or on behalf of Owner which is (i) in written or machine readable form and conspicuously marked as "CONFIDENTIAL" or "PROPRIETARY"; or (ii) disclosed orally but designated as Confidential Information by a written notice given within thirty (30) days after the oral disclosure which identifies the information orally disclosed, the place and date of the oral disclosure and the names of the employees or representatives of Disclosee to whom the oral disclosure was made. Each party as Disclosee acknowledges that the other party as Owner considers its Confidential Information to contain valuable trade secrets.

2. ***Exceptions.*** Notwithstanding anything to the contrary set forth in Paragraph 1, the term "Confidential Information" shall not include (i) information that is or becomes generally available to the public other than as a result of a disclosure by the Disclosee or by its representatives; (ii) information that becomes available to the Disclosee on a nonconfidential basis from a source other than Owner or any person acting on Owner's behalf, provided that this source is not prohibited from disclosing this information to the Disclosee by a legal, contractual, or fiduciary obligation to the Owner or to any other person; (iii) information disclosed by Owner to persons other than Disclosee in the absence of any restriction on further disclosure; (iv) information that was in the possession of the Disclosee prior to being furnished to the Disclosee or its representatives by the Owner or any person acting on its behalf, provided that the source of this information was not prohibited from disclosing the information to the Disclosee by a legal, contractual, or fiduciary obligation to the Owner or to any other person; (v) information which, after notice to Owner providing a reasonable opportunity to contest disclosure, Disclosee is legally obligated to disclose by reason of lawful subpoena, court or governmental order, law, rule, or regulation; (vi) information independently developed for the Disclosee by persons who had no knowledge of or access to the Confidential Information, as established by documentary evidence, and (vii) information approved for release by written authorization of the Owner. Information disclosed under this Agreement shall not be deemed to be within the foregoing exceptions merely because such information in embraced by more general knowledge in the public domain or in Disclosee's possession. In addition, no combination of features shall be deemed to be within the foregoing exceptions merely because individual features are in the public domain or in Disclosee's possession, unless the combination itself and its principle of operation are in the public domain or in Disclosee's possession.

3. *Nondisclosure; Protective Measures; Ownership of Improvements.* Until such time as the subject matter thereof shall cease to be Confidential Information in accordance with Paragraph 2 above, (a) Disclosee shall not disclose Confidential Information to any other person, firm, or entity (except for disclosure to Disclosee's employees as provided in Paragraph 4), or use it for its own benefit except to facilitate the discussions with Owner referred to above; and (b) Disclosee shall employ all reasonable measures to safeguard the Confidential Information from inadvertent disclosure including without limitation all measures that Disclosee employs to protect its own information of like importance. In addition, Disclosee agrees not to reverse engineer or attempt to reverse engineer any computer programs or devices supplied by Owner in connection with such discussions. In the event that the Disclosee shall conceive of or develop any improvements, further developments, or new applications as a consequence of the disclosure of the Confidential Information to the Disclosee, the Owner shall be deemed the owner of all such improvements, developments, and applications, and the Disclosee agrees promptly to disclose fully to Owner any and all such improvements, developments, and applications, and to cause to be executed and delivered to Owner at its request such assignments and/or other documents as are necessary in order to transfer such rights to, and vest them in, Owner.

4. *Disclosure to Employees.* Disclosee may disclose the Confidential Information to its responsible employees but only to the extent necessary to facilitate the discussions referred to above, and Disclosee undertakes to ensure by agreement, instruction, or otherwise that all such employees deal with Confidential Information strictly in accordance with Disclosee's obligations under this Agreement.

5. *Return of Materials.* All written or machine readable matter containing Confidential Information delivered by Owner to Disclosee or created by Disclosee shall be and remain the property of Owner, and all such written or machine readable matter and any and all copies thereof shall be promptly returned to Owner upon written request or destroyed at Owner's option.

6. *Nonlicense.* Nothing contained herein shall be construed as granting or conferring on Disclosee any rights by license or otherwise, express or implied, under any patent, copyright, trademark, trade secret, character, publicity, or other like right of Owner created or acquired prior to, on, or after the date of this Agreement.

7. *Term.* The parties agree to hold such Disclosure and Requirements in confidence and to use it only for the purpose contemplated by this Agreement for a period of three (3) years from the date of disclosure.

8. *Relationship.* No agency, partnership, joint venture, or other relationship is created by this Agreement.

9. *Injunction; Attorneys' Fees.* The parties acknowledge that injunctive relief shall be appropriate for the enforcement of each Owner's rights with respect to its Confidential Information. In the event of any legal action to enforce the provisions of this Agreement the court shall be entitled in its discretion to award to the prevailing party its reasonable attorneys' fees with respect to such action, in addition to any other relief or costs granted or allowed in the action.

10. *Governing Law.* This Agreement shall be governed by and construed in accordance with the internal substantive laws of the State of Massachusetts, U.S.A.

(without giving effect to such state's conflict of laws rules). Each party irrevocably consents to the nonexclusive personal jurisdiction of the state and federal courts within or for Suffolk County, Boston, MA, U.S.A., for purposes of any action to enforce or interpret this Agreement.

11. ***Entire Agreement.*** This Agreement constitutes the entire agreement of the parties regarding the subject matter hereof and may not be modified except by written instrument signed by an authorized representative of each party.

IN WITNESS WHEREOF, the parties hereto have caused this Agreement to be executed by their duly authorized representatives as of the date first written above.

SPC   PP

By: _____   By: _____
Name: Cyrus Daftary   Name: PP-President
Title: CEO   Title: CEO
Date: 3/1/02   Date: 3/1/02

SPC - Business Plan[1]

http://www.spc.com

This Business Plan contains confidential and proprietary information belonging exclusively to SPC. This is subject to a Confidentiality Agreement signed by the recipient. Recipients may not disclose, reproduce, or share this Business Plan with a third party unless such third party has executed a Confidentiality Agreement directly with SPC.

Edit History
5/1/02 version 0.5a

---

[1] The following document is an example of a business plan. The plan is provided as a guide only. The plan that you create for your company will require information specific to your industry and your company. The information contained in your business plan should be based on accurate information, real market information, and your best estimate of projections and forecasts.

MISSION STATEMENT

SPC will be the premier computer supplier to e-businesses around the world, including portal companies, e-commerce companies, and educational institutions, with a reputation for high quality products and impeccable customer service.

CONFIDENTIALITY AGREEMENT

This Agreement is entered into as of the 1st day of March, 2002, by and between Suffolk Personal Computers, LLC ("SPC") and Undersigned Investor ("U-I").

SPC is seeking outside funding for its Business Plan. The U-I acknowledges that SPC has furnished the contents of this Business Plan and certain proprietary data relating to the business affairs and operations of SPC for study and evaluation by the U-I for possibly investing in SPC. SPC is willing to permit the U-I to make these observations subject to the U-I's agreement with the following terms and conditions. In consideration of the obligations herein and other valuable consideration, the parties agree as follows:

1.   Confidentiality. U-I acknowledges that it will be provided or come into contact with information that is confidential and/or proprietary information of SPC ("Confidential Information") and U-I agrees:

(a)   that it will maintain the Confidential Information in confidence, using such degree of care as is appropriate to avoid unauthorized use or disclosure, but not less than a reasonable degree of care;

(b)   that it will not disclose any Confidential Information, except with SPC's prior written consent or as otherwise provided herein;

(c)   that upon completion of the parties' discussions or other engagement, or at any time SPC may so request, U-I will promptly deliver to SPC, or, at SPC's option, will destroy all memoranda, notes, records, reports, media, and other documents and materials (and all copies thereof) regarding or including any Confidential Information which U-I may then possess or have under its control; and

(d)   Confidential Information is and shall remain the sole property of SPC. U-I shall gain no interest or rights in or to Confidential Information by virtue of its being disclosed to U-I for the limited purposes contemplated hereunder.

2.   Confidential Information. For purposes of this Agreement, Confidential Information shall include all technology and business information of SPC, including but not limited to:

(a)   processes, methodologies, data, knowledge, know-how, computer software, source code, object code, and documentation;

(b)   information relating to planned or existing computer systems and systems architecture, methods of processing, and operational methods;

(c)   customer lists, sales, profits, organizational restructuring, new business initiatives, business strategies, and financial information;

(d)   confidential information of third parties with which a party conducts business; and

(e)   other information marked "Confidential" and/or "Proprietary".

Notwithstanding the foregoing, Confidential Information shall not include information that (i) is or becomes generally known to the public not as a result of a disclosure by U-I, (ii) is rightfully in the possession of U-I prior to disclosure by SPC, or (iii) is received by U-I in good faith and without restriction from a third party, not under a confidentiality obligation and having the right to make such disclosure.

3.   Permitted Disclosures. U-I shall be permitted to disclose Confidential Information only as

App. A-11

follows:

(a)   to officers, directors, employees, and agents of U-I ("Personnel") having a need to know such information in connection with the discussions or business dealings between the parties in connection with the SPC Business Plan. U-I shall instruct all such Personnel as to their obligations under this Agreement, and that they shall be bound by the terms and conditions hereof. U-I shall be responsible for compliance by its Personnel with the terms of this Agreement; and

(b)   if disclosure is required by law; however, U-I shall notify SPC in writing in advance of such disclosure, and provide SPC with copies of any related information so that it may take appropriate action to protect the Confidential Information.

4.   Remedies. U-I acknowledges that the disclosure of Confidential Information may cause irreparable injury to SPC. SPC may, therefore, be entitled to injunctive relief upon a disclosure or threatened disclosure of any Confidential Information, without a posting of a bond by SPC. Without limitation of the foregoing, U-I shall advise SPC immediately in the event that it learns or has reason to believe that any of its Personnel who has had access to Confidential Information has violated or intends to violate the terms of this Agreement, and will reasonably cooperate with PwC in regaining possession of the Confidential Information and seeking injunctive relief. This provision shall not in any way limit such other remedies as may be available to SPC at law or in equity.

5.   Non-compete. U-I agrees that during the period that it is observing or otherwise receiving information regarding the SPC Business Plan from SPC, and for a period of twelve (12) months thereafter, U-I will not develop or market, or have developed for it or any U-I client, a system which is similar to the process and system being developed by SPC in connection with the SPC Business Plan.

6.   General. Unless otherwise set forth in a separate agreement signed by the parties, neither party shall have an obligation to enter into any business relationship as a result of the exchange of information or discussions between them pursuant to this Agreement. The failure of either party to enforce any provision of this Agreement shall not be construed as a waiver or limitation of such party's right to subsequently enforce and compel strict compliance with every provision of this Agreement. If any term or provision of this Agreement shall be invalid or unenforceable to any extent, the remainder of this Agreement shall be valid and enforced to the fullest extent permitted by law. This Agreement and performance hereunder shall be governed by the law of the State of Massachusetts. This Agreement sets forth the entire agreement of the parties with respect to the subject matter hereof. This Agreement may not be amended or modified except pursuant to a written agreement signed by the parties hereto.

ACKNOWLEDGED AND AGREED:

By: U-I   By: SPC

Name: U-I President   Name: Cyrus Daftary

Title: CEO President   :   Title: CEO

Date: 3/1/02   Date: 3/1/02

This is a Business Plan. It does not imply an offering of securities.

DISCLAIMER

SPC makes no express or implied representation or warranty as to the accuracy or completeness of this information, or, in the case of projections, as to their attainability, or the accuracy or completeness of the assumptions from which they are derived, and it is expected that each interested party will pursue its own independent investigation. The projections are not representations and warranties concerning the SPC. It must be recognized that the projections of the SPC's future performance are necessarily subject to a high degree of uncertainty and may vary materially from actual results. Statements herein are made on the date of delivery hereof.

SPC expressly disclaims any and all liability for the contents of or omissions from this Plan. Market data and industry information contained in the Plan are derived from various trade publications and industry sources and company estimates. Such sources and estimates are inherently imprecise.

This Business Plan, and the information contained herein, shall be kept confidential. The recipient agrees not to disclose to any person any information contained herein, the fact that the recipient obtained confidential information concerning the SPC. Any reproduction or distribution of this confidential business plan, in whole or in part, or the divulgence of any of its contents without the prior written consent of the SPC, is prohibited.

SPC BSINESS PLAN

1.   **EXECUTIVE SUMMARY** **9**

   1.1   INVESTMENT OBJECTIVE...9

   1.2   BUSINESS STRATEGY 9

   1.3   OPERATIONS AND MANAGEMENT...9

   1.4   SCHEDULE 10

   1.5   FINANCIAL PROJECTIONS...10

   1.6   INVESTOR RETURNS 10

2.   **THE SPC OPPORTUNITY** **11**

3.   **SERVICE DESCRIPTION** **12**

   3.1   OVERVIEW..12

   3.2   SPC CUSTOMER EXPERIENCE...13

   3.3   SPC TARGET MARKET AND CUSTOMERS......................................13

   3.4   PROJECTED CUSTOMER GROWTH..14

   3.5   PRICING 14

4.   **BUSINESS DEVELOPMENT AND MARKETING**.................................**15**

   4.1   SALES STRATEGY 15

   4.2   MARKETING 15

   4.3   PUBLIC RELATIONS 16

   4.4   COMPETITION 17

   4.5   RISKS 17

5.   **OPERATIONS**..**18**

   5.1   STAFFING...18

   5.2   LOCATION OF BUSINESS...19

   5.3   EMPLOYEE OWNERSHIP 19

6.   **SPC MANAGEMENT AND ADVISORS**...**20**

   6.1   BOARD OF DIRECTORS 20

   6.2   MANAGEMENT 20

7.   **FINANCIAL PROJECTIONS** **21**

   7.1   ASSUMPTIONS 21

8.   **RETURN ON INVESTMENT**..**22**

   8.1   GROWTH OPPORTUNITIES...22

   8.2   CONCLUSION 22

App. A-15

9.   CALENDAR..**23**

1. EXECUTIVE SUMMARY

1.1   INVESTMENT OBJECTIVE

SPC seeks initial funding of $50 million to build infrastructure and staff for deployment of SPC's systems and services over a twelve month period. SPC seeks three strategic investors who will bring customer relationships and technological solutions to the Company.

1.2   BUSINESS STRATEGY

SPC is a business-to-business Solutions Provider (ASP) of made-to-order hardware and software. SPC allows its customers to simply and effectively purchase hardware, software, installation, and maintenance services via its website, allowing customers to avoid investing large sums in in-house infrastructure and operational support. Customers can order machines tailored to their organization's needs.

With SPC's unique pricing model, customers can purchase new machines with minimal expense. SPC provides a predictable cost structure that allows customers to expand their businesses quickly and efficiently.

1.3   OPERATIONS AND MANAGEMENT

SPC, is a Limited Liability Company, organized under the laws of the State of Delaware with its principal place of business in Boston, Massachusetts. SPC has been in existence as an LLC since January 2, 2002. SPC has operated its website (http://www.spc.com) since March 2002, and the domain name is registered along with twenty other names. SPC's application for the SPC trademark was accepted by the United States Patent and Trademark office on August 8, 2002. Additionally, SPC has ten patents approved by the USPTA. SPC's patentable technology has already been successfully deployed for major high technology firms.

The SPC management and development team is assembled and has a five-year working history. SPC has also engaged PricewaterhouseCoopers as its Audit and Tax Firm. The law firm of Krieger and McGuire has also been retained as outside legal counsel.

1.4   SCHEDULE

Table 1: Major Milestones for SPC's First Twelve Months of Operations

Date	Milestone
Jan 2003	Identify and contact Strategic Investors
Feb 2003	Finalize terms of first round financing
Mar 2003	Product offering complete and deployed with first customer
	Financing Complete
	Launch of Marketing Web site
Apr 2003	Build-out complete of new offices in Boston & Cambridge
	Customers: 20
	Full-time employees: 15
Oct 2003	Customers: 65
	Full-time employees: 55
Jan 2004	Customers: 100
	Initial Public Offering to enable acquisition strategy
	Full-time employees: 85

1.5   FINANCIAL PROJECTIONS

Table 2: Financial Projections

	2002	2003	2004
Total Revenue (US$ millions)	15.4	61.4	211.7
Net Profit (pre-tax) (US$ millions)	1.5	40.4	184.4
Net Profit Margin (after tax)	-10%	40%	52%

Fiscal Year 2002 begins January 1, 2002

1.6   INVESTOR RETURNS

Based upon projected revenues and profits, and valuations of similar companies, SPC estimates that initial investors will recognize a 1,000% return on investment within the first twelve months of operations. This investment will be realized through SPC's initial public offering that will be used to raise additional funds for the company's growth in the business-to-business solutions provider market.

2.   THE SPC OPPORTUNITY

The time is right for SPC to fundamentally change the way computers are delivered on
the Web.

- The online buying trend is exploding — analysts predict significantly increased
  online buying by businesses by 2004.
- Customer service is a key differentiator in today's market.
- Automated purchasing and build-to-order machines bring in large numbers of
  customers.
- From the SPC corporate perspective, these automated processes bring efficiencies,
  including centralized control that enables better management reporting and
  monitoring of customers' needs.

3.   SERVICE DESCRIPTION

3.1   OVERVIEW

SPC has developed several patentable systems, based on prior patents (Fig. 1-5).

Figure 1	Figure 2	Figure 3	Figure 4	Figure 5
Omitted from Business Plan	Omitted from Business Plan	Omitted from Business Plan	Omitted from Business Plan	Omitted from Business Plan

App. A-20

3.2 SPC CUSTOMER EXPERIENCE

SPC customers must maintain complete control of their machines. Therefore, SPC will create a Help Desk service and other customer tools.

Training and Customer Service

New SPC customers receive on-site, hands-on training. Customers work with SPC Account Managers who are available to assist with any technical issues or feature requests. The SPC also offers comprehensive 24-hour support, both automated and human.

3.3 SPC TARGET MARKET AND CUSTOMERS

SPC will initially target large to mid-sized customers who are either Internet pure-plays or are bricks and mortar transformers in the following lines of business:

- Portal Companies

- E-commerce Companies

- Educational Institutions

These customers display the following characteristics

- Expect to keep their infrastructure and operational costs low by leveraging technology, so actively seek out Internet solutions;

- Require high-quality customer service — the market for online B2B goods is flooded with options, and this market has expressed that the key differentiator is service level;

- Have significant funds available in their IT and e-business budgets;

- Are eager to show savvy use of Internet procurement — if it's a model they rely on when selling to others, they must use it themselves;

- Are highly educated technologically — they know what they want and are particular about finding the right machinery and software; and

- Prefer the flexibility of build-to-order options.

SPC is poised to succeed in this new medium for the following reasons:

- A superior product that will meet and exceed customer expectations;

- Tremendous demand from niche industries;

- First-class management team;

- Strategic alliances and strong industry relationships.

App. A-21

3.4   PROJECTED CUSTOMER GROWTH

Table 3: Projected Number of New SPC Customers

Year End	Mid-size	Large
2002	50	50
2003	200	150
2004	1000	600

3.5   PRICING

SPC's unique pay-per-use pricing scheme provides a primary benefit to our customers. Our patented system allows us to charge customers for the use of their systems — we charge customers when they turn on their machines. The cost per thousand impressions (CPM) pricing schedule is as follows:

Table 4: Current Pricing

Page Views per month	Cost per CPM per month FY 1	Cost per CPM per month FY 2	Cost per CPM per month FY 3
0 - 5 million	$25	$22.5	$20
5 - 10 million	$20	$17.5	$15
10 - 15 million	$15	$12.5	$10
> 15 million	$10	$8.5	$7

SPC's cost per CPM is a maximum of $5 per CPM per month, guaranteeing a gross profit from inception of the service. This pricing model is flexible, to allow SPC to remain competitive with a goal of 100% customer retention.

4.   BUSINESS DEVELOPMENT AND MARKETING

SPC's business development team will focus initially on establishing customer relationships with 5 mid-sized and 5 large Web businesses. SPC has already successfully deployed one large contract with Suffolk University Law School.

4.1   SALES STRATEGY

Currently there are no companies competing in this space. Failure to capitalize on this opportunity could allow companies like IBM, Dell, or Gateway to be formidable competitors. The sales strategy is multifold. Initial sales channels will be through traditional and online means, below, as well as through the development of strategic go-to-market partnerships.

- Some advertisements, in electronics trade publications, etc.
- Small sales staff, who will take up leads from ads, trade shows, etc.;
- Help desk fields sales calls initially, routing inquiries to sales staff;
- Listing on popular business and personal portals (B2B electronics sites, Yahoo!, etc.)

Partnership Development

SPC's key to developing a business customer base will be through strategic partnerships with companies that are already offering segments of the Internet Infrastructure services for a Web site. SPC proposes to partner with the following types of companies to gain access to an active customer base:

- Publishing Companies
- Internet Infrastructure Companies
- Traditional Application Service Providers
- Software Companies
- Internet Service Providers
- Web Development Companies
- Financial Institutions
- Academic Institutions

SPC's Business Development Team will use its existing business and personal relationships with these companies to initiate discussions, and form strategic partnerships for selling opportunities.

4.2   MARKETING

The exhaustive research conducted by Forrestors and Gartner Group is relied upon extensively in SPC's Business Plan. Copies of the research analysis and findings are available upon request.

4.2.1   Marketing Communications

The marketing strategy has two components — an online strategy and a traditional bricks and mortar strategy. A successful execution of strategy will provide education to our target market about our offerings and our Web site, driving inquiries. After our soft

App. A-23

launch in April 2002 and once we achieve our initial customer goals, SPC will hard launch — press releases to both online and traditional media outlets. Target for hard launch is March 2003.

4.2.2 Branding

SPC's cogent message to its business customers is clear: *SPC manages and delivers your hardware needs more effectively at lower costs, so you can concentrate on your core business.*

We accurately represent the Company as being made up of the most intelligent, most experienced professionals in the world. SPC is committed to delivering reliable, high-performance, innovative solutions with complete customer service.

4.2.3 Product and Service Promotion

SPC will use a variety of media to promote its site, including print, direct, and online marketing. A mix of media and promotion are contemplated on both local and regional levels, such as

- e-mail direct marketing (viral marketing)
- Targeted Internet Advertising (banner advertising, intersital ads)
- Push Technology/channel broadcasting (webcasting)
- Newspapers/Magazines/Trade Journals and Associations (print and electronic media)
- Conferences/Events/Sponsorships/Trade Shows

4.2.2 Web site

SPC launched its Web site (www.SPC.com) on March 1, 2002. The site will be simple and straightforward, outlining the benefits of the company's services to the customer, and promoting SPC as "the smartest customer-oriented people organization on the web."

4.2.3 Software Demo

SPC will create a password-protected, online demo of its services, which it will make available to qualified leads.

4.2.4 Advertising and Trade Shows

SPC will rely primarily on its business development staff and strategic partnerships to identify and win new customers. A modest marketing budget will support them in their effort. Advertising in trade magazines will be used to create awareness of SPC, and the company will establish a presence at two major trade shows a year.

4.3   PUBLIC RELATIONS

Public Relations will be the primary tool used to create the buzz about SPC. The Company will use its Chairman and CEO, Cyrus Daftary, as a primary spokesperson and "character" of the Web. Cyrus, who is the chief architect of SPC's technology and is the former Chief Technology Officer at PwC, is a well-known industry expert and has spoken at numerous conferences including Suffolk Law School, Massachusetts Bar Association, and Rhode Island Bar Association.

SPC will promote its first-mover advantage as an ASP and ride the excitement surrounding this growing market segment.

4.4 COMPETITION

SPC is unique in the marketplace in targeting this service business. However, potential competitors could come from several directions of the vertical integration of the delivery of other solutions.

- Internet Service Providers

- Large Web Development Companies

- Application Software Companies

Ultimately, SPC is in position to succeed in this marketplace because we are 100% dedicated to a single aspect of the delivery of hardware from businesses to consumers. In fact the management of the multiple vendor relationships is a core foundation of SPC's service offerings.

4.5 RISKS

Given the exponential growth of content and traffic on the Web, the risks faced by SPC are small in relation to the increasing demand for its services. PricewaterhouseCoopers has been engaged as an audit and tax firm. Additionally, the law firm of Krieger and McGuire has been selected as the outside counsel to assess any potential legal risks and manage all legal issues on behalf of SPC.

5.   OPERATIONS

5.1   STAFFING

SPC's staff will be kept to a minimum when operations begin. We are confident that with a staff of less than 100 persons, we can create a profitable business managing and distributing machines for 50 customers. However, our rapid expansion plans will require additional staffing after the first six months of operation.

5.1.1 Management

- Chief Executive Officer: Responsible for determining the strategic direction of the company, delivering return on investment to investors, identifying new business opportunities, and winning new accounts for SPC.

- Vice President of Services: Responsible for product definition, customer service and training, PR, and Marketing.

- Vice President of Technology: Responsible for application and operational development, and quality assurance.

- Vice President of Finance and Administration: Responsible for managing the relationships with strategic investors. Manages capital structures and financial needs of SPC. Manages legal aspects of the company and human resources.

- Vice President of Marketing: Responsible for marketing, public relations, and business development.

- President/COO: Responsible for overall day-to-day operations of the company, including marketing, services, and technology.

5.1.2 Technology

- Director of Application Development: Responsible for development of front-end and back-end of new software offerings.

- Director of Web Technologies: Responsible for front-end development of new software offerings.

- Chief Privacy Officer: Responsible for ensuring privacy measures are implemented and customer data are secured from internal and external exposure.

- Systems Architect: Responsible for design and implementation of systems schema.

- Senior Server Engineer: Responsible for design, development, and integration of back-end software.

- Director of Operational Development: Responsible for the development of new systems and architectures for the management and delivery of content for our customers.

- Director of Operations: Responsible for the day-to-day operations of SPC's technical infrastructure.

- Manager of Networking/Security: Responsible for security and operation of the SPC network. Defines standards and best practices while continuously monitoring the health of the network.

- Quality Assurance Manager: Responsible for the quality of software produced by the applications development group and for the quality of services provided by the operational development group. Establishes standards and processes for the delivery of services.

- Documentation Manager: Responsible for documenting all systems and processes used by the company.

5.1.3 Marketing/Business Development

- Senior Sales Representative: Responsible for identifying new sales opportunities and closing contracts with customers.

- Partner Development Representative: Responsible for identifying strategic partners and defining contracts for strategic partnerships.

- Marketing Manager: Oversees public relations, marketing, and advertising efforts.

5.1.4 Account Management and Production

- Director of Account Management: Responsible for overseeing account manager and ensuring satisfaction of all customers.

- Account Manager: Responsible for managing individual customers, ensuring satisfaction of assigned customers.

- Manager of Training: Responsible for training new customers on use of SPC's services.

- User Interface Designer: Responsible for the design and information architecture of the service for ease-of-use and efficient task completion.

5.1.5 Finance and Administration

- Controller: Responsible for managing day to day expenditures and cash flows.

- Human Resources Manager: Manages and supports the COO in recruiting and building a strong team of the smartest Web professionals in the World.

- Accounts Receivable

- Accounts Payable

5.1.6 Marketing

- Marketing and PR Manager: Responsible for marketing efforts and public relations.

5.2   LOCATION OF BUSINESS

SPC principal office will be located in Boston, with satellite offices in Cambridge, MA.

5.3   EMPLOYEE OWNERSHIP

As an incentive for long-term employees, SPC has reserved 20% of the company's shares for ownership by employees, including executives, issued as stock options over a four year vesting period.

6.   SPC MANAGEMENT AND ADVISORS

6.1   BOARD OF DIRECTORS

- Cyrus Daftary, Chairman and CEO, SPC

- Mike Rustad, CEO Rustad Technologies

- Todd Krieger, VP General Counsel, Bose Corporation.

The remaining two Board positions will be filled by Strategic Investors.

6.2   MANAGEMENT

- SPC's management team is assembled and has already successfully deployed their first solution for an online education portal, funded by a major player in the Internet industry. The team has a five-year history of working together and has built hardware and software infrastructure for some of the most recognizable names on the Web.

7.   FINANCIAL PROJECTIONS

The financials demonstrate that SPC will be operating profitably within its first seven months of operations. The results are summarized below:

Table 5 : Financial Projections

	2002	2003	2004
Total Revenue (US$ millions)	15.4	61.4	211.7
Net Profit (pre-tax) (US$ millions)	1.5	40.4	184.4
Net Profit Margin (after tax)	-10%	40%	52%

Fiscal Year 2002 begins January 1, 2002

By the twelfth month of operations, the Company will realize annualized revenues of $31 million and a net profit of $13 million, a margin of over 40%. This tremendous upside in profitability is possible because once the infrastructure is in place, costs are shared across large numbers of our customers.

For the first year of operations, SPC will realize total revenues of $15.3 million, with a net loss of $1.5 million. In the second year of operation, revenues are projected to quadruple as we leverage the infrastructure against a greater number of large and mid-sized customers. The large margins of 40% and 50% projected for the year 2003 and 2004 are feasible because of SPC's revolutionary technology and publishing methods.

7.1 ASSUMPTIONS

- Financing is received by March 1, 2003.
- Intellectual property is transferred from founders to SPC by March 31, 2003.
- First day of operations is April 1, 2003. Company begins receiving revenue on the first day of operations, from our first customer, Suffolk Law School.
- Fiscal Year begins on January 1.

8.   RETURN ON INVESTMENT

SPC's current valuation of $100 million is justified by its revenue projections and desirable profit margins forecast for the next three years. Based upon analysis of similar companies within the industry (see Table 6), SPC can conservatively expect to have a valuation of $1 to $3 billion within twelve months of operation. Investors would realize a tenfold return on their investment within twelve months.

8.1   GROWTH OPPORTUNITIES

SPC's entry into the hardware market is a "foot in the door" to providing any number of services to our customers. SPC anticipates growing revenues through the development and hosting of additional standard and custom solutions for our customers.

In early 2003, SPC will raise additional funds through an initial public offering in order to acquire additional companies. We will focus on acquiring operations that minimize our bottom line and provide more vertical integration with our partners and vendors.

Table 6: Market Capitalization of Comparable Internet Infrastructure Companies

Company	Most Recent Annualized Revenues	Current Market Capitalization
Company 1	N/A	$25 billion
Company 2	$76 million	$11 billion
Company 3	$6.4 million	$1 billion
Company 4	$33.2	$0.9 billion

8.2   CONCLUSION

The way computers are sold on the Web will change significantly in the next three years. SPC has the idea, the technology, and the team to revolutionize the way the Web is used. With unique software and hardware and existing customer base, SPC is set to become dominant in the marketplace. Investment by a complementary set of strategic partners is all that is needed to complete the picture and launch this company to the market leader position.

9.   CALENDAR

Date	Milestone
Jan 2003	Identify and contact Strategic Investors
	Obtain Angel Investment funds
	Full-time employees: 5
Feb 2003	Determine terms of first round financing
	Obtain letters of intent from strategic investors
	CEO to present at Harvard University Internet Conference
	Management Recruiting of VP Finance
	Sign lease on office space
Mar 1, 2003	Product offering complete and deployed with first customer,
	Suffolk Law Shool
	Financing Complete
	Hire VP of Business Development
	Launch of Marketing Web site
	Customers: 1
Mar 15, 2003	Money received from strategic investors.
Apr 1, 2003	Build-out complete of new offices
	Customers: 65
	Full-time employees: 26
Oct 2003	Secondary production facility operational at vendors facilities in Waltham
Jan 2004	Customers: 75
	Initial Public Offering to enable acquisition strategy
	Full-time employees: 100

App. A-31

APPENDIX B

INTERNET RESOURCES FOR LAWYERS: LEGAL RESEARCH, ISSUES, AND PRACTICE[1]

With the tremendous growth of the Internet, the search is on for ways to incorporate web technology into the legal profession. To date, the Internet has been useful for the legal profession as a research tool, a method of disseminating traditional materials, and communicating with the outside world. The purpose of this Appendix is to provide you with a starting point for your legal research on the Internet.

Please keep in mind that the following list of World Wide Web locations is only a tiny fraction of the useful legal resources that can be found on the Internet. This Appendix is not meant to be exhaustive, nor is it comprehensive in scope. It is offered as an example of the types of information one can find on the web, as well as an introductory, organizational tool for locating selected law-related resources. The web site addresses listed have recently been verified for accuracy.[2] However, keep in mind that the Internet is a somewhat fluid mass of information, and web site locations are often modified.

OVERVIEW..**APP. B-2**

GENERAL LAW SITES...**APP. B-4**

U.S. GOVERNMENT...**APP. B-6**

STATE GOVERNMENT ....**APP. B-8**

AREAS OF LAW..**APP. B-9**

BUSINESS..**APP. B-26**

INTERNET ....**APP. B-28**

SAMPLE LAW FIRM HOME PAGES..**APP. B-30**

---

[1] Special thanks to Yasir Fadil, a graduate of Northeastern University, for his assistance in updating the URLs.

[2] The URLs listed below were current as of May 12, 2002.

FINDING A LAWYER ON THE WEB ....APP. B-32

MISCELLANEOUS...APP. B-32

OVERVIEW

WHAT IS THE INTERNET?

The Internet is a giant network that interconnects many smaller groups of linked computer networks (a network of networks). The Internet enables users to access files stored on computer servers anywhere in the world as long as they are part of the Internet. As you may know, the Internet has experienced phenomenal growth in recent years as the number of web sites (URLs) has rapidly increased, thereby increasing the amount of information available on the Internet.

This hypergrowth has in turn increased the availability of legal materials on the Internet. This Appendix will direct you to some of the resources currently available on the Internet. Please keep in mind that there are literally thousands upon thousands of documents added to the Internet everyday. Consequently, it is impossible for one to have a current list of every URL. Search engines help always help you find a desired site.

Generally speaking, there are three ways to find legal-related materials on the Internet. First, you can search legal mailing lists/newsgroups. Second, you can purchase a legal Internet directory. Finally, you can use Internet search engines, which may be described as crawlers, indexes, spiders, or worms. The most popular search engines are AltaVista, Google, HotBot, Northern Light, and Yahoo!

UNDERSTANDING SEARCH ENGINES

If you find yourself at the very beginning of an issue with little or no information, the following search engines available on the Internet will help you retrieve documents relating to your search request.

A. YAHOO!

YAHOO! is one of the best ways to access information because of the sheer size of its database and strength of its search engine. Yahoo! functions like a "yellow pages" of the Internet. It is divided into various categories, including Government:Law, and numerous web sites are listed under each category. If you are unsure of the correct category, you can simply input several key terms and search both the categories and all sites. It is important to note that site links are placed on Yahoo at the discretion of its administrators. Therefore, unlike other search engines that canvas the entire net, Yahoo! has, by its very nature, "edited" what is made available. Yahoo! can be found at http://www.yahoo.com.

B. ALTAVISTA

In contrast to Yahoo!, AltaVista enables you to search millions of web pages by term(s). You can conduct a simple search by inputting a search term or a more advanced search that utilizes Boolean search logic. The Boolean search logic on the web is similar to that of LEXIS and Westlaw. AltaVista can be found at http://www.altavista.com.

C. GOOGLE

Google has built a powerful search engine that gives users access to its proprietary index comprising more than two billion URLs. At the heart of Google's technology is its PageRank™ technology and hypertext-matching analysis. These technologies allow Google to maintain its leadership position in the search industry by continually innovating its search capabilities. In the spring of 2002 Google reached a strategic agreement with AOL, whereby Google will provide its search technology to AOL.

D. FINDLAW, A LEGAL SEARCH ENGINE

Just as Yahoo! is the starting point for many searches on the Internet, FindLaw is probably one of the best starting points for conducting legal Internet research. FindLaw can be found at http://www.findlaw.com. FindLaw was purchased by Westlaw®, which is another step toward the commercialization of search engines. FindLaw also owns another search engine called LawCrawler. LawCrawler uses intelligent agents combined with the AltaVista search engine and database and other legal code and case law databases to retrieve information geared toward the specific needs of legal professionals. LawCrawler has an official license to use AltaVista Search. LawCrawler provides legal researchers with precision by enabling them to focus their searches on sites with legal information and within specific domains. Law Crawler can be found at http://www.findlaw.lawcrawler.com.

E. HIEROS GAMOS, A LEGAL SEARCH ENGINE

Although there are numerous other legal search engines, Hieros Gamos is another legal search engine that deserves special mention. Hieros Gamos, a site maintained by a collection of law firms, contains many of the links referenced in FindLaw and Cornell's LII but adds many other original documents. These documents include over 200 practice areas, numerous "Doing Business" guides, as well as other types of material that are not commonly available on the Internet. Hieros Gamos can be found at http://www.hg.org.

F. OTHER SEARCH ENGINES

Beaucoup! has assembled a home page that links users to over 2,500 search engines on the Internet. Keep in mind that various search engines will retrieve different search results, depending on how the algorithm is encoded. Therefore, one should try the same search request using various search engines to truly get an accurate feel for what exists on the Internet. Beaucoup! can be found at http://www.beaucoup.com.

G. METASEARCHERS

Dogpile, MetaCrawler, and Search.com are three of the most popular metasearchers that allow web site visitors to search the most popular search engines simultaneously with a click of the mouse.

GENERAL LAW SITES

The following sites can be used as gateways to law-related resources. Of most importance is the organizational structure these sites impose on the web. They each provide an impressive array of links to legal information, and their user-friendly subject arrangements provide easy navigation throughout the Internet.

American Law Sources On-Line   http://www.lawsource.com/also
Their stated purpose is to "provide a comprehensive, uniform, and useful compilation of links to all on-line sources of American law that are available without charge." Focus is on U.S., Canadian, and Mexican federal and state legal resources.

FindLaw   http://www.findlaw.com
Emerging as the favorite gateway to legal resources. Well-organized, comprehensive arrangement of law sites, including primary and secondary sources. Site for the LawCrawler search engine.

Hieros Gamos   http://www.hg.org
Billed as the largest comprehensive legal site, with over 50,000 links to U.S. federal and state law, legal organizations, and every government in the world. Also includes links in over 200 practice areas, 300-plus discussion groups, and 50 "Doing Business" guides.

Internet Lawyer   http://www.internetlawyer.com
Incorporates various legal research needs, including but not limited to basic legal research needs, fact-finding research, legal Internet column, and legal technology briefs. Internet Lawyer is published by GoAhead Publications.

Law Crawler   http://www.findlaw.lawcrawler.com
LawCrawler uses intelligent agents combined with the AltaVista search engine and database and other legal code and case law databases to retrieve information geared toward the specific needs of legal professionals. Law-Crawler has an official license to use AltaVista Search. LawCrawler provides legal researchers with precision by enabling them to focus their searches on sites with legal information and within specific domains.

LawLinks: The Internet Legal   **http://lawlinks.com**
  Resource Center

  Aspires to provide a place for all people interested in the law to congregate
  and obtain information. Users can conduct research, generate referrals, purchase legal products, collaborate, and recruit. Separate "Centers" for attorneys or consumers.

Legal Information Institute at   **http://www.law.cornell.edu**
  Cornell University

  An award-winning pioneer in the electronic dissemination of legal materials. Provides useful background commentary and full text of U.S. Supreme
  Court and N.Y. court decisions, the UCC, the U.S. Code, and selected state
  and federal laws. Also noted for its extensive links to law-related sources
  worldwide.

Legal Computer Solutions, Inc.   **http://www.lcsweb.com**

  Contains, among other things, a very comprehensive legal virtual library. The
  various links include those to current, essential legal resources, secondary
  sources, and professional information.

Legal Media Group   **http://www.legalmediagroup.com**
                                          /Default.asp?

  LegalMediaGroup.com brings together the resources of Euromoney Institutional Investor's legal publishing division in a single web portal. Choose one
  of their channels for news, analysis, features, and discussion, plus LMG's
  magazines, legal-market guides, and supplements.

Rominger Legal Services On-Line   **http://www.romingerlegal.com/**
  Research Page

  This site acts as a one-stop search option for search engines like Findlaw,
  DivorceNet, Lycos, AltaVista, and Yahoo! It also contains links to various
  sources like Federal Links, Professional Directories, and Non-Legal
  Resources.

Seamless Website   **http://www.seamless.com**

  This web site is broken down into four parts. The first section, The Chamber,
  contains news and information about Seamless and its clients. The second
  section, The Commons, contains original works on a broad range of legal topics. The third section, entitled The Shingle, features homepages of lawyers,
  legal associations, and legal service providers. The final section, entitled The
  Cross Road, links this site to 1,000 other legal sites.

Virtual Law Library   **http://www.law.indiana.edu/law/v-lib**
                                          /lawindex.html

  A collection of materials and pointers to law-related Internet sources.
  Includes U.S. and state government links, law journals, legal organizations,
  law firms, law schools, and publishers.

WashLaw   **http://lawlib.wuacc.edu**

Maintained by the staff of the Washburn Law Library, this is one of the most extensive legal sites currently available on the web. It links to law schools; law firms; international, state, and federal materials; directories; news sources; and much more.

U.S. GOVERNMENT

General Government Sites

The federal government has tens of thousands of web sites. Gov.Bot is a good starting point for locating government resources and documents online.

GPO Access   **http://www.access.gpo.gov**

This web server for the Government Printing Office is the source for most electronic government documents, including the *Congressional Record,* CFR, *Federal Register,* congressional bills, U.S. Code, agency publications, and much more. Reliable because it is the official publisher.

GPO Access Searching Tips   **http://www.ll.georgetown.edu/wtaylor/**
                                        gposrch.html

Library of Congress   **http://www.loc.gov**

Extremely versatile site features the *American Memory* and the *American Treasures* projects, which provide documents, photographs, motion pictures, and sound recordings from the Library's collections and exhibits. It also provides search capabilities for the library catalog, direct access to THOMAS (full text of U.S. House and Senate documents), the Global Legal Information Network, the U.S. Copyright Office, as well as links to other Internet research sources.

Federal Web Locator   **http://www.law.vill.edu/fed-agency**
                                        /fedwebloc.html

One of the most impressive collection of links to federal government web sites. Lists over 550 separate government information sites.

Administrative/Executive Branch

Department of Commerce	http://www.doc.gov
Department of Justice	http://www.usdoj.gov
Department of Labor	http://www.dol.gov
Department of Treasurer	http://www.ustreas.gov
Environmental Protection Agency	http://www.epa.gov
Federal Communications Commission	http://www.fcc.gov
Federal Trade Commission	http://www.ftc.gov

FedLaw: General Services Administration   http://www.legal.gsa.gov
FedWorld   http://www.fedworld.gov
Internal Revenue Service   http://www.irs.ustreas.gov
Pension Benefit Guaranty Corp.   http://www.pbgc.gov
Securities and Exchange Commission   http://www.sec.gov
U.S. Government Information   http://www-libraries.colorado.edu/ps/gov/us
                                             /federal.htm
U.S. International Trade Commission   http://www.usitc.gov
U.S. Trade Representation   http://ustr.gov
White House   http://www.whitehouse.gov

Courts/Judicial Branch

Administrative Office of the Federal Courts   http://supct.uscourts.gov
Court Rules   http://www.law.cornell.edu/rules
District of Columbia Circuit   http://www.ll.georgetown.edu:80/Fed-Ct
                                             /cadc.html
Federal Appellate Courts   http://www.ljx.com/cgi-bin/cir
Federal Circuit Court   http://www.law.emory.edu/fedcircuit
First Circuit   http://www.law.emory.edu:80/1circuit
Second Circuit   http://lawtouro.edu:80/abouttlc/2ndcircuit
Third Circuit   http://www.law.vill.edu/Fed-Ct/ca03.html
Fourth Circuit   http://law.emory.edu:80/4circuit/
Fifth Circuit   http://www.law.utexas.edu:80/us5th/us5th.html
Sixth Circuit   http://www.law.emory.edu:80/6circuit
Seventh Circuit   http://www.law.emory.edu:80/7circuit
Eighth Circuit   http://www.wulaw.wustl.edu:80/8thcir
Ninth Circuit   http://ming.law.vill.edu:80/Fed-Ct/ca09.html
Tenth Circuit   http://www.law.emory.edu:80/10circuit
Eleventh Circuit   http://www.law.emory.edu:/11circuit/index.html
Federal Court Locator   http://www.law.vill.edu/
Federal Court Finder   http://www.law.emory.edu/FEDCTS
Federal Judicial Center   http://fjc.gov
FedLaw   http://fedlaw.gsa.gov
FLITE Supreme Court Database   http://www.fedworld.gov/supcourt/index.htm
Oyez Oyez Supreme Court Resource   http://oyez.at.nwu.edu/oyezhtml
U.S. Federal Courts Finder   http://www.law.emory.edu/FEDCTS
U.S. Federal Courts Home Page   http://www.uscourts.gov
U.S. Supreme Court   http://www.law.cornell.edu/supct
                                           http://www.usscplus.com/
U.S. Supreme Court Oral Arguments   http://oyez.at.nwu.edu/oyez.html
Virtual Court Web Site   http://www.courtbar.org

Legislative Branch/Federal Materials

THOMAS   http://thomas.loc.gov

"In the spirit of Thomas Jefferson, a service of the U.S. Congress through its Library." Access to the legislative documents of both the House and Senate, plus links to many other government sources.

Code of Federal Regulations (CFR)	http://law.house.gov//cfr.htm
Congressional Bill Tracker	http://www.unipress.com/will-t-bill.html
Congressional Law Library	http://law.house.gov
Congressional Record	http://www.access.gpo.gov/su_docs/aces /aces150.html
Congress.Org	http://www.congress.org
Congressional Quarterly	http://www.cq.com
Electronic Federal Resources	http://www.bna.com
Federal Judicial Nominations	http://www.yale.edu/law/library/nom/
Federal Register	http://www.nara.gov/fedreg/
Federal Rules of Civil Procedure	http://www.law.cornell.edu/rules/frcp /overview.htm
Federal Rules of Evidence	http://www.law.cornell.edu/rules/fre /overview.html
Judicial Clerkships	http://www.judicialclerkships.com/
Judicial Nominations Database	http://www.law.umich.edu/currentstudents /careerservices/nomdb.htm
Legal Careers at Martindale.com	http://careers.martindale.com
Library of Congress	http://lcweb.loc.gov http://thomas.loc.gov
Senate Judiciary Committee Nomination Central	http://judiciary.senate.gov/nominations.cfm
Social Security Online	http://www.ssa.gov/
UCC Articles 1-9	http://www.cornell.edu/ucc/ucc.table.html
U.S. Code	http://www4.law.cornell.edu/uscode/ http://www.law.cornell.edu/uscode
United States Constitution	http://www.law.cornell.edu/constitution /constitution.overview.html
U.S. Supreme Court Collection	http://supct.law.cornell.edu/supct/
U.S. Tax Code	http://www.fourmilab.ch/ustax/ustax.html
U.S. Treasury	http://www.ustreas.gov
U.S. Government Electronic Commerce Policy	http://www.ecommerce.gov
U.S. Federal Government Agencies	http://www.lib.lsu.edu/gov/fedgov.html
U.S. House of Representatives	http://www.house.gov
U.S. Senate	http://www.senate.gov

STATE GOVERNMENT

General Sources

American National Standards Institute (ANSI)	http://www.ansi.org/
Boston Public Library State & Local Gov	http://www.bpl.org

Council of State Governments	http://www.csg.org
Data Interchange Standards Association (DISA)	http://www.disa.org/
Massachusetts Municipal Association	http://www.mma.org
Municipal Codes Online	http://www.spl.org/selectedsites/municode.html
National Center for State Courts	http://www.ncsconline.org
National Conference of Commissioners on Uniform State Laws	http://www.law.upenn.edu/bll/ulc/ulc_frame.htm
National Conference of State Legislatures	http://www.ncsl.org
State & Territorial Laws	http://www.legal.gsa.gov/intro5.htm
State Caselaw & Statutes via Hieros Gamos	http://www.hg.org/usstates.html http://www.hg.org/govt.html
State Court Directory	http://www.piperinfo.com/state/index.cfm
State Court Locator	http://vls.law.vill.edu/Locator/statecourt/
State Documents Checklist	http://gateway.library.uiuc.edu/doc/StateList /check/check.htm
State Law and Legislative Materials	http://www.washlaw.edu/
State Tax Forms	http://www.sm-b.com
State Web Locator	http://www.infoctr.edu/swl/

AREAS OF LAW

Antitrust

ABA, Section of Antitrust Law	http://www.abanet.org/antitrust/home.html
Antitrust Policy	http://www.antitrust.org
Department of Justice Antitrust Division	http://www.usdoj.gov
University of Chicago	http://www.lib.uchicago.edu/~llou/antitrust.html

Associations and Organizations

American Bar Association	http://www.abanet.org
American Association of Law Libraries	http://www.aallnet.org
Boston Bar Association	http://www.bostonbar.org
Massachusetts Bar Association	http://www.massbar.org

Banking and Bankruptcy

*AAA*dir:Directory of World Banks	http://aaadir.com
ABI World	http://www.abiworld.org
Banking Law	http://www.hg.org/banking.html
Bankruptcy Creditor's Service	http://bankrupt.com
Bankruptcy Law	http://www.hg.org/bankrpt.html

Cornell's Legal Information Institute	http://www.law.cornell.edu/topics/banking.html
FDIC	http://www.fdic.gov
Federal Reserve	http://www.federalreserve.gov/
Internet Bankruptcy Library	http://bankrupt.com
KnowX	http://knowx.com
Mortgage Calculator	http://www.mortgage-calc.com/
Mortgage 101	http://mortgage101.com
Office of the Comptroller of Currency	http://www.occ.treas.gov/
Universal Currency Converter	http://www.xe.net/currency
U.S. Bankruptcy Court S.D.N.Y.	http://www.nysb.uscourts.gov
World Bank	http://www.worldbank.org

Criminal Law

Criminal Law	http://www.hg.org/crime.html
Kelley Blue Book	http://kbb.com
Yahoo!	http://www.yahoo.com/Society_and_Culture/Crime/

Divorce

| DivorceNet | http://www.divorcenet.com/ |
| KnowX | http://knowx.com |

E-Commerce

Business 2.0	http://www.business2.com
BusinessWeek ebiz	http://www.businessweek.com/ebiz
E-commerce	http://fullcoverage.yahoo.com/Full_Coverage/Tech/Electronic_Commerce
E-Commerce Times	http://www.ecommercetimes.com
Internet World	http://internetworld.com
NewsLinx	http://www.newslinx.com/newstopics/e_commerce_news.html
NY Times E-Commerce	http://www.nytimes.com/library/tech/reference/indexcommerce.html
Red Herring	http://www.herring.com
Upside	http://www.upside.com
Wired News	http://www.wired.com/news/
Yahoo! Technology	http://story.news.yahoo.com/news?tmpl=index&cid=738&/

Environmental Law

Alpha Analytical Labs	http://www.alphalab.com/alphaweb/index.cfm

A full-service environmental analytical lab home page.

Australian Environmental Law	http://law.anu.edu.au/acel/
CIESIN (Consortium for International Earth Science Information Network)	http://www.ciesin.org
EnviroSense—Comon Sense Solutions to Environmental Problems	http://es.epa.gov
Environmental Law Around the World	http://www.igc.org/igc/gateway/
Environmental Law Information Center	http://www.hg.org/envirus.html
Environmental Protection Agency	http://www.epa.gov
Environmental Sciences Division, Oak Ridge National Laboratory (ORNL)	http://www.esd.ornl.gov
Greenpeace Multilateral Environmental Treaties	http://www.greenpeace.org/~intlaw
Indiana University	http://www.law.indiana.edu/v-lib/vlib.asp
NEIRC	http://www.gwu.edu/~greenu

National Environmental Information Resources Center is a partnership among George Washington University, the Institute for the Environment, and the EPA.

Pace Global Environmental Law Network	http://www.law.pace.edu
United Nations	http://www.unep.org http://www.undp.org/env.html
United Nations Scholar's Workstation	http://www.library.yale.edu/un/index.html
U.S. Geological Survey Home Page	http://info.er.usgs.gov

European Union

Community Research & Development	http://www.cordis.lu
Cyber-Rights & Cyber-Liberties (UK)	http://www.cyber-rights.org/
ECHO (European Commission)	http://www2.echo.lu
Europa	http://www.europa.eu.int
European Commission Legal Advisory Board	http://europa.eu.int/ISPO/legal/en/lab/labdef.html
European Internet Forum	http://europa.eu.int/ISPO/policy/eif /i_Welcome.html
European Internet Forum	http://www.cordis.lu/infosec/src/ets.htm
European Parliament	http://www.europarl.eu.int
European Union	http://www.eurunion.org
Law of Electronic and Internet Commerce in Germany	http://www.kuner.com/
Security of Telecommunications and Information Systems	http://www.cordis.lu/infosec/

Human Rights

Amnesty International	http://www.amnesty.org
Australian Human Rights Info Centre	http://www.austlii.edu.au/ahric

DIANA   http://www.yale.edu/lawweb/avalon/diana
                                               /index.html

Hieros Gamos   http://www.hg.org/human.html

Human Rights Web   http://www.hrweb.org/

International Committee of the Red Cross   http://www.icrc.org/

OAS Inter-American Court of Human Rights   http://www1.umn.edu/humanrts/iachr/iachr.html

University of Minnesota   http://www.umn.edu/humanrts

U.S. Dept. of State Foreign Affairs   http://dosfan.lib.uic.edu/

Immigration

American Immigration Center   http://www.us-immigration.com

Immigration Forms   http://www.wave.net/upg/immigration
                                               /forms.html

Immigration Law   http://www.visalaw.com/

Immigration Lawyers on the Web   http://www.ilw.com

Intellectual Property

ABA Section—Intellectual Property Law   http://www.hg.org.intell.html

American Intellectual   http://www.aipla.org/
   Property Law Association

Copyright Act   http://www.law.cornell.edu/usc/17

Copyright Office   http://lcweb.loc.gov//copyright

Copyright Regulations   http://www.law.cornell.edu/copyright/regulations
                                               /regs.overview.html

Copyright Rights   http://sunsite.berkeley.edu/Copyright/

Cyberlaw and Cyberlex   http://cyberlaw.com

IBM patent server   http://www.patents.ibm.com/ibm.html

Intellectual Property Owners   http://www.ipo.org/

International Trademark Association   http://www.inta.org/

Federal Courts Finder—Emory University   http://www.law.emory.edu/FEDCTS/

Franklin Pierce Law Center   http://www.fplc.edu

General Laws (U.S. House)   http://www.legal.gsa.gov/legal1g.htm

Lanham Act   http://www.inta.org/about/lanham.shtml

Law Journal   http://www.law.duke.edu/journals/dlj/

Official Gazette   http://www.micropat.com

Patent Act   http://www.law.cornell.edu/patent
                                               /patent.table.html

Patent FAQ   http://www.uspatentinfo.com/patentfaq.html

Patent Images   http://www.uspto.gov/patft/images.htm

Texas Intellectual Property Journal   http://www.utexas.edu/law/journals/tiplj/

Title 37 of CFR	http://www.law.cornell.edu/copyright/regulations/regs.overview.html
Trademark Act	http://www.lectlaw.com/files/inp25.htm
Tradesecrets	http://execpc.com
United States Patent Office	http://www.uspto.gov
Universal Copyright Convention	http://www.unesco.org/culture/laws/copyright/html_eng/page1.shtml
USC Title 17—Copyrights	http://www.law.cornell.edu/usc/17/
US Court of Appeals for the Federal Circuit	http://www.fedcir.gov/
Wacky Patents	http://colitz.com/site/wacky.htm
Yahoo!	http://www.yahoo.com/Government/Law/Intellectual_Property/

International and Foreign Law

Australasian Legal Information Institute	http://www.austlii.edu.au
Electronic Embassy	http://www.embassy.org
Electronic Frontier Canada's Legal Resources	http://insight.mcmaster.ca/org/efc/pages/legal.html
FindLaw	http://www.findlaw.com
Foreign and International Law	http://www.washlaw.edu/forint/forintmain.html
Foreign & International Law, J.W. Long Law Library, Willamette University	http://www.willamette.edu/law/longlib/forint.htm
Foreign Government Sites	http://www.hg.org/govt.html
GODORT Foreign Law Links	http://www.library.northwestern.edu/govpub/resource/internat/foreign.html
Guide to Electronic Resources for International Law/American Society of International Law	http://www.asil.org/resource/home.htm
Hieros Gamos	http://www.hg.org
International Court of Justice	http://www.icj.org
International Law Locator	http://vls.law.vill.edu/compass/international/
International Trade Law	http://ra.irv.uit.no
International Trade Law Monitor	http://www.wto.org/english/res_e/links_e/law_e.htm
Legal Group for the Internet in Canada	http://www.catalaw.com/logic/
Multilaterals Project of Fletcher School of Law & Diplomacy	http://www.tufts.edu/fletcher/multilaterals.html
OAS Inter-American Court of Human rights	http://www.umn.edu/humanrts/iachr
OECD	http://www.oecd.org
Organization of American States	http://www.sice.oas.org
United Nations	http://www.un.org
University of Chicago	http://www.lib.uchicago.edu/~llou
U.S. Department of State	http://www.state.gov

U.S. House of Reps. (Foreign Laws & Treaties)   http://www.house.gov/
U.S. International Trade Commission   http://www.usitc.gov
War Crimes Tribunal   http://www.igc.org/balkans/tribunal.html
Washlaw   http://lawlib.wuacc.edu
World List   http://www.law.osaka-u.ac.jp/legal-info/worldlist
                                                /worldlst.htm

Labor and Employment

AFL-CIO Homepage   http://www.aflcio.org
Bureau of Labor Statistics   http://stats.bls.gov
Center for Mobility, CMR Salary Calculator   http://www.homefair.com/homefair/calc
                                                /salcalc.html
Department of Labor   http://www.dol.gov
DOL Pension Welfare Benefits Admin.   http://www.dol.gov/dol/pwba
OSHA   http://www.osha.gov
Pension Benefits Guaranty Corporation   http://www.pbgc.gov
Social Security Administration   http://www.ssa.gov

Law Schools and Legal Education

Jurist: Law Professors on the Web   http://www.law.pitt.edu/hibbitts/jurist.htm
Law Student Web   http://www.siu.edu/~lsr/1L2L3L.htm
Virtual Law Library   http://www.law.indiana.edu/v-lib/
Index of Law-Related Journals   http://www.usc.edu/dept/law-lib/legal
                                                /journals.html
University of Akron McDowell Law Center   http://www3.uakron.edu/law/
University of Alabama School of Law   http://www.law.ua.edu/
Albany Law School Union University   http://www.als.edu/
Arizona State University   http://www.law.asu.edu/
University of Arizona College of Law   http://www.law.arizona.edu/
University of Arkansas School of Law   http://law.uark.edu/
University of Arkansas at Little Rock   http://www.ualr.edu/~lawschool/index.html
  School of Law
University of Baltimore School of Law   http://law.ubalt.edu/index.html
Basic Legal Citation   http://www.law.cornell.edu:80/citation
                                                /citation.table.html
Baylor University School of Law   http://law.baylor.edu/
Belfast Law School (UK)   http://www.law.qub.ac.uk/
Birmingham Law School   http://www.bsol.com/
Boston College Law School   http://infoeagle.bc.edu/bc_org/avp/law/lwsch/
Boston University School of Law   http://www.bu.edu/law/

Brigham Young University, J. Reuben Clark	http://www.law2.byu.edu/Law_School/
Brooklyn Law School	http://www.brooklaw.edu
University of Buffalo Law School	http://www.law.buffalo.edu/site/index.html
Catholic University of America	http://www.law.cua.edu
Cal Northern School of Law	http://www.calnorthern.edu/
University of California at Berkeley School of Law	http://www.law.berkeley.edu/
University of California at Davis School of Law	http://www.ucdavis.edu/
University of California—Los Angeles	http://www.law.ucla.edu/index1.html
University of California, Hastings College of the Law	http://www.uchastings.edu
California Western School of Law	http://www.cwsl.edu/
Campbell University—Norman Adrian Wiggins School of Law	http://webster.campbell.edu/
Capital University Law School	http://www.law.capital.edu/
Case Western Reserve Law School	http://lawwww.cwru.edu
Chicago-Kent College of Law	http://www.kentlaw.edu/
University of Chicago College of Law	http://www.law.uchicago.edu/
University of Cincinnati College of Law	http://www.law.uc.edu/
City University of New York Law School	http://www.cuny.edu/
Cleveland State University	http://www.law.csuohio.edu/
University of Colorado	http://www.colorado.edu/law/
Columbia University School of Law	http://www.law.columbia.edu/
University of Connecticut School of Law	http://www.law.uconn.edu/
Cornell School of Law	http://www.law.cornell.edu
Creighton University School of Law	http://culaw2.creighton.edu/
University of Dayton	http://www.law.udayton.edu/
University of Detroit Mercy School of Law	http://www.law.udmercy.edu/
Université de Montréal	http://www.droit.umontreal.ca/
Denver University	http://www.law.du.edu/
DePaul University College of Law	http://www.law.depaul.edu/
District of Columbia School of Law	http://209.218.190.36/
Drake University Law School	http://www.law.drake.edu
Duke University School of Law	http://www.law.duke.edu
Duquesne University	http://www.law.duq.edu/
Emory University School of Law	http://www.law.emory.edu
Faulkner University, Jones School of Law	http://www.faulkner.edu/law/
Fletcher School of Law and Diplomacy	http://fletcher.tufts.edu/
University of Florida College of Law	http://www.law.ufl.edu/
Florida State University College of Law	http://law.fsu.edu/
Fordham University School of Law	http://law.fordham.edu/
Franklin Pierce Law Center	http://www.fplc.edu/

George Mason University School of Law	http://www.gmu.edu/departments/law/
George Washington University Nationa Law Center	http://www.law.gwu.edu l
University of Georgia School of Law	http://www.lawsch.uga.edu/
Georgia State University College of Law	http://law.gsu.edu/
Georgetown University Law Library	http://www.ll.georgetown.edu/
Glendale University College of Law	http://www.glendalelaw.edu
Golden Gate University School of Law	http://www.ggu.edu/schools/law/index.html
Gonzaga University School of Law	http://law.gonzaga.edu/
Hamline University School of Law	http://web.hamline.edu/law/
Harvard Law School	http://www.law.harvard.edu/
Hofstra University School of Law	http://www.hofstra.edu/law
University of Houston Law Center	http://www.law.uh.edu
Howard University School of Law	http://www.law.howard.edu
University of Hawaii, William S. Richardson School of Law	http://www.hawaii.edu/law/
Humphreys College	http://www.humphreys.edu/law.htm
HytelNet	http://www.ucm.es/INET/hytelnet_html /start.html
University of Idaho College of Law	http://www.uidaho.edu/law/
University of Illinois College of Law	http://www.law.uiuc.edu/
University of Iowa—College of Law	http://www.law.uiowa.edu/
Indiana University—Indianapolis School of Law	http://indylaw.indiana.edu/
Indiana University School of Law	http://www.law.indiana.edu/
John Marshall Law School	http://www.jmls.edu
University of Kansas School of Law	http://www.law.ukans.edu/
University of Kentucky College of Law	http://www.uky.edu/Law/
University of LaVerne College Law	http://law.ulv.edu/
Universität Mainz (Germany)	http://radbruch.jura.uni-mainz.de/index-ie.html
Legal Information Institute/Cornell Law School	http://www.law.cornell.edu/index.html
Legal Information Services (UK)	http://www.law.warwick.ac.uk/
Lewis and Clark College Northwestern	http://www.lclark.edu/LAW/
Louisiana State University Law Center	http://www.law.lsu.edu/indexflash.asp
Loyola Law School	http://lls.edu/
Loyola University School of Law—Chicago	http://www.luc.edu/schools/law/
Loyola University School of Law— New Orleans	http://law.loyno.edu/
Marquette University	http://www.mu.edu/dept/law/index.html
University of Maryland School of Law	http://www.law.umaryland.edu/
Massachusetts School of Law	http://www.mslaw.edu
University of Massachusetts at Amherst Department of Legal Studies	http://www.umass.edu/legal/
McGeorge School of Law University of the Pacific	http://www.mcgeorge.edu/

University of Memphis, Cecil C. Humphreys	http://www.law.memphis.edu/
Mercer University Law School	http://www.law.mercer.edu/
University of Miami School of Law	http://www.law.miami.edu/
University of Michigan Law School	http://www.law.umich.edu/
Michigan State University—Detroit College of Law	http://www.law.msu.edu/
University of Minnesota Law School	http://www.law.umn.edu/
Mississippi College School of Law	http://law.mc.edu/
University of Mississippi School of Law	http://www.olemiss.edu/depts/law_school/
University of Missouri Columbia	http://www.law.missouri.edu/
University of Missouri—Kansas City	http://www.law.umkc.edu
University of Montana School of Law	http://www.umt.edu/law/
University of Nebraska College of Law	http://www.unl.edu/lawcoll/index.shtml
New England School of Law	http://www.nesl.edu/
New York Law School	http://www.nyls.edu
New York University School of Law	http://www.law.nyu.edu/
NOCALL-Northern Association of Law Libraries	http://law.wuacc.edu/nocall//home.html
University of North Dakota School of Law	http://www.law.und.nodak.edu/
University of New Mexico School of Law	http://lawschool.unm.edu/
North Carolina Central University	http://www.nccu.edu/law/
University of North Carolina School of Law	http://www.law.unc.edu/
Northeastern University School of Law	http://www.slaw.neu.edu
Northern Illinois University College of Law	http://www3.niu.edu/claw/index.htm
Northern Kentucky University Salmon P. Chase College of Law	http://www.nku.edu/~chase/
Northwestern University School of Law	http://www.law.northwestern.edu/
Notre Dame Law School	http://www.nd.edu/~ndlaw/
Nova Southeastern University	http://www.nsulaw.nova.edu
Ohio Northern University-Petit College of Law	http://www.law.onu.edu/
Ohio State University College of Law	http://www.osu.edu/units/law/
Oklahoma City University	http://www.okcu.edu/law/
University of Oklahoma Law Center	http://www.law.ou.edu/
University of Oregon School of Law	http://www.law.uoregon.edu
Pace	http://www.law.pace.edu/
University of Pennsylvania Law School	http://www.law.upenn.edu/
Pepperdine University School of Law	http://law.pepperdine.edu/
University of Pittsburgh School of Law	http://www.law.upenn.edu/
Regent University Law School	http://www.regent.edu/acad/schlaw/
University of Richmond	http://law.richmond.edu
Roger Williams University	http://law.rwu.edu/
Rutgers University Law School	http://www.newark.rutgers.edu/law/

Rutgers, The State University of New Jersey	http://www-camlaw.rutgers.edu/
Universität Saarbrücken Lehrstuhl für Rechtsinformatik (Germany)	http://www.jura.uni-sb.de/
Saint Louis University School of Law	http://lawlib.slu.edu/
Cumberland School of Law Samford University	http://www.samford.edu/schools/law/
University of San Diego School of Law	http://www.acusd.edu/~usdlaw/
University of San Francisco School of Law	http://www.usfca.edu/law/
San Joaquin College of Law	http://www.sjcl.org/
Santa Clara University School of Law	http://www.scu.edu/law/
Seattle University Law School	http://www.law.seattleu.edu/
University of South Carolina School of Law	http://www.law.sc.edu/
University of South Dakota School of Law	http://www.usd.edu/law/
South Texas College of Law	http://www.stcl.edu
Southern California Assoc. of Law Libraries	http://www.aallnet.org/chapter/scall/
University of Southern California Law Center	http://www.usc.edu/dept/law-lib/index.html
Southern Illinois University School of Law	http://www.law.siu.edu/
Southern Methodist University School of Law	http://www.law.smu.edu/indexie.htm
Southern New England School of Law	http://www.snesl.edu/
Southern University Law Center	http://www.subr.edu/
Southwestern University School of Law	http://www.swlaw.edu/main.html
Saint John's University School of Law	http://www.law.stjohns.edu/law/law
St. Louis University School of Law	http://law.slu.edu/
St. Thomas University School of Law	http://www.stu.edu/lawschool/
Stanford Law School	http://lawschool.stanford.edu/index.shtml
Stetson University College of Law	http://www.law.stetson.edu
Seton Hall University School of Law	http://law.shu.edu/
Suffolk University School of Law	http://www.law.suffolk.edu
Syracuse University College of Law	http://www.law.syr.edu/
University of Tennessee College of Law	http://www.law.utk.edu/
Temple University School of Law	http://www2.law.temple.edu/
University of Texas — Austin	http://www.utexas.edu/law/
Texas Southern University	http://www.tsu.edu/
Texas Tech University School of Law	http://www.law.ttu.edu/
Texas Wesleyan Law School	http://law.txwes.edu/
Thomas Jefferson School of Law	http://www.jeffersonlaw.edu
Thomas M. Cooley Law School	http://www.cooley.edu
University of Toledo College of Law	http://law.utoledo.edu/
Touro College Jacob D. Fuchsberg Law Center	http://www.tourolaw.edu/
University of Trento School of Law (Italy)	http://www.gelso.unitn.it/
Tulane Law School	http://www.law.tulane.edu
University of Tulsa College of Law	http://www.utulsa.edu/law/

The Law Faculty of University of Tromsø-IRV (Norway)	http://ananse.irv.uit.no/uk/uk.htm
University of Utah College of Law	http://www.law.utah.edu/
Vanderbilt University School of Law	http://law.vanderbilt.edu/
Vermont Law School	http://www.vermontlaw.edu/
Villanova University School of Law	http://vls.law.vill.edu/
University of Virginia School of Law	http://www.law.virginia.edu/
University of Waikato School of Law (New Zealand)	http://www.waikato.ac.nz/law/
Wake Forest University School of Law	http://www.law.wfu.edu/
Washburn University	http://www.washlaw.edu/
Washington College of Law/ The American University	http://www.wcl.american.edu/
Washington University School of Law	http://www.wulaw.wustl.edu
University of Washington School of Law	http://www.law.washington.edu/
Washington and Lee University School of Law	http://www.law.wlu.edu/
Wayne State University—Law School	http://www.law.wayne.edu/
University of West Los Angeles	http://www.uwla.edu/flash/UWLA_flash.html
West Virginia University	http://www.wvu.edu/academics.html
Western New England College School of Law	http://www.law.wnec.edu/
Western State University College of Law	http://www.wsulaw.edu/
Whittier College School of Law	http://www.law.whittier.edu/
Widener University School of Law	http://www.law.widener.edu/
College of William and Mary	http://www.wm.edu/
William Mitchell School of Law	http://www.wmitchell.edu/
William S. Boyd School of Law	http://www.law.unlv.edu/
Willamette University College of Law	http://www.willamette.edu/wucl/
University of Wisconsin	http://www.wisc.edu
University of Wyoming	http://uwadmnweb.uwyo.edu/Law/default.HTM
Yale Law School	http://www.law.yale.edu/
Yeshiva University—Benjamin N. Cardozo	http://www.cardozo.yu.edu

Legal Forms, Memos, and Briefs

Law Journal Extra	http://gort.ucsd.edu/newjour/l/msg00340.html
'Lectric Law Library	http://www.lectlaw.com//form.html
Realty Law Net	http://members.tripod.com/~LegalMessenger/legal_forms.htm
Brief Reporter	http://www.briefreporter.com

Legal and Business News Sources

American Journalism Review Newslink	http://newslink.org/menu.html
BNA	http://www.bna.com

Business Week Online	http://www.businessweek.com/index.html
Chicago Tribune	http://www.chicago.tribune.com
CNN Interactive	http://www.cnn.com
Commercial News Services on the Net	http://www.jou.ufl.edu/commres/webjou.htm
Court TV	http://www.courttv.com
Edgar	http://www.sec.gov/edgar.shtml
Encyclopedia of Law & Economics	http://encyclo.findlaw.com
Federal Communications Law Journal	http://www.law.indiana.edu./fclj/
Federal Legislative Information	http://thomas.loc.gov/
Forbes	http://www.forbes.com
Harvard Journal of Law & Technology	http://studorg.law.harvard.edu/jolt
Industry Solutions Home Page	http://www.microsoft.com/ms.htm
Intellectual Property Magazine	http://www.ipmag.com
Journal of On-Line Law	http://www.wm.edu/law/publications/jol/
Law Journal EXTRA!	http://gort.ucsd.edu/newjour/l/msg00340.html
Los Angeles Times	http://www.latimes.com
Microsoft Legal Industry Page	http://www.microsoft.com/malaysia/staylegal /resources/industry.htm
MSNBC	http://www.msnbc.com/news/
NASD	http://www.nasdr.com http://www.newspage.com
Newspapers Online	http://newspapers.com
New York Times	http://www.nytimes.com
NPR	http://www.npr.org
PointCast	http://www.pointcast.com/
PR Newswire	http://www.prnewswire.com
Red Herring Online	http://redherring.com
Reuters	http://www.reuters.com
Richmond Journal of Law & Technology	http://www.urich.edu/~jolt/
Securities in the Electronic Age	http://www.legalwks.com/books/securities /description.shtml
Small Business Association	http://www.sbaonline.sba.gov
Texas Intellectual Property Journal	http://www.utexas.edu/law/journals/tiplj/
United States Law Week	http://www.law.harvard.edu/library/research _guides/united_states_law_week.htm
USA Today	http://www.usatoday.com
Wall Street Journal	http://online.wsj.com
Wall Street Journal Interactive	http://online.wsj.com/public/us
Washington Post	http://washingtonpost.com

Legal Publishers

Aspen Law & Business	http://www.aspenpublishers.com

Bureau of National Affairs	http://www.bna.com
Lawyers Cooperative Publishing	http://www.westgroup.com/
LEXIS-NEXIS	http://www.lexis-nexis.com
Martindale Hubble	http://www.martindale.com
Matthew Bender	http://www.bender.com
Prentice Hall	http://vig.prenhall.com/
Shepard's	http://lexisnexis.com/shepards/
Westlaw	http://web2.westlaw.com/signon/default.wl

Litigation

The Expert Pages	http://www.expertpages.com
Expert Witnesses	http://www.washlaw.edu/expert.html
	http://www.nocall.org/experts.htm
Reference Manual on Scientific Evidence from the Federal Judiciary Center	http://www.fjc.gov/pubs.html
Sentencing Commission Federal Sentencing Guidelines Update Newsletter	http://www.fjc.gov
Uniform Acts	http://www.kentlaw.edu
Verbatim Reporters Center (court reporters)	http://www.verbatimreporters.com

Medical and Health Sources

American Cancer Society	http://www.cancer.org
American Medical Association	http://www.ama-assn.org
Center for Health Administration Studies	http://gopher.chas.uchicago.edu

The Center, located at the University of Chicago, offers health and demographic statistics as well as an annotated index of local and national health policy related data.

Centers for Disease Control	http://www.cdc.gov
Department of Health and Human Services	http://www.os.dhhs.gov
Drug Formulary	http://www.intmed.mcw.edu/drug.html
Health Care Financing Administration	http://www.hcfa.gov
Health Info	http://www.pobox.com/~subhas/health.html
Medical Education Information Center	http://medic.med.uth.tmc.edu/
Medical Matrix Hypermedia Guide to Internet Health and Medicine Related Resources	http://www.medmatrix.org/index.asp
Medical Resources by Subject	http://www.medic8.com/MedicalSubjects.htm
Mediconsult.com, Inc. (Virtual Medical Center)	http://www.mediconsult.com.my/
Medscape	http://www.medscape.com
MedWeb	http://www.medweb.emory.edu/MedWeb/
National Cancer Institute	http://cis.nci.nih.gov/
National Institute of Health	http://www.nih.gov/
National Library of Medicine	http://www.nlm.nih.gov

National Library of Medicine Medline Database	http://medlineplus.gov
New York Academy of Medicine:	http://www.nyam.org
Organizing Medical Networked Information	http://omni.ac.uk
Virtual Hospital	http://vh.radiology.uiowa.edu
Web of Addictions	http://www.well.com/www/woa
World Health Organization	http://www.who.int/home-page/

Professional Responsibility

ABA/BNA Lawyers' Manual on Professional Conduct	http://www.bna.com/prodhome/bus/MOPC.html
ABA Center for Professional Responsibility	http://www.abanet.org/cpr/home.html
American Legal Ethics Library	http://www.law.cornell.edu/ethics
Law Journal Extra-Professional Responsibility	http://attorneypages.com/inpractice /legalethics.htm
Legalethics.com	http://www.legalethics.com
Legal Ethical Opinion Database	http://www.attorneyshoppinglinks.com /edu_01.html
Massachusetts Ethics Opinions	http://www.state.ma.us/obcbbo
Massachusetts Ethics Rules	http://www.state.ma.us/obcbbo http://www.massbar.org/rules/
NetEthics	http://www.computerbar.org/netethic/netnav.htm
State Legal Advertising Restrictions	http://www.wld.com/direct/restrict.htm

Real Estate

The American Real Estate and Urban Economics Association	http://www.areuea.org
American Real Estate Society	http://www.aresnet.org
Boston.com	http://realestate.boston.com/
KnowX	http://www.knowx.com
Nareit	http://www.nareit.com
New York Times, Real Estate	http://www.nytimes.com/pages/realestate/
Real Estate ABC	http://www.realestateabc.com
Realtor	http://www.realtor.com
Yahoo! Real Estate	http://realestate.yahoo.com

Research and Writing

Citation Format

| Beyond the MLA Handbook | http://english.ttu.edu/kairos/1.2/inbox/mla.html |

Features citation format for Internet sources.

| The Bluebook | http://www.law.cornell.edu/citation /citation.table.html |

Citing Electronic Information	http://www-libraries.colorado.edu/ps/gov/gd/cite.htm
	http://www.mla.org/

Periodical Indexes

CARL Uncover	http://www.ulib.iupui.edu/erefs/carl.html
Index to Legal Periodicals	http://tarlton.law.utexas.edu/tallons/content_search.html
Legal Periodical Indexes	http://ublib.buffalo.edu/libraries/units/law/guides_handouts/periodicals.html
Locating Legal Periodical Articles	http://library.law.smu.edu/resguide/periodical.htm

Securities

American Stock Exchange	http://www.amex.com
EDGAR	http://www.sec.gov/edgarhp.htm
Nasdaq Stock Exchange	http://www.nasdaq.com
New York Stock Exchange	http://www.nyse.com
Quicken Financial Network (stock valuation)	http://www.quicken.com/
Securities and Exchange Commission	http://www.sec.gov
Security APL Quote Server	http://www.asianet.net/engin119.html
StockMaster	http://www.stockmaster.com
Wall Street Research Net	http://www.wsrn.com

Taxation

ABA Tax Section	http://www.abanet.org/tax
AccountingNet	http://accountingnet.com
American Accounting Association	http://www.aaa-edu.org
American Institute of CPAs (AICPA)	http://www.aicpa.org
American Taxation Association	http://www.atasection.org/
Association for Computers and Taxation	http://www.taxact.org
Bureau of National Affairs	http://www.bna.com
California Franchise Tax Board	http://www.ftb.ca.gov/index.html
California Legislative Information	http://www.leginfo.ca.gov/
CCH Incorporated	http://www.cch.com
Citizens for Tax Justice	http://www.ctj.org
Code of Federal Regulations	http://www.access.gpo.gov/nara/cfr
Commerce Clearing House	http://tax.cch.com
Commission of European Union	http://europa.eu.int/index-en.htm
Crossborder Tax and Transactions	http://www.crossborder.com/
Current Legal Resources	http://www.currentlegal.com

Equipment Leasing Association   http://www.elaonline.com

Estate Planning Legal Research Guide   http://www.law.ukans.edu/library/este_res.htm

Ernst & Young   http://www.ey.com/global/gcr.nsf/International
                                                /Welcome_-_Tax

Estate Plannig Gateways   http://www.estateplanninglinks.com/

Euro   http://europa.eu.int/euro

Fairmark   http://www.fairmark.com/

Federal Tax Law   http://www.taxsites.com/federal.html

Federation of Tax Administrators   http://www.taxadmin.org

Findlaw—Tax Section   http://www.findlaw.com/01topics/35tax
                                                /sites.html

Forms, Instructions & Publications Directory   http://www.taxsites.com/forms.html

House Ways and Means Committee   http://www.house.gov/ways_means

Institute of Property Taxation   http://www.ipt.org

Internal Revenue Bulletin   http://www.irs.ustreas.gov/prod/bus_info
                                                /bullet.html

The Internal Revenue Code On Line   http://www.fourmilab.ch/ustax/ustax.html

Internet Tax Freedom Act   http://cox.house.gov/nettax

IRS Forms   http://www.irs.ustreas.gov/prod/forms_pubs
                                                /index.html
                                                http://www.fedworld.gov/taxsear.html

IRS Home Page   http://www.irs.ustreas.gov

IRS Newsstand   http://www.irs.ustreas.gov/prod/news/index.html

IRS Regulations   http://www.irs.gov/tax_regs/regs.html

IRS Topic Index   http://www.irs.ustreas.gov/prod
                                                /search/site_tree.html

Joint Committee on Taxation   http://www.house.gov/jct

Law Journal Extra   http://gort.ucsd.edu/newjour/l/msg00340.html

Michigan Probate & Estate Planning Jrnl   http://www.icle.org/sections/probate/journal
                                                /about.htm

Multistate Tax Commission   http://www.mtc.gov

National Conference of State Legislatures   http://www.ncsl.org/

The Office of Tax Policy   http://www.otpr.org

Pillsbury, Madison and Sutro LLP Tax Page   http://pillsburylaw.com/

Policy and Tax Reform Groups Directory   http://www.taxsites.com/policy.html

Presidential Tax Returns   http://www.taxhistory.org/presidential

Research Institute of America   http://checkpoint.riag.com

Revenue Rulings   http://www.taxlinks.com

RIA   http://www.riahome.com

RIA Estate Planner's Alert   http://www.riahome.com/default.asp

Roth IRA Website Home Page   http://www.rothira.com/

Senate Finance Committee   http://www.senate.gov/~finance

State & Local Tax Professionals   http://www.willyancey.com/tax-salt.htmState &
Local Taxes Directory   http://www.taxsites.com/state.html

State Tax Agencies	http://www.taxsites.com/agencies.html
State Tax Forms	http://www.sm-b.com
State Tax Links	http://www.taxsites.com/state.html
Tax Analyst	http://www.tax.org/
Tax Analysts' Discussion Groups	http://www.tax.org/Discuss/discussion.htm
Tax and Accounting Academia	http://www.taxsites.com/academia.html
Tax and Accounting Sites Directory	http://www.taxsites.com
Tax Associations Directory	http://www.taxsites.com/associations.html
Tax Help, Tips, and Articles Directory	http://www.taxsites.com/help.html
Tax Library (Thompson Publishing Group)	http://taxlibrary.com
Tax Notes News Wire	http://www.tax.org/taxwire/taxwire.htm
Tax Planet	http://www.taxplanet.com
Tax Professional's Corner (IRS)	http://www.irs.ustreas.gov/taxpros/display /0,,i1%3D5%26genericId%3D7151,00.html
Tax Prophet	http://www.taxprophet.com
Tax Protestor's Hall of Fame	http://www.bus.ucf.edu/ckelliher/tax/examples /tax_protesters_hall_of_fame.htm
Tax Publishers & CPE Directory	http://www.taxsites.com/publishers.html
Tax Resources	http://pages.prodigy.net/agkalman/
The Tax Scam Bulletin Board	http://www.taxprophet.com/hot/Trustscam.htm
Tax Sites	http://www.taxsites.com
Tax Software Directory	http://www.taxsites.com/software.html
Tax Treaties—Danziger's FDI	http://www.danzigerfdi.com
Tax Treaties— Schmidt Enterprises, LLC	http://www.taxsites.com/international.html
The Tax Warrior	http://www.taxwarrior.com
TaxWeb	http://www.taxweb.com/taxforms.html
Thomas Legislative Information	http://thomas.loc.gov
Trust and Trustees	http://www.trusts-and-trustees.com/main2.htm
U.K. Presidency of European Union	http://presid.fco.gov.uk
United States General Accounting Office	http://www.gao.gov
U.S. Tax Code	http://www.fourmilab.ch/ustax/ustax.html
Various Tax Links	http://www.sm-b.com/nn/useful.htm
Will Yancey's Home Page	http://www.willyancey.com
Yahoo!	http://yahoo.com/government/taxes
Yahoo! Yellow Pages—Tax Preparers	http://yp.yahoo.com/py/yploc.py?Pyt=&clr =ypBrowse&ycat=7737258&desc =Legal+and+Financial

Torts

Center for Food Safety & Applied Nutrition	http://vm.cfsan.fda.gov/index.html
Centers for Disease Control and Prevention	http://www.cdc.gov/

Food and Drug Administration	http://www.fda.gov
Internet Grateful Med	http://wwwindex.nlm.nih.gov/databases /freemedl.html
National Cancer Institute	http://www.nci.nih.gov
National Institutes of Health	http://www.nih.gov
Occupational Safety & Health Administration	http://www.osha.gov
Office of Human Radiation Experiments	http://tis.eh.doe.gov/ohre

BUSINESS

Barron's Online	http://www.barrons.com
Barron's Online: Market Surveillance	http://www.corpfinet.com
Business Information Server (Dun & Bradstreet)	http://www.dnb.com/
Business Know-How	http://www.businessknowhow.com
Business Law Today	http://www.abanet.org
Business Plans	http://www.bplans.com
Business Resource Center	http://www.morebusiness.com
Census Bureau	http://www.census.gov
CNNfn: the Financial Network	http://www.cnnfn.com
CommerceNet	http://www.commerce.net
Consumer Price Index	http://www.bls.gov/bls/newsrels.htm
Ebusinessforum.com	http://www.ebusinessforum.com
The Forbes 500 Annual Directory	http://www.forbes.com
Hoover's Online	http://www.hoovers.com
Idea Cafe	http://www.businessownersideacafe.com
IHateFinancialPlanning.com	http://www.IhateFinancialPlanning.com
International Business Resources Page	http://ciber.bus.msu.edu/
International Small Business Consortium	http://www.isbc.com
Internet Business Resources	http://www.oak-ridge.com
Investor Education and Assistance	http://www.sec.gov/oiea1.htm
Market Research Center	http://www.asiresearch.com
Marketing Resource Center	http://www.marketingsource.com
Maryland Business Information Network	http://www.mdbusiness.state.md.us
National Federation of Independent Business	http://www.nfibonline.com
Small Business Administration Online	http://www.sbaonline.sba.gov
Small Business Advisor	http://www.isquare.com
Small Business Journal	http://www.tsbj.com
STAT-USA	http://www.stat-usa.gov

A giant, fee-based subscription service providing economic, business, and social/environmental program data produced by more than 50 federal sources.

Thomas Register	http://www.thomasregister.com/index.html
Young Entrepreneurs' Organization	http://www.yeo.org

People and Company Finders

Many of these sites permit the user to search by name, street address, or phone number. They supply a variety of data about individuals and businesses, such as e-mail addresses, financial information, profiles, and maps and directions.

American Business Information	http://www.lookupusa.com
Bigbook	http://bigbook.com
Database America	http://home.taegu.net/~p789284/peopl.htm
Four11	http://people.yahoo.com/
Infospace	http://www.infospace.com

> Includes maps, radius searching, and phone/add directory for the United States and some foreign countries.

Internet Address Finder	http://www.iaf.net
Internet Who's Who	http://www.whoswho-online.com/
Phone White Pages	http://www.switchboard.com http://www.angelfire.com/webfind/index.html http://www.555-1212.com
Reverse Directory	http://people.yahoo.com/
Social Security Death Index	http://www.ancestry.com/search/main.htm
Stalker's Home Page	http://www.glr.com/stalk.html

> Combines several people finder search sites, plus additional privacy info.

Switchboard	http://www.switchboard.com
Webgator: Investigative Resources on the Web	http://www.virtualgumshoe.com/
WhoWhere	http://whowhere.com
Yellow Pages	http://www.yellowpages.com.au/ http://www.yellowpages.co.nz/ http://search.yell.com/search/DoSearch http://www.switchboard.com http://www.bigfoot.com http://people.yahoo.com/

Online Brokers

Accutrade	http://www.accutrade.com
Ameritrade	http://www.ameritrade.com
Bidwell & Co.	http://www.bidwell.com
Brown & Co.	http://www.brownco.com
BuyAndHold	http://www.buyandhold.com
Charles Schwab	http://www.schwab.com
CNN Money	http://money.cnn.com/best/brokers/
Datek	http://www.datek.com
Discover Brokerage	http://www.online.msdw.com/new_site.html
Ditech	http://www.ditech.com
E*Trade	http://www.etrade.com

e-Sider   http://www.e-sider.com/cgi-pub/isadll.dll/AN
                                       /PUBINDEX

Interactive Brokers   http://www.interactivebrokers.com/index.html

Jack White & Co.   http://www.jackwhiteco.com

Merrill Lynch   http://www.ml.com

Quick & Reilly   http://www.quickandreilly.com

Scottsdale Securities   http://www.scottrade.com

Suretrade   http://www.suretrade.com

Waterhouse Securities   http://www.waterhouse.com

Web Street   http://www.webstreet.com.au/default.htm

INTERNET

Current Awareness

Law Library Resource Xchange   http://www.llrx.com

LegalOnline   http://legal-online.org/

Scout Report   http://wwwscout.cs.wisc.edu/scout/report/

Internet Legal Research Guides

The Internet Lawyer   http://www.internetlawyer.com

Internet Legal Resource Guide   http://www.ilrg.com/lsahq
                                       http://www.studylaw.com

The Legal List   http://www.speculativebubble.com/terms
                                       /legall.shtml

Law-Related Discussion Lists

LawLists by Lyonett Louis-Jacques   http://www.lib.uchicago.edu/~llou/lawlists
                                       /info.html

LISZT:Directory of E-Mail Discussion Lists   http://www.liszt.com

Search Engines

AOL   http://netfind.aol.com

AltaVista   http://altavista.com

Ask Jeeves   http://askjeeves.com

CNN Webspace Search Engine   http://cnn.com/SEARCH/index.html

Dog Pile   http://www.dogpile.com

Excite   http://www.excite.com

Galaxy   http://www.galaxy.com

Google	http://www.google.com
HomeWiz—Home Page Search Engine	http://www.800go.com/homewiz/homewiz.html
HotBot	http://hotbot.lycos.com/
Infoseek	http://infoseek.go.com/
Internet Sleuth—Legal Information	http://web.bilkent.edu.tr/Search/Sleuth/lega.html
Jump City	http://www.jumpcity.com/NEWHOME.html
LawCrawler	http://www.findlaw.lawcrawler.com
LookSmart	http://www.looksmart.com
Lycos	http://www.lycos.com
MegaGo	http://www.megago.com
Mega Spider	http://www.megaspider.com
MetaCrawler	http://www.metacrawler.com
Meta Spider	http://www.metaspider.com
National Directory	http://www.nationaldirectory.com
News Index—Current News Search Engine	http://www.newsindex.com
Northern Light	http://www.northernlight.com
OpenText	http://www.opentext.com
Snap	http://nbci.msnbc.com/nbci.asp
Starting Point	http://archive.ncsa.uiuc.edu/SDG/Software /Mosaic/StartingPoints /NetworkStartingPoints.html
Teoma	http://www.teoma.com
Webcrawlers	http://www.webcrawler.com
Yahoo!	http://www.yahoo.com
Yellow Pages	http://www.yellowpages.com

Master Sites for Search Engines

These sites incorporate many search engines into one page of links. Some allow for combined searching with more than one search engine at a time.

All-in-One Internet Search   http://www.allonesearch.com/all1srch.html

   Links to 800 search engines. Allows user to search all at once.

Beaucoup!   http://www.beaucoup.com

   Links to over 2,500 search engines. Allows user to search all search engines at once.

800go.com   http://800go.com

   Links to 12 search engines. Allows user to search all at once. The engines searched include Lycos, WebCrawler, Google, AltaVista, Infoseek, Teoma, Yahoo!, MegaSpider, Fast, Open Directory, MetaSpider, and Yellow Pages.

SavySearch   http://www.gocee.com/eureka/savvy.htm

   Links to 11 separate engines. Allows user to search all at once. The engines searched include Lycos, Excite, HotBot, WebCrawler, Google, Galaxy, AltaVista, Thunderstone, NationalDirectory, Infoseek, and Teoma.

SAMPLE LAW FIRM HOME PAGES

Alston & Bird	http://www.alston.com
Andrews & Kurth	http://www.akllo.com
Arent Fox	http://www.arentfox.com
Arnold & Porter	http://www.arnoldporter.com
Baker & Mckenzie	http://www.bakerinfo.com
Baker Botts	http://www.bakerbotts.com
Bingham Dana	http://www.bingham.com
Brobeck, Phleger & Harrison	http://www.brobeck.com
Buchanan Ingersoll	http://www.bipc.com
Carr & Ferrell	http://www.carr-ferrell.com
Cleary, Gottlieb, Steen & Hamilton	http://www.cgsh.com
Clifford Chance	http://www.cliffordchance.com
Cooley Godward	http://www.cooley.com
Coudert Brothers	http://www.coudert.com
Covington & Burling	http://www.cov.com
Cravath, Swaine & Moore	http://www.cravath.com
Davis Polk & Wardwell	http://www.dpw.com
Day, Berry & Howard	http://www.dbh.com
Debevoise & Plimpton	http://www.debevoise.com
Dechert	http://www.dechert.com
Dickstein Shapiro Morin & Oshinsky	http://www.dsmo.com
Dow, Lohnes & Albertson	http://www.dlalaw.com
Duane Morris	http://www.duanemorris.com
Edwards & Angell	http://www.ealaw.com
Faegre & Benson	http://www.faegre.com
Family Law Advisor	http://www.divorcenet.com/law/fla.html
Fenwick & West	http://www.fenwick.com
Fish & Richardson	http://www.fr.com
Foley, Hoag & Eliot	http://www.fhe.com
Folley & Lardner	http://www.foleylardner.com
Fried Frank Harris Shriver & Jacobson	http://www.ffhsj.com
Fulbright & Jaworski	http://www.fulbright.com
Gibson, Dunn & Crutcher	http://www.gdclaw.com
Glovsky & Koenig	http://www.searchboston.com/profiles/G /Glovsky_and_Koenig.shtml
Gray Cary Ware & Freidenrich	http://www.graycary.com
Greenberg Traurig	http://www.gtlaw.com
Gunderson Dettmer Stough Villeneuve Franklin & Hachigian	http://www.gunder.com
Hale & Dorr	http://www.haledorr.com
Heller Ehrman White & Mcauliffe	http://www.hewm.com

Hill & Barlow	http://www.hillbarlow.com
Holland & Knight	http://www.hklaw.com
Howrey Simon Arnold & White	http://www.howrey.com
Hunton & Williams	http://www.hunton.com
Jenkens & Gilchrist	http://www.jenkens.com
Jones, Day, Reavis & Pogue	http://www.jonesday.com
Katten Muchin Zavis	http://www.kmz.com
Kilpatrick Stockton	http://www.kilstock.com
King & Spalding	http://www.kslaw.com
Kirkland & Ellis	http://www.Kirkland.com
Kutak Rock	http://www.kutackrock.com
Lane Powell Spears Lubersky	http://www.lanepowell.com
Latham & Watkins	http://www.lw.com
Leboeuf, Lamb, Green & Macrae	http://www.luce.com
Lucash, Gesmer & Updegrove	http://www.lgu.com
Mayer, Brown, Rowe & Maw	http://www.mayerbrown.com
McCutchen, Doyle, Brown & Enersen	http://www.mccutchen.com
McDermott, Will & Emery	http://www.mwe.com
McGuirewoods	http://www.mcguirewoods.com
Milberg Weiss Bershad Hynes & Lerach	http://www.milberg.com
Mintz Levin Cohn Ferris Glovsky and Popeo	http://www.mintz.com
Morgan, Lewis & Bockius	http://www.morganlewis.com
Morrison & Foerster	http://www.mofo.com
Orrick, herrington & Sutcliffe	http://www.orrick.com
Patton Boggs	http://www.pattonboggs.com
Peabody & Brown	http://www.peabodybrown.com
Pepper & Corazzini	http://www.commlaw.com
Pepper Hamilton	http://www.pepperlaw.com
Perkins Coie	http://www.perkinscoie.com
Pillsbury Winthrop	http://www.pillsburywinthrop.com
Piper Marbury Rudnick & Wolfe	http://www.piperrudnick.com
Preston Gates & Ellis	http://www.prestongates.com
Pual, Weiss, Rifkind, Wharton & Garrison	http://www.pualweiss.com
Ropes & Gray	http://www.ropesgray.com
Schulte Roth & Zabel	http://www.srz.com
Shaw Pittman	http://www.shawpittman.com
Shearman & Sterling	http://www.shearman.com
Sidley Austin Brown & Wood	http://www.sidley.com
Simpson Thacher & Bratlett	http://www.simpsonthacher.com
Skadden, Arps, Slate, Meagher & Flom	http://www.skadden.com
Squire, Sanders & Dempsey	http://www.ssd.com
Sullivan & Cromwell	http://www.sullcrom.com

Tax Prophet	http://www.taxprophet.com
Testa, Hurwitz & Thibeault	http://www.tht.com
Troutman Sanders	http://www.troutmansanders.com
Venture Law Group	http://www.vlg.com
Weil, Gotshal & Manges	http://www.weil.com
Wilson Sonsini Goodrich & Rosati	http://www.wsgr.com

FINDING A LAWYER ON THE WEB

ABA	http://www.abanet.org/
Finding an Attorney in Your Area	http://www.lawyershop.com/
Findlaw	http://www.findlaw.com
FindLaw for The Public	http://consumer.pub.findlaw.com/
Law Journal EXTRA!	http://gort.ucsd.edu/newjour/l/msg00340.html
Lawyers.com	http://www.lawyers.com
Martindale Hubble	http://www.martindale.com
Over True	http://www.overture.com/
Westlaw Legal Directory	http://directory.westlaw.com/

MISCELLANEOUS

Amazon Bookstore	http://www.amazon.com
Building/Designing a Law Firm Web Page	http://www.lawfirmwebshop.com/onlineresources.html
	http://www.1st-tech.com
	http://www.dir.state.tx.us/egov/Surveys/State_Survey/app_a.htm
	http://www.brickbuilt.com
	http://ccrich.com/
	http://www.collegehill.com/
	http://www.virtual411.com/
	http://www.s6000.com/dci
	http://www.inherent.com
	http://internet-assist.net
	http://www.internetlawyer.com
	http://www.intranetix.com
	http://www.juris-net.com
	http://www.lawgirl.com
	http://www.webcounsel.com
	http://www.romingerlegal.com/WPdesign.htm
CD Now	http://www.cdnow.com
City Search (local events)	http://www.citysearch.com
Department of Housing and Urban Development	http://www.huduser.org
Free E-mail Service	http://bigfoot.com
	http://hotmail.com
	http://juno.com
	http://login.mail.lycos.com
	http://mail.yahoo.com

Internet Index	http://new-website.openmarket.com/intindex /index.cfm
Jobs—Online Search	http://www.careermag.com
	http://www.careerweb.com
	http://www.dice.com
	http://www.flipdog.com
	http://www.headhunter.net/index.htm
	http://www.hotjobs.com
	http://www.jobbankusa.com
	http://www.job-hunt.org
	http://jobsmart.org
	http://www.jobweb.com
	http://www.monster.com
	http://www.nationjob.com
Movie Links	http://www.movielink.com
Public Mailing Lists	http://paml.net
United States Post Office Zipcode Lookup	http://www.usps.gov/ncsc

GLOSSARY*

Absolute path: A designation of the location of a file that is given in relation to the root directory; it includes the root directory and the descending series of subdirectories leading to the end file.

Abuse of process: A tort action for misusing legal process.

Access code: The password, which the user must type in to get access into a computer system.

Access contract: An online contract with an information provider such as America Online or Prodigy. Access contracts have been validated by the Uniform Computer Information Transactions Act.

Acceptance (of goods):   Occurs when a buyer signifies that it is taking goods. Acceptance may also occur by inaction, by failing to reject goods. Finally, acceptance occurs when the buyer does an act inconsistent with the ownership of goods.

Acceptance testing: Software license agreements set up performance tests, and if the software complies with the test criteria, there is acceptance. Acceptance testing is the functional equivalent of inspection in the sale of goods.

Active server page (ASP):   A specification for a web page that is dynamically created by the web server and contains both HTML and scripting code.

Active X: A model for writing programs so that other programs and the operating system can call them. ActiveX technology is used with Microsoft Internet Explorer to make interactive web pages that look and behave like computer programs, rather than static pages.

Address resolution: Translation of an Internet address into its physical address (media access control [MAC] or Ethernet address).

Adhesion contract: A contract in which the weaker party adheres to the terms of the more powerful party. Shrinkwrap license agreements are adhesion contracts, as are contracts to rent automobiles, purchase insurance, or purchase utilities or telephone service.

ADP (automatic data processing):   The processing of information by means of a computer.

Agency: The law of agency is based on a relationship in which an agent is represented by a principal. A principal acts through an agent, who is therefore liable for acts on the principal's behalf. Relationships of agency cover the liability of the employer for the employee's actions. The common law definition of agency was originally termed "master and servant," also sometimes referred to as the principle of *respondeat superior*. A principal may be liable for the torts of an agent committed within the scope of duties. Likewise, a principal may be liable for contracts entered into by agents. Courts distinguish between employment relationships of agency where one person has the right to direct the actions of another and the independent contractor relationship.

Anonymous FTP: To transfer files using anonymous FTP, you must log in as "guest" or "anonymous" and enter your e-mail address as the password. By using the special user ID of "anonymous," the network user will bypass local security checks and will grant access to publicly accessible files on the remote system. Many of these sites are provided by corporations,

---

* We would like thank Manish Vashisht, of PricewaterhouseCoopers, for his written, editorial, and strategic contributions to this Glossary.

universities, and government agencies. The publicly available files are usually in a directory called "pub," which is isolated from the files used by other users on the system and will not accept uploads from anonymous users.

ANSI (American National Standards Institute):   The U.S. member of the International Standards Organization (ISO) and the International Electrotechnical Commission (IEC). ANSI develops standards for many things, only some having to do with computers, such as properties of diskettes, programming languages, etc. ASCII is an ANSI character set. ANSI standards are voluntary.

Anticybersquatting Consumer Protection Act (ACPA):   An act passed "to protect consumers and American businesses, to promote the grown of online commerce, and to prohibit the bad-faith and abusive registration of distinctive marks as Internet domain names with the intent to profit from the goodwill associated with such marks—cybersquatting." S. Rep. No. 106-140, at 4. The ACPA protects distinctive as well as famous trademarks from cybersquatters.

Antitrust guidelines (for collaborations among competitors):   The Federal Trade Commission and the U.S. Department of Justice issued guidelines on specific circumstances in which antitrust issues relate to competitor collaborations. Competitor collaboration is an agreement, other than a merger, to engage in economic activity between competitors.

AOL (America Online):   One of the largest providers of online services. AOL offers e-mail, interactive newspapers and magazines, conferencing, software files, computing support, and online classes, in addition to full Internet and World Wide Web access.

API (application program interface):   An interface between the operating system and application programs, which includes the way the application programs communicate with the operating system and the services the operating system makes available to the programs.

Appellate court: The court where civil or criminal actions are brought if review of a trial court decision is sought. In the United States, courts are divided into state and federal courts. Each state has trial courts, intermediate appellate courts, and a state supreme court. At the federal level, the federal district court is the trial court and the U.S. Court of Appeals is the appellate court. Bankruptcy decisions are tried in special bankruptcy courts and the decisions are reviewed by U.S. courts of appeals. There are 11 U.S. circuit courts as well as the D.C. Circuit. The U.S. Supreme Court is the highest appellate court. A party seeking appellate review at the U.S. Supreme Court will file a writ of certiorari. The U.S. Supreme Court accepts approximately 125 cases each session from the thousands of writs of certiorari.

Applet: A little application. An applet can be a utility or other simple program. On the World Wide Web, there are often applets written in Java attached to HTML documents.

Application program: Software that performs specific tasks, such as Word, PowerPoint, or Excel.

Application software: Software that solves problems or performs specific functions. WordPerfect, Word, and Excel are examples of application software, as are computer games.

ARPANET: The Department of Defense's Advanced Research Projects Agency Network (ARPA) connected computers around the United States. A Wide Area Network (WAN) developed in the 1960s by the Advanced Research Projects Agency of the U.S. Department of Defense that linked government sites, academic research sites, and industrial sites around the world. ARPANET was the testing ground and original backbone of the Internet. ARPANET was the inventor of packet switching technology that became part of the Internet infrastructure.

ASCII (American Standard Code for Information Interchange):   A code in which each alphanumeric character is represented as a number from 0 to 127, translated into a 7-bit binary code for the computer. Most microcomputers and printers use ASCII; because of this, text-only files can be transferred easily between different kinds of computers.

Assignment: A contract to transfer property rights or interests. Assignments involve an assignor or an assignee of property interests. The e-business will seek to obtain assignments on intellectual property rights. In copyright law, copyrights may be transferred to another party. A "transfer of copyright ownership" is an assignment. Assignments may transfer any or all of the rights of a copyright holder. 17 U.S.C. § 101. Nonassignment clauses may restrict assignment. Patent licenses are personal and cannot be assigned. 11 U.S.C. § 365(c)(1)(A). Nonexclusive patent licenses are deemed to be personal and therefore non-assignable. Trademarks, trade secrets, and copyrights are freely assignable. Registered marks may be assigned "with the good will of the business in which the mark is used, or with that part of the good will of the business connected with the use of and symbolized by the mark." 15 U.S.C. § 1060. Patents are not assigned unless recorded in the USPTO.

Attenuation: The weakening of a transmission signal that occurs over time and distance. Attenuation is measured in dB/km (decibels per kilometer).

Authentication: Verification of identity as a security measure. Passwords and digital signatures are forms of authentication.

Authoring tool: Software that allows developers to create multimedia presentations or World Wide Web pages. Typically, these tools automate some of the more difficult parts of generating program source codes so that developers can work on a higher, more abstract level.

B2B e-commerce (business-to-business electronic commerce): Businesses engaging in traditional business activities using the online world as the primary means.

Backbone: In a hierarchical network, the backbone is the top level, employing high-speed data transmission and serving as a major access point; smaller networks connect to the backbone.

Back end: A smaller, friendlier computer (called the front end) that does the main processing but interacts with the user.

Backup: An extra copy of a file kept for safety. The Copyright Act does not consider it an infringing act to make a backup copy or archival copy of software. 17 U.S.C. § 117(a).

Backward compatible: A version of software able to coexist with older versions that may have been installed on the machine previously and able to read files of the older version.

Bandwagon standardization: A process whereby subsequent entrants to the market adopt the standard of an existing firm.

Bandwidth: The amount of data that can be sent through a network connection, measured in bits per second (bps). High bandwidth allows fast transmission or high-volume transmission.

Banner: A graphic display on a web page used for advertisement. A banner ad is linked to an advertiser's web page.

Baud: A baud equals one bit per second. Bits refer to the rate of data transmission.

Bayh-Dole Act of 1980: Statute that provides ground rules for technology transfer. Universities, for example, may retain title to inventions developed through government funding. Universities file patents for inventions they wish to own.

BBS (bulletin board service): Usually requires users to dial in through telephone lines to access specialized information or services.

Berne Convention: International Convention for the Protection of Literary and Artistic Works formed in Berne, Switzerland, in 1886. The United States is a signatory to the Berne Convention.

Binary code: A system of numbers having 2 as its base and using 0s and 1s for its notation. Computers use binary code because it works well with digital electronics.

Bios: Basic input/output system.

Bit: Binary digit with values of "0" and "1." The bit per second rate defines how information is transmitted.

Blurring: A form of trademark dilution in which the plaintiff's mark is weakened.

Bluetooth: A technology that enables communication between the Internet and devices such as PDAs.

Boot: The process of loading a computer's operating system.

Breach of contract: A breakdown of contract, which entitles the nonbreaching party to damages. The contract breacher must compensate the nonbreaching parties for damages caused by the breach.

Broadband: A transmission medium that can carry signals from multiple independent network carriers on a single coaxial or fiber optic cable by establishing different bandwidth channels. Broadband technology can support a wide range of frequencies and is used to transmit data, voice, and video over long distances.

Broadcast: A transmission sent to many unspecified receivers at a time by means of a computer network, radio waves, or satellite. A broadcast is sent to everyone who has the equipment to receive it. On an Ethernet, a broadcast packet is one that is transmitted to all hosts on the network.

Buffer: A reserved area of memory for temporarily holding data. A buffer can hold data being sent from a high-speed device to a low-speed device until the slower device can accept the input; for example, to hold data sent to a printer until the printer is ready for it.

Bundled software: Software that comes free with the purchase of new hardware, usually a variety of basic programs and sometimes an encyclopedia, sample computer games, or other multimedia software.

Bus: A set of conductors that connect the functional units in a computer. It is called a bus because it travels to all destinations. There are local buses that connect elements within the CPU and buses that connect the computer to external memory and peripherals. Most personal computers use 32-bit buses both internally and externally.

Business method patent: In *State Street Bank v. Signature Financial Group,* 149 F.3d 1368 (Fed. Cir. 1998), the Federal Circuit held that a programmed computer using a mathematical algorithm was patentable as long it produced a useful, concrete, and tangible result. The business method was for the computation of interest in mutual funds through a hub-and-spoke method.

Business process reengineering (BPR): Making radical changes in an organization from the ground up in an effort to improve performance and make more efficient use of resources. The concept of BPR generally includes the use of computers and information technology to organize data, project trends, etc.

Business software alliance (BSA): An alliance of software publishers created to fight software piracy in countries around the world, by educating the public and getting laws passed.

Business torts: The body of law covering tort liability that arises out of commercial and consumer contracts. Business tort claims are generally brought by competitors and others injured by anti-competitive, predatory, or fraudulent business practices. Business torts include banking torts, lender liability, interference with economic relationships, fraud or misrepresentation, trade secrets litigation, and employment law.

Byte: The amount of memory space used to store one character, which is usually 8 bits.

Cable modem: A cable modem is an external device that hooks up to a computer. Instead of getting an Internet connection through a telephone connection (or another system), a connection is established through a local cable network company (the same place a cable TV connection comes from).

Cache: A temporary storage area for frequently accessed or recently accessed data. Having certain data stored in cache speeds up the operation of the computer.

Caveat emptor: "Let the buyer beware." In modern law, warranties have displaced this doctrine that the buyer purchases goods at his or her peril. Warranty law gives the buyer remedies for goods that are not at least merchantable, fair average, or fit for their ordinary purpose.

Central processing unit (CPU): Control unit of computer used for internal memory storage.

Certificate: A document issued by a trusted third-party, certificate authority, to identify the holder.

Certificate authority (CA): An authority in a network that issues and manages security credentials and public keys for message encryption. As part of a public key infrastructure (PKI), a CA checks with a registration authority (RA) to verify information provided by the requestor of a digital certificate. If the RA verifies the requestor's information, the CA can then issue a certificate.

Chat room: A real-time electronic forum; a virtual room where visitors can meet others and share ideas on a particular subject. There are chat rooms on the Internet and other online services.

CHI (computer-human interaction): An interdisciplinary field combining education, information science, graphic art, industrial design, mechanical engineering, psychology, artificial intelligence, etc., to understand how human beings process information so that products can better be designed to enhance usability.

CGI script (Common Gateway Interface script): A program that is run on a Web server, in response to input from a browser. The CGI script is the link between the server and a program running on the system, for example, a database.

Cipher: An algorithm or code that can be used to encrypt data.

Circumvention technology: Designed to permit access to a work but preventing copying of the work.

Clickwrap contract: A contract to use software in exchange for payment, derived entirely over the Internet.

Client/server: An architecture in which one computer can get information from another. The client is the computer that asks for access to data, software, or services. The server, which can be anything from a personal computer to a mainframe, supplies the requested data or services for the client.

Cluster: A group of sectors on a disk that is treated as a unit.

Communications Decency Act of 1996: Congress enacted this statute to provide immunity for Internet Service Providers who blocked and screened offensive materials. The federal statute has been expanded judicially to immunize providers against torts committed on web sites, bulletin boards, and listservs. Section 230 creates a federal immunity for any cause of action that would make service providers vicariously or indirectly liable for the torts of third parties.

Communications protocol: A standard way of regulating data exchange between computers, including the rules for data transmission and the formatting of messages. Some communications protocols are TCP/IP, DECnet, AppleTalk, SNA, and IPX/SPX.

Compensatory damages: A remedy that seeks to restore the injured party to the position it ws in prior to the wrong. A nonbreaching party is entitled to compensatory damages for the lost value of a bargain. An aggrieved party may seek recovery for incidental and consequential damages in addition to lost profits. Compensatory damages are traditionally classified into economic and noneconomic damages or pain and suffering. Compensatory damages may be sought in a wide variety of civil actions. The form of damages may be different depending on the body of law. Compensatory damages for the breach of contract generally take the form of purely economic or commercial losses. Tort damages, on the other hand, may include recovery for personal injury including noneconomic damages and punitive damages. Noneconomic damages are popularly known as "pain and suffering" damages. Tort remedies are traditionally classified as compensatory and punitive damages. Punitive damages are separate from compensatory damages and are awarded for the societal purposes of punishment of the defendant and deterrence. Compensatory damages restore the plaintiff to the position it was in prior to the wrong, whereas punitive damages punish and deter the defendant and others. Compensatory damages under tort law frequently take the form of past and future loss of earnings, past and future medical expenses, as well as "pain and suffering."

Competitive intelligence: Information that is used for analyzing a company's strategic position in the industry.

Competitive strategy: A strategy of a company aimed at increasing its competitiveness. It can be offensive or defensive.

Compiler: A computer program that translates a high-level programming language into machine language.

Computer-aided design (CAD): Software that assists designers in visualizing and assembling designs.

Computer Fraud and Abuse Act: Federal statute that prohibits anyone from "intentionally access[ing] a protected computer without authorization, and as a result of such conduct causes, damage." 18 U.S.C. § 1030(a)(5)(C).

Consequential damages: Damages not resulting directly from the wrong committed. These damages result from the act but are not direct or immediate. Personal injuries may be a form of consequential damages in a breach of warranty lawsuit. Consequential damages may be limited or excluded unless the limitation or exclusion is unconscionable.

Consortium: The loss of consortium originally referred to the marital or sexual relationship between the husband and wife. Consortium damages may also be sought for the loss of father/child or other familial relationships caused by the defendant's wrongdoing.

Constructive fraud: A court will presume fraud from the transaction, relationship of parties, and other circumstances as opposed to proof of actual fraud. Constructive fraud may be presumed from the circumstances.

Contributory infringement: Requires knowledge of the infringing activity and substantial participation in the primary infringing activity.

CONTU (Commission on New Technological Uses of Copyright): A national commission formed by Congress in the late 1970s to recommend the proper application of copyright law to new technology.

Cookie: A cookie is a set of data that a web site server gives to a browser the first time the user visits the site, which is updated with each return visit. The remote server saves the information the cookie contains about the user and the user's browser does the same, as a text file stored in the Netscape or Explorer system folder. Not all browsers support cookies.

COPPA (Children's On-Line Privacy Protection Act): Federal statute administered by the Federal Trade Commission governing how e-businesses can collect and use children's personal information.

Corporate entity: A business organization that is distinct from its shareholders. This organization has power to act in its own name. A corporation separate from that owning it, having the right to sue and be sued under its own name.

Contingent fees: Under the American system, contingent-fee lawyers are paid only if they are successful. A contingent fee agreement will generally cover terms such as allocation of expenses, the percentage of the award allocated to the plaintiff's attorney and the plaintiff, and allocation of the cost of expert witnesses. The customary contingent fee is two-thirds to the plaintiff and one-third to the defendant. In many jurisdictions, the parties may enter into contingent fees for different percentages depending on the difficulty of the case.

Contort: Term coined by Grant Gilmore in *Death of Contract* to refer to conduct on the borderline between contract law and tort law. Professor Gilmore's thesis was that the traditional division between contract and tort law is breaking down. The traditional contract law doctrine prohibits the plaintiff from seeking punitive damages in a strictly contractual cause of action. In recent years, a plaintiff will plead independent torts, such as fraud, to seek punitive damages in a contract case. Courts have validated tort causes of action in contract law. Gilmore advocated the merger of contract and tort law into a subject he called "contorts." Contort causes of action may be seen in insurance bad-faith cases, medical malpractice, and a wide variety of business tort cases. Empirical studies confirm that punitive damages are skyrocketing in contort type cases.

Contract: An agreement between two or more parties that is enforced by a court. Oral contracts or agreements are generally enforceable. However, all states have a statute of frauds, which requires writing for certain categories of cases. Article 2 of the Uniform Commercial Code requires a writing for the sale of goods that is $500 or greater. Article 2A of the Uniform Commercial Code governing the lease of goods requires a writing for leases for $1,000 or greater. A sales contract, for example, is an agreement for the seller to tender conforming goods and the buyer to pay for them. Contract is a broad field of law encompassing real estate, goods, services, licenses, online contracts, and performance contracts. Article 2 of the Uniform Commercial Code governs contracts for the sale of goods. However, most contracts are governed by the common law. The common law is general law as distinct from state law codes such as the Uniform Commercial Code or federal statutes governing contracts such as the Magnuson-Moss Act. A web site contract is an agreement by the web site visitor to adhere to the terms and the services of the site. An electronic contract is an enforceable agreement in which computers, without human review, transmit the offer and acceptance.

Copyright: Federal copyright law protects the copyright holder, giving him or her the exclusive right to make copies, prepare derivative works, control the distribution of the original and derivative works, and control performance or display of protected works.

Cyberlaw: Relatively new field of Internet and computer law. The field includes new areas such as the responsibility of Internet Service Providers and bulletin-board system operators for the material that passes through or is stored on their systems and the framework for international electronic commerce, and a new look at traditional areas such as intellectual property rights and copyright and censorship.

Daemon: A UNIX program that runs continuously in the background, until it is activated by a particular event. This word is often used to refer to programs that handle e-mail.

Damages: A plaintiff in a civil lawsuit seeks damages for losses or injuries due to the defendant's wrongdoing. Damages take the form of monetary awards and are traditionally classified into three categories: economic damages (out-of-pocket losses), noneconomic damages (pain and suffering or nonpecuniary damages), and punitive damages (designed to punish the defendant and deter others).

Data Protection Directive (EC Data Protection Directive): The EC Data Directive requires all of the countries of the European Union to develop protections for the use of personal data. The Directive does not permit the transfer of personal data without adequate data protection.

Debugging: Finding and removing errors, or bugs, from a computer program or system.

Defendant: The party in a lawsuit who is sued by the plaintiff, who initiates the lawsuit. The plaintiff alleges that the defendant has breached a contract or violated a legal duty owed him or her and seeks damages. A criminal law defendant is prosecuted on behalf of the state, whereas a private party sues a civil law defendant.

Deposition: Written documentation of a party's answers to questions used in preparation of a trial. The questions are answered under oath and can be used to impeach the witness's testimony at trial. Relevant depositional testimony is admissible at trial.

Digital contracts: A report published by The Institute for Information Law, Amsterdam, discussing the formation and validity of online contracts.

Digital Millennium Copyright Act (DMCA): Enacted in 1998 to implement the WIPO Copyright Treaty of 1996. The DMCA creates a safe harbor for ISPs and creates criminal and civil sanctions for the circumvention of copyright protection systems.

Digital signature: An electronic signature that can be used to authenticate the identity of the sender of a message or the signer of a document, and possibly to ensure that the original content of the message or document that has been sent is unchanged. Digital signatures are easily transportable, cannot be imitated by someone else, and can be automatically time-stamped.

Dilution: The lessening of the capacity of a trademark to identify and distinguish goods or services. Dilution may occur through the blurring of a mark or the tarnishment of a mark. Tarnishment occurs when a mark is associated with an inferior or offensive product or service.

Discovery: Refers to the pretrial collection of facts or documents relevant to a lawsuit. The parties to a lawsuit have a wide variety of techniques to gather facts to support their cases. Interrogatories are written questions served on the opposing party. Answers to written interrogatories may be admitted into evidence if the judge determines that they are relevant to the issue being tried. An injured plaintiff in a products liability lawsuit will seek information on product design, prior product failures, and the history of designs. An injured plaintiff in a sex discrimination case may depose witnesses or the defendant. A deposition is an interview of a witness with a court reporter and counsel for both sides present. Witnesses who are being deposed are sworn to tell the truth and may be prosecuted for perjury for untruthful statements. Statements made in depositions are transcribed and used in the trial to impeach a witness whose story has changed.

DMZ (demilitarized zone): The portion of the network that is shared with other Internet users, such as web servers. It is a portion of the network LAN and the Internet that protects the LAN.

Domain: A domain is an Internet address in letter form. Domain names must have at least two parts: the part on the left, which names the organization, and the part on the right, which identifies the highest subdomain, such as the country (.fr for France, .uk for United Kingdom) or the type of organization (.com for commercial, .edu for educational). Directory levels can be indicated in other parts. The domain name server translates the IP address into the domain name.

DoS (denial of service): A type of hacker attack in which a web site is bombarded with fake or illegal requests. This ties up all the resources and leaves the site unable to handle legitimate requests.

Download: To transfer files or data from one computer to another. To download means to receive; to upload means to transmit.

Downstream: The direction of information passed between servers. It can be in the form of data that move from a server to an individual computer. It is important to note that downstream differs from upstream due to different transfer rates. For example, cable modems transfer data up to 30 Mbps downstream, but only 128 kbps to 2 Mbps upstream.

DSL (digital subscriber line or digital subscriber loop): High-speed data transmission protocols that are compatible with regular copper telephone wire. DSL is typically used to provide a continuous, high-speed connection directly to an Internet Service Provider. There are several different types of DSL (ADSL, SDSL, UADSL, etc.), and many of them make it possible to talk on the telephone and use the Internet at the same time. Also called high-speed DSL (HDSL).

DUN (dial-up networking): DUN is a built-in program of Windows that dials a modem and lets a computer connect to the Internet. Despite having slower speeds, it is the method used most often for Internet access, because it uses standard telephone lines, which are available almost anywhere.

Duty of care: There is a general duty of care to avoid negligence. The radius of the risk generally determines the duty of care. The greater the danger, the greater the duty of care.

E-commerce: The use of computers and electronic communications in business transactions. E-commerce may include the use of electronic data interchange, electronic money exchange, Internet advertising, web sites, online databases, computer networks, and point-of-sale computer systems.

Economic damages: Any expense that is commercial and does not include injury to the person. For example, a consumer may recover the costs of repair and replacement of defective products.

Economic Espionage Act of 1996: Federal statute providing criminal and civil penalties for the theft of trade secrets, 18 U.S.C. § 1831. To qualify for trade secret protection, the owner must "have taken reasonable measures to keep such information secret; and the information derives independent economic value, actual or potential from not being generally known to, and not being readily ascertainable through proper means by the public." *Id.* at § 1839.

ECPA (Electronic Communications Privacy Act): A law that prohibits phone tapping, interception of e-mail, and other privacy violations except under special law enforcement situations usually requiring a warrant.

EDI (electronic data interchange): Conversion of a transmitted document into a format readable by the receiving computer.

EDP (electronic data processing): Data processing using electronic machines (computers).

.edu: A top-level domain name used for educational web sites.

Effects test: Test for personal jurisdiction employed in *Calder v. Jones,* 465 U.S. 783 (1984). The effect test finds personal jurisdiction where an intentional tort is directed to the plaintiff, causing injury where the plaintiff lives.

Electronic commerce directive: Validates electronic contracts in member states. Took effect on January 10, 2002.

Electronic signature: Transformation of a message that allows the recipient to verify the source and integrity of the message.

E-mail: A service that sends messages on computers via local or global networks.

E-mail address: The address that gives the source or destination of an e-mail message.

Encryption: A means of putting data into a secret code so they are unreadable except by authorized users.

Entity (choice of): The following are examples of legal entities: sole proprietorships, general and limited partnerships, C corporations, S corporations, limited liability companies, and trusts. A C corporation is a general corporation, versus an S corporation, which is generally a small entity. The e-business will need to choose a legal entity to structure its business for purposes of tax law, securities law, and general liability concerns.

E-Sign (Electronic Signatures in Global and National Commerce Act): President Clinton signed this federal statute on July 1, 2000. E-Sign validates contracts executed by electronic signatures as well as e-records. Consumers must be given adequate consent to perform electronic transactions. Section 101(a) of E-Sign validates signatures or contracts executed electronically.

Ethernet: A very common and very fast method of networking computers in a LAN. Ethernet will handle about 10 million bits-per-second and can be used with almost any kind of computer.

Extranet: The part of a company or organization's internal computer network that is available to outside users, for example, information services for customers.

Extraterritoriality: If conduct occurs within a state, the state has jurisdiction to prosecute the offences. If conduct is outside a state, a state cannot assert subject matter jurisdiction. In international e-commerce, comity requires that a national state refrain from exercising jurisdiction for wrongdoing not committed within its borders.

FAQs (frequently asked questions): Compilations of frequently asked questions on a particular topic and their answers. Technical personnel who routinely receive the same question many times may develop FAQs.

FDDI (fiber distributed data interface): An ANSI standard for 100 Mbit/s data transmission through fiber optic cable, in a token ring setup. Many local area networks can be linked together with a backbone that uses FDDI.

Federal powers: The Constitution grants powers to the federal government. Federal law will displace or preempt state law. Tort law is generally state law.

Federal Trademark Dilution Act (FTDA): Federal remedy for cybersquatting amending Trademark Act of 1946 (Lanham Act). The trademark dilution remedy of the FTDA applies only to "famous marks." The plaintiff must prove that its mark is a famous mark to be entitled to protection. Famousness is proven by general name recognition among the consuming public.

Fiber optics: The use of light to transmit data, video, and voice. Fiber optic cable has much higher bandwidth and carries signal much longer distances than wire cable. It is also lighter, easier to install, and provides better security.

Filed/filing a claim: To prepare and bring a document to a court for the purposes of initiating a lawsuit. Also to prepare and bring the document to a court so that the court will have a record of the document. The parties file a complaint, which begins the litigation process.

Filtering software: Application software that blocks objectionable materials over the Internet or the LAN.

Filters: A program or section of code that is designed to examine each input or output request for certain qualifying criteria and then process or forward it accordingly. This term was used in UNIX systems and is now used in other operating systems. A filter is "pass-through" code that takes input data, makes some specific decision about it and possible transformation of the data, and passes them on to another program in a kind of pipeline. Usually, a filter does no input/output operation on its own. Filters are sometimes used to remove or insert headers or control characters in data.

Finger: A UNIX command that enables a user to find another user's login name and e-mail address, and sometimes other information; it is necessary to know the name of the computer where the other person has an account.

Firewall: A firewall architecture that employs two routers to filter and transfer information between an organization's internal network and the Internet.

Firmware: Software stored in ROM or PROM; essential programs that remain even when the system is turned off. Firmware is easier to change than hardware but more permanent than software stored on disk.

Fixation: A work must be fixed in form to be entitled to copyright protection. Computer software is fixed even if not stored permanently.

Flat panel display: A type of video display that is relatively thinner than the desktop monitor. Most commonly used in laptops and a few new desktops.

Flow chart: A graphic representation of the analysis and solution of a problem in which symbols are used to represent operations and the data flow.

Frame: (1) A variable-length packet of data that is transmitted in frame relay technology. (2) One complete scan of the computer display screen. (3) In video or film, a single picture of a series that, displayed in sequence, creates the illusion of motion. (4) In computer graphics, the boundary that surrounds a graphic image. (5) On World Wide Web pages, a bordered area that acts as an independent browser window.

Framing: Displaying content from another web site while still maintaining advertisements from the original site.

Freeware: Software available free of charge, but which is copyrighted by the developer, which retains the right to control its redistribution and to sell it in the future. Freeware is different from free software, which has no restrictions on use, modification, or redistribution.

Frivolous lawsuit: A lawsuit filed without a basis in fact for nuisance purposes. Trial judges may punish frivolous lawsuits by assessing sanctions for pleadings not made in good faith.

Frolic of his own: A principal was historically not liable when an employee committed wrongdoing by departing from his employment duties.

FTP (file transfer protocol):   The Internet standard high-level protocol for transferring files from one machine to another over TCP/IP networks. FTP uses ports 20 and 21. FTP is commonly used to download programs and other files to a computer from other servers. It is also used to transfer web page files.

Gag order: An order barring a party from leaking information about a trial to reporters or anyone outside the confines of the courtroom. Also, an order against a party in court to prevent that party from interrupting while the court is in session.

Gateway: A device that connects two computer networks that use different protocols. It translates between protocols so that computers on the connected networks can exchange data. For example, commercial online services often have gateways for sending e-mail to Internet addresses.

GIF (graphics interchange format):   A format used for displaying bitmap images on World Wide Web pages, usually called a "gif" because .gif is the filename extension. These files use compression and can have 256 colors. JPEG and GIF are commonly used for images on the web; JPEG is considered best for photos and GIF for other graphic images.

Gigabyte: One billion bytes. Abbreviated GB, Gbyte, or G-byte.

Gopher: Through Gopher, a user can access files from many different computers by looking through hierarchical menus to find specific topics. A document may be a text, sound, image, or other type file. Gopher sites can now be accessed through the World Wide Web.

Gramm-Leach-Bliley Act: Federal statute requiring financial institutions to provide notice about their privacy practices to their customers. The FTC rule implementing the Act.

Gray market: A marketplace where goods are bought internationally and then resold to customers domestically, usually at a price far below the domestic price.

Gross negligence: Negligence beyond garden variety or ordinary negligence. One legal scholar stated that gross negligence could not be defined with precision and stated it was "negligence with an epithet." In Texas, punitive damages were once recoverable for gross negligence. Today, most jurisdictions require the plaintiff to prove that the defendant was either intentionally or recklessly negligent in injuring the plaintiff.

Groupware: Software for people working together on a project. Groupware makes it possible for several people to work on the same file at once, via a network. It also helps with scheduling meetings and other kinds of group planning. Lotus Notes is a popular groupware package.

GSM (global system for mobile communications):   A world standard for digital cellular communications.

GUI (graphical user interface):   An interface that has pictures as well as words on the screen. Originally invented by Xerox, the idea was expanded and popularized by Apple Computers. With windows, icons, pull-down menus, and the mouse, the graphical user interface is easier to learn and work with.

Hacker: (1) One who is knowledgeable about computers and creative in computer programming, usually implying the ability to program in assembly language or low-level languages. A hacker can mean an expert programmer who finds special tricks for getting around obstacles and stretching the limits of a system. (2) To some people it means an unconventional programmer or one who is not formally trained.

Hard disk: The main device that a computer uses to store information. Hard disks are rigid aluminum or glass disks about 3.5 inches in diameter in a personal computer, and smaller in a laptop. They are coated with ferromagnetic material and rotate around a central axle. A read/write head transfers data magnetically. A hard disk drive for a personal computer may contain as many as eight hard disks, rotating around the same axle.

Hardware: The physical part of a computer system; the machinery and equipment.

Harmless error: An error in the trial that did not affect the outcome of the judgment. A trivial error that does not substantially impact the outcome or prejudice the parties.

Header: (1) Text that appears at the top of every page in a document, which can be set up with a template in word processing and page layout programs. (2) The part of a communications packet that contains control information for the packet, such as source, destination, input sequence number, and priority level.

Hit: One visit to a World Wide Web page by a user. Many servers have counters on their home pages to tell how much traffic they are getting.

Home page: The first page on a World Wide Web site, to which supporting pages are linked.

Host: A computer connected to a network that provides data and services to other computers.

HTML (Hypertext Mark-up Language): The language used to create World Wide Web pages, with hyperlinks and markup for text formatting (different heading styles, bold, italic, numbered lists, insertion of images, etc.). The HTML coding language allows nonvisible information about a web page to be recorded in the source code.

HTTP (Hypertext Transfer Protocol): The protocol most often used to transfer information from World Wide Web servers to browsers, which is why Web addresses begin with http://. Also called Hypertext Transport Protocol.

Hub: A point where communication lines are brought together to exchange data. LANs (local area networks) use pieces of equipment called hubs to connect PCs.

Hung: Referring to a state in which a system is up and running but for some reason cannot complete a process; the system can do some things but is not fully functional.

Hyperlink: A link in an HTML document that leads to another World Wide Web site, or another place within the same document. Hyperlinks are usually underlined or shown in a different color from the surrounding text. Sometimes hyperlinks are pictures.

Incompatible: Not able to work together. Can be said of hardware/hardware, software/software, or hardware/software combinations.

Information Privacy: Aspects of privacy law that involve the right of individuals on the Internet to determine when, how, and to what extent they choose to share their personal information with others.

Information superhighway: A global, high-speed communications network that will carry voice, data, video, and other forms of information all over the world, and that will make it possible for people to send e-mail, get up-to-the-minute news, and access business, government, and educational information. The Internet is already providing many of these features, via telephone networks, cable TV services, online service providers, and satellites.

Information technology (IT): The technology of data processing and information management.

Infringement: Occurs when intellectual property rights are violated. Copyright infringement occurs when a defendant violates any of the exclusive rights of the copyright owner.

Input device: A peripheral device used to enter commands or information into a computer, such as a keyboard, mouse, joystick, modem, scanner, or touch screen.

Input/output (I/O): Transfer of data into a computer and from the computer to the outside world.

In rem jurisdiction: The Anticybersquatting Consumer Protection Act (ACPA) has an *in rem* jurisdiction provision over domain names where personal jurisdiction is not possible. One of the problems of prosecuting cybersquatting is the difficulty of locating cybersquatters who register names using aliases. The *in rem* remedy of the ACPA was to alleviate the problem of the anonymous cybersquatter. The *in rem* remedy allows a trademark owner to file an action against the domain name itself provided that the plaintiff proves it exercised due diligence in trying to locate the owner of the domain name. See, e.g., *Lucent Technologies, Inc. v. Lucentsucks.com,* 95 F. Supp. 2d 528 (E.D. Va. 2000). Courts have been reluctant to allow the *in rem* proceeding without proof that locating the defendant would be impossible.

Intellectual Property Law: The law of patents, trademarks, copyright, and trade secrets. Generally, it relates to intangible property that is in the nature of intellectual output, i.e., works of authorship, inventions, etc.

Intentional infliction of emotional distress: The intentional infliction of emotional distress is sometimes referred to as the tort of outrage. For the defendant to be liable for the intentional infliction of emotional distress, the misconduct must be extreme and outrageous. This tort is frequently pleaded in sexual harassment cases where the defendant intentionally or recklessly causes the plaintiff to suffer severe emotional distress. The law is more apt to recognize emotional distress claims where the conduct is far beyond the boundaries of acceptable behavior. The courts will also consider the plaintiff's vulnerability, age, and disparity in power when determining whether the conduct was sufficiently outrageous.

Intentional torts: Intent is the desire to bring about a result. A defendant who deliberately commits harm is responsible for the actual injury incurred. A plaintiff proves the defendant's intent by showing that it was the defendant's purpose to bring about a desired result or the result was substantially certain to follow from the defendant's actions. Battery is an example of an intentional tort. Battery is when the defendant intends to cause harmful or offensive conduct to another person. Assault is a closely related intentional tort where the person intends to cause harmful or offensive conduct and places the plaintiff in "imminent apprehension" or fear of being battered. Assault is the harm that is caused from the distress of being threatened with immediate bodily harm.

Interactive: A term for computer programs that accept input from the user while they are running; for example, a game that waits for the user to take an action, then responds to that action. The interaction between computer and user may take place through typed commands, voice commands, mouse clicks, or other means of interfacing. The opposite of interactive processing is batch processing, where all the commands are given before the program starts to run.

Interrogatories: A set or series of questions sent to the opposing party with relevant information pertaining to a specific case. Such questions are usually answered under oath. The information sought may be used in court.

Internet: A group of networks interconnected via routers. This worldwide information highway comprises thousands of interconnected computer networks and reaches millions of people in many different countries.

Internet community: A group of people with similar interests who are organized on a web site where they can chat and collaborate.

Internet Engineering Task Force (IETF): The main standards organization for the Internet. The IETF is a large international body of network designers, vendors, and researchers working to expand and improve the way the Internet functions.

InterNIC (Internet Network Information Center): A group of three organizations, which together provide services for NSFNet. General Atomics handles information services, AT&T handles directory and database services, and Network Solutions, Inc. (NSI) handles registration services. Network addresses and domain names for the Internet are assigned by InterNIC through NSI.

InterNIC (NSFnet Internet Network Information Center): Consortium that developed the registration system for domain name addresses. InterNIC was the successor to ICANN.

Interoperability: The ability of software and hardware on different machines to communicate.

IP address: The Internet Protocol address; a numeric address such as 10.2.9.27 that the domain name server translates into a domain name.

ISDN (Integrated Services Digital Network): Digital telecommunications lines that can transmit both voice and digital network services up to 128K and are much faster and more reliable than high-speed analog modems. Many telephone companies offer ISDN lines.

ISOP: Incentive Stock Option Plan recognized by the Internal Revenue Code.

ISP (Internet Service Provider): A company that provides individuals and with companies access to the Internet at speeds ranging from 300 bps to OC-3, and other related services such as web site building and hosting.

JAVA: A cross-platform programming language from Sun Microsystems that can be used to create animations and interactive features on World Wide Web pages. Java programs are embedded into HTML documents.

John Doe subpoena: Issued to Internet Service Providers to unveil anonymous Internet tortfeasors.

Joint and several liability: The liability of joint tortfeasors where the plaintiff has the option to sue either or both of them. If a co-defendant is insolvent, the solvent party is liable for the entire judgment. If a co-defendant is sued as an individual, it may seek contribution from the co-defendant. Tort reformers seek to eliminate the doctrine of joint and several liability.

Joint tortfeasor: Two or more persons contribute to the harm or damages in a tort case. Joint tortfeasors produce a single indivisible injury, and their liability is joint and several.

JPEG (Joint Photographic Experts Group): A format for storing high-quality color and grayscale photographs in bitmap form; also the group that developed the format. JPEG provides compression by segmenting the picture into small blocks that are divided to get the desired ratio; the process is reversed to decompress the image. JPEG uses the JPEG file interchange format, or JFIF.

Judgment: The final determination by the court of the rights of the parties. In a criminal proceeding, the judgment will include the sentencing of the defendant. The judgment is the conclusion of law based on the facts presented in the court record.

Judgment notwithstanding the verdict (JNOV): A motion made after a verdict to vacate a judgment. The moving party requests the court to set aside the verdict because it is entitled to judgment as a matter of law.

Kbps: Kilobits per second. Thousand bits per second. A data transfer rate.

Kernel: The essential part of a program or operating system that performs the basic functions.

Lanham Act: Federal statute establishing the trademark registration system in the United States. Trademarks that distinguish goods from others are registered on the principal register of the United States Patent and Trademark Office. A trademark may not be registered if it comprises "immoral, deceptive or scandalous matter; or matter which may disparage or false suggest a connect with persons, living or dead, institutions, beliefs, or national symbols, or bring them into contempt or disrepute." Lanham Act § 2(a), 15 U.S.C. § 1052(a).

LAN (local area network): A group of PCs and other computer devices, generally within a single building, that are connected together. Computers on a LAN can exchange information and share resources.

Leased line: A dedicated line that is leased exclusively to connect two points, 24 hours a day, 7 days a week. A leased line gives the highest-speed connection.

Legacy system: An information system that has been in use for a long time, usually on a mainframe or minicomputer.

Liability: A debt or obligation imposed by law.

Liable: A court finding that a person is responsible for a wrong committed. The party found liable in a lawsuit must pay money damages.

License: A principal means of transferring value in contrast to a sale or a lease. Unlike a sale, title does not pass from the licensor to a licensee. A lease, like a license, grants a right to use. However, leases are for tangible goods as opposed to licenses, which are for intangible information such as software. A license is a grant by a licensor to a licensee to use computer software, copyrighted information, patents, or other information for a term. Licenses come in a large number of flavors. Examples include software licenses, patent licenses, trademark licenses, affiliate licenses, and content licenses. Licenses may also be structured as exclusive, semi-exclusive, or exclusive license agreements.

License, end user: A license that gives a user the right to use a particular kind of software and specifies the conditions under which it may be used; for example, how many copies may be made, whether or not it may be distributed to other users, and whether it can be modified by the user.

Link: (1) A connector; anything that connects two or more things. (2) A pointer in an HTML document that leads to another World Wide Web site, or to another place within the same document; also called a hyperlink. Linked text is usually underlined or shown in a different color from the surrounding text. Sometimes graphics are links or contain links. Clicking on them activates links. (3) A pointer embedded in a database record that refers to data or the location of data in another record.

Listserv: The most common kind of mail list. Listservs are common on the Internet.

Load: (1) To copy a program into memory so it can be run. (2) To put a disk or tape into a drive so it can be used. (3) To put data onto a disk so they can be used.

Log: A record of a computer's or application's activity, used for system information, backup, and recovery.

Logic bomb: A lockout feature implemented in software programs whereby the program will shut down unless it receives a license or a security key from the programmer.

Logon/login: The process of connecting to a network or remote system.

Logoff: The act of disconnecting from a network or remote system.

Machine language: The language that is actually read and understood by the computer. Machine language consists of instructions, written in binary code, that a computer can execute directly. Each machine language statement corresponds to one machine action. An operation that requires one machine language instruction in one computer may require several instructions in another computer.

Macro: One instruction that represents a sequence of simpler instructions.

Magnetic tape: A data storage medium used for backup. The tape is made of a thin plastic strip with a magnetizable oxide coating on one side. To read or write, the tape drive winds the tape from one reel to another, causing it to move past a read/write head. Tapes are available in reels and cartridges of various sizes. The data are written in blocks with interblock gaps between them. To find a specific block of data on the tape the computer must read everything in front of it.

Mailbox: A box that holds incoming mail; a box for electronic mail is a file where mail messages are stored until the addressee opens and reads them.

Mailing list: An e-mail discussion forum. Participants subscribe to a list, receive copies of messages sent by other members, and can e-mail their own comments. In some mailing lists there is a moderator who receives all mail, screens it, and decides which messages to pass on. Unmoderated lists simply redirect all mail received to the list of recipients. Mailing lists may be highly technical, or social and recreational.

Mainframe: A mainframe originally meant the cabinet containing the central processor unit of a very large computer. After minicomputers became available, the word *mainframe* came to refer to the large computer itself, e.g., IBM mainframe.

Malice: A state of mind in which there is hatred or hostility toward another person. Punitive damages historically required the defendant to manifest ill will and hatred against the defendant. Malice is an aggravating factor in determining the size of punitive damages in many states.

Malpractice: Failure of a professional to meet a minimum standard of care usual in a professional. An intolerable lack of skill displayed by the medical and legal professions, engineers, computer scientists, or any other professional. Expert testimony is generally required to establish malpractice.

Mbps: Megabits per second.

Medical malpractice: A branch of the law that originally applied to the standard of care of physicians and surgeons. Today, medical malpractice has largely shifted to hospitals and other caregivers. The standard of care in medical malpractice is that of similar professionals in similar specialties. A psychiatrist, for example, is held to the standard of a reasonable psychiatrist. Information security professionals may be held to a professional standard of care that parallels what is expected of a physician.

Memory: Also called main memory. The working space used by the computer to hold the program that is currently running, along with the data it needs, and to run programs and process data. The main memory is built from RAM chips. The amount of memory available determines the size of programs that can be run, and whether more than one program can be run at once. Main memory is temporary, and is lost when the computer is turned off.

Metatags: Metatags are HTML tags that provide information that describes the content of the web pages a user will be viewing. Search engines have recognized that web site owners and administrators can use this resource to control their positioning and descriptions in search engine results. Many search engines have now incorporated reading metatags as part of their indexing formulas. In *Brookfield Communications, Inc. v. West Coast Entertainment Corp.,* 174 F.3d 1036 (9th Cir. 1999), the defendant's use of trademarks in the metatags constituted trademark infringement.

Microbrowser: An Internet browser designed for use with a wireless handheld device such as a mobile phone. Microbrowsers have small file sizes to accommodate the low memory available to handheld devices and the low-bandwidth constraints of the wireless-handheld networks.

Microchip: Also called microelectronic or integrated circuit. A microelectronic device comprises many miniature transistors and other electronic components on a single thin rectangle of silicon or sapphire. A microchip can contain dozens, hundreds, or millions of electronic components.

MIME (multipurpose Internet mail extensions): Extensions to the Internet mail format that allow it to carry multiple types of data (binary, audio, video, graphics, etc.) as attachments to e-mail messages.

Minimum contacts: The Due Process Clause of the U.S. Constitution requires that no defendant shall be haled into count unless the defendant has "certain minimum contacts [with the state] . . . such that the maintenance of the suit does not offend traditional notions of fair play and substantial justice." *International Shoe Co. v. Washington,* 326 U.S. 310, 316 (1945).

Misappropriation: "Acquisition of a trade secret of another by a person who knows or has reason to know that the trade secret was acquired by improper means; or disclosure or use of a trade secret of another without express or implied consent." Uniform Trade Secrets Act, § 1.

Misrepresentation: Misrepresentation is sometimes referred to as fraud or the tort of deceit. The elements of a fraud or misrepresentation claim are (1) a misrepresentation of material fact, (2) made willfully to deceive, recklessly, without knowledge, or mistakenly, (3) was unjustifiably relied on by the plaintiff under the circumstances, and (4) caused damage as a proximate cause. Misrepresentation claims may be classified as intentional or negligent fraud depending on whether the claim is based on intent or negligence.

Modem (modulator/demodulator): A simple analog data communications device for transmitting data over a POTS (plain old telephone service) line. Digital signals are converted to analog signals and vice versa. Modems are used to send data signals (digital) over the telephone network, which is usually analog. The modem modulates the digital data of computers into analog signals to send over the telephone lines, then demodulates back into digital signals to be read by the computer on the other end; thus the name "modem" for MOdulator/DEModulator.

MPEG (Motion Picture Expert Group): Group that sets standards for compressing and storing video, audio, and animation in digital form. MPEG is another compression method. MPEG-1 is a standard for CD-ROM video and audio. MPEG-2 is a standard for full-screen, broadcast quality video. MPEG-4 is a standard for video telephony.

MP3: MP3 stands for Motion Picture Experts Group, Audio Layer 3. A popular music download format. MP3 produces CD-quality music in a compressed file that can be transferred quickly and played on any multimedia computer with MP3 player software.

MS-DOS (Microsoft disk operating system): A personal computer operating system from Microsoft. It is a single-user system that runs one program at a time because of limited memory.

MTA (Madrid Trademark Agreement): An international treaty allowing trademark owners to file a single application in a member country and use that single application to secure rights in all other member countries.

Multimedia: Multimedia is communication that uses any combination of different media. Multimedia may include text, spoken audio, music, images, animation, and video. The large amounts of data required for computer multimedia files makes CD-ROMs a good option for storage, but there are other ways of receiving multimedia communications, such as the World Wide Web. Multimedia programs are often interactive, and include games, sales presentations, encyclopedias, and more.

Multiprocessing: Using two or more processors in the same computer, or two or more computers connected together, to execute more than one program or instruction at the same time.

Navigate: To find one's way around on the World Wide Web by following hypertext links from document to document, and from computer to computer.

NCCUSL (National Conference of Commissioners on United State Laws): A national group of state representatives working to unify state laws.

NDAs: Nondisclosure agreements signed by employees. (See Appendix A for a sample NDA.)

Negligence: Negligence is the failure to use ordinary care. The elements of negligence are duty, breach, risky conduct, causation, and damages. The plaintiff must show cause in fact and proximate cause to recover for negligence. The general standard is the failure of a person to follow a reasonable course of conduct. Negligence is a branch of tort law that evolved in the nineteenth century to protect plaintiffs from unreasonable or unsafe practices conducted without intent but nevertheless dangerous to society. The legal definition of negligence is some act or omission by which the defendant fails to exercise the due care of a reasonable person in the circumstances. The standard of care may be set by statute, industry practices, usages of trade, or common law decisions. The standard of care takes into account age, infirmities, and other characteristics of the defendant.

Negligent hiring or retention of employees: Employers are increasingly held to be liable for the negligent hiring, retention, or supervision of employees.

Netiquette: The etiquette of the Internet.

'Net search: A group of Internet search engines that allows one to search if one does not know the URL of the information sought.

Network: A group of interconnected computers, including the hardware and software used to connect them.

NIC (network interface card): The circuit board or other form of computer hardware that serves as the interface between a computer (or other form of data terminal equipment) and the communications network; in ADSL, a common NIC is an Ethernet NIC, which serves as the interface to the ADSL modem from the computer.

NNTP (Network News Transfer Protocol): Internet protocol for connecting to usenet newsgroups and posting messages.

Node: A computer or a terminal connected to a network.

Nonexludability: A characteristic of a public good whereby the creator of the good is unable to prevent those who do not pay for the good from consuming it.

Nonrivalrous: A characteristic of a public good whereby additional consumers of the good do not deplete the supply of the good available to others.

NQO: Nonqualified stock option.

Object code: Digital instructions in "1s" and "0s" readable by a computer.

OEM (original equipment manufacturer): A company that manufactures a product and sells it to a reseller.

Online: Connected to the Internet or other online service that demands the use of a modem by the user; or, referring to a user who has an account, which gives access to the Internet or other online service.

Open source software: Software in which the program source code is openly shared with developers and users. Benefits of OSS are that developers can customize programs, and these innovations, in turn, are shared within the programming community so that everyone learns from each other. Linux is one popular example.

Operating system (OS): The main control program of a computer that schedules tasks, manages storage, and handles communication with peripherals. Its main part, called the kernel, is always present. The operating system presents a basic user interface when no applications are open, and all applications must communicate with the operating system.

OSI (open systems interconnection, or open systems interconnect): A model developed by ISO (International Organization for Standardization) to allow computer systems made by different vendors to communicate with each other. The goal of OSI is to create a worldwide open systems networking environment in which all systems can interconnect. Most communications protocols today are based on the OSI model.

Outsourcing: Paying an outside contractor to provide certain services that they may specialize in, such as software development.

Package: An application program or group of programs developed for the general public. Rather than being custom designed for a specific user or company, the software is designed to meet the needs of a variety of users.

Packet: A unit of data formatted for transmission on a network. Data are broken up into packets for sending over a packet switching network. Each packet has a header containing its source and destination, a block of data content, and an error-checking code. All the data packets are reassembled once they have arrived.

Packet switching: A technology for sending packets of information over a network.

Parameter: In computing, a value sent to a program or operation by the user.

Password: A secret sequence of letters and other symbols needed to log in to a computer system as an authorized user. When a user enters a password, it appears as a line of asterisks ******* so no one can read it.

Patch: A quick modification of a program, which is sometimes a temporary fix until a problem can be solved more thoroughly.

Path: The exact directions to a file on a computer. These directions are usually described by means of the hierarchical filing system from the top down, stating the drive, directory, any subdirectories, the file itself, and its filename extension if it has one.

PC (personal computer): There are many kinds of personal computers; PC usually refers to personal computers that conform to the standard of the IBM PC.

PCS (personal communication services): Wireless communications services that use the digital technology for transmission and reception.

PCT (Patent Cooperation Treaty): An international treaty signed in 1970, which allows a patent applicant in a member country to delay subsequent member country applications for up to 30 months while still maintaining the original priority date.

Peripheral: Any piece of hardware connected to a computer; any part of the computer outside the CPU and working memory. Examples of peripherals are keyboards, mice, monitors, printers, scanners, disk and tape drives, microphones, speakers, joysticks, plotters, and cameras.

Per se **rule:** A concept of antitrust law applied to practices such as price fixing or bid rigging. The *per se* rule applies to agreements likely to harm competition with no procompetitive impact. Agreements not challenged as *per se* illegal are examined under the fact-specific rule of reason.

PGP (pretty good privacy): An encryption program based on RSA (Rivest-Shamir-Adleman) public-key cryptography. PGP allows users to exchange files and messages, with both privacy and authentication, over all kinds of networks. The messages are unreadable unless the receiver has an encryption key.

PICS (Platform for Independent Content Section): A cross-industry working group whose goal is to facilitate the development of technologies to give users of interactive media, such as the Internet, control over the kinds of material to which they and their children have access. PICS members believe that individuals, groups, and businesses should have easy access to the widest possible range of content selection products, and a diversity of voluntary rating systems.

Piracy: The illegal copying of software for personal or commercial use.

Platform: The type of operating system (Windows, DOS, Unix) or computer (PIII) on which software can run.

Plug-in: An accessory program that enhances a main application, e.g., Internet Explorer plug-in.

Point-to-point protocol (PPP): A protocol for communication between computers using TCP/IP, over standard telephone lines, ISDN, and other high-speed connections.

Port: A socket at the back of a computer used to plug in external devices such as a modem, mouse, scanner, or printer. A logical channel identified for network communications.

Portable software: Software that can be used on more than one hardware platform and easily switched from one to another.

Posting: Transmitting a message for distribution to a newsgroup.

Premises liability: Historically based on the conditions of land. A plaintiff's rights depended on whether he or she was classified as a trespasser, licensee, or invitee. These traditional categories are breaking down in favor of a general principle that the premise owners must exercise reasonable care for all visitors. Business invitees are owed the highest standard of care. A high technology company that has telecommuting employees creates difficult issues as to whether the company is liable for natural and artificial conditions at its employee's home. For example, does a telecommuter in Vermont expose a company to vicarious premises liability? If a telecommuting employee has a business invitee to his home and the visitor slips and falls, is the employer liable?

Privacy: The common law tort of privacy was first defined by Samuel Warren and Louis Brandeis in "The Right to Privacy," 4 *Harvard Law Review* 193 (1890). Warren and Brandeis argued that individuals had a legally protectible "right to be left alone." The common law tort has developed to protect citizens from intrusion upon seclusion, the right of publicity, and the disclosure of private facts.

Private key: Private key is a form of cryptography in which sender and receiver have the same key or similar keys.

Products liability: The branch of law that redresses injuries caused by defective products. Products liability cases generally fall into manufacturing defect, design defect, or failure to warn or inadequate warnings. The vast majority of states recognize the doctrine of strict products liability and have adopted some version of § 402A of the Restatement (Second) of Torts. Strict liability focuses on the defectiveness of the product rather than the conduct of the defendant. The plaintiff need not prove negligence, only that a defective product was placed in the stream of commerce, which caused his or her injuries. Strict liability, like negligence, requires proximate cause to be established by the plaintiff. The idea underlying proximate cause is that a defendant will not be liable for aberrant or bizarre consequences, only for damages that are reasonably foreseeable.

Programming: Designing and writing a computer program. The programmer must decide what the program needs to do, develop the logic of how to do it, and write instructions for the computer in a programming language that the computer can translate into its own language and execute.

Protocol: A communication protocol is a set of rules or standards designed so that computers can exchange information with a minimum of errors.

Proxy: A special software program that runs on a firewall gateway server, intercepts the communications sent across the Internet, and repackages it so that it can be sent to a secure internal network.

PSTN (public switched telephone network): A voice and data communications service, which uses switched lines.

Public key: Public key is a form of cryptography in which each user has a public key and a private key. Messages are sent encrypted with the receiver's public key; the receiver decrypts them using the private key. Using this method, the private key never has to be revealed to anyone other than the user.

Questions of fact: In jury cases, the jury determines the facts and the judge determines questions of law. A judge will decide whether the defendant owes a duty to the plaintiff as a question of law, whereas the jury determines whether the defendant breached the duty. The amount of damages suffered by the plaintiff is a question of fact, as is whether the defendant intentionally injured the plaintiff. In trials by judges, the trial judge decides both questions of law and fact.

Questions of law: A judge determines whether a contract or a clause in the contract is unconscionable as a matter of law. It is for the judge to determine the admissibility of evidence, which is a question of law.

RAM (random access memory): The working memory of the computer. RAM is the memory used for storing data temporarily while working on them, running application programs, etc.

Registry: The entity that maintains all official records regarding registrations of a top-level domain (TLD). There is one registry for each TLD, such as ".com," ".org," and ".edu."

Restatements of law: Restatements are projects by the American Law Institute, an elected group of top judges, legal academics, and lawyers. The Restatements summarize and derive general principles of law. One of the most successful Restatements was the Restatement (Second) of Torts published in 1965. The Restatement of the Law (Third), Torts is the undertaking to update the Restatement (Second) of Torts. The Restatement dealing with products liability has proven to be the most controversial because of its retreat from the principle of strict products liability.

Restatement (Third) of Unfair Competition: Restatement covering trade secrets. Most states follow the Uniform Trade Secrets Act.

Reversal or reversed judgment: A reversal occurs when an appellate court overturns the decision of the lower court. Many cases are reversed as a result of the improper introduction of evidence or procedural errors. A court has the power to modify a lower court's judgment in part. For example, a court may uphold compensatory damages but reverse the punitive damages. A losing party may file an appeal to a higher court if the reviewing court is not the final court. For example, a court of appeals decision to reverse a judgment may be appealed to the state supreme court.

Router: A device that finds the best path for a data packet to be sent from one network to another. A router stores and forwards electronic messages between networks, first determining all possible paths to the destination address and then picking the most expedient route, based on the traffic load and the number of hops.

RSA (Rivest-Shamir-Adleman): RSA is an Internet encryption and authentication system that uses an algorithm developed in 1977 by Ron Rivest, Adi Shamir, and Leonard Adleman. The RSA algorithm is the most commonly used encryption and authentication algorithm and is included as part of the web browsers from Netscape and Microsoft. It is also part of Lotus Notes, Intuit's Quicken, and many other products. The encryption system is owned by RSA Security.

Rule of reason: A test used in antitrust law that balances the procompetitive benefits of an activity against the anticompetitive effects.

Safe harbor for copyright: The Digital Millennium Copyright Act immunizes service providers from copyright infringement when acting as a conduit.

SAN (storage area network): A high-speed, special-purpose network (or subnetwork) that interconnects different kinds of data storage devices with associated data servers on behalf of a larger network of users. Typically, a storage area network is part of the overall network of computing resources for an enterprise.

Scientific expert testimony: Scientific evidence is admissible only if the principle upon which it is based has general acceptance in the field to which it belongs. In *Daubert v. Merrell Dow*

Pharmaceuticals, Inc., 509 U.S. 579 (1993), the U.S. Supreme Court ruled that all scientific evidence must have a grounding in the methods and procedures of science. Scientific evidence is also limited by the relevance standard.

SDMI (secure digital music initiative):   A forum that brings together more than 180 companies and organizations representing information technology, consumer electronics, security technology, the worldwide recording industry, and Internet service providers. The sole purpose of this forum is to provide consumers with convenient access to music both online and in new emerging digital distribution systems, enable copyright protection for artists' works, and promote the development of new music-related business and technologies.

Search engine: A program on the Internet that allows users to search for files and information, such as Yahoo!, Google, and AltaVista. Users searching for a specific web site can either type it into a web browser to access the site directly or utilize a "search engine" to search for a specific web site by keywords and phrases. Listings or results are the end result of a search. There are two types of search engines: human powered and web-crawler. Human-powered search engines produce human-compiled listings. Web crawlers "read" individual web pages by reading much of the text in the HTML source code and store the text they find in each page. See *Playboy Enterprises, Inc. v. Welles,* 78 F. Supp. 2d 1066 (S.D. Ca. 1999).

Security software: A component that can be used to restrict access to the computer system from the Internet.

Server: The computer in a client/server architecture that supplies files or services. The computer that requests services is called the client. The client may request file transfer, remote logins, printing, or other available services.

Service provider: A provider of online services or network access or the operator of facilities for these activities.

SET: Security standard used by credit card companies such as VISA.

Settlement: An agreement between the parties to end a dispute or controversy. Nine out of ten lawsuits are settled between the parties out of court prior to a full trial. Settlements are also important after a verdict and prior to a case going to an appeal. A growing number of products liability defendants require settlements to be confidential as a condition of resolving the dispute outside of court. Some agreements take the form of a confidential settlement in which the plaintiff's counsel is forbidden to share information obtained in discovery about product defects with other counsel. Another modern trend is the global settlement or class action, which adjudicates a large number of claims. In recent years, global settlements have been approved in asbestos products liability cases, silicon breast implant litigation, and tobacco cases.

SLIP (Serial Line Internet Protocol):   Software that uses the Internet Protocol (TCP/IP) over a serial line. SLIP makes it possible for a computer to communicate with other computers by means of a dial-up connection; for example, a serial port hooked to a modem that makes a connection between two local area networks or is used to access the Internet and World Wide Web.

Smart card: A plastic card the size of a credit card that has an embedded microprocessor for storing information, used for banking, medical alerts, etc. Inserting it into a reading device connected with a main computer uses it.

Smart money: A term referring to punitive or exemplary damages. Smart money was used to compensate for the "smarts suffered by the injured person." Smart money also refers to the deterrent function of punitive damages. Smart money is assessed to encourage the defendant to change his or her conduct.

Smart phones: Cell phones that can connect to the Internet.

SMS (short messaging system or short message service):   A feature that allows users to receive or transmit short text messages using a wireless phone. Using SMS, a short alphanumeric message, up to 160 characters, can be transmitted to a mobile phone, which displays the message as a pager would.

Software: The computer program that tells a computer's hardware what to do. System software is the operating system that controls the basic functioning capabilities of the computer, network software enables multiple computers to communicate with one another, and language software is used to develop programs.

Software piracy: Copying, installing, or using a software program without paying for the software access license.

Source code: A computer program written by a programmer in a source language. Source code is input to a compiler or assembler, to derive machine code.

Spamming: The practice of sending copies of a message to many different newsgroups, with no regard to whether the subject matter is appropriate; or sending the same message by e-mail to large numbers of people indiscriminately. Sometimes spams are advertisements. Spamming is considered very unethical because it not only wastes everyone's time but also costs money. The sender of the messages does not pay the cost; the sites of the recipient and others on the route pay it.

SSL (Secure Sockets Layer): A protocol from Netscape Communications Corporation, designed to provide secure communications on the Internet.

Stand-alone workstation: A workstation that can do its own processing independent of a server or host system.

Storage: A device into which data can be placed, held, and later retrieved. Refers to memory, disks, diskettes, magnetic tape, and other media for holding data.

Stricken/stricken from the record: A court's decision to delete evidence from the written transcript of a court proceeding. A jury may be instructed to disregard the proffered evidence.

Sub rosa: Confidential, secretive.

Subsidiary: A corporation in which the stock is owned or controlled by another corporation called the parent corporation. Parent corporations may be liable for the torts of their subsidiaries in some circumstances.

SUP: HTML tags indicating superscript type.

Supreme Court: The highest court where civil or criminal actions are brought if review of an appellate court decision is sought. Many states have intermediate appellate courts and all jurisdictions have a state supreme court. The U.S. Supreme Court may review federal and state cases provided that the court accepts the party's writ of certiorari. Certiorari is a writ issued by the Supreme Court to an inferior federal or state court. The writ requires the lower court to transmit the record and proceedings so that it may review it. The Supreme Court (as well as appellate court) makes its decision solely based on the record versus hearing live witnesses or opening up discovery.

Surfing: Traveling from site to site, exploring the Internet.

Switch: A communications device that controls the operation and routing of a signal path. A networking device that can send packets directly to a port, associated with a given network address.

T-1: Internet connection of 1.54 megabits per second.

T-3: Internet connection of 45 megabits per second.

TCP/IP: The Transmission Control Protocol (TCP) on top of the Internet Protocol (IP). These protocols were developed by DARPA to enable communication between different types of computers and computer networks. The Internet Protocol is a connectionless protocol, which provides packet routing. TCP is connection-oriented and provides reliable communication and multiplexing.

Terminal: A device that acts as the point of communication between user and computer. Usually a terminal is a screen and keyboard with no intelligence of its own, which is connected to a main computer and used for simple data entry and retrieval.

Thin client: A simple client machine or program that performs very little processing. In the thin client/server arrangement, most of the application processing is done in the server. The advantage of a thin client is simpler hardware and simpler maintenance; the maintenance for applications is done on the server.

Thread: A series of messages related to a specific topic on a newsgroup or a mailing list.

Thumbnail pictures: A small version of a larger image file. Use by Internet search engines constitutes fair use.

Time sharing: A computer environment that allows multiple users to work independently at the same time, usually from separate terminals. Time-sharing resembles multitasking (one user, many tasks) in that the processor takes turns between the different tasks, giving each task a tiny amount of time, so that it appears the different tasks are running at the same time.

Tort: A private wrong or injury that does not arise out of contractual relationships. Tort also refers to the branch of law that compensates the plaintiff for personal injuries and other consequences of the defendant's wrongdoing. The three traditional branches of tort law are intentional torts, negligence, and strict liability. Tort law is a flexible body of law that evolves to meet new societal dangers. Tort also refers to the branch of law that is concerned with redressing wrongs committed with or without force. Intentional torts may be committed against the person or property. Negligent torts stem from the violation of a duty of care fixed by law, outside of contractual relations.

Tort reform: Tort reform is a political movement that began in the 1970s to counter the expansion of tort remedies to new causes of action. The fields of products liability and medical malpractice are the usual targets of tort reformers rather than the field of business torts. Every state has enacted at least one tort restriction since the 1970s.

Tortious conduct: Wrongful, injurious conduct that does not stem from contracts. An act or omission that subjects the defendant to liability. Tortious conduct may be intentionally or negligently inflicted. In addition, tortious conduct may be based on strict liability.

Touchpoint: Channels through which users profit.

Trademarks: Words, designs, or phrases that identify the source of goods or services. Trademarks are protected by the federal Lanham Act and may also be protected by state registrations. Trademarks registered in the United States Patent and Trademark Office provide protection in the United States. Trademark protection must be sought in countries where the e-business is selling goods or rendering services.

Traffic: The amount of data traveling across a network.

Trespass to chattels: When one party intermeddles or intentionally uses personal property without authorization. See Restatement (Second) of Torts § 217(b)(1) (1965). The tort of trespass to chattels has been applied to the transmission of unsolicited bulk e-mails. See *America Online, Inc. v. LCGM, Inc.,* 46 F. Supp. 2d 444 (E.D. Va. 1998).

Trial court: The court where civil or criminal actions are first commenced. At the state level these are often referred to as municipal, circuit, superior, district, or county courts. At the federal level these courts are referred to as U.S. District Courts. Appellate courts review trial verdicts or judgments.

TRIPs (Agreement of Trade-Related Aspects of Intellectual Property Rights): An international treaty that relies on national treatment and nondiscrimination principles to set minimum standards for international protection of intellectual property.

Trojan horse: A program that appears to be useful and harmless but which has harmful side effects, such as destroying data or breaking security on the system on which it is run. It is similar to a virus except that it does not propagate itself as a virus does.

Unfair or deceptive acts or practices: The Federal Trade Commission Act prohibits "unfair or deceptive acts or practices." The FTC's rules cover advertising, marketing, and promotional activities for the Internet. Disclosures are required to prevent deception and must be presented "clearly and conspicuously." The FTC's Deception Policy Statement states that an ad is deceptive if it contains a statement or omits information that is likely to mislead consumers acting reasonably under the circumstances and is "material" or important to a consumer's decision to buy or use the product.

Uniform Computer Information Transaction Act (UCITA): Model state statute developed by the National Conference of Commissioners on Uniform State Law to govern "computer information transactions." As of July 2001, UCITA has only been enacted in Maryland and Virginia. Article 2B of the UCC was the predecessor to UCITA but was abandoned when the American Law Institute withdrew from the project. UCITA applies to a wide variety of Internet-related contracts, including access contracts, shrinkwrap agreements, browseware agreements, and other online contracts.

Uniform Domain Name Dispute Resolution Policy (UDRP): The World Intellectual Property Organization (WIPO) developed a policy for the arbitration of domain name disputes. A plaintiff may choose which provider to submit its dispute to. WIPO is a popular provider because its decisions tend to be pro-plaintiff, whereas e-Resolution is the most pro-defendant provider. To succeed under the UDRP policy, a plaintiff must prove that the domain name registered by the respondent is identical or confusingly similar to a trademark or service mark in which the plaintiff has rights, that the respondent has no rights or legitimate interests in respect of the domain name, and that the domain name has been registered and is being used in bad faith. It is considered to be bad faith when a respondent offers to sell the domain name to the complainant for consideration in excess of costs.

Uniform Electronic Transactions Act (UETA): Model state statute developed by the National Conference of Commissioners on Uniform State Law. UETA validates digital signatures and electronic records in a wide range of substantive fields of the law. The majority of states have adopted UETA.

UNIX: A multiuser, multitasking operating system developed by AT&T's Bell Laboratories. It was originally designed for minicomputers, then revised for use on mainframes and personal computers. There are now many versions of UNIX, which can be used on many different platforms. UNIX is written in the C programming language, which was also developed at AT&T.

Upload: To transfer files or data from one computer to another. To download means to receive; to upload means to transmit.

Upstream: The direction of data moving from a client to a Web server. It can also be defined as the reference to actual data that are moving from individual computers to servers. It is important to note that upstream differs from downstream due to different transfer rates; for example, cable modems transfer data up to 30 Mbps downstream, but only 128 kbps to 2 Mbps upstream.

URL (uniform resource locator): An Internet address that tells a browser where to find an Internet resource. For example, the URL for Suffolk University Law School is http://www.law.suffolk.edu/.

Usenet: A giant public bulletin board system on the Internet for news and electronic mail. Graduate students at Duke University and the University of North Carolina, using the UUCP communications protocol, started Usenet in 1979. It now has over 12,000 discussion areas, which cover every imaginable topic, and is read by millions of people all over the world. Messages and news articles are posted and users respond by e-mail.

User interface (UI): The means by which a user interacts with a computer. The interface includes input devices such as a keyboard, mouse, stylus, or microphone; the computer screen and what appear on it; the way commands are given, etc. With a command-line interface, only text appears on the screen, and the user must type in commands; with a graphical user interface, windows, mice, menus, and icons are used to communicate with the computer.

Validation: The evaluation of software at the end of its development, to make sure it meets the requirements of the intended user(s). The process of checking data to make sure they are correct and presented in the proper format.

Value-added tax (VAT): The VAT is a tax system followed by the European Union, which collects taxes from the supplier. The taxing authority is the member state where the supplier is located.

Vendor: A company that specializes in the development and sale of computer software or hardware.

Verdict: The decisions handed down by juries. A jury verdict in a criminal case is required to be unanimous in most states. In many civil cases, a simple majority of the juror votes may be sufficient.

Vicarious liability: Indirect legal liability for the torts of another. The concept of vicarious liability is juxtaposed against direct liability. A principal is vicariously liable for the acts of an agent committed within the scope of his or her duties. Since the nineteenth century, corporations have been vicariously liable for punitive damages arising out of an employee's wrongdoing. In copyright law, vicarious liability refers to infringement where the principal benefits financially and assists the direct infringer.

Videoconferencing: The face-to-face communication between two or more people through computers using web cameras, software, microphones, speakers, and communication lines to transmit compressed audio and video data.

Virtual reality: A computer simulation of reality, using 3D graphics and sound effects, often with user interfaces such as special goggles and gloves, to create a lifelike environment for entertainment, experimentation, and training.

Virus: A program that infects a computer by attaching itself to another program and propagating itself when that program is executed. Files downloaded over the Internet can infect a computer, as may the installation of new software or floppy disks that are infected with viruses. Viruses can destroy files or wipe out an entire hard drive.

VPN (virtual private network): An Internet-based system for information communication and enterprise interaction. A VPN uses the Internet for network connections between people and information sites. However, it includes stringent security mechanisms so that sending private and confidential information is as secure as in a traditional closed system.

VRML (Virtual Reality Markup Language): A programming language used to create the illusion of three-dimensional objects for onscreen virtual reality environments. The computer shows an apparently three-dimensional object from a certain position, then creates the illusion of movement by gradually changing the viewpoint. The objects can be programmed to respond to mouse clicks.

WAN (wide area network): A network in which computers are connected to each other over a long distance, using telephone lines and satellite communications.

WAP (wireless application protocol): A global standard for developing applications over wireless communication networks.

Watermarks: Invisible marks embedded in source data that can be traced to discover illegal copying of digital material.

Web (World Wide Web or WWW):   A hypermedia-based system for browsing Internet sites. It is named the web because it is made up of many sites linked together; users can travel from one site to another by clicking on hyperlinks. Text, graphics, sound, and video can all be accessed with browsers like Mosaic, Netscape, or Internet Explorer.

Web cast: Broadcasting information over the World Wide Web.

Web master: The person who administers a web site. The web master is often also the designer of some or all of the site's pages.

Web publishing: Creating hypertext documents and making them available on the World Wide Web. Web documents can include many different media, and often have text, pictures, animated graphics, sound and movie clips, and interactive forms. Web pages can also contain hyperlinks to other documents, electronic mail links, and search engines.

Web site: A server computer that makes documents available on the World Wide Web. Each web site is identified by a host name.

Whois: An Internet directory service that can be used to find information about users registered on a server, or other information about the network.

WML (Wireless Markup Language):   An XML-based markup language, designed for specifying the content and user interfaces of narrowband wireless devices, such as pagers and cellular phones.

Workstation: A one-person computer more powerful and faster than most personal computers, typically used for graphics, scientific computing, CAD, CAE, and other applications requiring high performance and memory.

World Wide Web Consortium (W3C):   Voluntary standard group that developed the P3P privacy protocol. Companies such as Cisco, IBM, and Microsoft are members of W3C.

Worm: A computer program that can make copies of itself and spread through connected systems, using up resources in affected computers or causing other damage.

XML (eXtensible Markup Language):   A programming language developed by the World Wide Web Consortium. XML allows web developers to create customized tags that will organize and deliver content more efficiently. XML is a metalanguage, containing a set of rules for constructing other markup languages. By allowing people to make up their own tags, it expands the amount and kinds of information that can be provided about the data held in documents.

INDEX

References are to Chapters (Ch.) and section numbers (§), or to the Appendixes.

ABA Cyberspace Jurisdictional Report, 7.03[F][2], 8.02[C][4]
Access contracts, 6.05[A]n436, 6.06[O]
Accrual v. cash accounting, 6.07[F]
ACEC, 6.07[B], 6.07[C][1]
ACPA, 4.03[K][4]
Active web site, 5.12[K][1]n825
Actual authority, 5.02[B][1][a]
Ad-blocking software applications, 2.07[A][6]
ADR, 8.04[B]
ADSL, 1.05[B][2]
Advanced Encryption Standard (AES), 3.02[A][7]
Advanced tunnels, 5.12[J]
Advertising
    ad-blocking software, 2.07[A][6]
    banner ads, 2.07[A][1], 4.03[K][8]
    checklist, 5.12[K][2], 9.02[G]
    children, to, 2.07[B][5]
    claim substantiation, 2.07[B][1][a]
    deception/unfairness, 2.07[B][1][b]
    e-mail marketing, 2.07[E]
    editorial content, 2.07[A][5]
    EU standards, 8.02[G][1]
    false/deceptive, 5.11[B]. *See also*
        False/deceptive advertising
    framing, 2.07[D]
    FTC guidelines, 6.09[K]
    ICC Guidelines, 8.02[G][2]
    insuring advertising injuries, 5.12[I]
    international issues, 8.02[G]
    international regulation, 5.11[B][1][d]
    interstitial advertisements, 2.07[A][2]
    introduction, 2.07[A]
    jurisdictional issues, 7.04[G][2]
    lawyers, 9.02[G][2]
    linking, 2.07[C]
    metatags, 2.07[F]
    misrepresentation, 2.07[B][2]
    NAD, 2.07[B][3]
    pop-up ads, 2.07[A][2]
    search engine priority, 2.07[A][5]
    web page sponsorship, 2.07[A][3]
Advisory Commission on Economic Commerce (ACEC), 6.07[B], 6.07[C][1]
Aegis Internet Insurance, 9.05[D][2]
Agency, 5.02[B][1]
Alternative dispute resolution (ADR), 8.04[B]
American International Group, 9.03[D][1]
Andean Pact countries, 8.01[B][3]n59
Anomaly, 3.03n216
ANSI X12, 6.02[A][2]
Antispam statutes, 5.01, 5.03[E]
Anticybersquatting Consumer Protection Act (ACPA), 4.03[K][4]
Antivirus programs, 10.03[E][2]
Antivirus protection, 3.06[E]
Apparent authority, 5.02[B][1][b]
Application gateway, 3.02[A][4][b]
Application service providers (ASPs), 8.04[C][6]
Arbitrary marks, 4.03[B][1][b][ii]
Arbitration, 8.04[B]
Arbitration clauses, 6.09[B]
Asportation, 5.11[B][3][c]n694
ASPs, 8.04[C][6]
Assault and battery, 5.03[A]
ATM card, 6.08[A][2]
Attorney
    advertising, 9.02[G][2]
    role of (checklist), 9.02[M][8]
Attribution procedures, 6.03[E][5]

Auction disputes, 9.04[B][2][a]
Author's tips. *See* Preventive law pointers
AUTOEXEC.BAT, 3.02[A][3]n84
Automated teller machine (ATM) card, 6.08[A][2]
Availability, 3.02[A][3]n80
Avoidable consequences, 5.08[B][1]

B2B models, 1.04[G], 6.02[A]
B2C models, 6.02[B]
B2G models, 6.02[C]
Back Orifice, 3.03[E]
Backdoor key, 4.02[G][2]
Backup, 3.02[A][1]
Bank loans, 2.03[A][4]
Banking card, 6.08[A][2]
Banner ads, 2.07[A][1], 4.03[K][8]
Basic tunnels, 5.12[J]
Bastion host, 3.02[A][4][c]
Battery, 5.03[A]
BBB, 9.04[B][2]
BBBOnline, 8.02[E]
BBS, 1.04[B]
Bedworth, Paul, 3.02[A][5]
Berne Convention, 8.02[B][2], 8.02[B][4][a][i][A]
Better Business Bureau (BBB), 9.04[B][2]
Bilateral contract, 6.04[B]
Biometric systems, 3.02[A][6]
Blocking software, 7.04[D], 10.04[B][8]
Blurring, 4.03[E][2][a][i]
BorderGuard, 3.02[B]
Breach of confidence, 4.04[A][2][b]
Breach of fiduciary duty, 5.04[D]
Bridges, 3.02[A][2]
Browser-side risks, 3.02[A][1]
Browsewrap agreements, 6.04[A][2][c]
Brussels Convention, 7.03[H][1]
Brussels Regulation, 7.03[H][3], 8.02[C][3]
Bubble Boy, 5.05[B]
Buffer flow attacks, 3.03[D]
Bugs/misconfiguration problems, 3.02[A][1]
Bulletin boards, 1.04[B]
Business defamation, 5.04[E]
Business plan (e-business model), Appendix A
Business organization, form. *See* Choice of business entity

Business-to-business (B2B) models, 1.04[G], 6.02[A]
Business-to-consumer (B2C) models, 6.02[B]
Business-to-government (B2G) models, 6.02[C]
Buy-side procurement, 1.04[H]n109

C corporation, 2.02[D][3][a]
CA, 6.03[E][3]
C2C models, 6.02[D]
Caching, 4.02[G][1][b]
Call-back protocol, 3.02[A][3]
Cash vs. accrual accounting, 6.07[F]
ccTLDs, 4.03[K][2], 8.02[B][4][c][ii][C]
Cease and desist letter, 2.08[D]
Central processing unit (CPU), 6.05[C][2]n470
CERT, 3.06[I], 9.02[M][5]
CERT/CC, 3.06[B]
Certicam, 3.02[E][1]
Certificate authority (CA), 3.02[A][10], 6.03[E][3]
Certification for Information System Security Professional (Cissp) certification exam, 3.05[D]
Certification mark, 4.03[C][3]
CFAA, 3.05[A][2], 10.02[A][9][d]
CGI scripts, 3.02[A][2]
CGL policies, 9.03[D]
Checklists
    advertisements, 5.12[K][2]
    advertising, 9.02[G]
    attorney advertising, 9.02[G][2]
    chief privacy officer, 5.12[K][11]
    choice of law/forum agreements, 5.12[K][10]
    copyright, 9.02[B][1]
    domain names, 9.02[B][3]
    e-business plans, 9.02[A]
    e-discovery, 5.12[K][12]
        e-mail and Internet usage, 9.02[M].
        See also E-mail and Internet usage
        checklist
    global planning, 9.02[R]
    employment-related torts, 5.12[K][5]
    employment systems, 9.02[K]
    framing, 9.02[B][7]
    information security, 9.02[N]

insurance, 9.03[E]
intentional torts, 5.12[K][3]
jurisdiction, 9.02[C]
jurisdictional risks, 5.12[K][1]
linking, 9.02[B][6]
moral rights, 9.02[B][8]
nondisclosure agreements, 4.04[B][1][a]
online contract formation, 9.02[I]
other terms/conditions, 5.12[K][9]
patents, 9.02[B][4]
payment systems, 9.02[J]
performance and remedies, 9.02[I]
privacy, 9.02[D]
privacy-based torts, 5.12[K][7]
privacy concerns, 5.12[K][8]
publication-based torts, 5.12[K][4]
regulatory issues, 9.02[L]
taxation, 9.02[H]
terms and conditions of use, 9.02[O]
third-party content, 9.02[E]
TOC agreement, 9.02[O]
torts, 9.02[F]
torts and customers, 5.12[K][6]
trade secrets, 9.02[B][5]
trademarks, 9.02[B][2]
UCITA, 9.02[P]
warranties, 9.02[I]
warranties checklist, 9.02[I]
web design and hosting, 9.02[I]
Chernobyl, 3.03[E]
Chief privacy officer, 5.12[K][11]
Children, advertising to, 2.07[B][5]
Children's Online Personal Protection Act
(COPPA), 2.07[B][5], 5.11[A],
6.03[A][2], 10.04
Children's Online Privacy Protection Rule,
6.03[A][2]
CHIPS, 6.08[A][3][b]
Choice of business entity
C corporation, 2.02[D][3][a]
corporation, 2.02[D][3]
general partnership, 2.02[D][2][a]
limited liability company, 2.02[D][3][c]
limited liability partnership, 2.02[D][2][c]
limited partnership, 2.02[D][2][b]
partnership, 2.02[D][2]
professional corporation, 2.02[D][3][d]
S corporation, 2.02[D][3][b]
sole proprietorship, 2.02[D][1]

Choice of forum, 5.12[K][10], 6.05[C][4],
6.09[E]
Choice of forum clauses, 6.03[H], 7.04[F] ,
8.04[C][13]
Choice of law, 5.12[K][10], 6.03[G],
6.05[C][4], 6.09[E], 7.02[C]
Choice of law clauses, 7.01[A][3], 7.04[F]
Chubb Technology Insurance Group,
9.03[D][2]
CISG, 8.02[I][1], [5], 8.04[C][5]
Cissp certification exam, 3.05[D]
Civil liability
checklists, 5.12[K]
corporate liability, 10.02[A][10]
employer liability. See Employer liability
immunities, 5.10[A]
negligence, 5.08. See also Negligence
overview, 5.01
preventive law pointers, 5.12
privacy, 5.07. See also Privacy
privileges, 5.10[B]
regulation. See Regulation
strict liability, 5.02[A][3], 5.09
torts. See Torts
Classical world system theory, 8.01[B][1]
ClickforCover.com, 9.05[D][9]
Clickfree agreements, 6.04[A][2][c]
Clickthrough agreements, 6.09[J]
Clickwrap agreements, 6.04[A][2][c], 6.09[C]
Clipper Chips, 1.02[B], 3.02[A][1]
Coined trademark, 4.03[B][1][b][i]
Cold site, 3.02[A][1][b]
Collective mark, 4.03[C][2]
Collective work, 4.02[C][9]
Commercial disparagement, 5.11[B][3][b]
Commercial general liability (CGL) policies,
9.03[D]
Communication theory, 7.02[C]
Communications Decency Act, 5.02[B][2][a]
Community trademark (CTM), 8.04[C][1]
Comparative negligence, 5.08[D][2]
Complete Insurance, 9.05[D][6]
Complex gateways, 3.02[A][4][c]
Compulsory license, 6.05[C][1]
Computer bulletin boards (BBS), 1.04[B]
Computer crimes, 3.03[C]
Computer Fraud and Abuse Act (CFAA),
3.05[A][2], 10.02[A][9][d]
Computer hardware, 6.05[C][2]n470

Computer malpractice, 5.09[B]
Computer networks/protocols, 1.04[E]
Computer viruses, 3.03[E], 5.05[B], 5.12[C]
Confidential information, 4.04[A]
Confidentiality agreement, 10.07[F]
Conflict of laws, 7.02[C]
Consideration, 6.04[B]
Consumer expectations test,
    5.02[A][3][a][ii]n89
Consumer-to-consumer (C2C) models,
    6.02[D]
Content and interactive service agreements,
    6.04[A][2][b]
Content licenses
    acceptance testing, 4.02[J][6][d]
    choice of law, 4.02[J][6][e]
    forum/dispute resolution, 4.02[J][6][e]
    franchise rules, 4.02[J][6][f]
    granting clause, 4.02[J][6][a]
    payment/royalty reports, 4.02[J][6][b]
    sample agreement, 4.02[J][a], 9.02[Q][4]
    warranties/infringement, 4.02[J][6][c]
Contract, 6.04. See also Electronic contracts
Contract of adhesion, 6.04[A][2][a]
Contributory negligence, 5.08[D][1]
Controversial web sites, 10.02[A][9][b]
Convention on Contracts for the International
    Sale of Goods (CISG), 8.02[I][1], [5],
    8.04[C][5]
COPPA, 2.07[B][5], 5.11[A], 6.03[A][2],
    10.04
COPS, 3.02[A][13]
Copyright
    application forms, 4.02[J][2], [4]
    checklists, 9.02[B][1], 9.02[Q][1][a]
    collective work, 4.02[C][9]
    constitutional/statutory authority, 4.02[B]
    content licenses, 4.02[J][6]. See also
        Content licenses
    contributory infringement, 4.02[D][2]
    Copyright Clearance Center, 9.05[C]
    defenses, 4.02[E]
    derivative works, 4.02[C][6]
    direct infringement, 4.02[D][1]
    disclaimers, 4.02[J][8]
    DMCA, 4.02[G]. See also DMCA
    EU directive, 8.02[B][4][a][i][C]
    exclusive rights, 4.02[C][4]
    fair use, 4.02[E][1], [2]

first sale doctrine, 4.02[C][5]
fixation, 4.02[C][4][c]
foreign published works, 4.06[B]
framing, 4.02[F][4]
global issues, 8.02[B][4][a]
infringement, 4.02[D], 9.05[A]
Internet searches, 4.02[J][5]
ISP liability, 4.02[G][1]
joint works, 4.02[C][2], [10]
linking, 4.02[F], 4.02[J][7]
notice, 4.02[C][7], [J][1]
online music, 4.02[C][11]
originality, 4.02[C][4][b]
overview, 4.01, 4.02[A]
registration, 4.02[J][2]-[4]
renewal/extension, 4.02[C][3]
software, 4.02[I]
SPA e-police, 3.05[B][3]
term, 4.02[C][1]
treaties, 8.02[B][4][a][i]
vicarious infringement, 4.02[D][3]
what is protected, 4.02[C][4][a]
work made for hire, 4.02[C][8]
Copyright and management systems,
    4.02[G][2]
Copyright notice, 4.02[C][7], [J][1]
Core countries, 8.01[B][3]
Corporate document retention policies,
    10.03[C]
Corporate espionage, 3.03[A][1]
Corporate liability
    civil liability, 10.02[A][10]
    crimes, 10.02[A][9]
Corporation, 2.02[D][3]
Council of the Union, 8.02[A]
Country-specific domain names, 2.06
CPO, 5.12[K][11]
CPU, 6.05[C][2]n470
Crawlers, 1.05[D]
Credit cards, 6.08[A][1]
Criteria-based authentication statutes,
    6.03[E][2][b]
Cryptography, 3.02[A][7], [8]
CSS, 4.02[G][4]n225
CTEA, 4.02[C][1]
CTM mark, 8.04[C][1]
Cultural/linguistic customization, 8.03[D]
Customized security products, 3.02[D]
CyberCash, 6.08[C]

Cybercrime, 8.02[N]
Cyberextortion, 3.03[B]
CyberGuard Firewall, 3.02[B]
CyberNotaries, 6.03[E][3]
Cyberscalpel, 1.05[F][1]n127
Cybersquatting, 4.03[K][6]
Cyberstalking, 5.03[A], 5.05[C]

D&O insurance, 9.03[C]
Daemons, 3.02[A][1][a]n49
Dark side hacker, 3.03[A]n261
Data diddling, 3.01n10
Data encryption standard (DES), 3.02[A][7]
Data Protection Directive, 8.04[C][12]
Debit cards, 6.08[A][2]
DDoS attack, 3.01, 3.03[D], 5.08[A]
Decentralized file-sharing system,
    4.02[C][11]
Deceptive Mail Prevention and Enforcement
    Act, 1.02[B]
Decryption, 3.02[A][9], 6.03[E][4]
Dedicated line, 1.04[D]
Deep linking, 4.02[F][2]
Defamation
    business, 5.04[E]
    defenses, 5.06[A][3]
    e-mail, 10.02[A][6]
    generally, 5.06[A]
    ISPs, 5.06[A][1][c]
    plaintiffs, 5.06[A][1][a]
    preventive law pointer, 5.12[D]
    public officials/public figures,
        5.06[A][1][b]
    retraction statutes, 5.06[A][2]
Defective software, 5.09[B]
Delicts, 8.02[F]
Denial-of-service (DOS) attacks, 3.03[A][3],
    3.03[D], 3.06[D]
Department of Commerce Internet use policy,
    App. 10-1
Derivative works, 4.02[C][6]
Demon, 3.02[A][1][a]n49
DES, 3.02[A][7]
Design defect, 5.02[A][3][a][ii]
Descriptive trademark, 4.03[B][1][b][iv]
Digital Millennium Copyright Act. See DMCA
Digital signature
    approval, 6.03[E][1][c]

authentication, 6.03[E][1][a]
ceremony, 6.03[E][1][b]
certificate authority, 6.03[E][3]
efficiency/logistics, 6.03[E][1][d]
generally, 3.02[A][9], 6.03[D], 6.04[C][2]
statutes, 6.03[E][2]
technology, 6.03[E][4]
Digital signature statutes, 6.03[E][2]
Dilution, 4.03[E][2], 4.03[K][5][b], [c],
    4.03[L][1][a][iv]
Direct linking, 2.07[C][2][a]
Direct taxes, 6.07[A]
Directed broadcast attack, 3.03[D]
Directors and officers liability insurance,
    9.03[C]
Disaster contingency plan, 3.03[I]
Disclaimers
    copyright, 4.02[J][8]
    preventive law pointer, 6.09[G]
    sample (web site), 2.08[A]
    warranties, 6.05[G][2][e]
Discovery, 5.12[K][12], 10.03[C], 10.07[D]
Discrimination, 5.03[C]
Distributed denial of service (DDoS) attack,
    3.01, 3.03[D], 5.08[A]
Distributed smurfing attacks, 3.03[D]
DMCA
    caching, 4.02[G][1][b]
    case law, 4.02[G][4]
    copyright and management systems,
        4.02[G][2]
    generally, 8.02[B][4][a][i][B]
    ISP liability, 4.02[G][1]
    libraries, 4.02[G][3]
    third-party links, 2.07[C][2][b]
Domain name
    ACPA, 4.03[K][4]
    case law, 4.03[K][5]
    checklists, 9.02[B][3], 9.03[Q][1][d]
    country level domain name disputes,
        8.02[B][4][c][ii][C]
    cybersquatting, 4.03[K][6]
    dispute resolution, 4.03[K][3],
        8.02[B][4][c][ii]
    disputes, 2.06[B][4]
    expiration, 2.06[B][4][e]
    generally, 2.06
    infringement, 2.06[B][4][a], [b]
    international issues, 8.02[B][4][c]

Domain name *(contd.)*
    levels (TLD/SLD), 2.06
    management of names/addresses,
        4.03[K][2]
    metatags, 4.03[K][7]
    preventive law pointer, 8.04[C][2]
    purchasing a name, 2.06[B][4][c]
    registering, 2.06[A], [B][2], 4.03[K][1], [2]
    registering in another domain,
        2.06[B][4][d]
    registering multiple names, 2.06[B][3]
    search engines, and, 2.06[B][4][f]
    trademarks, 2.06[B][1]
    UDRP policy/rules, 4.03[K][3],
        8.02[B][4][c][ii][B]
    value, 2.06[B]
Domain name service (DNS), 4.03[K][1]n493
Domestic Internet disputes, 7.03[J]
DOS attacks, 3.03[A][3], 3.03[D], 3.06[D]
DOS operating systems, 3.02[A][3]
*Dot Com Disclosures: Information About
        Online Advertising*, 5.11[A]
DSA, 3.02[A][7]
Dual-homed host, 3.02[A][4][c]

E-business, 1.01
E-business models
    business-to-business (B2B), 6.02[A]
    business-to-consumer (B2C), 6.02[B]
    business-to-government (B2G), 6.02[C]
    consumer-to-consumer (C2C), 6.02[D]
    government-to-consumer (G2C), 6.02[E]
E-business plan, 9.02[A], Appendix A
E-cash, 6.08[C]
E-commerce, 1.01
E-commerce laws. *See* Electronic contracts
E-delinquents, 3.03[A][3]
E-discovery, 5.12[K][12], 10.03[C],
        10.07[D]
E-mail. *See also* E-mail and Internet usage
    generally, 1.04[A]
    marketing, 2.07[E]
    opt-in vs. opt-out, 2.07[E][2]
    preventive law pointer, 5.12[F]
    retention of, 10.03[C]
    risks, 10.02
    smoking gun, 5.12[K][12], 10.03[C]
    spam, 5.03[E], 5.11[B][1][c]

    unsolicited, 2.07[E][3], 5.03[E],
        5.11[B][1][c], 6.03[A][3]
E-mail and Internet usage
    checklist, 9.02[M]
    defamation, 10.02[A][6]
    ex-employee access, 10.02[A][2], 10.07[A]
    fraud, 10.02[A][7]
    hostile workplace, 10.02[A][1]
    identity theft, 10.02[A][4]
    independent contractors, 10.02[B][2][b]
    intellectual property infringement,
        10.02[A][8]
    message filters, 10.04[B][12][b]
    monitoring of employees, 10.03[D],
        10.04[B][8], 10.06[B], 10.06[C][2]
    netiquette, 10.04[B][12][d]
    obscene materials, 10.02[A][9][b]
    off-hours usage, 10.06[C][1]
    overview, 10.01
    policy. *See* E-mail and Internet usage
        policies
    pornography, 10.02[A][9][b]
    preventive law pointers, 10.07
    risk management, 10.03. *See also* Risk
        management
    spell checks, 10.04[B][12][c]
    standard message signatures,
        10.04[B][12][a]
    telecommuters, 10.02[B][2][a]
    trade secrets, 10.02[A][5]
    unlawful interception of electronic
        communication, 10.02[A][9][c]
E-mail and Internet usage checklist
    disaster recovery, 9.02[M][5]
    e-mail monitoring checklist,
        9.02[M][7]
    generally, 9.02[M][1]
    information security and usage procedures,
        9.02[M][3]
    internal corporate investigations,
        9.02[M][6]
    role of counsel, 9.02[M][8]
    systems administrators, 9.02[M][7]
    training and education, 9.02[M][4]
    usage disclosures, 9.02[M][2]
E-mail and Internet usage policies
    conscious delay, 10.04[B][11]
    contact person, 10.04[B][13]
    copying/publishing, 10.04[B][6]

Department of Commerce Internet use policy, App. 10-1
implementation, 10.04[B][12], 10.06
legal audits, 10.04[A][1]
legal autopsies/near misses, 10.04[A][2]
monitoring of e-mail/Internet usage, 10.04[B][8]
other clauses, 10.04[B][10]
permitted users, 10.04[B][5]
purpose/background of policy, 10.04[B][3]
sample policy, 10.05
scope, 10.04[B][4]
table of contents, 10.04[B][2]
telecommuters, 10.04[B][9]
third-party rights, 10.04[B][7]
title, 10.04[B][1]
web site activities/jurisdiction, 10.04[A][3]
E-mail flooding, 3.01n13
E-mail marketing, 2.07[E]
E-mail notice, 10.07[E]
E-mail smoking guns, 5.12[K][12], 10.03[C]
E-mail threat, 5.03[A]
E-mailbox rule, 6.04[B][1]
E-Sign, 6.03[E]
East West Insurance, 9.03[D][3]
Eavesdropping, 3.02[A][1]
eBay, 3.05[B][1]
ECC, 3.02[E][1]
ECHELON, 3.03[A][1]
Economic Espionage Act (EEA), 3.05[A][2], 4.04[A][3], 8.02[N][1]
Economic loss, 5.02[A][3][b]
ECPA, 3.05[A][1], 10.02[A][9][c]
EDI, 1.04[H]n108
EDIFACT, 6.02[A][2]
EEA, 3.05[A][2], 4.04[A][3], 8.02[N][1]
Effects test, 7.03[D]
eHackerInsurance.com, 9.05[D][12]
802.11, 1.05[F][5]n133
Electro-hippies collectives, 3.03[A][4]
Electronic authentication initiatives, 6.03[E][6]
Electronic bulletin boards, 1.04[B]
Electronic checks, 6.08[D]
Electronic commerce, 1.04[G]
Electronic Communications Privacy Act (ECPA), 3.05[A][1], 10.02[A][9][c]
Electronic contracts
    attribution procedure, 6.03[E][5]
    checklists, 9.02[I]
    children's online privacy protection rule, 6.03[A][2]
    choice of forum clauses, 6.03[H]
    choice of law, 6.03[G], 6.05[C][4], 6.09[E]
    CISG, 8.02[I][1], [5], 8.04[C][5]
    digital signatures. See Digital signatures
    e-business models, 6.02. See also E-business models
    e-mailbox rule, 6.04[B][1]
    E-Sign, 6.03[E]
    electronic authentication initiatives, 6.03[E][6]
    formation of contract, 6.04[A]
    FTC, 6.03[A]
    industry standards, 6.03[B]
    legal proof issues, 6.04[C]
    License agreements, 6.06. See also License agreements
    Magnuson-Moss Act, 6.03[A][1], 6.09[A]
    payment systems, 6.08. See also Payment systems
    preventive law pointers, 6.09
    privacy, 6.03[F]
    taxation, 6.05. See also Taxation
    telemarketing sales rule, 6.03[A][3]
    UCC. See UCC
    UCITA, 6.05. See also UCITA
    UETA, 6.04[D]. See also UETA
    UNCITRAL Model Law, 8.02[I][1]
Electronic data interchange (EDI), 6.02[A][1], [2], 6.04[A][1]
Electronic discovery, 5.12[K][12], 10.07[D]
Electronic graffiti, 3.03[A][3]
Electronic negotiable instruments, 6.08[A][3]
Electronic Privacy Information Center (EPIC), 3.03[K]
Electronic self-help remedy, 6.05[L][7]
Electronic Signatures in Global and National Commerce Act (E-Sign), 6.03[E]
Electronic stalking, 5.03[A], 5.05[C]
Elliptic curve cryptography (ECC), 3.02[E][1]
Employer liability
    checklists, 5.12[K][5]
    direct liability, 5.02[B][1]
    imputed liability, 5.02[B][2]
    independent contractors, 5.02[B][2][b]
    joint tortfeasors, 5.02[B][3]
    telecommuting, 5.11[C]

Employer liability *(contd.)*
  vicarious liability, 5.02[B][2]
Employment issues, 8.02[L], 9.02[K]
Encryption, 3.02[A][7], [11]
Enfopol 38, 8.02[E]
Enron, 10.01
Ensurancebusiness.com, 9.05[D][9]
Entrepreneurs in residence, 2.03[A][6][c]
EPC, 8.02[B][4][d][ii]
EPIC, 3.03[K]
Ethical hackers, 3.03[A]n261, 270
European Commission, 8.02[A]
European Council, 8.02[A]
European Parliament, 8.02[A]
European Patent Convention (EPC),
  8.02[B][4][d][ii]
European Union
  advertising standards, 8.02[G][1]
  Article 81 of EC Treaty, 8.04[C][11][a]
  Article 82 of EC Treaty, 8.04[C][11][b]
  competition concerns, 8.02[A]
  competition law, 8.04[C][11]
  Copyright Directive, 8.02[B][4][a][i][C]
  Cybercrime Convention, 8.02[N][3]
  Data Protection Directive, 8.04[C][12]
  Database Directive, 8.02[B][7]
  Distance Selling Directive, 8.02[I][3]
  Electronic Commerce Directive,
    8.02[I][4]
  Electronic Signature Directive, 8.02[I][2]
  jurisdiction, 7.03[F][1], 7.03[H][3]
  major legal institutions, 8.02[A]
  proposed Directive on Financial Services,
    8.02[P]
  protection of personal data, 5.07[D]
  Regulation on Jurisdiction and Judgments,
    8.03[C][2]
  VAT, 6.07[I][1], 8.02[H]
Evolution of Internet law, 1.02[B]
Export controls on encryption, 3.02[A][11]
Export/import, 8.03[B], 8.04[C][8]
Extranet, 1.04[D], 3.02[A][1][a]

Face recognition, 3.02[A][6]
Failure to warn, 5.02[A][3][a][iii]
Fair use
  copyright, 4.02[E][1], [2]

trademarks, 4.03[G][2]
False/deceptive advertising
  conversion, 5.11[B][3][c]
  FTC, 5.11[B][1][a]
  little FTC acts, 5.11[B][1][b], 5.11[B][2]
  private attorneys general, 5.11[B][2]
  RICO, 5.11[B][3]
  section 5(a) of FTCA, 5.11[B][1][a][i]
  spam, 5.11[B][1][c]
  trade libel/commercial disparagement,
    5.11[B][3][b]
  UDTPA, 5.11[B][1][b], 5.11[B][2]
  unfair competition, 5.11[B][3][a]
False light, 5.07[B][4]
Fanciful marks, 4.03[B][1][b][i]
Federal Communications Commission (FCC),
  5.11[G]
Federal/local grant programs, 2.03[A][2]
Federal Trade Commission, 2.07[B][1]. *See
  also* FTC
Federal Trademark Dilution Act (FTDA),
  4.03[E][2][a]
Federal Wiretap Statute, 8.02[N][2]
FEDWIRE, 6.08[A][3][b]
Fibre channel, 3.02[A][1][b]
Fiduciary duty, 5.04[D]
File server, 1.04[D]
File Transfer Protocol (FTP), 1.04[E][3]
Fingerprint authentication, 3.02[A][6]
Firewall
  administrators, 3.02[A][4][e]
  application gateway, 3.02[A][4][b]
  host-based, 3.02[A][4]
  hybrid, 3.02[A][4][c]
  mass-market product, as, 3.02[B]
  packet filters, 3.02[A][4][a]
  problems, 3.02[A][4][d]
  proxy server, 3.02[A][4][b]
  router-based, 3.02[A][4]
FireWall-1, 3.02[B]
First sale doctrine, 4.02[C][5],
  6.04[A][2][a]
Fixation, 4.02[C][4][c]
Flaming, 5.03[A]
Foreign taxpayers, 6.07[A]
Forgers, 3.03[H]
Form of business entity, 6.07[J]. *See also*
  Choice of business entity

Forum non conveniens, 7.04[C]

Forum selection clauses, 6.03[H], 7.04[F],
    8.04[C][13]

Framing
    advantages, 2.07[D][1]
    checklists, 9.02[B][7], 9.02[Q][1][g]
    copyright, 4.02[F][4]
    legal issues, 2.07[D][2]
    other web sites, 2.07[D][3][b]
    protecting your web site, 2.07[D][3][a]

Fraud, 5.04[A], 10.02[A][7]

FTC
    adjudication, 5.11[A][5][a][iv]
    advertising, 2.07[B][1], 6.09[K]
    civil investigation demands,
        5.11[A][5][a][ii]
    consumer protection powers, 5.11[A][5]
    COPPA rule, 6.03[A][2], 10.04
    enforcement activity, 5.11[A][5][a][vi]
    false/deceptive advertising, 5.11[B][1][a]
    generally, 5.11[A], 6.03[A]
    Gramm-Leach-Bliley Act, 5.11[A][3]
    information policy, 5.11[A][1]
    online profiling, 5.11[A][2]
    rulemaking, 5.11[A][5][a][v]
    section 6(b) powers, 5.11[A][5][a][iii]
    subpoena power, 5.11[A][5][a][i]
    telemarketing sales rule, 6.03[A][3]
    unfairness doctrine, 5.11[B][1][a][i]
    web site, 5.11[A]

FTDA, 4.03[E][2][a]

FTP, 1.04[E][3]

Full warranty, 6.03[A][1]

Functional trade dress, 4.03[C][5]

Funding a startup
    bank loans, 2.03[A][4]
    corporate funds, 2.03[A][5]
    federal/local grant programs, 2.03[A][2]
    friends and family, 2.03[A][1]
    SBA, 2.03[A][3]

venture capital, 2.03[A][6]

G2C models, 6.02[E]

Gambling, 5.11[C]

Garden leave, 8.02[L]

Gateway modes, 3.02[A][2]

Gateways, 3.02[A][2]

General jurisdiction, 7.02[A]

General partnership, 2.02[D][2][a]

General public figure, 5.06[A][1][b]

General statutes, 6.03[E][2][b]

Generic marks, 4.03[B][1][b][v]

Global e-business legal planning, 9.02[R]

Global issues. *See* International issues

Global jurisdictional issues. *See* Jurisdictional
    issues

Global legal marketplace, 8.01

Going online
    benefits of, 2.02[C]
    domain names. *See* Domain names
    management support, 2.02[B]
    preparation, 2.02[A]
    web site. *See* Web site

Government-to-consumer (G2C) models,
    6.02[E]

Gramm-Leach-Bliley Act (GLBA), 3.03[K],
    5.11[A][3]

Grant programs, 2.03[A][2]

gTLDs, 4.03[K][2], 8.02[B][4][c][ii][C]

Hacker, 3.03[A]

Hacker insurance, 3.06[C]

Hacktivism, 3.03[A][4]

Hague Convention on Jurisdiction and
    Foreign Judgments, 7.03[H][4],
    8.02[C][1]

Hand geometry, 3.02[A][6]

Hardware, 6.05[C][2]n470

Health Insurance Portability & Accountability
    Act (HIPAA), 3.03[K], 5.11[A][4]

History, 1.02[B]

Hoaxbusters, 3.05[B][2]n493

Hold harmless clauses, 3.06[G], 10.03[A][1]

Home page, 1.05[D]n121

Host-based firewalls, 3.02[A][4]

Hostile workplace, 5.03[C], 10.02[A][1]

Hot site, 3.02[A][1][b]

HTML, 1.04[F]

HTTP, 1.04[E]n72

Hybrid gateways, 3.02[A][4][c]

Hybrid virus-worm infections, 3.03[F]

Hyperlinking. *See* Linking

Hypertext Markup Language (HTML),
    1.04[F]

IANA, 4.03[K][2]
ICANN, 2.06, 2.06[B][2], 4.03[K][2]
ICC, 6.03[B][2], 8.02[G][2]
ICC commercial crime bureau, 3.05[B][4]
ICC cybercrime unit, 8.02[N][1]
Identity systems, 1.05[F][6]
Identity theft, 10.02[A][4]
IDS, 3.03[D]
Immunities, 5.10[A]
Impact analysis, 2.02[B]
Implied warranty of merchantability,
    6.03[A][1], 6.05[G][2][b]
Import/export, 8.03[B], 8.04[C][8]
Impostors, 3.03[H]
Improper means test, 4.04[A][1][c]
Imputed liability, 5.02[B][2]
In rem jurisdiction, 7.02[D], 7.04[B]
Indemnification, 10.03[A][1]
Indemnification checklist, 9.02[Q][1][h]
Identity theft, 5.05[A]
Independent contractors, 5.02[B][2][b],
    10.02[B][2][b], 10.07[C]
Indirect taxes, 6.07[A]
Industry standards, 5.08[B][1], 6.03[B],
    8.02[Q]
Inevitable disclosure, 4.04[B][5]
Information security checklist, 9.02[N]
Information security systems, 3.04
Infringement
    copyright, 4.02[D], [E], 4.02[J][6][c],
        9.05[A]
    domain names, 4.03[K][5][a]
    e-mail, 10.02[A][8]
    patents, 4.05[E]
    trademark, 4.03[E], 9.05[A]
Instant messaging, 3.03[A][2]
Insurance
    advertising injuries, 5.12[I]
    CGL policies, 9.03[D]
    checklist, 9.03[E]
    directors & officers, 9.03[C]
    generally, 9.03[A], [B]
    international business, 8.03[C]
    Internet insurance companies, 9.03[D],
        9.05[D]
    risk management, 10.03[H]
Insurance Information Institute, 9.05[D][7]
InsuranceSTOP.com, 9.05[D][13]
InsureTrust.com, 9.03[D][4], 9.05[D][1]

Integrated Services Digital Network (ISDN),
    1.05[B][3]
Integrity of data, 3.03[G]
Intellectual property
    checklists, 9.02[B], 9.02[Q][2]
    copyright. *See* Copyright
    globalization, 4.06
    international issues, 8.02[B]
    jurisdictional issues, 7.04[G][6]
    overview, 4.01
    patents. *See* Patents
    trade secrets. *See* Trade secrets
    trademarks. *See* Trademarks
    WIPO, 4.06[A]
Intentional infliction of emotional distress,
    5.03[B]
International Information Systems Security
    Certification Consortium [(ISC)2],
    3.05[D]
Intentional interference with business
    contracts, 5.04[C]
Intentional torts, 5.02[A][1], 5.03
Interactivity, 7.03[E]
Interference with business contracts, 5.04[C]
International Chamber of Commerce (ICC),
    6.03[B][2], 8.02[G][2]
International Internet disputes, 7.03[G],
    7.03[H][4]
International Internet Surf Day, 5.11[F][2][c]
International issues
    advertising, 8.02[G]
    consumer protection, 8.02[O]
    cybercrime, 8.02[N]
    delicts, 8.02[F]
    dispute resolution, 8.04[A], [B]
    domain names, 8.02[B][4][c]
    employment issues, 8.02[L]
    Europe. *See* European Union
    financial services, 8.02[P]
    import/export, 8.03[B], 8.04[C][8]
    insuring against cyber risks, 8.03[C]
    intellectual property, 8.02[B]
    jurisdiction, 8.02[C]
    linguistic/cultural customization, 8.03[D]
    linking, 8.02[B][6]
    moral rights, 8.02[B][8]
    most favored nation status, 8.02[B][3]
    national treatment, 8.02[B][2]
    online contract formation, 8.02[I]

orders for goods and services, 8.03[A]
payment systems, 8.02[K]
preventive law pointers, 8.04[C]
privacy, 8.02[D]
products liability, 8.02[J]
regulatory issues, 8.02[M]
standards, 8.02[Q]
taxation, 6.07[G]-[H], 8.02[H]
third-party content, 8.02[E]
torts, 8.02[F]
withholding tax, 6.07[G]
International jurisdictional issues, 7.03[F],
    8.02[C]. *See also* Jurisdictional issues
International Shoe, 7.02[B][1]
International standards, 8.02[Q]
International taxation, 6.07[G]-[H], 8.02[H]
Internet, 1.03
Internet advertising, 9.02[G]. *See also*
    Advertising
Internet banking, 6.08[B]
Internet connections
    ADSL, 1.05[B][2]
    cable modems, 1.05[B][2]
    ISDN, 1.05[B][3]
    modem, 1.05[B][1]
    T1/T3 lines, 1.05[B][4]
Internet connections satellite, 1.05[E][6]
Internet copyright searches, 4.02[J][5]
Internet Corporation for Assigned Numbers
    and Names (ICANN), 2.06,
    2.06[B][2], 4.03[K][2]
Internet-enabled devices, 1.05[F][2]
Internet gambling, 5.11[C]
Internet insurance companies, 9.03[D],
    9.05[D]
Internet payment systems. *See* Payment
    systems
Internet publicity, 5.06[B]
Internet-related patents, 4.05[F][2]
Internet resources (for lawyers), Appendix B
    Internet roadmap
    impact analysis, 2.02[B]
    legal risks, 2.02[B]
    marketing and sales objectives, 2.02[B]
    measuring success, 2.02[B]
    proof of concept, 2.02[B]
Internet Scanner, 3.02[A][13]
Internet security. *See* Security
Internet service providers. *See* ISPs

Internet stock fraud, 5.11[F][2][b]
Internet Tax Freedom Act (ITFA), 6.07[B],
    6.07[C][1]
Internet taxation, 6.07. *See also* Taxation
Internet2, 1.05[F][1]
Internetins.com, 9.05[D][11]
InterNIC, 2.06[B][2]
InterNIC Registrar Directory, 4.03[K][1]n493
Interstitial advertising, 2.07[A][2]
Intranet, 1.04[D], 3.02[A][1][a]
Intrusion detection system (IDS), 3.03[D]
Invisible infringement, 4.03[K][7]
IP number/address, 2.06
IP spoofing, 3.01n8
(ISC)2, 3.05[D]
ISDN, 1.05[B][3]
ISPs
    contracts, 6.04[A][2][b]
    copyright liability, 4.02[G][1]
    defamation, 5.06[A][1][c]
    generally, 1.05[A]
    imputed liability, 5.02[B][2][a]
    negligence, 5.08[D][4]
ITFA, 6.07[B], 6.07[C][1]
ITFA moratorium, 6.07[B]

Japan Information Processing Development
    Center (JIPDEC), 8.02[E]
Joint tortfeasors, 5.02[B][3]
Joint works, 4.02[C][2], [10]
Jurisdictional issues
    ABA report, 7.03[F][2], 8.02[C][4]
    ALI/UNIDROIT proposals, 7.01
    Brussels Convention, 7.03[H][1]
    Brussels Regulation, 7.03[H][3],
        8.02[C][3]
    case law, 7.04[G]
    checklists, 5.12[K][1], 9.02[C]
    choice of law, 7.03[K]
    choice of law clauses, 7.01[A][3], 7.04[F]
    conflict of laws, 7.02[C]
    crimes/regulatory activity, 7.04[G][5]
    effects test, 7.03[D]
    EU regulation, 8.02[C][2]
    European Union, 7.03[F][1], 7.03[H][3]
    forum non conveniens, 7.04[C]
    general jurisdiction, 7.02[A]
    Hague Convention, 7.03[H][4], 8.02[C][1]

Jurisdictional issues *(contd.)*
  in rem jurisdiction, 7.02[D], 7.04[B],
    7.04[G][7]
  intellectual property, 7.04[G][6]
  interactivity, 7.03[E]
  international conventions, 7.03[H]
  international issues, 7.03[F], 8.02[C]
  International Shoe, 7.02[B][1]
  long-arm statutes, 7.02[E]
  Lugano Convention, 7.03[H][2]
  minimizing exposure, 7.03[I], 8.04[C][10]
  minimum contacts test, 7.01[C],
    7.02[B][1], 7.04[E]
  online contracts, 7.04[G][4]
  overview, 7.01
  personal jurisdiction, 7.01[B], 7.02,
    7.04[A]
  preventive law pointers, 7.04
  purposeful availment, 7.03[A]-[C]
  reasonableness test, 7.03[E][1]
  relatedness test, 7.03[C][1]
  service of process abroad, 8.02[C][2]
  sliding-scale analysis *(Zippo)*, 7.03[D], [E]
  specific jurisdiction, 7.02[B]
  subject matter jurisdiction, 7.01[A]
  tort-like behavior, 7.04[G][3]
  web page advertisements, 7.04[G][2]

Key words in banner ads, 4.03[K][8]
Kill files, 5.03[A]n161, 10.04[B][8]

LAN, 3.02[A][1][a]
Lawyers
  advertising, 9.02[G][2]
  role of, 9.02[M][8]
Leased line, 1.04[E]n178
Legal audit, 10.04[A][1]. *See also* Checklists,
    Web site intellectual property audit
Letter rogatory, 8.02[C][2]
Lex fori, 7.03[K]
Lex loci delicti, 7.03[K]
Libel, 5.06[A]. *See also* Defamation
Libraries, 4.02[G][3]
License agreements
  access contracts, 6.06[O]
  assignment, 6.06[J]
  confidentiality, 6.06[L]

  disabling devices, 6.06[G]
  export restrictions, 6.06[M]
  granting clause, 6.06[A]
  indemnification, 6.06[I]
  integration/merger clause, 6.06[N]
  licensee's rights, 6.06[K]
  scope, 6.06[C], [D]
  term for payment, 6.06[B]
  termination clause, 6.06[F], 6.09[H]
  updates, 6.06[E]
  warranties, 6.06[H]
Licenses. *See also* Electronic contracts
  anticompetitive conduct, 8.02[A][2]
  contract provisions, 6.06. *See also* License
    agreements
  copyright, 4.02[J][6]. *See also* Content
    licenses
  negotiations, 6.09[F]
  patents, 4.05[F][2][c]
  UCITA, 6.05. *See also* UCITA
  unconscionability, 6.05[E][2]
Likelihood of confusion test, 4.03[E][1]
Limited liability company (LLC),
    2.02[D][3][c], 6.07[J]
Limited liability partnership, 2.02[D][2][c]
Limited partnership, 2.02[D][2][b]
Limited purpose public figure, 5.06[A][1][b]
Limited statutes, 6.03[E][2][b]
Limited warranty, 6.03[A][1]
Linguistic/cultural customization, 8.03[D]
Linking
  checklists, 9.02[B][6], 9.02[Q][1][g]
  copyright, 4.02[F], 4.02[J][7]
  deep, 4.02[F][2]
  direct, 2.07[C][2][a]
  international issues, 8.02[B][6]
  introduction, 2.07[C][1]
  legal implications, 2.07[C][2]
  precautions, 2.07[C][3]
  samples, 2.08[E], [F]
  third-party links, 2.07[C][2][b]
Little FTC acts, 5.11[B][1][b], 5.11[B][2]
LLC, 2.02[D][3][c], 6.07[J]
Local area network (LAN), 3.02[A][1][a]
Local grant programs, 2.03[A][2]
Log files, 3.02[A][13]
Logic bomb, 5.12[C]n800
Long-arm statutes, 7.02[E]
Lugano Convention, 7.03[H][2]

MAC virus, 5.12[C]n795
Macro, 5.12[C]n797
Madrid Protocol, 4.03[H][3]
Magnuson-Moss Act, 6.03[A][1], 6.09[A]
Mailbox rule, 6.04[B][1]
Mailing lists, 1.04[C]
Mainframes, 1.04[F][1]n85
Management/organizational issues, 2.02[B].
    See also Internet roadmap
Manufacturing defect, 5.02[A][3][a][i]
Marketing and sales objectives, 2.02[B]
Marketing through e-mail, 2.07[E]
Mass-market licenses, 6.04[A][2]
Mass-market security products, 3.02[B]
Mass-market transactions, 6.05[A]n433
Megabyte, 1.04[F][4]n87
Melissa, 3.03[E]
Message board, 6.03[E][4]
Metatag, 1.05[D]n124, 2.07[F], 4.03[K][7],
    [L][1]
Metatag binding, 4.03[K][7]
MFN status, 8.02[B][3]
Micro browser, 1.05[F][2]n129
Minimum contacts test, 7.01[C], 7.02[B][1],
    7.04[E]
Mirror image caching, 4.02[G][1][b]
Misappropriation, 5.04[B], 5.07[B][2]
Misconfiguration problems, 3.02[A][1]
Misrepresentation, 5.04[A]
Modem, 1.05[B][1]
Monitoring of employees, 10.03[D],
    10.04[B][8], 10.06[B], 10.06[C][2]
Moral rights, 4.02[H][1], 8.02[B][8],
    9.02[B][8]
Most favored nation (MFN) status,
    8.02[B][3]
Multi-homed host, 3.02[A][4][c]
Music, 4.02[C][11]

NAD, 2.07[B][3]
NAP, 1.04n152
Napster, 1.02[B], 4.02[C][11], 4.02[D],
    [D][3]
NASD online regulation, 5.11[F][2][d]
National advertising division (NAD),
    2.07[B][3]
National treatment, 8.02[B][2]
Natural disasters, 3.03[I]

Navigating the Web, 1.05[D]
NDA, 2.03[A][5], 4.04[A][4], 4.04[B][1],
    10.03[A][2], 10.07[C][1]
Negligence
    assumption of risk, 5.08[D][3]
    comparative, 5.08[D][2]
    contributory, 5.08[D][1]
    defenses, 5.08[D]
    duty and breach, 5.02[A][2][a]
    generally, 3.05[C], 5.08[A]
    industry standards, 5.08[B][1]
    ISPs, 5.08[D][4]
    premise liability, 5.08[C]
    professional standard of care, 5.08[B][3]
    proximate cause, 5.02[A][2][b]
    statutory standard of care, 5.08[B][2]
    telecommuting, 5.11[D]
Negligent security, 8.02[F]n389
NET, 1.02[B], 3.05[A]
Net Secure, 9.05[D][3]
Netiquette, 4.02[F][1]n130, 10.02[B][12][d]
NetSP Gateway, 3.02[B]
Netspionage, 3.03[A][1]
Network access point (NAP), 1.04n152
Network eavesdropping, 3.02[A][1]
Network security, 3.02[A][1]
Newsgroups, 1.04[B]
Niche portal, 1.05[E]n125
Nimda, 3.03[F]
No Electronic Theft Act (NET), 1.02[B],
    3.05[A]
Nonutilitarian website vandalism, 3.03[A][3]
Noncompetition agreements, 4.04[B][5]
Nondisclosure agreement (NDA), 2.03[A][5],
    4.04[A][4], 4.04[B][1], 10.03[A][2],
    10.07[C][1]
Norton Disklock 3.5, 3.02[A][5]
Norton's For Your Eyes Only, 3.02[A][5]
Norton's Internet Security 2002, 3.02[B]
NSI, 2.06[B][2], 4.03[K][2]

Obscene materials, 10.02[A][9][b]
Obtaining redress in Internet disputes,
    7.03[G], 7.03[H][4], 7.03[J]
OECD guidelines, 6.03[B][1]
Offeror/offeree, 6.04[B]
Office of Internet Enforcement (OIE),
    5.11[F][2][e]

Online dispute resolution, 9.04
Online gambling, 5.11[C]
Online identity, 1.05[F][6]
Online loan approval patent, 4.05[F][2][a]
Online music, 4.02[C][11]
Online profiling, 5.11[A][2]
Online service providers (OSPs), 1.04[A]
Online stalking, 5.03[A], 5.05[C]
Operating systems, 3.02[A][3]
Opt-in e-mail, 2.07[E][2]
Opt-out e-mail, 2.07[E][2]
Organizational/management issues, 2.02[B].
 See also Internet roadmap
Originality, 4.02[C][4][b]
OSPs, 1.04[A]
Outrage, 5.03[B]
Owner-distributed security products, 3.02[C]

P3P, 5.07[D]
Packet filters, 3.02[A][4][a]
Packet switches, 3.02[A][2]
Parody, 4.03[G][3]
Partnerships, 2.02[D][2], 6.07[J]
Passing off, 4.03[L][1][a][ii]
Passive web site, 5.12[K][1]n825
Passphrase, 3.02[A][5]
Passport, 1.05[F][6]
Passwords, 3.02[A][5]
Patent
 appeals, 4.05[B][2]
 basic rules, 4.05[A]
 checklists, 9.02[B][4], 9.02[Q][1][i]
 counsel, 4.05[B][2]
 drawings, 4.05[C][2]
 examiners, 4.05[B][1], 4.05[C][4]
 infringement, 4.05[E]
 international issues, 8.02[B][4][d]
 Internet-related, 4.05[F][2]
 licensing, 4.05[F][2][c]
 nonobviousness, 4.05[A]
 oath, 4.05[C][3]
 online loan approval, 4.05[F][2][a]
 overview, 4.01, 4.05, 4.05[A]
 prosecution of, 4.05[B][2]
 push technologies, 4.05[F][1]
 reverse auction, 4.05[F][2][a]
 software, 4.05[D]
 specifications, 4.05[C][1]

 State Street, 4.05[F][2][b]
 treaties, 8.02[B][4][d][i], [ii]
Patent Act, 4.05[A]
Patent Cooperation Treaty (PCT),
  8.02[B][4][d][i], 8.04[C][3]
PATRIOT Act, 3.05[A][2], 7.04[G][5]
PayAssurance.com, 9.05[D][10]
Payment systems
 checklists, 9.02[J]
 credit cards, 6.08[A][1]
 debit cards, 6.08[A][2]
 e-cash, 6.08[C]
 electronic checks, 6.08[D]
 electronic negotiable instruments,
  6.08[A][3]
 Internet banking, 6.08[B]
 wire transfers, 6.08[A][3][b]
PC caching, 4.02[G][1][b]
PC card, 1.05[F][4]n132
PC virus, 5.12[C]n794
PCT, 8.02[B][4][d][i], 8.04[C][3]
PDA, 1.05[F][4]
Performance and remedies checklist, 9.02[I]
Periphery countries, 8.01[B][5]
Permanent establishment, 6.07[A]
Personal digital assistant (PDA), 1.05[F][4]
Personal Information Protection and
  Electronic Documents Act (PIPED),
  8.02[E]
Personal jurisdiction, 7.01[B], 7.02, 7.04[A]
PGP, 5.12[J]
Phone phreaks, 3.03[A]
Phonorecord, 4.02[J][1]
Physical security, 3.02[A][14]
Piggybacking, 3.01n9
Ping of Death, 3.03[D]
PIPED, 8.02[E]
PKI, 3.02[A][8], 6.03[E][3]
Platforms, 1.05[E]
Pop-up ads, 2.07[A][2]
Pornography, 10.02[A][9][b]
Portals, 1.05[E]
Premise liability, 5.08[C]
Premises liability, 8.02[F]n389
Prescriptive-approach digital signature
  statutes, 6.03[E][2][a]
Prescriptive jurisdiction, 8.02[C]
Pretty Good Privacy (PGP), 5.12[J]
Preventive law pointers. *See also* Samples

antivirus protection, 3.06[E]
arbitration clauses, 6.09[B]
blocking software, 7.04[D]
choice of law, 6.09[E], 7.04[F]
clickthrough agreements, 6.09[J]
clickwrap/webwrap licenses, 6.09[C]
communications policy, 5.12[A]
cookie warnings, 5.12[E]
Copyright Clearance Center (CCC),
    9.05[C]
copyright infringement, 9.05[A]
credit cards, 6.09[I]
CTM mark, 8.04[C][1]
DDS protection, 3.06[D]
defamation, 5.12[D]
disclaimers, 6.09[G]
distance contracts, 8.04[C][4]
domain name, 8.04[C][2]
e-mail notice, 10.07[E]
e-mail policy, 5.12[F]
electronic discovery, 10.07[D]
EU competition law, 8.04[C][11]
EU Data Protection Directive, 8.04[C][12]
forum non conveniens, 7.04[C]
forum selection clauses, 8.04[C][13]
hacker insurance, 3.06[C]
hold harmless clauses, 3.06[G]
imports/exports, 8.04[C][8]
in rem jurisdiction, 7.04[B]
independent contractors, 10.07[C]
insurance coverage, 9.05[D]
insuring advertising injuries, 5.12[I]
international sales contracts, 8.04[C][5]
license negotiations, 6.09[F]
localizing web sites, 8.04[C][9]
Magnuson-Moss Act, 6.09[A]
minimizing risk of jurisdiction,
    8.04[C][10]
minimum contacts, 7.04[E]
Patent Cooperation Treaty, 8.04[C][3]
personal jurisdiction, 7.04[A]
preventing misuse of Internet, 5.12[B]
privacy policy, 5.12[G], [H]
regulation, 8.04[C][7]
security, 3.06
software licensing agreements, 8.04[C][6]
telecommuters, 10.07[B]
telecommuting, 5.12[J]

terminating ex-employees' e-mail,
    10.07[A]
termination clause (license agreements),
    6.09[H]
trademark infringement, 9.05[A]
trademark usage, 9.05[B]
UCITA, 6.09[D]
viruses, 5.12[C]
Web advertisements, FTC guidelines,
    6.09[K]
wireless LAN risks, 3.06[J]
Privacy
    checklists, 5.12[K][7], [8], 9.02[D]
    corporate criminal, 3.03[K]
    EU Directive on Protection of Personal
        Data, 5.07[D]
    false light, 5.07[B][4]
    generally, 5.07[A]
    health information, 5.11[A][4]
    independent contractors, 5.07[B][1],
        10.02[B][2][b]
    international issues, 8.02[D]
    misappropriation, 5.07[B][2]
    online contracts, 6.03[F]
    preventive law pointers, 3.06[F], 5.12[G],
        5.12[H]
    right of publicity, 5.07[B][3]
    risk management, 10.03[G]
    sample policy statement, 2.08[C]
    self-regulatory guidelines, 5.07[A]
    statutory regulation, 5.07[C]
    unreasonable intrusion upon seclusion,
        5.07[B][1]
Privacy and Personal Information Act (New
    South Wales), 10.03[D]
Private corporate policing, 3.05[B]
Private systems, 1.04[D]
Privileges, 5.10[B]
Product liability, 5.02[A][3], 5.09
Professional corporation, 2.02[D][3][d]
Professional Insurance Agents, Ltd.,
    9.05[D][5]
Professional malpractice, 3.05[D]
Proprietary information, 4.04[A]
Proxy server, 3.02[A][4][b]
Proxy server caching, 4.02[G][1][b]
PTC.i Solutions, 9.05[D][8]
Public domain, 4.04[A]
Public figure doctrine, 5.06[A][1][b]

Public key cryptography, 3.02[A][8], 6.03[E][4]
Public key infrastructure (PKI), 6.03[E][3]
Publicity. *See* Rights of publicity
Publicity rights clearance checklist, 9.02[Q][1][e]
Publishing, 1.04[F]. *See also* Web site
Pull technologies, 4.05[F][1]
Purpose availment, 7.03[A]-[C]
Push technologies patents, 4.05[F][1]

Quasi *in-rem* jurisdiction, 7.02[D]

Racial harassment, 5.03[C]
RAT, 3.01
Reasonableness test, 7.03[E][1]
Recreational hackers, 3.03[A][3]
Redress, obtaining, in Internet disputes, 7.03[G], 7.03[H][4], 7.03[J]
Regulation
    advertising, of, 5.11[B], [G]. *See also* False/deceptive advertising
    checklists, 9.02[L]
    FCC, 5.11[G]
    FTC. *See* FTC
    international issues, 8.02[M]
    online gambling, 5.11[C]
    preventive law pointer, 8.04[C][7]
    securities, 5.11[F]. *See also* Securities regulation
    successor liability, 5.11[E]
    telecommuting, 5.11[D]
Regulation S-P, 5.11[A][3]
Relatedness test, 7.03[C][1]
Replication, 4.02[G][1][b]
Respondeat superior, 5.02[B][1], [2]
Retention of e-mail messages, 10.03[C], 10.07[D]
Retinal scans, 3.02[A][6]
Retraction statutes, 5.06[A][2]
Reverse auction patent, 4.05[F][2][a]
Reverse engineering, 4.04[A][1][c]
Right of publicity, 4.02[H][2], 5.07[B][3]
Risk management. *See also* Checklist
    antivirus programs, 10.03[E][2]
    electronic monitoring of employees, 10.03[D]
    employee training/supervision, 10.03[B], 10.06[C]
    generally, 9.01
    indemnification/hold harmless clauses, 10.03[A][1]
    information security, 10.03[E]
    insurance, 10.03[H]
    nondisclosure agreements, 10.03[A][2]
    privacy, 10.03[G]
    reallocating risks of loss, 10.03[A]
    reducing regulatory enforcement actions, 10.03[F]
    retention of e-mail messages, 10.03[C], 10.07[D]
    smoking guns, 5.12[K][12], 10.03[C]
    usage policies, 10.04. *See also* E-mail and Internet usage policies
Router-based firewalls, 3.02[A][4]
Routers, 3.02[A][2]
RSA, 3.02[A][7], [8]
Rule 10b-5 violation, 5.11[F][2][b]

S corporation, 2.02[D][3][b]
Salami, 3.01n12
Sales and marketing objectives, 2.02[B]
Sales and use tax, 6.07[D][1]-[5]
Samples
    cease and desist letter, 2.08[D]
    confidentiality agreement, 10.07[F]
    content license, 4.02[J][9], 9.02[Q][4]
    Department of Commerce Internet usage policy, App 10-1
    information security guidelines, 3.04[D][1]
    legal disclaimer (web site), 2.08[A]
    linking agreement, 2.08[F]
    linking term/conditions, 2.08[E]
    nondisclosure agreement, 10.07[C][1]
    notice to users, 3.06[H]
    privacy policy statement, 2.08[B]
    security policy, 2.08[C]
    terms of service, 2.08[H][1][b]
    web site hosting terms, 2.08[G]
SAN, 3.02[A][1][b]
SATAN, 3.02[A][13]
Satellite connections, 1.05[E][6]
SBA, 2.03[A][3]
Screen-locking programs, 3.02[A][1][a]
Screen-saver, 3.04[D]n434

Screenblanker, 3.04[D]n434
Screened host, 3.02[A][4][c]
Screenlock, 3.04[D]n434
Search engine priority, 2.07[A][5]
Search engines, 1.05[D]
SEC, 5.11[F][1], 5.11[F][2][e], 8.02[M]
Second level domain (SLD), 2.06
SecurID, 3.02[A][5]
Securities & Exchange Commission (SEC),
    5.11[F][1], 5.11[F][2][e], 8.02[M]
Securities Act of 1933, 5.11[F][2][a]
Securities Exchange Act of 1934,
    5.11[F][2][b]
Securities regulation
  Internet stock fraud, 5.11[F][2][b]
  NASD online regulation, 5.11[F][2][d]
  OIE, 5.11[F][2][e]
  online securities litigation, 5.11[F][2][e]
  other federal laws, 5.11[F][2][c]
  Rule 10b-5 violation, 5.11[F][2][b]
  Regulation S-P, 5.11[A][3]
  SEC, 5.11[F][1], 8.02[M]
  Securities Act of 1933, 5.11[F][2][a]
  Securities Exchange Act of 1934,
    5.11[F][2][b]
Security
  biometric systems, 3.02[A][6]
  bridges, 3.02[A][2]
  certificate authority, 3.02[A][10]
  computer crimes, 3.03[C]
  customized security products, 3.02[D]
  digital signature, 3.02[A][9]
  DOS attacks, 3.03[D], 3.06[D]
  ECC, 3.02[E][1]
  encryption, 3.02[A][7]
  export controls on encryption, 3.02[A][11]
  firewalls, 3.02[A][4]
  forgers/importers, 3.03[H]
  hackers, 3.03[A]
  hacktivism, 3.03[A][4]
  information security system, 3.04
  information warfare, 3.03[B]
  integrity of data, 3.03[G]
  LAN, 3.02[A][1][a]
  mass-market security products, 3.02[B]
  natural disasters, 3.03[I]
  negligence, 3.05[C]
  network, 3.02[A][1]
  operating systems, 3.02[A][3]
  overview, 3.01
  owner-distributed security products,
    3.02[C]
  passphrase, 3.02[A][5]
  passwords, 3.02[A][5]
  physical, 3.02[A][14]
  policy, 3.03, 3.04[D]
  preventive law pointers, 3.06
  privacy, 3.03[K]
  private corporate policing, 3.05[B]
  professional malpractice, 3.05[D]
  protective legislation, 3.05[A]
  public-key cryptography, 3.02[A][8]
  routers/gateways, 3.02[A][2]
  sample guidelines, 3.04[D][1]
  sample policy, 2.08[C]
  SAN, 3.02[A][1][b]
  smart cards, 3.02[E][2]
  social engineering, 3.03[J]
  telecommuting, 5.12[J]
  trade secrets, 4.04[B][3]
  viruses, 3.03[E]
  VPN, 3.02[A][12]
Security audit products, 3.02[A][13]
Security First Network Bank, 6.08[B]
Seed capital, 2.03[A][6][a]
Self-help electronic repossession remedy,
    6.05[L][7]
Sell-side sites, 1.04[H]n110
Semi-periphery Internet countries,
    8.01[B][4]
Server, 1.04[D]
Service mark, 4.03[C][1]
Service of process abroad/on foreign
    defendants, 7.03[H][4], 8.02[C][2]
Servicewrap licenses, 6.04[A][2][a]
Sex-related blackmail, 3.03[A][1]
Sexpionage, 3.03[A][1]
Sexual harassment, 5.03[C]
Shoulder surfing, 3.02[A][1][a]
Shrinkwrap agreements, 3.04[C],
    6.04[A][2][a]
Signature-enabling statutes, 6.03[E][2][c]
Single key cryptography, 6.03[E][4]
Single sign-on program, 1.05[F][6]
Site license agreement, 6.06
Skil test, 5.11[B][2]
Slander, 5.06[A]. *See also* Defamation
SLD, 2.06

Sliding-scale analysis (*Zippo*), 7.03[D], [E]

Small Business Administration (SBA), 2.03[A][3]

Smart card, 6.08[C]

Smoking guns, 5.12[K][12], 10.03[C]

Smurf attacks, 3.03[D]

Snaith Insurance, 9.05[D][4]

Sniffer, 3.03[G]

Snuffle, 3.02[A][11]

Social engineering, 3.02[A][1][a], 3.03[J]

Software copyrights, 4.02[I]

Software filtering, 10.04[B][8]

Software publishers' software police, 3.05[B][3]

Sole proprietorship, 2.02[D][1]

Sonny Bono Copyright Term Extension Act (CTEA), 4.02[C][1]

Sovereign immunity, 5.10[A]

SPA e-police, 3.05[B][3]

Spam, 1.04[D]n65, 5.03[E], 5.11[1][c]

Specific jurisdiction, 7.02[B]

Spiders, 1.05[D], 4.03[K][7]

Spoofing, 2.07[E][3]

Startup, funding. *See* Funding a startup

State antidilution statutes, 4.03[E][2][b]

Statute of Frauds, 6.05[F][1]

Sterilizing an employee, 8.02[L]

Stock fraud, 5.11[F][2][b]

Storage area network (SAN), 3.02[A][1][b]

Streaming, 4.02[K]

Streaming media, 4.02[K]

Strict liability, 5.02[A][3], 5.09

Subject matter jurisdiction, 7.01[A]

Substantial presence, 6.07[A]

Successor liability, 5.11[E]

Suggestive trademark, 4.03[B][1][b][iii]

Surf Control, 10.04[B][8]

Survivability, , 3.02[A][3]n80

SWIFT, 6.08[A][3][b]

Switch, 3.02[A][2]

Symmetrical cryptography, 3.02[A][7]

SYN flooding, 3.03[D]

System caching, 4.02[G][1][b]

T1 line, 1.05[B][4]

T3 line, 1.05[B][4]

Tarnishment, 4.03[E][2][a][ii]

Tax treaties, 6.07[H]

Taxable nexus, 6.07[A]

Taxation

    cash vs. accrual, 6.07[F]

    characterization of revenue (products vs. service), 6.07[E]

    checklists, 9.02[H]

    direct taxes, 6.07[A]

    factors to consider, 6.07[B]

    federal, 6.07[C][2]

    foreign taxpayers, 6.07[A]

    form of business entity, 6.07[J]

    indirect taxes, 6.07[A]

    international, 6.07[G]-[H]

    international issues, 8.02[H]

    introduction, 6.07[A]

    ITFA, 6.07[C][1]

    ITFA moratorium, 6.07[B]

    sales and use tax, 6.07[D][1]-[5]

    state, 6.07[D]

    tax treaties, 6.07[H]

    value-added tax (VAT), 6.07[I][1]

    web servers, 6.07[I][2]

    withholding tax, 6.07[G]

TCP/IP, 1.04[E]n71

TCP SYN flooding, 3.03[D]

TCP3270, 1.04[E][2]

Techinsurance.com, 9.03[D][4]

Telecommuting, 5.11[C], 5.12[J], 10.02[B][2][a], 10.04[B][9], 10.07[B]

Telemarketing sales rule, 6.03[A][3]

Telnet, 1.04[E][1]

Terms and conditions of use checklist, 9.02[O]

Terms of Service Agreement, 2.08[H][I]

Third-party content, 8.02[E], 9.02[E]

Third-party links, 2.07[C][2][b]

Time bomb, 5.12[C]n800

Timeline, 1.02[B]

Tips. *See* Preventive law pointers

Title VII claims, 5.03[C]

TLD, 2.06, 8.02[B][4][c]

TOC agreement, 9.02[O]

Top level domain (TLD), 2.06, 8.02[B][4][c]

Torts

    assault and battery, 5.03[A]

    branches, 5.02[A]

    breach of fiduciary duty, 5.04[D]

    business defamation, 5.04[E]

    checklists, 5.12[K][3]-[6], 9.02[F]

computer viruses, 5.05[B]
cyberstalking, 5.03[A], 5.05[C]
defamation, 5.06. *See also* Defamation
employer liability. *See* Employer liability
false advertising, 5.11[B][3]
flaming, 5.03[A]
fraud, 5.04[A]
identity theft, 5.05[A]
intentional, 5.02[A][1], 5.03
intentional infliction of emotional distress,
   5.03[B]
interference with business contracts,
   5.04[C]
international issues, 8.02[F]
jurisdictional issues, 7.04[G][3]
misappropriation, 5.04[B], 5.07[B][2]
misrepresentation, 5.04[A]
privacy, 5.07[B]
right of publicity, 5.07[B][3]
spamming, 5.03[E]
Title VII claims, 5.03[C]
trade secrets, 4.04[A][2]
trespass, 5.03[D], [E]
unfair competition, 5.04[B]
Trade dress, 4.03[C][5]
Trade libel, 5.11[B][3][b]
Trade name, 4.03[C][4]
Trade secrets
breach of confidence, 4.04[A][2][b]
checklists, 9.02[B][5], 9.02[Q][1][f]
confidentiality of trials, 4.04[B][3]
criminal prosecution, 4.04[A][3]
defined, 4.04[A][1][b]
e-mail, 10.02[A][5]
employee's duty, 4.04[A][1][f]
improper means test, 4.04[A][1][c]
inevitable disclosure, 4.04[B][5]
international issues, 8.02[B][5]
misappropriation, 4.04[A][1][a], [e]
noncompetition agreements, 4.04[B][5]
nondisclosure agreements, 4.04[A][4],
   [B][1]
overview, 4.01, 4.04[A]
protecting, 4.04[A][5]
reasonable efforts to protect, 4.04[A][1][d],
   4.04[B][3]
Restatement of Torts, 4.04[A][2][a]
reverse engineering, 4.04[A][1][c]
statute of limitations, 4.04[A][1][e]

UTSA, 4.04[A][1], 9.02[B][5]
web site, 4.04[B][2]
Trademarks
abandonment, 4.03[J]
ACPA, 4.03[K][4]
actual use, 4.03[H][2][a]
arbitrary marks, 4.03[B][1][b][ii]
blurring, 4.03[E][2][a][i]
checklists, 9.02[B][2], 9.02[Q][1][b], [c]
coined phrases, 4.03[B][1][b][i]
concurrent use, 4.03[D]
cybersquatting, 4.03[K][6]
defenses, 4.03[G]
descriptive marks, 4.03[B][1][b][iv]
dilution, 4.03[E][2], 4.03[K][5][b], [c],
   4.03[L][1][a][iv]
domain names, 2.06[B][1], 4.03[K]. *See
   also* Domain names
fair use, 4.03[G][2]
fanciful marks, 4.03[B][1][b][i]
federal dilution, 4.03[E][2][a],
   4.03[K][5][b]
generic terms, 4.03[B][1][b][v]
global issues, 8.02[B][4[b]
infringement, 4.03[E], 4.03[K][5][a],
   9.05[A]
intent to use, 4.03[H][2][b]
key words in banner ads, 4.03[K][8
likelihood of confusion test, 4.03[E][1]
links, 2.07[C][2]
metatags, 4.03[K][7], [L][1]
overview, 4.01, 4.03[A]
protecting, 4.03[I]
registration, 4.03[H]
searches, 4.03[H][1]
state dilution, 4.03[E][2][b], 4.03[K][5][c]
suggestive marks, 4.03[B][1][b][iii]
tarnishment, 4.03[E][2][a][ii]
unfair competition, 4.03[F],
   4.03[L][1][a][ii]
usage, 9.05[B]
Traffic data, 8.02[E]
Transactional jurisdiction. *See* Jurisdictional
   issues
Transitory digital network communications,
   4.02[G][1][a]
Trespass, 5.03[D], [E]
TRIPS, 8.02[B], 8.02[B][2],
   8.02[B][4][a][i][A]

Trojan horses, 3,03[E], 5.12[C]798
TruSecure, 9.05[D][14]
TRUSTe, 5.12[K][8]
Tunnel, 1.04[E]n80, 5.12[J]
Typosquatters, 4.03[K][6]

UCC
    Article 1, 6.03[G][1], [2]
    Article 2, 6.03[C]
    Article 3, 6.08[A][3][a]
    Article 4, 6.08[A][3][a]
    Article 4A, 6.08[A][3][b]
    choice of law, 6.03[G][1], [2]
    electronic contract formation rule,
        6.04[B][2]
    electronic negotiable instruments,
        6.08[A][3]
    wire transfers, 6.08[A][3][b]
UCITA
    cancellation, 6.05[L][2]
    canons of construction, 6.05[H]
    choice of forum, 6.05[C][4][b]
    choice of law, 6.02[G][3], 6.05[C][4][a]
    definitions, 6.05[C][3]
    disabling device, 6.05[L][7]
    disclaimers, 6.05[G][2][e]
    electronic contracting rules, 6.05[F]
    failure of essential purpose, 6.05[E][3]
    fundamental public policies,
        6.05[L][5]
    licensing rules, 6.05[D]
    liquidated damages, 6.05[L][6]
    material breach, 6.05[L][3]
    overview, 6.05[A]
    performance standards, 6.05[J]
    preventive law pointer, 6.09[D],
        8.04[C][6]
    procedural protection for licensees,
        6.05[E][1]
    remedies, 6.05[L]
    scope, 6.05[C]
    self-help electronic repossession remedy,
        6.05[L][7]
    Statute of Frauds, 6.05[F][1]
    statute of limitations, 6.05[L][8]
    structure/function, 6.05[B]
    tender/acceptance/rejection/revocation,
        6.05[K]

transfer of interests and rights, 6.05[I]
unconscionable license agreements,
        6.05[E][2]
warranties, 6.05[G]
UDP flooding, 3.03[D]
UDRP policy/rules, 4.03[K][3][a], [b],
        8.02[B][4][c][ii][B]
UDTPA, 5.11[B][1][b], 5.11[B][2], 5.11[C]
UETA
    admissibility in evidence, 6.04[D][7]
    automated transactions, 6.04[D][8]
    effect of change or error, 6.04[D][5]
    electronic records, 6.04[D][4]
    purpose, 6.04[D][1]
    receipt of electronic records, 6.04[D][9]
    retention of records, 6.04[D][6]
    scope, 6.04[D][2]
    validation of electronic signatures,
        6.04[D][3]
UNCITRAL Model Law on Electronic
        Commerce, 8.02[I][1]
Unconscionability, 6.05[E][2]
Unfair advertising, 2.07[B][1][b]
Unfair competition, 4.03[F], 4.03[L][1][a][ii],
        5.04[B]
Unfairness doctrine, 5.11[B][1][a][i]
Uniform Commercial Code. See UCC
Uniform Computer Information Transactions
        Act. See UCITA
Uniform Deceptive Trade Practices Act
        (UDTPA), 5.11[B][1][b], 5.11[B][2],
        5.11[C]
Uniform domain name dispute resolution
        policy (UDRP), 4.03[K][3],
        8.02[B][4][c][ii][B]
Uniform Electronic Transactions Act. See UETA
Uniform resource locator (URL),
        1.05[D]n121, 2.07[C][2]
Uniform Trade Secrets Act (UTSA),
        4.04[A][1], 9.02[B][5]
Unilateral contract, 6.04[B]
UNIX, 1.04[E] n67, 5.12[C]796
UNIX-based operating systems, 3.02[A][3]
Unreasonable intrusion upon seclusion,
        5.07[B][1]
Unsolicited bulk e-mail, 2.07[E][3], 6.03[A][3]
URL, 1.05[D]n121, 2.07[C][2]
Usage. See E-mail and Internet usage
Use tax, 6.07[D][1]-[5]

USENET, 1.04[B]
UTSA, 4.04[A][1], 9.02[B][5]

Value added tax (VAT), 6.07[A], 6.07[I][1],
    8.02[H]
VARA moral rights, 4.02[H][1]
VAT, 6.07[A], 6.07[I][1], 8.02[H]
Venture capital (VC), 2.03[A][6]
Vicarious liability, 5.02[B][2]
Virtual private networks (VPN), 1.04[D],
    3.02[A][12]
Virus-worm hybrids, 3.03[F]
Viruses, 3.03[E], 3.06[E], 5.05[B], 5.12[C]
Visual Artists Right Act, 4.02[H][1]
Voice browsing, 1.05[F][3]
VPN, 1.04[D], 3.02[A][12]

WAP, 1.05[F][2]
Warranties, 6.03[A][1], 6.05[G], 6.09[A]
Warranties checklist, 9.02[I]
Web advertisements. See Advertising
Web authoring tools, 2.05[A][1]
Web browser, 1.05[C]
Web bug, 5.07[A]
Web design and hosting checklist, 9.02[I]
Web pads, 1.05[F][5]
Web page advertisements, 7.04[G][2]
Web page sponsorship, 2.07[A][3]
Web site
    active/passive, 5.12[K][1]n825
    content, 2.04[C]
    internal v. external development, 2.05[A]
    organizing, 2.04[B]
    purpose of, 2.04
    questions to ask, 2.04[A]
    sample disclaimer, 2.08[A]
    updating, 2.05[B]

validating purpose, 2.04[D]
Web site development checklist, 9.02[Q][3]
Web site hosting terms, 2.08[G]
Web site intellectual property audit
    clearance of publicity rights, 9.02[Q][1][e]
    copyright, 9.02[Q][1][a]
    domain names, 9.02[Q][1][d]
    indemnification checklist, 9.02[Q][1][h]
    licensing intellectual property, 9.02[Q][2]
    linking or framing agreements,
        9.02[Q][1][g]
    patents, 9.02[Q][1][i]
    sample content license agreement,
        9.02[Q][4]
    trade secrets, 9.02[Q][1][f]
    trademarks, 9.02[Q][1][b], [c]
    web site development, 9.02[Q][3]
Web site trade secrets, 4.04[B][2]
Webwrap agreements, 3.04[C], 6.04[A][2][c],
    6.09[C]
WIPO, 4.06[A]
WIPO Arbitration and Mediation Center,
    8.02[B][4][c][ii][A]
WIPO copyright treaties, 8.02[B][4][a][i][B]
Wire transfers, 6.08[A][3][b]
Wireless LAN risks, 3.06[J]
Wiretapping, 10.02[A][9][c]
Withholding tax, 6.07[G]
WML, 1.05[F][2]
Work made for hire, 4.02[C][8]
World Intellectual Property Organization
    (WIPO), 4.06[A]
World system theory, 8.01[B][1]
World Wide Web, 1.05[D]n119
Worm, 3.06[E], 5.12[C]799

Zippo sliding-scale analysis, 7.03[D], [E]
Zombie, 3.01